The firstwriter.com
Writers' Handbook
2025

The firstwriter.com
Writers' Handbook
2025

EDITOR
J. PAUL DYSON

Published in 2024 by JP&A Dyson
27 Old Gloucester Street, London WC1N 3AX, United Kingdom
Copyright JP&A Dyson

https://www.jpandadyson.com
https://www.firstwriter.com

ISBN 978-1-909935-52-5

All rights reserved. No part of this publication may be reproduced or transmitted in any form or by any means, or stored in any retrieval system without prior written permission. firstwriter.com, the firstwriter.com logo, and the firstwriter.com oval are trademarks of JP&A Dyson trading as firstwriter.com. Whilst every effort is made to ensure that all information contained within this publication is accurate, no liability can be accepted for any mistakes or omissions, or for losses incurred as a result of actions taken in relation to information provided. Unless otherwise stated, firstwriter.com is not associated with and does not endorse, recommend, or guarantee any of the organisations or persons listed within this publication. Inclusion does not constitute recommendation.

**Registered with the IP Rights Office
Copyright Registration Service
Ref: 3491388659**

Foreword

The firstwriter.com Writers' Handbook returns for its 2025 edition with over 1,500 listings of literary agents, literary agencies, publishers, and magazines that have been updated in firstwriter.com's online databases between 2022 and 2024. This includes revised and updated listings from the previous edition and over 350 new entries.

Previous editions of this handbook have been bought by writers across the United States, Canada, and Europe; and ranked in the United Kingdom as the number one bestselling writing and publishing directory on Amazon. The 2024 edition continues this international outlook, giving writers all over the English-speaking world access to the global publishing markets.

Finding the information you need is made quick and easy with multiple tables, a detailed index, and unique paragraph numbers to help you get to the listings you're looking for.

The variety of tables helps you navigate the listings in different ways, and includes a Table of Authors, which lists over 6,000 authors and tells you who represents them, or who publishes them, or both.

The number of genres in the index has expanded to over 900. So, for example, while there was only one option for "Romance" in previous editions, you can now narrow this down to Historical Romance, Fantasy Romance, Supernatural / Paranormal Romance, Contemporary Romance, Diverse Romance, Erotic Romance, Feminist Romance, Christian Romance, or even Amish Romance.

The handbook also provides free online access to the entire current firstwriter.com databases, including over 2,200 magazines, over 2,400 literary agents and agencies, over 2,700 book publishers that don't charge fees, and constantly updated listings of current writing competitions, with typically more than 50 added each month.

For details on how to claim your free access please see the end of this book.

Included in the subscription

A subscription to the full website is not only free with this book, but comes packed with all the following features:

Advanced search features

- Save searches and save time – set up to 15 search parameters specific to your work, save them, and then access the search results with a single click whenever you log in. You can even save multiple different searches if you have different types of work you are looking to place.
- Add personal notes to listings, visible only to you and fully searchable – helping you to organise your actions.
- Set reminders on listings to notify you when to submit your work, when to follow up, when to expect a reply, or any other custom action.
- Track which listings you've viewed and when, to help you organise your search – any listings which have changed since you last viewed them will be highlighted for your attention.

Daily email updates

As a subscriber you will be able to take advantage of our email alert service, meaning you can specify your particular interests and we'll send you automatic email updates when we change or add a listing that matches them. So if you're interested in agents dealing in romantic fiction in the United States you can have us send you emails with the latest updates about them – keeping you up to date without even having to log in.

User feedback

Our agent, publisher, and magazine databases all include a user feedback feature that allows our subscribers to leave feedback on each listing – giving you not only the chance to have your say about the markets you contact, but giving a unique authors' perspective on the listings.

Save on copyright protection fees

If you're sending your work away to publishers, competitions, or literary agents, it's vital that you first protect your copyright. As a subscriber to firstwriter.com you can do this through our site and save 10% on the copyright registration fees normally payable for protecting your work internationally through the Intellectual Property Rights Office (https://www.CopyrightRegistrationService.com).

Monthly newsletter

When you subscribe to firstwriter.com you also receive our monthly email newsletter – described by one publishing company as "the best in the business" – including articles, news, and interviews for writers. And the best part is that you can continue to receive the newsletter even after you stop your paid subscription – at no cost!

For details on how to claim your free access please see the back of this book.

Contents

Foreword v
Contents vii
Glossary of Terms ix

Guidance

The Writer's Roadmap 1
Why Choose Traditional Publishing 3
Formatting Your Manuscript 5
Protecting Your Copyright 7
Should You Self-Publish 11
The Self Publishing Process 13

Tables

Table of US Literary Agencies 15
Table of UK Literary Agencies 17
Table of US Literary Agents 19
Table of UK Literary Agents 23
Table of Canadian Literary Agents 27
Table of US Magazines 29
Table of UK Magazines 31
Table of Canadian Magazines 33
Table of US Book Publishers 35
Table of UK Book Publishers 37
Table of Canadian Book Publishers 39
Table of Authors 41

Listings

Literary Agents and Agencies 79
Magazines 199
Book Publishers 253

Claim your free access to **www.firstwriter.com**: *See p.403*

Index

Index 321

Free Access

Get Free Access to the firstwriter.com Website 403

Glossary of Terms

This section explains common terms used in this handbook, and in the publishing industry more generally.

Academic
Listings in this book will be marked as targeting the academic market only if they publish material of an academic nature; e.g. academic theses, scientific papers, etc. The term is not used to indicate publications that publish general material aimed at people who happen to be in academia, or who are described as academic by virtue of being educated.

Adult
In publishing, "adult" simply refers to books that are aimed at adults, as opposed to books that are aimed at children, or young adults, etc. It is not a euphemism for pornographic or erotic content. Nor does it necessarily refer to content which is unsuitable for children; it is just not targeted at them. In this book, most ordinary mainstream publishers will be described as "adult", unless their books are specifically targeted at other groups (such as children, professionals, etc.).

Advance
Advances are up-front payments made by traditional publishers to authors, which are off-set against future royalties.

Agented
An *agented* submission is one which is submitted by a literary agent. If a publisher accepts only *agented* submissions then you will need a literary agent to submit the work on your behalf.

Author bio
A brief description of you and your life – normally in relation to your writing activity, but if intended for publication (particularly in magazines) may be broader in scope. May be similar to *Curriculum Vitae* (CV) or résumé, depending on context.

Bio
See *Author bio*.

Curriculum Vitae
A brief description of you, your qualifications, and accomplishments – normally in this context in relation to writing (any previous publications, or awards, etc.), but in the case of nonfiction proposals may also include relevant experience that qualifies you to write on the subject. Commonly abbreviated to "CV". May also be referred to as a résumé. May be similar to *Author bio*, depending on context.

CV
See *Curriculum Vitae*.

International Reply Coupon
When submitting material overseas you may be required to enclose *International Reply Coupons*, which will enable the recipient to send a response and/or return your material at your cost. Not applicable/available in all countries, so check with your local Post Office for more information.

IRC
See *International Reply Coupon*.

Manuscript
Your complete piece of work – be it a novel, short story, or article, etc. – will be referred to as your manuscript. Commonly abbreviated to "ms" (singular) or "mss" (plural).

MS
See *Manuscript*.

MSS
See *Manuscript*.

Professional
Listings in this book will be marked as targeting the professional market if they publish material serving a particular profession: e.g. legal journals, medical journals, etc. The term is not used to indicate publications that publish general material aimed at a notional "professional class".

Proposal
A proposal is normally requested for nonfiction projects (where the book may not yet have been completed, or even begun). Proposals can consist of a number of components, such as an outline, table of contents, CV, marketing information, etc. but the exact requirements will vary from one publisher to another.

Query
Many agents and publishers will prefer to receive a query in the first instance, rather than your full *manuscript*. A query will typically consist of a cover letter accompanied by a *synopsis* and/or sample chapter(s). Specific requirements will vary, however, so always check on a case by case basis.

Recommendation
If an agent is only accepting approaches by recommendation this means that they will only consider your work if it comes with a recommendation from an established professional in the industry, or an existing client.

RoW
Rest of world.

SAE
See *Stamped Addressed Envelope*. Can also be referred to as SASE.

SASE
Self-Addressed Stamped Envelope. Variation of SAE. See *Stamped Addressed Envelope*.

Simultaneous submission
A simultaneous submission is one which is sent to more than one market at the same time. Normally you will be sending your work to numerous different magazines, agents, and publishers at the same time, but some demand the right to consider it exclusively – i.e. they don't accept simultaneous submissions.

Stamped Addressed Envelope
Commonly abbreviated to "SAE". Can also be referred to as Self-Addressed Stamped Envelope, or SASE. When supplying an SAE, ensure that the envelope and postage is adequate for a reply or the return of your material, as required. If you are submitting overseas, remember that postage from your own country will not be accepted, and you may need to provide an *International Reply Coupon*.

Synopsis
A short outline of your story. This should cover all the main characters and events, including the ending. It is not the kind of "teaser" found on a book's back cover. The length of synopsis required can vary, but is generally between one and three pages.

TOC
Table of Contents. These are often requested as part of nonfiction proposals.

Unagented
An unagented submission is one which is not submitted through a literary agent. If a publisher accepts unagented submissions then you can approach them directly.

Unsolicited mss
A manuscript which has not been requested. Many agents and publishers will not accept unsolicited mss, but this does not necessarily mean they are closed to approaches – many will prefer to receive a short *query* in the first instance. If they like the idea, they will request the full work, which will then be a solicited manuscript.

The Writer's Roadmap

With most objectives in life, people recognise that there is a path to follow. Whether it is career progression, developing a relationship, or chasing your dreams, we normally understand that there are foundations to lay and baby steps to take before we'll be ready for the main event.

But for some reason, with writing (perhaps because so much of the journey of a writer happens in private, behind closed doors), people often overlook the process involved. They often have a plan of action which runs something like this:

1. Write novel.
2. Get novel published.

This is a bit like having a plan for success in tennis which runs:

1. Buy tennis racket.
2. Win Wimbledon.

It misses out all the practice that is going to be required; the competing in the minor competitions and the learning of the craft that will be needed in order to succeed in the major events; the time that will need to be spent gaining reputation and experience.

In this roadmap we'll be laying out what we think is the best path to follow to try and give yourself the best shot of success in the world of writing. You don't necessarily have to jump through all the hoops, and there will always be people who, like Pop Idol or reality TV contestants, get a lucky break that propels them to stardom without laying any of the foundations laid out below, but the aim here is to limit your reliance on luck and maximise your ability to shape your destiny yourself.

1: Write short material

Writers will very often start off by writing a novel. We would advise strongly against this. It's like leaving school one day and applying for a job as a CEO of an international corporation the next. Novels are the big league. They are expensive to produce, market, and distribute. They require significant investment and pose a significant financial risk to publishers. They are not a good place for new writers to try and cut their teeth. If you've already written your novel that's great – it's great experience and you'll have learned a lot – but we'd recommend shelving it for now (you can always come back to it later) and getting stuck into writing some short form material, such as poetry and short fiction.

This is what novelist George R. R. Martin, author of *A Game of Thrones*, has to say on the subject:

> "I would also suggest that any aspiring writer begin with short stories. These days, I meet far too many young writers who try to start off with a novel right off, or a trilogy, or even a nine-book series. That's like starting in at rock climbing by tackling Mt Everest. Short stories help you learn your craft."

You will find that writing short material will improve your writing no end. Writing short fiction allows you to play with lots of different stories and characters very quickly. Because you will probably only spend a few days on any given story you will quickly gain a lot of experience with plotting stories and will learn a lot about what works, what doesn't work, and what you personally are good at. When you write a novel, by contrast, you may spend years on a single story and one set of characters, making this learning process much slower.

Your writing will also be improved by the need to stick to a word limit. Writers who start their career by writing a novel often produce huge epics, the word counts of which they wear as a badge of honour, as if they demonstrate their commitment to and enthusiasm for writing. What they actually demonstrate is a naivety about the realities of getting published. The odds are already stacked against new writers getting a novel published, because of the cost and financial risk of publishing a novel. The bigger the novel, the more it will cost to print, warehouse, and distribute. Publishers will not look at a large word count and be impressed – they will be terrified. The longer the novel, the less chance it has of getting published.

A lengthy first novel also suggests that the writer has yet to learn one of the most critical skills a writer must possess to succeed: brevity. By writing short stories that fit the limits imposed by competitions and magazines you will learn this critical skill. You will learn to remove unnecessary words and passages, and you will find that your writing becomes leaner, more engaging, and more exciting as a result. Lengthy first novels are often rambling and sometimes boring – but once you've been forced to learn how to "trim the fat" by writing short stories, the good habits you've got into will transfer across when you start writing long form works, allowing you to write novels that are pacier and better to read. They will stand a better chance of publication not just because they are shorter and cheaper to produce, but they are also likely to be better written.

2: Get a professional critique

It's a good idea to get some professional feedback on your work at some point, and it's probably better to do this sooner, rather than later. There's no point spending a long time doing something that doesn't quite work if a little advice early on could have got you on the right track sooner. It's also a lot cheaper to get a short story critiqued than a whole novel, and if you can learn the necessary lessons now it will both minimise the cost and maximise the benefit of the advice.

Should you protect the copyright of short works before showing them to anyone?

This is a matter of personal preference. We'd suggest that it certainly isn't as important to register short works as full novels, as your short works are unlikely to be of much financial value to you. Having said that, films do sometimes get made which are based on short stories, in which case you'd want to have all your rights in order. If you do choose to register your short works this can be done for a relatively small amount online at https://www.copyrightregistrationservice.com/register.

3: Submit to competitions and magazines, and build a list of writing credits

Once you have got some short works that you are happy with you can start submitting them to competitions and small magazines. You can search for competitions at https://www.firstwriter.com/competitions and magazines at https://www.firstwriter.com/magazines. Prize money may not be huge, and you probably won't be paid for having your work appear in the kind of small literary magazines you will probably be approaching at first, but the objective here is to build up a list of writing credits to give you more credibility when approaching agents and publishers. You'll be much more likely to grab their attention if you can reel off a list of places where you have already been published, or prizes you have won.

4: Finish your novel and protect your copyright

Okay – so you've built up a list of writing credits, and you've decided it's time to either write a novel, or go back to the one you had already started (in which case you'll probably find yourself cutting out large chunks and making it a lot shorter!). Once you've got your novel to the point where you're happy to start submitting it for publication you should get it registered for copyright. Unlike the registration of short works, which we think is a matter of personal preference, we'd definitely recommend registering a novel, and doing so before you show it to anybody. That *includes* family and friends. Don't worry that you might want to change it – as long as you don't rewrite it to the point where it's not recognisable it will still be protected – the important thing is to get it registered without delay. You can protect it online at https://www.copyrightregistrationservice.com/register.

If you've already shown it to other people then just register it as soon as you can. Proving a claim to copyright is all about proving you had a copy of the work before anyone else, so time is of the essence.

5: Editing

These days, agents and publishers increasingly seem to expect manuscripts to have been professionally edited before being submitted to them – and no, getting your husband / wife / friend / relative to do it doesn't count. Ideally, you should have the whole manuscript professionally edited, but this can be expensive. Since most agents and publishers aren't going to want to see the whole manuscript in the first instance you can probably get away with just having the first three chapters edited. It may also be worth having your query letter and synopsis edited at the same time.

6: Submit to literary agents

There will be many publishers out there who will accept your submission directly, and on the face of it that might seem like a good idea, since you won't have to pay an agent 15% of your earnings.

However, all the biggest publishers are generally closed to direct submissions from authors, meaning that if you want the chance of getting a top publisher you're going to need a literary agent. You'll also probably find that their 15% fee is more than offset by the higher earnings you'll be likely to achieve.

To search for literary agents go to https://www.firstwriter.com/Agents. Start by being as specific in your search as possible. So if you've written a historical romance select "Fiction", "Romance", and "Historical". Once you've approached all the agents that specifically mention all three elements broaden your search to just "Fiction" and "Romance". As long as the new results don't specifically say they don't handle historical romance, these are still valid markets to approach. Finally, search for just "Fiction", as there are many agents who are willing to consider all kinds of fiction but don't specifically mention romance or historical.

Don't limit your approaches to just agents in your own country. With more and more agents accepting electronic queries it's now as easy to approach agents in other countries as in your own, and if you're ignoring either London or New York (the two main centres of English language publishing) you're cutting your chances of success in two.

7: Submit directly to publishers

Once you're certain that you've exhausted all potential agents for your work, you can start looking for publishers to submit your work directly to. You can search for publishers at https://www.firstwriter.com/publishers. Apply the same filtering as when you were searching for agents: start specific and gradually broaden, until you've exhausted all possibilities.

8: Self-publishing

In the past, once you got to the point where you'd submitted to all the publishers and agents who might be interested in your book, it would be time to pack away the manuscript in the attic, chalk it up to experience, and start writing another. However, these days writers have the option to take their book directly to market by publishing it themselves.

Before you decide to switch to self-publishing you must be sure that you've exhausted all traditional publishing possibilities – because once you've self-published your book you're unlikely to be able to submit it to agents and publishers. It will probably take a few years of exploring the world of traditional publishing to reach this point, but if you do then you've nothing to lose by giving self-publishing a shot. See our guide to self-publishing for details on how to proceed.

Why Choose Traditional Publishing

When **firstwriter.com** first started, back in 2001, there were only two games in town when it came to getting your book published: traditional publishing, and vanity publishing – and which you should pick was a no-brainer. Vanity publishing was little more than a scam that would leave you with an empty bank account and a house full of unsold books. If you were serious about being a writer, you had to follow the traditional publishing path.

Since then, there has been a self-publishing revolution, with new technologies and new printing methods giving writers a genuine opportunity to get their books into the market by themselves. So, is there still a reason for writers to choose traditional publishing?

The benefits of traditional publishing

Despite the allure and apparent ease of self-publishing, the traditional path still offers you the best chance of making a success of being a writer. There are rare cases where self-published writers make staggering fortunes and become internationally renowned on the back of their self-published books, but these cases are few and far between, and a tiny drop in the rapidly expanding ocean of self-published works. The vast majority of successful books – and the vast majority of successful writers – have their homes firmly in the established publishing houses. Even those self-published authors who find success usually end up moving to a traditional publisher in the end.

This is because the traditional publishers have the systems, the market presence, and the financial clout to *make* a book a bestseller. While successful self-published authors often owe their success in no small part to a decent dose of luck (a social media comment that goes viral; the right mention on the right media outlet at the right time), traditional publishers are in the business of engineering that success. They might not always succeed, but they have the marketing budgets and the distribution channels in place to give themselves, and the book they are promoting, the best possible chance.

And it's not just the marketing and the distribution. Getting signed with a traditional publisher brings a whole team of people with a wealth of expertise that will all work towards the success of the book. It will provide you with an editor who may have experience of working on previous bestsellers, who will not only help you get rid of mistakes in your work but may also help you refine it into a better book. They will help make sure that the quality of your content is good enough to make it in the marketplace.

The publishers will source a professional cover designer who will make your book look the part on the shelves and on the pages of the bookselling websites. They will have accountants who will handle the technicalities of tax regimes both home and abroad. They will have overseas contacts for establishing foreign publishing rights; translations; etc. They may even have contacts in the film industry, should there be a prospect of a movie adaptation. They will have experts working on every aspect of your book, right down to the printing and the warehousing and the shipping of the physical products. They will have people to manage the ebook conversion and the electronic distribution. As an author, you don't need to worry about any of this.

This means you get more time to simply be a writer. You may have to go on book tours, but even these will be organised for you by PR experts, who will also be handling all the press releases, etc.

And then there's the advances. Advances are up-front payments made by traditional publishers to authors, which are off-set against future royalties. So, an author might receive a $5,000 advance before their book is published. When the royalties start coming in, the publisher keeps the first $5,000 to off-set the advance. The good news for the author is that if the book flops and doesn't make $5,000 in royalties they still get to keep the full advance. In an uncertain profession, the security of an advance can be invaluable for an author – and of course it's not something available to self-published authors.

The drawbacks of traditional publishing

The main downside of traditional publishing is just that it's so hard to get into. If you choose to self-publish then – provided you have enough perseverance, the right help and advice, and perhaps a little bit of money – you are guaranteed to succeed and see your book in print and for sale. With traditional publishing, the cold hard fact is that most people who try will not succeed.

And for many of those people who fail it may not even be their fault. That aspect of traditional publishing which can bring so many benefits as compared to self-publishing – that of being part of a team – can also be part of its biggest drawback. It means that you have to get other people to buy into your book. It means that you have to rely on other people being competent enough to spot a bestseller. Many failed to spot the potential of the Harry Potter books. How many potential bestsellers never make it into print just because none of the professionals at the publishers' gates manage to recognise their potential?

So if you choose traditional publishing your destiny is not in your own hands – and for some writers the lack of exclusive control can also be a problem. Sometimes writers get defensive when editors try to tinker with their work, or annoyed when cover artists don't realise their vision the way they expect. But this is hardly a fair criticism of traditional publishing, as most writers (particularly when they are starting out) will benefit from advice from experienced professionals in the field, and will often only be shooting themselves in the foot if they insist on ignoring it.

The final main drawback with traditional publishing is that less of the sale price of each copy makes it to the writer. A typical royalty contract will give the writer 15%. With a self-published book, the author can expect to receive much more. So, all other things being equal, the self-published route can be more profitable – but, of course, all things are not equal. If self-publishing means lower sales (as is likely), then you will probably make less money overall. Remember, it's better to have 15% of something than 50% of nothing.

Conclusion

In conclusion, our advice to writers would be to aim for traditional publishing first. It might be a long shot, but if it works then you stand a much better chance of being successful. If you don't manage to get signed by an agent or a publisher then you still have the option of self-publishing, but make sure you don't get tempted to resort to self-publishing too soon – most agents and publishers won't consider self-published works, so this is a one-way street. Once you've self-published your work, you probably won't be able to change your mind and go back to the traditional publishers with your book unless it becomes a huge hit without them. It's therefore important that you exhaust all your traditional publishing options before making the leap to self-publishing. Be prepared for this to take perhaps a few years (lots of agents and publishers can take six months just to respond), and make sure you've submitted to everyone you can on *both* sides of the Atlantic (publishing is a global game these days, and you need to concentrate on the two main centres of English-language publishing (New York and London) equally) before you make the decision to self-publish instead.

Formatting Your Manuscript

Before submitting a manuscript to an agent, magazine, or publisher, it's important that you get the formatting right. There are industry norms covering everything from the size of your margins to the font you choose – get them wrong and you'll be marking yourself out as an amateur. Get them right, and agents and editors will be far more likely to take you seriously.

Fonts

Don't be tempted to "make your book stand out" by using fancy fonts. It *will* stand out, but not for any reason you'd want. Your entire manuscript should be in a monospaced font like Courier (not a proportional font, like Times Roman) at 12 points. (A monospaced font is one where each character takes up the same amount of space; a proportional font is where the letter "i" takes up less space than the letter "m".)

This goes for your text, your headings, your title, your name – everything. Your objective is to produce a manuscript that looks like it has been produced on a simple typewriter.

Italics / bold

Your job as the author is to indicate words that require emphasis, not to pick particular styles of font. This will be determined by the house style of the publisher in question. You indicate emphasis by underlining text; the publisher will decide whether they will use bold or italic to achieve this emphasis – you shouldn't use either in your text.

Margins

You should have a one inch (2.5 centimetre) margin around your entire page: top, bottom, left, and right.

Spacing

In terms of line spacing, your entire manuscript should be double spaced. Your word processor should provide an option for this, so you don't have to insert blank lines manually.

While line spacing should be double, spaces after punctuation should be single. If you're in the habit of putting two spaces after full stops this is the time to get out of that habit, and remove them from your manuscript. You're just creating extra work for the editor who will have to strip them all out.

Do not put blank lines between paragraphs. Start every paragraph (even those at the start of chapters) with an indent equivalent to five spaces. If you want a scene break then create a line with the "#" character centred in the middle. You don't need blank lines above or below this line.

Word count

You will need to provide an estimated word count on the front page of your manuscript. Tempting as it will be to simply use the word processor's word counting function to tell you exactly how many words there are in your manuscript, this is not what you should do. Instead, you should work out the maximum number of characters on a line, divide this number by six, and then multiply by the total number of lines in your manuscript.

Once you have got your estimated word count you need to round it to an approximate value. How you round will depend on the overall length of your manuscript:

- up to 1,500 words: round to the nearest 100;
- 1,500–10,000 words: round to the nearest 500;
- 10,000–25,000 words: round to the nearest 1,000;
- Over 25,000 words: round to the nearest 5,000.

The reason an agent or editor will need to know your word count is so that they can estimate how many pages it will make. Since actual pages include varying amounts of white space due to breaks in paragraphs, sections of speech, etc. the formula above will actually provide a better idea of how many pages will be required than an exact word count would.

And – perhaps more importantly – providing an exact word count will highlight you immediately as an amateur.

Layout of the front page

On the first page of the manuscript, place your name, address, and any other relevant contact details (such as phone number, email address, etc.) in the top left-hand corner. In the top right-hand corner write your approximate word count.

If you have registered your work for copyright protection, place the reference number two single lines (one double line) beneath your contact details. Since your manuscript will only be seen by agents or editors, not the public, this should be done as discreetly as possible, and you should refrain from using any official seal you may have been granted permissions to use. (For information on registering for copyright protection see "Protecting Your Copyright", below.)

Place your title halfway down the front page. Your title should be centred and would normally be in capital letters. You can make it bold or underlined if you want, but it should be the same size as the rest of the text.

From your title, go down two single lines (or one double line) and insert your byline. This should be centred and start with the word "By", followed by the name you are writing under. This can be your name or a pen name, but should be the name you want the work published under. However, make sure that the name in the top left-hand corner is your real, legal name.

From your byline, go down four single lines (or two double lines) and begin your manuscript.

Layout of the text

Print on only one side of the paper, even if your printer can print on both sides.

In the top right-hand corner of all pages except the first should be your running head. This should be comprised of the surname used in your byline; a keyword from your title, and the page number, e.g. "Myname / Mynovel Page 5".

Text should be left-aligned, *not* justified. This means that you should have a ragged right-hand edge to the text, with lines ending at different points. Make sure you don't have any sort of hyphenation function switched on in your word processor: if a word is too long to fit on a line it should be taken over to the next.

Start each new chapter a third of the way down the page with the centred chapter number / title, underlined. Drop down four single lines (two double lines) to the main text.

At the end of the manuscript you do not need to indicate the ending in any way: you don't need to write "The End", or "Ends", etc. The only exception to this is if your manuscript happens to end at the bottom of a page, in which case you can handwrite the word "End" at the bottom of the last page, after you have printed it out.

Protecting Your Copyright

Protecting your copyright is by no means a requirement before submitting your work, but you may feel that it is a prudent step that you would like to take before allowing strangers to see your material.

These days, you can register your work for copyright protection quickly and easily online. The Intellectual Property Rights Office operates a website called the "Copyright Registration Service" which allows you to do this:

- *https://www.CopyrightRegistrationService.com*

This website can be used for material created in any nation signed up to the Berne Convention. This includes the United States, United Kingdom, Canada, Australia, Ireland, New Zealand, and most other countries. There are around 180 countries in the world, and over 160 of them are part of the Berne Convention.

Provided you created your work in one of the Berne Convention nations, your work should be protected by copyright in all other Berne Convention nations. You can therefore protect your copyright around most of the world with a single registration, and because the process is entirely online you can have your work protected in a matter of minutes, without having to print and post a copy of your manuscript.

What is copyright?

Copyright is a form of intellectual property (often referred to as "IP"). Other forms of intellectual property include trade marks, designs, and patents. These categories refer to different kinds of ideas which may not exist in a physical form that can be owned as property in the traditional sense, but may nonetheless have value to the people who created them. These forms of intellectual property can be owned in the same way that physical property is owned, but – as with physical property – they can be subject to dispute and proper documentation is required to prove ownership.

The different types of intellectual property divide into these categories as follows:

- **Copyright:** copyright protects creative output such as books, poems, pictures, drawings, music, films, etc. Any work which can be recorded in some way can be protected by copyright, as long as it is original and of sufficient length. Copyright does not cover short phrases or names.
- **Trade marks:** trade marks cover words and/or images which distinguish the goods or services of one trader from another. Unlike copyright, trade marks can cover names and short phrases.
- **Designs:** designs cover the overall visual appearance of a product, such as its shape, etc.
- **Patents:** patents protect the technical or functional aspects of designs or inventions.

The specifics of the legal protection surrounding these various forms of intellectual property will vary from nation to nation, but there are also generally international conventions to which a lot if not most of the nations of the world subscribe. The information provided below outlines the common situation in many countries but you should be aware that this may not reflect the exact situation in every territory.

The two types of intellectual property most relevant to writers are copyright and trade marks. If a writer has written a novel, a short story, a poem, a script, or any other piece of writing then the contents themselves can be protected by copyright. The title, however, cannot be protected by copyright as it is a name. An author may therefore feel that they wish to consider protecting the title of their work by registering it as a trade mark, if they feel that it is particularly important and/or more valuable in itself than the cost of registering a trade mark.

If a writer wants to register the copyright for their work, or register the title of their work as a trade mark, there are generally registration fees to be paid. Despite the fact that copyright covers long works that could be hundreds of thousands of words long, while trade marks cover single words and short phrases, the cost for registering a trade mark is likely to be many times higher than that for registering a work for copyright protection. This is because trade marks must be unique and are checked against existing trade marks for potential conflicts. While works to be registered for copyright must also not infringe existing works, it is not practical to check the huge volume of new works to be registered for copyright against the even larger volume of all previously copyrighted works. Copyright registration therefore tends to simply archive the work in question as proof of the date at which the person registering the work was in possession of it.

In the case of both copyright and trade marks the law generally provides some protection even without any kind of registration, but registration provides the owner of the intellectual property with greater and more enforceable protection. In the case of copyright, the creator of a work usually automatically owns the copyright as soon as the work is recorded in some way (i.e. by writing it down or recording it electronically, etc.), however these rights can be difficult to prove if disputed, and therefore many countries (such as the United States) also offer an internal country-specific means of registering works. Some countries, like the United Kingdom, do not offer any such means of registration, however an international registration is available through the Intellectual Property Rights Office's Copyright Registration Service, and can be used regardless of any country-specific provisions. This can help protect copyright in all of the nations which are signatories of the Berne Convention.

In the case of trade marks, the symbol "™" can be applied to any mark which is being used as a trade mark, however greater protection is provided if this mark is registered, in which case the symbol "®" can be applied to the mark. It is often illegal to apply the "®" symbol to a trade mark which has not been registered. There are also options for international registrations of trade marks, which are administered by the World Intellectual Property Organization, however applications cannot be made to the WIPO directly – applications must be made through the relevant office of the applicant's country.

Copyright law and its history

The modern concept of copyright can be traced back to 1710 and the "Statute of Anne", which applied to England, Scotland, and Wales. Prior to this Act, governments had granted monopoly rights to publishers to produce works, but the 1710 Act was the first time that a right of ownership was acknowledged for the actual creator of a work.

From the outset, the attempt to protect the creator's rights was beset with problems due to the local nature of the laws, which applied in Britain only. This meant that lots of copyrighted works were reproduced without the permission of the author in Ireland, America, and in European countries. This not only hindered the ability of the London publishers to sell their legitimate copies of their books in these territories, but the unauthorised reproductions would also find their way into Britain, harming the home market as well.

A natural progression for copyright law was therefore its internationalisation, beginning in 1846 with a reciprocal agreement between Britain and Prussia, and culminating in a series of international treaties, the principal of which is the Berne Convention, which applies to over 160 countries.

Traditionally in the United Kingdom and the United States there has been a requirement to register a work with an official body in order to be able to claim copyright over it (Stationers Hall and the US Library of Congress respectively), however this has been changed by the Berne Convention, which requires signatory countries to grant copyright as an automatic right: i.e. the creator of a work immediately owns its copyright by virtue of creating it and recording it in some physical way (for instance by writing it down or making a recording of it, etc.). The United Kingdom and the United States have both been slow to fully adopt this approach. Though the United Kingdom signed the Berne Convention in 1887, it took 100 years for it to be fully implemented by the Copyright Designs and Patents Act 1988. The United States did not even sign the convention until 1989.

In the United States the US Library of Congress continues to provide archiving services for the purposes of copyright protection, but these are now optional. US citizens no longer need to register their work in order to be able to claim copyright over it. It is necessary, however, to be able to prove when the person who created it did so, and this is essentially the purpose of the registration today. In the United Kingdom, Stationers Hall has ceased to exist, and there is no longer any state-run means of registering the copyright to unpublished works, leaving the only available options as independent and/or international solutions such as the copyright registration service provided by the IP Rights Office.

Registering your work for copyright protection

Registering your work for copyright protection can help you protect your rights in relation to your work. Generally (particularly if you live in a Berne Convention country, as most people do) registration will not be compulsory in order to have rights over your work. Any time you create a unique original work you will in theory own the copyright over it, however you will need to be able to prove when you created it, which is the purpose of registering your work for copyright protection. There are other ways in which you might attempt to prove this, but registration provides better evidence than most other forms.

There are a range of different options for protecting your copyright that vary depending on where you live and the kind of coverage you want. Some countries, like the United States, provide internal means of registering the copyright of unpublished works, however the scope of these will tend to be restricted to the country in question. Other countries, like the United Kingdom, do not offer any specific government-sponsored system for registering the copyright of unpublished works. An international option is provided by the Intellectual Property Rights Office, which is not affiliated to any particular government or country. As long as you live in a Berne Convention country you should be able to benefit from using their Copyright Registration Service. You can register your work with the Intellectual Property Rights Office regardless of whether or not there are any specific arrangements in your home country (you may even choose to register with both to offer your work greater protection). Registration with the Intellectual Property Rights Office should provide you with protection throughout the area covered by the Berne Convention, which is most of the world.

Registering your work for copyright protection through the Intellectual Property Rights Office is an online process that can be completed in a few minutes, provided you have your file in an accepted format and your file isn't too large (if your file is too large and cannot be reduced you may have to split it and take out two or more registrations covering it). There is a registration fee to pay ($45 / £25 / €40 at the time of writing) per file for registration, however if you are a subscriber to **firstwriter.com** you can benefit from a 10% discount when you start the registration process on our site.

When registering your work, you will need to give some consideration to what your work actually consists of. This is a straightforward question if your work is a novel, or a screenplay, but if it is a collection of poetry or short stories then the issue is more difficult. Should you register your collection as one file, or register each poem separately, which would be more expensive? Usually, you can answer this question by asking yourself what you propose to do with your collection. Do you intend to submit it to publishers as a collection only? Or do you intend to send the constituent parts separately to individual magazines? If the former is the case, then register the collection as a single work under the title of the collection. If the latter is the case then this could be unwise, as your copyright registration certificate will give the name of the collection only – which will not match the names of the individual poems or stories. If you can afford to, you should therefore register them separately. If you have so many poems and / or stories to register that you cannot afford to register them all separately, then registering them as a collection will be better than nothing.

Proper use of the copyright symbol

The first thing to note is that for copyright there is only one form of the symbol (©), unlike trade marks, where there is a symbol for registered trade marks (®) and a symbol for unregistered trade marks (™).

To qualify for use of the registered trade mark symbol (®) you must register your trade mark with the appropriate authority in your country, whereas the trade mark symbol (™) can be applied to any symbol you are using as a trade mark. Use of the copyright symbol is more similar to use of the trade mark symbol, as work does not need to be registered in order to use it.

You can place the copyright symbol on any original piece of work you have created. The normal format would be to include alongside the copyright symbol the year of first publication and the name of the copyright holder, however there are no particular legal requirements regarding this. While it has historically been a requirement in some jurisdictions to include a copyright notice on a work in order to be able to claim copyright over it, the Berne Convention does not allow such restrictions, and so any country signed up to the convention no longer has this requirement. However, in some jurisdictions failure to include such a notice can affect the damages you may be able to claim if anyone infringes your copyright.

A similar situation exists in relation to the phrase "All Rights Reserved". This phrase was a requirement in order to claim international copyright protection in countries signed up to the 1910 Buenos Aires Convention. However, since all countries signed up to the Buenos Aires Convention are now also signed up to the Berne Convention (which grants automatic copyright) this phrase has become superfluous. The phrase continues to be used frequently but is unlikely to have any legal consequences.

The Berne Convention

The Berne Convention covers 162 of the approximately 190 countries in the world, including most major nations. Countries which are signed up to the convention are compelled to offer the same protection to works created in other signatory nations as they would to works created in their own. Nations not signed up to the Berne Convention may have their own arrangements regarding copyright protection.

You can check if your country is signed up to the Berne Convention at the following website:

- *https://www.CopyrightRegistrationService.com*

The status of your country should be shown automatically on the right side of the screen. If not, you can select your country manually from the drop-down menu near the top right of the page.

Should You Self-Publish

Over recent years there has been an explosion in self-published books, as it has become easier and easier to publish your book yourself. This poses writers with a new quandary: continue to pursue publication through the traditional means, or jump into the world of self-publishing? As the rejections from traditional publishers pile up it can be tempting to reach for the control and certainty of self-publishing. Should you give into the temptation, or stick to your guns?

Isn't it just vanity publishing?

Modern self-publishing is quite different from the vanity publishing of times gone by. A vanity publisher would often pose or at least seek to appear to be a traditional publisher, inviting submissions and issuing congratulatory letters of acceptance to everyone who submitted – only slowly revealing the large fees the author would have to pay to cover the cost of printing the books.

Once the books were printed, the vanity publisher would deliver them to the author then cut and run. The author would be left with a big hole in their pocket and a mountain of boxes of books that they would be unlikely to ever sell a fraction of.

Modern self-publishing, on the other hand, is provided not by shady dealers but by some of the biggest companies involved in the publishing industry, including Penguin and Amazon. It doesn't have the large fees that vanity publishing did (depending on the path you choose and your own knowledge and technical ability it can cost almost nothing to get your book published); it *does* offer a viable means of selling your books (they can appear on the biggest bookselling websites around the world); and it *doesn't* leave you with a house full of unwanted books, because modern technology means that a copy of your book only gets printed when it's actually ordered.

That isn't to say that there aren't still shady characters out there trying to take advantage of authors' vanity by charging them enormous fees for publishing a book that stands very little chance of success, but it does mean that self-publishing – done right – can be a viable and cost effective way of an author taking their book to market.

The benefits of self-publishing

The main benefit of self-publishing, of course, is that the author gets control of whether their book is published or not. There is no need to spend years submitting to countless agents and publishers, building up countless heartbreaking rejection letters, and possibly accepting in the end that your dreams of publication will never come true – you can make them come true.

And this need not be pure vanity on the author's part. Almost every successful book – even such massive hits as *Harry Potter* – usually build up a string of rejections before someone finally accepts them. The professionals that authors rely on when going through the traditional publishing process – the literary agents and the editors – are often, it seems, just not that good at spotting what the public are going to buy. How many potential bestsellers might languish forever in the slush pile, just because agents and editors fail to spot them? What if your book is one of them? The traditional publishing process forces you to rely on the good judgment of others, but the self-publishing process enables you to sidestep that barrier and take your book directly to the public, so that readers can decide for themselves.

Self-publishing also allows you to keep control in other areas. You won't have an editor trying to change your text, and you'll have complete control over what kind of cover your book receives.

Finally, with no publisher or team of editors and accountants taking their slice, you'll probably get to keep a lot more of the retail price of every book you sell. So if you can sell the same amount of books as if you were traditionally published, you'll stand to make a lot more money.

The drawbacks of self-publishing

While self-publishing can guarantee that your book will be available for sale, it cannot guarantee that it will actually sell. Your self-published book will probably have a much lower chance of achieving significant sales than if it had been published traditionally, because it will lack the support that a mainstream publisher could bring. You will have no marketing support, no established position in the marketplace, and no PR – unless you do it yourself. You will have to arrange your own book tours; you will have to do your own sales pitches; you will have to set your own pricing structure; and you will have to manage your own accounts and tax affairs. If you're selling through Amazon or Smashwords or Apple (and if you're not, then why did you bother self-publishing in the first place?) you're going to need to fill in the relevant forms with the IRS (the US tax office) – whether you're a US citizen or not. If you're not a US citizen then you'll have to register with the IRS and complete the necessary tax forms, and potentially other forms for claiming treaty benefits so that you don't get taxed twice (in the US and your home country). And then of course you'll also have to register for tax purposes in your home nation and complete your own tax return there (though you would also have to do this as a traditionally published author).

It can all get very complicated, very confusing, and very lonely. Instead of being able to just be a writer you can find yourself writing less and less and becoming more and more embroiled in the business of publishing a book.

And while it's great to have control over your text and your cover, you'd be ill advised to ignore the value that professionals such as editors and cover designers can bring. It's tempting to think that you don't need an editor – that you've checked the book and had a friend or family member check it too, so it's probably fine – but a professional editor brings a totally different mindset to the process and will check things that won't have even occurred to you and your reader. Without a professional editor, you will almost certainly end up publishing a book which is full of embarrassing mistakes, and trust me – there is no feeling quite as deflating as opening up the first copy of your freshly printed book to see an obvious error jump out – or, even worse, to have it pointed out in an Amazon review, for all to see.

The cover is also incredibly important. Whether for sale on the shelf or on a website, the cover is normally the first point of contact your potential reader has with your book, and will cause them to form immediate opinions about it. A good cover can help a book sell well, but a bad one can kill its chances – and all too often self-published books have amateurish covers that will have readers flicking past them without a second glance.

Claim your free access to www.firstwriter.com: See p.403

Finally, the financial benefits of self-publishing can often be illusory. For starters, getting a higher proportion of the retail price is pretty irrelevant if you don't sell any copies. Fifty per cent of nothing is still nothing. Far better to have 15% of something. And then there's the advances. Advances are up-front payments made by traditional publishers to authors, which are off-set against future royalties. So, an author might receive a $5,000 advance before their book is published. When the royalties start coming in, the publisher keeps the first $5,000 to off-set the advance. The good news for the author is that if the book flops and doesn't make $5,000 in royalties they still get to keep the full advance. In an uncertain profession, the security of an advance can be invaluable for an author – and of course it's not something available to self-published authors.

Conclusion

Self-publishing can seem like a tempting shortcut to publication, but in reality it has its own challenges and difficulties. For the moment at least, traditional publishing still offers you the best shot of not only financial success, but also quality of life as a writer. With other people to handle all the other elements of publishing, you get to concentrate on doing what you love.

So we think that writers should always aim for traditional publishing first. It might be a long shot, but if it works then you stand a much better chance of being successful. If you don't manage to get signed by an agent or a publisher then you still have the option of self-publishing, but make sure you don't get tempted to resort to self-publishing too soon – most agents and publishers won't consider self-published works, so this is a one-way street. Once you've self-published your work, you probably won't be able to change your mind and go back to the traditional publishers with your book unless it becomes a huge hit without them. It's therefore important that you exhaust all your traditional publishing options before making the leap to self-publishing. Be prepared for this to take perhaps a few years (lots of agents and publishers can take six months just to respond), and make sure you've submitted to everyone you can on *both* sides of the Atlantic (publishing is a global game these days, and you need to concentrate on the two main centres of English-language publishing (New York and London) equally) before you make the decision to self-publish instead.

However, once you have exhausted all options for traditional publishing, modern self-publishing does offer a genuine alternative path to success, and there are a growing number of self-published authors who have managed to sell millions of copies of their books. If you don't think traditional publishing is going to be an option, we definitely think you should give self-publishing a shot.

For directions on your path through the traditional publishing process see our Writers' Roadmap, above.

If you're sure you've already exhausted all your options for traditional publishing then see below for our quick guide to the self-publishing process.

The Self Publishing Process

Thinking about self-publishing your book? Make sure you go through all these steps first – and in the right order! Do them the wrong way round and you could find yourself wasting time and/or money.

1. Be sure you want to self-publish

You need to be 100% sure that you want to self-publish, because after you've done it there is no going back. Publishers and literary agents will not normally consider books that have been self-published, so if you wanted to get your book to print the old fashioned way you should stop now and rethink. Make absolutely sure that you've exhausted every possible opportunity for traditional publishing before you head down the self-publishing path.

For more information, see "Why choose traditional publishing?" and "Should you self-publish?", above.

2. Protect your copyright

Authors often wonder about what stage in the process they should protect their copyright – often thinking that it's best to leave it till the end so that there are no more changes to make to the book after it is registered.

However, this isn't the case. The key thing is to protect your work before you let other people see it – or, if you've already let other people see it, as soon as possible thereafter.

Don't worry about making small changes to your work after registering it – as long as the work is still recognisable as the same piece of work it will still be protected. Obviously, if you completely change everything you've written then you're going to need another registration, as it will effectively be a different book, but if you've just edited it and made minor alterations this won't affect your protection.

You can register you copyright online at https://www.copyrightregistrationservice.com.

3. Get your work edited

Editing is a vital step often overlooked by authors who self-publish. The result can often be an amateurish book littered with embarrassing mistakes. Any professionally published book will go through an editing process, and it's important that the same applies to your self-published book. It's also important to complete the editing process before beginning the layout, or you could find yourself having to start the layout again from scratch.

4. Choose your self-publishing path

Before you can go any further you are going to need to choose a size for your book, and in order to do that you are going to need to choose a self-publishing path.

There are various different ways of getting self-published, but in general these range from the expensive hands off approach, where you pay a company to do the hard work for you, to the cheap DIY approach, where you do as much as you can yourself.

At the top end, the hands off approach can cost you thousands. At the bottom end, the DIY approach allows you to publish your book for almost nothing.

5. Finalise your layout / typesetting

Before you can finalise your layout (often referred to in the industry as "typesetting") you need to be sure that you've finalised your content – which means having your full work professionally edited and all the necessary changes made. If you decide to make changes after this point it will be difficult and potentially costly, and will require you to go through many of the following steps all over again.

You also need to have selected your path to publication, so that you know what page sizes are available to you, and what page margins you are going to need to apply. If you create a layout that doesn't meet printing requirements (for instance, includes text too close to the edge of the page) then you will have to start the typesetting process all over again.

6. Organise your ISBN

Your book needs to have an ISBN. If you are using a self-publishing service then they may provide you with one of their own, but it is likely to come with restrictions, and the international record for your book will show your self-publishing service as the publisher.

You can acquire your own ISBNs directly from the ISBN issuer, but they do not sell them individually, so you will end up spending quite a lot of money buying more ISBNs than you need. You will, however, have control of the ISBN, and you will be shown as the publisher.

Alternatively, you can purchase a single ISBN at a lower price from an ISBN retailer. This should give you control over the ISBN, however the record for the book will show the ISBN retailer as the publisher, which you may not consider to be ideal.

Whatever you choose, you need to arrange your ISBN no later than this point, because it needs to appear in the preliminary pages (prelims) of your book.

7. Compile your prelims

Your prelims may include a variety of pages, but should always include a title page, a half title page, and an imprint/copyright page. You might then also include other elements, such as a foreword, table of contents, etc. You can only compile your table of contents at this stage, because you need to know your ISBN (this will be included on the copyright/imprint page) and the page numbers for your table of contents. You therefore need to make sure that you are happy with the typesetting and have no further changes to make before compiling your prelims.

8. Create your final press proof

Depending on the self-publishing path you have chosen, you may be able to use a Word file as your final document. However, you need to be careful. In order to print your book it will have to be converted into a press-ready PDF at some point. If a self-publishing service is doing this for you then you will probably find that they own the PDF file that is created, meaning you don't have control over your own press files. Some services will impose hefty charges (hundreds or even more than a thousand dollars) to release these press files.

It might also be the case that you won't get to see the final PDF, and therefore won't get chance to check it for any errors introduced by the conversion process. If it's an automated system, it may also be difficult to control the output you get from it.

We'd suggest that it's best to produce your own PDF files if possible. To do this you will need a copy of Adobe Acrobat Professional, and you will need to be familiar with the correct settings for creating print ready PDFs. Be careful to embed all fonts and make sure that all images are at 300 DPI.

9. Create your cover

Only once your press proof is finalised can you complete your cover design. That's because your cover includes not only the front cover and the back cover, but also (critically) the spine – and the width of the spine will vary according to the number of pages in your final press proof. In order to complete your cover design you therefore need to know your page size, your page count (including all prelims), and your ISBN, as this will appear on the back cover. You also need to get a barcode for your ISBN.

10. Produce your book

Once your cover and press proof are ready you can go through whichever self-publishing path you have chosen to create your book. With some pathways the production of a print proof can be an optional extra that is only available at an extra cost – but we'd recommend standing that cost and getting a print version of your book to check. You never know exactly how it's going to come out until you have a physical copy in your hand.

If you're happy with the proof you can clear your book for release. You don't need to do anything to get it on online retailers like Amazon – they will automatically pick up the ISBN and add your book to their websites themselves.

11. Create an ebook version

In the modern day, having an ebook version of your book is imperative. Ebooks account for a significant proportion of all book sales and are a particularly effective vehicle for unknown and self-published authors.

There are various different file formats used by the different platforms, but .epub is emerging as a standard, and having your book in .epub format should enable you to access all the platforms with a single file.

12. Distribute your ebook

Unlike with print books, you will need to act yourself to get your ebooks into sales channels. At a minimum, you need to ensure that you get your ebook available for sale through Amazon, Apple, and Google Play.

Table of US Literary Agencies

3 Seas Literary Agency	L001
Above the Line Agency	L003
Ahearn Agency, Inc, The	L011
Alive Literary Agency	L018
Ambassador Speakers Bureau & Literary Agency	L019
Ayesha Pande Literary	L036
Barone Literary Agency	L043
Baror International, Inc.	L044
Bent Agency, The	L058
Betsy Amster Literary Enterprises	L063
Bradford Literary Agency	L075
Brattle Agency LLC, The	L080
Bright Agency (US), The	L083
Browne & Miller Literary Associates	L089
CAA (Creative Artists Agency, LLC)	L097
Carol Mann Agency	L105
Carolyn Jenks Agency	L107
Chase Literary Agency	L118
Cyle Young Literary Elite	L149
Cynthia Cannell Literary Agency	L150
Dana Newman Literary, LLC	L152
Darhansoff & Verrill Literary Agents	L156
Diana Finch Literary Agency	L167
Don Congdon Associates, Inc.	L175
Donald Maass Literary Agency	L176
Doug Grad Literary Agency	L177
Dunham Literary, Inc.	L179
Dunow, Carlson & Lerner Agency	L184
Ekus Group, The	L193
Elaine Markson Literary Agency	L195
Evan Marshall Agency, The	L202
Fairbank Literary Representation	L208
Felicia Eth Literary Representation	L214
Flannery Literary	L228
Frances Collin Literary Agent	L237
Frances Goldin Literary Agency, Inc.	L238
Friedrich Agency LLC, The	L245
Garamond Agency, Inc., The	L253
Ginger Clark Literary	L260
Glass Literary Management LLC	L262
Global Lion Intellectual Property Management, Inc.	L264
Gurman Agency, LLC	L285
Harold Ober Associates, Inc.	L298
HG Literary	L310
High Line Literary Collective	L312
Inscriptions Literary Agency	L323
Irene Goodman Literary Agency (IGLA)	L324
Jeff Herman Agency, LLC, The	L331
Joelle Delbourgo Associates, Inc.	L334
Joy Harris Literary Agency, Inc.	L340
Kathryn Green Literary Agency, LLC	L354
Kimberley Cameron & Associates	L369
KT Literary	L377
Langtons International	L384
Leigh Feldman Literary	L393
Liza Dawson Associates	L405
Looking Glass Literary & Media Management	L406
Lotus Lane Literary	L407
MacGregor & Luedeke	L414
McCormick Literary	L436
Metamorphosis Literary Agency	L444
Mildred Marmur Associates, Ltd.	L450
Movable Type Management	L464
Nelson Literary Agency, LLC	L477
Olswanger Literary LLC	L490
Paradigm Talent and Literary Agency	L498
Paul S. Levine Literary Agency	L502
Perry Literary	L509
Regina Ryan Books	L531
Richard Curtis Associates, Inc.	L536
also	L298
Root Literary	L547
Rosenberg Group, The	L549
Rubin Pfeffer Content, LLC	L552
Rudy Agency, The	L553
Sarah Jane Freymann Literary Agency	L564
Selectric Artists	L573
Sheree Bykofsky Associates, Inc.	L579
Sterling Lord Literistic, Inc.	L597
Sternig & Byrne Literary Agency	L598
Strachan Literary Agency	L602
Stringer Literary Agency LLC, The	L603
Strothman Agency, The	L607
Stuart Krichevsky Literary Agency, Inc.	L609
Susan Schulman Literary Agency	L610
Victoria Sanders & Associates LLC	L642
Wallace Literary Agency, The	L024
Wordserve Literary	L673
Zack Company, Inc, The	L678

Table of UK Literary Agencies

A.M. Heath & Company Limited, Author's Agents ... L002
Aevitas Creative Management (ACM) UK ... L007
Agency (London) Ltd, The ... L009
AHA Talent Ltd ... L010
Alan Brodie Representation ... L013
Alice Williams Literary ... L017
Andrew Nurnberg Associates, Ltd ... L024
Anne Clark Literary Agency ... L028
Antony Harwood Limited ... L029
AVAnti Productions & Management ... L035
Bath Literary Agency ... L049
Bent Agency (UK), The ... L057
 also ... L058
BKS Agency, The ... L065
Blake Friedmann Literary Agency Ltd ... L066
Bookseeker Agency ... L070
Bright Agency (UK), The ... L082
Brotherstone Creative Management ... L085
C&W (Conville & Walsh) ... L096
CAA (London) ... L098
 also ... L097
Canterbury Literary Agency ... L101
Caroline Sheldon Literary Agency ... L106
 also ... L546
Colwill & Peddle ... L131
Coombs Moylett & Maclean Literary Agency ... L139
Curtis Brown ... L146
Darley Anderson Agency, The ... L157
David Godwin Associates ... L158
David Higham Associates Ltd ... L159
DHH Literary Agency Ltd ... L166
DunnFogg ... L182
Eddison Pearson Ltd ... L188
Elaine Steel ... L196
Emily Sweet Associates ... L199
Eunice McMullen Children's Literary Agent Ltd ... L201
Feldstein Agency, The ... L213
Felicity Bryan Associates ... L215
Fillingham Weston Associates ... L222
for Authors, A ... L231
FRA (Futerman, Rose, & Associates) ... L236
Fraser Ross Associates ... L240
Frog Literary Agency ... L246
Good Literary Agency, The ... L269
Graham Maw Christie Literary Agency ... L271
Greene & Heaton Ltd ... L276
Greyhound Literary ... L278
Hanbury Agency, The ... L290
Hannah Sheppard Literary Agency ... L291
Hardman & Swainson ... L294
Janklow & Nesbit UK Ltd ... L330
JFL Agency ... L332
Jo Unwin Literary Agency ... L333
Johnson & Alcock ... L335
Jonathan Clowes Ltd ... L336
Jonathan Pegg Literary Agency ... L337
Judith Murdoch Literary Agency ... L341
Judy Daish Associates Ltd ... L342
Julie Crisp Literary Agency ... L343
Kane Literary Agency ... L348
Kate Barker Literary, TV, & Film Agency ... L352
Kate Nash Literary Agency ... L353
Keane Kataria Literary Agency ... L358
Ki Agency Ltd ... L364
Knight Features ... L373
Kruger Cowne ... L376
Laxfield Literary Associates ... L387
Lewinsohn Literary ... L397
Limelight Management ... L400
Lindsay Literary Agency ... L401
Liverpool Literary Agency, The ... L404
Lutyens and Rubinstein ... L410
Madeleine Milburn Literary, TV & Film Agency ... L420
Marsh Agency, The ... L426
Mic Cheetham Literary Agency ... L445
MMB Creative ... L455
Northbank Talent Management ... L482
Originate Literary Agency ... L492
Perez Literary & Entertainment ... L506
Portobello Literary ... L521
Rachel Mills Literary ... L527
Rebecca Carter Literary ... L529
Redhammer ... L530
Robert Smith Literary Agency Ltd ... L539
Robertson Murray Literary Agency ... L541
Rochelle Stevens & Co. ... L543
Rocking Chair Books ... L544
Rogers, Coleridge & White Ltd ... L546
Rupert Crew Ltd ... L554
Ruppin Agency, The ... L555
Sayle Literary Agency, The ... L565
Sebes & Bisseling ... L572
Shaw Agency, The ... L576
Sheil Land Associates Ltd ... L577
Shesto Literary ... L580
Sophie Hicks Agency ... L591
Spring Literary ... L594
StoryWise ... L601
SYLA – Susan Yearwood Literary Agency ... L616
Tennyson Agency, The ... L622
Teresa Chris Literary Agency Ltd ... L623
Theseus Agency, The ... L627
Two Piers Literary Agency, The ... L636
Valerie Hoskins Associates ... L640
Viney Agency, The ... L643
Watson, Little Ltd ... L647
Whispering Buffalo Literary Agency ... L657
YMU Books ... L676
Zeno Agency ... L680

Table of US Literary Agents

Abellera, Lisa L369	Carr, Heather L245	Ekus, Sally L194
Acheampong, Kwaku L004	Carr, Jamie L108	also L193
also L107	Carr, Michael L109	Ellor, Zabé L198
Adams, Lisa L253	Carson, Lucy L245	Ericka T. Phillips L200
Ahearn, Pamela G. L011	Chanchani, Sonali L115	Esersky, Gareth L105
Alekseii, Keir L015	Chase, Farley L119	Eth, Felicia L214
Ambrosi, Beniamino L020	also L118	Evans, Stephany L206
Amling, Eric L021	Cheney, Elyse L121	also L036
also L156	Chiotti, Danielle L123	Fabien, Samantha L207
Amster, Betsy L063	Christensen, Erica L125	also L547
Andrade, Hannah L023	also L444	Fairbank, Sorche Elizabeth L208
also L075	Chromy, Adam L464	Fazzari, Hillary L210
Arms, Victoria Wells L031	Cichello, Kayla L127	also L075
also L310	Clark, Ginger L260	Feldman, Leigh L211
Bajek, Lauren L037	Cloughley, Amy L369	also L393
also L405	Cobb, Jon L310	Feldmann, Kait Lee L212
Baker-Baughman, Bernadette L642	Collin, Frances L237	also L377
Balow, Dan L039	Combemale, Chris L133	Ferguson, T.S. L218
Barbara, Stephen L041	also L597	Figueroa, Melanie L221
Barone, Denise L043	Comparato, Andrea L134	also L547
Baror, Danny L044	also L323	Finch, Diana L224
Baror-Shapiro, Heather L044	Concepcion, Cristina L135	also L167
Barr, Anjanette L045	also L175	Flannery, Jennifer L228
also L179	Congdon, Michael L175	Flum, Caitie L405
Bartlett, Bruce L003	Cooper, Gemma L140	Flynn, Amy Thrall L229
Bauman, Erica L050	also L058	Foster, Roz L238
Baumer, Jan L051	Cooper, Maggie L141	Fox, Aram L234
Beck, Rachel L405	Crandall, Becca L142	Frankel, Valerie L239
Bell, Madison Smartt L036	also L107	Freedman, Robert L241
Bent, Jenny L059	Cross, Claudia L143	Freese, Sarah Joy L673
also L058	Curry, Michael L176	Freymann, Sarah Jane L242
Berdinsky, Kendall L060	Curtis, Richard L536	also L564
Bernardi, Amanda L062	Cusick, John L148	Friedman, Claire L243
also L312	Dail, Laura L151	Friedman, Jessica L597
Bewley, Elizabeth L597	Danaczko, Melissa L153	Friedman, Rebecca L244
Blasdell, Caitlin L405	also L609	Friedrich, Molly L245
Boeving, Keely L673	Danko, Margaret L154	Fuentes, Sarah L247
Boker, Sidney L067	also L312	Galvin, Lori L252
Borstel, Stefanie Sanchez Von L071	Darga, Jon Michael L155	Geiger, Ellen L255
Bowlin, Sarah L073	Darhansoff, Liz L156	also L238
Bowman, Hannah L405	Datz, Arielle L184	Gerecke, Jeff L195
Bradford, Laura L076	Dawson, Liza L162	Getzler, Josh L256
also L075	also L405	also L310
Brailsford, Karen L077	Decker, Stacia L184	Ghahremani, Lilly L257
Brattesani, Hannah L079	Delbourgo, Joelle L334	Gilbert, Tara L258
also L245	Derviskadic, Dado L164	also L377
Brewer, Amy L081	Devereux, Allison L165	Gisondi, Katie L261
also L444	Deyoe, Cori L001	Glass, Alex L262
Brooks, Savannah L084	Dickerson, Donya L168	Goetz, Adria L265
also L377	Dijkstra, Sandra L169	also L377
Brophy, Philippa L597	Dominguez, Adriana L174	Goff, Ellen L267
Brouckaert, Justin L087	Doraswamy, Priya L407	also L310
Brown, Megan L088	Draper, Claire L178	Goldstein, Veronica L268
Bucci, Chris L090	Duduit, Del L149	Goloboy, Jennifer L176
Bukowski, Danielle L092	Dunham, Jennie L180	Goodman, Irene L324
also L597	also L179	Grad, Doug L177
Burkhart, Megan L149	Dunow, Henry L184	Graham, Stacey L272
Burl, Emelie L610	Eaglin, Adam L185	also L001
Bykofsky, Sheree L579	Eason, Lynette L186	Grajkowski, Kara L273
Byrne, Jack L598	Eberly, Chelsea L187	also L001
Cameron, Kimberley L369	Egan-Miller, Danielle L089	Grajkowski, Michelle L274
Campos, Vanessa L100	Eisenbraun, Nicole L191	also L001
Cannell, Cynthia L150	also L260	Granger, David L275
Cappello, Victoria L102	Eisenmann, Caroline L192	Green, Kathryn L354
also L058	also L238	Greer, Rima L003
Capron, Elise L104	Ekus, Lisa L193	Grimm, Katie L279
Carlson, Jennifer L184		also L175

Claim your free access to www.firstwriter.com: See p.403

Grossman, Loren R.	L280	Lakosil, Natalie	L379	Nadol, Jen	L472
also	L502	also	L406	Napolitano, Maria	L473
Gruber, Pam	L281	Landis, Sarah	L381	also	L377
also	L312	also	L597	Nasson, Melissa	L552
Guinsler, Robert	L283	Langton, Linda	L384	Necarsulmer, Edward	L184
also	L597	Latshaw, Katherine	L386	Nelson, Kristin	L478
Gunic, Masha	L284	Lazin, Sarah	L388	also	L477
Gurman, Susan	L286	Lechon, Shannon	L390	Newman, Dana	L152
also	L285	Lerner, Betsy	L184	Nguyen, Kiana	L176
Haggerty, Taylor	L287	Levine, Paul S.	L395	Nichols, Mariah	L479
also	L547	also	L502	Niumata, Erin	L480
Hakim, Serene	L288	Levitt, Sarah	L396	Nolan, Laura	L481
also	L036	Lewis, Alison	L398	Norman, Bryan	L018
Haley, Jolene	L289	also	L238	Nyen, Renee	L483
also	L176	Lightner, Kayla	L399	also	L377
Hall, Tessa Emily	L149	also	L036	O'Brien, Lee	L484
Hannigan, Carrie	L292	Liss, Laurie	L403	also	L406
also	L310	also	L597	O'Neill, Molly	L487
Hansen, Stephanie	L293	Lovell, Jake	L409	also	L547
also	L444	Luedeke, Amanda	L414	Ogtrop, Kristin van	L489
Harmsworth, Esmond	L297	Maass, Donald	L176	Olswanger, Anna	L491
Harper, Logan	L299	MacGregor, Chip	L414	also	L490
Harris, Erin	L300	Mack, Kate	L415	Orloff, Edward	L436
Harris, Joy	L340	MacKenzie, Joanna	L416	Orsini, Mark	L493
Harrison, Nick	L673	also	L477	Ostashevsky, Luba	L036
Harwell, Hilary	L301	MacLeod, Lauren	L418	Ostby, Kristin	L494
also	L377	also	L607	Ostler, Bruce	L495
Haug, Jack	L302	Madan, Neeti	L419	Pages, Saribel	L496
Hawk, Susan	L303	also	L597	Pande, Ayesha	L497
Hensley, Chelsea	L307	Maffei, Dorian	L369	also	L036
also	L377	Maltese, Alyssa	L422	Parker, Elana Roth	L499
Herman, Deborah Levine	L331	also	L547	Patterson, David	L609
Herman, Jeff	L331	Mann, Carol	L105	Patterson, Emma	L501
Hernando, Paloma	L308	Marini, Victoria	L423	Perel, Kim	L505
Heymont, Lane	L309	also	L312	also	L312
Hoffman, Scott	L316	Marmur, Mildred	L424	Perry, Joseph	L509
Hogrebe, Christina	L317	also	L450	Pestritto, Carrie	L511
Hosier, Erin	L184	Marr, Jill	L425	Pfeffer, Rubin	L513
Hwang, Annie	L322	Marshall, Evan	L202	also	L552
also	L036	Marshall, Jen	L427	Phelan, Beth	L514
Jackson, Amanda Hepp	L327	Marsiglia, Caroline	L428	Phillips, Aemilia	L515
Jackson, Eleanor	L184	Massie, Maria	L430	also	L609
Jackson, Jennifer	L176	Matson, Peter	L597	Pine, Gideon	L518
Jackson, Lisa	L018	Matte, Rebecca	L431	Plant, Zoe	L519
Jacobson, Rachel	L328	also	L075	also	L058
also	L018	Mattson, Jennifer	L432	Posner, Marcy	L522
Jenks, Carolyn	L107	Maurer, Shari	L433	Praeger, Marta	L524
Johnson, Greg	L673	also	L603	Prasanna, Tanusri	L525
Jones, Barbara	L338	McBride, Juliana	L435	Queen, Pilar	L436
also	L609	McCarthy, Bridget	L436	Ramer, Susan	L528
Kahn, Jody	L346	McClure, Cameron	L176	also	L175
Kantor, Camille	L349	McCormick, David	L436	Reed, Adam	L340
also	L369	McDonald, Caitlin	L176	Reid, Janet	L532
Kardon, Julia	L350	McGowan, Matt	L238	Reino, Jessica	L534
also	L310	McNicol, Andy	L437	also	L444
Karinch, Maryann	L351	McQuilkin, Rob	L438	Richesin, Nicki	L184
also	L553	Megibow, Sara	L439	Richter, Rick	L537
Kean, Taylor Martindale	L357	also	L377	Roberts, Soumeya Bendimerad	L540
Kellerman, Carly	L360	Mehren, Jane von	L440	also	L310
also	L018	Mendia, Isabel	L441	Robinson, Quressa	L542
Kenny, Julia	L361	Mileo, Jessica	L451	Rofe, Jennifer	L545
also	L184	Miller, Tom	L405	Root, Holly	L548
Kerr, Kat	L176	Milusich, Grace	L453	also	L547
Kerr, Kathleen	L363	also	L406	Rosenberg, Barbara Collins	L550
also	L018	Miranda, Caroline	L454	also	L549
Kim, Jennifer	L366	also	L175	Ross, Whitney	L551
Knigge, Sheyla	L372	Moore, Mary C.	L457	also	L312
also	L312	Moore, Penny	L458	Rushall, Kathleen	L556
Kotchman, Katie	L374	Moorhead, Max	L459	Rutman, Jim	L558
also	L175	Morris, Natascha	L461	also	L597
Kracht, Elizabeth	L369	Mortimer, Michele	L462	Ryan, Regina	L531
Krichevsky, Stuart	L609	also	L156	Salazar, Des	L559
Krienke, Mary	L375	Murgolo, Karen	L467	also	L444
also	L597	Muscato, Nate	L469	Salvo, Katie	L560
Kye-Casella, Maura	L175	Mustelier, James	L471	also	L444
		also	L058		

Sanchez, Kaitlyn	L561
also	L075
Sanders, Rayhane	L562
Sanders, Victoria	L642
Sant, Kelly Van	L563
also	L377
Schelling, Christopher	L573
Schulman, Susan	L610
Schwartz, Hannah	L609
Schwartz, Steve	L568
also	L564
Seidman, Yishai	L184
Shreve, Jeff	L569
Signorelli, Michael	L582
Silbersack, John	L058
Silver, Janet	L584
Siobhan, Aiden	L587
Sluytman, Antoinette Van	L588
also	L406
Soler, Shania N.	L589
also	L444
Soloway, Jennifer March	L590
Sorg, Arley	L592
also	L377
Stephens, Jenny	L596
also	L597
Stewart, Douglas	L599
also	L597
Stoloff, Sam	L238
Stone, Geoffrey	L600
also	L553
Strachan, Laura	L602
Stringer, Marlene	L604
also	L603
Strong, Catharine	L606
Strothman, Wendy	L608
also	L607
Sutherland, Kari	L611
also	L377
Sweren, Becky	L615
Symonds, Laurel	L617
also	L377
Takikawa, Marin	L618
also	L245
Tannenbaum, Amy	L620
Terlip, Paige	L624
Testerman, Kate	L625
also	L377
Thayer, Henry	L626
Tibbets, Anne	L630
also	L176
Tran, Jennifer Chen	L633
also	L262
Trussell, Caroline	L635
also	L444
Udden, Jennifer	L637
Uh, Cindy	L097
Usselman, Laura	L639
also	L609
Vance, Lisa Erbach	L641
Watson, Mackenzie Brady	L609
Watterson, Jessica	L648
Weiman, Paula	L649
Weiss, Alexandra	L650
Weitzner, Tess	L651
also	L238
Weltz, Jennifer	L653
Westin, Erin Casey	L654
Whatnall, Michaela	L655
Whelan, Maria	L656
Whitwham, Alice	L658
Wickers, Chandler	L659
also	L609
Wilson, Desiree	L667
also	L406
Wong-Baxter, Jade	L238
Wyckoff, Joanne	L105
Young, Cyle	L149
Zack, Andrew	L678
Zacker, Marietta B.	L679
Zeppieri, Marisa	L602
Zuraw-Friedland, Ayla	L681
also	L238

Table of UK Literary Agents

Adams, Seren L005
Ahearne, Clementine L012
Alcock, Michael L014
  also L335
Anderson, Darley L022
  also L157
Andrew, Nelle L025
  also L527
Andrew-Lynch, Davinia L026
  also L146
Andrews, Gina L027
  also L009
Apostolides, Zoe L139
Armstrong, Susan L032
  also L096
Arnold, Frances L543
Atyeo, Charlotte L034
  also L278
Ayris, Matilda L096
Bagnell, Becky L401
Bal, Emma L038
  also L420
Barker, Kate L352
Barnard, Arthur L042
  also L009
Barr, Nicola L046
  also L057
Bartholomew, Jason L047
  also L065
Bates, Tim L048
Baxter, Veronique L052
  also L159
Begum, Salma L053
  also L278
Bell, Eva L054
Belton, Maddy L055
  also L420
Bennett, Laura L056
  also L404
Benson, Ian L009
Berlyne, John L061
  also L680
Biltoo, Nicola L009
Blakey, Simon L009
Blofeld, Piers L577
Blunt, Felicity L146
Bolger, Maeve L068
  also L007
Bolton, Camilla L069
  also L157
Boulton, Hannah L009
Bovill, Imogen L072
Brace, Samantha L074
Brannan, Maria L078
  also L278
Brodie, Alan L013
Brotherstone, Charlie L086
  also L007
  also L085
Buckley, Louise L091
  also L291
Burke, Kate L093
  also L066
Burns, Camille L094
Burton, Kate L096
Calder, Rachel L565
Campbell, Charlie L099

  also L278
Caprio, Alice L103
  also L215
Carroll, Megan L110
  also L647
Carter, Rebecca L111
  also L529
Cartey, Claire L112
Caskie, Robert L113
Chang, Nicola L116
  also L159
Charnace, Edwina de L117
  also L455
Cheetham, Mic L120
  also L445
Cho, Catherine L124
  also L096
  also L380
Christie, Jennifer L126
  also L271
Churchill, Julia L002
Clark, Anne L028
Clarke, Caro L128
  also L521
Clarke, Catherine L129
  also L215
Cochran, Alexander L130
  also L096
Coleridge, Gill L546
Colwill, Charlotte L132
  also L131
Conrad, Claire Paterson L136
  also L330
Conville, Clare L137
  also L096
Coombes, Clare L138
  also L404
Copeland, Sam L546
Cox, Peter L530
Crossland, Annette L231
Crowley, Sheila L144
  also L146
Curran, Sabhbh L145
  also L146
Daish, Judy L342
Davies, Elinor L160
  also L420
Davis, Meg L364
DeBlock, Liza L163
DeFrees, Allison L096
Delamere, Hilary L009
Dillsworth, Elise L170
  also L159
Dixon, Isobel L171
  also L066
Dodd, Saffron L172
Doherty, Broo L166
Dolby, Trevor L173
  also L007
Drury, Ian L577
Dunn, Ben L181
  also L159
Dunnicliffe, Neil L183
  also L594
Durbridge, Stephen L009
Edenborough, Sam L189
  also L278

Edwards, Max L190
  also L007
Edwards, Stephen L546
Ellis-Martin, Sian L197
  also L066
Elliston, Tracey L342
Evans, Ann L336
Evans, Bethan L009
Evans, David L203
  also L159
  also L266
  also L270
Evans, Kate L204
Evans, Kiya L205
  also L470
Fairweather, Natasha L546
Faulks, Holly L209
  also L276
Fawcett, Lucy L577
Feldstein, Paul L213
Feldstein, Susan L213
Fellows, Abi L216
  also L166
Ferguson, Hannah L217
  also L294
Fergusson, Julie L219
Fillingham, Janet L222
Finan, Ciara L223
  also L146
Finch, Alison L332
Finch, Rebeka L225
  also L157
Finegan, Stevie L226
  also L680
Finn, Emma L096
Fitzgerald, Bea L227
  also L567
Fitzpatrick, Kara L013
Fogg, Jack L230
  also L182
Forrester, Jemima L232
  also L159
Foster, Clara L233
  also L007
Francis, Will L330
Fraser, Lindsey L240
Gahan, Isobel L250
Galustian, Natalie L251
  also L278
Garrett, Georgia L546
Gauntlett, Adam L254
Geller, Jonny L146
Gillam, Bianca L259
  also L680
Glenister, Emily L263
  also L166
Glover, Georgia L159
Godman, Susannah L410
Godwin, David L158
Goff, Anthony L266
  also L159
Goodall, Bill L231
Gordon, Andrew L270
  also L159
Greenstreet, Katie L277
Grunewald, Hattie L282
Haines, Katie L009

Hamilton, Bill	L002
Hammam, Samar	L544
Hanbury, Margaret	L290
Hardman, Caroline	L295
also	L294
Hare, Jessica	L296
also	L009
Harwood, Antony	L029
Hawn, Molly Ker	L304
also	L057
Hayden, Viola	L305
also	L146
Headley, David H.	L306
also	L166
Heaton, Carol	L276
Heller, Jenny	L541
Hewson, Andrew	L335
Hewson, Jenny	L546
Hickman, Emily	L311
also	L009
Hicks, Sophie	L591
Hobbs, Victoria	L314
also	L002
Hodges, Jodie	L315
Holloway, Sally	L318
also	L215
Holroyd, Penny	L319
Hordern, Kate	L320
Hornsley, Sarah	L321
also	L470
Hoskins, Valerie	L640
Howard, Amanda Fitzalan	L010
Illingworth, Harry	L166
Irvine, Lucy	L325
Irving, Dotti	L326
also	L278
Jamieson, Molly	L329
also	L315
Jones, Cara	L546
Jones, Philip Gwyn	L339
also	L278
Jones, Rebecca	L546
Kahn, Ella Diamond	L345
Kaliszewska, Joanna	L347
also	L065
Kania, Carrie	L096
Kataria, Kiran	L358
Kavanagh, Jade	L355
also	L157
Kavanagh, Simon	L356
also	L445
Keane, Sara	L358
Keen, Mariam	L657
Kelleher, Sophie	L359
also	L009
Kendrick, Tristan	L546
Keren, Eli	L362
Killingley, Jessica	L365
also	L065
Kinnersley, Jonathan	L009
Kirby, Robert	L370
Knatchbull, Kelly	L371
Kreitman, Julia	L009
Kremer, Lizzy	L159
Laluyaux, Laurence	L546
Lambert, Sophie	L380
also	L096
Land, Sonia	L577
Langlee, Lina	L382
Langton, Becca	L383
also	L157
Langtry, Elena	L385
also	L139
Lazar, Veronica	L035
Leach, Saskia	L389
also	L353
Leeke, Jessica	L391
also	L420
Lees, Jordan	L392
Leon, Nina	L394
also	L506
Lindsay, Fiona	L400
Lineberry, Isabel	L402
also	L506
Little, Mandy	L647
Lloyd, Jonathan	L146
Lord, Dominic	L332
Loughman, Morwenna	L408
also	L065
Luck, Lucy	L096
Lutyens, Alice	L146
Lyon, Rebecca	L411
also	L577
MacDonald, Emily	L412
Macdougall, Laura	L413
Maclean, Jamie	L417
also	L139
Maidment, Olivia	L421
also	L420
Marland, Matthew	L546
Martin, Olivia	L429
Maw, Jane Graham	L434
also	L271
McLay, Gill	L049
McMullen, Eunice	L201
Merullo, Annabel	L443
Michel, Caroline	L446
Middleton, Leah	L447
Milburn, Madeleine	L449
also	L420
Mills, Rachel	L452
also	L527
Molloy, Jess	L456
also	L146
Montgomery, Caroline	L554
Morrell, Imogen	L460
also	L276
Moylett, Lisa	L139
Mozley, Jack	L465
also	L506
Mulcahy, Ivan	L455
Mundy, Toby	L466
also	L007
Munson, Oli	L002
Murdoch, Judith	L341
Murray, Hilary	L541
Murray, Judith	L468
also	L276
Mushens, Juliet	L470
Nash, Justin	L474
also	L353
Nash, Kate	L353
Neely, Rachel	L476
Nelson, Zoe	L546
Nicklin, Susie	L426
Nundy, Sarah	L024
Nurnberg, Andrew	L024
O'Grady, Niamh	L486
O'Shea, Amy	L488
also	L271
Pass, Marina de	L500
Pearson, Clare	L188
Peddle, Kay	L503
also	L131
Pegg, Jonathan	L337
Pelham, Imogen	L504
Perez, Kristina	L507
also	L506
Perotto-Wills, Martha	L508
also	L057
Petty, Rachel	L512
Pickering, Juliet	L516
also	L066
Pierce, Rosie	L517
also	L146
Pike, Richard	L096
Plitt, Carrie	L520
also	L215
Power, Anna	L523
also	L335
Preston, Amanda	L526
Purdy, Rufus	L636
Rees, Florence	L002
Reilly, Milly	L533
also	L131
Riccardi, Francesca	L535
also	L353
Ripley-Duggan, Louise	L538
also	L627
Ritchie, Rebecca	L002
Robertson, Charlotte	L541
Robinson, Peter	L546
Roderick, Nemonie Craven	L336
Rose, Guy	L236
Ross, Kathryn	L240
Ruppin, Jonathan	L555
Rutherford, Laetitia	L557
also	L647
Sang, Angelique Tran Van	L215
Scarfe, Rory	L566
Schmidt, Leah	L009
Schofield, Hannah	L567
Scoular, Rosemary	L570
Seager, Chloe	L571
also	L420
Seymour, Charlotte	L575
also	L335
Shaw, Kate	L576
Sheldon, Caroline	L106
Sheppard, Hannah	L578
also	L291
Shestopal, Camilla	L581
also	L580
Silk, Julia	L583
also	L278
Silver, Lydia	L157
Simons, Tanera	L585
also	L157
Simpson, Cara Lee	L586
Smith, Anne	L539
Smith, Emily	L009
Smith, Robert	L539
Smith-Bosanquet, Jake	L096
Spackman, James	L593
also	L065
Standen, Yasmin	L348
Steed, Hayley	L595
also	L330
Stevens, Rochelle	L543
Straus, Peter	L546
Strong, Amy	L605
Summerhayes, Cathryn	L146
Sutherland-Hawes, Alice	L612
Swainson, Joanna	L613
also	L294
Sweeney, Sallyanne	L455
Sweet, Emily	L614
also	L007
also	L199
Talbot, Emily	L619
also	L315
Thompson, Paul	L070
Thorneycroft, Euan	L628
also	L002
Thwaites, Steph	L629
also	L146
Tillett, Tanya	L009

Todd, Hannah...............L631	White, Pat...............L546	Wilson, Ed...............L668
also...............L420	Wild, Gary...............L332	*also*...............L335
Topping, Antony...............L632	Williams, Alice...............L660	Winchester, Donald...............L647
also...............L276	*also*...............L017	Wise, Gordon...............L146
Turner, Matthew...............L546	Williams, Katie...............L661	Wood, Caroline...............L669
Unwin, Jo...............L638	*also*...............L009	*also*...............L215
also...............L333	Williams, Laura...............L662	Woodhouse, James...............L670
Viney, Charlie...............L644	*also*...............L276	Woods, Bryony...............L671
also...............L007	Williams, Sarah...............L663	Woollard, Jessica...............L672
also...............L643	*also*...............L591	*also*...............L159
Waldie, Zoe...............L546	Williams, Victoria...............L013	Yearwood, Susan...............L616
Wallace, Clare...............L157	Williamson, Jo...............L664	Yeoh, Rachel...............L675
Walsh, Caroline...............L645	*also*...............L029	*also*...............L420
also...............L159	Wills, James...............L666	Young, Claudia...............L677
Walsh, Kate...............L646	*also*...............L647	*also*...............L276
Watson, Rebecca...............L640	Wilson, Claire...............L546	
Weston, Kate...............L222		

Table of Canadian Literary Agents

Armada, Kurestin L030	Hiyate, Sam L313	Trudel, Jes L634
also L547	Kim, Julia L367	Wells, Karmen L652
Arthurson, Wayne L033	Kimber, Natalie L368	Willms, Kathryn L665
Bhasin, Tamanna L064	Kong, Kelvin L344	
Cavanagh, Claire L114	Mihell, Natasha L448	
Chevais, Jennifer L122	Motala, Tasneem L463	
Foxx, Kat L235	Telep, Trisha L621	

Table of US Magazines

2River View, The	M001
30 North	M002
32 Poems	M003
417 Magazine	M004
aaduna	M005
AARP The Magazine	M006
About Place Journal	M007
Account, The	M009
African American Review	M014
also	P250
African Voices	M015
Agni	M016
Agricultural History	M017
Air & Space Quarterly	M018
Alaska Quarterly Review	M019
Alfred Hitchcock Mystery Magazine	M020
American Book Review	M022
American Short Fiction	M023
Arboreal	M027
Art Papers	M031
Asimov's Science Fiction	M033
Atlanta Magazine	M035
Atlanta Review	M036
Atlantic Northeast	M037
Babybug	M041
Bacopa Literary Review	M042
Baffler, The	M043
Barren Magazine	M047
Bear Deluxe Magazine, The	M052
Belmont Story Review	M054
Beloit Fiction Journal	M055
Better Homes and Gardens	M057
Better Than Starbucks	M058
Big Fiction	M061
Birds & Blooms	M062
Black Belt	M063
Black Moon Magazine	M064
Black Warrior Review	M066
Blue Earth Review	M067
Blue Mesa Review	M068
Bluegrass Unlimited	M069
Boston Review	M071
Bowhunter	M072
Boyfriend Village	M073
also	M066
Cafe Irreal, The	M078
Carolina Woman	M080
CharlottesvilleFamily	M082
Chautauqua Literary Journal	M083
Cheshire	M084
also	M105
Cincinnati Review, The	M086
Cobblestone	M087
Coil, The	M089
also	P020
Cola	M090
Commonweal	M091
Concho River Review	M092
Conjunctions	M093
Conjunctions Online	M094
also	M093
Cowboys & Indians	M101
Crab Orchard Review	M102
Crazyhorse / Swamp Pink	M104
Cream City Review	M105
Creative Nonfiction	M106
Creem	M107
Cruising World	M109
CutBank	M111
Deep Overstock Magazine	M116
Ecotone	M127
El Portal	M129
Ellery Queen Mystery Magazine	M130
Entrepreneur	M131
Fabula Argentea	M134
Fate	M136
Faultline	M137
Fee: Foundation for Economic Education	M138
Feminist Studies	M139
Fiction	M140
First For Women	M142
First Line, The	M143
Five Points	M144
Flyfishing & Tying Journal	M146
also	P021
Folio	M147
Fourth River, The	M153
Fresh Words – An International Literary Magazine	M154
Fugue	M155
Funeral Business Solutions	M156
Funny Times	M157
Gargoyle Online	M161
also	P340
Georgia Review, The	M163
Gertrude	M164
also	P179
Ginosko Literary Journal	M165
Glacier, The	M166
Go World Travel Magazine	M167
Graywolf Lab	M172
also	P193
Gulf Coast: A Journal of Literature and Fine Arts	M173
Half Mystic Journal	M175
also	P197
Hanging Loose	M177
Harper's Magazine	M178
Harpur Palate	M179
Heavy Traffic	M181
Helix, The	M183
Horse & Rider	M188
Hotel Amerika	M189
Hudson Review, The	M190
Hunger Mountain	M191
I-70 Review	M192
Idaho Review	M193
Identity Theory	M194
Image	M195
Indiana Review	M196
Kenyon Review, The	M210
Kerning	M211
also	P453
Leisure Group Travel	M216
Literary Mama	M220
Lost Lake Folk Opera Magazine	M227
also	P406
Louisiana Literature	M228
MacGuffin, The	M229
Magazine of Fantasy & Science Fiction, The	M230
Manoa	M233
marie claire	M234
Marlin	M236
Massachusetts Review, The	M237
Meetinghouse	M238
Metropolis Magazine	M239
Michigan Quarterly Review	M240
Mid-American Review	M241
Midsummer Dream House	M242
Midway Journal	M243
Missouri Review, The	M245
MQR Mixtape	M248
also	M240
Mystery Magazine	M250
Nashville Review	M251
New England Review	M255
New Orleans Review	M257
Oakland Arts Review, The	M264
Obsidian: Literature in the African Diaspora	M265
Old Red Kimono	M267
Oyez Review	M272
Pacifica Literary Review	M273
Paris Review, The	M275
Pensacola Magazine	M281
Pleiades	M285
Ploughshares	M286
Preservation Magazine	M297
Qu Literary Magazine	M302
Rabble Review	M303
Radar Poetry	M305
Reactor	M307
Redbook Magazine	M310
River Hills Traveler	M313
River Styx	M314
Rock & Gem	M316
Ruralite	M318
Saddlebag Dispatches	M319
SAIL Magazine	M320
Savannah Magazine	M322
Scifaikuest	M323
also	P220
Second Factory	M328
also	P466
Seventeen	M329
Shenandoah	M331
Sierra	M336
Sinister Wisdom	M337
Soho Review, The	M339
SOMA	M340
South Carolina Review	M344
Southern Humanities Review	M345
Southern Review, The	M346
Southern Theatre	M347
Southwest Review	M348
Spa Magazine	M350
Spitball	M353
Story Unlikely	M356
Strange Horizons	M357
Strategic Finance	M358
Studio One	M360
Successful Meetings	M361
Sunshine Artist	M363
Sunspot Literary Journal	M364
Tahoma Literary Review	M368
Thin Air Magazine	M374
Third Coast	M375
Threepenny Review, The	M377
Tributaries	M380
also	M153

Tusculum Review, The M381	Waccamaw M394	Yellow Mama Webzine M411
UCity Review M382	West Branch M400	Yes Poetry Magazine M412
Vagabond City M386	Westchester Magazine M402	Zoetrope: All-Story M418
Vestal Review M388	WestWard Quarterly M403	Zone 3 .... M419
Virginia Quarterly Review, The M389	Wine Enthusiast M406	
Virginia Wine & Country Life M390	Yale Review, The M409	
Virginia Wine & Country Weddings M391	Yankee Magazine M410	

Table of UK Magazines

Abridged	M008
Accountancy Age	M010
Accountancy Daily	M011
also	P127
Acumen	M012
AdventureBox	M013
Allegro Poetry Magazine	M021
Amethyst Review	M024
Architectural Review, The	M029
Art Monthly	M030
Art Quarterly	M032
Astronomy Now	M034
Atrium	M038
Auroras & Blossoms PoArtMo Anthology	M039
Authentic Shorts	M040
also	P241
Balance	M044
Bandit Fiction	M045
Banipal	M046
BBC Doctor Who Magazine	M048
BBC History Magazine	M049
BBC Science Focus	M050
Beano, The	M051
Bella	M053
Best of British	M056
BFS Horizons	M059
BFS Journal	M060
Black Static	M065
Bookseller, The	M070
Britain Magazine	M075
Business Traveller	M076
Butcher's Dog	M077
Campaign	M079
Chapman	M081
also	P099
Cheshire Life	M085
Cocoa Girl	M088
Conversation (UK), The	M095
Corridor of Uncertainty, The	M097
Cotswold Life	M098
Country Smallholding	M100
Critical Quarterly	M108
Crystal Magazine	M110
Dark Horse, The	M114
Dawntreader, The	M115
also	P236
Derbyshire Life	M117
Descent	M118
Devon Life	M119
Dorset	M121
Dream Catcher	M123
Dumfries and Galloway Life	M125
Economist, The	M126
Essex Life	M132
Facts & Fiction	M135
Flaneur	M145
Fortean Times: The Journal of Strange Phenomena	M148
Fortnightly Review, The	M149
Forty20	M150
also	P402
Foundation: The International Review of Science Fiction	M151
Fourteen Poems	M152
Future Fire, The	M158
Garden Answers	M159
Garden News	M160
Geographical Journal, The	M162
Good Homes	M168
Good Ski Guide, The	M169
Granta	M171
Gutter Magazine	M174
Hampshire Life	M176
Healthy	M180
Hedgerow: A Journal of Small Poems	M182
Here Comes Everyone	M184
Hertfordshire Life	M185
History Today	M186
Homes & Antiques	M187
Ink Sweat and Tears	M197
Inque	M198
Insurance Age	M199
International Piano	M200
Interzone	M201
Irish Pages	M203
Jazz Journal	M206
Journal, The	M207
Kent Life	M209
Kids Alive!	M212
Lake, The	M213
Lancashire Life	M214
Leisure Painter	M217
Lighthouse	M218
Linguist, The	M219
Litro Magazine	M221
London Grip	M222
London Grip New Poetry	M223
also	M222
London Magazine, The	M224
London Review of Books	M225
Long Poem Magazine	M226
Magma	M231
marie claire (UK)	M235
MiniWorld Magazine	M244
Modern Poetry in Translation	M246
Moving Worlds: A Journal of Transcultural Writings	M247
My Weekly	M249
NB Magazine	M252
Neon	M253
New Accelerator, The	M254
New Internationalist	M256
New Statesman	M258
New Welsh Reader	M259
Norfolk & Suffolk Bride	M260
Norfolk Magazine	M261
North, The	M262
Northern Gravy	M263
OK! Magazine	M266
Orbis International Literary Journal	M269
Oxford Poetry	M270
Oxford Review of Books	M271
Panorama	M274
Park Home and Holiday Living	M276
Passionfruit Review, The	M277
PC Gamer	M278
PC Pro	M279
Pennine Ink Magazine	M280
People's Friend Pocket Novels	M282
also	M283
People's Friend, The	M283
Pilot	M284
PN Review	M287
Poetry London	M289
Poetry Review, The	M290
Poetry Wales	M291
Political Quarterly, The	M292
Popshot Quarterly	M293
Power Cut Lite	M294
Practising Midwife, The	M295
Present Tense	M296
also	P132
Pride	M298
Prole	M299
Pulsar Poetry Magazine	M300
Pushing Out the Boat	M301
Racecar Engineering	M304
Rail Express	M306
Reach	P236
Reader, The	M308
Red Magazine	M309
Rialto, The	M311
Riposte	M312
Rugby World	M317
Sailing Today	M321
Scots Magazine, The	M324
Scottish Farmer, The	M325
Scottish Field	M326
Scribble	M327
Shearsman	M330
Ships Monthly Magazine	M332
Shooter Literary Magazine	M333
Shoreline of Infinity	M334
Shorts Magazine	M335
Snowflake Magazine	M338
Somerset Life	M341
South	M343
Speciality Food	M351
Spelt Magazine	M352
Square Mile Magazine	M354
Structo Magazine	M359
Suffolk Magazine	M362
Supplement, The	M365
Sussex Life	M366
Swimming Pool News	M367
Take a Break's Take a Puzzle	M370
Tears in the Fence	M371
That's Life!	M373
This England	M376
Tocher	M378
Uncut	M383
Under the Radar	M384
also	P317
Viz	M392
Vogue	M393
Walk Magazine	M395
Wallpaper	M397
Wasafiri	M398
Welsh Country	M399
White Review, The	M404
Woman & Home	M407
Yachting Monthly	M408
Yorkshire Life	M413
Yorkshire Women's Life Magazine	M414
Your Cat	M415
Yours	M416
Yours Fiction – Women's Special Series	M417

Table of Canadian Magazines

Angela Poetry Magazine M025	Diver..M120	On Spec..M268
Antigonish Review, The..................................M026	Ekphrastic Review, The..................................M128	Temz Review, The M372
Arc M028	Event M133	Understorey Magazine.....................................M385
Brick M074	Fiddlehead, The M141	Vallum M387
Cottage Life...M099	Grain Literary Magazine................................M170	Windsor Review...M405
Dalhousie Review, The M113	Malahat Review, The.....................................M232	

Table of US Book Publishers

23 House Publishing	P001
4 Color Books	P131
4RV Biblical Based	P004
4RV Children's Corner	P004
4RV Fiction	P004
4RV Nonfiction	P004
4RV Poetry	P003
also	P004
4RV Publishing	P004
4RV Tenacious	P005
also	P004
4RV Tweens & Teens	P004
4RV Young Adult	P004
A-R Editions	P006
Aardwolf Press	P007
ABC-CLIO	P008
also	P071
ABC-CLIO / Greenwood	P008
Able Muse Press	P009
Abuzz Press	P010
AdventureKEEN	P013
Afterglow Books	P014
Albert Whitman & Company	P015
Algonquin Books	P016
also	P519
Algonquin Young Readers	P017
also	P519
Alternating Current Press	P020
Amato Books	P021
American Mystery Classics	P023
also	P345
Andrews McMeel Publishing	P026
Anhinga Press	P027
Applause	P184
Arcadia Publishing	P031
Arte Publico Press	P033
Arthur A. Levine Books	P399
Asabi Publishing	P034
Ascend Books, LLC	P035
Astra House	P036
also	P037
Astra Publishing House	P037
Astra Young Readers	P038
also	P037
Astragal Press	P184
AUWA Books	P043
Avon Books	P045
Backbeat Books	P046
also	P184
Baen Books	P049
Bald and Bonkers Network LLC	P050
Banter Press	P053
Baobab Press	P054
Barbour Publishing	P056
Basalt Books	P057
also	P501
Basic Books	P058
Basic Health Publications, Inc.	P059
also	P462
Baylor University Press	P060
becker&mayer! books	P367
Bentley Publishers	P061
Berrett-Koehler Publishers	P063
Bess Press	P064
Blue Poppy Enterprises	P074
Blue Star Press	P075
BOA Editions, Ltd.	P076
Books of Chapel Hill	P079
also	P519
Bramble	P080
also	P456
C&T Publishing	P088
Calkins Creek	P091
also	P037
Candlemark & Gleam	P092
Captivate Press	P095
Celadon Books	P097
Charisma House	P100
Charles River Press	P101
Charlesbridge Publishing	P102
Charlesbridge Teen	P103
also	P102
Chelsea House Publishers	P105
Cherry Lake Publishing Group	P106
Chronicle Books LLC	P111
Clarkson Potter	P131
Cleis Press	P115
Coaches Choice	P116
College Press Publishing	P117
Cornell Maritime Press	P123
also	P398
Coyote Arts	P125
Crabtree Publishing	P126
Crosley-Griffith	P088
Crossway	P128
Crown	P129
also	P131
Crown Publishing Group, The	P131
Currency	P131
Dancing Girl Press	P133
Darby Creek	P264
DAW Books	P135
also	P037
Del Rey	P137
Denis Kitchen Publishing Company Co., LLC	P138
DeVorss & Company	P139
DK Publishing	P141
Down East Books	P184
Dreamspinner Press	P144
DSP Publications	P145
also	P144
Eerdmans Books for Young Readers	P148
Enslow Publishers, Inc.	P154
Evan-Moor Educational Publishers	P157
FalconGuides	P184
Farrar, Straus & Giroux	P161
Fathom Books	P162
Feminist Press, The	P163
Filter Press	P166
Focal Press	P441
Forge	P169
also	P456
Fortress Press	P170
Free Spirit Publishing	P174
Friends United Press	P175
FrontLine	P176
FunStitch Studio	P088
Gale	P177
Geared Up Publications	P178
also	P398
Gertrude Press	P179
Glass Poetry Press	P183
Globe Pequot Press, The	P184
Gold SF	P185
also	P186
Goodman Beck Publishing	P187
Grand Central Publishing	P196
Graywolf Press	P193
Greenhaven Publishing	P177
Greenway Music Press	P006
Hachette Book Group	P196
Half Mystic Press	P197
Harlequin Desire	P202
Harmony Ink Press	P205
also	P144
Harvard Common Press	P367
Harvard University Press	P206
Hawthorne Books	P209
Hell's Hundred	P213
also	P417
Henry Holt & Co.	P215
High Tide Press	P217
Hippo Park	P218
also	P037
Hippocrene Books, Inc.	P219
Hiraeth Books	P220
Host Publications	P224
IDW Publishing	P228
Idyll Arbor	P229
Ig Publishing	P230
IgKids	P231
also	P230
Imagine Publishing	P234
also	P102
Indiana University Press	P235
Information Today, Inc.	P238
International Society for Technology in Education (ISTE)	P242
Jain Publishing Company, Inc.	P244
Jamii Publishing	P245
Jewish Lights Publishing	P462
Johns Hopkins University Press, The	P250
Kane Press	P251
also	P037
Kansas City Star Quilts	P088
Kar-Ben Publishing	P264
Kensington Publishing Corp.	P253
KidHaven Press	P177
Kore Press	P256
Langmarc Publishing	P259
Leapfrog Press	P263
Lerner Publishing Group	P264
Libraries Unlimited	P008
Liguori Publications	P267
Little Bigfoot	P391
Little, Brown and Company	P196
Llewellyn Worldwide Ltd	P269
Loft Press, Inc.	P270
Loyola Press	P272
LSU Press	P273
Lucent Books	P177
LW Books	P276
also	P398
Lyons Press	P184
Lyrical Press	P277
also	P253
M. Evans & Company	P278
Margaret K. McElderry Books	P281
MB Media	P283
Mcbooks Press	P184

Claim your free access to www.firstwriter.com: See p.403

MCD Books	P284
Medical Physics Publishing	P288
Menasha Ridge Press	P290
also	P013
Merriam Press	P293
Milkweed Editions	P296
MineditionUS	P298
also	P037
Minnesota Historical Society Press	P299
Minotaur Books	P300
Missouri Historical Society Press	P302
MIT Press, The	P303
Monacelli Press, The	P304
Moody Publishers	P305
Morgan Kaufmann Publishers	P150
Muddy Boots	P184
Mysterious Press, The	P309
also	P345
NAHB BuilderBooks	P310
Native Ink Press	P311
NBM Publishing	P312
New Harbinger Publications	P314
Nightfire	P316
also	P456
No Starch Press, Inc.	P318
Oghma Creative Media	P321
Oh MG Press	P322
also	P283
Ohio State University Press, The	P323
Ohio University Press	P324
Ooligan Press	P328
Orchard Books	P399
Pacific Press Publishing Association	P334
Paycock Press	P340
Pelican Publishing Company	P031
Penzler Publishers	P345
Perseus Books	P196
Peter Lang Publishing	P348
Peter Pauper Press	P350
Phoenix Moirai	P351
Picador	P353
Pinata Books	P355
also	P033
Pineapple Press	P356
also	P184
Praeger	P008
Press 53	P361
Prometheus	P184
Prufrock Press	P363
Purdue University Press	P364
Pureplay Press	P365
Quill Driver Books	P368
Quirk Books	P369
R D Publishers	P370
Rand McNally	P371
Red Feather	P375
also	P398
Rocky Nook	P379
Safari Press	P386
Saguaro Books, LLC	P388
Sasquatch Books	P391
Scarlet	P393
also	P345
Schiffer Craft	P394
also	P398
Schiffer Fashion Press	P395
also	P398
Schiffer Kids	P396
also	P398
Schiffer Military History	P397
also	P398
Schiffer Publishing	P398
Scholastic	P399
Seaworthy Publications	P403
Sentient Publications	P404
Shipwreckt Books Publishing Company	P406
Siloam	P408
Sinister Stoat Press	P410
Skip Jack Press	P184
Slope Editions	P411
Soho Crime	P416
also	P417
Soho Press	P417
Soho Teen	P418
also	P417
Spout Press	P420
Spruce Books	P391
St Martin's Press	P422
St. Martin's Essentials	P423
St. Martin's Griffin	P424
St. Martin's Publishing Group	P425
Stackpole Books	P184
Stanford University Press	P427
Stash Books	P088
Steerforth Press	P428
Steward House Publishers	P429
Stipes Publishing	P431
Storey Publishing	P519
Sunbelt Publications, Inc.	P433
Sweetgum Press	P438
Tailwinds Press	P439
Ten Speed Press	P444
also	P131
Texas A&M University Press	P445
Thames & Hudson Inc.	P446
Tidewater Publishers	P449
also	P398
Tilbury House Publishers	P450
also	P106
Toad Hall Editions	P453
Toon Books	P454
also	P037
Tor	P455
also	P456
Tor Publishing Group	P456
Tor Teen	P457
also	P456
Tor.com Publishing	P458
also	P456
Torrey House Press, LLC	P459
Turner Publishing	P462
Turtle Press	P463
Two Fine Crows Books	P464
TwoDot	P184
Tyndale House Publishers, Inc.	P465
Ugly Duckling Presse	P466
Union Park Press	P184
Unity	P473
University of Akron Press, The	P475
University of Alaska Press	P476
University of California Press	P478
University of Georgia Press	P479
University of Iowa Press	P480
University of Maine Press	P481
University of Massachusetts Press	P482
University of Michigan Press, The	P483
University of Nevada Press	P484
University of North Texas Press	P485
University of Pennsylvania Press	P486
University of Tennessee Press	P487
University of Texas Press	P488
University of Virginia Press	P489
University of Wisconsin Press, The	P490
University Press of Colorado	P491
Unseen Press	P492
Utah State University Press	P491
VanderWyk & Burnham	P494
Vinspire Publishing	P497
Voyageur Press	P367
W.W. Norton & Company, Inc.	P500
Walter Foster Publishing	P367
Washington State University Press	P501
Watson-Guptill Publications	P131
Wayne State University Press	P504
Wesleyan University Press	P506
Whitford Press	P508
also	P398
Wisdom Publications	P512
Wolfpack Publishing	P513
WordCrafts Press	P514
WordSong	P516
also	P037
Workman Publishing	P519
also	P037
Yes Poetry Chapbooks	M412
YesYes Books	P521
Zebra	P253
Zibby Books	P522

Table of UK Book Publishers

404 Ink	P002
Ad Hoc Fiction	P011
Adlard Coles	P012
Allison & Busby Ltd	P019
Amber Books Ltd	P022
Ammonite Press	P024
And Other Stories	P025
Apa Publications Group	P029
Arachne Press	P030
Armchair Traveller at the bookHaus, The	P208
Ashgate Publishing Limited	P441
Aurora Metro Press	P039
Authentic Ideas	P040
also	P241
Authentic Life	P041
also	P241
Autumn Publishing Ltd	P042
also	P232
Avon	P044
Bad Press Ink	P047
Badger Learning	P048
Barbican Press	P055
Berghahn Books Ltd	P062
BFI Publishing	P065
also	P071
Bird Eye Books	P066
also	P190
Birlinn Ltd	P067
Blackstaff Press	P068
also	P119
Bloodaxe Books	P069
Bloodhound Books	P070
Bloomsbury Academic	P071
Bloomsbury Professional	P072
Blue Jeans Books	P073
also	P435
Boathooks Books	P077
also	P435
Bookouture	P078
Breedon Books	P081
Brewin Books	P081
Brewin Books Ltd	P081
Bright Press	P082
also	P367
British Academy, The	P083
British Museum Press, The	P084
Brown, Son & Ferguson, Ltd	P086
Burning Eye Books	P087
Cadno	P089
also	P190
Candy Jar Books	P093
Canterbury Press	P094
Cassell	P096
CGI (Chartered Governance Institute) Publishing	P098
Chambers	P249
Chapman Publishing	P099
Chartered Institute of Personnel and Development (CIPD) Publishing	P104
Chicken House Publishing	P399
Child's Play (International) Ltd	P107
Choc Lit	P108
also	P248
ChristLight Books	P110
also	P435
Cinnamon Press	P112
Claret Press	P113
Classical Comics	P114
Collins	P118
Colourpoint Educational	P119
Comma Press	P120
Compassiviste Publishing	P121
Countryside Books	P124
Creative Essentials	P326
Crime & Mystery Club	P326
Croner-i Limited	P127
Dahlia Books	P132
Daunt Books Publishing	P134
Dedalus Ltd	P136
Dodo Ink	P142
Doubleday (UK)	P143
Duncan Petersen Publishing Limited	P146
Dynasty Press	P147
Elliott & Thompson	P149
Elsevier Ltd	P150
Encyclopedia Britannica (UK) Ltd	P151
Engram Books	P152
also	P435
Enitharmon Editions	P153
EPTA Books	P155
also	P435
Essence Press	P156
Everything With Words	P158
Facet Publishing	P159
Fairlight Books	P160
Fighting High	P165
Fircone Books Ltd	P271
Firefly	P167
Fiscal Publications	P168
Frances Lincoln Children's Books	P367
Free Association Books Ltd	P173
Frontline Books	P343
Goldsmiths Press	P186
Goss & Crested China Club	P189
Graffeg	P190
Graffeg Childrens	P191
also	P190
Granta Books	P192
Guinness World Records	P194
Guppy Books	P195
Hammersmith Books	P198
Handspring Publishing	P199
also	P246
Happy Yak	P200
also	P367
Hardie Grant UK	P201
Harlequin Mills & Boon Ltd	P203
Hashtag Press	P207
Haus Publishing	P208
Hay House Publishers	P210
Hazel Press	P211
Hearing Eye	P212
Henley Hall Press	P214
High Stakes Publishing	P216
also	P326
History into Print	P081
History Press, The	P221
Hodder & Stoughton Ltd	P222
Hodder Faith	P222
HopeRoad	P223
Howgate Publishing	P225
Hunt End Books	P081
Icon Books Ltd	P227
Igloo Books Limited	P232
Indigo Dreams Publishing	P236
Influx Press	P237
Inkandescent	P240
Integrity Media	P241
InterVarsity Press (IVP)	P243
Jessica Kingsley Publishers	P246
also	P249
JMD Media / DB Publishing	P247
Joffe Books	P248
John Murray Press	P249
Jordan Publishing	P265
Kamera Books	P326
Kates Hill Press, The	P252
Kitchen Press	P254
Kogan Page Ltd	P255
Korero Press	P257
Kube Publishing	P258
Lantana Publishing	P260
Laurence King Publishing	P261
Leamington Books	P262
LexisNexis	P265
Lightning Books	P266
Logaston Press	P271
Lund Humphries Limited	P274
Lutterworth Press, The	P275
Macmillan Children's Books	P279
Manilla Press	P280
Marion Boyars Publishers	P282
McGraw Hill EMEA	P285
McNidder & Grace	P286
Medina Publishing	P289
Mensch Publishing	P291
Methuen Publishing Ltd	P294
Metro Publications Ltd	P295
Mills & Boon	P297
Mirror Books	P301
Mudfog Press	P306
Murdoch Books UK Ltd	P308
Nell James Publishers	P313
New Walk Editions	P315
Nicholas Brealey Publishing	P222
Nine Arches Press	P317
Nosy Crow	P319
Old Street Publishing Ltd	P325
Oldcastle Books	P326
Oldcastle Books Group	P326
Oneworld Publications	P327
Orenda Books	P329
Ouen Press	P331
Out-Spoken Press	P332
Oxbow Books	P333
Parthian Books	P336
Patrician Press	P337
Pavilion Books	P338
Pavilion Poetry	P339
Peepal Tree Press	P341
Pen & Ink Designs Publishing	P342
Pen & Sword Books Ltd	P343
Peter Lang	P346
also	P347
Peter Owen Publishers	P349
Phillimore	P221
Piatkus Books	P352
Piccadilly Press	P354
Plexus Publishing Limited	P357
Pluto Press	P358
Pocket Mountains	P359

Claim your free access to www.firstwriter.com: See p.403

Table of UK Book Publishers

Polygon	P360
also	P067
Prestel Publishing Ltd	P362
also	P344
Psychology Press	P441
Pulp! The Classics	P326
Quadrant Books	P366
Quarto Group, Inc., The	P367
Ransom Publishing Ltd	P373
Remember When	P343
Renard Press Ltd	P376
Richards Publishing	P081
Rose and Crown Books	P381
also	P435
Routledge	P441
Ruby Fiction	P384
also	P108
RYA (Royal Yachting Association)	P385
Salt Publishing	P389
Saqi Books	P390
Scala Arts & Heritage Publishers	P392
Scholastic UK	P400
also	P399
SCM Press	P401
Scratching Shed Publishing	P402
Seren Books	P405
Sigma Press	P407
Singing Dragon	P409
also	P246
SmashBear Publishing	P412
Smokestack Books	P413
Society for Promoting Christian Knowledge (SPCK)	P414
Society of Genealogists	P415
Sparsile Books	P419
SRL Publishing	P421
Stainer & Bell Ltd	P426
Stewed Rhubarb Press	P430
Sunberry Books	P434
also	P435
Sunpenny Publishing	P435
Sweet & Maxwell	P436
Sweet Cherry Publishing	P437
Tall-Lighthouse	P440
Taylor & Francis Group	P441
Telegram Books	P390
Templar Books	P442
Thinkwell Books, UK	P447
Thistle Publishing	P448
Tiny Owl	P451
Tippermuir Books	P452
Tor	P455
Torva	P460
Troika Books	P461
Ulverscroft Ltd	P467
Unbound Press	P468
Unicorn	P469
also	P470
Unicorn Publishing Group	P470
Uniform	P471
also	P470
Unify	P472
also	P470
Universe	P474
also	P470
Valley Press	P493
Vane Women Press	P495
Velocity Press	P496
Virago Books	P498
W.W. Norton & Company Ltd	P499
Watkins Publishing	P503
Weidenfeld & Nicolson	P505
Wharncliffe Books	P343
Wide-Eyed Editions	P509
also	P367
Wild Places Publishing	P510
Windhorse Publications Ltd	P511
Words & Pictures	P515
also	P367
Wordsworth Editions	P518
Yale University Press (London)	P520
ZigZag Education	P523

Table of Canadian Book Publishers

Anvil Press Publishers P028
Arsenal Pulp Press P032
Broadview Press P085
Caitlin Press Inc. P090
Fernwood Publishing P164
Goose Lane Editions P188

Icehouse P226
    also P188
Ravenstone P374
Rocky Mountain Books P378
Roseway P382
    also P164

University of Alberta Press P477
Whitecap Books Ltd P507

*Claim your free access to **www.firstwriter.com**: See p.403*

Table of Authors

Aaddam, Safia El L574
Abbott, Diane L066
   also L516
Abbott, Rachel L159
Abdaal, Ali L204
Abdoo, Matt L155
Abdur-Rashid, Tasneem L166
   also L216
Abe, Naoko L096
Abe, Sally L163
Abeysekara, Shalini L329
Abrahams, Jodie L512
Abramović, Marina L566
Abrams, Brooke L416
   also L477
Abrams, Rebecca L557
   also L647
Acker, Tanya L334
Ackerley, J. R. L159
Ackerman, Ruthie L440
Ackroyd, Claire L321
Ackroyd, Peter L577
Acosta, Carlos L215
   also L669
Acton, Johnny L215
   also L318
Adair, Gilbert L066
Adams, Char L087
Adams, Gaar L096
   also L380
Adams, Guy L099
   also L278
Adams, Luci L110
   also L647
Adams, Nathaniel L184
Adams, Nicola L512
Adams, Nicole L146
   also L517
Adams, Poppy L468
Adams, R.G. L557
Adams, Rebecca L616
Adams, Richard L052
   also L159
Adams, Tim L007
   also L466
Adams, Tom L110
   also L647
Adams, William Lee L190
Adamson, Jean L110
   also L647
Adcock, Siobhan L184
Addison, Katherine L598
Adebisi, Maria Motunrayo L157
Adee, Sally L215
   also L520
Adelman, Juliana L276
   also L460
Adesina, Precious L209
   also L276
Adlam, Emily L526
Admans, Jaimie L526
Adner, Ron L297
Adshead, Gwen L096
   also L380
Aedin, M. Jules P144
Afrika, Tatamkhulu L066
Agbaimoni, Luke L086

Agbaje, Foluso L166
   also L263
Agbaje-Williams, Ore L116
   also L159
Agg, Henry L146
   also L223
   also L517
Agnew, Katie L159
Aguirre, Lauren L087
Ahlqvist, Emma L141
Ahluwalia, Jassa L282
Ahmadi, Arvin L058
   also L059
Ahmed, Emad L567
Ahmed, Imran L566
Ahmed, K Anis L099
   also L278
Ahmed, Saladin L176
Ahmed, Samira L129
   also L215
Ahmed, Sara L116
   also L159
Ahmed, Tufayel L586
Ahsan, Shahnaz L096
Ahuvia, Aaron L297
Aile, Rhianne P144
Ailes, Kat L159
   also L232
Ainsworth, Eve L662
Akala, ... L376
Akbar, Sam L677
Akehurst, Nigel L096
Akers, Mary L066
Akhtar, Amina L090
Akilah, Shani L066
   also L197
Akin, Sara L229
Akpan, Paula L166
   also L216
Akumiah, Heather L333
Al-Hassan, Alwia L392
Al-Sabawi, Dina L612
Alabed, Bana L392
Alagiah, George L290
Alais, Saskia L066
   also L516
Alameda, Courtney L148
Albano, Laurie L043
Albert, Elisa L073
Albert, Maria P144
Albert, Michele L011
Alberti, Fay Bound L254
Albuquerque, Telênia L050
Alcántara, Jacqueline L174
Alder, Mark L468
Alderman, Naomi L052
   also L159
Aldern, Clayton Page L276
   also L632
Alderson, Sarah L526
Alderton, Dolly L096
   also L137
Aldred, James L007
   also L173
   also L466
Aldred, Tanya L099
   also L278

Aldridge, Arthur L539
Alegre, Susie L086
Alexander, Becky L099
   also L278
Alexander, Claire L470
Alexander, Jane L105
Alexander, Keir L096
Alexander, Piers L096
Alexander, Rose L110
   also L647
Alexander, Tracy L159
Alford, Allison M. L467
Alghariz, Ahmed L229
Ali, Kasim L066
   also L516
Ali, Moeen L099
   also L278
Ali, Nimco L566
Ali, Rahaman L086
Ali-Afzal, Aliya L470
Alker, Elizabeth L159
   also L270
Alkon, Amy L063
Allan, Jennifer Lucy L251
   also L278
Allan, Jo L240
Allbeury, Ted L066
Allen, Anthea L086
Allen, Denise L644
Allen, Diane L341
Allen, Dwight L063
Allen, Jeremy L251
   also L278
Allen, Katie L295
Allen, Matt L566
Allen, Nikki L066
   also L093
Allen, P. David L334
Allen, Preston L184
Allen, Rachael L159
Allen, Wendy L557
   also L647
Allen, Will L063
Allen-Paisant, Jason L159
Allison, John L364
Allman, Esme L005
Allnutt, Luke L470
Allore, John L090
Allport, Alan L159
   also L270
   also L608
Allueva, Oscar L313
Almond, David L129
   also L215
Alonge, Amen L276
   also L632
Alonso, Kassten P209
Alpsten, Ellen L446
Alsadir, Nuar L159
Altman, Mara L184
Altmann, Danny L282
Alvarez, Jennifer Lynn L334
Amaka, Rosanna L116
Amati, Federica L676
Ambridge, Ben L215
   also L318
Ambrose, David L644

Table of Authors

Amidon, Stephen ... L184
Amna, Dur E Aziz ... L584
Amos, Shawn ... L458
Amuah, Marie-Claire ... L470
Ana Aranda ... L174
Anastasiu, Heather ... L334
Anatole, Alexina ... L131
 also ... L533
Anaxagorou, Anthony ... L276
 also ... L677
Anderson, Brett ... L086
Anderson, Cynthia ... L184
Anderson, Devery ... L297
Anderson, G V ... L096
Anderson, Geraint ... L159
Anderson, Ho Che ... L313
Anderson, Jill ... L236
Anderson, Michelle Collins ... L603
Anderson, Michelle Wilde ... L608
Anderson, Pamela ... L469
Anderson, R. J. ... L159
 also ... L645
Anderson, Ros ... L066
 also ... L197
Anderson, Sorrel ... L240
Anderson-Wheeler, Claire ... L032
 also ... L096
Andrade, Tonio ... L608
Andres, Alan ... L440
Andress, David ... L644
Andrew, Kelly ... L159
 also ... L645
Andrew, Kerry ... L159
 also ... L672
Andrew, Sally ... L066
 also ... L171
Andrews, Abi ... L159
Andrews, Casey Jay ... L146
 also ... L456
Andrés López ... L174
Angelico, Karen ... L096
 also ... L380
Angelou, Maya ... P498
Angwin, Roselle ... P236
Anie, Sussie ... L470
Ann, Rebecca ... L612
Annukka, Sui ... L146
 also ... L456
Anselmo, Lisa ... L334
Anshaw, Carol ... L159
 also ... L266
Antalek, Robin ... L096
Ante, Romalyn ... L066
 also ... L171
Anthony, Carl Sferrazza ... L469
Antiglio, Dominique ... L526
Antrobus, Raymond ... L116
Aplin, Ollie ... L096
Appachana, Anjana ... L429
Appiah, Krystle Zara ... L470
Appleby, Steven ... L096
Applestone, Jessica ... L184
Applestone, Josh & Jessica ... L184
Apps, Peter ... L276
 also ... L632
Appy, Christian G. ... L608
Aquila, Richard ... L184
Araujo, Jess J. ... L063
Arbuthnott, Gill ... L240
Arcanjo, JJ ... L392
Archbold, Tim ... L240
Archer, Amy ... L325
Archer, Deborah N. ... L608
Archer, Juliet ... P108
Archer, Micha ... L513

Archer, Rosie ... L110
 also ... L647
Arditti, Michael ... L159
Ardizzone, Edward ... L159
Are, Carolina ... L166
 also ... L216
Areguy, Fitsum ... L367
Arikha, Alba ... L443
Ariyo, Lopè ... L086
Arlen, Michael ... L159
Armstrong, Addison ... L153
 also ... L609
Armstrong, Dorothy ... L254
Armstrong, Graeme ... L066
 also ... L516
Armstrong, Jesse ... L333
 also ... L638
Armstrong, Karen ... L129
 also ... L215
Armstrong, Ross ... L470
Armstrong, Thomas ... L334
Arnold, Elana K. ... L513
Arnold, Luke ... L096
Arnott, Paul ... L644
Aron, Elaine N. ... L063
Arrowsmith, Simon ... L348
Arsenault, Mark ... L582
Arsenault, Ray ... L608
Arsén, Isa ... L090
Arthur, Karen ... L166
 also ... L216
Arvedlund, Erin ... L297
Arvin, Eric ... P144
Aryan, Stephen ... L470
Asare, Tobi ... L278
 also ... L583
Asbridge, Thomas ... L159
 also ... L270
Asgarian, Roxanna ... L609
Ash, Lamorna ... L159
 also ... L672
Ash, Lucy ... L129
 also ... L215
Ashcroft, Frances ... L215
 also ... L520
Ashe, Lucy ... L276
 also ... L632
Asher, Jane ... L566
Ashley, Trisha ... L341
 also ... P052
Ashling, Mickie B. ... P144
Ashon, Will ... L096
Ashton, James ... L007
 also ... L466
Ashton, Paul ... L066
Ashworth, Jenn ... L159
 also ... L266
Aspden, Rachel ... L129
 also ... L215
Atherton, Carol ... L034
 also ... L278
Athwal, Sarbjit Kaur ... L539
Atkin, Polly ... L128
 also ... L521
Atkins, Dani ... L066
 also ... L093
Atkins, Jennifer ... L159
Atkins, Lucy ... L468
Atkinson, Kate ... P143
Atkinson, Ros ... L677
Atleework, Kendra ... L584
Atogun, Odafe ... L007
 also ... L466
Attah, Ayesha Harruna ... L574
Attlee, Helena ... L632

Attlee, James ... L129
 also ... L215
Attwell, Ciara ... L321
Atwood, Margaret ... P498
Au, Sara ... L334
Augar, Philip ... L007
 also ... L466
Ault, Sandi ... L063
Austin, Sophie ... L294
 also ... L295
Austin, Stephanie ... L623
Austro, Ben ... L531
Avery, Mark ... L215
 also ... L318
Avillez, Joana ... L415
Awwad, Aysha ... L619
Axat, Federico ... L574
Aye, MiMi ... L066
 also ... L516
Ayoade, Richard ... L333
 also ... L638
Ayscough, Aaron ... L481
Azam, Sa'ad ... L276
 also ... L460
Azerrad, Michael ... L388
 also ... L481
Azzam, Abdul Rahman ... L066
 also ... L171
Azzopardi, Trezza ... L066
 also ... L516
Babakar, Mevan ... L276
 also ... L632
Babalola, Bolu ... L066
 also ... L516
Bacchus-Garrick, Nadine ... L204
Bacon, Beth ... L184
Badr, Ahmed ... L515
 also ... L609
Baer, Kate ... L416
 also ... L477
Baer, Prof Marc David ... L254
Baggini, Julian ... L159
Baggot, Mandy ... L157
 also ... L585
Bailey, Connie ... P144
Bailey, Louis ... L521
Bailey, Samantha M. ... L058
 also ... L059
Bailey, Susanna ... L619
Bainbridge, John ... L537
Bainbridge, Rebecca ... L676
Bakar, Faima ... L110
 also ... L647
Baker, Harriet ... L159
Baker, Kevin ... L184
Baker, Modern ... L215
 also ... L669
Baker, Richard Anthony ... L539
Baker, Stephen ... L096
Baker, Tina ... L052
 also ... L159
Balbirer, Nancy ... L184
Baldree, Travis ... L226
 also ... L680
Bale, Anthony ... L052
 also ... L159
Balen, Katya ... L129
 also ... L215
Balfe, Abigail ... L619
Balfour, Alice ... L240
Balfour, Sandy ... L066
 also ... L171
Ball, Jesse ... L615
Ballantine, Carol ... L209
 also ... L276
Ballantine, Poe ... P209

Access more listings online at www.firstwriter.com

Ballantyne, Iain	L048	
Ballantyne, Lisa	L096	
also	L380	
Balls, Katy	L159	
also	L270	
Balmer, Delia	L539	
Balter, Dave	L297	
Bamberger, Alan	L621	
Bamford, Emma	L069	
also	L157	
Bang, Michelle	L209	
also	L276	
Banissy, Michael	L443	
Banks, Gina	L416	
also	L477	
Bannan, Sarah	L591	
also	L663	
Bannon, Tia	L005	
Banta, Isabel	L108	
Barbarisi, Daniel	L440	
Barber, Antonia	L159	
also	L645	
Barcenilla, Lerah Mae	L325	
Barclay, Humphrey	L332	
Barclay, Jennifer	L294	
also	L295	
Barclay, Theo	L190	
Bareham, Lindsey	L159	
also	L270	
Bareilles, Sara	L481	
Barker, Larry	L236	
Barker, Raffaella	L276	
also	L468	
Barker, Xanthi	L131	
also	L533	
Barley, Nigel	L159	
also	L266	
Barnard, Joanna	L470	
Barnard, Robert	L159	
Barnes, Hannah	L007	
also	L466	
Barnes, Juliet	L539	
Barnett, Daniel	L652	
Barnett, Fiona	L364	
Barnett, Laura	L468	
Barnett, Rob	L537	
Barnett, Ross	L190	
Barnhardt, Wilton	L184	
Barnsley, Rhiannon	L476	
Barokka, Khairani	L166	
also	L216	
Barr, Damian	L096	
also	L137	
Barr, James	L129	
also	L215	
Barr, Lois	L063	
Barr-Green, Craig	L146	
also	L250	
Barranco, Jené Ray	L440	
Barrell, Tony	L096	
Barrett, Colin	L096	
Barrett, Justin L.	L297	
Barrett, Kerry	L526	
Barrett, Natasha S.	L427	
Barrett, Paddy	L278	
also	L583	
Barri, Zahra	L053	
also	L278	
Barrie, Amanda	L539	
Barrie, David	L129	
also	L215	
Barron, Kay	L215	
also	L669	
Barroux,	L240	
Barrow, Alex	L619	
Barrow, Cathy	L467	
Barrow-Belisle, Michele	L043	
Barrowcliffe, Mark	L468	
Barrows, Annie	L162	
also	L405	
Barry, Kevin	L096	
Barry, Rebecca Rego	L334	
Barry, Shannon Lee	L259	
also	L680	
Barsoux, Jean-Louis	L297	
Barter, Catherine	L662	
Bartkowski, Frances	L334	
Bartlett, Ciaran	L603	
Bartlett, Graham	L166	
also	L306	
Bartlett, Jamie	L446	
Bartlett, Lilly	L294	
also	L295	
Bartlett, Neil	L096	
also	L137	
Bartlett, Rosamund	L129	
also	L215	
Bartlett, Steven	L376	
Barton, John	L129	
also	L215	
Bartsch, Shadi	L608	
Barve, Nivedita	L005	
Basey, Lucy	L616	
Bashe, Patricia Romanowski	L388	
Basilières, Michel	L313	
Baskaran, Lucía	L574	
Baskerville, Katie	L166	
also	L216	
Bason, Christian	L297	
Basra, Gurki	L114	
Basu, Kaushik	L159	
also	L270	
Basu, Laura	L521	
Batchelor, John	L129	
also	L215	
Bateman, Jackie	L294	
Bateman, Sonya	L176	
Bates, Stephen	L644	
Batmanghelidjh, Camila	L446	
Batsha, Nishant	L108	
Battenfield, Jackie	L184	
Battersby, Matilda	L321	
Battle, Nick	L236	
Battle-Felton, Yvonne	L159	
also	L170	
Bauer, Ann	L297	
Bauer, Belinda	L052	
also	L159	
Bauer, Charlotte	L276	
also	L468	
Bauer, Douglas	L184	
Bauman, Whitney	L676	
Baume, Sara	L096	
Baumgartner, Alice	L608	
Baur, Becky	L619	
Bausch, Richard	L184	
Bautista-Carolina, Suhaly	L108	
Baxter, John	L539	
Baxter, Lily	L623	
Bay, Samara	L469	
Bayley, Chloe	L146	
also	L223	
Bayley, Stephen	L086	
Bayliss, Andrew J.	L254	
Bays, Jill	L426	
Bazalgette, Felix	L159	
Beadle, William	L539	
Beale, Susan	L215	
also	L669	
Beard, Richard	L096	
Beardsall, Jonny	L215	
also	L318	
Beashel, Amy	L282	
Beasley, Heidi Lauth	L204	
Beasley, Robert	L539	
Beatley, Meaghan	L574	
Beaton, E. J.	L343	
Beaton, Roderick	L215	
also	L520	
Beaty, Zoe	L333	
Beauman, Francesca	L096	
also	L137	
Beaumont, Matt	L096	
also	L137	
Bechtel, Greg	L033	
Becker, Robin	L532	
Becnel, Rexanne	L011	
Bedell, Elaine	L446	
Bee, J Y	L348	
Bee, Peta	L539	
Beech, Ella	L159	
also	L645	
Beech, Louise	L166	
also	L263	
Beers, Laura	L159	
also	L270	
Beetner, Eric	L033	
Beezmohun, Sharmilla	L053	
also	L278	
Begbie, Hannah	L052	
also	L159	
Begg, Paul	L539	
Begin, Mary Jane	L537	
Behr, Rafael	L566	
Beilock, Sian	L608	
Beirne, Liam	L332	
Beirne, Olivia	L321	
Bekins, Alix	P144	
Belim, Victoria	L099	
also	L278	
Bell, Alex	L294	
Bell, Alice	L146	
also	L226	
also	L517	
also	L680	
Bell, Anna	L294	
Bell, Annie	L159	
Bell, Darcey	L468	
Bell, Emma J.	L282	
Bell, Gary	L566	
Bell, Ginny	L623	
Bell, Johanna	L066	
also	L093	
Bell, Juliet	L278	
also	L583	
Bellamacina, Greta	L096	
also	L137	
Bellamy, Tomas	L066	
also	L516	
Belle, Jennifer	P498	
Beller, Elizabeth	L469	
Bellezza, Audrey	L334	
Belton, Catherine	L215	
also	L520	
Benavides, Lucía	L574	
Bendavid, Marc	L073	
Bender, Aimee	L159	
also	L184	
also	L266	
Benedictus, Leo	L096	
also	L380	
Benjamin, David	L297	
Benjamin, Ruha	L396	
Benn, Tom	L066	
also	L171	
Benner, Erica	L129	
also	L215	
Bennett, Anne	L341	

Bennett, Cathy	L043
Bennett, John	L539
Bennett, Joshua	L469
Bennett, M A	L623
Bennett, Maggie	L341
Bennett, Margot	L159
Bennett, Nic	L129
also	L215
Bennett, Nicki	P144
Bennett, SJ	L099
also	L278
Benoist, Jessica	L050
Benoist, Melissa	L050
Benson, Christine Melanie	L440
Benson, Harry	L443
Benson, Jendella	L066
also	L516
Benson, Michael	L388
Benson, Patrick	L096
also	L137
Bentley, Dorothy	L634
Benton, Janet	L440
Benton, Megan	L584
Benyon, Kaddy	L146
also	L517
Beorn, Waitman	L334
Berend, Nora	L254
Beresford, Jason	L240
Beresiner, Sophie	L204
Berg, Meliz	L066
also	L516
Berger, Joe	L159
also	L645
Bergman, Ronen	L566
Bergstrom, Abigail	L204
Berk, Sheryl	L537
Berney, Jennifer	L184
Bernières, Louis De	L215
also	L669
Bernstein, Ariel	L063
Bernstein, Sarah	L159
Berridge, Elizabeth	L159
Berriman, Amanda	L333
also	L638
Berriman, Mandy	L096
Berry, Anne	L341
Berry, Christine	L029
Berry, Jedediah	L297
Berry, Mary	L215
also	L669
Berson, Josh	L053
also	L278
Bertrand, Lynne	L229
Bertschinger, Claire	L129
also	L215
Berwin, Margot	L313
Bestwick, Simon	L364
Betke-Brunswick, Will	L141
Betley, Christian Piers	L236
Betts, Paul	L129
also	L215
Bez,	L251
also	L278
Bhadreshwar, Nina	L215
also	L669
Bhaskar, Michael	L096
also	L380
Bhathena, Tanaz	L184
Bhatia, Rahul	L007
also	L466
Bhatt, Chetan	L294
also	L295
Bhattacharya, Santanu	L159
also	L672
Bhojwani, Kaamna	L367
Bibra, Suleena	L444
Bickerdike, Jennifer Otter	L646
Bickers, Tessa	L159
also	L232
Bickerton, Chris	L007
also	L466
Biden, Hunter	L481
Biehler, L.	L477
Bigg, Marieke	L362
Biglow, Sarah	L043
Bilston, Brian	L333
also	L638
Binge, Nicholas	L096
Bingham, Frances	L336
Binkowski, Brooke	L621
Birch, Carol	L445
Birch, Ian	L066
also	L516
Birch, James	L096
also	L137
Birch, Will	L388
Bird, A.L.	L526
Bird, Brandon	L184
Bird, Michael	L129
also	L215
Birkhead, Tim	L215
also	L520
Birkhold, Matthew H.	L087
Birrell, Rebecca	L159
Bishop, Gary John	L058
also	L059
Bishop, Patrick	L443
Bishop, Sienna	P144
Bissonnette, Zac	L155
Black, Fiona	L128
also	L521
Black, George	L184
Black, Lea	L184
Black, Leona Nichole	L278
also	L583
Black, Louise Soraya	L110
also	L647
Black, Robin	L184
Black, Sue	P143
Black, Vanessa	L096
Blackburn, Simon	L129
also	L215
Blackburn, Victor Lloret	L574
Blackery, Emma	L096
Blackhurst, Chris	L644
Blackhurst, Jenny	L557
Blackmore, Neil	L052
also	L159
Blackmore, Rachel	L066
also	L516
Blackwell, Scarlett	P144
Blaine, Jamie	L018
Blaise, S.	P144
Blaize, Immodesty	L096
also	L137
Blake, Jenny	L388
Blake, Lucy	L297
Blake, Matt	L278
also	L326
Blake, Victoria	L623
Blakeman, Rob	P081
Blakeway, Jill	L481
Blanch, Lesley	L446
Blass, Tom	L048
Blaxill, Gina	L157
Bleeker, Emily	L603
Blessed, Brian	L048
Blight, David W.	L608
Bliss, Laura	L396
Block, Amanda	L333
also	L638
Block, Cierra	L226
also	L680
Blom, Jen K	L603
Bloodworth, James	L159
also	L270
Bloom, Emily	L609
also	L639
Bloom, Valerie	L188
Bloor, Thomas	L240
Blow, Charles	L469
Blue, Maame	L574
Blue-Williams, Steven	P144
Bluestein, Greg	L087
Blum, Andrew	L215
also	L318
Blunden, Edmund	L159
Blunt, James	L443
Blunt, Katherine	L609
also	L639
Bobelian, Michael	L184
Bock, Kenneth	L481
Bodanis, David	L096
Boden, Margaret	L159
also	L266
Boehme, Jillian	L477
Boehmer, Elleke	L129
also	L215
Boff, Jonathan	L159
also	L270
Bofkin, Lee	L096
Bohan, Suzanne	L334
Boissoneault, Lorraine	L184
Bojanowski, Marc	L396
Bolchover, David	L566
Boleyn, Darcie	L526
Bolingbroke-Kent, Antonia	L504
Bonasia, Lynn Kiele	L334
Bond, Caroline	L468
Bond, Charlotte	L096
also	L130
Bond, Tara	L157
Bongers, Charles	L313
Bonnaffons, Amy	L184
Bonnet, Didier	L297
Bonnett, Alastair	L029
Bono, Giacomo	L297
Bono, Katie	L634
Bonsu, Osei	L086
Booker, Simon	L443
Booles, Gill	L128
also	L521
Booth, Anne	L333
also	L638
Booth, Kevin	L539
Booth, Owen	L278
also	L583
Booth, Stephen	L623
Booth, Tom	L537
Bootle, Emily	L209
also	L276
Booy, Simon van	L096
Borba, Michele	L334
Borders, Lisa	L297
Bordo, Susan	L238
Borgh, Kate van der	L146
also	L517
Bornstein, Robert	L334
Borum, Jeremy	L644
Boss, Shira	L184
Bossiere, Zoë	L141
Bostock-Smith, Adam	L332
Bostwick, Marie	L162
also	L405
Bosworth, Patricia	L469
Botchway, Stella	L129
also	L215

Bothwick, Justine	L074
Bouazzaoui, Soraya	L333
Boudreau, Hélène	L418
Bouk, Dan	L440
Bounds, Jon	L294
also	L613
Bouquet, Cyril	L297
Bourgeois, Francis	L676
Bourgon, Lyndsie	L609
Bourke, Jordan	L677
Bourne-Taylor, Hannah	L096
also	L380
Bowdler, Michelle	L184
Bowen, Innes	L007
also	L466
Bowen, Sesali	L184
Bowers, Nadia	L184
Bowie, Nikolas	L608
Bowie, Sarah	L157
Bowker, John	L129
also	L215
Bowlby, Will	L086
Bowles, Peter	L446
Bowman, Akemi Dawn	L458
Boy, Clerkenwell	L086
Boyce, Kim	L063
Boyce, Lee	L591
also	L663
Boycott, Rosie	L446
Boyd, Elizabeth Reid	L334
Boyd, Pattie	L446
Boym, Svetlana	L184
Boyne, John	P143
Boytchev, Oggy	L294
also	L613
Bozeman, Darby	L567
Bracewell, Michael	L029
Bradbury, Megan	L096
also	L380
Bradbury-Haehl, Nora	L334
Braddon, Paul	L294
also	L613
Brade, Scarlett	L066
also	L093
Bradford, Chris	L644
Bradford, Maria	L159
also	L170
Bradley, Anna	L603
Bradley, Christina	L526
Bradley, Mark	L157
Bradley, Mark Philip	L608
Bradley, Vicki	L069
also	L157
Bradshaw, John	L096
Brady, Ali	L416
also	L477
Brady, Fern	L146
also	L456
Brager, Sol	L515
also	L609
Bragg, G.B.	L184
Bragg, Melvyn	L446
also	L577
Bragg, Sara	L157
also	L585
Brahin, Lisa	L665
Brahmachari, Sita	L512
Braithwaite, E. R.	L159
Bramley, Cathy	L294
Brammer, Mikki	L159
also	L232
Bramwell-Lawes, Stephanie	L676
Brandom, Helen	L401
Brandon, Ruth	L007
also	L466
Brar, Amman	L116
Bratton, Susan	L440
Braude, Mark	L615
Braun, Gabriella	L504
Braver, Gary	L297
Bravo, Lauren	L159
also	L232
Bray, Carys	L052
also	L159
Bray, Natalie	L146
also	L517
Braybrooke, Neville	L159
Brazier, Lucy	L276
also	L632
Brazil, Kevin	L159
Breathnach, Kevin	L096
Breen, Benjamin	L184
Brellend, Kay	L110
also	L647
Brencher, Hannah	L609
Brennan, Kevin	L048
Brennan, Marie	L226
also	L680
Brenner, Helene	L063
Breslin, Theresa	L159
also	L645
Brett, Luce	L278
also	L583
Brewer, Katie	L616
Brewster, Bill	L388
Brickell, Christopher	L129
also	L215
Bridges, Chris	L567
Bridgestock, R.C.	L166
also	L306
Bridget,	L276
Bridgewater, Marcus	L007
also	L466
Bridle, James	L632
Brier, Bob	L162
also	L405
Brigden, Susan	L129
also	L215
Briggs, Andy	L066
also	L093
Briggs, Carolyn S.	L297
Brignull, Irena	L129
also	L215
Brill, Francesca	L215
also	L669
Briner, Karen	L063
Briscoe, Constance	L022
also	L157
Brizec, Isabelle	L348
Broach, Elise	L184
Broadstock, Daniel	L392
Brock, Jared	L440
Brockett, Catheryn J.	L063
Brockmeier, Kevin	L184
Brody, Frances	L341
Brook, Rhidian	L215
also	L669
Brooke, Amanda	L567
Brooke, Anne	P144
Brooke-Hitching, Edward	L099
also	L278
Brooke-Smith, James	L215
also	L318
Brooke-Taylor, Tim	L332
Brooker, Charlie	L333
also	L638
Brooker, Will	L086
Brookes, Adam	L129
also	L215
Brookes, Catherine	L526
Brooks, Elizabeth	L294
also	L396
also	L613
Brooks, Michael	L096
Brooks, Mike	L096
Broom, Isabelle	L294
Broome, Iain	L096
also	L380
Broomfield, Mark	L294
also	L613
Brothers, The Wild Swimming	L096
Brotherson, Corey	L676
Brotherton, Marcus	L537
Brottman, Mikita	L184
Broudie, Ian	L086
Broughton, Frank	L388
Brovig, Dea	L096
also	L380
Browder, Bill	L096
Brower, Elena	L427
Brown, Anne Greenwood	L334
Brown, Archie	L215
also	L318
Brown, Benita	L623
Brown, Bethany	P144
Brown, Dan	P052
Brown, Danielle	L157
Brown, David W.	L184
Brown, Derren	P052
Brown, Don	L414
Brown, Glen	L052
also	L159
Brown, Ian	L332
Brown, Jackson P.	L329
Brown, Kate	L388
Brown, Larisa	L215
also	L318
Brown, Martin	L159
also	L645
Brown, Michelle Poirier	L033
Brown, Nora Anne	L066
also	L516
Brown, Stacia	L184
Brown, Steve	L512
Brown, Symeon	L116
Brown, Tom	L166
also	L306
Brown, Waka	L458
Brown, Whitney	L048
Browne, David	L184
Browne, Gay	L334
Browne, Hester	L159
Browne, Janet	L159
also	L266
Browne, Nm	L445
Brownfield, HF	L612
Brownlee, Lucie	L333
also	L638
Brownlie, Rebecca	L226
also	L680
Brownlow, Mike	L159
also	L645
Brubach, Holly	L469
Bruder, Jessica	L159
also	L266
Brueckmann, Alex	L313
Brueggemann, Wibke	L333
Brume, Rukky	L159
also	L232
Brumm, Michael	L229
Bruno, Debra	L297
Brusatte, Anne	L440
Brusatte, Stephen	L440
Bryan, Jonathan	L446
Bryan, Lynne	L276
also	L468

Bryan, Mike	L644	Bushe, Fran	L333	Canepa-Anson, Abi	L586
Bryant, Anabelle	L603	Busk, Michael	L313	Cannon, Joanna	L032
Bryant, Arthur	L159	Bustamante, Andrew	L537	*also*	L096
Brynard, Karin	L066	Bustamante, Mónica	L063	Caporn, Sam	L567
also	L171	*also*	L184	Cardwell, Diane	L087
Bryson, Bill	P143	Butchart, Pamela	L401	Carey, Anna	L148
Bublitz, Jacqueline	L586	Butcher, Jim	L176	Carey, Edward	L066
Buccola, Allison	L184	Butcher, Sally	L052	*also*	L171
Buchan, Elizabeth	L468	*also*	L159	Carey, John	L159
Buchan, Ursula	L215	Butler, Dave	L313	*also*	L270
also	L520	Butler, Dawn	P460	Carey, Linda	L364
Buchanan, Kyle	L537	Butler, Letty	L096	Carey, Louise	L364
Buchanan, Tracy	L294	Butler-Adams, William	L591	Carey, Mike	L364
also	L295	*also*	L663	Cargill-Martin, Honor	L157
Buck, Libby	L537	Butler-Bowdon, Tom	L215	Carlin, Aine	L677
Buck, Louisa	L096	*also*	L318	Carlisle, Tom	L392
also	L137	Butterfield, Charlotte	L567	Carlson, Craig	L334
Buck, Tobias	L007	Butterfield, Lanisha	L157	Carlson, Leland	L048
also	L466	Butterwick, Caroline	L166	Carnac, James	L539
Bucknall, Ella	L159	*also*	L216	Carnegie, Jo	L526
Bucksbaum, Sydney	L155	Butterworth, Nick	L052	Carney, Mark	L446
Budde, Mariann Edgar	L481	*also*	L159	Carney, Scott	L481
Bueno, Julia	L215	Button, Tara	L297	Carol, James	L069
also	L520	Byers, Michael	L584	*also*	L157
Bulger, Ralph	L539	Byrne, Emma	L215	Carpenter, Elisabeth	L294
Bull, Andy	L099	*also*	L520	*also*	L295
also	L278	Byrne, Jason	L276	Carr, Joe P.	L063
Bull, Jessica	L470	*also*	L632	Carr, John Dickson	L159
Bullen, Chiara	L227	Byrne, Monica	L238	Carr, Robyn	L162
Bullock, Maggie	L427	Byrnes, Jonathan	L297	*also*	L405
also	L440	Cabot, Meg	L294	Carrasco, Katrina	L184
Bullock-Prado, Gesine	L481	Cadigan, Pat	L445	Carrey, Jim	L469
Bunn, Davis	L414	Cagan, Kayla	L148	Carroll, E. Jean	L388
Bunting, Erin	L066	Cahill, James	L066	Carson, Paul	L157
also	L516	*also*	L171	Carter, Andrea	L166
Bunting, Jo Facer & Erin	L066	Cain, Cheryl	P435	*also*	L306
also	L516	Cain, Hamilton	L184	Carter, Bill	L184
Bunzl, Peter	L029	Cain, Kelly	L444	Carter, Chris	L022
Buoro, Stephen	L116	Caine, Michael	L446	*also*	L157
Burfoot, Ella	L240	Cairns, Angela	L616	Carter, Erika	L184
Burger, Ariel	L334	Calder, Emma	L446	Carter, Laura	L157
Burgess, Anthony	L159	Calder, Hannah	L621	*also*	L585
Burgess, Zoe	L209	Calder, Jill	L240	Carter, Paul	L334
also	L276	Calidas, Tamsin	L446	Carter, Steven	L063
Burgis, Tom	L096	Callaghan, Helen	L468	Carthew, Natasha	L066
also	L380	Callaghan, Jo	L032	*also*	L516
Burhardt, Majka	L297	*also*	L096	Cartmel, Andrew	L226
Burke, Kevin	L469	Callaghan, Louise	L190	*also*	L680
Burke, Stephen	L215	Callahan, Eliza Barry	L159	Cartner-Morley, Jess	L159
also	L669	Calleja, Jen	L005	Carty-Williams, Candice	L333
Burke, Wren	L276	Callow, Simon	L290	*also*	L638
also	L468	Calvin, Michael	L566	Carver, Will	L166
Burnell, Mark	L159	Calvo, Paco	L159	*also*	L306
also	L266	*also*	L672	Casale, Alexia	L506
Burnet, Graeme Macrae	L066	Cambanis, Thanassis	L608	*also*	L507
also	L171	Cameron, Bill	L532	Casares, Whitney	L467
Burnett, R. S.	L159	Cameron, Josephine	L148	Casely-Hayford, Augustus	L446
also	L232	Cameron, Lucy	L282	Casemore, Shawn	L297
Burnford, Sheila	L159	Cameron, Stella	L162	Casey, Anne-Marie	L159
Burnham, Amanda	L122	*also*	L405	Cassidy, Cathy	L022
Burns, Jimmy	L443	Cammaratta, Natalie	L444	Casson, John	L539
Burns, Karen	L063	Campbell, Al	L364	Castellani, Christopher	L584
Burstell, Ed	L254	Campbell, Alan	L445	Castillo-Speed, Lillian	L063
Burston, Paul	L166	Campbell, Jen	L099	Castle, Barbara	L159
also	L306	*also*	L278	Castle, Jill	L334
Burt, Caroline	L159	Campbell, John	L278	Castro, Orsola De	L204
also	L270	*also*	L339	Catchpool, Michael	L188
Burtka, David	L481	Campbell, Karen	L333	Cathcart, Brian	L443
Burton, Jessie	L470	*also*	L638	Cathrall, Sylvie	L448
Burton, Matthew	L129	Campbell, Susan	L334	Cathro, Grant	L332
also	L215	Campbell, Tom	L276	Catron, Mandy	L238
Burton, Sarah	L362	*also*	L632	Caudevilla, Fernando	L621
Bush, Stephen	L007	Campbell-Johnston, Rachel	L096	Caulfield, Timothy	L090
also	L466	*also*	L137	Causley, Charles	L159
Bushby, Karl	L215	Campbell-Smith, Judy	L603	Cave, Holly	L032
also	L318	Canellos, Peter	L608	*also*	L096

Cave, Kathryn L159
also L645
Cave, Lucie L526
Cavendish, Lucy L215
also L669
Caveney, Graham L215
also L318
Cayton-Holland, Adam L184
Cecchi-Dimegli, Paola L297
Cecil, Lila L313
Centeno, Nicole L440
Central, Climate L184
Cenziper, Debbie L334
Cerrotti, Rachael L334
Cervantes, Angela L174
Cervantes, Fernando L215
also L520
Chadwick, Angela L586
Chadwick, Elizabeth L066
also L171
Chaffin, Joshua L007
also L466
Chaiton, Sam L665
Chakkalakal, Tess L608
Chakrabortty, Aditya L159
also L270
Chalice, Lucy L364
Challen, David L333
also L638
Challis, Sarah L215
also L669
Chalmers, Ashley L146
also L223
Chalmers, John L329
Chamarette, Jenny L521
Chamberlain, Laura L110
also L647
Chamberlain, Mary L470
Chambers, Kimberley L048
Chan, Eliza L096
Chan, Vanessa L116
also L159
Chance, Rebecca L526
Chancellor, Bryn L184
Chandler, Adam L396
Chandler, HS L295
Chandler, Natalie L163
Chandler-Wilde, Helen L591
also L663
Chang, Catherine L567
Chang, Fran L066
also L516
Chapel, Janey P144
Chapin, Ted L388
Chapman, Gary L539
Chapman, Jason L159
also L645
Chapman, Peter L215
also L318
Chapman, Simon L240
Chapman, Sital Gorasia L401
Chapple, Matt L677
Charbonneau, Joelle L184
Charles, Georgina L146
also L456
Charles, Shavone L515
also L609
Charlesworth, Kate L364
Charlesworth, Monique L443
Charlier, Marj L334
Charlton, Paul L332
Charlton, Richard L443
Charlton-Dailey, Rachel L128
also L521
Charmley, John L129
also L215
Charney, Noah L184
Charter, David L644
Charters, Charlie L644
Charters, Shirley L539
Chase, Eve L159
Chase, James Hadley L159
Chase, Paula L184
Chater, Nick L129
also L215
Chatterjee, Pratap L238
Chaupoly, Ratha L481
Chawdhary, Sunita L325
Chawla, Seerut K. L159
also L232
Chayka, Kyle L192
Chayka, Meghan L665
Che, Hannah L086
Cheek, Mavis L446
Cheetham, Jo L333
also L638
Cheetham, Tracey L236
Chen, Angela L609
also L639
Chen, Chengde L236
Chen, Tiffany L086
Chen, Wendy L073
Cheng, Ken L146
also L456
Cheng, Linda L148
Chenoweth, Emily L184
Chern, Lina L416
also L477
Chernoff, Marc and Angel L537
Chernoff, Scott L155
Cheshire, Simon L294
Chess, K L184
Chester, Fliss L614
Chetty, Darren L333
Chien, Windy L427
Chigudu, Simukai L215
also L520
Child, Heather L343
Child, Lee L022
also L157
also P052
Childress, Mark L184
Childs, Tera Lynn L058
also L059
Chin, Rita Zoey L141
Chin-Quee, Tony L155
Chin-Tanner, Wendy L108
Chinn, Adrienne L294
also L613
Chinn, Carl P081
Chislett, Helen L446
Chiu, Christina L184
Chiusolo, Samantha L212
also L377
Cho, Catherine L124
also L096
also L380
Choate, Judith L467
Choi, Anne Soon L582
Chong, Camille L325
Choo, Yangsze L058
also L059
Chotzinoff, Robin L063
Chowdhury, Ajay L557
Chown, Marcus L215
also L520
Christensen, Julia F. L204
Christensen, Ulrik L297
Christgau, Robert L388
Christian, Timothy L313
Christiansen, Morten H. L129
also L215
Christianson, John L334
Christie, Emma L295
Christie-Miller, Amelia L614
Christopher, Adam L184
Chu, Deborah L676
Chu, Vikki L212
also L377
Chubb, Mimi L184
Chun, Ye L192
Chung, Bonnie L099
also L278
Chung, Julien L229
Church, Daniel L364
Churchill, Amanda L073
Ciccarelli, Kristen L477
Ciccone, Carla L609
also L639
CityLab, Bloomberg L396
Claesson, Jonas L336
Clair, Kassia St L504
Claire, Sophie L110
also L647
Clammer, Paul L644
Clancy, Christi L522
Clancy, Christina L522
Clare, Tim L096
also L380
Clark, Eliza L333
Clark, Emma Chichester L159
also L645
Clark, Lloyd L644
Clark, Nicky L566
Clark, Nicola L254
Clark, Tara L. L334
Clark, Tiana L108
Clark-Flory, Tracy L108
Clark-Junkins, Margot L334
Clarke, Arthur C. L159
Clarke, Cassandra Rose L184
Clarke, Chris L086
Clarke, Clare L086
Clarke, John L539
Clarke, Kevin L236
Clarke, Lucy L468
Clarke, Maxine Beneba L032
also L096
Clarke, Norie L066
also L516
Clarke, Robert L539
Clarke, Roger L096
also L137
Clarke, Rosie L341
Classon, Carrie L440
Clements, Abby L294
Clements, Ellie L333
Clements, Rory L623
Clerk, Carol L539
Cliff, Aimee L131
also L533
Cliff, Nigel L184
Cliffe-Minns, Louise L348
Clifford, David L189
also L278
Clifford, Frank L063
Clifton, Rita L446
Clinning, Shauna L506
also L507
Clive, Lady Mary L159
Cloepfil, Georgia L609
also L639
Coburn, Broughton L388
Cochrane, Lauren L086
Cockell, Charles L276
also L632
Cody, Liza L129
also L215

Claim your free access to ***www.firstwriter.com****: See p.403*

Coe, Jonathan	L215
also	L669
Coe, Reuben	L278
also	L326
Coe, Sebastian	L446
Coelho, Mário	L226
also	L680
Coetzee, J. M.	L159
also	L266
Coffelt, Nancy	L184
Coffey, Laura	L146
also	L456
Coffin, Jaed	L184
Coggan, Helena	L364
Cohen, Cole	L184
Cohen, Joshua	L297
Cohen, Julie	L623
Cohen, Marina	L148
Cohen, Miriam	L184
Cohen, Rob	L063
Cohen, Sir Ronald	L566
Cohen, Tal	L122
Cohu, Will	L215
also	L669
Colail, J. M.	P144
Colbert, Jaimee Wriston	L184
Coldwell, Paul	L254
Cole, Chloe	L108
Cole, Daniel	L032
also	L096
Cole, David	L238
Cole, Jessi	L477
Cole, Julia	L066
also	L516
Cole, Martina	L022
also	L157
Coleman, Ashley M.	L444
Coleman, Rowan	L282
Coleman, Sarah J.	L110
also	L647
Coles, Richard	L048
Colgan, Annette	L074
Colgan, Jenny	L333
also	L638
Colino, Stacey	L440
Colins, Katy	L470
Collard, Paul Fraser	L166
also	L306
Collett, Ryan	L282
Collier, Deryn	L033
Collier, Michael	L584
Collins, Christina	L401
Collins, David	L099
also	L278
Collins, Kathleen	L159
Collins, Sophie	L159
Collins-Dexter, Brandi	L582
Collison, Martha	L677
Colville, Zoë	L099
also	L278
Colwell, Chip	L608
Colyer, Howard	L166
Colón, Angel Luis	L155
Comite, Florence	L239
Compton, Martyn	L539
Compton, Michelle	L539
Conaboy, Chelsea	L153
also	L609
Conis, Elena	L608
Connelly, Charlie	L159
Connelly, Jaymz	P144
Conner, Cliff	L238
Connolly, Hannah	L146
also	L223
Connor, Alan	L159
also	L270
Connor, Erin	L567
Conroy, Natalia	L446
Conroy, Paul	L443
Constantine, Liv	L058
also	L059
Conte, Marie Le	L504
Conti-Brown, Peter	L608
Conway, James	L166
also	L306
Conybeare, Catherine	L608
Cook, Emma	L468
Cook, Gloria	L069
also	L157
Cook, Jesselyn	L087
Cook, Judy	L539
Cook, Melinda Chiu	L603
Cook, Peter	L159
Cook, Sue	L066
also	L516
Cooke, Jack	L677
Cooke, Pan	L537
Cooke, Trish	L159
also	L645
Coolidge, Jennifer	L096
also	L380
Coombs, Howard	L341
Cooper, Artemis	L129
also	L215
Cooper, Brendan	L048
Cooper, Caren	L609
Cooper, Carol	L074
Cooper, Emily S.	L159
Cooper, Emma	L526
Cooper, Jilly	P052
Cooper, Mark	L644
Cooper, Natasha	L159
Cooper, Roxie	L321
Cooper, Yvette	L096
also	L380
Copeland, Rashawn	L414
Copp, Lucy Tandon	L157
Corbin, Pam	L276
also	L632
Corbishley, Nicky	L614
Corby, Gary	L532
Corey, Deborah Joy	L184
Cornelius, Olivia Jordan	L204
Cornell, Paul	L184
Cornish, Jack	L254
Cornwell, Bernard	L159
also	L266
Corrigan, Caroline	L073
Costello, Jamie	L052
also	L159
Costello, Tara	L110
also	L647
Costeloe, Diney	L341
Cotterell, T.A.	L215
also	L669
Coulter, Kendra	L090
Coulter-Cruttenden, Dawn	L392
Courcy, Anne de	L066
also	L171
Courogen, Carrie	L184
Court, Dilly	L623
Courtauld, Sarah	L129
also	L215
Courter, Gay	L334
Cousens, Sophie	L157
Cousins, Bryony	L110
also	L647
Cove-Smith, Chris	L159
Cowan, Ashley	L114
Cowan, Nancy	L334
Cowan-Hall, Paige	L146
also	L223
Coward, Joseph	L209
Cowell, Cressida	L052
also	L159
Cowell, Emma	L066
also	L093
Cowen, Rob	L159
also	L672
Cowen, Tyler	L440
Cowing, Emma	L676
Cowley, Jason	L159
also	L270
also	M258
Cox, Carl	L591
also	L663
Cox, Helen	L294
also	L613
Crabtree, James	L007
also	L466
Craddock, Jeremy	L294
also	L613
Craig, Amanda	L029
also	L537
Craig, Andrew	L254
Craig, Holly	L157
also	L355
Craig, Jeremy	L184
Craig, Robin	L276
also	L460
Crampton, Caroline	L096
also	L380
Crane, Marisa	L141
Craven, M.W.	L166
also	L306
Crawford, Frances	L333
also	L638
Crawford, Katherine Scott	L334
Crawford, Robyn	L415
Crawford, Ryan	L612
Crawford, Susan	L087
Crenshaw, Kimberlé	L469
Crewe, Candida	L029
Crewe, Ivor	L159
also	L270
Crewe, Lesley	L236
Crisell, Hattie	L504
Crispell, Susan	L058
also	L059
Critchley, Simon	L336
Croce, Melissa	L155
Crocker, Bridget	L418
Croft, Adam	L443
Cronin, Marianne	L032
also	L096
Crooks, Jacqueline	L116
Crosby, Polly	L470
Crosby, Sarah	L591
also	L663
Cross, A J	L069
also	L157
Cross, Charles R.	L388
also	L481
Cross, Robin	L644
Crosskey, N.J.	L614
Crossley, Becki Jayne	L612
Crouch, Gabby Hutchinson	L332
Crowe, Duncan	L099
also	L278
Crowe, Sara	L066
also	L294
also	L516
also	L613
Crowl, Jonathan	L584
Crowley, Cath	L129
also	L215
Crowley, Katherine	L184
Crowley, Vivianne	L557

Crumpton, Nick L052	Dash, Mona L128	Deas, Stephen L096
also L159	*also* L521	*also* L130
Cryer, Bob L443	David, Donna L401	Deb, Mimi L476
Cullen, Dave L184	David, Iona L204	deBlanc-Knowles, Jaime L184
Cullen, James L297	David, Stuart L294	DeBlieu, Jan L063
Cullins, Ashley L155	*also* L613	DeCurtis, Anthony L388
Cumberbatch, Judy L240	Davidson, Carey L440	Dederer, Claire L096
Cummings, Les L539	Davies, Kate L468	*also* L380
Cummins, Fiona L096	Davies, Katie L096	Deen, Sophie L619
also L380	*also* L137	Deepak, Sharanya L276
Cundy, David L063	Davies, Martin L623	*also* L460
Cunliffe, John L159	Davies, Nicola L052	Deeren, R.S. L087
also L266	*also* L159	Deighton, Len L048
Cunnell, Howard L096	Davies, Russell L276	Delahaye, Michael L166
also L380	*also* L632	Delaney, Tish L159
Cunningham, Emily L574	Davies, Sara P052	Delany, Ella L153
Cunningham, Joshua L294	Davies, Sharron L294	*also* L609
Cunningham, Sue H L512	*also* L295	Delderfield, R. F. L159
Curran, Avery L276	Davies, Tom L282	Demacque-Crockett, Pepsi L048
also L460	Davis, Anna L276	Dempsey-Multack, Michelle L334
Curran, John L166	*also* L632	Denizet-Lewis, Benoit L087
also L306	Davis, Daniel M. L294	Dennis, Essie L227
Curran, Kim L227	*also* L295	Dennis, Roy L029
Curry, Tim L155	*also* L396	Dent, Lizzy L282
Curtis, Cheyenne L184	Davis, Danielle L229	Denton, Kady MacDonald L159
Curtis, James L159	Davis, Elizabeth L184	*also* L645
Curtis, Lauren Aimee L005	Davis, James L401	Denton, Rebecca L282
Curtis, Norma L341	Davis, Kevan L677	DePoy, Phillip L532
Cuthew, Lucy L333	Davis, Lisa Marie P144	Depp, Daniel L364
Cutler, Georgina L321	Davis, Lydia L468	DePree, Hopwood L427
Cyca, Michelle L609	Davis, Margaret Leslie L063	Derbyshire, Jonathan L007
also L639	Davis, Matthew L582	*also* L466
Cyd, Leela L063	Davison, Caroline L294	Derrible, Sybil L334
Czerski, Helen P460	*also* L613	DeSilva, Jeremy L297
Dabscheck, David L297	Dawar, Niraj L297	Desombre, Auriane L458
Dabydeen, David L029	Dawnay, Gabby L619	Despres, Mk Smith L229
Dahl, Roald L159	Dawson, Delilah S. L184	Dessa, ... L238
also L266	Dawson, Ella L108	Dettmar, Kevin L388
Dahlia, Fia L114	Dawson, J.R. L226	Detwiler-George, Jacqueline L275
Daiches, David L159	*also* L680	Devan, K L166
Daitz, Ben L481	Dawson, Mark L443	*also* L216
Dale, Aaron L166	Dawson, Rachel L276	Deverell, William L087
also L216	*also* L460	Devine, Rachel L476
Dale, Katie L325	Dawson, Tim L332	Devlin, Naomi L048
Daley, David L440	Day, Alex L110	deVos, Kelly L506
Dallin, Sara L048	*also* L647	*also* L507
Daly, Jim L401	Day, Anna L662	Dewar, Elaine L313
Daly, Tess P052	Day, Becca L166	Dey, Iain L099
Dangarembga, Tsitsi L116	*also* L263	*also* L278
also L159	Day, Martin L332	Dhairyawan, Rageshri L209
Dangor, Achmat L066	Day, Rosie L676	*also* L276
also L171	Day, Sarah L470	Dhaliwal, Sharan L166
Daniel Fishel L174	Day, Susie L159	*also* L216
Daniels, Benjamin L215	*also* L645	Dhand, A. A. L166
also L669	Dayal, Sandeep L297	*also* L306
Dannatt, Richard L644	Daykin, Chloe L129	Dhand, Roxane L282
Dapin, Mark L184	*also* L215	Dhillon, Preeti L166
Dar, Azma L166	Daykin, Lizzie L232	*also* L216
also L216	Daykin, Sarah L232	Diamond, David J. L063
Darcy, Dame L184	Deacon, Caroline L240	Diamond, Lucy L159
Dare, Bill L332	Deakin, Leona L276	Diamond, Martha O. L063
Dargie, Michael L313	*also* L662	Diamond, Rebekah L087
Dark, Alice Elliott L184	Dean, Abigail L470	Diaz, Juano L096
Darlington, Miriam L096	Dean, Ellie L623	*also* L380
also L137	Dean, Jason L069	Dick, Gethan L278
Darnton, Tracy L029	*also* L157	*also* L339
Dart, Michael L184	Dean, Peter J. L440	Dick, Morgan L159
Darwent, Heather L166	Dean, Will L066	*also* L232
also L263	*also* L093	Dickason, Christie L646
Darwin, Emma L294	DeAngelo, Darcie L608	Dickenson, Lisa L294
also L613	Dear, Ian L426	Dickie, Gloria L608
Das, Rijula L574	Dearden, Lizzie L159	Dickie, John L129
Das, Subhadra L116	*also* L270	*also* L215
Daseler, Graham L007	Dearman, Lara L096	Dickinson, Margaret L022
also L466	*also* L380	*also* L157

Dickinson, Miranda	L294
DiDonato, Tiffanie	L239
Diell, Rose	L557
also	L647
Diffee, Matt	L537
Difford, Chris	L096
also	L137
DiFranco, Ani	L388
Digance, Richard	L236
Dillamore, Lucy	L159
also	L645
Dillon, Alena	L184
Dillon, Lucy	L159
Dillsworth, LM	L470
Dimbleby, Jonathan	L052
also	L159
DiMicco, Dan	L297
Dinan, Nicola	P143
Dine, Michael	L007
also	L466
Dirie, Waris	P498
Ditum, Sarah	L294
also	L295
also	L396
Divin, Sue	L662
Dixon, Heather	L184
Dixon, Phyllis	L603
Do, Tuyen	L066
also	L516
Dobbie, Peter	L236
Dobkin, Adin	L615
Docton, Becky	L166
also	L306
Dodd, Chris	L099
also	L278
Dodd, Emily	L240
Dodsworth, Laura	L566
Doherty, Berlie	L052
also	L159
Dohrn, Zayd Ayers	L481
Doig, Andrew	L295
Dolan, Naoise	L159
Dominczyk, Dagmara	L481
Domingo, Sareeta	L159
Domoney, David	L159
also	L270
Domínguez, Iñaki	L621
Don, Lari	L240
Donahue, Helen	L609
Donahue, Peter	P209
Donaldson, Carol	L294
also	L613
Done, Stephen	L074
Donkin, Susie	L526
Donkor, Michael	L066
also	L516
Donlea, Charlie	L603
Donnelly, Joe	L521
Donnelly, Liza	L415
Donovan, Joan	L582
Donovan, Kim	L567
Donwood, Stanley	L159
also	L672
Dooey-Miles, Samantha	L128
also	L521
Doran, Gregory	L445
Doran, Phil	L063
Dore, Madeleine	L481
Dorey, Martin	L048
Dorey-Stein, Beck	L615
Dorion, Christiane	L240
Dorn, Barry C.	L297
Dorsey, Candas Jane	L033
Doshi, Avni	L574
Dotson, Drew	L122
Doty, Max	L078
also	L278
Dougherty, Karla	L334
Doughty, Anne	L341
Doughty, Louise	L029
Douglas, Alton	P081
Douglas, Ashley	L521
Douglas, Claire	L470
Douglas, Keighley	L401
Douglas, Ray	L238
Douglass, Chloe	L619
Douglass, Olivia	L005
Doust, Kelly	L159
Dowling, Clare	L022
also	L157
Dowling, Finuala	L066
also	L171
Dowling, Mike	L443
Downes, Lawrence	L184
Downes, Melvyn	L676
Downey, Allyson	L184
Downham, Jenny	L129
also	L215
Downing, David	L644
Downs-Barton, Karen	L159
also	L170
Dowswell, Paul	L644
Doyle, Hannah	L526
Doyle, Hayley	L069
also	L157
Doyle, Lisa	L058
also	L059
Dozal, Gabriel	L515
also	L609
Drake, Alicia	L159
Drake, Monica	P209
Drake, Patrick	L276
also	L632
Drayton, Joanne	L364
Dreilinger, Danielle	L427
Dreisinger, Baz	L295
Drew, Brian	P081
Drew, Kimberly	L108
Dreyfus, Nancy	L334
Dreyfuss, Emily	L582
Dring, Helen	L662
Driscoll, Clive	L539
Driscoll, Rachel Louise	L321
Drucker, Ali	L087
Druckman, Charlotte	L481
Druitt, Tobias	L129
also	L215
Drummond, Elizabeth	L567
Dryburgh, Nicole	L240
Duane, Diane	L364
duBois, Jennifer	L184
DuBois, Laurent	L608
Duchene, Remmy	P144
Duckworth, Charlotte	L294
also	L295
Duckworth, Chloe	L567
Dudley, Renee	L615
Duduit, Del	L149
Duenwald, Sarah	L396
Duffy, Lisa	L477
Duffy, Maureen	L336
Duggan, Audrey	P081
Duggan, Helena	L392
Duguid, Sarah	L159
Duke, Kim	L276
also	L677
Dumaine, Brian	L087
Dumond, Susie	L108
Dunant, Sarah	P498
Dunaway, Suzanne	L063
Dunbar, Helene	L418
Dunbar, Michaela	L591
also	L663
Duncan, Mike	L184
Duncan, Oonagh	L313
Dunham, Lacey	L108
Dunk, Anja	L614
Dunlop, Nic	L646
Dunlop, Rory	L096
also	L137
Dunn, Jane	L676
Dunn, John	L007
also	L466
Dunn, Jon	L048
Dunn, Katherine	L096
also	L380
Dunn, Lily	L276
Dunn, Rosie	L539
Dunn, Roxy	L586
Dunn, Suzannah	L276
also	L632
Dunne, Jacob	L086
Dunne, Patrick	L157
Dunne, Peter	L096
also	L137
Dunning, Mari Ellis	L276
also	L662
Duns, Jeremy	L276
also	L632
Duong, Stephanie	L367
Duplessis, Trevor	L033
Durant-Rogers, Annabel	L325
Durantez, Miriam Gonzalez	L443
Durkin, Hannah	L190
Durrant, Sabine	L468
Dusen, Kodie Van	L448
Dychtwald, Maddy	L440
Dye, Kerry Douglas	L058
also	L059
Dyer, Nick	L063
Dyson, DK	L184
Dyson, Ed	L332
Dyson, Katherine	L526
Dzukogi, Saddiq	L053
also	L278
D'Aguiar, Fred	L052
also	L159
D'Angour, Armand	L007
also	L466
Eagland, Jane	L240
Eagle, Judith	L325
Eakin, Hugh	L469
East, Philippa	L321
Eastham, Kate	L341
Easthope, Lucy	L333
also	L638
Easton, Rosa Kwon	L334
Eastwood, Owen	L566
Eaton, Ellie	L184
Eaves, Ed	L619
Eaves, Will	L215
also	L520
Echols, Damien	L184
Eddo-Lodge, Reni	L215
also	L520
Edelstein, Ilana	L297
Eden, Caroline	L159
also	L672
Eden, Polly	L332
Eden, Scott	L275
Eden, Simon David	L294
also	L613
Edge, Suzie	L166
also	L263
Edger, Stephen	L166
also	L263

Edgers, Geoff	Emswiler, James P.	L063	Faith, Paloma	L676
Eding, Stephanie	L444	Emswiler, Mary Ann	L063	Falafel, Olaf	L276
Edmonds, David	L052	Eng, Tan Twan	L159	also	L632
also	L159	also	L672	Falase-Koya, Alex	L612
Edmundson, Mark	L238	English, Richard	L159	Falaye, Deborah	L058
Edric, Robert	L029	also	L270	also	L059
Edwards, Alan	L146	Engstrom, Doug	L477	Falconer, Morgan	L582
also	L223	Ennes, Hiron	L096	Falk, Seb	L159
Edwards, Eve	L159	Epel, Naomi	L063	also	L270
also	L645	Epstein, Alex	L063	Fallanca, Vittoria	L276
Edwards, Georgie	L539	Epstein, Jenny	L321	also	L460
Edwards, Nick	L215	Epstein, Katherine C.	L297	Fallon, D'Arcy	P209
also	L669	Erades, Guillermo	L574	Fallon, Felice	L066
Edwards, Rachel	L294	Errett, Benjamin	L313	also	L171
also	L613	Erskine, Barbara	L066	Fallon, Rebecca	L146
Edwards, Russell	L539	also	L171	also	L517
Edwards, Scott V.	L608	Erskine, Fiona	L470	Famurewa, Jimi	L504
Edwards, Yvvette	L053	Eschmann, Reese	L477	Farber, Jim	L388
also	L278	Esden, Trish	L603	Farbman, David	L297
Eerkens, Mieke	L396	Esfandiari-Denney, Eve	L159	Farias, Miguel	L294
Egan, Kerry	L159	Esiri, Allie	L096	also	L295
Eglinton, Mark	L086	also	L137	Farjeon, Eleanor	L159
Egner, Jeremy	L537	Esler, Gavin	L159	Farjeon, J. Jefferson	L159
Ehrenhaft, Daniel	L184	also	L270	Farmelo, Graham	L007
Eijk, Maggy Van	L662	Espluga, Eudald	L574	also	L466
Eilberg-Schwartz, Penina	L615	Esposito, Mark	L297	Farmer, Addy	L157
El-Arifi, Saara	L470	Estate, Donald J. Sobol	L184	Farmer, Penelope	L096
El-Arifi, Sally	L163	Estate, Jim Carroll	L184	also	L137
El-Baghdadi, Iyad	L007	Estate, John Steptoe	L184	Farmer, Penny	L539
also	L466	Estate, Joseph Mitchell	L184	Farooqi, Saad T.	L313
Elder, Charity	L334	Estate, Scott O'Dell	L184	Farquhar, Michael	L058
Eldon, Sindri	L676	Estate, William Lee Miller	L184	also	L059
Eldred, Ava	L325	Esterhammer, Karin	L063	Farrant, Natasha	L129
Elkins, J. Theron	L063	Estima, Christine	L090	also	L215
Elkins-Tanton, Linda T.	L440	Etherington, Jan	L332	Farrarons, Emma	L392
Elledge, Jonn	L276	Ettlinger, Marion	L184	Farrell, Chris	L334
also	L632	Evangelou, Gabriela	L276	Farrell, Marchelle	L278
Ellen, Tom	L157	also	L677	also	L583
Ellender, Lulah	L251	Evangelou, Lucia	L276	Farrelly, Seán	L512
also	L278	also	L677	Farren, Tracey	L066
Ellenson, Ruth Andrew	L063	Evans, Claire	L396	also	L171
Ellin, Abby	L582	Evans, Clio	L226	Farrer, Maria	L470
Ellingwood, Ken	L087	also	L680	Farrier, David	L215
Elliott, Bobby	L236	Evans, James	L086	also	L520
Elliott, Laura	L521	Evans, Justin	L582	Fashola, Abimbola	L612
Elliott, Lexie	L522	Evans, Kate	L204	Faulke, Kathryn	L066
Elliott, Rebecca	L557	Evans, Marina	L506	also	L171
Elliott, Simon	L644	also	L507	Faulks, Ben	L159
Ellis, David	M039	Evans, Maz	L052	also	L645
Ellis, Giselle	P144	also	L159	Faurot, Jeannette	L063
Ellis, Rhian	L184	Evans, Rowan	L159	Favereau, Marie	L184
Ellis, Samantha	L468	Evans, Rowland	P435	Fawcett, Edmund	L129
Ellory, Anna	L166	Evans, Stephanie	L532	also	L215
also	L216	Evans, Stewart P.	L539	Fearnley, James	L215
Ellsworth, Loretta	L063	Evelyn, Alex	L157	also	L669
Elo, Elisabeth	L297	Everson, Katie	L333	Fearnley-Whittingstall, Hugh	L276
Eloise, Marianne	L110	also	L638	also	L632
also	L647	Ewan, C. M.	L069	Fearnley-Whittingstall, Jane	L276
Elster, Katherine Crowley & Kathy	L184	also	L157	also	L632
Elster, Kathy	L184	Ewing, Barbara	L445	Fears, Mina	L058
Elven, Lucie	L005	Ewing, Hope	L609	also	L059
Ely, Neil	L429	Excell, Becky	L614	Fedewa, Marilyn	L334
Elysia, Kate	L539	Eyre, Banning	L388	Feeney, Zoe	L662
Emberley, Michael	L537	Eyre, Kirsty	L278	Fein, Louise	L295
Emerson, Tracey	L086	also	L583	Feldman, Matthew	L364
Emery, Léa Rose	L204	Eyre-Morgan, Lloyd	L429	Feldman, Ruth	L396
Emily, Rachel	L401	Facelli, Victoria	L609	Feldman, Stephanie	L184
Emmanuel-Jones, Wilfred	L254	also	L639	Felicelli, Anita	L153
Emmerichs, Sharon	L506	Facer, Jo	L066	also	L609
also	L507	also	L516	Femi, Caleb	L333
Emmerson, Miranda	L294	Fagan, Sinéad	L332	Feng, Linda Rui	L192
also	L295	Fairbairn, Emily	L676	Fennell, David	L166
Emmett, Jonathan	L159	Fairhead, James	L215	also	L306
also	L645	also	L318	Fenstersock, Alison	L388
Emmons, Robert	L297	Fairless, Chelsea	L609	Ferguson, Kitty	L364
Empson, Clare	L282	Faith, Adelaide	L005		

Claim your free access to www.firstwriter.com: See p.403

Fergusson, Adam ... L099
   also ... L278
Fernandes, Sujatha ... L574
Fernandez, Carla ... L141
   also ... L440
Fernie, Ewan ... L336
Fernie, Gabrielle ... L662
Fernández-Armesto, Felipe ... L159
   also ... L270
Ferrars, Elizabeth ... L159
Ferrazzi, Keith ... L297
Ferreira, Becky ... L396
Ferrera, America ... L415
Ferrier, Rebecca ... L096
Ferris, Paul ... L236
Ferry, Georgina ... L215
   also ... L318
Fetuga, Rakaya ... L005
Feuer, Michael ... L334
Fewery, Jamie ... L099
   also ... L278
Fido, Martin ... L539
Field, Anji Loman ... L332
Field, Jean ... P081
Field, Ophelia ... L159
Field, Patricia ... L415
Fields, Helen ... L294
   also ... L295
Fields-Meyer, Tom ... L063
Filby, Eliza ... L007
   also ... L466
Filer, Nathan ... L096
   also ... L380
Filochowski, Jan ... L215
   also ... L318
Finch, Louise ... L401
Finch, Paul ... L066
   also ... L093
Fine, Anne ... L159
   also ... L266
Fine, Cordelia ... L159
   also ... L270
Finger, Aria ... L481
Finkel, Eugene ... L294
   also ... L295
Finkelstein, Danny ... L007
   also ... L466
Finkemeyer, Pip ... L159
   also ... L232
Finlay, Linda ... L623
Finlay, Mick ... L333
   also ... L638
Finnerty, Deirdre ... L166
   also ... L216
Finney, Kathryn ... L609
Finnigan, Louise ... L662
Fiorato, Marina ... L623
Fiore, Rosie ... L294
Firdaus, A P ... L278
   also ... L583
Firnhaber-Baker, Justine ... L254
Fischer, Becca ... L313
Fischer, Bronwyn ... L313
Fischer, Neal E ... L087
Fishell, Katy ... L415
Fisher, Helen ... L468
Fisher, Kerry ... L157
Fisher, Lucy ... L190
Fisher, Richard ... L204
Fishkin, Shelley Fisher ... L238
Fishman, Boris ... L184
Fisk, Nicholas ... L159
Fisk, Pauline ... L159
Fitz, Caitlin ... L608
Fitz-Simon, Christopher ... L276

Fitzgerald, Bea ... L227
   also ... L567
Fitzgerald, Ronan ... L005
Fitzgibbon, Theodora ... L159
Fitzhigham, Tim ... L644
Fitzmaurice, Ruth ... L591
   also ... L663
Fitzpatrick, Noel ... L676
FitzSimons, Amanda ... L427
Flahive, Grace ... L032
   also ... L096
Flannery-Schroeder, Ellen ... L334
Flavin, Teresa ... L240
Flavius, Selina ... L616
Fleet, Rebecca ... L215
   also ... L669
Fleming, Anna ... L029
Fleming, Caroline ... L048
Fleming, Leah ... L341
Fleming, Noah ... L297
Flemington, Sara ... L313
Fletcher, Carrie Hope ... L294
Fletcher, Catherine ... L129
   also ... L215
Fletcher, Corina ... L159
   also ... L645
Fletcher, Giovanna ... L294
Fletcher, Susan ... L229
Fletcher, Tom ... L086
Flicker, Felix ... L276
   also ... L632
Flint, Emma ... L333
   also ... L638
Flint, Sarah ... L341
Flitter, Emily ... L184
Flood, Ciara ... L240
Flood, CJ ... L129
   also ... L215
Flood, Nancy Bo ... L229
Flood, Patrick ... L443
Florence, Kelly ... L652
Flower, Sarah ... L539
Flyn, Cal ... L096
   also ... L380
Flynn, Caroline ... L444
Fogerty, John ... L481
Fogtdal, Peter ... P209
Folds, Ben ... L481
Foley, Hannah ... L240
Fong-Torres, Ben ... L388
Fonteyn, Margot ... L159
Footz, Nona ... L537
Force, Amy de la ... L321
Ford, Catt ... P144
Ford, Fiona ... L066
   also ... L093
Ford, Ford Madox ... L159
Ford, Jack ... L022
   also ... L157
Ford, JR ... L141
Ford, JR and Vanessa ... L537
Ford, Kate ... L591
   also ... L663
Ford, Kelly J ... L090
Ford, Lauren ... L110
   also ... L647
Ford, Martyn ... L157
Ford, Matthew ... L278
   also ... L339
Ford, Nicola ... L294
   also ... L613
Ford, Phil ... L332
Ford, Richard T ... L608
Ford, Vanessa ... L141
Foreman, Freddie ... L539
Foroohar, Darya ... L313

Forrest, Susanna ... L468
Forster, Julia ... L096
   also ... L380
Fort, Adrian ... L443
Fortgang, Laura Berman ... L334
Fortin, Sue ... L282
Forward, Susan ... L334
Fossen, Delores ... L058
   also ... L059
Foster, Alex Cody ... L582
Foster, Chad E. ... L297
Foster, Charles ... L159
   also ... L672
Foster, Fred ... L159
   also ... L232
Foster, Helen ... L539
Foster, Kennedy ... L532
Fowler, Karen Joy ... L159
   also ... L266
Fowler, Yara Rodrigues ... L504
Fowles, Sam ... L096
   also ... L380
Fox, Alix ... L066
   also ... L516
Fox, Becci ... L539
Fox, Catherine ... L159
   also ... L266
Fox, Debbie ... L313
Fox, Emily Jane ... L440
Fox, Essie ... L166
   also ... L306
Fox, Jared ... L582
Fox, Jeffrey ... L579
Fox, Kit ... L609
Foxwood, Rowan ... L325
Frahm, Eckart ... L254
Frainier, Lizzie ... L676
Fram, John ... L153
   also ... L609
Frances, Claire ... L476
Francis, Pauline ... L129
   also ... L215
Francis, Vievee ... L584
Francis, Will ... L048
Franco, Marisa ... L087
Frank, Anita ... L166
   also ... L306
Frank, Matthew ... L159
   also ... L270
Frank, Meryl ... L582
Frankel, Rebecca ... L297
Franklin, Emily ... L297
Franklin, Jonathan ... L443
Franklin, Mariel ... L116
   also ... L159
Franklin, Sarah ... L066
   also ... L516
Frankopan, Peter ... L129
   also ... L215
Franks, Dominic ... L163
Franse, Astrid ... L539
Fransman, Karrie ... L096
   also ... L380
Fraser, Caro ... L341
Fraser, Christa ... L584
Fraser, Emma ... L341
Fraser, Henry ... L566
Fraser, Jennifer Petersen ... L043
Fraser, Jill ... P081
Fraser, Liz ... L278
   also ... L583
Fraser-Cavassoni, Natasha ... L086
Frears, Ella ... L677
Frederick, Brendan ... L184
Freedman, Harry ... L294
   also ... L613

Freedman, Lawrence	L129	
also	L215	
Freeman, Gwen	P081	
Freeman, Joanne B.	L608	
Freeman, Mark	L282	
Freeman, Philip	L334	
Freeman, Roxy	L066	
also	L516	
Freeman, Sara	L096	
also	L380	
Freeman, Seth	L297	
Freemantle, Brian	L336	
Freestone, P. M.	L159	
also	L645	
Freitas, Irena	L174	
French, John	L236	
French, Tana	L022	
also	L157	
French, Vivian	L240	
Freston, Tom de	L159	
Freud, Emily	L623	
Freud, Esther	L096	
also	L137	
Frey, Pia	L184	
Fricas, Katie	L609	
Fridland, Valerie	L615	
Fridriksdottir, Johanna Katrin	L190	
Fried, Seth	L184	
Friedberg, Brian	L582	
Friedlander, Omer	L584	
Friedman, Joe	L240	
Friedman, Tova	L254	
Friend, William	L392	
Frisby, Dominic	L215	
also	L318	
Frizzell, Nell	P052	
Froh, Jeffrey	L297	
Front, Rebecca	L099	
also	L278	
Frost, Claire	L157	
also	L585	
Fry, Hannah	P460	
Fry, Stephen	L159	
also	L266	
Frye, Joe	L448	
Frye, Lacey-Anne	P144	
Fulcher, Stephen	L539	
Fuller, Adam Hossein	L122	
Fullerton, Jean	L066	
also	L093	
Fulton, Patricia	L313	
Furniss, Clare	L129	
also	L215	
Furniss, Jo	L392	
Furnivall, Kate	L623	
Fury, John	L566	
Fury, Paris	L566	
Fury, Tyson	L566	
Gabbay, Tom	L099	
also	L278	
Gacioppo, Amaryllis	L005	
Gailey, Georgia	L259	
also	L680	
Gailey, Samuel W.	L297	
Galbraith, James K.	L608	
Galen, Shana	L416	
also	L477	
Galer, Dustin	L665	
Galfard, Christophe	L276	
also	L632	
Galgut, Damon	L215	
also	L669	
Gallagher, Patrick	L332	
Gallant, Mavis	L159	
Gallardo, Adriana	L515	
also	L609	
Galleymore, Frances	P236	
also	P236	
Galligan, John	L416	
also	L477	
Gallon, Harry	L504	
Galloway, Janice	L066	
also	L516	
Galloway, Steven	L184	
Galway, Caitlin	L367	
Gamble, Ed	P052	
Gamble, Ione	L204	
Game, Shannah	L467	
Gamp, Gary	L282	
Gandhi, Arun	P370	
Ganeshram, Ramin	L440	
Ganguly, Chandra	L276	
also	L468	
Ganjei, Babak	L146	
also	L456	
Gannon, Emma	P460	
Gannon, Ted	L332	
Gapper, John	L007	
also	L466	
Garber, Stephanie	L058	
also	L059	
Garcia, Rhonda J	L652	
Garcia, Rogelio	L418	
Gardam, Jane	L159	
also	L645	
Gardner, Elysa	L388	
Gardner, Hazel	L512	
Gardner, Michael and Ava	L537	
Gardner, Sally	L129	
also	L215	
Garelick, Rhonda	L469	
Garfield, Bob	L440	
Garland, Emma	L209	
Garland, Sarah	L159	
also	L645	
Garner, Ian	L099	
also	L278	
Garner, Paula	L148	
Garnett, Eve	L159	
Garrard, Nicola	L166	
also	L216	
Garrison, Reve	P144	
Garroni, Lauren	L609	
Garthwaite, Annie	L504	
Gartner, John	L184	
Gaspard, Terry	L334	
Gastaldi, Federico	L229	
Gate, Darren	L240	
Gates, Susan	L159	
also	L645	
Gathorne-Hardy, Jonathan	L159	
Gatrell, Peter	L215	
also	L520	
Gattis, Ryan	L159	
Gatwood, Olivia	L609	
Gaudet, John	L334	
Gautier, Amina	L184	
Gavin, Gareth	L276	
also	L460	
Gavin, Jamila	L052	
also	L159	
Gay, Ross	L162	
also	L405	
Gaylord, Joshua	L184	
Gayton, Sam	L401	
Gbadamosi, Gabriel	L096	
also	L380	
Gearhart, Sarah	L087	
Gearing, Tessa	L325	
Geary, Karl	L096	
also	L380	
Geary, Valerie	L184	
Gebbia, Karen	L229	
Gee, Poppy	L184	
Geer, Yvette	L043	
Gehr, Richard	L388	
Geissinger, J. T.	L058	
also	L059	
Gendron, Alice	L282	
George, Jessica	L159	
also	L232	
George, Nelson	L388	
George, Susan	L236	
George-Warren, Holly	L481	
Georgescu, Irina	L048	
Geras, Adèle	L159	
also	L645	
Gerber, Michael	L184	
Gerner, Marina	L282	
Geronimus, Arline T	L469	
Gerritsen, Tess	P052	
Getten, Kereen	L612	
Gettleman, Jeffrey	L087	
Ghadiali, Ashish	L254	
Ghelani, Divya	L166	
also	L216	
Ghosh, Mina Ikemoto	L157	
Gibbons, Moyette	L567	
Gibbs, Tessa	L110	
also	L647	
Gibson, Jasper	L096	
also	L137	
Gibson, Marina	L254	
Gibson, Marion	L396	
Gibson, Michael	L007	
also	L466	
Gibson, Miles	L336	
Gibson, Paula Rae	P236	
Gibson, Rebecca	L146	
also	L456	
Gibson, Sarah	L029	
Gibson, Susannah	L159	
also	L270	
Gibson, Tamika	L612	
Giddens, Rhiannon	L481	
Gidney, Craig Laurance	L226	
also	L680	
Giesecke, Annette	L396	
Gifford, Lisa	L332	
Gilani, Nadia	L166	
also	L216	
Gilbert, Bob	L029	
Gilbert, Kenny	L418	
Gilbert-Collins, Susan	L334	
Gildea, Robert	L129	
also	L215	
Giles, Caro	L048	
Giles, Harry Josephine	L128	
also	L521	
Gilkey, David	L440	
Gill, Elizabeth	L341	
Gill, Flora	L086	
Gill, Josie	L131	
also	L533	
Gill, Nikita	L116	
Gill, Romy	L048	
Gill, Roy	L240	
Gill, Rupinder	L313	
Gill, Seema	P236	
Gillespie, Keith	L236	
Gillespie, Tyler	L418	
Gillett, Ed	L086	
Gillies, Andrea	L468	
Gilligan, Ruth	L096	
also	L380	
Gillingham, Erica	L166	
also	L216	
Gilliss, Meghan	L073	

Gilman, David	L066	
also	L171	
Gilmour, Jesse	L313	
Giltrow, Helen	L276	
Gimblett, Francis	L276	
also	L677	
Gimson, Andrew	L159	
also	L270	
Gingold, Alfred	L184	
Gion, Joel	L251	
also	L278	
Giorno, John	L469	
Giron, Maria	L005	
Gittell, Noah	L087	
Gittins, Rob	L332	
Giudici, Amelia	L103	
also	L215	
Giugni, Lilia	L644	
Gladstone, Xanthe	L614	
Glanfield, Jenny	L066	
also	L197	
Glasfurd, Guinevere	L052	
also	L159	
Glass, Emma	L116	
Glass, Seressia	L058	
also	L059	
Glasser, Ralph	L159	
Glazebrook, Olivia	L504	
Gleason, Mat	L621	
Gleeson, Claire	L278	
also	L583	
Gleiberman, Owen	L184	
Glen, Joanna	L032	
also	L096	
Glendinning, Victoria	L159	
also	L270	
Glenn, Ebony	L212	
also	L377	
Glenny, Misha	L096	
also	L137	
Glickman, Adina	L612	
Glogovac, Michelle	L334	
Glover, Jane	L290	
Glover, Jonathan	L129	
also	L215	
Glover, Julian	L007	
also	L466	
Glover, Kimberley	L616	
Gnuse, A.J.	L032	
also	L096	
Goacher, Lucy	L567	
Godfrey, Joline	L063	
Gold, Mara	L276	
also	L460	
Gold, Robert	L470	
Goldbach, Eliese Colette	L295	
also	L396	
Goldberg, Danny	L481	
Goldberg, Ron	L418	
Goldblatt, Amanda	L192	
Goldblatt, David	L215	
also	L318	
Goldie, Alison	L539	
Golding, Julia	L159	
also	L645	
Goldman, Dan	L537	
Goldreich, Anna	L005	
Goldsmith, William	L325	
Goldstein, Brandt	L184	
Golio, Gary	L184	
Golombok, Susan	L215	
also	L520	
Gomez, Erica	L612	
Gonsalves, Florence	L477	
Gonzales, Gina	L612	
Gonzalez, Clarissa Trinidad	L367	
Gonzalez, Nicky	L073	
Goodall, Lewis	L677	
Goodan, Chelsey	L467	
Goodavage, Clifton Hoodl Maria	L105	
Goodhart, David	L007	
also	L466	
Goodhind, Jean G	L048	
Goodman, Elyssa	L153	
also	L609	
Goodman, Lee	L532	
Goodman, Matthew	L184	
Goodman, Tanya Ward	L063	
Goodwin, Matthew	L086	
Goodwin, Sarah	L662	
Goran, Michael I.	L063	
Gordon, Kat	L215	
also	L669	
Gordon, Lyndall	L066	
also	L171	
Gordon, Marianne	L364	
Gorman, Michele	L294	
also	L295	
Gornall, Jonathan	L048	
Gosden, Chris	L129	
also	L215	
Gosling, Paula	L468	
Gosling, Victoria	L468	
Gothelf, Jeff	L297	
Gottesman, Jane	L388	
Gottlieb, Eli	L184	
Goudeau, Jessica	L609	
Goudge, Elizabeth	L159	
Gough, Julian	L099	
also	L278	
Gould-Bourn, James	L294	
also	L613	
Govani, Shinan	L313	
Gover, Janet	L278	
also	L583	
Gowan, Lee	L313	
Gower, Jon	L278	
also	L339	
Graetz, Michael	L608	
Graff, Andrew J.	L141	
Graham, Bre	L204	
Graham, Caroline	L159	
also	L266	
Graham, Elyse	L396	
Graham, Sarah	L278	
also	L583	
Graham, Wade	L087	
also	L396	
Gramazio, Holly	L052	
also	L159	
Granados, Marlowe	L159	
Grandin, Temple	L184	
Grange, Pippa	L566	
Granger, Ann	L066	
also	L171	
Grant, Ann E.	L334	
Grant, Carrie	L086	
Grant, Colin	L032	
also	L380	
Grant, David	L086	
Grant, Jules	L096	
also	L130	
Grant, Kester	L159	
also	L645	
Grant, Oliver	L662	
Grant, Stephen Starring	L275	
Gratification, Delayed	L048	
Graudin, Ryan	L159	
also	L645	
Graver, Elizabeth	L184	
Gray, Annie	L048	
Gray, Casey	L184	
Gray, Kate	L470	
Graydon, Samuel	L007	
also	L466	
Grayson, Jonathon	L334	
Graystone, C.C.	L448	
Graziosi, Barbara	L129	
also	L215	
Greanais, Margaret	L537	
Greathouse, J.T.	L226	
also	L680	
Greeley, Molly	L276	
also	L662	
Green, Catherine	L566	
Green, Charlotte	L539	
Green, Christopher	L539	
Green, Dominic	L159	
Green, Erin	L166	
also	L306	
Green, Ian	L445	
Green, Lauren	L108	
Green, Linda	L159	
also	L266	
Green, Peter	L159	
Green, Robin	L388	
Greenan, Tracy	L114	
Greenberg, Hindi	L063	
Greene, Andy	L537	
Greene, Brenda	L334	
Greene, Daniel B.	L226	
also	L680	
Greene, Graham	L159	
also	L266	
Greene, Ronnie	L297	
Greene, Vanessa	L294	
Greenfeld, Karl Taro	L469	
Greenhalgh, Huho	L362	
Greenhouse, Linda	L608	
Greenland, Seth	L184	
Greenlee, Sabrina	L440	
Greenlees, Paula	L295	
Greenwald, Charlie	L229	
Greenwald, Tommy	L229	
Greenwood, Kirsty	L294	
Greer, Germaine	P498	
Gregersen, Elaine	L333	
also	L638	
Gregerson, Linda	L584	
Gregoire, Sheila	L414	
Gregor, James	L192	
Gregory, Alexis	L166	
also	L216	
Gregory, Norma	L325	
Greifeld, Bob	L469	
Grey, Andrew	P144	
Grey, Stella	L468	
Grey, Tamsin	L333	
also	L638	
Gribbin, John	L159	
also	L270	
Grice, Allan	L539	
Grierson, Bruce	L238	
Griffin, Anne	L032	
also	L091	
also	L096	
Griffin, Nicholas	L615	
Griffin, Stephen	L236	
Griffith, Gabriella	L066	
also	L516	
Griffiths, Jay	L159	
also	L672	
Griffiths, Kareen	L512	
Grigorescu, Alexandra	L313	
Grigson, Geoffrey	L159	
Grigson, Jane	L159	
Grist, Mark	L333	
Groskop, Viv	P460	

Gross, Daniel	L440	
Gross, Gwendolen	L184	
Gross, Neil	L427	
Grosshans, Beth A	L334	
Groth, Olaf	L297	
Grotz, Jennifer	L584	
Groves, Annie	L623	
Grunenwald, Jill	L416	
also	L477	
Grynbaum, Michael	L469	
Gubicza, Jen	L212	
also	L377	
Gude, Erik	L537	
Gudowska, Malwina	L204	
Guess, Jessica	L652	
Guile, Alison	L619	
Guillory, Sarah	L612	
Guillén, Mauro	L440	
Guinness, Jack	L470	
Gulvin, Jeff	L646	
Gunaratne, Guy	L096	
also	L380	
Gunn, Alastair	L294	
also	L295	
Gunn, Kirsty	L096	
also	L137	
Guo, Nadia	L313	
Gupta, Kamal	L313	
Gupta, Sunetra	L297	
Guralnick, Peter	L537	
Gurney, Karen	L278	
also	L583	
Guron, Ravena	L612	
Gutierrez, Katie	L032	
also	L096	
Gutierrez, Rudy	L184	
Gutiérrez-Glik, Andrea	L481	
Gutteridge, Toby	L392	
Gwin, Minrose	L440	
Gwinn, Saskia	L034	
also	L278	
Gwynne, John	L343	
Hackett, Lily	L209	
Hackman, Rose	L609	
Hackworthy, Kate	L526	
Haddad, Rana	L336	
Haefele, John	L598	
Hafdahl, Meg	L652	
Hafiza, Radiya	L612	
Hahn, Taylor	L108	
Haig, Francesca	L470	
Haig, Matt	L096	
also	L137	
Haines, Lise	L297	
Hakakian, Roya	L566	
Hakes, Jasmin 'Iolani	L073	
Hakim, Yalda	L566	
Hale, Kathleen	L184	
Hale, Lisa	L184	
Hale, Steven	L418	
Hales, Gabrielle	L086	
Haley, Guy	L329	
Halfon, Simon	L048	
Hall, Araminta	L159	
Hall, Catherine	L215	
also	L669	
Hall, Clare Leslie	L282	
Hall, Eddie	L048	
Hall, Jake	L209	
also	L276	
Hall, Joanna	L468	
Hall, Julie L.	L334	
Hall, Lori Inglis	L032	
also	L096	
Hall, Simon	L215	
also	L318	
Hall, Wes	L313
Hallberg, David	L469
Halliburton, Rachel	L007
also	L466
Halliday, G.R.	L069
also	L157
Halliday, Thomas	L129
also	L215
Halligan, Liam	L007
also	L466
Halliwell, Ed	L426
Halls, Ben	L586
Halls, Stacey	L470
Halperin, Shirley	L388
Hamby, Chris	L297
Hamel-Akré, Jessica	L204
Hamilton, A.B.	L007
also	L233
Hamilton, Bridget Helen	L325
Hamilton, Christine	L539
Hamilton, Henrietta	L074
Hamilton, James	L215
also	L520
Hamilton, Karen	L096
also	L380
Hamilton, Lou	L096
also	L137
Hamilton-Bannis, Karissa	L676
Hamilton-McKenzie, Isaac	L512
Hamlyn, Lili	L005
Hammer, Alison	L416
also	L477
Hammond, Ryan	L157
Hampton, Leah	L184
Hamya, Jo	L159
Hancock, Penny	L159
also	L232
Handrick, Michael	L166
also	L216
Handy, Charles	L007
also	L466
Hankinson, Andrew	L007
also	L466
Hanley, James	L159
Hannah, James	L032
also	L096
Hannan, Tony	L048
Hannibal, Mary Ellen	L184
Hannig, Anita	L609
Hannity, Mary	L159
Hansen, Brooks	L584
Hansen, Kim-Julie	L086
Hansford, Andrew	L539
Haque, Sarah	L204
Haran, Maeve	L468
Harcourt, Isabella	L567
Harcourt, Lou Morgan / Maggie	L470
Harding, Charlie	L388
Harding, Debora	L096
also	L137
Harding, Emily	L334
Harding, Kate	L334
Hardman, Isabel	L159
also	L270
Hardy, Alyssa	L184
Hardy, Chips	L566
Hardy, Edward	L240
Hardy, Elle	L392
Hardy, Reina	L396
Hare, Bernard	L290
Harford, Tim	L215
also	L318
Hargreaves, Mary	L157
also	L585
Harlan, Charlie	L227
Harley, Belinda	L468
Harman, Alice	L157
Harman, Sophie	L159
also	L270
Harmer, Joyce Efia	L157
Harper, Candida	L159
also	L645
Harper, Elodie	L470
Harper, Mireille	L166
also	L216
Harper, Peter	L677
Harper, Tim	L159
also	L270
Harrar, George	L297
Harris, Ali	L159
Harris, Anstey	L321
Harris, Ben	L332
Harris, James	L619
Harris, Neil Patrick	L481
Harris, Oliver	L052
also	L159
Harris, Sarah	L348
Harris, Will	L116
Harris, Windy Lynn	L184
Harrison, Katy	L166
also	L263
Harrison, M John	L445
Harrison, Michael	L644
Harrison, Phil	L276
also	L468
Hart, Alice	L677
Hart, B. H. Liddell	L159
Hart, Ericka	L427
Hart, Gracie	L341
Hartema, Laura	L334
Hartley, Gabrielle	L087
also	L427
Hartley, Jack	L429
Hartley, Sarah	L066
also	L516
Hartnett, Angela	L048
Harvey, Alyxandra	L603
Harvey, Clare	L623
Hashimoto, Reiko	L086
Haslam, David	L066
also	L516
Hasler, Susan	L162
also	L405
Haslett, Emma Forsyth	L066
also	L516
Haspiel, James	L539
Hassan, Ramsey	L512
Hatch, Evie	L276
also	L460
Hatfield, Ruth	L401
Hattrick, Alice	L159
Hatzistefanis, Maria	L566
Hauck, Paul	L022
Hauck, Rachel	L414
Hauser, Ethan	L184
Havelin, Karen	L574
Hawdon, Lindsay	L032
also	L096
Hawke, Sam	L343
Hawkins, Ed	L034
also	L278
Hawkins, Paula	L159
also	P052
Hawkins, Scott	L405
Hawley, Ellen	L063
Hay, Suzanne	L043
Hayder, Mo	L052
also	L159
Haydock, Sophie	L470
Hayes, Erica	L603
Hayes, Larry	L401

Hayes, Nick L159
also L672
Hayes, Patrick P081
Haynes, Dana L532
Hayward, Cathy L074
Hayward, Julie L209
also L276
Hayward, Will L646
Hazel, James L190
Hazell, Lottie L159
also P143
Hazzard, Oli L159
He, Joan L148
Healey, Cherry L676
Healy, Claire Marie L159
Heap, Sue L188
Heard, Gerald L159
Hearn, Julie L129
also L215
Hearn, Sam L619
Hearne, Kevin L184
Heath, Sue L526
Heath-Stubbs, John L159
Heather, Peter L129
also L215
Heatherington, Emma L321
Heaton, Natalie L526
Hecker, Tim L215
also L520
Heckler, Kimberly L334
Hedges, Kristi L334
Hedrick, Lucy L603
Hehir, Sarah L676
Heidicker, Christian McKay L148
Heisenfelt, Ann L239
Heisz, Jennifer L090
Helen, Elizabeth L226
also L680
Hellenga, Robert L184
Heller, Miranda Cowley L032
also L096
Heller, Ted L239
Hellisen, CL L128
also L521
Heminsley, Alexandra L096
also L380
Hemnani, Ritu L229
Henderson, Alexis L058
also L059
Henderson, Caspar L029
Henderson, Emma L052
also L159
Henderson, Jordan L566
Henderson, Joseph M. L297
Henderson, Julietta L032
also L096
Hendricks, Steve L184
Hendrie, James L332
Hendrix, Grady L226
also L680
Hendrix, Michael L537
Hendry, Ali L166
also L216
Hendry, Diana L240
Hendry, Sharon L086
Hendy, Paul L236
Henley, Amelia L282
also L566
Henley, Marian L063
Hennigan, Jane L163
Henry, Joe L184
Hepburn, Jessica L086
Hepinstall, Becky L184
Hepworth, David L644
also P052
Herbert, James L159
also L266
Heritage, Stuart L276
also L632
Herlich, Taryn L448
Herrick, Holly L334
Herrick, Richard P101
Herriot, James L159
Herron, Mick L159
Herron, Rita L058
also L059
Herst, Charney L063
Herz, Rachel L418
Hess, Alex L190
Hess, Elizabeth L388
Hesse, Josiah L481
Hewitt, Deborah L159
also L232
Hewitt, Gavin L129
also L215
Hewitt, JM L557
Hewlett, Rosie L159
also L232
Heyam, Kit L209
also L276
Hibberd, James L537
Hibbert, Christopher L159
Hicks, Dan L086
Hicks, Josh L512
Higginbotham, Adam L096
also L380
Higgins, Carter L229
Higgins, Chris L240
Higgins, David L099
also L278
Higham, Tom L294
also L613
Hill, Charlie P236
Hill, Justin L644
Hill, Kat L276
also L460
Hill, Louis L129
also L215
Hill, Maisie L278
also L583
Hill, Matt Rowland L096
also L380
Hill, Nathan L159
also L266
Hill, Susan L577
Hill, Will L099
also L278
Hillman, Jonathan L007
also L466
Hilsum, Lindsey L215
also L520
Hilton, Lisa L166
also L306
Hilton, Wendy L011
Hincenbergs, Sue L476
Hine, Lewis L591
also L663
Hirsch, Heather L440
Hirschman, Leigh Ann L063
Hirshman, Linda L469
Hirst, Chris L159
also L270
Hirst, Lindsay L325
Hise, Brian Van L074
Hitch, Julian L276
also L632
Hitchman, Beatrice L276
Hitzmann, Sue L579
Ho, Karen L515
also L609
Ho-Yen, Polly L157
Hoban, Russell L159
also L270
Hobhouse, Penelope L129
also L215
Hobsbawm, Eric L159
also L270
Hodes, Martha L608
Hodge, Gavanndra L159
Hodges, Kate L066
also L516
Hodges, Michael L096
also L137
Hodgkin, Emily Jane L184
Hodgkinson, Leigh L159
also L645
Hodgkinson, Thomas W L099
also L278
Hodgman, George L184
Hodgson, Antonia L096
also L137
Hodgson, Jesse L159
also L645
Hoffman, Paul L159
also L266
Hoffman, Roy L334
Hogan, Edward L052
also L159
Hogan, Faith L341
Hogan, Michael L066
also L516
Hogerton, Sam L114
Hogg, James L048
Hogg, Nicholas L099
also L278
Hoggarth, Janet L644
Hogge, Fred L086
Hoghton, Anna L159
also L645
Hohenegger, Beatrice L184
Holborn, Stark L364
Holden, Amanda L108
Holding, Michael L034
also L278
Holland, James P052
Holland, Merlin L096
also L137
Hollander, Julia L276
also L468
Hollinger, David L608
Hollingshead, Iain L099
also L278
Hollingsworth, Mark L644
Holloway, JS P435
Holloway-Smith, Wayne L276
also L677
Holmes, Andrew L276
also L632
Holmes, Becky L048
also L333
also L638
Holmes, David L566
Holmes, J.M. L096
also L380
Holmes, Kelly L376
Holmes, Lucy-Anne L333
also L638
Holmes, Marianne L074
Holmes, Natasha L110
also L647
Holness, Nevin L146
also L250
Holt, Debby L623
Holwell, Hannah-Marie L329
Hone, David L190

Hong, Euny ... L159	Hoyland, Graham ... L644	Ince, Robin ... L644
Hong, Liu ... L159	Hu, Tung-Hui ... L396	Ingalls, Bea ... L512
also ... L672	Huang, Yuji ... L159	Innes, Kirstin ... L086
Hood, Christopher M. ... L184	Huang, Yunte ... L608	Inverne, James ... L566
Hood, Evelyn ... L074	Huband, Sally ... L029	Iqbal, Anam ... L567
Hooper, Meredith ... L159	Huber, Sam ... L469	Irankunda, Pacifique ... L608
also ... L645	Huchu, Tendai ... L426	Ireland, Amelia ... L166
Hoopes, Alex ... L108	Hudson, Kerry ... L066	*also* ... L263
Hope, Anna ... L215	*also* ... L516	Ireland, Perrin ... L396
also ... L669	Hudson, Lexy ... L325	Irving, Ellie ... L034
Hope, Maggie ... L341	Hudson, Michael ... L238	*also* ... L278
Hopkins, Angela Palm ... L584	Huerta, Lizz ... L515	Irwin, J D (Julie) ... L240
Hopkins, Megan ... L512	*also* ... L609	Isaacs, Robert ... L058
Hopkinson, Simon ... L159	Huggins, James Byron ... L414	*also* ... L059
also ... L266	Hughes, Alrene ... L341	Iselin, Josie ... L184
Hopper, Jill ... L029	Hughes, Benjamin ... L619	Issa, Hanan ... L166
Hopwood, Sharon ... L401	Hughes, Egan ... L069	*also* ... L216
Hora, Gulchehra ... L190	*also* ... L157	Issa, Islam ... L254
Horn, Ariel ... L063	Hughes, Gwyneth ... L196	Ivey, Bill ... L388
Horn, John ... L297	Hughes, Langston ... L159	Ivey, Felicitas ... P144
Horn, Trevor ... L159	Hughes, Richard ... L159	Izadi, Shahroo ... L591
also ... L270	Hugo, Ilze ... L184	*also* ... L663
Hornak, Francesca ... L336	Hui, Angela ... L116	J, Sailor ... L148
Hornby, Emma ... L341	Huizing, Alyssa ... L665	J. Weston Phippen ... L582
Hornby, Gill ... L215	Humble, Catherine ... L005	Jack, Albert ... L539
also ... L669	Hummer, Maria ... L662	Jack, Belinda ... L129
Horne, Eileen ... L096	Humphrey, Nicholas ... L007	*also* ... L215
also ... L380	*also* ... L466	Jack, Valerie ... L166
Hornsley, Sarah ... L321	Hung, Daisy J. ... L276	Jackie, ... L063
also ... L470	*also* ... L460	Jackman, Wayne ... L332
Horowitz, Sarah ... L155	Hunt, Alice ... L129	Jackson, Alex ... L614
Horrocks, Allison ... L418	*also* ... L215	Jackson, Andrew ... L644
Horwitz, Jesse ... L087	Hunt, Kenya ... L204	Jackson, Barry ... L537
Hosier, Erin ... L184	Hunt, Lynn ... L238	Jackson, Corrie ... L623
Hosken, Andrew ... L099	Hunter, ... L623	Jackson, Erik Forrest ... L334
also ... L278	Hunter, Becky ... L321	Jackson, Jeffrey H. ... L537
Hoskins, Hayley ... L110	Hunter, Lisa ... L063	Jackson, Jeremy ... L184
also ... L647	Hunter-Gault, Charlayne ... L469	Jackson, Julian ... L159
Hoskins, Tansy ... L159	Huntley, Alex ... L313	*also* ... L270
also ... L270	Hurcom, Sam ... L254	Jackson, Lawrence ... L615
Hosy-Pickett, Leigh ... L566	Hurley, Michael ... L278	Jackson, Steve ... L414
Hough, Richard ... L159	*also* ... L339	Jackson, Tiffany D. ... L058
Houghton, Eleanor ... L163	Hurlock, Kathryn ... L129	*also* ... L059
Houghton, Emily ... L321	*also* ... L215	Jackson, Tom ... L614
Hounsom, Lucy ... L052	Husain, Masud ... L159	Jacob, Catherine ... L157
also ... L159	*also* ... L672	Jacob, Margaret ... L238
Hourston, Alex ... L276	Hussain, Anika ... L612	Jacobs, John Hornor ... L184
also ... L632	Hussain, Iqbal ... L325	Jacobs, Melissa ... L063
House, Richard ... L215	Huston, Allegra ... L215	Jacobs, Naomi ... L539
also ... L669	*also* ... L669	Jacobson, Gavin ... L007
Housley, Sarah ... L276	Hutchins, Chris ... L539	*also* ... L466
also ... L460	Hutchinson, Dave ... L096	Jacques, Juliet ... L209
Hovitz, Helaina ... L334	Hutchinson, Lindsey ... L341	Jade, Holly ... L526
Howard, A. G. ... L058	Hutchinson, Michael ... L034	Jaeger, Meredith ... L058
also ... L059	*also* ... L278	*also* ... L059
Howard, Alex ... L129	Hutchison, Barry ... L240	Jaffe, Janet ... L063
also ... L215	Hutson, Shaun ... L364	Jaffe, Sarah ... L609
also ... L341	Hutton, Robert ... L215	*also* ... L639
Howard, Ayanna ... L396	*also* ... L318	Jaffe, Steven ... L238
Howard, David ... L276	Hutton, Rosalinda ... L539	Jager, Liz De ... L470
Howard, Minna ... L341	Hyatt, Michael ... L018	Jahanshahi-Edlin, Gabby ... L131
Howard, Sally ... L504	Hyatt, Oli ... L392	*also* ... L533
Howard, Scott Alexander ... L276	Hyde, Deborah ... L074	Jahshan, Elias ... L110
also ... L662	Hyland, Tara ... L157	*also* ... L647
Howell, C.R. ... L586	Hyslop, Leah ... L066	Jai, Sophie ... L166
Howell, Daniel ... L146	*also* ... L516	*also* ... L216
also ... L456	Høeg, Mette Leonard ... L278	Jakeman, Jo ... L504
Howells, Debbie ... L470	*also* ... L339	Jakubait, Muriel ... L539
Howes, Emily ... L032	Iacopelli, Jennifer ... L612	James, Alice ... L445
also ... L096	Iannotta, Jessica ... L440	James, Blair ... L005
Howes, Theresa ... L470	Idehen, Joshua ... L053	James, Cate ... L240
Howie, Vicki ... L348	*also* ... L278	James, Charlee ... L444
Howkins, John ... L644	Iglesias, Gabino ... L153	James, Charlie Hamilton ... L007
Hoy, Chris ... L566	*also* ... L609	*also* ... L173
Hoyer, Katja ... L007	Ilott, Terry ... L236	James, Cormac ... L066
also ... L466	Imdad, Ali ... L470	*also* ... L171

James, Ed	L166
also	L306
James, Heidi	L278
also	L583
James, Kendra	L440
James, Liza St.	L005
James, Lynsey	L321
James, Nikola	L539
James, Peter	L066
also	L171
James, Rachel McCarthy	L609
also	L639
James-Mackey, Tess	L612
Janakievska, Irina	L614
January, Sativa	L584
Jardine, Lis	L325
Jarman, Julia	L159
also	L645
Jarrett, Gene	L608
Jarrett-Macauley, Delia	L053
also	L278
Jasmine, Lucretia Tye	L415
Jasmon, Sarah	L215
also	L520
Jayaraman, Saru	L396
Jayatissa, Amanda	L153
also	L609
Jaye, Lola	L341
Jeans, Crystal	L032
also	L096
Jebara, Mohamad	L615
Jebelli, Joseph	L215
also	L520
Jecks, Michael	L294
also	L613
Jedrowski, Tomasz	L066
also	L171
Jefferies, Dinah	L294
also	L295
Jeffries, Sabrina	L011
Jeffries, Sheila	L341
Jeffries, Stuart	L278
also	L339
Jellicoe, Alexandra	L066
also	L516
Jeng, Sarah Zachrich	L416
also	L477
Jenkins, Sophie	L341
Jenkins, Tiffany	L007
also	L466
Jenner, Genevieve	L614
Jennings, Charles	L276
Jennings, Elizabeth	L159
Jensen, Helga	L166
also	L306
Jensen, Louise	L282
Jensen, Nancy McSharry	L396
Jensen, Oskar Cox	L294
also	L613
Jesmond, Jane	L526
Jewell, Hannah	L644
Jimenez, Claire	L440
Joachimsthaler, Erich	L297
Joan,	L276
Jobin, Matthew	L184
Joffe, Daron	L184
Johansen, Signe	L591
also	L663
John Parra	L174
John, D.B.	L276
also	L632
John, Lauren St	L129
also	L215
Johncock, Benjamin	L066
also	L516
Johns, Chris	L313
Johnson, Betsey	L415
Johnson, Daniel Brock	L608
Johnson, Katerina	L204
Johnson, Milly	L159
Johnson, R. Dean	L609
Johnson, Rebecca May	L159
Johnson, Sophie Lucido	L609
Johnson, Sylvia	L333
also	L638
Johnson-Schlee, Sam	L276
also	L460
Johnston, C.R.	L114
Johnston, John J	L190
Johnston, Riley	L333
Johnstone, Leigh	L074
Johnstone, Stuart	L294
also	L613
Jolly, Joanna	L007
also	L466
Jonasson, Ragnar	L166
also	L306
Jones, Amy	L090
Jones, Arden	L329
Jones, Becca	L477
Jones, Booker T	L388
Jones, Carol	L341
Jones, Carys	L163
Jones, Colin	L129
also	L215
Jones, Diana Wynne	L052
also	L159
Jones, Faith	L615
Jones, Ginger	L278
also	L583
Jones, Harold	L159
Jones, Ioan Marc	L362
Jones, Lizzie Huxley	L166
also	L216
Jones, Lora	L476
Jones, Lucy	L159
also	L672
Jones, Luke	L096
Jones, Mary	L184
Jones, Michael	L644
Jones, Noah Z	L184
Jones, Owen	L159
also	L270
Jones, Peter	L401
Jones, Rob Lloyd	L096
also	L137
Jones, Russell	L128
also	L521
Jones, Ruth	P052
Jones, Sandie	L157
also	L585
Jones, Sarah	L539
Jones, Shane	L073
Jones, Simon	L099
also	L278
Jones, Vanessa	L329
Jonker, Joan	L022
Jooste, Pamela	L341
Joplin, Laura	L388
Jordan, Amie	L157
Jordan, Don	L644
Jordan, Elise	L469
Jory, Chloe	L477
Joseph, Anjali	L468
Joseph, Anthony	L159
also	L170
Joseph, Jay	L401
Joseph, R.J.	L448
Joshi, Vijay	L129
also	L215
Joy, David	L184
Joyce, Helen	L295
Joyce, Rachel	L096
also	L137
also	P143
Jr., Frank Wheeler,	L184
Jr., Henry Louis Gates	L469
Jubber, Nick	L215
also	L520
Judd, Alan	L159
also	L266
Jukes, Helen	L159
also	L672
Jukes, Matthew	L646
Juliet Menéndez	L174
June, Valerie	L184
Jung, Grace	L334
Juric, Sam	L313
Jónasson, Jón Atli	L166
Júliusdóttir, Katrín	L166
also	L306
Kadri, Sadakat	L096
also	L137
Kahn-Harris, Keith	L276
also	L632
Kaiser, Menachem	L584
Kalia, Ammar	L005
Kallmayer, Line	L005
Kam, Jennifer Wolf	L506
also	L507
Kamal, Isabella	L603
Kambalu, Samson	L557
Kaminski, Theresa	L334
Kane, Ashlyn	P144
Kane, Karen	L184
Kaner, Hannah	L470
Kapil, Bhanu	L116
Kaplan, Bonnie J	L481
Kaplan, Hester	L184
Kapur, Manu	L297
Kar-Purkayastha, Ishani	L294
also	L295
Kara, Lesley	L526
Kardas-Nelson, Mara	L608
Karim, Noaah	L367
Karim-Cooper, Farah	L086
Karlie, Logan	L146
also	L223
Kashner, Sam	L415
Kasket, Elaine	L294
also	L295
Kassalow, Jordan	L440
Kastens, Alegra	L537
Kate, Jessica	L414
Katz, Ani	L184
Katz, Emily	L063
Katz, Rachelle	L334
Katzenbach, Jon	L297
Kaufman, Andrew	L313
Kaufman, Charlotte	L515
also	L609
Kaufman, Kenn	L608
Kaufman, Sashi	L418
Kaufman, Sophie Monks	L591
also	L663
Kaufmann, Miranda	L644
Kaur, Hardeep	L512
Kavan, Anna	L159
Kavanagh, Anthony	L166
also	L263
Kavanagh, Emma	L069
also	L157
Kavasch, E. Barrie	L063
Kawa, Abraham	L096
also	L137
Kawatski, Deanna	L621
Kaye, M. M.	L159

Access more listings online at www.firstwriter.com

Keane, Jessie	L159	
also	L232	
Keane, Molly	L159	
Kearney, Fionnuala	L321	
Keating, Fiona	L276	
also	L460	
Keay, Anna	L159	
also	L270	
Keay, John	L159	
also	L270	
Keeler, Christine	L539	
Keen, Andrew	L007	
also	L466	
Keen, Greg	L146	
also	L456	
Keenan, David	L096	
also	L137	
Keenan, Jillian	L615	
Keer, Jenni	L091	
also	L567	
Keiser, Jake	L615	
Keller, Jon	L184	
Keller, Joy	L063	
Kelley, Ann	L240	
Kelley, Nancy	L166	
also	L216	
Kelly, Greta	L122	
Kelly, Helena	L215	
also	L318	
Kelly, Jacqueline	L522	
Kelly, Jason	L579	
Kelly, Jim	L623	
Kelly, Joseph	L334	
Kelly, Louise	L240	
Kelly, Nicola	L096	
also	L380	
Kelly, Rachel	L105	
Kelly, Ruth	L392	
Kelly, Stephen	L334	
Kelly, Thomas Forrest	L608	
Kelman, Stephen	L052	
also	L096	
also	L137	
also	L159	
Kelsey, Anita	L539	
Kemp, Laura	L159	
Kempton, Beth	L294	
also	L295	
Kenani, Stanley	L215	
also	L669	
Kendrick, Erika J.	L522	
Kennedy, Brynne S.	L334	
Kennedy, James	L148	
Kennedy, John	L066	
also	L093	
Kennedy, Jonathan	L159	
also	L672	
also	P460	
Kennedy, Nancy	L334	
Kennedy, Paul	L159	
also	L270	
Kennedy, Sean	P144	
Kennedy-McGuinness, Siobhan	L539	
Kennedy-Moore, Eileen	L063	
Kenney, John	L090	
Kenward, Louise	L521	
Kenyon, Rachel Tawil	L063	
Kernick, Simon	L526	
Kerr, Emily	L526	
Kerseviciute, Laura	L226	
also	L680	
Kershaw, Robert	L644	
Kershaw, Scott	L392	
Kertzer, David	L608	
Kessler, Brad	L184	
Kessler, Diana	L166	
Kessler, Liz	L129	
also	L215	
Key, Amy	L215	
Keyes, Sidney	L159	
Keys, Barbara	L159	
also	L270	
also	L608	
Khalili, Nasser David	L566	
Khambete-Sharma, Vedashree	L276	
also	L468	
Khan, Amana Fontanella	L096	
also	L380	
Khan, Ausma Zehanat	L477	
Khan, Hiba Noor	L110	
also	L647	
Khan, Imran	L290	
also	L676	
Khan, Katie	L470	
Khan, Sara	L236	
Khan, Sulmaan Wasif	L159	
also	L270	
Khan, Sunnah	L574	
Khatib, Sulaiman	L615	
Khoo, Rachel	L159	
Khoury, Caroline	L066	
also	L093	
Khoury, Philip	L614	
Khurana, Vijay	L278	
also	L339	
Kidd, Jess	L032	
also	L096	
Kiefer, Christian	L184	
Kiel, Fred	L297	
Kiernan, Olivia	L032	
also	L096	
Kildaire, V.B.	P144	
Kilkerr, Justine	L032	
also	L096	
Killam, Kasley	L297	
Killham, Nina	L146	
also	L223	
Kim, Angela Jia	L481	
Kim, Catherine	L584	
Kim, Erin Rose	L506	
also	L507	
Kim, Michelle	L313	
Kim, Sang	L367	
Kimble, Megan	L609	
Kimm, Gabrielle	L276	
Kimmerer, Robin Wall	L396	
Kimmerle, Erin	L537	
Kimutai, Kiprop	L586	
Kinavey, Hilary	L334	
Kincade, Sierra	L416	
also	L477	
Kincaid, Shay	P144	
Kinchen, Rosie	L096	
also	L380	
King, Claire	L052	
also	L159	
King, Clive	L159	
also	L645	
King, Danny James	L146	
also	L456	
King, Ella	L526	
King, Esme	L276	
also	L468	
King, Evie	L333	
also	L638	
King, Lizzie	L677	
King, Tracy	P143	
King, Vanessa	L677	
Kingori, Patricia	L278	
also	L339	
Kingsbury, Karen	L018	
Kingsford, Eliza	L440	
Kingsley, Sean	L334	
Kingsolver, Barbara	L238	
Kingston, Holly	L294	
Kingstone, Heidi	L539	
Kinnings, Max	L276	
also	L632	
Kino, Shilo	L586	
Kinsella, Ana	L005	
Kinsella, Sophie	P052	
Kirby, Annie	L032	
also	L096	
Kirby, Brian	L539	
Kirby, Tim	L539	
Kirk, David	L276	
also	L632	
Kirkbride, Jasmin	L096	
also	L130	
Kirshenbaum, Binnie	L159	
also	L266	
Kirsten, Max	L646	
Kispert, Peter	L192	
Kissick, Lucy	L343	
Kisska, Kristin	L603	
Kitamura, Katie	L096	
also	L137	
Kitchen, Bert	L159	
also	L645	
Kitchin, C. H. B.	L159	
Kite, Gerad	L096	
also	L137	
Kittleson, Gail	P514	
Kjærgaard, Rikke Schmidt	L276	
also	L632	
Klaussmann, Liza	L215	
also	L669	
Klein, Linda Kay	L440	
Kleine, Andrea	L184	
Kleman, Kim	L297	
Kletter, Dana	L584	
Klidonas, Caroline	L227	
Kline, Harriet	L096	
also	L137	
Kling, Rebecca	L141	
also	L537	
Knickerbocker, Alyssa	L584	
Knight, Caedis	L526	
Knight, John	L539	
Knight, Rebecca Dinerstein	L276	
also	L468	
Knight, Ronnie	L539	
Knopman, Jaime	L467	
Knox, Joseph	L276	
also	L632	
Knox-Mawer, June	L159	
Koch, Richard	L215	
also	L318	
Kochanski, Halik	L159	
also	L270	
Kochhar, Atul	L086	
Koekkoek, Taylor	L184	
Koh, Karen	L416	
also	L477	
Kohda, Claire	L032	
also	L096	
Kolaya, Chrissy	L184	
Kolbeck, Liz	L616	
Kole, William J.	L537	
Komisar, Erica	L440	
Komlos, David	L297	
Komolafe, Peter	L282	
Konditor,	L066	
also	L516	
Kondor, Luke	L364	
Koonar, Sohan	L313	
Kooper, Zoya	L512	
Korman, Amanda	L184	

Korn, Gabrielle	L184
Korpon, Nik	L184
Koryang, Amari	L048
Kosik, Alison	L440
Koska, Anna	L614
Koslow, Connie	L011
Koslowski, Chris	L087
Kot, Danuta	L623
Kova, Elise	L058
also	L059
Kraatz, Jeramey	L148
Kramer, J. Kasper	L184
Krantz, Laura	L481
Krastev, Ivan	L007
also	L466
Krause, Jennifer	L440
Krauze, Gabriel	L333
also	L638
Kray, Reg	L539
Kray, Roberta	L539
Kress, Nancy	L582
Kressley, Carson	L481
Kriegsman, Ali	L615
Krimpas, Titania	L401
Kriss, Sam	L426
Kristjansson, Snorri	L190
Kristoff, Jay	L159
also	L645
Kronman, Anthony	L608
Krug, Cassidy	L515
also	L609
Kudei, Sonya	L276
Kuhlmann, Arkadi	L313
Kulp, Dan	P514
Kuo, Fifi	L159
also	L645
Kuo, Michelle	L238
Kuritzkes, Justin	L184
Kurtz, Catherine	L166
also	L216
Kuyken, Willem	L334
Kuznetsova, Maria	L184
Kwak, Chaney	L584
Kwak, Gene	L073
Kwakye, Chelsea	L215
also	L520
Kwon, Mya	L074
Kynge, James	L215
also	L318
Kyriacou, Eleni	L166
also	L216
LaBarge, Emily	L159
LaBarge, Melanie	L073
Labbe, Marguerite	P144
Lacey, Stephen	L159
also	L266
Lachlan, M.D.	L468
Lagos, Leah	L481
Lagrève, Manon	L276
also	L632
Lahti, Christine	L481
Lake, Joanne	L566
Lam, Andrew	L297
Lam, L.R.	L470
Lamanna, Gina	L321
Lamb, Nicola	L614
Lambert, Charles	L066
also	L171
Lambrianou, Tony	L539
Lamm, August	L209
also	L276
Lammy, David	L159
also	L270
Lamond, Caroline	L166
also	L263
Lampard, Frank	L566
Lampl, Peter	L215
also	L318
Lancaster, Mike	L401
Lancaster, Simon	L215
also	L318
Land, Ali	L470
Landau, Camille	L063
Landau, Deb Miller	L537
Landdeck, Katherine Sharp	L427
Landman, Tanya	L240
Landry, Sandra	L011
Lane, Jennifer	L034
also	L278
Lane, Johanna	L184
Lane, Lizzie	L048
Lane, Mitch	L614
Lane, Neil	L537
Lang, Michael	L388
Lang, Nico	L537
Langan, Sarah	L184
Lange, Richard	L184
Langley, Philippa	L644
Langmead, Oliver K.	L096
Langrish, Katherine	L129
also	L215
Languirand, Mary	L334
Lankina, Tomila	L215
also	L318
Lanza, Robert	L582
Lapena, Shari	P052
Lapidus, Jennifer	L481
Lapine, Missy Chase	L334
Lappé, Anna	L238
Larocca, Amy	L469
Larsen, Melissa	L108
Larsen, Reif	L468
Larson, Carlton F. W.	L608
Larwood, Kieran	L392
Lashinsky, Adam	L297
Laski, Marghanita	L159
Laskow, Sarah	L184
Lassoued, Alex	L282
Laszlo, Mary de	L341
Latham, Martin	L096
also	L380
Lattimore, Ashton	L108
Laurie, Hugh	L159
also	L266
Lavelle, Amy	L526
also	L567
Lavender, Eleanor	L159
also	L645
Lavery, Grace	L215
also	L520
Law, Catherine	L341
Law, Phyllida	L215
also	L669
Lawler, Liz	L566
Lawless, James	P236
Lawrence, Ann	L159
Lawrence, Caroline	L188
Lawrence, Derek	L537
Lawrence, Lee	L566
Lawrence, Natalie	L159
also	L672
Lawrie, Lucy	L294
also	L613
Laws, Chloe	L146
also	L223
Laws, Peter	L294
also	L613
Lawson, Michael	L078
also	L278
Lawson, Persia	L096
also	L137
Lawton, Graham	L007
also	L466
Lay, Carol	L063
Lazar, Jen	L584
Lazenby, John	L644
LB, Jade	L333
LDN, Iggy	L209
Leach, David	L313
Leach, Robert	P236
Leach, Tim	L215
also	L669
Leadbeater, Charles	L007
also	L466
Leadbeater, Cory	L073
Leader, Samuel	L584
Leaf, Clifton	L297
Leake, Elisabeth	L159
also	L270
Leaver, Kate	L159
also	L232
LeCraw, Holly	L184
Lee, Carol Ann	L539
Lee, Graham	L159
also	L270
Lee, Hali	L141
Lee, Jenny	L677
Lee, Jeremy	L159
Lee, John	L539
Lee, Julia	L162
also	L405
Lee, Kyo	L367
Lee, Louise	L333
also	L638
Lee, Lyla	L458
Lee, Marianne	L333
also	L638
Lee, Mirinae	L184
Lee, Patrick	L532
Lee, Robert G.	P514
Lee, Sam	L086
Lee, Sarah	L066
also	L093
Lee, Shannon	L440
Lee, Shu Han	L614
Lee, Sophia	L458
Lee, Tommy	L184
Lee, Tony	L332
Lee-Kennedy, Brydie	L504
Leech, Frances	L007
also	L466
Leeds, Thomas	L166
also	L216
Leendertz, Lia	L376
Lees, Georgina	L526
Lefler, Anna	L063
Legend, The Urban	L392
Leger, Arizona	L566
Leggo, Michael	L166
Lehnen, Christine	L294
Leider, Jerry	L236
Leiggi, Miranda	L612
Leiper, Kate	L240
Leitch, Maurice	L644
Leith, William	L276
also	L632
Leivaditaki, Marianna	L086
Lelic, Simon	L215
also	L669
Lemmey, Huw	L116
Lenier, Sue	L236
Lennon, Joan	L240
Lennon, Patrick	L157
Lennox, Judith	L290
Lennox, Lee	L512
Lent, James	L619

Leonard, Mark	L007
also	L466
Leonard, S.V.	L166
also	L263
Lepard, Dan	L276
also	L632
Lepucki, Edan	L184
Lerner, Claire	L334
Leslie, Barbra	L313
Leslie, Ian	L007
also	L466
Lesniak, Caroline	L603
Lesser, Elizabeth	L184
Lessore, Nathanael	L157
Lester, Jem	L662
Letemendia, Claire	L313
Lethbridge, Lucy	L129
also	L215
Lette, Kathy	L166
Letwin, Oliver	L007
also	L466
Levene, Alysa	L215
also	L318
Levin, Angela	L539
Levin, Daniel	L615
Levine, Irene S.	L334
Levinson, Adam Valen	L440
Levitt, Alexandra	L334
Levitt, Theresa	L192
Levy, Ashley Nelson	L073
Levy, Paul	L099
also	L278
Levy-Chehebar, Esther	L108
Lewis, Beth	L166
also	L306
Lewis, Damien	L159
also	L270
Lewis, Dan	L515
also	L609
Lewis, Daniel	L608
Lewis, David	L603
Lewis, Gwyneth	L029
Lewis, Ian	L074
Lewis, Jacqui	L087
Lewis, Jenny	L114
Lewis, Jerry Lee	L184
Lewis, Lisa L	L334
Lewis, Richard Leslie	L332
Lewis, Robert	L276
also	L632
Lewis, Robin	L184
Lewis, Ted	L159
Lewis-Oakes, Rebecca	L619
Lewis-Stempel, John	P143
Ley, Rebecca	L096
also	L380
Leyes, Emilie	L239
Li, Junheng	L297
Li, Maggie	L619
Li, Wenying	L521
Liang, Holan	L557
Liardet, Francis	L333
also	L638
Libaire, Jardine	L468
Libby, Gillian	L416
also	L477
Lida, David	L184
Lierow, Bernie	L388
Lierow, Diane	L388
Liftig, Anya	L184
Light, Alan	L481
Light, Daniel	L159
also	L270
Lightbown, Chris	L539
Lightfoot, Freda	L526
Lihou, Rose	L512
Lillie, Vanessa	L108
Lilly, Pamela	L440
Lim, Audrea	L609
Lim, Roselle	L058
also	L059
Lima, Ananda	L073
Lin, Patty	L155
Linden, Rachel	L414
Linder, Seth	L539
Lindop, Grevel	L644
Lindsay, Chantelle	L166
also	L216
Lindsay, Jack	L159
Lindsay, Keith R.	L236
Lindstrom, Eric	L276
Linfoot, Jane	L526
Lingard, Joan	L159
also	L240
Linic, Claire and Alan	L418
Linkner, Josh	L297
Linscott,	L623
Linton, Marisa	L325
Lipinski, Emily	L313
Lippert-Martin, Kristen	L148
Lippett, Ben	L614
Lippman, Thomas	L532
Lipscomb, Suzannah	L215
also	L520
Lipska, Barbara K.	L297
Lipson, Molly	L005
Liptrot, Amy	L029
Lister, David	L577
Lister, Kat	L066
also	L516
Lister, Simon	L086
Lister-Kaye, John	L129
also	L215
Listfield, Emily	L239
Listi, Brad	L184
Litchfield, David R. L.	L539
Littke, Lael	L598
Little, Hannah	L096
Little, Mary Ann	L334
Little, Tess	L215
also	L520
Littler, Richard	L066
also	L516
Littlewood, Clayton	L066
also	L516
Litvinoff, Emanuel	L159
Litvinova, Natalia	L574
Litwitchure,	L333
also	L638
Lively, Penelope	L159
Livesey, Finbarr	L215
also	L318
Livings, Liam	L282
Livingston, A. A.	L122
Livingston, Dan	L122
Llewellyn, David	L336
Llewellyn-Jones, Lloyd	L254
Lloyd, Heather K.	L440
Lloyd, John	L007
also	L466
Lloyd, Saci	L052
also	L159
Lo, Anita	L481
Lo, Catherine	L609
Lo, Malinda	L294
Lobato, Bruna Dantas	L073
Lobenstine, Margaret	L063
Loccoriere, Dennis	P236
Locke, Angela	P236
Lockwood, Greg	L215
also	L318
Lodder, Matt	L190
Loder, Kurt	L388
Lodge, Jo	L159
also	L645
Logan, T M	L069
also	L157
Logan, William Bryant	L184
Loh, Jonathan	L129
also	L215
Loiseau, Benoît	L005
Lomas, Tim	L297
Lombard, Jenny	L184
London, Clare	P144
London, Julia	L058
also	L059
Long, John	L440
Long, Kieran	L276
also	L632
Long, Mary	L539
Long, Tony	L539
Longmuir, Fiona	L278
also	L583
Lord, Annie	L521
Lord, Craig	L294
also	L295
Lorincz, Holly	L414
Losada, Isabel	L007
also	L466
Lott, Tim	L159
also	L645
Louie, Nicole	L567
Louis, Lia	L470
Lovatt, Elizabeth	L166
also	L216
Love, Ryan	L364
Lovell, Julia	L159
also	L672
Lovelock, James	L196
Lovett, Jo	L321
Lovric, Michelle	L034
also	L278
Lowe, Jack	L048
Lowe, Katie	L470
Lowe, Rebecca	L215
also	L520
Lowe, Stephen	L236
Lowenthal, Mark	L063
Lowkis, Carmella	L476
Lowndes, Leil	L184
Loxton, Alice	L294
also	L295
Loyn, David	L644
Loynd, Michael	L609
Lozada, Evelyn	L414
Lucas, Anneke	L313
Lucas, Fiona	L526
Lucas, Geralyn	L334
Lucas, Rachael	L526
Lucía Franco	L174
Lukate, Johanna	L362
Lumani, Violet	L155
Lumley, Joanna	L159
also	L266
Lumsden, Katie	L091
Lumsden, Richard	L159
also	L232
Lunde, Julie	L515
also	L609
Lunden, Jennifer	L609
Lunn, Natasha	L215
also	L520
Lupo, Kesia	L052
also	L159
Lury, Max	L159
Lusk, Sean	L166
also	L306
Lutz, John	L392

luxx, lisa ... L166
also ... L216
Lycett, Andrew ... L007
also ... L466
Lyman, Monty ... L644
also ... P460
Lyman, Robert ... L644
Lynch, Courtney ... L297
Lynch, Karen ... L444
Lynch, P J ... L096
also ... L137
Lynch, Sean ... L297
Lynes, S. E. ... L052
also ... L159
Lynn, Dame Vera ... L159
also ... L270
Lynskey, Dorian ... L276
also ... L632
Lyon, Joshua ... L184
Lyons, David B. ... L294
also ... L613
Lyons, Zoe ... L166
also ... L306
Lyttelton, Celia ... L096
also ... L137
López, Lucas Sogas ... L429
Ma, Lulee ... L512
MacAlister, Katie ... L274
MacArthur, Robin ... L184
MacBird, Bonnie ... L099
also ... L278
Macciochi, Jenna ... L204
MacColl, Jean ... L539
Macculloch, Diarmaid ... L129
also ... L215
MacDonald, Chris ... L470
MacDonald, Dee ... L526
MacDonald, Fraser ... L029
Macdonald, Malcolm Ross ... L159
Macdonald, Marianne ... L159
Mace, Guy ... L603
Macfarlane, Robert ... L159
also ... L672
MacGillivray, Kirsten ... L336
Macher, Tom ... L584
Machin, Anna ... L215
also ... L318
Machray, Elle ... L476
Macias, Maryann Jacob ... L477
MacInnes, Eric ... L236
Mackay, Janis ... L240
Mackenzie, Caroline ... L032
also ... L096
MacKenzie, Debora ... L190
Mackenzie, Polly ... L007
also ... L466
Mackenzie, Rebecca ... L468
Mackichan, Doon ... L333
also ... L638
Mackie, Mary ... L110
also ... L647
Mackintosh, Anneliese ... L066
also ... L516
Mackintosh, Sophie ... L159
Mackler, Lauren ... L334
MacLachlan, Patricia ... L513
MacLean, David Stuart ... L184
MacLean, Natalie ... L313
Maclean, Will ... L096
MacLeod, Ken ... L445
Macleod, Tatty ... L146
also ... L456
MacNeice, Louis ... L159
Macneil, Kevin ... L294
also ... L613
MacQuarrie, Kim ... L388
MacRae, L. A. ... L276
Macwhirter, L J ... L240
Madden, Anne ... L184
Madden, Gary ... L007
also ... L466
Maddocks, Fiona ... L215
also ... L520
Madeleine, Laura ... L364
Madison, Juliet ... L334
Madson, Devin ... L343
Maestas, Carrie ... L074
Maestripieri, Dario ... L297
Magan, Manchan ... L159
also ... L672
Magazine, Rookie ... L415
Magee, David ... L297
Mager, Kim ... L537
Maggar, Carina ... L209
also ... L276
Maglaque, Erin ... L159
Magson, Adrian ... L166
also ... L306
Maguire, Aileen ... L005
Maguire, Gráinne ... L146
also ... L456
Maguire, Laurie ... L129
also ... L215
Mahmood, Imran ... L069
also ... L157
Mahmoud, Doma ... L396
Mahnke, Aaron ... L537
Mahoney, Dennis ... L184
Mahoney, Gretel ... L539
Mahoney, Mary ... L418
Mahood, Katy ... L096
also ... L380
Maidment, Eleanor ... L677
Maines, Nicole ... L418
Maisonet, Illyanna ... L467
Majka, Sara ... L396
Major, Cesca ... L157
Major, Tim ... L096
also ... L130
Makepeace, Mark ... L007
also ... L466
Malakin, Dan ... L392
Malchik, Antonia ... L396
Malhotra, Aseem ... L566
Malik, Kenan ... L007
also ... L466
Malik, Shiv ... L096
also ... L380
Malik, Tania ... L184
Mallinder, Stephen ... L251
also ... L278
Malloy, Lauretta ... L467
Malone, Ailbhe ... L066
also ... L516
Malone, Nana ... L427
Malossi, Dan ... L122
Man, John ... L129
also ... L215
Manawer, Hussain ... L566
Mance, Henry ... L215
also ... L520
Mancini, Ruth ... L276
also ... L468
Mandanna, Sangu ... L458
Mandelbaum, Paul ... L063
Manes, Eileen ... L634
Mangan, Lucy ... L066
also ... L516
Manicka, Rani ... L157
Mann, Michael ... L146
also ... L184
also ... L250
Mannah, Foday ... L159
also ... L170
Manning, Ivy ... L063
Manning, Joseph ... L608
Manning, Olivia ... L159
Mannix, Kathryn ... L159
also ... L270
Manuel, Rob ... L276
also ... L632
Manuelpillai, Arji ... L053
also ... L278
Manzoor, Sarfraz ... L159
also ... L270
Mapp, Rue ... L141
Maqhubela, Lindiwe ... L110
also ... L647
Mara, Andrea ... P052
Mararike, Shingi ... L099
also ... L278
Marber, Ian ... L526
Marcelo Verdad ... L174
March, Char ... P236
March, Kerstin ... L334
Marcum, Andrea ... L440
Marcus, Ben ... L468
Marcus, Greil ... L159
also ... L266
Marcus, Halimah ... L073
Marcus, Leonard J. ... L297
Maria Hinojosa ... L174
Marin, Hugo Huerta ... L155
Maris, Kathryn ... L159
Mark, Jan ... L159
also ... L645
Mark, Monica ... L254
Mark, Sabrina Orah ... L073
Marks, Ann ... L155
Marks, Jeff ... L532
Marlow, Jane ... L332
Marlow, Natalie ... L166
also ... L216
Marlowe, Deb ... L011
Marney, Ellie ... L159
also ... L645
Marnham, Patrick ... L052
also ... L159
Marple, Mieke ... L313
Marquand, David ... L159
also ... L266
Marquardt, Tanya ... L184
Marquart, Debra ... L184
Marquis, Christopher ... L440
Marr, Elle ... L058
also ... L059
Marr, Sarah K ... L215
also ... L669
Marra, Anthony ... L584
Marren, Gemma ... L333
also ... L638
Marriott, Zoe ... L348
Marrone, Amanda ... L537
Marrouat, Cendrine ... M039
Marrs, Sandra ... L329
Marsden, Paul ... L236
Marsden, Sam ... L676
Marsh, David J. ... L334
Marsh, Katie ... L099
also ... L278
also ... L294
Marshall, Alex ... L184
Marshall, Helen ... L364
Marston, Ama ... L440
Marston, Stephanie ... L440
Martelli, Joan ... L239
Marten, Helen ... L159

Martin, Barry	L058
also	L059
Martin, Chuck	L334
Martin, Gina	P052
Martin, Jessica	L141
Martin, Kristen	L108
Martin, Melissa	L063
Martin, Robert	L297
Martin, S.I.	L644
Martinez, Amanda Rose	L584
Martinez, Claudia Guadalupe	L174
Martínez, Lucía Alba	L574
Marufu, Aneesa	L325
Marut, Lama	L334
Marvin, Cate	L184
Marwood, Alex	L557
Marx, Paul	L236
Marz, Leigh	L440
Marz, Megan	L005
Masciola, Carol	L334
Mashigo, Mohale	L096
Masing, Anna Sulan	L209
also	L276
Maslo, Lina	L229
Mason, Amanda	L278
also	L583
Mason, Mark	L644
Mason, Ruthy	L282
Mason, Simon	L159
also	L266
Massey, Katy	L333
also	L638
Masters, Ben	L159
also	L672
Masters, Oksana	L190
also	L582
Masters, S R	L294
also	L613
Matharu, Taran	L470
Matheson, Hugh	L099
also	L278
Matheson, Spencer	L584
Matson, Suzanne	L184
Matthews, Beryl	L066
also	L093
Matthews, L V	L069
also	L157
Matthews, Owen	L007
also	L466
Matthews, Sadie	L159
Matthewson, Janina	L677
Matthiesen, Toby	L129
also	L215
Matyjaszek, Kasia	L240
Maugham, Jolyon	L276
also	L632
Maur, Melissa Auf der	L469
Maurier, Daphne du	P498
Mauro, Laura	L190
Mavison, Dar	P144
Mavity, Roger	L086
Maw, Laura	L005
Mawdsley, Evan	L159
also	L266
Maxwell, Abi	L184
May, Emi-Lou	L325
May, Kiirsten	L313
May, Peter	L159
also	L266
Maya Wei-Haas	L174
also	L615
Mayeda, Andrew	L665
Mayer, Mark	L584
Mayer, Shannon	L226
also	L680
Mayhew, Emily	L504
Mayne, Maurice	L539
Mazarura, Rufaro Faith	L159
also	L232
Mazhirov, Anna	L584
Mazur, Grace Dane	L297
Mazzola, Anna	L470
Mañas, José Ángel	L621
McAllister, Gillian	L157
McAndrew, Tony	L236
McArdle, Elaine	L297
Mcauley, Paul	L445
McAuley, Roisin	L644
McBride, Hazel	L146
also	L223
McBride, Matthew	L184
McBride, Regina	L252
McBride, Shane	L155
McCarraher, Lucy	P435
McCarron, Marina	L567
McCarthy, Andrew	L469
McCarthy, Helen	L159
also	L270
McCaughrean, Geraldine	L052
also	L159
McCaulay, Diana	L557
also	L647
McCausland, Elly	L086
McCausland, Jeffrey D.	L297
McCay, Layla	L166
also	L216
McClorey, Kelly	L073
McClure, Jesse	L591
also	L663
McCluskey, Laura	L146
also	L517
McCorkle, Jill	L184
McCormack, Una	L190
McCormick, Neil	L099
also	L278
McCracken, Elizabeth	L159
also	L184
also	L266
McCrum, Robert	L096
also	L137
McCulloch, Amy	L470
McCullough, Kelly	L598
McCurdy, Janelle	L333
McDaniel, W. Caleb	L608
McDavid, Cathy	L274
McDermid, Val	L159
McDiarmid, Jessica	L090
McDonald, Chris	L166
also	L306
McDonald, Ed	L096
also	L130
McDonald, Keza	L190
McDonald, Margaret	L512
McDonald-Gibson, Charlotte	L096
also	L380
McDonnell, Evelyn	L388
McDonnell, Patrick	L184
McDougall, Claire	L297
Mcdougall, James	L129
also	L215
Mcdougall, Sophia	L129
also	L215
McDowell, Colin	L526
McDowell, Marta	L058
also	L059
McFadden, Bernice	L153
also	L609
McFarland, Keith	L297
McGarrity, Michael	L522
McGee, James	L276
also	L632
McGilchrist, Iain	L159
also	L266
McGill, C.E.	L032
also	L096
McGilloway, Brian	L166
also	L306
McGinty, Sean	L184
McGivering, Jill	L341
McGlasson, Claire	L662
McGoran, Jon	L184
McGough, Roger	L619
McGowan, Anthony	L099
also	L278
McGowan, Julie	P435
Mcgrath, Chris	L129
also	L215
McGrath, Robyn	L229
McGrath, Will	L184
Mcgregor, Richard	L215
also	L318
McGuckin, Briana Una	L090
McGuffey, Charmaine	L239
McGuire, Ian	L468
McHugh, Laura	L468
McInerney, Kerry	L276
also	L460
McIvor, Michelle	L665
McKay, Rebecca Taylor	L276
also	L662
Mckechnie, Sam	L096
also	L137
McKellar, Danica	L481
McKenna, Juliet E.	L190
McKenzie, Elizabeth	L159
also	L266
McKinley, Barry	L099
also	L278
McKinley, Tamara	L623
McKinney, Jason Lee	P514
McKinney, Meagan	L011
McKowen, Laura	L108
Mclaughlin, Cressida	L294
Mclaughlin, Rosanna	L159
McLaughlin, Tom	L159
also	L645
McLean, Lenny	L539
McLeod, Ella	L146
also	L250
McLeod, Kembrew	L388
Mcloughlin, Kate	L129
also	L215
McMahon, Tony	L236
McManus, Jane	L090
McManus, Sarah	L364
McMorland, Jane	L623
McMullan, Thomas	L159
McMullen, John	P101
McNally, Dennis	L388
Mcnamara, Ali	L294
McNamara, Luna	L282
McNeil, Jean	L052
also	L159
McNeil, Joanne	L073
McNeur, Catherine	L608
McNuff, Anna	L226
also	L680
McNulty, Eric J.	L297
McNulty, Phil	L591
also	L663
McOmber, Adam	L184
Mcphee, Susy	L294
McPherson, Ben	L468
Mcpherson, Kira	L586
McPhillips, Fiona	L476
McQueer, Chris	L504

McSweeney, Siobhan	L333	
also	L638	
McTague, Tom	L007	
also	L466	
Mda, Zakes	L066	
also	L171	
Mead, Peter	L007	
also	L173	
Meadows, Jodi	L418	
Meals, Roy	L334	
Meaning, Jack	L254	
Medaglia, Mike	L544	
Medel, Elena	L574	
Medhurst, Jennifer	L376	
Medinger, Gez	L282	
Mednick, Sara C.	L481	
Medrano, Emma	L166	
also	L263	
Medved, Lisa	L526	
Medved, Maureen	L313	
Medwed, Daniel	L238	
Meehan, Andrew	L591	
also	L663	
Meekings, S. K.	L506	
also	L507	
Meggitt-Phillips, Jack	L333	
Mehmood, Jamal	L005	
Mehr, Bob	L184	
Mehri, Momtaza	L116	
Melisse, Shane	L053	
also	L278	
Melkonian, Sir Vartan	L236	
Meller, Gill	L276	
also	L632	
Meller, Rachel	L166	
Mellon, Mary	L313	
Melrose, Fiona	L333	
also	L638	
Meltzer, Marisa	L427	
Mencimer, Stephanie	L238	
Mendelsohn, Joshua	L087	
Menon, Anand	L007	
also	L466	
Mensah, Elvin James	L470	
Menzies, Jean	L166	
also	L263	
Mercado, Richard	L612	
Mercer, Alison	L341	
Merciel, Liane	L603	
Mercurio, Peter	L609	
also	L639	
Meredith, Martin	L129	
also	L215	
Merrell, Susan Scarf	L184	
Merritt, Chris	L166	
also	L306	
Mertens, Maggie	L396	
Meslow, Scott	L537	
Mesrati, Mohamed	L336	
Messinger, Jonathan	L416	
also	L477	
Metcalfe, Anna	L116	
also	L159	
Metcalfe, Daniel	L007	
also	L466	
Meyer, Deon	L066	
also	L171	
Meyer, Rachelle	L122	
Meyers, Jeff	P209	
Meyler, Deborah	L184	
Mhaoileoin, Niamh Ni	L586	
Michael, Darcy	L537	
Michaelson, Christopher	L297	
Middlemiss, LaRonda Gardner	L444	
Middleton, Lia	L066	
also	L093	
Miers, Thomasina	L276	
also	L632	
Mihell, Natasha	L313	
Mikhail, Alain	L608	
Milan, Joe	L087	
Milchman, Jenny	L184	
Miles, David	L362	
Miles, Rosalind	L644	
Miliband, Ed	L159	
also	L270	
Mill, Anna	L096	
Millar, Louise	L159	
Miller, Barnabas	L184	
Miller, Beth	L341	
Miller, Catherine	L282	
Miller, Chris	L007	
also	L466	
Miller, Daphne	L184	
Miller, Harland	L096	
also	L137	
Miller, Kei	L159	
Miller, Paddy	L297	
Miller, Paul	L184	
Miller, Richard J.	L184	
Miller, Siobhan	L294	
Miller, Tamara L.	L252	
Millman, Janie	L166	
also	L306	
Mills, Liberty	L146	
also	L223	
Mills, Major Scotty	L392	
Mills, SSG Travis	L537	
Millward, Myfanwy	L159	
also	L645	
Milman, Oliver	L215	
also	L318	
Milne, Gemma	L662	
Milner, Kate	L159	
also	L645	
Milusich, Janice	L444	
Min, Juli	L032	
also	L096	
Mina, Denise	L184	
Mincemeyer, Damascus	L122	
Minchilli, Domenico	L063	
Minchilli, Elizabeth Helman	L063	
Minetor, Randi	L531	
Ming, Ann	L539	
Minor, Wendell	L229	
Minson, Shona	L131	
also	L533	
Minton, Jenny	L427	
Mir, Moin	L099	
also	L278	
Mir, Saima	L166	
also	L216	
Miralles, Nina-Sophia	L066	
also	L516	
Mirza, Munira	L007	
also	L466	
Misick, Michael	L236	
Misra, Jaishree	L341	
Mitchell, Charlotte	L251	
also	L278	
Mitchell, Emma	L066	
also	L516	
Mitchell, Gladys	L159	
Mitchell, Kara	L537	
Mitchell, Katie	L141	
Mitchell, Malcolm	L537	
Mitchell, Marie	L131	
also	L533	
Mitchell, Sarah	L052	
also	L159	
Mitton, Tony	L159	
also	L645	
Miéville, China	L445	
Moats, David	L251	
also	L278	
Moaveni, Azadeh	L427	
Modafferi, Christine	L329	
Modan, Rutu	L238	
Moffatt, Hannah	L157	
Mogel, Wendy	L063	
Moggach, Lottie	L276	
also	L632	
Mohammadi, Kamin	L468	
Mohamud, Ayaan	L157	
Moldavsky, Goldy	L058	
also	L059	
Molesworth, Helen	L254	
Molho, Tony	L608	
Molin, Meghan Scott	L416	
also	L477	
Molinaro, Joanne	L086	
Monaghan, Paddy	L539	
Monday, T. T.	L184	
Mone, Gregory	L184	
Monette, Sarah	L598	
Monroe, Jack	L376	
Monroe, Jo	L470	
Monroe, Katrina	L416	
also	L477	
Montalban, Vanessa	L477	
Monteleone, Joey	P514	
Montell, Amanda	L184	
Monterey, Emmett de	L096	
Montgomery, Heather L.	L229	
also	L380	
Montoya, Maria Clara	L621	
Montrose, Sharon	L063	
Moolla, Zeena	L166	
also	L216	
Mooney, Sinéad	L005	
Moor, Becka	L619	
Moor, Zewlan	L229	
Moorcroft, Sue	L066	
also	L516	
Moore, Elizabeth S	L166	
also	L306	
Moore, James	L539	
Moore, Kate	L011	
Moore, Marianne	L504	
Moore, Moira	L598	
Moore, Richard	L043	
Moore, Sally	L313	
Moore, Sam	L155	
Moore, Victoria	L159	
Moore-Fitzgerald, Sarah	L333	
also	L638	
Moorer, Allison	L481	
Moorhead, Kr	L294	
Moorhouse, Tom	L129	
also	L215	
Mooro, Alya	L504	
Morain, Daniel	L077	
Morales, Bonnie Frumkin	L063	
Morales, Gerardo Ivan	L174	
Morales, Zoraida Rivera	L229	
Moran, Katy	L129	
also	L215	
Mordue, Mark	P209	
Morelli, Laura	L058	
also	L059	
Moreno, Heidi	L174	
Morgan, Abi	L108	
Morgan, Alistair	L215	
also	L669	
Morgan, Angie	L297	
Morgan, Ann	L396	
Morgan, Christine	L376	

Morgan, Elian J	L103	
also	L215	
Morgan, Joan	L388	
Morgan, Michelle	L539	
Morgan, Nick	L297	
Morgan, Pete	L159	
Morgan, Phoebe	L069	
also	L157	
Morgan-Witts, Max	L236	
Morita, Jennifer	L252	
Morland, Paul	L007	
also	L466	
Morpurgo, Michael	L052	
also	L159	
Morpuss, Guy	L190	
Morris, Amelia	L073	
Morris, Caroline	L539	
Morris, Elizabeth	L574	
Morris, Jackie	L159	
also	L672	
Morris, Jim	L297	
Morris, Joel H	L058	
also	L059	
Morris, Jonathan	L332	
Morris, Kevin	L440	
Morris, Mandy	L481	
Morris, Priscilla	L096	
also	L380	
Morris, Sir Derek	L236	
Morris, Zana	L539	
Morrison, Jonathan	L189	
also	L278	
Morrison, Kate	L468	
Morrisroe, Rachel	L157	
Morrow, Bradford	L184	
Mort, Sophie	L204	
Morten, Anais	P144	
Mortimer, Grace	L066	
also	L516	
Morton, Brian	L184	
Morton, Catriona	L333	
Morton, Kate	L159	
Morton, Rochelle	L539	
Mosimann, Anton	L099	
also	L278	
Moskowitz, Eric	L608	
Mosler, Layne	L184	
Mosqueda, Andrea	L418	
Moss, Adam	L469	
Moss, Alan	L539	
Moss, Emma-Lee	L116	
also	L159	
Moss, Sarah	L184	
Moss, Tara	L090	
Mossman, Kate	L644	
Mostyn, Nicola	L032	
also	L096	
Mottershead, Heather	L567	
Motum, Markus	L392	
Motz, Anna	L254	
Mountain, David	L614	
Moussa, Tarek El	L155	
Mowll, Joshua	L096	
also	L137	
Moynes, Riley E	L665	
Mucha, Laura	L159	
also	L504	
also	L645	
Muchamore, Robert	L188	
Muchemi-Ndiritu, Irene	L574	
Mufleh, Luma	L087	
Muir, Evie	L166	
also	L216	
Muir-Wood, Robert	L096	
also	L380	
Mukendi, Tanya	L614	
Mukerji, Ritu	L184
Muldoon, Eilidh	L240
Mulgan, Geoff	L007
also	L466
Mulholland, Aefa	L128
also	L521
Mulholland, Marc	L215
also	L318
Mullender, Rosie	L333
also	L638
Munda, Rosaria	L477
Munder, Chrissy	P144
Mundy, Simon	L096
also	L380
Munhóz, Carolina	L448
Murad, Nadia	L096
also	L380
Murgatroyd, Erin	L110
also	L647
Murguia, Bethanie	L229
Muroki, Mercy	L566
Murphy, Bernadette	L467
Murphy, Julie	L148
Murphy, Kimberly Shannon	L184
Murphy, Martina	L294
also	L295
Murphy, Mary	L188
Murphy, Meagan B	L481
Murphy, Peter	L236
Murray, Andrew	L348
Murray, Annie	L022
also	L157
Murray, Struan	L146
also	L250
Murray, Victoria Christopher	L162
also	L405
Murrin, Alan	L215
also	L669
Musgrove, Myra	L184
Musolino, Julien	L294
Musson, Hester	L470
Mutch, Barbara	L341
Mutyora, Jade	L166
also	L216
Myers, Benjamin	L159
also	L672
Myers, Rebecca	L099
also	L278
Myint, Arnold	L155
Mykura, Kim	L506
also	L507
Myrie, Clive	L007
also	L466
Nadel, Barbara	L557
also	L647
Nadel, Dan	L388
Nadel, Jennifer	L215
also	L669
Nadelson, Scott	P209
Naghdi, Yasmine	L612
Nagle, Emily	L348
Nair, Anita	L426
Nakate, Vanessa	L215
also	L520
Nance, Sarafina	L153
also	L609
Nancollas, Tom	L215
also	L520
Napper, Paul	L440
Narayan, Natasha	L129
also	L215
Nasimi, Shabnam	L566
Natapoff, Alexandra	L238
Nathan, Debbie	L184
Nathan, Einat	L481
Nathan, L.M.	L146
also	L223
Nathans, Benjamin	L608
Naudus, Natalie	L058
also	L059
Naughtie, James	L129
also	L215
Nava, Eva Wong	L157
Nava, Yolanda	L063
Navai, Ramita	L096
also	L380
Nawaz, Maajid	L566
Nawaz, Sabina	L481
Nawotka, Ed	L184
Nayeri, Farah	L515
also	L609
Naylor, Helen	L294
also	L295
Nazemian, Abdi	L148
Neal, Jennifer	L131
also	L533
Neale, Kitty	L341
Neate, Bobbie	L539
Nehring, Cristina	L334
Neima, Luke	L005
Nellums, Eliza	L090
Nelson, Alissa Jones	L676
Nelson, Caleb Azumah	L005
Nelson, Fraser	L159
also	L270
Nelson, Selene	L376
Nemerever, Micah	L192
Neri, Greg	L184
Nero, Paul	L539
Network, Real Sports Entertainment	L537
Neuwith, Robert	L184
Newberry, Sheila	L341
Newbery, Linda	L129
also	L215
Newhouse, Alana	L184
Newlands, Tom	L096
also	L380
Newman, Catherine	P143
Newman, Cathy	L276
also	L632
Newman, Grace	L110
also	L647
Newman, Judith	L239
Newman, Nathan	L086
Newman, Peter	L470
Newsome, Amy	L614
Newson, Louise	L096
also	L380
Newstead, Briana J	L110
also	L647
Newton, Hollie	L096
also	L380
Ng, Jasmine	L448
Nguyen, Kevin	L073
Niala, JC	L128
also	L521
Nice, Nicola	L334
Nicholson, Christopher	L066
also	L171
Nicholson, Joy	L063
Nicholson, Judge Chris	L236
Nicholson, Lindsay	L566
Nicholson, Norman	L159
Nicolau, Maria	L574
Nicolson, Juliet	L096
also	L137
Niedzviecki, Hal	L313
Niekerk, Marlene van	L066
also	L171
Nies, Judith	L063

Nimmo, Jenny	L159
also	L645
Ninan, TN	L129
also	L215
Nison, Rebecca	L313
Nissenson, Carol	L634
Nissley, Jennifer	L477
Nitzberg, Mark	L297
Niño, Oliver	L481
Noakes, Grace	L567
Noakes, Laura	L157
Noble, Carrie Anne	P514
Noble, Kim	L539
Noble, LeeAnet	L467
Noelle, Marisa	L348
Nolan, Hayley	L163
Noni, Lynette	L477
Noonan, Danny	L074
Nooney, Laine	L396
Norberg, Johan	L159
also	L270
Nord, Camilla	L215
also	L520
Norfolk, Lawrence	L066
also	L171
Norman, Charity	L052
also	L159
Norminton, Gregory	L066
also	L171
Norms, Leena	L282
Norrie, Kirsten	L336
Norris, Barney	L662
Norris, Mary	L469
Norris, Richard	L251
also	L278
Norris, Susie	L063
North, Darden	P514
North, L. C.	L526
Northedge, Charlotte	L096
also	L380
Norton, Chris and Emily	L537
Norton, Madeleine	L146
also	L517
Norton, Preston	L058
also	L059
Norton, Sheila	L110
also	L647
Norwood, Robin	L364
Nott, David	L159
also	L270
Noxon, Christopher	L063
Noyce, Eleanor	L521
Null, Matthew Neill	L584
Numan, Gary	L048
Nunez, Sigrid	L159
also	L266
Nusbaum, Howard	L297
Nutt, Amy Ellis	L608
Nuttall, Jenni	L295
also	L396
Nwanoku, Chi-chi	L446
Nwoka, Okezie	L515
also	L609
Nyquist, Katy	L226
also	L680
Nzelu, Okechukwu	L586
O'Callaghan, Jennifer	L334
O'Connor, Joseph	L066
also	L171
O'Connor, Scott	L184
O'Dair, Marcus	L096
also	L380
O'Dell, Emily J.	L334
O'Donnell, Lisa	L032
also	L096
O'Flanagan, Sheila	L066
also	L171
O'Grady, Colleen	L334
O'Leary, Beth	L157
also	L585
O'Neill, Louise	L470
O'Neill, Luke	L190
O'Reilly, Barry	L297
O'Reilly, Callie Rae	L114
O'Reilly, Kaite	L066
also	L171
O'Reilly, Noel	L166
also	L306
O'Reilly, Sally	L333
also	L638
O'Riordan, Valerie	L166
O'Shea, Priya	L333
also	L638
O'Sullivan, Tara	L146
also	L456
Oates, Nathan	L096
also	L380
Obergefell, Jim	L334
Obidike, Jennifer	L204
Oborne, Peter	L159
also	L270
Ochota, Mary-Ann	L276
also	L632
Ochs, Sara	L066
also	L093
Odell, Jenny	L192
also	L215
also	L520
Oermann, Robert K.	L388
Offill, Jenny	L468
Ogene, Timothy	L005
Ogunbiyi, Ore	L215
also	L520
Ogundiran, Tobi	L096
Oh, Temi	L468
Ohajura, Michael	L644
Ohanesian, Aline	L184
Ohartghaile, Ciara	L276
also	L677
Oldfield, Elizabeth	L096
also	L380
Olding, Catriona	L566
Olivarez, José	L515
also	L609
Oliver, Abi	L022
also	L157
Oliver, Aimee	L329
Oliver, Diane	L159
also	L170
Oliver, Joshua	L146
also	L223
Olorunnipa, Toluse	L077
Olsen, Erik	L166
also	L216
Olson, Liesl	L608
Olson, Toby	P209
Omand, David	L007
also	L466
Omond, Tam	L557
Omotoso, Yewande	L159
also	L170
Oness, Elizabeth	L184
Ooi, Yen	L166
also	L216
Opie, Frederick Douglass	L418
Oppenheimer, Mark	L469
Orchard, Erica Mary	L240
Ord, Charlotte	L278
also	L583
Ordorica, Andrés N.	L128
also	L521
Orion, Ell	L313
Ormerod, Jan	L159
Orr, David	L184
Orr, Elaine Neil	L334
Orsted, Brad	L313
Orzel, Chad	L184
Osborn, Cate	L537
Osborn, Christopher	L276
also	L632
Osei, Adjoa	L129
also	L215
Oshman, Michal	L566
Oskis, Andrea	L146
also	L223
Osman, Richard	L470
Ostrander, Madeline	L609
also	L639
Ostrovsky, Arkady	L007
also	L466
Oswald, James	L470
Otheguy, Emma	L174
Otis, Mary	L073
Ovenden, Richard	L129
also	L215
Overton, Iain	L276
also	L632
Owen, Antonia	L236
Owen, D. Wystan	L584
Owen, Joanne	L129
also	L215
Owen, Nick	P081
Owen, Nikki	L282
Owen, Orla	L032
also	L096
Owen, Polly	L619
Owen, Tom	L236
Owens, Jay	L190
Owens, Laurie	L159
Owens, Susan	L159
also	L270
Owens, Zahra	P144
Owolade, Tomiwa	L007
also	L466
Oyebanji, Adam	L226
also	L680
Oza, Janika	L073
Ozbek, Sara-Ella	L209
O'Brien, Beth	L401
O'Brien, Fiona	L110
also	L647
O'Brien, Kate	L159
O'Brien, Vanessa	L427
O'Connell, John	L276
also	L632
O'Connor, Bryce	L226
also	L680
O'Connor, Sean	L468
O'Dell, Tawni	L162
also	L405
O'Donnell, Cardy	L332
O'Donnell, Leeanne	L066
also	L197
O'donnell, Svenja	L215
also	L669
O'Donoghue, Deborah	L159
also	L232
O'gorman, Colm	L215
also	L669
O'Hara, Mary	L236
O'Keeffe, Ciarán	L236
O'Leary, Laurie	L539
O'Neill, Eric M.	L615
O'Neill, Penelope	L512
O'Neill, Poppy	L676
O'Regan, Marie	L364
O'Reilly, Miriam	L236

Pacat, C. S.	L159	
also	L645	
Paccione, Angela V.	L297	
Packer, Ann	L073	
Packer, Nigel	L294	
Padamsee, Nicolas	L209	
also	L276	
Padua, Sydney	L096	
also	L137	
Padwa, Lynette	L063	
Pagan, Matthew A.	L367	
Page, Elliot	P143	
Page, Janice	L239	
Page, Jonathan	L586	
Page, Louise	L146	
also	L250	
Page, Robin	L609	
also	L639	
Page, Sally	L585	
Paine, Tom	L184	
Paley, Dan	L229	
Paling, Chris	L048	
Pallant, Stuart	L512	
Palma, Raul	L440	
Palmer, Alan	L426	
Palmer, Andrew	L073	
Palmer, Lindsey J.	L334	
Palmer, Marnie	L539	
Palmer, Soraya	L609	
also	L639	
Palà, Gemma Ruiz	L574	
Panagos, Angelique	L526	
Panay, Panos	L537	
Panciroli, Elsa	L215	
also	L520	
Panek, Richard	L184	
also	L275	
Pang, Camilla	L254	
Paniz, Neela	L063	
Pannu, Suk	L254	
Panton, Gary	L333	
Pantony, Ali	L321	
Paphides, Pete	L276	
also	L632	
Paphitas, Theo	L539	
Paphitis, Zoe	L236	
Papillon, Buki	L470	
Papineau, David	L048	
Paradis, Michel	L184	
Parazynski, Scott	L414	
Paris, B.A.	L069	
also	L157	
Paris, Helen	L468	
Park, Haejin	L212	
also	L377	
Park, James	L155	
Park, Patricia	L297	
Parker, Andrew	L644	
Parker, Anna	L276	
also	L460	
Parker, Anna Chapman	L005	
Parker, D. G.	P144	
Parker, Della	L341	
Parker, Derek	L159	
Parker, Geoffrey	L276	
Parker, Julia	L159	
Parker, Nina	L066	
also	L516	
Parker, Paula K.	P514	
Parker, Richard	L440	
Parker, Sam	L504	
Parkin, Claire	L333	
also	L638	
Parks, Alan	L066	
also	L171	
Parks, Shoshi	L087	
Parlato, Terri	L603	
Parmar, Sandeep	L159	
Parr, Helen	L159	
also	L270	
Parry, Julia	L295	
Parsons, Charlotte	L623	
Parsons, Vic	L131	
also	L533	
Parten, Bennett	L608	
Partington, Richard	L159	
also	L270	
Pascali-Bonaro, Debra	L184	
Pashby, Laura	L295	
Pass, Nina De	L662	
Pastan, Rachel	L184	
Patel, Jyoti	L209	
also	L276	
Patel, Neel	L209	
also	L276	
Patel, Rupal	L254	
Paterson, Judy	L240	
Patis, Vikki	L166	
also	L263	
Patrick, Den	L343	
Patrick, Phaedra	L157	
Patrikarakos, David	L392	
Pattison, Justine	L566	
Pattison, Nell	L470	
Paul, Deepa	L333	
also	L638	
Paul, Joanne	L254	
Paul, Marilyn	L440	
Paul-Choudhury, Sumit	L190	
Paula, Ju De	L074	
Pavey, Jo	L048	
Pavliscak, Pamela	L087	
Pawson, Stuart	L623	
Payleitner, Jay	L414	
Payne, Robert	L159	
Payne, Rogba	L392	
Payne, Val	L677	
Payton, Theresa	L334	
Peacock, Justin	L184	
Peacock/Gillian, Caro	L623	
Peak, James	L099	
also	L278	
Peall, Philippa	L166	
also	L216	
Pearce, AJ	L333	
also	L638	
Pearce, Daisy	L392	
Pearce, Fred	L159	
also	L672	
Pearce, Michelle	L334	
Pearce, Philippa	L159	
Pearl, Mariane	L574	
Pearlberg, Jamie	L184	
Pearlstein, Howard	L634	
Pears, Iain	L215	
also	L669	
Pearse, Lesley	L048	
Pearson, Harry	L159	
also	L270	
Pearson, Nancy	L665	
Pearson, Patricia	L388	
Pearson, Roger	L129	
also	L215	
Peate, Claire	L146	
also	L223	
Peaty, Adam	L566	
Pechey, Ben	L110	
also	L647	
Pedder, Cato	L052	
also	L159	
Peel, Kit	L096	
also	L137	
Peel, Megan	L096	
also	L137	
Peeples, Scott	L334	
Peisner, David	L481	
Pelham, Nicolas	L007	
also	L466	
Pendleton, Madeline	L537	
Penman, Sharon	L445	
Penn, Thomas	L129	
also	L215	
Pennington, John	L074	
Pennock, Matthew	L313	
Penny, Eleanor	L159	
Pepper, Penny	L166	
also	L216	
Percy, Ely	L096	
Pereira, Lindsay	L114	
Perera, Anna	L644	
Perera, Kishani	L063	
Peridot, Kate	L401	
Perrine, Liz	L603	
Perrottet, Tony	L184	
Perry, Andrew	L251	
also	L278	
Perry, Anne	L364	
Perry, Matteson	L615	
Perry, Rebecca	L005	
Perry, Rob	L282	
Persichetti, James	L477	
Peters, Cash	L063	
Peters, Shawn	L537	
Peterson, Amy	L609	
Peterson, Carla	L238	
Peterson, Gilles	L159	
also	L270	
Peterson, Holly	L469	
Pettegree, Andrew	L129	
also	L215	
Pettigrew, Nick	L190	
Petty, Kate Reed	L159	
also	L266	
Peyton, Katie	L313	
Ph.D., Annie Rogers,	L184	
Ph.D., Chad Orzel,	L184	
Philby, Charlotte	L052	
also	L159	
Phillips, Emily	L504	
Phillips, Gin	P209	
Phillips, Jonathan	L129	
also	L215	
Phillips, Leigh	L007	
also	L466	
Phillips, Marie	L276	
also	L632	
Phillips, Max	L184	
Phillips, Riaz	L116	
Phillips, Tom	L276	
also	L632	
Phillips, Trevor	L566	
Philpott, William	L644	
Piazza, Jo	L032	
Pichon, Liz	L159	
also	L645	
Piddington, Catherine	L526	
Pielichaty, Helena	L240	
Piepenburg, Erik	L155	
Pierce, Karen	L665	
Pierce, Molly	L603	
Pierce, Wendell	L481	
Piercey, Joshua	L074	
Pierre, DBC	L096	
also	L137	
Pierson, Melissa Holbrook	L184	
Pilcher, Eleanor	L567	

Table of Authors

Pilgrim, Alake L146
  also L250
Pilling, Ann P236
Pilling, David L215
  also L318
Pimenta, Dominic L190
Pimsleur, Julia L334
Pinborough, Sarah L052
  also L159
Pinchbeck, Dan M L096
  also L130
Pinchin, Karen L609
Pincus, Steven L608
Pine, Courtney L159
  also L170
Pinede, Nadine L229
Pinfield, Matt L481
Piper, Brittany L467
Pirmohamed, Alycia L521
Pishiris, Christina L159
  also L232
Pitcher, Annabel L129
  also L215
Pitt, Leah L146
  also L517
Pizzolatto, Nic L184
Plackett, Jon L096
  also L380
Plass, Adrian L022
Platt, Jo L069
  also L157
Plessis, Lauren du L166
  also L216
Pliego, Ande L567
Plummer, Deborah L297
Plummer, Dr. Deborah L440
Plunkett, Tammy L122
Pockrus, Matthew L584
Pocock, Joanna L005
Poet, George The L086
Poffenroth, Mary L007
  also L466
Pointer, Anna L526
Pokwatka, Aimee L184
Polichetti, Daria L184
Polk, Sam L238
Pollen, Samuel L612
Pollero, Gianna L333
Pollock, Allyson L426
Polo, Claudia L574
Polonsky, Rachel L129
  also L215
Polt, Richard L184
Pompeo, Joe L427
Ponseca, Nicole L481
Pope, Dan L297
Pope, Kelly Richmond L582
Popkey, Miranda L468
Popper, Robert L333
  also L638
Portero, Alana S. L574
Posner, Gerald L469
Possanza, Amelia L396
Poster, Jem L362
Postman, Andrew L239
Potter, Nick L215
  also L669
Potter, Rupert L074
Potter, Vanessa L295
Pouncey, Maggie L184
Powell, Anthony L159
  also L266
Powell, Des L159
  also L270
Powell, Gareth L L096

Powell, Huw L096
  also L137
Powell, Karen L066
  also L197
Powell, Margaret L159
Powell, Melissa L329
Powell, Rosalind L066
  also L516
Powers, Ann L388
Powers, Jessica L184
Powers, Lindsay L087
Powers, Michael P144
Powling, Chris L159
  also L645
Poynor, Elizabeth L481
Prasad, Maya L458
Pratchett, Terry P143
Pratt, Laura L665
Pratt, Wendy L128
  also L521
Prempeh, Charlene L096
  also L380
Prentice, Andrew L129
  also L215
Pressman, Gene L427
  also L440
Presto, Greg L537
Preston, Caroline L184
Preston, Elizabeth L396
Preto, Nicki Pau L458
Price, Alfred L426
Price, David Mark L644
Price, Katie L290
Price, Laura L096
  also L380
Price, Lauren L294
  also L613
Pride, Christine L032
  also L096
Prideaux, Sue L129
  also L215
Priest, Cherie L184
Pringle, Paul L427
Prins, Mark L184
Prior, Hazel L022
  also L157
Pritchett, Georgia L333
  also L638
Prizant, Barry L063
Prochaska, Elizabeth L096
  also L380
Procter, Alice L677
Proudman, Charlotte L254
Prum, Eric L481
Prusa, Carolyn L141
Pryce, Nicola L623
Przewlocki, Kiki L621
Ptacin, Mira L153
  also L609
Pufahl, Shannon L159
  also L266
Pugh, Tom L644
Puhak, Shelley L609
Pullen, Nicholas L448
Pulley, D. M. L184
Pullin, Jim L332
Punwani, Seema L114
Purbrick, Martin L507
  also L680
Purcell, Laura L470
Purcell, Sebastian L297
Purdie, Kathryn L159
  also L645
Purdy, Rebekah L043
Purington, Carol L184
Purington, Susan Todd & Carol L184

Purkayastha, Ian L415
Purkiss, Diane L129
  also L215
Purkiss, Sue L240
Purser, Ann L159
Purvis, Xenobe L209
  also L276
Pylväinen, Hanna L584
Pyo, Rejina L677
Quach, Michelle L058
  also L059
Quaintrell, Philip C L294
  also L613
Quantick, David L336
Quantock, Grace L166
  also L216
Quatro, Jamie L096
  also L380
Quigley, Joan L184
Quinn, Anthony J. L166
  also L306
Quinn, Bonnie L078
  also L278
Quinn, Daniel P370
Quinn, Josephine L129
  also L215
Quinn, Karina Lickorish L005
Quintana, Jenny L166
  also L306
Qureshi, Jasmine L166
  also L216
Qureshi, Sadiah L159
  also L270
R, Rebecca L612
Raab, Nathan L440
Radcliffe, Jenny L007
  also L173
Radecki, Barbara L313
Rader, Mark L184
Rader, Peter L469
Radeva, Sabina L052
  also L159
Radford, Sian L226
  also L680
Radio, National Public L481
Radloff, Jessica L537
Radojevic, Monika L166
  also L216
Rady, Martyn L254
Radzinsky, Edvard L099
  also L278
Raeff, Anne L297
Raeside, Julia L034
  also L278
Raheem, Zara L574
Rahim, Shoaib L367
Rajan, Amol L159
  also L270
Ralat, José R. L515
  also L609
Ramadorai, Tarun L278
  also L339
Ramani, Madhvi L159
  also L645
Ramirez, Reyes L515
Ramirez, Steve L396
Ramos, Joanne L032
  also L096
Ramoutar, Shivi L276
  also L632
Ramsay, Adam L128
  also L521
Ramsay, Eileen L623
Ramsay, Francesca L209
  also L276

Ramsden, James L677
Ramsden, Rosie L677
Rana, Swéta L190
Randall, Emily L325
Randolph, Ladette L584
Rankin, Joan L159
Ransom, Amy L278
  also L583
Ransom, Jon L166
  also L216
Ransom, Sue L099
  also L278
Rao, Anthony L440
Raphael, Amy L099
  also L278
Rappaport, Captain Elliot L215
  also L318
Rath, Emily L226
  also L680
Rattle, Kayleigh L676
Ravella, Shilpa L215
  also L318
Rawlence, Ben L096
  also L380
Rawsthorn, Alice L007
  also L466
Rawsthorne, Paula L096
  also L137
Ray, Cate L074
Ray, Janisse L238
Ray, Jonathan L468
Ray, Reagan Lee L263
Ray, Reagan Lee L166
  also L263
Raygorodetsky, Gleb L334
Rayner, Abigail L050
Rayner, Catherine L159
  also L645
Rayner, Gordon L539
Rayner, Jacqui L159
  also L645
Razak, Melody L215
  also L669
Razzouk, Assaad L007
  also L466
Rea, Julie L066
  also L516
Read, Herbert L159
Reading, Anna L557
  also L647
Readman, Angela L504
Realf, Maria L468
Rebain, Erik L418
Rebelle, Josey L333
  also L638
Reddy, Jini L166
  also L216
Redgold, Eliza L334
Redmond, Markus L122
Redworth, Glyn L215
  also L318
Reed, Harris L646
Reed, Nigel L048
Reed, Richard L276
  also L632
Reeder, Lydia L609
Reekles, Beth L157
Rees, Owen L129
  also L215
Rees-Mogg, Jacob L254
Reese, Ashanté L396
Reeve, Alex L215
  also L520
Reeves, Benjamin L582
Reeves, Gemma L005
Reeves, James L159

Reeves, Jordan L148
Reeves, Megan L566
Reeves, Richard L007
  also L466
Regan, Katy L159
Rege, Devika L574
Regel, Hannah L159
Reginato, James L469
Reich, Susanna L184
Reichard, Raquel L515
  also L609
Reichert, Michael L334
Reid, Aimee L229
Reid, Andrew L470
Reid, Ebony L096
  also L380
Reid, Fil L616
Reid, Mike L539
Reifler, Nelly L184
Reihana, Victoria L609
Reilly, Frances L539
Reilly, Martina L294
  also L295
Reilly, Winifred L063
Reimer, Heidi L184
Reiss, Benjamin L608
Relth, Michael L537
Renan, Daphna L608
Rendell, Matt L557
Renner, James L184
  also L334
Rensburg, Laure Van L470
Rensten, John L544
Renwick, Chris L159
  also L270
Resnik, Judith L608
Rettig, Liz L236
Revell, Tim L007
  also L466
Reyes, Ana L209
  also L276
Reyes, Paul L184
Reyes, Ruben L515
  also L609
Reynolds, Allie L066
  also L093
Reynolds, Brittlestar aka Stewart L033
Reynolds, David L215
  also L318
Reynolds, Gretchen L238
Reynolds, Sheri L522
Rhian Parry L110
  also L647
Rhodeen, Pen L615
Rhodes, David L022
  also L157
Rhodes, Kate L623
Rhodes-Courter, Ashley L334
Rhush, Becky L166
  also L263
Rhyno, Greg L313
Rhys, Gruff L336
Riaz, Farrah L226
  also L680
Ricciardi, David L537
Rice, Lynette L155
Rice, Sam L276
  also L632
Richard, Alison F. L608
Richard, Will L110
  also L647
Richards, Andrea L063
Richards, Dan L215
  also L520
Richards, David L644

Richards, Julian L129
  also L215
Richards, Steve L159
  also L270
Richardson, Hamilton L251
  also L278
Richardson, Lisa L157
Richardson, Susan L034
  also L278
Richey, Warren L532
Richmond, Gillian L526
Richter, Jennifer Ann L229
Rickards, Lynne L240
Ricketts, Peter L007
  also L466
Rickman, Eloise L215
  also L520
Rid, Thomas L129
  also L215
Ridgard, Sarah L052
  also L159
Ridgeley, Andrew L048
Rieder, Travis L440
Rieder, Travis N. L440
Rien, Paige L334
Riesman, Robert L184
Rifaat, Laila L325
Rigby, Lyn L539
Rijswijk, Honni Van L184
Riley, Alex L215
  also L520
Riley, Catherine L096
  also L380
Riley, CE L096
  also L380
Riley, Charlotte Lydia L215
  also L520
Riley, Christina L128
  also L521
Riley, Gillian L426
Riley, Mary-Jane L623
Rimer, Alexandra L334
Rimington, Celesta L477
Rinaldi, Nicholas L184
Rio, Alice L254
Rio, M. L. L052
  also L159
  also L184
Ripley, Amanda L297
Risen, Alexandra L313
Ritz, The L086
Rivers, Carol L341
Rix, Jamie L240
Rix, Megan L188
Rixon, Charlotte L294
  also L295
  also L396
Roahen, Sara L297
Robb, Jackie L332
Robbie, Lou L321
Roberton, Fiona L159
  also L645
Roberts, Adam L364
Roberts, Barbara L297
Roberts, Bethan L052
  also L159
Roberts, Caroline L294
Roberts, Gareth L294
  also L295
Roberts, I. D. L096
  also L130
Roberts, Jillian L334
Roberts, Michele P498
Roberts, Nadim L609
  also L639

Roberts, Patrick	L294
also	L613
Roberts, Richard Owain	L557
also	L647
also	P336
Roberts, Sophy	L096
also	L380
Roberts, Victoria L.	L297
Robertson, Al	L032
also	L096
Robertson, Annie	L066
also	L516
Robertson, Catherine	L577
Robertson, Debora	L048
Robertson, Ian	L215
also	L318
Robertson, Ritchie	L129
also	L215
Robertson, Tatsha	L334
Robinson, Alan	L110
also	L647
Robinson, Ava	L108
Robinson, Callum	L096
also	L380
Robinson, Ellie	L157
Robinson, Jane	L052
also	L159
Robinson, Keith	L619
Robinson, Lucy	L159
Robinson, Nicole	L166
also	L263
Robinson, Roger	L053
also	L278
Robinson-Textor, Marisa	L184
Robson, David	L215
also	L520
Robson, Laura Brooke	L477
Rocero, Geena	L155
Roche, Helen	L159
also	L270
Roche, Juno	L166
also	L216
Rockman, Seth	L608
Rockwell, Marsheila (Marcy)	L033
Roden, Claudia	L159
Rodriguez, Prisca Dorcas Mojica	L515
also	L609
Roe, Duncan	L566
Roelen, Keetie	L146
also	L223
Roffey, Monique	L066
also	L171
Roffman, Karin	L469
Rogan, Eugene	L129
also	L215
Rogers, Annie	L184
Rogers, Jodi	L440
Rogers, Rebecca	L278
also	L583
Rogerson, Phoenicia	L364
Rogoff, Seth	L239
Rogoyska, Jane	L159
also	L270
Rojstaczer, Stuart	L184
Rollock, Nicola	L215
also	L520
Romano, Angela	P144
Romano, Tricia	L184
Romeo, Lisa	L334
Romero-Montalvo, Leon	L166
Romm, James	L469
Ronald, Terry	L566
Ronan, Kelsey	L090
Ronson, Mark	L469
Ronson, Stephen	L392
Ronstadt, Linda	L184
Rooney, Graeme	L332
Rooney, Rachel	L159
also	L645
Root, Neil	L007
also	L173
Roper, Jane	L184
Roper, Richard	L662
Rosa, Brunello	L159
also	L270
Rose, Alex	L184
Rose, Clare	L131
also	L533
Rose, Jacqui	L022
also	L157
Rose-Innes, Henrietta	L066
also	L171
Rosen, Michael J.	L229
Rosenberg, Allegra	L141
Rosenberg, Jane	L254
Rosenthall, Olivia	L005
Rosoff, Meg	L129
also	L215
Ross, Craig	L297
Ross, John J.	L297
Ross, Kenneth G.	L236
Ross, Leone	L116
also	L159
Ross, Marissa A.	L184
Rossi, Alan	L005
Rot, Noble	L048
Rotert, Rebecca	L184
Roth, Eileen	L063
Rothkopf, David	L297
Rothstein, Marilyn Simon	L334
Rourke-Mooney, Beck	L418
Rouss, Shannan	L184
Roux, Abigail	P144
Rowan, Anthea	L278
also	L326
Rowan, Iain	L166
Rowan, Isabella	P144
Rowland, Katherine	L184
Rowson, Jonathan	L007
also	L466
Roy, Jacqueline	L131
also	L533
Roy, Lena	L184
Roz, Emily	L614
Ruane, Rose	L333
also	L638
Rubel, David	L184
Rubenhold, Hallie	P143
Rubin, Miri	L129
also	L215
Rubinstein, William D.	L539
Rublack, Ulinka	L129
also	L215
Ruck, Adam	L215
also	L669
Rucklidge, Julia J.	L481
Ruddock, Neil 'Razor'	L048
Rude, Curt	L043
Ruderman, Anne	L608
Rudge, Penny	L215
also	L669
Rudnick, Paul	L297
Ruettimann, Laurie	L297
Ruffles, Lydia	L096
also	L137
Rufus, Anneli	L481
Rumble, Taylor-Dior	L005
Rumfitt, Alison	L096
Rush, Lyndsay	L416
also	L477
Russakoff, Dale	L334
Russell, Craig	L297
Russell, Gary	L332
Russell, Gerri	L011
Russell, Karen	L468
Russell, Rupert	L159
also	L270
Russell, Thaddeus	L469
Russell-Brown, Katheryn	L174
Russell-Pavier, Nick	L294
also	L613
Russell-Walling, Edward	L215
also	L669
Russo, Francine	L440
Rustin, Susanna	L294
also	L295
Rutgers, Leonard	L189
also	L278
Rutherford, Geo	L537
Rutherford, Robert	L166
also	L306
Rutt, Stephen	L029
Rutter, Bethany	L333
Rutter, Thomas	L005
Ruzickova, Zuzana	L662
Rwizi, C. T.	L343
Ryan, Elliot	L066
also	L516
Ryan, Joan	L184
Ryan, Mark	L539
Ryan, Mike	P101
Ryan, Morgan	L058
also	L059
Ryan, Robin	L440
Ryan, Romla	L048
Ryle, Matthew	L614
Ryrie, Alec	L129
also	L215
Ryrie, Charlie	L677
Sachdeva, Anjali	L396
Sachsse, Emma	L122
Sacks, Alexandra	L469
Sadowski, Michael	L334
Sadr, Ehsaneh	L477
Safi, Aminah Mae	L418
Sagar, Andy	L619
Sahota, Kohinoor	L110
also	L647
Saint, Jennifer	L470
Saintclare, Celine	L282
Salam, Anbara	L282
Salinari, Karla	L334
Salter, Cassidy Ellis	L226
also	L680
Salu, Michael	L005
Samadder, Rhik	L096
also	L380
Samanani, Farhan	L215
also	L520
Samawi, Mohammed Al	L615
Samet, Elizabeth	L469
Sampson, Scott	L297
Sampson, Steve	P144
Sams, Saba	L116
also	L159
Samson, Polly	L096
also	L137
Samuels, Robert	L077
Samuels, Talia	L166
also	L263
Sancton, Julian	L087
Sandenbergh, Roberta	L334
Sanders, Ella Frances	L209
Sanders, Rob	L229
Sanderson, Jane	L159
also	L270
Sandor, Steven	L033
Sandoval, Richard	L184

Sands, Lynsay	L058	
also	L059	
Sansom, C. J.	L276	
also	L632	
Sansom, Clive	L159	
Sansom, William	L276	
Santlofer, Jonathan	L440	
Santos, Madrid	L174	
Santos, Marisa de los	L184	
Santos, Vanessa	L005	
Santos, Yaffa S.	L574	
Sanz, Marta	L574	
Saoudi, Lias	L251	
also	L278	
Sapiro, Mike	L467	
Sappington, Adam	L063	
Saro-Wiwa, Noo	L159	
also	L170	
Sarsfield, Margie	L141	
Sasson, Jean	L162	
also	L405	
Sassoon, Donald	L007	
also	L466	
Sassoon, Joseph	L129	
also	L215	
Satterly, Tom	L414	
Saunders, Dan	L566	
Saunders, Karen	L240	
Sautoy, Marcus du	L276	
also	L632	
Savage, Jon	L215	
also	L318	
Savage, Marjorie Barton	L063	
Savage, Vanessa	L470	
Savanh, Victoria	L108	
Savaş, Ayşegül	L073	
Savill, David	L096	
also	L380	
Sawyer, Jamie	L096	
also	L130	
Sawyer, R. Keith	L297	
Saxey, E.	L096	
also	L130	
Sayers, Dorothy L.	L159	
Scanlan, Kathryn	L159	
Scanlon, Suzanne	L294	
also	L295	
also	L396	
Scarlett, Fiona	L091	
also	L096	
also	L380	
Schaitkin, Alexis	L184	
Schapira, Kate	L427	
Scheer, Kodi	L184	
Scheff, Sue	L334	
Schelter, Kate	L415	
Schemel, Patty	L184	
Schenker, Sarah	L539	
Schesventer, Faith Williams	L157	
also	L383	
Scheynius, Lina	L005	
Schiavone, Tony	P101	
Schickel, Erika	L481	
Schickler, David	L184	
Schiffer, Zoë	L609	
also	L639	
Schiller, Rebecca	L278	
also	L583	
Schiot, Molly	L184	
Schmidt, Heidi Jon	L184	
Schmitt, Sally	L184	
Schmitz, Anthony	L063	
Schmitz, Elisa A.	L334	
Schmitz, Kathryn	L090	
Schneider, Indyana	L276	
also	L468	
Schneider, M.D. Edward	L063	
Schneiderhan, Caitlin	L148	
Schonfeld, David	L515	
also	L609	
Schories, Pat	L184	
Schorr, Melissa	L334	
Schroeder, Kate	L537	
Schulman, Michael	L469	
Schulte, Anitra Rowe	L444	
Schultz, Claire	L007	
also	L233	
Schultz, Ellen E.	L334	
Schultz, Emily	L090	
Schultz, William Todd	L184	
Schuneman, Kyle	L063	
Schurman, Bradley	L297	
Schwartz, A. Brad	L609	
also	L639	
Schwartz, Lynne Sharon	P209	
Schwartzel, Erich	L469	
Schwarz, Viviane	L677	
Scott, Alev	L276	
also	L632	
Scott, Anika	L557	
Scott, Caroline	L623	
Scott, Eddie	L276	
also	L460	
Scott, Helen	L166	
also	L216	
Scott, Izabella	L159	
Scott, Marina	L153	
also	L609	
Scott, Nikola	L294	
also	L295	
Scott, Paul	L159	
Scott, Su	L614	
Scott-Brown, Sophie	L005	
Scull, Luke	L096	
also	L130	
Seabright, Paul	L129	
also	L215	
Seal, Clare	L278	
also	L583	
Seal, Rebecca	L276	
also	L632	
Seale, Yasmine	L096	
also	L137	
Sebastian, Laura	L148	
Sebastian, Tim	L677	
Sebold, Alice	L159	
also	L266	
Seddon, Delphine	L512	
Seddon, Holly	L096	
also	L380	
Sedgwick, Mark	L007	
also	L466	
Sediment, Paul Keers:	L276	
Seeber, Claire	L362	
Seesequasis, Coltrane	L033	
Sefton, Joanne	L295	
Segall, Laurie	L615	
Seiden, Josh	L297	
Seiffert, Rachel	L052	
also	L159	
Seliger, Mark	L388	
Selinger, Hannah	L537	
Selleck, Tom	L440	
Selman, Victoria	L166	
also	L306	
Semple, David	L332	
Senapathy, Kavin	L090	
Senior, Antonia	L159	
also	L270	
Sentelik, Ian	P144	
Serafinowicz, James	L332	
Setchfield, Nick	L343	
Setoodeh, Ramin	L415	
Sevilla, Cate	L644	
Seville, Jane	P144	
Sewell, Zakia	L215	
also	L520	
Sexton, Tara	L110	
also	L647	
Seymour, Ingrid	L058	
also	L059	
Seymour, Jeff	L477	
Seymour, John	L159	
Seymour, Miranda	L159	
also	L266	
Seymour, Richard	L426	
Shabi, Rachel	L159	
also	L270	
Shackelford, Elizabeth	L469	
Shackle, Mike	L096	
also	L130	
Shadbolt, Nigel	L007	
also	L466	
Shah, Mira V.	L069	
also	L157	
Shah, Oliver	L007	
also	L466	
Shah, Sarupa	L616	
Shaha, Alom	L129	
also	L215	
Shahid, Humaira Awais	L584	
Shakur, Maurice "Mopreme"	L155	
Shalmiyev, Sophia	L108	
Shames, Terry	L532	
Shanker, Samara	L444	
Shannon, George	L063	
Shanté, Angela	L444	
Shapiro, Alan	L584	
Shapow, Nathan	L539	
Share, Amber	L087	
also	L415	
Sharkey, Lauren	L282	
Sharma, Babita	L392	
also	L566	
Sharma, Nina	L141	
Sharma, Priya	L096	
Sharot, Tali	L096	
also	L380	
Sharp, Cathy	L341	
Sharratt, Nick	L159	
also	L266	
Shavit, Shabtai	L615	
Shaw, Ali	L032	
also	L096	
Shaw, Christine	L426	
Shaw, Dale	L677	
Shaw, L C	L058	
also	L059	
Shaw, Liam	L129	
also	L215	
Shaw, Martin	L159	
also	L672	
Shaw, Matthew	L251	
also	L278	
Shaw, Rebecca	L069	
also	L157	
Shea, Kieran	L184	
Sheibani, Jion	L619	
Shelby, Jeff	L184	
Sheldrake, Merlin	L159	
also	L672	
Shenk, Joshua Wolf	L184	
Shepard, Molly D.	L440	
Shephard, Sarah	L034	
also	L278	
Shepherd, Megan	L159	
also	L645	

Shepherd-Robinson, Laura	L276	
also	L632	
Sheppard, Kathleen	L396	
Sher, Antony	L445	
Sherbill, Sara	L334	
Sheridan, Nick	L157	
Sherlock, Alison	L341	
Sherratt, Mel	L166	
also	L306	
Shertok, Heidi	L567	
Sherwood, Kim	L032	
also	L096	
Shetterly, Margot Lee	L609	
Shev, Wyatt	L043	
Shi, Qian	L619	
Shields, Lauren	L396	
Shih, David	L609	
also	L639	
Shimotakahara, Leslie	L313	
Shingler, Tina	L278	
also	L326	
Shireen, Nadia	L333	
also	L638	
Shoneyin, Lola	L159	
also	L672	
Short, Philip	L052	
also	L159	
Shorter, Louise	L392	
Shortt, Rupert	L048	
Shoulder, Jack	L141	
SHRM,	L297	
Shrubsole, Guy	L029	
Shuker, Carl	L504	
Shuldiner, Joseph	L481	
Shumaker, Heather	L334	
Shute, Jenefer	L184	
Shuttle, Penelope	L159	
Siadatan, Tim	L614	
Sidibe, Gabourey	L615	
Sidley, Kate	L415	
Siegel, Bernie	P370	
Signer, Rachel	L481	
Sikes, Kaitlin M	L229	
Silber, Alexandra	L334	
Silva, Hannah	L557	
also	L647	
Silva, Ingrid	L184	
Silvani, Celia	L567	
Silver, Elizabeth L.	L073	
Silver, Josh	L401	
Silver, Marisa	L184	
Simanowitz, Jenny	L333	
also	L638	
Simants, Kate	L052	
also	L159	
Simenon, Georges	L254	
Simmonds, Natali	L526	
Simmons, Cécile	L034	
also	L278	
Simmons, Gail	L096	
also	L380	
Simmons, Kristen	L416	
also	L477	
Simmons, Sylvie	L388	
Simons, Tom	L526	
Simpson, Catherine	L294	
also	L613	
Simpson, John	L376	
also	P144	
Simpson, Travis	L603	
Sims, Cat	L676	
Sinclair, Alexander	L539	
Sinclair, Jenna Hilary	P144	
Sinclair, Pete	L332	
Sinclair, Safiya	L584	
Singleton, Calah	L226	
also	L680	
Sinotok, Karen	L159	
also	L232	
Sipal, Susan	L011	
Sirdeshpande, Rashmi	L096	
Sissay, Lemn	L096	
also	L137	
Sites, Kevin	L582	
Sitoy, Lakimbini	L544	
Sittenfeld, Curtis	P143	
Sivasundaram, Sujit	L159	
also	L270	
Skelton, Matthew	L129	
also	L215	
Skibsted, Jens Martin	L297	
Skinner, Dan	P144	
Skinner, Keith	L539	
Skinner, Richard	L096	
also	L137	
Skoda, Amélie	L166	
also	L216	
Skuy, David	L313	
Skye, Ione	L184	
Skye, Sasha	P144	
Slade, Emma	L294	
Slahi, Mohamedou	L184	
Slapper, Emily	L476	
Slater, Alexander	L512	
Slater, Kim	L069	
also	L157	
Slater, KL	L069	
also	L157	
Slater, Sean	L069	
also	L157	
Slater, Sofia	L096	
also	L137	
Slatter, Angela	L364	
Slattery-Christy, David	L539	
Slim, Pamela	L334	
Sliwa, Joanna	L334	
Sloan, Nate	L388	
Slocombe, Penelope	L333	
also	L638	
Slovo, Gillian	P498	
Small, Mark	L141	
Smalls, Chris	L427	
Smith, Alexander McCall	L159	
also	L645	
Smith, Bruce	L444	
Smith, Danny	L294	
also	L613	
Smith, David	L174	
Smith, Emma	L129	
also	L215	
Smith, Freddie	L239	
Smith, Jean	L096	
also	L130	
Smith, Jon	L566	
Smith, Julia Ridley	L141	
Smith, Karen Ingala	L294	
also	L295	
Smith, Kate G.	L157	
also	L585	
Smith, Len	L539	
Smith, Lisa	L116	
also	L159	
Smith, Luanne G.	L603	
Smith, Mark B.	L159	
also	L270	
Smith, Mark David	L122	
Smith, Max Sydney	L504	
Smith, Michael	L251	
also	L278	
Smith, Nicholas Boys	L376	
Smith, Nikki	L096
also	L380
Smith, Patti	L184
Smith, Paul	L332
Smith, Rita	L539
Smith, Robin Callender	L236
Smith, Rt. Hon Iain Duncan	L236
Smith, Sherry	L184
Smith, Talmon Joseph	L073
Smith, Tiffany Watt	L215
also	L520
Smith, Victoria	L294
also	L295
Smith-Barton, Emma	L333
also	L638
Smoke, Ben	L131
also	L533
Smokler, Kevin	L184
Smolyansky, Julie	L481
Smythe, James	L276
also	L662
Snider, Laura	L444
Snow, Anna	L043
Snow, Philippa	L504
Snyder, Christopher A.	L334
So, Cynthia	L612
Sobiech, Laura	L334
Sokol, Josh	L396
Sole, Linda	L341
Soli, Tatjana	L184
Solomon, Jemma	L676
Solomon, Marc	L297
Solomons, Natasha	L032
also	L096
Somers, Jeff	L532
Somerville, Christopher	P143
Somerville, Zoe	L557
Something, Airy	L676
Sommer, Tim	L537
Sommerville, Anniki	L091
Sopel, Jon	L566
Sorrel, O.R.	L329
Sosna-Spear, Quinn	L148
Soundar, Chitra	L612
South, Alex	L096
also	L380
South, Mary	L159
South, Miss	L295
Southgate, Laura	L005
Southon, Emma	L644
Southwell, Gareth	L294
Sowa, Pat	L157
Sowemimo, Annabel	L131
also	L533
Spall, Shane	L557
Spanbauer, Tom	P209
Spangler, Brie	L609
Spark, Muriel	L159
Sparks, Kerrelyn	L274
Sparks, Lily	L184
Spector, Shira	L184
Spector, Tim	L096
also	L380
Spencer, Ashley	L155
Spencer, Dan	L586
Spencer, Elisabeth	L294
also	L295
Spencer, Mimi	L276
also	L632
Spencer, Sonja	P144
Spencer, Tom	L392
Sperling, Jason	L155
Spielman, Lori Nelson	L058
also	L059
Spiers, Johanna	L526
Spiller, Nancy	L063

Spiller, Tatton	L034	
also	L278	
Spoelman, Colin	L469	
Spohr, Kristina	L159	
also	L270	
Spooner, Meagan	L159	
also	L645	
Spotswood, Stephen	L022	
Spraggs, Gillian	L364	
Spring, Howard	L159	
Spring, Marianna	L007	
also	L173	
Spring, Olivia	L005	
Springer, Lisa	L477	
Springer, Nancy	L662	
Springsteen, Jennifer	L416	
also	L477	
Spurling, Hilary	L159	
also	L266	
Stacey, Alex	L614	
Stadlen, Lexi	L129	
also	L215	
Staff, P. A.	L392	
Stafford, Rebecca	L522	
Stamm, Julie M.	L334	
Stanley, Jessica	L159	
Stanley, Kelli	L184	
Stapleton, Susannah	L048	
Starcher, Allison Mia	L063	
Starkie, Allan	L539	
Starling, Boris	L470	
Starling, Hollie	L294	
also	L613	
Staub, Leslie	L229	
Stauffer, Rainesford	L108	
Stavinoha, Peter L.	L334	
Steadman, Catherine	L069	
also	L157	
Stears, Marc	L129	
also	L215	
Stedman, M L	L032	
also	L096	
Steele, Emma	L157	
also	L585	
Steele, Fraser	L332	
Steele, Jaxx	P144	
Steele, Jonathan	L577	
Steer, Dugald	L240	
Stefanovich-Thomson, Alexis	L367	
Stegert, Ali	L325	
Stein, Gertrude	L159	
Stein, Judith E.	L615	
Stein, Leigh	L184	
Steiner, Ben	L196	
Steiner, Guenther	P052	
Steinman, Louise	L063	
Steinmetz, Greg	L469	
Stephens, Isaiah	L537	
Steptoe, Javaka	L184	
Sterling, Michelle	L096	
also	L380	
Sterling, Michelle Min	L096	
also	L380	
Sterling, Siena	L644	
Stern, Adam Philip	L582	
Stern, Bill	L063	
Stern, Lindsay	L184	
Sterne, Jayne	L539	
Stevens, Andrew	L091	
Stevens, Georgina	L619	
Stevens, Mark	L096	
also	L137	
Stevenson, Mark	L644	
Stevenson, Talitha	P498	
Stewart, Andrea	L470	
Stewart, Cameron	L539	
Stewart, Dave	L376	
Stewart, Heather Grace	L444	
Stewart, Jude	L184	
Stewart, Maryon	L334	
Stewart, Polly	L276	
also	L468	
Stewart, Sam	L325	
Stewart, Sarah	L521	
Stieger, Allison	L313	
Stillman, Deanne	L582	
Stimson, Lora	L066	
also	L516	
Stinchcombe, Paul	L236	
Stirling, Joss	L159	
also	L645	
Stirling, Richard	L166	
Stock, Kathleen	L295	
Stockwin, Julian	L066	
also	L171	
Stohn, Stephen	L313	
Stoker, Sean	L005	
Stokes, Stacy	L416	
also	L477	
Stokes-Chapman, Susan	L470	
Stone, Jennifer	L282	
Stone, Robert	L440	
Stoppard, Miriam	L215	
also	L520	
Storey, Erik	L022	
also	L157	
Storey, Neil R.	L539	
Storey, Rosie	L159	
also	L232	
Storm, Jaelyn	P144	
Storti, Kara	L513	
Stott, Dean	L566	
Stott, Peter	L159	
also	L270	
Stovell, Sarah	L282	
Stowe, Hannah	L159	
also	L672	
Strachan, Claudia	L539	
Strachan, Hew	L159	
also	L266	
Straight, Susan	L184	
Strasser, Emily	L584	
Strathie, Chae	L240	
Strauss, Elissa	L108	
Strawson, John	L159	
Strayed, Cheryl	L584	
Strelow, Michael	P209	
Strong, Count Arthur	L276	
also	L632	
Strong, Jeremy	L159	
also	L266	
Strong, Lynn Steger	L073	
Strong, Roy	L129	
also	L215	
Stroud, Clover	P143	
Stroud, Jonathan	L052	
also	L159	
Stryker, Susan	L440	
Stuart, Andrea	L099	
also	L278	
Stuart, Jesse	L364	
Stuart, Kimberly	L414	
Stuart, Nancy Rubin	L334	
Stuart-Smith, Sue	L215	
also	L669	
Stubblefield, Robert	L532	
Studer, Kate Pawson	L603	
Stults, Shannon	L444	
Sturge, Georgina	L204	
Sturgeon, Nicola	L159	
also	L270	
Sturtevant, Dana	L334	
Subko, C.J.	L078	
also	L278	
Sudbury, Rowena	P144	
Suggars, Philip	L189	
also	L278	
Suleyman, Mustafa	L096	
also	L380	
Sullivan, Deirdre	L157	
Sullivan, Joy	L416	
also	L477	
Sullivan, Mecca Jamilah	L584	
Sullivan-Craver, Sharon	L043	
Summers, Julie	L129	
also	L215	
Sumrow, Melanie	L537	
Sung, Crystal	L567	
Surrey, Ellen	L229	
also	L513	
Sussman, Fiona	L294	
Sutcliff, Rosemary	L159	
Sutherland, Fae	P144	
Sutherland, Jacqueline	L276	
also	L468	
Sutherland, John	L662	
Sutherland, Krystal	L129	
also	L215	
Sutter, James L.	L159	
also	L645	
Sutton, Henry	L215	
also	L669	
Swaby, Rachel	L609	
Swain, Heidi	L526	
Swan, Annalyn	L096	
also	L137	
Swan, Karen	L526	
Swan, Shanna	L440	
Swarup, Shubhangi	L574	
Sweeney, Cynthia D'Aprix	L184	
Sweeney, Emma Claire	L052	
also	L159	
Sweezey, Mathew	L297	
Swift, Katherine	L215	
also	L669	
Swift, Vivian	L184	
Swiss, Deborah J.	L334	
Sword, Harry	L251	
also	L278	
Sword-Williams, Stefanie	L204	
Sydnor, Charisma	L481	
Sylva, Tasha	L159	
also	L232	
Sylvester, Simon	L032	
also	L096	
Symes, Sally	L159	
also	L645	
Sypeck, Jeff	L334	
Szarlan, Chrysler	L416	
also	L477	
Szewczyk, Jesse	L155	
Szwed, John	L388	
Sánchez, María	L574	
Sánchez-Andrade, Cristina	L574	
Sóuter, Ericka	L334	
Tachna, Ariel	P144	
Tagouri, Noor	L108	
Tait, Amelia	L204	
Tait, Vanessa	L159	
also	L645	
Takaoka, Shannon	L184	
Tallis, Raymond	L007	
also	L466	
Tamani, Liara	L184	
Tangka, Eulalie	L146	
also	L223	
Tangorra, Zahra	L108	
Tania de Regil	L174	

Tanner, Sophie	L526	
Tanzer, Ben	L416	
also	L477	
Tanzer, Eliska	L294	
also	L613	
Tarlo, Emma	L614	
Tarlow, Ellen	L229	
also	L513	
Tassier, Troy	L506	
also	L507	
Tate, Dizz	L159	
Tate, June	L341	
Tawney, Cyril	P236	
Tawse, Daniel	L401	
Tay, Tania	L567	
Taylor, A. J. P.	L159	
Taylor, Andrew	L276	
also	L632	
Taylor, Annie	L166	
also	L263	
Taylor, Benjamin	L608	
Taylor, Bob	L539	
Taylor, Colin	L048	
Taylor, Jessica	L566	
Taylor, Jordyn	L477	
Taylor, Katie	L614	
Taylor, Katrina	L184	
Taylor, Larime	L621	
Taylor, Lili	L469	
Taylor, Lulu	L159	
Taylor, Marsali	L623	
Taylor, Nick	L184	
Taylor, Sarah Stewart	L297	
Taylor, Vanessa	L254	
Taylor-Pitt, Paul	L166	
also	L216	
Tchaikovsky, Adrian	L445	
Teague, David	L184	
Telfer, CeCe	L582	
Telfer, Tori	L184	
Tempest, Daisy	L146	
also	L223	
Tempest, Kae	L116	
also	L159	
Temple, John	L334	
Temple, Rob	L470	
Templeton, Rebecca	L166	
also	L263	
Tennyson, Tre	L313	
Terrana, Diane	L313	
Tey, Josephine	L159	
Thai, Kim	L515	
also	L609	
Thammavongsa, Souvankham	L073	
Thample, Rachel de	L677	
Thanenthiran-Dharuman, Sureka	L159	
also	L232	
Thanhauser, Sofi	L609	
also	L639	
Thao, Dustin	L058	
also	L059	
Theall, Michelle	L582	
Thebo, Mimi	L157	
Theise, Terry	L063	
Theodoridou, Natalia	L032	
also	L096	
Thernstrom, Melanie	L184	
Thom, Alessandra	L005	
Thomas Hertog	P460	
Thomas, Cathy	L215	
also	L520	
Thomas, David	L414	
Thomas, Dylan	L159	
also	L270	
Thomas, Frances	L159	
also	L645	
Thomas, James	L251	
also	L278	
Thomas, Jo	L166	
also	L306	
Thomas, June	L141	
Thomas, Michelle	L096	
also	L380	
Thomas, Scarlett	L052	
also	L159	
Thomas, Stacey	L163	
Thompson, Anne Bahr	L440	
Thompson, Felicity Fair	L236	
Thompson, Jean	L184	
Thompson, Jo	L099	
also	L278	
Thompson, Kate	L066	
also	L093	
Thompson, Lara	L032	
also	L096	
Thompson, Lisa	L254	
Thompson, Shirley	P081	
Thompson, Tade	L096	
also	L130	
Thomson, Pat	L159	
also	L645	
Thomson-Spires, Nafissa	L096	
also	L380	
Thorne, Rebecca	L166	
also	L263	
Thurley, Simon	L159	
also	L270	
Ticktin, Allie	L440	
Tidy, Bill	L236	
Tierney, Sarah	L294	
also	L613	
Tiffany, Kaitlyn	L609	
also	L639	
Tiffany, Terri	P435	
Tilburg, Christopher Van	L334	
Tilney, Georgie	L276	
also	L677	
Timms, Barry	L619	
Tinari, Leah	L537	
Tinglof, Christina Baglivi	L063	
Tinline, Phil	L159	
also	L270	
Tinniswood, Adrian	L215	
also	L318	
Tipler, Eric	L467	
Tipping, Liz	L470	
Tirado, Vincent	L506	
also	L507	
Tishby, Noa	L615	
Tivnan, Tom	L099	
also	L278	
Tizzard, Gemma	L278	
also	L583	
Tobin, Max	L429	
Todd, G X	L069	
also	L157	
Todd, Richard	L184	
Todd, Ruby	L584	
Todd, Susan	L184	
Tomasi, Claire	L612	
Tomba, Neil	L537	
Tomba, Sheree	L537	
Tomlinson, David	L184	
Tomlinson, Theresa	L159	
also	L645	
Tonge, Samantha	L157	
Tonkin, Peter	L159	
Toon, Nigel	L159	
also	L672	
Torday, Piers	L096	
also	L137	
Torjussen, Mary	L066	
also	L093	
Tosti-Kharas, Jennifer	L297	
Toumine, Ana	L448	
Towns, Krista	L665	
Townshend, Pete	L566	
Tracey, Kevin	L467	
Tracini, Joe	L190	
Trail, Gayla	L481	
Tran, Ly Ky	L396	
Tran, Phuc	L396	
Travis, Nigel	L215	
also	L318	
Treave, Hannah	L066	
also	L093	
Tregebov, Michael	L621	
Tregenza, Sharon	L401	
Treggiden, Katie	L591	
also	L663	
Tregoning, John	L295	
Tremlett, Caroline	L048	
Trenhaile, John	L066	
also	L093	
Trenow, Liz	L294	
also	L295	
Trigell, Jonathan	L526	
Trinidad, Miguel	L481	
Trivelli, Joe	L614	
Trogen, Kari	L512	
Trueblood, Amy	L506	
also	L507	
Trueblood, Amy True / Amy	L507	
also	L680	
Truman, Sally Ann	L166	
also	L263	
Truong, Monique	L584	
Truss, Lynne	L159	
also	L266	
Tse, Terence	L297	
Tsong, Jing Jing	L513	
Tuama, Pádraig Ó	L096	
also	L137	
Tucker, Chelsea	L334	
Tucker, Jacqueline	L619	
Tucker, Nancy	L282	
Tudor, Kael	L619	
Tuffin, Stephen	L333	
also	L638	
Tuke, Amanda	L166	
Tundun, Ola	L166	
also	L263	
Tunstall, KT	L676	
Turkot, Joseph	L058	
also	L059	
Turman, Lawrence	L184	
Turnbull, Ann	L159	
also	L645	
Turner, A. K.	L052	
also	L159	
Turner, Brian	L544	
Turner, Chris	L313	
Turner, David	L567	
Turner, Emily	L226	
also	L680	
Turner, Jane	L096	
also	L380	
Turner, Jon Lys	L096	
also	L137	
Turner, Luke	L251	
also	L278	
Turner, Robin	L251	
also	L278	
Turner, Ronnie	L166	
also	L263	
Turner, Rosie	L166	
also	L216	

Turner, Sarah	L294	
also	L396	
Turns, Anna	L526	
Twitchell, James	L184	
Tyce, Harriet	L052	
also	L159	
Tyler, L.C.	L166	
also	L306	
Tyler, Simon	L159	
also	L270	
Tyson, Neil deGrasse	L184	
Uddin, Zakia	L005	
Ujifusa, Steven	L615	
Underwood, Jack	L159	
Unger, Craig	L469	
Unsworth, Emma Jane	L096	
also	L137	
Unwin, Lucy	L619	
Uose, Hanna Thomas	L116	
also	L159	
Upchurch, Gail	L325	
Updale, Eleanor	L129	
also	L215	
Upson, Nicola	L052	
also	L159	
Urban, Madeleine	P144	
Urwin, Jack	L066	
also	L516	
Urwin, Rosamund	L159	
also	L270	
Urzaiz, Begoña Gómez	L574	
Usher, M.D.	L334	
Usmani, Sumayya	L614	
Utley, Robert	L184	
Uzor, Kenechi	L005	
Vachon, Dana	L469	
Vadaketh, Sudhir Thomas	L007	
also	L466	
Vaidhyanathan, Siva	L238	
Valby, Karen	L184	
Valentine, Jenny	L052	
also	L159	
Valentine, Rachel	L401	
Valerie, Julie	L334	
Vallance, Sarah	L396	
VanBrakle, Khadija L.	L507	
VanBrakle, Khadijah	L506	
also	L507	
Vanderbilt, Tom	L215	
also	L318	
VanderLugt, Dana	L229	
Vannicola, Joanne	L313	
Vara, Geeta	L557	
Varaidzo,	L116	
also	L159	
Vardalos, Nia	L481	
Varga, Anne-Marie	L066	
also	L093	
Variyar, Rajasree	L470	
Varnes, Allison	L537	
Varoufakis, Yanis	L159	
also	L270	
also	L608	
Varouxakis, Georgios	L007	
also	L466	
Varricchio, Alex	L313	
Varshney, Vani	L448	
Vasagar, Jeevan	L007	
also	L466	
Vaughan, Carson	L609	
Vaughan, Laura	L032	
also	L096	
Vaughan, Sarah	L159	
Vaughn, Lauren Roedy	L122	
Vaz, Katherine	L184	
Veen, Johanna van	L506	
also	L507	
Velasquez, Eric	L513	
Vellekoop, Maurice	L313	
Velton, Sonia	L470	
Veltri, Michael	L297	
also	L440	
Venis, Linda	L063	
Ventura, MPH Emily	L063	
Vera, Marisel	L063	
Verde, Eva	L166	
also	L216	
Verdick, Elizabeth	L063	
Vernon, P.J.	L090	
Veselka, Vanessa	L073	
Veste, Luca	L066	
also	L093	
Vian, Maddy	L619	
Vicedo, Marga	L297	
Vick, Christopher	L129	
also	L215	
Vickers, Zachary Tyler	L584	
Victoire, Stephanie	L159	
also	L170	
Videen, Hana	L099	
also	L278	
Vieira, Toby	L336	
Viera, Rebecca Lynn	L334	
Viertel, Jack	L615	
Vieten, Cassandra	L467	
Vigurs, Kate	L099	
also	L278	
Vilden, Lynx	L481	
Vince, Ian	L276	
also	L632	
Vincent, John	L276	
also	L632	
Vincent, Sarah St.	L184	
Vincent, Yvonne	L364	
Vines, Stephen	L506	
also	L507	
Vinti, Lucia	L619	
Virdi, R.R.	L226	
also	L680	
Vitiello, Cory	L313	
Vitkus, Jessica	L388	
Vladic, Sara	L537	
Vladislavic, Ivan	L066	
also	L171	
Vlock, Deb	L532	
Voake, Steve	L096	
also	L137	
Vogel, Sarah	L609	
Vogl, James	L007	
also	L466	
Volanthen, John	L566	
Volpatt, Michael	L334	
Vondriska, Meg	L087	
Voors, Barbara	L336	
Vorhaus, John	L063	
Voskuil, Hannah	L063	
Vossler, Tom	L297	
Vyner, Harriet	L096	
also	L137	
Waal, Edmund De	L215	
also	L669	
Wabuke, Hope	L073	
Waddell, James	L007	
also	L466	
Waddell, Martin	L159	
also	L645	
Wade, Christine	L184	
Wade, Claire	L526	
Wade, Lizzie	L396	
Wade, Michael	L297	
Wadham, Lucy	L159	
also	L266	
Wagner, Adam	L276	
also	L632	
Wagner, Benjamin	L239	
Wagner, Kate	L192	
Wagner, Tony	L297	
Wainwright, Martha	L481	
Wainwright, Tom	L646	
Wait, Rebecca	L294	
also	L295	
Waite, Elizabeth	L157	
Waite, Evan	L087	
Wakeling, Kate	L240	
Wald, Elijah	L388	
Waldon, Laura	L184	
Walk, Weird	L333	
also	L638	
Walker, Alice	L159	
also	L266	
Walker, Andy	L313	
Walker, Angharad	L333	
Walker, Casey	L184	
Walker, Darren	L469	
Walker, Jennie	L276	
also	L632	
Walker, Kandace Siobhan	L166	
also	L216	
Walker, Kay	L313	
Walker, Martin	L215	
also	L669	
Walker, Owen	L007	
also	L466	
Walker, Sarai	L276	
Walker, Sophie	L282	
Walker, Tash	L096	
also	L380	
Walker-Edwards, Ryan	L429	
Walker-Figueroa, Devon	L584	
Wallace, Mike	L238	
Wallace, Rosie	L240	
Wallace, Wanda	L440	
Walle, Mark Van de	L184	
Waller, Sharon Biggs	L148	
Wallis, Max	L096	
also	L137	
Wallman, Sue	L401	
Walmsley-Johnson, Helen	L066	
also	L516	
Walsh, Bridget	L066	
also	L171	
Walsh, Bryan	L087	
Walsh, Catherine	L567	
Walsh, Claire	L591	
also	L663	
Walsh, Jill Paton	L052	
also	L159	
Walsh, Joanna	L159	
Walsh, Melanie	L159	
also	L645	
Walsh, Rosie	L159	
Walsh, Stephen	L159	
also	L266	
Walter, B P	L294	
also	L613	
Walter, Natasha	P498	
Walters, Louise	L294	
Walters, Minette	L159	
also	L232	
Walters, Vanessa	L159	
also	L232	
Walters, Victoria	L294	
Waltham, David	L215	
also	L318	
Walton, Charles	L129	
also	L215	

Walton, Jo	L598
Walton, Samantha	L215
also	L520
Wang, Dan	L007
also	L466
Wang, Rona	L458
Wangtechawat, Pim	L163
Wappler, Margaret	L184
Ward, Amanda Eyre	L096
also	L137
Ward, Becky	L364
Ward, Catherine	L325
Ward, Jacqueline	L468
Ward, Miranda	L159
Ward, Rachel	L321
Wark, Kirsty	L215
also	L669
Warner, Valentine	L048
Warren, Alyssa	L662
Warren, Dakota	L676
Warren, Rossalyn	L204
Warren, Özlem	L131
also	L533
Warrick, Eva	L005
Warwick, Christopher	L539
Warwick, Hugh	L029
Washington, Brigid	L467
Washington, Janelle	L174
Wason, Wendy	L099
also	L278
Wass, John	L297
Wasserstein, Bernard	L159
also	L270
Wassmer, MJ	L226
also	L680
Wastvedt, Patricia	L468
Waterhouse, Keith	L159
Waters, Sarah	L468
also	P498
Wathieu, Luc	L297
Watkin, Sean	L392
Watkins, Ali Marie	L087
Watkins, Tionne	L481
Watson, Amy	L155
Watson, Angus	L226
also	L680
Watson, Christie	L096
also	L380
Watson, Jesse Joshua	L513
Watson, Richard Jesse	L513
Watson, S J	L096
also	L137
Watson, Stephanie Venn	L467
Watson, Sue	L294
Watson, Tom	L566
Watt, Holly	L159
also	L270
also	L297
Watters, Aisling	L159
also	L170
Watts, Anne	L066
also	L171
Watts, Jonathan	L096
also	L380
Wayne, Jemma	L066
also	L516
Weatherby, Alison	L325
Weatherford, Carole Boston	L513
Weatherford, Jeffery Boston	L513
Weatherley, Anna-Lou	L022
also	L157
Weaver, Christian	L116
also	L159
Weaver, Pam	L110
also	L647
Weaver, Tim	L069
also	L157
Webb, Andrew	L276
also	L632
Webb, Caroline	L440
Webb, Catherine	L364
Webb, Clive	L215
also	L318
Webb, Justin	L007
also	L466
Webb, Ralf	L005
Webb, Veronica	L467
Webber, Imogen Lloyd	L313
Weber, Charlotte Fox	L254
Webster, Hayley	L333
also	L638
Webster, Lucy	L146
also	L456
Webster, Molly	L537
Webster, Rachel J.	L522
Webster-Hein, Michelle	L192
Wecker, Helene	L238
Wedell-Wedellsborg, Thomas	L297
Weduwen, Arthur Der	L129
also	L215
Wee, Lisa	L212
also	L377
Weeks, Lee	L022
Weetman, Frances	L007
also	L466
Wegert, Tessa	L090
Wegman, Jesse	L469
Weil, Jonathan	L129
also	L215
Weinberg, Elizabeth	L184
Weingarten, Lynn	L058
also	L059
Weinman, Jaime	L665
Weinman, Sarah	L515
also	L609
Weir, Keziah	L427
Weise, Jillian	L184
Weiss, Jan Merete	L184
Weissman, Michaele	L184
Weitzman, Elizabeth	L184
Welch, Caroline	L334
Weldon, Glen	L440
Weller, Monica	L539
Welliver, Melissa	L325
Wells, Diana	L063
Wells, Emma J.	L048
Wells, Ione	L209
also	L276
Wells, Kate	L526
Welman, Kimberley	L609
Wels, Susan	L334
Welsh, Natalie	L539
Wendig, Chuck	L184
Wenham-Jones, Jane	L623
Wesley, Mary	L052
also	L159
Wesson, Rob	L440
West, A. J.	L166
also	L263
also	L306
West, Genevieve	L469
West, Kate	L005
West, Kathleen	L416
also	L477
West, Kevin	L415
Westhead, Jessica	L313
Weston-Davies, Wynne	L539
Wetherell, Sam	L159
also	L270
Wetzel, Paige	L537
Weymouth, Adam	L096
also	L380
Weze, Clare	L166
also	L216
Whalen, Marybeth	L405
Wharton, Edith	P498
Whatley, Claire	L146
also	L456
Wheatcroft, Geoffrey	L007
also	L466
Wheeler, Frank	L184
Whelan, David	L504
Whipple, Dorothy	L159
Whipple, Tom	L591
also	L663
Whitaker, Helen	L321
Whitaker, Phil	L159
also	L270
White, Adam	L254
White, Alison	L294
also	L295
White, Elizabeth	L334
White, Elizabeth "Barry"	L334
White, Jim	L591
also	L663
White, Kali	L184
White, Kristin M.	L334
White, Mark	L236
White, Sam	L362
White, Shane	L608
White, Sophie	L157
also	L585
White, Steve	L282
White, T. H.	L159
White, Tiare	L063
Whitehart, Jacqueline	L401
Whitehead, Harry	L066
also	L171
Whitehead, Kylie	L504
Whiteley, Aliya	L190
Whitelock, Anna	L129
also	L215
Whitfield, Clare	L166
also	L306
Whitlam, Dan	L146
also	L223
also	L517
Whitmarsh, Tim	L129
also	L215
Whitney, Rebecca	L032
also	L096
Whittaker, K.J.	L129
also	L215
Whittle, Kerry	L074
Whyman, Kathleen	L166
also	L263
Whynott, Doug	L531
Wicker, Alden	L415
Wiedemann, Elettra	L481
Wiegle, Matt	L184
Wiggins, Bethany	L603
Wiggins, Marianne	L184
Wigglesworth, Gary	L226
also	L680
Wigham, Jasmine	L226
also	L680
Wight, Jen	L034
also	L278
Wightwick, Charlotte	L476
Wijeratne, Yudhanjaya	L226
also	L680
Wikholm, Catherine	L294
also	L295
Wilcox, Christina	L515
also	L609

Wilde, Lori L058
also L059
Wilder, Robyn L276
also L632
Wilder, Thornton L159
Wilding, Rose L204
Wilentz, Amy L184
Wiles, Will L276
also L632
Wiley, G.S. P144
Wiley, Richard P209
Wilford, Hugh L215
also L318
Wilhide, Elizabeth L159
also L266
Wiliam, Sioned L099
also L278
Wilkin, Sam L215
also L318
Wilkinson, Annie L341
Wilkinson, Corban L184
Willard, Barbara L159
Willcox, Toyah L236
Willetts, Imogen L215
also L318
Williams, Charles L159
Williams, Cristin L506
also L507
Williams, David Michael L598
Williams, Elizabeth Lewis L521
Williams, Gray L470
Williams, Hattie L470
Williams, James L007
also L466
Williams, Jen L470
Williams, Jeremy L110
also L557
also L647
Williams, Jessie L007
also L233
Williams, Josh L481
Williams, Karl L539
Williams, Kat L146
also L250
Williams, Rusty L155
Williams, Sophie L131
also L533
Williams, Zoe L096
also L380
Williamson, Lisa L129
also L215
Williamson, Sophie L603
Willingham, Dan L297
Willner, Nina L609
Wilson, Antoine L096
also L380
Wilson, Barrie L334
Wilson, Ben L096
also L137
Wilson, C.L. L274
Wilson, Casey L469
Wilson, Catelyn L226
also L680
Wilson, Catherine L254
Wilson, Claire L166
also L306
Wilson, Elspeth L128
also L521
Wilson, Eric L427
Wilson, Jacqueline L159
also L645
Wilson, Jason L276
also L632
Wilson, Joe L401
Wilson, Jon L159
also L270
Wilson, Miranda L644
Wilson, Ryan L295
Wilson, S.M. L321
Wilson, Samantha L294
also L613
Wilson-Lee, Edward L066
also L171
Wilton, Peter L539
Wilton, Robert L096
also L137
Wincer, Penny L278
also L583
Windo, Nick Clark L470
Winn, Alice L096
also L380
Winnett, Robert L539
Winning, Josh L506
also L507
Winstone, Keely L007
also L466
Winter, Kate L526
Winter, L. C. L166
also L263
Winter, Molly Roden L313
Winter, Tom L470
Winters, Ben H. L334
Winters, Ed L282
Winton, Tim L052
also L159
Wirkus, Tim L184
Wise, Greg L215
also L669
Witt, Chris L063
Witynski, Karen L063
Wixey, Matt L096
Wodicka, Tod L096
also L380
Woghiren, Annabelle L227
Wojtowycz, David L159
also L645
Wolf, Cristina L066
also L197
Wolf, Hope L159
also L270
Wolf, Steve D. L063
Wolfarth, Joanna L333
also L638
Wolfe, Sean Fay L537
Wolff, Isabel L096
also L137
Wolff, Mishna L184
Wolitzer, Hilma L184
Wollock, David L063
Wolmar, Christian L007
also L466
Womack, James L190
Womack, Jonathan P101
Womack, Marian L096
Womack, Rowena P101
Won, Annie L513
Won, Brian L513
Wong, Andrew L066
also L516
Wong, Dalton L526
Wong, Kelvin L440
Wong, Regina L677
Wood, Alisson L184
Wood, Alistair L644
Wood, Andy L254
Wood, Aubrey L184
Wood, Benjamin L468
Wood, Bill L103
also L215
Wood, Brian L566
Wood, Charlotte L052
also L159
Wood, Eleanor L295
Wood, Mary L341
Wood, Michael L129
also L215
Wood, Olivia L032
also L096
Wood, Patricia L522
Woodham, Simon L236
Woodhead, Matt L146
also L250
Woodhouse, Joe L614
Woodhouse, Mike L099
also L278
Wooding, Lucy L129
also L215
Woods, Billy L184
Woods, Carolyn L159
also L270
Woods, Kell L343
Woods, Neil L254
Woods, Tom L512
Woodward, Kelly L392
Woodward, Keren L048
Wooldridge, Michael L215
also L520
Woolf, Rebecca L184
Woolhouse, Alex L110
also L647
WoonHeng, Chia L086
Worrad, Jim L190
Worsley, Kate L052
also L159
Worsley, Lucy L129
also L215
Worthington, Everett L297
Woster, Sara L184
Wozencraft, Kim L184
Wrack, Suzanne L190
Wright, Ben L086
Wright, Claire L091
Wright, David L276
also L677
Wright, John C. L598
Wright, Ronald L184
Wright, Tappy L236
Wroblewski, David L184
Wroe, Jo Browning L032
also L096
Wroe, Simon L032
also L096
Wu, Duncan L644
Wuebben, Jon L334
Wullschläger, Jackie L276
Wyndham, John L159
Wyness, Gill L662
Wynne, Clive D. L440
Wythe, James L215
also L669
Wämberg, Jessica L129
also L215
Xie, Jenny L073
Xinran L052
also L159
Yakobi, Rohullah L646
Yallop, Jacqueline L048
Yallop, Olivia L190
Yamada, Taichi L159
also L672
Yang, Jeff L184
Yang, Kelly L146
also L250
Yang, Susie L276
also L468
Yano, Naomi L313
Yates, Jon L007
also L466

Yates, Kieran L215	Young, Lola L282	Zgheib, Yara L584
also L520	Young, Lucy L215	Zha, Zed L665
Yeboah, Stephanie L282	*also* L669	Zhang, Angel Di L155
Yeung, Adelle L612	Young, Robyn L276	Zhang, Lijia L615
Yeung, Bernice L609	*also* L632	Zhao, Katie L458
Yi, Charlyne L153	Young, Sergey L297	Zheutlin, Peter L334
also L609	Younger, Bella L662	Zichermann, Gabe L334
Yin, Mandy L116	Youngson, Anne L468	Ziegesar, Peter von L396
also L159	Yousefzada, Osman L096	Ziegler, Alan L184
Yip, Vern L481	*also* L137	Ziegler, Sheryl Gonzalez L427
Yokoi, Tomoko L297	Yu, Howard L297	Ziepe, Laura L294
Yoo, David L184	Yunis, Alia L184	Ziminski, Andrew L276
Yoon, Helen L229	Zackman, Gabra L334	*also* L632
also L513	Zadeh, Joe L276	Zin, Sara L609
Yoon, Jenna L458	*also* L460	Zmith, Adam L096
Yoshino, Kenji L184	Zahawi, Nadhim L566	*also* L380
Young, Alora L418	Zamani, Payam L615	Zolidis, Don L148
Young, Cyle L149	Zambreno, Kate L159	Zook, Kristal L481
Young, David L166	Zandri, Vincent L414	Zorian-Lynn, Joanne L539
also L254	Zarei, Fatemeh L448	Zorn, Justin L440
also L306	Zarkadakis, George L096	Zuckerman, Jocelyn C L388
Young, Dawn L063	*also* L130	Zuk, Marlene L418
Young, Emma L007	Zarrow, Rachel L108	Zurcher, Andrew L254
also L466	Zaza, Agatha L074	Zuritsky, Elisa L239
Young, Erin L276	Zehr, Dan L297	Zweibel, Alan L481
also L632	Zeleski, Allen L236	Ægisdottir, Eva Björg L166
Young, Eris L096	Zeller, Tom L609	*also* L306
also L130	Zenk, Molly L043	Şode, Yomi L053
Young, Hester L297	Zeschky, Clare L603	*also* L278
Young, Liam Patrick L251	Zetterberg, Ally L157	
also L278	*also* L585	

Literary Agents and Agencies

For the most up-to-date listings of these and hundreds of other literary agents and agencies, visit https://www.firstwriter.com/Agents

To claim your free access to the site, please see the back of this book.

L001 3 Seas Literary Agency
Literary Agency
PO Box 444, Sun Prairie, WI 53590
United States
Tel: +1 (608) 332-3430

https://www.threeseasagency.com
https://www.facebook.com/3-Seas-Literary-Agency-75205869856/
https://twitter.com/threeseaslit?lang=en

ADULT > **Fiction** > *Novels*
  Fantasy; Romance; Science Fiction; Thrillers; Women's Fiction

CHILDREN'S > **Fiction** > *Middle Grade*

YOUNG ADULT > **Fiction** > *Novels*

How to send: Query Manager
How not to send: Email

Accepts queries through online submission system only. See website for full guidelines.

Literary Agents: Cori Deyoe; Stacey Graham (**L272**); Kara Grajkowski (**L273**); Michelle Grajkowski (**L274**)

L002 A.M. Heath & Company Limited, Author's Agents
Literary Agency
6 Warwick Court, Holborn, London, WC1R 5DJ
United Kingdom
Tel: +44 (0) 20 7242 2811

submissions@amheath.com

https://amheath.com
https://twitter.com/AMHeathLtd
https://www.instagram.com/a.m.heath

Professional Body: The Association of Authors' Agents (AAA)

Fiction > *Novels*

Nonfiction > *Nonfiction Books*

Send: Query; Synopsis; Writing sample
How to send: Online submission system
How not to send: Post; Email

Handles general commercial and literary fiction and nonfiction. Submit work with cover letter, synopsis, and writing sample up to 10,000 words, via online submission system only. No paper submissions or submissions by email. Aims to respond within six weeks.

Agency Assistant: Jessica Lee

Agency Assistant / Associate Agent: Florence Rees

Literary Agents: Julia Churchill; Bill Hamilton; Victoria Hobbs (**L314**); Oli Munson; Rebecca Ritchie; Euan Thorneycroft (**L628**)

L003 Above the Line Agency
Literary Agency; Consultancy
468 N. Camden Drive, #200, Beverly Hills, CA 90210
United States
Tel: +1 (310) 859-6115

abovethelineagency@gmail.com

http://www.abovethelineagency.com

Professional Body: Writers Guild of America (WGA)

ADULT > **Scripts**
  Film Scripts; *TV Scripts*

CHILDREN'S > **Scripts**
  Film Scripts; *TV Scripts*

Send: Query
How to send: Online submission system

Costs: Offers services that writers have to pay for.

Send query via online web system only. Represents writers and directors; feature films, movies of the week, animation. Offers consultations at a rate of $200 per hour.

Literary Agents: Bruce Bartlett; Rima Greer

L004 Kwaku Acheampong
Literary Agent
United States

carolyn@carolynjenksagency.com

https://www.carolynjenksagency.com/agent/Kwaku-Acheampong

Literary Agency: Carolyn Jenks Agency (**L107**)

ADULT
  Fiction > *Novels*
  Nonfiction > *Nonfiction Books*

NEW ADULT
  Fiction > *Novels*
  Nonfiction > *Nonfiction Books*

Send: Query; Writing sample
How to send: In the body of an email

Looking for fiction and nonfiction across most genres, though he has a special passion for new adult.

L005 Seren Adams
Literary Agent
United Kingdom

SAdams@unitedagents.co.uk

https://www.unitedagents.co.uk/sadamsunitedagentscouk
https://twitter.com/serenadams

Literary Agency: United Agents

Fiction > *Novels*
  High Concept; Literary

Nonfiction > *Nonfiction Books*
  Crime; Narrative Nonfiction; Nature

Send: Query; Synopsis; Pitch; Market info
How to send: Email

I am looking for literary novels, novellas and stories set anywhere in the world. Increasingly I am drawn to fiction with a distinctive and off-kilter voice which holds my attention, often wryly funny and/or full of feeling, usually inflected with strangeness, intensity or longing of some kind. While I tend not to read historical fiction or genre fiction, I enjoy books which are primarily literary but draw upon other genres; I would love to find an unforgettable high-concept literary novel which could become an instant classic. I also love realist novels which explore moral, philosophical or political questions, complex relationships, and/or troubling memories. I will always be interested in novels about intimacy, desire, love and loss. I am excited by big ideas books with a radical edge, and keen to see proposals that are doing something new within an established non-fiction genre, such as nature writing. I also love literary true crime. I enjoy anything with a compelling story and investigative elements based on meticulous and sensitive research.

Author Estates: The Estate of Dornford Yates; The Estate of Maurice Baring OBE

Authors: Esme Allman; Tia Bannon; Nivedita Barve; Jen Calleja; Lauren Aimee Curtis;

Olivia Douglass; Lucie Elven; Adelaide Faith; Rakaya Fetuga; Ronan Fitzgerald; Amaryllis Gacioppo; Maria Giron; Anna Goldreich; Lili Hamlyn; Catherine Humble; Blair James; Liza St. James; Ammar Kalia; Line Kallmayer; Ana Kinsella; Molly Lipson; Benoît Loiseau; Aileen Maguire; Megan Marz; Laura Maw; Jamal Mehmood; Sinéad Mooney; Luke Neima; Caleb Azumah Nelson; Timothy Ogene; Anna Chapman Parker; Rebecca Perry; Joanna Pocock; Karina Lickorish Quinn; Gemma Reeves; Olivia Rosenthall; Alan Rossi; Taylor-Dior Rumble; Thomas Rutter; Michael Salu; Vanessa Santos; Lina Scheynius; Sophie Scott-Brown; Laura Southgate; Olivia Spring; Sean Stoker; Alessandra Thom; Zakia Uddin; Kenechi Uzor; Eva Warrick; Ralf Webb; Kate West

L006 Alex Adsett
Literary Agent; Consultant
Australia

https://alexadsett.com.au/literary-agency/
https://querymanager.com/query/AlexAdsettQueries
https://twitter.com/alexadsett

Literary Agency: Alex Adsett Literary (**L016**)

ADULT
  Fiction > *Novels*
    Commercial; Crime; Fantasy; Historical Romance; Literary; Mystery; Romantasy; Romantic Comedy; Romantic Mystery; Science Fiction
  Nonfiction > *Nonfiction Books*: Narrative Nonfiction
YOUNG ADULT > **Fiction** > *Novels*

Does not want:

> **Fiction** > *Novels*: Urban Fantasy

Send: Query; Author bio; Synopsis
How to send: Query Manager; By referral

Costs: Offers services that writers have to pay for. Provides commercial and strategic advice to authors and independent publishers, particularly regarding publishing contracts.

An Australian literary agent and publishing consultant, who has been working in the publishing and bookselling industry for almost twenty-five years. She is always seeking amazing manuscripts, with a focus on fiction and narrative non-fiction, especially SFF, crime and romance, for all ages from picture books to adults.

L007 Aevitas Creative Management (ACM) UK
Literary Agency
43 Great Ormond Street, London, WC1N 3HZ
United Kingdom

ukenquiries@aevitascreative.com

https://aevitascreative.com/home/acm-uk/
https://twitter.com/AevitasCreative
https://www.facebook.com/AevitasCreative/

Literary Agency: Aevitas
Professional Body: The Association of Authors' Agents (AAA)

UK branch of a US agency, founded in 2019, representing writers and brands throughout the world.

Authors: Tim Adams; James Aldred; James Ashton; Odafe Atogun; Philip Augar; Hannah Barnes; Rahul Bhatia; Chris Bickerton; Innes Bowen; Ruth Brandon; Marcus Bridgewater; Tobias Buck; Stephen Bush; Joshua Chaffin; James Crabtree; Graham Daseler; Jonathan Derbyshire; Michael Dine; John Dunn; Armand D'Angour; Iyad El-Baghdadi; Graham Farmelo; Eliza Filby; Danny Finkelstein; John Gapper; Michael Gibson; Julian Glover; David Goodhart; Samuel Graydon; Rachel Halliburton; Liam Halligan; A.B. Hamilton; Charles Handy; Andrew Hankinson; Jonathan Hillman; Katja Hoyer; Nicholas Humphrey; Gavin Jacobson; Charlie Hamilton James; Tiffany Jenkins; Joanna Jolly; Andrew Keen; Ivan Krastev; Graham Lawton; Charles Leadbeater; Frances Leech; Mark Leonard; Ian Leslie; Oliver Letwin; John Lloyd; Isabel Losada; Andrew Lycett; Polly Mackenzie; Gary Madden; Mark Makepeace; Kenan Malik; Owen Matthews; Tom McTague; Peter Mead; Anand Menon; Daniel Metcalfe; Chris Miller; Munira Mirza; Paul Morland; Geoff Mulgan; Clive Myrie; David Omand; Arkady Ostrovsky; Tomiwa Owolade; Nicolas Pelham; Leigh Phillips; Mary Poffenroth; Jenny Radcliffe; Alice Rawsthorn; Assaad Razzouk; Richard Reeves; Tim Revell; Peter Ricketts; Neil Root; Jonathan Rowson; Donald Sassoon; Claire Schultz; Mark Sedgwick; Nigel Shadbolt; Oliver Shah; Marianna Spring; Raymond Tallis; Sudhir Thomas Vadaketh; Georgios Varoufakis; Jeevan Vasagar; James Vogl; James Waddell; Owen Walker; Dan Wang; Justin Webb; Frances Weetman; Geoffrey Wheatcroft; James Williams; Jessie Williams; Keely Winstone; Christian Wolmar; Jon Yates; Emma Young

Company Director / Senior Agent: Charlie Viney (**L644**)

Literary Agents: Trevor Dolby (**L173**); Max Edwards (**L190**); Clara Foster (**L233**); Maria Cardona Serra (**L574**); Emily Sweet (**L614**)

Senior Agents / Vice Presidents: Charlie Brotherstone (**L086**); Toby Mundy (**L466**)

L008 Thais Afonso
Associate Agent
Rio de Janeiro
Brazil

https://www.azantianlitagency.com
https://www.azantianlitagency.com/about-us/thais-afonso

Literary Agency: Azantian Literary Agency

ADULT > **Fiction** > *Novels*
    Commercial; Contemporary Romance; Cyberpunk; Fantasy; Folklore, Myths, and Legends; Gothic; Horror; LGBTQIA; Mystery; Romantic Comedy; Science Fiction; Speculative; Suspense; Thrillers; Women's Fiction
YOUNG ADULT > **Fiction** > *Novels*
    Fantasy; Horror; Mystery; Romantasy; Science Fiction; Speculative; Supernatural / Paranormal Thrillers; Thrillers

Does not want:

> **Fiction** > *Novels*: Grimdark

Closed to approaches.

Intends to represent marginalized authors, and she's especially seeking to uplift BIPOC born and raised in the Global South. An Afro-Brazilian lesbian, she currently lives and works out of Rio de Janeiro, Brazil.

L009 The Agency (London) Ltd
Literary Agency
24 Pottery Lane, Holland Park, London, W11 4LZ
United Kingdom

info@theagency.co.uk
submissions@theagency.co.uk

http://www.theagency.co.uk

Professional Body: The Association of Authors' Agents (AAA)

ADULT > **Scripts**
    Film Scripts; *TV Scripts*; *Theatre Scripts*
CHILDREN'S > **Fiction**
    Middle Grade; *Novels*; *Picture Books*
TEEN > **Fiction** > *Novels*
YOUNG ADULT > **Fiction** > *Novels*

Send: Query; Synopsis; Writing sample
How to send: Email

Represents writers and authors for film, television, radio and the theatre. Also represents directors, producers, composers, and film and television rights in books, as well as authors of children's books from picture books to teen fiction. More likely to consider material from script writers if it has been recommended by a producer, development executive or course tutor. If this is the case send CV, covering letter and details of your referee by email. Do not email more than one agent at a time. For directors, send CV, showreel and cover letter by email. For children's authors, send query by email with synopsis and first three chapters (middle grade, teen, or Young Adult) or complete ms (picture books). All submissions should be sent directly to the relevant agent. Film, TV and theatre writers and composers should also CC the submissions email address.

Associate Agents: Arthur Barnard (**L042**); Sophie Kelleher (**L359**)

Literary Agents: Gina Andrews (**L027**); Ian Benson; Nicola Biltoo; Simon Blakey; Maeve Bolger (**L068**); Hannah Boulton; Hilary Delamere; Stephen Durbridge; Bethan Evans; Katie Haines; Jessica Hare (**L296**); Emily Hickman (**L311**); Jonathan Kinnersley; Julia Kreitman; Leah Schmidt; Emily Smith; Tanya Tillett; Katie Williams (**L661**)

L010 AHA Talent Ltd
Literary Agency
22-23 James Street, Covent Garden, London, WC2E 8NS
United Kingdom
Tel: +44 (0) 20 7250 1760

mail@ahacreatives.co.uk

https://www.ahatalent.co.uk
https://twitter.com/AHAcreatives

Scripts
Film Scripts; *Radio Scripts*; *TV Scripts*; *Theatre Scripts*

Send: Query; Author bio; Writing sample

Handles actors and creatives. Send query with CV/bio, and examples of your work.

Literary Agent: Amanda Fitzalan Howard

L011 The Ahearn Agency, Inc
Literary Agency
3436 Magazine St., #615, New Orleans, LA 70115
United States
Tel: +1 (504) 589-4200
Fax: +1 (504) 589-4200

pahearn@aol.com

http://www.ahearnagency.com

Fiction > *Novels*
Suspense; Women's Fiction

Closed to approaches.

Send one page query with SASE, description, length, market info, and any writing credits. Accepts email queries without attachments. Response in 2-3 months.

Specialises in women's fiction and suspense. No nonfiction, poetry, juvenile material or science fiction.

Authors: Michele Albert; Rexanne Becnel; Wendy Hilton; Sabrina Jeffries; Connie Koslow; Sandra Landry; Deb Marlowe; Meagan McKinney; Kate Moore; Gerri Russell; Susan Sipal

Literary Agent: Pamela G. Ahearn

L012 Clementine Ahearne
Literary Agent; Company Director
United Kingdom

clementine.ahearne@ila-agency.co.uk

Literary Agency: ILA (Intercontinental Literary Agency)

Closed to approaches.

L013 Alan Brodie Representation
Literary Agency
Paddock Suite, The Courtyard, 55 Charterhouse Street, London, EC1M 6HA
United Kingdom
Tel: +44 (0) 20 7253 6226

ABR@alanbrodie.com

https://www.alanbrodie.com
https://www.facebook.com/Alan-Brodie-Representation-Ltd-407206926050145/
https://twitter.com/abragency
https://www.instagram.com/abragency/?hl=en

Scripts
Film Scripts; *Radio Scripts*; *TV Scripts*; *Theatre Scripts*

Send: Query; Author bio
Don't send: Writing sample; Full text
How to send: By referral

Handles scripts only. No books. Approach with preliminary letter, recommendation from industry professional, and CV. Do not send a sample of work unless requested. No fiction, nonfiction, or poetry.

Literary Agents: Alan Brodie; Kara Fitzpatrick; Victoria Williams

L014 Michael Alcock
Literary Agent
United Kingdom

michael@johnsonandalcock.co.uk

http://www.johnsonandalcock.co.uk/michael-alcock

Literary Agency: Johnson & Alcock (**L335**)

Nonfiction > *Nonfiction Books*
Arts; Biography; Current Affairs; Food; Health; History; Popular Science

Send: Query; Writing sample; Synopsis

Client list covers non-fiction mainly in the fields of history and biography, current affairs, food, health, the arts and popular science.

L015 Keir Alekseii
Associate Agent
United States

http://www.azantianlitagency.com/pages/team-ka.html
https://querymanager.com/query/keiralekseii
https://querymanager.com/query/keiralekseii/BIPOC

Literary Agency: Azantian Literary Agency

ADULT > **Fiction** > *Novels*
Fantasy; Horror; Science Fiction

YOUNG ADULT > **Fiction** > *Novels*
Contemporary; Fantasy; Horror; Science Fiction

How to send: Query Manager

An educator and anti-GBV activist born and raised in Trinidad and Tobago, a twin island country in the West Indies. She is a writer, gamer, lover of folklore, and former research scientist. As a neurodivergent, queer woman of color, she is invested in discovering engaging work with similar representation, and is passionate about creating space for voices not often recognized. She is especially interested in stories from BIPOC who are born and raised in the Global South.

She is seeking YA & Adult SFFH and YA contemporary novels. She is ONLY open to receiving queries from writers who identify as belonging to a marginalized or underrepresented community.

L016 Alex Adsett Literary
Literary Agency
PO Box 694, Tugun, QLD 4224
Australia

alexadsett@alexadsett.com.au

https://alexadsett.com.au
https://twitter.com/alexadsett
http://www.facebook.com/Alexadsett.publishing
https://www.instagram.com/alexadsett

ADULT
Fiction > *Novels*
Commercial Women's Fiction; Commercial; Crime; Fantasy; Literary; Mystery; Romance; Romantic Comedy; Science Fiction

Nonfiction > *Nonfiction Books*: Narrative Nonfiction

CHILDREN'S > **Fiction**
Chapter Books; *Middle Grade*
YOUNG ADULT > **Fiction** > *Novels*

How to send: Query Manager; Email

Only represents authors in Australia, New Zealand, the Pacific or SE Asia, not USA or Europe. Only accepts submissions by invitation or referral, or from authors from an under-represented background – First Nations, authors of colour, authors from marginalised cultures, neuroatypical authors, authors with disability, or authors from varied socio-economic circumstances.

Consultant / Literary Agent: Alex Adsett (**L006**)

Literary Agents: Rochelle Fernandez (**L220**); Lisa Fuller (**L248**); Abigail Nathan (**L475**)

L017 Alice Williams Literary
Literary Agency
United Kingdom
Tel: +44 (0) 20 7385 2118

submissions@alicewilliamsliterary.co.uk

https://www.alicewilliamsliterary.co.uk
https://twitter.com/alicelovesbooks
http://instagram.com/agentalicewilliams

Professional Body: The Association of Authors' Agents (AAA)

CHILDREN'S
  Fiction
    Middle Grade; *Novels*; *Picture Books*
  Nonfiction > *Nonfiction Books*

YOUNG ADULT
  Fiction > *Novels*
  Nonfiction > *Nonfiction Books*

Closed to approaches.

A specialist literary agency proudly representing writers and illustrators of picture books, young fiction, middle-grade, YA and non-fiction.

Literary Agent: Alice Williams (**L660**)

L018 Alive Literary Agency
Literary Agency
5001 Centennial Blvd #50742, Colorado Springs, CO 80908
United States

https://aliveliterary.com

Nonfiction > *Nonfiction Books*
  Lifestyle; Personal Development; Religion

How to send: By referral

Accepts queries from referred authors only. Works primarily with well-established, best-selling, and career authors.

Authors: Jamie Blaine; Michael Hyatt; Karen Kingsbury

Literary Agents: Lisa Jackson; Rachel Jacobson (**L328**); Carly Kellerman (**L360**); Kathleen Kerr (*L363*); Bryan Norman

L019 Ambassador Speakers Bureau & Literary Agency
Literary Agency
United States
Tel: +1 (615) 370-4700

info@ambassadorspeakers.com

https://www.ambassadorspeakers.com

Fiction > *Novels*: Christianity

Nonfiction > *Nonfiction Books*: Christianity

Send: Query
How to send: Email

Represents select authors and writers who are published by religious and general market publishers in the US and Europe. Send query by email with short description.

L020 Beniamino Ambrosi
Literary Agent
United States

beniamino@cheneyagency.com
submissions@cheneyagency.com

https://www.cheneyagency.com/beniamino-ambrosi

Literary Agency: The Cheney Agency

Fiction in Translation > *Novels*: Literary

Fiction > *Novels*: Literary

Nonfiction in Translation > *Nonfiction Books*

Nonfiction > *Nonfiction Books*

Represents English-language nonfiction and literary fiction, and authors in translation.

L021 Eric Amling
Literary Agent; Foreign Rights Director
United States

submissions@dvagency.com

https://www.dvagency.com/aboutus

Literary Agency: Darhansoff & Verrill Literary Agents (**L156**)

Fiction > *Novels*: Literary

Nonfiction > *Nonfiction Books*
  Art Criticism; Cookery

Poetry > *Poetry Collections*

Business Manager and Foreign Rights Director, coordinating relationships with subagents across all major territories. As an agent, he is currently considering literary fiction, poetry, art criticism and cookbooks.

L022 Darley Anderson
Literary Agent
United Kingdom

https://www.darleyanderson.com/our-team

Literary Agency: The Darley Anderson Agency (**L157**)

ADULT > **Fiction** > *Novels*
  Romance; Thrillers

CHILDREN'S > **Fiction** > *Novels*: Animals

How to send: Email; Post

Looking specifically for thrillers with a strong central character set in America or Ireland or other internationally appealing locations and tear-jerking love stories. He is looking specifically for children's books featuring an original series character and animal stories. Email submissions should be sent to the agent's assistant.

Authors: Constance Briscoe; Chris Carter; Cathy Cassidy; Lee Child; Martina Cole; Margaret Dickinson; Clare Dowling; Jack Ford; Tana French; Paul Hauck; Joan Jonker; Annie Murray; Abi Oliver; Adrian Plass; Hazel Prior; David Rhodes; Jacqui Rose; Stephen Spotswood; Erik Storey; Anna-Lou Weatherley; Lee Weeks

L023 Hannah Andrade
Literary Agent
United States

https://bradfordlit.com/hannah-andrade-agent/
https://twitter.com/hhandrade93
https://querymanager.com/hannahandrade

Literary Agency: Bradford Literary Agency (**L075**)

ADULT
  Fiction > *Novels*: Mystery
  Nonfiction > *Nonfiction Books*
    Commercial; Crime; Investigative Journalism; Narrative Nonfiction

CHILDREN'S > **Fiction**
  Graphic Novels: General
  Middle Grade: General, and in particular: Dark Humour; Folklore, Myths, and Legends; Ghost Stories; Historical Fiction
YOUNG ADULT > **Fiction**
  Graphic Novels: General
  Novels: General, and in particular: Dark Fantasy; Folklore, Myths, and Legends; Historical Fiction; Mystery

Closed to approaches.

Likes to think of herself as an editorial-focused agent and is particularly eager to acquire BIPOC/underrepresented voices. She is prioritizing stories of joy where identity isn't the focus and is especially excited about stories rooted in history, mythology, and legends, particularly those that are lesser-known or underrepresented in traditional publishing.

Very interested in stories that explore the intricacies of multicultural identities. She loves stories of immigration (not relegated to America) and of first/second generation Americans who struggle balancing the values of their country with the culture and heritage of their parents (as in the tv shows Ramy or Gentefied). As a Mexican-American, she would particularly love to see the stories that she grew up with showcased in new and creative ways.

L024 Andrew Nurnberg Associates, Ltd
Literary Agency
43 Great Russell Street, London, WC1B 3PD
United Kingdom
Tel: +44 (0) 20 3327 0400

info@nurnberg.co.uk
submissions@nurnberg.co.uk

http://www.andrewnurnberg.com
https://twitter.com/nurnberg_agency
https://www.instagram.com/andrewnurnbergassociates/?hl=en

Professional Body: The Association of Authors' Agents (AAA)

ADULT
  Fiction > *Novels*
  Nonfiction > *Nonfiction Books*
CHILDREN'S > Fiction > *Novels*

Does not want:

> ADULT > Scripts
>   *Film Scripts*; *Radio Scripts*; *TV Scripts*; *Theatre Scripts*
> CHILDREN'S > Fiction > *Picture Books*

Send: Query; Synopsis; Writing sample
How to send: Email

Handles adult fiction and nonfiction, and children's fiction. No poetry, children's picture books, or scripts for film, TV, radio or theatre. Send query by email with one-page synopsis and first three chapters or 50 pages as attachments.

Literary Agency: The Wallace Literary Agency

Literary Agents: Sarah Nundy; Andrew Nurnberg

L025 Nelle Andrew
Literary Agent
United Kingdom

nelle@rmliterary.co.uk

Literary Agency: Rachel Mills Literary (**L527**)

Fiction > *Novels*
  Commercial; Crime; Family; Historical Fiction; Literary; Magical Realism; Political Thrillers; Psychological Thrillers; Romantic Comedy; Speculative; Suspense; Thrillers; Women's Fiction
Nonfiction > *Nonfiction Books*
  History; Literary Memoir; Narrative Nonfiction; Politics

Send: Author bio; Synopsis; Writing sample
How to send: Email

Interested in excellent writing, compelling plots, diverse and unexpected voices and thoroughly engrossing reads. She loves books that are as escapist as they are explorative; as transportive as they are reflective. Her tastes are omnivorous. She particularly loves literary/commercial crossover fiction, psychological thrillers and suspense, intense or funny family dramas, savvy romantic comedies; gasp out loud crime and thriller, rich historical and even magical realism but that has to be done really well. She is interested in speculative and cross genre writing as well as clever female fiction. Mostly she wants stories that make her care as well as compel her to read on. In narrative nonfiction, she loves literary memoir, historical and smart politics but mainly it has to be non fiction for people who don't generally read non-fiction – aka, slightly zeitgeist, illuminative and ultimately a gripping read. She does not do straight sci-fi/Fantasy/children's and YA although that does not mean she wouldn't look at an adult novel with a child protagonist. She does not do short stories and collections or poetry. She does not do espionage thrillers either but she would be interested in a political thriller like HOUSE OF CARDS.

L026 Davinia Andrew-Lynch
Literary Agent
United Kingdom

Literary Agency: Curtis Brown (**L146**)

L027 Gina Andrews
Literary Agent
United Kingdom

gandrews@theagency.co.uk

https://theagency.co.uk/the-agents/gina-andrews/

Literary Agency: The Agency (London) Ltd (**L009**)

L028 Anne Clark Literary Agency
Literary Agency
United Kingdom

submissions@anneclarkliteraryagency.co.uk
https://www.anneclarkliteraryagency.co.uk

Professional Body: The Association of Authors' Agents (AAA)

CHILDREN'S
  Fiction > *Middle Grade*
  Nonfiction > *Nonfiction Books*
YOUNG ADULT
  Fiction > *Novels*
  Nonfiction > *Nonfiction Books*

Closed to approaches.

Handles fiction for children and young adults. Send query by email only with the following pasted into the body of the email (not as an attachment): for fiction, include brief synopsis and first 3,000 words; for nonfiction, send short proposal and the text of three sample pages. No submissions by post. See website for full guidelines.

Literary Agent: Anne Clark

L029 Antony Harwood Limited
Literary Agency
103 Walton Street, Oxford, OX2 6EB
United Kingdom
Tel: +44 (0) 1865 559615

mail@antonyharwood.com
http://www.antonyharwood.com

Fiction > *Novels*
Nonfiction > *Nonfiction Books*

Send: Query; Synopsis; Writing sample; Self-Addressed Stamped Envelope (SASE)
How to send: Email; Post

Handles fiction and nonfiction in every genre and category, except for screenwriting and poetry. Send brief outline and first 50 pages by email, or by post with SASE.

Authors: Christine Berry; Alastair Bonnett; Michael Bracewell; Peter Bunzl; Amanda Craig; Candida Crewe; David Dabydeen; Tracy Darnton; Roy Dennis; Louise Doughty; Robert Edric; Anna Fleming; Sarah Gibson; Bob Gilbert; Caspar Henderson; Jill Hopper; Sally Huband; Gwyneth Lewis; Amy Liptrot; Fraser MacDonald; Stephen Rutt; Guy Shrubsole; Hugh Warwick

Literary Agents: Antony Harwood; Jo Williamson (**L664**)

L030 Kurestin Armada
Literary Agent
Canada

https://www.rootliterary.com/agents
https://querymanager.com/query/kurestinarmada
https://www.publishersmarketplace.com/members/kurestinarmada/

Literary Agency: Root Literary (**L547**)

ADULT > Fiction > *Novels*
  Fantasy; High / Epic Fantasy; Historical Romance; Horror; Romance; Romantasy; Science Fiction; Space Opera; Speculative; Spy Thrilllers; Upmarket; Westerns

CHILDREN'S > Fiction
  Chapter Books: General
  Graphic Novels: General
  Middle Grade: Adventure; Comedy / Humour; Contemporary; Fantasy; Historical Fiction; Literary; Mystery; Science Fiction; Upmarket
  Picture Books: Comedy / Humour

How to send: Query Manager

I love working with creators to form a roadmap for the rest of their career. Talking to people with projects that are ambitious, strange, personal, and just outrageously fun is the spark that keeps me going. I'm here to be their advocate and make sure they can keep writing for years and years to come.

L031 Victoria Wells Arms
Literary Agent
United States

victoria@hgliterary.com

https://www.hgliterary.com/victoria
https://twitter.com/VWArms
https://querymanager.com/query/VictoriaWellsArms

Literary Agency: HG Literary (**L310**)
Professional Bodies: Association of American

Literary Agents (AALA); Society of Children's Book Writers and Illustrators (SCBWI)

ADULT
Fiction > *Novels*

Nonfiction > *Nonfiction Books*: Food

CHILDREN'S > Fiction
Middle Grade; *Picture Books*
YOUNG ADULT > Fiction > *Novels*

Closed to approaches.

Represents authors of children's books of all ages, select adult authors, food authors, and many talented picture book illustrators.

L032 Susan Armstrong
Literary Agent
United Kingdom
Tel: +44 (0) 20 7393 4200

susan.submissions@cwagency.co.uk
susan.armstrong@cwagency.co.uk

https://cwagency.co.uk/agent/susan-armstrong
https://twitter.com/SusanW1F

Literary Agency: C&W (Conville & Walsh) (**L096**)

Fiction > *Novels*
Book Club Fiction; Contemporary; Crime; Family Saga; Fantasy; Gothic; Historical Fiction; Horror; Literary; Magical Realism; Science Fiction; Speculative; Suspense; Thrillers; Upmarket Commercial Fiction; Women's Fiction

Nonfiction in Translation > *Nonfiction Books*
Anthropology; Astronomy; Folklore, Myths, and Legends; Narrative Nonfiction; Paleontology; Supernatural / Paranormal

How to send: Word file email attachment

I love to see literary fiction, book group/upmarket commercial women's fiction, contemporary stories, family dramas, historical, crime, thrillers and suspense. I'm also keen to see high-quality magical realism and speculative fiction i.e. books with an edge of SFF, horror, gothic or 'otherness'. I enjoy novels that blend genres, are unusual in setting or circumstance, have unexpected twists, have a little darkness, pull at the heart-strings, and/or contain some sort of moral dilemma. Books that make me laugh are always welcome!

In terms of non-fiction, I'm keen to see accessible, narrative-led projects in the following areas: anthropology, palaeontology, astronomy, mythology, the supernatural and anything that's unusual or surprising about the world we live in.

So that's the writing, but what about the writer? There are no prerequisites except that I'm always looking for authors who want a long-term career and in return I will do everything to help shape, edit and sell their books along with offering support and guidance.

I'm not currently taking on new YA/children's books or espionage thrillers.

I am open to submissions from anyone anywhere in the world but I particularly love to hear from British, Irish, Greek and ANZ writers.

Authors: Claire Anderson-Wheeler; Jo Callaghan; Joanna Cannon; Holly Cave; Maxine Beneba Clarke; Daniel Cole; Marianne Cronin; Grace Flahive; Joanna Glen; A.J. Gnuse; Anne Griffin; Katie Gutierrez; Lori Inglis Hall; James Hannah; Lindsay Hawdon; Miranda Cowley Heller; Julietta Henderson; Emily Howes; Crystal Jeans; Jess Kidd; Olivia Kiernan; Justine Kilkerr; Annie Kirby; Claire Kohda; Caroline Mackenzie; C.E. McGill; Juli Min; Nicola Mostyn; Lisa O'Donnell; Orla Owen; Jo Piazza; Christine Pride; Joanne Ramos; Al Robertson; Ali Shaw; Kim Sherwood; Natasha Solomons; M L Stedman; Simon Sylvester; Natalia Theodoridou; Lara Thompson; Laura Vaughan; Rebecca Whitney; Olivia Wood; Jo Browning Wroe; Simon Wroe

L033 Wayne Arthurson
Literary Agent
Canada

https://www.therightsfactory.com/Agents/Wayne-Arthurson

Literary Agency: The Rights Factory

ADULT
Fiction > *Novels*
Crime; Fantasy; Literary; Science Fiction

Nonfiction > *Nonfiction Books*
Memoir; Narrative Nonfiction

YOUNG ADULT
Fiction > *Novels*
Crime; Fantasy; Literary; Science Fiction

Nonfiction > *Nonfiction Books*
Memoir; Narrative Nonfiction

Currently building his list of talent, looking specifically for YA or adult literary, crime and SFF and narrative nonfiction and memoir. He's actively seeking works by Indigenous writers.

Authors: Greg Bechtel; Eric Beetner; Michelle Poirier Brown; Deryn Collier; Candas Jane Dorsey; Trevor Duplessis; Brittlestar aka Stewart Reynolds; Marsheila (Marcy) Rockwell; Steven Sandor; Coltrane Seesequasis

L034 Charlotte Atyeo
Literary Agent
United Kingdom

charlotte@greyhoundliterary.co.uk

https://greyhoundliterary.co.uk/agent/charlotte-atyeo/
https://twitter.com/EverSoBookish

Literary Agency: Greyhound Literary (**L278**)

ADULT
Fiction > *Novels*: Literary

Nonfiction > *Nonfiction Books*
General, and in particular: Biography; Equality; Feminism; Gender Issues; Memoir; Music; Nature; Sport

CHILDREN'S
Fiction > *Picture Books*

Nonfiction
Middle Grade; *Nonfiction Books*
YOUNG ADULT > Fiction > *Novels*

Does not want:

Nonfiction > *Nonfiction Books*
Religion; Self Help

Send: Query; Synopsis; Writing sample; Outline
How to send: Email
How not to send: Post

Represents non-fiction authors as well as a select number of children's and fiction authors. She is primarily looking for original and brilliantly written general non-fiction, biography and memoir, sport, music, nature writing, and feminism, gender and equality issues. She is not currently taking on books about religion, self-help or memoirs that deal with abuse and/or trauma. When it comes to children's books, she is open to submissions of picture books and non-fiction (particularly from authors with expert knowledge of their subject). She is especially excited to hear from author/illustrators and from under-represented voices. On the adult fiction side, she is taking on a small number of literary novels. (She is not looking for crime and thriller, romance, or SFF.)

Authors: Carol Atherton; Saskia Gwinn; Ed Hawkins; Michael Holding; Michael Hutchinson; Ellie Irving; Jennifer Lane; Michelle Lovric; Julia Raeside; Susan Richardson; Sarah Shephard; Cécile Simmons; Tatton Spiller; Jen Wight

L035 AVAnti Productions & Management
Literary Agency
124 City Road, The City, London, EC1V 2NX
United Kingdom
Tel: +44 (0) 7999 193311

avantiproductions@live.co.uk

https://www.avantiproductions.co.uk

Scripts > *Film Scripts*

Send: Full text
How to send: Email
How not to send: Post

Costs: Author covers sundry admin costs.

Talent and literary representation. Open to screenplay submissions for short films and feature films, but no theatre scripts.

Literary Agent: Veronica Lazar

L036 Ayesha Pande Literary
Literary Agency
United States
Tel: +1 (212) 283-5825

queries@pandeliterary.com

https://www.pandeliterary.com

A New York based boutique literary agency with a small and eclectic roster of clients. Submit queries via form on website. No poetry, business books, cookbooks, screenplays or illustrated children's books.

Literary Agents: Madison Smartt Bell; Stephany Evans (**L206**); Serene Hakim (**L288**); Annie Hwang (**L322**); Kayla Lightner (**L399**); Luba Ostashevsky; Ayesha Pande (**L497**)

L037 Lauren Bajek
Junior Agent
United States

querylauren@lizadawson.com

https://www.lizadawsonassociates.com/lauren-bajek

Literary Agency: Liza Dawson Associates (**L405**)

Fiction > *Novels*
Fantasy; Horror; Literary; Science Fiction; Speculative; Upmarket

Nonfiction > *Nonfiction Books*
Crafts; Nature; Science

Send: Query; Writing sample
How to send: In the body of an email

Currently building a select list of fiction and nonfiction, with an emphasis in SFFH, upmarket speculative fiction, craft/DIY nonfiction, and science/nature nonfiction. Across the board, she is drawn to literary prose, queer and anticolonial perspectives, unusual or hybrid forms, and an ambitious sense of imagination. She is always interested in animal cognition, translation, and sentient houses.

L038 Emma Bal
Literary Agent
United Kingdom

https://madeleinemilburn.co.uk/looking-for/emma-bal-what-im-looking-for/

Literary Agency: Madeleine Milburn Literary, TV & Film Agency (**L420**)

Nonfiction > *Nonfiction Books*
Arts; Cookery; Food; Investigative Journalism; Memoir; Narrative Nonfiction; Nature; Science; Travel

Looking for non-fiction across the arts, humanities and sciences; narrative non-fiction; investigative journalism: cookery and food writing; travel and nature writing; memoir; illustrated projects.

L039 Dan Balow
Literary Agent
United States

vseem@stevelaube.com

https://stevelaube.com/what-i-am-looking-for/

Literary Agency: The Steve Laube Agency

Nonfiction > *Nonfiction Books*: Christianity

Send: Query; Proposal; Writing sample
How to send: Email attachment
How not to send: Post; In the body of an email

Represents nonfiction works mainly to Christian-themed publishers. No fiction.

L040 Gaia Banks
Literary Agent

Literary Agency: Sheil Land Associates Ltd (**L577**)

L041 Stephen Barbara
Literary Agent
United States

submissions@inkwellmanagement.com

https://www.inkwellmanagement.com
https://www.inkwellmanagement.com/staff/stephen-barbara
https://twitter.com/Stephen_Barbara

Literary Agency: InkWell Management

ADULT
  Fiction > *Novels*
  Nonfiction > *Nonfiction Books*

YOUNG ADULT > **Fiction** > *Novels*

Send: Query; Writing sample
How to send: Email

Selective in taking on new clients but remains excited to discover great new writers and would be thrilled to find a novel that hits big on an emotional level or, if nonfiction, changes the way he thinks about the world.

L042 Arthur Barnard
Associate Agent
United Kingdom

abarnard@theagency.co.uk

https://theagency.co.uk/the-agents/arthur-barnard/

Literary Agency: The Agency (London) Ltd (**L009**)

Scripts
Film Scripts; TV Scripts; Theatre Scripts

Send: Query; Writing sample
How to send: Email

Started working at the agency in 2019, after graduating with a degree in English from The University of Cambridge. In 2020 he began work as an assistant, expanding his knowledge across television, film and theatre. He currently holds the position of associate agent and is starting to build his own list of clients.

L043 Barone Literary Agency
Literary Agency
United States

DSBLawyer@outlook.com

https://www.baroneliterary.com

ADULT > **Fiction** > *Novels*
Erotic Romance; Historical Fiction; Horror; Romance; Women's Fiction

NEW ADULT > **Fiction** > *Novels*

YOUNG ADULT > **Fiction** > *Novels*

Does not want:

> **NEW ADULT** > **Fiction** > *Novels*
> Science Fiction; Supernatural / Paranormal
>
> **YOUNG ADULT** > **Fiction** > *Novels*
> Science Fiction; Supernatural / Paranormal

Closed to approaches.

Closed to submissions as at July 2023. Check website for current status.

Send query online form on website. Include synopsis and first three chapters. No plays, screenplays, picture books, middle grade, science fiction, paranormal, or nonfiction.

Authors: Laurie Albano; Michele Barrow-Belisle; Cathy Bennett; Sarah Biglow; Jennifer Petersen Fraser; Yvette Geer; Suzanne Hay; Richard Moore; Rebekah Purdy; Curt Rude; Wyatt Shev; Anna Snow; Sharon Sullivan-Craver; Molly Zenk

Literary Agent: Denise Barone

L044 Baror International, Inc.
Literary Agency
P.O. Box 868, Armonk, NY 10504-0868
United States

https://barorint.com

ADULT
  Fiction > *Novels*
  Commercial; Fantasy; Historical Fiction; Literary; Science Fiction; Suspense; Thrillers

  Nonfiction > *Nonfiction Books*

CHILDREN'S > **Fiction** > *Middle Grade*

YOUNG ADULT > **Fiction** > *Novels*

Closed to approaches.

Specialises in the international and domestic representation of literary works in both fiction and non-fiction ranging in genre including commercial fiction, literary, historical, suspense, thrillers, narrative, science fiction, fantasy, young adult, middle grade and more.

Literary Agents: Danny Baror; Heather Baror-Shapiro

L045 Anjanette Barr
Literary Agent
United States

query@dunhamlit.com

https://www.dunhamlit.com/anjanette-barr.html
https://aalitagents.org/author/anjanettebarr/
https://www.facebook.com/BookBarrista
https://twitter.com/bookbarrista
https://www.instagram.com/bookbarrista/
https://www.linkedin.com/in/anjanette-barr-34193765/
https://youtube.com/AnjanetteBarrtheBookBarr

Literary Agency: Dunham Literary, Inc. (**L179**)
Professional Bodies: Association of American Literary Agents (AALA); Society of Children's Book Writers and Illustrators (SCBWI)

ADULT
Fiction > *Novels*
General, and in particular: Gothic; Magical Realism

Nonfiction > *Nonfiction Books*
Arts; Biography; Culture; Folklore, Myths, and Legends; History; Memoir; Nature; Popular Science; Poverty; Religion

CHILDREN'S > **Fiction** > *Picture Books*

Send: Query; Writing sample
How to send: In the body of an email
How not to send: Google Docs shared document; Email attachment

She loves genre and popular fiction with substance, and literary and non-fiction titles infused with living ideas that leave readers with a new desire to immerse themselves in the subject matter. In non-fiction she is looking for well-researched biography written in beautiful literary prose, popular science and other disciplines titles that make lay-people enchanted and invested in topics previously over their heads, and memoir with the ability to connect diverse readers. She's also interested in books that shed light on poverty and justice in a new way. She prefers picture books that are winsome and pleasant to read aloud. Particular interests are the exploration of culture, history, faith, myth, fine arts, and nature. She has a soft spot for gothic novels and magical realism. As a mother of four, she's is especially fond of books that can be read aloud and shared with the whole family.

L046 Nicola Barr
Literary Agent
United Kingdom

https://www.thebentagency.com
https://www.thebentagency.com/nicola-barr
https://twitter.com/NicolaBarr123

Literary Agency: The Bent Agency (UK) (**L057**)

ADULT
Fiction > *Novels*
Commercial Women's Fiction; Commercial; Crime; Literary; Social Issues; Upmarket Commercial Fiction

Nonfiction > *Nonfiction Books*
Comedy / Humour; Europe; Feminism; Houses and Homes; Sport

YOUNG ADULT > **Fiction** >
Novels: Contemporary

Closed to approaches.

I have over the years represented many bestselling commercial fiction authors, Richard & Judy bestsellers, and award-winning crime fiction and commercial women's fiction. I am still very much on the lookout for upmarket commercial well-written fiction in these areas, particularly if they speak to a social issue, shine a light on a true-life injustice, have an atypical hero or heroine. I adore literary fiction, whether experimental or traditional, and will certainly not turn away a novel for seeming lack of… anything happening.

But, whether you are writing commercial fiction or literary fiction, I am endlessly fascinated by dysfunctional or unusual families, oddballs, women struggling and women achieving, the disenfranchised, outsiders. I embrace fiction that explores the darker side of life, but do respond well to points of view that don't take the world too seriously.

In YA, I'm most passionate about grounded contemporary.

I'm a committed Londoner, but was born and raised in Northern Ireland, then studied at the University of Glasgow. I am actively looking to build on the brilliant Irish, Northern Irish and Scottish writers I already have. I do have a natural tendency to be drawn to working-class voices and regional stories. I also love nothing more than getting stuck in editorially on a story if I see brilliance there.

Like many in these odd times, I find myself increasingly drawn to non-fiction that allows for a collective vent. In the past year or so I have represented books on housing, Europe, feminism, millennials, sexual harassment. I love illustrators, cartoonists. I love sport and comedy and I might even show an interest in your food blog. As long as it doesn't mention cupcakes.

L047 Jason Bartholomew
Literary Agent
United Kingdom

https://www.thebksagency.com/submissions

Literary Agency: The BKS Agency (**L065**)

Fiction > *Novels*
Crime; Thrillers

Nonfiction > *Nonfiction Books*
Biography; Current Affairs; History; Memoir; Narrative Nonfiction; Politics

Send: Query; Outline; Author bio
How to send: Online submission system

Originally from America. Spent ten years working in New York publishing, primarily for Hachette Book Group USA. He moved to Hachette UK in 2008 where he was the Rights Director across Hodder & Stoughton, Headline Publishing Group, Quercus Books, and John Murray Press.

L048 Tim Bates
Senior Agent
United Kingdom

tbates@pfd.co.uk

https://petersfraserdunlop.com/agent/tim-bates/

Literary Agency: Peters Fraser + Dunlop

Fiction > *Novels*

Nonfiction > *Nonfiction Books*
Commercial; Food; Narrative Nonfiction; Nature; Popular Culture; Sport

Send: Query; Synopsis; Writing sample; Proposal; Author bio
How to send: Email
How not to send: Post

Represents a wide range of authors and is particularly interested in pop culture, narrative and serious non-fiction, food-writing, nature and the outdoors, sport and commercial non-fiction and fiction of all forms.

Authors: Iain Ballantyne; Tom Blass; Brian Blessed; Kevin Brennan; Whitney Brown; Leland Carlson; Kimberley Chambers; Richard Coles; Brendan Cooper; Sara Dallin; Len Deighton; Pepsi Demacque-Crockett; Naomi Devlin; Martin Dorey; Jon Dunn; Caroline Fleming; Will Francis; Irina Georgescu; Caro Giles; Romy Gill; Jean G Goodhind; Jonathan Gornall; Delayed Gratification; Annie Gray; Simon Halfon; Eddie Hall; Tony Hannan; Angela Hartnett; James Hogg; Becky Holmes; Amari Koryang; Lizzie Lane; Jack Lowe; Gary Numan; Chris Paling; David Papineau; Jo Pavey; Lesley Pearse; Nigel Reed; Andrew Ridgeley; Debora Robertson; Noble Rot; Neil 'Razor' Ruddock; Romla Ryan; Rupert Shortt; Susannah Stapleton; Colin Taylor; Caroline Tremlett; Valentine Warner; Emma J. Wells; Keren Woodward; Jacqueline Yallop

L049 Bath Literary Agency
Literary Agency
5 Gloucester Road, Bath, BA1 7BH
United Kingdom

john.mclay@btinternet.com

https://www.bathliteraryagency.com
https://twitter.com/BathLitAgency
http://instagram.com/bathlitagency

Professional Body: The Association of Authors' Agents (AAA)

CHILDREN'S
Fiction
  Middle Grade; *Picture Books*
Poetry > *Picture Books*

YOUNG ADULT
Fiction > *Novels*
Nonfiction > *Nonfiction Books*

Send: Query; Synopsis; Writing sample; Full text; Self-Addressed Stamped Envelope (SASE)
How to send: Email; Post

Handles fiction and nonfiction for children, from picture books to Young Adult. Send query by email or by post with SAE for reply and return of materials if required, along with the first three chapters (fiction) or the full manuscript (picture books). See website for full details.

Literary Agent: Gill McLay

L050 Erica Bauman
Literary Agent
United States

https://aevitascreative.com/agents/
https://querymanager.com/query/EricaBauman

Literary Agency: Aevitas

ADULT > Fiction
  Graphic Novels: General
  Novels: Commercial; Folklore, Myths, and Legends; Magic; Romantic Comedy; Speculative

CHILDREN'S > Fiction > *Graphic Novels*

YOUNG ADULT > Fiction > *Graphic Novels*

How to send: Query Manager

Open to submissions the first week of every month. Most interested in commercial novels that feature an exciting premise and lyrical, atmospheric writing; imaginative, genre-blending tales; speculative worlds filled with haunting, quietly wondrous magic; fresh retellings of mythology, ballet, opera, and classic literature; sharply funny rom-coms; graphic novels for all ages; fearless storytellers that tackle big ideas and contemporary issues; and working with and supporting marginalized authors and stories that represent the wide range of humanity.

Authors: Telênia Albuquerque; Jessica Benoist; Melissa Benoist; Abigail Rayner

L051 Jan Baumer
Literary Agent
United States

jan@foliolit.com

https://www.foliolit.com/agent/jan-baumer

Literary Agency: Folio Literary Management, LLC

Nonfiction > *Nonfiction Books*
  Business; Comedy / Humour; Cookery; Health; Memoir; Narrative Nonfiction; Parenting; Prescriptive Nonfiction; Religion; Self Help; Spirituality; Wellbeing

Closed to approaches.

Interests as an agent are largely nonfiction, specifically spirituality, religion, self-help, health and wellness, parenting, memoir, and business with a spirituality or self-help angle. Response only if interested. If no response in 60 days, assume rejection.

L052 Veronique Baxter
Literary Agent; Company Director
United Kingdom

veroniquemanuscripts@davidhigham.co.uk
childrenssubmissions@davidhigham.co.uk

https://www.davidhigham.co.uk/agents-dh/veronique-baxter/

Literary Agency: David Higham Associates Ltd (**L159**)

ADULT
Fiction > *Novels*
  Book Club Fiction; Comedy / Humour; Crime; Domestic; Family Saga; High Concept; Historical Fiction; Horror; Literary; Speculative; Thrillers

Nonfiction > *Nonfiction Books*
  Crime; Current Affairs; Feminism; Food; History; Memoir; Psychology; Travel

CHILDREN'S > Fiction > *Middle Grade*
  Comedy / Humour; High Concept; Mystery

Send: Query; Synopsis; Writing sample
How to send: Email

In fiction, looking for: Literary fiction of all kinds including historical, horror and speculative; multi-generational novels; High concept book club fiction; Devil-in-the-detail domestic dramas; Crime and thrillers – particularly those set in unusual places or that take the genre conventions and do something a bit different with them; fictionalised true crime (gravitating towards the darker end of the spectrum); Caustic, funny novels.

In nonfiction, looking for true crime, history, current affairs, travel, food, psychology, feminism and memoir.

In children's, looking for high concept stories told with humour and heart, and mysteries and whodunnits at the older end.

Agency Assistant: Sara Langham

Authors: Richard Adams; Naomi Alderman; Tina Baker; Anthony Bale; Belinda Bauer; Hannah Begbie; Neil Blackmore; Carys Bray; Glen Brown; Sally Butcher; Nick Butterworth; Jamie Costello; Cressida Cowell; Nick Crumpton; Nicola Davies; Jonathan Dimbleby; Berlie Doherty; Fred D'Aguiar; David Edmonds; Maz Evans; Jamila Gavin; Guinevere Glasfurd; Holly Gramazio; Oliver Harris; Mo Hayder; Emma Henderson; Edward Hogan; Lucy Hounsom; Diana Wynne Jones; Stephen Kelman; Claire King; Saci Lloyd; Kesia Lupo; S. E. Lynes; Patrick Marnham; Geraldine McCaughrean; Jean McNeil; Sarah Mitchell; Michael Morpurgo; Charity Norman; Cato Pedder; Charlotte Philby; Sarah Pinborough; Sabina Radeva; Sarah Ridgard; M. L. Rio; Bethan Roberts; Jane Robinson; Rachel Seiffert; Philip Short; Kate Simants; Jonathan Stroud; Emma Claire Sweeney; Scarlett Thomas; A. K. Turner; Harriet Tyce; Nicola Upson; Jenny Valentine; Jill Paton Walsh; Mary Wesley; Tim Winton; Charlotte Wood; Kate Worsley; Xinran

L053 Salma Begum
Literary Agent
United Kingdom

salma@greyhoundliterary.co.uk

https://greyhoundliterary.co.uk
https://greyhoundliterary.co.uk/agents/salma-begum

Literary Agency: Greyhound Literary (**L278**)

Fiction > *Novels*
  General, and in particular: High Concept; Horror; Literary; Romance; Time Travel; Urban

Nonfiction > *Nonfiction Books*
  General, and in particular: Journalism; Memoir; Music; Social Media

Poetry > *Poetry Collections*

Send: Query; Synopsis; Writing sample
How to send: Email

Seeking confident, immersive, ambitious, narrative-driven writing. She works under the tenet that quality need not be to the sacrifice of commercial success. Her submission wishlist includes a sweeping love story set against a gritty urban backdrop; ingenious tales of time travel; and a masterfully crafted multi-generational epic. In non-fiction, she is looking for subject experts, journalists and memoirists who appreciate long-form literature and can breathe life into an idea, an event, a memory. Her non-fiction wishlist includes interrogations of social media use and its sometimes-devastating consequences as explored in the Netflix docudrama The Social Dilemma; captivating music writing such as Grime Kids by DJ Target and On Michael Jackson by Margo Jefferson; and ground-shifting journalism like Empire of Pain by Patrick Radden Keefe. She has published the work of a number of prize-winning poets. As an agent, her preference is for the colloquial, rhythmic, or playful, written with the ambition of forming a cohesive collection. She is keen to work with spoken word poets who are looking to bring their work to the page.

Authors: Zahra Barri; Sharmilla Beezmohun; Josh Berson; Saddiq Dzukogi; Yvvette Edwards; Joshua Idehen; Delia Jarrett-Macauley; Arji Manuelpillai; Shane Melisse; Roger Robinson; Yomi Ṣode

L054 Eva Bell
Literary Agent
United Kingdom

https://saylescreen.com/about-us/

Literary Agency: Sayle Screen Ltd

Scripts
 Film Scripts; TV Scripts; Theatre Scripts

How to send: By referral

Predominantly represents writers and writer/directors working across film, tv and theatre. Also represents script editors/script execs as well as dramatic rights in fiction and non-fiction books. Taste is varied across genres and tone, but the linking factor is always characterful storytellers that have a unique point of view or perspective on the worlds they are inviting their audience into.

L055 Maddy Belton
Literary Agent
United Kingdom

https://www.madeleinemilburn.co.uk/agents/maddy-belton/
https://twitter.com/MadsPhyllis

Literary Agency: Madeleine Milburn Literary, TV & Film Agency (**L420**)

ADULT > Fiction > *Novels*
 Contemporary Fantasy; Cozy Fantasy; Dark; Fairy Tales; Fantasy; Folklore, Myths, and Legends; High / Epic Fantasy; Historical Fiction; LGBTQIA; Romance; Science Fiction; Thrillers

CHILDREN'S
 Fiction > *Middle Grade*
  Comedy / Humour; Fantasy; Magic
 Nonfiction > *Nonfiction Books*

YOUNG ADULT > Fiction > *Novels*
 Contemporary Fantasy; Cozy Fantasy; Fantasy; High / Epic Fantasy; LGBTQIA; Romance

Send: Outline; Author bio; Market info; Marketing Plan; Writing sample
How to send: Email

SFF across all genres for all ages, including: grim dark, thriller, historical, romance, cosy fantasy, sci-fi, epic, YA fantasy, dark academia, contemporary fantasy, fantasy middle-grade, mythology, fairy tale and queer fantasy. Inspiring children's non-fiction.

L056 Laura Bennett
Associate Agent; Editor
United Kingdom

https://www.liverpool-literary.agency/about

Literary Agency: The Liverpool Literary Agency (**L404**)

ADULT > Fiction > *Novels*
 Dystopian Fiction; Fantasy; Post-Apocalyptic; Science Fiction; Steampunk; Urban Fantasy

YOUNG ADULT > Fiction > *Novels*
 Dystopian Fiction; Fantasy; Post-Apocalyptic; Science Fiction; Steampunk; Urban Fantasy

Closed to approaches.

L057 The Bent Agency (UK)
Literary Agency
Greyhound House, 23/24 George Street, Richmond, TW9 1HY
United Kingdom

info@thebentagency.com

https://www.thebentagency.com
https://www.instagram.com/thebentagency/

Professional Body: The Association of Authors' Agents (AAA)
Literary Agency: The Bent Agency (**L058**)

ADULT
 Fiction
  Graphic Novels; *Novels*
 Nonfiction > *Nonfiction Books*

CHILDREN'S > Fiction
 Chapter Books; *Graphic Novels*; *Middle Grade*

YOUNG ADULT
 Fiction
  Graphic Novels; *Novels*
 Nonfiction > *Nonfiction Books*

Send: Query
How to send: Email; Query Manager

UK office of established US agency. See website for individual agent interests and contact details and approach appropriate agent. Do not send submissions to general agency email address. See website for full submission guidelines.

Associate Agent: Martha Perotto-Wills (**L508**)

Literary Agent: Nicola Barr (**L046**)

Literary Agent / Managing Director: Molly Ker Hawn (**L304**)

L058 The Bent Agency
Literary Agency
PO Box 55772, Birmingham, AL 35205
United States

info@thebentagency.com

https://www.thebentagency.com
https://www.instagram.com/thebentagency/

ADULT
 Fiction
  Graphic Novels; *Novels*
 Nonfiction > *Nonfiction Books*

CHILDREN'S > Fiction
 Chapter Books; *Graphic Novels*; *Middle Grade*

YOUNG ADULT
 Fiction
  Graphic Novels; *Novels*
 Nonfiction > *Nonfiction Books*

Send: Query
How to send: Email; Query Manager

Accepts email or Query Manager queries only. See website for agent bios and specific interests and email addresses, then query one agent only. See website for full submission guidelines.

Authors: Arvin Ahmadi; Samantha M. Bailey; Gary John Bishop; Tera Lynn Childs; Yangsze Choo; Liv Constantine; Susan Crispell; Lisa Doyle; Kerry Douglas Dye; Deborah Falaye; Michael Farquhar; Mina Fears; Delores Fossen; Stephanie Garber; J. T. Geissinger; Seressia Glass; Alexis Henderson; Rita Herron; A. G. Howard; Robert Isaacs; Tiffany D. Jackson; Meredith Jaeger; Elise Kova; Roselle Lim; Julia London; Elle Marr; Barry Martin; Marta McDowell; Goldy Moldavsky; Laura Morelli; Joel H. Morris; Natalie Naudus; Preston Norton; Michelle Quach; Morgan Ryan; Lynsay Sands; Ingrid Seymour; L C. Shaw; Lori Nelson Spielman; Dustin Thao; Joseph Turkot; Lynn Weingarten; Lori Wilde

Company Director / Literary Agent: Gemma Cooper (**L140**)

Literary Agency: The Bent Agency (UK) (**L057**)

Literary Agent / President: Jenny Bent (**L059**)

Literary Agent / Vice President: Victoria Cappello (*L102*)

Literary Agents: James Mustelier (**L471**); Zoe Plant (**L519**); John Silbersack

L059 Jenny Bent
Literary Agent; President
United States

queries@thebentagency.com

https://www.thebentagency.com/jenny-bent

Literary Agency: The Bent Agency (**L058**)

ADULT
 Fiction > *Novels*
  Commercial; Domestic Suspense; Grounded Fantasy; High Concept; Horror; Literary; Romance; Romantic Comedy; Speculative; Upmarket Women's Fiction

Nonfiction > *Nonfiction Books*
Lifestyle; Self Help

YOUNG ADULT > **Fiction** > *Novels*
General, and in particular: Contemporary; Fantasy; Magic; Romantic Comedy; Suspense

Does not want:

> **Fiction** > *Novels*
> Cozy Mysteries; High / Epic Fantasy; Science Fiction

Send: Query; Writing sample
How to send: Email
How not to send: Post

I'm currently looking for literary and commercial fiction and young adult fiction as well as select non-fiction in the areas of self-help and lifestyle. My client list is diverse and I welcome submissions from BIPOC authors.

In adult fiction, I'm looking for high concept, upmarket women's fiction; grounded fantasy; speculative fiction and horror (I particularly love a good ghost story, along the lines of writing by Simone St. James and Jennifer McMahon); and domestic suspense, but the bar is very high in suspense right now so it has to be an extremely creative concept. I also rep some romance and rom-com, but no other genre fiction: I'm not a good choice for high fantasy, cozy mystery, or sci-fi.

In young adult fiction, I'm pretty open to genre — I love fantasy, rom-coms, suspense, contemporary, almost anything except for sci-fi. I do notice that my YA taste does tend to skew towards older readers, more in a crossover direction.

In general, I tend to prefer plot-driven books to character-driven ones and pacing is very important to me. I also love novels — for adults or young adults — that have an element of magic or fantasy to them or that take me into a world that is new to me, whether real or imaginary. And while I love books to be dark and weird in terms of content, I find that I am more drawn to traditional, rather than experimental, methods of structure and storytelling.

In nonfiction, I am looking for authors with a unique approach and a very large existing platform. I'm not generally the right choice for memoir or narrative non-fiction, but I'm always open to hearing a pitch just in case.

All of the books that I represent speak to the heart in some way: they are linked by genuine emotion, inspiration, and great writing and storytelling. I love books that make me laugh, make me cry, or ideally do both.

Authors: Arvin Ahmadi; Samantha M. Bailey; Gary John Bishop; Tera Lynn Childs; Yangsze Choo; Liv Constantine; Susan Crispell; Lisa Doyle; Kerry Douglas Dye; Deborah Falaye; Michael Farquhar; Mina Fears; Delores Fossen; Stephanie Garber; J. T. Geissinger; Seressia Glass; Alexis Henderson; Rita Herron; A. G. Howard; Robert Isaacs; Tiffany D. Jackson; Meredith Jaeger; Elise Kova; Roselle Lim; Julia London; Elle Marr; Barry Martin; Marta McDowell; Goldy Moldavsky; Laura Morelli; Joel H. Morris; Natalie Naudus; Preston Norton; Michelle Quach; Morgan Ryan; Lynsay Sands; Ingrid Seymour; L C. Shaw; Lori Nelson Spielman; Dustin Thao; Joseph Turkot; Lynn Weingarten; Lori Wilde

L060 Kendall Berdinsky
Literary Agent
United States

kberdinsky@dystel.com

https://www.dystel.com
https://www.dystel.com/kendall-berdinsky
https://querymanager.com/query/kendallb
https://twitter.com/klberdinsky

Literary Agency: Dystel, Goderich & Bourret LLC

Fiction > *Novels*
Book Club Fiction; Psychological Thrillers; Upmarket Romance

Nonfiction > *Nonfiction Books*: Narrative Nonfiction

How to send: Query Manager

Interested in seeing upmarket romance, book club fiction, psychological thrillers, and narrative nonfiction. Overall, she is looking for work from underrepresented communities with new stories to tell.

L061 John Berlyne
Literary Agent
United Kingdom

http://zenoagency.com/about-us/

Literary Agency: Zeno Agency (**L680**)

ADULT > **Fiction** > *Novels*
Crime; Fantasy; Historical Fiction; Horror; Science Fiction; Space Opera; Thrillers; Urban Fantasy

YOUNG ADULT > **Fiction** > *Novels*

Closed to approaches.

L062 Amanda Bernardi
Literary Agent
United States

https://www.highlineliterary.com
https://www.highlineliterary.com/agent-amanda
https://querymanager.com/query/3002
https://www.instagram.com/amandabernardibooks

Literary Agency: High Line Literary Collective (**L312**)

Nonfiction > *Nonfiction Books*
Arts; Cookery; Design; Environment; Health; Houses and Homes; Investigative Journalism; Nature; Parenting; Popular Culture; Popular History; Popular Science; Social Justice; Sociology; Sport; Wellbeing

How to send: Query Manager

Actively building her client list and works exclusively with non-fiction. She is interested in platform- or expertise-driven cookbooks, home & design, art, investigative journalism, social justice, pop science, wellness, social science, sports, health, pop history, parenting, nature, environmentalism, pop culture and anything that advances our community dialogue towards a better tomorrow. She is looking for projects that are thoughtful, actionable, and engaging for a general audience.

L063 Betsy Amster Literary Enterprises
Literary Agency
607 Foothill Blvd #1061, La Canada Flintridge, CA 91012
United States

b.amster.assistant@gmail.com

http://amsterlit.com

Fiction > *Novels*
Literary; Mystery; Thrillers; Upmarket Commercial Fiction; Upmarket Women's Fiction

Nonfiction
Gift Books: General
Nonfiction Books: Biography; Career Development; Cookery; Gardening; Health; History; Lifestyle; Medicine; Narrative Nonfiction; Nutrition; Parenting; Popular Culture; Psychology; Self Help; Social Issues; Travel; Women's Issues

How to send: Email
How not to send: Post

A full-service literary agency based in Los Angeles, California. No romances, screenplays, poetry, westerns, fantasy, horror, science fiction, techno thrillers, spy capers, apocalyptic scenarios, political or religious arguments, or self-published books. See website for full guidelines.

Authors: Amy Alkon; Dwight Allen; Will Allen; Jess J. Araujo; Elaine N. Aron; Sandi Ault; Lois Barr; Ariel Bernstein; Kim Boyce; Helene Brenner; Karen Briner; Catheryn J. Brockett; Karen Burns; Mónica Bustamante; Joe P. Carr; Steven Carter; Lillian Castillo-Speed; Robin Chotzinoff; Frank Clifford; Rob Cohen; David Cundy; Leela Cyd; Margaret Leslie Davis; Jan DeBlieu; David J. Diamond; Martha O. Diamond; Phil Doran; Suzanne Dunaway; Nick Dyer; J. Theron Elkins; Ruth Andrew Ellenson; Loretta Ellsworth; James P. Emswiler; Mary Ann Emswiler; Naomi Epel;

Alex Epstein; Karin Esterhammer; Jeannette Faurot; Tom Fields-Meyer; Joline Godfrey; Tanya Ward Goodman; Michael I. Goran; Hindi Greenberg; Ellen Hawley; Marian Henley; Charney Herst; Leigh Ann Hirschman; Ariel Horn; Lisa Hunter; Jackie; Melissa Jacobs; Janet Jaffe; Emily Katz; E. Barrie Kavasch; Joy Keller; Eileen Kennedy-Moore; Rachel Tawil Kenyon; Camille Landau; Carol Lay; Anna Lefler; Margaret Lobenstine; Mark Lowenthal; Paul Mandelbaum; Ivy Manning; Melissa Martin; Domenico Minchilli; Elizabeth Helman Minchilli; Wendy Mogel; Sharon Montrose; Bonnie Frumkin Morales; Yolanda Nava; Joy Nicholson; Judith Nies; Susie Norris; Christopher Noxon; Lynette Padwa; Neela Paniz; Kishani Perera; Cash Peters; Barry Prizant; Winifred Reilly; Andrea Richards; Eileen Roth; Adam Sappington; Marjorie Barton Savage; Anthony Schmitz; M.D. Edward Schneider; Kyle Schuneman; George Shannon; Nancy Spiller; Allison Mia Starcher; Louise Steinman; Bill Stern; Terry Theise; Christina Baglivi Tinglof; Linda Venis; MPH Emily Ventura; Marisel Vera; Elizabeth Verdick; John Vorhaus; Hannah Voskuil; Diana Wells; Tiare White; Chris Witt; Karen Witynski; Steve D. Wolf; David Wollock; Dawn Young

Literary Agent: Betsy Amster

L064 Tamanna Bhasin
Assistant Agent
Canada

https://www.therightsfactory.com
https://www.therightsfactory.com/Agents/tamanna-bhasin
https://querymanager.com/query/tbhasin

Literary Agency: The Rights Factory

ADULT > Fiction > *Novels*
  Fantasy; Historical Fiction; Romance

YOUNG ADULT > Fiction > *Novels*
  Fantasy; Historical Fiction

Closed to approaches.

Her dedication to diverse narratives shines through as a literary agent—where she now combines her love for reading with her expertise in spotting compelling manuscripts across genres.

L065 The BKS Agency
Literary Agency
Pennine Place, 2A Charing Cross Road, London, WC2H 0FH
United Kingdom

https://www.thebksagency.com
https://www.facebook.com/thebksagency
https://twitter.com/ThebksAgency

Professional Body: The Association of Authors' Agents (AAA)

A literary management agency based in London. Founded in 2018 by three friends, each of whom has spent over two decades working across the biggest publishing houses in London and New York.

Literary Agents: Jason Bartholomew (**L047**); Joanna Kaliszewska (**L347**); Jessica Killingley (**L365**); Morwenna Loughman (**L408**); James Spackman (**L593**)

L066 Blake Friedmann Literary Agency Ltd
Literary Agency
15 Highbury Place, London, N5 1QP
United Kingdom
Tel: +44 (0) 20 7387 0842

info@blakefriedmann.co.uk

http://www.blakefriedmann.co.uk
https://twitter.com/BlakeFriedmann
https://www.instagram.com/blakefriedmannliteraryagency/

Professional Body: The Association of Authors' Agents (AAA)

Fiction > *Novels*

Nonfiction > *Nonfiction Books*

Send: Query; Synopsis; Writing sample
How to send: Word file email attachment

Always on the lookout for exciting new work and welcomes submissions from both published and debut authors, across many genres, and from any background. No submissions originated, written or edited by Artificial Intelligence (AI) technology.

Associate Agent: Sian Ellis-Martin (**L197**)

Authors: Diane Abbott; Gilbert Adair; Tatamkhulu Afrika; Mary Akers; Shani Akilah; Saskia Alais; Kasim Ali; Ted Allbeury; Nikki Allen; Ros Anderson; Sally Andrew; Romalyn Ante; Graeme Armstrong; Paul Ashton; Dani Atkins; MiMi Aye; Abdul Rahman Azzam; Trezza Azzopardi; Bolu Babalola; Sandy Balfour; Johanna Bell; Tomas Bellamy; Tom Benn; Jendella Benson; Meliz Berg; Ian Birch; Rachel Blackmore; Scarlett Brade; Andy Briggs; Nora Anne Brown; Karin Brynard; Erin Bunting; Jo Facer & Erin Bunting; Graeme Macrae Burnet; James Cahill; Edward Carey; Natasha Carthew; Elizabeth Chadwick; Fran Chang; Norie Clarke; Julia Cole; Sue Cook; Anne de Courcy; Emma Cowell; Sara Crowe; Achmat Dangor; Will Dean; Tuyen Do; Michael Donkor; Finuala Dowling; Barbara Erskine; Jo Facer; Felice Fallon; Tracey Farren; Kathryn Faulke; Paul Finch; Fiona Ford; Alix Fox; Sarah Franklin; Roxy Freeman; Jean Fullerton; Janice Galloway; David Gilman; Jenny Glanfield; Lyndall Gordon; Ann Granger; Gabriella Griffith; Sarah Hartley; David Haslam; Emma Forsyth Haslett; Kate Hodges; Michael Hogan; Kerry Hudson; Leah Hyslop; Cormac James; Peter James; Tomasz Jedrowski; Alexandra Jellicoe; Benjamin Johncock; John Kennedy; Caroline Khoury; Konditor; Charles Lambert; Sarah Lee; Kat Lister; Richard Littler; Clayton Littlewood; Anneliese Mackintosh; Ailbhe Malone; Lucy Mangan; Beryl Matthews; Zakes Mda; Deon Meyer; Lia Middleton; Nina-Sophia Miralles; Emma Mitchell; Sue Moorcroft; Grace Mortimer; Christopher Nicholson; Marlene van Niekerk; Lawrence Norfolk; Gregory Norminton; Joseph O'Connor; Sheila O'Flanagan; Kaite O'Reilly; Sara Ochs; Leeanne O'Donnell; Nina Parker; Alan Parks; Karen Powell; Rosalind Powell; Julie Rea; Allie Reynolds; Annie Robertson; Monique Roffey; Henrietta Rose-Innes; Elliot Ryan; Lora Stimson; Julian Stockwin; Kate Thompson; Mary Torjussen; Hannah Treave; John Trenhaile; Jack Urwin; Anne-Marie Varga; Luca Veste; Ivan Vladislavic; Helen Walmsley-Johnson; Bridget Walsh; Anne Watts; Jemma Wayne; Harry Whitehead; Edward Wilson-Lee; Cristina Wolf; Andrew Wong

Literary Agent: Juliet Pickering (**L516**)

Literary Agent / Managing Director: Isobel Dixon (**L171**)

Senior Agent: Kate Burke (**L093**)

L067 Sidney Boker
Literary Agent
United States

https://inkwellmanagement.com/staff/sidney-boker

Literary Agency: InkWell Management

YOUNG ADULT > Fiction
  Graphic Novels: General
  Novels: Fantasy; Historical Fiction; Science Fiction

Loves to read young adult, fantasy, sci-fi, historical, and graphic novels, and almost anything with a strong female lead.

L068 Maeve Bolger
Literary Agent
United Kingdom

mbolger@theagency.co.uk

https://theagency.co.uk
https://theagency.co.uk/the-agents/maeve-bolger/

Literary Agency: The Agency (London) Ltd (**L009**)

Scripts
  Film Scripts; *Radio Scripts*; *TV Scripts*; *Theatre Scripts*

Send: Writing sample
How to send: Email

Trained at RADA and worked as a Stage Manager before becoming an agent in 2016. She represents Sound Designers, Composers,

Musical Directors, Set and Costume Designers, Lighting Designers and Directors in Theatre, alongside a list of Writers across all disciplines.

L069 Camilla Bolton
Literary Agent; Managing Director
United Kingdom

camilla@darleyanderson.com

https://www.darleyanderson.com/our-team
https://twitter.com/CamillaJBolton

Literary Agency: The Darley Anderson Agency (**L157**)

Fiction > *Novels*
  Book Club Fiction; Crime; Mystery; Suspense; Thrillers; Women's Fiction

How to send: Email attachment

Looking for accessible and commercial crime, thrillers, mysteries, suspense and women's fiction.

Authors: Emma Bamford; Vicki Bradley; James Carol; Gloria Cook; A J Cross; Jason Dean; Hayley Doyle; C. M. Ewan; G.R. Halliday; Egan Hughes; Emma Kavanagh; T M Logan; Imran Mahmood; L V Matthews; Phoebe Morgan; B.A. Paris; Jo Platt; Mira V. Shah; Rebecca Shaw; KL Slater; Kim Slater; Sean Slater; Catherine Steadman; G X Todd; Tim Weaver

L070 Bookseeker Agency
Literary Agency
United Kingdom

bookseller@blueyonder.co.uk

https://bookseekeragency.com
https://twitter.com/BookseekerAgent

Fiction > *Novels*

Poetry > *Any Poetic Form*

Send: Query; Synopsis; Writing sample
How to send: Email

Handles fiction and (under some circumstances) poetry. No nonfiction. Send query by email outlining what you have written and your current projects, along with synopsis and sample chapter (novels).

Literary Agent: Paul Thompson

L071 Stefanie Sanchez Von Borstel
Literary Agent
United States

https://www.fullcircleliterary.com/our-agents/stefanie-von-borstel/

Literary Agency: Full Circle Literary, LLC
Professional Bodies: Society of Children's Book Writers and Illustrators (SCBWI); Association of American Literary Agents (AALA)

ADULT > **Nonfiction** > *Nonfiction Books*
  Activism; Inspirational

CHILDREN'S
  Fiction > *Middle Grade*
    Contemporary; Historical Fiction

  Poetry > *Novels in Verse*
    Contemporary; History

How to send: By referral

Represents children's books from toddler to tween and select adult nonfiction. In adult nonfiction, her focus is on activism and inspiration.

L072 Imogen Bovill
Literary Agent
United Kingdom

Imogen@abnerstein.co.uk

http://abnerstein.co.uk

Literary Agency: Abner Stein

L073 Sarah Bowlin
Senior Agent
Los Angeles
United States

https://aevitascreative.com/agents/
https://querymanager.com/query/S_Bowlin_queries

Literary Agency: Aevitas

Fiction > *Novels*
  General, and in particular: Literary

Nonfiction > *Nonfiction Books*
  General, and in particular: Comedy / Humour; Dance; Food History; History; Narrative Nonfiction; Popular Culture; Wine

Closed to approaches.

Focused on bold, diverse voices in fiction and nonfiction. She's especially interested in stories of strong or difficult women and unexpected narratives of place, of identity, and of the shifting ways we see ourselves and each other. She's also interested in food history, wine, and dance.

Authors: Elisa Albert; Marc Bendavid; Wendy Chen; Amanda Churchill; Caroline Corrigan; Meghan Gilliss; Nicky Gonzalez; Jasmin 'Iolani Hakes; Shane Jones; Gene Kwak; Melanie LaBarge; Cory Leadbeater; Ashley Nelson Levy; Ananda Lima; Bruna Dantas Lobato; Halimah Marcus; Sabrina Orah Mark; Kelly McClorey; Joanne McNeil; Amelia Morris; Kevin Nguyen; Mary Otis; Janika Oza; Ann Packer; Andrew Palmer; Ayşegül Savaş; Elizabeth L. Silver; Talmon Joseph Smith; Lynn Steger Strong; Souvankham Thammavongsa; Vanessa Veselka; Hope Wabuke; Jenny Xie

L074 Samantha Brace
Literary Agent
United Kingdom

sbrace@pfd.co.uk

https://petersfraserdunlop.com/agent/samantha-brace/

Literary Agency: Peters Fraser + Dunlop

Fiction > *Novels*
  Book Club Fiction; Coming of Age; Crime; Family; Historical Fiction; Literary; Mystery; Psychological Suspense; Thrillers

Send: Query; Synopsis; Writing sample; Author bio
How to send: Email
How not to send: Post

I'm looking for anything a bit dark and twisty. I'm desperate for psych-suspense and thrillers with a sinister twist. I also love a mysterious family drama – weave together a moody historical setting with a few dark family secrets and I'm hooked. I also like historical fiction, coming of age stories, and literary fiction, but I always prefer a mystery at the heart. No children's, YA, fantasy, or sci-fi.

Authors: Justine Bothwick; Annette Colgan; Carol Cooper; Stephen Done; Henrietta Hamilton; Cathy Hayward; Brian Van Hise; Marianne Holmes; Evelyn Hood; Deborah Hyde; Leigh Johnstone; Mya Kwon; Ian Lewis; Carrie Maestas; Danny Noonan; Ju De Paula; John Pennington; Joshua Piercey; Rupert Potter; Cate Ray; Kerry Whittle; Agatha Zaza

L075 Bradford Literary Agency
Literary Agency
5694 Mission Center Road # 347, San Diego, CA 92108
United States
Tel: +1 (619) 521-1201

bradfordassistant@bradfordlit.com

https://bradfordlit.com

ADULT
  Fiction
    Graphic Novels: General
    Novels: Contemporary Romance; Erotic Romance; Fantasy; Historical Romance; Literary; Mystery; Romance; Romantasy; Romantic Comedy; Romantic Suspense; Science Fiction; Supernatural / Paranormal Romance; Thrillers; Upmarket Commercial Fiction; Women's Fiction
  Nonfiction > *Nonfiction Books*
    Biography; Business; Comedy / Humour; Cookery; Food; History; Memoir; Parenting; Popular Culture; Relationships; Self Help; Social Issues

CHILDREN'S > **Fiction**
  Graphic Novels; *Novels*; *Picture Books*
YOUNG ADULT > **Fiction** > *Novels*

How to send: Query Manager

Represents a wide range of fiction and nonfiction. Select a particular agent at the agency to submit to, and submit to only one agent at a time.

Literary Agents: Hannah Andrade (**L023**); Laura Bradford (**L076**); Hillary Fazzari (**L210**); Rebecca Matte (**L431**); Kaitlyn Sanchez (**L561**)

L076 Laura Bradford
Literary Agent
United States

https://bradfordlit.com/about/laura-bradford/
https://querymanager.com/query/laurabradford
http://www.twitter.com/bradfordlit

Literary Agency: Bradford Literary Agency (**L075**)
Professional Bodies: Association of American Literary Agents (AALA); Romance Writers of America (RWA); Society of Children's Book Writers and Illustrators (SCBWI)

ADULT
  Fiction
    Graphic Novels: General
    Novels: Contemporary Romance; Erotic Romance; Historical Fiction; Historical Romance; Mystery; Romance; Romantic Suspense; Speculative; Thrillers; Women's Fiction
  Nonfiction > *Nonfiction Books*

CHILDREN'S > **Fiction** > *Middle Grade*

YOUNG ADULT > **Fiction** > *Novels*

How to send: Query Manager

Interested in romance (historical, romantic suspense, category, contemporary, erotic), speculative fiction, women's fiction, mystery, thrillers, young adult, upper middle grade, illustration as well as some select non-fiction.

L077 Karen Brailsford
Consulting Agent
United States

https://aevitascreative.com/agents
https://querymanager.com/query/KarenBrailsford

Literary Agency: Aevitas

Nonfiction > *Nonfiction Books*
  Arts; Biography; Entertainment; Health; Memoir; Spirituality; Wellbeing

Send: Query; Author bio; Market info; Writing sample
How to send: Online submission system

Based in Los Angeles and is especially interested in arts and entertainment, memoir, biography, health and wellness, spirituality and works of non-fiction that inspire and shine a light on contemporary conditions.

Authors: Daniel Morain; Toluse Olorunnipa; Robert Samuels

L078 Maria Brannan
Literary Agent
United Kingdom

maria@greyhoundliterary.co.uk

https://greyhoundliterary.co.uk/agents/maria-brannan

Literary Agency: Greyhound Literary (**L278**)

ADULT
  Fiction > *Novels*
    General, and in particular: Book Club Fiction; Commercial; Fantasy; Gothic; High Concept; Horror; Romance; Romantic Comedy; Soft Science Fiction; Speculative; Thrillers; Upmarket
  Nonfiction > *Nonfiction Books*
    Biography; History; Nature; Science

NEW ADULT > **Fiction** > *Novels*
  General, and in particular: Book Club Fiction; Commercial; Fantasy; High Concept; Horror; Romance; Romantic Comedy; Soft Science Fiction; Speculative; Thrillers; Upmarket

YOUNG ADULT > **Fiction** > *Novels*
  General, and in particular: Book Club Fiction; Commercial; Fantasy; High Concept; Horror; Romance; Romantic Comedy; Soft Science Fiction; Speculative; Thrillers; Upmarket

Send: Query; Synopsis; Outline; Writing sample
How to send: Email

Has very wide ranging tastes in fiction and is interested in writing for adult, new adult/crossover and YA readers. She loves character-driven novels with a commercial bent that spark imagination or discussion and is always looking for stories that explore under-represented and diverse experiences with authenticity and sensitivity. She has a passion for genre fiction – especially all kinds of fantasy, whether that be epic, cosy, dark or romantic– that has memorable characters and vivid world-building; horror with a unique concept or perspective that can send a chill down your spine; and softer, genre-crossing science fiction that explores the experience of being human. She is also keen on voice-led and emotive reading group and upmarket fiction; love stories and rom-coms that make you fall for both the leads; unnerving, twisty crime writing; thrillers with a great hook that will leave you floored and anything with a high concept, speculative or gothic edge. On the nonfiction side, she is drawn to anything that draws the reader into the immediacy and tangibility of an author's personal experiences; history and biography that explores overlooked or underrepresented people and events; and nature and science writing that evokes fascination and wonder in the reader, books that intrigue and act as a door into underexplored or unfamiliar worlds.

Authors: Max Doty; Michael Lawson; Bonnie Quinn; C.J. Subko

L079 Hannah Brattesani
Literary Agent
United States

http://www.friedrichagency.com/about-alternate-2/

Literary Agency: The Friedrich Agency LLC (**L245**)

Fiction > *Novels*
  Arts; Comedy / Humour; Dark; Environment; Food; Horror; Literary; Upmarket

Nonfiction
  Essays: Comedy / Humour
  Nonfiction Books: Comedy / Humour; Environment; Narrative Nonfiction

Send: Query; Writing sample
How to send: In the body of an email

I'd love to see literary novels that use humor in dark and/or interesting ways, playful horror (think Grady Hendrix), smart and funny upmarket fiction, and narrative non-fiction and essay collections that can make me laugh.

L080 The Brattle Agency LLC
Literary Agency
PO Box 380537, Cambridge, MA 02238
United States

submissions@thebrattleagency.com

https://thebrattleagency.com

Fiction
  Graphic Novels: General
  Novels: Literary

Nonfiction > *Nonfiction Books*
  American History; Art History; Culture; European History; Music; Politics; Sport

Closed to approaches.

Accepts submissions only during one-month reading periods. See website for details.

L081 Amy Brewer
Senior Agent
United States

https://www.metamorphosisliteraryagency.com/about
https://querymanager.com/query/1379

Literary Agency: Metamorphosis Literary Agency (**L444**)

Fiction > *Novels*
  General, and in particular: Book Club Fiction; Comedy / Humour; LGBTQIA; Romance; Women's Fiction

Closed to approaches.

For the last few years, she has been learning all she can about social media optimization and platform building in the publishing industry.

Her experience in the mental health field and yoga training help her guide and assist clients with stress and anxiety in this highly competitive industry.

L082 The Bright Agency (UK)
Literary Agency
103-105 St John's Hill, London, SW11 1SY
United Kingdom
Tel: +44 (0) 20 7326 9140

mail@thebrightagency.com
literarysubmissions@thebrightagency.com

https://thebrightagency.com
https://thebrightagency.com/uk/submissions/new

Media Company: The Bright Group International Limited
Professional Body: The Association of Authors' Agents (AAA)

CHILDREN'S
  Fiction
    Chapter Books; *Graphic Novels*; *Middle Grade*; *Picture Books*
  Nonfiction > *Nonfiction Books*

Send: Query; Synopsis; Writing sample
How to send: Email

We love seeing new work, and we'd love to see yours. Talent is exciting, and when you help it grow, it's incredible. We're proud of our ability to discover and establish new artists and authors. We're also proud that we still represent people who were with us when we first opened, and who've truly bloomed over the years. Could you be next?

L083 The Bright Agency (US)
Literary Agency
157 – A First Street, C/O – Bright Group US Inc #339, Jersey City, NJ 07302
United States
Tel: +1 (646) 525 9040

mail@thebrightagency.com
literarysubmissions@thebrightagency.com

https://thebrightagency.com
https://thebrightagency.com/us/submissions/new

Media Company: The Bright Group International Limited

CHILDREN'S
  Fiction
    Chapter Books; *Graphic Novels*; *Middle Grade*; *Picture Books*
  Nonfiction > *Nonfiction Books*

Send: Query; Synopsis; Writing sample
How to send: Email

We love seeing new work, and we'd love to see yours. Talent is exciting, and when you help it grow, it's incredible. We're proud of our ability to discover and establish new artists and authors. We're also proud that we still represent people who were with us when first opened, and who've truly bloomed over the years. Could you be next?

L084 Savannah Brooks
Literary Agent
United States

https://www.sblitagent.com
https://ktliterary.com/about/
https://twitter.com/SBLitAgent
https://querymanager.com/query/1346

Literary Agency: KT Literary (**L377**)

ADULT > **Fiction** > *Short Fiction Collections*
  Contemporary; Horror; Mystery; Romantic Comedy; Speculative; Suspense; Thrillers
CHILDREN'S > **Fiction**
  Chapter Books; *Middle Grade*; *Picture Books*
YOUNG ADULT
  Fiction > *Novels*
  Nonfiction > *Nonfiction Books*

Closed to approaches.

Represents all of kid lit and adult contemporary and spec fiction, romcoms, thrillers/mystery/suspense, and horror. She's especially interested in stories that teach her something new, add to a larger sociopolitical conversation, and highlight underrepresented identities and cultures.

L085 Brotherstone Creative Management
Literary Agency
Mortimer House, 37-41 Mortimer Street, London, W1T 3JH
United Kingdom

submissions@bcm-agency.com
info@bcm-agency.com

http://bcm-agency.com

Fiction > *Novels*
  Commercial; Literary
Nonfiction > *Nonfiction Books*

Send: Query; Writing sample; Synopsis
How to send: Email

Always on the search for talented new writers. Send query by email. For fiction, include the first three chapters or 50 pages and 2-page synopsis. For nonfiction, include detailed outline and sample chapter. No children's and young adult fiction, sci-fi and fantasy novels or unsolicited short story and poetry collections, or scripts.

Senior Agent / Vice President: Charlie Brotherstone (**L086**)

L086 Charlie Brotherstone
Senior Agent; Vice President
United Kingdom

https://charliebrotherstone.com
https://www.aevitascreative.com/agent/charlie-brotherstone
https://bcm-agency.com/about/

Literary Agencies: Aevitas Creative Management (ACM) UK (**L007**); Brotherstone Creative Management (**L085**)

Fiction > *Novels*
  Commercial; Literary
Nonfiction > *Nonfiction Books*

Represents an eclectic list of authors, from academics, journalists, musicians, online creators and food writers, through to novelists of commercial and literary fiction and including numerous New York Times and Sunday Times bestsellers.

Authors: Luke Agbaimoni; Susie Alegre; Rahaman Ali; Anthea Allen; Brett Anderson; Lopè Ariyo; Stephen Bayley; Osei Bonsu; Will Bowlby; Clerkenwell Boy; Will Brooker; Ian Broudie; Hannah Che; Tiffany Chen; Chris Clarke; Clare Clarke; Lauren Cochrane; Jacob Dunne; Mark Eglinton; Tracey Emerson; James Evans; Tom Fletcher; Natasha Fraser-Cavassoni; Flora Gill; Ed Gillett; Matthew Goodwin; Carrie Grant; David Grant; Gabrielle Hales; Kim-Julie Hansen; Reiko Hashimoto; Sharon Hendry; Jessica Hepburn; Dan Hicks; Fred Hogge; Kirstin Innes; Farah Karim-Cooper; Atul Kochhar; Sam Lee; Marianna Leivaditaki; Simon Lister; Roger Mavity; Elly McCausland; Joanne Molinaro; Nathan Newman; George The Poet; The Ritz; Chia WoonHeng; Ben Wright

L087 Justin Brouckaert
Literary Agent
New York
United States

https://aevitascreative.com/agents/
https://querymanager.com/query/justinbrouckaert

Literary Agency: Aevitas

Nonfiction > *Nonfiction Books*
  Current Affairs; History; Internet Culture; Narrative Nonfiction; Politics; Science; Sport

Send: Author bio; Outline; Market info; Writing sample
How to send: Query Manager

Actively seeking narrative nonfiction in the areas of history, current affairs, sports, internet culture, politics, and science.

Authors: Char Adams; Lauren Aguirre; Matthew H. Birkhold; Greg Bluestein; Diane Cardwell; Jesselyn Cook; Susan Crawford; R.S. Deeren; Benoit Denizet-Lewis; William Deverell; Rebekah Diamond; Ali Drucker; Brian Dumaine; Ken Ellingwood; Neal E. Fischer; Marisa Franco; Sarah Gearhart; Jeffrey Gettleman; Noah Gittell; Wade Graham; Gabrielle Hartley; Jesse Horwitz; Chris Koslowski; Jacqui Lewis; Joshua Mendelsohn; Joe Milan; Luma Mufleh; Shoshi

Parks; Pamela Pavliscak; Lindsay Powers; Julian Sancton; Amber Share; Meg Vondriska; Evan Waite; Bryan Walsh; Ali Marie Watkins

L088 Megan Brown
Literary Agent
United States

jsanders@stevelaube.com

https://stevelaube.com/what-im-looking-for-megan-brown/

Literary Agency: The Steve Laube Agency

Nonfiction
  Nonfiction Books: Bible Studies; Christian Living; Christianity; Evangelism; Family; Military; Spirituality
  Reference: Christianity

Send: Proposal
How to send: Email

I am interested in nonfiction books. Specifically, I am most excited about pursuing projects in Bible study, reference, theology, Christian living and devotionals, spiritual formation, the integration of work and faith, marriage and family, church life, ministry, leadership, evangelism, and missions.

L089 Browne & Miller Literary Associates
Literary Agency
United States

mail@browneandmiller.com

https://www.browneandmiller.com
https://www.facebook.com/browneandmiller
https://twitter.com/BrowneandMiller

Fiction > *Novels*: Commercial

Nonfiction > *Nonfiction Books*: Commercial

Closed to approaches.

Handles books for the adult commercial book markets. No children's, young adult, science fiction, fantasy, horror, short stories, poetry, screenplays, or academic works. Send query only by email. No attachments.

Literary Agent: Danielle Egan-Miller

L090 Chris Bucci
Senior Agent
New York
United States

https://aevitascreative.com/agents/

Literary Agency: Aevitas

Fiction > *Novels*
  Commercial; Historical Fiction; History; Literary; Mystery; Popular Culture; Popular Science; Thrillers

Nonfiction > *Nonfiction Books*
  Narrative Nonfiction; Politics; Sport

Send: Author bio; Outline; Market info; Writing sample
How to send: Online submission system

Based in the New York Metropolitan area. Represents a broad range of fiction and nonfiction.

Authors: Amina Akhtar; John Allore; Isa Arsén; Timothy Caulfield; Kendra Coulter; Christine Estima; Kelly J. Ford; Jennifer Heisz; Amy Jones; John Kenney; Jessica McDiarmid; Briana Una McGuckin; Jane McManus; Tara Moss; Eliza Nellums; Kelsey Ronan; Kathryn Schmitz; Emily Schultz; Kavin Senapathy; P.J. Vernon; Tessa Wegert

L091 Louise Buckley
Literary Agent
United Kingdom

http://zenoagency.com
https://hs-la.com/louise-buckley/
https://twitter.com/LouiseMBuckley
https://www.instagram.com/louise_buckley_literary_agent

Literary Agency: Hannah Sheppard Literary Agency (**L291**)

Fiction > *Novels*
  Book Club Fiction; Commercial; Contemporary; Cozy Fantasy; Cozy Mysteries; Crime; Dark Academia; Disabilities; Gothic; Historical Fiction; Horror; Literary; Magic; Supernatural / Paranormal; Thrillers; Upmarket; Witches

Nonfiction > *Nonfiction Books*
  Motherhood; Neuroscience; Science

Closed to approaches.

I like literary and book-club novels that focus on the underdog, the repressed, the suppressed, especially novels that represent working-class people or children going through difficult circumstances. I am known for representing Irish literary and book-club fiction and I would very much welcome submissions from Irish authors writing upmarket fiction featuring characters that I can't help but root for. I would LOVE to see some cosy fantasy. Think witches, magical bookshops, talking cats. I am a big crime and thriller fan and welcome submissions in this area. At the moment I am especially enjoying reading cosy or humorous crime. I would love to see some dark academia. More generally, I would also love to see novels with a disabled protagonist or someone (like me) who is living with an invisible disability. In non-fiction, I would love to see any submissions that focus on motherhood, especially through the lens of a scientific or neurological perspective.

Authors: Anne Griffin; Jenni Keer; Katie Lumsden; Fíona Scarlett; Anniki Sommerville; Andrew Stevens; Claire Wright

L092 Danielle Bukowski
Literary Agent
United States

https://www.sll.com/our-team

Literary Agency: Sterling Lord Literistic, Inc. (**L597**)

Fiction > *Novels*

Nonfiction > *Nonfiction Books*

Send: Query; Synopsis; Writing sample
How to send: Online submission system

Represents fiction for adults, from smart bookclub to literary, and select nonfiction, Particularly looking for narratives from writers traditionally excluded from the publishing industry. For fiction, she likes books that balance plot with voice, have a strong sense of place, a unique hook, and are stylistically bold; for nonfiction, she's looking for work grounded in the author's personal interest, rigorously reported and researched, and will expand the reader's view of the world.

L093 Kate Burke
Senior Agent
United Kingdom

kate@blakefriedmann.co.uk

http://blakefriedmann.co.uk/kate-burke
https://twitter.com/kbbooks

Literary Agency: Blake Friedmann Literary Agency Ltd (**L066**)

Fiction > *Novels*
  Book Club Women's Fiction; Contemporary; Crime; Dark; Family; Gothic; High Concept Thrillers; Historical Fiction; Mystery; Thrillers; Women's Fiction

Does not want:

> **Fiction** > *Novels*
>   Political Thrillers; Spy Thrilllers

Send: Query; Synopsis; Writing sample
How to send: Word file email attachment

My list is made up of everything I like to read – gripping fiction featuring characters you can't get enough of and whom you don't want to part with at the end of a novel. I love dark stories but also uplifting love stories, too, and I'm keen to find more stories set in unusual or far-flung places. I love to learn more about a place and its inhabitants as I think fiction is all about escapism!

In terms of what I'm looking for: on the crime side, I love dark thrillers that keep me turning the page long into the night and that surprise me with plot twists and interesting narrative structures; crime series featuring new and fresh lead investigators; high-concept thrillers (contemporary or historical) that have a 'what if?' plot structure and say something about our society now or then.

On the historical fiction side, I love stories which combine a great sense of place and time (ideally, post-1800, please) with a mystery. I'm also a huge fan of anything set in a spooky old house so Gothic, atmospheric historical thrillers are also top of my wishlist!

Contemporary-wise, I love novels which have a discussable issue at their heart – and could work well for a heated book club discussion – as well as sweeping family stories about mothers, sisters and daughters (set anywhere in the world).

In case it's helpful to know what I don't represent: non-fiction, children's and young adult books, science fiction, fantasy, spy, conspiracy or political thrillers.

Authors: Nikki Allen; Dani Atkins; Johanna Bell; Scarlett Brade; Andy Briggs; Emma Cowell; Will Dean; Paul Finch; Fiona Ford; Jean Fullerton; John Kennedy; Caroline Khoury; Sarah Lee; Beryl Matthews; Lia Middleton; Sara Ochs; Allie Reynolds; Kate Thompson; Mary Torjussen; Hannah Treave; John Trenhaile; Anne-Marie Varga; Luca Veste

L094 Camille Burns
Literary Agent
United Kingdom

https://dkwlitagency.co.uk
https://dkwlitagency.co.uk/agents/
https://querymanager.com/query/Camille

Literary Agency: Diamond Kahn and Woods (DKW) Literary Agency Ltd

ADULT
  Fiction > *Novels*
    Fantasy; Historical Fiction; Romance; Speculative
  Nonfiction > *Nonfiction Books*: Culture

CHILDREN'S
  Fiction > *Middle Grade*
  Nonfiction > *Nonfiction Books*: Culture

YOUNG ADULT > **Fiction** > *Novels*
  General, and in particular: Romance

Closed to approaches.

In MG, I am drawn to stories with lots of heart and written in a lyrical tone which convey a sense of wonder and warmth, and which would not be amiss as a modern classic. I am also very keen to see stories that hover on the cusp between MG and teen, with darker themes and complex plotting, particularly when combined with action-packed sequences and acerbic wit. In YA, I'm open to seeing all genres, whether literary or commercial, but tend to be drawn to stories with a strong romantic component. I'm also keen to see stories with a strong cast of characters, which encapsulate the thrill, angst and drama of growing up. I am on the lookout for a select few adult fiction projects, particularly romance, fantasy, speculative or historical fiction. I would also love to see proposals for smart and accessible non-fiction (children's or adult) which teach us about the world we live in, which shine a light on a culture (including workplace culture etc), which are empowering, or which encourage deep thinking and fundamental shifts in perspective.

L095 Kate Bussert
Literary Agent

Literary Agency: Bret Adams Ltd

L096 C&W (Conville & Walsh)
Literary Agency
Cunard House, 15 Regent Street, London, SW1Y 4LR
United Kingdom
Tel: +44 (0) 20 7393 4200

https://cwagency.co.uk
https://twitter.com/cwagencyuk
https://instagram.com/cwagencyuk

Professional Body: The Association of Authors' Agents (AAA)

ADULT
  Fiction > *Novels*
  Nonfiction > *Nonfiction Books*

CHILDREN'S > **Fiction** > *Novels*

YOUNG ADULT > **Fiction** > *Novels*

Send: Query; Synopsis; Writing sample; Proposal; Author bio; Market info; Outline
How to send: Word file email attachment

See website for agent profiles and submit to one particular agent only. Send submissions by email as Word files only. No postal submissions. For fiction, submit the first three sample chapters of the completed manuscript (or about 50 pages) with a synopsis. For nonfiction, send 30-page proposal. No poetry or scripts, or picture books. See website for full guidelines.

Author / Literary Agent: Catherine Cho (**L124**)

Author Estate: The Estate of Francis Bacon

Authors: Naoko Abe; Gaar Adams; Gwen Adshead; Shahnaz Ahsan; Nigel Akehurst; Dolly Alderton; Keir Alexander; Piers Alexander; G V Anderson; Claire Anderson-Wheeler; Karen Angelico; Robin Antalek; Ollie Aplin; Steven Appleby; Luke Arnold; Will Ashon; Stephen Baker; Lisa Ballantyne; Damian Barr; Tony Barrell; Colin Barrett; Kevin Barry; Neil Bartlett; Sara Baume; Richard Beard; Francesca Beauman; Matt Beaumont; Greta Bellamacina; Leo Benedictus; Patrick Benson; Mandy Berriman; Michael Bhaskar; Nicholas Binge; James Birch; Vanessa Black; Emma Blackery; Immodesty Blaize; David Bodanis; Lee Bofkin; Charlotte Bond; Simon van Booy; Hannah Bourne-Taylor; Megan Bradbury; John Bradshaw; Kevin Breathnach; Michael Brooks; Mike Brooks; Iain Broome; The Wild Swimming Brothers; Dea Brovig; Bill Browder; Louisa Buck; Tom Burgis; Letty Butler; Jo Callaghan; Rachel Campbell-Johnston; Joanna Cannon; Holly Cave; Eliza Chan; Tim Clare; Maxine Beneba Clarke; Roger Clarke; Daniel Cole; Jennifer Coolidge; Yvette Cooper; Caroline Crampton; Marianne Cronin; Fiona Cummins; Howard Cunnell; Miriam Darlington; Katie Davies; Lara Dearman; Stephen Deas; Claire Dederer; Juano Diaz; Chris Difford; Rory Dunlop; Katherine Dunn; Peter Dunne; Hiron Ennes; Allie Esiri; Penelope Farmer; Rebecca Ferrier; Nathan Filer; Grace Flahive; Cal Flyn; Julia Forster; Sam Fowles; Karrie Fransman; Sara Freeman; Esther Freud; Gabriel Gbadamosi; Karl Geary; Jasper Gibson; Ruth Gilligan; Joanna Glen; Misha Glenny; A.J. Gnuse; Colin Grant; Jules Grant; Anne Griffin; Guy Gunaratne; Kirsty Gunn; Katie Gutierrez; Matt Haig; Lori Inglis Hall; Karen Hamilton; Lou Hamilton; James Hannah; Debora Harding; Lindsay Hawdon; Miranda Cowley Heller; Alexandra Heminsley; Julietta Henderson; Adam Higginbotham; Matt Rowland Hill; Michael Hodges; Antonia Hodgson; Merlin Holland; J.M. Holmes; Eileen Horne; Emily Howes; Dave Hutchinson; Crystal Jeans; Luke Jones; Rob Lloyd Jones; Rachel Joyce; Sadakat Kadri; Abraham Kawa; David Keenan; Nicola Kelly; Stephen Kelman; Amana Fontanella Khan; Jess Kidd; Olivia Kiernan; Justine Kilkerr; Rosie Kinchen; Annie Kirby; Jasmin Kirkbride; Katie Kitamura; Gerad Kite; Harriet Kline; Claire Kohda; Oliver K. Langmead; Martin Latham; Persia Lawson; Rebecca Ley; Hannah Little; P J Lynch; Celia Lyttelton; Caroline Mackenzie; Will Maclean; Katy Mahood; Tim Major; Shiv Malik; Mohale Mashigo; Robert McCrum; Ed McDonald; Charlotte McDonald-Gibson; C.E. McGill; Sam Mckechnie; Anna Mill; Harland Miller; Juli Min; Emmett de Monterey; Priscilla Morris; Nicola Mostyn; Joshua Mowll; Robert Muir-Wood; Simon Mundy; Nadia Murad; Ramita Navai; Tom Newlands; Louise Newson; Hollie Newton; Juliet Nicolson; Charlotte Northedge; Marcus O'Dair; Lisa O'Donnell; Nathan Oates; Tobi Ogundiran; Elizabeth Oldfield; Orla Owen; Sydney Padua; Kit Peel; Megan Peel; Ely Percy; Jo Piazza; DBC Pierre; Dan M Pinchbeck; Jon Plackett; Gareth L Powell; Huw Powell; Charlene Prempeh; Laura Price; Christine Pride; Elizabeth Prochaska; Jamie Quatro; Joanne Ramos; Ben Rawlence; Paula Rawsthorne; Ebony Reid; CE Riley; Catherine Riley; I. D. Roberts; Sophy Roberts; Al Robertson; Callum Robinson; Lydia Ruffles; Alison Rumfitt; Rhik Samadder; Polly Samson; David Savill; Jamie Sawyer; E. Saxey; Fíona Scarlett; Luke Scull; Yasmine Seale; Holly Seddon; Mike Shackle; Priya Sharma; Tali Sharot; Ali Shaw; Kim Sherwood; Gail Simmons; Lemn Sissay; Richard Skinner; Sofia Slater; Jean Smith;

Nikki Smith; Natasha Solomons; Alex South; Tim Spector; M L Stedman; Michelle Sterling; Michelle Min Sterling; Mark Stevens; Mustafa Suleyman; Annalyn Swan; Simon Sylvester; Natalia Theodoridou; Michelle Thomas; Lara Thompson; Tade Thompson; Nafissa Thomson-Spires; Piers Torday; Pádraig Ó Tuama; Jane Turner; Jon Lys Turner; Emma Jane Unsworth; Laura Vaughan; Steve Voake; Harriet Vyner; Tash Walker; Max Wallis; Amanda Eyre Ward; Christie Watson; S J Watson; Jonathan Watts; Adam Weymouth; Rebecca Whitney; Zoe Williams; Antoine Wilson; Ben Wilson; Robert Wilton; Alice Winn; Matt Wixey; Tod Wodicka; Isabel Wolff; Marian Womack; Olivia Wood; Jo Browning Wroe; Simon Wroe; Eris Young; Osman Yousefzada; George Zarkadakis; Adam Zmith

Literary Agents: Susan Armstrong (**L032**); Matilda Ayris; Kate Burton; Alexander Cochran (**L130**); Clare Conville (**L137**); Allison DeFrees; Emma Finn; Carrie Kania; Sophie Lambert (**L380**); Lucy Luck; Richard Pike; Jake Smith-Bosanquet

L097 CAA (Creative Artists Agency, LLC)

Literary Agency
2000 Avenue of the Stars, Los Angeles, CA 90067, 405 Lexington Avenue, 22nd Floor, New York, NY 10174
United States
Tel: +1 (424) 288-2000
Fax: +1 (424) 288-2900

https://www.caa.com

Literary Agency: CAA (London) (**L098**)

Literary Agent: Cindy Uh

L098 CAA (London)

Literary Agency
United Kingdom

https://www.caa.com
https://www.caa.com/entertainmenttalent/publishing

Literary Agency: CAA (Creative Artists Agency, LLC) (**L097**)
Professional Body: The Association of Authors' Agents (AAA)

ADULT
  Fiction > *Novels*
  Nonfiction > *Nonfiction Books*
CHILDREN'S > **Fiction** > *Picture Books*

Represents award-winning and bestselling storytellers across a wide range of disciplines. Our authors include media personalities, musicians, actors, political figures, trendsetters, and more. We take an active role in every step of the book process, from developing the concept to amplifying author platforms and launching industry-leading book tours.

L099 Charlie Campbell

Literary Agent
United Kingdom

charlie@greyhoundliterary.co.uk

https://greyhoundliterary.co.uk/agent/charlie-campbell/
https://twitter.com/ScapegoatCC

Literary Agency: Greyhound Literary (**L278**)

Fiction > *Novels*
  Commercial; Crime; Literary; Thrillers

Nonfiction > *Nonfiction Books*
  Commercial; Economics; Literary; Sport; Travel

Send: Query; Synopsis; Writing sample
How to send: Email

Represents a wide range of fiction and non-fiction, both literary and commercial. He is looking for original work and to build long-lasting and significant careers for his clients.

Authors: Guy Adams; K Anis Ahmed; Tanya Aldred; Becky Alexander; Moeen Ali; Victoria Belim; SJ Bennett; Edward Brooke-Hitching; Andy Bull; Jen Campbell; Bonnie Chung; David Collins; Zoë Colville; Duncan Crowe; Iain Dey; Chris Dodd; Adam Fergusson; Jamie Fewery; Rebecca Front; Tom Gabbay; Ian Garner; Julian Gough; David Higgins; Will Hill; Thomas W. Hodgkinson; Nicholas Hogg; Iain Hollingshead; Andrew Hosken; Simon Jones; Paul Levy; Bonnie MacBird; Shingi Mararike; Katie Marsh; Hugh Matheson; Neil McCormick; Anthony McGowan; Barry McKinley; Moin Mir; Anton Mosimann; Rebecca Myers; James Peak; Edvard Radzinsky; Sue Ransom; Amy Raphael; Andrea Stuart; Jo Thompson; Tom Tivnan; Hana Videen; Kate Vigurs; Wendy Wason; Sioned Wiliam; Mike Woodhouse

L100 Vanessa Campos

Literary Agent
United States

Vanessa@d4eo.com

https://www.d4eoliteraryagency.com/p/vanessa-campos.html
https://querymanager.com/query/Vanessa_Reads
https://twitter.com/VanessaShares

Literary Agency: D4EO Literary Agency

Nonfiction > *Nonfiction Books*
  Business; Entrepreneurship; Self Help

Send: Outline; Table of Contents; Writing sample; Marketing Plan
How to send: Query Manager

Looking to help bring more diverse voices to the business, entrepreneurship, and self-help publishing space.

L101 Canterbury Literary Agency

Literary Agency
43 Nunnery Fields, Canterbury, Kent, CT1 3JT
United Kingdom
Tel: +44 (0) 7947 827860

francesca@canterburyliteraryagency.com

http://www.canterburyliteraryagency.com

Fiction > *Novels*

Nonfiction > *Nonfiction Books*
  Autobiography; Biography; Women's Interests

"We are based in the UK, and actively welcome submissions from writers based in the United States and Canada. We sell to publishers in the UK an in the United States and Canada, and we sell translation rights worldwide.

Founded in 2011, we pride ourselves on being a literary agency devoted to the needs of writers. We welcome all kinds of submissions, including fiction, non-fiction, memoirs, collections of short stories and collections of poems. Our aim is to respond to all submissions in no more than two weeks. We will do all we can to give you the best chance of a literary career.

We believe in transparency and friendliness and we realise that, as a writer trying to get your literary career started, you may often feel the literary world is not very friendly to you; we will be friendly and positive and will do all we can to help you.

Also, we will get back to you. At a time when you are more likely to get an email reply from Charles Dickens than from most literary agencies, we aim to get back to you within two weeks. We reply to ALL emails we receive.

We are very well connected with publishers, we understand what needs to happen with a book to take it from a draft stage to being accepted by a publisher and we spare no effort for our writer clients."

Writers should be aware that there seems to a be a strong connection between this agency and The Conrad Press, a fee-charging publishing service. Listings for both were submitted within 17 minutes of each other at around 1am of the same morning, and their logos are almost identical. The postal address provided for this agency is the same address as was originally provided for The Conrad Press (which has subsequently been changed).

The agency website states that Francesca Garratt carries out editing work for The Conrad Press, and the other agent, Helen Komatsu, is listed as an editor at Conrad Press on her LinkedIn profile.

Oddly, her profile makes no mention of being a literary agent (at this agency or otherwise), despite apparently having been involved with the agency since 2011 and her LinkedIn profile containing changes as recent as 2018, when she became an editor at Conrad Press. The agency website describes her as "a highly experienced writer and literary agent", who "has been involved with the publishing industry for more than twenty years", however her LinkedIn profile lists only PR and marketing roles prior to becoming an editor with Conrad Press in 2018. The majority of that time (over 22 years) was spent in a marketing role working for a PR firm operated by the same person who now runs Conrad Press.

A post-pandemic interview with Helen Komatsu where she discusses her past and present career also fails to make any mention of work as a literary agent (https://www.careershifters.org/success-stories/from-business-owner-to-portfolio-career).

The agency website states that she is a published author, "having written books for the Financial Times organisation, Pearson and Reuters and other well-respected publishing houses", however searches on Amazon return no results for her name. She may, of course, have published under a different name.

Given the close connection between this agency and The Conrad Press, writers should be aware of the possibility that this agency may simply be a front for The Conrad Press, intended to generate customers for their publishing services.

Writers should also note that the agency states that "Our authors prefer us to keep their names confidential". This is highly irregular and raises red flags. Agencies routinely publish lists of their clients and authors appreciate publicity. If the agency has been in operation since 2011 you would expect them to have a number of clients, and the idea that every single one of those clients would want to have their association with this agency kept secret for some reason is both hard to believe, and, if true, suspicious in itself.

In light of these concerns, we would advise against approaching this agency.

Update: *On April 2, 2023, we were contacted by James Essinger, the person who runs Conrad Press, who asked us to include the following clarification: "Helen Komatsu co-authored several books with me some years ago when her name was Helen Wylie. Here is one: https://www.amazon.com/Seven-Deadly-Skills-Competing/dp/1861523742/ref=sr_1_1?crid=3Q3ZPTPTYQ5&keywords=Essinger+Wylie&qid=1680394116&sprefix=essinger+wylie%2Caps%2C173&sr=8-1"*

L102 Victoria Cappello
Literary Agent; Vice President
United States

Literary Agency: The Bent Agency (**L058**)

Closed to approaches.

L103 Alice Caprio
Literary Agent
United Kingdom

https://felicitybryan.com/fba-agent/alice-caprio/

Literary Agency: Felicity Bryan Associates (**L215**)

ADULT > **Fiction** > *Novels*
Book Club Fiction; Commercial; Fantasy; High Concept; Romance

CHILDREN'S > **Fiction** > *Middle Grade*
General, and in particular: Adventure; Fantasy; Romance

YOUNG ADULT > **Fiction** > *Novels*
General, and in particular: Fantasy; Romance

Does not want:

> **CHILDREN'S** > **Fiction** > *Middle Grade*
> Hard Science Fiction; High / Epic Fantasy
>
> **YOUNG ADULT** > **Fiction** > *Novels*
> Hard Science Fiction; High / Epic Fantasy

Send: Query; Synopsis; Writing sample
How to send: Online submission system

I am actively building a list that spans middle grade and YA fiction across all genres, commercial adult fiction, and romance and fantasy for all ages. I am on the hunt for stories that are smart, commercial and bold; books with fresh and exciting concepts whose voices can cross borders and speak out about important topics in an accessible and authentic manner. In YA, I'm open to all genres and particularly interested in character-driven stories with lively storytelling, a strong emotional core and attention-grabbing premises. On the adult side, I am looking for page-turning fiction with irresistible characters and a strong hook, from commercial to book club fiction. I am also open to working with authors within the romance and fantasy genres who have previously self-published, particularly if they have a TikTok or online presence. I'm not the best agent for hard sci-fi and hefty epic/military fantasy with multiple-POVs. I'm not open to picture books and illustrated fiction.

Authors: Amelia Giudici; Elian J Morgan; Bill Wood

L104 Elise Capron
Literary Agent
United States

https://dijkstraagency.com/agent-page.php?agent_id=Capron
https://querymanager.com/query/DijkstraCapron

Literary Agency: Sandra Dijkstra Literary Agency

Fiction > *Novels:* Literary

Nonfiction > *Nonfiction Books*
Culture; History; Memoir; Narrative Nonfiction; Science

How to send: Query Manager; By referral

Most interested in well-written narrative non-fiction (particularly trade-friendly history, cultural studies, and science) as well as character-driven literary fiction. While she will consider memoir, please note that she is very selective in this genre.

L105 Carol Mann Agency
Literary Agency
New York, NY
United States
Tel: +1 (212) 206-5635

submissions@carolmannagency.com

https://www.carolmannagency.com

Send: Query; Author bio; Writing sample
How to send: In the body of an email
How not to send: Email attachment; Post; Phone

Send query by email only, including synopsis, brief bio, and first 25 pages, all pasted into the body of your email. No attachments. No submissions by post, or phone calls. Allow 3-4 weeks for response.

Authors: Jane Alexander; Clifton Hoodl Maria Goodavage; Rachel Kelly

Literary Agents: Gareth Esersky; Carol Mann; Joanne Wyckoff

L106 Caroline Sheldon Literary Agency
Literary Agency
71 Hillgate Place, London, W8 7SS
United Kingdom
Tel: +44 (0) 20 7727 9102

info@carolinesheldon.co.uk

https://www.carolinesheldon.co.uk

Literary Agency: Rogers, Coleridge & White Ltd (**L546**)

ADULT > **Fiction** > *Novels*

CHILDREN'S > **Fiction**
Board Books; Chapter Books; Early Readers; Middle Grade; Novels; Picture Books

Closed to approaches.

Interested in fiction and all types of children's books. Send query by email only, addressed to appropriate agent. Do not send submissions to their individual email addresses.

Literary Agent: Caroline Sheldon

L107 Carolyn Jenks Agency
Literary Agency
30 Cambridge Park Drive, #5115, Cambridge, MA 02140
United States

https://www.carolynjenksagency.com
https://www.facebook.com/carolynjenksagency
https://twitter.com/TheJenksAgency

Company Director / Literary Agent: Carolyn Jenks

Literary Agents: Kwaku Acheampong (**L004**); Becca Crandall (**L142**)

L108 Jamie Carr
Literary Agent
United States

http://www.thebookgroup.com/jamie-carr

Literary Agency: The Book Group

Fiction > *Novels*
  Commercial Women's Fiction; Literary; Upmarket Commercial Fiction

Nonfiction > *Nonfiction Books*
  Culture; Finance; Food; Journalism; Judaism; Millennial; Narrative Nonfiction

Send: Query; Writing sample
How to send: In the body of an email

Represents novelists, short story writers, journalists, activists, and food and culture writers. Most interested in adult literary and upmarket commercial fiction and narrative nonfiction, she is drawn to writing that is voice-driven, highly transporting, from unique perspectives and marginalized voices, and that seeks to disrupt or reframe what appears to be known.

Authors: Isabel Banta; Nishant Batsha; Suhaly Bautista-Carolina; Wendy Chin-Tanner; Tiana Clark; Tracy Clark-Flory; Chloe Cole; Ella Dawson; Kimberly Drew; Susie Dumond; Lacey Dunham; Lauren Green; Taylor Hahn; Amanda Holden; Alex Hoopes; Melissa Larsen; Ashton Lattimore; Esther Levy-Chehebar; Vanessa Lillie; Kristen Martin; Laura McKowen; Abi Morgan; Ava Robinson; Victoria Savanh; Sophia Shalmiyev; Rainesford Stauffer; Elissa Strauss; Noor Tagouri; Zahra Tangorra; Rachel Zarrow

L109 Michael Carr
Literary Agent
United States

http://www.veritasliterary.com
https://querymanager.com/query/MichaelCarr

Literary Agency: Veritas Literary Agency

Fiction > *Novels*
  Fantasy; Historical Fiction; Science Fiction; Women's Fiction

Nonfiction > *Nonfiction Books*

Send: Query; Writing sample
How to send: Query Manager

L110 Megan Carroll
Literary Agent
United Kingdom

https://www.watsonlittle.com/agent/megan-carroll/
https://twitter.com/MeganACarroll

Literary Agency: Watson, Little Ltd (**L647**)

ADULT > **Fiction** > *Novels*
  Book Club Fiction; Coming of Age; Commercial; Contemporary; Dark Humour; Family; High Concept; Romance; Romantasy; Upmarket Romance; Upmarket

CHILDREN'S
  Fiction > *Middle Grade*
    Adventure; Comedy / Humour; Contemporary; Fantasy

  Nonfiction > *Nonfiction Books*

YOUNG ADULT > **Fiction** > *Novels*
  Book Club Fiction; Comedy / Humour; Commercial; Contemporary; High / Epic Fantasy; Horror; Romance; Romantasy; Thrillers; Upmarket Romance

Send: Query; Synopsis; Writing sample
How to send: Word file email attachment
How not to send: PDF file email attachment

Keen to see all kinds of love stories from the very commercial through to upmarket/reading group for adults and YA readers, both contemporary and in the 'romantasy' space. She'd especially love to see those familiar romance tropes – enemies to lovers, friends to lovers, love triangles, forbidden love etc. – with underrepresented characters at the centre. Also actively looking for upmarket fiction and would love to see high concept love stories, layered family drama, coming of age narratives, contemporary stories about life today and darkly comic novels that explore a specific time, place or experience. In YA, she is keen to see contemporary stories with humour, and romance at the heart – fun and emotional novels that appeal to the interests and issues of the teenage readers. She'd also love to see thrillers and horror stories for this age group too, as well as epic fantasy as long as there is a thread of romance throughout. On the younger end, she is looking for funny, contemporary middle grade and is keen to find original adventure stories in both fantasy and realistic settings.

Authors: Luci Adams; Tom Adams; Jean Adamson; Rose Alexander; Rosie Archer; Faima Bakar; Louise Soraya Black; Kay Brellend; Laura Chamberlain; Sophie Claire; Sarah J. Coleman; Tara Costello; Bryony Cousins; Alex Day; Marianne Eloise; Lauren Ford; Tessa Gibbs; Natasha Holmes; Hayley Hoskins; Elias Jahshan; Hiba Noor Khan; Mary Mackie; Lindiwe Maqhubela; Erin Murgatroyd; Grace Newman; Briana J. Newstead; Sheila Norton; Fiona O'Brien; Ben Pechey; Rhian Parry; Will Richard; Alan Robinson; Kohinoor Sahota; Tara Sexton; Pam Weaver; Jeremy Williams; Alex Woolhouse

L111 Rebecca Carter
Literary Agent
United Kingdom

https://rebeccacarterliteraryagent.wordpress.com/
https://twitter.com/RebeccasBooks

Literary Agency: Rebecca Carter Literary (**L529**)

ADULT
  Fiction > *Novels*
    Crime; Experimental

  Nonfiction > *Nonfiction Books*
    Biography; Creative Nonfiction; Cultural Commentary; Design; Environment; History; Memoir; Politics; Social Commentary; Technology; Travel

CHILDREN'S
  Fiction > *Novels*
  Nonfiction > *Nonfiction Books*

L112 Claire Cartey
Literary Agent
United Kingdom

claire@holroydecartey.com

https://www.holroydecartey.com/about.html
https://www.holroydecartey.com/submissions.html

Literary Agency: Holroyde Cartey

CHILDREN'S
  Fiction
    Novels; *Picture Books*
  Nonfiction > *Nonfiction Books*

Send: Synopsis; Full text
How to send: Email attachment

I have worked in children's publishing for over twenty years as Art Director at Hodder Children's Books and in design for Random House. I am looking for author and illustrator proposals for picture books, young fiction and non-fiction. In illustration I'm also looking for creative brand building potential in markets outside of publishing.

L113 Robert Caskie
Literary Agent
United Kingdom

robert@robertcaskie.com
submissions@robertcaskie.com

https://www.robertcaskie.com
https://twitter.com/rcaskie1

Literary Agency: Robert Caskie Ltd

Fiction > *Novels*
Book Club Fiction; Commercial; Literary

Nonfiction > *Nonfiction Books*
Memoir; Narrative Nonfiction; Nature; Politics; Social Issues

Send: Query; Writing sample; Proposal
How to send: Email

Interested in fiction and nonfiction writing that stimulates debate, comments on the world around us, and invokes an emotional response. Currently closed to fiction submissions, but still welcomes nonfiction submissions.

L114 Claire Cavanagh

Assistant Agent
Canada

https://www.therightsfactory.com
https://www.therightsfactory.com/Agents/claire-cavanagh
https://querymanager.com/query/2784

Literary Agency: The Rights Factory

Fiction > *Novels*
Commercial Women's Fiction; Commercial; LGBTQIA; Literary

Nonfiction > *Nonfiction Books*
Culture; Fashion; Films; Memoir; Music; Popular Culture; Society; Sub-Culture; TV

How to send: Query Manager

Currently seeking non-fiction projects on a range of topics including pop culture/celebrity, gift books, memoir/hybrid memoir, biography, history, art, fashion, cultural criticism, and society/culture. She is always keen to dive into niche topics and sub-cultures, including pop culture obsessions and analyses or insights into real or imagined communities. She gravitates towards insightful projects on a less explored topic particularly when done with humour and any subject which is meticulously researched and/or explores forgotten or hidden figures particularly from underrepresented communities.

Authors: Gurki Basra; Ashley Cowan; Fia Dahlia; Tracy Greenan; Sam Hogerton; C.R. Johnston; Jenny Lewis; Callie Rae O'Reilly; Lindsay Pereira; Seema Punwani

L115 Sonali Chanchani

Literary Agent
United States

sonali@foliolit.com

https://www.foliolit.com/agents-1/sonali-chanchani

Literary Agency: Folio Literary Management, LLC

Professional Body: Association of American Literary Agents (AALA)

Fiction > *Novels*
Book Club Fiction; Coming of Age; Family; Friends; Literary Mystery; Literary; Speculative; Thrillers; Women's Fiction

Nonfiction > *Nonfiction Books*
Culture; Ethnic Groups; Gender; Investigative Journalism; Narrative Nonfiction; Politics; Social Class; Social Justice; Society

Send: Query; Writing sample
How to send: In the body of an email

In fiction, she is looking for literary fiction and book club fiction with a strong, distinctive voice. She's particularly interested in smart, funny coming of age novels; braided narratives of friendship or family; literary mysteries; and atmospheric stories with a speculative or fabulist twist. She loves novels that subvert dominant cultural narratives and engage with themes of identity, belonging, community, inheritance, and diaspora. In nonfiction, she is looking for narratives and collections that illuminate some aspect of our society or culture with an eye towards social justice. She is especially drawn to investigative journalism and deeply researched narratives that advance our current conversations about race, class, gender, and politics.

L116 Nicola Chang

Literary Agent
United Kingdom

nicolachang@davidhigham.co.uk
nicolasubmissions@davidhigham.co.uk

https://www.davidhigham.co.uk/agents-dh/nicola-chang/

Literary Agency: David Higham Associates Ltd (**L159**)

Fiction
Novels: General, and in particular: Friends; Historical Fiction; Literary Thrillers; Literary; Romance; Saga
Short Fiction Collections: General

Nonfiction > *Nonfiction Books*
Cookery; Food

Poetry > *Any Poetic Form*

Send: Query; Writing sample
How to send: Email

On the lookout for precise, perspicacious books that examine and play with selfhood and the nature of identity; novel approaches to love stories; fiction set in decades gone by; stories that unspool over generations; literary thrillers; fiction about friends; writing with a global, transnational sensibility; places and characters not often represented in literature; stories concerning community and society; select short story collections; cookbooks—beautiful, timeless texts and recipes that are returned to again and again; food writing—what we do and don't think about when we are in the kitchen, around the dining table, on the sofa and eating out.

Authors: Ore Agbaje-Williams; Sara Ahmed; Rosanna Amaka; Raymond Antrobus; Amman Brar; Symeon Brown; Stephen Buoro; Vanessa Chan; Jacqueline Crooks; Tsitsi Dangarembga; Subhadra Das; Melissa Franklin; Nikita Gill; Emma Glass; Will Harris; Angela Hui; Bhanu Kapil; Huw Lemmey; Momtaza Mehri; Anna Metcalfe; Emma-Lee Moss; Riaz Phillips; Leone Ross; Saba Sams; Lisa Smith; Kae Tempest; Hanna Thomas Uose; Varaidzo; Christian Weaver; Mandy Yin

L117 Edwina de Charnace

Literary Agent
United Kingdom

https://mmbcreative.com/agents/edwina-de-charnace/

Literary Agency: MMB Creative (**L455**)

Fiction in Translation > *Novels*

Fiction > *Novels*
Dark Humour; East Asia; Family Saga; Horror; Psychological Thrillers; Romantasy

Nonfiction in Translation > *Nonfiction Books*

Nonfiction > *Nonfiction Books*
Art History; East Asia; Investigative Journalism; Literature; Personal Development; Self Help

Send: Query; Author bio; Synopsis; Writing sample
How to send: Email

Her Korean heritage and upbringing in Asia explain her soft spot for writing from or about East Asia in both original English and in translation. At the top of her present wishlist are family sagas, stories spanning multiple generations, horror amplified (rather than lightened) by dark humour, fantasy with romance (rather than romance with fantasy), socially-inflected psychological thrillers, expert-led non-fiction in self-help/personal development, investigative journalism on topics related to the beauty industry (like plastic surgery) and writing by academics on art history and non-canonical literature.

L118 Chase Literary Agency

Literary Agency
11 Broadway, Suite 1010, New York, NY 10004
United States
Tel: +1 (212) 477-5100

farley@chaseliterary.com

https://chaseliterary.com
https://twitter.com/FarleyChase
https://www.publishersmarketplace.com/members/farleychase/

Fiction
Graphic Novels: General
Novels: Commercial; Contemporary; Fantasy; High Concept; Historical Fiction; Horror; Literary

Nonfiction
Illustrated Books: Arts; Photography
Nonfiction Books: Biography; Business; Comedy / Humour; Current Affairs; History; Journalism; Memoir; Nature; Science; Self Help

Send: Query; Writing sample
How to send: Email

In fiction I'm looking for literary or commercial projects in either contemporary, historical, or fantasy settings. I'm open to anything with a strong sense of place, voice, and, especially, character and plot. I agree with Lorrie Moore who wrote 'We don't often know what intimate life consists of until novels tell us.' If you have a high-concept, character-driven fantasy, sci-fi, or horror novel please try me.

In nonfiction I'm keen to see memoir, natural history, science, current affairs, journalism, history, humor, and biography. Original business and self-help books stemming from expertise are also of serious interest.

I'm interested in visually-driven, lllustrated and graphic books. Whether they involve photography, comics, illustrations, or art, I'm taken by creative storytelling with visual elements, four color or black and white.

Literary Agent: Farley Chase (**L119**)

L119 Farley Chase
Literary Agent
United States

https://chaseliterary.com
https://aalitagents.org/author/farleychase/
https://www.linkedin.com/in/farley-chase-76b3b832/
https://twitter.com/FarleyChase

Literary Agency: Chase Literary Agency (**L118**)
Professional Body: Association of American Literary Agents (AALA)

L120 Mic Cheetham
Literary Agent
United Kingdom

Mic@miccheetham.co.uk

Literary Agency: Mic Cheetham Literary Agency (**L445**)

L121 Elyse Cheney
Literary Agent
United States

https://www.cheneyagency.com/elyse-cheney

Literary Agency: The Cheney Agency

L122 Jennifer Chevais
Associate Agent
Canada

https://www.therightsfactory.com/Agents/Jennifer-Chevais/
https://querymanager.com/query/JChevais
https://twitter.com/jchevais

Literary Agency: The Rights Factory

Fiction
Graphic Novels: General
Novels: General, and in particular: Fantasy; Horror; Science Fiction; Thrillers; Upmarket

Nonfiction > *Nonfiction Books*
General, and in particular: Memoir

Does not want:

> **Nonfiction** > *Nonfiction Books*: Warfare

How to send: Query Manager

Currently building her list of authors specialising in fantasy, science fiction, and horror, but she also has a soft spot for thrillers, upmarket fiction, memoir, graphic novels, and many more.

Authors: Amanda Burnham; Tal Cohen; Drew Dotson; Adam Hossein Fuller; Greta Kelly; A. A. Livingston; Dan Livingston; Dan Malossi; Rachelle Meyer; Damascus Mincemeyer; Tammy Plunkett; Markus Redmond; Emma Sachsse; Mark David Smith; Lauren Roedy Vaughn

L123 Danielle Chiotti
Literary Agent
United States

danielle.submission@gmail.com

https://www.upstartcrowliterary.com/agents/danielle-chiotti

Literary Agency: Upstart Crow Literary

ADULT
Fiction > *Novels*
Literary; Upmarket Commercial Fiction

Nonfiction > *Nonfiction Books*
Comedy / Humour; Cookery; Current Affairs; Food; Lifestyle; Memoir; Narrative Nonfiction; Relationships; Wine

CHILDREN'S > **Fiction** > *Middle Grade*

YOUNG ADULT > **Fiction** > *Novels*

How to send: Email

For adult fiction, she is seeking upmarket commercial fiction and literary fiction. She prefers books that explore deep emotional relationships in an interesting or unusual way.

For middle grade and YA: She is actively seeking fresh young adult and middle grade fiction across all genres. She is drawn toward gorgeous writing and strong, flawed characters. Her dream project for young readers is one that challenges and inspires, with a compelling voice that will make her stay up all night reading.

For nonfiction: she is looking for compelling, voice-driven projects that shed a humorous or thought-provoking light on a previously unknown topic in the areas of narrative nonfiction/memoir, lifestyle, relationships, humor, current events, food, wine, and cooking.

L124 Catherine Cho
Literary Agent; Author
United Kingdom

https://www.paperliterary.com/submissions-catherine/
https://twitter.com/catkcho

Literary Agencies: Paper Literary; C&W (Conville & Walsh) (**L096**)
Literary Agent: Sophie Lambert (**L380**)

ADULT
Fiction > *Novels*
Book Club Fiction; Family; Folklore, Myths, and Legends; High Concept; Historical Fiction; Literary; Magical Realism; Multicultural; Relationships; Speculative; Suspense

Nonfiction > *Nonfiction Books*: Narrative Nonfiction

YOUNG ADULT > **Fiction** > *Novels*: Fantasy

Send: Query; Synopsis; Writing sample

Originally from Kentucky. After a background in law and public affairs, she began her publishing career in New York at Folio Literary Management before moving to London.

L125 Erica Christensen
Senior Agent
United States

https://www.metamorphosisliteraryagency.com/about
https://querymanager.com/query/ericachristensen
https://twitter.com/literaryerica

Literary Agency: Metamorphosis Literary Agency (**L444**)

ADULT > **Fiction** > *Novels*
Romance; Thrillers

YOUNG ADULT > **Fiction** > *Novels*
Contemporary; Romance

Does not want:

> **ADULT** > **Fiction** > *Novels*
> Historical Romance; Supernatural / Paranormal Romance
>
> **YOUNG ADULT** > **Fiction** > *Novels*
> Historical Romance; Supernatural / Paranormal Romance

Closed to approaches.

Only open to SUBSIDIARY RIGHTS queries for established Romance and Thriller authors (Self-Published/Indie and Traditional) who retain the subsidiary rights (audio, foreign, gaming, film/tv) for their book(s). The book(s) must have a minimum of 50 reviews. Please include your Amazon author page and Goodreads page in the Bio section.

L126 Jennifer Christie

Literary Agent
United Kingdom

http://www.grahammawchristie.com/about1.html

Literary Agency: Graham Maw Christie Literary Agency (**L271**)

Nonfiction > *Nonfiction Books*
General, and in particular: Business; Comedy / Humour; Economics; History; Memoir; Personal Development; Personal Experiences; Philosophy; Popular Science; Psychology; Science; Social Issues

Send: Outline; Author bio; Market info; Writing sample
How to send: Email

Interests are wide ranging, from popular science, philosophy and humour to business and memoir.

L127 Kayla Cichello

Literary Agent
United States

kayla.submission@gmail.com

https://www.upstartcrowliterary.com/agents/kayla-cichelloa
https://twitter.com/SeriousKayla

Literary Agency: Upstart Crow Literary

ADULT > **Fiction** > *Novels*
Contemporary Romance; Upmarket

CHILDREN'S > **Fiction**
Middle Grade: General
Picture Books: Comedy / Humour

YOUNG ADULT > **Fiction** > *Novels*
Commercial; Dark Humour; Literary; Magical Realism; Mystery; Romance; Romantic Comedy; Suspense

Closed to approaches.

Open to picture books through YA and illustrators, and select adult manuscripts in the upmarket and contemporary romance categories. She is searching for those voices that make her laugh and keep the page turning.

L128 Caro Clarke

Literary Agent
United Kingdom

submissions@portobelloliterary.co.uk

https://www.portobelloliterary.co.uk

Literary Agency: Portobello Literary (**L521**)

Fiction > *Novels*
Crime; Fantasy; Literary; Speculative

Nonfiction
Essays: General
Nonfiction Books: Cookery; Culture; Food; Intersectional Feminism; LGBTQIA; Memoir; Narrative Nonfiction; Nature; Popular Science; Travel

Send: Synopsis; Author bio; Writing sample
How to send: Email
How not to send: Post

I am actively building a list of authors writing fiction and non-fiction. I have very broad taste in fiction and I'm attracted to excellent writing, clever plots, unusual settings and complex characters. I love all types of stories from niche literary novels, to speculative fiction and fantasy, gripping crime and novels with wide appeal. I am partial to fiction that transports you, steals your heart and makes you think. On the non-fiction side, I'm looking for narrative non-fiction, memoir, popular science, big ideas, travel, culture, essays, queer culture and intersectional feminism. I'm also interested in food writing and cookbooks. I have a particular soft spot for nature writing of any type. What I look for in non-fiction are fascinating topics, a unique perspective or one that disrupts the status quo and an engaging voice. Most of all, I'm looking for writers who are passionate about the topic of their book.

Authors: Polly Atkin; Fiona Black; Gill Booles; Rachel Charlton-Dailey; Mona Dash; Samantha Dooey-Miles; Harry Josephine Giles; CL Hellisen; Russell Jones; Aefa Mulholland; JC Niala; Andrés N. Ordorica; Wendy Pratt; Adam Ramsay; Christina Riley; Elspeth Wilson

L129 Catherine Clarke

Literary Agent; Managing Director
United Kingdom

https://felicitybryan.com/fba-agent/catherine-clarke/

Literary Agency: Felicity Bryan Associates (**L215**)

ADULT > **Nonfiction** > *Nonfiction Books*
Biography; History; Memoir; Nature; Philosophy

CHILDREN'S > **Fiction** > *Novels*

I have been building a list of adult non-fiction and children's fiction writers since 2001. In non-fiction, I particularly love history and philosophy and biography, especially from authors who have the academic credentials or expertise but also have the ambition and vision and writerly skill to make us see their subjects in a new light, or to overturn received wisdom. I also love outstanding nature writing with a dash of compelling memoir.

Authors: Samira Ahmed; David Almond; Karen Armstrong; Lucy Ash; Rachel Aspden; James Attlee; Katya Balen; James Barr; David Barrie; Rosamund Bartlett; John Barton; John Batchelor; Erica Benner; Nic Bennett; Claire Bertschinger; Paul Betts; Michael Bird; Simon Blackburn; Elleke Boehmer; Stella Botchway; John Bowker; Christopher Brickell; Susan Brigden; Irena Brignull; Adam Brookes; Matthew Burton; John Charmley; Nick Chater; Morten H. Christiansen; Liza Cody; Artemis Cooper; Sarah Courtauld; Cath Crowley; Chloe Daykin; John Dickie; Jenny Downham; Tobias Druitt; Natasha Farrant; Edmund Fawcett; Catherine Fletcher; CJ Flood; Pauline Francis; Peter Frankopan; Lawrence Freedman; Clare Furniss; Sally Gardner; Robert Gildea; Jonathan Glover; Chris Gosden; Barbara Graziosi; Thomas Halliday; Julie Hearn; Peter Heather; Gavin Hewitt; Louis Hill; Penelope Hobhouse; Alex Howard; Alice Hunt; Kathryn Hurlock; Belinda Jack; Lauren St John; Colin Jones; Vijay Joshi; Liz Kessler; Katherine Langrish; Lucy Lethbridge; John Lister-Kaye; Jonathan Loh; Diarmaid Macculloch; Laurie Maguire; John Man; Toby Matthiesen; James Mcdougall; Sophia Mcdougall; Chris Mcgrath; Kate Mcloughlin; Martin Meredith; Tom Moorhouse; Katy Moran; Natasha Narayan; James Naughtie; Linda Newbery; TN Ninan; Adjoa Osei; Richard Ovenden; Joanne Owen; Roger Pearson; Thomas Penn; Andrew Pettegree; Jonathan Phillips; Annabel Pitcher; Rachel Polonsky; Andrew Prentice; Sue Prideaux; Diane Purkiss; Josephine Quinn; Owen Rees; Julian Richards; Thomas Rid; Ritchie Robertson; Eugene Rogan; Meg Rosoff; Miri Rubin; Ulinka Rublack; Alec Ryrie; Joseph Sassoon; Paul Seabright; Alom Shaha; Liam Shaw; Matthew Skelton; Emma Smith; Lexi Stadlen; Marc Stears; Roy Strong; Julie Summers; Krystal Sutherland; Eleanor Updale; Christopher Vick; Charles Walton; Arthur Der Weduwen; Jonathan Weil; Anna Whitelock; Tim Whitmarsh; K.J. Whittaker; Lisa Williamson; Michael Wood; Lucy Wooding; Lucy Worsley; Jessica Wärnberg

L130 Alexander Cochran

Literary Agent
United Kingdom

alexander.submissions@cwagency.co.uk
alexander.cochran@cwagency.co.uk

https://cwagency.co.uk/agent/alexander-cochran

Literary Agency: C&W (Conville & Walsh) (**L096**)

Fiction > *Novels*
Crime; Dark Thrillers; Fantasy; Literary; Science Fiction; Speculative; Thrillers

Nonfiction > *Nonfiction Books*
  Current Affairs; History; Narrative Nonfiction

How to send: Email

I'm actively building my list and am always on the lookout for new writers of speculative fiction, literary fiction, crime and thriller and serious non-fiction. My tastes range widely, and in fiction I'm particularly interested in dark thrillers and crime novels, sci-fi and fantasy that push boundaries or cross genres, but are rooted in the believable, playful literary fiction, and novels that don't shy away from the darker aspects of humanity. On the non-fiction side, I tend towards the serious, and I am looking for books with big ideas that subvert our assumptions, serious histories, and narrative non-fiction with a focus on contemporary events and issues.

Authors: Charlotte Bond; Stephen Deas; Jules Grant; Jasmin Kirkbride; Tim Major; Ed McDonald; Dan M Pinchbeck; I. D. Roberts; Jamie Sawyer; E. Saxey; Luke Scull; Mike Shackle; Jean Smith; Tade Thompson; Eris Young; George Zarkadakis

L131 Colwill & Peddle
Literary Agency
London
United Kingdom

https://www.colwillandpeddle.com
http://instagram.com/colwillandpeddle
https://twitter.com/colwillpeddle

Professional Body: The Association of Authors' Agents (AAA)

Authors: Alexina Anatole; Xanthi Barker; Aimee Cliff; Josie Gill; Gabby Jahanshahi-Edlin; Shona Minson; Marie Mitchell; Jennifer Neal; Vic Parsons; Clare Rose; Jacqueline Roy; Ben Smoke; Annabel Sowemimo; Özlem Warren; Sophie Williams

Literary Agents: Charlotte Colwill (**L132**); Kay Peddle (**L503**); Milly Reilly (**L533**)

L132 Charlotte Colwill
Literary Agent
United Kingdom

Charlotte@colwillandpeddle.com
submissions@colwillandpeddle.com

https://www.colwillandpeddle.com/about

Literary Agency: Colwill & Peddle (**L131**)

ADULT > Fiction > *Novels*
  General, and in particular: Comedy / Humour; Historical Fiction; Literary Horror; Literary; Romance; Science Fiction

CHILDREN'S
  Fiction > *Novels*

  Nonfiction
    Middle Grade: Real Life Stories
    Nonfiction Books: General

YOUNG ADULT
  Fiction > *Novels*
    Contemporary; Fantasy; High Concept

  Nonfiction > *Nonfiction Books:* Real Life Stories

Send: Query; Synopsis; Writing sample; Author bio; Market info; Outline

Looking for adult fiction and children's fiction and non-fiction.

Always looking for fiction with a unique voice and compelling story, with something new to say. Loves unusual perspectives, dark twists and sharp writing. Particularly on the lookout for smart romance with an edge, page-turning historical dramas, literary horror or science fiction with a contemporary resonance and literary fiction that is funny and moving, with a brand new hook.

In children's books she is open to both fiction and non-fiction for all ages, from picture books to Young Adult. At the moment she is really looking for a funny and engaging author/illustrator with a fresh new series for young readers (5+), middle grade fiction with a new hook, brilliant world-building and characters we haven't seen before, and in YA she's looking for homegrown fantasy fiction, high concept contemporary stories and books about unusual relationships. In children's non-fiction she'd love to see books that tackle curriculum subjects in a brand new and super engaging way, and real life stories for middle grade and YA readers.

L133 Chris Combemale
Associate Agent
United States

https://www.sll.com/our-team

Literary Agency: Sterling Lord Literistic, Inc. (**L597**)

Fiction > *Novels*
  Literary; Upmarket Commercial Fiction

Nonfiction
  Essays: Economics; Food; Popular Science; Technology
  Nonfiction Books: Cultural Criticism; Food; Narrative Nonfiction; Philosophy; Popular Science; Technology

Send: Query; Synopsis; Proposal; Writing sample
How to send: Online submission system

Looking for a broad range of literary fiction and upmarket commercial fiction with an unexpected hook. In non-fiction he is interested in narrative nonfiction, cultural criticism/essay, and expert-driven projects across subject areas with special attention to technology, food, pop-science, philosophy, and any book that asks big questions about forces of change.

L134 Andrea Comparato
Literary Agent
United States

andrea@inscriptionsliterary.com

https://inscriptionsliterary.com/agents/
https://aalitagents.org/author/acomparato/
https://www.publishersmarketplace.com/members/inscriplit/
https://querymanager.com/query/InscriptionsLit_Query

Literary Agency: Inscriptions Literary Agency (**L323**)
Professional Body: Association of American Literary Agents (AALA)

ADULT
  Fiction > *Novels*
    Mystery; Suspense

  Nonfiction > *Nonfiction Books:* Memoir

CHILDREN'S
  Fiction
    Middle Grade; Picture Books
  Scripts > *Film Scripts*

How to send: Query Manager; Email

All manuscript submissions should be sent through Query Manager. Screenplay / Script submissions by email.

L135 Cristina Concepcion
Literary Agent; Foreign Rights Manager
United States

dca@doncongdon.com

Literary Agency: Don Congdon Associates, Inc. (**L175**)

Fiction > *Novels*

Nonfiction > *Nonfiction Books*
  Current Affairs; Narrative Nonfiction

How to send: Email

Represents writers of adult fiction, history, current events and narrative non-fiction.

L136 Claire Paterson Conrad
Literary Agent; Company Director
United Kingdom

http://www.janklowandnesbit.co.uk/node/671

Literary Agency: Janklow & Nesbit UK Ltd (**L330**)

Fiction > *Novels*
  Commercial; Experimental; Feminism; Literary

Nonfiction > *Nonfiction Books*
  Biology; Creative Nonfiction; Environment; Nature; Popular Science

Send: Query; Synopsis; Writing sample; Outline
How to send: Email
How not to send: Post

In fiction, I work across upmarket commercial to literary fiction and mistrust pigeon-holing books into genres. I'm actively looking to take on distinctive fiction which is voice or character driven; a strong hook or unusual perspective is always a bonus. I'm currently keen to find an all-consuming multi-generational novel or gripping love stories, particularly if it's warm-hearted and wise. I'd also like to find more novels that make you laugh out loud, and fiction that subverts the norm, even in subtle ways. I love beautifully written literary fiction that has a strong sense of place, feminist fiction with a revisionary twist and experimental novels that play with structure or form, especially when this is used to illuminate the complexities of human experience. I'd particularly like to hear from novelists who have started writing later in life.

In non-fiction, currently, I'm looking for writers who show us new ways of looking at things or help us understand the world better, or books that start conversations and change minds. I'm also passionate about finding and amplifying voices from under-represented backgrounds. I'm looking for memoir and narrative non-fiction by writers, journalists or historians who can retell fascinating stories or little-known periods of history. I'm searching for good food writing and books about the food system, or books that highlight our need to protect and care for our precious planet, especially nature writing. I'm looking for books that are a call to arms for other issues of our day, ones that challenge orthodoxies in ways that aren't necessarily prescriptive. I'd love to find more good popular science writing, written by great communicators. Lastly, I'm a huge fan of non-fiction that melds genres.

L137 Clare Conville

Literary Agent
United Kingdom
Tel: +44 (0) 20 7393 4203

elizabeth.milne@cwagency.co.uk

https://cwagency.co.uk/agent/clare-conville

Literary Agency: C&W (Conville & Walsh) (**L096**)

Fiction
Novels: Commercial; Literary
Short Fiction Collections: General

Nonfiction > *Nonfiction Books*
Arts; History; Memoir; Nature

How to send: Email

Reading is her hobby as well as her profession and she loves literary and literary/commercial novels, memoir, short stories and exceptional voice-driven non-fiction. Areas of special interest are history, nature and art and she also enjoys reading comic books. She is passionate about finding original voices and loves working with new writers. She looks for strong, unique perspectives and dark humour across both fiction and non-fiction.

Authors: Dolly Alderton; Damian Barr; Neil Bartlett; Francesca Beauman; Matt Beaumont; Greta Bellamacina; Patrick Benson; James Birch; Immodesty Blaize; Louisa Buck; Rachel Campbell-Johnston; Roger Clarke; Miriam Darlington; Katie Davies; Chris Difford; Rory Dunlop; Peter Dunne; Allie Esiri; Penelope Farmer; Esther Freud; Jasper Gibson; Misha Glenny; Kirsty Gunn; Matt Haig; Lou Hamilton; Debora Harding; Michael Hodges; Antonia Hodgson; Merlin Holland; Rob Lloyd Jones; Rachel Joyce; Sadakat Kadri; Abraham Kawa; David Keenan; Stephen Kelman; Katie Kitamura; Gerad Kite; Harriet Kline; Persia Lawson; P J Lynch; Celia Lyttelton; Robert McCrum; Sam Mckechnie; Harland Miller; Joshua Mowll; Juliet Nicolson; Sydney Padua; Kit Peel; Megan Peel; DBC Pierre; Huw Powell; Paula Rawsthorne; Lydia Ruffles; Polly Samson; Yasmine Seale; Lemn Sissay; Richard Skinner; Sofia Slater; Mark Stevens; Annalyn Swan; Piers Torday; Pádraig Ó Tuama; Jon Lys Turner; Emma Jane Unsworth; Steve Voake; Harriet Vyner; Max Wallis; Amanda Eyre Ward; S J Watson; Ben Wilson; Robert Wilton; Isabel Wolff; Osman Yousefzada

L138 Clare Coombes

Literary Agent
United Kingdom

https://www.liverpool-literary.agency/about

Literary Agency: The Liverpool Literary Agency (**L404**)

Fiction > *Novels*
General, and in particular: Crime; Historical Fiction; Psychological Thrillers; Women's Fiction

Closed to approaches.

Would love to see historical fiction, crime fiction, psychological thrillers and women's fiction, but as a new agent, she is open to all great writing with a strong hook in any area (excluding non-fiction, children's and YA).

L139 Coombs Moylett & Maclean Literary Agency

Literary Agency
120 New Kings Road, London, SW6 4LZ
United Kingdom

info@cmm.agency

https://cmm.agency
https://www.instagram.com/cmmlitagency/
https://www.facebook.com/cmmlitagency/

Professional Body: The Association of Authors' Agents (AAA)

ADULT
Fiction > *Novels*
Chick Lit; Commercial; Contemporary; Crime; Historical Fiction; Horror; Literary; Mystery; Suspense; Thrillers; Women's Fiction

Nonfiction > *Nonfiction Books*
General, and in particular: Biography; Crime; Current Affairs; Environment; Food; History; How To; Lifestyle; Narrative Nonfiction; Politics; Popular Science; Self Help

YOUNG ADULT > **Fiction** > *Novels*

Closed to approaches.

Send query with synopsis and first three chapters via online form. No submissions by email, fax or by post. No poetry, plays or scripts for film and TV. Whole books and postal submissions will not be read.

Literary Agents: Zoe Apostolides; Elena Langtry (**L385**); Jamie Maclean (**L417**); Lisa Moylett

L140 Gemma Cooper

Literary Agent; Company Director
United States

http://www.thebentagency.com/gemma-cooper

Literary Agency: The Bent Agency (**L058**)

CHILDREN'S
Fiction
Chapter Books; *Graphic Novels*; *Illustrated Books*; *Middle Grade*
Nonfiction > *Nonfiction Books*
History; Science

YOUNG ADULT
Fiction > *Novels*
Contemporary; Family; Friends; High Concept; Magic; Romantic Comedy; Supernatural / Paranormal Romance

Nonfiction > *Nonfiction Books*

Does not want:

> **YOUNG ADULT** > **Fiction** > *Novels*: High / Epic Fantasy

Closed to approaches.

Represents authors and author / illustrators who write chapter books, middle-grade, and young adult fiction and nonfiction, as well as select webcomic adaptations. No adult fiction or nonfiction, or children's picture books, other than by existing clients.

L141 Maggie Cooper

Literary Agent
Boston, MA
United States

https://aevitascreative.com/agents/
https://querymanager.com/query/cooper

Literary Agency: Aevitas

Fiction > *Novels*
Cozy Fantasy; Fabulism; Feminist Romance; Historical Fiction; LGBTQIA; Literary; Magical Realism

Nonfiction > *Nonfiction Books*
Climate Science; Creative Nonfiction; Culture; Food; Gender; Social Justice; Sustainable Living

Closed to approaches.

I'm seeking imaginative, genre-bending literary fiction; beautifully told queer stories; and smart, feminist vacation reads. I love retellings of classic stories, epistolary novels, and well-earned happy endings. I don't typically work on "hard" science fiction and fantasy, although I'm drawn to stories that blend the realist and speculative in the traditions of magical realism, fabulism, or otherwise—and right now, I'm very open to seeing cozy or quirky fantasy, especially if it overlaps with my other interests. I'm particularly attracted to structural innovation, language that makes the reader pause over its peculiar specificity, and books that make our world a weirder, kinder, and/or more joyful place.

In nonfiction, I'm looking for graphic projects with a literary sensibility, self-aware creative nonfiction, and projects with a quirky, joyful, or humorous bent. Across genres, I'm always interested in food, literary culture, gender, sustainability and climate crisis, social justice, schools and education, and projects that engage our current cultural moment, whether directly or slantwise.

Authors: Emma Ahlqvist; Will Betke-Brunswick; Zoë Bossiere; Rita Zoey Chin; Marisa Crane; Carla Fernandez; JR Ford; Vanessa Ford; Andrew J. Graff; Rebecca Kling; Hali Lee; Rue Mapp; Jessica Martin; Katie Mitchell; Carolyn Prusa; Allegra Rosenberg; Margie Sarsfield; Nina Sharma; Jack Shoulder; Mark Small; Julia Ridley Smith; June Thomas

L142 Becca Crandall
Literary Agent
United States

carolyn@carolynjenksagency.com

https://www.carolynjenksagency.com/agent/BECCA-CRANDALL

Literary Agency: Carolyn Jenks Agency (**L107**)

ADULT
Fiction
Graphic Novels; *Novels*
Nonfiction > *Nonfiction Books*

CHILDREN'S > **Fiction**
Middle Grade; *Picture Books*
YOUNG ADULT > **Fiction** > *Novels*

Closed to approaches.

L143 Claudia Cross
Literary Agent; Partner
United States

https://www.foliolit.com/agents-1/claudia-cross

Literary Agency: Folio Literary Management, LLC

Closed to approaches.

L144 Sheila Crowley
Literary Agent
United Kingdom

crowleyofficesubmissions@curtisbrown.co.uk

https://curtisbrown.co.uk
https://curtisbrown.co.uk/agent/sheila-crowley

Literary Agency: Curtis Brown (**L146**)

Fiction > *Novels*
Book Club Fiction; Commercial; Family; Mystery; Romance; Saga; Suspense; Thrillers

Nonfiction > *Nonfiction Books*

Send: Query; Author bio; Writing sample; Proposal
How to send: Email

I represent a wide range of authors from award-winning novelists to million-copy-selling non-fiction writers. Authors are at the centre of everything I do as an agent – one of the best things about the job is working closely with writers across all stages of the publishing process. I am looking for the best new talent in bookclub and commercial fiction, be that an epic romance, family drama, transporting saga or a page-turning thriller. As well as helping debut authors launch a publishing career, I'm also interested in taking on published writers who may want to reinvigorate their career or change direction.

L145 Sabhbh Curran
Literary Agent
United Kingdom

sabhbh.curran@curtisbrown.co.uk

http://submissions.curtisbrown.co.uk/agents/

Literary Agency: Curtis Brown (**L146**)

Fiction > *Novels*
Book Club Fiction; Dark; Historical Fiction; Literary; Psychological Suspense

Nonfiction > *Nonfiction Books*
Art History; Arts; Current Affairs; Fashion; Food; History; Mind, Body, Spirit; Narrative Nonfiction; Popular Culture; Popular Science; Psychology; Travel

Send: Query; Synopsis; Writing sample; Proposal
How to send: Email

I am on the hunt for literary, book club fiction and psychological suspense fiction. What I look for is well-crafted and stylish prose, complex characterisations and probably at least a hint of darkness: obsessive friendships and relationships; loneliness; trauma; dysfunctional families; the strangeness of urban life. I'm also drawn to beautifully written, researched and evoked historical fiction.

In non-fiction, I'm particularly keen to hear from chefs, mixologists and food writers but I am also interested in narrative non-fiction, history, travel writing, current affairs, popular science, psychology, MBS, fashion and popular culture. I would like to hear from non-fiction writers (especially journalists and activists) who speak to a younger audience. I have a real soft spot for anything related to art or art history, whatever the genre.

L146 Curtis Brown
Literary Agency
Cunard House, 15 Regent Street, London, SW1Y 4LR
United Kingdom
Tel: +44 (0) 20 7393 4400

info@curtisbrown.co.uk

https://www.curtisbrown.co.uk
http://submissions.curtisbrown.co.uk/

Professional Body: The Association of Authors' Agents (AAA)
Literary Agency: United Talent Agency (UTA)

ADULT
Fiction > *Novels*
General, and in particular: Commercial Women's Fiction; Crime; Erotic; Historical Fiction; Horror; Literary; Memoir; Romance; Thrillers

Nonfiction > *Nonfiction Books*

Scripts
Film Scripts; *TV Scripts*; *Theatre Scripts*

CHILDREN'S > **Fiction**
Early Readers: General
Middle Grade: General, and in particular: Fantasy; Science Fiction
Picture Books: General

YOUNG ADULT > **Fiction** > *Novels*
General, and in particular: Fantasy; Science Fiction

Send: Query; Synopsis; Writing sample

Costs: Offers services that writers have to pay for. Offers writing courses.

Renowned and long-established London agency. Handles general fiction and nonfiction, and scripts. Also represents directors, designers, and presenters. Also offers services such as writing courses for which authors are charged.

Authors: Nicole Adams; Henry Agg; Casey Jay Andrews; Sui Annukka; Craig Barr-Green; Chloe Bayley; Alice Bell; Kaddy Benyon; Kate van der Borgh; Fern Brady; Natalie Bray; Ashley Chalmers; Georgina Charles; Ken

Cheng; Laura Coffey; Hannah Connolly; Paige Cowan-Hall; Alan Edwards; Rebecca Fallon; Babak Ganjei; Rebecca Gibson; Nevin Holness; Daniel Howell; Logan Karlie; Greg Keen; Nina Killham; Danny James King; Chloe Laws; Tatty Macleod; Gráinne Maguire; Michael Mann; Hazel McBride; Laura McCluskey; Ella McLeod; Liberty Mills; Struan Murray; L.M. Nathan; Madeleine Norton; Tara O'Sullivan; Joshua Oliver; Andrea Oskis; Louise Page; Claire Peate; Alake Pilgrim; Leah Pitt; Keetie Roelen; Eulalie Tangka; Daisy Tempest; Lucy Webster; Claire Whatley; Dan Whitlam; Kat Williams; Matt Woodhead; Kelly Yang

Literary Agent / President: Jonathan Lloyd

Literary Agents: Davinia Andrew-Lynch (*L026*); Felicity Blunt; Sheila Crowley (**L144**); Sabhbh Curran (**L145**); Ciara Finan (**L223**); Jonny Geller; Viola Hayden (**L305**); Alice Lutyens; Jess Molloy (**L456**); Rosie Pierce (**L517**); Cathryn Summerhayes; Steph Thwaites (**L629**); Gordon Wise

L147 Curtis Brown (Australia) Pty Ltd

Literary Agency
Australia

submission@curtisbrown.com.au

https://www.curtisbrown.com.au

Professional Body: Australian Literary Agents' Association (ALAA)

Fiction > *Novels*

Nonfiction > *Nonfiction Books*

How to send: Email
How not to send: Post

Accepts submission from within Australia and New Zealand only, during March, June, and October. No fantasy, sci-fi, stage/screenplays, poetry, self-help books, children's picture books, early reader books, young adult books, comic books, short stories, cookbooks, educational, corporate books or translations. Send query by email with synopsis up to two pages and first three chapters. See website for full guidelines.

Literary Agents: Clare Forster; Grace Heifetz; Fiona Inglis; Pippa Masson; Tara Wynne

L148 John Cusick

Literary Agent; Vice President
United States

https://www.foliojr.com/john-cusick
https://www.publishersmarketplace.com/members/JohnC/
https://twitter.com/johnmcusick

Literary Agencies: Folio Literary Management, LLC; Folio Jr.

ADULT > **Fiction** > *Novels*
Fantasy; Horror; Romance; Romantic Comedy; Science Fiction; Suspense; Thrillers

CHILDREN'S > **Fiction** > *Middle Grade*
Comedy / Humour; Contemporary; Fantasy; Science Fiction; Speculative

YOUNG ADULT > **Fiction** > *Novels*
Comedy / Humour; Contemporary; Fantasy; Science Fiction; Speculative

Send: Query; Writing sample
How to send: Email

I'm seeking unique voices in middle-grade, young adult, and young adult/adult-crossover fiction. I want stories that move readers, moments that make me look up and say "Wow, yes. I've felt that."

I want compelling page-turners that create life-long readers, stories that will inspire fandoms, characters readers will cosplay as, obsess over, and never forget. I want #ownvoices stories of all styles and genres, and am particularly interested in sci-fi, fantasy, and genre fiction from under-represented voices. I love the strange, iconoclastic, and unusual. Send me the books kids will sneak / steal / borrow in secret. Those intimate, dangerous, life-saving stories.

I love proactive protagonists, kids and teens chasing a dream or a hero who swings in with a song in her heart and a knife in her teeth. I am not seeking picture book authors or illustrators, or non-fiction, at this time.

Authors: Courtney Alameda; Kayla Cagan; Josephine Cameron; Anna Carey; Linda Cheng; Marina Cohen; Paula Garner; Joan He; Christian McKay Heidicker; Sailor J; James Kennedy; Jeramey Kraatz; Kristen Lippert-Martin; Julie Murphy; Abdi Nazemian; Jordan Reeves; Caitlin Schneiderhan; Laura Sebastian; Quinn Sosna-Spear; Sharon Biggs Waller; Don Zolidis

L149 Cyle Young Literary Elite

Literary Agency
United States

https://cyleyoung.com
https://www.facebook.com/cyle61?fref=ts
https://twitter.com/cyleyoung

Author / Junior Agent: Del Duduit

Author / Literary Agent: Cyle Young

Junior Agent: Megan Burkhart

Literary Agent: Tessa Emily Hall

L150 Cynthia Cannell Literary Agency

Literary Agency
United States

info@cannellagency.com

https://cannellagency.com
https://twitter.com/cynthiacan
https://www.facebook.com/CynthiaCannellLiteraryAgency/
https://www.linkedin.com/company/cynthia-cannell-literary-agency/about/

Professional Body: Association of American Literary Agents (AALA)

Fiction > *Novels*

Nonfiction > *Nonfiction Books*
Biography; Contemporary; Memoir; Personal Development; Spirituality

Closed to approaches.

Full-service literary agency based in New York. Represents fiction, memoir, biography, self-improvement, spirituality, and nonfiction on contemporary issues. No screenplays, children's books, illustrated books, cookbooks, romance, category mystery, or science fiction. Send query by email only, including brief description of the project, relevant biographical information, and any publishing credits. No attachments or submissions by post. Response not guaranteed.

Literary Agent: Cynthia Cannell

L151 Laura Dail

Literary Agent; President
United States

http://www.ldlainc.com/about
http://twitter.com/lcdail
http://aaronline.org/Sys/PublicProfile/2176649/417813

Literary Agency: Laura Dail Literary Agency
Professional Body: Association of American Literary Agents (AALA)

Closed to approaches.

L152 Dana Newman Literary, LLC

Literary Agency
1900 Avenue of the Stars, 19th Floor, Los Angeles, CA 90067
United States

dananewmanliterary@gmail.com

https://www.dananewman.com
https://twitter.com/DanaNewman
https://www.linkedin.com/in/dananewman/
https://www.instagram.com/danamnewman/

Fiction > *Novels*
Literary; Suspense; Thrillers; Upmarket

Nonfiction > *Nonfiction Books*
Biography; Business; Current Affairs; Fitness; Health; History; Literary; Memoir; Mind, Body, Spirit; Narrative Nonfiction; Parenting; Popular Culture; Psychology; Social Issues; Sport; Technology; Wellbeing; Women's Interests

Send: Query; Outline; Author bio
How to send: Email

We are interested in practical nonfiction (business, health and wellness, mind/body/spirit, psychology, parenting, technology) by authors with smart, unique perspectives and established platforms who are committed to actively marketing and promoting their books.

We love compelling, inspiring narrative nonfiction in the areas of memoir, biography, history, pop culture, current affairs/women's interest, social trends, and sports/fitness. A favorite genre is literary nonfiction: true stories, well told, that read like a novel you can't put down.

On the fiction side we consider a select amount of literary fiction, upmarket fiction, and suspense/thriller. We look for character-driven stories written in a distinctive voice that are emotionally truthful.

Submissions are accepted via email only.

Literary Agent: Dana Newman

L153 Melissa Danaczko
Literary Agent
United States

mdquery@skagency.com

http://skagency.com
http://skagency.com/agents/melissa-danaczko/

Literary Agency: Stuart Krichevsky Literary Agency, Inc. (**L609**)

Fiction > *Novels*
Book Club Fiction; Commercial; Contemporary; Family; Friends; Historical Fiction; International; Literary; Magic; Psychological Thrillers; Sub-Culture

Nonfiction > *Nonfiction Books*
History; Memoir; Science

Focuses on literary and commercial fiction and gravitates towards plot-driven novels with a fresh perspective, energetic writing and deep sense of place. Favorite categories include historical fiction, psychological thrillers, and contemporary book club fiction. She has a soft spot for novels with international settings, unreliable narrators, elements of magic, dysfunctional families, intense friendships, and unique subcultures. She is also representing select history, science, memoir and idea-driven non-fiction. In all categories, it's a big plus if a book can introduce her to a new world, make her think differently about one she already knows or tap into the cultural climate.

Authors: Addison Armstrong; Chelsea Conaboy; Ella Delany; Anita Felicelli; John Fram; Elyssa Goodman; Gabino Iglesias; Amanda Jayatissa; Bernice McFadden; Sarafina Nance; Mira Ptacin; Marina Scott; Charlyne Yi

L154 Margaret Danko
Literary Agent
United States

https://www.highlineliterary.com/agent-margaret
https://querymanager.com/query/margaretdanko

Literary Agency: High Line Literary Collective (**L312**)

Fiction > *Novels*
Family; Historical Fiction; Horror; Literary; Magical Realism; Romantic Comedy; Suspense; Upmarket; Women's Fiction

Nonfiction > *Nonfiction Books*
Comedy / Humour; Cookery; Crime; Environment; Lifestyle; Mental Health; New Age; Politics; Popular Science; Spirituality

Closed to approaches.

Actively looking for attention-grabbing voices especially historical fiction with a dash of magical realism, literary and upmarket suspense or horror, narratives with a deep sense of place and history, quirky and heartwarming family stories, and women's fiction and rom-coms full of charm and whimsy. She is also accepting nonfiction in the areas of humor, lifestyle, new age and general spirituality, popular science especially in environmental and human sciences, mental health/wellness, politics and true crime that challenge established conventions, and select cooking projects with an emphasis on new takes on tradition, especially within the Latine diaspora.

L155 Jon Michael Darga
Senior Agent
New York
United States

https://aevitascreative.com/agents/
https://querymanager.com/query/jonmichaeldarga

Literary Agency: Aevitas

Fiction > *Novels*: Commercial

Nonfiction > *Nonfiction Books*
Biography; Cookery; History; Photography; Popular Culture

Send: Author bio; Outline; Pitch; Market info; Writing sample
How to send: Online submission system

Represents both nonfiction and fiction. He is most interested in voice-driven pop culture writing and histories that re-cast the narrative by emphasizing unexpected or unheard voices.

Authors: Matt Abdoo; Zac Bissonnette; Sydney Bucksbaum; Scott Chernoff; Tony Chin-Quee; Angel Luis Colón; Melissa Croce; Ashley Cullins; Tim Curry; Sarah Horowitz; Patty Lin; Violet Lumani; Hugo Huerta Marin; Ann Marks; Shane McBride; Sam Moore; Tarek El Moussa; Arnold Myint; James Park; Erik Piepenburg; Lynette Rice; Geena Rocero; Maurice "Mopreme" Shakur; Ashley Spencer; Jason Sperling; Jesse Szewczyk; Amy Watson; Rusty Williams; Angel Di Zhang

L156 Darhansoff & Verrill Literary Agents
Literary Agency
275 Fair Street, Suite 17D, Kingston NY, 12401
United States
Tel: +1 (845) 514-2070

submissions@dvagency.com
info@dvagency.com

https://www.dvagency.com

ADULT
  Fiction > *Novels*
  Nonfiction > *Nonfiction Books*

YOUNG ADULT > **Fiction** > *Novels*

Send: Query; Writing sample
How to send: In the body of an email
How not to send: Post

Response only if interested. If no response within eight weeks, assume rejection.

Foreign Rights Director / Literary Agent: Eric Amling (**L021**)

Literary Agents: Liz Darhansoff; Michele Mortimer (**L462**)

L157 The Darley Anderson Agency
Literary Agency
Estelle House, 11 Eustace Road, London, SW6 1JB
United Kingdom
Tel: +44 (0) 20 7385 6652

https://darleyanderson.com
https://twitter.com/DA_Agency
https://www.instagram.com/darleyanderson_agency/

Professional Body: The Association of Authors' Agents (AAA)

Fiction > *Novels*
Commercial; Crime; Historical Fiction; Romance; Romantasy; Romantic Comedy; Thrillers

Send: Query; Synopsis; Writing sample
How to send: Online submission system; Post

We specialise in commercial, page-turning, conversation-starting fiction. We're talking heart stopping thrillers, 'have you read this yet?!' books, laugh out loud rom-coms, steamy romances, addictive crime, sweeping love stories, breathtaking romantasy and glamorous regency dramas, to name but a few.

Associate Agent: Rebeka Finch (**L225**)

Authors: Maria Motunrayo Adebisi; Mandy Baggot; Emma Bamford; Gina Blaxill; Tara

Bond; Sarah Bowie; Mark Bradley; Vicki Bradley; Sara Bragg; Constance Briscoe; Danielle Brown; Lanisha Butterfield; Honor Cargill-Martin; James Carol; Paul Carson; Chris Carter; Laura Carter; Lee Child; Martina Cole; Gloria Cook; Lucy Tandon Copp; Sophie Cousens; Holly Craig; A J Cross; Jason Dean; Margaret Dickinson; Clare Dowling; Hayley Doyle; Patrick Dunne; Tom Ellen; Alex Evelyn; C. M. Ewan; Addy Farmer; Kerry Fisher; Jack Ford; Martyn Ford; Tana French; Claire Frost; Mina Ikemoto Ghosh; G.R. Halliday; Ryan Hammond; Mary Hargreaves; Alice Harman; Joyce Efia Harmer; Polly Ho-Yen; Egan Hughes; Tara Hyland; Catherine Jacob; Sandie Jones; Amie Jordan; Emma Kavanagh; Patrick Lennon; Nathanael Lessore; T M Logan; Imran Mahmood; Cesca Major; Rani Manicka; L V Matthews; Gillian McAllister; Hannah Moffatt; Ayaan Mohamud; Phoebe Morgan; Rachel Morrisroe; Annie Murray; Eva Wong Nava; Laura Noakes; Beth O'Leary; Abi Oliver; B.A. Paris; Phaedra Patrick; Jo Platt; Hazel Prior; Beth Reekles; David Rhodes; Lisa Richardson; Ellie Robinson; Jacqui Rose; Faith Williams Schesventer; Mira V. Shah; Rebecca Shaw; Nick Sheridan; Rashmi Sirdeshpande; KL Slater; Kim Slater; Sean Slater; Kate G. Smith; Pat Sowa; Catherine Steadman; Emma Steele; Erik Storey; Deirdre Sullivan; Mimi Thebo; G X Todd; Samantha Tonge; Elizabeth Waite; Anna-Lou Weatherley; Tim Weaver; Sophie White; Ally Zetterberg

Literary Agent / Managing Director: Camilla Bolton (**L069**)

Literary Agents: Darley Anderson (**L022**); Jade Kavanagh (**L355**); Becca Langton (**L383**); Lydia Silver; Tanera Simons (**L585**); Clare Wallace

L158 David Godwin Associates

Literary Agency
2nd Floor, 40 Rosebery Avenue, Clerkenwell, London, EC1R 4RX
United Kingdom
Tel: +44 (0) 20 7240 9992

submissions@davidgodwinassociates.co.uk

http://www.davidgodwinassociates.com

Professional Body: The Association of Authors' Agents (AAA)

Fiction > *Novels*

Nonfiction > *Nonfiction Books*

Send: Query; Synopsis; Writing sample
How to send: Email

Handles a range of nonfiction and fiction. Send query by email with synopsis and first 30 pages. No poetry. No picture books, except for existing clients.

Literary Agent: David Godwin

L159 David Higham Associates Ltd

Literary Agency
6th Floor, Waverley House, 7-12 Noel Street, London, W1F 8GQ
United Kingdom
Tel: +44 (0) 20 7434 5900

reception@davidhigham.co.uk
submissions@davidhigham.co.uk
childrenssubmissions@davidhigham.co.uk

https://davidhigham.co.uk
https://twitter.com/DHAbooks
https://www.linkedin.com/company/david-higham-associates-limited
https://www.instagram.com/davidhighambooks/?hl=en

Professional Body: The Association of Authors' Agents (AAA)

We are always on the lookout for exciting new voices. From pioneering non-fiction, to meticulously-plotted thrillers, life-changing love stories, and bold literary debuts, we are committed to storytelling in all forms. We are keen to hear from writers from under-represented backgrounds.

Agency Assistant: Sara Langham

Associate Agent: David Evans (**L203**)

Author / Editor-in-Chief: Jason Cowley

Authors: Rachel Abbott; J. R. Ackerley; Richard Adams; Ore Agbaje-Williams; Katie Agnew; Sara Ahmed; Kat Ailes; Naomi Alderman; Tracy Alexander; Elizabeth Alker; Rachael Allen; Jason Allen-Paisant; Alan Allport; Nuar Alsadir; Geraint Anderson; R. J. Anderson; Kelly Andrew; Kerry Andrew; Abi Andrews; Carol Anshaw; Michael Arditti; Edward Ardizzone; Michael Arlen; Thomas Asbridge; Lamorna Ash; Jenn Ashworth; Jennifer Atkins; Julian Baggini; Harriet Baker; Tina Baker; Anthony Bale; Katy Balls; Antonia Barber; Lindsey Bareham; Nigel Barley; Robert Barnard; Kaushik Basu; Yvonne Battle-Felton; Belinda Bauer; Felix Bazalgette; Ella Beech; Laura Beers; Hannah Begbie; Annie Bell; Aimee Bender; Margot Bennett; Joe Berger; Sarah Bernstein; Elizabeth Berridge; Santanu Bhattacharya; Tessa Bickers; Rebecca Birrell; Neil Blackmore; James Bloodworth; Edmund Blunden; Margaret Boden; Jonathan Boff; Maria Bradford; E. R. Braithwaite; Mikki Brammer; Lauren Bravo; Carys Bray; Neville Braybrooke; Kevin Brazil; Theresa Breslin; Glen Brown; Martin Brown; Hester Browne; Janet Browne; Mike Brownlow; Jessica Bruder; Rukky Brume; Arthur Bryant; Ella Bucknall; Anthony Burgess; Mark Burnell; R. S. Burnett; Sheila Burnford; Caroline Burt; Sally Butcher; Nick Butterworth; Eliza Barry Callahan; Paco Calvo; John Carey; John Dickson Carr; Jess Cartner-Morley; Anne-Marie Casey; Barbara Castle; Charles Causley; Kathryn Cave; Aditya Chakrabortty; Vanessa Chan; Jason Chapman; Eve Chase; James Hadley Chase; Seerut K. Chawla; Emma Chichester Clark; Arthur C. Clarke; Lady Mary Clive; J. M. Coetzee; Kathleen Collins; Sophie Collins; Charlie Connelly; Alan Connor; Peter Cook; Trish Cooke; Emily S. Cooper; Natasha Cooper; Bernard Cornwell; Jamie Costello; Chris Cove-Smith; Cressida Cowell; Rob Cowen; Ivor Crewe; Nick Crumpton; John Cunliffe; James Curtis; Roald Dahl; David Daiches; Tsitsi Dangarembga; Nicola Davies; Susie Day; Lizzie Dearden; Tish Delaney; R. F. Delderfield; Kady MacDonald Denton; Lucy Diamond; Morgan Dick; Lucy Dillamore; Lucy Dillon; Jonathan Dimbleby; Berlie Doherty; Naoise Dolan; Sareeta Domingo; David Domoney; Stanley Donwood; Kelly Doust; Karen Downs-Barton; Alicia Drake; Sarah Duguid; Fred D'Aguiar; Caroline Eden; David Edmonds; Eve Edwards; Kerry Egan; Jonathan Emmett; Tan Twan Eng; Richard English; Eve Esfandiari-Denney; Gavin Esler; Maz Evans; Rowan Evans; Seb Falk; Eleanor Farjeon; J. Jefferson Farjeon; Ben Faulks; Felipe Fernández-Armesto; Elizabeth Ferrars; Ophelia Field; Anne Fine; Cordelia Fine; Pip Finkemeyer; Nicholas Fisk; Pauline Fisk; Theodora Fitzgibbon; Corina Fletcher; Margot Fonteyn; Ford Madox Ford; Charles Foster; Fred Foster; Karen Joy Fowler; Catherine Fox; Matthew Frank; Melissa Franklin; P. M. Freestone; Tom de Freston; Stephen Fry; Mavis Gallant; Jane Gardam; Sarah Garland; Eve Garnett; Susan Gates; Jonathan Gathorne-Hardy; Ryan Gattis; Jamila Gavin; Jessica George; Adèle Geras; Susannah Gibson; Andrew Gimson; Guinevere Glasfurd; Ralph Glasser; Victoria Glendinning; Julia Golding; Elizabeth Goudge; Caroline Graham; Holly Gramazio; Marlowe Granados; Kester Grant; Ryan Graudin; Dominic Green; Linda Green; Peter Green; Graham Greene; John Gribbin; Jay Griffiths; Geoffrey Grigson; Jane Grigson; Araminta Hall; Jo Hamya; Penny Hancock; James Hanley; Mary Hannity; Isabel Hardman; Sophie Harman; Candida Harper; Tim Harper; Ali Harris; Oliver Harris; B. H. Liddell Hart; Alice Hattrick; Paula Hawkins; Mo Hayder; Nick Hayes; Lottie Hazell; Oli Hazzard; Claire Marie Healy; Gerald Heard; John Heath-Stubbs; Emma Henderson; James Herbert; James Herriot; Mick Herron; Deborah Hewitt; Rosie Hewlett; Christopher Hibbert; Nathan Hill; Chris Hirst; Russell Hoban; Eric Hobsbawm; Gavanndra Hodge; Leigh Hodgkinson; Jesse Hodgson; Paul Hoffman; Edward Hogan; Anna Hoghton; Euny Hong; Liu Hong; Meredith Hooper; Simon Hopkinson; Trevor Horn; Tansy Hoskins; Richard Hough; Lucy Hounsom; Yuji Huang; Langston Hughes; Richard Hughes; Masud Husain; Julian Jackson; Julia Jarman; Elizabeth Jennings; Milly Johnson; Rebecca May Johnson; Diana Wynne Jones; Harold Jones; Lucy Jones; Owen Jones; Anthony Joseph;

Alan Judd; Helen Jukes; Anna Kavan; M. M. Kaye; Jessie Keane; Molly Keane; Anna Keay; John Keay; Stephen Kelman; Laura Kemp; Jonathan Kennedy; Paul Kennedy; Sidney Keyes; Barbara Keys; Sulmaan Wasif Khan; Rachel Khoo; Claire King; Clive King; Binnie Kirshenbaum; Bert Kitchen; C. H. B. Kitchin; June Knox-Mawer; Halik Kochanski; Jay Kristoff; Fifi Kuo; Emily LaBarge; Stephen Lacey; David Lammy; Marghanita Laski; Hugh Laurie; Eleanor Lavender; Ann Lawrence; Natalie Lawrence; Elisabeth Leake; Kate Leaver; Graham Lee; Jeremy Lee; Damien Lewis; Ted Lewis; Daniel Light; Jack Lindsay; Joan Lingard; Emanuel Litvinoff; Penelope Lively; Saci Lloyd; Jo Lodge; Tim Lott; Julia Lovell; Joanna Lumley; Richard Lumsden; Kesia Lupo; Max Lury; S. E. Lynes; Dame Vera Lynn; Louis MacNeice; Malcolm Ross Macdonald; Marianne Macdonald; Robert Macfarlane; Sophie Mackintosh; Manchan Magan; Erin Maglaque; Foday Mannah; Olivia Manning; Kathryn Mannix; Sarfraz Manzoor; Greil Marcus; Kathryn Maris; Jan Mark; Ellie Marney; Patrick Marnham; David Marquand; Helen Marten; Simon Mason; Ben Masters; Sadie Matthews; Evan Mawdsley; Peter May; Rufaro Faith Mazarura; Helen McCarthy; Geraldine McCaughrean; Elizabeth McCracken; Val McDermid; Iain McGilchrist; Elizabeth McKenzie; Tom McLaughlin; Thomas McMullan; Jean McNeil; Rosanna Mclaughlin; Anna Metcalfe; Ed Miliband; Louise Millar; Kei Miller; Myfanwy Millward; Kate Milner; Gladys Mitchell; Sarah Mitchell; Tony Mitton; Victoria Moore; Pete Morgan; Michael Morpurgo; Jackie Morris; Kate Morton; Emma-Lee Moss; Laura Mucha; Benjamin Myers; Fraser Nelson; Norman Nicholson; Jenny Nimmo; Johan Norberg; Charity Norman; David Nott; Sigrid Nunez; Peter Oborne; Diane Oliver; Yewande Omotoso; Jan Ormerod; Laurie Owens; Susan Owens; Kate O'Brien; Deborah O'Donoghue; C. S. Pacat; Derek Parker; Julia Parker; Sandeep Parmar; Helen Parr; Richard Partington; Robert Payne; Fred Pearce; Philippa Pearce; Harry Pearson; Cato Pedder; Eleanor Penny; Gilles Peterson; Kate Reed Petty; Charlotte Philby; Liz Pichon; Sarah Pinborough; Courtney Pine; Christina Pishiris; Anthony Powell; Des Powell; Margaret Powell; Chris Powling; Shannon Pufahl; Kathryn Purdie; Ann Purser; Sadiah Qureshi; Sabina Radeva; Amol Rajan; Madhvi Ramani; Joan Rankin; Catherine Rayner; Jacqui Rayner; Herbert Read; James Reeves; Katy Regan; Hannah Regel; Chris Renwick; Steve Richards; Sarah Ridgard; M. L. Rio; Fiona Roberton; Bethan Roberts; Jane Robinson; Lucy Robinson; Helen Roche; Claudia Roden; Jane Rogoyska; Rachel Rooney; Brunello Rosa; Leone Ross; Rupert Russell; Saba Sams; Jane Sanderson; Clive Sansom; Noo Saro-Wiwa; Dorothy L. Sayers; Kathryn Scanlan; Izabella Scott; Paul Scott; Alice Sebold; Rachel Seiffert; Antonia Senior; John Seymour; Miranda Seymour; Rachel Shabi; Nick Sharratt; Martin Shaw; Merlin Sheldrake; Megan Shepherd; Lola Shoneyin; Philip Short; Penelope Shuttle; Kate Simants; Karen Sinotok; Sujit Sivasundaram; Alexander McCall Smith; Lisa Smith; Mark B. Smith; Mary South; Muriel Spark; Kristina Spohr; Meagan Spooner; Howard Spring; Hilary Spurling; Jessica Stanley; Gertrude Stein; Joss Stirling; Rosie Storey; Peter Stott; Hannah Stowe; Hew Strachan; John Strawson; Jeremy Strong; Jonathan Stroud; Nicola Sturgeon; Rosemary Sutcliff; James L. Sutter; Emma Claire Sweeney; Tasha Sylva; Sally Symes; Vanessa Tait; Dizz Tate; A. J. P. Taylor; Lulu Taylor; Kae Tempest; Josephine Tey; Sureka Thanenthiran-Dharuman; Dylan Thomas; Frances Thomas; Scarlett Thomas; Pat Thomson; Simon Thurley; Phil Tinline; Theresa Tomlinson; Peter Tonkin; Nigel Toon; Lynne Truss; Ann Turnbull; A. K. Turner; Harriet Tyce; Simon Tyler; Jack Underwood; Hanna Thomas Uose; Nicola Upson; Rosamund Urwin; Jenny Valentine; Varaidzo; Yanis Varoufakis; Sarah Vaughan; Stephanie Victoire; Martin Waddell; Lucy Wadham; Alice Walker; Jill Paton Walsh; Joanna Walsh; Melanie Walsh; Rosie Walsh; Stephen Walsh; Minette Walters; Vanessa Walters; Miranda Ward; Bernard Wasserstein; Keith Waterhouse; Holly Watt; Aisling Watters; Christian Weaver; Mary Wesley; Sam Wetherell; Dorothy Whipple; Phil Whitaker; T. H. White; Thornton Wilder; Elizabeth Wilhide; Barbara Willard; Charles Williams; Jacqueline Wilson; Jon Wilson; Tim Winton; David Wojtowycz; Hope Wolf; Charlotte Wood; Carolyn Woods; Kate Worsley; John Wyndham; Xinran; Taichi Yamada; Mandy Yin; Kate Zambreno

Chair / Literary Agent: Anthony Goff (**L266**)

Company Director / Literary Agent: Veronique Baxter (**L052**)

Literary Agents: Nicola Chang (**L116**); Elise Dillsworth (**L170**); Jemima Forrester (**L232**); Georgia Glover; Andrew Gordon (**L270**); Lizzy Kremer; Caroline Walsh (**L645**); Jessica Woollard (**L672**)

L160 Elinor Davies
Associate Agent
United Kingdom

https://www.madeleinemilburn.co.uk
https://www.madeleinemilburn.co.uk/agents/elinor-davies/
https://twitter.com/Elinor22Mair

Literary Agency: Madeleine Milburn Literary, TV & Film Agency (**L420**)

Fiction > *Novels*
Book Club Fiction; Commercial; Cozy Mysteries; Crime; Culture; Family; Friends; High Concept; Historical Fiction; Magical Realism; Mystery; Romance; Social Commentary; Society; Supernatural / Paranormal Thrillers; Upmarket; Women's Fiction

Send: Query; Synopsis; Writing sample
How to send: Online submission system

I'm looking for commercial to upmarket stories that span compulsive to comforting reads. A clear hook is a must. An addictive premise that can be summed up in just a few words but will stay in the reader's mind. I am all about books that stir big emotions whether that's sobbing or laughing hysterically, filling me up with love and/or longing. I'm especially keen to find healing fiction. Books that tackle big themes such as love, death and human connection in an uplifting way are my favourite, and if they feature a 'curio' or magical realist element, even moreso! I'm obsessed with love stories of all kinds – whether that's romantic, familial or friendship. I'm keen to find authors writing sweeping love stories that are guaranteed to break your heart. Equally, stories that feel akin to a telenovela, full of drama, twists and passion. I'd also love to find a family love story, ideally intergenerational and heartwarming. I'm dying to find a smart, high-concept crime novel that is big, ambitious and international. I'm also eager for something that deals with an obscure crime that we've not seen delved into in books before (although nothing too dark or violent please!) I especially love crime books that have the reader rooting for the criminal throughout. I'm still on the lookout for unpredictable, direct narrators in this space. Light mysteries and cosy crime are also welcome but must have a fresh angle or a setting we haven't yet seen explored. On the darker end, I enjoy supernatural thrillers and books with a supernatural element that can lean into horror. In women's fiction I'm drawn to novels full of social commentary that sit comfortably in the book club space. I'd also love to find historical novels that delve into society and culture in the second half of the twentieth century (1950s onwards). Otherwise, I like historical-set novels to be a backdrop to something else – for example, a love story or a crime that can be real or imagined.

L161 Bonnie Davis
Literary Agent

Literary Agency: Bret Adams Ltd

L162 Liza Dawson
Senior Agent; President
United States

queryliza@lizadawsonassociates.com

https://www.lizadawsonassociates.com/liza-dawson

Literary Agency: Liza Dawson Associates (**L405**)

Professional Bodies: The Authors Guild; Mystery Writers of America (MWA)

Fiction > *Novels*
Book Club Fiction; Contemporary; Historical Fiction; Literary; Mystery; Social Class; Spy Thrilllers; Thrillers

Nonfiction > *Nonfiction Books*
Comedy / Humour; Culture; Environment; Ethnic Groups; Finance; Memoir; Narrative History; Politics; US Southern States; Women's Issues

Closed to approaches.

She specializes in: Smart, plot-driven bestselling fiction. Memorable, confidently-written, literary fiction. Page-turning thrillers that teach you about spycraft, foreign intrigue or an unusual career. Mysteries – featuring brainy detectives. Literary fiction for book clubs. Breakout historical novels. In nonfiction, she is drawn to cross-cultural and women's issues written by experts. She is looking for narrative history, memoirs about women and men who have escaped from closed, repressive societies and books by journalists and poets who are trying to make sense of exotic locations, race, the environment, Wall Street, Washington, and the South. Humor and tenderness are a plus, and she has a weakness for cartoonists and quirky humor.

Authors: Annie Barrows; Marie Bostwick; Bob Brier; Stella Cameron; Robyn Carr; Ross Gay; Susan Hasler; Julia Lee; Victoria Christopher Murray; Tawni O'Dell; Jean Sasson

L163 Liza DeBlock
Literary Agent
United Kingdom

submissions@mushens-entertainment.com

https://www.mushens-entertainment.com/liza-deblock

Literary Agency: Mushens Entertainment

Fiction > *Novels*
Grounded Fantasy; High Concept; Historical Fiction; Literary; Romantasy; Speculative; Thrillers; Upmarket; Urban Fantasy; Vampires; Werewolves; Witches

Nonfiction > *Nonfiction Books*
Cookery; Popular Science; Social History

Send: Query; Synopsis; Writing sample
How to send: Email

Looking for both fiction and non fiction.

For fiction, she is interested in adult only – do not send her children's, middle grade, or YA. She is looking for historical fiction that is well researched, immerses readers in the era, and looks at overlooked characters from the past, or perhaps gives a new spin on someone we think we know. On the literary and upmarket side, she is looking for novels infused with emotions that capture the human experience and make readers think. If your literary novel is something that A24 productions might turn into a movie, this is her taste. When it comes to fantasy, she loves urban and grounded fantasy (no sci-fi please!), and is always happy to look at anything with a vampire, werewolf, witches, warlocks, fairies, and perhaps a sinister selkie or two. She is also very much looking for romantasy and is the best person at the agency to submit that too. For thrillers, send her anything set in an exotic location, high-concept, or things with a speculative twist. She loves when characters are put in situations she would never want to be in, and then they have to get out of it.

On the non fiction side, she is looking for books that teach her something new or reframe a topic from an alternative point of view. This can include cookery, pop science, and social history.

Please do not send her: novellas or unfinished manuscripts, sci-fi, horror, erotica, graphic novels, children's books, middle grade, or poetry.

Authors: Sally Abe; Natalie Chandler; Sally El-Arifi; Dominic Franks; Jane Hennigan; Eleanor Houghton; Carys Jones; Hayley Nolan; Stacey Thomas; Pim Wangtechawat

L164 Dado Derviskadic
Literary Agent
United States
Tel: +1 (212) 400-1494

dado@foliolitmanagement.com

http://foliolit.com/dado-derviskadic

Literary Agency: Folio Literary Management, LLC

Nonfiction > *Nonfiction Books*
Art History; Biography; Cookery; Cultural History; Fashion; Films; Food; Health; Motivational Self-Help; Nutrition; Philosophy; Popular Culture; Popular Science; Psychology; Religion; Spirituality; Sub-Culture

Send: Query; Writing sample; Proposal
How to send: In the body of an email

I am primarily interested in: cultural history; biography; art history; film; religion and spirituality; psychology; philosophy; pop science and motivational self-help; health and nutrition; pop culture and subcultures; fashion; and food narrative and cookbooks.

L165 Allison Devereux
Literary Agent
United States

https://www.cheneyagency.com/allison-devereux

Literary Agency: The Cheney Agency

L166 DHH Literary Agency Ltd
Literary Agency
23-27 Cecil Court, London, WC2N 4EZ
United Kingdom
Tel: +44 (0) 20 3990 2452

enquiries@dhhliteraryagency.com

https://www.dhhliteraryagency.com

Professional Body: The Association of Authors' Agents (AAA)

ADULT
Fiction > *Novels*
Nonfiction > *Nonfiction Books*

CHILDREN'S > **Fiction** > *Novels*

YOUNG ADULT > **Fiction** > *Novels*

Send: Query; Synopsis; Writing sample
How to send: Email
How not to send: Post

Accepts submissions by email only. No postal submissions. See website for specific agent interests and email addresses and approach one agent only. Do not send submissions to generic "enquiries" email address.

Authors: Tasneem Abdur-Rashid; Foluso Agbaje; Paula Akpan; Carolina Are; Karen Arthur; Khairani Barokka; Graham Bartlett; Katie Baskerville; Louise Beech; R.C. Bridgestock; Tom Brown; Paul Burston; Caroline Butterwick; Andrea Carter; Will Carver; Paul Fraser Collard; Howard Colyer; James Conway; M.W. Craven; John Curran; Aaron Dale; Azma Dar; Heather Darwent; Becca Day; Michael Delahaye; K Devan; Sharan Dhaliwal; A. A. Dhand; Preeti Dhillon; Becky Docton; Suzie Edge; Stephen Edger; Anna Ellory; David Fennell; Deirdre Finnerty; Essie Fox; Anita Frank; Nicola Garrard; Divya Ghelani; Nadia Gilani; Erica Gillingham; Erin Green; Alexis Gregory; Michael Handrick; Mireille Harper; Katy Harrison; Ali Hendry; Lisa Hilton; Amelia Ireland; Hanan Issa; Valerie Jack; Sophie Jai; Ed James; Helga Jensen; Ragnar Jonasson; Lizzie Huxley Jones; Jón Atli Jónasson; Katrín Júlíusdóttir; Anthony Kavanagh; Nancy Kelley; Diana Kessler; Catherine Kurtz; Eleni Kyriacou; Caroline Lamond; Thomas Leeds; Michael Leggo; S.V. Leonard; Kathy Lette; Beth Lewis; Chantelle Lindsay; Elizabeth Lovatt; Sean Lusk; Zoe Lyons; Adrian Magson; Natalie Marlow; Layla McCay; Chris McDonald; Brian McGilloway; Emma Medrano; Rachel Meller; Jean Menzies; Chris Merritt; Janie Millman; Saima Mir; Zeena Moolla; Elizabeth S. Moore; Evie Muir; Jade Mutyora; Noel O'Reilly; Valerie O'Riordan; Erik Olsen; Yen Ooi; Vikki Patis; Philippa Peall; Penny Pepper; Lauren du Plessis; Grace Quantock; Anthony J. Quinn; Jenny Quintana; Jasmine Qureshi; Monika Radojevic; Jon Ransom; Reagan Lee Ray; Jini Reddy; Becky Rhush; Nicole Robinson; Juno Roche; Leon Romero-Montalvo; Iain Rowan; Robert Rutherford; Talia Samuels; Helen

Scott; Victoria Selman; Mel Sherratt; Amélie Skoda; Richard Stirling; Annie Taylor; Paul Taylor-Pitt; Rebecca Templeton; Jo Thomas; Rebecca Thorne; Sally Ann Truman; Amanda Tuke; Ola Tundun; Ronnie Turner; Rosie Turner; L.C. Tyler; Eva Verde; Kandace Siobhan Walker; A. J. West; Clare Weze; Clare Whitfield; Kathleen Whyman; Claire Wilson; L. C. Winter; David Young; lisa luxx; Eva Björg Ægisdottir

Company Director / Literary Agent: Emily Glenister (**L263**)

Literary Agent / Managing Director: David H. Headley (**L306**)

Literary Agents: Broo Doherty; Abi Fellows (**L216**); Harry Illingworth

L167 Diana Finch Literary Agency

Literary Agency
116 West 23rd Street, Suite 500, New York, NY 10011
United States
Tel: +1 (917) 544-4470

http://dianafinchliteraryagency.blogspot.com
https://dianafinchliteraryagency.submittable.com/submit
https://www.facebook.com/DianaFinchLitAg/

Nonfiction > *Nonfiction Books*
Adventure; Business; Environment; History; Lifestyle; Mathematics; Memoir; Narrative Nonfiction; Politics; Science

How to send: Submittable

The agency is closed to all fiction submissions, and taking only nonfiction queries, including memoir, until further notice.

Literary Agent: Diana Finch (**L224**)

L168 Donya Dickerson

Literary Agent
United States

https://www.aevitascreative.com
https://www.aevitascreative.com/agent/donya-dickerson
https://querymanager.com/query/3213

Literary Agency: Aevitas

Nonfiction > *Nonfiction Books*
Business; History; Parenting; Personal Development; Popular Culture; Science; Self Help; Technology

How to send: Query Manager

Focuses primarily on nonfiction in the categories of business, personal development, self-help, pop culture, science, technology, history, and parenting. She is looking for breakthrough thinking, experts with a fresh voice, and new approaches to solving the problems people face daily. She is especially drawn to books that help others be their best self and succeed in both their professional and personal lives. She is based in New York.

L169 Sandra Dijkstra

Literary Agent
United States

https://www.dijkstraagency.com/sandra-dijkstra.php
https://querymanager.com/query/DijkstraCapron

Literary Agency: Sandra Dijkstra Literary Agency

Fiction > *Novels*
Commercial; Literary

Nonfiction > *Nonfiction Books*
Business; Current Affairs; History; Politics; Religion; Science

How to send: By referral

Agent to authors in the arenas of nonfiction (including history, politics, current affairs, business, and science), and quality fiction which crosses over between literary and commercial, her mission is to champion authors whose books make a difference.

L170 Elise Dillsworth

Literary Agent
United Kingdom

elise@elisedillsworthagency.com

https://www.davidhigham.co.uk/agents-dh/elise-dillsworth/

Literary Agencies: Elise Dillsworth Agency (EDA); David Higham Associates Ltd (**L159**)

Fiction > *Novels*
General, and in particular: International; Literary

Nonfiction > *Nonfiction Books*
General, and in particular: Autobiography; International; Literary; Memoir

Represents literary and general fiction and non-fiction – especially autobiography and memoir, with a keen aim to reflect writing that is international.

Authors: Yvonne Battle-Felton; Maria Bradford; Karen Downs-Barton; Anthony Joseph; Foday Mannah; Diane Oliver; Yewande Omotoso; Courtney Pine; Noo Saro-Wiwa; Stephanie Victoire; Aisling Watters

L171 Isobel Dixon

Literary Agent; Managing Director
United Kingdom

isobeldixon@blakefriedmann.co.uk

http://blakefriedmann.co.uk/isobel-dixon
https://twitter.com/isobeldixon

Literary Agency: Blake Friedmann Literary Agency Ltd (**L066**)

Fiction > *Novels*
Contemporary; Crime; Historical Fiction; Literary; Thrillers

Nonfiction > *Nonfiction Books*
Biography; Memoir; Narrative History

Closed to approaches.

Interests are wide-ranging and her clients' work includes contemporary, historical and literary fiction, crime and thrillers, memoir, biography and narrative history.

Authors: Sally Andrew; Romalyn Ante; Abdul Rahman Azzam; Sandy Balfour; Tom Benn; Karin Brynard; Graeme Macrae Burnet; James Cahill; Edward Carey; Elizabeth Chadwick; Anne de Courcy; Achmat Dangor; Finuala Dowling; Barbara Erskine; Felice Fallon; Tracey Farren; Kathryn Faulke; David Gilman; Lyndall Gordon; Ann Granger; Cormac James; Peter James; Tomasz Jedrowski; Charles Lambert; Zakes Mda; Deon Meyer; Christopher Nicholson; Marlene van Niekerk; Lawrence Norfolk; Gregory Norminton; Joseph O'Connor; Sheila O'Flanagan; Kaite O'Reilly; Alan Parks; Monique Roffey; Henrietta Rose-Innes; Julian Stockwin; Ivan Vladislavic; Bridget Walsh; Anne Watts; Harry Whitehead; Edward Wilson-Lee

L172 Saffron Dodd

Literary Agent
United Kingdom

submissions@ashliterary.com

https://ashliterary.com/#saffronwishlist
https://querymanager.com/query/saffronashliterary

Literary Agency: ASH Literary

CHILDREN'S > *Fiction* > *Middle Grade*
Adventure; Contemporary; Fantasy; Magic

YOUNG ADULT > *Fiction* > *Novels*
Fantasy; Mystery; Romantic Comedy; Thrillers

Send: Query; Synopsis; Writing sample
How to send: Query Manager; Email

I'm looking for fully realised, immersive, and creative worlds with standout characters. I love middle-grade fantasy and I'm looking for something filled with adventure, magic, and intrigue, with a strong and distinct voice. In contemporary middle-grade, I'm looking for witty and sharp protagonists with something to say and an interesting perspective on the world. In YA, I lean towards fantasy but would also love a solid mystery thriller or a shenanigan filled rom-com that does or says something new. I'm also keen to see stories set in the UK during the transitional period between sixth form/college and university. Above all, I'm keen to see work from historically excluded and underrepresented writers in the UK.

L173 Trevor Dolby
Literary Agent
United Kingdom

https://aevitascreative.com/agents/#agent-7410

Literary Agency: Aevitas Creative Management (ACM) UK (**L007**)

Nonfiction > *Nonfiction Books*
  Biography; Comedy / Humour; Memoir; Military History; Narrative History; Nature; Popular Culture; Popular Science

Closed to approaches.

Looking for popular science with a clear relevance to everyday life, narrative history, military history, humour, biography, popular culture, natural history and great memoirs by passionate people whose lives have been well lived.

Authors: James Aldred; Charlie Hamilton James; Peter Mead; Jenny Radcliffe; Neil Root; Marianna Spring

L174 Adriana Dominguez
Senior Agent; Partner
United States

https://aevitascreative.com/agents/
https://querymanager.com/query/2243

Literary Agency: Aevitas

ADULT > **Nonfiction** > *Nonfiction Books*: Narrative Nonfiction

CHILDREN'S
  Fiction
    Middle Grade; Picture Books
  Nonfiction > *Nonfiction Books*

How to send: Query Manager

Interested in illustrators with fresh, unmistakable styles, platform-driven narrative nonfiction from children to adult, and select children's fiction from picture books to middle grade.

Authors: Jacqueline Alcántara; Ana Aranda; Andrés López; Angela Cervantes; Daniel Fishel; Irena Freitas; John Parra; Juliet Menéndez; Lucía Franco; Marcelo Verdad; Maria Hinojosa; Claudia Guadalupe Martinez; Maya Wei-Haas; Gerardo Ivan Morales; Heidi Moreno; Emma Otheguy; Katheryn Russell-Brown; Madrid Santos; David Smith; Tania de Regil; Janelle Washington

L175 Don Congdon Associates, Inc.
Literary Agency
88 Pine Street, Suite 730, New York, NY 10005
United States
Tel: +1 (212) 645-1229

dca@doncongdon.com
https://doncongdon.com

Professional Body: Association of American Literary Agents (AALA)

Fiction > *Novels*
Nonfiction > *Nonfiction Books*

Send: Query; Synopsis; Writing sample
How to send: Email; Query Manager

Send query by email (no attachments) or by Query Manager, per agent preference. Include one-page synopsis, relevant background info, and first chapter, all within the body of the email if submitting by email. Include the word "Query" in the subject line. See website for full guidelines. No unsolicited MSS.

Foreign Rights Manager / Literary Agent: Cristina Concepcion (**L135**)

Literary Agents: Michael Congdon; Katie Grimm (**L279**); Katie Kotchman (**L374**); Maura Kye-Casella; Caroline Miranda (**L454**); Susan Ramer (**L528**)

L176 Donald Maass Literary Agency
Literary Agency
1000 Dean Street, Suite 331, Brooklyn, NY 11238
United States
Tel: +1 (212) 727-8383

info@maassagency.com
http://www.maassagency.com

Professional Body: Association of American Literary Agents (AALA)

ADULT
  Fiction > *Novels*
  Nonfiction > *Nonfiction Books*

YOUNG ADULT > **Fiction** > *Novels*

Send: Query; Synopsis; Writing sample
How to send: Email
How not to send: Post; Phone; Social Media

Welcomes all genres, in particular science fiction, fantasy, mystery, suspense, horror, romance, historical, literary and mainstream novels. Send query to a specific agent, by email, with "query" in the subject line. No queries by post, phone, or social media. See website for individual agent interests and email addresses.

Authors: Saladin Ahmed; Sonya Bateman; Jim Butcher

Literary Agents: Michael Curry; Jennifer Goloboy; Jolene Haley (**L289**); Jennifer Jackson; Kat Kerr; Donald Maass; Cameron McClure; Caitlin McDonald; Kiana Nguyen; Anne Tibbets (**L630**)

Vice President: Katie Shea Boutillier

L177 Doug Grad Literary Agency
Literary Agency
156 Prospect Park West, #3L, Brooklyn, NY 11215
United States
Tel: +1 (718) 788-6067

doug.grad@dgliterary.com
http://www.dgliterary.com
https://www.facebook.com/DGLit

Fiction
  Graphic Novels: General
  Novels: Comedy / Humour; Crime; Historical Fiction; Mystery; Romance; Science Fiction; Thrillers; Westerns; Women's Fiction
Nonfiction
  Illustrated Books: Comedy / Humour; Photography
  Nonfiction Books: Adventure; Biography; Business; Cars; Comedy / Humour; Cookery; Crime; Dogs; Films; Gardening; Health; History; How To; Journalism; Language; Memoir; Military; Music; Politics; Religion; Self Help; Sport; Theatre; Travel

Send: Query
Don't send: Writing sample
How to send: Email
How not to send: Post; Phone

Send query letter by email. Do not include sample material until requested.

Literary Agent: Doug Grad

L178 Claire Draper
Literary Agent
United States

https://querymanager.com/query/draper_claire

Literary Agency: Azantian Literary Agency

ADULT
  Fiction > *Novels*
    Feminism; LGBTQIA; Romance

  Nonfiction > *Nonfiction Books*
    General, and in particular: Arts; Cookery; Crafts; Feminism; Home Improvement; LGBTQIA; Media; Memoir; Parenting; Plants

CHILDREN'S > **Fiction**
  Graphic Novels; Middle Grade
YOUNG ADULT > **Fiction**
  Graphic Novels; Novels

How not to send: Query Manager

Prefers to work with queer and BIPOC creators. Likes lighthearted, emotional, hopeful, adventurous reads. Largely genre-agnostic, but prefers books with a fast pace, high stakes, and strong emotional development for the main character(s). Does not want to see books from authors writing identity-based books not of their own identity.

L179 Dunham Literary, Inc.
Literary Agency
United States

query@dunhamlit.com

https://www.dunhamlit.com

ADULT
  Fiction > *Novels*

  Nonfiction > *Nonfiction Books*: Narrative Nonfiction

CHILDREN'S > Fiction
  Novels; Picture Books

Send: Query; Writing sample
Don't send: Full text
How to send: By referral; Online pitch events; Conferences
How not to send: Post; Fax; Phone; Email attachment; Google Docs shared document; Social Media

Handles quality fiction and nonfiction for adults and children. Send query by email only. See website for full guidelines. No approaches by post, phone or fax. No email attachments or links to Google docs.

Literary Agents: Anjanette Barr (**L045**); Jennie Dunham (**L180**)

L180 Jennie Dunham
Literary Agent
United States

https://www.dunhamlit.com/jennie-dunham.html
https://aalitagents.org/author/jenniedunham/
https://twitter.com/JennieDunhamLit
https://www.linkedin.com/in/jennie-dunham-11028b140/
https://www.facebook.com/JennieDunhamLit
https://www.instagram.com/jenniedunhamlit

Literary Agency: Dunham Literary, Inc. (**L179**)
Professional Bodies: Association of American Literary Agents (AALA); Society of Children's Book Writers and Illustrators (SCBWI)

ADULT
  Fiction
    Graphic Novels: General
    Novels: Comedy / Humour; Historical Fiction; LGBTQIA; Literary; Mystery; Thrillers; Women's Fiction
  Nonfiction > *Nonfiction Books*
    Biography; Current Affairs; Family; History; Memoir; Narrative Nonfiction; Parenting; Politics; Relationships; Science; Technology

CHILDREN'S > Fiction
  Middle Grade; Picture Books
NEW ADULT
  Fiction > *Novels*
  Nonfiction > *Nonfiction Books*
YOUNG ADULT > Fiction > *Novels*

Send: Query; Writing sample
Don't send: Full text
How to send: In the body of an email
How not to send: Post; Fax; Phone; Email attachment

Represents literary fiction and non-fiction for adults and children.

L181 Ben Dunn
Literary Agent
United Kingdom

https://dunnfogg.co.uk
https://dunnfogg.co.uk/about-us/

Literary Agency: DunnFogg (**L182**)

Fiction > *Novels*
  Book Club Fiction; Speculative; Thrillers; Women's Fiction

Nonfiction > *Nonfiction Books*
  High Concept; Memoir; Narrative Nonfiction; Nature; Popular Science

How to send: Online submission system

I am happy to consider submissions in the following areas:

Fiction: off-beat thriller, reading group, speculative, issue-led women's fiction.

Non-fiction: Memoir, narrative-led non-fiction, nature writing, media tie-in (TV, Radio, Social Media, Podcast), pop-science, and big ideas.

For fiction, I enjoy off-beat characters, unusual plots and writing that extends the margins of what is traditionally expected within a genre. I am drawn to unique voices, and often novels written with humour, not 'funny' novels per se, but writing that stands out as different and unexpected.

For non-fiction, I made my start in publishing just as it was embracing popular culture. This led me into a career of following and anticipating trends, and I have continued that course into my time as an agent.

L182 DunnFogg
Literary Agency
PO Box 78047, London, N4 9LP
United Kingdom

https://dunnfogg.co.uk

Professional Body: The Association of Authors' Agents (AAA)

Fiction > *Novels*

Nonfiction > *Nonfiction Books*

Send: Query; Author bio; Synopsis; Writing sample
How to send: Online submission system

A high-profile independent literary agency that specialises in quality and commercial non-fiction and fiction. Set up in 2021, the agency represents numerous award-winning, bestselling and renowned writers and artists.

Literary Agents: Ben Dunn (**L181**); Jack Fogg (**L230**)

L183 Neil Dunnicliffe
Literary Agent
United Kingdom

neil@springliterary.com

https://www.springliterary.com/about

Literary Agency: Spring Literary (**L594**)

L184 Dunow, Carlson & Lerner Agency
Literary Agency
27 West 20th Street, Suite 1103, New York, NY 10011
United States
Tel: +1 (212) 645-7606

mail@dclagency.com

https://www.dclagency.com

Professional Body: Association of American Literary Agents (AALA)

ADULT
  Fiction > *Novels*
    Commercial; Literary

  Nonfiction > *Nonfiction Books*

CHILDREN'S > Fiction
  Chapter Books; Early Readers; Middle Grade

Send: Query; Writing sample; Self-Addressed Stamped Envelope (SASE)
How to send: In the body of an email; Post
How not to send: Email attachment

Represents literary and commercial fiction, a wide range of nonfiction, and children's literature for all ages. Prefers queries by email, but will also accept queries by post with SASE. No attachments. Does not respond to all email queries.

Author Estates: The Estate of Donald J. Sobol; The Estate of Jim Carroll; The Estate of John Steptoe; The Estate of Joseph Mitchell; The Estate of William Lee Miller

Authors: Nathaniel Adams; Siobhan Adcock; Preston Allen; Mara Altman; Stephen Amidon; Cynthia Anderson; Jessica Applestone; Josh & Jessica Applestone; Richard Aquila; Beth Bacon; Kevin Baker; Nancy Balbirer; Wilton Barnhardt; Jackie Battenfield; Douglas Bauer; Richard Bausch; Aimee Bender; Jennifer Berney; Tanaz Bhathena; Brandon Bird; George Black; Lea Black; Robin Black; Michael Bobelian; Lorraine Boissoneault; Amy Bonnaffons; Shira Boss; Michelle Bowdler; Sesali Bowen; Nadia Bowers; Svetlana Boym; G.B. Bragg; Benjamin Breen; Elise Broach; Kevin Brockmeier; Mikita Brottman; David W. Brown; Stacia Brown; David Browne; Allison Buccola; Mónica Bustamante; Hamilton Cain; Katrina Carrasco; Bill Carter; Erika Carter; Adam Cayton-Holland; Climate Central; Bryn Chancellor; Joelle Charbonneau; Noah Charney; Paula Chase; Emily Chenoweth; K Chess; Mark

Childress; Christina Chiu; Adam Christopher; Mimi Chubb; Cassandra Rose Clarke; Nigel Cliff; Nancy Coffelt; Jaed Coffin; Cole Cohen; Miriam Cohen; Jaimee Wriston Colbert; Deborah Joy Corey; Paul Cornell; Carrie Courogen; Jeremy Craig; Katherine Crowley; Dave Cullen; Cheyenne Curtis; Mark Dapin; Dame Darcy; Alice Elliott Dark; Michael Dart; Elizabeth Davis; Delilah S. Dawson; Alena Dillon; Heather Dixon; Lawrence Downes; Allyson Downey; Mike Duncan; DK Dyson; Ellie Eaton; Damien Echols; Daniel Ehrenhaft; Rhian Ellis; Katherine Crowley & Kathy Elster; Kathy Elster; Donald J. Sobol Estate; Jim Carroll Estate; John Steptoe Estate; Joseph Mitchell Estate; Scott O'Dell Estate; William Lee Miller Estate; Marion Ettlinger; Marie Faverau; Stephanie Feldman; Boris Fishman; Emily Flitter; Brendan Frederick; Pia Frey; Seth Fried; Steven Galloway; John Gartner; Amina Gautier; Joshua Gaylord; Valerie Geary; Poppy Gee; Michael Gerber; Alfred Gingold; Owen Gleiberman; Brandt Goldstein; Gary Golio; Matthew Goodman; Eli Gottlieb; Temple Grandin; Elizabeth Graver; Casey Gray; Seth Greenland; Gwendolen Gross; Rudy Gutierrez; Kathleen Hale; Lisa Hale; Leah Hampton; Mary Ellen Hannibal; Alyssa Hardy; Windy Lynn Harris; Ethan Hauser; Kevin Hearne; Robert Hellenga; Steve Hendricks; Joe Henry; Becky Hepinstall; Emily Jane Hodgkin; George Hodgman; Beatrice Hohenegger; Christopher M. Hood; Erin Hosier; Ilze Hugo; Josie Iselin; Jeremy Jackson; John Hornor Jacobs; Matthew Jobin; Daron Joffe; Mary Jones; Noah Z. Jones; David Joy; Frank Wheeler, Jr.; Valerie June; Karen Kane; Hester Kaplan; Ani Katz; Jon Keller; Brad Kessler; Christian Kiefer; Andrea Kleine; Taylor Koekkoek; Chrissy Kolaya; Amanda Korman; Gabrielle Korn; Nik Korpon; J. Kasper Kramer; Justin Kuritzkes; Maria Kuznetsova; Johanna Lane; Sarah Langan; Richard Lange; Sarah Laskow; Holly LeCraw; Mirnae Lee; Tommy Lee; Edan Lepucki; Elizabeth Lesser; Jerry Lee Lewis; Robin Lewis; David Lida; Anya Liftig; Brad Listi; William Bryant Logan; Jenny Lombard; Leil Lowndes; Joshua Lyon; Robin MacArthur; David Stuart MacLean; Anne Madden; Dennis Mahoney; Tania Malik; Michael Mann; Tanya Marquardt; Debra Marquart; Alex Marshall; Cate Marvin; Suzanne Matson; Abi Maxwell; Matthew McBride; Jill McCorkle; Elizabeth McCracken; Patrick McDonnell; Sean McGinty; Jon McGoran; Will McGrath; Adam McOmber; Bob Mehr; Susan Scarf Merrell; Deborah Meyler; Jenny Milchman; Barnabas Miller; Daphne Miller; Paul Miller; Richard J. Miller; Denise Mina; T. T. Monday; Gregory Mone; Amanda Montell; Bradford Morrow; Brian Morton; Layne Mosler; Sarah Moss; Ritu Mukerji; Kimberly Shannon Murphy; Myra Musgrove; Debbie Nathan; Ed Nawotka; Greg Neri; Robert Neuwith; Alana Newhouse; Scott O'Connor; Aline Ohanesian; Elizabeth Oness; David Orr; Chad Orzel; Tom Paine; Richard Panek; Michel Paradis; Debra Pascali-Bonaro; Rachel Pastan; Justin Peacock; Jamie Pearlberg; Tony Perrottet; Annie Rogers, Ph.D.; Chad Orzel, Ph.D.; Max Phillips; Melissa Holbrook Pierson; Nic Pizzolatto; Aimee Pokwatka; Daria Polichetti; Richard Polt; Maggie Pouncey; Jessica Powers; Caroline Preston; Cherie Priest; Mark Prins; D. M. Pulley; Carol Purington; Susan Todd & Carol Purington; Joan Quigley; Mark Rader; Susanna Reich; Nelly Reifler; Heidi Reimer; James Renner; Paul Reyes; Robert Riesman; Honni Van Rijswijk; Nicholas Rinaldi; M. L. Rio; Marisa Robinson-Textor; Annie Rogers; Stuart Rojstaczer; Tricia Romano; Linda Ronstadt; Jane Roper; Alex Rose; Marissa A. Ross; Rebecca Rotert; Shannan Rouss; Katherine Rowland; Lena Roy; David Rubel; Joan Ryan; Richard Sandoval; Marisa de los Santos; Alexis Schaitkin; Kodi Scheer; Patty Schemel; David Schickler; Molly Schiot; Heidi Jon Schmidt; Sally Schmitt; Pat Schories; William Todd Schultz; Kieran Shea; Jeff Shelby; Joshua Wolf Shenk; Jenefer Shute; Ingrid Silva; Marisa Silver; Ione Skye; Mohamedou Slahi; Patti Smith; Sherry Smith; Kevin Smokler; Tatjana Soli; Lily Sparks; Shira Spector; Kelli Stanley; Leigh Stein; Javaka Steptoe; Lindsay Stern; Jude Stewart; Susan Straight; Cynthia D'Aprix Sweeney; Vivian Swift; Shannon Takaoka; Liara Tamani; Katrina Taylor; Nick Taylor; David Teague; Tori Telfer; Melanie Thernstrom; Jean Thompson; Richard Todd; Susan Todd; David Tomlinson; Lawrence Turman; James Twitchell; Neil deGrasse Tyson; Robert Utley; Karen Valby; Katherine Vaz; Sarah St. Vincent; Christine Wade; Laura Waldon; Casey Walker; Mark Van de Walle; Margaret Wappler; Elizabeth Weinberg; Jillian Weise; Jan Merete Weiss; Michaele Weissman; Elizabeth Weitzman; Chuck Wendig; Frank Wheeler; Kali White; Matt Wiegle; Marianne Wiggins; Amy Wilentz; Corban Wilkinson; Tim Wirkus; Mishna Wolff; Hilma Wolitzer; Alisson Wood; Aubrey Wood; Billy Woods; Rebecca Woolf; Sara Woster; Kim Wozencraft; Ronald Wright; David Wroblewski; Jeff Yang; David Yoo; Kenji Yoshino; Alia Yunis; Alan Ziegler; Jaime deBlanc-Knowles; Jennifer duBois

Literary Agents: Jennifer Carlson; Arielle Datz; Stacia Decker; Henry Dunow; Erin Hosier; Eleanor Jackson; Julia Kenny (**L361**); Betsy Lerner; Edward Necarsulmer; Nicki Richesin; Yishai Seidman

L185 Adam Eaglin
Literary Agent
United States

https://www.cheneyagency.com/adameaglin

Literary Agency: The Cheney Agency

L186 Lynette Eason
Literary Agent
United States

ehumphries@stevelaube.com

https://stevelaube.com/what-i-am-looking-for-lynette-eason/

Literary Agency: The Steve Laube Agency

ADULT
  Fiction > *Novels*
    Christianity; Contemporary Women's Fiction; Historical Fiction; Mystery; Romantic Suspense; Speculative; Thrillers

  Nonfiction > *Nonfiction Books*: Christianity

YOUNG ADULT
  Fiction > *Novels*: Christianity

  Nonfiction > *Nonfiction Books*: Christianity

Send: Query; Writing sample
How to send: Email
How not to send: Post

I am looking for Christian authors wishing to write and sell to the Christian market. This means that I'm searching for clients who adhere to the teachings of Christ and Scripture. I'm looking to represent authors of all types of Christian fiction. I'm also interested in YA nonfiction and may be interested in some adult nonfiction, depending on the topic. I am not looking for children's books.

L187 Chelsea Eberly
Literary Agent; Company Director
United States

https://www.greenhouseliterary.com/the-team/chelsea-eberly/
https://twitter.com/chelseberly
https://www.publishersmarketplace.com/members/ChelseaEberly/
https://querymanager.com/query/ChelseaEberly

Literary Agency: The Greenhouse Literary Agency

ADULT > **Fiction** > *Novels*
  Book Club Women's Fiction; Upmarket Women's Fiction

CHILDREN'S
  Fiction
    Graphic Novels: General
    Middle Grade: Adventure; Comedy / Humour; Fantasy; Folklore, Myths, and Legends; Magical Realism; Mystery
    Picture Books: General

  Nonfiction
    Nonfiction Books; *Picture Books*

YOUNG ADULT
  Fiction
    Graphic Novels: Comedy / Humour; Contemporary; Fantasy; Magical Realism; Romance

Novels: Commercial; Fantasy; Feminism; Literary; Mystery; Romance; Social Justice; Thrillers
Nonfiction > *Graphic Nonfiction*
General, and in particular: History

Does not want:

CHILDREN'S > **Fiction** > *Middle Grade*: Horror
YOUNG ADULT > **Fiction** > *Novels*: Horror

Send: Query; Author bio; Writing sample; Proposal
How to send: By referral

Represents authors of middle grade, young adult, graphic novels, and women's fiction, as well as illustrators who write picture books.

L188 Eddison Pearson Ltd
Literary Agency
West Hill House, 6 Swain's Lane, London, N6 6QS
United Kingdom
Tel: +44 (0) 20 7700 7763

enquiries@eddisonpearson.com

https://www.eddisonpearson.com
https://linktr.ee/ClarePearson
https://eddisonpearson.blog
https://www.linkedin.com/in/clare-pearson-epla
https://twitter.com/ClarePearson_EP

Professional Body: The Association of Authors' Agents (AAA)

CHILDREN'S
  Fiction
    Novels: Contemporary; Historical Fiction
    Picture Books: General
  Poetry > *Any Poetic Form*
YOUNG ADULT > **Fiction** > *Novels*

Send: Query; Writing sample
How to send: Email
How not to send: Social Media; Post

A London-based literary agency providing a personal service to a small stable of talented authors, mainly of books for children and young adults. Send query by email only for auto-response containing up-to-date submission guidelines and email address for submissions. No submissions or enquiries by post.

Authors: Valerie Bloom; Michael Catchpool; Sue Heap; Caroline Lawrence; Robert Muchamore; Mary Murphy; Megan Rix

Literary Agent: Clare Pearson

L189 Sam Edenborough
Literary Agent; Foreign Rights Director
United Kingdom

sam@greyhoundliterary.co.uk

https://greyhoundliterary.co.uk/agent/sam-edenborough/
https://twitter.com/SamEdenborough

Literary Agency: Greyhound Literary (**L278**)

Fiction > *Novels*
Cyberpunk; Fantasy; Folklore, Myths, and Legends; Hard Science Fiction; Horror; Speculative; Upmarket

Nonfiction > *Nonfiction Books*
Classical Music; Culture; History; Jazz; Music; Science

Send: Synopsis; Outline; Writing sample
How to send: Email

A life-long reader of speculative fiction. He loves hard SF and cyberpunk that explores the biggest questions about what it means to be human; fantasy with wit, brilliantly deep world-building and characters with an edge. He is interested in upmarket, folkloric or horror-tinged fiction. He is also looking for fiction and non-fiction which engages with landscape or the sea in a profound and original way; books about jazz and classical music and musicians; work by historians and novelists who challenge us to rethink comfortable assumptions about an era or a culture; and writing by scientists who are able to communicate complex ideas to a wide readership with verve.

Authors: David Clifford; Jonathan Morrison; Leonard Rutgers; Philip Suggars

L190 Max Edwards
Literary Agent
United Kingdom

max@appletreeliterary.co.uk

https://aevitascreative.com/agents/#agent-7412
http://appletreeliterary.co.uk/about/
https://querymanager.com/query/2619

Literary Agency: Aevitas Creative Management (ACM) UK (**L007**)

Fiction > *Novels*
Commercial; Crime; Fantasy; High Concept; Science Fiction

Nonfiction > *Nonfiction Books*
History; Journalism; Memoir; Nature

Closed to approaches.

In non-fiction, he is looking for experts telling a new story for a trade audience; incredible memoirs and untold histories; journalists looking to take their stories long-form; and smart and original ideas. In fiction, he is looking for commercial and genre novels, and is a massive fan of novels that mix genres in a unique way. He's a sucker for high concepts, smart plots and unique characters – twists and turns, good (and bad) guys with depth and life.

Authors: William Lee Adams; Theo Barclay; Ross Barnett; Louise Callaghan; Hannah Durkin; Lucy Fisher; Johanna Katrin Fridriksdottir; James Hazel; Alex Hess; David Hone; Gulchehra Hora; John J. Johnston; Snorri Kristjansson; Matt Lodder; Debora MacKenzie; Oksana Masters; Laura Mauro; Una McCormack; Keza McDonald; Juliet E. McKenna; Guy Morpuss; Luke O'Neill; Jay Owens; Sumit Paul-Choudhury; Nick Pettigrew; Dominic Pimenta; Swéta Rana; Joe Tracini; Aliya Whiteley; James Womack; Jim Worrad; Suzanne Wrack; Olivia Yallop

L191 Nicole Eisenbraun
Literary Agent
United States

nme@gingerclarkliterary.com

https://gingerclarkliterary.com/About
https://gingerclarkliterary.com/Submissions
http://aaronline.org/Sys/PublicProfile/51483163/417813

Literary Agency: Ginger Clark Literary (**L260**)
Professional Body: Association of American Literary Agents (AALA)

CHILDREN'S > **Fiction** > *Middle Grade*
General, and in particular: Fairy Tales
YOUNG ADULT > **Fiction** > *Novels*
General, and in particular: Fairy Tales

Send: Query; Writing sample
How to send: Email

Looking for middle grade and young adult in all genres. She is particularly interested in great fairytale retellings with colorful twists and stories that tackle difficult subjects in unexpected ways.

L192 Caroline Eisenmann
Senior Agent; Vice President
United States

ce@goldinlit.com

https://goldinlit.com/agents/

Literary Agency: Frances Goldin Literary Agency, Inc. (**L238**)
Professional Body: Association of American Literary Agents (AALA)

Fiction > *Novels*
Literary; Social Issues; Upmarket

Nonfiction
  Essays: General
  Nonfiction Books: Biography; Cultural Criticism; History; Literary Memoir; Sub-Culture

How to send: Email

Particularly drawn to novels that engage with social issues, stories about obsession, and work that centers around intimacy and its discontents. Her nonfiction interests include deeply reported narratives (especially those that take the reader into the heart of a subculture), literary memoir, cultural criticism, essay collections, and history and biography with a surprising point of view.

Authors: Kyle Chayka; Ye Chun; Linda Rui Feng; Amanda Goldblatt; James Gregor; Peter Kispert; Theresa Levitt; Micah Nemerever; Jenny Odell; Kate Wagner; Michelle Webster-Hein

L193 The Ekus Group
Literary Agency
57 North Street, Hatfield, MA 01038
United States
Tel: +1 (212) 794-1082

info@lisaekus.com

https://ekusgroup.com

Nonfiction > *Nonfiction Books*: Cookery

How to send: Online submission system

Handles cookery books only. Submit proposal through submission system on website.

Literary Agent: Lisa Ekus

Senior Agent: Sally Ekus (**L194**)

L194 Sally Ekus
Senior Agent
United States

sally@ekusgroup.com

https://ekusgroup.com
https://ekusgroup.com/people/sally-ekus/
https://www.jvnla.com/our-team.php
https://aalitagents.org/author/sallylisaekus-com/
https://www.linkedin.com/in/sally-ekus-b8116554/
https://www.instagram.com/sallyekus/

Literary Agencies: The Ekus Group (**L193**); The Jean V. Naggar Literary Agency
Professional Body: Association of American Literary Agents (AALA)

Nonfiction > *Nonfiction Books*
Cookery; Health; Lifestyle; Wellbeing

Send: Query; Proposal; Author bio; Market info; Marketing Plan; Table of Contents
How to send: Email

Represents a wide range of culinary, health, wellness, and lifestyle talent, from first-time cookbook authors to seasoned chefs, RDs, professional food writers, bloggers, online creators, and journalists.

L195 Elaine Markson Literary Agency
Literary Agency
116 West 23rd Street, 5th flr, New York, NY 10011
United States

gagencyquery@gmail.com

https://www.marksonagency.com

Fiction > *Novels*

Nonfiction > *Nonfiction Books*
Literary Agent: Jeff Gerecke

L196 Elaine Steel
Literary Agency
49 Greek Street, London, W1D 4EG
United Kingdom
Tel: +44 (0) 1273 739022

es@elainesteel.com

https://www.elainesteel.com

Professional Body: The Association of Authors' Agents (AAA)

Fiction > *Novels*

Nonfiction > *Nonfiction Books*

Scripts
Film Scripts; Radio Scripts; TV Scripts; Theatre Scripts

Send: Query; Author bio; Outline
Don't send: Full text
How to send: Email

Represents writers and directors in film, television, stage and radio as well as book writers. Send query by email with CV and outline, along with details of experience. No unsolicited mss.

Authors: Gwyneth Hughes; James Lovelock; Ben Steiner

L197 Sian Ellis-Martin
Associate Agent
United Kingdom

sian@blakefriedmann.co.uk

http://blakefriedmann.co.uk/sianellis-martin
https://twitter.com/sianellismartin

Literary Agency: Blake Friedmann Literary Agency Ltd (**L066**)

Fiction > *Novels*
Coming of Age; Commercial; Contemporary; Crime; Ethnic Groups; Family Saga; Family; Friends; Historical Fiction; LGBTQIA; Literary; Love; Relationships; Romance; Romantic Comedy; Sex; Sexuality; Social Class; Thrillers

Nonfiction > *Nonfiction Books*
Cookery; Food; History; Love; Narrative Nonfiction; Politics; Popular Culture; Relationships

Does not want:

Fiction > *Novels*: Police Procedural

Send: Query; Synopsis; Writing sample
How to send: Email attachment

I'm building a list of fiction and non-fiction across genres. I'm keen to hear from authors who feel their voice is underrepresented in publishing and it's important to me to work with authors and books from a wide variety of backgrounds.

Authors: Shani Akilah; Ros Anderson; Jenny Glanfield; Leeanne O'Donnell; Karen Powell; Cristina Wolf

L198 Zabé Ellor
Literary Agent
United States

https://www.jdlit.com/zabe-ellor
https://querymanager.com/query/ZabeEllor
https://twitter.com/ZREllor

Literary Agency: The Jennifer DeChiara Literary Agency

ADULT
Fiction
Graphic Novels: General
Novels: Commercial; Fantasy; Mystery; Science Fiction; Thrillers; Upmarket Contemporary Fiction
Nonfiction > *Nonfiction Books*
History; Science

CHILDREN'S > **Fiction**
Graphic Novels: General
Middle Grade: Adventure; Comedy / Humour; Speculative
YOUNG ADULT > **Fiction**
Graphic Novels: General
Novels: General, and in particular: Contemporary; Fantasy; Mystery; Romance; Science Fiction; Thrillers

Closed to approaches.

For fiction, send a query, a 1-2 page synopsis, and the first 25 pages of your project. For nonfiction, send a query and a sample chapter. For graphic novels, send a query with a link to your portfolio website. I strive to respond to all queries in 12-14 weeks.

L199 Emily Sweet Associates
Literary Agency
United Kingdom

http://www.emilysweetassociates.com

Professional Body: The Association of Authors' Agents (AAA)

Types: Fiction; Nonfiction
Subjects: Biography; Commercial; Cookery; Current Affairs; History; Literary
Markets: Adult

Send: Query
Don't send: Full text

No Young Adult or children's. Query through form on website in first instance.

Literary Agent: Emily Sweet (**L614**)

L200 Ericka T. Phillips
Literary Agent
United States

https://www.stephanietadeagency.com/aboutus

Literary Agency: Stephanie Tade Literary Agency

Nonfiction > *Nonfiction Books*
  Buddhism; Health; Mind, Body, Spirit; Spirituality

Interested in non-fiction authors working in the Buddhist and mindfulness arena with a focus on health and spiritual well-being. She has a passion for developing projects and building platforms that help amplify the voices of women of color and black women writers in particular. She is experienced in platform development, marketing, and publicity and helps authors translate their message into brand strategy.

L201 Eunice McMullen Children's Literary Agent Ltd
Literary Agency
Low Ibbotsholme Cottage, Off Bridge Lane, Troutbeck Bridge, Windermere, Cumbria, LA23 1HU
United Kingdom
Tel: +44 (0) 1539 448551

eunice@eunicemcmullen.co.uk

https://www.eunicemcmullen.co.uk

CHILDREN'S > Fiction
  Middle Grade; *Novels*; *Picture Books*
TEEN > Fiction > *Novels*

Closed to approaches.

Most of my clients have been with me a considerable time so my list tends not to change. The agency is no longer accepting new submissions.

Literary Agent: Eunice McMullen

L202 The Evan Marshall Agency
Literary Agency
1 Pacio Court, Roseland, NJ 07068-1121
United States
Tel: +1 (973) 287-6216

evan@evanmarshallagency.com

https://www.evanmarshallagency.com

Professional Body: Association of American Literary Agents (AALA)

Types: Fiction; Nonfiction
Markets: Adult; Young Adult

Closed to approaches.

Represents all genres of adult and young-adult full-length fiction. New clients by referral only.

Literary Agent: Evan Marshall

L203 David Evans
Associate Agent
United Kingdom

davidevans@davidhigham.co.uk

https://www.davidhigham.co.uk/agents-dh/david-evans/

Literary Agency: David Higham Associates Ltd (**L159**)
Literary Agent: Andrew Gordon (**L270**)
Literary Agent / Chair: Anthony Goff (**L266**)

ACADEMIC > Nonfiction > *Nonfiction Books*
ADULT
  Fiction
    Novels: Literary
    Short Fiction: Literary

  Nonfiction > *Nonfiction Books*
    Culture; History; Journalism; Nature; Philosophy; Politics; Science

Closed to approaches.

Looking for literary fiction of style and ambition. He admires novelists who create memorable and unsettling voices, and short story writers with a keen sense of the poetic and absurd. In non-fiction, he enjoys projects of rigour, clarity and passion that can make small ideas radiate and big ideas graspable. He is particularly looking for works of academic research or journalistic investigation written for a wide readership, across areas such as culture, philosophy, politics, history, science, nature.

L204 Kate Evans
Literary Agent
United Kingdom
Tel: +44 (0) 20 7344 1047

kevans@pfd.co.uk

https://petersfraserdunlop.com/agent/kate-evans/
https://twitter.com/kateeevans

Literary Agency: Peters Fraser + Dunlop

Fiction > *Novels*
  General, and in particular: Family Saga; Literary Suspense; Romance

Nonfiction > *Nonfiction Books*
  Cookery; Economics; Food; History; Literary; Memoir; Narrative Nonfiction; Nature; Personal Development; Philosophy; Politics; Popular Culture; Popular Science; Science; Social Issues

Does not want:

> **Fiction** > *Novels*
>   Hard Science Fiction; High / Epic Fantasy

Send: Query; Synopsis; Writing sample; Proposal; Author bio
How to send: Email
How not to send: Post

I am actively looking for exciting new voices across both fiction and non-fiction.

I'm interested in non-fiction that says something about the way we live- from beautiful narrative non-fiction with a strong voice to passionate manifestos from experts in their fields. Whether it's popular science, big ideas, nature writing, memoir, fresh approaches to history or insightful takes on pop culture, I am drawn to writing that makes social, political, and economic issues accessible and engaging.

I read very widely in fiction but the common thread that runs through most novels I love is a sharply observed take on relationships and strong characters I'll think about long after I've left them on the page. I want a book I can gleefully, greedily consume- that kind of crying in public, ignoring your friends level compulsiveness... but I also want it to be beautifully put together.

I would love to see more literary suspense, a funny-sad family drama and I am forever on the lookout for a great love story.

I am largely genre-agnostic and if you're using genre (crime, horror, speculative) in an interesting way underpinned by exceptional writing I'd love to see it. Having said this, I'm probably not the best agent for hard SFF or YA.

Authors: Ali Abdaal; Nadine Bacchus-Garrick; Heidi Lauth Beasley; Sophie Beresiner; Abigail Bergstrom; Orsola De Castro; Julia F. Christensen; Olivia Jordan Cornelius; Iona David; Léa Rose Emery; Kate Evans; Richard Fisher; Ione Gamble; Bre Graham; Malwina Gudowska; Jessica Hamel-Akré; Sarah Haque; Kenya Hunt; Katerina Johnson; Jenna Macciochi; Sophie Mort; Jennifer Obidike; Georgina Sturge; Stefanie Sword-Williams; Amelia Tait; Rossalyn Warren; Rose Wilding

L205 Kiya Evans
Associate Agent
United Kingdom

kiya@mushens-entertainment.com
submissions@mushens-entertainment.com

https://www.mushens-entertainment.com/kiya-evans
https://twitter.com/kiyarosevans

Literary Agency: Mushens Entertainment
Literary Agent: Juliet Mushens (**L470**)

Fiction > *Novels*
  Book Club Fiction; Commercial; Feminism; Gothic; Grounded Science Fiction; High Concept Romance; Historical Fiction; Horror; LGBTQIA; Literary; Magical Realism; Mystery; Psychological Thrillers; Romance; Romantasy; Romantic Comedy; Speculative; Thrillers; Upmarket

Nonfiction > *Nonfiction Books*
  Culture; Narrative Nonfiction; Popular History; Society

Send: Query; Synopsis; Writing sample; Proposal

I'm looking for compelling fiction and narrative non-fiction which is commercial, literary, or something that feels like the best of both. Above all, I'm drawn to strong voices, honest, memorable writing, and books which confidently explore interesting, universal dynamics and experiences. I love a book that makes me cry or swoon (or both!).

L206 Stephany Evans
Literary Agent
United States

https://www.pandeliterary.com/about-pandeliterary
https://twitter.com/firerooster
http://aaronline.org/Sys/PublicProfile/2176670/417813

Literary Agency: Ayesha Pande Literary (**L036**)
Professional Bodies: Association of American Literary Agents (AALA); Romance Writers of America (RWA); Mystery Writers of America (MWA); The Agents Round Table (ART)

Fiction > *Novels*
Commercial; Crime; Literary; Mystery; Romance; Thrillers; Upmarket Women's Fiction; Women's Fiction

Nonfiction > *Nonfiction Books*
Fitness; Food and Drink; Health; Lifestyle; Memoir; Narrative Nonfiction; Running; Spirituality; Sustainable Living; Wellbeing

Closed to approaches.

L207 Samantha Fabien
Literary Agent
United States

https://www.rootliterary.com/agents
https://www.publishersmarketplace.com/members/samfabien/
https://twitter.com/samanthashnh
https://aalitagents.org/author/samanthashnh/
https://querymanager.com/query/samanthafabien

Literary Agency: Root Literary (**L547**)
Professional Body: Association of American Literary Agents (AALA)

ADULT > **Fiction** > *Novels*
Book Club Fiction; Commercial; Contemporary Romance; Fantasy; High Concept; Horror; Mystery; Romantic Comedy; Speculative; Suspense; Thrillers; Upmarket; Women's Fiction

CHILDREN'S > **Fiction** > *Middle Grade*

YOUNG ADULT > **Fiction** > *Novels*

Send: Query; Synopsis; Writing sample
How to send: Query Manager

I live for the rollercoaster of emotions that characters and stories can take me on. Whether I'm swooning or gasping, I want to feel strongly enough about a project that I desperately need to share it with the world.

L208 Fairbank Literary Representation
Literary Agency
21 Lyman Street, Waltham, MA 02452
United States
Tel: +1 (617) 576-0030

queries@fairbankliterary.com

https://fairbankliterary.com
https://www.publishersmarketplace.com/members/SorcheFairbank/
http://www.twitter.com/FairbankLit

ADULT
  Fiction > *Novels*
    International; Literary

  Nonfiction
    Gift Books: General
    Nonfiction Books: Comedy / Humour; Crafts; Design; Food; Lifestyle; Memoir; Narrative Nonfiction; Popular Culture; Wine

CHILDREN'S > **Fiction**
  Middle Grade; *Picture Books*

Send: Query; Writing sample
How to send: In the body of an email; Online contact form; Post
How not to send: Email attachment; Phone

Clients range from first-time authors to international best-sellers, prize winning-journalists to professionals at the top of their fields. Tastes tend toward literary and international fiction; voice-y novels with a strong sense of place; big memoir that goes beyond the me-moir; topical or narrative nonfiction with a strong interest in women's voices, global perspectives, and class and race issues; children's picture books & middle grade from illustrator/artists only; quality lifestyle books (food, wine, and design); pop culture; craft; and gift and humor books. Most likely to pick up works that are of social or cultural significance, newsworthy

Literary Agent: Sorche Elizabeth Fairbank

L209 Holly Faulks
Literary Agent
United Kingdom

http://greeneheaton.co.uk/agents/holly-faulks/
https://twitter.com/hollycfaulks

Literary Agency: Greene & Heaton Ltd (**L276**)

Fiction > *Novels*
Literary; Social Commentary; Thrillers; Upmarket

Nonfiction > *Nonfiction Books*
Current Affairs; Language; Lifestyle; Memoir; Politics; Popular Science; Society

Send: Synopsis; Writing sample
How to send: Email

I am actively building a list of fiction and non-fiction clients. In non-fiction I am looking for writing on current affairs, language, lifestyle and popular science as well as memoir. I am also looking for literary and upmarket commercial fiction.

In fiction I read widely across genre and am usually drawn to voice-led novels set in the real world, particularly if they engage with the complexities of human experience. That may be an insular, personal experience, a focus on family relationships or an exploration of a wider community or world. I like writing that is witty and sharp but that maintains warmth. I'd also love to find some fresh new voices in the thriller space, particularly ones with incisive social commentary.

Most of the non-fiction I work on is socially and politically engaged and I'm always looking for more writers in this area exploring new subjects. As in fiction, I'm drawn to books that explore the way we live, particularly in the modern world. I studied languages at university so I'm always keen to find books about the spoken word, and more particularly about the way it relates to the way we experience the world. I'd also like to hear from academics interested in writing a book for general readers, whatever their expertise!

Authors: Precious Adesina; Carol Ballantine; Michelle Bang; Emily Bootle; Zoe Burgess; Joseph Coward; Rageshri Dhairyawan; Emma Garland; Lily Hackett; Jake Hall; Julie Hayward; Kit Heyam; Juliet Jacques; Iggy LDN; August Lamm; Carina Maggar; Anna Sulan Masing; Sara-Ella Ozbek; Nicolas Padamsee; Jyoti Patel; Neel Patel; Xenobe Purvis; Francesca Ramsay; Ana Reyes; Ella Frances Sanders; Ione Wells

L210 Hillary Fazzari
Literary Agent
United States

https://bradfordlit.com
https://bradfordlit.com/hillary-fazzari-agent/
https://querymanager.com/query/3240
https://aalitagents.org/author/hillaryfazzari/
https://twitter.com/HillaryFazzari

Literary Agency: Bradford Literary Agency (**L075**)
Professional Body: Association of American Literary Agents (AALA)

ADULT
  Fiction > *Novels*
    Dystopian Fiction; Romance; Romantasy; Romantic Comedy; Science Fiction

  Nonfiction > *Nonfiction Books*
    Classics / Ancient World; Commercial; Feminism; History; Medieval; Women

CHILDREN'S > Fiction
  Graphic Novels; Middle Grade
NEW ADULT > Fiction > *Novels*
  Dystopian Fiction; Romance; Romantasy; Romantic Comedy; Science Fiction

YOUNG ADULT > Fiction
  Graphic Novels: General
  Novels: Commercial; Dark Academia; Dystopian Fiction; High Concept; Historical Fiction; Romantasy; Romantic Comedy

How to send: Query Manager

A highly editorial agent, she is looking for high concept, high stakes stories with deep character development and gorgeous, commercial prose. Overall, she acquires primarily Middle Grade and YA, and is open to any genre in those areas, including graphic novels (but only with illustrators attached). In New Adult and Adult, she acquires more selectively and is open to unsolicited queries in: Rom-coms and rom-com adjacent material (including relevant genre mashups); Romantasy and other SFF/romance mashups (including romantic dystopian); and very select narrative nonfiction that focuses on history.

L211 Leigh Feldman
Literary Agent
United States

Literary Agency: Leigh Feldman Literary (**L393**)

L212 Kait Lee Feldmann
Literary Agent
United States

kait@ktliterary.com
querykait@ktliterary.com

https://www.kaitfeldmann.com
https://www.kaitfeldmann.com/mswl
https://ktliterary.com/agents

Literary Agency: KT Literary (**L377**)

CHILDREN'S > Fiction
  Graphic Novels; Picture Books

Send: Query; Full text
How to send: Email attachment; Links to material online

Costs: Offers services that writers have to pay for.

I represent illustrators and illustrator-authors who are primarily interested in working on picture books and graphic novels. We'd be a good match if you enjoy wholesome chaos. Let's make books for the kids who get in trouble for their imagination, the next generation of mad scientists, supervillains, and witches at the end of the street.

Authors: Samantha Chiusolo; Vikki Chu; Ebony Glenn; Jen Gubicza; Haejin Park; Lisa Wee

L213 The Feldstein Agency
Literary Agency; Editorial Service; Consultancy
52 Ashley Drive, Bangor, Northern Ireland, BT20 5RD
United Kingdom
Tel: +44 (0) 2891 312485

submissions@thefeldsteinagency.co.uk

https://www.thefeldsteinagency.co.uk
https://twitter.com/feldsteinagency

Fiction > *Novels*

Nonfiction > *Nonfiction Books*

Does not want:

> Fiction > *Novels*
>   Fantasy; Historical Fiction; Romance; Science Fiction

Send: Query; Synopsis; Proposal; Author bio
How to send: Word file email attachment; PDF file email attachment

Costs: Offers services that writers have to pay for. Offers editing, ghostwriting, and consultancy services.

Handles adult fiction and nonfiction only. No children's, young adult, romance, science fiction, fantasy, poetry, scripts, short stories, or already-published works (including self-published). For fiction, please email a cover letter, a 1-2 page synopsis of your novel, and a brief biography. For non-fiction, please email a cover letter, a detailed proposal, and a brief biography. No reading fees or evaluation fees. The only instance in which an author would be charged a fee is for ghost-writing.

Consultant / Literary Agent: Paul Feldstein

Editor / Literary Agent: Susan Feldstein

L214 Felicia Eth Literary Representation
Literary Agency
555 Bryant Street, Suite 350, Palo Alto, CA 94301
United States

feliciaeth.literary@gmail.com

https://ethliterary.com

ADULT
  Fiction
    Novels: Historical Fiction; Literary; Magical Realism; Multicultural; Suspense
    Short Fiction Collections: General

  Nonfiction > *Nonfiction Books*
    Business; Cookery; Journalism; Memoir; Parenting; Popular Culture; Popular Science; Psychology; Social Issues; Sport; Travel; Women's Issues

YOUNG ADULT > Fiction > *Novels*

Send: Query; Author bio; Outline
How to send: Email; Post

Costs: Author covers sundry admin costs.

Send query by email or by post with SASE, including details about yourself and your project. Send sample pages upon invitation only.

Literary Agent: Felicia Eth

L215 Felicity Bryan Associates
Literary Agency
2a North Parade Avenue, Banbury Road, Oxford, OX2 6LX
United Kingdom
Tel: +44 (0) 1865 513816

submissions@felicitybryan.com

https://felicitybryan.com

Professional Body: The Association of Authors' Agents (AAA)

Fiction > *Novels*

Nonfiction > *Nonfiction Books*

Send: Query; Synopsis; Proposal; Writing sample
How to send: Online submission system
How not to send: Post

As an agency we are always searching for talented new writers. Whether you write beautifully crafted literary fiction, immersive middle-grade novels, or fascinating and informative non-fiction, we would love the opportunity to consider your work. We look for ambitious, confident writing that feels fresh and distinctive, and we welcome voices from all backgrounds. There is no expectation for writers to have existing connections to the publishing industry or a formal creative writing qualification. We take the time to carefully read and review every submission we receive.

Associate Agent: Sally Holloway (**L318**)

Authors: Carlos Acosta; Johnny Acton; Sally Adee; Samira Ahmed; David Almond; Ben Ambridge; Karen Armstrong; Lucy Ash; Frances Ashcroft; Rachel Aspden; James Attlee; Mark Avery; Modern Baker; Katya Balen; James Barr; David Barrie; Kay Barron; Rosamund Bartlett; John Barton; John Batchelor; Susan Beale; Jonny Beardsall; Roderick Beaton; Catherine Belton; Erica Benner; Nic Bennett; Louis De Bernières; Mary Berry; Claire Bertschinger; Paul Betts; Nina Bhadreshwar; Michael Bird; Tim Birkhead; Simon Blackburn; Andrew Blum; Elleke Boehmer; Stella Botchway; John Bowker; Christopher Brickell; Susan Brigden; Irena Brignull; Francesca Brill; Rhidian Brook; James Brooke-Smith; Adam Brookes; Archie Brown; Larisa Brown; Ursula Buchan; Julia Bueno; Stephen Burke; Matthew Burton; Karl Bushby; Tom Butler-Bowdon; Emma Byrne; Lucy Cavendish; Graham Caveney; Fernando Cervantes; Sarah Challis; Peter Chapman; John Charmley; Nick Chater; Simukai Chigudu; Marcus Chown; Morten H. Christiansen; Liza

Cody; Jonathan Coe; Will Cohu; Artemis Cooper; T.A. Cotterell; Sarah Courtauld; Cath Crowley; Benjamin Daniels; Chloe Daykin; John Dickie; Jenny Downham; Tobias Druitt; Will Eaves; Reni Eddo-Lodge; Nick Edwards; James Fairhead; Natasha Farrant; David Farrier; Edmund Fawcett; James Fearnley; Georgina Ferry; Jan Filochowski; Rebecca Fleet; Catherine Fletcher; CJ Flood; Pauline Francis; Peter Frankopan; Lawrence Freedman; Dominic Frisby; Clare Furniss; Damon Galgut; Sally Gardner; Peter Gatrell; Robert Gildea; Amelia Giudici; Jonathan Glover; David Goldblatt; Susan Golombok; Kat Gordon; Chris Gosden; Barbara Graziosi; Catherine Hall; Simon Hall; Thomas Halliday; James Hamilton; Tim Harford; Julie Hearn; Peter Heather; Tim Hecker; Gavin Hewitt; Louis Hill; Lindsey Hilsum; Penelope Hobhouse; Anna Hope; Gill Hornby; Richard House; Alex Howard; Alice Hunt; Kathryn Hurlock; Allegra Huston; Robert Hutton; Belinda Jack; Sarah Jasmon; Joseph Jebelli; Lauren St John; Colin Jones; Vijay Joshi; Nick Jubber; Helena Kelly; Stanley Kenani; Liz Kessler; Amy Key; Liza Klaussmann; Richard Koch; Chelsea Kwakye; James Kynge; Peter Lampl; Simon Lancaster; Katherine Langrish; Tomila Lankina; Grace Lavery; Phyllida Law; Tim Leach; Simon Lelic; Lucy Lethbridge; Alysa Levene; Suzannah Lipscomb; John Lister-Kaye; Tess Little; Finbarr Livesey; Greg Lockwood; Jonathan Loh; Rebecca Lowe; Natasha Lunn; Diarmaid Macculloch; Anna Machin; Fiona Maddocks; Laurie Maguire; John Man; Henry Mance; Sarah K Marr; Toby Matthiesen; James Mcdougall; Sophia Mcdougall; Chris Mcgrath; Richard Mcgregor; Kate Mcloughlin; Martin Meredith; Oliver Milman; Tom Moorhouse; Katy Moran; Alistair Morgan; Elian J Morgan; Marc Mulholland; Alan Murrin; Jennifer Nadel; Vanessa Nakate; Tom Nancollas; Natasha Narayan; James Naughtie; Linda Newbery; TN Ninan; Camilla Nord; Jenny Odell; Ore Ogunbiyi; Adjoa Osei; Richard Ovenden; Joanne Owen; Svenja O'donnell; Colm O'gorman; Elsa Panciroli; Iain Pears; Roger Pearson; Thomas Penn; Andrew Pettegree; Jonathan Phillips; David Pilling; Annabel Pitcher; Rachel Polonsky; Nick Potter; Andrew Prentice; Sue Prideaux; Diane Purkiss; Josephine Quinn; Captain Elliot Rappaport; Shilpa Ravella; Melody Razak; Glyn Redworth; Owen Rees; Alex Reeve; David Reynolds; Dan Richards; Julian Richards; Eloise Rickman; Thomas Rid; Alex Riley; Charlotte Lydia Riley; Ian Robertson; Ritchie Robertson; David Robson; Eugene Rogan; Nicola Rollock; Meg Rosoff; Miri Rubin; Ulinka Rublack; Adam Ruck; Penny Rudge; Edward Russell-Walling; Alec Ryrie; Farhan Samanani; Joseph Sassoon; Jon Savage; Paul Seabright; Zakia Sewell; Alom Shaha; Liam Shaw; Matthew Skelton; Emma Smith; Tiffany Watt Smith; Lexi Stadlen; Marc Stears; Miriam Stoppard; Roy Strong; Sue Stuart-Smith; Julie Summers; Krystal Sutherland; Henry Sutton; Katherine Swift; Cathy Thomas; Adrian Tinniswood; Nigel Travis; Eleanor Updale; Tom Vanderbilt; Christopher Vick; Edmund De Waal; Martin Walker; David Waltham; Charles Walton; Samantha Walton; Kirsty Wark; Clive Webb; Arthur Der Weduwen; Jonathan Weil; Anna Whitelock; Tim Whitmarsh; K.J. Whittaker; Hugh Wilford; Sam Wilkin; Imogen Willetts; Lisa Williamson; Greg Wise; Bill Wood; Michael Wood; Lucy Wooding; Michael Wooldridge; Lucy Worsley; James Wythe; Jessica Wärnberg; Kieran Yates; Lucy Young

Company Directors / Literary Agents: Carrie Plitt (**L520**); Caroline Wood (**L669**)

Literary Agent / Managing Director: Catherine Clarke (**L129**)

Literary Agents: Alice Caprio (**L103**); Angelique Tran Van Sang

L216 Abi Fellows
Literary Agent
United Kingdom

af.submission@dhhliteraryagency.com

https://www.dhhliteraryagency.com
https://www.dhhliteraryagency.com/abi-fellows

Literary Agency: DHH Literary Agency Ltd (**L166**)

ADULT
Fiction > *Novels*
   General, and in particular: Dark; Historical Fiction; Literary; Romantic Comedy

Nonfiction > *Nonfiction Books*
   General, and in particular: Commercial; Culture; History; Literary Memoir; Self Help

CHILDREN'S > **Fiction** > *Middle Grade*
YOUNG ADULT > **Fiction** > *Novels*

Does not want:

> **Fiction** > *Novels*
>   Cookery; Fantasy; Horror; Science Fiction

Send: Query; Synopsis; Proposal; Writing sample; Outline; Market info
How to send: Email

For fiction, please send your cover letter, one-page synopsis and first three chapters. For non-fiction, please send a proposal (including overview of book's main idea, information about you the author / why you are the person to write the book, an outline of full book with chapter breakdowns / descriptions and sources, a sample chapter and, if these are available to you, media links, advance praise, comparable titles).

Authors: Tasneem Abdur-Rashid; Paula Akpan; Carolina Are; Karen Arthur; Khairani Barokka; Katie Baskerville; Caroline Butterwick; Aaron Dale; Azma Dar; K Devan; Sharan Dhaliwal; Preeti Dhillon; Anna Ellory; Deirdre Finnerty; Nicola Garrard; Divya Ghelani; Nadia Gilani; Erica Gillingham; Alexis Gregory; Michael Handrick; Mireille Harper; Ali Hendry; Hanan Issa; Sophie Jai; Lizzie Huxley Jones; Nancy Kelley; Catherine Kurtz; Eleni Kyriacou; Thomas Leeds; Chantelle Lindsay; Elizabeth Lovatt; Natalie Marlow; Layla McCay; Saima Mir; Zeena Moolla; Evie Muir; Jade Mutyora; Erik Olsen; Yen Ooi; Philippa Peall; Penny Pepper; Lauren du Plessis; Grace Quantock; Jasmine Qureshi; Monika Radojevic; Jon Ransom; Jini Reddy; Juno Roche; Helen Scott; Amélie Skoda; Paul Taylor-Pitt; Rosie Turner; Eva Verde; Kandace Siobhan Walker; Clare Weze; lisa luxx

L217 Hannah Ferguson
Literary Agent
United Kingdom

hannah@hardmanswainson.com
submissions@hardmanswainson.com

https://www.hardmanswainson.com/agent/hannah-ferguson/
https://twitter.com/AgentFergie

Literary Agency: Hardman & Swainson (**L294**)

Fiction > *Novels*
   General, and in particular: Book Club Fiction; Commercial; Crime; Literary; Thrillers; Women's Fiction

Nonfiction > *Nonfiction Books*: Narrative Nonfiction

Send: Query; Synopsis; Full text
How to send: Email

Represents women's fiction, from the more literary to the very commercial. Likes book club reads that really capture a reader's attention or heart. Always on the lookout for great crime and thrillers and interesting non-fiction.

L218 T.S. Ferguson
Literary Agent
United States

http://www.azantianlitagency.com/pages/team-tf.html
https://querymanager.com/query/TSFerguson

Literary Agency: Azantian Literary Agency

CHILDREN'S > **Fiction**
   Graphic Novels: General
   Middle Grade: General, and in particular: Adventure; Dark; Fairy Tales; Folklore, Myths, and Legends; High Concept; Horror; LGBTQIA
YOUNG ADULT > **Fiction**
   Graphic Novels: General

Novels: General, and in particular: Adventure; Dark; Fairy Tales; Folklore, Myths, and Legends; High Concept; Horror; LGBTQIA

Does not want:

> **CHILDREN'S > Fiction >** *Middle Grade*
>   Hard Science Fiction; Sport
> **YOUNG ADULT > Fiction >** *Novels*
>   Hard Science Fiction; Sport

How to send: Query Manager

Looking for young adult and middle grade fiction across all genres that combines high-concept, hooky stories with writing and voice that feel standout. An addicting, page-turning quality is always a plus! He has a special place in his heart for dark and edgy stories (including but not limited to horror), fairy tales, mythology, action-adventure, LGBTQ stories, graphic novels, and stories by and about under-represented voices. He is not the best fit for sports-centric stories, high sci-fi, or non-fiction.

L219 Julie Fergusson
Literary Agent
United Kingdom

http://thenorthlitagency.com/our-friends-in-the-north/
https://twitter.com/julie_fergusson

Literary Agency: The North Literary Agency

Fiction > *Novels*
  Book Club Fiction; Domestic Suspense; Literary; Psychological Thrillers; Romantic Comedy; Speculative

Closed to approaches.

Looking for fiction across a range of genres, particularly psychological thrillers, domestic suspense, near-future speculative, romcoms, reading group and literary fiction. No submissions from authors who live in North America.

L220 Rochelle Fernandez
Literary Agent
Australia

rochelle@alexadsett.com.au

https://alexadsett.com.au/literary-agency/
https://querymanager.com/query/3065

Literary Agency: Alex Adsett Literary (**L016**)

ADULT
  Fiction > *Novels*
    Commercial; Crime; Fantasy; Mystery; Romantic Comedy; Science Fiction
  Nonfiction > *Nonfiction Books*: Memoir

CHILDREN'S > Fiction
  Middle Grade; *Picture Books*

How to send: Query Manager

Seeking well written manuscripts of any genre with a compelling premise and three dimensional, interesting characters. Based in Sydney, she is passionate about hearing and seeing diverse stories that represent the wonderful multicultural multifaceted society that comprises Australia.

L221 Melanie Figueroa
Literary Agent
United States

https://www.melaniefigueroa.com
https://www.rootliterary.com/agents
https://querymanager.com/query/melaniefigueroa
https://twitter.com/wellmelsbells/
https://www.linkedin.com/in/melaniefigueroa
https://www.instagram.com/wellmelsbells/

Literary Agency: Root Literary (**L547**)
Professional Body: Association of American Literary Agents (AALA)

ADULT > Fiction > *Novels*
  Commercial; Contemporary; Family Saga; Fantasy; Historical Fiction; Horror; Literary; Magical Realism; Mystery; Speculative; Suspense; Thrillers; Upmarket; Women's Fiction

CHILDREN'S > Fiction > *Middle Grade*
  Contemporary; Fantasy; Historical Fiction; Literary; Mystery; Science Fiction

YOUNG ADULT > Fiction > *Novels*
  Contemporary; Fantasy; Historical Fiction; Literary; Mystery; Romance; Science Fiction

How to send: Query Manager

I want to work with the kind of stories that both create and sustain life-long readers—books that make me sigh with contentment, learn something new, or take delight in the unexpected. Those stories stay with you, and they're a gift I want to help give readers by lifting up the voices of talented and hard-working creatives.

L222 Fillingham Weston Associates
Literary Agency
20 Mortlake High Street, London, SW14 8JN
United Kingdom
Tel: +44 (0) 20 8748 5594

info@fillinghamweston.com
submissions@fillinghamweston.com

https://www.fillinghamweston.com
https://www.facebook.com/Fillingham-Weston-Associates-117304691662209
https://twitter.com/fwa_litagency
https://www.instagram.com/fillinghamwestonassociates/

ADULT > Scripts
  Film Scripts; *TV Scripts*; *Theatre Scripts*

CHILDREN'S > Scripts
  Film Scripts; *TV Scripts*; *Theatre Scripts*

YOUNG ADULT > Scripts
  Film Scripts; *TV Scripts*; *Theatre Scripts*

Send: Query; Author bio
Don't send: Full text; Writing sample
How to send: Email

Represents writers and directors for stage, film and TV, as well as librettists, lyricists and composers in musical theatre. Does not represent books. See website for full submission guidelines.

Literary Agents: Janet Fillingham; Kate Weston

L223 Ciara Finan
Literary Agent
United Kingdom
Tel: + 44 (0) 207 393 4357

ciara.finan@curtisbrown.co.uk

https://curtisbrown.co.uk
https://curtisbrown.co.uk/agent/ciara-finan

Literary Agency: Curtis Brown (**L146**)

Fiction > *Novels*
  Book Club Fiction; Cozy Fantasy; Crime; Fantasy; Historical Fiction; Politics; Psychological Thrillers; Romance; Romantasy; Romantic Comedy; Thrillers

Nonfiction > *Nonfiction Books*
  Beauty; Commercial; Economics; Feminism; Health; History; Politics; Relationships

Send: Query; Synopsis; Writing sample; Proposal
How to send: Email

I am looking for fantasy, romantasy, dark academia, rom-coms and romance, book club fiction, psychological thrillers, historical fiction and commercial non-fiction. I'm particularly interested in finding and championing stories by writers from underrepresented backgrounds and communities.

Authors: Henry Agg; Chloe Bayley; Ashley Chalmers; Hannah Connolly; Paige Cowan-Hall; Alan Edwards; Logan Karlie; Nina Killham; Chloe Laws; Hazel McBride; Liberty Mills; L.M. Nathan; Joshua Oliver; Andrea Oskis; Claire Peate; Keetie Roelen; Eulalie Tangka; Daisy Tempest; Dan Whitlam

L224 Diana Finch
Literary Agent
United States

dianafinchagent@gmail.com

http://dianafinchliteraryagency.blogspot.com/
https://dianafinchliteraryagency.submittable.com/submit
https://aalitagents.org/author/dianagent/
https://twitter.com/DianaFinch

Literary Agency: Diana Finch Literary Agency (**L167**)
Professional Body: Association of American Literary Agents (AALA)

How to send: Submittable

L225 Rebeka Finch
Associate Agent
United Kingdom

rebeka@darleyanderson.com

https://darleyanderson.com
https://darleyanderson.com/team/rebeka-finch/
https://twitter.com/Beka_finch
https://www.instagram.com/rebeka.finch/

Literary Agency: The Darley Anderson Agency (**L157**)

ADULT > *Fiction* > *Novels*
Commercial; Romance; Romantasy; Romantic Comedy; Women's Fiction

NEW ADULT > *Fiction* > *Novels*
Commercial; Romance; Romantasy; Romantic Comedy; Women's Fiction

How to send: Email attachment

I am on the hunt for commercial romantic and romantasy fiction, specifically for BookTok hungry new adult/20+ markets. I want books with romance at the very heart of the narrative. Messy, cheesy, heartbreaking, relatable, I want the characters and their story to engross me completely and have me reaching for it time and time again.

L226 Stevie Finegan
Literary Agent
United Kingdom

finegan@zenoagency.com

http://zenoagency.com/news/stevie-finegan/
https://twitter.com/StevieFinegan

Literary Agency: Zeno Agency (**L680**)

ADULT
Fiction
Graphic Novels: Feminism; LGBTQIA
Novels: High / Epic Fantasy; Soft Science Fiction
Nonfiction > *Nonfiction Books*
Feminism; Mental Health; Politics; Social Issues

CHILDREN'S > **Fiction**
Early Readers; *Middle Grade*; *Picture Books*

Closed to approaches.

Authors: Travis Baldree; Alice Bell; Cierra Block; Marie Brennan; Rebecca Brownlie; Andrew Cartmel; Mário Coelho; J.R. Dawson; Clio Evans; Craig Laurance Gidney; J.T. Greathouse; Daniel B. Greene; Elizabeth Helen; Grady Hendrix; Laura Kerseviciute; Shannon Mayer; Anna McNuff; Katy Nyquist; Adam Oyebanji; Bryce O'Connor; Sian Radford; Emily Rath; Farrah Riaz; Cassidy Ellis Salter; Calah Singleton; Emily Turner; R.R. Virdi; MJ Wassmer; Angus Watson; Gary Wigglesworth; Jasmine Wigham; Yudhanjaya Wijeratne; Catelyn Wilson

L227 Bea Fitzgerald
Literary Agent; Author
United Kingdom

beasubmissions@theblairpartnership.com

https://www.theblairpartnership.com/literary-agents/bea-fitzgerald/
https://twitter.com/Bea_a_Bea

Literary Agency: LBA Books Ltd
Literary Agent: Hannah Schofield (**L567**)

ADULT > *Fiction* > *Novels*
Fantasy; Romantasy; Science Fiction

YOUNG ADULT > *Fiction* > *Novels*
Fantasy; Science Fiction

Send: Pitch; Market info; Author bio; Synopsis; Writing sample
How to send: Word file email attachment; PDF file email attachment

I represent fantasy and sci-fi, while also working as the agency's digital lead. My tastes vary but rather consistently I enjoy voice and character led stories with propulsive writing and strong worldbuilding. Across all genres, I'd love to see work by underrepresented writers.

Authors: Chiara Bullen; Kim Curran; Essie Dennis; Charlie Harlan; Caroline Klidonas; Annabelle Woghiren

L228 Flannery Literary
Literary Agency
United States

jennifer@flanneryliterary.com

https://flanneryliterary.com

CHILDREN'S
Fiction > *Middle Grade*
Nonfiction > *Nonfiction Books*

YOUNG ADULT > *Fiction* > *Novels*

Closed to approaches.

Send query by email, with the word "Query" in the subject line. Include first 5-10 pages of your novel or full picture book text. Deals exclusively in children's and young adults' fiction and nonfiction, including picture books. See website for full guidelines.

Literary Agent: Jennifer Flannery

L229 Amy Thrall Flynn
Senior Agent
United States

https://www.aevitascreative.com
https://www.aevitascreative.com/agent/amy-thrall-flynn
https://querymanager.com/query/flynn

Literary Agency: Aevitas

CHILDREN'S > **Fiction**
Chapter Books; *Early Readers*; *Middle Grade*; *Picture Books*
YOUNG ADULT > *Fiction* > *Novels*

Closed to approaches.

Represents writers and illustrators of fiction and nonfiction for children, from picture books to young adult novels.

Authors: Sara Akin; Ahmed Alghariz; Lynne Bertrand; Michael Brumm; Julien Chung; Danielle Davis; Mk Smith Despres; Susan Fletcher; Nancy Bo Flood; Federico Gastaldi; Karen Gebbia; Charlie Greenwald; Tommy Greenwald; Ritu Hemnani; Carter Higgins; Lina Maslo; Robyn McGrath; Wendell Minor; Heather L. Montgomery; Zewlan Moor; Zoraida Rivera Morales; Bethanie Murguia; Dan Paley; Nadine Pinede; Aimee Reid; Jennifer Ann Richter; Michael J. Rosen; Rob Sanders; Kaitlin M Sikes; Leslie Staub; Ellen Surrey; Ellen Tarlow; Dana VanderLugt; Helen Yoon

L230 Jack Fogg
Literary Agent
United Kingdom

https://dunnfogg.co.uk
https://dunnfogg.co.uk/about-us/

Literary Agency: DunnFogg (**L182**)

Fiction > *Novels*
Literary; Psychology; Speculative; Suspense

Nonfiction > *Nonfiction Books*
Business; Crafts; Design; Food; Investigative Journalism; Memoir; Narrative Nonfiction; Nature; Psychology; Sociology; Sport

How to send: Online submission system

In fiction, I'm drawn to books which combine compelling storytelling, engaging characters and strong plotting, whether they be considered commercial or literary. I particularly love novels of ambition and scope, which are full of big-hearted characters and aren't afraid to entertain. In non-fiction, my tastes are broad, and I read widely in the areas of memoir, current affairs, politics, biography, sport, history, psychology, pop science, food and nature writing. I'm especially drawn to great narrative non-fiction which has a deep focus and then expands outwards to explain a whole culture or subculture.

L231 A for Authors
Literary Agency
73 Hurlingham Road, Bexleyheath, Kent, DA7 5PE
United Kingdom
Tel: +44 (0) 1322 463479

enquiries@aforauthors.co.uk

http://aforauthors.co.uk

Fiction > *Novels*
Commercial; Crime; Historical Fiction; Literary; Thrillers

How to send: Word file email attachment; PDF file email attachment

Query by email only. Include synopsis and first three chapters (or up to 50 pages) and short author bio. All attachments must be Word format documents. No submissions by post or by downloadable link.

Literary Agents: Annette Crossland; Bill Goodall

L232 Jemima Forrester
Literary Agent
United Kingdom

jemimaforrester@davidhigham.co.uk

https://www.davidhigham.co.uk/agents-dh/jemima-forrester/

Literary Agency: David Higham Associates Ltd (**L159**)

Fiction > *Novels*
Book Club Fiction; Commercial; Crime; Fantasy; High Concept; Historical Fiction; Literary; Magic; Psychological Suspense; Speculative; Thrillers; Upmarket; Women's Fiction

Nonfiction > *Nonfiction Books*
Comedy / Humour; Feminism; Lifestyle; Popular Culture

Send: Query; Synopsis; Writing sample
How to send: Email

Actively growing her list of commercial and upmarket fiction and has wide-ranging tastes within this space. She is looking for: book club and accessible literary fiction; crime and thrillers; upmarket historical fiction; psychological suspense; women's fiction; speculative/high-concept novels; novels with a lightly magical or fantastical edge. She loves distinctive narrative voices, well-paced plots with a great hook, and complex female characters. She's often drawn to humour, quirky or unusual narrators, moral dilemmas and stories about sisters. In non-fiction, she is looking for innovative lifestyle and popular-culture projects, unique personal stories and humour.

Authors: Kat Ailes; Tessa Bickers; Mikki Brammer; Lauren Bravo; Rukky Brume; R. S. Burnett; Seerut K. Chawla; Lizzie Daykin; Sarah Daykin; Morgan Dick; Pip Finkemeyer; Fred Foster; Jessica George; Penny Hancock; Deborah Hewitt; Rosie Hewlett; Jessie Keane; Kate Leaver; Richard Lumsden; Rufaro Faith Mazarura; Deborah O'Donoghue; Christina Pishiris; Karen Sinotok; Rosie Storey; Tasha Sylva; Sureka Thanenthiran-Dharuman; Minette Walters; Vanessa Walters

L233 Clara Foster
Literary Agent
United Kingdom

https://www.aevitascreative.com/agent/clara-foster

https://querymanager.com/query/2979

Literary Agency: Aevitas Creative Management (ACM) UK (**L007**)

ADULT > **Fiction** > *Novels*
Book Club Fiction; Folklore, Myths, and Legends; Historical Romance; Literary; Romance; Romantasy; Romantic Mystery; Upmarket

YOUNG ADULT > **Fiction** > *Novels*
High Concept; Romance

How to send: Query Manager

Looking to represent writers across genre fiction, upmarket, and reading-group, as well as select non-fiction. She is editorially-focused and works closely with clients in the lead up to submission to publishers.

In fiction, she is looking for stories in the upmarket/book-club sweet spot where literary and genre-fiction meet, intensely emotional literary women, and just about anything written with beautiful prose, a high-stakes plot, and/or a folkloric, legendary, or mythical grounding. She loves a romance in any genre—fantasy, historical, mystery, or a combination of all three—and will, no matter how dark a book gets in the middle, always gravitate towards a happy ending.

She is also looking for projects in the YA/Crossover space. Much like her taste in adult fiction, she wants to see clever world-building, emotional (and flawed) characters, and preferably a romantic sub-plot—or main plot. Here however she would like to find writing from authors who push the boundaries even further: new twists on old tropes, high concepts (an idea you can pitch in a sentence), and perspectives we rarely get to see.

In Non-fiction, she would like to find highly practical guides aimed squarely at women with the intention of filling crucial gaps in our collective knowledge.

Authors: A.B. Hamilton; Claire Schultz; Jessie Williams

L234 Aram Fox
Literary Agent
United States

https://www.mmqlit.com/about/

Literary Agency: Massie & McQuilkin

Fiction > *Novels*
Commercial; Literary

Nonfiction > *Nonfiction Books*
History; Memoir; Narrative Nonfiction; Nature; Politics

Send: Query; Writing sample; Proposal; Synopsis; Author bio
How to send: In the body of an email

Represents a mix of fiction and nonfiction. His favorite novelists, commercial as well as literary, put immersive storytelling front and center. In nonfiction, he's looking for powerful memoir, natural history, deeply reported narrative nonfiction, and world-class explainers and advice-givers.

L235 Kat Foxx
Assistant Agent
Canada

https://www.therightsfactory.com
https://www.therightsfactory.com/Agents/kat-foxx
https://querymanager.com/query/KatFoxx

Literary Agency: The Rights Factory

ADULT
Fiction > *Novels*
Book Club Fiction; Commercial; Gothic; Historical Fantasy; Historical Fiction; Magical Realism; Mystery; Nostalgia; Romance; Romantic Comedy; Supernatural / Paranormal Horror; Suspense; Thrillers

Nonfiction > *Nonfiction Books*
Childbirth; Classics / Ancient World; Crime; Food; Memoir; Motherhood; Parenting; Pregnancy; Travel; Wine; Witchcraft; Witches

YOUNG ADULT > **Fiction** > *Novels*
Gothic; Historical Fantasy; Historical Fiction; Magical Realism; Mystery; Romance; Romantic Comedy; Supernatural / Paranormal Horror; Suspense; Thrillers

Closed to approaches.

Building her list of exceptionally talented authors in commercial and book club fiction as well as some select nonfiction topics. In fiction, she's looking for Adult and YA thriller/mystery/suspense, gothic and supernatural horror, historical fiction (preferably pre-20th century), historical fantasy/magical realism (less magicians / wizards / kings / queens and more witches, ghosts, time travel, past lives, etc.), and romcom and romance (light spice). She also enjoys anything nostalgic and anything to do with past lives and soul connections, haunted houses, ancestry, and midwifery/natural childbirth. She *loves* creepy, scary stories that make her eyes water and give her goosebumps! Across ages and genres, stories that normalize blended, single-parent, adoptive, racially and/or culturally diverse, and same-sex relationships and families are high on her list. For nonfiction, she is seeking compelling memoirs that read like fiction, motherhood/natural pregnancy and childbirth/midwifery/planned unassisted births, single parenthood (especially if paired with overcoming an abusive relationship with the other parent), past life/reincarnation, the "brotherhood" mentality of law enforcement, narcissistic abuse recovery, true crime, wine/food/travel, a history of witches and witchcraft, and ancient locations/civilizations.

L236 FRA (Futerman, Rose, & Associates)
Literary Agency
91 St Leonards Road, London, SW14 7BL
United Kingdom
Tel: +44 (0) 20 8255 7755

guy@futermanrose.co.uk

http://www.futermanrose.co.uk

Professional Body: The Association of Authors' Agents (AAA)

Nonfiction > *Nonfiction Books*
General, and in particular: Entertainment; Media; Music; Politics; Sports Celebrity

Send: Query
Don't send: Full text
How to send: Email

We have a strong reputation for non-fiction, especially books about show business, the music profession and politics, and in recent years we've had particular success with sports biographies and memoirs. We have successfully placed film and TV rights to many of our authors' works with major studios and producers, in some cases even ahead of the book rights.

Authors: Jill Anderson; Larry Barker; Nick Battle; Christian Piers Betley; Tracey Cheetham; Chengde Chen; Kevin Clarke; Lesley Crewe; Richard Digance; Peter Dobbie; Bobby Elliott; Paul Ferris; John French; Susan George; Keith Gillespie; Stephen Griffin; Paul Hendy; Terry Ilott; Sara Khan; Jerry Leider; Sue Lenier; Keith R. Lindsay; Stephen Lowe; Eric MacInnes; Paul Marsden; Paul Marx; Tony McAndrew; Tony McMahon; Sir Vartan Melkonian; Michael Misick; Max Morgan-Witts; Sir Derek Morris; Peter Murphy; Judge Chris Nicholson; Antonia Owen; Tom Owen; Mary O'Hara; Ciarán O'Keeffe; Miriam O'Reilly; Zoe Paphitis; Liz Rettig; Kenneth G. Ross; Robin Callender Smith; Rt. Hon Iain Duncan Smith; Paul Stinchcombe; Felicity Fair Thompson; Bill Tidy; Mark White; Toyah Willcox; Simon Woodham; Tappy Wright; Allen Zeleski

Literary Agent: Guy Rose

L237 Frances Collin Literary Agent
Literary Agency
PO Box 33, Wayne, PA 19087-0033
United States
Tel: +1 (610) 254-0555
Fax: +1 (610) 254-5029

queries@francescollin.com

http://www.francescollin.com

Fiction > *Novels*
Fantasy; Historical Fiction; Literary; Science Fiction; Women's Fiction

Nonfiction > *Nonfiction Books*
Biography; Culture; History; Memoir; Narrative Nonfiction; Nature; Travel

Send: Query
How to send: Email
How not to send: Email attachment; Phone; Fax

Prefers queries by email (no attachments). No queries by phone or fax.

Literary Agent: Frances Collin

L238 Frances Goldin Literary Agency, Inc.
Literary Agency
214 W 29th St., Suite 1006, New York, NY 10001
United States

agency@goldinlit.com

http://www.goldinlit.com

Professional Body: Association of American Literary Agents (AALA)

Types: Fiction; Nonfiction; Poetry; Translations
Formats: Film Scripts
Subjects: Arts; Autobiography; Commercial; Crime; Culture; Current Affairs; Entertainment; History; Legal; Literary; Nature; Philosophy; Politics; Science; Society; Sport; Technology; Thrillers; Travel
Markets: Adult; Children's; Young Adult

Closed to approaches.

Submit to one agent only. See website for specific agent interests and preferred method of approach. No screenplays, romances (or most other genre fiction), and only rarely poetry. No work that is racist, sexist, ageist, homophobic, or pornographic.

Associate Agent: Jade Wong-Baxter

Authors: Susan Bordo; Monica Byrne; Mandy Catron; Pratap Chatterjee; David Cole; Cliff Conner; Dessa; Ray Douglas; Mark Edmundson; Shelley Fisher Fishkin; Bruce Grierson; Michael Hudson; Lynn Hunt; Margaret Jacob; Steven Jaffe; Barbara Kingsolver; Michelle Kuo; Anna Lappé; Daniel Medwed; Stephanie Mencimer; Rutu Modan; Alexandra Natapoff; Carla Peterson; Sam Polk; Janisse Ray; Gretchen Reynolds; Siva Vaidhyanathan; Mike Wallace; Helene Wecker

Literary Agents: Roz Foster; Alison Lewis (**L398**); Tess Weitzner (**L651**); Ayla Zuraw-Friedland (**L681**)

President / Senior Agent: Sam Stoloff

Senior Agents / Vice Presidents: Caroline Eisenmann (**L192**); Ellen Geiger (**L255**); Matt McGowan

L239 Valerie Frankel
Literary Agent
Brooklyn, NY
United States

https://www.aevitascreative.com/agent/valerie-frankel

Literary Agency: Aevitas

ADULT
Fiction > *Novels*
Mystery; Romance; Thrillers

Nonfiction > *Nonfiction Books*
Business; Health; Lifestyle; Memoir; Wellbeing

YOUNG ADULT > **Fiction** > *Novels*

Closed to approaches.

Literary agent based in Brooklyn, New York. Has 35 years of editorial experience, and has collaborated with celebrities, public figures, and experts on more than thirty books, including two #1 New York Times bestsellers. She's interested in non-fiction (memoir, health and wellness, business, lifestyle) and fiction (thriller, mystery, romance, YA).

Authors: Florence Comite; Tiffanie DiDonato; Ann Heisenfelt; Ted Heller; Emilie Leyes; Emily Listfield; Joan Martelli; Charmaine McGuffey; Judith Newman; Janice Page; Andrew Postman; Seth Rogoff; Freddie Smith; Benjamin Wagner; Elisa Zuritsky

L240 Fraser Ross Associates
Literary Agency
42 Hadfast Road, Cousland, Midlothian, EH22 2NZ
United Kingdom

fraserrossassociates@gmail.com

http://www.fraserross.co.uk

ADULT
Fiction > *Novels*
Nonfiction > *Nonfiction Books*

CHILDREN'S > **Fiction** > *Picture Books*

Send: Query; Synopsis; Proposal; Writing sample; Full text
How to send: Email; Post

Send query by email or by post, including CV, the first three chapters and synopsis for fiction, or a one page proposal and the opening chapter and a further two chapter outlines for nonfiction. For picture books, send complete MS, without illustrations. No poetry, playscripts, screenplays, or individual short stories.

Authors: Jo Allan; Sorrel Anderson; Gill Arbuthnott; Tim Archbold; Alice Balfour; Barroux; Jason Beresford; Thomas Bloor; Ella

Burfoot; Jill Calder; Simon Chapman; Judy Cumberbatch; Caroline Deacon; Emily Dodd; Lari Don; Christiane Dorion; Nicole Dryburgh; Jane Eagland; Teresa Flavin; Ciara Flood; Hannah Foley; Vivian French; Joe Friedman; Darren Gate; Roy Gill; Edward Hardy; Diana Hendry; Chris Higgins; Barry Hutchison; J D (Julie) Irwin; Cate James; Ann Kelley; Louise Kelly; Tanya Landman; Kate Leiper; Joan Lennon; Joan Lingard; Janis Mackay; L J Macwhirter; Kasia Matyjaszek; Eilidh Muldoon; Erica Mary Orchard; Judy Paterson; Helena Pielichaty; Sue Purkiss; Lynne Rickards; Jamie Rix; Karen Saunders; Dugald Steer; Chae Strathie; Kate Wakeling; Rosie Wallace

Literary Agents: Lindsey Fraser; Kathryn Ross

L241 Robert Freedman
Literary Agent; President
United States

Literary Agency: Robert A. Freedman Dramatic Agency, Inc.

Scripts > *Theatre Scripts*

L242 Sarah Jane Freymann
Literary Agent
United States

sarah@sarahjanefreymann.com

http://www.sarahjanefreymann.com/?page_id=3872

Literary Agency: Sarah Jane Freymann Literary Agency (**L564**)

ADULT
  Fiction > *Novels*
    Literary; Mainstream

  Nonfiction > *Nonfiction Books*
    Alternative Health; Cookery; Health; Journalism; Lifestyle; Memoir; Men's Issues; Multicultural; Narrative Nonfiction; Nature; Parenting; Psychology; Science; Self Help; Spirituality; Travel; Women's Issues

YOUNG ADULT > **Fiction** > *Novels*

Send: Query; Writing sample
How to send: In the body of an email; Post
How not to send: Email attachment

In nonfiction, interested in spiritual, psychology, self-help, women/men's issues, books by health experts (conventional and alternative), cookbooks, narrative non-fiction, natural science, nature, memoirs, cutting-edge journalism, travel, multicultural issues, parenting, lifestyle. In fiction, interested in sophisticated mainstream and literary fiction with a distinctive voice. Also looking for edgy Young Adult fiction.

L243 Claire Friedman
Literary Agent
United States

http://www.inkwellmanagement.com/staff/claire-friedman

Literary Agency: InkWell Management

ADULT
  Fiction > *Novels*
    Book Club Fiction; Commercial; Romance; Speculative; Suspense; Thrillers; Upmarket

  Nonfiction > *Nonfiction Books*: Narrative Nonfiction

CHILDREN'S > **Fiction** > *Novels*

YOUNG ADULT > **Fiction** > *Novels*
  Book Club Fiction; Commercial; Romance; Speculative; Suspense; Thrillers; Upmarket

Send: Query; Writing sample
How to send: In the body of an email

Actively seeking upmarket and commercial fiction in the adult and YA categories, with a special focus on book club fiction, thrillers and suspense, romance, and anything with a speculative edge.

L244 Rebecca Friedman
Literary Agent
United States

queries@rfliterary.com

https://rfliterary.com/about/
https://twitter.com/rebeccalitagent

Literary Agency: Rebecca Friedman Literary Agency

ADULT
  Fiction > *Novels*
    Commercial; Contemporary Romance; Literary; Suspense; Women's Fiction

  Nonfiction > *Nonfiction Books*
    Journalism; Memoir

YOUNG ADULT > **Fiction** > *Novels*

Send: Query; Writing sample
How to send: Email

Interested in commercial and literary fiction with a focus on literary novels of suspense, women's fiction, contemporary romance, and young adult, as well as journalistic non-fiction and memoir. Most of all, she is looking for great stories told in strong voices.

L245 The Friedrich Agency LLC
Literary Agency
United States

https://www.friedrichagency.com

Fiction > *Novels*

Nonfiction > *Nonfiction Books*

Send: Query; Writing sample
How to send: Email

See website for agent bios and individual contact details, then submit to one by email only. See website for full guidelines.

Associate Agent: Marin Takikawa (**L618**)
Literary Agents: Hannah Brattesani (**L079**); Heather Carr; Lucy Carson; Molly Friedrich

L246 Frog Literary Agency
Literary Agency; Editorial Service
United Kingdom
Tel: +44 (0) 7221 660990

hello@frogliterary.agency
submissions@frogliterary.agency

https://www.frogliterary.agency
https://twitter.com/frogliterary
http://www.instagram.com/frogliterary

Nonfiction > *Nonfiction Books*

Closed to approaches.

Costs: Offers services that writers have to pay for.

LGBTQIA+ writers only. No submissions from heterosexuals. Writing need not have a queer focus, so heterosexual content may be accepted if it is written by someone who says they are gay. However, the same content would be rejected if the person who wrote it says they are straight. Also offers editorial services to writers, which may be considered a conflict of interest. Always exercise caution when contacting agencies that offer paid-for services that claim to improve your chances of being accepted by agencies, as the agency may merely be a front for generating business for the editorial service.

L247 Sarah Fuentes
Literary Agent
United States

https://www.unitedtalent.com
https://www.unitedtalent.com/bio/sarah-fuentes

Literary Agency: United Talent Agency (UTA)

Fiction > *Novels*
  Comedy / Humour; Dark; Literary; Speculative; Upmarket

Nonfiction > *Nonfiction Books*
  Cultural Criticism; History; Investigative Journalism; Literary Memoir; Popular Science; Social History

Send: Query; Full text; Proposal
How to send: Online submission system

Across genres she is looking for sharp and distinct contemporary voices, compelling prose, and singular points of view. In fiction she's interested in novels that dig into the complicated inner workings of relationships and bring readers deep in the messy minds of their characters, and particularly those that wrestle with class, sexuality, race, and power in all its forms. She also loves a twist of humor, a dark bent, or a speculative or uncanny edge. In nonfiction, she's drawn to idea-driven narratives that help explain how we see and construct the world around us or that bring some hidden architecture into view. Her interests span literary memoir, popular science, investigative journalism, history (social, intellectual, and overlooked histories in particular), and cultural criticism and essays.

L248 Lisa Fuller
Literary Agent
Australia

https://alexadsett.com.au
https://alexadsett.com.au/literary-agency/

Literary Agency: Alex Adsett Literary (**L016**)

ADULT > **Fiction** > *Novels*: Speculative

CHILDREN'S > **Fiction** > *Novels*

YOUNG ADULT > **Fiction** > *Novels*

Interested in Own Voices works, YA, children's literature and all things speculative fiction.

L249 Eugenie Furniss
Literary Agent

eugeniefurniss@42mp.com

https://www.42mp.com/agents
https://twitter.com/Furniss

Literary Agency: 42 Management and Production

Fiction > *Novels*
  Comedy / Humour; Crime; Historical Fiction

Nonfiction > *Nonfiction Books*
  Biography; Finance; Memoir; Politics; Popular History

Closed to approaches.

Drawn to crime in all its guises and historical fiction. On the nonfiction front seeks biography and popular history, and politics.

L250 Isobel Gahan
Associate Agent
United Kingdom
Tel: +44 (0) 207 393 4411

isobel.gahan@curtisbrown.co.uk

https://curtisbrown.co.uk
https://curtisbrown.co.uk/agent/isobel-gahan

CHILDREN'S
  Fiction
    Graphic Novels: Coming of Age; Fantasy; Historical Fantasy; Science Fiction; Space Opera
    Middle Grade: Fantasy; Historical Fantasy; Science Fiction; Space Opera
  Nonfiction > *Nonfiction Books*

YOUNG ADULT
  Fiction
    Graphic Novels: Coming of Age; Fantasy; Historical Fantasy; Science Fiction; Space Opera

    Novels: Fantasy; Historical Fantasy; Science Fiction; Space Opera
  Nonfiction > *Nonfiction Books*

Closed to approaches.

I'm currently building my own list, looking for YA and middle grade fantasy, sci-fi, graphic novels and non-fiction. I read widely, but I have a particular love for fantasy and especially plots with ambitious world-building and immersive mythologies. I also enjoy coming-of-age stories that explore growing up, particularly in graphic novel form. I read widely in adult fantasy and sci-fi and I love historical fantasy and ambitious space-operas that explore the universe.

Authors: Craig Barr-Green; Nevin Holness; Michael Mann; Ella McLeod; Struan Murray; Louise Page; Alake Pilgrim; Kat Williams; Matt Woodhead; Kelly Yang

L251 Natalie Galustian
Literary Agent
United Kingdom

natalie@greyhoundliterary.co.uk

https://greyhoundliterary.co.uk/agent/natalie-galustian/
https://twitter.com/natgalustian

Literary Agency: Greyhound Literary (**L278**)

Fiction
  Novels: Literary
  Short Fiction: Literary

Nonfiction
  Essays: General
  Nonfiction Books: Arts; Biography; Comedy / Humour; Commercial; Cookery; Drama; History; Memoir; Music; Narrative Nonfiction

Send: Query; Synopsis; Writing sample; Outline
How to send: Email
How not to send: Post

Represents narrative and commercial non-fiction as well as literary fiction. She is primarily looking for strong new voices in non-fiction across musical, visual, dramatic and culinary arts, history, memoir, biography, essays and humour, along with some select fiction and short stories of literary quality.

Author Estates: The Estate of Alan Rickman; The Estate of Alfred H. Mendes

Authors: Jennifer Lucy Allan; Jeremy Allen; Bez; Lulah Ellender; Joel Gion; Stephen Mallinder; Charlotte Mitchell; David Moats; Richard Norris; Andrew Perry; Hamilton Richardson; Lias Saoudi; Matthew Shaw; Michael Smith; Harry Sword; James Thomas; Luke Turner; Robin Turner; Liam Patrick Young

L252 Lori Galvin
Senior Agent
Boston
United States

https://aevitascreative.com/agents/
https://querymanager.com/query/QueryLoriGalvin

Literary Agency: Aevitas

Fiction > *Novels*
  Domestic Suspense; Mystery; Psychological Thrillers

Nonfiction > *Nonfiction Books*
  Cookery; Food; Memoir

Send: Author bio; Query; Synopsis; Writing sample; Pitch; Market info
How to send: Query Manager

Represents both adult fiction (especially domestic suspense, psychological thrillers and mysteries) and nonfiction (memoir, food writing, and cookbooks).

Authors: Regina McBride; Tamara L. Miller; Jennifer Morita

L253 The Garamond Agency, Inc.
Literary Agency
United States

query@garamondagency.com

https://garamondagency.com
http://www.facebook.com/garamondagency/
https://twitter.com/@garamondagency

Nonfiction > *Nonfiction Books*
  General, and in particular: Business; History; Narrative Nonfiction; Politics; Psychology; Science; Sociology

Does not want:

Nonfiction > *Nonfiction Books*: Memoir

Send: Query
Don't send: Proposal
How to send: Email
How not to send: Email attachment

Represents only adult, nonfiction projects.

Do not send proposals for children's books, young adult, fiction, poetry, or memoirs.

Query first if you have any questions about whether this is the right agency for your work.

Send email containing a short description of your project before forwarding your proposal. Please send brief queries only. No attachments. Unsolicited attachments will be deleted unread.

Literary Agent: Lisa Adams

L254 Adam Gauntlett
Literary Agent
United Kingdom
Tel: +44 (0) 20 7344 1032

agauntlett@pfd.co.uk

https://petersfraserdunlop.com/agent/adam-gauntlett/
https://twitter.com/albioneye

Literary Agency: Peters Fraser + Dunlop

ADULT
  Fiction > *Novels*
    Crime; High Concept; Historical Fiction; Thrillers; Upmarket Commercial Fiction

  Nonfiction > *Nonfiction Books*
    Crime; History; Memoir; Narrative Nonfiction; Popular Science; Psychology

CHILDREN'S > **Fiction** > *Middle Grade*

Send: Query; Synopsis; Writing sample; Proposal; Author bio
How to send: Email
How not to send: Post

Looking for upmarket-commercial fiction, series crime and thrillers, historical fiction, high-concept fiction, middle grade, narrative non-fiction, true crime, memoir, popular science/psychology and serious history. Drawn to strong female leads, original voices, quirky and endearing narrators, and well-executed plot twists.

Authors: Fay Bound Alberti; Dorothy Armstrong; Prof Marc David Baer; Andrew J. Bayliss; Nora Berend; Ed Burstell; Nicola Clark; Paul Coldwell; Jack Cornish; Andrew Craig; Wilfred Emmanuel-Jones; Justine Firnhaber-Baker; Eckart Frahm; Tova Friedman; Ashish Ghadiali; Marina Gibson; Sam Hurcom; Islam Issa; Lloyd Llewellyn-Jones; Monica Mark; Jack Meaning; Helen Molesworth; Anna Motz; Camilla Pang; Suk Pannu; Rupal Patel; Joanne Paul; Charlotte Proudman; Martyn Rady; Jacob Rees-Mogg; Alice Rio; Jane Rosenberg; Georges Simenon; Vanessa Taylor; Lisa Thompson; Charlotte Fox Weber; Adam White; Catherine Wilson; Andy Wood; Neil Woods; David Young; Andrew Zurcher

L255 Ellen Geiger
Senior Agent; Vice President
United States

https://goldinlit.com/agents/

Literary Agency: Frances Goldin Literary Agency, Inc. (**L238**)

Fiction > *Novels*
  Culture; Historical Fiction; Literary Thrillers; Multicultural

Nonfiction > *Nonfiction Books*
  Biography; History; Investigative Journalism; Multicultural; Politics; Psychology; Religion; Social Issues; Women's Issues

Closed to approaches.

Represents a broad range of fiction and non-fiction. She has a lifelong interest in multicultural and social issues embracing change. History, biography, progressive politics, psychology, women's issues, religion and serious investigative journalism are special interests.

In fiction, she loves a good literary thriller, and novels in general that provoke and challenge the status quo, as well as historical and multicultural works. She is drawn to big themes which make a larger point about the culture and times we live in, such as Barbara Kingsolver's Poisonwood Bible. She is not the right agent for New Age, romance, how-to or right-wing politics.

L256 Josh Getzler
Literary Agent; Partner
United States

josh@hgliterary.com

https://www.hgliterary.com/josh
https://twitter.com/jgetzler
http://www.publishersmarketplace.com/members/jgetzler/
http://aaronline.org/Sys/PublicProfile/2902758/417813
http://queryme.online/Getzler

Literary Agency: HG Literary (**L310**)
Professional Body: Association of American Literary Agents (AALA)

ADULT
  Fiction > *Novels*
    Crime; Historical Fiction; Mystery; Thrillers; Upmarket; Women's Fiction

  Nonfiction > *Nonfiction Books*
    Business; History; Politics

CHILDREN'S > **Fiction** > *Middle Grade*
  Comedy / Humour; Contemporary

Closed to approaches.

L257 Lilly Ghahremani
Literary Agent
United States

https://www.fullcircleliterary.com/our-agents/lilly-ghahremani/
https://querymanager.com/query/LillyFCL
https://twitter.com/Wonderlilly

Literary Agency: Full Circle Literary, LLC

ADULT > **Nonfiction**
  Gift Books: High Concept; Photography
  Illustrated Books: General

CHILDREN'S
  Fiction
    Middle Grade: Comedy / Humour; Culture; Middle East
    Picture Books: Comedy / Humour; Culture; Middle East
  Nonfiction > *Nonfiction Books*

YOUNG ADULT > **Fiction** > *Novels*: Middle East

Closed to approaches.

Seeks to partner up with creatives who have done their homework on the industry, their place in it, and have a concept that stays with her. Wants: Children's books that infuse traditional cultural wisdoms in a modern, relatable way; Children's nonfiction books by experts; Funny but smart picture books that surprise; Books for kids of any age that center disabled characters without necessarily being about disability; High-concept gift books with illustration/photography included; Picture book, middle grade, and YA with Middle Eastern characters, settings, or themes; and Joyous middle grade.

L258 Tara Gilbert
Literary Agent
United States

https://taragilbert.com
https://querymanager.com/query/TaraGilbert
https://ktliterary.com/about/
https://www.publishersmarketplace.com/members/tsgilbert/
https://twitter.com/Literary_Tara
https://www.pinterest.com/tarashilohgilbert/
https://www.instagram.com/literary.tara/
https://www.facebook.com/taragilbertlitagent

Literary Agency: KT Literary (**L377**)

ADULT > **Fiction** > *Novels*
  Historical Fantasy; Horror; Low Fantasy; Romance; Speculative; Upmarket

CHILDREN'S > **Fiction** > *Graphic Novels*

YOUNG ADULT > **Fiction** > *Novels*
  Comedy / Humour; Contemporary; Fantasy; Horror; Romance; Romantic Comedy

Closed to approaches.

Their passion is working with LGBTQ+, BIPOC, Neurodiverse, body diverse, and underrepresented authors and illustrators, focusing on fiction and graphic novels for MG, YA, and adults.

L259 Bianca Gillam
Literary Agent
United Kingdom

https://zenoagency.com
https://zenoagency.com/agents/bianca-gillam/

Literary Agency: Zeno Agency (**L680**)

Fiction > *Novels*
  Romantasy; Romantic Comedy; Thrillers; Women's Fiction

Nonfiction > *Nonfiction Books*: Narrative Nonfiction

Closed to approaches.

When open, I am looking for: Romantasy, Rom-coms with an edge, women's fiction with a strong hook and deep emotional narrative (think Taylor Jenkins-Reid), atmospheric thrillers with a strong sense of place (think In My Dreams I Hold a Knife by Ashley

Winstead). My primary focus is fiction, but I am open to a select number of narrative non-fiction projects, with a focus on stories that have particular relevance for young women (think I'm Glad My Mom Died by Jeannette McCurdy), or are so gripping they read like fiction (think Educated by Tara Westover).

Authors: Shannon Lee Barry; Georgia Gailey

L260 Ginger Clark Literary
Literary Agency
554 Boston Post Road, Suite 513, Orange, CT 06477
United States
Tel: +1 (646) 396-0903

info@GingerClarkLiterary.com

https://gingerclarkliterary.com
https://www.instagram.com/clarkliterary/
https://twitter.com/ClarkLiterary

Literary Agents: Ginger Clark; Nicole Eisenbraun (**L191**)

L261 Katie Gisondi
Literary Agent
United States

http://www.ldlainc.com/about
https://querymanager.com/query/2696
https://www.manuscriptwishlist.com/mswl-post/katie-gisondi/
https://twitter.com/GisondiKatie

Literary Agency: Laura Dail Literary Agency

ADULT > Fiction
  Graphic Novels: Fantasy; High Concept; Romance
  Novels: Cozy Mysteries; Fantasy; High Concept; Mystery; Romance; Romantasy; Romantic Comedy
CHILDREN'S > Fiction
  Graphic Novels: Fantasy; High Concept; Romance
  Middle Grade: Adventure; Fantasy; High Concept
YOUNG ADULT > Fiction
  Graphic Novels: Fantasy; High Concept; Romance
  Novels: Adventure; Fantasy

How to send: Query Manager
How not to send: Email; Social Media; Phone; Post

In all genres I prioritize diversity and marginalized voices. Specifically, I would love to see more Indigenous, Native American, and First Nations, as well as Latinx, disabled, chronically ill, and trans/nonbinary/queer stories and voices. In general, I am looking for commercial fiction and non-fiction with a clear, distinct voice and a unique hook.

L262 Glass Literary Management LLC
Literary Agency
138 West 25th Street, 10th Floor, New York, NY 10001
United States
Tel: +1 (646) 237-4881

info@glassliterary.com

https://glassliterary.com
https://www.facebook.com/glassliterary
https://www.publishersmarketplace.com/members/GlassLiterary/

ADULT
  Fiction > *Novels*
  Nonfiction > *Nonfiction Books*
CHILDREN'S
  Fiction > *Novels*
  Nonfiction > *Nonfiction Books*

Send: Query
How to send: Online contact form

Represents fiction and nonfiction for adults and children. Send query through online contact form. Prefers queries that describe your book concisely; are well-written and typo-free; show an understanding of the marketplace and where your book would fit into it; and, for nonfiction, show why you are the best person to be writing the book you're proposing. Response not guaranteed unless interested.

Literary Agents: Alex Glass; Jennifer Chen Tran (**L633**)

L263 Emily Glenister
Literary Agent; Company Director
United Kingdom

eg.submission@dhhliteraryagency.com

http://www.dhhliteraryagency.com/emily-glenister.html
http://www.twitter.com/emily_glenister

Literary Agency: DHH Literary Agency Ltd (**L166**)

Fiction
  Novels: Book Club Fiction; Commercial; Contemporary; Crime; Ghost Stories; Gothic; Historical Fiction; Horror; Magical Realism; Psychological Thrillers; Romance; Romantic Comedy; Upmarket Commercial Fiction; Urban Fantasy
  Short Fiction Collections: Ghost Stories; Horror
Nonfiction > *Nonfiction Books*
  Autobiography; Biography; Crime; History; Medicine; Memoir; Popular Culture; Royalty; Women

Does not want:

  Fiction > *Novels*: Police Procedural

Send: Query; Synopsis; Writing sample
How to send: Word file email attachment

Looking for female-led commercial fiction; upmarket commercial fiction; diverse and unique voices; crime and psychological thrillers; witty, contemporary and observant romcoms; epic love stories; smart and quick-witted historical fiction; gothic fiction (historical OR contemporary); female focus and dual timeline narrative; book club fiction; magical realism and urban fantasy; fun retellings (not Greek mythology, please); horror novel / ghost story; short story collections with a ghost / horror theme. In nonfiction: historical (monarchy, medicine or women); pop culture; biographies, autobiographies and memoirs; true crime.

Authors: Foluso Agbaje; Louise Beech; Heather Darwent; Becca Day; Suzie Edge; Stephen Edger; Katy Harrison; Amelia Ireland; Anthony Kavanagh; Caroline Lamond; S.V. Leonard; Emma Medrano; Jean Menzies; Vikki Patis; Reagan Lee Ray; Reagan Lee Ray; Becky Rhush; Nicole Robinson; Talia Samuels; Annie Taylor; Rebecca Templeton; Rebecca Thorne; Sally Ann Truman; Ola Tundun; Ronnie Turner; A. J. West; Kathleen Whyman; L. C. Winter

L264 Global Lion Intellectual Property Management, Inc.
Literary Agency
PO BOX 669238, Pompano Beach, FL 33066
United States
Tel: +1 (754) 222-6948

queriesgloballionmgt@gmail.com

https://globallionmanagement.com
https://www.facebook.com/GlobalLionMgt/
https://twitter.com/globallionmgt
https://www.instagram.com/globallionmgt/

Fiction > *Novels*
  Commercial; Fantasy; Science Fiction

Nonfiction > *Nonfiction Books*
  Arts; Business; Commercial; Education; Film Industry; Self Help; TV; Technology

Send: Query; Synopsis; Writing sample; Author bio
How to send: Online submission system

Currently looking for commercial fiction, fantasy, science fiction, and intriguing studies of interesting subjects, art, and "making of" books on the film and television industry. Will not turn down anything with sharp prose, modern takes on classic concepts, a great mystery to solve or intriguing characters.

L265 Adria Goetz
Literary Agent
United States

https://ktliterary.com/submissions/
https://querymanager.com/query/adriastreasuretrove
https://adriagoetz.wpcomstaging.com/manuscript-wishlist/

Literary Agency: KT Literary (**L377**)

ADULT > Fiction > *Novels*
Cozy Fantasy; Romantic Comedy; Thrillers; Upmarket

CHILDREN'S > **Fiction**
Graphic Novels; *Middle Grade*; *Picture Books*

Send: Query; Synopsis; Writing sample; Full text
How to send: Query Manager

Seeking picture books (especially by author-illustrators), middle grade fiction, graphic novels, and adult fiction—particularly rom coms, thrillers, upmarket fiction, and cozy fantasy.

L266 Anthony Goff
Literary Agent; Chair
United Kingdom

submissions@davidhigham.co.uk

https://www.davidhigham.co.uk/agents-dh/anthony-goff/

Literary Agency: David Higham Associates Ltd (**L159**)

ADULT
Fiction > *Novels*
Commercial; Literary

Nonfiction > *Nonfiction Books*
Commercial; Literary

CHILDREN'S > Fiction > *Novels*

Closed to approaches.

Represents many high-profile and successful authors of literary and commercial fiction and non-fiction, and also several children's writers.

Associate Agent: David Evans (**L203**)

Authors: Carol Anshaw; Jenn Ashworth; Nigel Barley; Aimee Bender; Margaret Boden; Janet Browne; Jessica Bruder; Mark Burnell; J. M. Coetzee; Bernard Cornwell; John Cunliffe; Roald Dahl; Anne Fine; Karen Joy Fowler; Catherine Fox; Stephen Fry; Caroline Graham; Linda Green; Graham Greene; James Herbert; Nathan Hill; Paul Hoffman; Simon Hopkinson; Alan Judd; Binnie Kirshenbaum; Stephen Lacey; Hugh Laurie; Joanna Lumley; Greil Marcus; David Marquand; Simon Mason; Evan Mawdsley; Peter May; Elizabeth McCracken; Iain McGilchrist; Elizabeth McKenzie; Sigrid Nunez; Kate Reed Petty; Anthony Powell; Shannon Pufahl; Alice Sebold; Miranda Seymour; Nick Sharratt; Hilary Spurling; Hew Strachan; Jeremy Strong; Lynne Truss; Lucy Wadham; Alice Walker; Stephen Walsh; Elizabeth Wilhide

L267 Ellen Goff
Associate Agent
United States

ellen@hgliterary.com

https://www.hgliterary.com/ellen

Literary Agency: HG Literary (**L310**)

ADULT
Fiction > *Novels*
Fantasy; Romance; Romantasy

Nonfiction > *Nonfiction Books*
General, and in particular: Food; Gender; Intersectional Feminism

CHILDREN'S > **Fiction**
Middle Grade; *Picture Books*

YOUNG ADULT
Fiction
Graphic Novels: General
Novels: General, and in particular: Ghost Stories; Gothic; Romance

Nonfiction > *Nonfiction Books*
General, and in particular: Food

List consists of authors writing for all age groups, from picture books to middle grade to young adult to adult, in both fiction and nonfiction. She also represents illustrators, for kidlit and adult projects, as well as graphic novelists. She is always hungry for stories celebrating girl power and intersectional feminism, but also narratives that don't shy away from asking questions about gender and exploring gender roles. She has a soft spot for southern stories that remind her of her home state of Kentucky, and is a perpetual sucker for a darn good love story. For picture books, she is only taking on new clients who are author-illustrators, and gravitates toward projects that highlight the sparse and simple. She is interested in all genres and formats of MG and YA, especially anything spooky, graphic novels, novels-in-verse, and projects that allow her to travel vicariously through place and time. In adult, she represents fantasy and romance and their intersection. She might be convinced on a nonfiction project if it involves food.

L268 Veronica Goldstein
Literary Agent
United States

https://www.unitedtalent.com
https://www.unitedtalent.com/bio/veronica-goldstein

Literary Agency: United Talent Agency (UTA)

Fiction > *Novels*
Autofiction; Contemporary; Culture; Experimental; Literary; Politics; Society; Speculative

Nonfiction > *Nonfiction Books*
Culture; Investigative Journalism; Memoir; Nature; Politics; Popular Culture; Science; Sociology; Technology

Send: Query; Full text; Proposal
How to send: Online submission system

In fiction, she looks for literary novels with an original, contemporary voice that balance the complexities of culture and politics with storytelling that explores the inner worlds of its characters in a way that challenges expectations and deepens the emotional stakes of the story. Autofiction, grounded speculative fiction, and experimental forms are always of interest. She's also looking for compelling critical takes on cultural and sociological trends and overlooked or misunderstood histories; investigative and issue-focused narrative nonfiction; and memoir that makes the personal political and vice versa. Pop culture, science, technology, politics, and writing about the natural world are always of interest.

L269 The Good Literary Agency
Literary Agency
United Kingdom

info@thegoodliteraryagency.org

https://www.thegoodliteraryagency.org
https://twitter.com/thegoodagencyuk

Professional Body: The Association of Authors' Agents (AAA)

ADULT
Fiction > *Novels*
General, and in particular: Cozy Mysteries; Romantic Comedy

Nonfiction > *Nonfiction Books*
General, and in particular: Health; Lifestyle

CHILDREN'S
Fiction > *Middle Grade*
General, and in particular: Contemporary; Fantasy

Nonfiction > *Nonfiction Books*
General, and in particular: Lifestyle

YOUNG ADULT
Fiction > *Novels*
General, and in particular: Contemporary Fantasy; Romance

Nonfiction > *Nonfiction Books*
General, and in particular: Lifestyle

Send: Query
Don't send: Full text

Focused on discovering, developing and launching the careers of writers of colour, disability, working class, LGBTQ+ and anyone who feels their story is not being told in the mainstream. Writers must be born or resident in Britain. No poetry, plays, or screenplays. Accepts submissions from the 1st to the 21st of each month only. See website for full guidelines and to submit via online form.

L270 Andrew Gordon
Literary Agent
United Kingdom

andrewgordon@davidhigham.co.uk

https://www.davidhigham.co.uk/agents-dh/andrew-gordon/

Literary Agency: David Higham Associates Ltd (**L159**)

Fiction > *Novels*
  Commercial; High Concept Crime; Literary; Thrillers

Nonfiction > *Nonfiction Books*
  Adventure; Biography; Business; Current Affairs; Economics; Films; History; Memoir; Music; Narrative Nonfiction; Politics; Popular Culture; Popular Science; Psychology; Sport

List is primarily non-fiction. On the lookout for Non-fiction: — history (whether narrative, popular or serious) — current affairs, politics and economics — biography and memoir — narrative and literary non-fiction including books that blur genre boundaries — sport and tales of adventure — popular culture, film and music — popular science and psychology — 'smart thinking' or ideas books — business books with a strong narrative (rather than 'how to'); and Fiction: — novels that grab the attention, whether literary or commercial — strong stories evocative of a period or place — big, brassy 'airport' thrillers and high-concept crime.

Associate Agent: David Evans (**L203**)

Author / Editor-in-Chief: Jason Cowley

Authors: Elizabeth Alker; Alan Allport; Thomas Asbridge; Katy Balls; Lindsey Bareham; Kaushik Basu; Laura Beers; James Bloodworth; Jonathan Boff; Caroline Burt; John Carey; Aditya Chakrabortty; Alan Connor; Ivor Crewe; Lizzie Dearden; David Domoney; Richard English; Gavin Esler; Seb Falk; Felipe Fernández-Armesto; Cordelia Fine; Matthew Frank; Susannah Gibson; Andrew Gimson; Victoria Glendinning; John Gribbin; Isabel Hardman; Sophie Harman; Tim Harper; Chris Hirst; Russell Hoban; Eric Hobsbawm; Trevor Horn; Tansy Hoskins; Julian Jackson; Owen Jones; Anna Keay; John Keay; Paul Kennedy; Barbara Keys; Sulmaan Wasif Khan; Halik Kochanski; David Lammy; Elisabeth Leake; Graham Lee; Damien Lewis; Daniel Light; Dame Vera Lynn; Kathryn Mannix; Sarfraz Manzoor; Helen McCarthy; Ed Miliband; Fraser Nelson; Johan Norberg; David Nott; Peter Oborne; Susan Owens; Helen Parr; Richard Partington; Harry Pearson; Gilles Peterson; Des Powell; Sadiah Qureshi; Amol Rajan; Chris Renwick; Steve Richards; Helen Roche; Jane Rogoyska; Brunello Rosa; Rupert Russell; Jane Sanderson; Antonia Senior; Rachel Shabi; Sujit Sivasundaram; Mark B. Smith; Kristina Spohr; Peter Stott; Nicola Sturgeon; Dylan Thomas; Simon Thurley; Phil Tinline; Simon Tyler; Rosamund Urwin; Yanis Varoufakis; Bernard Wasserstein; Holly Watt; Sam Wetherell; Phil Whitaker; Jon Wilson; Hope Wolf; Carolyn Woods

L271 Graham Maw Christie Literary Agency

Literary Agency
37 Highbury Place, London, N5 1QP
United Kingdom
Tel: +44 (0) 7971 268342

submissions@grahammawchristie.com

http://www.grahammawchristie.com
https://twitter.com/litagencygmc
https://www.instagram.com/litagencygmc/

Professional Body: The Association of Authors' Agents (AAA)

Nonfiction > *Nonfiction Books*

Send: Query; Outline; Author bio; Market info; Marketing Plan; Writing sample
How to send: Email

No fiction, poetry, or scripts. Send query with one-page summary, a paragraph on the contents of each chapter, your qualifications for writing it, details of your online presence, market analysis, what you could do to help promote your book, and a sample chapter or two.

Junior Agent: Amy O'Shea (**L488**)

Literary Agents: Jennifer Christie (**L126**); Jane Graham Maw (**L434**)

L272 Stacey Graham

Literary Agent
United States

stacey@threeseaslit.com

https://www.threeseasagency.com/agents/stacey-graham
http://querymanager.com/Stacey3Seas

Literary Agency: 3 Seas Literary Agency (**L001**)

ADULT
  Fiction
    Graphic Novels: General
    Novels: Comedy / Humour; Commercial; Mystery; Popular Culture; Romantic Comedy
  Nonfiction > *Nonfiction Books*
    Antiques; Commercial; Cookery; Crafts; How To; Lifestyle; Pets

YOUNG ADULT > **Fiction** > *Graphic Novels*

How to send: Query Manager

Currently looking to expand her list with adult romance (referral only); quirky, fascinating nonfiction with strong commercial appear and a great platform; graphic novels for adult / young adult; mystery; commercial fiction; humour; and pop culture.

L273 Kara Grajkowski

Literary Agent
United States

threeseasagency.kara@gmail.com

https://www.threeseasagency.com/agents/kara-grajkowski
https://querymanager.com/query/2761

Literary Agency: 3 Seas Literary Agency (**L001**)

CHILDREN'S > **Fiction** > *Novels*: Contemporary

YOUNG ADULT > **Fiction** > *Novels*: Contemporary

Closed to approaches.

Looking for contemporary middle grade fiction; contemporary young adult fiction; and own voices.

L274 Michelle Grajkowski

Literary Agent
United States

michelle@threeseaslit.com

https://www.threeseasagency.com/agents/michelle-grajkowski
http://querymanager.com/Michelle3Seas
http://aaronline.org/Sys/PublicProfile/2176701/417813

Literary Agency: 3 Seas Literary Agency (**L001**)

Professional Body: Association of American Literary Agents (AALA)

ADULT
  Fiction > *Novels*
    Romance; Women's Fiction
  Nonfiction > *Nonfiction Books*

CHILDREN'S > **Fiction** > *Middle Grade*

How to send: Query Manager

Primarily represents romance, women's fiction, young adult and middle grade fiction along with select nonfiction projects with a terrific message. She is currently looking for fantastic writers with a voice of their own.

Authors: Katie MacAlister; Cathy McDavid; Kerrelyn Sparks; C.L. Wilson

L275 David Granger

Literary Agent
New York
United States

https://aevitascreative.com/agents/

Literary Agency: Aevitas

Nonfiction > *Nonfiction Books*
  Celebrity; Culture; Food; Journalism; Politics

Closed to approaches.

Represents primarily non-fiction and is obsessed with topics across an extremely wide spectrum – politics; food culture; actual innovation in design, tech and science; fame. What binds these things is a yen for intensely original ideas and writing that pushes boundaries.

Authors: Jacqueline Detwiler-George; Scott Eden; Stephen Starring Grant; Richard Panek

L276 Greene & Heaton Ltd
Literary Agency
T18, West Wing, Somerset House, Strand, London, WC2R 1LA
United Kingdom

submissions@greeneheaton.co.uk
info@greeneheaton.co.uk

http://www.greeneheaton.co.uk
https://twitter.com/greeneandheaton

Professional Body: The Association of Authors' Agents (AAA)

Fiction > *Novels*

Nonfiction > *Nonfiction Books*

Does not want:

> CHILDREN'S > Fiction > *Picture Books*

Send: Query; Synopsis; Writing sample
Don't send: Full text
How to send: Email
How not to send: Post

Send query by email only, including synopsis and three chapters or approximately 50 pages. No submissions by post. No response unless interested. Handles all types of fiction and nonfiction, but no scripts or children's picture books.

Author Estates: The Estate of Julia Darling; The Estate of Sarah Gainham

Authors: Juliana Adelman; Precious Adesina; Clayton Page Aldern; Amen Alonge; Anthony Anaxagorou; Peter Apps; Lucy Ashe; Sa'ad Azam; Mevan Babakar; Carol Ballantine; Michelle Bang; Raffaella Barker; Charlotte Bauer; Emily Bootle; Lucy Brazier; Bridget; Lynne Bryan; Zoe Burgess; Wren Burke; Jason Byrne; Tom Campbell; Charles Cockell; Pam Corbin; Robin Craig; Avery Curran; Russell Davies; Anna Davis; Rachel Dawson; Leona Deakin; Sharanya Deepak; Rageshri Dhairyawan; Patrick Drake; Kim Duke; Lily Dunn; Suzannah Dunn; Mari Ellis Dunning; Jeremy Duns; Jonn Elledge; Gabriela Evangelou; Lucia Evangelou; Olaf Falafel; Vittoria Fallanca; Hugh Fearnley-Whittingstall; Jane Fearnley-Whittingstall; Christopher Fitz-Simon; Felix Flicker; Christophe Galfard; Chandra Ganguly; Gareth Gavin; Helen Giltrow; Francis Gimblett; Mara Gold; Molly Greeley; Jake Hall; Phil Harrison; Evie Hatch; Julie Hayward; Stuart Heritage; Kit Heyam; Kat Hill; Julian Hitch; Beatrice Hitchman; Julia Hollander; Wayne Holloway-Smith; Andrew Holmes; Alex Hourston; Sarah Housley; David Howard; Scott Alexander Howard; Daisy J. Hung; Charles Jennings; Joan; D.B. John; Sam Johnson-Schlee; Keith Kahn-Harris; Fiona Keating; Vedashree Khambete-Sharma; Gabrielle Kimm; Esme King; Max Kinnings; David Kirk; Rikke Schmidt Kjærgaard; Rebecca Dinerstein Knight; Joseph Knox; Sonya Kudei; Manon Lagrève; August Lamm; William Leith; Dan Lepard; Robert Lewis; Eric Lindstrom; Kieran Long; Dorian Lynskey; L. A. MacRae; Carina Maggar; Ruth Mancini; Rob Manuel; Anna Sulan Masing; Jolyon Maugham; James McGee; Kerry McInerney; Rebecca Taylor McKay; Gill Meller; Thomasina Miers; Lottie Moggach; Cathy Newman; Mary-Ann Ochota; Ciara Ohartghaile; Christopher Osborn; Iain Overton; John O'Connell; Nicolas Padamsee; Pete Paphides; Anna Parker; Geoffrey Parker; Jyoti Patel; Neel Patel; Marie Phillips; Tom Phillips; Xenobe Purvis; Shivi Ramoutar; Francesca Ramsay; Richard Reed; Ana Reyes; Sam Rice; C. J. Sansom; William Sansom; Marcus du Sautoy; Indyana Schneider; Alev Scott; Eddie Scott; Rebecca Seal; Paul Keers: Sediment; Laura Shepherd-Robinson; James Smythe; Mimi Spencer; Polly Stewart; Count Arthur Strong; Jacqueline Sutherland; Andrew Taylor; Georgie Tilney; Ian Vince; John Vincent; Adam Wagner; Jennie Walker; Sarai Walker; Andrew Webb; Ione Wells; Robyn Wilder; Will Wiles; Jason Wilson; David Wright; Jackie Wullschläger; Susie Yang; Erin Young; Robyn Young; Joe Zadeh; Andrew Ziminski

Literary Agents: Holly Faulks (**L209**); Carol Heaton; Imogen Morrell (**L460**); Judith Murray (**L468**); Antony Topping (**L632**); Laura Williams (**L662**); Claudia Young (**L677**)

L277 Katie Greenstreet
Literary Agent
United Kingdom

submissions@paperliterary.com

Literary Agency: Paper Literary

Fiction > *Novels*
Book Club Fiction; Commercial; Family; Historical Fiction; Literary Suspense; Psychological Suspense; Romance; Upmarket

Nonfiction > *Nonfiction Books*: Memoir

I'm building a list of quality commercial and upmarket/book club fiction, with a select number of memoirs and non-fiction projects also in the mix.

L278 Greyhound Literary
Literary Agency
United Kingdom

info@cclagents.com

https://greyhoundliterary.co.uk

Professional Body: The Association of Authors' Agents (AAA)

ADULT
Fiction > *Novels*
Commercial; Literary

Nonfiction > *Nonfiction Books*
General, and in particular: Biography; Comedy / Humour; Cookery; History; Lifestyle; Memoir; Music; Politics; Sport; Wellbeing

CHILDREN'S
Fiction > *Novels*
Nonfiction > *Nonfiction Books*

Send: Query; Synopsis; Writing sample
How to send: Email

Author Estates: The Estate of Alan Rickman; The Estate of Alfred H. Mendes

Authors: Guy Adams; K Anis Ahmed; Tanya Aldred; Becky Alexander; Moeen Ali; Jennifer Lucy Allan; Jeremy Allen; Tobi Asare; Carol Atherton; Paddy Barrett; Zahra Barri; Sharmilla Beezmohun; Victoria Belim; Juliet Bell; SJ Bennett; Josh Berson; Bez; Leona Nichole Black; Matt Blake; Owen Booth; Luce Brett; Edward Brooke-Hitching; Andy Bull; Jen Campbell; John Campbell; Bonnie Chung; David Clifford; Reuben Coe; David Collins; Zoë Colville; Duncan Crowe; Iain Dey; Gethan Dick; Chris Dodd; Max Doty; Saddiq Dzukogi; Yvvette Edwards; Lulah Ellender; Kirsty Eyre; Marchelle Farrell; Adam Fergusson; Jamie Fewery; A P Firdaus; Matthew Ford; Liz Fraser; Rebecca Front; Tom Gabbay; Ian Garner; Joel Gion; Claire Gleeson; Julian Gough; Janet Gover; Jon Gower; Sarah Graham; Karen Gurney; Saskia Gwinn; Ed Hawkins; David Higgins; Maisie Hill; Will Hill; Thomas W. Hodgkinson; Nicholas Hogg; Michael Holding; Iain Hollingshead; Andrew Hosken; Michael Hurley; Michael Hutchinson; Mette Leonard Høeg; Joshua Idehen; Ellie Irving; Heidi James; Delia Jarrett-Macauley; Stuart Jeffries; Ginger Jones; Simon Jones; Vijay Khurana; Patricia Kingori; Jennifer Lane; Michael Lawson; Paul Levy; Fiona Longmuir; Michelle Lovric; Bonnie MacBird; Stephen Mallinder; Arji Manuelpillai; Shingi Mararike; Katie Marsh; Amanda Mason; Hugh Matheson; Neil McCormick; Anthony McGowan; Barry McKinley; Shane Melisse; Moin Mir; Charlotte Mitchell; David Moats; Jonathan Morrison; Anton Mosimann; Rebecca Myers; Richard Norris; Charlotte Ord; James Peak; Andrew Perry; Bonnie Quinn; Edvard Radzinsky; Julia Raeside; Tarun Ramadorai; Amy Ransom; Sue Ransom; Amy Raphael; Hamilton Richardson; Susan Richardson; Roger Robinson; Rebecca Rogers; Anthea Rowan; Leonard Rutgers; Lias Saoudi; Rebecca Schiller; Clare Seal; Matthew Shaw; Sarah Shephard; Tina Shingler; Cécile Simmons; Michael Smith; Tatton Spiller;

Andrea Stuart; C.J. Subko; Philip Suggars; Harry Sword; James Thomas; Jo Thompson; Tom Tivnan; Gemma Tizzard; Luke Turner; Robin Turner; Hana Videen; Kate Vigurs; Wendy Wason; Jen Wight; Sioned Wiliam; Penny Wincer; Mike Woodhouse; Liam Patrick Young; Yomi Ṣode

Chair: Patrick Janson-Smith

Foreign Rights Director / Literary Agent: Sam Edenborough (**L189**)

Literary Agents: Charlotte Atyeo (**L034**); Salma Begum (**L053**); Maria Brannan (**L078**); Charlie Campbell (**L099**); Natalie Galustian (**L251**); Dotti Irving (**L326**); Philip Gwyn Jones (**L339**); Julia Silk (**L583**)

L279 Katie Grimm

Literary Agent
United States

http://doncongdon.com/agents.shtml#agent-03
https://querymanager.com/query/KGRIMM

Literary Agency: Don Congdon Associates, Inc. (**L175**)

ADULT
  Fiction
    Graphic Novels: General
    Novels: Historical Fiction; Literary; Mystery; Speculative; Upmarket Women's Fiction
    Short Fiction Collections: General
  Nonfiction > *Nonfiction Books*
    History; Memoir; Narrative Nonfiction; Science; Social Issues

YOUNG ADULT > **Fiction** > *Novels*
  Contemporary; High Concept; Speculative

Closed to approaches.

She represents vivid literary fiction (be it voicey, historical, speculative, or mysterious), up-market women's fiction, cohesive short story collections, and graphic novels. In young adult, she loves compelling and heartbreaking contemporary novels and speculative high-concepts rooted in science and history. In middle grade, she enjoys novels with a heartfelt, timeless quality, and stories that explore the magic of our world or those imagined. For non-fiction, she is looking for memoirs and narratives that explore greater social issues, dark and weird times in human history, the personal impact of science, and any off-beat topic explored through an academic lens.

L280 Loren R. Grossman

Literary Agent
United States
Tel: +1 (310) 314-2113
Fax: +1 (310) 450-0181

lrg@ix.netcom.com

https://paulslevinelit.com/loren-r-grossman/

Literary Agency: Paul S. Levine Literary Agency (**L502**)

Nonfiction > *Nonfiction Books*
  Archaeology; Architecture; Arts; Autobiography; Education; Gardening; Genealogy; Health; Legal; Medicine; Science; Sociology; Technology

Send: Query
How to send: Email; Post

Send one-page query, preferably by email (though snail mail is acceptable). No query-related phone calls.

L281 Pam Gruber

Literary Agent
United States

https://www.highlineliterary.com/agent-pam
https://querymanager.com/query/Pam_Gruber
https://www.instagram.com/pjgruber/
https://twitter.com/Pamlet606

Literary Agency: High Line Literary Collective (**L312**)

ADULT
  Fiction > *Novels*
    Coming of Age; Commercial; Folklore, Myths, and Legends; Grounded Fantasy; Literary; Speculative
  Nonfiction > *Nonfiction Books*: Narrative Nonfiction

CHILDREN'S > **Fiction**
  Graphic Novels: General
  Middle Grade: Coming of Age; Commercial; Folklore, Myths, and Legends; Grounded Fantasy; Literary; Speculative

YOUNG ADULT > **Fiction**
  Graphic Novels: General
  Novels: Coming of Age; Commercial; Folklore, Myths, and Legends; Grounded Fantasy; Literary; Speculative

How to send: Query Manager

Actively looking for adult, young adult, and middle grade fiction with literary voices and commercial hooks. In all categories, she is particularly interested in finding grounded fantasy that feels like folklore, stories exploring an under-represented mythology, twisty speculative fiction, fantastical realism, and coming-of-age stories (any age). She is also open to graphic novels (chapter book, middle grade, and YA only), preferably with art attached. In nonfiction, she is drawn to a more narrative style, with an honest, relatable voice that has something to say about life or can fascinate her with new information about the world.

L282 Hattie Grunewald

Literary Agent
United Kingdom

https://www.theblairpartnership.com/literary-agents/hattie-grunewald/
https://twitter.com/hatteatime

Literary Agency: The Blair Partnership

Fiction > *Novels*
  Book Club Fiction; Commercial; Crime; Historical Fiction; Thrillers; Upmarket

Nonfiction > *Nonfiction Books*
  Lifestyle; Mental Health; Personal Development

Closed to approaches.

Represents commercial and upmarket fiction, including women's fiction, crime and thriller, historical and book club fiction. Also represents some non-fiction in the areas of lifestyle and personal development.

Authors: Jassa Ahluwalia; Danny Altmann; Amy Beashel; Emma J. Bell; Lucy Cameron; Rowan Coleman; Ryan Collett; Tom Davies; Lizzy Dent; Rebecca Denton; Roxane Dhand; Clare Empson; Sue Fortin; Mark Freeman; Gary Gamp; Alice Gendron; Marina Gerner; Clare Leslie Hall; Amelia Henley; Louise Jensen; Peter Komolafe; Alex Lassoued; Liam Livings; Ruthy Mason; Luna McNamara; Gez Medinger; Catherine Miller; Leena Norms; Nikki Owen; Rob Perry; Celine Saintclare; Anbara Salam; Lauren Sharkey; Jennifer Stone; Sarah Stovell; Nancy Tucker; Sophie Walker; Steve White; Ed Winters; Stephanie Yeboah; Lola Young

L283 Robert Guinsler

Senior Agent
United States

https://www.sll.com/our-team

Literary Agency: Sterling Lord Literistic, Inc. (**L597**)

Nonfiction > *Nonfiction Books*

Send: Query; Synopsis; Writing sample
How to send: Online submission system

His general curiosity in all things has allowed him the opportunity to represent a wide variety of prize-winning and New York Times bestselling nonfiction authors and projects. Most every avenue of the nonfiction spectrum can be found on his list. As well, he has been a champion of LGBTQ+ voices his entire career.

L284 Masha Gunic

Associate Agent
United States

http://www.azantianlitagency.com/pages/team-mg.html
https://querymanager.com/query/MashaGunic

Literary Agency: Azantian Literary Agency

CHILDREN'S > **Fiction** > *Middle Grade*
  Adventure; Comedy / Humour; Contemporary; Fantasy; Historical Fiction; Horror

YOUNG ADULT > Fiction > *Novels*
  Commercial; Contemporary; Fantasy; High Concept; Historical Fiction; Literary; Magical Realism; Mystery; Science Fiction; Space Opera; Thrillers

Closed to approaches.

Represents middle grade and young adult novels.

L285 Gurman Agency, LLC
Literary Agency
United States

https://gurmanagency.com

Professional Body: Writers Guild of America (WGA)

Scripts > *Theatre Scripts*

How to send: By referral

Represents playwrights, directors, choreographers, composers and lyricists. New clients by referral only, so prospective clients should seek a referral rather than querying. No queries accepted.

Literary Agent: Susan Gurman (*L286*)

L286 Susan Gurman
Literary Agent
United States

Literary Agency: Gurman Agency, LLC (**L285**)

L287 Taylor Haggerty
Literary Agent
United States

submissions@rootliterary.com
taylor@rootliterary.com

https://www.rootliterary.com/agents
https://www.publishersmarketplace.com/members/taylorhaggerty/
https://twitter.com/tayhaggerty

Literary Agency: Root Literary (**L547**)

ADULT > **Fiction** > *Novels*
  Book Club Fiction; Commercial; Romance

TEEN > **Fiction** > *Novels*
  Book Club Fiction; Commercial; Romance

Send: Query; Writing sample
How to send: In the body of an email

I represent commercial fiction for teens and adults – particularly in the romance and book club spaces. I gravitate toward smart, funny, voice-driven projects and welcome all the longing, pining, heart-breaking and heart-mending emotional rollercoasters you want to send my way. I have a tendency to fall for books that blur the lines between genres and am a big novelty seeker as a reader, so always love to be surprised by the fresh and unexpected!

L288 Serene Hakim
Literary Agent
United States

https://www.pandeliterary.com/about-pandeliterary
https://twitter.com/serenemaria
http://aaronline.org/Sys/PublicProfile/52119398/417813

Literary Agency: Ayesha Pande Literary (**L036**)
Professional Body: Association of American Literary Agents (AALA)

ADULT > **Fiction** > *Novels*
  Culture; International; Literary

CHILDREN'S > **Fiction** > *Middle Grade*: Fantasy

YOUNG ADULT > **Fiction** > *Novels*
  Contemporary; Culture; International

Closed to approaches.

Represents authors in a variety of genres, from MG fantasy to adult literary fiction to contemporary YA. Particularly interested in both YA and adult fiction that has international themes, highlights a variety of cultures, and focuses on underrepresented and/or marginalized voices. At the moment, she is mostly focusing on YA/MG and taking on adult writers more selectively. Specifically, she's looking for writing that explores different meanings of identity, home, and family, and in general would love to find more Middle Eastern writers.

L289 Jolene Haley
Literary Agent
United States

https://www.jolenehaley.com
http://maassagency.com/jolene-haley/
https://querymanager.com/query/QueryJolene
https://twitter.com/JoleneHaley
https://www.instagram.com/jolenehaleybooks/

Literary Agency: Donald Maass Literary Agency (**L176**)

ADULT
  Fiction > *Novels*
    Cozy Mysteries; Crime; Ghost Stories; Mystery; Romantic Comedy; Romantic Suspense

  Nonfiction > *Nonfiction Books*
    Crime; Magic; Mind, Body, Spirit; Spirituality; Witchcraft

CHILDREN'S > **Fiction** > *Middle Grade*
  Adventure; Comedy / Humour; Contemporary; Family; Horror; Magic; Magical Realism; Mystery

YOUNG ADULT > **Fiction** > *Novels*
  Adventure; Coming of Age; Contemporary; Folklore, Myths, and Legends; Ghost Stories; Horror; Magical Realism; Mystery; Romance; Tarot; Thrillers; Witches

How to send: Query Manager

Has been in the publishing industry since 2012 on both the publisher and agency sides in editorial, marketing, publicity, contracts, and agent positions.

L290 The Hanbury Agency
Literary Agency
Suite 103, 88 Lower Marsh, London, SE1 7AB
United Kingdom

enquiries@hanburyagency.com

http://www.hanburyagency.com
https://www.facebook.com/HanburyAgency/
https://twitter.com/hanburyagency
https://www.instagram.com/the_hanbury_agency/

Fiction > *Novels*

Nonfiction > *Nonfiction Books*
  Current Affairs; History; Popular Culture

Closed to approaches.

Closed to submissions as at August 2019. Check website for current status.

No film scripts, plays, poetry, books for children, self-help. Not accepting fantasy, science fiction, or misery memoirs. Send query by post with brief synopsis, first 30 pages (roughly), and your email address and phone number. No submissions by email. Do not include SAE, as no material is returned. Response not guaranteed, so assume rejection if no reply after 8 weeks.

Authors: George Alagiah; Simon Callow; Jane Glover; Bernard Hare; Imran Khan; Judith Lennox; Katie Price

Literary Agent: Margaret Hanbury

L291 Hannah Sheppard Literary Agency
Literary Agency
United Kingdom

https://hs-la.com
https://twitter.com/hannah_litagent
https://instagram.com/hannah_litagent
https://www.facebook.com/hannahsheppard.editor

Professional Body: The Association of Authors' Agents (AAA)

ADULT
  Fiction > *Novels*
    Crime Thrillers; Family; Friends; High Concept; Horror; Romantasy; Speculative Romance; Speculative; Thrillers

  Nonfiction > *Nonfiction Books*
    Feminism; Narrative Nonfiction

CHILDREN'S > **Fiction**
  Graphic Novels: General
  Middle Grade: Comedy / Humour; Ghost Stories; Horror; Romance; Romantasy
YOUNG ADULT > **Fiction** > *Graphic Novels*

Send: Query; Synopsis; Writing sample
How to send: Online submission system

I represent both adult and children's fiction (as well as a small amount of non-fiction) and, more than anything, I want to be entertained by a great story while caring deeply about your characters. In general, I love bold, distinctive voices, intriguing stories with a strong hook and flawed characters with something to learn. I want characters who are truly diverse – let's be inclusive, body positive and joyful in our representation. I also like big, mind-bending ideas and combinations of genres that feel fresh and create something new…

Literary Agents: Louise Buckley (**L091**); Hannah Sheppard (*L578*)

L292 Carrie Hannigan

Literary Agent; Partner
United States

carrie@hgliterary.com

https://www.hgliterary.com/carrie
http://queryme.online/Hannigan

Literary Agency: HG Literary (**L310**)
Professional Body: Association of American Literary Agents (AALA)

ADULT > **Nonfiction** > *Nonfiction Books*

CHILDREN'S
  Fiction
    Graphic Novels: General
    Novels: Comedy / Humour; Contemporary; Fantasy
  Nonfiction > *Nonfiction Books*

Closed to approaches.

L293 Stephanie Hansen

Senior Agent
United States

https://www.metamorphosisliteraryagency.com/about
https://querymanager.com/query/Query_Metamorphosis

Literary Agency: Metamorphosis Literary Agency (**L444**)
Professional Body: Association of American Literary Agents (AALA)

ADULT
  Fiction > *Novels*: Thrillers
  Nonfiction > *Nonfiction Books*

YOUNG ADULT > **Fiction** > *Novels*
  Contemporary; Thrillers

How to send: Query Manager

Represents authors with their debut novels and New York Times-bestsellers and has brokered deals with small presses, mid-size publishers, major publishing houses, foreign publishers, audio producers, gaming app companies, reading app companies, and film producers. Looks for Thrillers (YA & Adult); YA contemporary with unexpected antagonists; Prose that flows as smoothly as poetry; Unforgettable plot twists; Well-rounded characters; and Non-fiction with heart.

L294 Hardman & Swainson

Literary Agency
S106, New Wing, Somerset House, Strand, London, WC2R 1LA
United Kingdom
Tel: +44 (0) 20 3701 7449

submissions@hardmanswainson.com

https://www.hardmanswainson.com
https://twitter.com/HardmanSwainson

Professional Body: The Association of Authors' Agents (AAA)

Send: Query; Proposal; Writing sample; Full text
How to send: Email

Agency launched June 2012 by former colleagues at an established agency. Represents a range of fiction and nonfiction. See website for full submission guidelines.

Authors: Sophie Austin; Jennifer Barclay; Lilly Bartlett; Jackie Bateman; Alex Bell; Anna Bell; Chetan Bhatt; Jon Bounds; Oggy Boytchev; Paul Braddon; Cathy Bramley; Elizabeth Brooks; Isabelle Broom; Mark Broomfield; Tracy Buchanan; Meg Cabot; Elisabeth Carpenter; Simon Cheshire; Adrienne Chinn; Abby Clements; Helen Cox; Jeremy Craddock; Sara Crowe; Joshua Cunningham; Emma Darwin; Stuart David; Sharron Davies; Daniel M. Davis; Caroline Davison; Lisa Dickenson; Miranda Dickinson; Sarah Ditum; Carol Donaldson; Charlotte Duckworth; Simon David Eden; Rachel Edwards; Miranda Emmerson; Miguel Farias; Helen Fields; Eugene Finkel; Rosie Fiore; Carrie Hope Fletcher; Giovanna Fletcher; Nicola Ford; Harry Freedman; Michele Gorman; James Gould-Bourn; Vanessa Greene; Kirsty Greenwood; Alastair Gunn; Tom Higham; Michael Jecks; Dinah Jefferies; Oskar Cox Jensen; Stuart Johnstone; Ishani Kar-Purkayastha; Elaine Kasket; Beth Kempton; Holly Kingston; Lucy Lawrie; Peter Laws; Christine Lehnen; Malinda Lo; Craig Lord; Alice Loxton; David B. Lyons; Kevin Macneil; Katie Marsh; S R Masters; Cressida Mclaughlin; Ali Mcnamara; Susy Mcphee; Siobhan Miller; Kr Moorhead; Martina Murphy; Julien Musolino; Helen Naylor; Nigel Packer; Lauren Price; Philip C Quaintrell; Martina Reilly; Charlotte Rixon; Caroline Roberts; Gareth Roberts; Patrick Roberts; Nick Russell-Pavier; Susanna Rustin; Suzanne Scanlon; Nikola Scott; Catherine Simpson; Emma Slade; Danny Smith; Karen Ingala Smith; Victoria Smith; Gareth Southwell; Elisabeth Spencer; Hollie Starling; Fiona Sussman; Eliska Tanzer; Sarah Tierney; Liz Trenow; Sarah Turner; Rebecca Wait; B P Walter; Louise Walters; Victoria Walters; Sue Watson; Alison White; Catherine Wikholm; Samantha Wilson; Laura Ziepe

Literary Agents: Hannah Ferguson (**L217**); Caroline Hardman (**L295**); Joanna Swainson (**L613**)

L295 Caroline Hardman

Literary Agent
United Kingdom

submissions@hardmanswainson.com
caroline@hardmanswainson.com

http://www.hardmanswainson.com/agents/caroline-hardman/

Literary Agency: Hardman & Swainson (**L294**)

Fiction > *Novels*
  Book Club Fiction; Crime; Historical Fiction; Literary; Thrillers; Upmarket Commercial Fiction

Nonfiction > *Nonfiction Books*
  Current Affairs; Feminism; Health; Human Biology; Lifestyle; Medicine; Memoir; Narrative Nonfiction; Personal Development; Popular Science; Psychology; Wellbeing

Send: Synopsis; Full text
How to send: Email

Direct submissions to the agent, but send to the submissions email address, not her individual email address.

Authors: Katie Allen; Sophie Austin; Jennifer Barclay; Lilly Bartlett; Chetan Bhatt; Tracy Buchanan; Elisabeth Carpenter; HS Chandler; Emma Christie; Sharron Davies; Daniel M. Davis; Sarah Ditum; Andrew Doig; Charlotte Duckworth; Miranda Emmerson; Miguel Farias; Louise Fein; Helen Fields; Eugene Finkel; Eliese Colette Goldbach; Michele Gorman; Paula Greenlees; Alastair Gunn; Dinah Jefferies; Helen Joyce; Ishani Kar-Purkayastha; Elaine Kasket; Beth Kempton; Craig Lord; Alice Loxton; Martina Murphy; Helen Naylor; Jenni Nuttall; Julia Parry; Laura Pashby; Vanessa Potter; Martina Reilly; Charlotte Rixon; Gareth Roberts; Susanna Rustin; Suzanne Scanlon; Nikola Scott; Joanne Sefton; Karen Ingala Smith; Victoria Smith; Miss South; Elisabeth Spencer; Kathleen Stock; John Tregoning; Liz Trenow; Rebecca Wait; Alison White; Catherine Wikholm; Ryan Wilson; Eleanor Wood

L296 Jessica Hare

Literary Agent
United Kingdom

jhare@theagency.co.uk

https://theagency.co.uk/the-agents/jessica-hare/
https://twitter.com/jcehare
https://instagram.com/jcehare

Literary Agency: The Agency (London) Ltd (**L009**)

CHILDREN'S
Fiction
  Board Books; *Chapter Books*; *Early Readers*; *Middle Grade*; *Picture Books*
Nonfiction > *Nonfiction Books*

Runs the Children's Books department. Represents established and emerging children's books authors and illustrators across every age range and genre.

L297 Esmond Harmsworth
Literary Agent; President
United States

https://aevitascreative.com/agents/
https://querymanager.com/query/Esmond_Harmsworth_Submissions

Literary Agency: Aevitas

Fiction > *Novels*
  Crime; Historical Fiction; Horror; Literary; Mystery; Suspense; Thrillers

Nonfiction > *Nonfiction Books*
  Business; Culture; History; Politics; Psychology; Science

Closed to approaches.

Represents serious nonfiction books on topics such as politics, psychology, culture, business, history and science. For fiction, he represents literary fiction, mystery and crime, thriller, suspense and horror, and historical novels.

Authors: Ron Adner; Aaron Ahuvia; Devery Anderson; Erin Arvedlund; Dave Balter; Justin L. Barrett; Jean-Louis Barsoux; Christian Bason; Ann Bauer; David Benjamin; Jedediah Berry; Lucy Blake; Didier Bonnet; Giacomo Bono; Lisa Borders; Cyril Bouquet; Gary Braver; Carolyn S. Briggs; Debra Bruno; Majka Burhardt; Tara Button; Jonathan Byrnes; Shawn Casemore; Paola Cecchi-Dimegli; Ulrik Christensen; Joshua Cohen; James Cullen; David Dabscheck; Niraj Dawar; Sandeep Dayal; Jeremy DeSilva; Dan DiMicco; Barry C. Dorn; Ilana Edelstein; Elisabeth Elo; Robert Emmons; Katherine C. Epstein; Mark Esposito; David Farbman; Keith Ferrazzi; Noah Fleming; Chad E. Foster; Rebecca Frankel; Emily Franklin; Seth Freeman; Jeffrey Froh; Samuel W. Gailey; Jeff Gothelf; Ronnie Greene; Olaf Groth; Sunetra Gupta; Lise Haines; Chris Hamby; George Harrar; Joseph M. Henderson; John Horn; Erich Joachimsthaler; Manu Kapur; Jon Katzenbach; Fred Kiel; Kasley Killam; Kim Kleman; David Komlos; Andrew Lam; Adam Lashinsky; Clifton Leaf; Junheng Li; Josh Linkner; Barbara K. Lipska; Tim Lomas; Courtney Lynch; Sean Lynch; Dario Maestripieri; David Magee; Leonard J. Marcus; Robert Martin; Grace Dane Mazur; Elaine McArdle; Jeffrey D. McCausland; Claire McDougall; Keith McFarland; Eric J. McNulty; Christopher Michaelson; Paddy Miller; Angie Morgan; Nick Morgan; Jim Morris; Mark Nitzberg; Howard Nusbaum; Barry O'Reilly; Angela V. Paccione; Patricia Park; Deborah Plummer; Dan Pope; Sebastian Purcell; Anne Raeff; Amanda Ripley; Sara Roahen; Barbara Roberts; Victoria L. Roberts; Craig Ross; John J. Ross; David Rothkopf; Paul Rudnick; Laurie Ruettimann; Craig Russell; SHRM; Scott Sampson; R. Keith Sawyer; Bradley Schurman; Josh Seiden; Jens Martin Skibsted; Marc Solomon; Mathew Sweezey; Sarah Stewart Taylor; Jennifer Tosti-Kharas; Terence Tse; Michael Veltri; Marga Vicedo; Tom Vossler; Michael Wade; Tony Wagner; John Wass; Luc Wathieu; Holly Watt; Thomas Wedell-Wedellsborg; Dan Willingham; Everett Worthington; Tomoko Yokoi; Hester Young; Sergey Young; Howard Yu; Dan Zehr

L298 Harold Ober Associates, Inc.
Literary Agency
286 Madison Avenue, 10th Floor, New York, NY 10017
United States
Tel: +1 (212) 759-8600

contact@haroldober.com

https://www.haroldober.com

Fiction > *Novels*

Nonfiction > *Nonfiction Books*

Closed to approaches.

Describes itself as one of the most storied and celebrated literary agencies in the country, representing some of the most iconic authors of the 20th Century.

Literary Agency: Richard Curtis Associates, Inc. (**L536**)

L299 Logan Harper
Literary Agent
United States

https://www.janerotrosen.com/agents

Literary Agency: Jane Rotrosen Agency

Fiction > *Novels*
  Book Club Fiction; Contemporary Romance; Crime; Domestic Suspense; Horror; Literary; Mystery; Psychological Thrillers; Romantic Comedy; Upmarket

Send: Query
How to send: Online contact form

Seeking a wide range of character-driven fiction and is particularly drawn to book club fiction, contemporary romance and romantic comedies, psychological thrillers, domestic suspense, horror, mystery/crime, upmarket and literary fiction.

L300 Erin Harris
Literary Agent; Vice President
United States

eharris@foliolitmanagement.com

https://www.publishersmarketplace.com/members/eharris/
https://twitter.com/ErinHarrisFolio

Literary Agency: Folio Literary Management, LLC
Professional Body: Association of American Literary Agents (AALA)

ADULT
Fiction > *Novels*
  Alternative History; Book Club Fiction; Contemporary; Fabulism; Fairy Tales; Family Saga; Folklore, Myths, and Legends; High Concept; Historical Fiction; Horror; Literary Mystery; Literary; Science Fiction; Suspense

Nonfiction > *Nonfiction Books*
  High Concept; Memoir; Narrative Nonfiction

Poetry > *Poetry Collections*

YOUNG ADULT > **Fiction** > *Novels*
  Contemporary; High Concept; Magic; Speculative; Suspense

Send: Query; Writing sample
How to send: In the body of an email

Passionate about books that interrogate our collective and personal histories with heart and intelligence; characters that make us feel and stories that make us think, even as they keep us feverishly turning pages; and book club and literary fiction that is high concept, whether it be contemporary, historical, or genre-bending (i.e. an accessible, elevated dash of fabulism, sci-fi, horror, suspense, alt. history, etc.)

L301 Hilary Harwell
Literary Agent
United States

https://ktliterary.com/submissions/
https://www.manuscriptwishlist.com/mswl-post/hilary-harwell/
https://querymanager.com/query/HilaryHarwell

Literary Agency: KT Literary (**L377**)

CHILDREN'S > **Fiction**
  Chapter Books; *Graphic Novels*; *Middle Grade*; *Picture Books*
YOUNG ADULT > **Fiction** > *Novels*

How to send: Query Manager

Seeking picture books, chapter books, graphic novels, middle grade and young adult fiction.

L302 Jack Haug
Associate Agent
United States

Literary Agency: Aevitas

L303 Susan Hawk
Literary Agent
United States

susanhawk.submission@gmail.com

http://www.upstartcrowliterary.com/agent/susan-hawk/

https://twitter.com/@susanhawk

Literary Agency: Upstart Crow Literary

CHILDREN'S
    Fiction
        Chapter Books; *Middle Grade*; *Picture Books*
    Nonfiction > *Nonfiction Books*

TEEN > **Fiction** > *Novels*

YOUNG ADULT > **Fiction** > *Novels*

How to send: Email

Represents work for children and teens only: picture books, chapter books, middle grade, and young adult, along with some non-fiction for young readers. She doesn't represent adult projects. Open to queries the first week of each month.

L304 Molly Ker Hawn

Literary Agent; Managing Director
United Kingdom

hawnqueries@thebentagency.com

http://www.thebentagency.com/molly-ker-hawn

http://www.twitter.com/mollykh

https://www.publishersmarketplace.com/members/mkhawn

Literary Agency: The Bent Agency (UK) (**L057**)

ADULT > **Fiction** > *Novels*
    Fantasy; Science Fiction; Speculative

CHILDREN'S
    Fiction
        Graphic Novels; *Middle Grade*
    Nonfiction > *Nonfiction Books*

YOUNG ADULT > **Fiction**
    Graphic Novels; *Novels*

Closed to approaches.

I'm looking for exceptional middle-grade and young adult fiction with global commercial appeal, as well as graphic novels for children and young adults with illustrations in place and fantasy, science fiction and speculative fiction for adults.

For children's and YA, I'm open to any genre and almost any topic. Contemporary, historical, fantasy, science fiction, romance, horror…I've loved and sold books that fit all those descriptions. For adult fantasy, science fiction and speculative fiction, I'm looking for fast-paced stories that would appeal to a broad audience, set either in new worlds or one that could be our own, with vividly drawn characters.

No matter the genre or age category, the writing needs to be polished and assured; the story needs to be captivating. I like to be astonished! I'm especially drawn to stories with a strong sense of place, told by authors who fundamentally understand the world they're writing about, whether it's real or imaginary.

L305 Viola Hayden

Literary Agent
United Kingdom
Tel: +44 (0)20 7393 4391

viola.hayden@curtisbrown.co.uk

https://curtisbrown.co.uk
https://curtisbrown.co.uk/agent/viola-hayden

Literary Agency: Curtis Brown (**L146**)

Fiction > *Novels*
    Book Club Fiction; Commercial; Crime; Historical Fiction; Suspense

Nonfiction > *Nonfiction Books*
    General, and in particular: Memoir; Narrative Nonfiction

Send: Query; Synopsis; Writing sample
How to send: Email
How not to send: Online submission system

I am looking for commercial and reading group fiction, but also narrative non-fiction and some memoir.

L306 David H. Headley

Literary Agent; Managing Director
United Kingdom

submission@dhhliteraryagency.com

http://www.dhhliteraryagency.com/david-h-headley.html
https://twitter.com/davidhheadley

Literary Agency: DHH Literary Agency Ltd (**L166**)

Fiction > *Novels*
    High / Epic Fantasy; High Concept; Space Opera

Send: Query; Synopsis; Writing sample
How to send: Email attachment

Looking for: character-driven debuts; sweeping stories with big universal themes; high concepts; expansive space operas; epic fantasy; thought-provoking stories; uplifting fiction; original narrative voices; and emotional journeys.

Authors: Graham Bartlett; R.C. Bridgestock; Tom Brown; Paul Burston; Andrea Carter; Will Carver; Paul Fraser Collard; James Conway; M.W. Craven; John Curran; A. A. Dhand; Becky Docton; David Fennell; Essie Fox; Anita Frank; Erin Green; Lisa Hilton; Ed James; Helga Jensen; Ragnar Jonasson; Katrín Júlíusdóttir; Beth Lewis; Sean Lusk; Zoe Lyons; Adrian Magson; Chris McDonald; Brian McGilloway; Chris Merritt; Janie Millman; Elizabeth S. Moore; Noel O'Reilly; Anthony J. Quinn; Jenny Quintana; Robert Rutherford; Victoria Selman; Mel Sherratt; Jo Thomas; L.C. Tyler; A. J. West; Clare Whitfield; Claire Wilson; David Young; Eva Björg Ægisdottir

L307 Chelsea Hensley

Associate Agent
United States

https://www.chelseahensley.com
https://ktliterary.com/agents
https://www.chelseahensley.com/mswl
https://querymanager.com/query/Chelseahensley

Literary Agency: KT Literary (**L377**)

ADULT > **Fiction** > *Novels*
    Fantasy; Supernatural / Paranormal Horror

CHILDREN'S > **Fiction**
    Middle Grade: Adventure; Fairy Tales; Fantasy; Folklore, Myths, and Legends; Historical Fiction; Mystery
    Picture Books: General

YOUNG ADULT > **Fiction** > *Novels*
    Contemporary Fantasy; Contemporary; Dark; Dystopian Fiction; Fantasy; High / Epic Fantasy; Historical Fiction; Mystery; Romance; Science Fiction; Thrillers

Closed to approaches.

In all areas I'm looking for lyrical prose, voice that comes off the page, intricate plots, complex emotional arcs, and immersive worlds. I'd love to see some ambitious works that play with form and narration as well as works that blend genre, aren't afraid to get a little weird, and surprise me. The bolder the better. I'm also eager to find authors who write across multiple genres and age categories, so if you have ambitions to write beyond the project you're currently querying, take a look at other areas of my wishlist and see if we may be a good fit for future works of yours, too.

L308 Paloma Hernando

Associate Agent
United States

submissions@einsteinliterary.com

https://www.einsteinliterary.com/staff/
https://twitter.com/AgentPaloma

Literary Agency: Einstein Literary Management

ADULT
    Fiction
        Graphic Novels: High / Epic Fantasy; LGBTQIA; Magic; Romance; Science Fiction
        Novels: High / Epic Fantasy; LGBTQIA; Magic; Romance; Science Fiction
    Nonfiction > *Nonfiction Books*
        General, and in particular: History; Media

CHILDREN'S
    Fiction > *Middle Grade*: Comedy / Humour

Nonfiction > *Nonfiction Books*
General, and in particular: History; Media

YOUNG ADULT > **Fiction**
Graphic Novels: High / Epic Fantasy; LGBTQIA; Magic; Romance; Science Fiction
Novels: High / Epic Fantasy; LGBTQIA; Magic; Romance; Science Fiction

Send: Query; Writing sample
How to send: In the body of an email
How not to send: Email attachment

Her favorite books often have a bit of magic in them, and she loves being able to dive into any world, real or invented, presented on the page. She is looking for both graphic novels and prose fiction for YA or adult, including more mature stories, particularly ones that deal with difficult emotions and nuanced characters. She loves romance, particularly queer romance, science fiction that feels fresh, high fantasy, and middle grade with a good sense of humor. She is interested in non-fiction for all ages, especially anything that digs into media analysis or an event in history. She loves a story with a strong voice and solid construction.

L309 Lane Heymont
President; Literary Agent
United States

https://www.thetobiasagency.com/lane-heymont
https://querymanager.com/query/1291
http://aaronline.org/Sys/PublicProfile/27203936/417813

Literary Agency: The Tobias Literary Agency
Professional Body: Association of American Literary Agents (AALA)

ADULT
Fiction > *Novels*
Commercial; Horror

Nonfiction > *Nonfiction Books*
Celebrity; Culture; History; Popular Culture; Science

YOUNG ADULT > **Fiction** > *Novels*: Horror

Send: Author bio; Query; Market info; Writing sample
How to send: Query Manager

Represents a broad range of commercial fiction and serious nonfiction. In fiction, he is especially interested in projects broadly defined as horror. This includes select young adult horror. He is always looking for projects by underrepresented voices both in horror, fiction in general, and nonfiction. In nonfiction, he focuses on the sciences, cultural studies, history, pop-culture, and celebrity projects.

L310 HG Literary
Literary Agency
6 West 18TH Street, Suite 7R, New York, NY 10011
United States

https://www.hgliterary.com
https://twitter.com/hgliterary
http://instagram.com/hgliterary

Associate Agents: Jon Cobb; Ellen Goff (**L267**)

Literary Agent: Victoria Wells Arms (**L031**)

Literary Agents / Partners: Josh Getzler (**L256**); Carrie Hannigan (**L292**)

Literary Agents / Vice Presidents: Julia Kardon (**L350**); Soumeya Bendimerad Roberts (**L540**)

L311 Emily Hickman
Literary Agent
United Kingdom
Tel: +44 (0) 20 7908 0977

ehickman@theagency.co.uk

https://theagency.co.uk/the-agents/emily-hickman/

Literary Agency: The Agency (London) Ltd (**L009**)

Scripts
Film Scripts; *TV Scripts*; *Theatre Scripts*

Represents a diverse list of writers and writer/directors across stage and screen, alongside the dramatic rights for a variety of fiction and non-fiction authors.

L312 High Line Literary Collective
Literary Agency
United States

https://www.highlineliterary.com

Standing at the cross-section between art and commerce, our agents facilitate thriving, vibrant careers for writers, artists and creators. From the moment we begin working with a client, we establish full-spectrum representation dedicated to each creator's unique needs. From audience engagement, to career orientation, to strategic long-term management, our holistic guidance charts your most successful publishing journey.

Literary Agents: Amanda Bernardi (**L062**); Margaret Danko (**L154**); Pam Gruber (**L281**); Sheyla Knigge (**L372**); Victoria Marini (**L423**); Kim Perel (**L505**); Whitney Ross (**L551**)

L313 Sam Hiyate
Literary Agent; President; Chief Executive Officer
Canada

shiyate@therightsfactory.com

https://www.therightsfactory.com/Agents/Sam-Hiyate
https://www.therightsfactory.com/submit-sam

Literary Agency: The Rights Factory

Fiction > *Novels*
Crime; Literary; Mystery; Thrillers; Upmarket Commercial Fiction

Nonfiction > *Nonfiction Books*
Business; Food; Health; Lifestyle; Memoir; Personal Development

Send: Query; Author bio; Writing sample
How to send: Email

Handles various categories, including memoir, literary and commercial fiction, narrative non-fiction and graphic novels. He's looking for works of all categories with distinct and compelling voices. He loved to discover and help new writers prepare their works for the market, and to help them build a career with their talent.

Authors: Oscar Allueva; Ho Che Anderson; Michel Basilières; Margot Berwin; Charles Bongers; Alex Brueckmann; Michael Busk; Dave Butler; Lila Cecil; Timothy Christian; Michael Dargie; Elaine Dewar; Oonagh Duncan; Benjamin Erretti; Saad T. Farooqi; Becca Fischer; Bronwyn Fischer; Sara Flemington; Darya Foroohar; Debbie Fox; Patricia Fulton; Rupinder Gill; Jesse Gilmour; Shinan Govani; Lee Gowan; Alexandra Grigorescu; Nadia Guo; Kamal Gupta; Wes Hall; Alex Huntley; Chris Johns; Sam Juric; Andrew Kaufman; Michelle Kim; Sohan Koonar; Arkadi Kuhlmann; David Leach; Barbra Leslie; Claire Letemendia; Emily Lipinski; Anneke Lucas; Natalie MacLean; Mieke Marple; Kiirsten May; Maureen Medved; Mary Mellon; Natasha Mihell; Sally Moore; Hal Niedzviecki; Rebecca Nison; Ell Orion; Brad Orsted; Matthew Pennock; Katie Peyton; Barbara Radecki; Greg Rhyno; Alexandra Risen; Leslie Shimotakahara; David Skuy; Allison Stieger; Stephen Stohn; Tre Tennyson; Diane Terrana; Chris Turner; Joanne Vannicola; Alex Varricchio; Maurice Vellekoop; Cory Vitiello; Andy Walker; Kay Walker; Imogen Lloyd Webber; Jessica Westhead; Molly Roden Winter; Naomi Yano

L314 Victoria Hobbs
Literary Agent
United Kingdom

https://amheath.com/agents/victoria-hobbs/
http://twitter.com/victoriajhobbs

Literary Agency: A.M. Heath & Company Limited, Author's Agents (**L002**)

Fiction > *Novels*
General, and in particular: Crime; Thrillers

Nonfiction > *Nonfiction Books*
General, and in particular: Cookery; Food;

Health; Narrative Nonfiction; Nature; Politics

Agency Assistant: Jessica Lee

L315 Jodie Hodges
Literary Agent
United Kingdom
Tel: +44 (0) 20 3214 0891

jhodges@unitedagents.co.uk

https://www.unitedagents.co.uk/jhodgesunitedagentscouk
http://twitter.com/jodiehodges31

Literary Agency: United Agents

CHILDREN'S > Fiction
  Comics: General
  Graphic Novels: General
  Middle Grade: Adventure; Comedy / Humour; Domestic; Fantasy; Historical Fiction
  Picture Books: General

Send: Query; Synopsis; Writing sample; Full text
How to send: Email attachment
How not to send: Post

I'll always be keen to see classic storytelling for 8-12s be it an adventure, a fantasy, historical, domestic, a comedy. Anything and everything to appeal to the both the voracious child reader I was and those children for whom books aren't an everyday part of life. Additionally, I'm always searching for children's book illustrators or writer/illustrators who know their own style and are attuned to the children's book market. I also represent creators of comics and graphic novels for children and very happy to see more.

Associate Agent: Molly Jamieson (**L329**)

Literary Agent: Emily Talbot (**L619**)

L316 Scott Hoffman
Literary Agent; Partner
United States

shoffman@foliolitmanagement.com

https://www.foliolit.com/agents-1/scott-hoffman

Literary Agency: Folio Literary Management, LLC

Nonfiction > *Nonfiction Books*
  Business; Fitness; Health; History; Psychology; Social Issues; Wellbeing

Closed to approaches.

Send query by email with first ten pages. Assume rejection if no response within six weeks.

L317 Christina Hogrebe
Literary Agent
United States

https://www.janerotrosen.com/
https://www.janerotrosen.com/contact-christina-hogrebe

Literary Agency: Jane Rotrosen Agency

Fiction > *Novels*
  Fantasy; Romance; Thrillers

How not to send: Online submission system

Drawn to the kind of fun, escapist stories that also spark lively debate in her book club, especially in the areas of fantasy, thriller, and romance, and would love to champion an author underrepresented in those categories.

L318 Sally Holloway
Associate Agent
United Kingdom

https://felicitybryan.com/fba-agent/sally-holloway/

Literary Agency: Felicity Bryan Associates (**L215**)

Nonfiction > *Nonfiction Books*
  Biography; Business; Contemporary; Economics; High Concept; History; Investigative Journalism; Literature; Narrative Nonfiction; Popular Culture; Popular Psychology; Popular Science

Send: Query; Proposal; Writing sample; Synopsis
How to send: Online submission system

I am always on the look-out for authors who can write with authority, wit and originality in the fields of 'Big Ideas', popular psychology, contemporary issues, economics and business (though not 'how to' books). I also like writers who can explain complex ideas entertainingly or who are able to transport me into a different world, in areas as diverse as popular science, history, biography, literature, popular culture. I would love to find more writers of narrative non-fiction who have important stories to tell, especially investigative journalists.

Authors: Johnny Acton; Ben Ambridge; Mark Avery; Jonny Beardsall; Andrew Blum; James Brooke-Smith; Archie Brown; Larisa Brown; Karl Bushby; Tom Butler-Bowdon; Graham Caveney; Peter Chapman; James Fairhead; Georgina Ferry; Jan Filochowski; Dominic Frisby; David Goldblatt; Simon Hall; Tim Harford; Robert Hutton; Helena Kelly; Richard Koch; James Kynge; Peter Lampl; Simon Lancaster; Tomila Lankina; Alysa Levene; Finbarr Livesey; Greg Lockwood; Anna Machin; Richard Mcgregor; Oliver Milman; Marc Mulholland; David Pilling; Captain Elliot Rappaport; Shilpa Ravella; Glyn Redworth; David Reynolds; Ian Robertson; Jon Savage; Adrian Tinniswood; Nigel Travis; Tom Vanderbilt; David Waltham; Clive Webb; Hugh Wilford; Sam Wilkin; Imogen Willetts

L319 Penny Holroyde
Literary Agent
United Kingdom

penny@holroydecartey.com

https://www.holroydecartey.com/about.html
https://www.holroydecartey.com/submissions.html

Literary Agency: Holroyde Cartey

CHILDREN'S
  Fiction
    Board Books; Chapter Books; Early Readers; Middle Grade; Picture Books
  Nonfiction > *Nonfiction Books*

Send: Synopsis; Full text
How to send: Email attachment

I've worked in publishing for nearly thirty years at publishers Walker Books in the UK and Candlewick Press in the US and then as an agent with Caroline Sheldon. I have a particular love for the picture book but am looking for authors and illustrators working across fiction and non-fiction for all ages.

L320 Kate Hordern
Literary Agent
United Kingdom

kate@khla.co.uk

https://twitter.com/katehordern

Literary Agency: Kate Hordern Literary Agency

ADULT
  Fiction > *Novels*
    General, and in particular: Book Club Fiction; Commercial; Crime; Historical Fiction; Psychological Suspense; Speculative; Upmarket Women's Fiction

  Nonfiction > *Nonfiction Books*
    History; Memoir

CHILDREN'S > Fiction > *Middle Grade*

I'm looking for fiction across the range, from bookclub through to psychological suspense, crime, speculative, historical, commercial and upmarket women's fiction, with a unique hook, whether that is a very special voice or a high-concept plot or compelling characters or a combination of these. In non-fiction I'm looking for history, where the author has the appropriate platform, and memoir. My middle-grade kids fiction list is currently closed to new submissions.

L321 Sarah Hornsley
Literary Agent; Author
United Kingdom

shornsley@pfd.co.uk

https://petersfraserdunlop.com/agent/sarah-hornsley/
https://twitter.com/SarahHornsley

Literary Agencies: Peters Fraser + Dunlop; Mushens Entertainment
Literary Agent: Juliet Mushens (**L470**)

Fiction > *Novels*
Book Club Fiction; Commercial; Historical Fiction; Romance; Speculative; Suspense; Thrillers; Women's Fiction

Nonfiction > *Nonfiction Books*

Send: Query; Synopsis; Writing sample; Proposal; Author bio
How to send: Email
How not to send: Post

I'm looking for adult commercial and book club fiction across all genres. I'm always on the look-out for a strong hook – a setting or scenario which captures my imagination straight away. Generally, I am drawn to strong, emotive writing matched with a gripping fast-paced plot. I am very hands-on editorially and am looking to only take on a few select really special writers this year. I'd love to find a really high-concept twisty thriller or suspense novel. Something that subverts my expectations and keeps me on the edge of my seat. I also never tire of exploring dark sibling relationships and as a mother myself I love a complex mother/daughter relationship. In general and women's fiction, I'm really keen to find something with heart and brilliant emotive storytelling. I absolutely adore historical fiction. I'm also a huge fan of romantic fiction and have had a number of authors shortlisted for the RNA Awards. I enjoy anything from genre-bending rom-coms and laugh-out-loud escapist spicy romance with fresh hooks to emotive epic love stories.

Authors: Claire Ackroyd; Ciara Attwell; Matilda Battersby; Olivia Beirne; Roxie Cooper; Georgina Cutler; Rachel Louise Driscoll; Philippa East; Jenny Epstein; Amy de la Force; Anstey Harris; Emma Heatherington; Emily Houghton; Becky Hunter; Lynsey James; Fionnuala Kearney; Gina Lamanna; Jo Lovett; Ali Pantony; Lou Robbie; Rachel Ward; Helen Whitaker; S.M. Wilson

L322 Annie Hwang

Literary Agent
United States

https://twitter.com/AnnieAHwang
https://www.publishersmarketplace.com/members/hwangan/

Literary Agency: Ayesha Pande Literary (**L036**)

Fiction > *Novels*: Literary

Nonfiction > *Nonfiction Books*: Narrative Nonfiction

Poetry > *Poetry Collections*

Closed to approaches.

Primarily represents voice-driven literary fiction that plays with genre, though she also takes on nonfiction and poetry on occasion. In particular, she is drawn to what she likes to think of as "literary fiction with teeth"— ambitious novels that are daring in their approach that also grapple with the complexities of the world with nuance and finesse.

L323 Inscriptions Literary Agency

Literary Agency
United States
Tel: +1 (636) 633-7846

https://inscriptionsliterary.com
https://querymanager.com/query/InscriptionsLit_Query

ADULT
Fiction > *Novels*
General, and in particular: Christian Romance; Contemporary Romance; Hardboiled Crime; Mystery; Science Fiction; Suspense

Nonfiction > *Nonfiction Books*
Christianity; Crime; Memoir

Scripts > *Film Scripts*

CHILDREN'S > **Fiction**
Middle Grade; *Picture Books*

Does not want:

> **CHILDREN'S** > **Fiction** > *Middle Grade*
> Dark Magic; Gender Issues; Science Fiction; Voodoo; Witchcraft

Send: Query; Synopsis; Writing sample; Full text; Pitch
How to send: Query Manager; Email

A boutique literary agency which offers representation services to authors who are both published and pre-published. Our mission is to form strong partnerships with our clients and build long-term relationships that extend from writing the first draft through the entire length of the author's career.

What is a boutique literary agency? A small, but mighty agency that has less than 12 agents. We specialize in quality, not quantity. We limit the amount of clients we take on, in order to give each client our full attention.

We are not looking for books containing: political agenda, controversies, AI content, alternative religion books, books labeled "Christian" that do not follow the standards of the Bible, Sci-Fi-Christian, illustrated children's books.

We are not looking for: Erotic, board books, baby or toddler books, lyrical books, SEL books, or topics in children's books that contradict basic Christian standards. We believe Christian values should always be portrayed in Children's fiction.

Submit literary submissions via QueryManager. Submit pitches for screenplay representation by email.

Literary Agent: Andrea Comparato (**L134**)

L324 Irene Goodman Literary Agency (IGLA)

Literary Agency
United States

https://www.irenegoodman.com
https://twitter.com/IGLAbooks
http://instagram.com/iglabooks
https://www.facebook.com/IreneGoodmanAgency

ADULT
Fiction > *Novels*
Historical Fiction; Mystery; Romance; Thrillers

Nonfiction > *Nonfiction Books*
Business; Cookery; France; Health; History; Judaism; Lifestyle; Politics; Popular Culture

YOUNG ADULT > **Fiction** > *Novels*

Closed to approaches.

Interests include business, health, politics and history, cookbooks, pop culture, Jewish interest, Francophilia, lifestyle, upmarket fiction, historical fiction, and mysteries. All non-fiction proposals should include an overview, descriptions of each chapter, comp titles, and a healthy platform. Fiction should include the first ten pages, a complete synopsis, and a total word count. If you are published by a commercial publisher, please tell me who published you and give me an idea of the sales history.

Literary Agent: Irene Goodman

L325 Lucy Irvine

Literary Agent
United Kingdom
Tel: +44 (0) 20 7344 1087

lirvine@pfd.co.uk

https://petersfraserdunlop.com/agent/lucy-irvine/

Literary Agency: Peters Fraser + Dunlop

ADULT > **Fiction** > *Novels*
Fantasy; Science Fiction

CHILDREN'S > **Fiction**
Chapter Books: General
Early Readers: General
Middle Grade: General, and in particular: Adventure; Commercial; Folklore, Myths, and Legends
Picture Books: General, and in particular: Comedy / Humour

YOUNG ADULT > **Fiction** > *Novels*
Fantasy; Historical Fiction; LGBTQIA; Mystery; Romance

Does not want:

Fiction > *Novels*: Grimdark

Send: Query; Synopsis; Writing sample; Proposal; Author bio
How to send: Email

My taste is generally very broad; I represent anything that falls under the Children's umbrella, from picture books to YA, as well as Science Fiction and Fantasy in the Adult market.

I'm being very selective with the picture books I take on at the moment, but am particularly looking here for funny stories with returnable potential and unexpected twists on popular themes.

My taste in middle-grade books veers towards the commercial; I'm drawn to quick-paced, adventurous narratives with series potential. I love stories set in worlds that pull you in and stay with you long after you've finished reading, and am particularly keen to see original worldbuilding and hooky, plot driven narratives. I would love to find something in the vein of Maria Kuznair's The Ship of Shadows or B.B. Alston's Amari and the Night Brothers. I'm also very drawn to reimagined folktales, myths, and legends, especially from voices traditionally under represented within publishing. Some middle-grade books I grew up on and adored include The Roman Mysteries, the Chronicles of Ancient Darkness, and the Percy Jackson series.

On the YA side, I love all kinds of genre fiction, from fantasy to historical to romance to murder mystery. I'm drawn to romances with a twist, and am particularly looking here for queer love stories. Fantasy wise I'm keen to see original world-building, and love anything that genre bends or offers a fresh take on traditional themes. I love my fantasies with a side of romance, or with characters that I can clearly see a fandom forming around. A few YA books I've recently loved include Hani and Ishu's Guide to Fake Dating, The Upper World, and The Other Ones. I am a perpetual fan of enemies/rivals to lovers, fake-dating, found-family, unexpected friendships, and platonic love stories.

Adult wise, I accept submissions in anything that falls under the SFF umbrella, from urban to epic fantasy, from space opera to steampunk, but am not the right person for anything too grimdark, or anything with graphic sexual violence. I would love to find something with the ambition and wit of Gideon the Ninth, or the scope and narrative-weaving of The Priory of the Orange Tree. I also recently read and loved Legends and Lattes and would love something in the cozy fantasy space.

I am always looking for diverse writers and protagonists across race, sexuality, gender, class, and disability.

Across the board, I'd love to find stories with casts of characters that make me feel as much as the Stranger Things characters make me feel (which is, to say, a lot).

Authors: Amy Archer; Lerah Mae Barcenilla; Sunita Chawdhary; Camille Chong; Katie Dale; Annabel Durant-Rogers; Judith Eagle; Ava Eldred; Rowan Foxwood; Tessa Gearing; William Goldsmith; Norma Gregory; Bridget Helen Hamilton; Lindsay Hirst; Lexy Hudson; Iqbal Hussain; Lis Jardine; Marisa Linton; Aneesa Marufu; Emi-Lou May; Emily Randall; Laila Rifaat; Ali Stegert; Sam Stewart; Gail Upchurch; Catherine Ward; Alison Weatherby; Melissa Welliver

L326 Dotti Irving
Literary Agent
United Kingdom

dotti@greyhoundliterary.co.uk

https://greyhoundliterary.co.uk/agents/dotti-irving

Literary Agency: Greyhound Literary (**L278**)

Nonfiction > *Nonfiction Books*: Narrative Nonfiction

Send: Query; Synopsis; Writing sample
How to send: Email

Primarily interested in narrative non-fiction, in books that tell a story that rings true and speaks to a wider world.

Authors: Matt Blake; Reuben Coe; Anthea Rowan; Tina Shingler

L327 Amanda Hepp Jackson
Associate Agent
United States

https://www.stephanietadeagency.com/aboutus

Literary Agency: Stephanie Tade Literary Agency

L328 Rachel Jacobson
Literary Agent
United States

https://aliveliterary.com/about/

Literary Agency: Alive Literary Agency (**L018**)

Nonfiction > *Nonfiction Books*

How to send: By referral

Enjoys helping authors hone their ideas, tap into their generative creativity, and share their message—because she wholeheartedly believes books can be a positive force for good in the world.

L329 Molly Jamieson
Associate Agent
United Kingdom
Tel: +44 (0) 20 3214 0973

mjamieson@unitedagents.co.uk

https://www.unitedagents.co.uk/mjamiesonunitedagentscouk

Literary Agency: United Agents
Literary Agent: Jodie Hodges (**L315**)

ADULT > **Fiction** > *Novels*
   Commercial; Fantasy; Folk Horror; Gothic; Horror; Romance; Science Fiction

CHILDREN'S > **Fiction** > *Novels*
   Fantasy; Science Fiction

Send: Query; Synopsis; Writing sample
How to send: Email

Has a particular interest in scifi and fantasy across both adult and children's books. She loves anything with high stakes, characters you would follow anywhere, big stories, expansive worldbuilding, breathless romance, and threads of adventure running throughout. She would be keen to see gothic horror and folk horror, stories that mess with your mind, rather than showcasing gratuitous violence.

Author Estates: The Estate of Algernon Blackwood; The Estate of R Austin Freeman; The Estate of Rafael Sabatini; The Estate of Sir Alan (A P) Herbert

Authors: Shalini Abeysekara; Jackson P. Brown; John Chalmers; Guy Haley; Hannah-Marie Holwell; Arden Jones; Vanessa Jones; Sandra Marrs; Christine Modafferi; Aimee Oliver; Melissa Powell; O.R. Sorrel

L330 Janklow & Nesbit UK Ltd
Literary Agency
66-67 Newman Street, Fitzrovia, London, W1T 3EQ
United Kingdom
Tel: +44 (0) 20 7243 2975

submissions@janklow.co.uk

http://www.janklowandnesbit.co.uk
https://twitter.com/JanklowUK

Professional Body: The Association of Authors' Agents (AAA)

ADULT
   Fiction > *Novels*
      General, and in particular: Commercial; Literary

   Nonfiction > *Nonfiction Books*

CHILDREN'S > **Fiction** > *Novels*

YOUNG ADULT > **Fiction** > *Novels*

Send: Query; Synopsis; Writing sample
How to send: Email

Send query by email, including informative covering letter providing background about yourself and your writing; first three chapters /

approx. 50 pages; a brief synopsis for fiction, or a full outline for nonfiction. For poetry, submit a short pitch and small sample of 3-5 poems.

Company Director / Literary Agent: Claire Paterson Conrad (**L136**)

Literary Agents: Will Francis; Hayley Steed (**L595**)

L331 The Jeff Herman Agency, LLC

Literary Agency
PO Box 1522, Stockbridge, MA 01262
United States
Tel: +1 (413) 298-0077

submissions@jeffherman.com
Jeff@Jeffherman.com

https://jeffherman.com

Nonfiction
Nonfiction Books: Business; Crime; Health; History; How To; Memoir; Multicultural; Narrative Nonfiction; Parenting; Psychology; Self Help; Spirituality
Reference: General

Send: Query; Pitch
Don't send: Proposal; Full text
How to send: Email; Post

Send query by post with SASE. With few exceptions, handles nonfiction only, with particular interest in the genres given above. No scripts or unsolicited MSS.

Literary Agents: Deborah Levine Herman; Jeff Herman

L332 JFL Agency

Literary Agency
60 St Martin's Lane, London, WC2N 4JS
United Kingdom
Tel: +44 (0) 20 3137 8182

representation@jflagency.com
agents@jflagency.com

http://www.jflagency.com

Scripts
Film Scripts; *Radio Scripts*; *TV Scripts*; *Theatre Scripts*

Send: Query
How to send: Email

Handles scripts only (for television, film, theatre and radio). Considers approaches from established writers with broadcast experience, but only accepts submissions from new writers during specific periods – consult website for details.

Authors: Humphrey Barclay; Liam Beirne; Adam Bostock-Smith; Tim Brooke-Taylor; Ian Brown; Grant Cathro; Paul Charlton; Gabby Hutchinson Crouch; Bill Dare; Tim Dawson; Martin Day; Ed Dyson; Polly Eden; Jan Etherington; Sinéad Fagan; Anji Loman Field; Phil Ford; Patrick Gallagher; Ted Gannon; Lisa Gifford; Rob Gittins; Ben Harris; James Hendrie; Wayne Jackman; Tony Lee; Richard Leslie Lewis; Jane Marlow; Jonathan Morris; Cardy O'Donnell; Jim Pullin; Jackie Robb; Graeme Rooney; Gary Russell; David Semple; James Serafinowicz; Pete Sinclair; Paul Smith; Fraser Steele

Literary Agents: Alison Finch; Dominic Lord; Gary Wild

L333 Jo Unwin Literary Agency

Literary Agency
United Kingdom

info@jounwin.co.uk

https://www.jounwin.co.uk

Professional Body: The Association of Authors' Agents (AAA)

ADULT
Fiction > *Novels*
Nonfiction > *Nonfiction Books*

CHILDREN'S > **Fiction** > *Novels*

YOUNG ADULT > **Fiction** > *Novels*

Closed to approaches.

Handles literary fiction, commercial women's fiction, comic writing, narrative nonfiction, Young Adult fiction and fiction for children aged 9+. No poetry, picture books, or screenplays, except for existing clients. Accepts submissions by email. Mainly represents authors from the UK and Ireland, and sometimes Australia and New Zealand. Only represents US authors in very exceptional circumstances. See website for full guidelines.

Authors: Heather Akumiah; Jesse Armstrong; Richard Ayoade; Zoe Beaty; Amanda Berriman; Brian Bilston; Amanda Block; Anne Booth; Soraya Bouazzaoui; Charlie Brooker; Lucie Brownlee; Wibke Brueggemann; Fran Bushe; Karen Campbell; Candice Carty-Williams; David Challen; Jo Cheetham; Darren Chetty; Eliza Clark; Ellie Clements; Jenny Colgan; Frances Crawford; Lucy Cuthew; Lucy Easthope; Katie Everson; Caleb Femi; Mick Finlay; Emma Flint; Elaine Gregersen; Tamsin Grey; Mark Grist; Becky Holmes; Lucy-Anne Holmes; Sylvia Johnson; Riley Johnston; Evie King; Gabriel Krauze; Jade LB; Louise Lee; Marianne Lee; Francis Liardet; Litwitchure; Doon Mackichan; Gemma Marren; Katy Massey; Janelle McCurdy; Siobhan McSweeney; Jack Meggitt-Phillips; Fiona Melrose; Sarah Moore-Fitzgerald; Catriona Morton; Rosie Mullender; Sally O'Reilly; Priya O'Shea; Gary Panton; Claire Parkin; Deepa Paul; AJ Pearce; Gianna Pollero; Robert Popper; Georgia Pritchett; Josey Rebelle; Rose Ruane; Bethany Rutter; Nadia Shireen; Jenny Simanowitz; Penelope Slocombe; Emma Smith-Barton; Stephen Tuffin; Weird Walk; Angharad Walker; Hayley Webster; Joanna Wolfarth

Literary Agent: Jo Unwin (**L638**)

L334 Joelle Delbourgo Associates, Inc.

Literary Agency
101 Park St., Montclair, Montclair, NJ 07042
United States
Tel: +1 (973) 773-0836

submissions@delbourgo.com

https://www.delbourgo.com

ADULT
Fiction > *Novels*
Commercial; Fantasy; Literary; Mystery; Science Fiction; Thrillers; Women's Fiction

Nonfiction
Nonfiction Books: Biography; Cookery; Current Affairs; Food; Health; History; Memoir; Mind, Body, Spirit; Narrative Nonfiction; Parenting; Popular Culture; Psychology; Science
Reference: Popular

CHILDREN'S
Fiction
Middle Grade; *Picture Books*
Nonfiction > *Middle Grade*

YOUNG ADULT > **Fiction** > *Novels*

Closed to approaches.

Costs: Author covers sundry admin costs.

A boutique literary agency based in the greater New York City area. We represent a wide range of authors writing for the adult trade market, from creative nonfiction to expert-driven nonfiction, commercial fiction to literary fiction, as well as middle grade fiction and nonfiction.

Authors: Tanya Acker; P. David Allen; Jennifer Lynn Alvarez; Heather Anastasiu; Lisa Anselmo; Thomas Armstrong; Sara Au; Rebecca Rego Barry; Frances Bartkowski; Audrey Bellezza; Waitman Beorn; Suzanne Bohan; Lynn Kiele Bonasia; Michele Borba; Robert Bornstein; Elizabeth Reid Boyd; Nora Bradbury-Haehl; Anne Greenwood Brown; Gay Browne; Ariel Burger; Susan Campbell; Craig Carlson; Paul Carter; Jill Castle; Debbie Cenziper; Rachael Cerrotti; Marj Charlier; John Christianson; Tara L. Clark; Margot Clark-Junkins; Gay Courter; Nancy Cowan; Katherine Scott Crawford; Michelle Dempsey-Multack; Sybil Derrible; Karla Dougherty; Nancy Dreyfus; Rosa Kwon Easton; Charity Elder; Chris Farrell; Marilyn Fedewa; Michael Feuer; Ellen Flannery-Schroeder; Laura Berman Fortgang; Susan Forward; Philip Freeman; Terry Gaspard; John Gaudet; Susan Gilbert-Collins; Michelle Glogovac; Ann E. Grant; Jonathon Grayson; Brenda Greene; Beth A. Grosshans; Julie L. Hall; Emily Harding; Kate Harding; Laura Hartema; Kimberly

Heckler; Kristi Hedges; Holly Herrick; Roy Hoffman; Helaina Hovitz; Erik Forrest Jackson; Grace Jung; Theresa Kaminski; Rachelle Katz; Joseph Kelly; Stephen Kelly; Brynne S. Kennedy; Nancy Kennedy; Hilary Kinavey; Sean Kingsley; Willem Kuyken; Mary Languirand; Missy Chase Lapine; Claire Lerner; Irene S. Levine; Alexandra Levitt; Lisa L. Lewis; Mary Ann Little; Geralyn Lucas; Lauren Mackler; Juliet Madison; Kerstin March; David J. Marsh; Chuck Martin; Lama Marut; Carol Masciola; Roy Meals; Cristina Nehring; Nicola Nice; Jennifer O'Callaghan; Emily J. O'Dell; Colleen O'Grady; Jim Obergefell; Elaine Neil Orr; Lindsey J. Palmer; Theresa Payton; Michelle Pearce; Scott Peeples; Julia Pimsleur; Gleb Raygorodetsky; Eliza Redgold; Michael Reichert; James Renner; Ashley Rhodes-Courter; Paige Rien; Alexandra Rimer; Jillian Roberts; Tatsha Robertson; Lisa Romeo; Marilyn Simon Rothstein; Dale Russakoff; Michael Sadowski; Karla Salinari; Roberta Sandenbergh; Sue Scheff; Elisa A. Schmitz; Melissa Schorr; Ellen E. Schultz; Sara Sherbill; Heather Shumaker; Alexandra Silber; Pamela Slim; Joanna Sliwa; Christopher A. Snyder; Laura Sobiech; Julie M. Stamm; Peter L. Stavinoha; Maryon Stewart; Nancy Rubin Stuart; Dana Sturtevant; Deborah J. Swiss; Jeff Sypeck; Ericka Sóuter; John Temple; Christopher Van Tilburg; Chelsea Tucker; M.D. Usher; Julie Valerie; Rebecca Lynn Viera; Michael Volpatt; Caroline Welch; Susan Wels; Elizabeth White; Elizabeth "Barry" White; Kristin M. White; Barrie Wilson; Ben H. Winters; Jon Wuebben; Gabra Zackman; Peter Zheutlin; Gabe Zichermann

Literary Agent: Joelle Delbourgo

L335 Johnson & Alcock
Literary Agency
West Wing, Somerset House, Strand, London, WC2R 1LA
United Kingdom
Tel: +44 (0) 20 7251 0125

http://www.johnsonandalcock.co.uk

Professional Body: The Association of Authors' Agents (AAA)

Send: Query; Synopsis; Writing sample
How to send: Email attachment
How not to send: Post

Send query by email to specific agent. Response only if interested. Include synopsis and first three chapters (approximately 50 pages).

Company Directors / Literary Agents: Andrew Hewson; Ed Wilson (**L668**)

Literary Agent / Managing Director: Anna Power (**L523**)

Literary Agents: Michael Alcock (**L014**); Charlotte Seymour (**L575**)

L336 Jonathan Clowes Ltd
Literary Agency
United Kingdom
Tel: +44 (0) 20 7722 7674

admin@jonathanclowes.co.uk

https://www.jonathanclowes.co.uk

Professional Body: The Association of Authors' Agents (AAA)

Fiction > *Novels*

Nonfiction > *Nonfiction Books*

Send: Query; Synopsis; Writing sample
How to send: Email
How not to send: Post

Send query with synopsis and three chapters (or equivalent sample) by email.

Authors: Frances Bingham; Jonas Claesson; Simon Critchley; Maureen Duffy; Ewan Fernie; Brian Freemantle; Miles Gibson; Rana Haddad; Francesca Hornak; David Llewellyn; Kirsten MacGillivray; Mohamed Mesrati; Kirsten Norrie; David Quantick; Gruff Rhys; Toby Vieira; Barbara Voors

Literary Agents: Ann Evans; Nemonie Craven Roderick

L337 Jonathan Pegg Literary Agency
Literary Agency
c/o Workshop, 47 Southgate Street, Winchester, SO23 9EH
United Kingdom
Tel: +44 (0) 1962 656101

submissions@jonathanpegg.com
info@jonathanpegg.com

https://jonathanpegg.com

Professional Body: The Association of Authors' Agents (AAA)

Fiction > *Novels*
  Historical Fiction; Literary; Suspense; Thrillers; Upmarket

Nonfiction
  Gift Books: Comedy / Humour
  Nonfiction Books: Biography; Business; Comedy / Humour; Current Affairs; History; Lifestyle; Memoir; Nature; Popular Psychology; Popular Science

Send: Query; Synopsis; Author bio; Market info; Writing sample
How to send: Email

Aims to read every submission and respond within a month, but cannot guarantee to do so in all cases.

Literary Agent: Jonathan Pegg

L338 Barbara Jones
Literary Agent
United States

bjquery@skagency.com

http://skagency.com/submission-guidelines/

Literary Agency: Stuart Krichevsky Literary Agency, Inc. (**L609**)

Closed to approaches.

L339 Philip Gwyn Jones
Literary Agent
United Kingdom

https://greyhoundliterary.co.uk/agents/philip-gwyn-jones
https://twitter.com/PGJPublishing

Literary Agency: Greyhound Literary (**L278**)

Fiction > *Novels*

Thirty-three years of experience as an editor and publisher, just over half of them in corporate publishing and just under half in independent publishing.

Authors: John Campbell; Gethan Dick; Matthew Ford; Jon Gower; Michael Hurley; Mette Leonard Høeg; Stuart Jeffries; Vijay Khurana; Patricia Kingori; Tarun Ramadorai

L340 Joy Harris Literary Agency, Inc.
Literary Agency
1501 Broadway, Suite 2605, New York, NY 10036
United States
Tel: +1 (212) 924-6269

contact@joyharrisliterary.com

https://www.joyharrisliterary.com

Professional Body: Association of American Literary Agents (AALA)

Types: Fiction; Nonfiction; Translations
Formats: Short Fiction
Subjects: Autobiography; Comedy / Humour; Commercial; Culture; Experimental; History; Literary; Media; Mystery; Satire; Spirituality; Suspense; Women's Interests
Markets: Adult; Young Adult

Closed to approaches.

Costs: Author covers sundry admin costs.

Send query by email, including sample chapter or outline. No poetry, screenplays, genre fiction, self-help, or unsolicited mss. See website for full guidelines.

Literary Agents: Joy Harris; Adam Reed

L341 Judith Murdoch Literary Agency
Literary Agency
19 Chalcot Square, London, NW1 8YA
United Kingdom
Tel: +44 (0) 20 7722 4197

jmlitag@btinternet.com

http://www.judithmurdoch.co.uk

Fiction > *Novels*
 Commercial; Crime; Literary

Send: Query; Synopsis; Writing sample
How to send: Post
How not to send: Email

Send query by post with SAE or email address for response, brief synopsis, and first three chapters. No science fiction, fantasy, children's stories, or email submissions.

Author Estates: The Estate of Catherine King; The Estate of Meg Hutchinson

Authors: Diane Allen; Trisha Ashley; Anne Bennett; Maggie Bennett; Anne Berry; Frances Brody; Rosie Clarke; Howard Coombs; Diney Costeloe; Norma Curtis; Anne Doughty; Kate Eastham; Leah Fleming; Sarah Flint; Caro Fraser; Emma Fraser; Elizabeth Gill; Gracie Hart; Faith Hogan; Maggie Hope; Emma Hornby; Alex Howard; Minna Howard; Alrene Hughes; Lindsey Hutchinson; Lola Jaye; Sheila Jeffries; Sophie Jenkins; Carol Jones; Pamela Jooste; Mary de Laszlo; Catherine Law; Jill McGivering; Alison Mercer; Beth Miller; Jaishree Misra; Barbara Mutch; Kitty Neale; Sheila Newberry; Della Parker; Carol Rivers; Cathy Sharp; Alison Sherlock; Linda Sole; June Tate; Annie Wilkinson; Mary Wood

Literary Agent: Judith Murdoch

L342 Judy Daish Associates Ltd
Literary Agency
2 St Charles Place, London, W10 6EG
United Kingdom
Tel: +44 (0) 20 8964 8811
Fax: +44 (0) 20 8964 8966

judy@judydaish.com

http://www.judydaish.com

Literary Agency: United Agents

Scripts
 Film Scripts; *Radio Scripts*; *TV Scripts*; *Theatre Scripts*

Represents writers, directors, designers and choreographers for theatre, film, television, radio and opera. No books or unsolicited mss.

Literary Agents: Judy Daish; Tracey Elliston

L343 Julie Crisp Literary Agency
Literary Agency; Editorial Service
United Kingdom

juliecrisp@gmail.com

http://www.juliecrisp.co.uk
https://querymanager.com/query/2079

Professional Body: The Association of Authors' Agents (AAA)

Fiction > *Novels*
 Fantasy; Magical Realism; Science Fiction; Speculative Horror

Closed to approaches.

Costs: Offers services that writers have to pay for.

Open to queries and actively looking for full length, adult, fantasy, science fiction, magical realism and speculative fiction.

Authors: E. J. Beaton; Heather Child; John Gwynne; Sam Hawke; Lucy Kissick; Devin Madson; Den Patrick; C. T. Rwizi; Nick Setchfield; Kell Woods

L344 K2 Literary
Literary Agency
Canada

https://k2literary.com
https://www.facebook.com/k2literary/
https://twitter.com/k2literary
https://instagram.com/k2literary

ADULT > **Fiction** > *Novels*

CHILDREN'S > **Fiction** > *Novels*

How to send: By referral

Currently accepts submissions by referral only. Unsolicited submissions, queries, submission emails, or phone calls will not be answered.

Literary Agent: Kelvin Kong

L345 Ella Diamond Kahn
Literary Agent
United Kingdom

http://dkwlitagency.co.uk/agents/
https://twitter.com/elladkahn

Literary Agency: Diamond Kahn and Woods (DKW) Literary Agency Ltd

ADULT
 Fiction > *Novels*
  Contemporary; Crime; Historical Fiction; Speculative; Upmarket

 Nonfiction > *Nonfiction Books*

CHILDREN'S > **Fiction** > *Middle Grade*

YOUNG ADULT > **Fiction** > *Novels*

Closed to approaches.

Represents upmarket contemporary and historical fiction, crime fiction, speculative fiction, and some non-fiction. She also represents a wide range of children's fiction for the 9-12 and YA age groups. She is passionate about finding and championing new voices, including those traditionally under-represented in publishing.

L346 Jody Kahn
Literary Agent
United States

jkahn@bromasite.com

http://brandthochman.com/agents

Literary Agency: Brandt & Hochman Literary Agents, Inc.

Fiction > *Novels*
 Comedy / Humour; Culture; Literary; Upmarket

Nonfiction > *Nonfiction Books*
 Culture; Food; History; Journalism; Literary Memoir; Narrative Nonfiction; Social Justice; Sport

Send: Query
How to send: Email

L347 Joanna Kaliszewska
Literary Agent
United Kingdom

https://www.thebksagency.com/about
https://www.thebksagency.com/submissions

Literary Agency: The BKS Agency (**L065**)

Fiction > *Novels*
 General, and in particular: Book Club Fiction; Crime; Literary; Thrillers; Upmarket Commercial Fiction

Looking for all types of fiction but particularly interested in reading group, upmarket commercial, literary, crime and thriller.

L348 Kane Literary Agency
Literary Agency
United Kingdom

submissions@kaneliteraryagency.com
getintouch@kaneliteraryagency.com

https://www.kaneliteraryagency.com
https://www.facebook.com/kaneliteraryagency/
https://twitter.com/YasminKane3
https://www.instagram.com/YasminKane3/

Professional Body: The Association of Authors' Agents (AAA)

Fiction > *Novels*
 Crime; Domestic Thriller; Noir; Police Procedural; Psychological Thrillers; Thrillers

Send: Query; Synopsis; Writing sample; Pitch; Market info
How to send: Email

Currently only looking for: crime fiction, thrillers, police procedurals, psychological thrillers, and domestic thrillers. Bring on the noir!

Authors: Simon Arrowsmith; J Y Bee; Isabelle Brizec; Louise Cliffe-Minns; Sarah Harris; Vicki Howie; Zoe Marriott; Andrew Murray; Emily Nagle; Marisa Noelle

Literary Agent: Yasmin Standen

L349 Camille Kantor
Literary Agent
United States

https://www.camillekantor.com
https://www.kimberleycameron.com/team/
https://querymanager.com/query/camillekantor/
https://www.instagram.com/lady_reads_alot/

https://twitter.com/CamilleKantor/
https://www.manuscriptwishlist.com/mswl-post/camille-kantor/

Literary Agency: Kimberley Cameron & Associates (**L369**)

Fiction > *Novels*
High Concept; Literary; Nature

Nonfiction > *Nonfiction Books*
Nature; Popular Science

How to send: Query Manager

Looking for titles, whether fiction or non-fiction, that will inspire the public to engage with nature while imparting fascinating knowledge about our planet and its inhabitants. She is particularly interested in popular science non-fiction work. Her fiction tastes include books that immerse the reader in descriptive but clear imagery and that have themes of nature-human interactions. She especially loves interesting, well-developed characters and high concept literary fiction that approaches philosophical topics about our relationship with our planet.

L350 Julia Kardon

Literary Agent; Vice President
United States

julia@hgliterary.com

https://www.hgliterary.com/julia
https://twitter.com/jlkardon
https://querymanager.com/query/JuliaKardon

Literary Agency: HG Literary (**L310**)

Fiction > *Novels*
Literary; Upmarket

Nonfiction > *Nonfiction Books*
History; Journalism; Memoir; Narrative Nonfiction

How to send: Query Manager

She is interested primarily in literary and upmarket fiction and memoir, and especially stories grappling with racial, religious, sexual or national identity, narrative nonfiction, journalism, and history. She does not represent thrillers, any children's literature or books about spirituality or Christianity.

L351 Maryann Karinch

Literary Agent
United States

mak@rudyagency.com

http://rudyagency.com

Literary Agency: The Rudy Agency (**L553**)

Fiction > *Novels*
Adventure; Crime; Historical Fiction; Mystery; Thrillers

Nonfiction > *Nonfiction Books*
General, and in particular: Business; Health; History; Investigative Journalism; Medicine; Sport

Send: Query
Don't send: Proposal; Full text
How to send: Email

Wants to see non-fiction projects from authors who are experts in their field, and that could be any field—business, investigative journalism, sports, history, health and medicine. Genre fiction is preferred. Grab her with your storytelling on the first page.

L352 Kate Barker Literary, TV, & Film Agency

Literary Agency
London,
United Kingdom
Tel: +44 (0) 20 7688 1638

kate@katebarker.net

https://www.katebarker.net

Professional Body: The Association of Authors' Agents (AAA)

Fiction > *Novels*
Book Club Fiction; Commercial; Contemporary; High Concept; Historical Fiction; Literary

Nonfiction > *Nonfiction Books*
History; Lifestyle; Memoir; Nature; Popular Psychology; Science; Wellbeing

Send: Query; Writing sample
How to send: Online submission system

I'm looking for commercial, literary and reading group novels: my taste in fiction is broad. I like strong stories, interesting settings (contemporary or historical) and high concept novels. I especially love books that make me cry. Please note that I do not represent science fiction, fantasy or books for children. Work in those genres will not be read. Non-fiction: I'm looking for smart thinking, history, memoir, popular psychology and science, nature writing, lifestyle and wellbeing. Big ideas and subjects that get people talking. I particularly enjoy helping experts translate their work for a general audience.

Literary Agent: Kate Barker

L353 Kate Nash Literary Agency

Literary Agency
United Kingdom

https://katenashlit.co.uk
https://www.facebook.com/KateNashLiteraryAgency/
https://twitter.com/katenashagent
https://www.youtube.com/channel/UCAugaYbUoZXD7wldntZ8DwQ

Professional Body: The Association of Authors' Agents (AAA)

ADULT
Fiction > *Novels*

Nonfiction > *Nonfiction Books*: Commercial

CHILDREN'S > **Fiction** > *Middle Grade*

YOUNG ADULT > **Fiction** > *Novels*

Send: Query; Synopsis; Writing sample; Pitch; Author bio
How to send: Online submission system

Open to approaches from both new and established authors. Represents general and genre fiction and popular nonfiction. No poetry, drama, or genre SFF. Send query via online submission form with synopsis and first chapter (fiction) or up to three chapters (nonfiction) pasted into the body of the email (no attachments).

Junior Agent: Saskia Leach (**L389**)

Literary Agent / Managing Director: Justin Nash (**L474**)

Literary Agents: Kate Nash; Francesca Riccardi (**L535**)

L354 Kathryn Green Literary Agency, LLC

Literary Agency
157 Columbus Avenue, Suite 510, New York, NY 10023
United States
Tel: +1 (212) 245-4225

query@kgreenagency.com
kathy@kgreenagency.com

https://www.kathryngreenliteraryagency.com
https://twitter.com/kathygreenlit

ADULT
Fiction > *Novels*
General, and in particular: Cozy Mysteries; Historical Fiction

Nonfiction > *Nonfiction Books*
General, and in particular: Comedy / Humour; History; Memoir; Parenting; Popular Culture

CHILDREN'S > **Fiction** > *Middle Grade*

YOUNG ADULT > **Fiction** > *Novels*

Does not want:

> **ADULT** > **Fiction** > *Novels*
> Fantasy; Science Fiction
>
> **CHILDREN'S** > **Fiction**
> *Middle Grade*: Fantasy; Science Fiction
> *Picture Books*: General
>
> **YOUNG ADULT** > **Fiction** > *Novels*
> Fantasy; Science Fiction

Closed to approaches.

Send query by email. Do not send samples unless requested. No science fiction, fantasy, children's picture books, screenplays, or poetry.

Literary Agent: Kathryn Green

L355 Jade Kavanagh
Literary Agent
United Kingdom

jade@darleyanderson.com

https://darleyanderson.com
https://darleyanderson.com/team/jade-kavanagh/
https://twitter.com/jadekav_
https://www.instagram.com/jade_kavanagh_agent/

Literary Agency: The Darley Anderson Agency (**L157**)

Fiction > *Novels*
Book Club Fiction; Dark; Horror; Psychological Suspense; Speculative; Suspense; Thrillers

How to send: Online submission system

My primary genres and areas of interest include, thriller, glam suspense, psychological suspense, horror, book club and speculative fiction with a darker edge.

Author: Holly Craig

L356 Simon Kavanagh
Literary Agent
United Kingdom

Simon@miccheetham.co.uk

Literary Agency: Mic Cheetham Literary Agency (**L445**)

L357 Taylor Martindale Kean
Literary Agent
United States

https://www.fullcircleliterary.com/our-agents/taylor-martindale-kean/
https://querymanager.com/query/TaylorFCL

Literary Agency: Full Circle Literary, LLC

CHILDREN'S > **Fiction** > *Middle Grade*
General, and in particular: Contemporary; Fantasy; Historical Fiction; Literary; Magical Realism

YOUNG ADULT > **Fiction** > *Novels*
General, and in particular: Fantasy; Magical Realism

Closed to approaches.

She is looking for young adult fiction and literary middle grade fiction, across all genres. She is interested in finding unique and unforgettable voices in contemporary, fantasy, historical and magical realism novels. She is looking for books that demand to be read. More than anything, she is looking for diverse, character-driven stories that bring their worlds vividly to life, and voices that are honest, original and interesting.

L358 Keane Kataria Literary Agency
Literary Agency
United Kingdom

info@keanekataria.co.uk

https://www.keanekataria.co.uk/submissions/

Fiction > *Novels*
Book Club Fiction; Commercial Women's Fiction; Contemporary; Cozy Mysteries; Historical Fiction; Romance; Saga

Send: Query; Synopsis; Writing sample
How to send: PDF file email attachment

Currently accepting submissions in the crime, domestic noir and commercial women's fiction genres. No thrillers, science fiction, fantasy or children's books. Send query by email only with synopsis and first three chapters. Attachments in PDF format only.

Literary Agents: Kiran Kataria; Sara Keane

L359 Sophie Kelleher
Associate Agent
United Kingdom
Tel: +44 (0) 20 7727 1346

skelleher@theagency.co.uk

https://theagency.co.uk/the-agents/sophie-kelleher/

Literary Agency: The Agency (London) Ltd (**L009**)
Literary Agent: Tanya Tillett

Scripts
Film Scripts; *TV Scripts*; *Theatre Scripts*

Joined the agency in January 2020, originally working as an assistant. In 2022, she covered an agent's maternity leave, expanding her knowledge as an agent across film, television and theatre. She now works as an associate agent with her own list of writers. Prior to her career in film and TV, she worked in publishing.

L360 Carly Kellerman
Literary Agent
United States

https://aliveliterary.com

Literary Agency: Alive Literary Agency (**L018**)

Nonfiction > *Nonfiction Books*

How to send: By referral

Has spent more than fifteen years helping writers find their voice and hone their message. With a professional background that spans editorial development and sales, she has a proven knack for finding the sweet spot between profoundly meaningful and commercially viable content. Her unique blend of business acumen and love for storytelling makes her an excellent advocate and guide for authors navigating the publishing world.

L361 Julia Kenny
Literary Agent
United States

https://www.dclagency.com

Literary Agency: Dunow, Carlson & Lerner Agency (**L184**)

Fiction > *Novels*
Dark; Literary; Suspense

Primarily works on fiction and has a soft spot for dark, literary suspense. She is on the lookout for writing that immediately draws her in, bold voices, "unlikeable" narrators, and stories that linger.

L362 Eli Keren
Associate Agent
United Kingdom
Tel: +44 (0) 20 3214 0775

ekeren@unitedagents.co.uk

https://www.unitedagents.co.uk/ekerenunitedagentscouk
https://twitter.com/EliArieh

Literary Agency: United Agents

Fiction > *Novels*
Commercial; Crime; Domestic Suspense; Historical Fiction; LGBTQIA; Literary; Magical Realism; Mystery; Speculative; Thrillers; Upmarket

Nonfiction > *Nonfiction Books*
General, and in particular: Cultural History; LGBTQIA; Popular Science

Closed to approaches.

In non-fiction, I am particularly interested in expert-led smart and engaging popular science. My own background is in chemistry, but I'm fairly omnivorous and happy to look at any non-fiction that grips me, be that science, cultural history or something unexpected. I enjoy books by writers completely obsessed with a niche subject who are skilled enough communicators to make the rest of the world fall in love with their passion too, whatever that passion might be. I am interested in any book that will change the world for the better. I'm probably not the right agent for books on religion or spirituality.

In fiction, I mostly work with commercial and upmarket fiction, not so much with the very literary. In commercial fiction, I'm interested in crime/thriller and domestic suspense with a strong hook and addictive storytelling. I love mysteries and whodunnits, and am also open to uplifting general fiction. I'm happy to look at historical fiction with a contemporary outlook. Towards the more literary side, I'm looking for books with plot and pace that set out to achieve something, change the way I see the world, challenge me and subvert my expectations. I don't typically work with science-fiction or fantasy, but am open to some grounded speculative fiction and magical realism. I don't work with holocaust novels.

I do not represent authors for children's and YA literature.

Authors: Marieke Bigg; Sarah Burton; Huho Greenhalgh; Ioan Marc Jones; Johanna Lukate; David Miles; Jem Poster; Claire Seeber; Sam White

L363 Kathleen Kerr
Literary Agent
United States

Literary Agency: Alive Literary Agency (**L018**)

L364 Ki Agency Ltd
Literary Agency
Primrose Hill Business Centre, 110 Gloucester Avenue, London, NW1 8HX
United Kingdom
Tel: +44 (0) 20 3214 8287

https://ki-agency.co.uk

Professional Bodies: The Association of Authors' Agents (AAA); Personal Managers' Association (PMA); Writers' Guild of Great Britain (WGGB)

Fiction > *Novels*

Nonfiction > *Nonfiction Books*
Leadership; Personal Coaching; Personal Development

Scripts
Film Scripts; *TV Scripts*; *Theatre Scripts*

Send: Synopsis; Writing sample
How to send: Email attachment

Represents novelists and scriptwriters in all media. No children's or poetry, or submissions from writers in the US or Canada. Send synopsis and first three chapters / first 50 pages by email.

Authors: John Allison; Fiona Barnett; Simon Bestwick; Al Campbell; Linda Carey; Louise Carey; Mike Carey; Lucy Chalice; Kate Charlesworth; Daniel Church; Helena Coggan; Daniel Depp; Joanne Drayton; Diane Duane; Matthew Feldman; Kitty Ferguson; Marianne Gordon; Stark Holborn; Shaun Hutson; Luke Kondor; Ryan Love; Laura Madeleine; Helen Marshall; Sarah McManus; Robin Norwood; Marie O'Regan; Anne Perry; Adam Roberts; Phoenicia Rogerson; Angela Slatter; Gillian Spraggs; Jesse Stuart; Yvonne Vincent; Becky Ward; Catherine Webb

Literary Agent: Meg Davis

L365 Jessica Killingley
Literary Agent
United Kingdom

https://www.thebksagency.com/about
https://www.thebksagency.com/submissions

Literary Agency: The BKS Agency (**L065**)

Fiction > *Novels*
Fantasy; High Concept; Speculative

Nonfiction > *Nonfiction Books*
Business; Personal Development

Send: Query; Outline; Author bio
How to send: Online submission system

I am looking for personal development, business and smart thinking from authors with strong platforms and engaged audiences. I am also currently open for original, high-concept, speculative adult fiction.

L366 Jennifer Kim
Literary Agent
United States

https://www.dijkstraagency.com
https://www.dijkstraagency.com/agent-page.php?agent_id=Kim
https://querymanager.com/query/JenniferKim

Literary Agency: Sandra Dijkstra Literary Agency

Fiction in Translation > *Novels*

Fiction > *Novels*
Culture; Family Saga; Fantasy; Ghost Stories; Gothic; Horror; Literary; Science Fiction; Speculative

Nonfiction > *Nonfiction Books*
History; Journalism; Music; Politics; Popular Culture

Does not want:

> **Fiction** > *Novels*
> Hard Science Fiction; High / Epic Fantasy

How to send: Query Manager

Most interested in literary fiction, speculative fiction, and translated fiction for the adult market, unusual history, journalism, politics, and pop-culture and music history. She is particularly drawn to eccentric and unusual stories and values a distinct narrative voice and a strong sense of place. She loves literary fiction with genre elements (horror, sci-fi, or fantasy), but isn't a great fit for high fantasy or straightforward science fiction. She's a fit for anything described as gothic, alternative, or weird, ghost stories that explore culture and trauma, family sagas (both blood and chosen), and anything that dismantles oppressive systems. As a third culture kid, she's interested in stories that reflect that experience.

Open to submissions during the first week of every month.

L367 Julia Kim
Assistant Agent
Canada

https://www.therightsfactory.com
https://www.therightsfactory.com/Agents/julia-kim
https://querymanager.com/query/3602

Literary Agency: The Rights Factory

Fiction > *Novels*
Crime; Historical Fiction; Horror; Literary; Mystery

Nonfiction > *Nonfiction Books*
Arts; Biography; Culture; Current Affairs; Films; Food; History; Lifestyle; Memoir; Politics; Popular Culture; TV; Women's Issues

How to send: Query Manager

Looking for literary fiction and select genre fiction (mystery, crime, horror, historical). She is also seeking a range of nonfiction topics including history, politics, current affairs, women's issues, biography and memoir, food and lifestyle, art and culture, film and TV, pop culture.

Authors: Fitsum Areguy; Kaamna Bhojwani; Stephanie Duong; Caitlin Galway; Clarissa Trinidad Gonzalez; Noaah Karim; Sang Kim; Kyo Lee; Matthew A. Pagan; Shoaib Rahim; Alexis Stefanovich-Thomson

L368 Natalie Kimber
Literary Agent
Canada

Literary Agency: The Rights Factory

ADULT
Fiction
Graphic Novels: General
Novels: Adventure; Commercial; Cookery; Historical Fiction; Literary; Science Fiction
Nonfiction > *Nonfiction Books*
Creative Nonfiction; Memoir; Popular Culture; Science; Spirituality; Sustainable Living

YOUNG ADULT > **Fiction** > *Novels*: Boy Books

Send: Query; Author bio; Writing sample
How to send: Email

L369 Kimberley Cameron & Associates
Literary Agency
1550 Tiburon Blvd #704, Tiberon, CA 94920
United States

info@kimberleycameron.com

https://www.kimberleycameron.com
https://www.facebook.com/kimberleycameronandassociates

https://twitter.com/K_C_Associates
https://www.instagram.com/kcandaliterary/

Fiction > *Novels*

Nonfiction > *Nonfiction Books*

How to send: Query Manager

See website for specific agent interests and submit to most suitable agent through their online submission system.

Literary Agents: Lisa Abellera; Kimberley Cameron; Amy Cloughley; Camille Kantor (**L349**); Elizabeth Kracht; Dorian Maffei

L370 Robert Kirby
Literary Agent; Company Director
United Kingdom

https://www.unitedagents.co.uk/rkirbyunitedagentscouk

Literary Agency: United Agents

Fiction > *Novels*
  Adventure; Commercial; Speculative

Nonfiction > *Nonfiction Books*
  Cultural History; Environment; Psychology; Science

Send: Synopsis; Writing sample
How to send: Email
How not to send: Post

I have an interest in science, psychology, cultural history and environmental issues. I enjoy gripping adventure fiction, speculative fiction and emotionally driven commercial fiction. Submissions should be sent to my assistant by via email, with a synopsis and first three chapters. Please do not send submissions via the post.

L371 Kelly Knatchbull
Literary Agent; Company Director
United Kingdom

Literary Agency: Sayle Screen Ltd

L372 Sheyla Knigge
Literary Agent
United States

https://www.highlineliterary.com/agent-sheyla
https://querymanager.com/query/sheylaknigge

Literary Agency: High Line Literary Collective (**L312**)

ADULT > **Fiction** > *Novels*
  Erotic; Fantasy; Folklore, Myths, and Legends; LGBTQIA; Magic

CHILDREN'S > **Fiction** > *Middle Grade*: Fantasy

YOUNG ADULT > **Fiction** > *Novels*: Romance

How to send: Query Manager

Very interested in books by marginalized creators who have yet to have the opportunity to have their voices heard particularly BIPOC, LGBTQIA, and other #OwnVoices as a fellow queer woman of color. She longs to see uplifting stories from these communities rather than ones that focus on the trauma that comes from being a part of them. She would love to see stories filled with myth, magic, and a healthy dose of smut when appropriate. Alternatively, she would love to see Percy Jackson-esque Middle Grade fiction; the type she can giggle along with as she reads them to her own children. Stories set in other lands, or other worlds tend to be her go to choice.

L373 Knight Features
Literary Agency
Trident Business Centre, 89 Bickersteth Road, London, SW17 9SH
United Kingdom

https://www.knightfeatures.com

Nonfiction > *Nonfiction Books*
  Business; Communication; Military

Send: Query; Synopsis; Writing sample; Market info
How to send: Online submission system

Send query with synopsis and three sample chapters. Include information on whether you envisage the book being illustrated, and details of the target market, the level at which it might be pitched, and the likely readership. Include information about any works in the same field which might be seen as competition for your book, or give some indication of how yours differs from these.

Company Directors: Samantha Ferris; Gaby Martin

Managing Director: Andrew Knight

L374 Katie Kotchman
Literary Agent
United States

https://doncongdon.com/agents
https://querymanager.com/query/Kkotchman
https://aalitagents.org/author/kkotchman/
https://twitter.com/kkotchman

Literary Agency: Don Congdon Associates, Inc. (**L175**)
Professional Body: Association of American Literary Agents (AALA)

Fiction > *Novels*
  American Midwest; Literary; Women's Fiction

Nonfiction > *Nonfiction Books*
  American Midwest; Business; Culture; Memoir; Motivational Self-Help; Narrative Nonfiction; Popular Culture; Popular Science; Psychology; Social Issues

How to send: Query Manager

In non-fiction, she specializes in narrative non-fiction (particularly memoir, popular science, pop culture, and social/cultural issues), business (all areas), and self-help that focuses on success, motivation, and psychology. She is actively seeking new nonfiction clients with built-in platforms from whom she can learn something new. In fiction, she's interested in representing women's fiction and literary fiction. In all areas, she's particularly interested in characters who struggle with dualities of nature and/or culture, as the topics of cognitive dissonance and those who straddle two different worlds fascinate her. She has soft spots for the Midwest, family secrets, and a good underdog story.

L375 Mary Krienke
Literary Agent
United States

https://www.sll.com/our-team

Literary Agency: Sterling Lord Literistic, Inc. (**L597**)

Fiction > *Novels*
  Culture; Disabilities; Literary; Mental Health; Sexuality; Upmarket

Nonfiction
  Illustrated Books: General
  Nonfiction Books: Culture; Disabilities; Health; Mental Health; Narrative Nonfiction; Prescriptive Nonfiction; Sexuality

Send: Query; Synopsis; Writing sample
How to send: Online submission system

Represents literary and upmarket fiction, narrative nonfiction, and select memoir, prescriptive, and illustrated projects. In both fiction and nonfiction, work that investigates culture, identity, sexuality, disability, and mental health is especially welcome.

L376 Kruger Cowne
Literary Agency
Unit 7C, Chelsea Wharf, 15 Lots Road, London, SW10 0QJ
United Kingdom
Tel: +44 (0) 20 7352 2277

hello@krugercowne.com

https://www.krugercowne.com
https://twitter.com/krugercowne
https://www.instagram.com/krugercowne/
https://www.facebook.com/krugercowne
https://www.linkedin.com/company/kruger-cowne
https://www.youtube.com/user/KrugerCowneTalent

Professional Body: The Association of Authors' Agents (AAA)

Nonfiction > *Nonfiction Books*
  General, and in particular: Celebrity; Entrepreneurship; Futurism; Journalism

How to send: Email

A talent management agency, with an extremely strong literary arm.

The majority of the works handled by the agency fall into the category of celebrity nonfiction. However, also regularly work with journalists, entrepreneurs and influencers on projects, with a speciality in polemics, and speculative works on the future.

Authors: Akala; Steven Bartlett; Kelly Holmes; Lia Leendertz; Jennifer Medhurst; Jack Monroe; Christine Morgan; Selene Nelson; John Simpson; Nicholas Boys Smith; Dave Stewart

L377 KT Literary
Literary Agency
United States

queries@ktliterary.com

https://ktliterary.com
https://twitter.com/ktliterary
https://www.instagram.com/ktliterary/

ADULT > Fiction > *Novels*

CHILDREN'S > Fiction > *Middle Grade*

YOUNG ADULT > Fiction > *Novels*

Send: Query
How to send: Query Manager; Email
How not to send: Post; Social Media

Please see each individual agent's bio for instructions on how to best query them. If QueryManager provides an accessibility issue, send an email addressed to the specific agent in question. No snail mail queries or pitches via social media.

Associate Agent: Chelsea Hensley (**L307**)

Authors: Samantha Chiusolo; Vikki Chu; Ebony Glenn; Jen Gubicza; Haejin Park; Lisa Wee

Foreign Rights Manager / Literary Agent: Maria Napolitano (**L473**)

Literary Agents: Savannah Brooks (**L084**); Kait Lee Feldmann (**L212**); Tara Gilbert (**L258**); Adria Goetz (**L265**); Hilary Harwell (**L301**); Renee Nyen (*L483*); Jas Perry (*L510*); Kelly Van Sant (**L563**); Arley Sorg (**L592**); Kari Sutherland (**L611**); Laurel Symonds (**L617**); Kate Testerman (*L625*)

Senior Agent / Vice President: Sara Megibow (**L439**)

L378 The Labyrinth Literary Agency
Literary Agency
India

submissions@labyrinthagency.com

http://www.labyrinthagency.com
https://www.instagram.com/labyrinthagency/
https://twitter.com/LabyrinthAgency
https://twitter.com/LabyrinthAgency

Fiction > *Novels*

Nonfiction > *Nonfiction Books*

Send: Synopsis; Writing sample; Author bio
How to send: Email

Costs: Offers services that writers have to pay for. Offers editorial and advice services to authors with whom they do not have a business relationship.

Literary Agent: Anish Chandy

L379 Natalie Lakosil
Literary Agent
United States

https://www.adventuresinagentland.com
https://www.lookingglasslit.com/natalie-lakosil
https://querymanager.com/query/natlak
https://aalitagents.org/author/natalie_lakosil/
https://twitter.com/Natalie_Lakosil
http://www.manuscriptwishlist.com/mswl-post/natalie-lakosil/

Literary Agency: Looking Glass Literary & Media Management (**L406**)
Professional Body: Association of American Literary Agents (AALA)

ADULT
  Fiction > *Novels*
    Cozy Mysteries; Crime; Thrillers; Upmarket Women's Fiction; Upmarket
  Nonfiction > *Nonfiction Books*

CHILDREN'S
  Fiction
    Chapter Books; *Middle Grade*; *Picture Books*
  Nonfiction
    Chapter Books; *Middle Grade*; *Picture Books*

YOUNG ADULT
  Fiction > *Novels*
  Nonfiction > *Nonfiction Books*

Closed to approaches.

Represents adult nonfiction, adult cozy mystery/crime, female-driven thrillers, upmarket women's/general fiction, illustrators, and all ages (picture book, chapter book, MG, YA) of children's literature, both fiction and nonfiction.

L380 Sophie Lambert
Literary Agent
United Kingdom
Tel: +44 (0) 20 7393 4200

sophie.lambert@cwagency.co.uk

https://cwagency.co.uk/agent/sophie-lambert

Literary Agency: C&W (Conville & Walsh) (**L096**)

Fiction > *Novels*
  Commercial; Crime; Literary; Thrillers

Nonfiction > *Nonfiction Books*
  Anthropology; Arts; Environment; Food; History; Memoir; Narrative Nonfiction; Nature; Travel

Closed to approaches.

I love fiction which is voice driven and introduces readers to different perspectives and singular narrators, as well as beautifully written literary fiction which has a strong sense of place, and commercial crime and thrillers which keep the reader on the edge of their seats and continually surprise and excite me. Where nonfiction is concerned I am drawn to narrative nonfiction which straddles genre and I'm especially interested in nature writing, travel, history, anthropology, art and the environment. I represent lots of memoir, as well as books by experts in their field and specialists. I would love to find a gorgeous, all-consuming love story, or a food writer who matches Bill Burford or Anthony Bourdain. Essentially, I'm looking for an exquisite writer to take me by the hand and show me a different way to see the world, whether that's through fiction or nonfiction.

Author / Literary Agent: Catherine Cho (**L124**)

Authors: Gaar Adams; Gwen Adshead; Karen Angelico; Lisa Ballantyne; Leo Benedictus; Michael Bhaskar; Hannah Bourne-Taylor; Megan Bradbury; Iain Broome; Dea Brovig; Tom Burgis; Tim Clare; Jennifer Coolidge; Yvette Cooper; Caroline Crampton; Fiona Cummins; Howard Cunnell; Lara Dearman; Claire Dederer; Juano Diaz; Katherine Dunn; Nathan Filer; Cal Flyn; Julia Forster; Sam Fowles; Karrie Fransman; Sara Freeman; Gabriel Gbadamosi; Karl Geary; Ruth Gilligan; Colin Grant; Guy Gunaratne; Karen Hamilton; Alexandra Heminsley; Adam Higginbotham; Matt Rowland Hill; J.M. Holmes; Eileen Horne; Nicola Kelly; Amana Fontanella Khan; Rosie Kinchen; Martin Latham; Rebecca Ley; Katy Mahood; Shiv Malik; Charlotte McDonald-Gibson; Emmett de Monterey; Priscilla Morris; Robert Muir-Wood; Simon Mundy; Nadia Murad; Ramita Navai; Tom Newlands; Louise Newson; Hollie Newton; Charlotte Northedge; Marcus O'Dair; Nathan Oates; Elizabeth Oldfield; Jon Plackett; Charlene Prempeh; Laura Price; Elizabeth Prochaska; Jamie Quatro; Ben Rawlence; Ebony Reid; CE Riley; Catherine Riley; Sophy Roberts; Callum Robinson; Rhik Samadder; David Savill; Fíona Scarlett; Holly Seddon; Tali Sharot; Gail Simmons; Nikki Smith; Alex South; Tim Spector; Michelle Sterling; Michelle Min Sterling; Mustafa Suleyman; Michelle Thomas; Nafissa Thomson-Spires; Jane Turner; Tash Walker; Christie Watson; Jonathan Watts; Adam Weymouth; Zoe Williams; Antoine Wilson; Alice Winn; Tod Wodicka; Adam Zmith

L381 Sarah Landis
Literary Agent
United States

https://www.sll.com/our-team

Literary Agency: Sterling Lord Literistic, Inc. (**L597**)

ADULT > **Fiction** > *Novels*
Fantasy; High Concept; Speculative; Thrillers

CHILDREN'S > **Fiction** > *Middle Grade*
Fantasy; High Concept; Speculative; Thrillers

Send: Query; Synopsis; Writing sample
How to send: Online submission system

Represents a wide range of fiction from middle grade to adult. She is particularly drawn to high-concept plots, big hooks, speculative fiction, twisty thrillers, novels with a strong emotional core, and sweeping fantasy. She is always on the lookout for new talent and narrative risk-takers.

L382 Lina Langlee
Literary Agent
United Kingdom

http://thenorthlitagency.com/our-friends-in-the-north/
https://twitter.com/LinaLanglee

Literary Agency: The North Literary Agency

ADULT > **Fiction** > *Novels*
General, and in particular: Commercial; Crime; Fantasy; High Concept; Horror; Literary; Romance; Science Fiction; Speculative; Thrillers

CHILDREN'S > **Fiction** > *Middle Grade*

YOUNG ADULT > **Fiction** > *Novels*

Closed to approaches.

Looking for books across genres: commercial/high concept fiction with a great hook (be that romance, crime, thriller or general fiction), accessible literary fiction, and intriguing speculative fiction, SFF & horror. Also looking for fun, fantastical, and moving Middle Grade, and "big emotion" Young Adult across genres. Actively welcomes authors from all backgrounds and would like to see more diverse stories and voices. She is less keen on political or gangland thrillers. As a general rule, she would not offer representation to US-based authors since they are better served by US-based agents, except in the very rare situation where their story ought to originate from the UK.

L383 Becca Langton
Literary Agent
United Kingdom

https://www.darleyanderson.com/our-team

Literary Agency: The Darley Anderson Agency (**L157**)

CHILDREN'S > **Fiction**
Graphic Novels: General
Middle Grade: General, and in particular: Adventure

TEEN > **Fiction** > *Novels*

YOUNG ADULT > **Fiction** > *Novels*
General, and in particular: Contemporary; Fantasy; LGBTQIA; Romantic Comedy

Closed to approaches.

Looking for new stories in all shapes and sizes, from middle grade and graphic novel to teen and YA fiction. Reads widely but loves books with compelling voices, twists and brave new ideas. In YA she would love to see some Queer fantasy, rom-coms with plenty of 'com' and contemporary stories told from a new perspective. For younger readers she love/hates the books that make her cry and is on the search for characters that stay with her long after the final page. High-stakes adventure stories are welcome as are graphic novels and books that make you want to read just one more chapter…

Author: Faith Williams Schesventer

L384 Langtons International
Literary Agency
United States

llangton@earthlink.net
langtonsinternational@gmail.com

https://langtonsinternational.com
https://www.facebook.com/LangtonsInternationalAgency

Fiction > *Novels*
Mystery; Thrillers; Women's Fiction

Nonfiction > *Nonfiction Books*
Business; Crime; Memoir

Literary agency based in New York, specializing in business, self-help, memoir, and true crime, as well as mystery, thrillers, women's and literary fiction.

Literary Agent: Linda Langton

L385 Elena Langtry
Literary Agent
United Kingdom

https://cmm.agency/about-us.php

Literary Agency: Coombs Moylett & Maclean Literary Agency (**L139**)

Fiction > *Novels*
Commercial Women's Fiction; Psychological Thrillers

Nonfiction > *Nonfiction Books*
Crime; Popular Science

How to send: Online submission system

L386 Katherine Latshaw
Literary Agent; Vice President
United States

klatshaw@foliolit.com

https://www.foliolit.com/agents-1/katherine-latshaw

Literary Agency: Folio Literary Management, LLC

ADULT
Fiction > *Novels*

Nonfiction
Essays: General
Illustrated Books: General
Nonfiction Books: Commercial; Cookery; Feminism; Health; Lifestyle; Memoir; Narrative Nonfiction; Popular Culture; Prescriptive Nonfiction; Wellbeing

CHILDREN'S > **Fiction** > *Middle Grade*

YOUNG ADULT > **Fiction** > *Novels*

How to send: Email

L387 Laxfield Literary Associates
Literary Agency
United Kingdom

submissions@laxfieldliterary.com
https://laxfieldliterary.com

Professional Body: The Association of Authors' Agents (AAA)

Fiction > *Novels*
Commercial; Literary

Nonfiction > *Nonfiction Books*
Creative Nonfiction; Memoir; Nature; Travel

Does not want:

> **Fiction** > *Novels*: Fantasy

Send: Query; Synopsis; Writing sample; Author bio; Outline
How to send: Word file email attachment

We are looking for fiction and non-fiction of the highest quality. We are keen to receive literary and commercial fiction. We are also looking for non-fiction, particularly creative non-fiction, travel writing, memoir and nature writing. We do not represent poetry, plays, children's books or YA.

L388 Sarah Lazin
Literary Agent
United States

https://www.aevitascreative.com/agent/sarah-lazin
http://lazinbooks.com/about-us/

Literary Agency: Aevitas

Nonfiction
Nonfiction Books: Biography; Current Affairs; Health; History; Journalism; Memoir; Parenting; Politics; Popular Culture; Social Issues
Reference: General

How to send: By referral

Represents a range of nonfiction writers working in fields such as popular culture, biography, history, politics, journalism, memoir, parenting, health, practical nonfiction, contemporary affairs, social issues, and general reference. She accepts submissions through referral only.

Authors: Michael Azerrad; Patricia Romanowski Bashe; Michael Benson; Will Birch; Jenny Blake; Bill Brewster; Frank Broughton; Kate Brown; E. Jean Carroll; Ted Chapin; Robert Christgau; Broughton Coburn; Charles R. Cross; Anthony DeCurtis; Kevin Dettmar; Ani DiFranco; Banning Eyre; Jim Farber; Alison Fensterstock; Ben Fong-Torres; Elysa Gardner; Richard Gehr; Nelson George; Jane Gottesman; Robin Green; Shirley Halperin; Charlie Harding; Elizabeth Hess; Bill Ivey; Booker T. Jones; Laura Joplin; Michael Lang; Bernie Lierow; Diane Lierow; Kurt Loder; Kim MacQuarrie; Evelyn McDonnell; Kembrew McLeod; Dennis McNally; Joan Morgan; Dan Nadel; Robert K. Oermann; Patricia Pearson; Ann Powers; Mark Seliger; Sylvie Simmons; Nate Sloan; John Szwed; Jessica Vitkus; Elijah Wald; Jocelyn C. Zuckerman

L389 Saskia Leach
Junior Agent
United Kingdom

https://katenashlit.co.uk
https://katenashlit.co.uk/people/
https://querymanager.com/query/Saskia
https://twitter.com/saskialeach_

Literary Agency: Kate Nash Literary Agency (**L353**)

Fiction > *Novels*

Closed to approaches.

Enjoys reading a wide range of genres and is fascinated by stories written from multiple perspectives. She also loves books which feature complex and dynamic characters.

L390 Shannon Lechon
Associate Agent
United States

http://www.azantianlitagency.com/pages/team-sl.html
https://querymanager.com/query/shannonlechon

Literary Agency: Azantian Literary Agency

ADULT
  Fiction > *Novels*
    Fantasy; Folklore, Myths, and Legends; Horror; Literary; Mystery; Romantasy; Science Fantasy; Social Issues; Speculative; Thrillers

  Nonfiction
    Graphic Nonfiction: Mental Health
    Nonfiction Books: Medicine; Memoir; Mental Health

CHILDREN'S > Fiction
  Graphic Novels: General
  Middle Grade: Comedy / Humour; Horror; Mystery; Speculative
YOUNG ADULT > Fiction
  Graphic Novels: Fantasy
  Novels: Dark; Fantasy; Gothic; Horror; Mystery; Science Fiction; Speculative; Thrillers

Closed to approaches.

Interested in experimental styles and unreliable narrators. Intense platonic interpersonal bonds are a particular favorite of hers. She likes underexplored magic systems and fantasy that doesn't care if you understand it or not.

L391 Jessica Leeke
Literary Agent
United Kingdom

info@madeleinemilburn.com

https://www.madeleinemilburn.co.uk
https://www.madeleinemilburn.co.uk/agents/jessica-leeke/
https://x.com/JessicaLeeke

Literary Agency: Madeleine Milburn Literary, TV & Film Agency (**L420**)

Fiction > *Novels*
  Book Club Fiction; Upmarket

How to send: Online submission system

Represents book club fiction with global appeal and upmarket general fiction.

L392 Jordan Lees
Literary Agent
United Kingdom

jordansubmissions@theblairpartnership.com

https://www.theblairpartnership.com/literary-agents/jordan-lees/
https://twitter.com/JordanHLees

Literary Agency: The Blair Partnership
ADULT
  Fiction > *Novels*
    Commercial; Crime; Dark; Detective Fiction; High Concept; Literary; Speculative; Thrillers; Upmarket

  Nonfiction > *Nonfiction Books*
    General, and in particular: Crime

CHILDREN'S > Fiction > *Middle Grade*
  General, and in particular: Crime; Detective Fiction; Fantasy; Horror; Science Fiction

Does not want:

  Fiction > *Novels*: Spy Thrilllers

Closed to approaches.

I primarily represent crime and thrillers, upmarket/literary fiction and some children's, as well as true crime and non-fiction written by journalists and experts in their respective fields. I'm typically drawn to writing with an upmarket edge, and I'm open to anything high-concept, speculative or which blends one genre with another.

Authors: Alwia Al-Hassan; Bana Alabed; JJ Arcanjo; Daniel Broadstock; Tom Carlisle; Dawn Coulter-Cruttenden; Helena Duggan; Emma Farrarons; William Friend; Jo Furniss; Toby Gutteridge; Elle Hardy; Oli Hyatt; Ruth Kelly; Scott Kershaw; Kieran Larwood; The Urban Legend; John Lutz; Dan Malakin; Major Scotty Mills; Markus Motum; David Patrikarakos; Rogba Payne; Daisy Pearce; Stephen Ronson; Babita Sharma; Louise Shorter; Tom Spencer; P. A. Staff; Sean Watkin; Kelly Woodward

L393 Leigh Feldman Literary
Literary Agency
United States

query@lfliterary.com
assistant@lfliterary.com

https://www.lfliterary.com

ADULT
  Fiction > *Novels*
    Historical Fiction; Literary

  Nonfiction > *Nonfiction Books*
    Memoir; Narrative Nonfiction

YOUNG ADULT > Fiction > *Novels*: Contemporary

Send: Query; Writing sample; Proposal
How to send: Email

Particularly interested in historical fiction, contemporary YA, literary fiction, memoir, and narrative nonfiction. No adult and YA paranormal, fantasy, science fiction, romance, thrillers, mysteries, or picture books. Send query by email with first ten pages or proposal. Only makes personal response if interested.

Literary Agent: Leigh Feldman (*L211*)

L394 Nina Leon
Associate Agent
United Kingdom

https://www.perezliterary.com/about-us/the-team/
https://querymanager.com/query/NinaLeon

Literary Agency: Perez Literary & Entertainment (**L506**)

ADULT > Fiction > *Novels*
  Adventure; Chick Lit; Commercial; Contemporary Romance; Contemporary; Crime; Fantasy; Gothic; Historical Fiction; Historical Romance; Horror; LGBTQIA; Literary; Magic; Magical Realism; Mystery; Romance; Romantasy; Romantic Suspense; Romantic Thrillers; Science Fiction; Supernatural / Paranormal Romance; Suspense; Thrillers; Upmarket; Urban Fantasy; Women's Fiction

CHILDREN'S > Fiction > *Middle Grade*
Contemporary; Fantasy; Historical Fiction; Mystery

NEW ADULT > Fiction > *Novels*
Fantasy; Romance

YOUNG ADULT > Fiction > *Novels*
Contemporary; Fantasy; Historical Fiction; Literary; Mystery; Romance; Supernatural / Paranormal Romance; Supernatural / Paranormal; Thrillers

How to send: Query Manager

Knew from a young age that the magic and power of stories was something she would always need in her life. She now proudly champions authors whose magic shines through every story they write. Works closely with her clients from day one. Editorially focused, she enjoys the collaborative back and forth of polishing a manuscript before guiding clients through the publishing process. Believes that all voices have value and deserve to be heard.

L395 Paul S. Levine
Literary Agent
United States

paul@paulslevinelit.com

Literary Agency: Paul S. Levine Literary Agency (**L502**)

L396 Sarah Levitt
Literary Agent
New York
United States

https://aevitascreative.com/agents/
https://querymanager.com/query/2585

Literary Agency: Aevitas

Fiction > *Novels*: Literary

Nonfiction > *Nonfiction Books*
Comedy / Humour; History; Journalism; Memoir; Narrative Nonfiction; Popular Culture; Popular Science

Closed to approaches.

Most interested in narrative nonfiction in the areas of popular science, big ideas, history, humor, pop culture, memoir, and reportage, in addition to voice-driven literary fiction with a bold plot and fresh, imaginative characters. She's excited by strong female and underrepresented voices, the strange and speculative, and projects that ignite cultural conversation.

Authors: Ruha Benjamin; Laura Bliss; Marc Bojanowski; Elizabeth Brooks; Adam Chandler; Bloomberg CityLab; Daniel M. Davis; Sarah Ditum; Baz Dreisinger; Sarah Duenwald; Mieke Eerkens; Claire Evans; Ruth Feldman; Becky Ferreira; Marion Gibson; Annette Giesecke; Eliese Colette Goldbach; Elyse Graham; Wade Graham; Reina Hardy; Ayanna Howard; Tung-Hui Hu; Perrin Ireland; Saru Jayaraman; Nancy McSharry Jensen; Robin Wall Kimmerer; Doma Mahmoud; Sara Majka; Antonia Malchik; Maggie Mertens; Ann Morgan; Laine Nooney; Jenni Nuttall; Amelia Possanza; Elizabeth Preston; Steve Ramirez; Ashanté Reese; Charlotte Rixon; Anjali Sachdeva; Suzanne Scanlon; Kathleen Sheppard; Lauren Shields; Josh Sokol; Ly Ky Tran; Phuc Tran; Sarah Turner; Sarah Vallance; Lizzie Wade; Peter von Ziegesar

L397 Lewinsohn Literary
Literary Agency
58 Old Compton Street, London, W1D 4UF
United Kingdom

queries@lewinsohnliterary.com

https://www.lewinsohnliterary.com
https://www.instagram.com/lewinsohnliterary

Professional Body: The Association of Authors' Agents (AAA)

Fiction
Graphic Novels: General
Novels: Family; Friends; Relationships; Romance; Romantic Comedy

Nonfiction
Gift Books: General
Illustrated Books: Cookery
Nonfiction Books: Memoir; Nature; Popular Culture

Closed to approaches.

We will be especially keen to read romcoms or anything with interesting relationship dynamics, be it about friendships, families, colleagues or romantic, tales set in cities or unusual places, even or especially if they seem outwardly mundane, memoir that elicits a strong emotional response and shines a light on the familiar in new ways, nature and pop culture writing that captures the zeitgeist but has timeless weight and resonance, and the occasional dabble with beautifully designed illustrated books, such as graphic novels, cookery, photo or gift books.

L398 Alison Lewis
Literary Agent
United States

atl@goldinlit.com

https://www.goldinlit.com/alison-lewis
https://twitter.com/atatelewis

Literary Agency: Frances Goldin Literary Agency, Inc. (**L238**)

Fiction > *Novels*: Literary

Nonfiction > *Nonfiction Books*
Cultural Criticism; History; Journalism; Literary Memoir; Science

Send: Query; Writing sample; Proposal
How to send: Email

Represents a wide range of nonfiction, spanning journalism, cultural criticism, history, science, literary memoir, and essays, as well as select literary fiction. She is particularly drawn to writers with a distinctive voice and perspective, a sense of social or political imagination and responsibility, scholars and researchers who can translate their expertise for a wide readership, and writers pushing the boundaries of form, preconceived ideas, and histories of representation in literature.

L399 Kayla Lightner
Literary Agent
United States

https://www.pandeliterary.com/our-team-pandeliterary
https://www.manuscriptwishlist.com/mswl-post/kayla-lightner/
https://twitter.com/LightnerKayla
https://www.linkedin.com/in/kayla-lightner-362406ab/

Literary Agency: Ayesha Pande Literary (**L036**)
Professional Body: Association of American Literary Agents (AALA)

Fiction
Graphic Novels: General
Novels: Book Club Fiction; Family Saga; Fantasy; Folklore, Myths, and Legends; Gothic; Historical Fiction; Literary; Magical Realism; Science Fiction; Speculative; Upmarket

Nonfiction > *Nonfiction Books*
Culture; Finance; Health; History; Internet Culture; Internet; Memoir; Mental Health; Narrative Nonfiction; Technology

Send: Pitch; Synopsis; Author bio; Writing sample
How to send: Online submission system

I love discovering diverse and fresh new perspectives across adult literary + upmarket fiction, non-fiction, and graphic novels. I'm particularly a fan of authors with singular voices that masterfully straddle the line between storytelling and teaching readers something new (about themselves, their communities, or the world we live in).

L400 Limelight Management
Literary Agency
10 Filmer Mews, 75 Filmer Road, London, SW6 7BZ
United Kingdom
Tel: +44 (0) 20 7384 9950

mail@limelightmanagement.com

https://www.limelightmanagement.com
https://www.facebook.com/pages/Limelight-Celebrity-Management-Ltd/399328580099859?fref=ts
https://twitter.com/Fionalimelight
https://www.youtube.com/channel/UCCmxquRk_blKqjR8jKRryFA

https://instagram.com/limelightcelebritymanagement/
https://www.linkedin.com/company-beta/11219861/

Professional Body: The Association of Authors' Agents (AAA)

Fiction > *Novels*
Commercial Women's Fiction; Crime; Historical Fiction; Mystery; Suspense; Thrillers

Nonfiction > *Nonfiction Books*
Arts; Autobiography; Biography; Business; Cookery; Crafts; Health; Nature; Popular Science; Sport; Travel

Send: Query; Synopsis; Writing sample; Author bio
How to send: Email

Always looking for exciting new authors. Send query by email with the word "Submission" in the subject line and synopsis and first three chapters as Word or Open Document attachments. Also include market info, and details of your professional life and writing ambitions. Film and TV scripts for existing clients only. See website for full guidelines.

Literary Agent / Managing Director: Fiona Lindsay

L401 Lindsay Literary Agency
Literary Agency
United Kingdom
Tel: +44 (0) 1420 831430

info@lindsayliteraryagency.co.uk

http://www.lindsayliteraryagency.co.uk
https://twitter.com/lindsaylit

Professional Body: The Association of Authors' Agents (AAA)

CHILDREN'S > *Fiction*
Middle Grade: General, and in particular: High / Epic Fantasy
Picture Books: General

YOUNG ADULT > *Fiction* > *Novels*
General, and in particular: Contemporary Romance; High Concept; Romantasy

Send: Query; Author bio; Pitch; Synopsis; Writing sample; Full text
How to send: Email

Send query by email only, including cover letter in the body of the email, single-page synopsis and first three chapters, or complete ms in the case of picture books. No submissions by post.

Authors: Helen Brandom; Pamela Butchart; Sital Gorasia Chapman; Christina Collins; Jim Daly; Donna David; James Davis; Keighley Douglas; Rachel Emily; Louise Finch; Sam Gayton; Ruth Hatfield; Larry Hayes; Sharon Hopwood; Peter Jones; Jay Joseph; Titania Krimpas; Mike Lancaster; Beth O'Brien; Kate Peridot; Josh Silver; Daniel Tawse; Sharon Tregenza; Rachel Valentine; Sue Wallman; Jacqueline Whitehart; Joe Wilson

Literary Agent: Becky Bagnell

L402 Isabel Lineberry
Junior Agent
United Kingdom

https://www.perezliterary.com
https://www.perezliterary.com/submit/submit-to-isabel/
https://querymanager.com/query/IsabelLineberry

Literary Agency: Perez Literary & Entertainment (**L506**)

NEW ADULT > *Fiction* > *Novels*
Contemporary Romance; Fantasy; Romantasy

YOUNG ADULT > *Fiction* > *Novels*
Contemporary Romance; Fantasy; Romantasy

How to send: Submittable

I represent YA and New Adult and am particularly interested in Contemporary Romance, Romantasy and Fantasy. I am always attracted to the character and voice first, so give me romantic tension that has me giggling, a villain who is as charming as they are evil or a group of characters who have me watching their conversations as if it's a tennis match.

L403 Laurie Liss
Literary Agent; Executive Vice President
United States

https://www.sll.com/our-team
http://aaronline.org/Sys/PublicProfile/2176754/417813

Literary Agency: Sterling Lord Literistic, Inc. (**L597**)
Professional Body: Association of American Literary Agents (AALA)

Fiction > *Novels*

Nonfiction > *Nonfiction Books*

Send: Query; Synopsis; Writing sample
How to send: Online submission system

L404 The Liverpool Literary Agency
Literary Agency
Liverpool
United Kingdom

submissions@liverpool-literary.agency

https://www.liverpool-literary.agency/
https://twitter.com/LiverpoolLit
https://www.instagram.com/liverpool_literary_agency/

Professional Body: The Association of Authors' Agents (AAA)

ADULT > *Fiction* > *Novels*

YOUNG ADULT > *Fiction* > *Novels*
Dystopian Fiction; Fantasy; Post-Apocalyptic; Science Fiction; Steampunk; Urban Fantasy

Closed to approaches.

Costs: Offers services that writers have to pay for. Also offers editorial services.

Literary agency based in Liverpool, focusing on helping writers from Northern England break into the publishing industry.

Associate Agent / Editor: Laura Bennett (**L056**)

Literary Agent: Clare Coombes (**L138**)

L405 Liza Dawson Associates
Literary Agency
121 West 27th Street, Suite 1201, New York, NY 10001
United States

lwu@lizadawson.com

https://www.lizadawsonassociates.com
https://twitter.com/LizaDawsonAssoc

Professional Body: Association of American Literary Agents (AALA)

Fiction > *Novels*

Nonfiction > *Nonfiction Books*

See website for specific agent interests and query appropriate agent directly. Specific agent submission guidelines and contact details are available on website.

Authors: Annie Barrows; Marie Bostwick; Bob Brier; Stella Cameron; Robyn Carr; Ross Gay; Susan Hasler; Scott Hawkins; Julia Lee; Victoria Christopher Murray; Tawni O'Dell; Jean Sasson; Marybeth Whalen

Junior Agent: Lauren Bajek (**L037**)

Literary Agents: Rachel Beck; Caitlin Blasdell; Hannah Bowman; Caitie Flum; Tom Miller

President / Senior Agent: Liza Dawson (**L162**)

L406 Looking Glass Literary & Media Management
Literary Agency
United States

https://www.lookingglasslit.com
https://twitter.com/LookingGlassLit
https://www.instagram.com/lookingglasslit/

We are a boutique agency with a full-service team of fierce advocates who support all facets of our clients' careers. Our priority is championing authors and books that reflect the diverse world around us. The books we work with leave lasting impressions that inspire growth, thought, and joy in the world.

Associate Agents: Grace Milusich (**L453**); Antoinette Van Sluytman (**L588**)

Literary Agents: Natalie Lakosil (**L379**); Lee O'Brien (**L484**); Desiree Wilson (**L667**)

L407 Lotus Lane Literary
Literary Agency
United States

contact@lotuslit.com

https://lotuslit.com

Fiction > *Novels*

Nonfiction > *Nonfiction Books*

Send: Query; Author bio; Synopsis; Writing sample
How to send: Email

Independent literary agency based in New Jersey, representing a diverse list of debut and seasoned authors. Handles adult fiction and nonfiction, and sells rights to the US, UK, Europe, and India.

Literary Agent: Priya Doraswamy

L408 Morwenna Loughman
Literary Agent
United Kingdom

https://www.thebksagency.com/about

Literary Agency: The BKS Agency (**L065**)

Fiction > *Novels*

Nonfiction > *Nonfiction Books*
Cookery; Lifestyle; Narrative Nonfiction; Popular Psychology; Popular Science

How to send: Online submission system

I am looking for narrative non-fiction, particularly across smart thinking, pop-science and pop-psychology – as well as lifestyle and cookery. I'm open to all types of fiction.

L409 Jake Lovell
Literary Agent
United States

https://www.dijkstraagency.com
https://www.dijkstraagency.com/agent-page.php?agent_id=Lovell
https://querymanager.com/query/jakelovell

Literary Agency: Sandra Dijkstra Literary Agency

Fiction > *Novels*
Dark; Gothic; Horror; Speculative; Supernatural / Paranormal; Thrillers; UFOs; Upmarket; Westerns

Nonfiction > *Nonfiction Books*
General, and in particular: History; Military; Westerns

Actively looking for adult fiction and non-fiction. He is interested in upmarket fiction, with an emphasis on: Gothic, horror, thrillers, westerns, and speculative fiction (supernatural, paranormal, UFOs, etc...; think Jordan Peele or 10 Cloverfield Lane). When it comes to fiction, he loves dark stories that cause readers to question turning off the lights before bed. Dark stories permeate through all cultures, backgrounds, and histories, and he wants to hear them. His tastes lean more in the vein of The Hunger by Alma Katsu, The Only Good Indians by Stephen Graham Jones, Tender is the Flesh by Agustina Bazterrica, and works by Paul Tremblay, Mona Awad, and Colson Whitehead. In general, he's especially drawn to character driven stories written in distinct and diverse voices.

On the non-fiction front, he is looking for captivating stories and perspectives that stay with readers and keep them coming back. He is especially interested in working with historians, up-and-coming scholars looking to transition to trade readership, journalists, doctors, veterans, and people with unique takes on important issues. Think: Freakonomics, Outliers, A Molecule Away From Madness, Columbine, American Sniper, Empire's Workshop, and The Fact of a Body.

Open to queries the first week of every month.

L410 Lutyens and Rubinstein
Literary Agency
17 Powis Mews, London, W11 1JN
United Kingdom
Tel: +44 (0) 20 7792 4855

submissions@lutyensrubinstein.co.uk

https://www.lutyensrubinstein.co.uk
https://twitter.com/LandRAgency
https://instagram.com/LandRAgency

Professional Body: The Association of Authors' Agents (AAA)

Fiction > *Novels*
Commercial; Literary

Nonfiction > *Nonfiction Books*

Send: Query; Synopsis; Writing sample
How to send: Email
How not to send: Post

Send up to 5,000 words or first three chapters by email with covering letter and short synopsis. No film or TV scripts, or unsolicited submissions by hand or by post.

Literary Agent: Susannah Godman

L411 Rebecca Lyon
Literary Agent
United Kingdom

https://www.sheiland.com/about

Literary Agency: Sheil Land Associates Ltd (**L577**)

Scripts
Film Scripts; TV Scripts; Theatre Scripts

L412 Emily MacDonald
Literary Agent
United Kingdom

emilymacdonald@42mp.com

https://www.42mp.com/agents
https://twitter.com/Ebh_mac

Literary Agency: 42 Management and Production

Fiction > *Novels*
Book Club Fiction; Crime; High Concept; Literary; Romantic Comedy; Thrillers; Upmarket

Nonfiction > *Nonfiction Books*
History; Memoir; Narrative Nonfiction; Nature; Regional; Scotland; Social Commentary

Closed to approaches.

Bring me a story with characters that never leave you and a narrative that pulls you in, keeping you in the world well after you've finished reading. I read across a wide-range and have a particular interest in; book club, high-concept crime/thriller, upmarket and literary fiction (with a real soft spot for witty romcoms with an unassailable hook!) In both fiction and non-fiction, I love stories woven into their natural landscape, where the setting is as central a character as those who drive the narrative. I'm actively looking for narrative non-fiction which immerses the reader into an untold true story (personal or historical), exploring a new point of view, and providing a compelling social commentary, with an investigative twist! I want to have my horizons expanded when I read. I'd also love to find a story which blends nature writing and memoir.

L413 Laura Macdougall
Literary Agent
United Kingdom

LMacdougall@unitedagents.co.uk

https://www.unitedagents.co.uk/lmacdougallunitedagentscouk
https://twitter.com/L_Macdougall
https://www.instagram.com/lmac_84/?hl=en
https://www.pinterest.co.uk/lmvmacdougall/

Literary Agency: United Agents

Fiction > *Novels*
Book Club Fiction; Comedy / Humour; Commercial; Crime; Family Saga; Family; Friends; Historical Fiction; LGBTQIA; Literary; Menopause; Romance; Saga

Nonfiction
Illustrated Books: General
Nonfiction Books: Culture; Ethnic Groups; Gardening; Gender; History; LGBTQIA; Midwifery; Narrative Nonfiction; Nature; Parenting; Philosophy; Politics; Popular Science; Psychology; Science; Scotland; Sexuality; Social Class; Sport

Send: Synopsis; Writing sample; Proposal
How to send: Email

I represent a diverse spectrum of commercial fiction – saga, romance, historical, book club and 'up-lit' – and literary fiction, ranging from the quirky to the daring and experimental. I've always been a big fan of historical fiction and also have a soft spot for novels that explore the complexities of relationships and family life.

My non-fiction list is equally varied, spanning illustrated books to parenting titles, history, popular philosophy and gardening. I also represent a fascinating wealth of narrative non-fiction, from Scottish nature writing to death, materials science, politics, manufacturing, midwifery and the recent history of gay bars. A writer who can successfully communicate their passion, whether that's about something niche or obscure or a global phenomenon, will always be of interest to me.

As a queer woman, I represent a large number of LGBTQ+ writers and I'm particularly keen to hear from those who also identify as LGBTQ+ and who are exploring the full spectrum of LGBTQ+ lives in their writing.

L414 MacGregor & Luedeke

Literary Agency
PO Box 1316, Manzanita, OR 97130
United States
Tel: +1 (503) 389-4803

submissions@macgregorliterary.com

http://www.macgregorandluedeke.com
https://twitter.com/MacGregorLit

Fiction > *Novels*
Christianity; Literary; Romance

Nonfiction > *Nonfiction Books*
Crime; Memoir; Self Help; Spirituality

Send: Query; Market info; Author bio; Writing sample
Don't send: Full text
How to send: Email

Costs: Author covers sundry admin costs.

The company has focused on specific niche markets — memoir, spirituality, self-help books, Christian and literary fiction, true crime, romance, as well as some specialty projects.

Authors: Don Brown; Davis Bunn; Rashawn Copeland; Sheila Gregoire; Rachel Hauck; James Byron Huggins; Steve Jackson; Jessica Kate; Rachel Linden; Holly Lorincz; Evelyn Lozada; Scott Parazynski; Jay Payleitner; Tom Satterly; Kimberly Stuart; David Thomas; Vincent Zandri

Literary Agent / President: Chip MacGregor

Literary Agent / Vice President: Amanda Luedeke

L415 Kate Mack

Literary Agent; Vice President; Company Director
United States

https://www.aevitascreative.com/agent/kate-mack

Literary Agency: Aevitas

Nonfiction
Illustrated Books: General
Nonfiction Books: Comedy / Humour; Culture; Fashion; History; Music

Closed to approaches.

She is most interested in cultural history, fashion, music, illustrated books for adults, strong female voices, and stories that give a voice to a person or community that's historically been silenced or ostracized.

Authors: Joana Avillez; Robyn Crawford; Liza Donnelly; America Ferrera; Patricia Field; Katy Fishell; Lucretia Tye Jasmine; Betsey Johnson; Sam Kashner; Rookie Magazine; Ian Purkayastha; Kate Schelter; Ramin Setoodeh; Amber Share; Kate Sidley; Kevin West; Alden Wicker

L416 Joanna MacKenzie

Literary Agent
United States

https://nelsonagency.com/joanna-mackenzie/
https://www.publishersmarketplace.com/members/JoannaMacKenzie/
https://twitter.com/joannamackenzie
https://www.facebook.com/joanna.topor.mackenzie

Literary Agency: Nelson Literary Agency, LLC (**L477**)

Fiction > *Novels*
Commercial; Family; Friends; Mystery; Speculative; Thrillers; Women's Fiction

Closed to approaches.

Interested in high-concept, twisty, unputdownable stories with a strong voice in the areas of women's fiction, thriller, and speculative; timely commercial fiction in which the personal intersects with the world at large, and/or that explores toxic friendships and complex, challenging family dynamics; Heartfelt and timeless stories that you want to re-read about identity, unlikely friendships, reinvention, second acts, and women finding their voices and power, especially with touches of magic or speculative; Voicey, confident, atmospheric mysteries set in close-knit communities; creepy islands and Midwest-set are a plus. Always looking for stories about the immigrant experience.

Authors: Brooke Abrams; Kate Baer; Gina Banks; Ali Brady; Lina Chern; Shana Galen; John Galligan; Jill Grunenwald; Alison Hammer; Sarah Zachrich Jeng; Sierra Kincade; Karen Koh; Gillian Libby; Jonathan Messinger; Meghan Scott Molin; Katrina Monroe; Lyndsay Rush; Kristen Simmons; Jennifer Springsteen; Stacy Stokes; Joy Sullivan; Chrysler Szarlan; Ben Tanzer; Kathleen West

L417 Jamie Maclean

Literary Agent
United Kingdom

https://cmm.agency/about-us.php

Literary Agency: Coombs Moylett & Maclean Literary Agency (**L139**)

Fiction > *Novels*
Erotic; Historical Crime; Mystery; Thrillers

Nonfiction > *Nonfiction Books*
Gender Politics; How To; Lifestyle; Relationships

Send: Synopsis; Writing sample
How to send: Online submission system

Specialises in both fiction and nonfiction and is particularly interested in sexual politics, relationship, lifestyle how-to's, erotica, thrillers, whodunit and historical crime.

L418 Lauren MacLeod

Senior Agent
United States

https://www.aevitascreative.com/agent/lauren-macleod
https://www.strothmanagency.com/about
https://querymanager.com/query/LMacLeod
https://twitter.com/Lauren_MacLeod
http://aaronline.org/Sys/PublicProfile/12259463/417813

Literary Agencies: Aevitas; The Strothman Agency (**L607**)
Professional Body: Association of American Literary Agents (AALA)

ADULT > **Nonfiction** > *Nonfiction Books*
Cookery; Crime; Food; History; Memoir; Narrative Nonfiction; Popular Culture

CHILDREN'S > **Fiction** > *Middle Grade*

YOUNG ADULT > **Fiction** > *Novels*

Send: Query
How to send: Email; Query Manager; By referral

Only accepting nonfiction queries for food writing, cookbooks, true crime, and pop culture without a referral. If you have a memoir, narrative nonfiction, or YA or MG fiction project and have been referred by a friend or client, make contact directly.

Authors: Hélène Boudreau; Bridget Crocker; Helene Dunbar; Rogelio Garcia; Kenny Gilbert; Tyler Gillespie; Ron Goldberg; Steven Hale; Rachel Herz; Allison Horrocks; Sashi Kaufman; Claire and Alan Linic; Mary Mahoney; Nicole Maines; Jodi Meadows; Andrea Mosqueda; Frederick Douglass Opie; Erik Rebain; Beck Rourke-Mooney; Aminah Mae Safi; Alora Young; Marlene Zuk

L419 Neeti Madan
Senior Agent
United States

https://www.sll.com/our-team

Literary Agency: Sterling Lord Literistic, Inc. (**L597**)

Fiction > *Novels*

Nonfiction > *Nonfiction Books*
  Journalism; Lifestyle; Memoir; Popular Culture

Send: Query; Synopsis; Writing sample
How to send: Online submission system

Her books run the gamut from the commercial to the cerebral. A true generalist, she is drawn to thoughtful writing on intriguing and important subjects, including memoir, journalism, popular culture, lifestyle, and the occasional novel. She is on the lookout for the types of books she loves as a reader—writing that breaks through barriers and elevates underrepresented voices, page-turners that keep her up until 3 AM, and irreverent books that makes her laugh.

L420 Madeleine Milburn Literary, TV & Film Agency
Literary Agency
The Factory, 1 Park Hill, London, SW4 9NS
United Kingdom
Tel: +44 (0) 20 7499 7550

submissions@madeleinemilburn.com
childrens@madeleinemilburn.com
info@madeleinemilburn.com

https://madeleinemilburn.co.uk
https://twitter.com/MMLitAgency
https://www.instagram.com/madeleinemilburn/?hl=en
https://www.facebook.com/MadeleineMilburnLiteraryAgency

Professional Body: The Association of Authors' Agents (AAA)

ADULT
  Fiction > *Novels*
  Nonfiction > *Nonfiction Books*

CHILDREN'S
  Fiction > *Novels*
  Nonfiction > *Nonfiction Books*

NEW ADULT
  Fiction > *Novels*
  Nonfiction > *Nonfiction Books*

TEEN
  Fiction > *Novels*
  Nonfiction > *Nonfiction Books*

YOUNG ADULT
  Fiction > *Novels*
  Nonfiction > *Nonfiction Books*

Send: Query; Synopsis; Pitch; Market info; Writing sample
How to send: Online submission system
How not to send: Post; Email

Represents award-winning and bestselling authors of adult and children's fiction and non-fiction. Submit via online submissions system. No submissions by post or by email.

Associate Agent: Elinor Davies (**L160**)

Company Director / Literary Agent: Madeleine Milburn (**L449**)

Literary Agents: Emma Bal (**L038**); Maddy Belton (**L055**); Jessica Leeke (**L391**); Olivia Maidment (**L421**); Hannah Todd (**L631**); Rachel Yeoh (**L675**)

Managing Director: Giles Milburn

Senior Agent: Chloe Seager (**L571**)

L421 Olivia Maidment
Literary Agent
United Kingdom

submissions@madeleinemilburn.com

https://www.madeleinemilburn.co.uk/agents/olivia-maidment/
https://twitter.com/liv_maidment

Literary Agency: Madeleine Milburn Literary, TV & Film Agency (**L420**)

Fiction > *Novels*
  Book Club Fiction; Contemporary; Family Saga; Family; Historical Fiction; Horror; Literary; Magical Realism; Speculative

Nonfiction > *Nonfiction Books*: Narrative Nonfiction

Send: Synopsis; Writing sample
How to send: Email
How not to send: Post

I represent literary, literary crossover, and book club fiction.

I am looking for smart, voice-led fiction with wide appeal. I really admire writers who have a commitment to craft and style, and I am drawn to books that utilise a strong hook or a unique voice. I love discovering authors who write with powerful themes and conversation-starting questions at the heart of their work combined with a compelling narrative and plot. I enjoy novels that investigate identity and explore or critique the way that we live, and fiction that uses individual stories to explore moments of wider societal change. I am open to both intimate, closely told novels and sweeping narratives that are epic in their scale and scope, and all that lies between. Above all, I want to see books that combine masterful writing, unforgettable characters, and thematic and emotional depth with well-crafted plot.

I also love literary leaning fiction that blends with elements of genre, in particular novels with shades of the speculative, magical realist, historical, or horror. For me, writing in this area needs to be grounded in the human stories at the heart of the novel, and I really enjoy books with big imaginations.

L422 Alyssa Maltese
Literary Agent
United States

https://www.alyssamaltese.com
https://www.rootliterary.com/agents
https://querymanager.com/query/alyssamaltese
https://www.publishersmarketplace.com/members/alyssamaltese/Alyssa Maltese

Literary Agency: Root Literary (**L547**)

ADULT
  Fiction > *Novels*
    Contemporary Romance; Domestic Suspense; Historical Fiction; Horror; Psychological Thrillers; Speculative

  Nonfiction > *Nonfiction Books*
    Animals; Mental Health; Narrative Nonfiction; Nature; Popular Culture; Prescriptive Nonfiction; Psychology; Science; Sex

YOUNG ADULT > **Fiction** > *Novels*
  Coming of Age; Contemporary; Fantasy; Historical Fiction; Horror; Romance; Speculative

Does not want:

> **ADULT** > **Fiction** > *Novels*: Supernatural / Paranormal Romance
>
> **YOUNG ADULT** > **Fiction** > *Novels*
> High / Epic Fantasy; Supernatural / Paranormal Romance

How to send: Query Manager

In the YA space, I'm seeking fiction that helps young readers discover their own voice and sense of self-worth. I love kids and have a background in early childhood education, and feel strongly that if a child is old enough to experience something, then they are old enough to read about it. I'm particularly drawn to contemporary coming-of-age stories with a healthy dose of angst. I'm open to genre elements (particularly speculative, fantasy, romance, historical), but in general I prefer fiction grounded in our world, so I'm not the best fit for straightforward fantasy. I'm also seeking YA horror. In this space, I love high stakes and work embedded with social commentary. I would be absolutely tickled to find a YA project exploring 2000s emo culture. (It's not a phase, mom!) If your book is set at Warped Tour or Bamboozle, I want to see it! In adult fiction, I'm casting a bit of a wider net. I'm looking for weird upmarket speculative novels. I'm also seeking commercial psychological thrillers, domestic suspense, and horror. Propulsive pacing is a must, and twists that really surprise me are a bonus! My very favorite kind of historical fiction is slice-of-life revealing untold stories of interesting women.

I'd also love some contemporary romance to round out my list. One of my favorite tropes is when love is reciprocated, but one or both love interests doesn't realize it... think enemies to lovers; best friends to lovers; sunshine and grumpy. My ideal romance is torturously slow burn with a healthy dose of angst and substantial emotional growth. In adult nonfiction, I'm seeking prescriptive and research-driven narrative nonfiction from authors with an established expertise and audience. Topics of interest in nonfiction include psychology, mental health, taboo topics such as death and sex, science pertaining to nature and animals, and pop culture. I am not accepting submissions for poetry, short story collections, screenplays, novellas, early reader books, chapter books, religious texts, picture books, graphic novels, or illustrations of any kind. I am not the best fit for high/epic fantasy, space operas, paranormal romance, crime fiction/detective novels, cozy mysteries, legal thrillers, romantic thrillers, pulp fiction, sick lit, stories set in mental hospitals, most things related to sports, grifter-themed stories, torture porn/gratuitous gore, or fairytale retellings (though I do have a soft spot for Arthurian legend).

L423 Victoria Marini

Literary Agent
United States

https://www.highlineliterary.com/agent-victoria
https://querymanager.com/query/2982
https://twitter.com/LitAgentMarini

Literary Agency: High Line Literary Collective (**L312**)

ADULT > Fiction > *Novels*
General, and in particular: Book Club Fiction; Contemporary; Fantasy; High Concept

YOUNG ADULT > Fiction > *Novels*
General, and in particular: Contemporary; Fantasy; High Concept

Closed to approaches.

Seeking Adult and Young Adult fiction across all genres with a particular emphasis on high concept contemporary fiction, genre adjacent book club fiction, and all things fantastical.

L424 Mildred Marmur

Literary Agent
United States

Literary Agency: Mildred Marmur Associates, Ltd. (**L450**)

L425 Jill Marr

Literary Agent
United States

https://www.dijkstraagency.com/agent-page.php?agent_id=Marr
https://querymanager.com/query/JillMarr

Literary Agency: Sandra Dijkstra Literary Agency

ADULT
Fiction > *Novels*
Commercial; Fantasy; Folklore, Myths, and Legends; Food; Gothic; Historical Fiction; Horror; Magical Realism; Mystery; Psychological Suspense; Romance; Romantasy; Romantic Comedy; Speculative; Thrillers; Upmarket

Nonfiction > *Nonfiction Books*
Comedy / Humour; Crime; Current Affairs; Health; History; Memoir; Music; Narrative Nonfiction; Nutrition; Politics; Popular Culture; Science; Social Commentary; Sport

CHILDREN'S > Fiction > *Picture Books*

Closed to approaches.

Looking for fiction and non-fiction by unrepresented voices, BIPOC and Latinx writers, disabled persons, and people identifying as LGBTQ+, among others. She is interested in commercial and upmarket fiction, with an emphasis on mysteries, thrillers, Gothic, horror, romantasy, romance, fantasy, speculative fiction, and historical fiction. She loves food-centric novels, no matter what the genre. She is looking to find more rom coms with a fresh voice, perspective and a strong hook. When it comes to suspense she likes it dark and psychological. Her tastes lean more in the vein of The Silent Patient, The Lost Apothecary or Mexican Gothic than Private Investigator and CIA stories. And she almost never takes on military or Western projects. However she is a sucker for novels with grounded magical realism, and is always looking for a new take on mythology or folklore. She is also looking for non-fiction by authors with a big, timely, smart message. She'd like to see work that does a deep dive into subcultures and social commentary as well as historical projects that look at big picture issues. She is looking for non-fiction projects in the areas of current events, true crime, science, history, narrative non-fiction, sports, politics, health and nutrition, pop culture, humor, music, and very select memoir.

L426 The Marsh Agency

Literary Agency
50 Albemarle Street, London, W1S 4BD
United Kingdom
Tel: +44 (0) 20 7493 4361

http://www.marsh-agency.co.uk

Professional Body: The Association of Authors' Agents (AAA)

Types: Fiction; Nonfiction
Subjects: Literary
Markets: Adult; Young Adult

Closed to approaches.

Not currently accepting unsolicited mss as at March 2018. Most new clients come through recommendations.

Authors: Jill Bays; Ian Dear; Ed Halliwell; Tendai Huchu; Sam Kriss; Anita Nair; Alan Palmer; Allyson Pollock; Alfred Price; Gillian Riley; Richard Seymour; Christine Shaw

Literary Agent: Susie Nicklin

L427 Jen Marshall

Literary Agent
New York
United States

https://www.aevitascreative.com/agent/jen-marshall
https://querymanager.com/query/JenMarshall
https://twitter.com/jenmarshall3

Literary Agency: Aevitas

ADULT
Fiction
Graphic Novels: General
Novels: Adventure; Commercial; Crime; Drama; Horror; Literary; Popular Culture; Romance

Nonfiction > *Nonfiction Books*
Arts; Business; Crime; Design; Fashion; Health; History; Investigative Journalism; Mathematics; Narrative Nonfiction; Popular Culture; Science; Social Justice; Technology

CHILDREN'S > Fiction > *Novels*

Closed to approaches.

Represents acclaimed and bestselling narrative nonfiction projects. Also represents select literary and commercial fiction projects. Areas of interest in nonfiction are wide-ranging: investigative journalism, untold histories, fashion and design, social justice, true crime, tech, business, science, cities, and pop culture. In fiction, she primarily seeks literary and commercial works for adults.

Authors: Natasha S. Barrett; Elena Brower; Maggie Bullock; Windy Chien; Hopwood DePree; Danielle Dreilinger; Amanda FitzSimons; Neil Gross; Ericka Hart; Gabrielle Hartley; Katherine Sharp Landdeck; Nana Malone; Marisa Meltzer; Jenny Minton; Azadeh Moaveni; Vanessa O'Brien; Joe Pompeo; Gene Pressman; Paul Pringle; Kate Schapira; Chris Smalls; Keziah Weir; Eric Wilson; Sheryl Gonzalez Ziegler

L428 Caroline Marsiglia

Literary Agent
United States

https://www.aevitascreative.com
https://www.aevitascreative.com/agent/caroline-marsiglia

Nonfiction > *Nonfiction Books*
Investigative Journalism; Memoir; Narrative Nonfiction; Self Help

Closed to approaches.

Primarily interested in non-fiction, focusing on investigative journalism, memoir, evidence-based self-help, and narrative non-fiction. Across all genres, she is eager to work with authors who share her dedication to creating a more diverse and accessible literary landscape.

L429 Olivia Martin
Associate Agent
United Kingdom
Tel: +44 (0) 20 3214 0778

omartin@unitedagents.co.uk

https://www.unitedagents.co.uk/omartinunitedagentscouk

Literary Agency: United Agents
Literary Agent: Charles Walker

Authors: Anjana Appachana; Neil Ely; Lloyd Eyre-Morgan; Jack Hartley; Lucas Sogas López; Max Tobin; Ryan Walker-Edwards

L430 Maria Massie
Literary Agent
United States

Literary Agency: Massie & McQuilkin

Fiction > *Novels:* Literary

Nonfiction > *Nonfiction Books*
Memoir; Narrative Nonfiction

Send: Query; Author bio; Writing sample
How to send: In the body of an email

Brings over two decades' worth of experience in representing authors and helping to make sure that they can be read around the world.

L431 Rebecca Matte
Literary Agent
United States

https://bradfordlit.com/about/rebecca-matte/
https://querymanager.com/query/RMatte
https://www.manuscriptwishlist.com/mswl-post/rebecca-matte/
https://twitter.com/rebeccalmatte

Literary Agency: Bradford Literary Agency (**L075**)

ADULT > **Fiction** > *Novels*
Disabilities; Fantasy; Queer Romance; Romance; Romantasy; Science Fiction

YOUNG ADULT > **Fiction** > *Novels*
Disabilities; Fantasy; Queer Romance; Romance; Romantasy; Science Fiction

How to send: Query Manager

Loves adult and YA science fiction/fantasy and queer romance. But no matter the setting—be it a far off kingdom beset by magic or around the corner in Brooklyn—she seeks out books that feature diverse, complex characters in deeply rooted relationships, platonic and romantic. A well-crafted romance will make her heart sing, while a beautifully detailed friendship will elevate any book to an instant favorite. She also gravitates towards inherently hopeful stories of self-discovery and reinvention at all ages, particularly those that center questions of gender and sexuality. She tries to bring magic to every moment of life, and loves books that do the same.

L432 Jennifer Mattson
Senior Agent
United States

jmatt@andreabrownlit.com

https://www.andreabrownlit.com/Team/Jennifer-Mattson
http://twitter.com/jannmatt
http://instagram.com/jennmattson
https://www.publishersmarketplace.com/members/JenMatt/
https://www.manuscriptwishlist.com/mswl-post/jennifer-mattson/
https://querymanager.com/query/JenniferMattson

Literary Agency: Andrea Brown Literary Agency, Inc.

CHILDREN'S > **Fiction** > *Middle Grade*

YOUNG ADULT > **Fiction** > *Novels*

Closed to approaches.

Represents authors, illustrators, and author-illustrators who bring a distinct point of view to their work, and who tell stories with multiple layers. In middle grade and YA both, her heart beats faster for stories that cascade from a mind-expanding premise. She also loves survival stories and losing herself in Dickensian sagas (WOLVES OF WILLOUGHBY CHASE!), and enjoys watching characters puzzle their way through problems. She has a special soft spot for middle grade about resilient kids sorting out the messiness of life.

L433 Shari Maurer
Literary Agent
United States

https://www.stringerlit.com
https://querymanager.com/query/1434
https://aalitagents.org/author/sharimaurer/

Literary Agency: The Stringer Literary Agency LLC (**L603**)
Professional Body: Association of American Literary Agents (AALA)

ADULT > **Nonfiction** > *Nonfiction Books*

Memoir; Narrative Nonfiction; Parenting; Popular Science

CHILDREN'S
Fiction
Middle Grade: Contemporary; Historical Fiction; Literary; Mystery
Picture Books: General

Nonfiction > *Middle Grade*

YOUNG ADULT
Fiction > *Novels*
Contemporary; Historical Fiction; Literary; Mystery

Nonfiction > *Nonfiction Books*

Send: Query; Synopsis; Writing sample; Pitch
How to send: Query Manager

L434 Jane Graham Maw
Literary Agent
United Kingdom

submissions@grahammawchristie.com

https://www.grahammawchristie.com/about

Literary Agency: Graham Maw Christie Literary Agency (**L271**)

Nonfiction > *Nonfiction Books*
General, and in particular: Activism; Memoir; Narrative Nonfiction; Psychology

Send: Outline; Author bio; Market info; Writing sample; Proposal; Pitch
How to send: Email

For general non-fiction she seeks out activists, psychologists, creatives, change-makers and thought-leaders. On the narrative/memoir side she is looking for beautifully crafted books that take the reader somewhere new – a time, a place, or an experience, while managing to be universally appealing. The topics her authors write about are often aligned to the changes readers are seeking post-pandemic.

L435 Juliana McBride
Literary Agent
United States

https://rfliterary.com/about/
https://querymanager.com/query/JulianaMcBride
https://twitter.com/julianaotabot
https://www.instagram.com/julianalovesbooks/
https://www.manuscriptwishlist.com/mswl-post/juliana-mcbride/

Literary Agency: Rebecca Friedman Literary Agency

ADULT > **Fiction** > *Novels*
Commercial; Literary

CHILDREN'S > **Fiction** > *Middle Grade*
Contemporary; Relationships; Speculative

YOUNG ADULT > **Fiction** > *Novels*

How to send: Submittable

Loves commercial and literary fiction, young adult novels, and middle grade novels; mostly grounded contemporary stories with a speculative element, and honest stories that explore relationships and make her laugh.

L436 McCormick Literary
Literary Agency
United States
Tel: +1 (212) 691-9726

queries@mccormicklit.com

http://mccormicklit.com

ADULT
  Fiction > *Novels*
    Commercial; Literary

  Nonfiction > *Nonfiction Books*
    Arts; Biography; Cookery; Cultural History; Memoir; Narrative Nonfiction; Politics

YOUNG ADULT > **Fiction** > *Novels*

Send: Query; Author bio; Writing sample
How to send: Email
How not to send: Email attachment

Send queries by email with short bio and ten sample pages, indicating in the subject line which agent you are querying (see website for individual agent interests). No attachments. Response only if interested.

Literary Agents: Bridget McCarthy; David McCormick; Edward Orloff; Pilar Queen

L437 Andy McNicol
Senior Agent
United States

https://www.aevitascreative.com
https://www.aevitascreative.com/agent/andy-mcnicol

Literary Agency: Aevitas

Nonfiction > *Nonfiction Books*

Closed to approaches.

Has represented New York Times bestselling books, including a #1 New York Times bestselling memoir and lifestyle brands.

L438 Rob McQuilkin
Literary Agent
United States

info@mmqlit.com

https://www.mmqlit.com/about/

Literary Agency: Massie & McQuilkin

Fiction > *Novels*

Nonfiction > *Nonfiction Books*
  Cultural Criticism; History; Memoir

Poetry > *Poetry Collections*

Send: Query; Author bio; Writing sample
How to send: Email

Specializes in fiction, memoir, history, cultural criticism, and poetry.

L439 Sara Megibow
Vice President; Senior Agent
United States

saraquery@ktliterary.com

Literary Agency: KT Literary (**L377**)

ADULT > **Fiction** > *Novels*
  Fantasy; Romance; Science Fiction

CHILDREN'S > **Fiction** > *Middle Grade*

YOUNG ADULT > **Fiction** > *Novels*

Send: Query
How to send: Email

Open to YA, MG, romance, and SFF. All queries will receive a response; general turn around time is about 3–6 weeks.

L440 Jane von Mehren
Literary Agent; Senior Partner
United States

https://aevitascreative.com/agents/

Literary Agency: Aevitas

Fiction > *Novels*
  Book Club Fiction; Historical Fiction; Literary

Nonfiction > *Nonfiction Books*
  Business; History; Memoir; Popular Culture; Science

Send: Query; Author bio; Market info; Writing sample
How to send: Online submission system

Interested in narratives in the areas of business, history, memoir, popular culture and science, books that help us live our best lives, literary, book club, and historical fiction.

Authors: Ruthie Ackerman; Alan Andres; Daniel Barbarisi; Jené Ray Barranco; Christine Melanie Benson; Janet Benton; Dan Bouk; Susan Bratton; Jared Brock; Anne Brusatte; Stephen Brusatte; Maggie Bullock; Nicole Centeno; Carrie Classon; Stacey Colino; Tyler Cowen; David Daley; Carey Davidson; Peter J. Dean; Maddy Dychtwald; Linda T. Elkins-Tanton; Carla Fernandez; Emily Jane Fox; Ramin Ganeshram; Bob Garfield; David Gilkey; Sabrina Greenlee; Daniel Gross; Mauro Guillén; Minrose Gwin; Heather Hirsch; Jessica Iannotta; Kendra James; Claire Jimenez; Jordan Kassalow; Eliza Kingsford; Linda Kay Klein; Erica Komisar; Alison Kosik; Jennifer Krause; Shannon Lee; Adam Valen Levinson; Pamela Lilly; Heather K. Lloyd; John Long; Andrea Marcum; Christopher Marquis; Ama Marston; Stephanie Marston; Leigh Marz; Kevin Morris; Paul Napper; Raul Palma; Richard Parker; Marilyn Paul; Dr. Deborah Plummer; Gene Pressman; Nathan Raab; Anthony Rao; Travis Rieder; Travis N. Rieder; Jodi Rogers; Francine Russo; Robin Ryan; Jonathan Santlofer; Tom Selleck; Molly D. Shepard; Robert Stone; Susan Stryker; Shanna Swan; Anne Bahr Thompson; Allie Ticktin; Michael Veltri; Wanda Wallace; Caroline Webb; Glen Weldon; Rob Wesson; Kelvin Wong; Clive D. Wynne; Justin Zorn

L441 Isabel Mendia
Associate Agent
United States

https://www.cheneyagency.com/isabel-mendia

Literary Agency: The Cheney Agency

Nonfiction > *Nonfiction Books*
  Climate Science; Cultural Criticism; History; Immigration; Narrative Journalism; Politics; Progressive Politics; Racism; Science

Send: Query; Self-Addressed Stamped Envelope (SASE)
How to send: Post; Email

Interested in representing a range of nonfiction, including cultural criticism, narrative reportage, science, and history. A native Spanish speaker, she is particularly interested in Latinx stories, and in writing that makes sense of first- and second-generation immigrant experiences. She is also attracted to projects that have a progressive political mission, and that are responding in some way to colonialism, capitalism, racism, and the climate crisis. She also loves pop culture, and projects that provide entertainment, humor, and hope.

L442 Meridian Artists
Literary Agency
43 Britain Street, Suite A02, Toronto, Ontario
M5A 1R7
Canada
Tel: +1 (416) 961-2777

info@meridianartists.com

https://www.meridianartists.com

Fiction > *Novels*

Nonfiction > *Nonfiction Books*

Scripts
  Film Scripts; *TV Scripts*

Send: Synopsis; Author bio; Writing sample
How to send: Online submission system

Offers premier full-service entertainment industry representation with principal offices in Toronto and Los Angeles. An established leader in the representation and management of Talent, Screenwriters, Directors, Authors, and Key Creatives.

L443 Annabel Merullo
Senior Agent
United Kingdom

amerullo@pfd.co.uk

https://petersfraserdunlop.com/agent/annabel-merullo/

Literary Agency: Peters Fraser + Dunlop

Fiction > *Novels*
  Commercial; Literary

Nonfiction > *Nonfiction Books*
  Commercial; Literary

Send: Query; Author bio; Synopsis; Writing sample; Proposal
How to send: Email

Represents literary and commercial writers of fiction and non-fiction. Only taking nonfiction submissions at this time.

Authors: Alba Arikha; Michael Banissy; Harry Benson; Patrick Bishop; James Blunt; Simon Booker; Jimmy Burns; Brian Cathcart; Monique Charlesworth; Richard Charlton; Paul Conroy; Adam Croft; Bob Cryer; Mark Dawson; Mike Dowling; Miriam Gonzalez Durantez; Patrick Flood; Adrian Fort; Jonathan Franklin

L444 Metamorphosis Literary Agency

Literary Agency
United States

info@metamorphosisliteraryagency.com

https://www.metamorphosisliteraryagency.com
https://www.facebook.com/metamorphosislitagent
https://twitter.com/MetamorphLitAg
https://www.linkedin.com/company/metamorphosis-literary-agency
https://www.instagram.com/metamorphosis_literary_agency/

ADULT
  Fiction > *Novels*
  Nonfiction > *Nonfiction Books*

YOUNG ADULT > **Fiction** > *Novels*

Send: Query; Author bio; Writing sample; Synopsis
How to send: Query Manager

Costs: Author covers sundry admin costs.

Our mission is to help authors become traditionally published. We represent well-crafted commercial fiction and nonfiction. We work with authors to ensure that every book is in the best presentable form. Our publishing connections come from experience, numerous conferences, hard work, and genuine care.

Assistant Agent: Des Salazar (**L559**)

Authors: Suleena Bibra; Kelly Cain; Natalie Cammaratta; Ashley M. Coleman; Stephanie Eding; Caroline Flynn; Charlee James; Karen Lynch; LaRonda Gardner Middlemiss; Janice Milusich; Anitra Rowe Schulte; Samara Shanker; Angela Shanté; Bruce Smith; Laura Snider; Heather Grace Stewart; Shannon Stults

Junior Agent: Caroline Trussell (**L635**)

Literary Agent: Shania N. Soler (**L589**)

Senior Agents: Amy Brewer (**L081**); Erica Christensen (**L125**); Stephanie Hansen (**L293**); Jessica Reino (**L534**); Katie Salvo (**L560**)

L445 Mic Cheetham Literary Agency

Literary Agency
62 Grafton Way, London, W1T 5DW
United Kingdom
Tel: +44 (0) 20 3976 7713

submissions@miccheetham.co.uk

https://miccheetham.com

Fiction > *Novels*

Nonfiction > *Nonfiction Books*

Send: Query; Outline; Writing sample; Author bio
How to send: Email

Agency with a deliberately small list. Only takes on two or three new writers each year. New writers are advised to acquaint themselves with the work of the writers currently represented by the agency before submitting their own work.

Authors: Carol Birch; Nm Browne; Pat Cadigan; Alan Campbell; Gregory Doran; Barbara Ewing; Ian Green; M John Harrison; Alice James; Ken MacLeod; Paul Mcauley; China Miéville; Sharon Penman; Antony Sher; Adrian Tchaikovsky

Literary Agents: Mic Cheetham (**L120**); Simon Kavanagh (**L356**)

L446 Caroline Michel

Literary Agent; Chief Executive Officer
United Kingdom
Tel: +44 (0) 20 7344 1000

cmichelsubmissions@pfd.co.uk

https://petersfraserdunlop.com/agent/caroline-michel/

Literary Agency: Peters Fraser + Dunlop

Fiction > *Novels*

Nonfiction > *Nonfiction Books*
  Biography; History; Science

Send: Query; Synopsis; Writing sample; Proposal; Author bio
How to send: Email
How not to send: Post

Loves everything and anything. She is endlessly curious about people's ideas, what's going on in the world and how to understand it, whether it's through history, fiction, biography, science. She is an eternal optimist and loves working with people who believe that everything is possible.

Authors: Ellen Alpsten; Jamie Bartlett; Camila Batmanghelidjh; Elaine Bedell; Lesley Blanch; Peter Bowles; Rosie Boycott; Pattie Boyd; Melvyn Bragg; Jonathan Bryan; Michael Caine; Emma Calder; Tamsin Calidas; Mark Carney; Augustus Casely-Hayford; Mavis Cheek; Helen Chislett; Rita Clifton; Sebastian Coe; Natalia Conroy; Chi-chi Nwanoku

L447 Leah Middleton

Literary Agent
United Kingdom

leah@marjacq.com

http://www.marjacq.com/leah-middleton.html

Literary Agency: Marjacq Scripts Ltd

Scripts
  Film Scripts; *TV Scripts*

Send: Full text; Synopsis; Author bio
How to send: Email

Open to submissions from screenwriters with at least one broadcast credit. Works with writers across genres and formats. Send one full screenplay written to format (feature or TV), a full synopsis (including spoilers!) and writing CV. No submissions from newer writers who haven't yet received their first credit.

L448 Natasha Mihell

Associate Agent
Canada

https://www.therightsfactory.com/Agents/Natasha-Mihell
https://querymanager.com/query/natasharf

Literary Agency: The Rights Factory

ADULT
  Fiction > *Novels*
    Fantasy; Horror; Science Fiction

  Nonfiction > *Nonfiction Books*
    Biography; Memoir

CHILDREN'S > **Fiction** > *Middle Grade*
  Fantasy; Horror; Science Fiction

YOUNG ADULT > **Fiction** > *Novels*
  Fantasy; Horror; Science Fiction

Closed to approaches.

Loves stories that sing, move, and shimmer, and most especially, those that are fearless in speaking their truths. She is a great fan of conceptual depth and courage and will consider any story that has clear heart and vision. She is always keen to support voices from the 2SLGBTQQIA+, BIPOC, #ownvoices, disabled and neurodiverse communities.

Authors: Sylvie Cathrall; Kodie Van Dusen; Joe Frye; C.C. Graystone; Taryn Herlich; R.J. Joseph; Carolina Munhóz; Jasmine Ng; Nicholas Pullen; Ana Toumine; Vani Varshney; Fatemeh Zarei

L449 Madeleine Milburn
Literary Agent; Company Director
United Kingdom

https://madeleinemilburn.co.uk/team-member/madeleine-milburn/
https://twitter.com/agentmilburn

Literary Agency: Madeleine Milburn Literary, TV & Film Agency (**L420**)

Fiction > *Novels*
General, and in particular: Book Club Fiction; Commercial; Crime; Family Saga; Historical Fiction; Literary; Romantic Mystery; Suspense; Thrillers; Upmarket

Send: Query; Pitch; Market info; Author bio; Synopsis; Writing sample
How to send: Email
How not to send: Post

Open to submissions from writers based in the UK and internationally, with strong ties in Canada and the US, and looking for upmarket and accessible literary fiction with a strong hook, compelling characters and propulsive storytelling. I'm looking to build on the crime and thriller side of my list with a big new suspense, and also looking for an epic multi-generational family drama, or a powerful love story with a mystery at its heart.

L450 Mildred Marmur Associates, Ltd.
Literary Agency
2005 Palmer Avenue, Suite 127, Larchmont, NY 10538
United States

https://aaronline.wildapricot.org/Sys/PublicProfile/2176773/417813

Fiction > *Novels*

Nonfiction > *Nonfiction Books*

Literary agent based in Larchmont, New York.

Literary Agent: Mildred Marmur (*L424*)

L451 Jessica Mileo
Literary Agent
United States

submissions@inkwellmanagement.com
https://inkwellmanagement.com/staff/jessica-mileo

Literary Agency: InkWell Management

ADULT
  Fiction > *Novels*
    Book Club Fiction; Commercial; High Concept; Romantic Comedy; Women's Fiction

  Nonfiction > *Nonfiction Books*
    Narrative Nonfiction; Prescriptive Nonfiction

CHILDREN'S > **Fiction**
  Graphic Novels; Novels

Send: Query; Writing sample
How to send: Email

Primarily focuses on children's books, children's graphic novels, women's fiction, rom-coms, commercial/book club fiction, and select prescriptive and narrative nonfiction. The projects she works with are high concept, commercial, and have a juicy hook. She is always looking for books that are from points of view of underrepresented folks in books and media, such as BIPOC and/or LGBTQIA+.

L452 Rachel Mills
Literary Agent; Company Director
United Kingdom

rachel@rmliterary.co.uk

https://twitter.com/bookishyogini

Literary Agency: Rachel Mills Literary (**L527**)

Nonfiction > *Nonfiction Books*
Biography; Commercial; Food; Narrative Nonfiction; Popular Science; Psychology; Upmarket; Wellbeing

Send: Query; Writing sample
How to send: Email

Very selectively looking for new clients writing commercial and upmarket non-fiction and wishing to develop their work into major global publishing and media brands. Areas of interest include psychology, popular science, well-being, narrative non-fiction, biography, food, sustainability, health, social media and platform led projects. She looks for projects which are international and will work on screen as well as in print.

L453 Grace Milusich
Associate Agent
United States

https://www.lookingglasslit.com
https://www.lookingglasslit.com/grace-milusich
https://querymanager.com/query/2859
https://twitter.com/gracemilusich
https://gracemilusich.weebly.com/

Literary Agency: Looking Glass Literary & Media Management (**L406**)

ADULT > **Fiction** > *Novels*
  Contemporary; Fantasy; Gothic; Mystery; Religion; Romantasy; Thrillers

YOUNG ADULT > **Fiction** > *Novels*
  Contemporary; Fantasy; Gothic; Mystery; Religion; Romantasy; Thrillers

Closed to approaches.

Interested in pursuing both YA and adult pieces (with a particular interest in pieces that narrow the gap between YA and adult). She is passionate about twisty fantasy, thrillers, and contemporary fiction featuring powerful/challenging themes. She would also like to see stories exploring religious trauma, unputdownable pacing, gothic or mysterious narratives, and complex characters. She is also a lover of the found family trope in all its forms. She is hoping to work on romantasy projects that feature BIPOC protagonists, and she is a sucker for morally grey or unlikeable characters too!

L454 Caroline Miranda
Literary Agent
United States

https://doncongdon.com/agents
https://querymanager.com/query/cmiranda
https://aalitagents.org/author/cmiranda/
https://twitter.com/rhymeswithline
https://www.linkedin.com/in/carolinemiranda/

Literary Agency: Don Congdon Associates, Inc. (**L175**)
Professional Body: Association of American Literary Agents (AALA)

ADULT
  Fiction
    Novels: Fantasy; Gothic; High Concept; Horror; Science Fiction; Speculative
    Short Fiction Collections: Speculative

  Nonfiction > *Nonfiction Books*
    History; Narrative Nonfiction; Science

CHILDREN'S > **Fiction** > *Middle Grade*
  Adventure; Coming of Age; Speculative

YOUNG ADULT > **Fiction** > *Novels*
  Adventure; Coming of Age; Speculative

Closed to approaches.

Represents diverse voices in speculative fiction, in both the children's and adult markets, as well as select nonfiction. In fiction, she is interested in representing gothic horror, science fiction, and fantasy. Within those genres, she particularly enjoys high-concept, plot-driven work with strong world-building, character development, and compelling emotional stakes. She is also seeking short stories in any speculative genre collected around a theme and with a strong sense of purpose. As for Middle Grade and Young Adult fiction, she gravitates to lovable casts of characters, coming-of-age stories, and adventure plots. In nonfiction, she is looking for engrossing narrative nonfiction with an intersectional perspective that guides readers through history or science in an approachable and deeply personal way.

L455 MMB Creative
Literary Agency
10 Bedford Square, London, WC1V 3RA
United Kingdom
Tel: +44 (0) 20 3582 9370
Fax: +44 (0) 20 3582 9377

nonfiction@mmbcreative.com
literaryfiction@mmbcreative.com
historicalfiction@mmbcreative.com
romance@mmbcreative.com

sciencefiction@mmbcreative.com
fantasy@mmbcreative.com
asiansubmissions@mmbcreative.com
horror@mmbcreative.com

https://mmbcreative.com

Professional Body: The Association of Authors' Agents (AAA)

Fiction > *Novels*
Allegory; Autofiction; Fabulism; Family Saga; Fantasy; Historical Fiction; Horror; Literary; Romance; Science Fiction

Nonfiction
Essays: General
Nonfiction Books: Art History; Autobiography; Economics; History; Literary Criticism; Personal Development; Politics; Psychology; Science; Self Help; Society

Send: Query; Synopsis; Author bio; Writing sample; Market info
How to send: Email

Represents actors, authors, stage and screen writers, presenters and voice over artists.

Literary Agents: Edwina de Charnace (**L117**); Ivan Mulcahy; Sallyanne Sweeney

L456 Jess Molloy
Literary Agent
United Kingdom
Tel: +44 (0) 20 7393 4281

jess.molloy@curtisbrown.co.uk

https://curtisbrown.co.uk
https://curtisbrown.co.uk/agent/jess-molloy

Literary Agency: Curtis Brown (**L146**)

Fiction > *Novels*
Crime; Fantasy; Ireland; Romance

Nonfiction > *Nonfiction Books*
Crime; Narrative Nonfiction; Psychology

I read broadly across fiction and narrative non-fiction. I am usually first pulled in by a unique concept or setting, but what keeps me reading are beautifully drawn, complex characters, relationships, and family dynamics. I enjoy reading fantasy and romance and I am particularly on the lookout for a story which has a slow burn at its heart, full of angst and drama. I have a deep love for Irish fiction both in terms of Irish writers, and novels set in Ireland. I enjoy crime fiction and true crime writing that subverts the genre and focuses on the victim or the fallout for their family. In terms of non-fiction, I enjoy issues led narrative writing with a personal story at its heart and particularly love hearing from underrepresented voices. I am also interested in psychology and therapy. My non-fiction reading varies broadly from comedians to experts and journalists, but what I am always looking for is an authentic voice that will teach me something fascinating or share a very personal journey with me.

Authors: Casey Jay Andrews; Sui Annukka; Fern Brady; Georgina Charles; Ken Cheng; Laura Coffey; Babak Ganjei; Rebecca Gibson; Daniel Howell; Greg Keen; Danny James King; Tatty Macleod; Gráinne Maguire; Tara O'Sullivan; Lucy Webster; Claire Whatley

L457 Mary C. Moore
Literary Agent
United States

https://www.aevitascreative.com/agent/mary-c-moore
https://querymanager.com/query/Mary_C_Moore

Literary Agency: Aevitas

Fiction > *Novels*
Book Club Fiction; Detective Fiction; Speculative; Upmarket

Closed to approaches.

Represents a wide range of fiction. She likes to work with clients long-term, and is comfortable representing multiple genres/age-ranges that an author is interested in, although prefers to begin a partnership in one genre before jumping to another. She is currently hoping to find layered and deeply satisfying upmarket fiction, bookclub fiction with light speculative elements, and smart female sleuth stories.

L458 Penny Moore
Literary Agent
United States

https://aevitascreative.com/agents/
https://querymanager.com/query/LiteraryPenny

Literary Agency: Aevitas

CHILDREN'S
Fiction
Middle Grade; *Picture Books*
Nonfiction > *Nonfiction Books*

YOUNG ADULT
Fiction > *Novels*
Nonfiction > *Nonfiction Books*

Send: Author bio; Query; Writing sample; Market info
How to send: Query Manager

Mainly represents children's literature, including picture books, middle grade, and young adult. She also has an interest in select platform nonfiction projects that speak to younger audiences. Though she's interested in all genres, she's specifically seeking inventive works featuring breakout voices and compelling plot lines that will make young readers feel seen and heard for the first time.

Authors: Shawn Amos; Akemi Dawn Bowman; Waka Brown; Auriane Desombre; Lyla Lee; Sophia Lee; Sangu Mandanna; Maya Prasad; Nicki Pau Preto; Rona Wang; Jenna Yoon; Katie Zhao

L459 Max Moorhead
Literary Agent
United States

max@mmqlit.com

http://www.mmqlit.com/about/

Literary Agency: Massie & McQuilkin

Fiction > *Novels*: Literary

Nonfiction > *Nonfiction Books*
Biography; Cultural History; Journalism; Memoir; Narrative Nonfiction; Politics

How to send: Email

Represents literary fiction and nonfiction in the areas of memoir, politics, journalism, cultural history, and biography. In fiction: he is drawn to beautiful writing, unforgettable characters, family stories, socially engaged writing, and compelling plots.

L460 Imogen Morrell
Literary Agent
United Kingdom

http://greeneheaton.co.uk/agents/imogen-morrell/
https://twitter.com/imogen_morrell

Literary Agency: Greene & Heaton Ltd (**L276**)

Fiction > *Novels*
Crime; Historical Fiction; Horror; LGBTQIA; Literary; Speculative; Thrillers; Upmarket

Nonfiction > *Nonfiction Books*
Arts; Culture; Environment; Food; History; Narrative Nonfiction; Nature; Politics

Send: Query; Synopsis; Writing sample
How to send: Word file email attachment

In non-fiction, I'm looking for proposals about history, culture, food, art, nature, the environment, politics, identity, usually with a strong narrative or personal element. In fiction, I'm looking for literary/upmarket fiction, historical fiction and fresh takes on genre writing (be it a thriller, horror, crime, or speculative novel). I love books that centre an edgy or surprising voice, are totally immersive or richly plotted, and socially or politically engaged. I'm always drawn to queer stories, set now and in the past, so please do send them my way.

Authors: Juliana Adelman; Sa'ad Azam; Robin Craig; Avery Curran; Rachel Dawson; Sharanya Deepak; Vittoria Fallanca; Gareth Gavin; Mara Gold; Evie Hatch; Kat Hill; Sarah Housley; Daisy J. Hung; Sam Johnson-Schlee; Fiona Keating; Kerry McInerney; Anna Parker; Eddie Scott; Joe Zadeh

L461 Natascha Morris
Senior Agent
United States

https://www.thetobiasagency.com/natascha-morris
https://querymanager.com/query/natascha

Literary Agency: The Tobias Literary Agency

CHILDREN'S > Fiction
 Graphic Novels; *Picture Books*
YOUNG ADULT > Fiction
 Graphic Novels; *Novels*

Closed to approaches.

Primarily looking for picture books, middle grade graphic novels and young adult across most genres, including graphic novels. She is also open to illustrator submissions.

L462 Michele Mortimer
Literary Agent
United States

submissions@dvagency.com
https://www.dvagency.com/aboutus

Literary Agency: Darhansoff & Verrill Literary Agents (**L156**)

ADULT
 Fiction > *Novels*
  Crime; Historical Fiction; Horror; Literary; Mystery; Romance; Thrillers; Upmarket Women's Fiction

 Nonfiction > *Nonfiction Books*
  Animals; Crime; Culture; Feminism; Memoir; Music; Narrative Nonfiction; Nature; Popular Culture; Sociology; Sport; Wellbeing
YOUNG ADULT > Fiction > *Novels*: Realistic

Send: Query; Writing sample
How to send: In the body of an email

Currently considers literary fiction; historical fiction; sophisticated genre (crime, mystery, thrillers, horror); upmarket character-rich women's fiction and smart romance; realism-based young adult fiction; memoirs, essays, and narrative nonfiction. Nonfiction interests include music, sports, wellness, the natural world, animal welfare, feminism, true crime, sociology, and culture both pop and serious.

L463 Tasneem Motala
Assistant Agent
Canada

https://www.therightsfactory.com/submissions
https://querymanager.com/query/2005

Literary Agency: The Rights Factory

ADULT > Fiction
 Graphic Novels; *Novels*; *Short Fiction Collections*

YOUNG ADULT > Fiction
 Graphic Novels; *Novels*; *Short Fiction Collections*

Closed to approaches.

I'm currently looking for character-driven young adult, adult, short story collections, and graphic novels written with a touch of magic. I'm also on the hunt for artists and illustrators who are interested in doing work for picture books, covers work, and graphic novels.

L464 Movable Type Management
Literary Agency
244 Madison Avenue, Suite 334, New York, NY 10016
United States
Tel: +1 (646) 431-6134

Submission@MovableTM.com

https://www.movabletm.com

Fiction > *Novels*: Commercial

Nonfiction > *Nonfiction Books*: Commercial

How to send: Email

Looking for authors of high quality commercial fiction and nonfiction with archetypal themes, stories, and characters, especially if they have strong film/TV potential. Response only if interested.

Literary Agent: Adam Chromy

L465 Jack Mozley
Literary Agent
United Kingdom

https://www.perezliterary.com/submit/submit-to-jack/

Literary Agency: Perez Literary & Entertainment (**L506**)

Fiction > *Novels*
 Alien Fiction; Alternative History; Dystopian Fiction; High Concept; Literary; Post-Apocalyptic; Science Fiction; Social Commentary; Speculative; Utopian Fiction

The son of a mining engineer and a poet, I naturally ended up with a doctorate in quantum physics and a love of Science Fiction, each using, as they do, a little of the extraordinary to understand the everyday.

SF's capacity to disrupt and subvert dominant perspectives is central to why I fell for it, and I encourage submissions from writers from underrepresented backgrounds.

What I look for above all else is the visceral impact of a story which leaves you changed. I first found this, in distilled form, in 2000AD Future Shocks, particularly those by Alan Moore, and I appreciate anything holding a Black Mirror up to our world, and to ourselves.

L466 Toby Mundy
Senior Agent; Vice President
United Kingdom

https://aevitascreative.com/agents/#agent-7413

Literary Agency: Aevitas Creative Management (ACM) UK (**L007**)

Fiction > *Novels*
 Literary; Thrillers

Nonfiction > *Nonfiction Books*
 Biography; Current Affairs; History; Memoir; Narrative Nonfiction; Popular Culture; Popular Science; Sport

Send: Query; Writing sample
How to send: Online submission system

Looking for gripping narrative nonfiction, and well written, mind-expanding works in the areas of history, biography, memoir, current affairs, sport, popular culture and popular science. Also represents a small number of thriller writers and literary novelists.

Authors: Tim Adams; James Aldred; James Ashton; Odafe Atogun; Philip Augar; Hannah Barnes; Rahul Bhatia; Chris Bickerton; Innes Bowen; Ruth Brandon; Marcus Bridgewater; Tobias Buck; Stephen Bush; Joshua Chaffin; James Crabtree; Graham Daseler; Jonathan Derbyshire; Michael Dine; John Dunn; Armand D'Angour; Iyad El-Baghdadi; Graham Farmelo; Eliza Filby; Danny Finkelstein; John Gapper; Michael Gibson; Julian Glover; David Goodhart; Samuel Graydon; Rachel Halliburton; Liam Halligan; Charles Handy; Andrew Hankinson; Jonathan Hillman; Katja Hoyer; Nicholas Humphrey; Gavin Jacobson; Tiffany Jenkins; Joanna Jolly; Andrew Keen; Ivan Krastev; Graham Lawton; Charles Leadbeater; Frances Leech; Mark Leonard; Ian Leslie; Oliver Letwin; John Lloyd; Isabel Losada; Andrew Lycett; Polly Mackenzie; Gary Madden; Mark Makepeace; Kenan Malik; Owen Matthews; Tom McTague; Anand Menon; Daniel Metcalfe; Chris Miller; Munira Mirza; Paul Morland; Geoff Mulgan; Clive Myrie; David Omand; Arkady Ostrovsky; Tomiwa Owolade; Nicolas Pelham; Leigh Phillips; Mary Poffenroth; Alice Rawsthorn; Assaad Razzouk; Richard Reeves; Tim Revell; Peter Ricketts; Jonathan Rowson; Donald Sassoon; Mark Sedgwick; Nigel Shadbolt; Oliver Shah; Raymond Tallis; Sudhir Thomas Vadaketh; Georgios Varouxakis; Jeevan Vasagar; James Vogl; James Waddell; Owen Walker; Dan Wang; Justin Webb; Frances Weetman; Geoffrey Wheatcroft; James Williams; Keely Winstone; Christian Wolmar; Jon Yates; Emma Young

L467 Karen Murgolo
Literary Agent
United States

https://www.aevitascreative.com/agent/karen-murgolo

https://querymanager.com/query/KarenMurgoloQueries

Literary Agency: Aevitas

Nonfiction > *Nonfiction Books*
Cookery; Health; Memoir; Narrative Nonfiction; Psychology; Science; Spirituality; Wellbeing

Send: Pitch; Author bio; Outline; Market info; Writing sample
How to send: Query Manager

Interested in authoritative health, wellness, science and psychology, spirituality, inspirational (or just really fun) memoirs; original cookbooks, and narratives that illuminate a compelling subject or start a conversation.

Authors: Allison M. Alford; Cathy Barrow; Whitney Casares; Judith Choate; Shannah Game; Chelsey Goodan; Jaime Knopman; Illyanna Maisonet; Lauretta Malloy; Bernadette Murphy; LeeAnet Noble; Brittany Piper; Mike Sapiro; Eric Tipler; Kevin Tracey; Cassandra Vieten; Brigid Washington; Stephanie Venn Watson; Veronica Webb

L468 Judith Murray
Literary Agent
United Kingdom

https://greeneheaton.co.uk
https://greeneheaton.co.uk/agents/judith-murray/

Literary Agency: Greene & Heaton Ltd (**L276**)

Fiction > *Novels*
Crime; Fantasy; Gothic; Historical Fiction; Horror; Literary; Romance; Romantasy; Romantic Comedy; Science Fiction; Thrillers

Nonfiction > *Nonfiction Books*
Biography; History; Literary; Memoir

Send: Query; Synopsis; Full text
How to send: Email

I love literary fiction and well-written genre fiction, including thrillers, crime, historical novels, gothic, clever horror (not too gory) science-fiction, fantasy, romantasy, rom-coms and epic love stories; and literary non-fiction including history, biography and memoir.

Authors: Poppy Adams; Mark Alder; Lucy Atkins; Raffaella Barker; Laura Barnett; Mark Barrowcliffe; Charlotte Bauer; Darcey Bell; Caroline Bond; Lynne Bryan; Elizabeth Buchan; Wren Burke; Helen Callaghan; Lucy Clarke; Emma Cook; Kate Davies; Lydia Davis; Sabine Durrant; Samantha Ellis; Helen Fisher; Susanna Forrest; Chandra Ganguly; Andrea Gillies; Paula Gosling; Victoria Gosling; Stella Grey; Joanna Hall; Maeve Haran; Belinda Harley; Phil Harrison; Julia Hollander; Anjali Joseph; Vedashree Khambete-Sharma; Esme King; Rebecca Dinerstein Knight; M.D. Lachlan; Reif Larsen; Jardine Libaire; Rebecca Mackenzie; Ruth Mancini; Ben Marcus; Ian McGuire; Laura McHugh; Ben McPherson; Kamin Mohammadi; Kate Morrison; Jenny Offill; Temi Oh; Sean O'Connor; Helen Paris; Miranda Popkey; Jonathan Ray; Maria Realf; Karen Russell; Indyana Schneider; Polly Stewart; Jacqueline Sutherland; Jacqueline Ward; Patricia Wastvedt; Sarah Waters; Benjamin Wood; Susie Yang; Anne Youngson

L469 Nate Muscato
Literary Agent
New York
United States

https://aevitascreative.com/agents/

Literary Agency: Aevitas

Fiction > *Novels*
Fantasy; Literary; Science Fiction

Nonfiction > *Nonfiction Books*
Arts; Education; Politics; Popular Culture; Sociology; Technology

Send: Author bio; Outline; Pitch; Market info; Writing sample
How to send: Online submission system

Drawn to nonfiction that illuminates the past and present—from arts and pop culture to education, politics, sociology, and technology—and envisions more just and equitable futures. He is also interested in select genre fiction with literary trappings, sci-fi/fantasy stories that leap into new worlds yet reveal something radical about our own.

Authors: Pamela Anderson; Carl Sferrazza Anthony; Samara Bay; Elizabeth Beller; Joshua Bennett; Charles Blow; Patricia Bosworth; Holly Brubach; Kevin Burke; Jim Carrey; Kimberlé Crenshaw; Hugh Eakin; Rhonda Garelick; Arline T. Geronimus; John Giorno; Karl Taro Greenfeld; Bob Greifeld; Michael Grynbaum; David Hallberg; Linda Hirshman; Sam Huber; Charlayne Hunter-Gault; Elise Jordan; Henry Louis Gates Jr.; Amy Larocca; Melissa Auf der Maur; Andrew McCarthy; Adam Moss; Mary Norris; Mark Oppenheimer; Holly Peterson; Gerald Posner; Peter Rader; James Reginato; Karin Roffman; James Romm; Mark Ronson; Thaddeus Russell; Alexandra Sacks; Elizabeth Samet; Michael Schulman; Erich Schwartzel; Elizabeth Shackelford; Colin Spoelman; Greg Steinmetz; Lili Taylor; Craig Unger; Dana Vachon; Darren Walker; Jesse Wegman; Genevieve West; Casey Wilson

L470 Juliet Mushens
Literary Agent
United Kingdom

submissions@mushens-entertainment.com

https://www.mushens-entertainment.com/juliet-mushens
https://twitter.com/mushenska

Literary Agency: Mushens Entertainment

Fiction > *Novels*
Book Club Fiction; Crime; Fantasy; Gothic; High Concept; Historical Fiction; Psychology; Science Fiction; Thrillers

Send: Query; Synopsis; Writing sample
How to send: Email

Looking for: crime, thriller, reading group fiction, gothic novels, historical fiction, and SFF. Do not send her: picture-books, MG, non-fiction, novellas, short stories/short story collections, screenplays, poetry collections or erotica. Please do not send her unfinished books. Unless she has specifically asked to see it, do not send her revised versions of earlier manuscripts she has rejected. Do not send her novels which her colleagues have rejected.

Associate Agent: Kiya Evans (**L205**)

Author / Literary Agent: Sarah Hornsley (**L321**)

Authors: Claire Alexander; Aliya Ali-Afzal; Luke Allnutt; Marie-Claire Amuah; Sussie Anie; Krystle Zara Appiah; Ross Armstrong; Stephen Aryan; Joanna Barnard; Jessica Bull; Jessie Burton; Mary Chamberlain; Katy Colins; Polly Crosby; Sarah Day; Abigail Dean; LM Dillsworth; Claire Douglas; Saara El-Arifi; Fiona Erskine; Maria Farrer; Robert Gold; Kate Gray; Jack Guinness; Francesca Haig; Stacey Halls; Lou Morgan / Maggie Harcourt; Elodie Harper; Sophie Haydock; Debbie Howells; Theresa Howes; Ali Imdad; Liz De Jager; Hannah Kaner; Katie Khan; L.R. Lam; Ali Land; Lia Louis; Katie Lowe; Chris MacDonald; Taran Matharu; Anna Mazzola; Amy McCulloch; Elvin James Mensah; Jo Monroe; Hester Musson; Peter Newman; Louise O'Neill; Richard Osman; James Oswald; Buki Papillon; Nell Pattison; Laura Purcell; Andrew Reid; Laure Van Rensburg; Jennifer Saint; Vanessa Savage; Boris Starling; Andrea Stewart; Susan Stokes-Chapman; Rob Temple; Liz Tipping; Rajasree Variyar; Sonia Velton; Gray Williams; Hattie Williams; Jen Williams; Nick Clark Windo; Tom Winter

L471 James Mustelier
Literary Agent
United States

http://www.thebentagency.com/james-mustelier
https://querymanager.com/query/1908

Literary Agency: The Bent Agency (**L058**)

ADULT

Fiction > *Novels*
Alternative History; Commercial; Dark Humour; Fantasy; Horror; Literary; Mystery; Science Fiction; Speculative

Nonfiction > *Nonfiction Books*
Commercial; Literary

CHILDREN'S > Fiction > *Middle Grade*
Fairy Tales; Folklore, Myths, and Legends; High / Epic Fantasy; Historical Fiction; Science Fiction

YOUNG ADULT > Fiction > *Novels*
Fairy Tales; Folklore, Myths, and Legends; High / Epic Fantasy; Historical Fiction; Science Fiction

Does not want:

Fiction > *Novels*
High / Epic Fantasy; Space Opera

Closed to approaches.

L472 Jen Nadol
Associate Agent
United States

Jen.Nadol@theunteragency.com

http://theunteragency.com

Literary Agency: The Unter Agency

Send: Pitch
How to send: Email

L473 Maria Napolitano
Literary Agent; Foreign Rights Manager
United States

maria@ktliterary.com

https://www.maria-regina.com
https://ktliterary.com/agents

Literary Agency: KT Literary (**L377**)

Fiction > *Novels*
Book Club Fiction; Commercial; High Concept; Romantic Comedy; Speculative; Thrillers; Upmarket

Represents a broad range of fiction, from commercial rom-coms to radical speculative fiction, subversive thrillers, and upmarket book club fiction. She is drawn to character-driven stories, unusual perspectives, genre-bending works, and supremely pitchable high concepts.

L474 Justin Nash
Literary Agent; Managing Director
United Kingdom

https://katenashlit.co.uk/people/
https://twitter.com/JustinNashLit

Literary Agency: Kate Nash Literary Agency (**L353**)

Fiction > *Novels*
Book Club Fiction; Crime; Fantasy; Folklore, Myths, and Legends; Historical Fiction; Science Fiction; Thrillers

Nonfiction > *Nonfiction Books*
General, and in particular: Classics / Ancient World; History; Medieval; Military; Travel

Looking for thrillers and crime fiction of all types; book club and historical fiction that moves me and makes me think (including novels featuring fantasy/mythology) and SF. In non-fiction, books which open up the conversation and take me on a journey.

L475 Abigail Nathan
Literary Agent
Sydney
Australia

https://alexadsett.com.au/literary-agency/
https://querymanager.com/query/AbigailNathanQueries

Literary Agency: Alex Adsett Literary (**L016**)

ADULT > Fiction > *Novels*
Commercial; Cozy Fantasy; Cozy Mysteries; Crime; Fantasy; Historical Romance; Mystery; Romance; Romantasy; Romantic Comedy; Romantic Mystery; Science Fiction; Thrillers

CHILDREN'S > Fiction > *Middle Grade*
YOUNG ADULT > Fiction > *Novels*

Closed to approaches.

Looking for engaging plots and convincing characters. Something that will keep her turning the pages and that will stay with her after she's finished reading. There are some rules and conventions it pays to follow, but something a bit weird or slightly (or very) unexpected will pique her interest, and characters that touch a nerve or worlds that make us question the status quo are always welcome. Above all, she's looking for great stories, told well – fiction in general and all things genre: sci-fi, fantasy, paranormal, horror, crime, thriller, romance (and any combination of those), for adult, YA or middle grade.

L476 Rachel Neely
Literary Agent
United Kingdom

submissions@mushens-entertainment.com

https://www.mushens-entertainment.com/rachel-neely

Literary Agency: Mushens Entertainment

Fiction > *Novels*
Book Club Fiction; Crime; Fantasy; Gothic; Historical Fiction; Romance; Romantic Comedy; Thrillers

Send: Query; Synopsis; Writing sample
How to send: Email

Looking for: dark academia, book club fiction, historical fiction, tragic love stories, rom-coms, fantasy, crime and thrillers. Would love to see: a commercial locked-room thriller, novels about cults, a voice-led serial-killer thriller, compelling dark academia, gothic historical fiction with a unique hook, a tragic love story, and anything that has an outsider trying to break into the world of the privileged and morally bankrupt.

Authors: Rhiannon Barnsley; Mimi Deb; Rachel Devine; Claire Frances; Sue Hincenbergs; Lora Jones; Carmella Lowkis; Elle Machray; Fiona McPhillips; Emily Slapper; Charlotte Wightwick

L477 Nelson Literary Agency, LLC
Literary Agency
1732 Wazee Street, Suite 207, Denver, CO 80202
United States
Tel: +1 (303) 292-2805

info@nelsonagency.com

https://nelsonagency.com

Professional Body: Association of American Literary Agents (AALA)

ADULT > Fiction > *Novels*

CHILDREN'S > Fiction
Middle Grade; *Picture Books*

YOUNG ADULT > Fiction > *Novels*

Send: Query; Author bio; Writing sample
How to send: Query Manager
How not to send: Post; Phone

View individual agent interests and submit to one agent only.

Authors: Brooke Abrams; Kate Baer; Gina Banks; L. Biehler; Jillian Boehme; Ali Brady; Lina Chern; Kristen Ciccarelli; Jessi Cole; Lisa Duffy; Doug Engstrom; Reese Eschmann; Shana Galen; John Galligan; Florence Gonsalves; Jill Grunenwald; Alison Hammer; Sarah Zachrich Jeng; Becca Jones; Chloe Jory; Ausma Zehanat Khan; Sierra Kincade; Karen Koh; Gillian Libby; Maryann Jacob Macias; Jonathan Messinger; Meghan Scott Molin; Katrina Monroe; Vanessa Montalban; Rosaria Munda; Jennifer Nissley; Lynette Noni; James Persichetti; Celesta Rimington; Laura Brooke Robson; Lyndsay Rush; Ehsaneh Sadr; Jeff Seymour; Kristen Simmons; Lisa Springer; Jennifer Springsteen; Stacy Stokes; Joy Sullivan; Chrysler Szarlan; Ben Tanzer; Jordyn Taylor; Kathleen West

Literary Agents: Joanna MacKenzie (**L416**); Kristin Nelson (**L478**)

L478 Kristin Nelson
Literary Agent
United States

https://nelsonagency.com/kristin-nelson/
https://twitter.com/agentkristinNLA
https://querymanager.com/query/1350

Literary Agency: Nelson Literary Agency, LLC (**L477**)
Professional Body: Association of American Literary Agents (AALA)

ADULT > Fiction > *Novels*
   Commercial; Fantasy; High Concept; Historical Fiction; Literary; Science Fiction; Speculative; Thrillers

YOUNG ADULT > Fiction > *Novels*

Closed to approaches.

My goal as an agent is simple: I want every client of mine to make a living solely from writing and 90% of my authors do without help from any other source of income.

L479 Mariah Nichols
Literary Agent
United States

https://www.mariahlovesliterary.com
https://www.d4eoliteraryagency.com/p/mariah-nichols.html
https://twitter.com/litagentmariah

Literary Agency: D4EO Literary Agency

ADULT
   Fiction > *Novels*
      Contemporary Romance; Psychological Thrillers; Romantic Comedy; Women's Fiction

   Nonfiction > *Nonfiction Books*
      Cookery; Diversity; How To; Lifestyle; Mental Health; Romance; Self Help

YOUNG ADULT > Fiction > *Novels*
   Contemporary Romance; Science Fiction; Supernatural / Paranormal Romance; Thrillers

Closed to approaches.

Interested in upmarket and commercial adult fiction focusing on women's fiction, psychological thrillers, and contemporary romance/rom-coms, along with representing young adult fiction with genres including science fiction, paranormal romance, thrillers, and contemporary romance. She is also wanting to represent nonfiction in categories such as cookbooks, memoirs, self-help, lifestyle, and how-to. Stories that showcase diversity and highlight mental health or special needs is something that she would especially like to see.

L480 Erin Niumata
Literary Agent; Senior Vice President
United States
Tel: +1 (212) 400-1494

erin@foliolit.com

https://www.foliolit.com/agents-1/erin-niumata
https://www.instagram.com/ecniumata/?hl=en
https://twitter.com/ecniumata?ref_src=twsrc%5Egoogle%7Ctwcamp%5Eserp%7Ctwgr%5Eauthor

Literary Agency: Folio Literary Management, LLC

Fiction > *Novels*
   Book Club Fiction; Commercial Women's Fiction; Commercial; Historical Fiction; Mystery; Romance; Romantic Comedy; Thrillers; Women's Fiction

Nonfiction > *Nonfiction Books*
   Commercial; Cookery; Memoir; Narrative Nonfiction; Prescriptive Nonfiction

Send: Query; Synopsis; Writing sample
How to send: In the body of an email

Looking for commercial nonfiction, from prescriptive and practical to narrative and memoir, as well as a select list of fiction including mysteries, rom-coms, and commercial women's fiction.

L481 Laura Nolan
Literary Agent; Senior Partner
United States

https://aevitascreative.com/agents/

Literary Agency: Aevitas
Professional Body: Association of American Literary Agents (AALA)

Nonfiction > *Nonfiction Books*
   Celebrity; Culture; Investigative Journalism; Medicine; Music; Performing Arts; Psychology; Sub-Culture

Send: Query; Writing sample
How to send: Online submission system

Represents investigative journalists, thought leaders, doctors, psychologists, musicians, and celebrities who inspire, entertain, educate and are striving to upend the culture. Seeks clients who are asking the "big" questions, exploring fascinating sub-cultures, and are paradigm-shifters in their fields, as well as performing artists who are successful in one medium but whose talents and passion translate into narrative.

Authors: Aaron Ayscough; Michael Azerrad; Sara Bareilles; Hunter Biden; Jill Blakeway; Kenneth Bock; Mariann Edgar Budde; Gesine Bullock-Prado; David Burtka; Scott Carney; Ratha Chaupoly; Charles R. Cross; Ben Daitz; Zayd Ayers Dohrn; Dagmara Dominczyk; Madeleine Dore; Charlotte Druckman; Aria Finger; John Fogerty; Ben Folds; Holly George-Warren; Rhiannon Giddens; Danny Goldberg; Andrea Gutiérrez-Glik; Neil Patrick Harris; Josiah Hesse; Bonnie J. Kaplan; Angela Jia Kim; Laura Krantz; Carson Kressley; Leah Lagos; Christine Lahti; Jennifer Lapidus; Alan Light; Anita Lo; Danica McKellar; Sara C. Mednick; Allison Moorer; Mandy Morris; Meagan B Murphy; Einat Nathan; Sabina Nawaz; Oliver Niño; David Peisner; Wendell Pierce; Matt Pinfield; Nicole Ponseca; Elizabeth Poynor; Eric Prum; National Public Radio; Julia J. Rucklidge; Anneli Rufus; Erika Schickel; Joseph Shuldiner; Rachel Signer; Julie Smolyansky; Charisma Sydnor; Gayla Trail; Miguel Trinidad; Nia Vardalos; Lynx Vilden; Martha Wainwright; Tionne Watkins; Elettra Wiedemann; Josh Williams; Vern Yip; Kristal Zook; Alan Zweibel

L482 Northbank Talent Management
Literary Agency
United Kingdom
Tel: +44 (0) 20 3973 0836

info@northbanktalent.com
fiction@northbanktalent.com
nonfiction@northbanktalent.com
childrens@northbanktalent.com

https://www.northbanktalent.com
https://twitter.com/NorthbankTalent
https://www.facebook.com/northbanktalent/
https://www.instagram.com/northbanktalent
https://www.linkedin.com/company/northbank-talent-management/
https://www.youtube.com/channel/UCKEAHOg6Y2G3NOy146k9y4A?view_as=subscriber

Professional Body: The Association of Authors' Agents (AAA)

ADULT
   Fiction > *Novels*
   Nonfiction > *Nonfiction Books*

YOUNG ADULT > Fiction > *Novels*

Send: Query; Synopsis; Writing sample
How to send: Email

Literary and talent agency based in central London. Actively seeking new clients. Send query by email with synopsis and first three chapters as Word or Open Document attachments to appropriate email address.

L483 Renee Nyen
Literary Agent
United States

Literary Agency: KT Literary (**L377**)

Closed to approaches.

L484 Lee O'Brien
Literary Agent
United States

leesubmissions@lookingglasslit.com

https://www.lookingglasslit.com/lee-obrien
https://twitter.com/leepaigeobrien
https://www.leepaigeobrien.com/

Literary Agency: Looking Glass Literary & Media Management (**L406**)

ADULT > Fiction > *Novels*
   Commercial; Fantasy; High Concept; LGBTQIA; Romantic Comedy; Thrillers

CHILDREN'S > Fiction > *Novels*
   Commercial; Fantasy; High Concept; LGBTQIA; Romantic Comedy; Thrillers

YOUNG ADULT > Fiction > *Novels*
   Commercial; Fantasy; High Concept; LGBTQIA; Romantic Comedy; Thrillers

Send: Query; Writing sample
How to send: Email

Focuses on MG, YA, and Adult, and he's interested in a range of genres, from fantasy to thrillers to romcoms. Within the genres he represents, he's especially looking for stories with a strong commercial hook or a compelling high-concept, and he loves anything full of twists and turns, an unforgettable cast of characters, or a mystery he can't put down. He's actively seeking diverse books and marginalized voices, and has a particular love for anything queer.

L485 Faith O'Grady
Literary Agent
108 Upper Leeson Street, Dublin 4
Ireland
Tel: + 353 1 637 5000
Fax: + 353 1 667 1256

info@lisarichards.ie

http://lisarichards.ie/writers#.YAgtljlxdaS

Literary Agency: The Lisa Richards Agency

ADULT
  Fiction > *Novels*

  Nonfiction > *Nonfiction Books*
    Biography; Comedy / Humour; History; Lifestyle; Memoir; Motorsports; Narrative Nonfiction; Popular Culture; Self Help

CHILDREN'S > Fiction
  Chapter Books; Middle Grade

Does not want:

> **ADULT**
>   Fiction > *Novels*
>   Horror; Science Fiction
>   **Scripts**
>   *Film Scripts; TV Scripts*
>   **CHILDREN'S > Fiction** > *Picture Books*

Send: Query; Writing sample; Self-Addressed Stamped Envelope (SASE); Proposal
How to send: Email

If sending fiction, please limit your submission to the first three or four chapters. If sending non-fiction, please send a detailed proposal about your book, a sample chapter and a cover letter. Every effort will be made to respond to submissions within 3 months of receipt.

L486 Niamh O'Grady
Literary Agent
United Kingdom

https://www.thesohoagency.co.uk/agent/niamh-ogrady

Literary Agency: The Soho Agency

Fiction > *Novels*
  Book Club Fiction; Comedy / Humour; Family; Literary; Relationships

Nonfiction > *Nonfiction Books*
  Comedy / Humour; Narrative Nonfiction

Send: Query; Synopsis; Writing sample
How to send: Email attachment

Actively looking for accessible literary and reading-group fiction, and narrative non-fiction. She is drawn to books with heart and humour, thought-provoking writing and distinctive, compelling voices. She particularly loves novels that explore family and relationships and wants to read stories that leave an emotional impact, with characters that stay with her long after the final page. She is keen to find new Irish and Northern writing talent.

L487 Molly O'Neill
Literary Agent
United States

submissions@rootliterary.com

https://www.rootliterary.com/agents
https://querymanager.com/query/mollyoneillbooks
https://www.publishersmarketplace.com/members/mollyoneillagent/
https://twitter.com/molly_oneill

Literary Agency: Root Literary (**L547**)

ADULT > Nonfiction > *Nonfiction Books*
  Creativity; Culture; Family; Friends; Narrative Nonfiction

CHILDREN'S > Fiction > *Middle Grade*
  General, and in particular: Comedy / Humour; Fabulism; Magical Realism

YOUNG ADULT > Fiction > *Novels*

How to send: Query Manager; Email

If I can visualize exactly how to form a web of connections around a book and its creator while I'm reading an early draft, then it's a fantastic signal that I also know how to help that author or artist build their way into a meaningful, and potentially lucrative, career.

L488 Amy O'Shea
Junior Agent
United Kingdom

submissions@grahammawchristie.com

https://www.grahammawchristie.com
https://www.grahammawchristie.com/about

Literary Agency: Graham Maw Christie Literary Agency (**L271**)

Nonfiction > *Nonfiction Books*
  Comedy / Humour; Crime; History; Lifestyle; Memoir; Prescriptive Nonfiction

Interested in a wide variety of non-fiction from prescriptions for thinking and living better by experts in their field, to humour, history, true crime and memoir whereby the author immerses the reader in a lived experience. In an ever-changing landscape, she is looking for books that bring fresh, practical and accessible solutions to their audience – anything that can teach us more about who we are and the world we share.

L489 Kristin van Ogtrop
Literary Agent
United States

https://inkwellmanagement.com/staff/kristin-van-ogtrop

Literary Agency: InkWell Management

Fiction > *Novels*: Literary

Nonfiction
  Illustrated Books: General
  Nonfiction Books: Lifestyle; Memoir; Prescriptive Nonfiction

Represents lifestyle, illustrated books, prescriptive nonfiction, literary fiction and memoir.

L490 Olswanger Literary LLC
Literary Agency
United States

https://www.olswanger.com

Literary Agent: Anna Olswanger (**L491**)

L491 Anna Olswanger
Literary Agent
United States

anna@olswangerliterary.com

https://www.olswanger.com
https://aalitagents.org/author/olswanger/
https://twitter.com/annaolswanger
https://www.facebook.com/AnnaOlswanger
https://www.instagram.com/annaolswanger
https://www.pinterest.com/olswanger/anna-olswanger-literary-agent/
https://www.linkedin.com/in/olswanger

Literary Agency: Olswanger Literary LLC (**L490**)
Professional Body: Association of American Literary Agents (AALA)

CHILDREN'S > Fiction
  Graphic Novels; Picture Books

How to send: Email

Has been an agent since 2005. Represents a wide variety of genres but is currently focused on illustrated books (picture books and graphic novels).

L492 Originate Literary Agency
Literary Agency
United Kingdom

https://twitter.com/OriginateLit
https://linktr.ee/nataliejerome

Professional Body: The Association of Authors' Agents (AAA)

L493 Mark Orsini
Literary Agent; Partner
United States

Literary Agency: Bret Adams Ltd

L494 Kristin Ostby
Literary Agent
United States

https://www.greenhouseliterary.com/the-team/kristin-ostby/
https://querymanager.com/query/kristinostby

Literary Agency: The Greenhouse Literary Agency

ADULT > **Fiction** > *Novels*
 Mystery; Upmarket

CHILDREN'S
 Fiction
  Chapter Books: Comedy / Humour
  Middle Grade: Adventure; Comedy / Humour; Contemporary; Cozy Mysteries; Friends; Historical Fiction; Light Fantasy; Mystery; Supernatural / Paranormal; Thrillers
 Poetry > *Novels in Verse*

YOUNG ADULT > **Fiction** > *Novels*
 Comedy / Humour; Contemporary; Cozy Mysteries; Friends; Historical Fiction; Historical Romance; Light Fantasy; Mystery; Romance; Speculative Romance; Supernatural / Paranormal; Thrillers

Closed to approaches.

Represents authors of middle grade and young adult fiction, as well as picture book author/illustrators. She is primarily seeking voice- and character-driven contemporary middle-grade and young adult fiction, with a focus on BIPOC creators. Not currently accepting picture book manuscripts, graphic novel scripts, issue books, or nonfiction. No manuscripts over 95,000 words.

L495 Bruce Ostler
Literary Agent; Partner
United States

Literary Agency: Bret Adams Ltd

L496 Saribel Pages
Literary Agent
United States

saribel@galltzacker.com

https://www.galltzacker.com
https://www.galltzacker.com/submissions.html
https://querymanager.com/query/2945
https://www.manuscriptwishlist.com/mswl-post/saribel-pages/

Literary Agency: Gallt & Zacker Literary Agency

CHILDREN'S > **Fiction**
 Graphic Novels: Adventure; Contemporary; Fantasy; Horror; Mystery; Speculative
 Picture Books: General

Closed to approaches.

Only seeking to represent picture books and graphic novels. Interested in contemporary, adventure, fantasy, speculative, horror, and mysteries. Accepts queries from the 1st to 7th of each month.

L497 Ayesha Pande
Literary Agent
United States

https://www.pandeliterary.com/about-pandeliterary
https://twitter.com/agent_ayesha
http://aaronline.org/Sys/PublicProfile/2455085/417813

Literary Agency: Ayesha Pande Literary (L036)
Professional Bodies: Association of American Literary Agents (AALA); The Agents Round Table (ART)

ADULT
 Fiction > *Novels*: Literary
 Nonfiction > *Nonfiction Books*
  Biography; Cultural Commentary; History; Memoir; Narrative Nonfiction

YOUNG ADULT > **Fiction** > *Novels*

Closed to approaches.

While her interests are wide-ranging and eclectic, she works mostly with literary fiction, narrative nonfiction across a broad range of topics including history and cultural commentary, memoir and biography, and the occasional work of young adult fiction. She is drawn to distinctive voices with a compelling point of view and memorable characters.

L498 Paradigm Talent and Literary Agency
Literary Agency
810 Seventh Avenue, Suite 205, New York, NY 10019
United States
Tel: +1 (212) 897-6400
Fax: +1 (310) 288-2000

books@paradigmagency.com

https://www.paradigmagency.com

Fiction > *Novels*

Nonfiction > *Nonfiction Books*

Scripts
 Film Scripts; *TV Scripts*; *Theatre Scripts*

Send: Query; Writing sample
How to send: In the body of an email

Talent and literary agency with offices in Los Angeles, New York, and London. Represents books in all areas and genres, as well as scriptwriters for film, TV, and theatre.

L499 Elana Roth Parker
Literary Agent
United States

http://www.ldlainc.com/submissions/
http://www.manuscriptwishlist.com/mswl-post/elana-roth-parker/
https://querymanager.com/query/queryelana
http://aaronline.org/Sys/PublicProfile/43775067/417813

Literary Agency: Laura Dail Literary Agency
Professional Body: Association of American Literary Agents (AALA)

ADULT > **Fiction** > *Novels*
 Commercial; Contemporary; Mystery; Romance; Romantic Comedy; Thrillers; Upmarket Women's Fiction

CHILDREN'S > **Fiction** > *Middle Grade*
 Adventure; Comedy / Humour; High / Epic Fantasy; High Concept

YOUNG ADULT > **Fiction** > *Novels*
 Adventure; Comedy / Humour; Commercial; High Concept; Romance

Closed to approaches.

Handles middle grade and young adult fiction. Closed to picture book submissions.

L500 Marina de Pass
Literary Agent
United Kingdom

https://www.thesohoagency.co.uk/agent/marina-de-pass
https://twitter.com/marinadepass

Literary Agency: The Soho Agency

ADULT
 Fiction > *Novels*
  General, and in particular: Animals; Book Club Fiction; Commercial; Contemporary; Crime; Dark Academia; Dogs; Family Saga; Folklore, Myths, and Legends; Historical Fiction; Literary; Police Procedural; Speculative; Spy Thrillers; Thrillers; Upmarket; Vikings Fiction

 Nonfiction > *Nonfiction Books*: Narrative Nonfiction

YOUNG ADULT > **Fiction** > *Novels*
 Mystery; Thrillers

Does not want:

> **ADULT** > **Fiction** > *Novels*: Science Fiction
>
> **YOUNG ADULT** > **Fiction** > *Novels*: Science Fiction

Send: Query; Synopsis; Writing sample
How to send: Email attachment

Looking for big stories, compelling writing and unforgettable characters. She reads across all genres in adult and YA fiction, except for straight sci-fi, and gravitates towards stories told through a female lens.

L501 Emma Patterson
Literary Agent
United States

epatterson@bromasite.com

Literary Agency: Brandt & Hochman Literary Agents, Inc.
Professional Body: Association of American Literary Agents (AALA)

Fiction > *Novels*
  Historical Fiction; Literary; Upmarket

Nonfiction > *Nonfiction Books*
  Investigative Journalism; Memoir; Narrative Nonfiction; Popular History

Send: Query
How to send: Email

Represents fiction ranging from dark, literary novels to historical and upmarket fiction; narrative non-fiction that includes memoir, investigative journalism, and popular history; and select children's projects. She is looking for fresh, lyrical, and voice-driven writing, suspenseful plots, emotional narratives, transporting settings, and unforgettable characters. Books that grapple with the dynamics of relationships (of all kinds, but especially from a female perspective), have a grounded speculative bent, or explore the current cultural landscape are all of perennial interest. Query by email only.

L502 Paul S. Levine Literary Agency
Literary Agency
1054 Superba Avenue, Venice, CA 90291-3940
United States
Tel: +1 (310) 450-6711
Fax: +1 (310) 450-0181

paul@paulslevinelit.com

https://paulslevinelit.com

ADULT
Fiction
  Graphic Novels: General
  Novels: Adventure; Legal; Mainstream; Mystery; Politics; Romance; Thrillers; Women's Fiction
Nonfiction > *Nonfiction Books*
  Business; Contemporary; How To; Legal; Mind, Body, Spirit; Politics; Popular Culture; Relationships; Self Help; Sport

CHILDREN'S
Fiction
  Graphic Novels; *Novels*
Nonfiction > *Nonfiction Books*

YOUNG ADULT
Fiction
  Graphic Novels; *Novels*
Nonfiction > *Nonfiction Books*

Send: Query
How to send: Email; Post
How not to send: Phone

Send query by email, or by post with SASE. No phone calls.

Literary Agents: Loren R. Grossman (**L280**); Paul S. Levine (**L395**)

L503 Kay Peddle
Literary Agent
United Kingdom

Kay@colwillandpeddle.com
submissions@colwillandpeddle.com

https://www.colwillandpeddle.com/about

Literary Agency: Colwill & Peddle (**L131**)

Nonfiction > *Nonfiction Books*
  Cookery; Current Affairs; Food; History; Journalism; Literary Memoir; Narrative Nonfiction; Nature; Politics; Popular Science; Social Justice; Travel

Send: Query; Proposal; Author bio; Market info; Writing sample; Outline; Pitch
How to send: Word file email attachment

Looking for books that spark discussion, that have the potential to change opinions and reveal hidden aspects of a familiar story. Interested in narrative nonfiction; literary memoir; cookery and food writing; travel writing; nature writing; journalism with a social justice angle; politics; current affairs; history and popular science.

L504 Imogen Pelham
Literary Agent
United Kingdom

imogen@marjacq.com

https://www.marjacq.com
https://www.marjacq.com/imogen-pelham.html

Literary Agency: Marjacq Scripts Ltd

Fiction > *Novels*
  Literary Thrillers; Literary; Upmarket; Women's Fiction

Nonfiction > *Nonfiction Books*
  General, and in particular: Arts; Cookery; Cultural Criticism; History; Investigative Journalism; Memoir; Psychology; Science; Social Issues

How to send: Email

Represents non-fiction which looks at serious subjects in innovative ways, and literary and upmarket fiction. In non-fiction, her list covers history, science, memoir, cookery, cultural criticism, social issues, and psychology. She is particularly interested in identity, the arts, and investigative journalism. She is drawn to books which have interesting takes on the everyday, which shine a light on an unexplored aspect of history or ourselves, and which encourage us to think more deeply about our place in the world. In fiction, she is looking for outstanding writing which shines a light on humanity, an unforgettable cast of characters, literary thrillers, and smart women's fiction.

Authors: Antonia Bolingbroke-Kent; Gabriella Braun; Kassia St Clair; Marie Le Conte; Hattie Crisell; Jimi Famurewa; Yara Rodrigues Fowler; Harry Gallon; Annie Garthwaite; Olivia Glazebrook; Sally Howard; Jo Jakeman; Brydie Lee-Kennedy; Emily Mayhew; Chris McQueer; Marianne Moore; Alya Mooro; Laura Mucha; Sam Parker; Emily Phillips; Angela Readman; Carl Shuker; Max Sydney Smith; Philippa Snow; David Whelan; Kylie Whitehead

L505 Kim Perel
Literary Agent
United States

https://www.highlineliterary.com/agent-kim

Literary Agency: High Line Literary Collective (**L312**)

Closed to approaches.

L506 Perez Literary & Entertainment
Literary Agency
49 Greek Street, London, W1D 4EG
United Kingdom
Tel: +44 (0) 20 7193 4792

assist@perezliterary

https://www.perezliterary.com
http://querymanager.com/KristinaPerez
https://www.instagram.com/perezliterary/
https://twitter.com/perez_literary
https://www.linkedin.com/company/perezliterary/
https://www.facebook.com/perezliterary

Professional Body: The Association of Authors' Agents (AAA)

ADULT
Fiction > *Novels*
  Book Club Fiction; Commercial; Crime; Thrillers; Upmarket

Nonfiction > *Nonfiction Books*
  Biography; Cultural History; Current Affairs; Feminism; Popular Science

YOUNG ADULT > **Fiction** > *Novels*
  Fantasy; Romance

Send: Query; Writing sample
How to send: Query Manager
How not to send: Email

A full-service agency dedicated to storytelling in all of its forms. We believe in the power of words to open minds and change lives. In today's fast moving marketplace, we are on the constant lookout for opportunities in both traditional and non-traditional media. We are committed to empowering our clients and helping them to formulate the best strategies to achieve their storytelling goals.

Associate Agent: Nina Leon (**L394**)

Authors: Alexia Casale; Shauna Clinning; Sharon Emmerichs; Marina Evans; Jennifer Wolf Kam; Erin Rose Kim; S. K. Meekings; Kim Mykura; Troy Tassier; Vincent Tirado; Amy Trueblood; Khadijah VanBrakle; Johanna van Veen; Stephen Vines; Cristin Williams; Josh Winning; Kelly deVos

Junior Agent: Isabel Lineberry (**L402**)

Literary Agent: Jack Mozley (**L465**)

Literary Agent / Managing Director: Kristina Perez (**L507**)

L507 Kristina Perez
Literary Agent; Managing Director
United Kingdom

https://www.perezliterary.com/about-us/the-team/
http://querymanager.com/KristinaPerez
https://twitter.com/kperezagent

Literary Agency: Perez Literary & Entertainment (**L506**)

ADULT
Fiction > *Novels*
Book Club Fiction; Commercial; Crime; Thrillers; Upmarket

Nonfiction > *Nonfiction Books*
Biography; Cultural History; Current Affairs; Feminism; Popular Science

YOUNG ADULT > Fiction > *Novels*
Fantasy; Romance

Send: Query; Writing sample
How to send: Query Manager

Being both an agent and an author allows her to fully guide her clients through every step of the publishing process. She loves launching debut authors' careers as well as working with mid-career authors looking for new challenges. She sees each client relationship as a true partnership in which they develop the right strategy for a client's career together. Author care is paramount and she prides herself on using her multifaceted understanding of the industry to help her clients achieve their goals. She is eager to work with writers from around the globe.

Authors: Alexia Casale; Shauna Clinning; Sharon Emmerichs; Marina Evans; Jennifer Wolf Kam; Erin Rose Kim; S. K. Meekings; Kim Mykura; Martin Purbrick; Troy Tassier; Vincent Tirado; Amy Trueblood; Amy True / Amy Trueblood; Khadija L. VanBrakle; Khadijah VanBrakle; Johanna van Veen; Stephen Vines; Cristin Williams; Josh Winning; Kelly deVos

L508 Martha Perotto-Wills
Associate Agent
United Kingdom

http://www.thebentagency.com/martha-perotto-wills
https://twitter.com/martha_again

Literary Agency: The Bent Agency (UK) (**L057**)

ADULT
Fiction > *Novels*
Fantasy; Horror; Literary; Science Fiction

Nonfiction > *Nonfiction Books*

YOUNG ADULT > Fiction > *Novels*

Closed to approaches.

Representing authors of adult literary fiction and sci-fi/fantasy/horror, as well as select adult non-fiction and young adult fiction. Particularly enjoys authorial confidence; unexpected, singular narrative voices; good, stylish sentences; humour/wit; knotty interpersonal relationships; and transportive writing that immerse the reader in a fully-formed world, whether fantastical, geographical, or emotional.

L509 Perry Literary
Literary Agency
United States

jperry@perryliterary.com
https://www.perryliterary.com

Nonfiction > *Nonfiction Books*
Business; Cookery; Crime; Journalism; Memoir; Narrative Nonfiction; Parenting; Popular Culture; Psychology; Science; Self Help; Sociology; Sport; Technology

Send: Query; Writing sample
How to send: In the body of an email

Send query by email with first ten pages in the body of the email (or full manuscript for picture books). No attachments. See website for full guidelines.

Literary Agent: Joseph Perry

L510 Jas Perry
Literary Agent

Literary Agency: KT Literary (**L377**)

Closed to approaches.

L511 Carrie Pestritto
Literary Agent
United States

http://www.ldlainc.com/about
http://aaronline.org/Sys/PublicProfile/53765008/417813
http://twitter.com/literarycarrie
https://literarycarrie.wixsite.com/blog
http://www.manuscriptwishlist.com/mswl-post/carrie-pestritto/

Literary Agency: Laura Dail Literary Agency
Professional Body: Association of American Literary Agents (AALA)

ADULT
Fiction > *Novels*
Chick Lit; Commercial; Cozy Mysteries; Historical Fiction; Literary; Mystery; Romance; Thrillers; Upmarket Women's Fiction

Nonfiction > *Nonfiction Books*
Biography; Memoir; Narrative Nonfiction

CHILDREN'S > Fiction > *Middle Grade*
Commercial; High Concept

YOUNG ADULT > Fiction > *Novels*
Contemporary; Fantasy; Historical Fiction; Horror; Mystery; Thrillers

Closed to approaches.

Loves the thrill of finding new authors with strong, unique voices and working closely with her clients. Always strives to help create books that will introduce readers to new worlds and is drawn in by relatable characters, meticulous world-building, and unusual, compelling premises.

L512 Rachel Petty
Literary Agent
United Kingdom

rachelsubmissions@theblairpartnership.com
https://www.theblairpartnership.com/literary-agents/rachel-petty/
https://twitter.com/Rachel_petty_

Literary Agency: The Blair Partnership

CHILDREN'S
Fiction
Chapter Books; *Early Readers*; *Middle Grade*; *Picture Books*
Nonfiction > *Nonfiction Books*

YOUNG ADULT
Fiction > *Novels*
Contemporary Romance; Diverse Romance; Fantasy; High Concept; Horror; Romance; Speculative; Thrillers

Nonfiction > *Nonfiction Books*

How to send: Email

Represents children's fiction and non-fiction, from picture books up to YA and crossover. Looking for ambitious storytelling, a bold approach to structure and voice and a fresh take on genre, and particularly interested in submissions from author/illustrators and people from underrepresented and marginalised communities. Looking for ROMANCE as the primary focus in anything YA – and would really like high concept, diverse contemporary YA romance of the sort that will launch a thousand ships. Likes horror and thrillers (or a combination of both, especially with a twist), hooky YA fantasy/speculative (but only with excellent world building with a simple, clever pitch), hilarious middle grade, bold graphic picture books, and anything that has the potential to jump off the page and onto the screen.

Authors: Jodie Abrahams; Nicola Adams; Sita Brahmachari; Steve Brown; Sue H Cunningham; Seán Farrelly; Hazel Gardner; Kareen Griffiths; Isaac Hamilton-McKenzie; Ramsey Hassan; Josh Hicks; Megan Hopkins; Bea Ingalls; Hardeep Kaur; Zoya Kooper; Lee Lennox; Rose Lihou; Lulee Ma; Margaret McDonald; Penelope O'Neill; Stuart Pallant; Delphine Seddon; Alexander Slater; Kari Trogen; Tom Woods

L513 Rubin Pfeffer
Literary Agent
United States

Literary Agencies: Rubin Pfeffer Content, LLC (**L552**); Aevitas

Authors: Micha Archer; Elana K. Arnold; Patricia MacLachlan; Kara Storti; Ellen Surrey; Ellen Tarlow; Jing Jing Tsong; Eric Velasquez; Jesse Joshua Watson; Richard Jesse Watson; Carole Boston Weatherford; Jeffery Boston Weatherford; Annie Won; Brian Won; Helen Yoon

L514 Beth Phelan
Literary Agent
United States

bethqueries@galltzacker.com
beth@galltzacker.com

https://www.galltzacker.com/submissions.html
https://querymanager.com/query/querybeth

Literary Agency: Gallt & Zacker Literary Agency

CHILDREN'S
Fiction > *Middle Grade*
 Contemporary; Fantasy

Nonfiction > *Middle Grade*

YOUNG ADULT
Fiction > *Novels*
 Contemporary; Fantasy

Nonfiction > *Nonfiction Books*

Closed to approaches.

Gravitates toward stories and characters that inspire, and anything with a touch of humor and the bittersweet. She is very interested in powerful and unique storytelling, offbeat contemporary fiction, immersive fantasy, and profoundly resonant voices. Open to queries from the 1st to the 7th of every month.

L515 Aemilia Phillips
Literary Agent
United States

apquery@skagency.com

http://skagency.com
http://skagency.com/agents/aemilia-phillips/

Literary Agency: Stuart Krichevsky Literary Agency, Inc. (**L609**)

Fiction > *Novels*
 General, and in particular: Culture; Dark; Literary; Magic; Politics; Social Justice

Nonfiction > *Nonfiction Books*
 Central America; Commercial; Cultural Criticism; Feminism; Journalism; Narrative Nonfiction; South America

How to send: Email

Works with a range of fiction and non-fiction writers. She is particularly interested in writers who push conventional boundaries in order to address cultural, political, and social justice issues. Interested in journalism, narrative non-fiction, literary fiction, and poetry, she looks for diverse, smart writing with an impactful story to tell. For non-fiction she's looking for driven, obsessed writers and topics that challenge the way we think about the world, with a particular interest in Latin American and feminist voices. She loves books that at first glance appear to be commercial, but that are also smart cultural critiques that force readers to examine new viewpoints. She's fascinated by darker, complex fictional characters who upend preconceptions, and stories with just a touch of magic.

Authors: Ahmed Badr; Sol Brager; Shavone Charles; Gabriel Dozal; Adriana Gallardo; Karen Ho; Lizz Huerta; Charlotte Kaufman; Cassidy Krug; Dan Lewis; Julie Lunde; Farah Nayeri; Okezie Nwoka; José Olivarez; José R. Ralat; Reyes Ramirez; Raquel Reichard; Ruben Reyes; Prisca Dorcas Mojica Rodriguez; David Schonfeld; Kim Thai; Sarah Weinman; Christina Wilcox

L516 Juliet Pickering
Literary Agent
United Kingdom

juliet@blakefriedmann.co.uk

http://blakefriedmann.co.uk/juliet-pickering
https://twitter.com/julietpickering

Literary Agency: Blake Friedmann Literary Agency Ltd (**L066**)

Fiction > *Novels*
 Book Club Fiction; Commercial; Literary

Nonfiction
 Illustrated Books: General
 Nonfiction Books: Cookery; Food; Narrative Nonfiction; Popular Culture; Relationships; Social History

Send: Query; Synopsis; Writing sample
How to send: Word file email attachment
How not to send: Post; Links to material online

Alongside literary, book club and commercial fiction, I represent non-fiction writers across the board, including memoir, pop culture, social history, writing on issues of race, gender and class, and cookery and food.

Authors: Diane Abbott; Saskia Alais; Kasim Ali; Graeme Armstrong; MiMi Aye; Trezza Azzopardi; Bolu Babalola; Tomas Bellamy; Jendella Benson; Meliz Berg; Ian Birch; Rachel Blackmore; Nora Anne Brown; Erin Bunting; Jo Facer & Erin Bunting; Natasha Carthew; Fran Chang; Norie Clarke; Julia Cole; Sue Cook; Sara Crowe; Tuyen Do; Michael Donkor; Jo Facer; Alix Fox; Sarah Franklin; Roxy Freeman; Janice Galloway; Gabriella Griffith; Sarah Hartley; David Haslam; Emma Forsyth Haslett; Kate Hodges; Michael Hogan; Kerry Hudson; Leah Hyslop; Alexandra Jellicoe; Benjamin Johncock; Konditor; Kat Lister; Richard Littler; Clayton Littlewood; Anneliese Mackintosh; Ailbhe Malone; Lucy Mangan; Nina-Sophia Miralles; Emma Mitchell; Sue Moorcroft; Grace Mortimer; Nina Parker; Rosalind Powell; Julie Rea; Annie Robertson; Elliot Ryan; Lora Stimson; Jack Urwin; Helen Walmsley-Johnson; Jemma Wayne; Andrew Wong

L517 Rosie Pierce
Literary Agent
United Kingdom

piercesubmissions@curtisbrowngroup.co.uk
rosie.pierce@curtisbrown.co.uk

https://curtisbrown.co.uk
https://curtisbrown.co.uk/agent/rosie-pierce

Literary Agency: Curtis Brown (**L146**)

Fiction > *Novels*
 Coming of Age; Commercial; Dark Academia; Family Saga; Friends; Ghost Stories; Horror; Literary; Mystery; Psychological Suspense; Romantic Comedy; Thrillers

Nonfiction > *Nonfiction Books*
 Alternative History; Celebrity; Internet; Memoir; Narrative Nonfiction; Popular Culture; Psychology

Send: Query; Synopsis; Proposal; Writing sample
How to send: Email

I read widely and across genres, and I am looking for both literary and commercial fiction. I love family dramas, ghost and horror stories, psychological suspense, murder mysteries, gripping thrillers, and big-hearted romantic comedies. In storytelling I am most often drawn to distinctive, original voices; vivid characterisation and world building; confident, engaging prose; and astute social observation. I particularly love to read about the relationships that shape – or even define – a life. I am looking for expansive, character-driven novels that explore complicated family dynamics, enduring friendships, love affairs, coming of age, the best and worst things we do for love. I am also always keen to read novels that explore occultism, séances, the uncanny, dark academia, and thrillers with emotional punch and nail-biting plot. And if a novel can make me laugh, I am sold. In non-fiction, I'd love to hear from writers who bring their expertise and/or experiences to the page in an accessible, compelling and original way. I am looking for narrative non-fiction, memoir, and books exploring pop and celebrity culture, alternative histories, psychology, the internet.

Authors: Nicole Adams; Henry Agg; Alice Bell; Kaddy Benyon; Kate van der Borgh; Natalie Bray; Rebecca Fallon; Laura McCluskey; Madeleine Norton; Leah Pitt; Dan Whitlam

L518 Gideon Pine
Literary Agent
United States

submissions@inkwellmanagement.com

https://inkwellmanagement.com/staff/gideon-pine

Literary Agency: InkWell Management

Fiction > *Novels*
  Horror; Literary; Mystery; Thrillers

Nonfiction > *Nonfiction Books*
  Crime; Health; History; Investigative Journalism; Narrative Nonfiction; Wellbeing

Send: Query; Writing sample
How to send: In the body of an email

Interested in representing writers in the nonfiction space with a focus on historical narrative nonfiction, true crime, health and wellness, and long form investigative journalism. He is also looking for voice-driven debut novels, including but not limited to the following genres: thriller, mystery, horror, or literary fiction.

L519 Zoe Plant
Literary Agent
United States

plantqueries@thebentagency.com

http://www.thebentagency.com/zoe-plant
https://www.twitter.com/zoeplant89

Literary Agency: The Bent Agency (**L058**)

ADULT > **Fiction** > *Novels*
  Commercial; Fantasy; Gothic; High Concept; Horror; Mystery; Science Fiction; Speculative; Thrillers

CHILDREN'S > **Fiction** > *Middle Grade*
  General, and in particular: Commercial

YOUNG ADULT > **Fiction** > *Novels*
  General, and in particular: Commercial; Horror; Magic; Science Fiction; Speculative; Thrillers

Closed to approaches.

I am looking for middle-grade and young adult fiction across all genres, as well as adult science fiction, fantasy, horror and speculative fiction. Across the board, my tastes lean towards commercial, entertaining, accessible books that also have something to say about the world. I am particularly interested in seeing submissions from writers from traditionally underrepresented backgrounds.

L520 Carrie Plitt
Literary Agent; Company Director
United Kingdom

https://felicitybryan.com/fba-agent/carrie-plitt/

Literary Agency: Felicity Bryan Associates (**L215**)

Fiction
  Novels: Book Club Fiction; Coming of Age; Family; Friends; Literary; Romance
  Short Fiction Collections: General

Nonfiction > *Nonfiction Books*
  History; Investigative Journalism; Memoir; Narrative Essays; Narrative Nonfiction; Nature; Popular Psychology; Popular Science; Social Issues; Travel

Send: Query; Synopsis; Proposal
How to send: Online submission system

I am actively building a list of non-fiction and fiction. In non-fiction, I love to represent expert authors who are passionate about their subject, who have something new to say, and who can convey their argument in a clear and invigorating manner. I have a particular interest in books about the issues our society faces today, narrative non-fiction, investigative journalism, popular science, popular psychology, big ideas, nature writing, history and travel. I also love book-length essays or cohesive essay collections, and memoirs that explore wider themes like freedom or education. In fiction, the books I represent range from the very literary to those you might read in a book club. Besides excellent writing, I am often drawn to emotionally complex novels; coming of age stories; sprawling narratives about love, friendship or families; and stories that capture the zeitgeist in some way – even when they are set in the past. I love a good short story collection, especially if the stories are linked together.

Authors: Sally Adee; Frances Ashcroft; Roderick Beaton; Catherine Belton; Tim Birkhead; Ursula Buchan; Julia Bueno; Emma Byrne; Fernando Cervantes; Simukai Chigudu; Marcus Chown; Will Eaves; Reni Eddo-Lodge; David Farrier; Peter Gatrell; Susan Golombok; James Hamilton; Tim Hecker; Lindsey Hilsum; Sarah Jasmon; Joseph Jebelli; Nick Jubber; Chelsea Kwakye; Grace Lavery; Suzannah Lipscomb; Tess Little; Rebecca Lowe; Natasha Lunn; Fiona Maddocks; Henry Mance; Vanessa Nakate; Tom Nancollas; Camilla Nord; Jenny Odell; Ore Ogunbiyi; Elsa Panciroli; Alex Reeve; Dan Richards; Eloise Rickman; Alex Riley; Charlotte Lydia Riley; David Robson; Nicola Rollock; Farhan Samanani; Zakia Sewell; Tiffany Watt Smith; Miriam Stoppard; Cathy Thomas; Samantha Walton; Michael Wooldridge; Kieran Yates

L521 Portobello Literary
Literary Agency
United Kingdom

info@portobelloliterary.co.uk
submissions@portobelloliterary.co.uk

https://www.portobelloliterary.co.uk
https://twitter.com/portyliterary
https://instagram.com/portyliterary

Professional Body: The Association of Authors' Agents (AAA)

Fiction > *Novels*

Nonfiction > *Nonfiction Books*

Send: Synopsis; Author bio; Writing sample
How to send: Email
How not to send: Post

Literary agency based in Edinburgh. Looking for clients and happy to chat to writers at any stage of their career. Response only if interested. No postal submissions, or submissions originated, written or edited by Artificial Intelligence (AI) technology.

Authors: Polly Atkin; Louis Bailey; Laura Basu; Fiona Black; Gill Booles; Jenny Chamarette; Rachel Charlton-Dailey; Mona Dash; Joe Donnelly; Samantha Dooey-Miles; Ashley Douglas; Laura Elliott; Harry Josephine Giles; CL Hellisen; Russell Jones; Louise Kenward; Wenying Li; Annie Lord; Aefa Mulholland; JC Niala; Eleanor Noyce; Andrés N. Ordorica; Alycia Pirmohamed; Wendy Pratt; Adam Ramsay; Christina Riley; Sarah Stewart; Elizabeth Lewis Williams; Elspeth Wilson

Literary Agent: Caro Clarke (**L128**)

L522 Marcy Posner
Literary Agent; Senior Vice President
United States

marcy@foliolit.com

https://www.foliolit.com/agents-1/marcy-posner
https://querymanager.com/query/marcyposner

Literary Agency: Folio Literary Management, LLC

ADULT
  Fiction > *Novels*
    Historical Fiction; Mystery; Psychological Suspense; Thrillers; Women's Fiction

  Nonfiction > *Nonfiction Books*
    Culture; Environment; Journalism; Narrative Nonfiction; Nature; Psychology; Social Issues; Women's Issues

CHILDREN'S > Fiction > *Middle Grade*
Contemporary; Fantasy; Historical Fiction; Mystery; Science Fiction

YOUNG ADULT > Fiction > *Novels*
Contemporary; Historical Fiction; Mystery; Romance

How to send: Query Manager
How not to send: Email

Looking for Thrillers, Psychological suspense, Historical fiction, Women's fiction, Mystery, YA (contemporary, historical, romance, mystery), Middle grade (contemporary, SFF, historical, mystery), Narrative non-fiction, Cultural/social issues, Journalism, Nature and ecology, Psychology and Women's issues. No longer accepts queries through email. Submit through online submission system only.

Authors: Christi Clancy; Christina Clancy; Lexie Elliott; Jacqueline Kelly; Erika J. Kendrick; Michael McGarrity; Sheri Reynolds; Rebecca Stafford; Rachel J. Webster; Patricia Wood

L523 Anna Power

Literary Agent; Managing Director
Bloomsbury House, 74-77 Great Russell Street, London, WC1B 3DA
United Kingdom

anna@johnsonandalcock.co.uk

http://www.johnsonandalcock.co.uk/anna-power

https://twitter.com/APowerAgent

Literary Agency: Johnson & Alcock (**L335**)

Fiction
Graphic Novels: General
Novels: Book Club Fiction; Crime; Historical Fiction; Literary; Suspense

Nonfiction > *Nonfiction Books*
Cultural Criticism; Current Affairs; Food; History; Memoir; Popular Science; Psychology

Send: Query; Synopsis; Writing sample
How to send: Email attachment
How not to send: Post

In fiction, she is looking for literary, book club and historical fiction, as well as suspense and crime. Whatever the genre, she looks for a distinctive and compelling voice, and worldbuilding that immerses the reader. She is drawn especially to a moral dilemma, stories about families and relationships, and novels that combine darkness and humour. She is also interested to see graphic novels which appeal to a crossover readership.

In non-fiction, she invites submissions of history, memoir, current affairs, cultural criticism, popular science, psychology and food writing; anything that communicates an author's passion in an inventive and inspiring way. She welcomes approaches from experts with new and surprising takes on their subject, which alter the way we think about and engage with the world.

L524 Marta Praeger

Literary Agent
United States

Literary Agency: Robert A. Freedman Dramatic Agency, Inc.

Scripts > *Theatre Scripts*

L525 Tanusri Prasanna

Literary Agent
United States

tpsubmissions@defliterary.com

https://www.defliterary.com/agent/tanusri-prasanna/

Literary Agency: DeFiore and Company

ADULT
Fiction > *Novels*: Diversity

Nonfiction > *Nonfiction Books*
Memoir; Narrative Nonfiction; Social Justice

CHILDREN'S
Fiction
Middle Grade: Coming of Age; Contemporary; School; Suspense
Picture Books: General

Nonfiction
Middle Grade; Picture Books

YOUNG ADULT
Fiction > *Novels*
Coming of Age; Contemporary; School; Suspense

Nonfiction > *Nonfiction Books*

Send: Pitch; Author bio; Synopsis; Full text
How to send: Email

Looks for accessible and wide-reaching, narrative nonfiction set against themes in social justice and representation, as well as memoirs and select fiction featuring diverse perspectives, contexts, and even storytelling styles. In the YA and middle-grade spaces, Drawn to contemporary coming-of-age stories, charming and relatable romances, ambitious world-building fantasies, and well-plotted, voice-driven suspense. She's also a big fan of stories set in schools or interesting neighborhoods told from fresh viewpoints. For picture books, her list includes both meaningful, lyrical, stories as well as ones that bring alive the wonder and complexity of our world with humor and heart. She's also interested in nonfiction that excites the imagination and curiosity of young readers.

Send a concise pitch, short bio, and a two-page synopsis if querying YA/MG fiction. For picture books, include the entire text in the body of your email. If querying an illustrated project, provide sample illustrations and links to your website / Instagram page.

L526 Amanda Preston

Literary Agent
United Kingdom

amandasubmissions@lbabooks.com

http://www.lbabooks.com/agent/amanda-preston/

Literary Agency: LBA Books Ltd

ADULT
Fiction > *Novels*
Book Club Fiction; Commercial; Crime; High Concept Thrillers; Historical Fiction; Romance

Nonfiction > *Nonfiction Books*
Contemporary; Crime; Environment; History; Memoir; Narrative Nonfiction; Nature; Psychology; Science; Wellbeing

YOUNG ADULT > Fiction > *Novels*
Contemporary; Historical Fiction; Speculative

Represents a wide range of best-selling and award-winning authors across fiction and non-fiction. On the hunt for a high-concept thriller which is character and plot driven, but also has a discussable issue at its heart. Would also love a novel where the location is as integral to the plot as the crime. Would love a new crime series. On the hunt for a glorious book club love story that is doing something a bit different and special. For nonfiction, would love more true crime. It can be contemporary or historical, an unsolved case or a different perspective on a well known case. Not looking for any child-related crime stories. Looking for narrative non-fiction predominately in science, the environment, psychology, nature writing, well-being and memoir.

Authors: Emily Adlam; Jaimie Admans; Sarah Alderson; Dominique Antiglio; Kerry Barrett; A.L. Bird; Darcie Boleyn; Christina Bradley; Catherine Brookes; Jo Carnegie; Lucie Cave; Rebecca Chance; Emma Cooper; Susie Donkin; Hannah Doyle; Katherine Dyson; Kate Hackworthy; Sue Heath; Natalie Heaton; Holly Jade; Jane Jesmond; Lesley Kara; Simon Kernick; Emily Kerr; Ella King; Caedis Knight; Amy Lavelle; Georgina Lees; Freda Lightfoot; Jane Linfoot; Fiona Lucas; Rachael Lucas; Dee MacDonald; Ian Marber; Colin McDowell; Lisa Medved; L. C. North; Angelique Panagos; Catherine Piddington; Anna Pointer; Gillian Richmond; Natali Simmonds; Tom Simons; Johanna Spiers; Heidi Swain; Karen Swan; Sophie Tanner; Jonathan Trigell; Anna Turns; Claire Wade; Kate Wells; Kate Winter; Dalton Wong

L527 Rachel Mills Literary

Literary Agency
M27, South Wing, Somerset House, Strand, London, WC2R 1LA
United Kingdom

https://www.rachelmillsliterary.co.uk
https://twitter.com/bookishyogini
https://www.instagram.com/rachelmillsliterary/

Professional Body: The Association of Authors' Agents (AAA)

How to send: Email

As an agency we are particularly interested in female voices, and in showcasing talent which deserves to be heard, regardless of age or background. We seek to work with authors whose careers we can help build over the long term, across multiple projects.

Company Director / Literary Agent: Rachel Mills (**L452**)

Literary Agent: Nelle Andrew (**L025**)

L528 Susan Ramer
Literary Agent
United States

dca@doncongdon.com

https://doncongdon.com/agents

Literary Agency: Don Congdon Associates, Inc. (**L175**)

Fiction > *Novels*
  Book Club Fiction; Contemporary; Literary; Upmarket

Nonfiction > *Nonfiction Books*
  Arts; Cultural History; Fashion; Food; Literary Memoir; Music; Narrative Nonfiction; Popular Culture; Social History; Women's Issues

How to send: Email

Looks for literary fiction, upmarket 'book club' fiction (contemporary and historical, American in particular), and narrative non-fiction. Is drawn to an authentic voice, unforgettable characters with an edge, and an unfamiliar, well-crafted story that is emotional in unpredictable ways. For non-fiction, her interests include social history, cultural history, smart pop culture (fashion, food, art, music), women's issues, and literary memoir with a distinctive theme. She particularly likes a narrative that combines a personal thread with reporting and analysis of a broader social or cultural issue. In everything, she appreciates a sense of humor, especially when it's on the dark side. No queries in the following categories: romance, sci-fi, fantasy, espionage, mysteries, politics, health/diet/fitness, self-help sports or children's (young adult, middle grade or picture book); and she does not represent screenplays.

L529 Rebecca Carter Literary
Literary Agency
c/o PEW Literary, 46 Lexington Street, London, W1F 0LP
United Kingdom

info@rebeccacarterliterary.com

https://www.rebeccacarterliterary.com
https://twitter.com/rebeccasbooks
https://www.instagram.com/rebeccacarterliteraryagent/

Professional Body: The Association of Authors' Agents (AAA)

Literary Agent: Rebecca Carter (**L111**)

L530 Redhammer
Literary Agency
United Kingdom

https://redhammer.info
https://www.facebook.com/RealLitopia
https://twitter.com/Litopia
https://www.linkedin.com/in/petecox/
https://studio.youtube.com/channel/UCmbrM2ciaxb4hHQFfnSeOpg

Fiction > *Novels*

Nonfiction > *Nonfiction Books*

Send: Pitch; Writing sample
How to send: Online submission system

Suggests aspiring writers join their writers' colony. Interested in hearing from previously published authors, self-published authors, celebrities, whistleblowers, and people with a unique life story.

Literary Agent: Peter Cox

L531 Regina Ryan Books
Literary Agency
United States

queries@reginaryanbooks.com

https://www.reginaryanbooks.com

Professional Body: Association of American Literary Agents (AALA)

ADULT > **Nonfiction**
  Nonfiction Books: Architecture; Birds; Business; Cookery; Crime; Diet; Environment; Gardening; Health; History; Leisure; Lifestyle; Narrative Nonfiction; Nature; Parenting; Politics; Psychology; Science; Spirituality; Sport; Sustainable Living; Travel; Wellbeing; Women's Issues
  Reference: Popular

CHILDREN'S > **Nonfiction** > *Picture Books*

Does not want:

  Nonfiction > *Nonfiction Books*: Religion

Send: Query; Proposal; Writing sample; Full text; Author bio; Market info; Marketing Plan
How to send: Word file email attachment

Costs: Offers services that writers have to pay for. Offers publishing consultation services and book packaging and production (print and electronic).

We are a Manhattan-based boutique literary agency primarily representing adult nonfiction. We also offer publishing consultation services and book packaging and production (print and electronic).

We are always looking for new and exciting books in our areas of interest, including well-written narrative nonfiction, architecture, history, politics, natural history (especially birds), true crime, science (especially the brain), the environment, women's issues, parenting, cooking, psychology, health, wellness, diet, business, non-religious contemporary spirituality, children's picture books, lifestyle, sustainability, popular reference, and leisure activities including sports, narrative travel, and gardening. We represent books that have something new to say, are well-written and that will, if possible, make the world a better place.

Authors: Ben Austro; Randi Minetor; Doug Whynott

Literary Agent: Regina Ryan

L532 Janet Reid
Literary Agent
United States

Janet@JetReidLiterary.com

http://www.jetreidliterary.com
http://jetreidliterary.blogspot.com/
https://queryshark.blogspot.com/
http://aaronline.org/Sys/PublicProfile/2176820/417813
https://www.publishersmarketplace.com/members/JanetReid/

Professional Bodies: Association of American Literary Agents (AALA); Mystery Writers of America (MWA)

Fiction > *Novels*
  Commercial; Crime; Domestic Suspense; Literary; Mystery; Thrillers

Nonfiction > *Nonfiction Books*
  Biography; History; Memoir; Narrative Nonfiction; Science

Send: Query; Writing sample; Author bio; Proposal
How to send: In the body of an email
How not to send: Email attachment

New York literary agent with a list consisting mainly of crime novels and thrillers, and narrative nonfiction in history and biography.

Authors: Robin Becker; Bill Cameron; Gary Corby; Phillip DePoy; Stephanie Evans; Kennedy Foster; Lee Goodman; Dana Haynes; Patrick Lee; Thomas Lippman; Jeff Marks; Warren Richey; Terry Shames; Jeff Somers; Robert Stubblefield; Deb Vlock

L533 Milly Reilly
Literary Agent
United Kingdom

submissions@colwillandpeddle.com

https://www.colwillandpeddle.com/about

Literary Agency: Colwill & Peddle (**L131**)

Fiction > *Novels*: Literary

Nonfiction > *Nonfiction Books*
Arts; Comedy / Humour; Food; Health; Medicine; Nature; Politics; Psychology; Society

Closed to approaches.

In non-fiction, my taste is broad. I'm on the look-out for informed, illuminating writing that challenges readers to think and live critically and imaginatively. Topics that interest me include food, art, comedy, the natural world, human behaviour and psychology, illness and medicine, and the social and political. I represent writers of memoir and creative non-fiction, where I'm particularly excited by bold, perceptive writing that interrogates the means of telling a story. When it comes to fiction, I'm drawn to brutally honest, character-driven stories that delve into inner lives and social dynamics. I like a story that deals with darkness and complexity but is not without hope, and writing that is playful and poetic.

Authors: Alexina Anatole; Xanthi Barker; Aimee Cliff; Josie Gill; Gabby Jahanshahi-Edlin; Shona Minson; Marie Mitchell; Jennifer Neal; Vic Parsons; Clare Rose; Jacqueline Roy; Ben Smoke; Annabel Sowemimo; Özlem Warren; Sophie Williams

L534 Jessica Reino
Senior Agent
United States

https://www.metamorphosisliteraryagency.com/about
https://querymanager.com/query/JessicaReino
https://twitter.com/jnrlitauthor

Literary Agency: Metamorphosis Literary Agency (**L444**)

ADULT
Fiction > *Novels*
General, and in particular: Contemporary Romance; Fantasy; Legal Thrillers; Mystery; Psychological Thrillers; Suspense; Women's Fiction

Nonfiction > *Nonfiction Books*
Comedy / Humour; Health; Parenting; Popular Culture; Sport

CHILDREN'S > *Fiction* > *Middle Grade*
General, and in particular: Horror

YOUNG ADULT > *Fiction* > *Novels*
Contemporary; Fantasy; Horror; Magical Realism; Romance; Science Fiction; Supernatural / Paranormal

Closed to approaches.

Looking for manuscripts that are well-written with a strong voice in order to make that emotional connection. Seeking MG, YA, Adult and nonfiction projects.

L535 Francesca Riccardi
Literary Agent
United Kingdom

https://katenashlit.co.uk/people/
https://twitter.com/friccar_

Literary Agency: Kate Nash Literary Agency (**L353**)

Fiction > *Novels*
Commercial; Crime; Detective Fiction; Family; Friends; Thrillers

Reads widely, especially across popular commercial genres, but is a particular fan of crime and thrillers, and loves a dogged detective or unusual sleuth. She also enjoys books about unusual family dynamics, toxic friendships and people keeping secrets.

L536 Richard Curtis Associates, Inc.
Literary Agency
286 Madison Avenue, 10th Floor, New York, NY 10017
United States
Tel: +1 (212) 759-8600

curtisagency@haroldober.com
contact@haroldober.com

https://www.haroldober.com/richard-curtis

Literary Agency: Harold Ober Associates, Inc. (**L298**)
Professional Body: Association of American Literary Agents (AALA)

Fiction > *Novels*

Nonfiction > *Nonfiction Books*

Closed to approaches.

Acquired in January 2022. Continues to administer advance, royalty and other payments for the thousands of backlist titles brought to readers since the agency was founded in 1979.

Literary Agent: Richard Curtis

L537 Rick Richter
Literary Agent; Senior Partner
United States

https://aevitascreative.com/agents/
https://querymanager.com/query/RickRichter

Literary Agency: Aevitas

ADULT
Fiction > *Novels*
Commercial; Horror; Psychological Thrillers

Nonfiction > *Nonfiction Books*
Celebrity Memoir; Crime; Food; History; Memoir; Music; Narrative Nonfiction; Politics; Popular Culture; Religion; Science; Self Help; Social Justice; Sports Celebrity

CHILDREN'S
Fiction
Chapter Books; Early Readers; Middle Grade; Picture Books
Nonfiction
Early Readers; Middle Grade; Picture Books
YOUNG ADULT
Fiction > *Novels*
Nonfiction > *Nonfiction Books*

Send: Author bio; Market info; Writing sample
How to send: Online submission system

Areas of interest include self-help, pop culture, memoir, history, thriller, true crime, political and social issues, narrative food writing, and faith. He has deep experience and interest in children's books.

Authors: John Bainbridge; Rob Barnett; Mary Jane Begin; Sheryl Berk; Tom Booth; Marcus Brotherton; Kyle Buchanan; Libby Buck; Andrew Bustamante; Marc and Angel Chernoff; Pan Cooke; Amanda Craig; Matt Diffee; Geoff Edgers; Jeremy Egner; Michael Emberley; Nona Footz; JR and Vanessa Ford; Michael and Ava Gardner; Dan Goldman; Margaret Greanais; Andy Greene; Erik Gude; Peter Guralnick; Michael Hendrix; James Hibberd; Barry Jackson; Jeffrey H. Jackson; Alegra Kastens; Erin Kimmerle; Rebecca Kling; William J. Kole; Deb Miller Landau; Neil Lane; Nico Lang; Derek Lawrence; Kim Mager; Aaron Mahnke; Amanda Marrone; Scott Meslow; Darcy Michael; SSG Travis Mills; Kara Mitchell; Malcolm Mitchell; Real Sports Entertainment Network; Chris and Emily Norton; Cate Osborn; Panos Panay; Madeline Pendleton; Shawn Peters; Greg Presto; Jessica Radloff; Michael Relth; David Ricciardi; Geo Rutherford; Kate Schroeder; Hannah Selinger; Tim Sommer; Isaiah Stephens; Melanie Sumrow; Leah Tinari; Neil Tomba; Sheree Tomba; Allison Varnes; Sara Vladic; Molly Webster; Paige Wetzel; Sean Fay Wolfe

L538 Louise Ripley-Duggan
Literary Agent
United Kingdom

https://www.theseus.agency/team

Literary Agency: The Theseus Agency (**L627**)

L539 Robert Smith Literary Agency Ltd
Literary Agency
12 Bridge Wharf, 156 Caledonian Road, London, N1 9UU
United Kingdom
Tel: +44 (0) 20 8504 0024

robert@robertsmithliteraryagency.com

https://www.robertsmithliteraryagency.com

Nonfiction > *Nonfiction Books*
Autobiography; Biography; Comedy / Humour; Crime; Current Affairs; Fitness; Health; History; Inspirational; Language; Military; Personal Development; Popular Culture; Real Life Stories; Warfare

Closed to approaches.

Email or post a covering letter, briefly describing the book you want to write and why you are well qualified to be its author. Do not submit proposals for novels, academic books, poetry, children's books, religious books or film / TV scripts.

Authors: Arthur Aldridge; Sarbjit Kaur Athwal; Richard Anthony Baker; Delia Balmer; Juliet Barnes; Amanda Barrie; John Baxter; William Beadle; Robert Beasley; Peta Bee; Paul Begg; John Bennett; Kevin Booth; Ralph Bulger; James Carnac; John Casson; Gary Chapman; Shirley Charters; John Clarke; Robert Clarke; Carol Clerk; Martyn Compton; Michelle Compton; Judy Cook; Les Cummings; Clive Driscoll; Rosie Dunn; Georgie Edwards; Russell Edwards; Kate Elysia; Stewart P. Evans; Penny Farmer; Martin Fido; Sarah Flower; Freddie Foreman; Helen Foster; Becci Fox; Astrid Franse; Stephen Fulcher; Alison Goldie; Charlotte Green; Christopher Green; Allan Grice; Christine Hamilton; Andrew Hansford; James Haspiel; Chris Hutchins; Rosalinda Hutton; Albert Jack; Naomi Jacobs; Muriel Jakubait; Nikola James; Sarah Jones; Christine Keeler; Anita Kelsey; Siobhan Kennedy-McGuinness; Heidi Kingstone; Brian Kirby; Tim Kirby; John Knight; Ronnie Knight; Reg Kray; Roberta Kray; Tony Lambrianou; Carol Ann Lee; John Lee; Angela Levin; Chris Lightbown; Seth Linder; David R. L. Litchfield; Mary Long; Tony Long; Jean MacColl; Gretel Mahoney; Maurice Mayne; Lenny McLean; Ann Ming; Paddy Monaghan; James Moore; Michelle Morgan; Caroline Morris; Zana Morris; Rochelle Morton; Alan Moss; Bobbie Neate; Paul Nero; Kim Noble; Laurie O'Leary; Marnie Palmer; Theo Paphitas; Gordon Rayner; Mike Reid; Frances Reilly; Lyn Rigby; William D. Rubinstein; Mark Ryan; Sarah Schenker; Nathan Shapow; Alexander Sinclair; Keith Skinner; David Slattery-Christy; Len Smith; Rita Smith; Allan Starkie; Jayne Sterne; Cameron Stewart; Neil R. Storey; Claudia Strachan; Bob Taylor; Christopher Warwick; Monica Weller; Natalie Welsh; Wynne Weston-Davies; Karl Williams; Peter Wilton; Robert Winnett; Joanne Zorian-Lynn

Literary Agents: Anne Smith; Robert Smith

L540 Soumeya Bendimerad Roberts
Literary Agent; Vice President
United States

soumeya@hgliterary.com

https://www.hgliterary.com/soumeya
https://querymanager.com/query/SBR
https://www.publishersmarketplace.com/members/SoumeyaRoberts/

Literary Agency: HG Literary (**L310**)
Professional Body: Association of American Literary Agents (AALA)

Fiction > *Novels*
Animals; Family; Literary; Motherhood; Nature; Postcolonialism; Social Commentary; Sub-Culture; Upmarket

Nonfiction > *Nonfiction Books*
Animals; Crafts; Design; Family; Lifestyle; Memoir; Motherhood; Narrative Nonfiction; Nature; Personal Essays; Social Commentary; Sub-Culture

Send: Query; Synopsis; Writing sample
How to send: Query Manager

Represents award-winning and best-selling authors in literary and upmarket fiction, narrative non-fiction, and memoir. She also represents a curated list across creative fields including design, craft, and lifestyle. She is seeking new voices in fiction and narrative nonfiction, especially stories about dynamic relationships between complex but sympathetic characters; families, siblings, and motherhood; social commentary; unconventional settings and subcultures; our relationship with land, nature, and animals; and controlled experiments with form. She is particularly, but not exclusively, interested in work that investigates or reflects on the post-colonial world, marginalized and liminal spaces, and narratives by people of color. In non-fiction, she is primarily looking for idea-driven or voice-forward memoirs, personal essay collections, and narrative non-fiction of all stripes. She is not looking for fantasy, science fiction, religious books, commercial romance, middle grade, young adult, or picture books.

L541 Robertson Murray Literary Agency
Literary Agency
3rd Floor, 37 Great Portland Street, London, W1W 8QH
United Kingdom
Tel: +44 (0) 20 7580 0702

info@robertsonmurray.com

https://robertsonmurray.com

Types: Fiction; Nonfiction
Subjects: Autobiography; Comedy / Humour; Commercial; Cookery; Current Affairs; History; Lifestyle; Literary; Science; Society; Sport
Markets: Adult; Children's; Young Adult

Closed to approaches.

No science fiction, academic books, scripts, or poetry. Submit online through form on website. No postal submissions. Currently closed to submissions of children's books as at April 2019. See website current status and for full guidelines.

Literary Agents: Jenny Heller; Hilary Murray; Charlotte Robertson

L542 Quressa Robinson
Literary Agent
United States

https://querymanager.com/query/1066
https://www.publishersmarketplace.com/members/QuressaRobinson/
https://twitter.com/qnrisawesome

Literary Agency: Folio Literary Management, LLC

ADULT
Fiction > *Novels*
Fantasy; Science Fiction

Nonfiction > *Nonfiction Books*
Commercial; Literary Memoir; Literary; Narrative Nonfiction; Popular Science; Westerns

CHILDREN'S > **Fiction** > *Middle Grade*
Contemporary; Fantasy; Literary; Science Fiction

YOUNG ADULT > **Fiction** > *Novels*
Contemporary; Fantasy; Romantic Comedy; Science Fiction

How to send: By referral

Looking for:

Modern-day blue stockings, BIPOC fangirls/fanboys, #blackgirlmagic, #carefreeblackgirls, #blackboyjoy, LGBTQ+, BIPOC falling in love, neuroatypical / neurodivergent, and disabled BIPOCs as leads.

Middle Grade (contemporary, literary, and SF/F). Cute, quirky, charming, and fun. Along the lines of Kiki's Delivery Service, Spirited Away, The Girl that Drank the Moon, the Pandava series, Hurricane Child.

Young adult (contemporary, Rom Coms, and SF/F) *I have TONS of SF/F on my current list so I am extremely selective with this genre*

Adult SF/F with strong genre-bending/crossover appeal. (Think the All Souls Trilogy by Deborah Harkness, The Night Circus by Erin Morgenstern, and The Age of Miracles by Karen Thompson Walker. I'm also a fan of Anne Bishop and Naomi Novik. More recent books that I've loved: Trail of Lightning, The Ten Thousand Doors of January, and Empire of Sand.)

Passion projects in narrative nonfiction with a strong literary voice and commercial appeal (Wild by Cheryl Strayed, Black Man in a White Coat by Damon Tweedy, When Breath Becomes Air by Paul Kalanithi). Would love to see non-whitewashed cowboy stories; pop science by women, specifically women of color; and literary, voice-driven memoir with commercial appeal.

#ownvoices and marginalized authors in all genres mentioned above. Inclusive narratives in all genres.

L543 Rochelle Stevens & Co.

Literary Agency
2 Terretts Place, Upper Street, London, N1 1QZ
United Kingdom
Tel: +44 (0) 20 7359 3900

info@rochellestevens.com

http://www.rochellestevens.com
http://twitter.com/TerrettsPlace
http://www.rochellestevens.com/submissions/#

Scripts
  Film Scripts; *Radio Scripts*; *TV Scripts*; *Theatre Scripts*

Send: Query; Author bio
How to send: By referral

Handles script writers for film, television, theatre, and radio. No longer handles writers of fiction, nonfiction, or children's books. See website for full submission guidelines.

Literary Agents: Frances Arnold; Rochelle Stevens

L544 Rocking Chair Books

Literary Agency
United Kingdom
Tel: +44 (0) 7809 461342

representme@rockingchairbooks.com

http://www.rockingchairbooks.com
https://twitter.com/rockingbooks
https://www.instagram.com/rockingchairbooks/

Professional Body: The Association of Authors' Agents (AAA)

Fiction
  Graphic Novels: General
  Novels: Commercial; Literary
Nonfiction > *Nonfiction Books*

Send: Query; Full text; Writing sample
How to send: Email

Founded in 2011 after the founder worked for five years as a Director at an established London literary agency. Send complete ms or a few chapters by email only. No Children's, YA or Science Fiction / Fantasy.

Authors: Mike Medaglia; John Rensten; Lakimbini Sitoy; Brian Turner

Literary Agent: Samar Hammam

L545 Jennifer Rofe

Senior Agent
United States

jennifer@andrebrownlit.com

https://www.andreabrownlit.com/Team/Jennifer-Rof%C3%A9
http://twitter.com/jenrofe
http://instagram.com/jenrofe
https://www.publishersmarketplace.com/members/jenrofe/
https://www.manuscriptwishlist.com/mswl-post/jennifer-rofe/
http://queryme.online/jenrofe

Literary Agency: Andrea Brown Literary Agency, Inc.

CHILDREN'S > **Fiction**
  Chapter Books: General
  Middle Grade: General, and in particular: Commercial; Contemporary; Fantasy; Historical Fiction; Literary; Magic
  Picture Books: General

Send: Query; Author bio; Writing sample
How to send: Query Manager

Always seeking distinct voices and richly developed characters. Middle grade has long been her soft spot and she's open to all genres in this category—literary, commercial, contemporary, magical, fantastical, historical, and everything in between. She especially appreciates stories that make her both laugh and cry, and that offer an unexpected view into the pre-teen experience. In picture books, she likes funny, character-driven projects; beautifully imagined and written stories; and milestone moments with a twist.

Not currently accepting queries for picture book or YA texts. However, if you write in multiple spaces, please query for one of the accepted categories and mention your other areas of interest.

L546 Rogers, Coleridge & White Ltd

Literary Agency
20 Powis Mews, London, W11 1JN
United Kingdom
Tel: +44 (0) 20 7221 3717

info@rcwlitagency.com

https://www.rcwlitagency.com
https://www.instagram.com/rcwliteraryagency/
https://twitter.com/RCWLitAgency

Professional Body: The Association of Authors' Agents (AAA)

ADULT > **Fiction** > *Novels*
  Commercial; Crime; Literary; Thrillers

CHILDREN'S > **Fiction** > *Novels*

YOUNG ADULT > **Fiction** > *Novels*

Send: Query; Writing sample; Synopsis; Proposal
How to send: Word file email attachment; PDF file email attachment

Submissions should include a covering letter telling us about yourself and the background to the book. In the case of fiction they should consist of the first three chapters or approximately the first fifty pages of the work to a natural break, and a brief synopsis. Non-fiction submissions should take the form of a proposal up to twenty pages in length explaining what the work is about and why you are best placed to write it. Attachments in either Word or PDF formats are acceptable, otherwise sample chapters or proposals can be pasted into the body of the submission email.

Literary Agency: Caroline Sheldon Literary Agency (**L106**)

Literary Agents: Gill Coleridge; Sam Copeland; Stephen Edwards; Natasha Fairweather; Georgia Garrett; Jenny Hewson; Cara Jones; Rebecca Jones; Tristan Kendrick; Laurence Laluyaux; Matthew Marland; Zoe Nelson; Peter Robinson; Peter Straus; Matthew Turner; Zoe Waldie; Pat White; Claire Wilson

L547 Root Literary

Literary Agency
United States

info@rootliterary.com
submissions@rootliterary.com

https://www.rootliterary.com
https://www.instagram.com/rootliterary/
https://twitter.com/RootLiterary
https://www.pinterest.com/rootliterary/_created/

We're a boutique, future-focused literary agency, representing award-winning, bestselling, and up-and-coming authors, illustrators, and graphic novelists. We're committed to helping our clients confidently define and redefine their vision of success while they build a lasting body of work and a meaningful career, and we do so by advocating, empowering, educating, negotiating, problem-solving, and revenue-generating in innovative ways to support our clients' creative work.

Literary Agents: Kurestin Armada (**L030**); Samantha Fabien (**L207**); Melanie Figueroa (**L221**); Taylor Haggerty (**L287**); Alyssa Maltese (**L422**); Molly O'Neill (**L487**); Holly Root (**L548**)

L548 Holly Root

Literary Agent
United States

https://www.rootliterary.com/agents
https://www.publishersmarketplace.com/members/hroot/

Literary Agency: Root Literary (**L547**)

Fiction > *Novels*

How to send: By referral

Currently only considering new submissions by referral.

L549 The Rosenberg Group

Literary Agency
United States

http://www.rosenberggroup.com
https://querymanager.com/query/QueryManagerRosenbergGroup

Professional Body: Association of American Literary Agents (AALA)

ACADEMIC > Nonfiction > *Nonfiction Books*

ADULT
  Fiction > *Novels*
    Romance; Women's Fiction

  Nonfiction > *Nonfiction Books*
    General, and in particular: Apiculture (Beekeeping); History; Psychology; Wine

How to send: Query Manager

Represents romance and women's fiction for an adult audience, nonfiction, and college textbooks.

Literary Agent: Barbara Collins Rosenberg (**L550**)

L550 Barbara Collins Rosenberg
Literary Agent
United States

Literary Agency: The Rosenberg Group (**L549**)

Closed to approaches.

L551 Whitney Ross
Literary Agent
United States

https://www.highlineliterary.com/agent-whitney
https://querymanager.com/query/WhitneyRoss

Literary Agency: High Line Literary Collective (**L312**)

ADULT
  Fiction > *Novels*
    General, and in particular: Contemporary; Fantasy; Romance; Science Fiction

  Nonfiction > *Nonfiction Books*
    Cookery; Design; Fashion

CHILDREN'S > Fiction > *Middle Grade*
YOUNG ADULT > Fiction > *Novels*

Closed to approaches.

Looking for middle grade, young adult, and adult fiction across all genres, with an emphasis on historical, SF and fantasy, romance, and contemporary fiction. She is also open to non-fiction submissions in the areas of design, cooking, and fashion.

L552 Rubin Pfeffer Content, LLC
Literary Agency
648 Hammond Street, Chestnut Hill, MA 02467
United States

info@rpcontent.com
http://www.rpcontent.com

Literary Agency: Aevitas

Types: Fiction; Nonfiction
Markets: Children's; Young Adult

Send: Query
Don't send: Full text
How to send: Email

Focuses on children's books and digital content for all ages and genres. Send query by email. See website for full guidelines.

Literary Agents: Melissa Nasson; Rubin Pfeffer (**L513**)

L553 The Rudy Agency
Literary Agency
United States
Tel: +1 (970) 577-8500

https://www.rudyagency.com

ADULT
  Fiction > *Novels*

  Nonfiction > *Nonfiction Books*
    Business; Health; History; Investigative Journalism; Legal; Medicine; Politics; Science; Sport

CHILDREN'S
  Fiction > *Picture Books*
  Nonfiction > *Illustrated Books*

YOUNG ADULT > Fiction > *Novels*

Send: Query
Don't send: Proposal; Full text
How to send: Email

Agency representing both fiction and nonfiction. Send query before sending proposal or manuscript. Approach only one agent.

Literary Agents: Maryann Karinch (**L351**); Geoffrey Stone (**L600**)

L554 Rupert Crew Ltd
Literary Agency
Southgate, 7 Linden Avenue, Dorchester, Dorset, DT1 1EJ
United Kingdom
Tel: +44 (0) 1305 260335

info@rupertcrew.co.uk
http://www.rupertcrew.co.uk

Professional Body: The Association of Authors' Agents (AAA)

Fiction > *Novels*
Nonfiction > *Nonfiction Books*

Closed to approaches.

Closed to submissions as at July 2023. Check website for current status.

Send query with SAE, synopsis, and first two or three consecutive chapters. International representation, handling volume and subsidiary rights in fiction and nonfiction properties. No Short Stories, Science Fiction, Fantasy, Horror, Poetry or original scripts for Theatre, Television and Film. Email address for correspondence only. No response by post and no return of material with insufficient return postage.

Literary Agent: Caroline Montgomery

L555 The Ruppin Agency
Literary Agency
London,
United Kingdom

submissions@ruppinagency.com

https://www.ruppinagency.com/
https://twitter.com/ruppinagency

Fiction > *Novels*
  Commercial; Crime; Historical Fiction; Literary; Mystery; Thrillers

Nonfiction > *Nonfiction Books*
  Memoir; Narrative Nonfiction; Nature; Science; Social Issues

Closed to approaches.

Literary agency set up by a former bookseller, offering writers a new perspective on finding the right publisher for their work. Keen to find writers with something to say about society today and particularly looking for storylines that showcase voices and communities that have tended to be overlooked by the publishing world, although that should deter no-one from sending their writing. No poetry, children's, young adult, graphic novels, plays and film scripts, self-help or lifestyle (including cookery, gardening, or interiors), religious or other esoteric titles, illustrated, academic, business or professional titles.

Literary Agent: Jonathan Ruppin

L556 Kathleen Rushall
Senior Agent
United States

kathleen@andreabrownlit.com

https://www.kathleenrushall.com
https://www.andreabrownlit.com/Team/Kathleen-Rushall
https://www.facebook.com/kathleen.rushall.5/
https://www.publishersmarketplace.com/members/KatRushall/
https://www.manuscriptwishlist.com/mswl-post/kathleen-rushall/

Literary Agency: Andrea Brown Literary Agency, Inc.

CHILDREN'S > Fiction
  Middle Grade: Animals; Astrology; Contemporary; Environment; Family Saga; High Concept; Magic; Romance; Tarot; Witches
  Picture Books: Animals; Astrology; Environment; Tarot; Witches
YOUNG ADULT > Fiction > *Novels*

Closed to approaches.

Represents a wide range of children's literature. She represents NYT bestselling and award-winning authors. She's drawn to empowering stories, and environmental and whimsical themes, particularly for the youngest set. She loves animals and books about their welfare and science. She's always interested in picture books that inspire emotional intelligence, self-awareness, and empathy.

L557 Laetitia Rutherford
Literary Agent
United Kingdom

https://www.watsonlittle.com/agent/laetitia-rutherford/
http://www.twitter.com/laetitialit

Literary Agency: Watson, Little Ltd (**L647**)

Fiction > *Novels*
Fabulism; Fantasy; Historical Fiction; Literary; Surreal; Upmarket

Nonfiction > *Nonfiction Books*
Cats; Comedy / Humour; Contemporary; Cookery; Food; How To; Nature

Send: Query; Synopsis; Writing sample
How to send: Email

I represent a broad and diverse list of authors in Fiction and contemporary Non-Fiction, ranging from multi-media artists, poets and academics writing for the mainstream, to bestselling and award-winning Crime authors, several with series in TV development. Unique voices with the power to bridge and communicate with wide audiences inspire me.

My current focus is on literary and upmarket fiction. For the moment, I am not looking from Crime fiction.

I am open to queries from writers with timely subject matter, propulsive narratives, and irresistible style whether accessible or more playful and ambitious of form. I am looking for fresh, bold, and beautiful voices, preferably contemporary settings, and with the international appeal that comes from a brilliant central idea or little heard cultural standpoint.

At the moment, I am particularly open to novels with surreal or fantastical or fabulist aspects, that throw universal storylines into the challenges of today (and tomorrow)'s complex world. I'd love to experience your characters' stories unfold in new and underexplored worlds or work or play.

If historical, let your novel speak for today.

The strength of your concept might jump out at me first, but I want to be hooked and excited by the vividness, originality and flair of your prose, its emotional power and capacity to move, provoke and entertain.

Tones of charm and humour also work well for me. I love cats, food and cooking, and nature, and I love how-to-live concepts from experts, activists or exciting new voices.

Author Estate: The Estate of Akemi Tanaka

Authors: Rebecca Abrams; R.G. Adams; Wendy Allen; Jenny Blackhurst; Ajay Chowdhury; Vivianne Crowley; Rose Diell; Rebecca Elliott; JM Hewitt; Samson Kambalu; Holan Liang; Alex Marwood; Diana McCaulay; Barbara Nadel; Tam Omond; Anna Reading; Matt Rendell; Richard Owain Roberts; Anika Scott; Hannah Silva; Zoe Somerville; Shane Spall; Geeta Vara; Jeremy Williams

L558 Jim Rutman
Vice President; Literary Agent
United States

https://www.sll.com/our-team
http://aaronline.org/Sys/PublicProfile/4090054/417813

Literary Agency: Sterling Lord Literistic, Inc. (**L597**)
Professional Body: Association of American Literary Agents (AALA)

Fiction > *Novels*: Literary

Nonfiction
Essays: General
Nonfiction Books: Biography; Films; History; Journalism; Literary Criticism; Music; Narrative Nonfiction; Sport

Send: Query; Synopsis; Writing sample
How to send: Online submission system

Represents adult literary fiction and non-fiction. In fiction, he is interested in audacious novels that test the form and prioritize language. His non-fiction interests are wide ranging, from history, journalism, music, film, sports, and biography, to traditional narrative approaches, criticism, and essays. He is often drawn to interdisciplinary and hybrid treatments, authorities seeking to complicate long held assumptions.

L559 Des Salazar
Assistant Agent
United States

https://www.metamorphosisliteraryagency.com
https://querymanager.com/query/3486

Literary Agency: Metamorphosis Literary Agency (**L444**)

ADULT > **Fiction** > *Novels*
Fantasy; Horror; LGBTQIA; Literary; Mystery; Romance; Science Fiction; Thrillers

NEW ADULT > **Fiction** > *Novels*

YOUNG ADULT > **Fiction** > *Novels*

Open to queries in January and July.

L560 Katie Salvo
Senior Agent
United States

https://www.metamorphosisliteraryagency.com/about
https://querymanager.com/query/KatieSalvo
https://www.metamorphosisliteraryagency.com/submissions

Literary Agency: Metamorphosis Literary Agency (**L444**)

ADULT
Fiction > *Novels*
LGBTQIA; Romance; Women's Fiction

Nonfiction > *Nonfiction Books*
Biography; History; LGBTQIA

CHILDREN'S > **Fiction** > *Middle Grade*

YOUNG ADULT > **Fiction** > *Novels*

Closed to approaches.

Has a background in literary criticism, philosophy, political theory, and history. She is particularly interested in representing women's fiction, romance, children's books, middle grade, young adult, LGBTQ+, and historical biography.

L561 Kaitlyn Sanchez
Literary Agent
United States

https://bradfordlit.com/kaitlyn-sanchez/
https://querymanager.com/query/2049
https://twitter.com/KaitlynLeann17

Literary Agency: Bradford Literary Agency (**L075**)

CHILDREN'S
Fiction
Graphic Novels: General
Middle Grade: Adventure; Comedy / Humour; Coming of Age; Friends; Magic
Picture Books: General

Nonfiction > *Nonfiction Books*

Closed to approaches.

Looking for children's books (picture books through middle grade) in all categories, including graphic novels, nonfiction, and illustration. She is incredibly eclectic in her tastes, with a great affinity for emotional stories as well as funny stories. Always looking for diversity in all forms, including but not limited to BIPOC, neurodiversity, and LGBTQ+. Loves working with artists, so she's always on the lookout for great illustrators, author-illustrators, and graphic novelists. Generally leans PG and PG-13 for most submissions, though some intensity here and there is fine.

L562 Rayhane Sanders
Literary Agent
United States

https://www.mmqlit.com
https://www.mmqlit.com/about/

Literary Agency: Massie & McQuilkin
Professional Body: Association of American Literary Agents (AALA)

Fiction > *Novels*
Culture; Ethnic Groups; Immigration; Sexuality

Nonfiction > *Nonfiction Books*
Culture; Ethnic Groups; Immigration; Sexuality

Send: Query; Writing sample
How to send: In the body of an email

She is particularly interested in representing a diversity of voices from around the world, and in fresh voices telling stories we haven't heard before. She is fond of immigrant tales and stories concerned with race, sexuality, cross-cultural themes, and notions of identity.

L563 Kelly Van Sant
Literary Agent
United States

https://www.penandparsley.com
https://querymanager.com/query/kellyvansant
https://www.manuscriptwishlist.com/mswl-post/kelly-van-sant/

Literary Agency: KT Literary (**L377**)

CHILDREN'S > *Fiction* > *Middle Grade*

YOUNG ADULT > *Fiction* > *Novels*

Closed to approaches.

Seeks young adult and middle grade fiction, with a particular interest in projects by marginalized creators.

L564 Sarah Jane Freymann Literary Agency
Literary Agency
United States

Submissions@SarahJaneFreymann.com

http://www.sarahjanefreymann.com

ADULT
Fiction > *Novels*
Commercial; Literary

Nonfiction > *Nonfiction Books*
Cookery; Design; Journalism; Lifestyle; Memoir; Narrative Nonfiction; Self Help; Spirituality

YOUNG ADULT > *Fiction* > *Novels*

Send: Query; Writing sample
How to send: In the body of an email; Post

Strongly prefers to receive queries by email. Include pitch letter and first ten pages pasted into the body of the email (no attachments). If approaching by post, include SASE or email address for response.

Literary Agents: Sarah Jane Freymann (**L242**); Steve Schwartz (**L568**)

L565 The Sayle Literary Agency
Literary Agency
1 Petersfield, Cambridge, CB1 1BB
United Kingdom
Tel: +44 (0) 1223 303035

info@sayleliteraryagency.com

http://www.sayleliteraryagency.com

Professional Body: The Association of Authors' Agents (AAA)

Fiction > *Novels*

Nonfiction > *Nonfiction Books*

Closed to approaches.

Established in 1896, we are an independent, full-service literary agency dedicated to representing the finest writers and experts in their fields. We work with experienced editors and publishers and in collaboration with dedicated co-agents to give these writers the best chance of success in a highly competitive and international industry.

Literary Agent: Rachel Calder

L566 Rory Scarfe
Literary Agent; Company Director
United Kingdom

https://www.theblairpartnership.com/literary-agents/rory-scarfe/

Literary Agency: The Blair Partnership

ADULT
Fiction > *Novels*: Commercial

Nonfiction > *Nonfiction Books*: Commercial

Scripts
Film Scripts; *TV Scripts*

CHILDREN'S
Fiction > *Novels*
Nonfiction > *Nonfiction Books*

Closed to approaches.

Represents clients across commercial fiction, children's fiction and non-fiction, as well as screenwriters and brands.

Authors: Marina Abramović; Imran Ahmed; Nimco Ali; Matt Allen; Jane Asher; Rafael Behr; Gary Bell; Ronen Bergman; David Bolchover; Michael Calvin; Nicky Clark; Sir Ronald Cohen; Laura Dodsworth; Owen Eastwood; Henry Fraser; John Fury; Paris Fury; Tyson Fury; Pippa Grange; Catherine Green; Roya Hakakian; Yalda Hakim; Chips Hardy; Maria Hatzistefanis; Jordan Henderson; Amelia Henley; David Holmes; Leigh Hosy-Pickett; Chris Hoy; James Inverne; Nasser David Khalili; Joanne Lake; Frank Lampard; Liz Lawler; Lee Lawrence; Arizona Leger; Aseem Malhotra; Hussain Manawer; Mercy Muroki; Shabnam Nasimi; Maajid Nawaz; Lindsay Nicholson; Catriona Olding; Michal Oshman; Justine Pattison; Adam Peaty; Trevor Phillips; Megan Reeves; Duncan Roe; Terry Ronald; Dan Saunders; Babita Sharma; Jon Smith; Jon Sopel; Dean Stott; Jessica Taylor; Pete Townshend; John Volanthen; Tom Watson; Brian Wood; Nadhim Zahawi

L567 Hannah Schofield
Literary Agent
United Kingdom

hannahsubmissions@lbabooks.com

http://www.lbabooks.com/agent/hannah-schofield/

Literary Agency: LBA Books Ltd

ADULT
Fiction > *Novels*
Book Club Fiction; Commercial; Historical Fiction; Romantasy; Romantic Comedy; Suspense; Thrillers; Women's Fiction

Nonfiction > *Nonfiction Books*
Crime; History; Memoir; Narrative Nonfiction; Personal Development; Social History

YOUNG ADULT > **Fiction** > *Novels*

How to send: Email

Represents a broad list of commercial and reading-group fiction, and select non-fiction.

Author / Literary Agent: Bea Fitzgerald (**L227**)

Authors: Emad Ahmed; Darby Bozeman; Chris Bridges; Amanda Brooke; Charlotte Butterfield; Sam Caporn; Catherine Chang; Erin Connor; Kim Donovan; Elizabeth Drummond; Chloe Duckworth; Moyette Gibbons; Lucy Goacher; Isabella Harcourt; Anam Iqbal; Jenni Keer; Amy Lavelle; Nicole Louie; Marina McCarron; Heather Mottershead; Grace Noakes; Eleanor Pilcher; Ande Pliego; Heidi Shertok; Celia Silvani; Crystal Sung; Tania Tay; David Turner; Catherine Walsh

L568 Steve Schwartz
Literary Agent
United States

http://www.sarahjanefreymann.com/?page_id=3872

Literary Agency: Sarah Jane Freymann Literary Agency (**L564**)

Fiction > *Novels*
Crime; Historical Fiction; Popular; Thrillers

Nonfiction > *Nonfiction Books*
Business; Comedy / Humour; Current Affairs; Psychology; Self Help; Sport; Travel

Send: Query; Writing sample
How to send: In the body of an email

Interested in popular fiction (crime, thrillers, and historical novels), world and national affairs, business books, self-help, psychology, humor, sports and travel.

L569 The Science Factory
Literary Agency
Scheideweg 34C, Hamburg, 20253
Germany
Tel: + 49 40 4327 4959; +44 (0) 20 7193 7296 (Skype)

info@sciencefactory.co.uk

https://www.sciencefactory.co.uk
https://twitter.com/sciencefactory

ACADEMIC > Nonfiction > *Nonfiction Books*
General, and in particular: Health; History; Mathematics; Medicine; Nature; Philosophy; Science; Technology

ADULT > Nonfiction > *Nonfiction Books*
General, and in particular: Health; History; Mathematics; Medicine; Nature; Philosophy; Science; Technology

Send: Query; Writing sample
Don't send: Full text
How to send: Email

Specialises in science, technology, medicine, and natural history, but will also consider other areas of nonfiction. Novelists handled only occasionally, and if there is some special relevance to the agency (e.g. a thriller about scientists, or a novel of ideas). See website for full submission guidelines.

Literary Agents: Jeff Shreve; Tisse Takagi; Peter Tallack

L570 Rosemary Scoular
Literary Agent
United Kingdom

https://www.unitedagents.co.uk/rscoularunitedagentscouk

Literary Agency: United Agents

Nonfiction > *Nonfiction Books*
Adventure; Arts; Food; History; Investigative Journalism; Memoir; Nature; Politics; Popular Science; Travel

Focuses on nonfiction, from food writing to history, popular science and nature, travel and adventure, politics and investigative journalism, the arts and memoir of all kinds.

L571 Chloe Seager
Senior Agent
United Kingdom

https://madeleinemilburn.co.uk/team-member/19023/

Literary Agency: Madeleine Milburn Literary, TV & Film Agency (**L420**)

CHILDREN'S
Fiction > *Middle Grade*
Nonfiction > *Middle Grade*
TEEN > **Fiction** > *Novels*
YOUNG ADULT
Fiction > *Novels*
Nonfiction > *Nonfiction Books*

Send: Query; Pitch; Market info; Author bio; Synopsis; Writing sample
How to send: Email
How not to send: Post

Actively looking for: Middle Grade age 7 and up; clean teen; young adult; non-fiction MG and YA.

L572 Sebes & Bisseling
Literary Agency
United Kingdom

https://sebesbisseling.co.uk

Fiction > *Novels*

Nonfiction > *Nonfiction Books*

Does not want:

> **Fiction** > *Novels*
> Fantasy; Horror; Romance; Science Fiction

Send: Query; Synopsis; Writing sample

London branch of a literary agency with offices in Amsterdam and Stockholm. Represents authors in the US, UK and in translation, for their book, digital and screen adaptation rights. Welcomes submissions from authors writing in English across all genres, except fantasy, scifi, horror, romance, poetry, YA, middle grade and picture books.

L573 Selectric Artists
Literary Agency
9 Union Square #123, Southbury, CT 06488
United States
Tel: +1 (347) 668-5426

query@selectricartists.com

https://www.selectricartists.com

ADULT
Fiction
Graphic Novels: General
Novels: Commercial; Domestic Thriller; Science Fiction
Nonfiction
Graphic Nonfiction: General
Nonfiction Books: Memoir; Narrative Nonfiction
YOUNG ADULT > **Fiction** > *Novels*
Fantasy; Science Fiction

Closed to approaches.

Some categories have become tougher to sell – memoir, YA fantasy, science fiction (both adult and YA), domestic thrillers – so the bar is set even higher since I already have good writers in those areas. But I'm always looking for commercial fiction, literary fiction, narrative nonfiction, graphic novels and graphic nonfiction, and new work from previously under-represented voices. Send query by email with your manuscript attached as a .doc, .pdf, or .pages file. Put the word "query" in the subject line. No queries by phone. Response only if interested.

Literary Agent: Christopher Schelling

L574 Maria Cardona Serra
Literary Agent
Spain

https://www.aevitascreative.com/agent/maria-cardona-serra
https://querymanager.com/query/MariaCardona_Queries

Literary Agency: Aevitas Creative Management (ACM) UK (**L007**)

Fiction > *Novels*
Literary; Romance; Upmarket Crime; Upmarket

Nonfiction > *Nonfiction Books*
Narrative Nonfiction; Women's Issues

Closed to approaches.

Focuses in upmarket and literary fiction by authors who write in English and Spanish. Maria is an editorially minded agent that works closely with her authors with a long-term career plan. She is passionate about international voices and is used to working with authors that live in different corners of the world. She reads broadly yet is particularly drawn by character-driven, heart-wrenching fiction, modern love stories, and genre-bending upmarket crime. She is always looking for that perfect line that makes her thrill, paying special attention to the voice on the page and is always up for a surprise in a manuscript, looking for stories she hasn't read before. She is also interested in narrative non-fiction about women's experiences.

Authors: Safia El Aaddam; Ayesha Harruna Attah; Federico Axat; Lucía Baskaran; Meaghan Beatley; Lucía Benavides; Victor Lloret Blackburn; Maame Blue; Emily Cunningham; Rijula Das; Avni Doshi; Guillermo Erades; Eudald Espluga; Sujatha Fernandes; Karen Havelin; Sunnah Khan; Natalia Litvinova; Lucía Alba Martínez; Elena Medel; Elizabeth Morris; Irene Muchemi-Ndiritu; Maria Nicolau; Gemma Ruiz Palà; Mariane Pearl; Claudia Polo; Alana S. Portero; Zara Raheem; Devika Rege; Yaffa S. Santos; Marta Sanz; Shubhangi Swarup; María Sánchez; Cristina Sánchez-Andrade; Begoña Gómez Urzaiz

L575 Charlotte Seymour
Literary Agent
United Kingdom

charlotte@johnsonandalcock.co.uk

http://www.johnsonandalcock.co.uk/charlotte-seymour

Literary Agency: Johnson & Alcock (**L335**)

Fiction > *Novels*
  Book Club Fiction; Crime; Literary; Suspense; Thrillers

Nonfiction > *Nonfiction Books*
  Arts; Cookery; Cultural History; Food; Journalism; Nature; Popular Science; Social History

Send: Query; Synopsis; Writing sample
How to send: Email

In fiction, looks for book club and literary fiction as well as outstanding character – and voice-driven crime, thriller and suspense. She loves writing that crosses boundaries, whether geographic or linguistic or in bringing a twist to a genre.

In non-fiction, she is interested in accessible, engaging writing on a range of subjects including popular science, social and cultural history, reportage, nature, the arts, food and cookery. She especially loves hybrid books, for example, when in a memoir, the personal is interwoven with a bigger story or subject.

L576 The Shaw Agency

Literary Agency
United Kingdom

https://www.theshawagency.co.uk

ADULT
  Fiction > *Novels*
    Commercial; Literary
  Nonfiction > *Nonfiction Books*
    Lifestyle; Narrative Nonfiction; Wellbeing

CHILDREN'S
  Fiction > *Novels*
  Nonfiction > *Nonfiction Books*

TEEN > **Fiction** > *Novels*

Closed to approaches.

Handles literary and commercial fiction, fact and fiction books for children (6+) and teenagers/young adults, and narrative non-fiction. Send query through online form with one-page synopsis, first 10 pages, and email address for response. See website for full guidelines.

Literary Agent: Kate Shaw

L577 Sheil Land Associates Ltd

Literary Agency
RM 9-25, LABS House, 15-19 Bloomsbury Way, London, WC1A 2TH
United Kingdom
Tel: +44 (0) 20 7405 9351
Fax: +44 (0) 20 7831 2127

submissions@sheilland.co.uk

https://www.sheilland.com
https://twitter.com/sheilland

ADULT
  Fiction > *Novels*
    Book Club Fiction; Commercial Women's Fiction; Contemporary; Crime; Family Saga; Fantasy; Ghost Stories; Historical Fiction; Horror; Literary; Mystery; Romance; Science Fiction; Thrillers
  Nonfiction
    Gift Books: Comedy / Humour
    Nonfiction Books: Biography; Cookery; Gardening; Lifestyle; Memoir; Mind, Body, Spirit; Personal Development; Politics; Popular Science; Psychology; Travel
  Scripts
    Film Scripts; *TV Scripts*; *Theatre Scripts*

CHILDREN'S
  Fiction > *Novels*
  Scripts
    Animation Scripts; *TV Scripts*

YOUNG ADULT > **Fiction** > *Novels*

Send: Query
Don't send: Full text
How to send: Email

A long-established literary, theatrical and film agency. Welcomes approaches from new clients of all backgrounds, whether they have been published already or are first time writers. Looks for literary fiction, commercial fiction and non-fiction. Also represents celebrities and journalists with a story to tell.

Authors: Peter Ackroyd; Melvyn Bragg; Susan Hill; David Lister; Catherine Robertson; Jonathan Steele

Literary Agents: Gaia Banks (**L040**); Piers Blofeld; Ian Drury; Lucy Fawcett; Sonia Land; Rebecca Lyon (**L411**)

L578 Hannah Sheppard

Literary Agent
United Kingdom

Literary Agency: Hannah Sheppard Literary Agency (**L291**)

L579 Sheree Bykofsky Associates, Inc.

Literary Agency
4326 Harbor Beach Boulevard, PO Box 706, Brigantine, NJ 08203
United States

shereebee@aol.com

http://www.shereebee.com

Nonfiction > *Nonfiction Books*
  Biography; Business; Comedy / Humour; Cookery; Current Affairs; Films; Games; Health; Multicultural; Music; Parenting; Personal Development; Psychology; Spirituality; Women's Interests

Send: Query
Don't send: Full text
How to send: Email
How not to send: Fax; Post

Send query by email only. Include one page query in the body of the email. No attachments.

Authors: Jeffrey Fox; Sue Hitzmann; Jason Kelly

Literary Agent: Sheree Bykofsky

L580 Shesto Literary

Literary Agency
United Kingdom

https://shesto-literary.com

Professional Body: The Association of Authors' Agents (AAA)

Fiction > *Novels*

Nonfiction > *Nonfiction Books*

Representing authors of fiction and nonfiction.

Literary Agent: Camilla Shestopal (**L581**)

L581 Camilla Shestopal

Literary Agent
United Kingdom

https://shesto-literary.com
https://shesto-literary.com/about/

Literary Agency: Shesto Literary (**L580**)

ADULT
  Fiction > *Novels*
    Crime; Ghost Stories; Historical Fiction; Horror; Mystery; Psychological Thrillers; Romantic Suspense; Supernatural / Paranormal; Suspense; Thrillers; Women's Fiction
  Nonfiction > *Nonfiction Books*
    General, and in particular: Memoir; Narrative Nonfiction; Self Help

CHILDREN'S > **Fiction** > *Middle Grade*

YOUNG ADULT > **Fiction** > *Novels*

Send: Query; Author bio; Synopsis; Writing sample; Proposal; Outline
How to send: Online contact form

Looking for: crime fiction (encompassing thriller, mystery, psychological thriller); supernatural suspense; Ghost stories; romantic suspense; historical fiction; women's fiction; children's (middle grade and YA only); horror; and non-fiction (including anything which is topical, appealing, accessible such as self-help, narrative and memoir).

Do not send science-fiction, fantasy, short stories, poetry collections, erotica, or picture books for children.

L582 Michael Signorelli

Literary Agent
United States

https://aevitascreative.com/agents/
https://querymanager.com/query/2593

Literary Agency: Aevitas

Fiction > *Novels*
  Commercial; Literary

Nonfiction > *Nonfiction Books*
  Culture; Current Affairs; History; Memoir; Politics; Science; Sport; Technology

Send: Pitch; Market info; Writing sample
How to send: Query Manager

Represents literary and commercial fiction as well as nonfiction in cultural history, current affairs, memoir, politics, science, sports, and technology.

Authors: Mark Arsenault; Anne Soon Choi; Brandi Collins-Dexter; Matthew Davis; Joan Donovan; Emily Dreyfuss; Abby Ellin; Justin Evans; Morgan Falconer; Alex Cody Foster; Jared Fox; Meryl Frank; Brian Friedberg; J. Weston Phippen; Nancy Kress; Robert Lanza; Oksana Masters; Kelly Richmond Pope; Benjamin Reeves; Kevin Sites; Adam Philip Stern; Deanne Stillman; CeCe Telfer; Michelle Theall

L583 Julia Silk

Literary Agent
United Kingdom

julia@greyhoundliterary.co.uk

https://greyhoundliterary.co.uk/agent/julia-silk/
https://twitter.com/juliasreading
https://www.instagram.com/juliasreading/
https://www.pinterest.co.uk/juliasreadingbo/my-favourite-books/

Literary Agency: Greyhound Literary (**L278**)

Fiction > *Novels*
  Commercial; Historical Fiction; Literary; Upmarket Crime; Upmarket Thrillers

Nonfiction > *Nonfiction Books*
  Crime; Health; Journalism; Lifestyle; Memoir; Narrative Nonfiction; Wellbeing

Send: Query; Writing sample
How to send: Email

In fiction she is looking for smart, compelling writing across the spectrum from commercial to literary, particularly when it opens a door into a previously inaccessible world or experience, exposes our flaws and hypocrisies in new ways, or upends expectations with wit and energy. She is also drawn to the combination of the acutely personal and the universal that makes great memoir, as well as the blurring of the lines of form and genre in books across categories such as true crime/memoir. She is a huge fan of upmarket crime and thrillers and is also on the lookout for immaculately voiced historical fiction. In narrative non-fiction she is keen to hear from journalists and experts illuminating new stories and previously unexplored subjects; on the practical side she represents a number of writers in health, wellbeing and lifestyle, and is interested in original evidence-based proposals in this area from experts with a strong platform. She loves to work with writers and on books that shape and change readers' view of the world.

Authors: Tobi Asare; Paddy Barrett; Juliet Bell; Leona Nichole Black; Owen Booth; Luce Brett; Kirsty Eyre; Marchelle Farrell; A P Firdaus; Liz Fraser; Claire Gleeson; Janet Gover; Sarah Graham; Karen Gurney; Maisie Hill; Heidi James; Ginger Jones; Fiona Longmuir; Amanda Mason; Charlotte Ord; Amy Ransom; Rebecca Rogers; Rebecca Schiller; Clare Seal; Gemma Tizzard; Penny Wincer

L584 Janet Silver

Literary Agent; Senior Partner
United States

https://aevitascreative.com/agents/

Literary Agency: Aevitas

Fiction > *Novels*: Literary

Nonfiction > *Nonfiction Books*: Creative Nonfiction

Poetry > *Poetry Collections*

Closed to approaches.

Represents a roster of bestselling and award-winning authors of literary fiction, creative nonfiction, and poetry.

Authors: Dur E Aziz Amna; Kendra Atleework; Megan Benton; Michael Byers; Christopher Castellani; Michael Collier; Jonathan Crowl; Vievee Francis; Christa Fraser; Omer Friedlander; Linda Gregerson; Jennifer Grotz; Brooks Hansen; Angela Palm Hopkins; Sativa January; Menachem Kaiser; Catherine Kim; Dana Kletter; Alyssa Knickerbocker; Chaney Kwak; Jen Lazar; Samuel Leader; Tom Macher; Anthony Marra; Amanda Rose Martinez; Spencer Matheson; Mark Mayer; Anna Mazhirov; Matthew Neill Null; D. Wystan Owen; Matthew Pockrus; Hanna Pylväinen; Ladette Randolph; Humaira Awais Shahid; Alan Shapiro; Safiya Sinclair; Emily Strasser; Cheryl Strayed; Mecca Jamilah Sullivan; Ruby Todd; Monique Truong; Zachary Tyler Vickers; Devon Walker-Figueroa; Yara Zgheib

L585 Tanera Simons

Literary Agent
United Kingdom

tanera@darleyanderson.com

https://www.darleyanderson.com/our-team
https://twitter.com/tanera_simons

Literary Agency: The Darley Anderson Agency (**L157**)

Fiction > *Novels*
  Book Club Fiction; Commercial; Historical Fiction; Romance; Romantic Comedy

How to send: Email attachment
How not to send: Post

Looking for romantic comedies, sweeping love stories, accessible book club fiction, historical/timeslip, and general commercial fiction.

Authors: Mandy Baggot; Sara Bragg; Laura Carter; Claire Frost; Mary Hargreaves; Sandie Jones; Beth O'Leary; Sally Page; Kate G. Smith; Emma Steele; Sophie White; Ally Zetterberg

L586 Cara Lee Simpson

Literary Agent
United Kingdom

clsimpson@pfd.co.uk

https://petersfraserdunlop.com/agent/cara-lee-simpson/

Literary Agency: Peters Fraser + Dunlop

Fiction > *Novels*
  General, and in particular: Book Club Fiction; Ethnic Groups; Family Saga; Gender; Literary; Relationships; Social Class; Speculative

Nonfiction > *Nonfiction Books*
  Memoir; Narrative Nonfiction; Nature; Real Life Stories; Social Commentary

Send: Query; Synopsis; Writing sample; Proposal; Author bio
How to send: Email

I am on the lookout for general fiction, immersive book club novels and literary fiction. I generally lean towards fiction that is accessible to a wide readership while remaining beautifully written, and I'm always interested in stories that explore gender, race, class, sexuality, and those which offer a profound look at relationship dynamics. I would love to find a traditional intergenerational family or friendship story (contemporary or historical), something sweeping in scope with a richly imagined setting, exploring an unusual event or unexpected setup. I would also love to find something speculative. I work on a select number of narrative non-fiction titles and am interested in memoirs and real-life stories, nature writing, and social commentaries told through an interesting lens and with a strong sense of personal journey.

Authors: Tufayel Ahmed; Jacqueline Bublitz; Abi Canepa-Anson; Angela Chadwick; Roxy Dunn; Ben Halls; C.R. Howell; Kiprop Kimutai; Shilo Kino; Kira Mcpherson; Niamh Ní Mhaoileoin; Okechukwu Nzelu; Jonathan Page; Dan Spencer

L587 Aiden Siobhan
Associate Agent
United States

asiobhan@ldlainc.com

https://aidensiobhan.com
http://www.ldlainc.com/about
https://querymanager.com/query/asiobhan
https://twitter.com/aiden_png
http://instagram.com/aiden.png

Literary Agency: Laura Dail Literary Agency

ADULT
  Fiction
    Graphic Novels: General
    Novels: Contemporary; Historical Fiction; LGBTQIA; Psychological Horror; Romance; Speculative; Supernatural / Paranormal
  Nonfiction > *Graphic Nonfiction*

CHILDREN'S > Fiction
  Graphic Novels: General
  Middle Grade: General, and in particular: Fantasy
YOUNG ADULT > Fiction
  Graphic Novels: General
  Novels: General, and in particular: Fantasy

How to send: Query Manager

Loves any story that is diverse, heartfelt, beautifully written, and makes them stay up reading until 3 A.M. Send them your trope-filled, high-stakes, addicting novels that will hook them so well they'll have to draw fan art (and they will)!

L588 Antoinette Van Sluytman
Associate Agent
United States

https://www.lookingglasslit.com/antoinette-van-sluytman
https://querymanager.com/query/2783
https://aalitagents.org/author/antoinette-van-sluytman/
https://twitter.com/antoinight
https://www.instagram.com/toni_vansluy
https://www.linkedin.com/in/antoinette-van-sluytman-83b5a423a/

Literary Agency: Looking Glass Literary & Media Management (**L406**)
Professional Body: Association of American Literary Agents (AALA)

ADULT > Fiction
  Graphic Novels: General
  Novels: Adventure; Dark Fantasy; High / Epic Fantasy; Historical Fiction; Horror; Science Fiction; Speculative
YOUNG ADULT > Fiction
  Graphic Novels; Novels

Closed to approaches.

Interested in all genres of speculative fiction, specifically cosmic horror, dark fantasy, epic fantasy, sci-fi, in addition to historical fiction. Antoinette maintains special interest in adult projects but is also open to select YA and graphic novels. In general she loves lyrical prose that challenges narrative conventions, ambitiously immersive worlds inspired by different cultures, morally gray and dysfunctional but lovable characters with fun dynamics, and new takes on old tropes. She is drawn to atmospheric and lyrical prose and complex philosophical/psychological themes across all genres. Some general themes she enjoys are adventures, antiheroines, quirky concepts you might find in an anime, dark fantasy, and anticolonialism. In historical fiction she's interested in finding stories inspired by non-western mythologies or about the untold stories of female heroines around the world.

L589 Shania N. Soler
Literary Agent
United States

https://www.metamorphosisliteraryagency.com
https://www.metamorphosisliteraryagency.com/submissions
https://querymanager.com/query/shaniansoler
https://x.com/beyond_literary

Literary Agency: Metamorphosis Literary Agency (**L444**)

ADULT > Fiction > *Novels*
  Book Club Fiction; Comedy / Humour; Dystopian Fiction; Folklore, Myths, and Legends; Gothic; High / Epic Fantasy; Historical Fiction; Horror; Low Fantasy; Magical Realism; Romance; Romantasy

CHILDREN'S > Fiction > *Middle Grade*

NEW ADULT > Fiction > *Novels*

YOUNG ADULT > Fiction > *Novels*

Closed to approaches.

Has been an avid book lover from the moment she picked up Richelle Mead's Vampire Academy. Ever since then, her TBR pile has steadily grown. Currently working on an MA at the University of Leeds, she has received her Bachelor of Arts in English from the University of Maine and plans to pursue a PhD in Japan, where she spent 7 months during her undergrad studying the language and culture.

L590 Jennifer March Soloway
Literary Agent
United States

soloway@andreabrownlit.com

https://querymanager.com/query/JenniferMarchSoloway
https://twitter.com/marchsoloway

Literary Agency: Andrea Brown Literary Agency, Inc.

ADULT > Fiction > *Novels*
  Commercial; Crime; Literary; Psychological Suspense

CHILDREN'S > Fiction
  Middle Grade: Adventure; Comedy / Humour; Contemporary; Fantasy; Ghost Stories; Mystery; Realistic
  Picture Books: General, and in particular: Comedy / Humour
YOUNG ADULT > Fiction > *Novels*
  Family; Literary; Mental Health; Psychological Horror; Relationships; Romance; Sexuality; Suspense; Thrillers

Send: Query
How to send: Email; By referral

Represents authors and illustrators of picture book, middle grade, and YA stories, and is actively building her list. Although she specializes in children's literature, she also represents adult fiction, both literary and commercial, particularly crime and psychological suspense projects.

Currently accepting queries by referral only.

L591 Sophie Hicks Agency
Literary Agency
4 Providence Yard, Ezra Street, London, E2 7RJ
United Kingdom
Tel: +44 (0) 20 3617 0997

info@sophiehicksagency.com

https://www.sophiehicksagency.com
https://twitter.com/SophieHicksAg
https://www.instagram.com/sophiehicksagency/

Professional Body: The Association of Authors' Agents (AAA)

ADULT
  Fiction > *Novels*
  Nonfiction > *Nonfiction Books*

CHILDREN'S > Fiction > *Novels*

Send: Query; Writing sample; Synopsis
How to send: Email

Welcomes submissions. Send query by email with sample pages attached as Word or PDF documents. See website for full guidelines and specific submissions email addresses. No poetry or scripts for theatre, film or television, and not currently accepting illustrated books for children.

Authors: Sarah Bannan; Lee Boyce; William Butler-Adams; Helen Chandler-Wilde; Carl Cox; Sarah Crosby; Michaela Dunbar; Ruth Fitzmaurice; Kate Ford; Lewis Hine; Shahroo Izadi; Signe Johansen; Sophie Monks Kaufman; Jesse McClure; Phil McNulty; Andrew Meehan; Katie Treggiden; Claire Walsh; Tom Whipple; Jim White

Literary Agents: Sophie Hicks; Sarah Williams (**L663**)

L592 Arley Sorg
Literary Agent
United States

https://arleysorg.com
https://ktliterary.com/submissions/
https://querymanager.com/query/QueryArley

Literary Agency: KT Literary (**L377**)

Fiction > *Novels*
Environment; Fantasy; Horror; Literary; Science Fiction; Speculative

Closed to approaches.

Primarily interested in adult speculative titles, including science fiction, fantasy, and horror with speculative/fantastic elements, literary speculative fiction, and climate fiction.

L593 James Spackman
Literary Agent
United Kingdom

https://www.thebksagency.com/about
https://www.thebksagency.com/submissions

Literary Agency: The BKS Agency (**L065**)

Fiction > *Graphic Novels*

Nonfiction
Graphic Nonfiction: General
Nonfiction Books: Culture; Music; Sport

Send: Query; Outline; Author bio
How to send: Online submission system

Looking for sport, music, culture and smart thinking.

L594 Spring Literary
Literary Agency
United Kingdom

submissions@springliterary.com

https://www.springliterary.com
https://twitter.com/springliterary
https://www.instagram.com/springliterary

CHILDREN'S > **Fiction** > *Picture Books*

YOUNG ADULT
Fiction > *Novels*
Nonfiction > *Nonfiction Books*

Send: Query; Synopsis; Writing sample; Author bio; Full text
How to send: Email

Specialises in children's and YA writing and illustration. Works with all the major publishing houses, plus entertainment companies, to ensure the best match for each book, author and illustrator.

Literary Agent: Neil Dunnicliffe (**L183**)

L595 Hayley Steed
Literary Agent
United Kingdom

https://www.janklowandnesbit.co.uk
https://janklowandnesbit.co.uk/agency/hayley-steed

Literary Agency: Janklow & Nesbit UK Ltd (**L330**)

Fiction > *Novels*
Book Club Fiction; Commercial; Dark Academia; Dark; Dystopian Fiction; Family; High Concept; Historical Fiction; Horror; Light Fantasy; Mystery; Romance; Romantasy; Romantic Comedy; Speculative; Thrillers; Women's Fiction

Send: Query; Synopsis; Writing sample
How to send: Email
How not to send: Post

I'm looking for commercial and book club fiction across all genres. I'm particularly drawn to a strong hook – a setting, scenario or a 'what if' that captures my attention immediately and leads the way into a gripping story. I love to find compelling and distinctive voices that draw me in but are matched with well-paced plots and commercial appeal. I'm always open to books that cross genres, or which feel a little different.

L596 Jenny Stephens
Literary Agent
United States

https://www.sll.com/our-team

Literary Agency: Sterling Lord Literistic, Inc. (**L597**)

ADULT > **Nonfiction**
Illustrated Books: General
Nonfiction Books: Cookery; Cultural Criticism; Environment; Food; History; Lifestyle; Narrative Nonfiction; Nature; Prescriptive Nonfiction; Social Justice; Wellbeing

CHILDREN'S > **Nonfiction**
Illustrated Books; Nonfiction Books

Send: Query; Synopsis; Writing sample
How to send: Online submission system

Represents nonfiction in a variety of categories including cookbooks; practical lifestyle projects; prescriptive books particularly in the wellness and mindfulness spaces; and narrative writing on environmental, social, and economic justice; natural sciences; history; food; and cultural criticism. For both adults and kids, she is often drawn to visual books that inform and explore through both text and image.

L597 Sterling Lord Literistic, Inc.
Literary Agency
594 Broadway, New York, NY 10012
United States
Tel: +1 (212) 780-6050
Fax: +1 (212) 780-6095

info@sll.com

https://www.sll.com

Send: Query; Synopsis; Writing sample
How to send: Online submission system

Select one agent to query and approach via online form on website.

Associate Agent: Chris Combemale (**L133**)

Chair / Literary Agent: Peter Matson

Executive Vice President / Literary Agent: Laurie Liss (**L403**)

Foreign Rights Director: Szilvia Molnar

Literary Agent / President: Philippa Brophy

Literary Agent / Vice President: Jim Rutman (**L558**)

Literary Agents: Elizabeth Bewley; Danielle Bukowski (**L092**); Jessica Friedman; Mary Krienke (**L375**); Sarah Landis (**L381**); Jenny Stephens (**L596**)

Senior Agents: Robert Guinsler (**L283**); Neeti Madan (**L419**)

L598 Sternig & Byrne Literary Agency
Literary Agency
2370 S. 107th Street, Apt 4, Milwaukee, Wisconsin 53227-2036
United States
Tel: +1 (414) 328-8034

jackbyrne@hotmail.com

https://sternig-byrne-agency.com

Professional Bodies: Science Fiction and Fantasy Writers of America (SFWA); Mystery Writers of America (MWA)

Fiction > *Novels*
Fantasy; Science Fiction

Closed to approaches.

Send brief query by post or email in first instance (if sending by email send in the body of the mail, do not send attachments). Will request further materials if interested. Currently only considering science fiction and fantasy. Preference given to writers with a publishing history.

Authors: Katherine Addison; John Haefele; Lael Littke; Kelly McCullough; Sarah Monette; Moira Moore; Jo Walton; David Michael Williams; John C. Wright

Literary Agent: Jack Byrne

L599 Douglas Stewart
Literary Agent; Vice President
United States

https://www.sll.com/our-team

Literary Agency: Sterling Lord Literistic, Inc. (**L597**)

ADULT
Fiction > *Novels*
Commercial; Literary

Nonfiction > *Nonfiction Books*: Narrative Nonfiction

CHILDREN'S
  Fiction > Novels
  Nonfiction > Nonfiction Books: Narrative Nonfiction
YOUNG ADULT
  Fiction > Novels
  Nonfiction > Nonfiction Books: Narrative Nonfiction

Send: Query; Synopsis; Writing sample
How to send: Online submission system

List consists of fiction and narrative nonfiction for all ages, from the innovatively literary to the unabashedly commercial, and includes multiple million-copy bestsellers and award-winners.

L600 Geoffrey Stone
Literary Agent
United States

gstone@rudyagency.com

http://rudyagency.com/

Literary Agency: The Rudy Agency (**L553**)

Nonfiction > *Nonfiction Books*
  Christian Living; Cookery; History; Sport

Send: Query
How to send: Email

Looking for proposals and manuscripts on history, sports, cooking, personal stories, and Christian living, and is open to a wide range of non-fiction and fiction that align with those interests.

L601 StoryWise
Literary Agency
41 Jubilee Road, Swanage, Dorset, BH19 2SE
United Kingdom

submissions@storywise.uk

https://storywise.uk
https://www.facebook.com/storywiseagency
https://twitter.com/StoryWiseAgency
https://www.instagram.com/storywiseagency/

Professional Body: The Association of Authors' Agents (AAA)

CHILDREN'S
  Fiction
    Middle Grade; *Picture Books*
  Nonfiction > *Nonfiction Books*

Closed to approaches.

Specialist children's literary agency representing bestselling and award-winning authors and illustrators of picture books, fiction and non-fiction.

L602 Strachan Literary Agency
Literary Agency
P.O. Box 2091, Annapolis, MD 21404
United States

Query@StrachanLit.com

http://www.strachanlit.com

Types: Fiction; Nonfiction
Subjects: Autobiography; Comedy / Humour; Commercial; Cookery; Crime; Gardening; Health; Lifestyle; Literary; Mystery; Personal Development; Religion; Suspense; Thrillers; Travel; Women's Interests
Markets: Adult; Children's; Young Adult

Closed to approaches.

Send query through online form on website, providing a brief description of your book as well as your biographical information and writing credits or professional experience. No samples or mss unless requested. No picture books, genre fiction, poetry, or screenplays.

Literary Agents: Laura Strachan; Marisa Zeppieri

L603 The Stringer Literary Agency LLC
Literary Agency
8429 Lorraine Road #408, Lakewood Ranch, FL 34202
United States

https://www.stringerlit.com
https://www.instagram.com/stringerlit/
https://www.pinterest.com/stringerlit/
https://www.facebook.com/StringerLit
https://twitter.com/MarleneStringer

Professional Bodies: Association of American Literary Agents (AALA); Mystery Writers of America (MWA); Society of Children's Book Writers and Illustrators (SCBWI); The Authors Guild; Women's Fiction Writers Association (WFWA)

ADULT > **Fiction** > *Novels*

CHILDREN'S > **Fiction**
  Middle Grade; *Picture Books*
YOUNG ADULT > **Fiction** > *Novels*

Send: Query; Synopsis; Pitch; Outline; Author bio
How to send: Query Manager

A full-service literary agency specializing in commercial fiction since 2008.

Authors: Michelle Collins Anderson; Ciaran Bartlett; Emily Bleeker; Jen K Blom; Anna Bradley; Anabelle Bryant; Judy Campbell-Smith; Melinda Chiu Cook; Phyllis Dixon; Charlie Donlea; Trish Esden; Alyxandra Harvey; Erica Hayes; Lucy Hedrick; Isabella Kamal; Kristin Kisska; Caroline Lesniak; David Lewis; Guy Mace; Liane Merciel; Terri Parlato; Liz Perrine; Molly Pierce; Travis Simpson; Luanne G. Smith; Kate Pawson Studer; Bethany Wiggins; Sophie Williamson; Clare Zeschky

Literary Agents: Shari Maurer (**L433**); Marlene Stringer (**L604**)

L604 Marlene Stringer
Literary Agent
United States

https://aalitagents.org/author/marlenes/
https://querymanager.com/query/StringerLit

Literary Agency: The Stringer Literary Agency LLC (**L603**)
Professional Body: Association of American Literary Agents (AALA)

ADULT > **Fiction** > *Novels*
  Commercial; Historical Fiction; Literary; Psychological Horror; Women's Fiction

YOUNG ADULT > **Fiction** > *Novels*
  Contemporary; Crime; Fantasy; Magical Realism; Mystery; Romance; Suspense; Thrillers

Does not want:

  Fiction > *Novels*: Erotic Romance

How to send: Query Manager

Open to Book club fiction that straddles the commercial/literary line; Historical fiction; Women's Fiction, both contemporary and historical; Older YA, both fantasy and contemporary; Crime Fiction; Thrillers of all types; Suspense; Mysteries of all types; Romance (except erotic); Psychological Horror; Magical Realism.

L605 Amy Strong
Assistant Agent
United Kingdom

https://lbabooks.com/agents/amy-strong

Literary Agency: LBA Books Ltd

Fiction > *Novels*
  Fairy Tales; Fantasy; Folklore, Myths, and Legends

Closed to approaches.

I am an avid reader with an eclectic taste in fiction. But my go-to genre is fantasy. I especially love books that draw on fairy tales or folklore – even better if they approach classic stories with a new twist.

L606 Catharine Strong
Associate Agent
United States

Literary Agency: Aevitas

L607 The Strothman Agency
Literary Agency
Box 255, Newcastle, ME 04553
United States

strothmanagency@gmail.com
info@strothmanagency.com

https://www.strothmanagency.com/
https://twitter.com/StrothmanAgency
https://www.facebook.com/StrothmanAgency/

Send: Query
How to send: Email; Query Manager
How not to send: Email attachment; Post

Only accepts electronic submissions. Physical query letters will be recycled unopened. Accepts referrals by email. Queries without referral must approach through Query Manager. Do not send entire manuscripts or attachments unless requested. All unrequested attachments will be deleted unread. Does not accept or respond to queries via fax or telephone.

Literary Agent / Partner: Wendy Strothman (**L608**)

Senior Agent: Lauren MacLeod (**L418**)

L608 Wendy Strothman
Literary Agent; Partner
United States

https://www.aevitascreative.com/agent/wendy-strothman
https://www.strothmanagency.com/about
https://querymanager.com/query/WStrothman
http://aaronline.org/Sys/PublicProfile/2176866/417813

Literary Agencies: Aevitas; The Strothman Agency (**L607**)
Professional Body: Association of American Literary Agents (AALA)

Nonfiction > *Nonfiction Books*
Current Affairs; History; Narrative Journalism; Narrative Nonfiction; Nature; Science

Closed to approaches.

Looking for books that matter, books that change the way we think about things we take for granted, that tell stories that readers can't forget, and advance scholarship and knowledge. History, narrative nonfiction, narrative journalism, science and nature, and current affairs.

Accepts referrals by email; otherwise approach through Query Manager.

Authors: Alan Allport; Michelle Wilde Anderson; Tonio Andrade; Christian G. Appy; Deborah N. Archer; Ray Arsenault; Shadi Bartsch; Alice Baumgartner; Sian Beilock; David W. Blight; Nikolas Bowie; Mark Philip Bradley; Thanassis Cambanis; Peter Canellos; Tess Chakkalakal; Chip Colwell; Elena Conis; Peter Conti-Brown; Catherine Conybeare; Darcie DeAngelo; Gloria Dickie; Laurent DuBois; Scott V. Edwards; Caitlin Fitz; Richard T. Ford; Joanne B. Freeman; James K. Galbraith; Michael Graetz; Linda Greenhouse; Martha Hodes; David Hollinger; Yunte Huang; Pacifique Irankunda; Gene Jarrett; Daniel Brock Johnson; Mara Kardas-Nelson; Kenn Kaufman; Thomas Forrest Kelly; David Kertzer; Barbara Keys; Anthony Kronman; Carlton F. W. Larson; Daniel Lewis; Joseph Manning; W. Caleb McDaniel; Catherine McNeur; Alain Mikhail; Tony Molho; Eric Moskowitz; Benjamin Nathans; Amy Ellis Nutt; Liesl Olson; Bennett Parten; Steven Pincus; Benjamin Reiss; Daphna Renan; Judith Resnik; Alison F. Richard; Seth Rockman; Anne Ruderman; Benjamin Taylor; Yanis Varoufakis; Shane White

L609 Stuart Krichevsky Literary Agency, Inc.
Literary Agency
118 East 28th Street, Suite 908, New York, NY 10016
United States
Tel: +1 (212) 725-5288
Fax: +1 (212) 725-5275

query@skagency.com

http://skagency.com

ADULT
Fiction > *Novels*
Nonfiction > *Nonfiction Books*

YOUNG ADULT
Fiction > *Novels*
Nonfiction > *Nonfiction Books*

Send: Query; Writing sample
How to send: In the body of an email

Send query by email with first few pages of your manuscript (up to 10) pasted into body of the email (no attachments). See website for complete submission guidelines and appropriate submission addresses for each agent.

Authors: Addison Armstrong; Roxanna Asgarian; Ahmed Badr; Emily Bloom; Katherine Blunt; Lyndsie Bourgon; Sol Brager; Hannah Brencher; Shavone Charles; Angela Chen; Carla Ciccone; Georgia Cloepfil; Chelsea Conaboy; Caren Cooper; Michelle Cyca; Ella Delany; Helen Donahue; Gabriel Dozal; Hope Ewing; Victoria Facelli; Chelsea Fairless; Anita Felicelli; Kathryn Finney; Kit Fox; John Fram; Katie Fricas; Adriana Gallardo; Lauren Garroni; Olivia Gatwood; Elyssa Goodman; Jessica Goudeau; Rose Hackman; Anita Hannig; Karen Ho; Lizz Huerta; Gabino Iglesias; Sarah Jaffe; Rachel McCarthy James; Amanda Jayatissa; R. Dean Johnson; Sophie Lucido Johnson; Charlotte Kaufman; Megan Kimble; Cassidy Krug; Dan Lewis; Audrea Lim; Catherine Lo; Michael Loynd; Julie Lunde; Jennifer Lunden; Bernice McFadden; Peter Mercurio; Sarafina Nance; Farah Nayeri; Okezie Nwoka; José Olivarez; Madeline Ostrander; Robin Page; Soraya Palmer; Amy Peterson; Karen Pinchin; Mira Ptacin; Shelley Puhak; José R. Ralat; Reyes Ramirez; Lydia Reeder; Raquel Reichard; Victoria Reihana; Ruben Reyes; Nadim Roberts; Prisca Dorcas Mojica Rodriguez; Zoë Schiffer; David Schonfeld; A. Brad Schwartz; Marina Scott; Margot Lee Shetterly; David Shih; Brie Spangler; Rachel Swaby; Kim Thai; Sofi Thanhauser; Kaitlyn Tiffany; Carson Vaughan; Sarah Vogel; Sarah Weinman; Kimberley Welman; Christina Wilcox; Nina Willner; Bernice Yeung; Charlyne Yi; Tom Zeller; Sara Zin

Literary Agents: Melissa Danaczko (**L153**); Barbara Jones (**L338**); Stuart Krichevsky; David Patterson; Aemilia Phillips (**L515**); Hannah Schwartz; Laura Usselman (**L639**); Mackenzie Brady Watson; Chandler Wickers (**L659**)

L610 Susan Schulman Literary Agency
Literary Agency
454 West 44th Street, New York, NY 10036
United States
Tel: +1 (212) 713-1633

Susan@Schulmanagency.com

https://twitter.com/SusanSchulman

Professional Body: Association of American Literary Agents (AALA)

ADULT
Fiction > *Novels*
General, and in particular: Commercial; Literary; Women's Fiction

Nonfiction > *Nonfiction Books*
Commercial; Creativity; Economics; Finance; Health; History; Legal; Literary; Memoir; Mind, Body, Spirit; Politics; Psychology; Social Issues; Writing

CHILDREN'S
Fiction
Board Books; Chapter Books; Middle Grade; Picture Books
Nonfiction > *Nonfiction Books*
History; Memoir; Popular Culture; Science

YOUNG ADULT > **Fiction** > *Novels*

Send: Query; Synopsis; Writing sample; Author bio
How to send: Email

Specializes in representing motion picture, television and allied rights, foreign rights, live stage including commercial theater, opera and dance adaptations, new media rights including e-book and digital applications, and other subsidiary rights on behalf of North American publishers and literary agents. The agency also represents its own clients domestically and internationally in all markets. The agency has a particular interest in fiction and non-fiction books for, by and about women and women's issues and interests, as well as all levels of children's books including picture books, middle-grade and young adult, history, science, pop culture, and memoir. Our primary interest however is in authors and their projects which explore big ideas about the world and being human. The agency's areas of focus include: commercial and literary fiction and non-fiction, specifically narrative memoir, politics, economics, social issues, history, urban planning, finance, law, health, psychology, body/mind/sprit, and creativity and writing.

Associate Agent: Emelie Burl

Literary Agent: Susan Schulman

L611 Kari Sutherland
Literary Agent
United States

kari@ktliterary.com

https://ktliterary.com/about/
https://querymanager.com/query/Kari_Sutherland_Query_Form
https://twitter.com/KariSutherland

Literary Agency: KT Literary (**L377**)

ADULT > **Fiction** > *Novels*: Upmarket

CHILDREN'S > **Fiction**
  Chapter Books; Graphic Novels; Middle Grade; Picture Books
YOUNG ADULT > **Fiction** > *Novels*

How to send: Query Manager

Middle grade and YA are at the heart of her list, but she also represents picture books, chapter books, graphic novels, and upmarket fiction.

L612 Alice Sutherland-Hawes
Literary Agent
United Kingdom

https://www.ashliterary.com/#about

Literary Agency: ASH Literary

Closed to approaches.

Authors: Dina Al-Sabawi; Rebecca Ann; HF Brownfield; Ryan Crawford; Becki Jayne Crossley; Alex Falase-Koya; Abimbola Fashola; Kereen Getten; Tamika Gibson; Adina Glickman; Erica Gomez; Gina Gonzales; Sarah Guillory; Ravena Guron; Radiya Hafiza; Anika Hussain; Jennifer Iacopelli; Tess James-Mackey; Miranda Leiggi; Richard Mercado; Yasmine Naghdi; Samuel Pollen; Rebecca R; Cynthia So; Chitra Soundar; Claire Tomasi; Adelle Yeung

L613 Joanna Swainson
Literary Agent
United Kingdom

submissions@hardmanswainson.com

http://www.hardmanswainson.com/agents/joanna-swainson/
https://twitter.com/JoannaSwainson

Literary Agency: Hardman & Swainson (**L294**)

Fiction > *Novels*
  Comedy / Humour; Commercial; Contemporary; Crime; Folk Horror; Ghost Stories; Historical Fiction; Horror; Literary; Speculative; Thrillers
Nonfiction > *Nonfiction Books*
  Folklore, Myths, and Legends; Memoir; Narrative Nonfiction; Nature; Popular History; Science

Send: Synopsis; Full text
How to send: Email
How not to send: Post

In fiction, I'm looking for complex, larger-than-life characters. I love crime and thrillers at both ends of the commercial / literary spectrum. I also love a good ghost story and accessible speculative fiction, as well as a bit of horror, especially folk horror. Whatever the genre, whether literary or commercial, historical or contemporary, thriller or crime, I'm looking for originality and distinctive voices. I especially like fiction threaded with humour – not necessarily of the laugh out loud kind, it's often much subtler than that, but you can't have too many arresting observations and insights. On the non-fiction front, I enjoy narrative non-fiction, especially popular history (and prehistory) and science. I'm very partial to a memoir. I also enjoy nature writing and am interested in folklore.

Authors: Jon Bounds; Oggy Boytchev; Paul Braddon; Elizabeth Brooks; Mark Broomfield; Adrienne Chinn; Helen Cox; Jeremy Craddock; Sara Crowe; Emma Darwin; Stuart David; Caroline Davison; Carol Donaldson; Simon David Eden; Rachel Edwards; Nicola Ford; Harry Freedman; James Gould-Bourn; Tom Higham; Michael Jecks; Oskar Cox Jensen; Stuart Johnstone; Lucy Lawrie; Peter Laws; David B. Lyons; Kevin Macneil; S R Masters; Lauren Price; Philip C Quaintrell; Patrick Roberts; Nick Russell-Pavier; Catherine Simpson; Danny Smith; Hollie Starling; Eliska Tanzer; Sarah Tierney; B P Walter; Samantha Wilson

L614 Emily Sweet
Literary Agent
United Kingdom

https://www.emilysweetassociates.com
https://www.aevitascreative.com/agent/emily-sweet

Literary Agencies: Emily Sweet Associates (**L199**); Aevitas Creative Management (ACM) UK (**L007**)

Nonfiction > *Nonfiction Books*
  Biography; Cookery; Current Affairs; Food and Drink; History; Lifestyle; Memoir

Send: Query; Synopsis
How to send: Online contact form

Particularly looks for exciting, original and useful cookery and lifestyle books, as well as innovative storytelling in the areas of history, memoir, biography, current affairs and topical non-fiction.

Authors: Fliss Chester; Amelia Christie-Miller; Nicky Corbishley; N.J. Crosskey; Anja Dunk; Becky Excell; Xanthe Gladstone; Alex Jackson; Tom Jackson; Irina Janakievska; Genevieve Jenner; Philip Khoury; Anna Koska; Nicola Lamb; Mitch Lane; Shu Han Lee; Ben Lippett; David Mountain; Tanya Mukendi; Amy Newsome; Emily Roz; Matthew Ryle; Su Scott; Tim Siadatan; Alex Stacey; Emma Tarlo; Katie Taylor; Joe Trivelli; Sumayya Usmani; Joe Woodhouse

L615 Becky Sweren
Senior Agent
United States

https://aevitascreative.com/agents/#agent-7413

Literary Agency: Aevitas

Nonfiction > *Nonfiction Books*
  Culture; History; Investigative Journalism; Memoir

Closed to approaches.

Authors: Jesse Ball; Mark Braude; Adin Dobkin; Beck Dorey-Stein; Renee Dudley; Penina Eilberg-Schwartz; Valerie Fridland; Nicholas Griffin; Lawrence Jackson; Mohamad Jebara; Faith Jones; Jillian Keenan; Jake Keiser; Sulaiman Khatib; Ali Kriegsman; Daniel Levin; Maya Wei-Haas; Eric M. O'Neill; Matteson Perry; Pen Rhodeen; Mohammed Al Samawi; Laurie Segall; Shabtai Shavit; Gabourey Sidibe; Judith E. Stein; Noa Tishby; Steven Ujifusa; Jack Viertel; Payam Zamani; Lijia Zhang

L616 SYLA – Susan Yearwood Literary Agency
Literary Agency
2 Knebworth House, Londesborough Road, Stoke Newington, London, N16 8RL
United Kingdom
Tel: +44 (0) 20 7503 0954

submissions@susanyearwoodagency.com

https://susanyearwoodagency.com

Professional Body: The Association of Authors' Agents (AAA)

ADULT
  Fiction > *Novels*
  Nonfiction > *Nonfiction Books*
CHILDREN'S > **Fiction** > *Novels*
YOUNG ADULT > **Fiction** > *Novels*

Send: Query; Author bio; Writing sample; Synopsis
How to send: Email attachment

Send query by email, including synopsis and first thirty pages as Word or PDF attachment.

Authors: Rebecca Adams; Lucy Basey; Katie Brewer; Angela Cairns; Selina Flavius; Kimberley Glover; Liz Kolbeck; Fil Reid; Sarupa Shah

Literary Agent: Susan Yearwood

L617 Laurel Symonds
Literary Agent
United States

https://ktliterary.com/about/
https://www.manuscriptwishlist.com/mswl-post/laurel-symonds/
https://twitter.com/laurelsymonds
https://www.facebook.com/laurelsymondsagent
https://www.linkedin.com/in/laurelsymonds/

Literary Agency: KT Literary (**L377**)

CHILDREN'S
Fiction
   Graphic Novels: General
   Middle Grade: General, and in particular: Contemporary; Fantasy; Historical Fiction; Literary
   Picture Books: General

Nonfiction > *Nonfiction Books*
   General, and in particular: Engineering; History; Mathematics; Science; Technology

YOUNG ADULT
Fiction
   Graphic Novels: General
   Novels: General, and in particular: Commercial; Contemporary; Fantasy; Historical Fiction
Nonfiction > *Nonfiction Books*
   General, and in particular: Engineering; History; Mathematics; Science; Technology

Closed to approaches.

I represent young adult and middle grade fiction, and I have a special interest in contemporary, historical fiction, and genre-blending fantasy. I look for engaging voices, commercial hooks, and immersive worlds. My YA tastes are pretty commercial but my middle grade tastes can skew more literary, and I'm especially interested in middle grade that might lend itself to illustration.

I also represent picture books, graphic novels, and other illustrated work, and I am open to new clients who are both authors and illustrators. My tastes are diverse, ranging from sophisticated to quirky to gently humorous. I especially appreciate a smart use of color and perspective.

Additionally, I represent select nonfiction for children and young adults, especially projects about STEM or history with age-appropriate hooks and series potential.

L618 Marin Takikawa
Associate Agent
United States

mtakikawa@friedrichagency.com

http://www.friedrichagency.com/marin
https://twitter.com/marintakikawa
https://www.instagram.com/marintakikawa

Literary Agency: The Friedrich Agency LLC (**L245**)

ADULT
Fiction > *Novels*
   Environment; Family Saga; Folklore, Myths, and Legends; Ghost Stories; Literary; Magical Realism; Social Issues; Speculative; Upmarket

Nonfiction > *Nonfiction Books*
   Cultural History; Narrative Nonfiction; Postcolonialism; Social History

YOUNG ADULT > Fiction > *Novels*
   Adventure; Contemporary; Dark; Gothic; Literary; Mystery; Speculative

Send: Query; Writing sample
How to send: In the body of an email
How not to send: Email attachment

For adult fiction, I'm always seeking innovative—both in idea and structure—literary/upmarket fiction that's lush, evocative, and full of heart(break). I'm also looking for family sagas, novels that subvert forms of power, specifically relating to colonialism/imperialism, and engages with social and environmental issues. I'm also particularly enamored by genre-bending works: speculative concepts, ghost stories, magical realism, and anything that plays with myth and folklore will always catch my eye! For YA, I'm looking for voice-driven and literary-leaning novels with the emotional breadth and depth in the tradition of authors like Emily X. R. Pan and Kelly Loy Gilbert—although I won't say no to sweeter contemporary YA (my comfort reads are Anna & the French Kiss, Love & Gelato, and Better Than the Movies)! I'm also excited by speculative concepts and am not afraid of going dark. Give me all your gothic, atmospheric, haunting books (especially with a sense of mystery and adventure)! Some of my recent favorite YA books are If You Could See the Sun by Ann Liang, All My Rage by Sabaa Tahir, and Firekeeper's Daughter by Angeline Boulley. In adult nonfiction, I gravitate toward community-oriented narrative nonfiction with engaging and insightful research or reportage, as well as social/cultural histories and criticisms. I'm also looking for narrative nonfiction that is intersectional, resistant, and radical in nature, that questions why we have the institutions, ideas, and systems we have in place. I often think about the legacies of colonialism, how it haunts and perpetuates in various forms in the modern age (such as the environment and in capitalism), but also about collective action/liberation and its sense of possibilities and what an equitable future could look like. I'd love to hear from you if your work is in this space.

L619 Emily Talbot
Literary Agent
United Kingdom

etalbot@unitedagents.co.uk
https://www.unitedagents.co.uk/etalbotunitedagentscouk

Literary Agency: United Agents
Literary Agent: Jodie Hodges (**L315**)

ADULT > Nonfiction > *Nonfiction Books*

CHILDREN'S > Fiction
   Middle Grade; *Picture Books*
YOUNG ADULT > Fiction > *Novels*

Send: Query; Synopsis; Writing sample

Represents hildren's illustrators and authors of picture books, middle grade, YA and non-fiction.

Authors: Aysha Awwad; Susanna Bailey; Abigail Balfe; Alex Barrow; Becky Baur; Gabby Dawnay; Sophie Deen; Chloe Douglass; Ed Eaves; Alison Guile; James Harris; Sam Hearn; Benjamin Hughes; James Lent; Rebecca Lewis-Oakes; Maggie Li; Roger McGough; Becka Moor; Polly Owen; Keith Robinson; Andy Sagar; Jion Sheibani; Qian Shi; Georgina Stevens; Barry Timms; Jacqueline Tucker; Kael Tudor; Lucy Unwin; Maddy Vian; Lucia Vinti

L620 Amy Tannenbaum
Literary Agent
United States

atannenbaum@janerotrosen.com

https://www.janerotrosen.com/agents
https://www.janerotrosen.com/contact-amy-tannenbaum

Literary Agency: Jane Rotrosen Agency

Fiction > *Novels*
   Commercial; Contemporary Romance; Historical Fiction; Literary; Psychological Suspense; Speculative; Thrillers; Women's Fiction

Send: Query
How to send: In the body of an email
How not to send: Email attachment

represents clients who write across a variety of genres including women's fiction, historical fiction, grounded speculative, contemporary romance, thriller and psychological suspense. She is particularly interested in those categories, as well as fiction that falls into the sweet spot between literary and commercial and works by marginalized voices.

L621 Trisha Telep
Associate Agent
Canada

https://www.therightsfactory.com/Agents/Trisha-Telep

Literary Agency: The Rights Factory

Closed to approaches.

L622 The Tennyson Agency
Literary Agency
109 Tennyson Avenue, New Malden, Surrey, KT3 6NA
United Kingdom
Tel: +44 (0) 20 8543 5939

agency@tenagy.co.uk

http://www.tenagy.co.uk

Types: Scripts
Formats: Film Scripts; Radio Scripts; TV Scripts; Theatre Scripts
Subjects: Drama
Markets: Adult

Closed to approaches.

Mainly deals in scripts for film, TV, theatre, and radio, along with related material on an ad-hoc basis. Handles writers in the European Union only. Send query with CV and outline of work. Prefers queries by email. No nonfiction, poetry, short stories, science fiction and fantasy or children's writing, or unsolicited MSS.

L623 Teresa Chris Literary Agency Ltd
Literary Agency
43 Musard Road, London, W6 8NR
United Kingdom
Tel: +44 (0) 20 7386 0633

teresachris@litagency.co.uk

http://www.teresachrisliteraryagency.co.uk

Professional Body: The Association of Authors' Agents (AAA)

Fiction > *Novels*
Commercial Women's Fiction; Commercial; Crime; Literary

Does not want:

> **Fiction** > *Novels*
> Fantasy; Horror; Science Fiction

Send: Query; Synopsis; Writing sample
How to send: Email

Welcomes submissions. Send submissions by email only, with first three chapters, and one-page synopsis. Specialises in crime fiction and commercial women's fiction. No poetry, short stories, fantasy, science fiction, horror, or children's fiction.

Authors: Stephanie Austin; Lily Baxter; Ginny Bell; M A Bennett; Victoria Blake; Stephen Booth; Benita Brown; Rory Clements; Julie Cohen; Dilly Court; Martin Davies; Ellie Dean; Linda Finlay; Marina Fiorato; Emily Freud; Kate Furnivall; Annie Groves; Clare Harvey; Debby Holt; Hunter; Corrie Jackson; Jim Kelly; Danuta Kot; Linscott; Tamara McKinley; Jane McMorland; Charlotte Parsons; Stuart Pawson; Caro Peacock/Gillian; Nicola Pryce; Eileen Ramsay; Kate Rhodes; Mary-Jane Riley; Caroline Scott; Marsali Taylor; Jane Wenham-Jones

L624 Paige Terlip
Literary Agent
United States

paige@andreabrownlit.com

https://www.andreabrownlit.com/agents.html
https://twitter.com/pterlip
https://www.instagram.com/pterlip/

Literary Agency: Andrea Brown Literary Agency, Inc.

ADULT
Fiction > *Novels*
Cozy Mysteries; Fantasy; High Concept; Magic; Psychological Suspense; Science Fiction; Thrillers; Upmarket

Nonfiction > *Nonfiction Books*
Mind, Body, Spirit; Narrative Nonfiction; Self Help

CHILDREN'S > **Fiction**
Chapter Books; Middle Grade; Picture Books

YOUNG ADULT > **Fiction** > *Novels*
High Concept; Magic

Closed to approaches.

Represents all categories of children's books from picture books to young adult, as well as select adult fiction and nonfiction. She is also actively building her list of illustrators and is especially looking for author-illustrators and graphic novel illustrators.

L625 Kate Testerman
Literary Agent
United States

Literary Agency: KT Literary (**L377**)

Closed to approaches.

L626 Henry Thayer
Literary Agent
United States

hthayer@bromasite.com

Literary Agency: Brandt & Hochman Literary Agents, Inc.
Professional Body: Association of American Literary Agents (AALA)

Fiction > *Novels*
General, and in particular: Literary

Nonfiction > *Nonfiction Books*
General, and in particular: American History; Arts; Basketball; Biography; Current Affairs; Films; History; Politics; Popular Culture; Popular Music; Science; Sport

Send: Query
How to send: Email

Primarily represents nonfiction, including biography, history, current affairs, international relations, politics, the arts and sciences, sports, and popular culture. He is looking for engaging stories that make complex ideas accessible to the curious reader and bold arguments that challenge the conventional wisdom. He is also interested in finding new, compelling voices in literary and genre fiction, especially novels that bridge the gap between the two. His wide-ranging interests, within the world of books and beyond it, include American history, popular music, film, and basketball. Query by email only.

L627 The Theseus Agency
Literary Agency
29 Rosslyn Hill, London, NW3 5UJ
United Kingdom
Tel: +44 (0) 20 4559 9421

info@theseus.agency

https://www.theseus.agency

Fiction > *Novels*

Nonfiction > *Nonfiction Books*

We help brands and writers pin-point, protect, and harness what makes them matter to the wider world.

We manage rights, brand and dealmaking. And we do it for any idea that lives in the public imagination, whether it started life as a book or script, a product, or a person.

By bringing together management, representation, and strategy, we balance long-term goals and short-term opportunities. We map plans for the future, while seeking out and striking innovative deals in the present, knowing that each is integral to the other.

Literary Agent: Louise Ripley-Duggan (**L538**)

L628 Euan Thorneycroft
Literary Agent
United Kingdom

https://amheath.com/agents/euan-thorneycroft/
http://twitter.com/EuanThorneycrof

Literary Agency: A.M. Heath & Company Limited, Author's Agents (**L002**)

Fiction > *Novels*
Adventure; Book Club Fiction; Commercial; Crime; Historical Fiction; Historical Mystery Fiction; Literary; Police Procedural; Psychological Suspense; Spy Thrilllers; Thrillers

Nonfiction > *Nonfiction Books*
History; Memoir; Nature; Politics; Science; Technology

How to send: Online submission system

I love novels with propulsive stories, fascinating characters, and great heart, whether it is commercial fiction or something more literary. I want first-in-class storytelling. And I want to be made to care. I love crossover literary/commercial fiction (Bookclub fiction). I read a lot of crime and thrillers from police procedurals to spy fiction, psychological suspense and full-throttle action adventure, and if they have a really unusual and imaginative hook, so much the better. Historical fiction is also a big passion of mine, and that might be a historical crime series. In non-fiction, I love memoirs in all shapes and sizes. I am also interested in working with experts in their field and helping them turn their ideas into something that will appeal to a broad readership. I am most interested in those ideas which can be told through stories and narratives, in the areas of history, science, technology, politics and nature.

Agency Assistant: Jessica Lee

L629 Steph Thwaites
Literary Agent
United Kingdom

thwaitesoffice@curtisbrown.co.uk
children's.submission@curtisbrown.co.uk

https://curtisbrown.co.uk
https://curtisbrown.co.uk/agent/steph-thwaites

Literary Agency: Curtis Brown (**L146**)

ADULT
  Fiction
    Novels: Book Club Fiction; Commercial; Family; Romantic Comedy; Thrillers
    Short Fiction Collections: General

  Nonfiction > *Nonfiction Books:* Commercial

CHILDREN'S > **Fiction** > *Middle Grade*

YOUNG ADULT > **Fiction** > *Novels*

Send: Query; Synopsis; Author bio; Writing sample
How to send: Email

Represents a broad range of writers from debut authors to literary estates, number one and Sunday Times bestselling authors and prize winners writing quality commercial fiction and non-fiction, short stories, YA novels and middle grade fiction. She is currently seeking commercial fiction, thrillers, book-group fiction, romantic comedy and family dramas.

L630 Anne Tibbets
Literary Agent
United States

http://maassagency.com/anne-tibbets/
https://querymanager.com/query/AnneTibbets

Literary Agency: Donald Maass Literary Agency (**L176**)

Fiction > *Novels*
  Cozy Mysteries; Domestic Mystery; Domestic; Fantasy; Horror; International; Literary Horror; Mystery; Police Procedural; Psychological Horror; Science Fiction; Suspense; Thrillers

Send: Author bio; Query; Synopsis; Writing sample
How to send: Query Manager
How not to send: Email

Represents adult commercial genre, primarily thrillers, mysteries, science fiction, fantasy, horror and select non-fiction.

L631 Hannah Todd
Literary Agent
United Kingdom

submissions@madeleinemilburn.com

https://madeleinemilburn.co.uk/team-member/hannah-todd/

Literary Agency: Madeleine Milburn Literary, TV & Film Agency (**L420**)

Fiction > *Novels*
  Commercial; Cozy Mysteries; Crime; High Concept Thrillers; LGBTQIA; Romance; Romantic Comedy; Saga; Thrillers; Women's Fiction

Send: Query; Pitch; Market info; Synopsis; Writing sample
How to send: Email attachment
How not to send: Post

Actively looking for: commercial fiction across all genres including women's fiction; spicy romance novels; clever thrillers; cosy crime; romantic comedies; sagas. If you can make her laugh, cry or fall in love then you're onto a winner!

L632 Antony Topping
Literary Agent
United Kingdom

http://greeneheaton.co.uk/agents/antony-topping/

Literary Agency: Greene & Heaton Ltd (**L276**)

Fiction > *Novels*
  Book Club Fiction; Contemporary; Crime; Historical Literary; Historical Thrillers; Thrillers; Upmarket

Nonfiction > *Nonfiction Books*
  Comedy / Humour; Food; History; Memoir; Music; Nature; Science

I represent historical thriller writers, contemporary and historical literary novelists, upmarket genre and bookclub fiction, science writers, food writers, historians, nature writers, music journalists, memoirists, and cultural critics.

Authors: Clayton Page Aldern; Amen Alonge; Peter Apps; Lucy Ashe; Helena Attlee; Mevan Babakar; Lucy Brazier; James Bridle; Jason Byrne; Tom Campbell; Charles Cockell; Pam Corbin; Russell Davies; Anna Davis; Patrick Drake; Suzannah Dunn; Jeremy Duns; Jonn Elledge; Olaf Falafel; Hugh Fearnley-Whittingstall; Jane Fearnley-Whittingstall; Christopher Fitz-Simon; Felix Flicker; Christophe Galfard; Stuart Heritage; Julian Hitch; Andrew Holmes; Alex Hourston; D.B. John; Keith Kahn-Harris; Max Kinnings; David Kirk; Rikke Schmidt Kjærgaard; Joseph Knox; Manon Lagrève; William Leith; Dan Lepard; Robert Lewis; Kieran Long; Dorian Lynskey; Rob Manuel; Jolyon Maugham; James McGee; Gill Meller; Thomasina Miers; Lottie Moggach; Cathy Newman; Mary-Ann Ochota; Christopher Osborn; Iain Overton; John O'Connell; Pete Paphides; Marie Phillips; Tom Phillips; Shivi Ramautar; Richard Reed; Sam Rice; C. J. Sansom; Marcus du Sautoy; Alev Scott; Rebecca Seal; Laura Shepherd-Robinson; Mimi Spencer; Count Arthur Strong; Andrew Taylor; Ian Vince; John Vincent; Adam Wagner; Jennie Walker; Andrew Webb; Robyn Wilder; Will Wiles; Jason Wilson; Erin Young; Robyn Young; Andrew Ziminski

L633 Jennifer Chen Tran
Literary Agent
United States

https://glassliterary.com/team/jennifer-chen-tran/
https://twitter.com/jenchentran
https://querymanager.com/query/jct

Literary Agency: Glass Literary Management LLC (**L262**)

ADULT > **Fiction**
  Graphic Novels: General
  Novels: Chick Lit; Commercial; Contemporary; Family Saga; Literary; Multicultural; Romance; Upmarket; Women's Fiction

CHILDREN'S > **Fiction** > *Middle Grade*
  Contemporary; Literary; Mystery

NEW ADULT > **Fiction** > *Novels*

YOUNG ADULT > **Fiction** > *Novels*
  Contemporary; Historical Fiction; Literary

Closed to approaches.

Works with a wide range of award-winning talent, including entrepreneurs, journalists, physicians, thought leaders, James Beard nominated chefs, and graphic novelists, among others. Deeply committed to amplifying voices from persons with disabilities, BIPOC, LGBTQ, underrepresented, marginalized, and neurodiverse communities.

L634 Jes Trudel
Assistant Agent
Canada

https://www.therightsfactory.com
https://www.therightsfactory.com/Agents/jes-trudel
https://querymanager.com/query/jestrudel
https://writingcommunity.ca/agentjestrudel/

Literary Agency: The Rights Factory

CHILDREN'S > Fiction
Board Books: General, and in particular: Commercial; High Concept
Chapter Books: General, and in particular: Commercial; High Concept
Middle Grade: General, and in particular: Adventure; Contemporary; Low Fantasy; Mystery; Romance; Speculative; Suspense; Thrillers
Picture Books: General, and in particular: Commercial; High Concept

YOUNG ADULT
Fiction > *Novels*
General, and in particular: Adventure; Contemporary; Low Fantasy; Mystery; Romance; Speculative; Suspense; Thrillers

Nonfiction > *Nonfiction Books*
General, and in particular: Arts; Entrepreneurship; Environment; Mental Health; Social Justice

Closed to approaches.

In Board Book, Picture Book and Chapter Book categories, I'm especially interested in high concept, commercial stories (I already have several clients who excel at quiet, lyrical stories). I love both kid characters and animal characters. I prefer lyrical over rhyming texts, but if you do have a rhyming story, please make sure the meter is perfect and the rhymes are not cliche/forced.

In Middle Grade and Young Adult, I especially like action/adventure, contemporary, mystery, romance, low fantasy, present or near future speculative, and suspense/thriller. I prefer kid characters in these categories, though I will still look at stories with anthropomorphized characters in MG. I'm not a fan of vampires, werewolves, aliens, zombies, ghosts, fairies, fae, or other supernatural creatures in MG or YA.

I'm eager to take on nonfiction projects across all age groups, especially related to mental health, DEI, social justice, arts, community building, environmentalism, and entrepreneurship.

Authors: Dorothy Bentley; Katie Bono; Eileen Manes; Carol Nissenson; Howard Pearlstein

L635 Caroline Trussell
Junior Agent
United States

https://www.metamorphosisliteraryagency.com/about
https://querymanager.com/query/2782
https://twitter.com/carolinejtrulit

Literary Agency: Metamorphosis Literary Agency (**L444**)

Fiction > *Novels*
Family; Fantasy; Horror; Magical Realism; Psychological Horror; Psychological Thrillers; Romance; Romantasy; Romantic Comedy; Thrillers; Urban Fantasy; Women's Fiction

Closed to approaches.

Open to queries in February, April, May, August, September and November. Looking for Thrillers (especially psychological thrillers); Romance (rom-coms, romantasy, enemies to lovers); Women's Fiction (especially focusing on sister dynamics/sisterhood); Adult Fantasy (particularly magical realism and urban fantasy); Adult Horror (especially psychological, haunted houses); and in any genre, stories that feature dynamic characters with non-visible disabilities and/or mental illness.

L636 The Two Piers Literary Agency
Literary Agency
Brighton
United Kingdom

hello@twopiersagency.com

https://twopiersagency.com
https://twitter.com/TwoPiersAgency
https://www.facebook.com/TwoPiersAgency
https://www.instagram.com/twopiersagency/

ADULT
Fiction > *Novels*
Nonfiction > *Nonfiction Books*

CHILDREN'S > Fiction > *Middle Grade*

YOUNG ADULT > Fiction > *Novels*

Closed to approaches.

Costs: Offers services that writers have to pay for. Sister company provides online novel-writing course.

Literary agency based in Brighton, which represents writers from all over the world and sells their work into the UK, US and international territories. An editorially focused agency that works closely with authors to produce manuscripts that are as strong as they can possibly be before submitting them to publishers.

Literary Agent: Rufus Purdy

L637 Jennifer Udden
Literary Agent
United States

https://www.ldlainc.com
https://querymanager.com/query/QueryJenniferUdden

Literary Agency: Laura Dail Literary Agency

Fiction > *Novels*
Fantasy; Historical Romance; Horror; Mystery; Psychological Horror; Romance; Romantasy; Science Fiction; Thrillers

How to send: Query Manager

Fantasy: from epic secondary world to historical or more contemporary fantasy, character-driven fantasy of all stripes with strong world building and a distinctive voice.

Science Fiction: science fiction of all stripes, particularly if there is a cross-genre element or an interesting hook.

Romance: innovative historical romance, sports romance, and romantasy.

Mystery/Thriller: Anything with a classic British feel, particularly if those tropes are subverted or there is a nontraditional narrator/setting.

Horror: Psychological and body horror, especially if there is a fresh take on an old trope.

L638 Jo Unwin
Literary Agent
United Kingdom

submissions@jounwin.co.uk

https://www.jounwin.co.uk/jo-unwin
https://twitter.com/jounwin

Literary Agency: Jo Unwin Literary Agency (**L333**)

ADULT > Fiction > *Novels*
Commercial Women's Fiction; Literary

CHILDREN'S > Fiction > *Middle Grade*

YOUNG ADULT > Fiction > *Novels*

Closed to approaches.

I represent authors of literary fiction, commercial women's fiction, Young Adult fiction and fiction for children aged 9+ but not younger (picture books only if written by established clients). I also represent comic writing and narrative non-fiction. Suffice to say I don't represent poetry or screenplays (unless written by my established clients).

Authors: Jesse Armstrong; Richard Ayoade; Amanda Berriman; Brian Bilston; Amanda Block; Anne Booth; Charlie Brooker; Lucie Brownlee; Karen Campbell; Candice Carty-Williams; David Challen; Jo Cheetham; Jenny Colgan; Frances Crawford; Lucy Easthope; Katie Everson; Mick Finlay; Emma Flint; Elaine Gregersen; Tamsin Grey; Becky Holmes; Lucy-Anne Holmes; Sylvia Johnson; Riley Johnston; Evie King; Gabriel Krauze; Louise Lee; Marianne Lee; Francis Liardet; Litwitchure; Doon Mackichan; Gemma Marren; Katy Massey; Siobhan McSweeney; Fiona Melrose; Sarah Moore-Fitzgerald; Rosie Mullender; Sally O'Reilly; Priya O'Shea; Claire Parkin; Deepa Paul; AJ Pearce; Robert Popper; Georgia Pritchett; Josey Rebelle; Rose

Ruane; Nadia Shireen; Jenny Simanowitz; Penelope Slocombe; Emma Smith-Barton; Stephen Tuffin; Weird Walk; Hayley Webster; Joanna Wolfarth

L639 Laura Usselman
Literary Agent
United States

luquery@skagency.com

http://skagency.com/agents/laura-usselman/

Literary Agency: Stuart Krichevsky Literary Agency, Inc. (**L609**)

Fiction > *Novels*: Literary

Nonfiction > *Nonfiction Books*
  General, and in particular: Business; Cultural Criticism; Legal; Memoir; Parenting

How to send: Email

Represents adult nonfiction and select literary fiction. Her favorite novels are written in distinctive prose and have memorable characters at their heart. For nonfiction, she is interested in thoughtful narrative nonfiction, restlessly curious idea books, and reported memoir. Special areas of interest include legal and business narratives, cultural criticism, and contemporary parenthood.

Authors: Emily Bloom; Katherine Blunt; Angela Chen; Carla Ciccone; Georgia Cloepfil; Michelle Cyca; Victoria Facelli; Sarah Jaffe; Rachel McCarthy James; Peter Mercurio; Madeline Ostrander; Robin Page; Soraya Palmer; Nadim Roberts; Zoë Schiffer; A. Brad Schwartz; David Shih; Sofi Thanhauser; Kaitlyn Tiffany

L640 Valerie Hoskins Associates
Literary Agency
20 Charlotte Street, London, W1T 2NA
United Kingdom
Tel: +44 (0) 20 7637 4490

info@vhassociates.co.uk

https://vhassociates.co.uk

Scripts
  Film Scripts; Radio Scripts; TV Scripts

Send: Query
How to send: Email

Small agency extremely limited as to the number of new clients that can be taken on. Allow up to eight weeks for response to submissions.

Literary Agents: Valerie Hoskins; Rebecca Watson

L641 Lisa Erbach Vance
Literary Agent
United States

queryvance@aaronpriest.com

https://aaronpriest.com
https://aaronpriest.com/member/lisa-erbach-vance/

Literary Agency: Aaron M. Priest Literary Agency

Fiction > *Novels*
  Comedy / Humour; Commercial; Domestic Suspense; Family; Friends; Ghost Stories; Literary; Psychological Suspense; Relationships; Romantic Comedy; Speculative; Supernatural / Paranormal; Thrillers

Nonfiction > *Nonfiction Books*: Narrative Nonfiction

Send: Query; Writing sample
How to send: In the body of an email
How not to send: Email attachment

Currently most interested in and actively seeking out fiction, literary or commercial, especially works featuring female characters, as well as some narrative non-fiction. Types of work include: Propulsive, emotionally engaging thrillers—domestic or international. Moody psychological and domestic suspense. Speculative fiction set in a recognizable near future. Ghost or supernatural stories that go beyond chills and speak to current culture but are not graphically violent. Observant, thoughtful fiction about families and friends, with fresh perspectives on modern relationships. Narratives with a witty or lovingly humorous spin, including rom-coms. Diverse and unique narrative voices that speak to the human condition and the world today; underrepresented voices of all backgrounds and identities.

L642 Victoria Sanders & Associates LLC
Literary Agency
440 Buck Road, Stone Ridge, NY 12484
United States
Tel: +1 (212) 633-8811

queriesvsa@gmail.com

http://www.victoriasanders.com

Types: Fiction; Nonfiction; Translations
Formats: Film Scripts; Theatre Scripts
Subjects: Adventure; Arts; Autobiography; Comedy / Humour; Commercial; Contemporary; Crime; Culture; Current Affairs; Fantasy; History; Legal; Literary; Literature; Music; Mystery; Politics; Psychology; Satire; Society; Suspense; Thrillers; Women's Interests
Markets: Adult; Children's; Young Adult

Closed to approaches.

Send one-page query describing the work and the author by email only, with the first 25 pages pasted into the body of the email. No attachments or submissions by post. Response usually between 1 and 4 weeks.

Literary Agents: Bernadette Baker-Baughman; Victoria Sanders

L643 The Viney Agency
Literary Agency
64 New Cavendish Street, London, W1G 8TB
United Kingdom

https://www.thevineyagency.com

Professional Body: The Association of Authors' Agents (AAA)

ADULT
  Fiction > *Novels*

  Nonfiction > *Nonfiction Books*
    Biography; Narrative Nonfiction

CHILDREN'S > **Fiction** > *Novels*

Closed to approaches.

A London-based literary agency founded in 2008. The agency represents a diverse range of authors primarily handling their book deals with publishers worldwide, and providing a full range of services including selling film and TV options to broadcasters and production companies. Represents over 100 authors, writing across many genres, including adult and children's fiction and a wide variety of narrative nonfiction and biography.

Company Director / Senior Agent: Charlie Viney (**L644**)

L644 Charlie Viney
Company Director; Senior Agent
21 Dartmouth Park Avenue, London, NW5 1JL
United Kingdom

Charlie@thevineyagency.com

https://www.aevitascreative.com/agent/charlie-viney
https://www.thevineyagency.com/about

Literary Agencies: The Viney Agency (**L643**); Aevitas Creative Management (ACM) UK (**L007**)

Fiction > *Novels*

Nonfiction > *Nonfiction Books*

I have been a literary agent since 2002 and founded the agency in 2008. The agency represents a diverse range of clients writing across a wide range of subjects. I first started in the book trade as a bookseller and then enjoyed a twenty-five-year career in general trade publishing, mostly working in international sales and marketing, later becoming a board director at a major British publishing house. Being a literary agent combines my love of books and an enjoyment of business while enabling me to work very closely with our wonderful authors and manage their careers across all media.

Authors: Denise Allen; David Ambrose; David Andress; Paul Arnott; Stephen Bates; Chris

Blackhurst; Jeremy Borum; Chris Bradford; Mike Bryan; David Charter; Charlie Charters; Paul Clammer; Lloyd Clark; Mark Cooper; Robin Cross; Richard Dannatt; David Downing; Paul Dowswell; Simon Elliott; Tim Fitzhigham; Lilia Giugni; Michael Harrison; David Hepworth; Justin Hill; Janet Hoggarth; Mark Hollingsworth; John Howkins; Graham Hoyland; Robin Ince; Andrew Jackson; Hannah Jewell; Michael Jones; Don Jordan; Miranda Kaufmann; Robert Kershaw; Philippa Langley; John Lazenby; Maurice Leitch; Grevel Lindop; David Loyn; Monty Lyman; Robert Lyman; S.I. Martin; Mark Mason; Roisin McAuley; Rosalind Miles; Kate Mossman; Michael Ohajura; Andrew Parker; Anna Perera; William Philpott; David Mark Price; Tom Pugh; David Richards; Cate Sevilla; Emma Southon; Siena Sterling; Mark Stevenson; Miranda Wilson; Alistair Wood; Duncan Wu

L645 Caroline Walsh
Literary Agent
United Kingdom

childrenssubmissions@davidhigham.co.uk
carolinewalsh@davidhigham.co.uk

https://www.davidhigham.co.uk/agents-dh/caroline-walsh/

Literary Agency: David Higham Associates Ltd (**L159**)

ADULT
Fiction > *Novels*
  Book Club Fiction; Commercial; Upmarket

Nonfiction > *Nonfiction Books*

CHILDREN'S
Fiction
  Board Books; Chapter Books; Middle Grade; Novels; Picture Books
Nonfiction > *Nonfiction Books*

Poetry > *Poetry Collections*

TEEN > **Fiction** > *Novels*

YOUNG ADULT > **Fiction** > *Novels*

Send: Query; Synopsis; Writing sample
How to send: Email

Many of my clients have gone on to write award-wining and bestselling books and their output covers the whole range of children's books, from pre-school board books, through picture books, poetry, middle-grade fiction, non-fiction and Teen/YA novels. I also represent a handful of adult fiction writers where my tastes are for upmarket book club fiction and classy commercial page-turners.

Authors: R. J. Anderson; Kelly Andrew; Antonia Barber; Ella Beech; Joe Berger; Theresa Breslin; Martin Brown; Mike Brownlow; Kathryn Cave; Jason Chapman; Emma Chichester Clark; Trish Cooke; Susie Day; Kady MacDonald Denton; Lucy Dillamore; Eve Edwards; Jonathan Emmett; Ben Faulks; Corina Fletcher; P. M. Freestone; Jane Gardam; Sarah Garland; Susan Gates; Adèle Geras; Julia Golding; Kester Grant; Ryan Graudin; Candida Harper; Leigh Hodgkinson; Jesse Hodgson; Anna Hoghton; Meredith Hooper; Julia Jarman; Clive King; Bert Kitchen; Jay Kristoff; Fifi Kuo; Eleanor Lavender; Jo Lodge; Tim Lott; Jan Mark; Ellie Marney; Tom McLaughlin; Myfanwy Millward; Kate Milner; Tony Mitton; Laura Mucha; Jenny Nimmo; C. S. Pacat; Liz Pichon; Chris Powling; Kathryn Purdie; Madhvi Ramani; Catherine Rayner; Jacqui Rayner; Fiona Roberton; Rachel Rooney; Megan Shepherd; Alexander McCall Smith; Meagan Spooner; Joss Stirling; James L. Sutter; Sally Symes; Vanessa Tait; Frances Thomas; Pat Thomson; Theresa Tomlinson; Ann Turnbull; Martin Waddell; Melanie Walsh; Jacqueline Wilson; David Wojtowycz

L646 Kate Walsh
Associate Agent
United Kingdom
Tel: +44 (0) 20 3214 0884

kwalsh@unitedagents.co.uk

https://www.unitedagents.co.uk/kwalshunitedagentscouk

Literary Agency: United Agents

Nonfiction > *Nonfiction Books*
  20th Century; Commercial; Current Affairs; History; Music; Popular Science

Send: Query; Synopsis; Writing sample
How to send: Email

Actively building her list. She's on the lookout mainly (although not exclusively) for commercial non-fiction, with a particular interest in music titles, history and broad-spectrum popular science, and anything that feels like a fresh and original way of looking at the world. She is especially drawn to 20th and 21st century affairs, and welcomes anything from anyone willing to speculate on what comes next.

Authors: Jennifer Otter Bickerdike; Christie Dickason; Nic Dunlop; Jeff Gulvin; Will Hayward; Matthew Jukes; Max Kirsten; Harris Reed; Tom Wainwright; Rohullah Yakobi

L647 Watson, Little Ltd
Literary Agency
Suite 315, ScreenWorks, 22 Highbury Grove, London, N5 2ER
United Kingdom
Tel: +44 (0) 20 7388 7529

office@watsonlittle.com
submissions@watsonlittle.com

https://www.watsonlittle.com
https://twitter.com/watsonlittle

Professional Body: The Association of Authors' Agents (AAA)

ADULT
Fiction > *Novels*
Nonfiction > *Nonfiction Books*

CHILDREN'S
Fiction > *Novels*
Nonfiction > *Nonfiction Books*

Send: Query; Author bio; Writing sample; Market info; Outline
How to send: Word file email attachment; PDF file email attachment; In the body of an email
How not to send: Post

Send query by email only with outline in the body of the email, and synopsis and sample material as Word document attachments (or PDF attachments, if illustrated), addressed to a specific agent. See website for full guidelines and details of specific agents. No scripts, poetry, or unsolicited MSS.

Author Estate: The Estate of Akemi Tanaka

Authors: Rebecca Abrams; Luci Adams; Tom Adams; Jean Adamson; Rose Alexander; Wendy Allen; Rosie Archer; Faima Bakar; Louise Soraya Black; Kay Brellend; Laura Chamberlain; Sophie Claire; Sarah J. Coleman; Tara Costello; Bryony Cousins; Alex Day; Rose Diell; Marianne Eloise; Lauren Ford; Tessa Gibbs; Natasha Holmes; Hayley Hoskins; Elias Jahshan; Hiba Noor Khan; Mary Mackie; Lindiwe Maqhubela; Diana McCaulay; Erin Murgatroyd; Barbara Nadel; Grace Newman; Briana J. Newstead; Sheila Norton; Fiona O'Brien; Ben Pechey; Anna Reading; Rhian Parry; Will Richard; Richard Owain Roberts; Alan Robinson; Kohinoor Sahota; Tara Sexton; Hannah Silva; Pam Weaver; Jeremy Williams; Alex Woolhouse

Literary Agents: Megan Carroll (**L110**); Mandy Little; Laetitia Rutherford (**L557**); James Wills (**L666**); Donald Winchester

L648 Jessica Watterson
Literary Agent
United States

https://www.dijkstraagency.com/agent-page.php?agent_id=Watterson
https://querymanager.com/query/jessicawatterson

Literary Agency: Sandra Dijkstra Literary Agency

ADULT
Fiction > *Novels*
  Fantasy; Romance

Nonfiction > *Nonfiction Books*
  Millennial; Popular Culture

CHILDREN'S > **Fiction** > *Novels*: Comedy / Humour

How to send: By referral

Most drawn to riveting and heart pounding romance. She loves fun, fresh voices and character driven stories that keep a reader turning the page because they need to know what happens next. Independent heroines are a must, in addition to well realized heroes who aren't alpha-holes. She also loves fantasy that will appeal to a broad readership, especially if it has some spice in it!

In the children's realm, she connects with anything that has heart and humor.

She does like the occasional pop-culture or millenial leaning non-fiction project.

She is only open to queries by referral at this time.

L649 Paula Weiman
Literary Agent
United States

submissions@ashliterary.com

https://ashliterary.com
https://ashliterary.com/#paulawishlist
https://querymanager.com/query/paulaashliterary

Literary Agency: ASH Literary

CHILDREN'S > *Fiction* > *Middle Grade*
Adventure; Contemporary

YOUNG ADULT > *Fiction* > *Novels*
Contemporary; Fantasy; High / Epic Fantasy; Magic; Romantic Comedy; Suspense; Thrillers

Closed to approaches.

I'm most actively seeking YA rom-coms at the moment. I want to see rom-coms with teeth, romances that are rooted in a larger social or cultural topic so the story has interest beyond the love story. My favorite tropes are fake dating and rivals-to-lovers where one character is way more into the rivalry than the other. In YA suspense, I want to see well-developed plots with beautiful prose, following teenagers who tackle systemic injustice and corrupt power systems. For YA thrillers I want heists, either contemporary or historical, where the team is trying to fight injustice or right a wrong from behind the scenes. In YA fantasy, I look for rich atmosphere and a propulsive plot, whether the stories are high fantasy or contemporary with a dash of magic. In middle grade, I want clever adventures with active narrators whose voice is so strong that they direct the plot. I'm also looking for contemporary middle grade that touches on grief and/or queer identity. I'm really eager for a middle grade story that tackles child labor rights or student activism.

L650 Alexandra Weiss
Associate Agent
United States

http://www.azantianlitagency.com/pages/team-awe.html
https://querymanager.com/query/AlexandraWeiss

Literary Agency: Azantian Literary Agency

ADULT
Fiction > *Novels*
Contemporary; Cozy Fantasy; High Concept; Literary; Mystery; Speculative; Thrillers

Nonfiction > *Nonfiction Books*
Animals; Climate Science; Environment; Gender; Internet; LGBTQIA; Media; Mental Health; Science; Space

CHILDREN'S > **Fiction**
Graphic Novels: General
Middle Grade: Contemporary; Fantasy; Horror; Suspense
Picture Books: General

YOUNG ADULT > **Fiction**
Graphic Novels: General
Novels: Coming of Age; Contemporary; Cozy Fantasy; Folklore, Myths, and Legends; Low Fantasy; Magical Realism; Romantic Comedy; Soft Science Fiction; Thrillers

How to send: Query Manager

Represents fiction and nonfiction picture books, middle grade, young adult, graphic novels, and a handful of genres within adult fiction and nonfiction.

L651 Tess Weitzner
Literary Agent
United States

tw@goldinlit.com

https://www.goldinlit.com
https://www.goldinlit.com/tess-weitzner
https://twitter.com/TessWeitzner

Literary Agency: Frances Goldin Literary Agency, Inc. (**L238**)

ADULT
Fiction > *Novels*
Horror; Literary; Magical Realism; Upmarket

Nonfiction > *Nonfiction Books:* Narrative Nonfiction

CHILDREN'S > *Fiction* > *Middle Grade:* Contemporary

YOUNG ADULT > *Fiction* > *Novels*

Send: Query; Writing sample; Proposal
How to send: Email

Primarily looking for upmarket fiction, literary fiction, and narrative nonfiction narrow and deep in scope that might play with unreliable narrators, interrogations of power and violence, reclamations of identity, or dark-as-night humor. Fresh takes on horror, magical realism, camp, and kitsch will always be met with zeal. In the children's space, she is looking for contemporary middle-grade and YA stories that are fun, engaging, and seemingly "quiet" that crack open larger questions or underrepresented experiences. As part of their brilliant storytelling, they respect young readers and approach tough topics with warmth, humor, and edge. She is not accepting queries in science fiction, fantasy, or picture books at this time.

L652 Karmen Wells
Literary Agent
Canada

karmen@therightsfactory.com

https://www.therightsfactory.com/Agents/Karmen-Wells
https://twitter.com/KarmenEdits

Literary Agency: The Rights Factory

Fiction > *Novels*
Comedy / Humour; Coming of Age; Commercial; Drama; Dystopian Fiction; High Concept; Horror; LGBTQIA; Literary; Popular Culture; Science Fiction

Nonfiction > *Nonfiction Books:* Narrative Nonfiction

Send: Query; Pitch; Author bio; Writing sample
How to send: Email

Looking for published or to-be-published books to represent to producers for film or TV adaptation.

Authors: Daniel Barnett; Kelly Florence; Rhonda J. Garcia; Jessica Guess; Meg Hafdahl

L653 Jennifer Weltz
Literary Agent
United States

Literary Agency: The Jean V. Naggar Literary Agency

Closed to approaches.

L654 Erin Casey Westin
Literary Agent
United States

https://querymanager.com/query/erincaseywestin
https://twitter.com/erincaseywestin

Literary Agency: Gallt & Zacker Literary Agency

CHILDREN'S > **Fiction**
Middle Grade; Picture Books
YOUNG ADULT
Fiction
Graphic Novels; Novels
Nonfiction > *Nonfiction Books*

Closed to approaches.

Open to queries from the 1st to the 7th of every month.

L655 Michaela Whatnall
Literary Agent
United States

mwhatnall@dystel.com

https://www.dystel.com/michaela-whatnall
https://querymanager.com/query/michaelawhatnall
https://twitter.com/mwhatnall

Literary Agency: Dystel, Goderich & Bourret LLC

ADULT
 Fiction
  Graphic Novels: General
  Novels: Contemporary; Grounded Fantasy; Historical Fiction; Speculative; Upmarket
  Nonfiction > *Nonfiction Books*: Narrative Nonfiction

CHILDREN'S
 Fiction
  Graphic Novels; *Middle Grade*; *Picture Books*
  Nonfiction > *Nonfiction Books*: Narrative Nonfiction

YOUNG ADULT > Fiction
  Graphic Novels: General
  Novels: General, and in particular: Adventure; Contemporary; Fantasy; Historical Fiction; Horror; Romantic Comedy; Science Fiction

How to send: Query Manager

Strong interest in children's literature, particularly middle grade and young adult fiction of all genres, including contemporary, fantasy, science fiction, historical, adventure, horror, and rom-com. In the adult fiction space, they are particularly seeking contemporary, speculative, and historical upmarket fiction, as well as character-driven, grounded fantasy. They are also open to select narrative nonfiction for both children and adults, graphic novels, and picture books.

L656 Maria Whelan
Literary Agent
United States

http://www.inkwellmanagement.com/staff/maria-whelan

Literary Agency: InkWell Management

Fiction > *Novels*
 Comedy / Humour; Commercial; Culture; Literary; Magical Realism; Speculative; Upmarket Women's Fiction

Nonfiction > *Nonfiction Books*
 General, and in particular: Cultural Commentary; Society

Send: Query; Writing sample
How to send: In the body of an email

Enjoys literary fiction, magical realism, upmarket women's fiction and humor, as well as non-fiction, revolving around peculiar topics especially overlooked facets of society.

L657 Whispering Buffalo Literary Agency
Literary Agency
97 Chesson Road, London, W14 9QS
United Kingdom
Tel: +44 (0) 20 7385 4655

info@whisperingbuffalo.com

https://www.whisperingbuffalo.com

ADULT
 Fiction > *Novels*
  Commercial; Literary
 Nonfiction > *Nonfiction Books*: Commercial

CHILDREN'S > Fiction > *Novels*

YOUNG ADULT > Fiction > *Novels*

Send: Query; Author bio; Synopsis; Writing sample; Proposal
How to send: Word file email attachment

Represents a growing stable of storytellers including individuals with a high media profile in a variety of fields. The agency is building its list and welcomes unsolicited submissions.

Literary Agent: Mariam Keen

L658 Alice Whitwham
Literary Agent
United States

https://www.cheneyagency.com/alice-whitwham

Literary Agency: The Cheney Agency

L659 Chandler Wickers
Literary Agent
United States

cw@skagency.com

http://skagency.com/agents/chandler-wickers/

Literary Agency: Stuart Krichevsky Literary Agency, Inc. (**L609**)

Fiction > *Novels*
 Coming of Age; Family Saga; Literary; Upmarket

Nonfiction > *Nonfiction Books*
 Adventure; History; Journalism; Popular Culture; Technology; Warfare

Send: Query; Writing sample; Proposal
How to send: In the body of an email
How not to send: Email attachment

Interested in representing adult fiction and non-fiction.

She is drawn to voice-driven literary and upmarket fiction with a strong sense of place, novels featuring darkly funny narrators, flawed protagonists, coming of age stories, and family sagas. She's especially excited about writing that plays with form, stories that explore visceral experiences of body and mind, and characters grappling with philosophical questions about faith and desire. In non-fiction, she looks for novelistic journalism, comprehensive histories, war reporting, wilderness adventures, and journeys to the edges of the Earth. As a San Francisco native and Brooklyn transplant she is keen on stories that intersect tech and pop culture, converge scholarly with personal narratives, and those that demystify a subculture or reveal an underbelly.

L660 Alice Williams
Literary Agent
United Kingdom

alice@alicewilliamsliterary.co.uk

https://twitter.com/alicelovesbooks
https://www.instagram.com/agentalicewilliams/

Literary Agency: Alice Williams Literary (**L017**)

L661 Katie Williams
Literary Agent
United Kingdom

https://theagency.co.uk/the-agents/katie-williams/

Literary Agency: The Agency (London) Ltd (**L009**)

Scripts
 Film Scripts: Comedy / Humour; Drama
 TV Scripts: Comedy / Humour; Drama
 Theatre Scripts: Comedy / Humour; Drama

Represents drama and comedy writers in television, theatre and film.

L662 Laura Williams
Literary Agent
United Kingdom

lwilliams@greeneheaton.co.uk

http://greeneheaton.co.uk/agents/laura-williams/
https://twitter.com/laurabirdland

Literary Agency: Greene & Heaton Ltd (**L276**)

ADULT
 Fiction > *Novels*
  20th Century; Comedy / Humour; Commercial; Crime; Dark; Friends; Ghost Stories; Gothic; Historical Fiction; Historical Mystery Fiction; Horror; LGBTQIA; Literary; Magic; Magical Realism; Mystery; Police Procedural; Psychological Thrillers; Romance; Romantic Comedy; Speculative; Upmarket Commercial Fiction; Witches

 Nonfiction > *Nonfiction Books*
  Crime; History; Memoir; Mental Health; Narrative Nonfiction; Popular Culture; Popular Science

CHILDREN'S > Fiction > *Middle Grade*: Contemporary

YOUNG ADULT > Fiction >
Novels: Contemporary

I have a broad list across different genres of fiction, alongside a smaller non-fiction and children's book list, and I'm always looking for new and exciting projects. I love working on literary fiction and upmarket commercial fiction, of all different kinds, and I'm always on the lookout for meditative or moving novels about modern life. I prefer warmth and heart to coldness or ennui, although I love novels with a bit of bite and sharpness to them. I love stories about female friendships or conversely groups of women who don't get on.

I am always looking for historical and period fiction, particularly early- or mid-twentieth century, which sheds light on untold stories, or historical mysteries or ambitious cross-centuries narratives. I'm also always on the lookout for a big tragic love story that will sweep me away and make me cry happy or sad tears. At the more commercial end of fiction, I love funny novels with warmth and romantic comedies with a bit of depth.

I'm keen on darkness and a claustrophobic feel in novels, from gothic to horror to murder mysteries to ghost stories to psychological thrillers to speculative/magical realist fiction to novels that feel like true crime, or intense and emotional narratives about dark things, and I think being truly scared by a story is one of the most difficult things a writer can achieve. I love weird and wonderful stories with unexpected twists, I love witches and cults and magic and being amazed by an author's imagination, but I also love brilliantly plotted conventional murder mysteries or procedurals, as long as there's something fresh and exciting about it.

Most of all I'm looking for novels I haven't read before – something unusual structurally or thematically, something that shines a light on a subject the author is passionate about, something that'll break my heart or raise my blood in an entirely new way. I don't want protagonists in novels to hold a mirror up to my own life, I want them to show me an open door into theirs. I'm always looking to promote diverse voices from across the globe, and I'm particularly keen on LGBTQI+ stories.

I also have a very small list of young adult and middle grade fiction, which I love working on. I'm looking for something that feels current and contemporary, with a real conversation at its core. I'm not currently looking for fantasy, or anything younger than middle grade.

On the non-fiction side, I love working on memoirs of extraordinary people, or narrative non-fiction about something the author feels passionately about. I've worked on many books about mental health, and I'm interested in untold stories across popular science, history and popular culture. I'd also really like to find a brilliant true crime book.

Authors: Eve Ainsworth; Catherine Barter; Anna Day; Leona Deakin; Sue Divin; Helen Dring; Mari Ellis Dunning; Maggy Van Eijk; Zoe Feeney; Gabrielle Fernie; Louise Finnigan; Sarah Goodwin; Oliver Grant; Molly Greeley; Scott Alexander Howard; Maria Hummer; Jem Lester; Claire McGlasson; Rebecca Taylor McKay; Gemma Milne; Barney Norris; Nina De Pass; Richard Roper; Zuzana Ruzickova; James Smythe; Nancy Springer; John Sutherland; Alyssa Warren; Gill Wyness; Bella Younger

L663 Sarah Williams
Literary Agent
United Kingdom

sarah@sophiehicksagency.com
williamsoffice@sophiehicksagency.com

http://www.sophiehicksagency.com/sarahwilliams

Literary Agency: Sophie Hicks Agency (**L591**)

Fiction > *Novels*
Commercial; Family Saga; Literary; Romance; Thrillers

Nonfiction > *Nonfiction Books*
Memoir; Nature; Science; Travel

Send: Synopsis; Writing sample; Outline

She is always on the lookout for creative, engaging storytellers and is currently hoping to hear from writers of narrative non-fiction of most types – memoir, travel, nature, science, and explorations of the intricacies of the human experience. In fiction, she would love to find a surprising and excellently plotted multi-generational family story, and is perpetually hoping for a sweeping love story with colliding geographies. A twisty thriller is always welcome.

Authors: Sarah Bannan; Lee Boyce; William Butler-Adams; Helen Chandler-Wilde; Carl Cox; Sarah Crosby; Michaela Dunbar; Ruth Fitzmaurice; Kate Ford; Lewis Hine; Shahroo Izadi; Signe Johansen; Sophie Monks Kaufman; Jesse McClure; Phil McNulty; Andrew Meehan; Katie Treggiden; Claire Walsh; Tom Whipple; Jim White

L664 Jo Williamson
Literary Agent
United Kingdom

jo@antonyharwood.com
mail@antonyharwood.com

http://antonyharwood.com/jo-williamson/

Literary Agency: Antony Harwood Limited (**L029**)

ADULT > Fiction > *Novels*
Contemporary Romance; Dark; Psychological Thrillers; Romantic Comedy; Women's Fiction

CHILDREN'S > Fiction
Middle Grade: Adventure; Comedy / Humour; Contemporary; Folklore, Myths, and Legends
Picture Books: General

YOUNG ADULT > Fiction > *Novels*: Romance

Looking for compelling stories with strong voices. More specifically, Middle Grade adventures that feel fresh, as well as laugh-out-loud fiction with an engaging central character and series potential. She loves myths and legends so is keen to find something that blends contemporary with mythology for MG readers. She is also looking for YA romance with a strong hook. She is actively building her list of adult fiction and would like to find women's fiction, dark psychological thrillers, or a contemporary and funny romantic adventure. Follow agency submission guidelines (see website) and approach via general agency email address.

L665 Kathryn Willms
Literary Agent
Canada

kathryn@therightsfactory.com

https://www.therightsfactory.com/Agents/Kathryn-Willms
https://www.therightsfactory.com/submit-kathryn
https://querymanager.com/query/2039

Literary Agency: The Rights Factory

Fiction > *Novels*
Hard Science Fiction; Literary; Speculative

Nonfiction
Gift Books: General
Nonfiction Books: Biography; Business; Culture; Environment; Food and Drink; Health; History; Lifestyle; Narrative Nonfiction; Nature; Personal Development; Psychology; Science; Social Justice; Wellbeing; Women's Issues

Send: Query; Author bio; Writing sample
How to send: Query Manager; Email attachment

Specializes in nonfiction. She is particularly interested in ambitious, unconventional, smart, and well-written book projects that contribute new perspectives, revel in the quirkiness of the world, and change the way we see it. She's passionate about work that translates specialist knowledge to the mainstream to push cultural conversations in new and surprising directions. She enthusiastically welcomes submissions from BIPOC and LGBTQ-2S creators. She is starting to acquire hard science fiction and speculative literary fiction. She's attracted to the same qualities in fiction and nonfiction: big ideas; ambitious and/or clever premises; a sense of humour; and engagement with the big questions of our times.

Authors: Lisa Brahin; Sam Chaiton; Meghan Chayka; Dustin Galer; Alyssa Huizing; Andrew Mayeda; Michelle McIvor; Riley E. Moynes; Nancy Pearson; Karen Pierce; Laura Pratt; Krista Towns; Jaime Weinman; Zed Zha

L666 James Wills
Literary Agent
United Kingdom

Literary Agency: Watson, Little Ltd (**L647**)

Closed to approaches.

L667 Desiree Wilson
Literary Agent
United States

https://www.lookingglasslit.com/desiree-wilson
https://desir.ee/submissions/
https://twitter.com/swindlesoiree

Literary Agency: Looking Glass Literary & Media Management (**L406**)

ADULT
  Fiction
    Graphic Novels: Contemporary; Fantasy; Horror; Magical Realism; Science Fiction; Speculative
    Novels: Contemporary; Fantasy; Horror; Magical Realism; Romantic Comedy; Science Fiction; Speculative; Thrillers; Upmarket
    Short Fiction: General

  Nonfiction > *Nonfiction Books*: Narrative Nonfiction

CHILDREN'S
  Fiction
    Graphic Novels: General
    Middle Grade: Gender; Horror; Mental Health
  Nonfiction > *Middle Grade*
    Engineering; History; Mathematics; Science; Technology

YOUNG ADULT > **Fiction**
  Graphic Novels: High Concept; Relationships
  Novels: Fairy Tales; Fantasy; High Concept; Horror; LGBTQIA; Romance; Romantic Comedy; Science Fiction; Urban Fantasy

Does not want:

  Fiction > *Novels*: Hard Science Fiction

Closed to approaches.

I represent upper middle grade, YA, and adult genre fiction, especially horror (and kid-horror), high-concept fantasy, speculative fiction, magical realism, and accessible or near-future science fiction. I am also looking for select middle grade nonfiction about history or STEM.

L668 Ed Wilson
Literary Agent; Company Director
United Kingdom
Tel: +44 (0) 20 7251 0125

ed@johnsonandalcock.co.uk

http://www.johnsonandalcock.co.uk/ed-wilson
https://twitter.com/literarywhore

Literary Agency: Johnson & Alcock (**L335**)

Fiction > *Novels*
  Commercial; Crime; Experimental; Fantasy; High Concept; Literary; Science Fiction; Speculative; Thrillers

Nonfiction > *Nonfiction Books*
  History; Memoir; Nature; Politics; Popular Culture; Sport

Send: Query; Synopsis; Writing sample
How to send: Email attachment

In fiction, he looks for anything with originality and style, and his list covers the full gamut from literary to commercial writing. He likes books with an imaginative setting, strong narrative voice, and compelling premise. He has an active SFF list, representing multiple award-winning authors, and is always on the lookout for new writers. Think of him for high concept writing, intelligent crime and thrillers, and books that transcend genre. Ed is not currently taking on any new YA or children's authors and does not represent plays or film scripts.

His non-fiction tastes cover a wide range: from serious politics and sweeping narrative history, to sport, natural history, quirky memoir and popular culture. He loves writers that find a new and inventive way into a well-known subject and works editorially with all his authors to make their books the best they can be.

L669 Caroline Wood
Literary Agent; Company Director
United Kingdom

https://felicitybryan.com/fba-agent/caroline-wood/

Literary Agency: Felicity Bryan Associates (**L215**)

Fiction > *Novels*
  Commercial; Crime; Literary; Romance; Thrillers

Nonfiction > *Nonfiction Books*
  Cookery; Memoir

I represent a range of fiction, from literary prize winners to commercial crime and thrillers. I'm looking for great storytelling, complex relationships and books that make me feel. I'm always keen to find strong, original debuts that will stand out from the crowd. Right now, I'm looking for a great love story – intimate or sweeping. I'm always attracted to books that are cinematic and a lot of the novels I represent are optioned for film and TV. In non-fiction, I represent primarily cookery and memoirs.

Authors: Carlos Acosta; Modern Baker; Kay Barron; Susan Beale; Louis De Bernières; Mary Berry; Nina Bhadreshwar; Francesca Brill; Rhidian Brook; Stephen Burke; Lucy Cavendish; Sarah Challis; Jonathan Coe; Will Cohu; T.A. Cotterell; Benjamin Daniels; Nick Edwards; James Fearnley; Rebecca Fleet; Damon Galgut; Kat Gordon; Catherine Hall; Anna Hope; Gill Hornby; Richard House; Allegra Huston; Stanley Kenani; Liza Klaussmann; Phyllida Law; Tim Leach; Simon Lelic; Sarah K Marr; Alistair Morgan; Alan Murrin; Jennifer Nadel; Svenja O'donnell; Colm O'gorman; Iain Pears; Nick Potter; Melody Razak; Adam Ruck; Penny Rudge; Edward Russell-Walling; Sue Stuart-Smith; Henry Sutton; Katherine Swift; Edmund De Waal; Martin Walker; Kirsty Wark; Greg Wise; James Wythe; Lucy Young

L670 James Woodhouse
Literary Agent
United Kingdom

enquiries@tiborjones.com

http://www.tiborjones.com/about/

Literary Agency: Tibor Jones & Associates

Fiction > *Novels*
  Africa; Commercial; Literary

Send: Query; Synopsis; Writing sample

Passionate about stories from Africa, but his interests range from strong commercial crime fiction to high-end literary work.

L671 Bryony Woods
Literary Agent
United Kingdom

submissions.bryony@dkwlitagency.co.uk

http://dkwlitagency.co.uk/agents/
https://twitter.com/BryonyWoods

Literary Agency: Diamond Kahn and Woods (DKW) Literary Agency Ltd

ADULT
  Fiction > *Novels*
    General, and in particular: Commercial; Dark Magic; Fairy Tales; Fantasy; Friends; Literary; Romance; Science Fiction; Upmarket Contemporary Fiction

  Nonfiction
    Essays: General
    Nonfiction Books: Memoir

CHILDREN'S > **Fiction** > *Middle Grade*
YOUNG ADULT > **Fiction** > *Novels*

Does not want:

> **Fiction** > *Novels*
>   Crime; Psychological Thrillers

Closed to approaches.

My reading taste is fairly eclectic, and covers commercial to literary and everything in between.

At the moment I'd particularly love to find some beautifully written, upmarket contemporary novels; books about friendships and platonic love; thought-provoking sci-fi or richly imagined fantasy worlds; brilliant, sweeping love stories on an epic canvas; found families, or novels about finding love in unexpected places; anything that truly makes me laugh; fairy tales, or anything darkly magical; books that surprise me; books that will break my heart; books that are full of hope.

I tend to avoid anything particularly gritty or depressing, so crime novels or harrowing psychological thrillers are likely to be a no. I also don't represent children's picture books, or poetry collections. The non-fiction side of my list is small, but I have been known to fall for a beautiful memoir or a moving collection of essays.

L672 Jessica Woollard

Literary Agent
United Kingdom

jessicawoollard@davidhigham.co.uk

https://davidhigham.co.uk
https://davidhigham.co.uk/agents-dh/jessica-woollard/

Literary Agency: David Higham Associates Ltd (**L159**)

Fiction > *Novels*: Literary

Nonfiction > *Nonfiction Books*
  Memoir; Narrative Nonfiction

How to send: Email

I represent a diverse range of narrative non-fiction and have always been attracted to memoir. I also represent some literary fiction – the way we relate to land often plays a key role here – and international literary fiction with a particular focus on Southeast Asia, Japan and Africa.

Authors: Kerry Andrew; Lamorna Ash; Santanu Bhattacharya; Paco Calvo; Rob Cowen; Stanley Donwood; Caroline Eden; Tan Twan Eng; Charles Foster; Jay Griffiths; Nick Hayes; Liu Hong; Masud Husain; Lucy Jones; Helen Jukes; Jonathan Kennedy; Natalie Lawrence; Julia Lovell; Robert Macfarlane; Manchan Magan; Ben Masters; Jackie Morris; Benjamin Myers; Fred Pearce; Martin Shaw; Merlin Sheldrake; Lola Shoneyin; Hannah Stowe; Nigel Toon; Taichi Yamada

L673 Wordserve Literary

Literary Agency
United States

admin@wordserveliterary.com

http://www.wordserveliterary.com
http://wordservewatercooler.com
https://twitter.com/WordServeLit
http://www.facebook.com/WordServeLiterary

ADULT
  Fiction > *Novels*
    Christianity; Historical Fiction; Legal; Literary; Mainstream; Romance; Supernatural / Paranormal; Suspense; Women's Fiction

  Nonfiction > *Nonfiction Books*
    Biography; Christianity; Current Affairs; Family; Finance; Health; History; Memoir; Military; Popular Culture; Psychology; Self Help; Women's Issues

CHILDREN'S > **Fiction**
  Middle Grade; Novels
YOUNG ADULT > **Fiction** > *Novels*

Send: Query; Writing sample
How to send: In the body of an email
How not to send: Email attachment

Represents books for the general and Christian markets. Nonfiction 40,000 – 100,000 words; fiction 60,000-120,000 words. No gift books, poetry, short stories, screenplays, children's picture books, science fiction or fantasy for any age. Email approaches only. See website for detailed submission guidelines. Submissions that disregard the submission guidelines may themselves be disregarded.

Literary Agents: Keely Boeving; Sarah Joy Freese; Nick Harrison; Greg Johnson

L674 Writer's Side

Literary Agency; Editorial Service
8 Chanan Singh Park, Delhi Cantt, New Delhi, 110010
India

kanishka500@gmail.com
kanishka@writersside.com

http://www.writersside.com

Fiction > *Novels*
  General, and in particular: Commercial; Literary

Nonfiction > *Nonfiction Books*
  General, and in particular: Business; Narrative Nonfiction

Send: Synopsis; Author bio; Writing sample
How to send: Word file email attachment

Costs: Offers services that writers have to pay for.

Describes itself as the number one literary agency in South Asia. Represents authors from India and abroad. Particularly interested in debut writing from India, Pakistan, Sri Lanka and Bangladesh. Also offers editorial services, but this is held separate from the literary agency and customers of the editorial service will not be represented by the agency.

Literary Agent: Kanishka Gupta

L675 Rachel Yeoh

Literary Agent
United Kingdom

submissions@madeleinemilburn.com

https://madeleinemilburn.co.uk/team-member/rachel-yeoh/

Literary Agency: Madeleine Milburn Literary, TV & Film Agency (**L420**)

Fiction > *Novels*
  Autofiction; Book Club Fiction; Literary; Magical Realism; Nature; Philosophy; Politics; Postcolonialism; Social Commentary; Upmarket

Nonfiction > *Nonfiction Books*: Memoir

Send: Query; Pitch; Market info; Author bio
How to send: Email

Actively looking for: literary, upmarket, book club, autobiographical fiction, political perspectives, social critiques, postcolonial literature, magical realism, nature writing, philosophical themes, classical retellings, character-driven stories, topical issues, narrative memoir, global voices, diaspora.

I am looking for global voices in literary, upmarket and book club fiction that tell compelling stories reflective of the human experience, as well as autobiographical fiction and narrative non-fiction.

L676 YMU Books

Literary Agency
180 Great Portland Street, London, W1W 5QZ
United Kingdom

https://www.ymugroup.com
https://books.ymugroup.com

Professional Body: The Association of Authors' Agents (AAA)

Nonfiction > *Nonfiction Books*
  Celebrity; Commercial

Closed to approaches.

A market-leading literary agency in premium brand and platform representation, working with writers and creators who excel in their genres.

Authors: Federica Amati; Rebecca Bainbridge; Whitney Bauman; Francis Bourgeois; Stephanie Bramwell-Lawes; Corey Brotherson; Deborah Chu; Emma Cowing; Rosie Day; Melvyn Downes; Jane Dunn; Sindri Eldon; Emily Fairbairn; Paloma Faith; Noel Fitzpatrick; Lizzie Frainier; Karissa Hamilton-Bannis; Cherry Healey; Sarah Hehir; Imran Khan; Sam Marsden; Alissa Jones Nelson;

Poppy O'Neill; Kayleigh Rattle; Cat Sims; Jemma Solomon; Airy Something; KT Tunstall; Dakota Warren

L677 Claudia Young
Literary Agent
United Kingdom

http://greeneheaton.co.uk/agents/claudia-young/
https://twitter.com/ClaudiaL_Young

Literary Agency: Greene & Heaton Ltd (**L276**)

Fiction > *Novels*
  Contemporary; Crime; Historical Fiction; Literary; Thrillers

Nonfiction > *Nonfiction Books*
  Comedy / Humour; Cookery; Food Journalism; Travel

Closed to approaches.

Interested in all types of writing, in particular cooking and food journalism, comedy and travel writing. Loves literary fiction, contemporary as well as historical novels, crime fiction and thrillers.

Authors: Sam Akbar; Anthony Anaxagorou; Ros Atkinson; Jordan Bourke; Aine Carlin; Matt Chapple; Martha Collison; Jack Cooke; Kevan Davis; Kim Duke; Gabriela Evangelou; Lucia Evangelou; Ella Frears; Francis Gimblett; Lewis Goodall; Peter Harper; Alice Hart; Wayne Holloway-Smith; Lizzie King; Vanessa King; Jenny Lee; Eleanor Maidment; Janina Matthewson; Ciara Ohartghaile; Val Payne; Alice Procter; Rejina Pyo; James Ramsden; Rosie Ramsden; Charlie Ryrie; Viviane Schwarz; Tim Sebastian; Dale Shaw; Rachel de Thample; Georgie Tilney; Regina Wong; David Wright

L678 The Zack Company, Inc
Literary Agency
United States

https://zackcompany.com
https://www.facebook.com/literaryagency
https://twitter.com/thezackcompany

Fiction
  Graphic Novels: General
  Novels: African American; Chick Lit; Comedy / Humour; Commercial Women's Fiction; Cozy Mysteries; Erotic; Fantasy; Hard Science Fiction; High / Epic Fantasy; Historical Fiction; Horror; International; Literary; Mystery; Native Americans; Post-Apocalyptic; Romance; Romantasy; Romantic Suspense; Science Fiction; Speculative Romance; Supernatural / Paranormal Romance; Suspense; Thrillers; Urban Fantasy; Women's Fiction

Nonfiction > *Nonfiction Books*
  Alternative Health; American History; Animals; Autobiography; Aviation; Biography; British History; Career Development; Childcare; Classics / Ancient World; Comedy / Humour; Cookery; Crime; Cultural History; Current Affairs; Diet; Economics; Entertainment; Entrepreneurship; Environment; European History; Films; Finance; Fitness; Food; Gardening; Health; Home Improvement; Inspirational; Investigative Journalism; Judaism; Leadership; Management; Medieval; Meditation; Memoir; Military History; Military; Mind, Body, Spirit; Music; National Security; Nature; Nutrition; Outdoor Activities; Painting; Parenting; Personal Development; Personal Finance; Pets; Politics; Popular Science; Relationships; Religion; Science; Secret Intelligence; Sex; Spirituality; Sports Celebrity; TV; Technology; Wellbeing; Women's Issues; Yoga

Send: Author bio; Synopsis; Full text; Proposal
How to send: Online submission system
How not to send: Post; Email

Requirements change frequently, so check the agency website before approaching. Approaches must be made via the form on the website.

Literary Agent: Andrew Zack

L679 Marietta B. Zacker
Literary Agent
United States

https://www.galltzacker.com/submissions.html
https://querymanager.com/query/querymarietta

Literary Agency: Gallt & Zacker Literary Agency

CHILDREN'S > **Fiction**
  Middle Grade; *Picture Books*
YOUNG ADULT
  Fiction
    Graphic Novels; *Novels*
  Nonfiction > *Nonfiction Books*

How to send: Query Manager

Open to queries from the 1st to the 7th of every month.

L680 Zeno Agency
Literary Agency
Primrose Hill Business Centre, 110 Gloucester Avenue, London, NW1 8HX
United Kingdom
Tel: +44 (0) 20 7096 0927

info@zenoagency.com

http://zenoagency.com

Professional Body: The Association of Authors' Agents (AAA)

Fiction > *Novels*
  General, and in particular: Fantasy; Horror; Science Fiction

Nonfiction > *Nonfiction Books*

London-based literary agency that works with writers, illustrators and photographers. We cover fiction, non-fiction and children's books, with a specialism in adult fantasy, science fiction and horror. We represent a top-drawer range of authors, both as primary agent and in association with a number of well-known agencies abroad. Our list comprises major brand-names, high profile award winners, talented debut authors and prestigious literary estates.

Authors: Travis Baldree; Shannon Lee Barry; Alice Bell; Cierra Block; Marie Brennan; Rebecca Brownlie; Andrew Cartmel; Mário Coelho; J.R. Dawson; Clio Evans; Georgia Gailey; Craig Laurance Gidney; J.T. Greathouse; Daniel B. Greene; Elizabeth Helen; Grady Hendrix; Laura Kerseviciute; Shannon Mayer; Anna McNuff; Katy Nyquist; Adam Oyebanji; Bryce O'Connor; Martin Purbrick; Sian Radford; Emily Rath; Farrah Riaz; Cassidy Ellis Salter; Calah Singleton; Amy True / Amy Trueblood; Emily Turner; R.R. Virdi; MJ Wassmer; Angus Watson; Gary Wigglesworth; Jasmine Wigham; Yudhanjaya Wijeratne; Catelyn Wilson

Literary Agents: John Berlyne (**L061**); Stevie Finegan (**L226**); Bianca Gillam (**L259**)

L681 Ayla Zuraw-Friedland
Literary Agent
United States

azf@goldinlit.com

https://www.goldinlit.com/ayla-zuraw-friedland
https://twitter.com/aylazeef

Literary Agency: Frances Goldin Literary Agency, Inc. (**L238**)

Fiction
  Graphic Novels: General
  Novels: Literary

Nonfiction > *Nonfiction Books*
  Arts; LGBTQIA; Social Class; Technology

Send: Query; Writing sample
How to send: Email

Interested in literary fiction and nonfiction that inspect big questions about queer identity, class, community, and art & technology through a personal lens. Please note that she does not represent Young Adult, Middle Grade, or Picture Books.

Magazines

For the most up-to-date listings of these and hundreds of other magazines, visit https://www.firstwriter.com/magazines

To claim your free access to the site, please see the back of this book.

M001 The 2River View
Online Magazine
Santa Rosa, CA 95404
United States

Belong@2river.org

https://www.2river.org
https://2river.submittable.com/submit

Poetry > *Any Poetic Form*

Send: Full text
How to send: Submittable

Costs: A fee is charged upon submission. $3 reading fee per submission.

Considers unpublished poems only. Submit via online submission system. See website for more details.

Editor-in-Chief: Richard Long

M002 30 North
Magazine
United States

https://30northliterarymagazine.com

Fiction > *Short Fiction*: Literary

Nonfiction > *Short Nonfiction*: Creative Nonfiction

Poetry > *Any Poetic Form*

Send: Full text
How to send: Submittable

Welcomes submissions from students and alumni of the college and from student artists and writers across the nation and world. We welcome creative writing in all genres, as well as visual art and songwriting.

M003 32 Poems
Magazine
Washington & Jefferson College, Department of English, 60 S. Lincoln Street, Washington, PA 15301
United States

submissions@32poems.com

http://32poems.com

Nonfiction > *Reviews*: Poetry as a Subject

Poetry > *Any Poetic Form*

Send: Full text
How to send: Submittable; Duosuma; Post

Costs: A fee is charged for online submissions. $3 fee for online submissions.

Welcomes submissions from January 1st to April 30th and from July 1st to October 31st. We respond quickly, often within a few weeks, and poets who have not received a response within 90 days are encouraged to query regarding their manuscript's status. As a rule, we publish shorter poems that fit on a single page, but we regularly make exceptions to accommodate remarkable work that runs a little longer. Please send no more than five poems (in a single document) and no more than one active submission at a time. We do not accept translations or work that has been previously published in print or online.

Editor: George David Clark

Managing Editor: Elisabeth Clark

M004 417 Magazine
Magazine
Whitaker Publishing, 2111 S. Eastgate Ave., Springfield, MO 65809
United States
Tel: +1 (417) 883-7417

https://www.417mag.com
http://facebook.com/417mag
http://instagram.com/417mag
http://twitter.com/417mag
http://pinterest.com/417magazine
https://www.linkedin.com/company/whitaker-publishing

Nonfiction > *Articles*
  Food; Lifestyle; Missouri; Outdoor Activities

Publishes material of local interest to southwest Missouri only. Potential contributors are advised to study the magazine before approaching.

M005 aaduna
Online Magazine
144 Genesee Street Suite 102-259, Auburn, NY 13021
United States

submissionsmanager@aaduna.org

https://www.aaduna.net
https://www.facebook.com/AadunaInc
https://aadunanotes.blogspot.com/
https://twitter.com/aadunaspeaks

Fiction
  Novel Excerpts; *Short Fiction*
Nonfiction > *Essays*

Poetry > *Any Poetic Form*

Send: Query; Author bio; Full text
How to send: Word file email attachment
How not to send: PDF file email attachment

Publishes fiction, poetry, and nonfiction. Primarily interested in providing a viable publishing platform for people of color. Submissions must be sent by email and writers are also strongly encouraged to send a copy by post as well, however this is no longer required. See website for full guidelines.

M006 AARP The Magazine
Magazine
c/o Editorial Submissions, 601 E St. NW, Washington, DC 20049
United States

pubspitches@aarp.org

https://www.aarp.org/magazine/

Nonfiction
  Articles: General, and in particular: Fitness; Food; Health; Investments; Nutrition; Personal Finance; Relationships; Travel
  Essays: Personal Essays

Send: Query
Don't send: Full text
How to send: Email

Magazine for those over 50. Rarely uses unsolicited ideas but will review those submitted in accordance with the guidelines on the website.

M007 About Place Journal
Magazine
PO Box 24, Black Earth, WI 53515-0424
United States

blackearthinstitute@gmail.com

https://aboutplacejournal.org
https://aboutplacejournal.submittable.com/submit

Fiction > *Short Fiction*: Literary

Nonfiction
 Essays: General
 Short Nonfiction: Creative Nonfiction

Poetry > *Any Poetic Form*

Closed to approaches.

Publishes poetry, fiction, and essays / creative nonfiction. Accepts submissions during specific submission windows. See website for details and for themes.

M008 Abridged
Print Magazine
United Kingdom

abridged@ymail.com

https://www.abridged.zone
https://www.facebook.com/profile.php?id=100042275333261
https://twitter.com/Abridged030

Poetry > *Any Poetic Form*
 Contemporary; Experimental

Aims to publish and exhibit contemporary/experimental poetry plus contemporary art. Each issue is themed. Themes focus on contemporary concerns in a rapidly changing society. We are offering an alternative and complete integration of poetry, art and design. We experiment continually.

M009 The Account
Online Magazine
United States

poetryprosethought@gmail.com

https://theaccountmagazine.com
https://theaccountajournalofpoetryprosethought.submittable.com/submit
https://twitter.com/TheAccountMag
https://www.facebook.com/TheAccountAJournalOfPoetryProseAndThought

Fiction > *Short Fiction*

Nonfiction > *Short Nonfiction*: Creative Nonfiction

Poetry > *Any Poetic Form*

Send: Full text

Accepts poetry, fiction, and creative nonfiction. Send 3-5 poems, essays up to 6,000 words, or fiction between 1,000 and 6,000 words, through online submission system. Each piece of work must be accompanied by an account between 150 and 500 words, giving voice to the artist's approach.

Editors: Brianna Noll, Poetry Editor; Jennifer Hawe, Nonfiction Editor; M. Milks, Fiction Editor; Tyler Mills, Editor-in-Chief; Christina Stoddard, Managing Editor/ Publicist

M010 Accountancy Age
Magazine
United Kingdom

https://www.accountancyage.com
https://www.twitter.com/accountancyage/
https://www.linkedin.com/groups?gid=2352548

PROFESSIONAL > **Nonfiction** > *Articles*
 Accounting; Business; Finance

Weekly magazine publishing articles on accountancy, business, and the financial world.

Editor: Aaran Fronda

M011 Accountancy Daily
Online Magazine
240 Blackfriars Road, London, SE1 8NW
United Kingdom

accountancynews@croneri.co.uk

https://www.accountancydaily.co
https://twitter.com/accountancylive

Book Publisher: Croner-i Limited (**P127**)

PROFESSIONAL > **Nonfiction** > *News*
 Accounting; Business; Finance

Specialises in technical analysis, news and comment on tax, accounting and audit for the accounting profession working across practice and business.

M012 Acumen
Magazine
4 Thornhill Bridge Wharf, Caledonian Road, London, N1 0RU
United Kingdom
Tel: +44 (0) 20 7278 6674

hello@acumen-poetry.co.uk

https://acumen-poetry.co.uk

Nonfiction
 Articles: Poetry as a Subject
 Essays: Poetry as a Subject
 Reviews: Books; Poetry as a Subject
Poetry in Translation > *Any Poetic Form*

Poetry > *Any Poetic Form*

Send: Full text
How to send: Online submission system; Email; Post

We aim to publish the best in new poetry and poetry translations, alongside articles, debate, comment and reviews of recent poetry publications. We publish new and established writers and are proud to have discovered many new voices. All poems are considered on merit. We welcome unpublished and unsubmitted poems, translations of poems, articles and debate on poetry covering a wide variety of topics and with different writing styles.

Editor: Patricia Oxley

M013 AdventureBox
Magazine
United Kingdom

contact@bayard-magazines.co.uk

https://bayard-magazines.co.uk/collections/all-products/products/adventurebox-magazine

Magazine Publisher: Bayard Magazines

CHILDREN'S > **Fiction** > *Early Readers*: Adventure

Magazine that aims to keep kids hooked on reading. This title was made for kids who have just begun to read independently. The distinctive format helps kids feel grown up and that they've arrived at the next step in their reading journey.

M014 African American Review
Magazine
United States

aileen.keenan@slu.edu

https://afamreview.org
https://twitter.com/afamreview

Book Publisher: The Johns Hopkins University Press (**P250**)

Fiction > *Short Fiction*: African American

Nonfiction
 Essays: African American; Arts; Culture; Films; Literature; Theatre; Visual Culture
 Interviews: African American
 Reviews: African American; Books
Poetry > *Any Poetic Form*: African American

How to send: Online submission system

Publishes insightful essays on African American literature, theatre, film, the visual arts, and culture; "Forgotten Manuscript" features; interviews; poetry; fiction; and book reviews.

Editor: Aileen Keenan

M015 African Voices
Magazine
325 Lafayette Avenue, C.F. Suite, Brooklyn, NY 11238
United States
Tel: +1 (212) 865-2982

https://africanvoices.com
https://africanvoices.submittable.com/submit/
https://www.facebook.com/africanvoicesmag
https://www.instagram.com/africanvoices/
https://x.com/africanvoices

Fiction
 Novel Excerpts; *Short Fiction*
Poetry > *Any Poetic Form*

Scripts > *Theatre Scripts*

How to send: Submittable

Costs: A fee is charged upon submission. $3.77 per submission.

An international, literary magazine devoted to the promotion of fiction, non-fiction, poetry and visual arts created by people of color. Published three times a year (2 print issues and 1 digital issue) and distributed throughout the United States and abroad. Encourages writers and artists to review sample copies before submitting work so they are familiar with the editorial style. Publishes short stories and poetry online on a monthly basis.

Open to submissions all year round. Prioritizes and publishes work from writers from the African Diaspora and people of color. Encourages people to submit work that is transgressive, creative and thought provoking. Accepts all genres and styles (i.e. speculative fiction, humor, mystery and drama). Short one to three act plays and novel excerpts are accepted as well. All styles of poetry are considered including avant-garde, free verse, haiku, light verse and traditional. All subject matter of poems are considered for publication.

No AI generated poems, short stories, essays or art. Submissions must be 100 percent created by human writers and artists.

M016 Agni

Magazine
Boston University, 236 Bay State Road,
Boston, MA 02215
United States

agni@bu.edu

https://agnionline.bu.edu
https://twitter.com/AGNIMagazine
https://facebook.com/agnimag

Fiction > *Short Fiction*

Nonfiction > *Essays*

Poetry > *Any Poetic Form*

Closed to approaches.

Costs: A fee is charged upon submission. $3 submission fee.

Submit one story, one essay, or up to five poems, and wait for reply before sending more. Accepts submissions by post with SASE or via online submission system. No submissions by email. Open to submissions between September 1 and December 15; and between February 15 and May 31.

Editor: Sven Birkerts

M017 Agricultural History

Magazine
Kennesaw State University, Dept. of History and Philosophy, 402 Bartow Ave., Kennesaw, GA 30144
United States

aghistory@kennesaw.edu

https://www.aghistorysociety.org/the-journal
https://read.dukeupress.edu/agricultural-history/pages/Submission_Guidelines
https://mc04.manuscriptcentral.com/aghistory

ACADEMIC > **Nonfiction** > *Articles*
Agriculture; History

Send: Full text

Publishes articles on all aspects of the history of agriculture and rural life with no geographical or temporal limits. Submit via online submission system. See website for full guidelines.

Editor: Albert Way

M018 Air & Space Quarterly

Magazine
United States

https://airandspace.si.edu/air-and-space-quarterly

Magazine Publisher / Book Publisher: Smithsonian Institution

Nonfiction > *Articles*
Aviation; Military Aviation; Space

Magazine exploring topics in aviation and space, from the earliest moments of flight to today.

M019 Alaska Quarterly Review

Magazine
United States

https://aqreview.org
https://alaskaquarterlyreview.submittable.com/submit
https://www.facebook.com/AlaskaQuarterlyReview/
https://www.youtube.com/channel/UCvtOaG2FJ7tuEs8Vsd-rbFQ
https://twitter.com/AQReview

Fiction
Novel Excerpts: Experimental; Traditional
Novellas: Experimental; Traditional
Short Fiction: Experimental; Traditional
Nonfiction > *Short Nonfiction*
Experimental; Literary; Traditional
Poetry > *Any Poetic Form*
Experimental; Traditional
Scripts > *Theatre Scripts*
Drama; Experimental; Traditional

Closed to approaches.

Costs: A fee is charged upon submission. $3 submission fee.

The editors invite submissions of fiction, short plays, poetry, photo essays, and literary nonfiction in traditional and experimental styles.

M020 Alfred Hitchcock Mystery Magazine

Magazine
6 Prowitt Street, Norwalk, CT 06855
United States

https://www.alfredhitchcockmysterymagazine.com

Fiction > *Short Fiction*
Courtroom Dramas; Crime; Mystery; Police Procedural; Suspense

How to send: Online submission system

Interested in nearly every kind of mystery: stories of detection of the classic kind, police procedurals, private eye tales, suspense, courtroom dramas, stories of espionage, and so on. Only requirement is that the story be about a crime (or the threat or fear of one).

Editor: Linda Landrigan

M021 Allegro Poetry Magazine

Online Magazine
United Kingdom

https://www.allegropoetry.org

Poetry > *Any Poetic Form:* Contemporary

Send: Full text; Author bio
How to send: In the body of an email

Biannual online poetry magazine. Accepts poetry submissions up to 40 lines by email between June 1 and July 31, and between December 1 and January 31. Each year the March issue is a general issue, and the September issue is a themed one.

M022 American Book Review

Magazine
United States
Tel: +1 (361) 248-8245

americanbookreview@gmail.com

https://www.americanbookreview.org
https://www.facebook.com/AmBookRev
https://www.youtube.com/user/AmericanBookReview

Book Publisher: University of Nebraska Press

Nonfiction > *Reviews*
Cultural Criticism; Fiction as a Subject; Literary Criticism; Poetry as a Subject

Closed to approaches.

Specializes in reviews of frequently neglected works of fiction, poetry, and literary and cultural criticism from small, regional, university, ethnic, avant-garde, and women's presses. In nonfiction, reviews important books of criticism, biographies, and cultural studies. No reviews of "how-to" or "self-help" books. Would consider a review of innovative children's literature, but not usually part of the preferred content. Prefers books that have been published in the past six months, but will review books that have been published in the past year. No unsolicited reviews.

M023 American Short Fiction
Magazine
United States

editors@americanshortfiction.org

https://americanshortfiction.org
https://americanshortfiction.submittable.com/submit
https://www.facebook.com/americanshortfiction
https://x.com/asfmag
https://www.instagram.com/americanshortfiction/

Fiction in Translation > *Short Fiction*

Fiction > *Short Fiction*

Send: Full text
How to send: Submittable
How not to send: Post

Costs: A fee is charged upon submission. $3 submission fee.

Has published, and continues to seek, short fiction by some of the finest writers working in contemporary literature, whether they are established or new or lesser-known authors. In addition to its triannual print magazine, also publishes stories online. Unsolicited submissions are accepted from September to December. Short fiction submitted to the magazine must be original and previously unpublished. All manuscripts must be written in English. Translations are acceptable but must be accompanied by a copy of the original text. Considers simultaneous submissions on the condition that if the manuscript is accepted for publication elsewhere, the author immediately withdraws the submission through the Submittable site. No poetry, plays, nonfiction, reviews, etc.

M024 Amethyst Review
Online Magazine
United Kingdom

editor@amethystmagazine.org
Sarah.Poet@gmail.com

https://amethystmagazine.org
https://www.facebook.com/AmethystReview/

Fiction > *Short Fiction*: Spirituality

Nonfiction > *Short Nonfiction*: Spirituality

Poetry > *Any Poetic Form*: Spirituality

Send: Full text; Author bio
How to send: Word file email attachment; In the body of an email

Publishes work that engages in some way with spirituality or the sacred. Submit up to five poems (of any length) and / or prose pieces of up to 2,000 words. Simultaneous submissions if notification of acceptance elsewhere is provided. No previously published work. Send submissions by email with author bio of around 50 words. See website for full guidelines.

Editor: Sarah Law

M025 Angela Poetry Magazine
Online Magazine
Wax Poetry and Art, Attn: Angela Poetry Magazine, 101-5170 Dunster Road, Suite 108, Nanaimo, BC, V9T 6M4,
Canada
Tel: +1 (250) 667-7748

info@waxpoetryart.com

http://waxpoetryart.com/angela/

Magazine Publisher: Wax Poetry and Art Network

Poetry > *Any Poetic Form*: Contemporary

How to send: Email

Accepts poetry submissions from everyone on Earth and orbiting spacecraft. Publishes poems that are curious, humorous, and generally on the lighter side of life. Read the Submissions page and follow the guidelines to submit.

M026 The Antigonish Review
Magazine
PO Box 5000, Antigonish, Nova Scotia, B2G 2W5
Canada
Tel: +1 (902) 867-3962
Fax: +1 (902) 867-5563

tar@stfx.ca

https://antigonishreview.com
https://twitter.com/antigonishrevie
https://www.facebook.com/The-Antigonish-Review-332083480162513/
https://www.linkedin.com/in/the-antigonish-review-7602052a

Fiction in Translation > *Short Fiction*: Literary

Fiction > *Short Fiction*: Literary

Nonfiction > *Essays*
   Creative Nonfiction; Culture; History; Memoir; Sport; Travel

Poetry in Translation > *Any Poetic Form*

Poetry > *Any Poetic Form*

Send: Full text
How to send: Submittable
How not to send: Post; Email

Costs: A fee is charged upon submission. $5 for prose; $3 for poetry.

Submit via online portal only. Submit no more than 2-3 poems (or 3-4 pages of poetry) and submit no more till a response is received. Considers poetry on any subject written from any point of view and in any form. For fiction, send only one story at a time. Also publishes poetry and prose translated into English from other languages (be sure to indicate source language). Also considers critical articles and essays that are fresh, vigorous, and free from jargon. Welcomes creative nonfiction. No email submissions, postal submissions, or simultaneous submissions.

M027 Arboreal
Online Magazine
United States

https://arborealmag.com
https://arboreal.submittable.com/submit
https://www.instagram.com/arborealmagazine/
https://twitter.com/arborealmag
https://www.facebook.com/ArborealMag
https://www.linkedin.com/company/arborealmag/

Fiction > *Short Fiction*

Nonfiction > *Essays*

Poetry > *Any Poetic Form*

How to send: Submittable

Online magazine that came about when two friends sought to create something of value, something for pure enjoyment, something to encourage creativity.

M028 Arc
Magazine
PO Box 269 Stn B, Ottawa, ON, K1P 6C4
Canada

arc@arcpoetry.ca
prose@arcpoetry.ca
coordinatingeditor@arcpoetry.ca

https://arcpoetry.ca
https://arcpoetry.submittable.com/submit
https://www.facebook.com/ArcPoetryMagazine/
https://x.com/arcpoetry
https://www.instagram.com/arcpoetrymag/
https://www.youtube.com/user/ArcPoetry

Nonfiction
   Articles: Poetry as a Subject
   Essays: Poetry as a Subject
   Interviews: Poetry as a Subject
   Reviews: Poetry as a Subject

Poetry > *Any Poetic Form*

Send: Full text; Pitch
How to send: Submittable; Email

Costs: A fee is charged upon submission in some cases. Poets based in the US must pay a submission fee of $2 per poem. If this fee is a barrier for anyone wishing to submit, poets may enquire about having the fee waived.

Accepts unsolicited submissions from poets at all stages of their writing careers during Spring and Fall submission periods, via Submittable. Send up to three poems, up to 360 lines in total. Also publishes essays, articles, interviews and reviews relating to poetry. Send pitches by email.

M029 The Architectural Review

Magazine
15 Bouverie Street, London, EC4Y 8DP
United Kingdom
Tel: +44 (0) 20 3953 2000

https://www.architectural-review.com

Magazine Publisher: EMAP Publishing

PROFESSIONAL > *Nonfiction* > *Articles*
Architecture; Design

Magazine of architecture and design aimed at professionals.

Editor: Paul Finch

M030 Art Monthly

Magazine
Peveril Garden Studios, 140 Great Dover Street, London, SE1 4GW
United Kingdom
Tel: +44 (0) 20 7240 0389

info@artmonthly.co.uk

http://www.artmonthly.co.uk
https://www.twitter.com/artmonthly
https://www.facebook.com/artmonthly
https://instagram.com/art_monthly_uk

Nonfiction
Articles: Arts
Interviews: Arts
Reviews: Arts

Magazine of contemporary visual art. Publishes in-depth features, interviews with artists, profiles on emerging artists and coverage of major trends and developments by independent critics.

M031 Art Papers

Magazine
PO Box 5748, Atlanta, GA 31107
United States
Tel: +1 (404) 588-1837
Fax: +1 (678) 999-7002

editor@artpapers.org
info@artpapers.org

https://www.artpapers.org
https://www.facebook.com/artpapers
https://twitter.com/artpapers
https://www.instagram.com/artpapers/

Nonfiction > *Articles*
Arts; Contemporary; Culture

The independent critical voice covering contemporary art and culture in the world today.

M032 Art Quarterly

Magazine
PO Box 4387, Chippenham, SN15 9NY
United Kingdom
Tel: +44 (0) 20 3757 9772

artquarterly@artfund.org

https://www.artfund.org/about-us/art-quarterly

Nonfiction > *Articles*: Arts

Arts magazine publishing features on artists, galleries and museums.

M033 Asimov's Science Fiction

Magazine
United States

asimovs@dellmagazines.com

https://www.asimovs.com
http://asimovs.magazinesubmissions.com/

Magazine Publisher: Dell Magazines

Fiction > *Short Fiction*
Fantasy; Science Fiction; Slipstream; Surreal

Poetry > *Any Poetic Form*
Fantasy; Science Fiction; Slipstream; Surreal

Does not want:

> **Fiction** > *Short Fiction*: Sword and Sorcery

How to send: Online submission system; Post

Seeks serious, character-orientated science fiction and (borderline) fantasy, slipstream, and surreal. The characters should always be the main focus, rather than the science. Humour will be considered. No simultaneous submissions, sword-and-sorcery, horror, explicit sex, violence, or works written, developed, or assisted by AI.

M034 Astronomy Now

Magazine
United Kingdom

https://astronomynow.com

Nonfiction
Articles: Astronomy
News: Astronomy

The UK's biggest astronomy magazine. Since 1987 it has been essential reading for astronomers in the UK and around the world. Each month, the magazine contains features, reviews, news and practical guides on all aspects of astronomy, from the latest scientific discoveries to advice for those discovering the night sky for the first time.

M035 Atlanta Magazine

Magazine
5901-A Peachtree Dunwoody Rd NE, Suite 350, Atlanta, GA 30328
United States
Tel: +1 (404) 527-5500

https://www.atlantamagazine.com
https://www.facebook.com/atlantamag
http://instagram.com/atlantamagazine
https://www.linkedin.com/company/atlantamagazine
https://twitter.com/atlantamagazine

Nonfiction
Articles: Arts; Atlanta; Culture; Design; Food and Drink; Gardening; Health; Lifestyle; Property / Real Estate; Travel; Wellbeing
News: Atlanta

Send: Query
How to send: Email

We focus on Atlanta and the metro region. We're looking for stories that haven't been told before, that help us see the city, the state, the region, and ourselves in new ways.

M036 Atlanta Review

Magazine
Suite 333, 686 Cherry St. NW, Atlanta, GA 30332-0161
United States

atlantareview@gatech.edu

http://atlantareview.com
https://atlantareview.submittable.com/submit
https://twitter.com/ATLReview
https://www.facebook.com/atlantareview
https://www.instagram.com/atlantareviewpojo/

Poetry > *Any Poetic Form*

Closed to approaches.

Costs: A fee is charged for online submissions. $3. Also runs competitions for which a fee is charged.

Accepts submissions of poetry between January 1 and June 1, and between September 15 and December 1. Submit online ($3 submission fee) or by post with SASE. Also runs competitions.

M037 Atlantic Northeast

Magazine
United States

https://atlanticnortheastmag.com
https://www.instagram.com/atlanticnemag/
https://twitter.com/AtlanticNEMag

Fiction > *Short Fiction*
Atlantic Northeast; Culture; History

Nonfiction > *Short Nonfiction*
Atlantic Northeast; Creative Nonfiction; Culture; History

Closed to approaches.

A magazine dedicated to exploring the history, culture, and spirit of the Northeastern United States and Canada.

M038 Atrium

Online Magazine
Worcestershire
United Kingdom

https://atriumpoetry.com
https://www.facebook.com/AtriumPoetry
https://twitter.com/Atrium_Poetry

Poetry > *Any Poetic Form*

Closed to approaches.

A poetry webzine based in Worcestershire, UK. A new poem is published twice a week, on Tuesdays and Fridays. Aims to publish poems that allow readers to think, feel and see things in a new way.

M039 Auroras & Blossoms PoArtMo Anthology
Online Magazine
United Kingdom

info@abpositiveart.com

https://abpositiveart.com
https://www.facebook.com/abpositiveart
https://twitter.com/ab_positiveart
https://www.youtube.com/channel/UCkAh-EnwcJbd865SEXJQsEw

ADULT
  Fiction > *Short Fiction*
  Nonfiction > *Essays*

TEEN
  Fiction > *Short Fiction*
  Nonfiction > *Essays*

Send: Query; Author bio; Writing sample
How to send: Email

Annual anthology sold in ebook format.

Editors / Poets: David Ellis; Cendrine Marrouat

M040 Authentic Shorts
Online Magazine
United Kingdom

enquiries@integrity-media.co.uk

http://integrity-media.co.uk

Book Publisher: Integrity Media (**P241**)

Fiction > *Short Fiction*

Send: Query; Outline; Full text
How to send: Email

An online platform for publishing short stories. We are open minded with regard to the subject of short stories and will consider submissions across all genres.

There is no perfect length for a short story, only the author can decide, but we would expect them to be no more than 7,000 to 8,000 words. This will allow them to be adaptable for online publication, either as a serialisation or under small collections of aligned works.

M041 Babybug
Magazine
United States

https://cricketmedia.com
https://cricketmedia.com/babybug-submission-guidelines/
https://cricketmag.submittable.com/submit

Magazine Publisher: Cricket Media, Inc.

CHILDREN'S
  Fiction > *Short Fiction*
  Nonfiction > *Short Nonfiction*
  Poetry > *Any Poetic Form*

Closed to approaches.

Publishes poetry, stories, and nonfiction (including activities and parent–child interaction) for children aged 6 months to 3 years. Stories should be up to six short sentences; poems should be rhythmic and rhyming and up to eight lines long.

M042 Bacopa Literary Review
Magazine
United States

https://writersalliance.org/bacopa-literary-review/

Fiction > *Short Fiction*: Literary

Nonfiction > *Short Nonfiction*: Creative Nonfiction

Poetry > *Any Poetic Form*

Closed to approaches.

Annual print journal publishing short stories, creative nonfiction, poetry, and prose poetry. Accepts submissions only through free annual contest.

M043 The Baffler
Magazine
234 5th Avenue, New York, NY 10001
United States
Tel: +1 (844) 523-4680

https://thebaffler.com
https://www.facebook.com/TheBafflerMagazine/
https://twitter.com/thebafflermag

Fiction > *Short Fiction*
  Comedy / Humour; Politics; Satire

Nonfiction > *Articles*
  Culture; Left Wing Politics

Poetry > *Any Poetic Form*

Send: Pitch
How to send: Online submission system

Describes itself as "America's leading voice of interesting and unexpected left-wing political criticism, cultural analysis, short stories, poems and art". Submit pitch using online form on website.

M044 Balance
Magazine
Wells Lawrence House, 126 Back Church Lane, London, E1 1FH
United Kingdom
Tel: +44 (0) 3451 232399
Fax: +44 (0) 20 7424 1001

helpline@diabetes.org.uk

https://www.diabetes.org.uk/balance

Nonfiction
  Articles: Diabetes; Exercise; Health; Recipes
  News: Diabetes

News articles and features of interest to people with diabetes.

M045 Bandit Fiction
Online Magazine
United Kingdom

https://banditfiction.com
https://www.facebook.com/banditfiction/
https://twitter.com/BanditFiction
https://www.instagram.com/banditfiction/
https://open.spotify.com/show/4roZtA65SdavXAwfflm1eE

Fiction > *Short Fiction*

Poetry > *Any Poetic Form*

We are digital publishers who believe in outstanding fiction. Our community is a place where readers and writers can grow and engage with the literary scene. Championing new, high quality and entertaining writing that is in touch with the craft of fiction, every piece of short fiction we publish is hand-picked by The Editor, edited alongside the author, and published direct to our website, always free to read. There are no limits on the genres, styles, perspectives or traditions we accept, and we aim to select pieces that represent something great about the current and future literary scene.

M046 Banipal
Magazine
1 Gough Square, London, EC4A 3DE
United Kingdom

editor@banipal.co.uk

http://www.banipal.co.uk
https://www.facebook.com/BanipalMagazine/
https://twitter.com/banipalmagazine

Fiction in Translation > *Short Fiction*

Nonfiction
  Interviews: Writing
  Reviews: Books

Poetry in Translation > *Any Poetic Form*

Send: Query
How to send: Email; Post

Contemporary Arab authors in English translations. Publishes new and established writers, and diverse material including translations, poetry, short stories, novel excerpts, profiles, interviews, appreciations, book reviews, reports of literary festivals, conferences, and prizes. Welcomes submissions by post, but queries only by email. Unsolicited email submissions with attachments will be automatically deleted. Response in 3-6 months.

M047 Barren Magazine

Magazine
United States

info@barrenmagazine.com
poetry@barrenmagazine.com
fiction@barrenmagazine.com
flashcnf@barrenmagazine.com
creativenonfiction@barrenmagazine.com

https://barrenmagazine.com
http://twitter.com/BarrenMagazine
http://facebook.com/BarrenMagazine
http://instagram.com/barrenmagazine

Fiction > *Short Fiction*

Nonfiction > *Nonfiction Books*: Creative Nonfiction

Poetry > *Any Poetic Form*

Closed to approaches.

An Alt.Lit Introspective.

A literary publication that features fiction, poetry, creative nonfiction, and photography for hard truths, long stares, and gritty lenses. We revel in the shadow-spaces that make up the human condition, and aim to find antitheses to that which defines us: light in darkness; beauty in ugliness; peace in disarray. We invite you to explore it with us.

Editor: Jason D. Ramsey

M048 BBC Doctor Who Magazine

Print Magazine
United Kingdom

dwm@panini.co.uk

https://doctorwhomagazine.com

Magazine Publisher: Panini UK

CHILDREN'S > **Nonfiction** > *Articles*
  Science Fiction; TV

Magazine for fans of Doctor Who, aged 6-12.

M049 BBC History Magazine

Magazine
United Kingdom
Tel: +44 (0) 117 300 8699

historymagazine@historyextra.com

https://www.historyextra.com
https://www.facebook.com/HistoryExtra
https://twitter.com/HistoryExtra
https://www.instagram.com/historyextra
https://www.youtube.com/channel/historyextra

Magazine Publisher: Immediate Media Co.

Nonfiction > *Articles*: History

Magazine publishing articles about history.

M050 BBC Science Focus

Magazine
Eagle House, Colston Avenue, Bristol, BS1 4ST
United Kingdom
Tel: +44 (0) 1173 008755

editorialenquiries@sciencefocus.com

https://www.sciencefocus.com
https://www.facebook.com/sciencefocus
https://twitter.com/sciencefocus
https://www.instagram.com/bbcsciencefocus
http://uk.pinterest.com/ScienceFocus
https://www.youtube.com/channel/UCS0P18FM3wfcKIS7Asy6cUQ

Magazine Publisher: Immediate Media Co.

Nonfiction
  Articles: Science
  News: Science

Send: Query
Don't send: Full text
How to send: Email

Publishes news and articles on science and technology. Accepts queries for articles only. Do not send completed articles. Does not accept submissions of news items.

M051 The Beano

Magazine
185 Fleet Street, London, EC4A 2HS
United Kingdom
Tel: +44 (0) 20 7400 1030

hello@beano.com

https://www.beano.com

Newspaper Publisher / Magazine Publisher: DC Thomson Media

CHILDREN'S > **Fiction** > *Cartoons*: Comedy / Humour

Publishes comic strips for children aged 6-12.

M052 The Bear Deluxe Magazine

Magazine
1881 NW Vaughn Street, Portland, OR 97209
United States
Tel: +1 (971) 235-2734

thebear@orlo.org
beardeluxe@orlo.org

https://orlo.org
https://www.facebook.com/pages/Bear-Deluxe-Magazine/115925931775159
https://twitter.com/orlobear

Fiction > *Short Fiction*

Nonfiction > *Articles*
  Arts; Culture; Environment

Poetry > *Any Poetic Form*

Send: Full text
How to send: Email

Magazine of the arts, culture and environment. Send submissions by email.

Editor: Tom Webb

M053 Bella

Magazine
The Lantern, 75 Hampstead Road, London, NW1 2PL
United Kingdom

Bella.Hotline@bauermedia.co.uk

https://www.bellamagazine.co.uk
https://twitter.com/#!/bellamagazineUK
http://facebook.com/bellamagazineUK
https://www.instagram.com/bellamagazineuk/

Magazine Publisher: Bauer Media Group

Nonfiction > *Articles*
  Celebrity; Diet; Fashion; Real Life Stories; Travel

Send: Query
How to send: Email

Human interest magazine for women, publishing articles on celebs, diet, style, travel, and real-life stories. Send query by email.

M054 Belmont Story Review

Magazine
United States

belmontstoryreview@gmail.com

https://belmontstoryreview.wixsite.com/website
https://belmontstoryreview.submittable.com/submit

Fiction > *Short Fiction*

Nonfiction > *Short Nonfiction*: Creative Nonfiction

Poetry > *Any Poetic Form*

Closed to approaches.

Established in 2016, the magazine aims to surprise and delight readers through an eclectic mix of storytelling which includes fiction, personal essay, poetry, songwriting, drama, graphic narrative, and photography; as well as creative reportage, including coverage of music, film, creativity and collaboration, and the intersection of faith and culture. "Faith" is not a specific religious perspective but a broad idea of faith is important for all selected publications.

We seek to publish new and established writers passionate about their craft, fearlessly encountering difficult ideas, seeking to explore human experience in all its broken blessedness.

M055 Beloit Fiction Journal

Magazine
Box 11, Beloit College, 700 College Street, Beloit, WI 53511
United States

https://www.beloit.edu/fiction-journal/
https://beloitfictionjournal.submittable.com/submit

Fiction > *Short Fiction*: Literary

Closed to approaches.

Costs: A fee is charged upon submission. $3 per submission.

Open to literary fiction on any subject or theme, up to 11,000 words. Also accepts flash fiction. Showcases new writers as well as established writers. Simultaneous submissions are accepted.

M056 Best of British

Magazine
Morton Way, Horncastle, Lincolnshire, LN9 6JR
United Kingdom

https://www.bestofbritishmag.co.uk
https://www.facebook.com/bestbritishmag/
https://twitter.com/bestofbritishuk

Magazine Publisher: Mortons Media Group

Nonfiction > *Articles*
  History; Nostalgia; United Kingdom

Describes itself as "the UK's premier nostalgia magazine", covering every aspect of life from the 1930s to today.

M057 Better Homes and Gardens

Magazine
1716 Locust St, Des Moines, IA 50309
United States

bhgeditor@dotdashmdp.com

https://www.bhg.com
https://www.facebook.com/mybhg/
https://twitter.com/bhg/
https://www.pinterest.com/bhg/
https://www.instagram.com/betterhomesandgardens/

Magazine Publisher: Dotdash Meredith

Nonfiction > *Articles*
  Cookery; Gardening; Home Improvement; Recipes

The fourth best-selling magazine in the United States. Publishes articles on gardening, home improvement, cleaning and organizing, and cooking and recipes.

M058 Better Than Starbucks

Magazine
PO Box 673, Mayo, FL 32066
United States
Tel: +1 (561) 719-8627

betterthanstarbucks2@gmail.com

https://www.betterthanstarbucks.org

ADULT
  Fiction > *Short Fiction*

  Nonfiction > *Short Nonfiction*: Creative Nonfiction

  Poetry in Translation > *Any Poetic Form*

  Poetry
    Any Poetic Form: Africa; Comedy / Humour; International
    Experimental Poetry: General
    Formal Poetry: General
    Free Verse: General
    Haiku: General
    Prose Poetry: General

CHILDREN'S > **Poetry** > *Any Poetic Form*

Closed to approaches.

Publishes African Poetry, International Poetry, Prose Poetry, Forms as well as Formal Poetry, Poetry Translations, Experimental Poetry and poetry for children. Encourages sentiment in poetry. Also publishes Fiction, Flash Fiction, Micro Fiction and Creative Nonfiction. Submitted opinion pieces will be considered.

Editor: Vera Ignatowitsch

M059 BFS Horizons

Magazine
United Kingdom

bfshorizons@britishfantasysociety.org
poetry@britishfantasysociety.org

https://britishfantasysociety.org
https://britishfantasysociety.org/get-in-touch/bfs-horizons/

Association: The British Fantasy Society

Fiction > *Short Fiction*
  Fantasy; Horror

Poetry > *Any Poetic Form*
  Fantasy; Horror

Send: Full text; Author bio
How to send: Word file email attachment; In the body of an email

We welcome short fiction submissions in any Fantasy or Horror genre or sub-genre, of 500 – 5000 words. In poetry, any form will be accepted. To be honest, rhyming poetry in iambic pentameters will be a hard sell. However, it would be good to see sonnets, Villanelles or the odd Rondeau, or any other form you care to tackle. Tip: Before submitting, read your poem out loud. Does it work? Check the metre. Does it scan? Look at your line lengths. Lengthy poems or sagas will be considered but should follow instead the submission guidelines for fiction.

M060 BFS Journal

Magazine
United Kingdom

kmanwaring@aub.ac.uk

https://www.britishfantasysociety.org/
https://britishfantasysociety.org/get-in-touch/bfs-journal/
https://twitter.com/BritFantasySoc

Association: The British Fantasy Society

ACADEMIC > **Nonfiction** > *Articles*: Fantasy

ADULT > **Nonfiction**
  Articles: Fantasy
  Interviews: Fantasy
  Reviews: Fantasy

How to send: Email

Fantasy journal devoted to non-fiction: interviews, academic articles, reviews and features.

M061 Big Fiction

Online Magazine
Seattle University, English Dept, c/o Juan Carlos Reyes, P.O. Box 222000, Seattle, WA 98122-1090
United States

editors@bigfiction.com

https://www.bigfictionmagazine.com

Fiction > *Novelettes*

Nonfiction
  Essays: General
  Reviews: Fiction as a Subject
  Short Nonfiction: Creative Nonfiction

Closed to approaches.

Costs: A fee is charged upon submission. $5 for novelettes; $3 for essays.

Literary magazine devoted to longer short fiction, between 7,500 and 20,000 words.

M062 Birds & Blooms

Magazine
1610 North 2nd Street, Suite 102, Milwaukee, WI 53212
United States

customercare@birdsandblooms.com

https://www.birdsandblooms.com
https://www.facebook.com/BirdsBlooms
https://twitter.com/birdsblooms
https://www.pinterest.com/birdsblooms/
https://www.instagram.com/birdsblooms/

Nonfiction > *Articles*
  Birds; Gardening

Send: Full text
How to send: Online submission system

Magazine for backyard / bird enthusiasts, covering how to improve your garden and attract birds. Conversational tone.

M063 Black Belt

Magazine
United States

https://blackbeltmag.com
https://www.instagram.com/blackbeltmag/
https://twitter.com/black_belt_mag
https://www.facebook.com/

BlackBeltMagazine/
https://www.linkedin.com/company/black-belt-magazine/

Nonfiction > *Articles*: Martial Arts

Magazine on martial arts for the experienced and inexperienced alike.

Editor-in-Chief: Robert Young

M064 Black Moon Magazine
Online Magazine
United States

blackmoonmageditors@gmail.com

http://www.blackmoonmag.com
https://www.facebook.com/BlackMoonMagazine
https://www.instagram.com/black.moon.mag/
https://twitter.com/Black_Moon_Mag

Fiction > *Short Fiction*

Nonfiction
 Interviews: Literature
 Reviews: Books

Poetry > *Any Poetic Form*

Send: Full text; Query; Author bio
How to send: Email attachment

Submit up to three short stories between 1,000 and 8,000 words, or up to five poems of up to five pages each. Also accepts book reviews and interviews with professionals in the writing community for online publication. No submissions in January or July.

M065 Black Static
Magazine
United Kingdom

blackstatic@ttapress.com

http://ttapress.com/blackstatic/

Magazine Publisher / Book Publisher: TTA Press

Fiction > *Short Fiction*
 Dark; Horror

Closed to approaches.

Always open to unsolicited submissions of new dark/horror stories up to a maximum of 10,000 words.

Editor: Andy Cox

M066 Black Warrior Review
Magazine
United States

blackwarriorreview@gmail.com
managingeditor.bwr@gmail.com

https://bwr.ua.edu
https://www.facebook.com/pages/Black-Warrior-Review/335215809212
https://twitter.com/BlackWarriorRev

Fiction
 Cartoons: General
 Short Fiction: General, and in particular: Experimental

Nonfiction
 Graphic Nonfiction; *Short Nonfiction*

Poetry
 Any Poetic Form; *Visual Poetry*

How to send: Submittable; Email

Costs: A fee is charged upon submission. $3. Black, indigenous, and incarcerated writers may submit by email for free.

Accepts short stories and nonfiction up to 7,000 words, up to three pieces of flash fiction up to 1,000 words or submit up to five poems up to 10 pages total. Accepts work that takes risk or is experimental, in lieu of convention and/or grammatical cleanliness. Seeks nonfiction pieces outside western traditions; pieces that defy any such categorization. Welcomes submissions of striking visual narratives (think: graphic novel or memoir in short form).

Online Magazine: Boyfriend Village (**M073**)

M067 Blue Earth Review
Magazine
136 Nelson Hall, Minnesota State University, Mankato, Mankato, MN 56001
United States

blueearthreview@gmail.com

https://blueearthreview.mnsu.edu
https://www.facebook.com/theblueearthreview/
https://twitter.com/BlueEarthReview

Fiction > *Short Fiction*

Nonfiction
 Essays: Personal Essays
 Short Nonfiction: Creative Nonfiction; Memoir

Poetry > *Any Poetic Form*

Send: Full text
How to send: Submittable

Publishes fiction, creative nonfiction and poetry. Interested in creative nonfiction (memoir and personal essay) with contemporary themes. No literary criticism. Submit up to five poems at a time.

M068 Blue Mesa Review
Magazine
Department of English Language and Literature, Humanities Building, Second Floor, MSC03 2170, 1 University of New Mexico, Albuquerque, NM 87131-0001
United States

https://bmr.unm.edu/
https://bluemesareview.submittable.com/submit
https://www.instagram.com/bluemesareview/

Fiction > *Short Fiction*

Nonfiction > *Short Nonfiction*: Creative Nonfiction

Poetry > *Any Poetic Form*

How to send: Submittable

We accept previously unpublished work in Fiction (up to 6,000 words), Nonfiction (up to 6,000 words), Poetry (up to 3 poems), and Visual Art. We have a rotating editorial board, so each issue is fresh and unique. In general, we are seeking strong voices and lively, compelling narratives with a fine eye for craft. We look forward to reading your best work!

M069 Bluegrass Unlimited
Magazine
311 W 2nd St, Owensboro, KY 42301
United States
Tel: +1 (800) 258-4727

https://www.bluegrassunlimited.com
https://www.facebook.com/BluegrassUnlimited/
https://www.instagram.com/bluegrassunlimited/
https://twitter.com/bgunlimitedmag
https://www.youtube.com/channel/UCxNYVomNcDI-5mrOy3KgoHA

Nonfiction
 Articles: Bluegrass
 Interviews: Bluegrass
 News: Bluegrass
 Reviews: Bluegrass

A print magazine that has been dedicated to the furtherance of bluegrass music for over 50 years.

Managing Editor: Dan Miller

M070 The Bookseller
Magazine
47 Bermondsey Street, London, SE1 3XT
United Kingdom
Tel: +44 (0) 20 7403 1818

https://www.thebookseller.com
http://twitter.com/thebookseller
http://www.facebook.com/TheBooksellerMagazine
http://www.linkedin.com/company/the-bookseller-magazine
https://www.instagram.com/_thebookseller/
https://www.youtube.com/channel/UCF5SoBkJKDO9CXtmr1eGW9Q

Magazine Publisher: The Stage Media Company Ltd

PROFESSIONAL > **Nonfiction** > *Articles*
 Book Publishing; Books

Magazine for the book business covering publishing, the book trade, retail, and libraries, publishing trade news and features.

M071 Boston Review
Print Magazine
PO Box 390568, Cambridge, MA 02139

United States
Tel: +1 (617) 356-8198

review@bostonreview.net

https://www.bostonreview.net
https://bostonreview.submittable.com/submit
https://www.facebook.com/bostonreview/
https://twitter.com/BostonReview/

Fiction > *Short Fiction*

Nonfiction
Essays: Culture; Politics
Reviews: Books

Poetry > *Any Poetic Form*

How to send: Submittable; Post

A political and literary forum—a public space for discussion of ideas, politics, and culture. Independent and nonprofit, animated by hope and committed to equality, we believe in the power of collective reasoning and imagination to create a more just world.

M072 Bowhunter
Magazine
United States

https://www.bowhunter.com
https://www.facebook.com/BowHunterMag/
https://twitter.com/BowHunterMag
https://www.instagram.com/bowhunter/
https://www.youtube.com/channel/UCyW-6pltixp7xZ4gD0GUrGw
https://www.pinterest.com/bowhunter0028/

Magazine Publisher: Outdoor Sportsman Group

Nonfiction > *Articles*
  Archery; Hunting

Magazine publishing articles relating to hunting with a bow and arrow.

M073 Boyfriend Village
Online Magazine
United States

https://bwr.ua.edu/about-boyfriend-village/

Magazine: Black Warrior Review (**M066**)

Fiction > *Short Fiction*

Nonfiction > *Short Nonfiction*

Poetry > *Any Poetic Form*

Closed to approaches.

Costs: A fee is charged upon submission. $3.

There is one submission category for all genres. Accepts fiction, poetry, nonfiction, hybrid, visual and multimedia art, as well as sound collage, video, games, and more.

M074 Brick
Magazine
P.O. Box 609, STN P, Toronto, ON, M5S 2Y4
Canada

info@brickmag.com

https://brickmag.com/
https://brickmag.submittable.com/submit
https://twitter.com/brickMAG
https://facebook.com/brickmagazine
https://instagram.com/brickliterary

Nonfiction
Essays: Arts; City and Town Planning; Dance; Food; History; Literature; Music; Photography; Science; Sport; Travel; Writing
Interviews: Arts; Literature; Performing Arts
Short Nonfiction: Literary; Memoir

Closed to approaches.

Send entire submission in first instance. Please read magazine before submitting. Accepts unsolicited nonfiction submissions on a variety of subjects during April and October each year. No unsolicited fiction or poetry.

M075 Britain Magazine
Magazine
The Chelsea Magazine Company, Jubilee House, 2 Jubilee Place, London, SW3 3QW
United Kingdom
Tel: +44 (0) 20 7349 3700

editor@britain-magazine.co.uk

https://www.britain-magazine.com
https://www.facebook.com/BritainMagazine/
https://www.instagram.com/britain_magazine/
https://twitter.com/BritainMagazine

Magazine Publisher: The Chelsea Magazine Company

Nonfiction > *Articles*
  Culture; History; Nature; Royalty; Travel; United Kingdom

Magazine of UK travel, culture, heritage and style, and the go-to publication for visitors fascinated by British history. Each issue is packed with tales of kings and queens, heroes and villains and the stories behind British castles, cathedrals, stately homes and gardens, countryside, and coastline.

M076 Business Traveller
Magazine
10 John Street, London, WC1N 2EB
United Kingdom
Tel: +44 (0) 20 7821 2700

mcaswell@businesstraveller.com
enquiries@panaceapublishing.com

https://www.businesstraveller.com
https://www.linkedin.com/groups/2136397
https://www.facebook.com/BusinessTraveller
https://www.twitter.com/BTUK
https://www.instagram.com/businesstravelleruk/

Nonfiction > *Articles*
  Business; Travel

The leading magazine around the world for the frequent corporate traveller. A consumer publication, it is aimed at entertaining business travellers, saving them money and making their travelling life easier. Each edition is packed with editorial on the latest news about airlines, airports, hotels and car rental.

Editor: Tom Otley

M077 Butcher's Dog
Print Magazine
United Kingdom

https://www.butchersdogmagazine.co.uk
https://butchersdogpoetry.submittable.com/submit
https://www.facebook.com/ButchersDogPoetry
https://twitter.com/butchersdogmag
https://www.instagram.com/butchersdogmag/

Poetry > *Any Poetic Form*

Closed to approaches.

Proudly edited and published in the heart of North East England. We print two unthemed poetry magazines each year in Spring and Autumn. Every issue features original cover artwork and contains a selection of up to twenty-five exceptional poems. Poems are selected on their merit in an anonymous reading process, supporting a more inclusive body of contemporary writing than the publishing industry currently represents.

M078 The Cafe Irreal
Magazine
United States

editors@cafeirreal.com

http://cafeirreal.alicewhittenburg.com

Types: Fiction
Formats: Short Fiction
Subjects: Literary
Markets: Adult

Closed to approaches.

Quarterly webzine publishing fantastic fiction resembling the work of writers such as Franz Kafka and Jorge Luis Borges. Send stories up to 2,000 in the body of an email. No simultaneous submissions.

M079 Campaign
Magazine
Bridge House, 69 London Road, Twickenham, TW1 3SP
United Kingdom

https://www.campaignlive.co.uk
https://www.facebook.com/campaignmag/
https://twitter.com/campaignmag
https://www.linkedin.com/groups/3614115/
https://www.instagram.com/campaignmagazine
https://www.youtube.com/CampaignLiveTV

Magazine Publisher: Haymarket Media Group

PROFESSIONAL > **Nonfiction**
Articles: Advertising; Business; Marketing; Media

News: Advertising; Business; Marketing; Media

Describes itself as the world's leading business media brand serving the marketing, advertising and media communities.

Editor: Claire Beale

Editor-in-Chief: Gideon Spanier

M080 Carolina Woman

Online Magazine
United States

articles@carolinawoman.com
info@carolinawoman.com

https://www.carolinawoman.com
https://www.facebook.com/profile.php?id=100063516732380
https://x.com/carolina_woman
https://www.linkedin.com/company/carolina-woman-inc.
http://www.pinterest.com/carolinawmag/
http://instagram.com/carolinawomanmagazine/

Nonfiction > *Articles*
Lifestyle; Women's Interests

Send: Pitch
How to send: Email

Lifestyle magazine for women. Generally does not accept unsolicited articles or hire freelance writers, but is open to article ideas by email.

M081 Chapman

Magazine
4 Broughton Place, Edinburgh, EH1 3RX
United Kingdom
Tel: +44 (0) 131 557 2207

chapman-pub@blueyonder.co.uk

http://www.chapman-pub.co.uk

Book Publisher: Chapman Publishing (**P099**)

Fiction > *Short Fiction*: Literary

Nonfiction > *Articles*: Literary Criticism

Poetry > *Any Poetic Form*

Closed to approaches.

Describes itself as Scotland's leading literary magazine, publishing new creative writing: poetry, fiction, discussion of cultural affairs, theatre, reviews and the arts in general, plus critical essays. It publishes international as well as Scottish writers and is a dynamic force for artistic and cultural change and development. Always open to new writers and ideas.

Fiction may be of any length, but average is around 3,000 words. Send one piece at a time. Poetry submissions should contain between four and ten poems. Single poems are not usually published.

Articles and reviews are usually commissioned and ideas should be discussed with the editor in advance.

All submissions must include an SAE or IRCs or email address for response. No submissions by email.

M082 CharlottesvilleFamily

Magazine
United States

sales@ivylifeandstylemedia.com

https://www.charlottesvillefamily.com
https://www.facebook.com/CharlottesvilleFamily
https://twitter.com/ChvilleFamily
https://www.linkedin.com/company/ivylifeandstylemedia/

Magazine Publisher: Ivy Life & Style Media

Nonfiction > *Articles*
Albemarle; Charlottesville; Education; Family; Food; Health; Houses and Homes; Leisure; Lifestyle; Parenting

Send: Query

Town and country living at its best! An award-winning quarterly magazine dedicated to serving families in Virginia's Charlottesville-Albemarle area with engaging feature stories on parenting, education, health and recreation as well as useful resources designed to help "Make Parenting Easier and Growing Up Fun".

M083 Chautauqua Literary Journal

Magazine
United States

chautauquajournal@gmail.com

https://chautauquajournal.wixsite.com/website
https://chautauqua.submittable.com/submit
https://www.instagram.com/chautauquajournal/
https://www.facebook.com/chautauqualiteraryjournal/
https://twitter.com/chautauqualit
http://chautauqualit.tumblr.com/

Fiction > *Short Fiction*

Nonfiction > *Short Nonfiction*: Creative Nonfiction

Poetry > *Any Poetic Form*

Closed to approaches.

Costs: A fee is charged upon submission. $2 submission fee.

Welcomes unsolicited submissions of poetry, flash, fiction, and creative nonfiction from February 15 to March 15 and from September 1 to September 30.

M084 Cheshire

Online Magazine
United States

infoccr00@gmail.com

https://uwm.edu/creamcityreview/i-o/
https://uwm.edu/creamcityreview/general/
https://creamcityreview.submittable.com/submit

Magazine: Cream City Review (**M105**)

Fiction > *Short Fiction*

Nonfiction > *Essays*

Poetry > *Any Poetic Form*

Closed to approaches.

Online magazine for writing that operates outside the printed page, including asemic writing, concrete poetry, interactive fiction and poetry, video, collage, hypertext essay, GIFpoetics, programmatic, gamic, and all hybrid and multimodal points along the way, things that capture process and procedure, lines and the signs between. Not interested in text-based work that engages very little with mixed and/or digital medium.

M085 Cheshire Life

Magazine
United Kingdom

Magazine Publisher: Great British Life

M086 The Cincinnati Review

Magazine
PO Box 210069, Cincinnati, Ohio 45221-0069
United States

editors@cincinnatireview.com

https://www.cincinnatireview.com/
https://facebook.com/CincinnatiReview
https://twitter.com/CincinnReview
https://www.youtube.com/channel/UCbDPomwAnBAddHtuKKh4HqA

Fiction in Translation > *Short Fiction*: Literary

Fiction > *Short Fiction*: Literary

Nonfiction > *Short Nonfiction*
Creative Nonfiction; Literary

Poetry in Translation > *Any Poetic Form*

Poetry > *Any Poetic Form*

Scripts
Film Scripts; Theatre Scripts

How to send: Online submission system

Submit up to ten pages of poetry, or up to forty pages of double-spaced fiction, or up to twenty pages of double-spaced literary nonfiction during September, December, or May.. Accepts micro submissions year-round, except when accepting contest submissions.

Editors: Michael Griffith; Kristen Iversen; Rebecca Lindenberg

M087 Cobblestone

Magazine
United States

cobblestone@cricketmedia.com

https://cricketmedia.com
https://cricketmedia.com/cobblestone-submission-guidelines/

Magazine Publisher: Cricket Media, Inc.

CHILDREN'S
Fiction > *Short Fiction*: American History

Nonfiction
  Articles: Activities; American History
  Puzzles: General

Poetry > *Any Poetic Form*: American History

Send: Query
Don't send: Full text
How to send: Email

American history magazine for kids ages 9 to 14 that knows that history doesn't have to be dull and dry. It can be vibrant and alive – and so much fun. That's why every page is a living, breathing guide to how Americans lived, worked, played, and died from the 1600s to today. Filled with fascinating true stories from all decades of our country's history, augmented with dramatic photographs and beautiful illustrations, this magazine is designed to take kids on a journey through history while it excites their imaginations and brings the past to life.

Editor: Meg Chorlian

M088 Cocoa Girl
Print Magazine
United Kingdom

admin@thecocoadream.com

https://www.cocoagirl.com
https://www.instagram.com/cocoagirlmag/

Magazine Publisher: Cocoa Publishing

CHILDREN'S
Nonfiction
  Articles: Black People; Culture
  Interviews: Black People; Culture
  Poetry > *Any Poetic Form*
    Black People; Culture

How to send: Email

Magazine for Black girls. This magazine gives Black children a voice whilst educating the community about the Black culture. Filled with inspiring and empowering content for children aged 7-11 years old. Particularly looking for children aged 7-11 to contribute as writers, poets, artists, and young journalists.

M089 The Coil
Online Magazine
United States

https://medium.com/the-coil
https://twitter.com/CoilMag
https://alternatingcurrent.submittable.com/submit

Book Publisher: Alternating Current Press (**P020**)

Fiction
  Novel Excerpts: General
  Short Fiction: Literary

Nonfiction
  Essays; *Interviews*; *Reviews*
Poetry > *Any Poetic Form*
  General, and in particular: History

How to send: Submittable

Independent online literary magazine.

M090 Cola
Print Magazine
United States

https://www.colaliteraryreview.com
https://colaliteraryreview.submittable.com/submit
https://twitter.com/ColaLitReview

Fiction > *Short Fiction*: Literary

Poetry > *Any Poetic Form*

Closed to approaches.

Costs: A fee is charged upon submission in some cases. $3 submission fee during spring submission period. Autumn submissions are free.

Annual print journal edited by graduate students. Publishes poetry and fiction. Submit 3-5 poems or pieces of flash fiction up to 1,000 words, or a longer short story up to 8,000 words (1,000 words to 5,000 words preferred), via online submission system. See website for full guidelines.

M091 Commonweal
Magazine
475 Riverside Drive, Room 244, New York, NY 10115
United States
Tel: +1 (212) 662-4200

editors@commonwealmagazine.org
poetryeditor@commonwealmagazine.org

https://www.commonwealmagazine.org
https://www.facebook.com/commonwealmagazine
https://twitter.com/commonwealmag

Nonfiction > *Articles*
  Culture; Politics; Religion

Poetry > *Any Poetic Form*

Closed to approaches.

Journal of opinion edited by Catholic lay people. Publishes articles on religion, literature, and the arts. More interested in articles which examine the links between "worldly" concerns and religious beliefs than churchy or devotional pieces. Submit pitches by email. Also publishes poetry. Submit through online submission system and include a short bio that could accompany your poem in print.

M092 Concho River Review
Magazine
United States

http://www.conchoriverreview.org
https://www.facebook.com/conchoriverreview

Fiction > *Short Fiction*

Nonfiction
  Essays: General
  Reviews: Books
  Short Nonfiction: Creative Nonfiction

Poetry > *Any Poetic Form*

Closed to approaches.

Costs: A fee is charged upon submission. $3 per submission.

Published biannually, welcomes submissions of high-quality fiction, nonfiction, poetry, and book reviews year-round.

Accepts only original work that has not been published previously.

Accepts submissions from writers residing outside the United States, however, international contributors should provide a domestic address to which a contributor's copy can be mailed.

M093 Conjunctions
Magazine
21 East 10th St., #3E, New York, NY 10003
United States

conjunctions@bard.edu

https://www.conjunctions.com
https://conjunctions.submittable.com/submit
http://www.facebook.com/pages/Conjunctions/133404885505
https://www.instagram.com/_conjunctions/
https://twitter.com/_conjunctions

Fiction > *Short Fiction*: Literary

Nonfiction > *Short Nonfiction*: Creative Nonfiction

Poetry > *Any Poetic Form*

Send: Full text; Self-Addressed Stamped Envelope (SASE)
How to send: Post; Submittable

Publishes short and long form fiction, poetry, and creative nonfiction. No academic essays or book reviews. Do not query or send samples – submit complete ms by post with SASE (year-round) or using online submission system (during specific online submission windows in autumn and winter). See website for full guidelines.

Editor: Bradford Morrow

Online Magazine: Conjunctions Online (**M094**)

M094 Conjunctions Online

Online Magazine
21 E 10th Street, #3E, New York, NY 10003
United States

http://www.conjunctions.com/online/
https://conjunctions.submittable.com/submit
http://www.facebook.com/pages/Conjunctions/133404885505
https://www.instagram.com/_conjunctions/
https://twitter.com/_conjunctions

Magazine: Conjunctions (**M093**)

Fiction > *Short Fiction*

Nonfiction > *Short Nonfiction*: Creative Nonfiction

Poetry > *Any Poetic Form*

Closed to approaches.

Weekly online magazine. No thematic restrictions. Postal submissions are accepted year-round, but online submissions are open only during specific windows.

M095 The Conversation (UK)

Online Magazine
Shropshire House (4th Floor), 11-20 Capper Street, London, WC1E 6JA
United Kingdom

uk-support@theconversation.com

https://theconversation.com
https://www.facebook.com/ConversationUK
https://twitter.com/ConversationUK
https://www.instagram.com/theconversationdotcom
https://www.linkedin.com/company/the-conversation-uk
https://newsie.social/@TheConversationUK

Nonfiction
Articles: Arts; Business; Culture; Economics; Education; Environment; Health; Politics; Science; Society; Technology
News: Arts; Business; Culture; Economics; Education; Environment; Health; Politics; Science; Society; Technology

How to send: Online submission system

Online magazine describing itself as "the world's leading publisher of research-based news and analysis... a unique collaboration between academics and journalists." Publishes news and articles researchers and academics currently employed by a university or research institution. This includes PhD students under supervision, but nor Masters students.

M096 Cornwall Life

Magazine

Magazine Publisher: Great British Life

M097 The Corridor of Uncertainty

Magazine
United Kingdom

clarky@corridorofuncertainty.com

https://www.corridorofuncertainty.com
https://twitter.com/clarkyfanzine
https://www.facebook.com/groups/10963081916

Nonfiction > *Articles*: Cricket

Unofficial England cricket fanzine.

Editor: James Buttler

M098 Cotswold Life

Magazine
United Kingdom

https://www.greatbritishlife.co.uk/magazines/cotswold/

Magazine Publisher: Great British Life

Nonfiction > *Articles*
Arts; Cotswolds; Countryside; Fashion; Food and Drink; Gardening; History; Interior Design; Property / Real Estate

Publishes articles on Cotswold property, interiors, gardens, arts, heritage, fashion, food & drink and countryside matters.

M099 Cottage Life

Magazine
99 Atlantic Avenue, Suite 400, Toronto, ON, M6K 3J8
Canada
Tel: +1 (416) 599-2000

edit@cottagelife.com

https://cottagelife.com
https://www.facebook.com/cottagelife/
https://x.com/cottagelife/
http://instagram.com/cottagelife/
http://pinterest.com/cottagelife/
http://youtube.com/user/CottagelifeMagazine/

Nonfiction > *Articles*
Architecture; Boats; Building / Construction; Design; Environment; Finance; How To; Lifestyle; Nature; Politics; Property / Real Estate

Send: Query
How to send: Email

The magazine has a strong service slant, combining useful "how-to" journalism with coverage of the people, trends, and issues in cottage country. We run columns and shorter features on subjects such as boating, real estate, building projects, cottage design and architecture, nature, personal cottage experience, and environmental, political, and financial issues of concern to cottagers. Depending on the subject, these can be anywhere from 1,000 to 1,800 words long. Our front-of-the-book department, Waterfront, features short news, humour, human interest, and service items, with a maximum length of 400 words. Our other front-of-book department, Workshop, is a place for "hammer and nails" DIY stories of the same length about maintaining a cottage. Major features range from 1,500 to 3,000 words and cover every aspect of cottage living—including profiles of cottagers, cottages, and cottage communities, investigations of relevant environmental and political issues, and in-depth service pieces that help readers solve common cottage problems. The fee varies with the length and complexity of the story, whether it's for digital or print, and the writer's experience. The editor and writer will agree on the fee when the story is assigned.

M100 Country Smallholding

Magazine
The Granary, Downs Court, Yalding Hill, Yalding, Kent, ME18 6AL
United Kingdom
Tel: +44 (0) 7725 829575

https://www.countrysmallholding.com/

Magazine Publisher: Kelsey Media

Nonfiction > *Articles*
Country Lifestyle; Countryside; Gardening; Self-Sufficiency; Smallholdings

Magazine for smallholders, small farmers and landowners, and those interested in both rural and urban self-sufficiency.

M101 Cowboys & Indians

Magazine
12801 North Central Expressway, Suite 565, Dallas, TX 75243
United States
Tel: +1 (386) 246-0179

editorial@cowboysindians.com

https://www.cowboysindians.com
https://www.facebook.com/cowboysindians/
http://pinterest.com/cowboysindians/
http://www.twitter.com/CI_Magazine
http://instagram.com/cowboysindiansmagazine#

Nonfiction > *Articles*
American West; Arts; Culture; Entertainment; Fashion; Food and Drink; Houses and Homes; Ranch Lifestyle; Ranches; Travel

Magazine focusing on the past and present of the American West, including both historical and lifestyle material.

M102 Crab Orchard Review

Magazine
United States

https://craborchardreview.siu.edu
https://craborchardreview.submittable.com/submit

Fiction > *Short Fiction*

Nonfiction > *Essays*

Poetry > *Any Poetic Form*

Closed to approaches.

Closed to submissions for the foreseeable future following the death of the editor in December 2019. Check website for current status.

M103 Crannog Magazine
Magazine
47 Dominick, St Lower, Galway, H91 X0AP
Ireland

hello@crannogmagazine.com
submissions@crannogmagazine.com

https://crannogmagazine.com
https://twitter.com/crannogm
https://www.facebook.com/crannogmagazine/

Book Publisher / Magazine Publisher: Wordsonthestreet (**P517**)

Fiction > *Short Fiction*: Literary

Poetry > *Any Poetic Form*

Send: Full text; Author bio
How to send: Online submission system
How not to send: Post

Costs: A purchase is required. Authors who have not previously been published in the magazine must purchase the current issue before submitting.

A literary magazine publishing fiction and poetry only. No reviews or nonfiction. Published twice yearly in March and September. Accepts submissions in May and November. Authors who have been previously published in the magazine are required to purchase a copy of the current issue (or take out a subscription); for authors who have not been previously published in the magazine this is a requirement. Send up to one story or up to three poems via online submission system.

M104 Crazyhorse / Swamp Pink
Magazine
Department of English, College of Charleston, 66 George Street, Charleston, SC 29424
United States
Tel: +1 (843) 953-4470

crazyhorse@cofc.edu

https://crazyhorse.cofc.edu
https://www.facebook.com/CrazyhorseLiteraryJournal
https://twitter.com/crazyhorselitjo

Fiction > *Short Fiction*

Nonfiction > *Short Nonfiction*: Creative Nonfiction

Poetry > *Any Poetic Form*

Closed to approaches.

Costs: A fee is charged upon submission. $3.00.

Publishes fiction, poetry, and nonfiction on a semi-monthly basis. Aims to publish exceptional work from writers at all stages of their careers. Particularly interested in submissions from writers of color and writers from marginalized and underrepresented communities. Submissions of fiction and nonfiction can be up to 7,500 words in length. Has published exceptional work that falls outside this range, but it is an unusual occurrence. For poetry, submit a set of 3-6 poems.

M105 Cream City Review
Magazine
Department of English, University of Wisconsin-Milwaukee, P.O. Box 413, Milwaukee, WI 53201
United States

infoccr00@gmail.com
poetryccr@gmail.com
fictionccr@gmail.com
nonfictionccr@gmail.com

https://uwm.edu/creamcityreview/
https://www.facebook.com/creamcityreview/
https://twitter.com/creamcityreview
https://www.instagram.com/cream_city_review/

Fiction > *Short Fiction*

Nonfiction > *Short Nonfiction*: Creative Nonfiction

Poetry > *Any Poetic Form*

Closed to approaches.

Send prose up to 20 pages, or up to five poems of any length. Open to submissions January 2 to March 2 and August 1 to October 1.

Online Magazine: Cheshire (**M084**)

M106 Creative Nonfiction
Magazine
United States

information@creativenonfiction.org

https://creativenonfiction.org
https://creativenonfiction.submittable.com/submit/
https://www.facebook.com/creativenonfiction
https://twitter.com/cnfonline
https://instagram.com/creativenonfiction/

Nonfiction > *Essays*
Creative Nonfiction; Memoir; Personal Essays

Closed to approaches.

Publishes all types of creative nonfiction, from immersion reportage to lyric essay to memoir and personal essays. See website for specific submission calls and their topics, or submit a pitch for a column year-round.

M107 Creem
Magazine
United States

editor@creem.com
info@creem.com

https://www.creem.com
https://instagram.com/creemmag
https://twitter.com/creemmag

Nonfiction
Articles: Rock Music
Reviews: Rock Music

How to send: Email

Revival of the magazine that describes itself as "America's only rock n' roll magazine".

M108 Critical Quarterly
Magazine
Newbury, Crediton, Devon, EX17 5HA
United Kingdom

CRIQ@wiley.com
CQpoetry@gmail.com
CQcriticism@gmail.com

http://onlinelibrary.wiley.com/journal/10.1111/(ISSN)1467-8705

Book Publisher: John Wiley & Sons, Inc.

Fiction > *Short Fiction*

Nonfiction > *Essays*
Culture; Literary Criticism

Poetry > *Any Poetic Form*

How to send: Online submission system

Internationally renowned for its unique blend of literary criticism, cultural studies, poetry and fiction. The journal addresses the whole range of cultural forms so that discussions of, for example, cinema and television can appear alongside analyses of the accepted literary canon. It is a necessary condition of debate in these areas that it should involve as many and as varied voices as possible, and the journal welcomes submissions from new researchers and writers as well as more established contributors.

Editor: Colin MacCabe

M109 Cruising World
Magazine
605 Chestnut Street, Suite 800, Chattanooga, TN 37450
United States
Tel: +1 (407) 628-4802

editor@cruisingworld.com

https://www.cruisingworld.com
https://www.facebook.com/cruisingworld/
https://twitter.com/cruisingworld/
https://www.instagram.com/cruisingworldmag
https://www.youtube.com/c/cruisingworld

Media Company: Bonnier Corporation

Nonfiction > *Articles*

Boats; Sailing

Send: Full text; Author bio
How to send: Word file email attachment

Magazine for owners of sailboats between 20 and 50 feet in length. Authors should familiarise themselves with the magazine before approaching.

M110 Crystal Magazine
Magazine
3 Bowness Avenue, Prenton, Birkenhead, CH43 0SD
United Kingdom
Tel: +44 (0) 1516 089736; +44 (0) 7769 790676

christinecrystal@hotmail.com

http://www.christinecrystal.blogspot.com

Fiction > *Short Fiction*
  Adventure; Comedy / Humour; Fantasy; Horror; Mystery; Romance; Science Fiction; Suspense; Thrillers; Westerns

Nonfiction
  Articles: Literature; Nature; Travel
  News: General

Poetry > *Any Poetic Form*

Send: Full text
How to send: Email

An A4, 40-page, spiral-bound, print only bi-monthly. With colour images. This magazine is intended for subscribers. They will receive six issues a year (£21). Non-Subscribers may send in work and purchase the issue it appears in for £3.50. This is the same price a subscriber would pay for one issue.

The magazine is very popular. Subscribers have emailed me saying they are disappointed not to be in the November issue. There is a Feedback page on the website.

Contents: stories, poems and articles. Letters – kind comments or none at all. News – an opportunity to share writing achievements and anything of interest to writers.

Also accepting fillers and very long stories which could be turned into serials.

Wordsmithing. Titters Tips Titillations. Pay special attention to the second item in each section because there you will find useful information on writing (the 'tips' part of the title).

Also Word Wise. In this issue we learn about the semicolon.

There are yearly Surprise Competitions with very low entry fee (£1.23) and small surprise gifts. There are pictures of previous prizes and winning entries on the website. Surprise Competitions are open to all. The 'Write a Sonnet' Surprise Competition is now closed. For the first time I have chosen a winner and a runner-up. The entries will appear in the January 2025 issue and also on the website.

Editor: Christine Carr

M111 CutBank
Magazine
University of Montana, English Dept, LA 133, Missoula, MT 59812
United States

editor.cutbank@gmail.com
cutbankonline@gmail.com
cutbankreview@gmail.com

http://www.cutbankonline.org
https://cutbank.submittable.com/submit
https://twitter.com/cutbankonline
http://instagram.com/cutbankmag
https://www.facebook.com/cutbanklitmag/

Fiction > *Short Fiction*

Nonfiction > *Short Nonfiction:* Creative Nonfiction

Poetry > *Any Poetic Form*

Closed to approaches.

Costs: A fee is charged upon submission. $5 reading fee.

Accepts poetry, fiction, creative nonfiction, and visual art submissions. Please only submit online; paper submissions will be recycled.

M112 Cyphers
Magazine
3 Selskar Terrace, Ranelagh, Dublin 6, D06 DW66
Ireland

letters@cyphers.ie

https://www.cyphers.ie

Fiction in Translation > *Short Fiction*

Fiction > *Short Fiction*

Poetry in Translation > *Any Poetic Form*

Poetry > *Any Poetic Form*

Send: Full text
How to send: Post
How not to send: Email

Publishes poetry and fiction in English and Irish, from Ireland and around the world. Translations are welcome. No unsolicited critical articles. Submissions by post only. Attachments sent by email will be deleted. See website for full guidelines.

M113 The Dalhousie Review
Magazine
Dalhousie University, Halifax, Nova Scotia, B3H 4R2
Canada

dalhousie.review@dal.ca

https://ojs.library.dal.ca/dalhousiereview

Fiction > *Short Fiction*

Nonfiction
  Essays: Literary

  Reviews: Books

Poetry > *Any Poetic Form*

Send: Full text
How to send: Email

Publishes fiction, poetry, essays, and book reviews. Submit up to five poems at a time. Query before submitting reviews. See website for full submission guidelines.

M114 The Dark Horse
Magazine
PO Box 8351, Irvine, KA12 2DD
United Kingdom

https://www.thedarkhorsemagazine.com
https://www.facebook.com/The-Dark-Horse-Magazine-184043168311270/
https://twitter.com/thedarkhorsemag

Poetry > *Any Poetic Form*

Send: Full text; Self-Addressed Stamped Envelope (SASE)
How to send: Post
How not to send: Email

International literary magazine committed to British, Irish and American poetry. Send submissions by post only, to UK or US editorial addresses. No simultaneous submissions. See website for full guidelines.

Editor: Gerry Cambridge

M115 The Dawntreader
Magazine
24 Forest Houses, Halwill, Beaworthy, Devon, EX21 5UU
United Kingdom

dawnidp@indigodreams.co.uk

https://www.indigodreams.co.uk/magazines

Book Publisher: Indigo Dreams Publishing (**P236**)

Fiction > *Short Fiction*
  Environment; Folklore, Myths, and Legends; Mysticism; Nature; Spirituality

Nonfiction > *Articles*
  Environment; Folklore, Myths, and Legends; Mysticism; Nature; Spirituality

Poetry > *Any Poetic Form*
  Environment; Folklore, Myths, and Legends; Mysticism; Nature; Spirituality

Send: Full text
How to send: Email attachment

A quarterly publication specialising in myth, legend; in the landscape, nature; spirituality and love; the mystic, the environment. Submit up to five poems (40 lines or fewer), and prose, articles, and local legends up to 1,000 words.

Editor: Ronnie Goodyer

M116 Deep Overstock Magazine
Magazine
United States

submissions@deepoverstock.com

https://deepoverstock.com/issues/
https://deepoverstock.com/submission-guidelines/

Book Publisher / Magazine Publisher: Deep Overstock Publishing

Fiction > *Short Fiction*

Send: Full text; Author bio
How to send: In the body of an email

Accepts fiction. Issues are themed. Check website for current theme. Prefers fiction to be under 6,000 words. Submissions over 3,000 words may not be considered. Submit one or two pieces of fiction per theme, or up to three if they are each under 1,000 words. Send up to seven poems per theme.

M117 Derbyshire Life
Magazine
United Kingdom

Magazine Publisher: Great British Life

M118 Descent
Magazine
PO Box 297, Kendal, LA9 9GQ
United Kingdom
Tel: +44 (0) 7354 794240

info@descentmagazine.co.uk

https://www.descentmagazine.co.uk
https://twitter.com/CavingMagazine
https://www.facebook.com/profile.php?id=100083468112084
https://www.instagram.com/descentcavingmagazine/

Magazine Publisher: Stalactite Publishing

Nonfiction > *Articles*: Caving and Potholing

Send: Query
How to send: Email; Post

Magazine written by cavers, for cavers. Contact with ideas prior to submission.

Editor: Chris Howes

M119 Devon Life
Magazine
United Kingdom

https://www.greatbritishlife.co.uk/magazines/devon/

Magazine Publisher: Great British Life

Nonfiction > *Articles*
  Arts; Countryside; Devon; Events; Food and Drink; History; Houses and Homes; Lifestyle; Travel; Walking

Celebrates all that is great about Devon. The people, the places, the food and drink spots, the walks, the countryside, the history, the beaches, the homes, the events, the arts scene…produced by those with inside knowledge of the best and brightest Devon has to offer.

M120 Diver
Magazine
216 East Esplanade St., North Vancouver, BC, V7L 1A3
Canada
Tel: +1 (604) 988-0711

mail@divermag.com

https://divermag.com
https://www.facebook.com/divermagazine

Nonfiction > *Articles*: Scuba Diving

North America's longest established scuba diving magazine.

M121 Dorset
Magazine
United Kingdom

Magazine Publisher: Great British Life

M122 Dorset Magazine
Magazine

Magazine Publisher: Archant

M123 Dream Catcher
Magazine
109 Wensley Drive, Leeds, LS7 2LU
United Kingdom

https://www.dreamcatchermagazine.co.uk

Fiction > *Short Fiction*

Nonfiction > *Interviews*

Poetry > *Any Poetic Form*

Send: Full text
How to send: Post

Send submissions by post, following guidelines on website. No electronic submissions.

M124 The Dublin Review
Magazine
Ireland

enquiry@thedublinreview.com

https://thedublinreview.com
https://twitter.com/thedublinreview
https://www.instagram.com/thedublinreview/
https://www.facebook.com/TheDublinReview/

Fiction > *Short Fiction*

Nonfiction
  Essays: General
  Short Nonfiction: Memoir

Send: Full text
How to send: Online submission system

Publishes essays, criticism, reportage, and fiction for a general, intelligent readership. No poetry. Accepts submissions via form on website.

M125 Dumfries and Galloway Life
Print Magazine
United Kingdom

Magazine Publisher: Great British Life

M126 The Economist
Magazine
The Adelphi, 1-11 John Adam Street, London, WC2N 6HT
United Kingdom

https://www.economist.com
https://www.facebook.com/theeconomist
https://www.instagram.com/theeconomist
https://www.twitter.com/theeconomist
https://www.linkedin.com/company/the-economist
https://www.youtube.com/user/economistmagazine

Nonfiction
  Articles: Business; Current Affairs; Finance; Politics
  News: Business; Current Affairs; Finance; Politics

Magazine covering economics, business, finance, politics, and current affairs.

M127 Ecotone
Magazine
Department of Creative Writing, University of North Carolina Wilmington, 601 South College Road, Wilmington, NC 28403-5938
United States

ecotone@uncw.edu

https://ecotonemagazine.org

Fiction > *Short Fiction*

Nonfiction > *Short Nonfiction*

Poetry > *Any Poetic Form*

Send: Full text

Publishes work from a wide range of voices. Particularly interested in hearing from writers historically underrepresented in literary publishing and in place-based contexts: people of colour, Indigenous people, people with disabilities, gender-nonconforming people, LGBTQIA+, women, and others. Check website for specific reading periods and submit prose up to 30 double-spaced pages or 3-5 poems by post with SAE or using online system ($3 charge). No hard copy submissions from outside the US.

Editor: David Gessner

M128 The Ekphrastic Review
Online Magazine
Canada

theekphrasticreview@gmail.com

https://www.ekphrastic.net

Fiction > *Short Fiction*

Nonfiction
  Articles: Arts
  Interviews: Literature
  Reviews: Literature
  Short Nonfiction: General

Poetry in Translation > *Any Poetic Form*: Arts

Poetry > *Any Poetic Form*: Arts

Send: Full text
How to send: Email

Costs: A fee is charged upon submission. $5 CAD submission fee.

Publishes poetry that responds to, explores, or is inspired by a piece of art, and fiction and nonfiction of any kind, including book interviews or profiles, and articles about ekphrastic writing. Accepts submissions in January, April, July and October only. Submissions sent in other months will be deleted unread.

Editor: Lorette C. Luzajic

M129 El Portal
Magazine
United States

el.portal@enmu.edu

https://elportaljournal.com
https://elportal.submittable.com/submit
https://twitter.com/elportaljournal

Fiction > *Short Fiction*

Nonfiction > *Short Nonfiction*: Creative Nonfiction

Poetry > *Any Poetic Form*

Send: Full text
How to send: Submittable

Accepts submissions of flash fiction up to 500 words, short stories and creative nonfiction up to 4,000 words, or up to five poems. Open reading periods run from July 1st to August 31st and from December 1st to January 31st.

M130 Ellery Queen Mystery Magazine
Magazine
6 Prowitt Street, Norwalk, CT 06855
United States
Tel: +1 (212) 686-7188 x 675

elleryqueenmm@dellmagazines.com

http://www.elleryqueenmysterymagazine.com
https://www.facebook.com/elleryqueenmm
https://twitter.com/eqmm
https://www.instagram.com/elleryqueenmm/
https://somethingisgoingtohappen.net/

Fiction > *Short Fiction*
  Crime; Mystery

How to send: Online submission system

Mystery magazine, publishing every kind of mystery short story: psychological suspense; deductive puzzle; private eye case; realistic to imaginative; hard-boiled to "cozies". However, no explicit sex or violence, or true crime. Always seeking original detective stories, and especially happy to review first stories by authors who have never before published fiction professionally (submit to the "Department of First Stories). No need to send query – unsolicited MSS welcome. Submit through online system (see website for details). Accepts postal submissions only from those with a prior publishing history with the magazine.

M131 Entrepreneur
Magazine
1651 East Fourth Street, Suite 125, Santa Ana, Ca 92701
United States

https://www.entrepreneur.com/
https://www.facebook.com/EntMagazine
https://twitter.com/entrepreneur
https://www.linkedin.com/company/entrepreneur-media
https://www.pinterest.com/entrepreneurmedia
https://www.instagram.com/entrepreneur/
https://www.youtube.com/user/EntrepreneurOnline

Nonfiction > *Articles*
  Business; Entrepreneurship; Finance; How To

Magazine for people who have started and are running their own business, providing news o current trends, practical how-to articles, features on combining work and life, etc. Runs features and several regular columns, as well as an inner magazine on start-ups.

M132 Essex Life
Magazine
United Kingdom

https://www.greatbritishlife.co.uk/magazines/essex/

Magazine Publisher: Great British Life

Nonfiction
  Articles: Essex; Fashion; Food and Drink; Gardening; Interior Design; Lifestyle; Nostalgia; Property / Real Estate; Travel; Walking
  Interviews: Celebrity; Essex

Magazine publishing material relating to Essex.

M133 Event
Magazine
PO Box 2503, New Westminster, BC, V3L 5B2
Canada
Tel: +1 (604) 527-5293

event@douglascollege.ca

https://www.eventmagazine.ca
https://eventmagazine.submittable.com/submit
https://twitter.com/EVENTmags
https://www.facebook.com/eventmagazine
http://www.youtube.com/channel/UCKuYlH5b3uRaitKO4lCk8zA?feature=watch

Fiction > *Short Fiction*

Nonfiction
  Reviews: Books
  Short Nonfiction: Creative Nonfiction

Poetry > *Any Poetic Form*

Closed to approaches.

One of Western Canada's longest-running literary magazines. Welcomes submissions in English from around the world during specific submission windows. Submissions must be entirely human created. No work written, developed, or assisted in any capacity by Artificial Intelligence.

M134 Fabula Argentea
Magazine
United States

FAsubmits@gmail.com
fabargmagazine@gmail.com

https://fabulaargentea.com

Fiction > *Short Fiction*

Send: Full text
How to send: Email attachment
How not to send: PDF file email attachment

Online magazine publishing fiction up to 8,000 words. Submit fiction up to 8,000 words as an email attachment.

M135 Facts & Fiction
Magazine
United Kingdom
Tel: +44 (0) 1773 822829

steel.carpet@tiscali.co.uk

http://www.factsandfiction.co.uk
https://petecastle.co.uk/fandf

Nonfiction
  Articles: Storytelling
  Interviews: Storytelling
  News: Storytelling
  Reviews: Storytelling

How to send: Email

The magazine for everyone interested in (oral) storytelling. Not a short story or poetry mag. We deal with storytelling as an oral art form, in many ways as a traditional art form – so articles and other material should reflect that.

Editor: Pete Castle

M136 Fate
Magazine
PO Box 774, Hendersonville, NC 28793
United States
Tel: +1 (612) 965-5515

Phyllis@fatemag.com

https://www.fatemag.com
https://www.youtube.com/channel/UCAjXG-tsjV5VJM-i-afsvqA
https://twitter.com/Fate_Magazine
https://instagram.com/fatemagazine

Nonfiction > *Articles*
  Mystery; Science; Supernatural / Paranormal

How to send: Post; Email

Magazine of mysterious and unexplained phenomena.

Editor-in-Chief: Phyllis Galde

M137 Faultline
Magazine
UCI Department of English, 435 Humanities Instructional Building, Irvine, CA 92697-2650
United States
Tel: +1 (949) 824-1573

faultline@uci.edu
ucifaultline@gmail.com

https://faultline.sites.uci.edu/
https://www.facebook.com/uci.faultline
https://twitter.com/faultline_journ

Fiction in Translation > *Short Fiction*

Fiction > *Short Fiction*

Nonfiction in Translation > *Short Nonfiction*: Creative Nonfiction

Nonfiction > *Short Nonfiction*: Creative Nonfiction

Poetry in Translation > *Any Poetic Form*

Poetry > *Any Poetic Form*

Closed to approaches.

Send up to five poems or up to 20 pages of fiction or creative nonfiction, between October 15 and December 15 only.

Fiction Editor: Sara Joyce Robinson

Poetry Editor: Lisa P. Sutton

M138 Fee: Foundation for Economic Education
Online Magazine
1776 Peachtree St. NW, Suite 710S, Atlanta, GA 30309
United States
Tel: +1 (404) 554-9980
Fax: +1 (404) 393-3142

submissions@fee.org

https://fee.org
https://fee.org/submissions

Nonfiction > *Articles*
  Culture; History; Philosophy; Politics

Send: Query; Full text

We welcome compelling, thoughtful articles exploring trends, principles, history, and ideas underlying a free society: private property, the rule of law, voluntary exchange, individual rights, morality, personal character, cultural evolution, self-responsibility, charity, mutual aid, and limitations on power.

M139 Feminist Studies
Magazine
677 Rome Hall, 801 22nd Street, NW, George Washington University, Washington, DC 20052
United States

info@feministstudies.org
submit@feministstudies.org
creative@feministstudies.org
art@feministstudies.org
review@feministstudies.org

http://www.feministstudies.org

ACADEMIC > **Nonfiction** > *Essays*
  Cultural Criticism; Literary Criticism

ADULT
  Fiction > *Short Fiction*: Feminism

  Nonfiction > *Articles*
    Arts; Culture; Feminism

  Poetry > *Any Poetic Form*: Feminism

Send: Full text; Proposal; Writing sample; Author bio
How to send: Email

Feminist journal publishing research and criticism, creative writing, art, essays, and other forms of writing and visual expression. See website for submission guidelines and specific submission email addresses.

M140 Fiction
Magazine
c/o Department of English, City College of New York, Convent Ave. at 138th Street, New York, NY 10031
United States

fictionmageditors@gmail.com

http://www.fictioninc.com
http://submissions.fictioninc.com/
http://instagram.com/fiction.magazine
https://twitter.com/fictionmag
https://www.facebook.com/fiction.mag/

Fiction in Translation > *Short Fiction*

Fiction > *Short Fiction*
  Experimental; Literary

Closed to approaches.

We publish literary and experimental fiction and translations of works previously unpublished in English. We favor stories of under 7,500 words. We do not accept unsolicited artwork, graphic stories, novel excerpts, or interviews. Reading period runs from October 15 to April 15 annually.

M141 The Fiddlehead
Magazine
Campus House, 11 Garland Court, University of New Brunswick, PO Box 4400, Fredericton NB, E3B 5A3
Canada
Tel: +1 (506) 453-3501

fiddlehd@unb.ca

https://thefiddlehead.ca
https://twitter.com/TheFiddlehd
http://www.facebook.com/pages/The-Fiddlehead-Atlantic-Canadas-International-Literary-Journal/174825212565312

Fiction
  Novel Excerpts; *Short Fiction*

Nonfiction > *Short Nonfiction*: Creative Nonfiction

Poetry > *Any Poetic Form*

Closed to approaches.

Publishes poetry, fiction, and creative nonfiction in a variety of styles, including experimental genres. Also publishes excerpts from longer works, and reviews. Submit up to six poems (up to 12 pages total), or a piece of fiction up to 6,000 words. All submissions must be original and unpublished. Prefers submissions through online submission system (January 1 to March 31 and September 15 to November 30 only), but will accept submissions by post all year round. See website for full details.

M142 First For Women
Magazine
270 Sylvan Avenue, Englewood Cliffs, NJ 07632
United States

contactus@firstforwomen.com

https://www.firstforwomen.com
https://www.facebook.com/firstforwomenmag
https://www.instagram.com/firstmag
https://www.pinterest.com/firstforwomen

Nonfiction > *Articles*
  Beauty; Diet; Fashion; Food; Health; Menopause; Personal Finance; Wellbeing

Magazine where active women in all eras of life come for the tools and inspiration that they need to look good, feel great and enjoy every aspect of their experiences.

M143 The First Line
Magazine
PO Box 250382, Plano, Texas 75025-0382
United States

submission@thefirstline.com

http://www.thefirstline.com

Fiction > *Short Fiction*

Nonfiction > *Essays*: Literary Criticism

Poetry > *Any Poetic Form*

Send: Full text; Self-Addressed Stamped Envelope (SASE)
How to send: Word file email attachment; Post
How not to send: PDF file email attachment; Google Docs shared document

Prefers submissions by email, but will also accept submissions by post with SASE. Prefers attachments as a Word or Word Perfect file. Stories must begin with the appropriate first line for that issue, as provided on the website. Occasionally accepts poems starting with the specified first line. Also accepts essays on your favourite first line from a book.

M144 Five Points
Magazine
Georgia State University, P.O. Box 3999, Atlanta, GA 30302-3999
United States

http://fivepoints.gsu.edu

Fiction in Translation > *Short Fiction*: Literary

Fiction > *Short Fiction*: Literary

Nonfiction in Translation > *Essays*

Nonfiction > *Short Nonfiction*
General, and in particular: Literary

Poetry in Translation > *Any Poetic Form*

Poetry > *Any Poetic Form*

Closed to approaches.

Costs: A fee is charged upon submission.

Welcomes unsolicited submissions of fiction, poetry, flash fiction, literary non-fiction, and translations in these genres. Submit through online submission system.

Editor: Megan Sexton

M145 Flaneur
Online Magazine
United Kingdom

editor@flaneur.me.uk

http://www.flaneur.me.uk

Nonfiction > *Articles*
Arts; Films; Food and Drink; Literature; Music; Politics; Sport; TV; Theatre; Travel

Send: Full text
How to send: In the body of an email

Online magazine of arts, culture, politics, and sport.

Editor: J Powell

M146 Flyfishing & Tying Journal
Magazine
United States

https://ftjangler.com

Book Publisher / Magazine Publisher: Amato Books (**P021**)

Nonfiction > *Articles*: Fly Fishing

Magazine for both new and veteran anglers, covering flyfishing and fly tying. Magazine is released quarterly, and each issue is appropriate to the given season.

M147 Folio
Magazine
United States

folio.editors@gmail.com

https://www.american.edu/cas/literature/folio/
https://foliolitjournal.submittable.com/submit
https://www.facebook.com/FolioLitJournal/
https://twitter.com/FolioLitJournal
https://www.linkedin.com/in/folio-literary-journal-a235a8b4
http://folio-lit-journal.tumblr.com/

Fiction > *Short Fiction*: Literary

Nonfiction > *Essays*: Creative Nonfiction

Poetry > *Any Poetic Form*

Closed to approaches.

Accepts submissions of fiction, nonfiction, and poetry on specific themes during specific submission windows. See website for details.

M148 Fortean Times: The Journal of Strange Phenomena
Magazine
Diamond Publishing Ltd, 2nd Floor, Saunders House, 52-53 The Mall, Ealing, W5 3AT
United Kingdom

hello@metropolis.co.uk

http://subscribe.forteantimes.com
https://www.instagram.com/forteantimes/
https://www.facebook.com/ForteanTimes
https://twitter.com/forteantimes

Magazine Publisher: Diamond Publishing

Nonfiction > *Articles*: Supernatural / Paranormal

Publishes accounts of strange phenomena, experiences, curiosities, mysteries, prodigies, and portents. No fiction or poetry.

Editor: David Sutton

M149 The Fortnightly Review
Online Magazine
United Kingdom

info@fortnightlyreview.co.uk

https://fortnightlyreview.co.uk

Fiction > *Short Fiction*

Nonfiction
Essays; Reviews
Poetry > *Any Poetic Form*

Send: Full text
How to send: Email

Online magazine publishing reviews, essays and reportage, fiction, and poetry.

Poetry Editors: Robert Archambeau; Peter Robinson

M150 Forty20
Magazine
47 Street Lane, Leeds, West Yorkshire, LS8 1AP
United Kingdom
Tel: +44 (0) 113 225 9797
Fax: +44 (0) 113 225 2515

editorial@forty-20.com
admin@scratchingshedpublishing.com

https://www.scratchingshedpublishing.com/magazine/
https://www.facebook.com/forty20magazine
https://twitter.com/forty20magazine

Book Publisher / Magazine Publisher: Scratching Shed Publishing (**P402**)

Nonfiction
Articles: Rugby League
Interviews: Rugby League
News: Rugby League

How to send: Email

The alternative voice of rugby league. Intelligent, thought-provoking, informative and fun, it covers rugby league at every level. Features thought-provoking articles by the game's most respected writers and best-known personalities, and face-to-face interviews with rugby league's most engaging characters, be they in the European Super League, Australasian NRL or anywhere else in the world.

M151 Foundation: The International Review of Science Fiction
Magazine
28 St John's Road, Guildford, GU2 7UH
United Kingdom

sff@beccon.org

https://www.sf-foundation.org/about-the-sff-journal

Nonfiction
Articles: Science Fiction

Reviews: Books; Science Fiction

Describes itself as the essential critical review of science fiction, publishing articles up to 6,000 words and reviews up to 1,500 words.

M152 Fourteen Poems
Print Magazine
United Kingdom

hello@14poems.com

https://www.fourteenpoems.com
https://twitter.com/fourteenpoems
http://instagram.com/14poems

Poetry > *Any Poetic Form*: LGBTQIA

Send: Full text; Author bio
How to send: PDF file email attachment; Word file email attachment

Print magazine published three times a year. Each issue includes work by fourteen LGBTQ+ poets, printing their queer takes on sex, love, race, gender and life in the LGBTQ+ global community.

M153 The Fourth River
Magazine
United States

4thriver@gmail.com

https://www.thefourthriver.com
https://twitter.com/thefourthriver
https://www.instagram.com/thefourthriver/
https://www.facebook.com/TheFourthRiver

Fiction > *Short Fiction*: Literary

Nonfiction > *Short Nonfiction*: Creative Nonfiction

Poetry > *Any Poetic Form*

Closed to approaches.

Costs: A fee is charged upon submission. $2 submission fee.

Print and digital literary magazine publishing creative writing that explores the relationship between humans and their environments, whether natural or man-made. Submit 3-5 poems or prose up to 4,000 words between July 1 and September 1 for print, or December 1 and February 1 for online, via online submission system. No submissions by email.

Online Magazine: Tributaries (**M380**)

M154 Fresh Words – An International Literary Magazine
Print Magazine; Online Magazine
United States

freshwordsmagazine@gmail.com

https://sites.google.com/view/freshwordsmagazine

Fiction > *Short Fiction*

Nonfiction
  Essays: Literature
  Interviews: General
  Reviews: Books
  Short Nonfiction: Travel

Poetry > *Any Poetic Form*

How to send: Email

We are open for submissions. We invite poems, short stories, essays, plays, diaries, excerpts from books (published or upcoming submitted by author only), book reviews, interviews and travelogues. Please send all submissions by email. See website for full guidelines.

M155 Fugue
Magazine
United States

fugue@uidaho.edu

https://fuguejournal.com
https://twitter.com/FugueJournal
https://www.instagram.com/fugue_journal/
https://www.facebook.com/fuguejournal/

Fiction > *Short Fiction*

Nonfiction
  Essays: General
  Reviews: Books

Poetry > *Any Poetic Form*

Closed to approaches.

Costs: A fee is charged upon submission. $3.

Submit 3 to 5 poems, up to two short shorts, one story, or one essay per submission. Accepts submissions online only, between August 15 and December 15. Submission service charges $3 per submission.

M156 Funeral Business Solutions
Magazine
1801 South Bay Street, Eustis, FL 32726-5666
United States
Tel: +1 (352) 242-8111

https://fbsmagazine.com
https://www.facebook.com/profile.php?id=100088592525602
https://www.linkedin.com/company/funeralbusinesssolutions/

Magazine Publisher: Radcliffe Media, Inc.

PROFESSIONAL > **Nonfiction**
  Articles: Funeral Industry
  Interviews: Funeral Industry
  News: Funeral Industry
  Reviews: Funeral Industry

Send: Full text
How to send: Email

Different from traditional association magazines or trade journals because it is specially-crafted to bring you the best industry specific business news and solutions that will help you to make effective business decisions for your staff, company, and client families.

Our magazine design and layout is purposefully easy to read and digest in short segments. We know that the average funeral professional has an unpredictable schedule and an effective business magazine gives the reader shorter editorials that get to the point without fluff.

Our writers provide actionable ideas and effective strategies that will help you, the industry professional, run a more profitable business. Issues are published every two months, giving you ample time to digest 8-12 articles, latest industry headlines, the included Funeral Home Success Stories, Vendor Company Spotlights, Industry Book Overviews and more.

Our goal is to never bore you or waste your precious time, so our editors consider each article, press release, and spotlight carefully to make sure it can in some way benefit a funeral director running a business.

At the end of each day, we are primarily a magazine of business solutions for an industry that our publisher, editors, and writers love.

Publisher: Timothy Totten

M157 Funny Times
Magazine
PO Box 18530, Cleveland Heights, OH 44118
United States
Tel: +1 (888) 386-6984

submissions@funnytimes.com
info@funnytimes.com

https://funnytimes.com
https://www.facebook.com/TheFunnyTimes

Fiction
  Cartoons: Business; Comedy / Humour; Current Affairs; Food; Pets; Politics; Relationships; Religion; Technology
  Short Fiction: Business; Comedy / Humour; Current Affairs; Food; Pets; Politics; Relationships; Religion; Technology

Send: Full text; Self-Addressed Stamped Envelope (SASE)
How to send: Email; Post

Send query with SASE and details of previous publishing history (where applicable). Publishes funny stories and cartoons only. No fax or email submissions.

Editor: Raymond Lesser, Susan Wolpert

M158 The Future Fire
Online Magazine
United Kingdom

fiction@futurefire.net
nonfiction@futurefire.net

http://futurefire.net

Fiction in Translation > *Short Fiction*

Fiction > *Short Fiction*

Crime; Environment; Feminism; LGBTQIA; Mystery; Noir; Postcolonialism; Speculative

Nonfiction > *Reviews*
Arts; Books; Films; Magazines

Poetry in Translation > *Any Poetic Form*

Poetry > *Any Poetic Form*
Environment; Feminism; LGBTQIA; Postcolonialism; Speculative

Send: Full text
How to send: Email attachment

Magazine of social political and speculative cyber fiction. Publishes short stories up to 17,500. Also publishes nonfiction reviews. Accepts email submissions for fiction; for reviews send query by email before submitting material. See website for full submission guidelines.

M159 Garden Answers
Magazine
Bauer Media, Media House, Lynch Wood, PE2 6EA
United Kingdom

https://www.gardenanswersmagazine.co.uk/
https://www.facebook.com/gardenanswers
https://twitter.com/GardenAnswers

Magazine Publisher: Bauer Media Group

Nonfiction > *Articles:* Gardening

A vibrant and inspiring gardening magazine filled with ingenious design ideas and exciting plant combinations guaranteed to make your garden beautiful.

M160 Garden News
Magazine
United Kingdom

https://www.gardennewsmagazine.co.uk
https://www.facebook.com/GardenNewsOfficial
https://twitter.com/GardenNewsmag

Magazine Publisher: Bauer Media Group

Nonfiction > *Articles:* Gardening

Weekly gardening magazine publishing tips, reminders, and expert advice.

Editor: Neil Pope

M161 Gargoyle Online
Online Magazine
3819 13th Street North, Arlington, VA 22201
United States
Tel: +1 (703) 380-4893

https://gargoylemagazine.com
https://gargoylemagazinepaycockpress.submittable.com/submit
https://www.facebook.com/profile.php?id=100063527378646

Book Publisher / Magazine Publisher: Paycock Press (**P340**)

Fiction > *Short Fiction*
Poetry > *Any Poetic Form*

Closed to approaches.

Dedicated to publishing work by unknown poets and fiction writers, as well as seeking out the overlooked or neglected. The mag was on something of an extended hiatus from 1990-1997 and then resurfaced. After 46 years and 76 issues the magazine has ended the print run and shifted to an online presence from mid-2022 onward.

M162 The Geographical Journal
Online Magazine
United Kingdom

https://rgs-ibg.onlinelibrary.wiley.com/journal/14754959

ACADEMIC > **Nonfiction** > *Articles:* Geography

How to send: Online submission system

Academic journal founded in 1893. In order to minimise environmental impact, online only from 2024.

M163 The Georgia Review
Magazine
706A Main Library, 320 S. Jackson St., The University of Georgia, Athens, GA 30602-9009
United States
Tel: +1 (800) 542-3481

https://thegeorgiareview.com
https://thegeorgiareview.submittable.com/submit
https://www.instagram.com/georgiareview/
https://www.facebook.com/thegeorgiareview/
https://twitter.com/home

Fiction > *Short Fiction:* Literary

Nonfiction
Essays: General
Reviews: Books

Poetry > *Any Poetic Form*

Closed to approaches.

Costs: A fee is charged upon submission in some cases. $3 for non-subscribers. Subscribers submit for free.

Publishes literary fiction, poetry (submit 6-10 pages of poetry or one long poem), essays and book reviews. Submissions accepted between August 15 and May 15 only. Submissions received between May 15 and August 15 are returned unread.

M164 Gertrude
Online Magazine
United States

EditorGertrudePress@gmail.com

https://www.gertrudepress.org

Book Publisher: Gertrude Press (**P179**)

Fiction > *Short Fiction*
General, and in particular: LGBTQIA

Nonfiction
Essays: Creative Nonfiction; LGBTQIA
Short Nonfiction: Creative Nonfiction; LGBTQIA; Memoir
Poetry > *Any Poetic Form*
General, and in particular: LGBTQIA

Closed to approaches.

Costs: A fee is charged upon submission. £3 submission fee.

Online LGBTQA journal publishing fiction, poetry, and creative nonfiction. Subject matter need not be LGBTQA-specific, and writers from all backgrounds are welcomed. Submit fiction or creative nonfiction up to 3,000 words, or up to five poems (no line limit, but under 40 lines preferred), via online submission system. For book reviews and interviews, email editor with proposal. See website for full guidelines.

Editor: Tammy

M165 Ginosko Literary Journal
Magazine
United States

https://ginoskoliteraryjournal.com
https://ginosko.submittable.com/submit/

Fiction > *Short Fiction*

Nonfiction > *Short Nonfiction:* Creative Nonfiction

Poetry > *Any Poetic Form*

Send: Full text
How to send: Submittable

Costs: A fee is charged upon submission. $3 submission fee.

Semi-annual literary journal accepting short fiction, poetry, creative nonfiction, social justice issues, and literary and spiritual insights.

Editor: Robert Cesaretti

M166 The Glacier
Online Magazine
United States

https://theglacierjournal.com
https://42miles.submittable.com/submit

Book Publisher: 42 Miles Press

Fiction > *Short Fiction*
General, and in particular: Experimental

Poetry > *Any Poetic Form*
General, and in particular: Lyrical

How to send: Submittable

Costs: A fee is charged upon submission. $3 per submission.

Online magazine published once a year, in the autumn. Publishes poetry, fiction, and visual art. Accepts simultaneous submissions, but no previously published work. Prefers lyric/associative poetry over straight narrative, but does not have a house style. Send up to seven poems, all within a single file. In fiction, prefers more experimental work to straight narrative. Likes fiction that gets to the point and that keeps burning in a reader's mind after the last word is read . . . 1300 words max. Send up to three stories, single or double spaced is fine.

M167 Go World Travel Magazine
Online Magazine
United States

submissions@goworldtravel.com

https://www.goworldtravel.com
https://www.facebook.com/Go.World.Travel
https://www.instagram.com/goworldtravelmagazine/
https://pinterest.com/goworldtravel/
https://twitter.com/GoWorldMagazine
https://www.youtube.com/user/GoWorldPublishing

Nonfiction > *Articles*: Travel

How to send: Email

A digital publication for world travelers. We work with journalists around the world, and partner with destination marketing organizations and other tourism and travel businesses to promote travel.

Editor: Heike Schmidt, Senior Editor

M168 Good Homes
Magazine
United Kingdom

info@goodhomesmagazine.com

https://www.goodhomesmagazine.com
https://www.facebook.com/GoodHomes
https://uk.pinterest.com/goodhomes/
https://twitter.com/GoodHomesMag
https://www.instagram.com/goodhomesmag/

Magazine Publisher: Media 10

Nonfiction > *Articles*
    Decorating; Interior Design

Magazine of decorating and interior design.

M169 The Good Ski Guide
Magazine
United Kingdom

https://www.goodskiguide.com/
https://www.facebook.com/goodskiguide.official
https://twitter.com/officialGSG
https://www.youtube.com/goodskiguideoffical

Nonfiction > *Articles*
    Skiing; Travel

Magazine of skiing and ski resorts.

M170 Grain Literary Magazine
Magazine
Saskatchewan Writers' Guild, PO Box 3986, Regina, SK S4P 3R9
Canada
Tel: +1 (306) 791-7740

grainmag@skwriter.com

https://grainmagazine.ca
https://grainmagazine.submittable.com/submit
https://www.facebook.com/GrainLitMag
https://x.com/GrainLitMag
https://instagram.com/grainlitmag

Fiction > *Short Fiction*

Nonfiction > *Short Nonfiction*: Literary

Poetry > *Any Poetic Form*

How to send: Submittable

An internationally acclaimed literary journal that publishes engaging, surprising, eclectic, and challenging writing and art by Canadian and international writers and artists. Nine-month reading period, September 15 to June 15.

M171 Granta
Magazine
12 Addison Avenue, Holland Park, London, W11 4QR
United Kingdom
Tel: +44 (0) 20 7605 1360

editorial@granta.com

https://granta.com

Fiction > *Short Fiction*

Nonfiction > *Short Nonfiction*

Poetry > *Any Poetic Form*

Closed to approaches.

Costs: A fee is charged upon submission. £3.50 for prose; £2 for poems.

Submit one story or essay, or up to four poems, via online submission system. £3.50 charge for prose submissions; £2 for poems. No specific length limits for prose, but most pieces are between 3,000 and 6,000 words. Unlikely to read anything over 10,000 words.

Editor: Sigrid Rausing

M172 Graywolf Lab
Online Magazine
United States

https://graywolflab.org

Book Publisher: Graywolf Press (**P193**)

Fiction > *Short Fiction*

Nonfiction > *Articles*
    Arts; Literature; Music; Visual Arts

Poetry > *Any Poetic Form*

Closed to approaches.

An online platform for interdisciplinary conversations and new writing. Each issue starts by gathering a small group of artists for a roundtable discussing a theme. Over several months, we invite responses to that conversation from more artists, writers, and thinkers.

M173 Gulf Coast: A Journal of Literature and Fine Arts
Magazine
University of Houston, Department of English, Roy G. Cullen Building, 3687 Cullen Boulevard, Room 203, Houston, Texas 77204-3013
United States
Tel: +1 (713) 743-3223

gulfcoastea@gmail.com
gcmagreviews@gmail.com

http://www.gulfcoastmag.org
https://www.facebook.com/GulfCoastJournal
https://twitter.com/Gulf_Coast
https://www.instagram.com/gulfcoastjournal/

Fiction in Translation > *Short Fiction*

Fiction > *Short Fiction*

Nonfiction
    Essays: Art Criticism
    Interviews: Literature
    Reviews: Books

Poetry in Translation > *Any Poetic Form*

Poetry > *Any Poetic Form*

How to send: Submittable

Costs: A fee is charged upon submission. $3 submission fee.

Submit up to five poems, or fiction or essays up to 7,000 words, by post or via online submission manager. For other material, send query by email to address on website. $3.00 submission fee. Accepts material September 1 to March 1, annually.

Editor: Luisa Muradyan Tannahill

M174 Gutter Magazine
Magazine
United Kingdom

contactguttermagazine@gmail.com

https://www.guttermag.co.uk/

Fiction > *Short Fiction*
    International; Literary; Scotland

Nonfiction > *Essays*
    Creative Nonfiction; International; Literary; Scotland

Poetry > *Any Poetic Form*
    International; Scotland

Closed to approaches.

Publishes poetry, short stories, and essays. Publishes work by writers born or living in Scotland alongside international writing. Send up to three poems up to 100 lines total or prose up to 2,500 words. Submit through online submission system. See website for full guidelines.

Editors: Colin Begg; Kate MacLeary; Laura Waddell

M175 Half Mystic Journal
Print Magazine
United States

hello@halfmystic.com

https://www.halfmystic.com

Book Publisher: Half Mystic Press (**P197**)

Fiction in Translation > *Short Fiction*
 Experimental; Music

Fiction > *Short Fiction*
 Experimental; Music

Nonfiction in Translation > *Short Nonfiction*
 Creative Nonfiction; Experimental; Music

Nonfiction > *Short Nonfiction*
 Creative Nonfiction; Experimental; Music

Poetry in Translation
 Any Poetic Form: Music
 Experimental Poetry: Music

Poetry
 Any Poetic Form: Music
 Experimental Poetry: Music

Closed to approaches.

Publishes all genres of poetry, prose, creative nonfiction, translations, and experimental work—as long as each piece pertains in some way to music. See website for the theme of the current issue.

M176 Hampshire Life
Magazine
United Kingdom

Magazine Publisher: Great British Life

M177 Hanging Loose
Magazine
PO Box 150608, Brooklyn, NY 11215
United States
Tel: +1 (857) 998-9473

highschool@hangingloosepress.com

https://www.hangingloosepress.com
https://www.facebook.com/hangingloosepress
https://twitter.com/HangingLooseNY

Fiction > *Short Fiction*

Poetry > *Any Poetic Form*

Send: Full text; Self-Addressed Stamped Envelope (SASE)
How to send: Email

Send up to six poems, or flash fiction, or short fiction (up to 1000 words). Potential contributors should familiarise themselves with the magazine before submitting. Includes regular section of High School writers. Send submissions by email. Allow up to three months for a response.

M178 Harper's Magazine
Magazine
666 Broadway, 11th Floor, New York, NY 10012
United States
Tel: +1 (212) 420-5720

letters@harpers.org
readings@harpers.org

https://harpers.org
https://twitter.com/Harpers
https://www.facebook.com/HarpersMagazine/
https://www.instagram.com/harpersmagazine/

Fiction > *Short Fiction*

Nonfiction
 Articles: Culture; Current Affairs; Environment; Journalism; Politics; Society
 Essays: Culture; Current Affairs; Environment; Politics; Society

Send: Query; Full text; Self-Addressed Stamped Envelope (SASE)
How to send: Post
How not to send: Email

Current affairs magazine publishing topical essays, and fiction. Considers unsolicited fiction MSS, however no unsolicited nonfiction (query in first instance). All queries and submissions must be sent by post.

M179 Harpur Palate
Magazine
Binghamton University, English Department, P.O. Box 6000, Binghamton, NY 13902-6000
United States

harpur.palate@gmail.com

https://harpurpalate.binghamton.edu
https://twitter.com/harpurpalate
https://www.instagram.com/harpurpalate
https://www.facebook.com/harpurpalate
https://harpurpalate.submittable.com/submit

Fiction > *Short Fiction*

Nonfiction > *Short Nonfiction*: Creative Nonfiction

Poetry > *Any Poetic Form*

Closed to approaches.

Submit up to three poems, up to five pages total; fiction up to 4,500 words; creative nonfiction up to 5,500 words; or three pieces of short prose up to 1,000 words each. Submit through online submission system.

M180 Healthy
Magazine
United Kingdom

healthy@therivergroup.co.uk

https://www.healthy-magazine.co.uk
https://www.facebook.com/HealthyMagazine
https://twitter.com/healthymag
http://instagram.com/healthymagdaily

Magazine Publisher: The River Group

Nonfiction > *Articles*
 Beauty; Fitness; Food; Health; Lifestyle

Magazine of holistic health and lifestyle. Send query by email in first instance.

Editor: Heather Beresford

M181 Heavy Traffic
Print Magazine
United States

info@heavytrafficmagazine.com

https://heavytrafficmagazine.com
https://twitter.com/heavytrafficmag
https://www.instagram.com/heavy_traffic_mag/

Fiction > *Short Fiction*

Send: Full text
How to send: Email

Fiction magazine with open submissions and no criteria. Send submissions by email.

M182 Hedgerow: A Journal of Small Poems
Print Magazine
United Kingdom

hedgerowsubmission@gmail.com

https://hedgerowhaiku.com
https://www.facebook.com/hedgerowpoems

Fiction > *Short Fiction*

Poetry
 Any Poetic Form; *Haibun*; *Haiga*; *Haiku*; *Prose Poetry*; *Senryu*; *Tanka*

Send: Full text
How to send: In the body of an email

A short-poetry journal dedicated to publishing an eclectic mix of new and established voices across the spectrum of the short poem, with particular attention to the constantly evolving forms of English-language haiku, senryu, tanka, haiga and haibun. Submissions of prose poems, other longer poems and sequences, as well as short stories also welcome. Please note—for consistency, the house style will inform both print and online presentation.

M183 The Helix
Magazine
United States

helixmagazine@gmail.com

https://helixmagazine.org

Fiction > *Short Fiction*

Nonfiction > *Short Nonfiction*

Poetry > *Any Poetic Form*

Send: Full text; Author bio
How to send: Submittable

Publishes fiction, creative nonfiction, poetry, plays, and art. Submit prose up to 3,000 words each, or up to four poems.

Editor: Victoria-Lynn Bell

M184 Here Comes Everyone
Magazine
United Kingdom

https://hcemagazine.com
https://www.facebook.com/HCEmagazine/
https://twitter.com/herecomesevery1

Fiction > *Short Fiction*

Nonfiction > *Articles*

Poetry > *Any Poetic Form*

Closed to approaches.

Biannual literature and arts magazine publishing poetry, fiction, articles, and artwork. Each issue is themed. See website for upcoming themes and to submit.

Editor: Raef Boylan

M185 Hertfordshire Life
Print Magazine
United Kingdom

Magazine Publisher: Great British Life

M186 History Today
Magazine
2nd Floor, 9 Staple Inn, London, WC1V 7QH
United Kingdom
Tel: +44 (0) 20 3219 7810

submissions@historytoday.com
admin@historytoday.com
enquiries@historytoday.com

https://www.historytoday.com

Nonfiction > *Articles*: History

Send: Query; Author bio
How to send: Email

Historical magazine publishing short articles (up to 1,000 words); mid-length articles (1,300-2,200 words) and feature articles (3,000 to 3,400 words). Send query by email with proposal and details of your career / academic background. See website for full guidelines.

M187 Homes & Antiques
Magazine
United Kingdom

https://www.homesandantiques.com
https://www.facebook.com/homesantiques
http://uk.pinterest.com/homesantiques
https://twitter.com/@homes_antiques
https://www.youtube.com/channel/UChlvNbVVoLcWle1xHnuAZlQ
https://www.instagram.com/homes_antiques

Magazine Publisher: Our Media

Nonfiction > *Articles*
   Antiques; Decorating; Interior Design

Magazine of home interest, antiques, and collectibles.

Editor: Angela Linforth

M188 Horse & Rider
Magazine
7500 Alamo Road NW, Albuquerque, NM 87120
United States

https://my.horseandrider.com
https://www.facebook.com/HorseandRider
https://www.pinterest.com/hrsrdrmag/
https://www.instagram.com/horseandridermag/
https://twitter.com/Horse_and_Rider

Magazine Publisher: Equine Network

Nonfiction > *Articles*
   American West; Horses; Travel

Provides all you need for today's Western horse life. Learn from top professional trainers, clinicians, and horse-keeping experts. Experience Western life. Travel to Western destinations and scenic trails. Your resource to live today's Western horse life.

M189 Hotel Amerika
Magazine
C/O The Department of Creative Writing, Columbia College Chicago, 600 South Michigan Avenue, Chicago, IL 60605
United States
Tel: +1 (312) 369-8175

http://www.hotelamerika.net

Fiction > *Short Fiction*: Literary

Nonfiction > *Essays*

Poetry > *Any Poetic Form*

Closed to approaches.

Costs: A fee is charged upon submission. $3.00.

Submissions will be considered between September 1 and April 1. Materials received after April 1 and before September 1 will not be considered.

Editor: David Lazar

M190 The Hudson Review
Magazine
33 West 67th Street, New York, NY 10023
United States
Tel: +1 (212) 650-0020

info@hudsonreview.com
https://hudsonreview.com
https://www.facebook.com/The-Hudson-Review-134346783271591/
https://twitter.com/TheHudsonReview

Fiction > *Short Fiction*

Nonfiction
   Articles: Contemporary Culture
   Essays: Arts; Dance; Films; Literary Criticism; Music; Theatre
   Reviews: Books

Poetry > *Any Poetic Form*

Send: Full text; Self-Addressed Stamped Envelope (SASE)
How to send: Post; Online submission system

Publishes fiction, poetry, essays, book reviews; criticism of literature, art, theatre, dance, film and music; and articles on contemporary cultural developments.

Accepts certain material at only certain times of year: poetry between April 1 and June 30; fiction between September 1 and November 30; and nonfiction between January 1 and March 31. MSS submitted out of season are returned if adequate return postage is provided only. MSS of subscribers are read year-round.

No specialisation in any particular type of writing – literary quality is the only criteria. Read a sample copy of the magazine for a flavour of the kinds of material published.

No simultaneous submissions. Electronic submissions for fiction only.

M191 Hunger Mountain
Magazine
36 College Street, Montpelier, VT 05602
United States

hungermtn@vcfa.edu

https://hungermtn.org

Fiction in Translation > *Short Fiction*: Literary

Fiction > *Short Fiction*: Literary

Nonfiction in Translation > *Short Nonfiction*: Creative Nonfiction

Nonfiction > *Short Nonfiction*: Creative Nonfiction

Poetry in Translation > *Any Poetic Form*

Poetry > *Any Poetic Form*

Closed to approaches.

Costs: A fee is charged upon submission.

Seeks to provide a platform for traditionally silenced voices, to expand representation in literature and to examine culture with a critical eye. Publishes fiction, nonfiction, poetry, hybrid work, and translations of all of these forms. Welcomes work that is genre-less and the traditional genres some magazines shun. Wants more speculative fiction. Doesn't believe in the divide between literary and genre fiction. Wants to read your science fiction, fantasy, magical realism, ecofabulism, irrealism and slipstream. Submit prose up to 5,000 words, or up to three flash pieces, or up to five poems, via online submission system.

Editor: Caroline Mercurio

M192 I-70 Review

Magazine
913 Joseph Drive, Lawrence, KS 66044
United States

i70review@gmail.com

http://i70review.fieldinfoserv.com

Fiction > *Short Fiction*

Poetry > *Any Poetic Form*

Send: Full text; Author bio
How to send: Word file email attachment

Accepts submissions of fiction and flash fiction or 3-5 poems, by email, during the reading period that runs from July 1 to December 31. Accepts simultaneous submissions. See website for full details.

M193 Idaho Review

Magazine
Boise State University, 1910 University Drive, Boise, Idaho 83725
United States

hannahphillips290@boisestate.edu

https://www.idahoreview.org
https://theidahoreview.submittable.com/submit
http://www.facebook.com/10213528569031037
http://twitter.com/idahoreview
http://www.instagram.com/theidahoreview

Fiction
Novel Excerpts: Literary
Short Fiction: Literary

Nonfiction
Essays: General
Short Nonfiction: Creative Nonfiction

Poetry > *Any Poetic Form*

Closed to approaches.

Costs: A fee is charged for online submissions. $3 to submit online.

Annual literary journal publishing poetry and fiction. No specific limit for fiction, but most of the stories accepted are under 25 double-spaced pages. For poetry, submit up to five poems. Accepts submissions by post with SASE, but prefers submissions through online submission system ($3 fee).

M194 Identity Theory

Online Magazine
United States

fiction@identitytheory.com
essays@identitytheory.com
poetry@identitytheory.com

http://www.identitytheory.com
https://identitytheory.submittable.com/submit

Fiction > *Short Fiction*

Nonfiction
Essays: Lyric Essays; Personal Essays
Interviews: General
Short Nonfiction: Creative Nonfiction; Memoir

Poetry > *Any Poetic Form*

Send: Full text
How to send: Submittable; Email

Online literary magazine publishing short fiction, including flash fiction and microfiction. Send fiction or essays up to 4,000 words through Submittable or through specific email address, or 3-5 unpublished poems in the body of an email.

Editor: Matt Borondy

M195 Image

Magazine
16915 SE 272nd St, Suite #100-213, Covington, WA 98042
United States
Tel: +1 (206) 659-6008

image@imagejournal.org

https://imagejournal.org
http://facebook.com/imagejournal
http://twitter.com/image_journal
https://www.instagram.com/image_journal

Fiction > *Short Fiction*
Culture; Literary; Religion; Spirituality

Nonfiction > *Essays*
Arts; Culture; Literature; Religion; Spirituality

Poetry > *Any Poetic Form*
Culture; Religion; Spirituality

Fosters contemporary art and writing that grapple with the mystery of being human by curating, cultivating, convening, and celebrating work that explores religious faith and faces spiritual questions. A vibrant thread in the fabric of culture, contributing to mainstream literary and artistic communities by demonstrating the vitality of contemporary art and literature invigorated by religious faith.

M196 Indiana Review

Magazine
United States

https://indianareview.iu.edu
https://indianareview.submittable.com/submit
https://twitter.com/indianareview
https://www.facebook.com/IndianaReview

Fiction in Translation > *Short Fiction*: Literary

Fiction > *Short Fiction*: Literary

Nonfiction in Translation > *Essays*

Nonfiction > *Essays*

Poetry in Translation > *Any Poetic Form*

Poetry > *Any Poetic Form*

Send: Full text
Don't send: Query
How to send: Submittable

Costs: A fee is charged upon submission. $3 per submission.

Send fiction or nonfiction up 6,000 words or 3-6 poems (up to 12 pages total) per submission, during specific submission windows only (see website for details). No submissions by post or by email – all submissions must be made through online submission manager ($3 fee). See website for full guidelines, and to submit.

M197 Ink Sweat and Tears

Online Magazine
United Kingdom

submissions@inksweatandtears.co.uk
interns@inksweatandtears.co.uk

https://inksweatandtears.co.uk
https://twitter.com/InkSweatTears
https://www.facebook.com/InkSweatandTears
https://www.instagram.com/insta.inksweatandtears/

Nonfiction > *Reviews*
Literature; Poetry as a Subject

Poetry
Any Poetic Form; *Haibun*; *Haiga*; *Haiku*; *Prose Poetry*

Send: Full text
How to send: Email

UK-based webzine publishing poetry, prose, prose-poetry, word and image pieces, and poetry reviews. Send 4-6 pieces of poetry (or 1-2 short prose/flash fiction works) by email only. Accepts unsolicited reviews of poetry and short story collections. See website for full guidelines.

Editor: Helen Ivory

M198 Inque

Magazine
United Kingdom

info@inquemag.com

https://inquemag.com
http://instagram.com/inquemag
http://twitter.com/inquemagazine

Fiction > *Short Fiction*: Literary

Nonfiction
Articles: Arts; Literature
Interviews: Arts; Literature

Annual literary magazine dedicated to extraordinary new writing. Documenting what is going to be an era-defining decade, it will run no advertising, have no web version, and only ever publish 10 issues. Contributors include Margaret Atwood, Max Porter, Joyce Carol Oates, Ocean Vuong, Tom Waits, Ben Lerner, Alexander Chee, Kae Tempest, and more.

M199 Insurance Age
Online Magazine
Infopro Digital, 133 Houndsditch, London, EC3A 7BX
United Kingdom
Tel: +44 (0) 20 7316 9000
Fax: +44 (0) 20 7681 3401

info@insuranceage.co.uk

https://www.insuranceage.co.uk
https://twitter.com/insuranceage
https://www.linkedin.com/company/insurance-age

PROFESSIONAL > Nonfiction
  Articles: Insurance
  News: Insurance

Publishes news and features on the insurance industry.

M200 International Piano
Magazine
United Kingdom

https://www.markallengroup.com/brands/international-piano/
https://twitter.com/IP_mag
https://www.facebook.com/internationalpiano/
https://www.instagram.com/internationalpianomagazine
https://www.youtube.com/channel/UCOKPU5skkhcvQRjXVkou10Q

Media Company: Mark Allen Group

ACADEMIC > Nonfiction > *Articles*: Piano

ADULT > Nonfiction > *Articles*: Piano

PROFESSIONAL > Nonfiction > *Articles*: Piano

Describes itself as the leading magazine for pianists and piano fans around the world. Wide-ranging reviews and in-depth features meet inspiring practical advice from top performers and teachers in this indispensable guide to the piano in all its forms, published 10 times per year.

Editor: Tim Parry

M201 Interzone
Magazine
United Kingdom

submissions@interzone.press
editors@interzone.press

https://interzone.press
https://interzone.press/submissions/

Magazine Publisher: MYY Press

Fiction in Translation > *Short Fiction*
  Fantasy; Horror; Science Fiction

Fiction > *Short Fiction*
  Fantasy; Horror; Science Fiction

Closed to approaches.

Publishes fantastika (including science fiction, fantasy, and horror) short stories up to 17,500 words. See website for full guidelines.

Editor / Publisher: Gareth Jelley

M202 Ireland's Own
Magazine
Channing House, Rowe Street, Wexford
Ireland
Tel: +353 1 7055 454

submissions@irelandsown.ie
info@irelandsown.ie

https://irelandsown.ie
https://www.facebook.com/irelandsown1902/
https://twitter.com/irelandsown1902

Fiction > *Short Fiction*: Ireland

Nonfiction > *Articles*
  Books; Cookery; Entertainment; Films; Health; History; Ireland; Literature; Science; Sport

How to send: Email

Magazine publishing stories and articles of Irish interest for the whole family, plus puzzles and games.

Editor: Sean Nolan

M203 Irish Pages
Magazine
129 Ormeau Road, Belfast, BT7 1SH
United Kingdom
Tel: +44 (0) 2890 434800

editor@irishpages.org
managingeditor@irishpages.org
sales@irishpages.org
gaeilge@irishpages.org

https://irishpages.org
https://twitter.com/irishpages
https://www.youtube.com/channel/UC08ArKYYmKVUpP5eHfEMz0w

Fiction in Translation > *Short Fiction*

Fiction > *Short Fiction*

Nonfiction in Translation
  Essays: General
  Short Nonfiction: Autobiography; Creative Nonfiction; History; Literary Journalism; Memoir; Nature; Religion; Science
Nonfiction
  Essays: General
  Short Nonfiction: Autobiography; Creative Nonfiction; History; Literary Journalism; Memoir; Nature; Religion; Science
Poetry in Translation > *Any Poetic Form*

Poetry > *Any Poetic Form*

Send: Full text
How to send: Post
How not to send: Email

Non-partisan and non-sectarian literary journal publishing writing from the island of Ireland and elsewhere in equal measure. Publishes work in English, and in the Irish Language or Ulster Scots with English translations or glosses. Accepts submissions throughout the year by post only with stamps, coupons or cash for return postage (no self-addressed envelope is needed). See website for more details.

M204 Island
Magazine
PO Box 4703, Hobart TAS 7000
Australia
Tel: +61 (0) 3 6234 1462

admin@islandmag.com

https://islandmag.com
https://island.submittable.com/submit

Fiction > *Short Fiction*
  General, and in particular: Experimental; Literary

Nonfiction
  Articles; *Essays*
Poetry > *Any Poetic Form*
  General, and in particular: Experimental; Literary

Closed to approaches.

Welcomes submissions of nonfiction, fiction and poetry from Australia, New Zealand and the Pacific, as well as from Australians living abroad. Will consider more traditional forms but has a strong interest in experimental and literary approaches to form and content. See website for details and to submit using online submission system.

Online Magazine: Island Online (**M205**)

M205 Island Online
Online Magazine
Australia

admin@islandmag.com
ben@islandmag.com

https://islandmag.com/online
https://island.submittable.com/submit
http://www.facebook.com/islandmagtas
http://instagram.com/islandmagtas
https://twitter.com/IslandMagTas

Magazine: Island (**M204**)

Fiction > *Short Fiction*
  Arts; Culture; Environment; Experimental; Literary; Nature; Society

Nonfiction > *Essays*
  Arts; Culture; Environment; Nature; Society

Closed to approaches.

Digital publishing platform operated in conjunction with longstanding print magazine.

Will consider more traditional forms but has a strong interest in experimental and literary approaches to form and content.

M206 Jazz Journal
Online Magazine
United Kingdom

editor@jazzjournal.co.uk

https://jazzjournal.co.uk

Nonfiction
Articles: Jazz
News: Jazz
Reviews: Jazz

The oldest English-language magazine dedicated to the coverage of jazz music. Published in print for seven decades and from 2019 as a web-only publication. Provides a rolling jazz news and review service with columns and features added on an ad-hoc, roughly monthly basis. Publishes approximately 70 reviews of newly issued jazz recordings per month.

M207 The Journal
Magazine
38 Pwllcarn Terrace, Blaengarw, Bridgend, CF32 8AS
United Kingdom

asamsmith@hotmail.com

https://thesamsmith.com
https://thesamsmith.com/the-journal/

Nonfiction
Interviews: Poetry as a Subject
Reviews: Poetry as a Subject

Poetry in Translation > *Any Poetic Form*

Poetry > *Any Poetic Form*

Closed to approaches.

Accepts poems in English, or translations into English (about 6 at a time). Also welcome are interviews with poets, reviews, appreciations or appraisals of current poetry scenes. If a reply is desired within the UK, enclose SAE.

Editor: Sam Smith

M208 Kavya Kishor
Online Magazine
Bangladesh

editor.kavyakishor@gmail.com

https://en.kavyakishor.com

Fiction > *Short Fiction*

Nonfiction
Articles; *Essays*; *Interviews*; *Reviews*
Poetry > *Any Poetic Form*

How to send: Email

An online literary magazine of English and Bengali language from Bangladesh.

M209 Kent Life
Magazine
United Kingdom

https://www.greatbritishlife.co.uk/magazines/kent/

Magazine Publisher: Great British Life

Nonfiction > *Articles*
Arts; Celebrity; Countryside; Culture; Food and Drink; Gardening; Houses and Homes; Kent; Lifestyle; Local History; Nature; Recipes; Travel; Walking Guides

Every month you'll find within our pages a wealth of fresh ideas on how you can best explore our area's glorious countryside, beautiful coastline, thriving towns and villages and fascinating history. Whether you want to sample great local food and drink, dip into our exciting arts scene or revel in the glorious natural beauty that surrounds us, we've got suggestions galore. You'll hear Kent voices loud and clear, too, of course, with our top-notch writers highlighting the energy and sheer diversity of our community via their stories and interviews, and our columnists adding their unique take on county life. Add to the mix our inspiring monthly features on gorgeous homes and gardens, our town guides, walk suggestions and fascinating stories from local history, and you've got an unmissable monthly blend of ideas, lifestyle, nature and personalities.

M210 The Kenyon Review
Magazine
102 W. Wiggin St., Gambier, OH 43022
United States
Tel: +1 (740) 427-5208
Fax: +1 (740) 427-5417

kenyonreview@kenyon.edu

https://kenyonreview.org
https://thekenyonreview.submittable.com/submit

Fiction in Translation
Novel Excerpts; *Short Fiction*
Fiction
Novel Excerpts; *Short Fiction*
Nonfiction in Translation > *Essays*

Nonfiction > *Essays*

Poetry in Translation > *Any Poetic Form*

Poetry > *Any Poetic Form*

Scripts > *Theatre Scripts*

Closed to approaches.

Submit through online submission system. Send short fiction up to 7,500 words, poetry up to six poems, or plays or excerpts up to 30 pages. Translations are also accepted, but author is responsible for permissions. No unsolicited interviews, book reviews, or artwork, or submissions by email or post.

M211 Kerning
Magazine
United States

hello@toadhalleditions.ink

https://www.toadhalleditions.ink/kerning-a-space-for-words

Book Publisher / Self Publishing Service / Magazine Publisher: Toad Hall Editions **(P453)**

Fiction > *Short Fiction*

Nonfiction
Essays: General
Short Nonfiction: Creative Nonfiction

Poetry > *Any Poetic Form*

How to send: Email

Costs: Invites donations. Choose to pay $7, $14, or no fee when submitting.

Publishes work by women and gender diverse people only.

M212 Kids Alive!
Magazine
The Salvation Army Territorial Headquarters, 1 Champion Park, London, SE5 8FJ
United Kingdom
Tel: +44 (0) 20 7367 4910

kidsalive@salvationarmy.org.uk

https://www.salvationist.org.uk/media/kidsalive

CHILDREN'S
Fiction > *Cartoons*: Christianity

Nonfiction > *Articles*: Christianity

Christian children's magazine publishing puzzles, comic strips, etc.

M213 The Lake
Online Magazine
United Kingdom

poetry@thelakepoetry.co.uk

http://www.thelakepoetry.co.uk

Poetry > *Any Poetic Form*

Send: Full text; Author bio
How to send: In the body of an email; Word file email attachment

Submit up to five poems within the body of an email or attach one Word document with POETRY SUBMISSION in the Subject line. Please also include a short third person biography (50 words max.). If you have a publication or personal web site then you can also include a link to the site. I will respond to all submissions within two to three weeks. If after that time you haven't heard from me let me know via email.

M214 Lancashire Life
Magazine
United Kingdom

https://www.lancashirelife.co.uk

Magazine Publisher: Great British Life

Nonfiction > *Articles*
Food and Drink; Lancashire; Property / Real Estate; Travel

Publishes articles, features, and pictures of Lancashire.

M215 Landfall
Magazine
Otago University Press, PO Box 56, Dunedin 9054
New Zealand
Tel: +64 (0) 3 479 4155

landfall@otago.ac.nz

https://www.otago.ac.nz/press/landfall/index.html
https://www.facebook.com/landfall.journal
https://twitter.com/landfallnz

Book Publisher: Otago University Press (**P330**)

Fiction > *Short Fiction*: Literary

Nonfiction
Articles: Arts; Culture; New Zealand
Essays: General
Reviews: Books; Local
Poetry > *Any Poetic Form*

Send: Full text; Author bio
How to send: Email

Publishes literary fiction and essays, poetry, extracts from work in progress, commentary on New Zealand arts and culture, work by visual artists including photographers, and reviews of local books.

M216 Leisure Group Travel
Magazine
United States

Jason@ptmgroups.com

https://leisuregrouptravel.com
https://www.facebook.com/LeisureGroupTravel
https://twitter.com/leisuregroup
https://www.linkedin.com/showcase/leisure-group-travel/

PROFESSIONAL > **Nonfiction** > *Articles*
Business; Travel

How to send: Email; Online contact form

Magazine aimed at group travel buyers. Submit news and press releases that relate to the group travel industry by email or through contact form on website.

M217 Leisure Painter
Magazine
The Maltings, West Street, Bourne, Lincolnshire, PE10 9PH
United Kingdom
Tel: +44 (0) 1778 395174

https://www.painters-online.co.uk

Magazine Publisher: Warners Group Publications

Nonfiction > *Articles*: Painting

Magazine offering artistic inspiration, guidance, tuition and encouragement for beginners and amateur artists. Includes features and step-by-step painting and drawing demonstrations.

M218 Lighthouse
Magazine
United Kingdom

subs.lighthouse@gmail.com
lighthouseprosesubmissions@gmail.com

https://storymachines.co.uk/portfolio/lighthouse/

Fiction > *Short Fiction*

Poetry > *Any Poetic Form*

Send: Full text
How to send: Email

A literary journal dedicated to publishing new writing and championing new writers. Aims to publish the best short fiction, poetry, and art emerging from the UK scene. No submissions generated by AI (Artificial Intelligence) or other machine learning means.

M219 The Linguist
Magazine
Chartered Institute of Linguists (CIOL), Thanet House, 231-232 Strand, London, WC2R 1DA
United Kingdom
Tel: +44 (0) 20 7940 3100

info@ciol.org.uk

https://www.ciol.org.uk/the-linguist

PROFESSIONAL > **Nonfiction** > *Articles*: Language

Magazine for language professionals.

M220 Literary Mama
Online Magazine
United States

LMinfo@literarymama.com
LMreviews@literarymama.com
LMnonfiction@literarymama.com
lmfiction@literarymama.com
LMreflections@literarymama.com
lmpoetry@literarymama.com

https://literarymama.com
http://www.facebook.com/litmama
http://twitter.com/literarymama
https://www.instagram.com/literary_mama/

Fiction > *Short Fiction*: Motherhood

Nonfiction
Essays: Creativity; Motherhood; Writing
Reviews: Books; Motherhood
Short Nonfiction: Creative Nonfiction; Motherhood
Poetry > *Any Poetic Form*: Motherhood

Closed to approaches.

Online magazine publishing fiction, poetry, creative nonfiction, and book reviews focusing on mother writers, and the complexities and many faces of motherhood. Accepts submissions in the text of emails only – no snail mail submissions. See website for full submission guidelines. Contact again if no response after three months.

M221 Litro Magazine
Magazine
90 York Way, London, N1 9AG
United Kingdom
Tel: +44 (0) 207 917 2887

editor@litro.co.uk
online@litro.co.uk
podcasts@litro.co.uk

https://www.litro.co.uk
https://www.facebook.com/Litromedia/
https://open.spotify.com/show/78fpfD5ejecJXXdsVHGJqb
https://www.instagram.com/litromedia/
https://twitter.com/litromagazine

Fiction > *Short Fiction*

Nonfiction > *Short Nonfiction*
Literary Journalism; Memoir; Travel

How to send: Submittable
How not to send: Email

Accepts short fiction, flash/micro fiction, nonfiction (memoir, literary journalism, travel narratives, etc), and original artwork (photographs, illustrations, paintings, etc) based on the designated monthly theme. Works translated into English are also welcome. See website for upcoming themes.

M222 London Grip
Online Magazine
United Kingdom

editor@londongrip.co.uk

https://londongrip.co.uk

Nonfiction
Articles: General, and in particular: Arts; Culture
Reviews: Books; Drama

How to send: Email

A wholly independent online cultural omnibus offering intelligent reviews of current shows, events and books and providing space for well-argued articles on a wide range of topics. Intended to act as an exhibition space for cross-media arts and includes an in-house poetry magazine with its own editor. The site's name reflects its place of origin rather than signalling any wish to focus on one city.

Online Magazine: London Grip New Poetry (**M223**)

M223 London Grip New Poetry
Online Magazine
United Kingdom

poetry@londongrip.co.uk

https://londongrip.co.uk

Online Magazine: London Grip (**M222**)

Nonfiction
  Articles: Poetry as a Subject
  Reviews: Poetry as a Subject

Poetry > *Any Poetic Form*

How to send: Email

Quarterly online poetry magazine. Poetry may be submitted in December/January, March/April, June/July, or September/October. Proposals for poetry reviews (or other articles on poetry) may be submitted at any time.

M224 The London Magazine
Magazine
11 Queen's Gate, London, SW7 5EL
United Kingdom
Tel: +44 (0) 20 7584 5977

editorial@thelondonmagazine.org
admin@thelondonmagazine.org

https://thelondonmagazine.org
https://thelondonmagazine.submittable.com/submit
https://www.facebook.com/thelondonmagazine1732/
https://twitter.com/thelondonmag
https://www.instagram.com/thelondonmagazine/?hl=en

Fiction > *Short Fiction*

Nonfiction > *Short Nonfiction*

Poetry > *Any Poetic Form*

Does not want:

> **Fiction** > *Short Fiction*
> Erotic; Fantasy; Science Fiction

Send: Full text
How to send: Submittable
How not to send: Post

Costs: A fee is charged upon submission in some cases. £3 fee per submission every other month. Free submissions in September, November, January, March, May, and July.

Send submissions through online submission system. Does not normally publish science fiction or fantasy writing, or erotica. No submissions by post. See website for full guidelines.

M225 London Review of Books
Magazine
28 Little Russell Street, London, WC1A 2HN
United Kingdom
Tel: +44 (0) 20 7209 1101

edit@lrb.co.uk

https://www.lrb.co.uk
https://www.facebook.com/LondonReviewOfBooks
https://twitter.com/lrb
https://www.youtube.com/londonreviewofbooks
https://www.instagram.com/londonreviewofbooks/

Nonfiction
  Articles: Anthropology; Arts; Biography; Classics / Ancient World; Culture; Economics; History; Legal; Literary Criticism; Literature; Memoir; Philosophy; Politics; Psychology; Science; Technology
  Reviews: General

Poetry > *Any Poetic Form*

Send: Full text; Proposal; Self-Addressed Stamped Envelope (SASE)
How to send: Email; Post

Publishes poems, reviews, reportage, memoir, articles, and blogposts. Send submissions by email or by post (with SAE).

M226 Long Poem Magazine
Magazine
20 Spencer Rise, London, NW5 1AP
United Kingdom

longpoemmagazine@gmail.com

http://longpoemmagazine.org.uk
https://www.facebook.com/groups/longpoemmagazine/
https://twitter.com/LongPoemMag

Nonfiction
  Essays: Poetry as a Subject
  Reviews: Books

Poetry > *Long Form Poetry*

Magazine dedicated to publishing long poems and sequences. Publishes unpublished poems of at least 75 lines (but no book length poems). Also publishes essays on aspects of the long poem and reviews of books featuring long poems or sequences. Send submissions by email as Word file attachments. Does not accept poems submitted in the body of emails. See website for full guidelines and submission months. Poems submitted outside submission months will be discarded.

M227 Lost Lake Folk Opera Magazine
Print Magazine
United States

https://shipwrecktbooks.press
https://shipwrecktbooks.submittable.com/submit

Book Publisher: Shipwreckt Books Publishing Company (**P406**)

Fiction > *Short Fiction*

Nonfiction > *Essays*

Poetry > *Any Poetic Form*

Scripts > *Theatre Scripts*

Send: Full text; Author bio
How to send: Submittable

Literary magazine published twice annually. Accepts short fiction (1000-6000 wds); one-act and other short plays or scenes (1000-6000 wds); essays and opinion (500-300 wds); poetry (no more than 10 poems or 10 pages).

M228 Louisiana Literature
Magazine
United States

lalit@selu.edu

http://www.louisianaliterature.org
https://twitter.com/LaLiterature
https://louisianaliterature.submittable.com/submit

Fiction > *Short Fiction*: Literary

Nonfiction > *Essays*: Creative Nonfiction

Poetry > *Any Poetic Form*

Send: Full text
How to send: Submittable

Literary journal publishing fiction, poetry, and creative nonfiction. Submit via online system available at the website.

Editor: Dr Jack Bedell

M229 The MacGuffin
Magazine
Schoolcraft College, 18600 Haggerty Road, Livonia, MI 48152
United States
Tel: +1 (734) 462-5327

macguffin@schoolcraft.edu

https://schoolcraft.edu/macguffin
https://themacguffin.submittable.com/submit

Fiction > *Short Fiction*

Nonfiction > *Short Nonfiction*: Creative Nonfiction

Poetry
  Any Poetic Form; *Experimental Poetry*; *Free Verse*

Send: Full text
How to send: Submittable

Publishes fiction, creative nonfiction, and poetry. Submit up to five poems or up to two pieces of prose via online submission system.

M230 The Magazine of Fantasy & Science Fiction
Magazine
PO Box 3447, Hoboken, NJ 07030
United States

fsfmag@fandsf.com

http://fandsf.com
https://fandsf.moksha.io/publication/fsf

Fiction > *Short Fiction*
  Fantasy; Science Fiction

Send: Full text; Self-Addressed Stamped Envelope (SASE)
How to send: Moksha; Post

We have no formula for fiction, but we like to be surprised by stories, either by the character insights, ideas, plots, or prose. The speculative element may be slight, but it should be present. We prefer character-oriented stories, whether it's fantasy, science fiction, horror, humor, or another genre. We encourage submissions from diverse voices and perspectives, and have published writers from all over the world. Do not query for fiction; submit the entire manuscript. We publish fiction up to 25,000 words in length. Please read the magazine before submitting. A sample copy (print edition) is available for $7.00 in the US and $17.50 elsewhere (to NJ address).

We do not accept simultaneous submissions. Please prepare your submission according to standard guidelines. If you're mailing your manuscript, put your name on each page, and enclose a self-addressed, stamped envelope. Writers are encouraged to submit their work electronically.

We prefer not to see more than one submission from a writer at a time.

Allow 8 weeks for a response.

Payment is 8-12 cents per word on acceptance. We buy first North American and foreign serial rights and an option on anthology rights. All other rights are retained by the author.

Our columns and non-fiction articles are assigned in-house. We do not accept freelance submissions in those areas.

M231 Magma
Magazine
23 Pine Walk, Carshalton, SM5 4ES
United Kingdom

info@magmapoetry.com
reviews@magmapoetry.com

https://magmapoetry.com
https://magmapoetry.submittable.com/submit
https://www.facebook.com/MagmaPoetry/

Nonfiction > *Reviews*: Poetry as a Subject

Poetry > *Any Poetic Form*

Closed to approaches.

Each issue has a different theme and different editors. The editorship circulates among the group that runs the magazine, with frequent guest editors. This allows for greater diversity of editorship, opportunities for mentoring new editors and publication of a very wide range of work.

Editor: Laurie Smith

M232 The Malahat Review
Magazine
Clearihue Bldg, Rm C318, University of Victoria, P.O. Box 1700, Stn CSC, Victoria, B.C. V8W 2Y2
Canada

malahat@uvic.ca

http://www.malahatreview.ca
https://twitter.com/malahatreview

Fiction > *Short Fiction*

Nonfiction
  Essays: Personal Essays
  Reviews: Books
  Short Nonfiction: Biography; Creative Nonfiction; History; Memoir; Narrative Nonfiction; Social Commentary; Travel

Poetry > *Any Poetic Form*

How to send: Submittable

Publishes poetry, short fiction, and creative nonfiction by new and established writers mostly from Canada, reviews of Canadian books, and the best writing from abroad. Submissions from Canadian writers are accepted year-round. Fiction and poetry submissions from international writers only accepted during specific windows.

M233 Manoa
Magazine
United States

manoaeds@hawaii.edu

https://manoajournal.org
https://www.instagram.com/manoa_journal/
https://www.facebook.com/manoajournal/
https://twitter.com/manoajournal

ACADEMIC > **Nonfiction** > *Essays*
  Asia; Culture; Literature; Pacific

ADULT
  Fiction in Translation > *Short Fiction*
    Asia; Pacific

  Fiction > *Short Fiction*
    Asia; Pacific

  Poetry in Translation > *Any Poetic Form*
    Asia; Pacific

  Poetry > *Any Poetic Form*
    Asia; Pacific

Closed to approaches.

A Pacific journal, however material does not need to be related to the Pacific, or by authors from the region.

M234 marie claire
Magazine
United States

pr@futurenet.com

https://www.marieclaire.com
https://www.facebook.com/MarieClaire
https://twitter.com/marieclaire
https://www.pinterest.com/MarieClaire
https://instagram.com/marieclairemag
https://www.youtube.com/c/MarieClaire

Magazine Publisher: Future

Nonfiction > *Articles*
  Beauty; Career Development; Celebrity; Culture; Fashion; Finance; Fitness; Food and Drink; Health; Horoscopes; Politics; Relationships; Sex; Travel; Women's Interests

Lifestyle magazine aimed at the younger working woman.

M235 marie claire (UK)
Magazine
Future PLC, 121 – 141 Westbourne Terrace, Paddington, London, W2 6JR
United Kingdom

https://www.marieclaire.co.uk
https://www.facebook.com/MarieClaireUK/
https://twitter.com/marieclaireuk
https://www.pinterest.co.uk/marieclaireuk/
https://www.instagram.com/marieclaireuk/

Magazine Publisher: Future

Nonfiction > *Articles*
  Beauty; Celebrity; Entertainment; Fashion; Hairstyles; Health; Lifestyle; Relationships; Sex

Glossy magazine for women.

M236 Marlin
Magazine
PO Box 8500, Winter Park, FL 32790-8500
United States

editor@marlinmag.com

https://www.marlinmag.com
https://www.facebook.com/marlinmag
https://twitter.com/MarlinMagazine
http://instagram.com/marlinmag/
http://www.youtube.com/MarlinMagazine/

Nonfiction > *Articles*
  Boats; How To; Offshore Gamefishing; Travel

Publishes articles, features, and news items relating to offshore fishing, destinations, personalities, fishery regulations, the boating industry and related topics, including how-to and technical information.

M237 The Massachusetts Review

Magazine
400 Venture Way, Hadley, MA 01035
United States
Tel: +1 (413) 545-2689
Fax: +1 (413) 577-0740

massrev@external.umass.edu

http://www.massreview.org
https://www.facebook.com/pages/The-Massachusetts-Review/40580092594
https://twitter.com/MassReview
http://instagram.com/themassachusettsreview?ref=badge
http://themassreview.tumblr.com/

Fiction in Translation > *Short Fiction*: Literary

Fiction > *Short Fiction*: Literary

Nonfiction in Translation > *Essays*
  Arts; Current Affairs; Drama; Literature; Music; Philosophy; Science

Nonfiction
  Articles: Arts; Current Affairs; Drama; Literature; Music; Philosophy; Science
  Essays: Arts; Current Affairs; Drama; Literature; Music; Philosophy; Science

Poetry in Translation > *Any Poetic Form*

Poetry > *Any Poetic Form*

Send: Full text; Self-Addressed Stamped Envelope (SASE)
How to send: Post; Online submission system; Email

Costs: A fee is charged for online submissions. $3.

Send one story of up to 25–30 pages or up to six poems of any length (though rarely publishes poems of more than 100 lines). White people may not submit between May 1 and September 30. Others may submit year-round, and may use email if the online submission system is closed. White people are not permitted to submit by email. Articles and essays of breadth and depth are considered, as well as discussions of leading writers; of art, music, and drama; analyses of trends in literature, science, philosophy, and public affairs. No plays, reviews of single books, or submissions by fax or email.

M238 Meetinghouse

Magazine
United States

submissions@meetinghousemag.org

https://www.meetinghousemag.org
https://twitter.com/meethousemag

Fiction > *Short Fiction*

Poetry > *Any Poetic Form*

Closed to approaches.

A literary magazine that provides a space for diverse voices to speak with one another. Submit up to two pieces of prose and up to five poems per submission.

M239 Metropolis Magazine

Magazine
United States
Tel: +1 (212) 934-2800

info@metropolismag.com

https://www.metropolismag.com/
https://www.facebook.com/MetropolisMag
https://metropoliseditorialaccount.submittable.com/submit
https://twitter.com/MetropolisMag
https://www.linkedin.com/company/metropolis-magazine
https://www.instagram.com/metropolismag/

Magazine Publisher: Sandow

Nonfiction > *Articles*
  Architecture; Arts; City and Town Planning; Culture; Design; Interior Design; Sustainable Living; Technology

Send: Pitch
How to send: Submittable

Magazine examining contemporary life through design: architecture, interior design, product design, graphic design, crafts, planning, and preservation.

M240 Michigan Quarterly Review

Magazine
3277 Angell Hall, 435 S. State Street, Ann Arbor, MI 48109-1003
United States
Tel: +1 (734) 764-9265

mqr@umich.edu

https://sites.lsa.umich.edu/mqr/
https://mqr.submittable.com/submit

Fiction in Translation > *Short Fiction*

Fiction > *Short Fiction*

Nonfiction
  Articles; *Essays*

Poetry in Translation > *Any Poetic Form*

Poetry > *Any Poetic Form*

Closed to approaches.

Costs: A fee is charged upon submission. $3 submission fee.

An interdisciplinary and international literary journal, combining distinctive voices in poetry, fiction, and nonfiction, as well as works in translation.

Online Magazine: MQR Mixtape (**M248**)

M241 Mid-American Review

Magazine
Department of English, Bowling Green State University, Bowling Green, OH 43403
United States
Tel: +1 (419) 372-2725

mar@bgsu.edu

https://casit.bgsu.edu/midamericanreview/

Fiction in Translation > *Short Fiction*: Literary

Fiction > *Short Fiction*: Literary

Nonfiction
  Essays: General
  Reviews: Books

Poetry in Translation > *Any Poetic Form*

Poetry > *Any Poetic Form*

How to send: Online submission system; Post

Accepts fiction, poetry, translations, and nonfiction (including personal essays, essays on writing, and short reviews). Submit by post with SASE or through online submission system.

M242 Midsummer Dream House

Magazine
4833 Santa Monica Ave #7341, San Diego, CA 92167
United States
Tel: +1 (619) 438 5129

editor@midsummerdream.house

https://midsummerdream.house
https://twitter.com/msdreamhouse
https://instagram.com/midsummerdream.house
https://midsummerdreamhouse.tumblr.com/
https://www.facebook.com/midsummerdream.house/

Fiction > *Short Fiction*
  Avant-Garde; Contemporary; Experimental; Literary; Traditional

Nonfiction > *Short Nonfiction*
  Avant-Garde; Contemporary; Experimental; Literary; Traditional

Poetry > *Any Poetic Form*
  Avant-Garde; Contemporary; Experimental; Literary; Traditional

Send: Full text
How to send: Email

An independent literary and arts magazine based in San Diego, California, that includes a wide variety of artistic and thought-provoking work, including the experimental and avant-garde.

M243 Midway Journal

Online Magazine; Editorial Service
United States

editors@midwayjournal.com

https://midwayjournal.com
https://www.facebook.com/midway.journal
https://twitter.com/MidwayJournal

https://www.instagram.com/the_midway_journal_/

Fiction > *Short Fiction*

Nonfiction
Essays: General
Interviews: General
Short Nonfiction: Creative Nonfiction

Poetry > *Any Poetic Form*

Send: Full text
How to send: Submittable

Costs: A fee is charged; Offers services that writers have to pay for. $2.50 for expedited submissions, available year-round. Free submissions during specific windows only. Also offers editorial services.

Aims to act as a bridge between aesthetics (and coasts), and create an engaging sense of place. Publishes work that aims to complicate and question the boundaries of genre, binary, and perspective. It offers surprises and ways of re-seeing, re-thinking, and re-feeling.

Fiction Editor: Ralph Pennel

Nonfiction Editor: Allie Mariano

Poetry Editor: Samantha Sharp

M244 MiniWorld Magazine
Magazine
The Granary, Downs Court, Yalding Hill,
Yalding, Kent, ME18 6AL
United Kingdom
Tel: +44 (0) 1959 543747

https://shop.kelsey.co.uk/miniworld-magazine
http://www.facebook.com/miniworldmagazine
https://twitter.com/MagMiniWorld

Magazine Publisher: Kelsey Media

Nonfiction > *Articles*: Mini Cars

Magazine devoted to the mini, including technical advice, tuning, restoration, social history, maintenance, etc.

M245 The Missouri Review
Magazine
453 McReynolds Hall, University of Missouri,
Columbia, MO 65211
United States

question@moreview.com

https://www.missourireview.com
https://www.facebook.com/themissourireview
https://twitter.com/missouri_review
https://www.instagram.com/themissourireview/

Fiction > *Short Fiction*

Nonfiction
Essays: General
Reviews: Books

Poetry > *Any Poetic Form*

Does not want:

Nonfiction > *Essays*: Literary Criticism

Send: Query; Self-Addressed Stamped Envelope (SASE); Full text
How to send: Post; Online submission system

Costs: A fee is charged for online submissions. $4 submission fee for online submissions.

Publishes poetry, fiction, and essays of general interest. No literary criticism. Submit by post with SASE, or via online system. There is a $4 charge for online submissions. Also considers omnibus reviews of 3-6 recently published books that share a common feature or address a similar topic. Especially interested in essays that respond to books from smaller presses and/or emerging authors

Editor: Speer Morgan

M246 Modern Poetry in Translation
Magazine
United Kingdom

editor@mptmagazine.com

http://modernpoetryintranslation.com
https://twitter.com/MPTmagazine
https://www.instagram.com/modernpoetryintranslation/

Poetry in Translation > *Any Poetic Form*

Send: Full text
How to send: Submittable

Respected poetry series originally founded by prominent poets in the sixties. New Series continues their editorial policy: translation of good poets by translators who are often themselves poets, fluent in the foreign language, and sometimes working with the original poet. Publishes translations into English only. No original English language poetry. Send submissions via online submission system.

M247 Moving Worlds: A Journal of Transcultural Writings
Magazine
School of English, University of Leeds, Leeds,
LS2 9JT
United Kingdom
Tel: +44 (0) 1133 434792
Fax: +44 (0) 1133 434774

mworlds@leeds.ac.uk

http://www.movingworlds.net
https://twitter.com/Moving_Worlds

ACADEMIC > **Nonfiction** > *Essays*
Culture; Literary Criticism; Literature; Multicultural

ADULT
Fiction in Translation > *Short Fiction*
General, and in particular: Experimental

Fiction > *Short Fiction*
General, and in particular: Experimental

Poetry in Translation > *Any Poetic Form*
General, and in particular: Experimental

Poetry > *Any Poetic Form*
General, and in particular: Experimental

Biannual international magazine for creative work as well as criticism, literary as well as visual texts, writing in scholarly as well as more personal modes, in English and translations into English. It is open to experimentation, and represents work of different kinds and from different cultural traditions. Its central concern is the transcultural.

Editors: Shirley Chew; Stuart Murray

M248 MQR Mixtape
Online Magazine
United States

https://sites.lsa.umich.edu/mqr/mqr-mixtape/
https://mqr.submittable.com/submit

Magazine: Michigan Quarterly Review (M240)

Fiction > *Short Fiction*

Poetry > *Any Poetic Form*

How to send: Submittable

Costs: A fee is charged upon submission. $3 submission fee.

An eclectic, online zine guest curated by university graduate students.

M249 My Weekly
Magazine
D C Thomson & Co Ltd, My Weekly, 2 Albert Square, Dundee, DD1 1DD
United Kingdom
Tel: +44 (0) 1382 223131

swatson@dcthomson.co.uk
kirstyn.smith@dcthomson.co.uk

https://www.myweekly.co.uk/
https://www.facebook.com/My-Weekly-199671216711852/
http://twitter.com/My_Weekly
https://www.instagram.com/my_weekly_magazine/

Newspaper Publisher / Magazine Publisher: DC Thomson Media

Fiction > *Short Fiction*

Nonfiction > *Articles*
Beauty; Cookery; Crafts; Fashion; Films; Food and Drink; Gardening; Health; Lifestyle; Personal Finance; Real Life Stories; TV; Travel; Women's Interests

Weekly women's magazine aged at the over-50s, publishing a mix of lifestyle features, true life stories, and fiction.

M250 Mystery Magazine
Magazine
United States

https://www.mysteryweekly.com
https://www.facebook.com/MysteryWeekly
https://twitter.com/MysteryWeekly
https://www.instagram.com/mystery_magazine/
https://www.linkedin.com/in/mystery-magazine-85598110a/

Fiction > *Short Fiction*: Mystery

Closed to approaches.

Submit mysteries between 2,500 and 7,500 words through online submission system available on website. No multiple submissions.

M251 Nashville Review
Magazine
United States

thenashvillereview@gmail.com
https://as.vanderbilt.edu/nashvillereview

Fiction in Translation > *Short Fiction*

Fiction
  Comics; *Short Fiction*
Nonfiction in Translation
  Essays: General
  Short Nonfiction: Creative Nonfiction; Memoir
Nonfiction
  Essays: General
  Short Nonfiction: Creative Nonfiction; Memoir
Poetry in Translation > *Any Poetic Form*

Poetry > *Any Poetic Form*

Send: Query; Author bio; Full text
How to send: Submittable

Submit short stories and novel excerpts up to 8,000 words, or three flash fiction pieces (1,000 words each), 1-3 poems (up to ten pages total), or creative nonfiction including memoir excerpts, essays, imaginative meditations, up to 8,000 words, via online submission system during the two annual reading periods: August and January. Art and comic submissions are accepted year-round. Looking for anything from one-page comics to excerpts from graphic novels, but no single-frame cartoons.

M252 NB Magazine
Magazine
United Kingdom

editor@nbmagazine.co.uk
https://nbmagazine.co.uk

Nonfiction > *Articles*: Book Publishing

Magazine and online platform for book lovers, book clubs and all round bibliophiles. Publishes articles and features on books and the book trade, as well as extracts from books.

M253 Neon
Magazine
United Kingdom

subs@neonmagazine.co.uk
https://www.neonmagazine.co.uk

Fiction > *Short Fiction*
  Dark; Literary; Speculative; Surreal

Poetry
  Any Poetic Form: Dark; Literary; Surreal
  Graphic Poems: Dark; Literary; Surreal

Closed to approaches.

Quarterly online magazine publishing stylised poetry and prose, particularly the new, experimental, and strange. Welcomes genre fiction. Dark material preferred over humour; free verse preferred over rhyme. Send work pasted into the body of an email with a biographical note and the word "Submission" in the subject line.

Editor: Krishan Coupland

M254 The New Accelerator
Online Magazine
United Kingdom

https://newaccelerator.substack.com

Fiction > *Short Fiction*: Science Fiction

Digital science fiction short story anthology. The aim of the anthology is to bring cutting-edge fiction to an eager and discerning global science fiction audience.

M255 New England Review
Magazine
Middlebury College, Middlebury, VT 05753
United States
Tel: +1 (802) 443-5075

nereview@middlebury.edu

https://www.nereview.com
https://newenglandreview.submittable.com/submit
https://www.facebook.com/NewEnglandReviewMiddlebury/
https://twitter.com/nerweb

Fiction
  Novel Excerpts; *Novellas*; *Short Fiction*
Nonfiction in Translation > *Essays*

Nonfiction
  Essays: Personal Essays
  Short Nonfiction: Arts; Cultural Criticism; Environment; Films; Literary Criticism; Travel
Poetry > *Any Poetic Form*

Scripts > *Theatre Scripts*: Drama

Closed to approaches.

Costs: A fee is charged for online submissions. $3 per submission.

Welcomes submissions in fiction, poetry, nonfiction, drama, and translation. Different submission windows for different categories of work. See website for details.

M256 New Internationalist
Magazine
United Kingdom

https://newint.org
https://twitter.com/newint
https://www.facebook.com/newint
https://www.instagram.com/newinternationalist

Nonfiction
  Articles: Civil Rights; Environment; Feminism; Politics; Social Issues; Social Justice
  News: Civil Rights; Environment; Feminism; Politics; Social Issues; Social Justice

How to send: Online submission system

Independent, non-profit magazine that has been producing in-depth journalism on human rights, politics, and social and environmental justice since 1973. Welcomes pitches for articles: stories range from features on under-covered topics around the world, important social movements and struggles in the fight for global justice, to radical opinion pieces with an international – or internationalist – perspective, making interesting and original arguments you wouldn't see elsewhere. Topics span social justice, global inequality, the environment, feminism and liberatory struggles, tech politics and more. Generally publishes articles of between 800-2000 words in length. Occasionally publishes investigative reports and in-depth features of up to 5000 words.

Editors: Vanessa Baird; Chris Brazier; Dinyar Godrej; David Ransom

M257 New Orleans Review
Online Magazine
United States

noreview@loyno.edu

https://www.neworleansreview.org
https://www.facebook.com/neworleans.review/
https://twitter.com/NOReview

Fiction > *Short Fiction*: Literary

Nonfiction
  Reviews: Literature
  Short Nonfiction: General

Poetry > *Any Poetic Form*

Send: Full text
How to send: Submittable

Costs: A fee is charged upon submission. $3 per submission.

A journal of contemporary literature and culture. Send one story or piece of nonfiction up to 5,000 words, or up to five poems via online submission system.

M258 New Statesman

Magazine
Studio 5 Salters House, 156 High Street, Hull, HU1 1NQ
United Kingdom

comments@newstatesman.co.uk

https://www.newstatesman.com
https://www.facebook.com/NewStatesman/
https://twitter.com/newstatesman
https://www.linkedin.com/company/new-statesman/
https://www.instagram.com/newstatesman

Nonfiction > *Articles*
Arts; Books; Business; Culture; Current Affairs; Politics

Describes itself as the leading progressive political and cultural magazine in the United Kingdom. Founded as a weekly review of politics and literature in 1913, it has notably recognised and published new writers and critics, as well as encouraged notable careers. Today, it is a vibrant print-digital hybrid.

Author / Editor-in-Chief: Jason Cowley

M259 New Welsh Reader

Print Magazine
PO Box 170, Aberystwyth, Ceredigion, SY23 1WZ
United Kingdom
Tel: +44 (0) 1970 628410

https://newwelshreview.com/new-welsh-reader
https://newwelshreview.com/about-us/submissions/submit-your-short-prose-and-fiction
https://newwelshreview.com/about-us/submissions/submit-your-poetry

Fiction > *Short Fiction*: Literary

Nonfiction
Essays: General
Short Nonfiction: Creative Nonfiction

Poetry > *Any Poetic Form*

Send: Full text
How to send: Online submission system

Focus is on Welsh writing in English, but has an outlook which is deliberately diverse, encompassing broader UK and international contexts. Submit through online submission system. Full details available on website.

Editor: Gwen Davies

M260 Norfolk & Suffolk Bride

Print Magazine
United Kingdom

https://www.greatbritishlife.co.uk/magazines/bride/

Magazine Publisher: Great British Life

Nonfiction > *Articles*
Fashion; Norfolk; Suffolk; Weddings

For engaged couples in the region. Filled with inspiration, information and advice, this annual publication is geared towards planning your wedding the local way. From fashion features and expert articles, to real weddings and venue listings, it makes easy work of your wedmin by providing everything you need to plan the perfect day. Glean ideas for your wedding in every aspect and connect with the local suppliers who can bring your vision to life.

M261 Norfolk Magazine

Magazine
United Kingdom

Magazine Publisher: Great British Life

M262 The North

Magazine
The Poetry Business, Campo House, 54 Campo Lane, Sheffield, S1 2EG
United Kingdom
Tel: +44 (0) 1144 384074

office@poetrybusiness.co.uk

https://poetrybusiness.co.uk

Poetry > *Any Poetic Form*: Contemporary

Closed to approaches.

Send up to 6 poems with SASE / return postage. We publish the best of contemporary poetry. No "genre" or derivative poetry. Submitters should be aware of, should preferably have read, the magazine before submitting. See our website for notes on submitting poems. No submissions by email. Overseas submissions may be made through online submission system.

Editors: Ann Sansom; Peter Sansom

M263 Northern Gravy

Magazine
United Kingdom

info@northerngravy.com
Submissions@NorthernGravy.com

https://northerngravy.com
https://www.facebook.com/NorthernGravy/
https://x.com/NorthGravy
https://www.instagram.com/northerngravy/

ADULT
Fiction > *Short Fiction*
Poetry > *Any Poetic Form*

CHILDREN'S > **Fiction** > *Short Fiction*

YOUNG ADULT > **Fiction** > *Short Fiction*

Closed to approaches.

Accepts submissions over three areas: Fiction, Poetry and Kid Lit (writing for Middle Grade and Young Adult audiences), from writers either born or currently residing in the UK or Ireland. Submit one story or up to four poems.

M264 The Oakland Arts Review

Magazine
United States

ouartsreview@oakland.edu

https://oar.submittable.com/submit
http://www.facebook.com/oarjournal
https://twitter.com/OARjournal
http://www.instagram.com/oaklandartsreview/

Fiction
Cartoons: Literary
Graphic Novels: Literary
Short Fiction: Literary

Nonfiction
Graphic Nonfiction: Memoir
Short Nonfiction: Creative Nonfiction

Poetry
Experimental Poetry; Formal Poetry; Free Verse
Scripts
Film Scripts; Radio Scripts; TV Scripts; Theatre Scripts

Send: Full text
How to send: Submittable

Literary journal publishing work by undergraduates around the world. Publishes fiction between 10 and 15 double spaced pages; creative nonfiction between 7 and 10 double spaced pages; comics of high literary quality; screenwriting; and both free verse and formal poetry (submit 3-5 poems). Submit through online submission system via website.

M265 Obsidian: Literature in the African Diaspora

Magazine
Illinois State University, Williams Hall Annex, Normal, IL 61790
United States

https://obsidianlit.org
https://obsidian.submittable.com/submit

Fiction > *Short Fiction*: African Diaspora

Poetry > *Any Poetic Form*: African Diaspora

Scripts > *Theatre Scripts*: African Diaspora

Send: Full text
How to send: Submittable

Publishes scripts, fiction, and poetry focused on Africa and her Diaspora. See website for submission guidelines and to submit via online submission system.

M266 OK! Magazine

Magazine
One Canada Square, Canary Wharf, London, E14 5AB

United Kingdom
Tel: +44 (0) 20 7293 3000

https://www.ok.co.uk

Magazine Publisher: Reach Magazines Publishing

Nonfiction
  Articles: Lifestyle; Women's Interests
  Interviews: Celebrity
  News: Celebrity

Celebrity magazine, welcoming ideas for features and interviews/pictures of celebrities.

Editor-in-Chief: Caroline Waterston

M267 Old Red Kimono
Magazine
Georgia Highlands College, 3175 Cedartown Hwy SE, Rome, GA 30161
United States

ORK@highlands.edu

https://sites.highlands.edu/old-red-kimono/

Fiction > *Short Fiction*

Poetry > *Any Poetic Form*

Send: Full text
How to send: Email

Annual student-edited literary magazine. Send 3-5 poems or short stories up to 2,000 words by post or by email. Submissions from contributors outside the university are considered between October and February each year.

Editor: Steven Godfrey

M268 On Spec
Magazine
Canada

onspecmag@gmail.com

https://www.onspec.ca

Fiction > *Short Fiction*
  Fantasy; Horror; Science Fiction; Speculative

Poetry > *Any Poetic Form*
  Fantasy; Horror; Science Fiction; Speculative

Closed to approaches.

Publishes speculative writing of all kinds, but nothing derivative. Try to avoid what you think are trends.

M269 Orbis International Literary Journal
Magazine
17 Greenhow Avenue, West Kirby, Wirral, CH48 5EL
United Kingdom

carolebaldock@hotmail.com

http://www.orbisjournal.com

Fiction in Translation > *Short Fiction*

Fiction > *Short Fiction*

Nonfiction > *Articles*
Poetry in Translation
  Any Poetic Form; *Prose Poetry*
Poetry
  Any Poetic Form; *Prose Poetry*

Send: Query; Full text; Author bio; Self-Addressed Stamped Envelope (SASE)
How to send: Post; International Email
How not to send: Domestic Email; Email attachment

Send four poems or prose up to 1,000 words by post with SASE. No submissions by email, unless from overseas, in which case two submissions maximum and no attachments.

Editor: Carole Baldock

M270 Oxford Poetry
Magazine
c/o Partus Press, 266 Banbury Road, Oxford, OX2 7DL
United Kingdom

editors@oxfordpoetry.co.uk
reviews@oxfordpoetry.co.uk

https://www.oxfordpoetry.com
https://www.instagram.com/oxford_poetry
https://www.facebook.com/OxfordPoetryMag/
https://twitter.com/oxfordpoetry

Book Publisher / Magazine Publisher: Partus Press

Nonfiction
  Articles: Literature
  Essays: Literature
  Interviews: Literature
  Reviews: Literature

Poetry in Translation > *Any Poetic Form*

Poetry > *Any Poetic Form*

How to send: Submittable

Costs: A fee is charged upon submission. £3 submission fee.

Publishes poems, interviews, reviews, and essays. Accepts unpublished poems on any theme and of any length during specific biannual submission windows, which are announced on the website. Send up to four poems by email. See website for full details. To suggest a book for review, email the reviews editor.

M271 Oxford Review of Books
Print Magazine; Online Magazine
Radcliffe Humanities Building, Radcliffe Observatory Quarter, Woodstock Road, Oxford, OX2 6GG
United Kingdom

orbeditor@gmail.com
orbpoetry@gmail.com

https://www.the-orb.org
https://www.facebook.com/this.is.the.ORB/
https://twitter.com/oxreviewofbooks
https://www.instagram.com/oxfordreviewofbooks/

Fiction > *Short Fiction*

Nonfiction
  Essays: Current Affairs
  Interviews: Activism; Classics / Ancient World; History; Philosophy; Poetry as a Subject; Politics
  Reviews: Books; Culture; Films; TV
Poetry > *Any Poetic Form*

Send: Pitch; Full text
How to send: Email

Publishes reviews of films, books, TV shows (think culture in the broadest sense); interviews with politicians, actors, philosophers, historians, poets, classicists, and activists; essays that provide a new and fresh take on current affairs; and poetry and fiction. Submit 3-4 poems, or pitches for prose, by email. Pitches are accepted on a rolling basis for online, and during specific windows for print. See website for more details.

M272 Oyez Review
Magazine
United States

oyezreview@gmail.com

https://medium.com/oyez-review/
https://www.facebook.com/OyezReview

Fiction > *Short Fiction*: Literary

Nonfiction > *Short Nonfiction*: Creative Nonfiction

Poetry > *Any Poetic Form*

An award-winning literary magazine published annually. There are no restrictions on style, theme, or subject matter. Though we consider it part of our mission to publish undiscovered writers, we also have a strong tradition of publishing some of today's best writers, including Charles Bukowski, James McManus, Carla Panciera, Sandra Kohler, and Saul Bennett.

Editor: Janet Wondra

M273 Pacifica Literary Review
Online Magazine
Seattle, WA
United States

pacificalitreview@gmail.com

http://www.pacificareview.com
https://pacificaliteraryreview.submittable.com/submit
https://www.facebook.com/PacificaLiteraryReview
https://twitter.com/PacificaReview

Fiction
  Novel Excerpts; *Short Fiction*
Nonfiction > *Short Nonfiction*: Creative Nonfiction

Poetry > *Any Poetic Form*

Send: Full text
How to send: Submittable

Costs: A fee is charged upon submission. $3 per submission.

Accepts poetry, fiction, creative non-fiction, and folios. Prose submissions must be under 5,000 words. Flash fiction submissions must be no more than 1000 words individually. Novel excerpts are acceptable but must be able to stand alone. For poetry, please submit no more than three poems in a single document. For flash fiction, please submit no more than three pieces in a single document.

Editor: Matt Muth

M274 Panorama
Online Magazine
London
United Kingdom

enquiries@panoramajournal.org

https://panoramajournal.org
https://www.facebook.com/panoramathejournaloftravelplaceandnature/
https://panoramajournal.submittable.com/submit
https://twitter.com/Panorama_J
https://www.linkedin.com/company/panorama-the-journal-of-travel-place-and-nature/
https://www.instagram.com/panorama_journal/

Fiction > *Short Fiction*
Literary; Nature; Travel

Nonfiction > *Short Nonfiction*
Literary; Nature; Travel

Poetry > *Any Poetic Form*
Literary; Nature; Travel

Send: Query; Author bio; Full text
How to send: Submittable

We publish contemporary, literary-themed travel works of nonfiction, fiction, poetry, illustration, as well as travel-themed photo essays and film stills. We are looking for exquisite, rich, surprising work capable of unbinding readers from their expectations and routines. Make us get lost on a journey in your hometown. Be the verbal cartographer of your own exile. Bring us the fictional realities of characters who take us places we can't go on our own. Offer us poetry that leaves us stranded in the natural world. Most of all, write evocative, experiential, descriptive prose that takes our readers with you, and confirms our belief in the power of place. We have a particular interest in travel memoir, real or imagined, but we invite memoir with an edge. This is not the place for traditional travel memoir: give us something different.

M275 The Paris Review
Magazine
544 West 27th Street, Floor 3, New York, NY 10001
United States
Tel: +1 (212) 343-1333

queries@theparisreview.org

https://www.theparisreview.org
https://theparisreview.submittable.com/submit
https://www.facebook.com/parisreview
https://twitter.com/parisreview
http://theparisreview.tumblr.com/

Fiction > *Short Fiction:* Literary

Nonfiction
Interviews; *Short Nonfiction*
Poetry > *Any Poetic Form*

Closed to approaches.

Send submissions through online submission system or by post. All submissions must be in English and previously unpublished, though translations are acceptable if accompanied by copy of the original text. Simultaneous submissions accepted as long as immediate notification is given of acceptance elsewhere.

M276 Park Home and Holiday Living
Magazine
The Granary, Downs Court, Yalding Hill, Yalding, Kent, ME18 6AL
United Kingdom
Tel: +44 (0) 1959 541444

phhc.ed@kelsey.co.uk

https://www.parkhomemagazine.co.uk

Magazine Publisher: Kelsey Media

Nonfiction > *Articles*
Caravans; Holiday Homes; Lifestyle

Magazine for those owning holiday caravans or living in residential park homes.

Editor: Alex Melvin

M277 The Passionfruit Review
Online Magazine
United Kingdom

editor@passionfruitreview.com

https://passionfruitreview.com
https://duotrope.com/duosuma/submit/the-passionfruit-review-1o4uh

Fiction > *Short Fiction:* Love

Nonfiction > *Short Nonfiction*
Creative Nonfiction; Love

Poetry > *Any Poetic Form:* Love

How to send: Duosuma

Costs: A fee is charged upon submission in some cases.

The theme for general submissions is love: the romantic, the familial, the platonic, the intimate, the lost, the young, the wretched. Above all, Passionfruit seeks to be a home for that which illuminates something of the human spirit – pieces that explore what love is (or isn't, or might be), when we love, how we love, what we love, and why we love.

Our focus is on poetry, but there are no particular restrictions on genre, type, or style – we will consider poetry, prose, and visual art for each issue.

M278 PC Gamer
Magazine
Quay House, The Ambury, Bath, BA1 1UA
United Kingdom

editors@pcgamer.com

https://www.pcgamer.com
https://steamcommunity.com/groups/pcgamer
https://twitter.com/pcgamer
https://www.facebook.com/pcgamermagazine/
https://www.youtube.com/user/pcgamer

Magazine Publisher: Future

Nonfiction
Articles: Computer and Video Games; Computers
News: Computer and Video Games; Computers
Reviews: Computer and Video Games; Computers

We are the global authority on PC games. We've been covering PC gaming for more than 20 years, and continue that legacy today with worldwide print editions and around-the-clock news, features, esports coverage, hardware testing, and game reviews.

Editor: Alan Dexter

M279 PC Pro
Magazine
Quay House, The Ambury, Bath, BA1 1UA
United Kingdom
Tel: +44 (0) 330 333 9493

customercare@subscribe.pcpro.co.uk

https://subscribe.pcpro.co.uk
https://www.facebook.com/pcpro
https://twitter.com/pcpro

Magazine Publisher: Future

ADULT > **Nonfiction** > *Articles:* Computers

PROFESSIONAL > **Nonfiction** > *Articles:* Computers

IT magazine for professionals in the IT industry and enthusiasts.

M280 Pennine Ink Magazine
Magazine
United Kingdom

g.laura.sheridan@gmail.com

https://pennineink.wordpress.com/submissions-to-pennine-ink/

Fiction > *Short Fiction*

Nonfiction > *Articles*

Poetry > *Any Poetic Form*

Send: Full text
How to send: Email

Publishes poetry, flash fiction, and articles from anywhere in the world. Submit a maximum of three pieces in total.

Editor: Laura Sheridan

M281 Pensacola Magazine

Magazine
21 E. Garden St., Ste. 205, Pensacola, FL 32502
United States
Tel: +1 (850) 433-1166
Fax: +1 (850) 435-9174

info@ballingerpublishing.com

http://www.pensacolamagazine.com
https://www.facebook.com/pensacolamagazine
https://www.instagram.com/pensacola_magazine/

Magazine Publisher: Ballinger Publishing

Nonfiction > *Articles*
Business; Culture; Entertainment; Fashion; Health; Lifestyle; Pensacola

Publishes articles and stories on business, entertainment, culture, fashion, healthcare, lifestyle and other topics important to the Northwest Florida community.

M282 People's Friend Pocket Novels

Magazine
United Kingdom

pfeditor@dcthomson.co.uk

https://www.thepeoplesfriend.co.uk

Magazine: The People's Friend (**M283**)

Fiction > *Novellas*
Family Saga; Romance

Send: Query
How to send: Email

Publishes romance and family fiction between 37,000 and 39,000 words, aimed at adults aged over 30. Send query by email See website for more information.

M283 The People's Friend

Magazine
United Kingdom

pfeditor@dcthomson.co.uk

https://www.thepeoplesfriend.co.uk

Newspaper Publisher / Magazine Publisher: DC Thomson Media

Fiction > *Short Fiction:* Women's Fiction

Nonfiction > *Nonfiction Books*
Cookery; Crafts; Lifestyle; Women's Interests

Publishes complete short stories (1,200-3,000 words (4,000 for specials)) and serials, focusing on character development rather than complex plots, plus 10,000-word crime thrillers. Also considers nonfiction from nature to nostalgia and from holidays to hobbies, and poetry. Guidelines available on website.

Magazine: People's Friend Pocket Novels (**M282**)

M284 Pilot

Magazine
United Kingdom

https://www.pilotweb.aero

Magazine Publisher: Kelsey Media

ADULT > **Nonfiction** > *Articles*
Air Travel; Piloting

PROFESSIONAL > **Nonfiction** > *Articles*
Air Travel; Piloting

Send: Full text
How to send: Email

Aimed at private, commercial and would-be flyers, including enthusiasts.

Editor: Philip Whiteman

M285 Pleiades

Magazine
Department of English, Martin 336, University of Central Missouri, 415 E. Clark St., Warrensburg, MO 64093
United States
Tel: +1 (660) 543-4268

pleiadespoetryeditor@gmail.com
pleiadesfictioninquiries@gmail.com
pleiadescnf@gmail.com
pleiadesreviews@gmail.com

https://pleiadesmag.com
https://twitter.com/pleiadesmag
https://www.facebook.com/UCMPleiades
http://websta.me/n/pleiades_magazine
https://www.pinterest.com/pleiadesUCM/

Fiction > *Short Fiction*

Nonfiction
Reviews: Books
Short Nonfiction: Creative Nonfiction

Poetry > *Any Poetic Form*

Closed to approaches.

Send submissions through online submission system during specific windows only.

M286 Ploughshares

Magazine
Emerson College, 120 Boylston St., Boston, MA 02116-4624
United States

https://www.pshares.org
http://facebook.com/ploughshares
http://www.pinterest.com/pshares
http://twitter.com/pshares
https://instagram.com/psharesjournal/

Fiction > *Short Fiction*

Nonfiction > *Short Nonfiction*

Poetry > *Any Poetic Form*

Closed to approaches.

Costs: A fee is charged for online submissions. $3 fee for online submissions, except for subscribers, who may submit for free.

Welcomes unsolicited submissions of fiction, poetry, and nonfiction during the regular reading period, which runs from June 1 to January 15. The literary journal is published four times a year: mixed issues of poetry and prose in the Spring and Winter, a prose issue in the summer, and a longform prose issue in the Fall, with two of the four issues per year guest-edited by a different writer of prominence.

Editor: Don Lee

M287 PN Review

Magazine
4th Floor, Alliance House, 30 Cross Street, Manchester, M2 7AQ
United Kingdom
Tel: +44 (0) 161 834 8730

PNRsubmissions@carcanet.co.uk

https://www.pnreview.co.uk

Nonfiction
Essays: Poetry as a Subject
Reviews: Poetry as a Subject

Poetry > *Any Poetic Form*

Send: Query; Full text
How to send: Email; Post

Poetry may be submitted during the months of June and December. Subscribers may submit by email; otherwise submissions should be by post. Queries for nonfiction submissions may be sent to the editor at any time, by email.

Editor: Michael Schmidt

M288 Poetry Ireland Review

Magazine
3 Great Denmark Street, Dublin 1, D01 NV63
Ireland
Tel: +353 (0)1 6789815

pir@poetryireland.ie
info@poetryireland.ie

https://www.poetryireland.ie
https://poetryireland.submittable.com/submit/

Nonfiction
Articles: Poetry as a Subject
Essays: Poetry as a Subject
Interviews: Poetry as a Subject

Poetry > *Any Poetic Form*

Send: Full text; Proposal
How to send: Post; Submittable

Send up to four poems through online submission system, or by post. Poetry is accepted from around the world but must be previously unpublished. No sexism or racism. Prose is generally commissioned; however, proposals are welcome. No unsolicited prose.

M289 Poetry London
Magazine
Goldsmiths, University of London, New Cross, London, SE14 6NW
United Kingdom

admin@poetrylondon.co.uk

https://poetrylondon.co.uk
https://poetrylondon.submittable.com/submit
https://twitter.com/Poetry_London
https://www.instagram.com/poetry_london/
https://www.facebook.com/poetrylondon
https://www.youtube.com/c/PoetryLondon

Poetry in Translation > *Any Poetic Form*

Poetry > *Any Poetic Form*

Send: Full text; Self-Addressed Stamped Envelope (SASE)
How to send: Submittable, Post

Send up to six poems via online submission system, or by post with SASE or adequate return postage (if within the UK) or email address for response (if overseas). Considers poems by both new and established poets. Also publishes book reviews.

M290 The Poetry Review
Magazine
The Poetry Society, 22 Betterton Street, London, WC2H 9BX
United Kingdom
Tel: +44 (0) 20 7420 9880

poetryreview@poetrysociety.org.uk

https://poetrysociety.org.uk/
https://thepoetrysociety.submittable.com/submit

Nonfiction
 Essays: Poetry as a Subject
 Reviews: Poetry as a Subject

Poetry in Translation > *Any Poetic Form*

Poetry > *Any Poetic Form*

Send: Full text
How to send: Submittable

Costs: A fee is charged upon submission in some cases. Non-members pay £2 to submit.

Describes itself as "one of the liveliest and most influential literary magazines in the world", and has been associated with the rise of the New Generation of British poets – Carol Ann Duffy, Simon Armitage, Glyn Maxwell, Don Paterson... though its scope extends beyond the UK, with special issues focusing on poetries from around the world. Send up to 6 unpublished poems, or literary translations of poems, through online submission system.

M291 Poetry Wales
Magazine
Suite 6, 4 Derwen Road, Bridgend, CF31 1LH
United Kingdom
Tel: +44 (0) 1656 663018

poetrywalessubmissions@gmail.com
info@poetrywales.co.uk
editor@poetrywales.co.uk

https://poetrywales.co.uk
https://poetrywales.submittable.com/submit
http://twitter.com/poetrywales
http://facebook.com/poetrywales
http://instagram.com/poetrywales

Nonfiction
 Articles: Poetry as a Subject
 Reviews: Books; Poetry as a Subject
Poetry > *Any Poetic Form*

Send: Full text
How to send: Submittable; Post; Email

Publishes poetry, features, and reviews from Wales and beyond. Submit via online submission system, or by post. If online form is not working, use email. Also runs competitions.

M292 The Political Quarterly
Magazine
Department of Politics, Birkbeck, University of London, Malet Street, London, WC1E 7HX
United Kingdom

submissions@politicalquarterly.net

https://politicalquarterly.org.uk
https://twitter.com/po_qu
https://www.facebook.com/PoliticalQuarterly

Nonfiction
 Articles: Politics
 Reviews: Books

How to send: Email

Magazine covering national and international politics. Accepts unsolicited articles.

M293 Popshot Quarterly
Magazine
United Kingdom

submit@popshotpopshot.com
hello@popshotpopshot.com

https://www.popshotpopshot.com
https://www.facebook.com/popshotmag
https://www.pinterest.com/popshotmag
https://www.instagram.com/popshotmag
https://twitter.com/popshotmag

Fiction > *Short Fiction*: Literary

Poetry > *Any Poetic Form*

Closed to approaches.

Publishes flash fiction, short stories, and poetry on the theme of the current issue (see website). Submit by email.

M294 Power Cut Lite
Magazine
United Kingdom

submissions@powercutmag.co.uk

https://powercutmag.co.uk
https://www.facebook.com/powercutmag
https://twitter.com/powercutmag
https://www.pinterest.co.uk/powercutmag/
https://www.linkedin.com/in/kristina-stevens-28790b294/
https://www.instagram.com/powercutmag/

Fiction > *Short Fiction*
 20th Century; Historical Fiction

Nonfiction
 Essays: 20th Century; Arts; Culture; Films; History; Literature; Photography
 Reviews: 20th Century; Films; Literature
Poetry > *Any Poetic Form*: 20th Century

Send: Full text
How to send: Email

Magazine exploring 20th century pop culture and focusing on 1930-1999. All work should be set in or explore this period. See website for submission guidelines.

M295 The Practising Midwife
Magazine
Saturn House, Mercury Rise, Altham Industrial Park, Altham, Lancashire, BB5 5BY
United Kingdom

info@all4maternity.com

https://www.all4maternity.com
https://twitter.com/all4maternity
https://www.facebook.com/all4maternity/

PROFESSIONAL > **Nonfiction**
 Articles: Midwifery
 News: Midwifery

Publishes accessible, authoritative and readable information for midwives, students and other professionals in the maternity services.

Editor-in-Chief: Alys Einion

M296 Present Tense
Print Magazine
United Kingdom

http://www.dahliapublishing.co.uk/present-tense-lit-mag

Book Publisher: Dahlia Books (**P132**)

Fiction > *Short Fiction*

Nonfiction > *Short Nonfiction*: Creative Nonfiction

Poetry > *Any Poetic Form*

Send: Full text
How to send: Online submission system

A literary magazine of new writing. Publishes poetry, flash fiction, short stories, and creative non-fiction with a strong sense of place.

M297 Preservation Magazine
Magazine
600 14th Street NW, Suite 500, Washington, DC 20005
United States
Tel: +1 (202) 588-6013

preservation@savingplaces.org
editorial@savingplaces.org

https://savingplaces.org/preservation-magazine

Nonfiction > *Articles*
  History; Travel

Send: Query
How to send: Phone; Email

Magazine publishing material on the preservation of historic buildings and neighbourhoods in the United States.

M298 Pride
Magazine
1 Garrat Lane, London, SW18 4AQ
United Kingdom
Tel: +44 (0) 20 3442 3310

editor@pridemagazine.com

http://pridemagazine.com
http://www.facebook.com/PrideMagazine
http://www.instagram.com/pridemaguk

Nonfiction
  Articles: Beauty; Career Development; Entertainment; Fashion; Hairstyles; Health; Lifestyle
  News: Ethnic Groups; Social Issues

Magazine aimed at black women. Publishes news, and articles and features on entertainment, hair, beauty, and fashion.

M299 Prole
Magazine
United Kingdom

submissionspoetry@prolebooks.co.uk
submissionsprose@prolebooks.co.uk

https://prolebooks.co.uk
https://facebook.com/Prole-236155444300
https://twitter.com/Prolebooks

Fiction > *Short Fiction*: Literary

Nonfiction > *Short Nonfiction*: Creative Nonfiction

Poetry > *Any Poetic Form*

Send: Full text
How to send: In the body of an email

We promote accessible literature of high quality. Anything that we publish will be intelligent, engaging and impact the reader in a variety of ways. It's the reader who comes first. We want to appeal to a wide audience and reconnect a broad readership with excellent examples of poetry and short prose. We do not accept previously published material, either in paper journals or e-zines. We will consider pieces that have been shared on personal sites or membership writing sites but ask you to remove them prior to submission. We do not accept simultaneous submissions.

M300 Pulsar Poetry Magazine
Online Magazine
90 Beechwood Drive, Camelford, Cornwall, PL32 9NB
United Kingdom
Tel: +44 (0) 1840 213633

pulsar.ed@btinternet.com

https://www.pulsarpoetry.com

Poetry > *Any Poetic Form*

Send: Full text; Self-Addressed Stamped Envelope (SASE)
How to send: In the body of an email; Domestic Post

The editor's preference is for hard hitting poems that have a message, meaning, and are well written. Not keen on deeply religious poems or de-dah de-dah poems where everything chimes annoyingly like a cheap clock. Please don't send poems about cute and cuddly kittens. Simultaneous submissions are not considered. Postal submissions from within the UK only.

Editor: David Pike

M301 Pushing Out the Boat
Magazine
United Kingdom

info@pushingouttheboat.co.uk

https://www.pushingouttheboat.co.uk

Fiction > *Short Fiction*: Literary

Poetry > *Any Poetic Form*

Scripts > *Theatre Scripts*

How to send: Online submission system

Magazine of prose, poetry and visual arts, based in North-East Scotland. Welcomes work in English, Doric or Scots. Submit via online submission system during open reading periods. See website for details.

M302 Qu Literary Magazine
Magazine
United States

qulitmag@queens.edu

http://www.qulitmag.com

Fiction > *Short Fiction*: Literary

Nonfiction > *Essays*

Poetry > *Any Poetic Form*

Scripts
  Film Scripts; *TV Scripts*; *Theatre Scripts*

Send: Full text
How to send: Submittable
How not to send: Email

Costs: A fee is charged upon submission. $2.50 per submission.

Literary journal published by a university MFA program. Editorial staff is comprised of current students. Publishes fiction, poetry, essays and script excerpts.

M303 Rabble Review
Online Magazine
United States

rabblereview420@gmail.com

https://rabblereview.com
https://www.instagram.com/rabble_review/
https://twitter.com/rabble_review

Fiction > *Short Fiction*

Nonfiction > *Essays*
  Creative Nonfiction; Cultural Criticism; Current Affairs; Literature; Politics

Poetry > *Any Poetic Form*

How to send: Online submission system

Unapologetically leftist in politics, we recognize the complete abolition of capitalism, coerced labor, and the State as absolute preconditions for human and artistic liberation. We want to capture the working class in its full spectrum, that is, we're committed to solidarity among workers of all races, genders, sexual orientations, abilities, and their intersections. By spreading accessible leftist thought, encouraging direct action, and providing a space for revolutionary aesthetics to develop we hope to do our part in the radicalization and ultimate liberation of the working class.

M304 Racecar Engineering
Magazine
The Chelsea Magazine Company, 111 Buckingham Palace Road, London, SW1 0DT
United Kingdom
Tel: +44 (0) 20 7349 3700

editorial@racecarengineering.com

https://www.racecar-engineering.com
https://www.facebook.com/RacecarEngineering/
https://twitter.com/RacecarEngineer

Magazine Publisher: The Chelsea Magazine Company

Nonfiction
  Articles: Engineering; Racecars
  News: Engineering; Racecars

Publishes news articles and in-depth features on racing cars and related products and technology. No material on road cars or racing drivers.

M305 Radar Poetry
Magazine
United States

radarpoetry@gmail.com

https://www.radarpoetry.com

Poetry > *Any Poetic Form*

Closed to approaches.

Costs: A fee is charged upon submission; Offers services that writers have to pay for. $3 submission fee, or optional $25 fee for submission with feedback.

Electronic journal of poetry and artwork, published quarterly. Interested in the interplay between poetry and visual media. Each issue features pairings of poetry and artwork, selected by the editors. Submit 3-5 original, previously unpublished poems through online submission system. Accepts submissions November 1 to January 1 (free), and March 1 to May 1 ($3) annually.

Editors: Rachel Marie Patterson; Dara-Lyn Shrager

M306 Rail Express
Magazine
United Kingdom
Tel: +44 (0) 1507 529529

RailExpressEditor@mortons.co.uk

https://www.railexpress.co.uk
https://www.facebook.com/RailExpressMag
https://www.instagram.com/railexpressmagazine/
https://twitter.com/railexpress

Magazine Publisher: Mortons Media Group

Nonfiction > *Articles*: Railways

Magazine publishing news and features on railways in the UK.

M307 Reactor
Online Magazine
United States

blogsubmissions@tor.com

https://reactormag.com
https://reactormag.com/submissions-guidelines/

Nonfiction
Articles: Fantasy; Science Fiction
Essays: Fantasy; Science Fiction
Reviews: Books; Fantasy; Science Fiction

Send: Pitch; Writing sample
How to send: Email

Most interested in pitches for essays, think pieces, list posts, reaction pieces, and reviews in the 1000-2500 word range (although also open to longer essays). If possible, please include 2-3 writing samples and/or links to your published work on other sites.

M308 The Reader
Magazine
The Mansion House, Calderstones Park, Liverpool, L18 3JB
United Kingdom
Tel: + 44 (0) 1517 292200

https://www.thereader.org.uk
https://www.thereader.org.uk/what-we-do/the-reader-magazine/
https://twitter.com/thereaderorg
https://www.facebook.com/thereaderorg
https://www.instagram.com/thereaderorg/

Nonfiction > *Articles*: Literature

Magazine of charity promoting shared reading through reading aloud groups. No longer publishes original fiction and poetry.

M309 Red Magazine
Magazine
30 Panton Street, London, SW1Y 4AJ
United Kingdom

https://www.redonline.co.uk
https://www.facebook.com/redmagazine/
https://twitter.com/RedMagDaily
https://www.pinterest.co.uk/redmagazine/
https://www.instagram.com/redmagazine/?hl=en
https://www.youtube.com/user/RedMagazineOnline

Magazine Publisher: Hearst Magazines UK

Nonfiction
Articles: Beauty; Decorating; Fashion; Fitness; Food; Hairstyles; Health; Interior Design; Parenting; Relationships; Sex; Travel; Wellbeing
Interviews: Women's Interests
Reviews: Books; Films; Music; TV

Magazine aimed at women in their thirties.

M310 Redbook Magazine
Online Magazine
300 W. 57th St., New York, NY 10019
United States

https://www.redbookmag.com
https://twitter.com/redbookmag
https://www.youtube.com/c/Redbook?sub_confirmation=1
https://www.facebook.com/REDBOOK
https://www.instagram.com/redbookmag/
https://www.pinterest.com/redbookmag/

Media Company: Hearst

Nonfiction > *Articles*
Beauty; Design; Family; Fitness; Food and Drink; Friends; Hairstyles; Home Improvement; Lifestyle; Make-Up; Nutrition; Parenting; Pets; Relationships; Sex

Former print magazine now published online only since 2019.

M311 The Rialto
Magazine
74 Britannia Road, Norwich, NR1 4HS
United Kingdom

info@therialto.co.uk

https://www.therialto.co.uk
https://therialto.submittable.com/submit
https://www.facebook.com/rialtopoetry/
https://twitter.com/RialtoPoetry
https://www.instagram.com/rialtopoetry/

Poetry > *Any Poetic Form*

Closed to approaches.

Send up to six poems with SASE or adequate return postage or submit through online submission system. No submissions by email.

Editor: Michael Mackmin

M312 Riposte
Print Magazine
United Kingdom

studio@ripostemagazine.com

https://www.ripostemagazine.com
https://x.com/RiposteMagazine
https://www.instagram.com/ripostemagazine/

Nonfiction
Articles: Arts; Business; Design; Environment; Music; Politics; Social Justice; Women
Essays: Arts; Business; Design; Environment; Music; Politics; Social Justice; Women
Interviews: Women

We profile bold and fascinating women who challenge power structures and stereotypes. Our interviews are honest rather than being full of media-trained responses as the women we feature candidly discuss their successes and failures, their work, their passions and perspectives. Essays and features cover a broad range of issues including art, design, music, business, innovation, politics, social justice and environmental issues.

M313 River Hills Traveler
Magazine
212 E Main Street, Neosho, MO 64850
United States
Tel: +1 (417) 451-3798

https://www.riverhillstraveler.com

Nonfiction
Articles: Boats; Camping; Fishing; Hunting; Lifestyle; Missouri; Outdoor Activities; Ozarks
News: Animals; Missouri; Nature; Ozarks; Travel

Magazine covering outdoor sports and nature in the southeast quarter of Missouri, the east and central Ozarks.

Managing Editor: Madeleine Link

Publisher: Jimmy Sexton

M314 River Styx
Online Magazine
3301 Washington Ave, Suite 2C, St. Louis,

MO 63103
United States

https://www.riverstyx.org
https://riverstyx.submittable.com/submit
https://twitter.com/riverstyxmag/
https://www.facebook.com/RiverStyxLiteraryMagazine/
https://www.linkedin.com/company/river-styx/
https://www.instagram.com/riverstyxmag/

Fiction > *Short Fiction*

Nonfiction > *Short Nonfiction*: Creative Nonfiction

Poetry > *Any Poetic Form*

Scripts > *Theatre Scripts*

How to send: Submittable
How not to send: Email; Post

Costs: A fee is charged upon submission. $3 submission fee.

A multicultural magazine of poetry, short fiction, creative nonfiction, short plays, and art. Seeks to publish work that is striking in its originality, energy, and craft, from both new and established writers.

M315 Riverbed Review
Online Magazine
Ireland

riverbedreview@gmail.com

https://riverbedreview.wordpress.com
https://www.instagram.com/riverbedreview/
https://twitter.com/RiverbedReview

Fiction > *Short Fiction*
  Literary; Rivers

Poetry > *Any Poetic Form*: Rivers

Closed to approaches.

Publishes original and unpublished stories and poems that are set around (or are about) a river — fictional or otherwise. Submissions are accepted from March 16 to May 16; and October 16 to December 16.

M316 Rock & Gem
Magazine
United States

https://www.rockngem.com
https://www.facebook.com/RockandGem/
https://www.instagram.com/rockandgemmagazine/
https://twitter.com/RandG_official/

Magazine Publisher: EG Media Investments

Nonfiction > *Articles*
  Fossils; Gems; How To; Lapidary; Minerals; Rock Collecting / Rockhounding; Rocks

First published in 1971 with the goal of serving the needs and goals of anyone with an interest in rocks, gems, minerals, fossils and general lapidary.

Editor-in-Chief: Pam Freeman

M317 Rugby World
Magazine
Unit 415, Winnersh Triangle, Eskdale Road, Winnersh, RG41 5TU
United Kingdom
Tel: +44 (0) 1225 442244

rugbyworldletters@futurenet.com
sarah.mockford@futurenet.com

https://www.rugbyworld.com
https://www.facebook.com/rugbyworldmagazine
https://www.youtube.com/user/rugbyworld08
https://twitter.com/rugbyworldmag

Magazine Publisher: Future

Nonfiction
  Articles: Rugby
  News: Rugby

Send: Query; Author bio; Synopsis

Magazine publishing news and articles related to rugby. Send idea with coverline, headline, and 50-word synopsis, along with brief resume of your experience.

Editor: Sarah Mockford

M318 Ruralite
Magazine
5625 NE Elam Young Parkway Suite 100, Hillsboro, OR 97124
United States
Tel: +1 (503) 357-2105

editor@pur.coop
info@pur.coop

https://www.ruralite.com
https://www.facebook.com/Ruralite
https://www.instagram.com/ruralitemag/
https://twitter.com/RuraliteMag
https://vimeo.com/showcase/5668282

Nonfiction > *Articles*
  Energy; Lifestyle; Photography; Recipes; Travel

Send: Pitch
How to send: Email

Serves members of publicly owned electric utilities, delivering engaging human-interest features, energy-related content, travel and photography tips, scrumptious recipes, reader submissions and important information about electric service.

M319 Saddlebag Dispatches
Magazine
United States

submissions@saddlebagdispatches.com

https://saddlebagdispatches.com

Fiction > *Short Fiction*: American West

Nonfiction > *Articles*: American West

Poetry > *Any Poetic Form*: American West

Send: Full text
How to send: Email

Publishes fiction, nonfiction, and poetry about the American West. Looks for themes of open country, unforgiving nature, struggles to survive and settle the land, freedom from authority, cooperation with fellow adventurers, and other experiences that human beings encounter on the frontier. Send submissions by email. See website for full guidelines.

M320 SAIL Magazine
Magazine
35 Industrial Park Road, Unit 10, Centerbrook, CT 06409
United States
Fax: +1 (860) 767-1048

sailmail@sailmagazine.com

https://www.sailmagazine.com
https://www.facebook.com/sailmag
https://twitter.com/sailmagazine
https://www.instagram.com/sailmagazine
https://pinterest.com/sailmagazine

Nonfiction > *Articles*
  Boats; Sailing

Sailing magazine covering boats, DIY, cruising, racing, equipment, etc.

Editor-in-Chief: Wendy Clarke

M321 Sailing Today
Magazine
The Chelsea Magazine Company, 111 Buckingham Palace Road, London, SW1 ODT
United Kingdom
Tel: +44 (0) 20 7349 3700

editor@sailingtoday.co.uk

https://www.sailingtoday.co.uk
https://www.facebook.com/sailingtoday/
https://twitter.com/SailingTodayMag
https://www.youtube.com/channel/UCah1Wlfp86HD0tpbhW1LP1Q

Nonfiction > *Articles*: Sailing

Practical magazine for cruising sailors. Offers a wealth of practical advice and a dynamic mix of in-depth boat, gear and equipment news.

M322 Savannah Magazine
Magazine
United States
Tel: +1 (912) 652-0293

https://www.savannahmagazine.com
https://www.facebook.com/SavannahMagazine
https://twitter.com/savmag
https://www.pinterest.com/savmagazine/
https://www.instagram.com/savannahmagazine/
https://www.youtube.com/user/SavannahMagazineLive

Nonfiction > *Articles*
Culture; Food; Health; Houses and Homes; Lifestyle; Savannah, GA; Weddings

Send: Query
How to send: Email
How not to send: Phone

Our mission is to celebrate the inimitable Savannah lifestyle and serve the city as thought leaders. We discover and uplift the talented individuals of the city's creative class. With smart, layered, inclusive content, we interpret Savannah's unique cultural identity — and become the change we want to see in the city.

M323 Scifaikuest
Print Magazine; Online Magazine
United States

gatrix65@yahoo.com

https://www.hiraethsffh.com/scifaikuest

Book Publisher / Ebook Publisher / Online Publisher: Hiraeth Books (**P220**)

Nonfiction > *Articles*
Biography; Creative Writing; Poetry as a Subject

Poetry
Haibun: Horror; Science Fiction
Haiku: Horror; Science Fiction
Senryu: Horror; Science Fiction
Tanka: Horror; Science Fiction

Send: Full text; Author bio
How to send: Email

Print and online magazine publishing science fiction and horror poetry in forms such as scifaiku, haibun, senryu, and tanka. Also publishes articles. See website for full submission guidelines.

M324 The Scots Magazine
Magazine
D.C. Thomson & Co. Ltd, 2 Albert Square, Dundee, DD1 1DD
United Kingdom
Tel: +44 (0) 1382 223131

mail@scotsmagazine.com

https://www.scotsmagazine.com
https://www.facebook.com/scotsmagazine/
https://twitter.com/ScotsMagazine
https://www.instagram.com/scots_magazine/
https://www.youtube.com/channel/UCQQRFhCCyaPvpY8uWpBmHtg?

Newspaper Publisher / Magazine Publisher: DC Thomson Media

Nonfiction > *Articles*
Folklore, Myths, and Legends; History; Outdoor Activities; Scotland; Wildlife

Send: Query
Don't send: Full text
How to send: Email

Scottish interest magazine publishing material covering history, folklore, wildlife, outdoor pursuits, Scottish personalities, etc.

Editor: John Methven

M325 The Scottish Farmer
Magazine
125 Fullarton Drive, Glasgow, G32 8FG
United Kingdom

https://www.thescottishfarmer.co.uk
https://www.facebook.com/scottishfarmer
https://twitter.com/scottishfarmer
https://www.instagram.com/scottishfarmernewspaper/
https://www.linkedin.com/company/17949188

Magazine Publisher / Newspaper Publisher: Newsquest Media Group

PROFESSIONAL > Nonfiction
Articles: Farming; Scotland
News: Farming; Scotland

Agricultural magazine publishing news and features on political, personal, and technological developments in farming, as well as rural and craft items. Approach with ideas by email or fax.

Editors: Alasdair Fletcher; Deputy Editor: Ken Fletcher

M326 Scottish Field
Magazine
Fettes Park, 496 Ferry Road, Edinburgh, EH5 2DL
United Kingdom
Tel: +44 (0) 1315 511000

editor@scottishfield.co.uk

https://www.scottishfield.co.uk
https://www.facebook.com/scottishfield
http://www.twitter.com/scottishfield

Nonfiction > *Articles*
Beauty; Culture; Fashion; Food and Drink; Gardening; Interior Design; Lifestyle; Outdoor Activities; Scotland; Travel

Lifestyle magazine publishing articles and features of general Scottish interest.

Editor: Richard Bath

M327 Scribble
Magazine
14 The Park, Stow on the Wold, Cheltenham, Glos., GL54 1DX
United Kingdom
Tel: +44 (0) 1451 831053

enquiries@parkpublications.co.uk

http://www.parkpublications.co.uk/scribble.html

Magazine Publisher: Park Publications

Fiction > *Short Fiction*

Send: Full text
How to send: Email; Post

Costs: A fee is charged upon submission. £5. Free for subscribers.

Accepts short stories on any subject from new and experienced writers. Each quarter prizes of £75, £25, and £15 will be awarded for the best three stories in the edition. These competitions are free to annual subscribers. See website for further details.

M328 Second Factory
Print Magazine
United States

https://uglyducklingpresse.org/about/submissions/
https://udp.submittable.com/submit

Book Publisher: Ugly Duckling Presse (**P466**)

Fiction > *Short Fiction*
General, and in particular: Experimental

Nonfiction > *Short Nonfiction*
General, and in particular: Experimental

Poetry > *Any Poetic Form*

Closed to approaches.

Publishes mainly poetry. Fiction and nonfiction will have a better chance if it is fairly short (more than 4 pages per contributor are not usually published) and if it has a fairly experimental and/or playful nature. 'Traditional' fiction and prose submissions are not as likely to be accepted, but open to surprises.

M329 Seventeen
Magazine
300 W. 57th St, 17th Fl. New York, NY 10019
United States

mail@seventeen.com

https://www.seventeen.com
https://www.youtube.com/user/SeventeenMagazine
https://www.instagram.com/seventeen/
https://www.facebook.com/seventeen/

Magazine Publisher: Hearst Magazines International

YOUNG ADULT > Nonfiction > *Articles*
Beauty; Celebrity; Fashion; Health; Lifestyle; Politics; Wellbeing

Fashion beauty and lifestyle magazine for young women in their late teens and early twenties.

M330 Shearsman
Print Magazine
PO Box 4239, Swindon, SN3 9FN
United Kingdom

editor@shearsman.com

https://www.shearsman.com
https://www.facebook.com/profile.php?id=100063797880717
https://twitter.com/ShearsmanBooks
https://www.pinterest.com/shearsmanbooks/pins

Book Publisher: Shearsman Books

Poetry > *Any Poetic Form*

Now operates two reading windows for submissions: March and September. Send submissions with SAE for return. If outside UK please send disposable MS and email address for response. Do not send IRCs. Email submissions accepted if submission is sent in body of email, not as an attachment. PDFs accepted through online upload system. Please study magazine or at least website before deciding whether or not to submit your work. Publishes poetry in the modernist tradition, plus some prose, including reviews.

M331 Shenandoah

Magazine
United States

shenandoah@wlu.edu

https://shenandoahliterary.org
https://www.facebook.com/ShenandoahLiterary
https://www.instagram.com/shenandoah_literary
https://twitter.com/ShenandoahWLU

Fiction in Translation
  Comics; *Novel Excerpts*; *Short Fiction*
Fiction
  Comics; *Novel Excerpts*; *Short Fiction*
Nonfiction in Translation
  Essays: General
  Short Nonfiction: Creative Nonfiction; Memoir
Nonfiction
  Essays: General
  Short Nonfiction: Creative Nonfiction; Memoir
Poetry in Translation > *Any Poetic Form*

Poetry > *Any Poetic Form*

Closed to approaches.

Aims to showcase a wide variety of voices and perspectives in terms of gender identity, race, ethnicity, class, age, ability, nationality, regionality, sexuality, and educational background. Considers short stories, essays, excerpts of novels in progress, poems, comics, and translations of all the above.

M332 Ships Monthly Magazine

Magazine
Kelsey Media, The Granary, Downs Court, Yalding Hil, Yalding, Kent, ME18 6AL
United Kingdom
Tel: +44 (0) 1959 543747

https://shipsmonthly.com

Magazine Publisher: Kelsey Media

ADULT > **Nonfiction** > *Articles*: Ships
PROFESSIONAL > **Nonfiction** > *Articles*
  Shipping; Ships

Magazine aimed at ship enthusiasts and maritime professionals. Publishes news and illustrated articles related to all kinds of ships, including reports on the ferry, cruise, new building and cargo ship scene as well as navies across the world.

Editor: Nicholas Leach

M333 Shooter Literary Magazine

Magazine
United Kingdom

submissions.shooterlitmag@gmail.com

https://shooterlitmag.com

Fiction > *Short Fiction*

Nonfiction
  Essays: General
  Short Nonfiction: Memoir

Poetry > *Any Poetic Form*

Send: Full text; Author bio
How to send: Email

Publishes literary fiction, poetry, creative nonfiction and memoir relating to specific themes for each issue. See website for current theme and full submission guidelines.

M334 Shoreline of Infinity

Magazine
United Kingdom

editor@shorelineofinfinity.com

https://www.shorelineofinfinity.com
https://duotrope.com/duosuma/submit/shoreline-of-infinity-6a37K
https://www.facebook.com/ShorelineOfInfinity/
https://twitter.com/shoreinf
https://www.youtube.com/channel/UCm2N3L9V2rvnkS5dCRzttCg
https://www.instagram.com/shoreinf/

Fiction > *Short Fiction*
  Fantasy; Science Fiction

Poetry > *Any Poetic Form*: Science Fiction

Closed to approaches.

Science Fiction magazine from Scotland. We want stories that explore our unknown future. We want to play around with the big ideas and the little ones. We want writers to tell us stories to inspire us, give us hope, provide some laughs. Or to scare the stuffing out of us. We want good stories: we want to be entertained. We want to read how people cope in our exotic new world, we want to be in their minds, in their bodies, in their souls.

M335 Shorts Magazine

Online Magazine
United Kingdom

editor.shorts@gmail.com

http://shortsmagazine.com

Fiction > *Short Fiction*

Nonfiction > *Essays*

Poetry > *Any Poetic Form*

Send: Full text; Author bio
How to send: Word file email attachment

Online magazine published four times a year, and includes short fiction, flash fiction, sci-fi, life writing, poetry, essays, science, research, opinion pieces, monologues, drama, top ten lists, photography, featured artists.

M336 Sierra

Print Magazine; Online Magazine
United States

https://www.sierraclub.org
https://www.sierraclub.org/sierra
https://www.facebook.com/SierraMagazine/
https://www.instagram.com/sierramagazine/
https://twitter.com/sierra_magazine
https://www.pinterest.com/sierramagazine/

Nonfiction
  Articles: Adventure; Climate Science; Culture; Environment; Narrative Nonfiction; Nature; Social Justice; Sustainable Living; Travel; Wildlife
  Reviews: Books; Films

Send: Query; Pitch
How to send: Online submission system

A quarterly national print and digital magazine publishing award-winning journalism and cutting-edge photography, art, and video dedicated to protecting the natural world. Looking for reported stories on a wide range of environmental and social justice issues from writers who can bring to our audience a broad array of perspectives and writing styles.

M337 Sinister Wisdom

Magazine
2333 McIntosh Road, Dover, FL 33527
United States
Tel: +1 (813) 502-5549

julie@sinisterwisdom.org

https://www.sinisterwisdom.org
http://sinisterwisdom.submittable.com/submit
https://www.facebook.com/SinisterWisdom
https://www.instagram.com/sinister_wisdom/
https://twitter.com/Sinister_Wisdom
https://www.youtube.com/channel/UCtbGssCcCgE4WIwjGYL_qDA
https://www.linkedin.com/company/sinister-wisdom

Fiction > *Short Fiction*: LGBTQIA

Nonfiction
Essays: LGBTQIA
Reviews: Books

Poetry > *Any Poetic Form*: LGBTQIA

Send: Full text; Author bio
How to send: Submittable; Post

Multicultural lesbian literary and art journal. Material may be in any style or form, or combination of forms. Submit five poems, two short stories or essays, OR one longer piece of up to 5,000 words. Prefers submissions via online submission system, but will accept submissions by post if necessary.

Editor: Julie R. Enszer

M338 Snowflake Magazine
Print Magazine
United Kingdom

info@snowflakeculture.com

https://www.snowflakeculture.com
https://twitter.com/SnowflakeMag
https://www.instagram.com/snowflake_magazine

Fiction > *Short Fiction*
General, and in particular: LGBTQIA

Nonfiction
Articles: General, and in particular: LGBTQIA
Essays: General, and in particular: LGBTQIA
Interviews: General, and in particular: LGBTQIA

Poetry > *Any Poetic Form*
General, and in particular: LGBTQIA

Closed to approaches.

Publishes art, poetry, essays, flash fiction, photography, interviews and articles that are either queer themed or from an artist who identifies as LGBTQ+ (or both).

M339 The Soho Review
Magazine
New York
United States

thesohoreview@gmail.com

https://thesohoreview.com

Fiction
Cartoons: Comedy / Humour
Jokes: General
Short Fiction: Comedy / Humour

Poetry > *Any Poetic Form*: Comedy / Humour

Send: Pitch
How to send: Email

Humor magazine based in New York. Constantly looking for jokes, cartoons, poems, and short stories. Pitch ideas by email.

M340 SOMA
Magazine
888 O'Farrell Street, Suite 103, San Francisco, CA 94109
United States

http://www.somamagazine.com
http://www.twitter.com/SOMAmagazine
http://www.facebook.com/SOMA.Magazine
http://www.youtube.com/user/somamagazine
http://www.myspace.com/somamagazine

Nonfiction > *Articles*
Arts; Design; Fashion; Films; Music

Magazine of music, film, the arts, fashion, design, architecture, and nightlife.

M341 Somerset Life
Magazine
United Kingdom

https://www.greatbritishlife.co.uk/magazines/somerset/

Magazine Publisher: Great British Life

Nonfiction
Articles: Food; Gardening; History; Houses and Homes; Lifestyle; Somerset; Travel
Reviews: Restaurants

Magazine that puts the gloss on life in Somerset. Every month it's packed with features about this picturesque part of England – from characters and personalities to heritage and traditions. We turn the focus on our towns and villages, and give comprehensive guides to enjoying life in Somerset – including what's on, restaurant reviews and topical features on major events.

M342 Sonder Magazine
Print Magazine
Dublin
Ireland

sonderlit@gmail.com

https://sonderlit.com
https://www.instagram.com/sonder_lit/
https://twitter.com/MagazineSonder
https://www.facebook.com/sonderlit
https://www.linkedin.com/company/sonder-magazine/
https://www.youtube.com/channel/UCm3GnFrr2QXkz14LeOe7IHA

Fiction > *Short Fiction*

Nonfiction > *Short Nonfiction*: Creative Nonfiction

Closed to approaches.

A Dublin-based print journal, focused on the idea of sonder, the self, and others: that existential feeling you get when you're walking down the street or sitting in the pub and are overcome by the realization that everyone you pass is just out there doing their own thing, thinking their own thoughts and living their own lives. Publishes short stories, flash fiction, and creative non-fiction, all based around the individual and how we interact with each other.

M343 South
Magazine
PO Box 9338, Wimborne, BH21 9JA
United Kingdom

south@southpoetry.org

http://www.southpoetry.org

Poetry > *Any Poetic Form*

Send: Full text
How to send: Post
How not to send: Email

Submit up to three poems up to 40 lines each by post (two copies of each), along with submission form available on website. No previously published poems (including poems that have appeared on the internet). Submissions are not returned. See website for full details. No translations or submissions by email.

Editors: Peter Keeble; Anne Peterson; Chrissie Williams

M344 South Carolina Review
Magazine
314 Strode Tower, Clemson, SC 29634
United States
Tel: +1 (864) 656-3151

km@clemson.edu

https://www.clemson.edu/caah/sites/south-carolina-review
https://thesouthcarolinareview.submittable.com/submit

Fiction > *Short Fiction*

Nonfiction
Essays: General
Reviews: Books
Short Nonfiction: Creative Nonfiction

Poetry > *Any Poetic Form*

Closed to approaches.

Publishes fiction and poetry primarily, but will also consider creative nonfiction, scholarly essays, and book reviews.

Editor: Wayne Chapman

M345 Southern Humanities Review
Magazine
9088 Haley Center, Auburn University, Auburn, AL 36849
United States
Tel: +1 (334) 844-9088

shr@auburn.edu

http://www.southernhumanitiesreview.com
https://www.facebook.com/southernhumanitiesreview

https://twitter.com/SouthernHReview
https://www.instagram.com/southernhumanitiesreview
https://www.youtube.com/channel/UCnywOlZbBtEX7OFYMUMSQsg

Fiction > *Short Fiction*

Nonfiction > *Essays*
Creative Nonfiction; Literary Journalism; Literary; Lyric Essays; Memoir; Personal Essays; Travel

Poetry > *Any Poetic Form*

Send: Full text
How to send: Submittable
How not to send: Post; Email

Costs: A fee is charged upon submission. $3 submission fee.

Submissions for all fiction and nonfiction are open from August 15 until November 1 in the fall and from January 15 until March 14 in the spring. Poetry submissions are open from August 24 until September 7 in the fall and from January 15 until March 14 in the spring. Nonfiction submissions are open year-round.

M346 The Southern Review

Magazine
338 Johnston Hall, Louisiana State University, Baton Rouge, LA 70803
United States
Tel: +1 (225) 578-6467
Fax: +1 (225) 578-6461

southernreview@lsu.edu

https://thesouthernreview.org
https://www.facebook.com/lsusouthernreview
https://twitter.com/southern_review
https://soundcloud.com/lsupress_and_tsr

Fiction in Translation > *Short Fiction*

Fiction > *Short Fiction*

Nonfiction in Translation > *Essays*

Nonfiction > *Essays*

Poetry in Translation > *Any Poetic Form*

Poetry > *Any Poetic Form*

Closed to approaches.

Costs: A fee is charged upon submission. $3 per submission.

Strives to discover and promote a diverse array of engaging, relevant, and challenging literature—including fiction, nonfiction, poetry, and translation from literary luminaries as well as the best established and emerging writers.

M347 Southern Theatre

Magazine
5710 N Gate City Blvd, Ste K Box 186, Greensboro, NC 27407
United States
Tel: +1 (336) 265-6148

info@setc.org

https://setc.org/publications/
https://www.facebook.com/setc.org/
https://twitter.com/setctweet
https://www.instagram.com/setc/
https://www.linkedin.com/company/setcorg

Nonfiction > *Articles*: Theatre

Magazine covering theatre around the nation and beyond. Published quarterly and sent to all individual and organizational members.

M348 Southwest Review

Magazine
3225 Daniel Avenue, Room G09, Heroy Science Hall Basement, Dallas, TX 75205-1437
United States
Tel: +1 (214) 768-1037
Fax: +1 (214) 768-1408

swr@smu.edu

https://southwestreview.com
https://southwestreview.submittable.com/submit
https://www.facebook.com/SouthwestRev/
https://twitter.com/SouthwestReview
https://www.instagram.com/southwest_review/

Fiction > *Short Fiction*

Nonfiction > *Articles*
Arts; Current Affairs; History; Literature; Music

Poetry > *Any Poetic Form*

Closed to approaches.

Costs: A fee is charged upon submission. $3 submission fee.

The third-longest-running literary quarterly in the United States.

M349 Southword Journal

Magazine
Frank O'Connor House, 84 Douglas Street, Cork
Ireland
Tel: +353 (0) 21 4322396

info@munsterlit.ie

http://www.munsterlit.ie/Southword%20Journal.html
https://www.facebook.com/Southword.Journal/
https://southword.submittable.com/submit/

Fiction > *Short Fiction*

Poetry > *Any Poetic Form*

Closed to approaches.

Accepts submissions during specific submission windows only. See website for details.

M350 Spa Magazine

Print Magazine
P.O. Box 278, Pilot Hill, CA 95664
United States
Tel: +1 (916) 467-9118

editor@spamagazine.com

https://spamagazine.com

PROFESSIONAL > **Nonfiction**
Articles: Business; Spas and Hot Tubs
News: Business; Spas and Hot Tubs

Magazine covering spas and hot tubs. Digital version is available for free by email. Print version is free to anyone in the pool and spa industry.

M351 Speciality Food

Magazine
United Kingdom
Tel: +44 (0) 1206 505981

holly.shackleton@artichokehq.com

https://www.specialityfoodmagazine.com
https://twitter.com/specialityfood
https://www.linkedin.com/company/speciality-food/
https://www.instagram.com/specialityfoodmagazine/

Media Company: Artichoke Media

PROFESSIONAL > **Nonfiction**
Articles: Business; Food and Drink
News: Business; Food and Drink

Trade magazine for the food and drink industry.

Editor: Holly Shackleton

M352 Spelt Magazine

Magazine
United Kingdom

Speltmagazine@gmail.com

https://speltmagazine.com

Nonfiction > *Short Nonfiction*
Creative Nonfiction; Farming; Rural Living

Poetry > *Any Poetic Form*
Farming; Rural Living

Closed to approaches.

Publishes poetry and creative non-fiction that has something to say about the rural experience. Send up to six poems or up to two pieces of creative nonfiction (up to 1,500 words each) in the body of an email.

M353 Spitball

Magazine
536 Lassing Way, Walton, KY 41094
United States

spitball5@hotmail.com

https://www.spitballmag.com

Fiction > *Short Fiction*: Baseball

Nonfiction
Reviews: Baseball; Books
Short Nonfiction: Baseball

Poetry > *Any Poetic Form*: Baseball

Send: Full text
How not to send: Email

Costs: A purchase is required. Potential contributors must purchase a sample copy ($7.50) before submitting.

Literary baseball magazine, publishing poems, fiction, prose, art, and book reviews relating to baseball. See website for full guidelines.

M354 Square Mile Magazine
Magazine
United Kingdom

https://squaremile.com
https://twitter.com/squaremile_com
https://www.facebook.com/squaremileuk/
https://instagram.com/squaremile_com

Magazine Publisher: Threadneedle Media

Nonfiction > *Articles*
  Arts; Books; Boxing; Cars; Comedy / Humour; Culture; Films; Fitness; Food and Drink; Formula One; Golf; Investments; London; Motorbikes; Music; Photography; Property / Real Estate; Pubs; Sport; TV; Technology; Travel; Whisky; Wine; Yachts

Luxury lifestyle magazine targeting wealthy men working in London's financial districts.

Editor: Martin Deeson

M355 The Stinging Fly
Magazine
PO Box 6016, Dublin 1
Ireland

stingingfly@gmail.com
submissions.stingingfly@gmail.com

https://stingingfly.org
https://www.facebook.com/StingingFly
http://twitter.com/stingingfly

Fiction in Translation > *Short Fiction*

Fiction
  Graphic Short Fiction; *Novel Excerpts*; *Short Fiction*
Nonfiction
  Essays: General
  Interviews: Books; Creative Writing
Poetry in Translation > *Any Poetic Form*

Poetry > *Any Poetic Form*

Closed to approaches.

A literary magazine, a book publisher, an education provider, and an online platform. Independent and not for profit. Aims to seek out, nurture, publish and promote the very best new Irish and international writing.

Publisher: Declan Meade

M356 Story Unlikely
Magazine
United States
Tel: +1 (563) 370-0217

storyunlikely@mailbox.org

https://www.storyunlikely.com

Fiction > *Short Fiction*
  General, and in particular: Adventure; Comedy / Humour; Crime; Drama; Fantasy; Historical Fiction; Horror; Literary; Mystery; Romance; Science Fiction; Suspense; Thrillers; Westerns

Nonfiction > *Short Nonfiction*
  General, and in particular: Creative Nonfiction; Memoir; Narrative Nonfiction

How to send: Email; Online submission system

Magazine submission period runs from February 2nd through September 29th. No restrictions on genre (seeking all types of stories; fiction and creative nonfiction). 10k word limit (15k for Members). 8 cents a word. Reprints are 1 cent a word (we cap payment at $200, or $400 for Members). All published stories are illustrated. No submission fee.

Editor: Danny Hankner

M357 Strange Horizons
Online Magazine
United States

management@strangehorizons.com

http://strangehorizons.com
https://strangehorizons.moksha.io/publication/strange-horizons/guidelines
https://www.facebook.com/groups/strangehorizons/
https://twitter.com/strangehorizons
https://www.patreon.com/strangehorizons

Fiction > *Short Fiction*
  Fantasy; Science Fiction; Slipstream; Speculative

Nonfiction
  Articles: Fantasy; Science Fiction; Slipstream; Speculative
  Essays: Fantasy; Science Fiction; Slipstream; Speculative
  Interviews: Fantasy; Science Fiction; Slipstream; Speculative
  Reviews: Fantasy; Science Fiction; Slipstream; Speculative
Poetry > *Any Poetic Form*
  Fantasy; Science Fiction; Slipstream; Speculative

Send: Full text
How to send: Moksha
How not to send: Email

Weekly online magazine of speculative fiction, poetry, and nonfiction on related topics. Submit via online submission system only.

M358 Strategic Finance
Magazine
United States

sfmag@imanet.org

https://sfmagazine.com

PROFESSIONAL > **Nonfiction** > *Articles*: Finance

Send: Query; Full text; Submission Form
How to send: Word file email attachment
How not to send: PDF file email attachment

Publishes articles that help financial professionals perform their jobs more effectively, advance their careers, grow personally and professionally, and make their organisations more profitable.

M359 Structo Magazine
Print Magazine; Online Magazine
United Kingdom

https://structomagazine.co.uk

Magazine Publisher: Structo Press

Fiction in Translation > *Short Fiction*

Fiction > *Short Fiction*

Poetry in Translation > *Any Poetic Form*

Poetry > *Any Poetic Form*

Closed to approaches.

Short stories of up to approximately 4,000 words will be considered, both original stories and new translations of non-English language texts; or up to three previously unpublished poems in English or new translations from other languages. Hybrid forms are welcome.

M360 Studio One
Print Magazine; Online Magazine
United States

studio1@csbsju.edu

https://digitalcommons.csbsju.edu/studio_one/
https://www.csbsju.edu/forms/MNDYVGOZ4Z

Fiction > *Short Fiction*

Nonfiction > *Short Nonfiction*: Creative Nonfiction

Poetry > *Any Poetic Form*

Closed to approaches.

Literary and visual arts magazine published each spring. Founded in 1976 as a print publication with a print run of between 400 and 600 copies. Also, online since 2012.

M361 Successful Meetings
Magazine
301 Route 17 N, Suite 1150, Rutherford, NJ 07070
United States
Tel: +1 (201) 902-1978

ledelstein@ntmllc.com

http://www.successfulmeetings.com

PROFESSIONAL > **Nonfiction** > *Articles*: Business

Magazine for multi-tasking meeting planners.

Editor: Loren Edelstein

M362 Suffolk Magazine
Magazine
United Kingdom

Magazine Publisher: Great British Life

M363 Sunshine Artist
Magazine
N7528 Aanstad Rd., Iola, WI 54945
United States
Tel: +1 (800) 597-2573

https://sunshineartist.com

Magazine Publisher: JP Media LLC

PROFESSIONAL > **Nonfiction** > *Reviews*
Arts; Crafts

Publishes reviews of fine art fairs, festivals, events, and small craft shows around the country, for professionals making a living through art shows.

Managing Editor: Melissa Jones

M364 Sunspot Literary Journal
Print Magazine; Online Magazine
Durham, NC
United States
Tel: +1 (919) 928-2245

Sunspotlit@gmail.com

https://sunspotlit.com
https://sunspotlit.submittable.com/submit

Fiction in Translation > *Short Fiction*

Fiction
Graphic Novels; Graphic Short Fiction; Novelettes; Novellas; Short Fiction
Nonfiction > *Essays*

Poetry in Translation > *Any Poetic Form*

Poetry > *Any Poetic Form*

Scripts
Film Scripts; Theatre Scripts

How to send: Submittable

Costs: Offers services that writers have to pay for; A fee is charged upon submission in some cases. Offers a poetry feedback service and competitions for which there is an entry fee.

Since launching in January of 2019, this journal has amplified diverse multinational voices. New works have been published in their original language side-by-side with English translations. Boundaries that exclude meaningful and important works have been broken by accepting extremely long-form pieces, a rarity in publishing today.

M365 The Supplement
Magazine
Atlantean Publishing, 4 Pierrot Steps, 71 Kursaal Way, Southend-on-Sea, Essex, SS1 2UY
United Kingdom

atlanteanpublishing@hotmail.com

https://atlanteanpublishing.wordpress.com/
https://atlanteanpublishing.fandom.com/wiki/The_Supplement

Book Publisher / Magazine Publisher: Atlantean Publishing

Fiction > *Short Fiction*

Nonfiction
Articles: General
News: Small Press
Reviews: Books; Films
Poetry > *Any Poetic Form*

Send: Full text; Self-Addressed Stamped Envelope (SASE)
How to send: Email; Post

Publishes small-press news and advertisements, reviews covering new publications from small presses, independent and mainstream books, films and much more beside, and various articles on an equally wide variety of topics — as well as the occasional poem or very short piece of fiction, often related to the non-fiction content.

Editor: David-John Tyrer

M366 Sussex Life
Magazine
United Kingdom

Magazine Publisher: Great British Life

M367 Swimming Pool News
Magazine
United Kingdom

jon@aqua-publishing.co.uk

https://www.swimmingpoolnews.co.uk

Magazine Publisher: Aqua Publishing

PROFESSIONAL > **Nonfiction** > *Articles*
Spas and Hot Tubs; Swimming Pools

How to send: Email

Informing the pool and spa industry since 1959. Covering the UK's wet leisure market, this magazine is the UK's longest running and most respected trade title. Produced bi-monthly, the magazine covers swimming pools, covers, enclosures, spas, swim spas, hot tubs, saunas, chemicals, accessories and much, much more!

M368 Tahoma Literary Review
Magazine
United States

poetry@tahomaliteraryreview.com
fiction@tahomaliteraryreview.com
nonfiction@tahomaliteraryreview.com

https://tahomaliteraryreview.com

Fiction > *Short Fiction*
Experimental; Literary

Nonfiction
Essays: General, and in particular: Experimental; Lyric Essays
Short Nonfiction: Narrative Nonfiction

Poetry
Formal Poetry; Free Verse; Long Form Poetry

Closed to approaches.

Costs: A fee is charged upon submission; Offers services that writers have to pay for. $4 for poetry and flash prose; $5 for longer prose. Critiques available for an additional fee.

Publishes poetry, fiction, and nonfiction. Charges $4 submission fee for short works; $5 submission fee for long works. Submit online through online submission system.

M369 Takahe
Magazine
New Zealand

https://www.takahe.org.nz
https://takahemagazine.submittable.com/submit
https://twitter.com/takahemagazine

Fiction > *Short Fiction*: Literary

Nonfiction
Essays: Cultural Criticism; New Zealand; South Pacific
Reviews: Books

Poetry > *Any Poetic Form*

How to send: Submittable

Exists to foster and promote art and literature that represents the diverse voices of Aotearoa New Zealand within the global context. It does this by publishing innovative prose, poetry, art, and critique by emerging and established writers and artists.

Art Editor: Andrew Paul Wood

Fiction Editor: Zoë Meager

Poetry Editor: Erik Kennedy

Reviews Editor: Sile Mannion

M370 Take a Break's Take a Puzzle
Magazine
Media House, Peterborough Business Park, Lynch Wood, Peterborough, PE2 6EA
United Kingdom

https://www.puzzleshq.com/puzzles-magazines/mixed/take-a-puzzle/

Magazine: Take a Break
Magazine Publisher: Bauer Media Group

Nonfiction > *Puzzles*

Magazine of puzzles.

M371 Tears in the Fence
Magazine
Flats, Durweston Mill, Mill Lane, Durweston, Blandford Forum, Dorset, DT11 0QD
United Kingdom

tearsinthefence@gmail.com

https://tearsinthefence.com

Fiction > *Short Fiction*

Nonfiction
  Essays: General
  Interviews: General
  Reviews: General
  Short Nonfiction: Creative Nonfiction

Poetry
  Any Poetic Form; *Prose Poetry*

Send: Full text
How to send: Email attachment; In the body of an email
How not to send: PDF file email attachment

International literary magazine publishing poetry, fiction, prose poems, essays, translations, interviews and reviews. Publishes fiction as short as 100 words or as long as 3,500. Maximum 6 poems per poet per issue. No simultaneous or PDF submissions, or previously published material. Send submissions by email as both an attachment and in the body of the email.

M372 The Temz Review
Online Magazine
London, ON
Canada

thetemzreview@gmail.com

https://www.thetemzreview.com

Fiction > *Short Fiction*: Literary

Nonfiction
  Interviews: Literature
  Reviews: Literature

Poetry > *Any Poetic Form*

Send: Full text; Query
How to send: Moksha; Email

Quarterly online magazine. Submit one piece of fiction or creative nonfiction (or more than one if under 1,000 words) or 1-8 poems via online submission system. For reviews and interviews, send query by email.

M373 That's Life!
Magazine
The Lantern, 75 Hampstead Road, London, NW1 2PL
United Kingdom

stories@thatslife.co.uk

http://www.thatslife.co.uk

Types: Nonfiction
Formats: Articles; News
Subjects: Lifestyle
Markets: Adult

Publishes nonfiction true life stories. See website for details.

M374 Thin Air Magazine
Print Magazine
United States

https://thinairmagazine.org
https://www.instagram.com/thinairmagazine/
https://twitter.com/thinairmagazine
https://www.facebook.com/thinairmagazine/

Fiction > *Short Fiction*: Literary

Nonfiction > *Short Nonfiction*

Poetry > *Any Poetic Form*

Send: Full text
How to send: Submittable

Costs: A fee is charged upon submission. $3 per submission.

A non-profit, graduate-student-run, literary magazine. Submit up to three poems, or prose up to 3,000 words.

M375 Third Coast
Magazine
United States

editors@thirdcoastmagazine.com

http://thirdcoastmagazine.com
https://thirdcoastmagazine.submittable.com/submit
http://facebook.com/thirdcoastmagazine
http://twitter.com/thirdcoastmag
http://instagram.com/thirdcoastmag

Fiction > *Short Fiction*

Nonfiction > *Short Nonfiction*: Creative Nonfiction

Poetry > *Any Poetic Form*

Scripts > *Theatre Scripts*

Closed to approaches.

Costs: A fee is charged upon submission. $3 submission fee.

All submissions should be sent via Submittable, through the portals of their respective genres. All attachments sent by email will be deleted, and any submissions sent via postal mail or social media will not be read. Accepts simultaneous submissions, but not multiple submissions; please submit no more than one manuscript at a time. No previously published works.

M376 This England
Magazine
185 Fleet Street, Holborn, London, EC4A 2HS
United Kingdom
Tel: +44 (0) 20 7400 1083

thisengland@dcthomson.co.uk
editor@thisengland.co.uk

https://www.thisengland.co.uk
https://www.dcthomson.co.uk/brands/this-england/
https://www.facebook.com/ThisEnglandMagazine/

Newspaper Publisher / Magazine Publisher: DC Thomson Media

Nonfiction > *Articles*
  Culture; England; History; Nature

Poetry > *Any Poetic Form*: England

The quarterly magazine for everyone who loves England's scenery, heritage, history and people. Launched in 1968 with the light-hearted slogan, "as refreshing as a pot of tea" and with a mission of "poetry not politics", it is packed with absorbing articles, beautiful photography and uplifting stories and poems celebrating all that is best about England.

M377 The Threepenny Review
Magazine
PO Box 9131, Berkeley, CA 94709
United States

wlesser@threepennyreview.com

https://www.threepennyreview.com

Fiction > *Short Fiction*: Literary

Nonfiction > *Articles*
  Arts; Culture; Literature

Poetry > *Any Poetic Form*

Closed to approaches.

National literary magazine with coverage of the visual and performing arts. Send complete MS by post with SASE or via online submission system. No previously published material, simultaneous submissions, or submissions from May to December. Prospective contributors are advised to read the magazine before submitting.

Editor: Wendy Lesser

M378 Tocher
Magazine
School of Scottish Studies Archives, University of Edinburgh, 29 George Square, Edinburgh, EH8 9LD
United Kingdom

scottish.studies.arhives@ed.ac.uk

https://www.ed.ac.uk/literatures-languages-cultures/celtic-scottish-studies/research/publications/in-house/tocher

ACADEMIC > Nonfiction > *Articles*
Culture; Folklore, Myths, and Legends; Music; Scotland

ADULT
Fiction in Translation > *Short Fiction*: Scotland

Fiction > *Short Fiction*: Scotland

The journal contains traditional Scottish songs, stories, music, customs, beliefs, local history, rhymes and riddles transcribed from tapes held in the sound archive.

M379 Tolka
Magazine
Ireland

https://www.tolkajournal.org
https://www.instagram.com/tolkajournal/
https://twitter.com/tolkajournal

Fiction > *Short Fiction*: Autofiction

Nonfiction
Essays: Personal Essays
Short Nonfiction: Memoir; Travel

Closed to approaches.

Biannual literary journal of non-fiction: publishing essays, reportage, travel writing, auto-fiction, individual stories and the writing that flows in between.

M380 Tributaries
Online Magazine
United States

https://www.thefourthriver.com
https://4thriver.submittable.com/submit

Magazine: The Fourth River (**M153**)

Fiction in Translation > *Short Fiction*

Fiction > *Short Fiction*

Nonfiction in Translation > *Short Nonfiction*

Nonfiction > *Short Nonfiction*

Poetry in Translation > *Any Poetic Form*

Poetry > *Any Poetic Form*

How to send: Submittable

Weekly online publication, showcasing the brief and the inspiring, that which sustains us and takes us through unexpected courses. Each week we will feature one short piece on our website. Submit one poem or up to 500 words of fiction or nonfiction prose, translations in any genre, and hybridity that addresses the mission. Multiple submissions are not accepted. Simultaneous submissions are fine as long as you notify us immediately. We do not accept previously published work.

M381 The Tusculum Review
Magazine
P.O. Box 5113, 60 Shiloh Rd, Greeneville, TN 37745-0595
United States
Tel: +1 (423) 636-7300 ext. 5420

review@tusculum.edu

https://ttr.tusculum.edu

Fiction > *Short Fiction*: Literary

Nonfiction
Essays: General
Reviews: Books

Poetry > *Any Poetic Form*

Scripts > *Theatre Scripts*: Drama

Send: Full text; Self-Addressed Stamped Envelope (SASE)
How to send: Submittable; Email; Post

Costs: A fee is charged for online submissions. $2.

We seek well-crafted writing that takes risks. We publish work in and between all genres: poetry, fiction, essays, and plays--we appreciate work in experimental and traditional modes. We accept prose submissions of less than 7,000 words (24 double-spaced pages) and poetry submissions under five pages. We publish scripts in the 10-minute format (10 pages) and book reviews of under two pages. Generally, no submissions by mail or email, but if Submittable is a hardship make contact by email. If you do not have internet access send submissions by post with SASE.

M382 UCity Review
Online Magazine
United States

editors@ucityreview.com

http://www.ucityreview.com
https://twitter.com/UCityReview

Poetry > *Any Poetic Form*

Closed to approaches.

Online magazine accepting submissions of poetry in February / March and August / September. Submit 10-12 poems in .doc or .docx format, by email.

M383 Uncut
Magazine
United Kingdom

editors@uncut.co.uk

http://www.uncut.co.uk
https://www.facebook.com/UncutMagazine/
https://www.instagram.com/uncut_magazine/
https://twitter.com/uncutmagazine/

Nonfiction
Articles: Films; Music
Reviews: Films; Music

Magazine covering film and music.

M384 Under the Radar
Magazine
United Kingdom

mail@ninearchespress.com

https://ninearchespress.com/magazine
https://ninearchespress.submittable.com/submit

Book Publisher: Nine Arches Press (**P317**)

Fiction > *Short Fiction*

Poetry > *Any Poetic Form*

How to send: Submittable

A magazine of new contemporary poetry and fiction. Submit up to six poems, or short fiction up to 2,500 words. Submit only previously unpublished work.

M385 Understorey Magazine
Magazine
Alexa McDonough Institute for Women, Gender and Social Justice, Mount Saint Vincent University, 166 Bedford Highway, Halifax, NS, B3M 2J6
Canada

editor@understoreymagazine.ca

https://understoreymagazine.ca

Fiction > *Short Fiction*
Feminism; Women's Issues; Women

Nonfiction > *Short Nonfiction*
Creative Nonfiction; Feminism; Women's Issues; Women

Poetry > *Any Poetic Form*
Feminism; Women's Issues; Women

Closed to approaches.

Publishes fiction, poetry, and creative nonfiction by Canadian women. Send prose up to 1,500 words or up to five poems by email. See website for full guidelines.

M386 Vagabond City
Online Magazine
United States

vagabondcitypoetry@gmail.com
vagabondcityfiction@gmail.com
vagabondcitynonfic@gmail.com
vagabondcityliterary@gmail.com

https://vagabondcitylit.com

Fiction > *Short Fiction*

Nonfiction
Essays: Creative Nonfiction
Interviews: General
Reviews: Books

Poetry > *Any Poetic Form*

Send: Full text
How to send: Email

Electronic magazine featuring poetry, fiction, art, creative nonfiction and essays by marginalised creators. Also publishes book reviews and interviews. Submit up to five pieces at a time in the body of an email or as a Word file attachment. See website for full guidelines.

M387 Vallum

Magazine
5038 Sherbrooke West, P.O. Box 23077 CP
Vendome Station, Montreal, Quebec, H4A 1T0
Canada

info@vallummag.com

https://vallummag.com
https://www.facebook.com/VallumMagazine
https://twitter.com/vallummag
https://www.instagram.com/vallummag/
https://soundcloud.com/vallum-magazine
https://www.youtube.com/channel/UCARH_nOH0vXwmpXSxzpgQZg

Nonfiction
  Essays; *Interviews*; *Reviews*
Poetry > *Any Poetic Form*: Contemporary

Closed to approaches.

Send 4-7 poems, essays of 4-6 pages, interviews of 3-5 pages, reviews of 1-3 pages, through online submission system only. No fiction, plays, movie scripts, memoir, or creative nonfiction. Check website for submission windows and themes.

M388 Vestal Review

Online Magazine
United States

info@vestalreview.org

https://www.vestalreview.net
https://vestalreview.submittable.com/submit
https://www.facebook.com/VestalReview/
https://www.instagram.com/vestalreview/
https://twitter.com/VestalReview

Fiction > *Short Fiction*

Nonfiction
  Interviews; *Reviews*

Send: Full text
How to send: Submittable

Publishes flash fiction up to 500 words. Accepts submissions between February 1 and May 31, and between August 1 and November 30. Also accepts proposals for interviews and reviews.

M389 The Virginia Quarterly Review

Magazine
5 Boar's Head Lane, PO Box 400223,
Charlottesville, VA 22904
United States
Tel: +1 (434) 924-3675
Fax: +1 (434) 924-1397

editors@vqronline.org

https://www.vqronline.org
https://www.facebook.com/vqreview
https://twitter.com/vqr

Fiction > *Short Fiction*

Nonfiction > *Short Nonfiction*
  Arts; Creative Nonfiction; Cultural Criticism; History; Literary Criticism; Politics

Poetry > *Any Poetic Form*

Does not want:

> **Fiction** > *Short Fiction*
>   Fantasy; Romance; Science Fiction

Closed to approaches.

Strives to publish the best writing they can find. Has a long history of publishing accomplished and award-winning authors, but they also seek and support emerging writers.

M390 Virginia Wine & Country Life

Magazine
United States

Concierge@ivypublications.com
editor@ivylifeandstylemedia.com

https://wineandcountrylife.com
https://www.facebook.com/WineAndCountryLife/
https://www.instagram.com/wineandcountrylife/
https://www.pinterest.com/wclifeva/

Magazine Publisher: Ivy Life & Style Media

Nonfiction > *Articles*
  Architecture; Arts; Beer Making; Country Lifestyle; Entertainment; Farm Equipment; Food and Drink; Gardening; Interior Design; Literature; Music; Virginia; Wine

Send: Query
How to send: Email

We tell the stories of the makers and celebrate the art of living well in the heart of Virginia Wine Country. Each luxury print magazine highlights Virginia wine, farm-to-table food, architecture, gardening, the arts and elegant entertaining, as well as Virginia craft drinks.

M391 Virginia Wine & Country Weddings

Magazine
4282 Ivy Road, Charlottesville, VA 22903
United States
Tel: +1 (434) 984-4713

Concierge@ivypublications.com

https://wineandcountryweddings.com

Magazine Publisher: Ivy Life & Style Media

Nonfiction > *Articles*
  Lifestyle; Virginia; Weddings

Send: Query
How not to send: Email

A uniquely curated magazine for creating the elegant country wedding in Jefferson's Virginia, one that will inspire couples as well as top event planners across the nation from New York City to Beverly Hills.

M392 Viz

Magazine
2nd Floor, Saunders House, 52-53 The Mall,
Ealing, W5 3TA
United Kingdom

hello@metropolis.co.uk

https://viz.co.uk
https://www.facebook.com/VizComic/
https://twitter.com/vizcomic

Magazine Publisher: Diamond Publishing

Fiction > *Cartoons*: Comedy / Humour

Nonfiction > *Articles*
  Comedy / Humour; Satire

Magazine of adult humour, including cartoons, spoof articles, etc.

M393 Vogue

Magazine
United Kingdom

https://www.vogue.co.uk
https://www.facebook.com/BritishVogue
https://www.instagram.com/britishvogue
https://twitter.com/BritishVogue
https://www.youtube.com/user/vogue

Media Company: Condé Nast

Nonfiction > *Articles*
  Arts; Beauty; Fashion; Lifestyle

Upmarket women's magazine. Generally commissions required pieces from known writers.

M394 Waccamaw

Online Magazine
United States

http://waccamawjournal.com
https://www.facebook.com/Waccamaw-A-Journal-of-Contemporary-Literature-164290950299653/
https://twitter.com/waccamawjournal
https://www.instagram.com/waccamawjournal/

Book Publisher: Athenaeum Press

Fiction > *Short Fiction*: Literary

Nonfiction > *Essays*

Poetry > *Any Poetic Form*

Closed to approaches.

Online literary journal publishing poems, stories, and essays. Submit prose up to 6,000 words or 3-5 poems between August 1 and September 8 annually. Submit via online submission system only.

M395 Walk Magazine

Magazine
United Kingdom

https://www.ramblers.org.uk/walkmag
https://twitter.com/walkmagazine

Nonfiction > *Articles*: Walking

Rambling magazine publishing features on any aspect of walking in Britain. No general travel articles.

M396 The Wallace Stevens Journal
Magazine
University of Antwerp, Prinsstraat 13, 2000 Antwerp
Belgium

https://www.press.jhu.edu/journals/wallace-stevens-journal

ACADEMIC > **Nonfiction**
  Articles: Biography; Literary Criticism; Poetry as a Subject
  Essays: Biography; Literary Criticism; Poetry as a Subject
  News: Literature
  Reviews: Books

ADULT > **Poetry** > *Any Poetic Form*

Send: Full text
How to send: Word file email attachment

Publishes articles and essays on all aspects of Wallace Stevens' poetry and life. Also accepts poetry inspired by the poet. See website for full submission guidelines.

Editor: Bart Eeckhout

M397 Wallpaper
Print Magazine; Online Magazine
United Kingdom

contact@wallpaper.com

https://www.wallpaper.com
https://www.instagram.com/wallpapermag
https://twitter.com/wallpapermag
https://www.facebook.com/wallpapermagazine
https://www.pinterest.co.uk/wallpapermag/
https://flipboard.com/@wallpapermag
https://foursquare.com/wallpapermag

Magazine Publisher: Future

Nonfiction > *Articles*
  Architecture; Arts; Beauty; Design; Fashion; Technology; Transport

Magazine of architecture, design, art, entertaining, beauty & grooming, transport, technology, fashion, and watches and jewellery.

M398 Wasafiri
Magazine
c/o School of English and Drama, Queen Mary, University of London, Mile End Road, London, E1 4NS
United Kingdom
Tel: +44 (0) 20 7882 2686

wasafiri@qmul.ac.uk

https://www.wasafiri.org
https://www.facebook.com/wasafiri.magazine
https://twitter.com/Wasafirimag
https://www.youtube.com/channel/UC4J-lxAIL8iBiaRR2AOpGFg
https://www.linkedin.com/groups/8343914/profile

Fiction > *Short Fiction*: Literary

Nonfiction
  Articles: Culture; Literature
  Essays: Culture; Literature
Poetry > *Any Poetic Form*

Send: Full text
How to send: Online submission system

The indispensable journal of contemporary African, Asian Black British, Caribbean and transnational literatures.

In over fifteen years of publishing, this magazine has changed the face of contemporary writing in Britain. As a literary magazine primarily concerned with new and postcolonial writers, it continues to stress the diversity and range of black and diasporic writers world-wide. It remains committed to its original aims: to create a definitive forum for the voices of new writers and to open up lively spaces for serious critical discussion not available elsewhere. It is Britain's only international magazine for Black British, African, Asian and Caribbean literatures. Get the whole picture, get the magazine at the core of contemporary international literature today.

Submit via online submissions portal only (see website).

M399 Welsh Country
Magazine
Aberbanc, Llandysul, Ceredigion, SA44 5NP
United Kingdom
Tel: +44 (0) 1559 372010

info@welshcountry.co.uk

https://www.welshcountry.co.uk

Nonfiction
  Articles: Arts; Crafts; Culture; Food and Drink; Gardening; History; Nature; Wales; Walking
  News: Wales

Magazine covering Welsh villages, history, wild life, walking and gardening. In addition we promote amazing local artisan Welsh food & drink producers, as well as a strong focus on the thriving Welsh arts & crafts scene.

M400 West Branch
Magazine
Stadler Center, Bucknell University, 1 Dent Drive, Lewisburg, PA 17837
United States

westbranch@bucknell.edu

https://westbranch.blogs.bucknell.edu

Fiction > *Short Fiction*

Nonfiction
  Essays; *Reviews*
Poetry > *Any Poetic Form*

Closed to approaches.

Send all submissions via online submission system, between August 1 and April 1 annually.

M401 West Essex Life
Magazine

Magazine Publisher: Archant

M402 Westchester Magazine
Magazine
2 Clinton Ave, Rye, NY 10580
United States
Tel: +1 (914) 345-0601

https://westchestermagazine.com
https://www.instagram.com/westchestermagazine/
https://twitter.com/WestchesterMag
https://www.facebook.com/WestchesterMagazine
https://www.linkedin.com/company/westchester-magazine/
https://www.tiktok.com/@westchestermag

Nonfiction > *Articles*
  Business; Food and Drink; Houses and Homes; Interior Design; Lifestyle; Property / Real Estate; Restaurants; Westchester County

Regional business lifestyle magazine covering Westchester County, New York.

M403 WestWard Quarterly
Magazine
PO Box 369, Hamilton, IL 62341
United States
Tel: +1 (800) 440-4043

editorwwq@mail.com

https://www.wwquarterly.com

Poetry > *Any Poetic Form*

How to send: Email; Post

We accept all styles of poetry and look for good imagery and grammar and a fresh outlook. If rhyming, we look for consistency and natural word order in the rhyme scheme. If metrical, we look for consistent scansion or "beat." If free verse, we look for some kind of rhythm, flow, and harmony that makes a poem differ from prose. We do not publish material with a negative or cynical outlook (possibly excepting in a humorous vein) or material with profanity or crudity. Additionally, poetry that is obscure (with references or meanings not readily accessible to most readers) is not likely to be acceptable for this magazine.

M404 The White Review
Magazine
A.103 Fuel Tank, 8-12 Creekside, London, SE8 3DX
United Kingdom

editors@thewhitereview.org

https://www.thewhitereview.org
http://www.facebook.com/thewhitereview
http://www.twitter.com/thewhitereview
http://www.instagram.com/thewhitereview

Fiction in Translation > *Short Fiction*: Literary

Fiction > *Short Fiction*: Literary

Nonfiction
  Essays: Arts; Literature
  Interviews: Arts; Literature
Poetry in Translation > *Any Poetic Form*

Poetry > *Any Poetic Form*

Closed to approaches.

Print and online arts and literature magazine. Publishes cultural analysis, reviews, and new fiction and poetry. Accepts submissions only in specific submission windows. Prose submissions should be a minimum of 1,500 words. See website for guidelines and submit by email.

M405 Windsor Review
Magazine
Department of English, University of Windsor, 401 Sunset Ave, Windsor, Ontario, N9B 3P4
Canada

thewindsorreview@uwindsor.ca

https://ojs.uwindsor.ca
https://ojs.uwindsor.ca/index.php/windsor_review

Fiction > *Short Fiction*

Nonfiction
  Essays: Literature
  Short Nonfiction: Creative Nonfiction

Poetry > *Any Poetic Form*

Closed to approaches.

Features poetry, fiction, creative nonfiction, and review essays. We welcome material from all writers, with a focus on new and emerging voices.

M406 Wine Enthusiast
Magazine
United States

https://www.wineenthusiast.com
https://www.instagram.com/wineenthusiast/
https://www.facebook.com/WineEnthusiast/
https://twitter.com/WineEnthusiast
https://www.pinterest.com/wineenthusiast/
https://www.tiktok.com/@wineenthusiast
https://www.youtube.com/@WineEnthusiastCatalog

Nonfiction > *Articles*: Wine

For more than 40 years we've been the premier source for all things wine, creating and delivering unique wine lifestyle products and content that inspires and empowers everyone to enjoy wine to its fullest. We started with a humble mission to make the wine experience accessible to everyone and have grown into a dynamic commerce and media company regarded around the world for our unmatched passion and expertise.

Editor: Tim Moriarty

M407 Woman & Home
Magazine
121-141 Westbourne Terrace, London, W2 6JR
United Kingdom
Tel: +44 (0) 20 3148 5000

https://www.womanandhome.com

Magazine Publisher: Future

Nonfiction > *Articles*
  Beauty; Fashion; Food; Health; Lifestyle; Travel; Wellbeing; Women's Interests

Our mission is to keep 40+ women informed on the subjects that matter to them, so they can live smarter, healthier and happier lives. We publish celebrity news for grown-ups, as well as informative, no-nonsense health and wellbeing features about subjects like the menopause. We speak to internationally renown experts to give up-to-date advice on dieting and weight-loss plans. We aim to delight you with delicious – and healthy – recipes. And to inspire your next holiday destinations with travel recommendations both near and far. We filter through the latest fashion and beauty noise to offer you advice on the trends you'll want to try, because they're flattering as well as stylish.

M408 Yachting Monthly
Magazine
United Kingdom

yachtingmonthly@futurenet.com

https://www.yachtingmonthly.com
http://www.youtube.com/user/YachtingMonthly
http://www.facebook.com/yachtingmonthlymag
http://twitter.com/yachtingmonthly

Magazine Publisher: Future

Nonfiction > *Articles*
  Sailing; Yachts

Magazine publishing articles and features on yachting and cruising.

M409 The Yale Review
Magazine
United States

theyalereview@yale.edu

https://yalereview.yale.edu
https://www.facebook.com/YaleReview/
https://www.instagram.com/yalereview/
https://twitter.com/YaleReview

Fiction > *Short Fiction*: Literary

Nonfiction > *Essays*
  Arts; Cultural Criticism; Films; History; Literary Criticism; Memoir; Music; Politics; TV

Poetry > *Any Poetic Form*

Closed to approaches.

Opens for submissions of poetry, nonfiction, and fiction in September of each year, via online submission system. Accepts pitches for essays and criticism on a rolling basis by email.

Editor: Meghan O'Rourke

M410 Yankee Magazine
Magazine
United States

https://newengland.com
https://www.facebook.com/YankeeMagazine/
https://www.instagram.com/yankeemagazine/
https://www.pinterest.com/yankeemagazine

Nonfiction > *Articles*
  Arts; Culture; Current Affairs; Food; History; Houses and Homes; Lifestyle; New England; Travel

Magazine covering the finest that New England has to offer, from home, food and travel coverage to arts and culture, current events, and history. Drawing readers from across generations and around the country, this magazine is New England's storyteller: exploring the future, present, and past of this fabled region, and sharing the lifestyle secrets that only the locals know. Through beautiful photos, artwork, and unforgettable stories, the magazine paints a portrait of New England that feels like home to all who live here and inspires people everywhere to discover the New England they dream of.

M411 Yellow Mama Webzine
Magazine
United States

crosmus@hotmail.com

http://blackpetalsks.tripod.com/yellowmama

Types: Fiction
Subjects: Horror; Literary
Markets: Adult

Send: Full text
How to send: Email

Webzine publishing fiction and poetry. Seeks cutting edge, hardboiled, horror, literary, noir, psychological / horror. No fanfiction, romance, swords & sorcery, fantasy, or erotica. Send submissions by email. See website for full guidelines.

M412 Yes Poetry Magazine
Online Magazine
United States

editor@yespoetry.com

https://www.yespoetry.com
https://twitter.com/yespoetry
https://yespoetry.tumblr.com/

Fiction > *Short Fiction*

Nonfiction
  Essays; *Interviews*; *Reviews*
Poetry > *Any Poetic Form*

Closed to approaches.

A lifestyle art publication that encourages deep analysis and thought, pushing for progressive change and identification.

Book Publisher: Yes Poetry Chapbooks

M413 Yorkshire Life
Magazine
United Kingdom

https://www.greatbritishlife.co.uk/magazines/yorkshire/

Magazine Publisher: Great British Life

Nonfiction
  Articles: Culture; Food and Drink; Houses and Homes; Lifestyle; Outdoor Activities; Travel; Walking; Yorkshire
  Interviews: Yorkshire

Magazine covering the people, places, history, arts, food and events of Yorkshire.

M414 Yorkshire Women's Life Magazine
Print Magazine
PO Box 113, Leeds, LS8 2WX
United Kingdom

ywleditorial@btinternet.com

https://www.yorkshirewomenslife.co.uk

Nonfiction > *Articles*
  Fashion; Lifestyle; Travel; Wellbeing; Women's Issues; Yorkshire

We believe every woman has a right to be who she wants to be; that's why our magazine is inclusive to everyone. Our title encourages and supports new women writers by providing a platform via the magazine to profile new women's writing. The title works with new writers while covering women focused issues both regionally and internationally.

M415 Your Cat
Magazine
United Kingdom

https://www.yourcat.co.uk
https://www.facebook.com/yourcatmagazine
https://www.twitter.com/yourcatmagazine
https://www.instagram.com/yourcatmagazine
https://www.youtube.com/YourCatYourDog

Magazine Publisher: Warners Group Publications

Nonfiction > *Articles*: Cats

Practical magazine covering the care of cats and kittens.

Editor:

M416 Yours
Magazine
The Lantern, 75 Hampstead Road, London, NW1 2PL
United Kingdom

yours@bauermedia.co.uk

https://www.yours.co.uk
https://www.facebook.com/Yoursmagazine
https://twitter.com/yoursmagazine
https://www.pinterest.com/yoursmagazine/

Magazine Publisher: Bauer Media Group

Nonfiction
  Articles: Beauty; Fashion; Finance; Fitness; Food; Gardening; Health; Pets; Recipes; Relationships; Travel
  Interviews: Celebrity
  Short Nonfiction: Real Life Stories; Women

How to send: Email; Post

Magazine for women over 50. Publishes tips and expert advice on a range of topics from travel to financial guidance as well as discovering the latest fashion trends, beauty, and health tips. Also exclusive celebrity interviews and recipes for healthy meals or hearty treats.

Fiction Editor: Marion Clarke

M417 Yours Fiction – Women's Special Series
Print Magazine
The Lantern, 75 Hampstead Road, London, NW1 2PL
United Kingdom

yours@bauermedia.co.uk

https://www.yours.co.uk/yours-fiction/

Magazine Publisher: Bauer Media Group

Fiction > *Short Fiction*
  General, and in particular: Ghost Stories; Historical Fiction; Mystery; Romance; Saga

Closed to approaches.

Publishes 26 stories per issue. Stories can be of any genre, but we especially keen on romance, murder mystery, historical fiction, ghost stories, sagas and stories to make you smile. Any length between 450 and 2,700 words.

M418 Zoetrope: All-Story
Magazine
916 Kearny Street, San Francisco, CA 94133
United States

info@all-story.com

https://store.all-story.com

Fiction > *Short Fiction*

Closed to approaches.

Magazine of short fiction.

M419 Zone 3
Magazine
United States

https://www.zone3press.com

Book Publisher / Magazine Publisher: Zone 3 Press

Fiction > *Short Fiction*
  Contemporary; Literary

Nonfiction > *Short Nonfiction*
  Contemporary; Creative Nonfiction; Literary

Poetry > *Any Poetic Form*

Closed to approaches.

Costs: A fee is charged upon submission. $3.

Publishes fiction, poetry, and creative nonfiction. Accepts submissions through online submission system between August 1 and April 1 annually. $3 submission fee.

Book Publishers

For the most up-to-date listings of these and hundreds of other book publishers, visit https://www.firstwriter.com/publishers

To claim your free access to the site, please see the back of this book.

P001 23 House Publishing
Book Publisher
United States
Fax: +1 (214) 367-4343

editor@23house.com

http://www.23house.com

Nonfiction > *Nonfiction Books*
  Ghosts; Regional

Currently looking for nonfiction, regional ghost story manuscripts. A prospective book should contain both the history and ghost stories of the specific region. The maximum word count is 65,000, and the minimum is 40,000 – photos, maps, and other visual aids are a major plus.

P002 404 Ink
Book Publisher
United Kingdom

hello@404ink.com

https://www.404ink.com
https://www.facebook.com/404ink/
http://instagram.com/404ink
https://twitter.com/404Ink

Fiction
  Novels; *Short Fiction Collections*
Nonfiction > *Nonfiction Books*
  General, and in particular: Inspirational; Politics; Social Issues

Poetry > *Poetry Collections*

Closed to approaches.

Publishes fiction, non-fiction, short stories and poetry. No children's books. Particularly likes humour, gritty women-led fiction, anti-heroes, parodies, the weird and wonderful, hard-hitting social issue non-fiction, inspirational stories and accessible political engagement. Would quite like to publish a crime book that's an unusual take on the genre.

P003 4RV Poetry
Publishing Imprint
249079 East 1000 Rd., Hydro, OK 73048
United States
Tel: +1 (405) 820-9640

president@4rvpublishingllc.com
vp-o_ad@4rvpublishingllc.com

http://www.4rvpublishing.com/poetry-submissions.html

Book Publisher: 4RV Publishing (**P004**)

Poetry > *Poetry Collections*

Send: Query; Synopsis; Full text
How to send: Email attachment

Poetry books should have at least 20 poems (one per page) that follow a general theme. Full manuscript should be submitted.

P004 4RV Publishing
Book Publisher
249079 East 1000 Road, Hydro, OK 73048
United States
Tel: +1 (405) 820-9640

Administrator@4rvpublishingllc.com

https://www.4rvpublishing.com
https://www.facebook.com/4RV-Publishing-LLC-20479523692/
https://twitter.com/4RV
https://www.youtube.com/user/4RVPublishingLLC

ADULT
  Fiction > *Novels*
    General, and in particular: Christianity; Fantasy; Romance; Science Fiction

  Nonfiction > *Nonfiction Books*

  Poetry > *Poetry Collections*

CHILDREN'S > **Fiction**
  Chapter Books; *Early Readers*; *Middle Grade*; *Picture Books*
TEEN > **Fiction** > *Novels*
YOUNG ADULT > **Fiction** > *Novels*

Does not want:

> **Fiction** > *Novels*: Erotic

Send: Query; Synopsis; Writing sample
How to send: Email attachment

Accepts most genres of fiction and nonfiction books for all ages, including nonfiction, mystery, romance, mainstream, western, Christian, and science-fiction, as well as children's books, middle grade and young adult novels. No poetry or graphic sex or violence. Language should not be overly profane or vulgar. Accepts submissions by email from the US, UK, and Australia. Not accepting children's books as at May 2022. See website for current status and full guidelines.

Publishing Imprints: 4RV Biblical Based; 4RV Children's Corner; 4RV Fiction; 4RV Nonfiction; 4RV Poetry (**P003**); 4RV Tenacious (**P005**); 4RV Tweens & Teens; 4RV Young Adult

P005 4RV Tenacious
Publishing Imprint
United States

president@4rvpublishingllc.com
vp-o_ad@4rvpublishingllc.com

http://www.4rvpublishing.com/tenacious-submissions.html

Book Publisher: 4RV Publishing (**P004**)

Fiction > *Novels*
  Adventure; Crime; Fantasy; Historical Fiction; Mystery; Romance; Science Fiction; Suspense; US Southern States; Women's Fiction

Nonfiction > *Nonfiction Books*

Send: Query; Synopsis; Writing sample
How to send: Email attachment

Genres wanted at this time include Action/Adventure, Science Fiction, Fantasy, Mystery/ Suspense/Crime, Romance (without graphic details), Nonfiction, Women's Lit, Southern-Lit, Historical Fiction.

P006 A-R Editions
Book Publisher
8401 Greenway Blvd, Suite 100, Middleton WI 53562
United States
Tel: +1 (608) 836-9000

info@areditions.com

https://www.areditions.com
https://www.facebook.com/areditions

Nonfiction > *Nonfiction Books*: Music

Send: Query; Proposal
How to send: Email; File sharing service

Publisher of modern critical editions of music based on current musicological research, aimed at scholars and performers. See website for submission guidelines.

Publishing Imprint: Greenway Music Press

P007 Aardwolf Press
Book Publisher
United States

aardwolfpress@aol.com

http://www.aardwolfpress.com

Fiction > *Novels*
  Fantasy; Horror; Science Fiction; Speculative

Does not want:

> **Fiction** > *Novels*
>   Hard Science Fiction; Space Opera

Send: Query; Outline; Writing sample
How to send: Email
How not to send: Email attachment

Small publisher of speculative fiction between 50,000 and 100,000 words. Send query by email with first five pages in the body of the text. No attachments, poetry, previously published books (including online in any form), children's, stories set mainly off the Earth or earlier than the 20th century, books about elves, dragons, wizards, quests for rings/jewels/swords etc. space opera or hard science fiction.

P008 ABC-CLIO
Book Publisher
1385 Broadway Fifth Floor, New York, NY 10018
United States
Tel: +1 (800) 368-6868
Fax: +1 (805) 968-1911

CustomerService@abc-clio.com

https://www.abc-clio.com/
https://www.facebook.com/ABCCLIO
https://twitter.com/ABC_CLIO
https://www.youtube.com/user/ABCCLIOLive
https://www.linkedin.com/company/abc-clio/

Book Publisher: Bloomsbury Academic (**P071**)

ACADEMIC > **Nonfiction** > *Reference*
  General, and in particular: History; Sociology

Publishes academic reference works and periodicals primarily on topics such as history and social sciences for educational and public library settings.

Publishing Imprints: ABC-CLIO / Greenwood; Libraries Unlimited; Praeger

P009 Able Muse Press
Book Publisher
United States

submission@ablemuse.com

https://www.ablemusepress.com
https://www.facebook.com/groups/eratosphere.ablemuse/
https://twitter.com/ablemuse
https://www.youtube.com/user/ablemuse
https://www.instagram.com/ablemusepress/
https://www.linkedin.com/in/alex-pepple-8657359/
https://www.pinterest.com/ablemuse/

Fiction > *Novels*

Nonfiction > *Nonfiction Books*

Poetry > *Poetry Collections*

Send: Full text
How to send: Online submission system; Email attachment
How not to send: In the body of an email

Publishes fiction and poetry. Prefers submissions via online form, but will also accept submissions by email with ms attached as a separate document. Do not paste material in the body of the email. See website for full details.

P010 Abuzz Press
Book Publisher
United States

https://www.abuzzpress.com

Fiction > *Novels*
  General, and in particular: Adventure; Christianity

Nonfiction
  Colouring Books: General
  Nonfiction Books: Adventure; Christianity; How To

How to send: Online submission system

Publishes nonfiction, adult colouring books, how-to, new age, and exceptional fiction. No poetry, short story collections, books with colour interiors, or illegal material. Send submissions via form on website.

P011 Ad Hoc Fiction
Book Publisher
United Kingdom

helpdesk@adhocfiction.com

https://www.adhocfiction.com
https://twitter.com/AdHocFiction

Fiction > *Short Fiction Collections*

An award winning small independent publisher specialising in short-short fiction since 2015. Publishes anthologies of micro fiction, novellas-in-flash, and individual collections of flash fiction by local and international authors.

P012 Adlard Coles
Publishing Imprint
United Kingdom

adlardcoles@bloomsbury.com

https://www.bloomsbury.com/uk/connect/contact-us/writing-for-bloomsbury/

Book Publisher: Bloomsbury Publishing Plc

Nonfiction > *Nonfiction Books*: Nautical

Send: Query; Synopsis; Writing sample; Outline; Market info; Author bio
How to send: Email

Nautical imprint of large international publisher. Happy to accept unsolicited submissions, but response only if interested. Send all submissions by email with the word "submission" in the subject line.

P013 AdventureKEEN
Book Publisher
United States
Tel: +1 (800) 678-7006
Fax: +1 (877) 374-9016

info@adventurewithkeen.com

https://adventurewithkeen.com
https://www.instagram.com/adventurewithkeen/
https://twitter.com/adventurekeen
https://www.facebook.com/adventurekeen/
https://www.pinterest.com/adventurekeen/
https://www.linkedin.com/company/adventurekeen

Nonfiction > *Nonfiction Books*
  Adventure; Local History; Nature; Outdoor Activities; Sport; Travel

A nonfiction publisher of books on a wide range of subjects, including adventure, outdoors, travel, nature, local history, sports, and more.

Publishing Imprint: Menasha Ridge Press (**P290**)

P014 Afterglow Books
Publishing Imprint
United States

https://bookpages.harlequin.com/afterglow-books/
https://harlequin.submittable.com/submit

Fiction > *Novels*: Romance

Does not want:

> **Fiction** > *Novels*
>   Historical Romance; Romantic Suspense; Supernatural / Paranormal Romance

Send: Full text; Synopsis; Writing sample
How to send: Submittable

Depth, relatability and sizzling spice, too: these characters are determined to live their best lives — and find the romance that makes them feel seen, unapologetically. In the pages of these books, characters from all walks of life, all types of diverse identities, will pursue their dreams and discover love isn't far behind.

Because everyone deserves a happily ever after that's true to who they are. Seeks books that are: proof that happy endings are meant for everyone; explicitly sexy with chemistry that pops; unique plots and strong emotional conflicts that embrace the world around us; and the journey of complex characters who aren't afraid to make mistakes or stand up for what they believe in. No paranormal, romantic suspense, dark or historical romances, or billionaires at this time.

P015 Albert Whitman & Company
Book Publisher
250 South Northwest Highway, Suite 320, Park Ridge, Illinois 60068
United States
Tel: +1 (800) 255-7675
Fax: +1 (847) 581-0039

submissions@albertwhitman.com

https://www.albertwhitman.com
https://www.facebook.com/AlbertWhitmanCompany
https://twitter.com/albertwhitman
https://instagram.com/albertwhitman
https://www.pinterest.com/albertwhitmanco/

CHILDREN'S > **Fiction**
  Middle Grade; *Picture Books*
YOUNG ADULT > **Fiction** > *Novels*

Send: Query; Full text
How to send: Email attachment

Publishes picture books, middle-grade fiction, and young adult novels. Will consider fiction and nonfiction manuscripts for picture books for children ages 1 to 8, up to 1,000 words; middle-grade novels up to 35,000 words for children up to the age of 12; and young adult novels up to 70,000 words for ages 12-18. See website for full submission guidelines.

Editor-in-Chief: Kathleen Tucker

P016 Algonquin Books
Publishing Imprint
PO Box 2225, Chapel Hill, NC 27515-2225
United States
Tel: +1 (919) 967-0108
Fax: +1 (919) 933-0272

inquiry@algonquin.com

https://www.hachettebookgroup.com/imprint/workman-publishing-company/algonquin-books/
http://twitter.com/algonquinbooks
http://facebook.com/AlgonquinBooks
http://instagram.com/algonquinbooks

Book Publisher: Workman Publishing (**P519**)

Fiction > *Novels*
Nonfiction > *Nonfiction Books*
Closed to approaches.

Publishes both fiction and nonfiction. Does not accept unsolicited submissions.

P017 Algonquin Young Readers
Publishing Imprint
United States

Book Publisher: Workman Publishing (**P519**)

P018 Allen & Unwin
Book Publisher
SYDNEY:, 83 Alexander St, Crows Nest, NSW 2065, MELBOURNE:, 406 Albert Street, East Melbourne, Vic 3002
Australia
Tel: +61 (0) 2 8425 0100

fridaypitch@allenandunwin.com

https://www.allenandunwin.com
https://www.allenandunwin.com/about/submission-guidelines/the-friday-pitch
https://www.facebook.com/AllenandUnwinBooks
https://twitter.com/AllenAndUnwin
http://instagram.com/allenandunwin

ADULT
  Fiction > *Novels*
  Nonfiction > *Nonfiction Books*
CHILDREN'S > **Fiction**
  Board Books; *Chapter Books*; *Early Readers*; *Middle Grade*; *Picture Books*
YOUNG ADULT > **Fiction** > *Novels*

Send: Query; Synopsis; Writing sample
How to send: Email

Publisher with offices in Australia, New Zealand, and the UK. Accepts queries by email. See website for detailed instructions.

Book Publisher: Murdoch Books Australia (**P308**)

P019 Allison & Busby Ltd
Book Publisher
11 Wardour Mews, London, W1F 8AN
United Kingdom
Tel: +44 (0) 20 3950 7834

susie@allisonandbusby.com

https://www.allisonandbusby.com
http://www.facebook.com/pages/Allison-Busby-Books/51600359534
https://twitter.com/allisonandbusby
https://www.youtube.com/channel/UCrYAc6ndJZWJWAONHCn8-Qw
https://www.tiktok.com/@allisonandbusby
https://www.instagram.com/allisonandbusby/

Fiction > *Novels*
  Contemporary; Crime; Fantasy; Historical Fiction; Mystery; Romance; Saga; Thrillers
Nonfiction
  Gift Books: General
  Nonfiction Books: Biography; Comedy / Humour; Crime; Memoir

How to send: Through a literary agent

Accepts approaches via a literary agent only. No unsolicited MSS or queries from authors.

Publishing Director: Susie Dunlop

P020 Alternating Current Press
Book Publisher
2525 Arapahoe Ave, Ste E4 #162, Boulder, CO 80302
United States

info@altcurrentpress.com

https://altcurrentpress.com

ADULT
  Fiction > *Novels*
  Nonfiction > *Nonfiction Books*
CHILDREN'S > **Fiction** > *Chapter Books*

Indie press dedicated to publishing and promoting incredible literature that challenges readers and has an innate sense of self, timelessness, and atmosphere:

Online Magazine: The Coil (**M089**)

P021 Amato Books
Book Publisher; Magazine Publisher
United States
Tel: +1 (800) 541-9498

customerservice@amatobooks.com

https://amatobooks.com

Nonfiction > *Nonfiction Books*
  Alaska; Fishing; Fly Fishing; History; How To; Hunting; Offshore Gamefishing; Walking

Magazine: Flyfishing & Tying Journal (**M146**)

P022 Amber Books Ltd
Book Publisher
United House, North Road, London, N7 9DP
United Kingdom
Tel: +44 (0) 20 7520 7600

editorial@amberbooks.co.uk
enquiries@amberbooks.co.uk

https://www.amberbooks.co.uk
https://www.facebook.com/amberbooks
https://twitter.com/AmberBooks
https://www.pinterest.co.uk/amberbooksltd/
https://www.instagram.com/amberbooksltd/

Nonfiction > *Illustrated Books*
  General, and in particular: History; Military

Send: Synopsis; Table of Contents; Writing sample; Author bio
Don't send: Full text
How to send: Post; Email

Publishes illustrated nonfiction books in a wide range of formats and subject areas for an international audience. Particularly interested in submissions on military topics, but not exclusively so, and welcomes good ideas on any nonfiction subject suitable for treatment as an illustrated book.

P023 American Mystery Classics
Publishing Imprint
United States

https://penzlerpublishers.com/product-category/american-mystery-classics/

Book Publisher: Penzler Publishers (**P345**)

Fiction > *Novels*: Mystery

Dedicated to reissuing classic American mystery fiction in new hardcover and paperback editions.

P024 Ammonite Press
Book Publisher
United Kingdom

https://www.ammonitepress.com
https://twitter.com/AmmonitePress
https://www.youtube.com/c/AmmonitePress
https://www.instagram.com/gmcpublications/

Nonfiction
  Gift Books: General
  Nonfiction Books: Biography; History; Personal Development; Photography; Popular Culture; Self Help; Wellbeing

Send: Synopsis; Writing sample

Publishes illustrated reference, guide and gift books that bring the worlds of photography and biography, pop culture and history, self-improvement and self-help into sharper focus.

Publisher: Jonathan Bailey

P025 And Other Stories
Book Publisher
Central Library, Surrey Street, Sheffield, S1 1XZ
United Kingdom

info@andotherstories.org

https://www.andotherstories.org
https://twitter.com/andothertweets
https://www.facebook.com/AndOtherStoriesBooks/
https://www.instagram.com/andotherpics/

Fiction in Translation > *Novels*: Literary

Fiction > *Novels*: Literary

Nonfiction in Translation > *Nonfiction Books*: Narrative Nonfiction

Nonfiction > *Nonfiction Books*: Narrative Nonfiction

Poetry > *Poetry Collections*

How to send: Through a literary agent

Our focus is on literary fiction and increasingly on non-fiction too, particularly narrative kinds of non-fiction. Also began publishing poetry collections in 2023.

P026 Andrews McMeel Publishing
Book Publisher
ATTN: Submissions (Please specify Books or Calendars), 1130 Walnut St., Kansas City, MO 64106
United States

corpcommunications@amuniversal.com

https://publishing.andrewsmcmeel.com

ADULT
Nonfiction
  Gift Books: General
  Nonfiction Books: Comedy / Humour; Food and Drink
  Puzzles: General

Poetry > *Poetry Collections*

CHILDREN'S
  Fiction > *Middle Grade*
  Nonfiction > *Nonfiction Books*

How to send: Online submission system; Post

A leading publisher of poetry, inspiration, humor, and children's books and licensed, popular calendars. We publish as many as 150 books and 200 calendars annually. We are happy to consider submissions from creators and literary agents via email or regular mail, but materials submitted by any other means will not be considered. Please keep in mind that we receive a high volume of submissions and we do not answer calls or visits regarding submissions.

P027 Anhinga Press
Book Publisher
PO Box 3665, Tallahassee, FL 32315
United States

info@anhinga.org

http://www.anhinga.org
https://twitter.com/Anhinga_Press
https://www.facebook.com/anhingapress

Poetry
  Chapbooks; *Poetry Collections*

A non-profit, 501(c)3 operating in Tallahassee, Florida. Since 1974 our mission has been to bring quality poetry to a broad audience by publishing poetry, sponsoring poetry events and educational activities, participating in writers conferences, working with area colleges, making our books available as textbooks for students, and networking with other arts organizations as a good citizen of the arts community and the community at large.

P028 Anvil Press Publishers
Book Publisher
P.O. Box 3008, MPO, Vancouver, B.C., V6B 3X5
Canada
Tel: +1 (604) 876-8710

info@anvilpress.com

https://www.anvilpress.com
https://www.facebook.com/Anvil-Press-115437275199047/
https://www.twitter.com/anvilpress
https://www.instagram.com/anvilpress_publishers/

Fiction > *Novels*

Nonfiction > *Nonfiction Books*
  Arts; Photography

Poetry > *Poetry Collections*

Scripts > *Theatre Scripts*: Drama

Send: Query; Synopsis; Writing sample; Author bio
Don't send: Full text
How to send: Email

Publisher designed to discover and nurture Canadian literary talent. Considers work from Canadian authors only.

Editor: Brian Kaufman

P029 Apa Publications Group
Book Publisher
7 Bell Yard, London, WC2A 2JR
United Kingdom
Tel: +44 (0) 20 7403 0284

london@insightguides.com

https://www.insightguides.com
https://www.facebook.com/InsightGuides
https://twitter.com/insightguides
https://instagram.com/insightguides
https://www.pinterest.com/insightguides
https://www.linkedin.com/company/insight-guides

Nonfiction > *Nonfiction Books*: Travel

We've spent more than 45 years helping travellers to plan their next adventures. As well as our popular guidebooks, we now offer you the opportunity to book tailor-made private tours completely personalised to your interests and needs.

P030 Arachne Press
Book Publisher
100 Grierson Road, London, SE23 1NX
United Kingdom
Tel: +44 (0) 20 8699 0206

https://arachnepress.com
https://arachnepress.submittable.com/submit
https://www.facebook.com/ArachnePress

Fiction > *Short Fiction Collections*

Poetry > *Poetry Collections*

Closed to approaches.

A small, independent publisher of award-winning short fiction, award winning poetry and (very) select non-fiction, for adults and children. Only accepts responses to call outs (mainly for inclusion in anthologies). No AI generated or AI assisted work. See website for full details and current calls.

P031 Arcadia Publishing
Book Publisher
United States

https://www.arcadiapublishing.com
https://www.facebook.com/ArcadiaPublishing
https://twitter.com/arcadiapub
http://pinterest.com/imagesofamerica/
https://www.instagram.com/arcadia_publishing

ADULT
  Fiction > *Novels*

  Nonfiction
    Nonfiction Books: Activities; American History; Antiques; Architecture; Arts; Autobiography; Biography; Business; Collectibles; Comedy / Humour; Cookery; Crafts; Crime; Design; Economics; Education; Engineering; Family; Fitness; Games; Gardening; Health; History; Hobbies; Houses and Homes; Language; Legal; Leisure; Literary Criticism; Medicine; Mind, Body, Spirit; Music; Nature; Performing Arts; Pets; Philosophy; Photography; Politics; Psychology; Recreation; Relationships; Religion; Science; Self Help; Sociology; Sport; Technology; Transport; Travel
    Reference: General

  Poetry > *Poetry Collections*

CHILDREN'S
  Fiction
    Board Books; *Chapter Books*; *Early Readers*; *Middle Grade*; *Picture Books*
  Nonfiction > *Nonfiction Books*

YOUNG ADULT > **Fiction** > *Novels*

How to send: Online submission system

Publishes books on over 70 different subjects of American history, including stories of true crime and passion in their crime series, past wars in military history books, and books on the history of sports. No fiction submissions.

Book Publisher: Pelican Publishing Company

P032 Arsenal Pulp Press
Book Publisher
202-211 East Georgia Street, Vancouver, BC, V6A 1Z6
Canada
Tel: +1 (604) 687-4233
Fax: +1 (604) 687-4283

submissions@arsenalpulp.com

https://arsenalpulp.com

ADULT
  Fiction
    Graphic Novels: General
    Novels: LGBTQIA; Literary
  Nonfiction
    Graphic Nonfiction: General
    Nonfiction Books: British Columbia; Crafts; Culture; LGBTQIA; Literary; Politics; Regional; Sociology; Youth Culture

CHILDREN'S
  Fiction > *Novels*
    Diversity; LGBTQIA

  Nonfiction > *Nonfiction Books*
    Diversity; LGBTQIA

YOUNG ADULT
  Fiction > *Novels*
    General, and in particular: LGBTQIA

  Nonfiction > *Nonfiction Books*: LGBTQIA

How to send: Email; Post

Publishes Books by BIPOC and LGBTQ2S+ authors, including young adult and children's; Literary fiction and non-fiction (no genre fiction, such as mysteries, thrillers, or romance); Political/sociological studies; Cultural studies; Regional non-fiction, especially British Columbia; Graphic novels and graphic non-fiction; Youth culture and young adult literature; Books for children, especially those that emphasize diversity; Craft books. Prefers submissions by email, but will accept submissions by post.

P033 Arte Publico Press
Book Publisher
University of Houston, 4902 Gulf Fwy, Bldg. 19, Room 100, Houston, TX 77204-2004
United States

submapp@uh.edu

https://artepublicopress.com
https://www.facebook.com/artepublico/
https://twitter.com/artepublico
https://www.instagram.com/artepublico/
https://www.pinterest.com/artepublico/
http://artepublicopress.tumblr.com/

  Fiction > *Novels*
    Central America; Culture; History; Politics; South America

  Nonfiction > *Nonfiction Books*
    Central America; Culture; History; Politics; South America

Send: Writing sample
How to send: Online submission system
How not to send: Post

Publisher of contemporary and recovered literature by US Hispanic authors.

Publishing Imprint: Pinata Books (**P355**)

P034 Asabi Publishing
Book Publisher
United States

https://www.asabipublishing.com

ADULT
  Fiction > *Novels*
    Crime; Erotic; Historical Fiction; Horror; LGBTQIA; Mystery; Noir; Thrillers

  Nonfiction > *Nonfiction Books*
    Autobiography; Biography; Memoir; Narrative Nonfiction; Outdoor Survival Skills; Travel

CHILDREN'S
  Fiction > *Novels*: Culture

  Nonfiction > *Nonfiction Books*
    Cultural History; Games

TEEN
  Fiction > *Novels*: Culture

  Nonfiction > *Nonfiction Books*
    Cultural History; Games

YOUNG ADULT
  Fiction > *Novels*: Culture

  Nonfiction > *Nonfiction Books*
    Cultural History; Games

Check website for submission windows. Submit query letter / proposal through form on website. No religious or spiritual books of any kind.

P035 Ascend Books, LLC
Book Publisher
11722 West 91st Street, Overland Park, Kansas 66214
United States
Tel: +1 (913) 948-5500

bsnodgrass@ascendbooks.com

http://ascendbooks.com
http://www.twitter.com/Ascend_Books

ADULT > **Nonfiction** > *Nonfiction Books*
  Entertainment; Sport

CHILDREN'S > **Fiction**
  Board Books; *Picture Books*

Send: Query; Self-Addressed Stamped Envelope (SASE)
How to send: Post
How not to send: Email

Highly specialised publishing company with a burgeoning presence in sports, entertainment and commemoration events. Send query by email.

Editor: Bob Snodgrass

P036 Astra House
Publishing Imprint
United States

Book Publisher: Astra Publishing House (**P037**)

P037 Astra Publishing House
Book Publisher
United States

https://astrapublishinghouse.com/

Dedicated to publishing books for children and adults that celebrate excellent storytelling, have a strong point of view, and introduce readers to new perspectives about their everyday lives as well as the lives of others.

Publishing Imprints: Astra House (*P036*); Astra Young Readers (*P038*); Calkins Creek (*P091*); DAW Books (**P135**); Hippo Park (*P218*); Kane Press (**P251**); MineditionUS (*P298*); Toon Books (*P454*); WordSong (**P516**)

P038 Astra Young Readers
Publishing Imprint
United States

Book Publisher: Astra Publishing House (**P037**)

P039 Aurora Metro Press
Book Publisher
80 Hill Rise, Richmond, TW10 6UB
United Kingdom
Tel: +44 (0) 20 8948 1427

submissions@aurorametro.com
editor@aurorametro.com

https://aurorametro.com
https://www.facebook.com/AuroraMetroBooks/
https://twitter.com/aurorametro

ADULT
 Fiction
  Novels; *Short Fiction*
 Nonfiction > *Nonfiction Books*
  Arts; Biography; History; Popular Culture; Travel; Wellbeing

 Scripts
  Film Scripts; *Theatre Scripts*
YOUNG ADULT > **Fiction** > *Novels*

Send: Query; Synopsis; Author bio; Writing sample

Publishes adult fiction, YA fiction, drama, and non-fiction biography and books about the arts and popular culture.

P040 Authentic Ideas
Publishing Imprint
85 Great Portland Street, First Floor, London, W1W 7LT
United Kingdom
Tel: +44 (0) 20 3745 0658

enquiries@integrity-media.co.uk

http://www.integrity-media.co.uk

Book Publisher: Integrity Media (**P241**)

Fiction > *Novels*
 Comedy / Humour; Crime; Drama; Fantasy; Horror; Literary; Mystery; Science Fiction; Thrillers

Send: Query; Synopsis; Writing sample
How to send: Email

Seeks to help up and coming authors to find their voice, display their creativity and deliver a novel of which they can be proud. It is our desire, that through this imprint our authors find their written voice and peace from their past. And through this imprint, a road for the future.

P041 Authentic Life
Publishing Imprint
85 Great Portland Street, First Floor, London, W1W 7LT
United Kingdom
Tel: +44 (0) 20 3745 0658

enquiries@integrity-media.co.uk

http://www.integrity-media.co.uk

Book Publisher: Integrity Media (**P241**)

Nonfiction > *Nonfiction Books*
 Autobiography; Biography; Health; Mental Health; Philosophy; Psychology; Self Help; Spirituality

Send: Query; Synopsis; Writing sample
How to send: Email

Focuses on relaying stories that cut to the heart of the society we all share. These are stories of normal individuals. Tales of hardship, suffering, injustice, endurance, strength, tenacity, resilience, faith and hope, that convey a picture of the world most of us witness and experience.

P042 Autumn Publishing Ltd
Publishing Imprint
Cottage Farm, Mears Ashby Road, Sywell, Northants, NN6 0BJ
United Kingdom
Tel: +44 (0) 1604 741116

customerservice@igloobooks.com

https://autumnpublishing.co.uk

Book Publisher: Igloo Books Limited (**P232**)

CHILDREN'S > **Nonfiction**
 Activity Books: General
 Nonfiction Books: English; Health; Mathematics; Nature; Science

Deals in books for babies and toddlers, activity books, early learning books, and sticker books. Publisher's philosophy is that children should enjoy learning with books, and to this end combines activity and learning by turning simple workbooks into activity books, allowing children to learn whilst they play.

Publishing Imprint: Byeway Books

P043 AUWA Books
Publishing Imprint
United States

https://auwabooks.com

Book Publisher: Macmillan Publishers

P044 Avon
Publishing Imprint
United Kingdom

https://corporate.harpercollins.co.uk/what-we-publish/avon/
https://www.facebook.com/AvonBooksUK/
https://twitter.com/AvonBooksUK

Book Publisher: HarperCollins UK

Fiction > *Novels*
 Commercial; Crime; Saga; Suspense; Thrillers

A commercial fiction division publishing predominantly crime, thrillers, suspense, feel-good general fiction, and saga.

P045 Avon Books
Publishing Imprint
United States

https://www.harpercollins.com
https://www.harpercollins.com/pages/avonromance
https://twitter.com/avonbooks
https://www.instagram.com/avonbooks/
https://www.facebook.com/avonromance

Book Publisher: HarperCollins

Fiction > *Novels*
 Contemporary Romance; Historical Romance; Romance; Romantic Comedy; Supernatural / Paranormal Romance

Publishing award-winning romance since 1941. Recognized for having pioneered the historical romance category and continues to publish in wide variety of other genres, including paranormal, urban fantasy, contemporary and regency.

P046 Backbeat Books
Book Publisher
United States

BackbeatSubmissions@rowman.com

http://www.backbeatbooks.com

Book Publisher: The Globe Pequot Press (**P184**)

Nonfiction > *Nonfiction Books*
 Autobiography; Biography; Business; History; Music; Musical Instruments

Send: Query; Outline; Table of Contents; Writing sample; Author bio; Market info; Marketing Plan
How to send: Email; Post

Founded in 1991, we have grown to become the world's leading imprint dedicated solely to music. Passionate fans and musicians know to look to our brand to find the highest quality titles on their favorite topics. Specifically, our books are known for their depth, spirit, and authority, offering a diverse range of titles—from biographies and memoirs, critical examinations, and histories to authoritative volumes on musical instruments and instruction—covering all areas of popular music and beyond.

Editor: Mike Edison

P047 Bad Press Ink
Book Publisher
United Kingdom

enquiries@badpress.ink

https://badpress.ink
https://www.facebook.com/BADPRESS.iNKPublishing
https://twitter.com/badpressink
https://www.youtube.com/user/iainparkebadpress

Fiction > *Novels*

Publishes alternative books and niche lifestyle fiction. Complete online submission process on website.

Editors: Pat Blayney; Iain Parke

P048 Badger Learning
Book Publisher
Unit 55 Oldmedow Road, Hardwick Industrial Estate, King's Lynn, Norfolk, PE30 4JJ
United Kingdom
Tel: +44 (0) 1553 816082

info@badger-publishing.co.uk

https://www.badgerlearning.co.uk
https://twitter.com/@BadgerLearning
https://en-gb.facebook.com/badger.learning

ACADEMIC > **Nonfiction** > *Nonfiction Books*
  English; History; Mathematics; Science
CHILDREN'S
  Fiction
    Chapter Books; *Early Readers*; *Middle Grade*
  Nonfiction > *Nonfiction Books*
TEEN
  Fiction > *Novels*
  Nonfiction > *Nonfiction Books*
YOUNG ADULT
  Fiction > *Novels*
  Nonfiction > *Nonfiction Books*

Publishes books for UK schools, particularly books to engage reluctant and struggling readers.

P049 Baen Books
Book Publisher
PO Box 1188, Wake Forest, NC 27588
United States
Tel: +1 (919) 570-1640
Fax: +1 (919) 570-1644

https://www.baen.com
https://www.baen.com/slush/index/submit
https://twitter.com/BaenBooks

Fiction > *Novels*
  Fantasy; Science Fiction

Send: Full text
How to send: Online submission system
How not to send: Email

Publishes only science fiction and fantasy. Interested in science fiction with powerful plots and solid scientific and philosophical underpinnings. For fantasy, any magical system must be both rigorously coherent and integral to the plot. Work must at least strive for originality. Prefers manuscripts between 100,000 and 130,000 words. No submissions via email. Full manuscripts can be submitted online, in rtf format, via an electronic submission system. Postal submission accepted from those who are unable to submit electronically.

P050 Bald and Bonkers Network LLC
Book Publisher
United States
Tel: +1 (208) 421-2330

admin@baldandbonkers.net

https://baldandbonkers.net
https://www.facebook.com/BaldandBonkers
https://twitter.com/PRF_Dakota
https://www.instagram.com/baldandbonkersnetwork/
https://baldandbonkersnetwork.tumblr.com/
https://www.youtube.com/c/BaldandBonkers

Fiction > *Novels*

Nonfiction > *Nonfiction Books*

Poetry > *Any Poetic Form*

How to send: Email

Founded on the premise of helping unknown authors gain the exposure they would from big time publishing outlets. Every author accepted is guaranteed one-on-one attention and an interview at book launch to help gain immediate exposure.

P051 Ballantine Books
Publishing Imprint

Book Publisher: Random House

P052 Bantam (UK)
Publishing Imprint

Book Publisher: Transworld Publishers

Authors: Trisha Ashley; Dan Brown; Derren Brown; Lee Child; Jilly Cooper; Tess Daly; Sara Davies; Nell Frizzell; Ed Gamble; Tess Gerritsen; Paula Hawkins; David Hepworth; James Holland; Ruth Jones; Sophie Kinsella; Shari Lapena; Andrea Mara; Gina Martin; Guenther Steiner

P053 Banter Press
Book Publisher
561 Hudson Street, #57, New York, NY 10014
United States

banter@wordsupply.com

https://www.banterpress.com

Nonfiction > *Nonfiction Books*
  Business; Communication; Marketing; Writing

Send: Query; Outline; Author bio; Writing sample; Market info; Marketing Plan
How to send: PDF file email attachment
How not to send: Post

We seek nonfiction authors who are active speakers and writers within their industry, especially those who do seminars or consulting. Currently, we're eager to see topics in business communication, writing, professional services marketing, personal branding, and marketing technology. We are open to works that have unfairly gone out of print.

Editor: David McClintock

P054 Baobab Press
Book Publisher
121 California Avenue, Reno, NV 89503
United States
Tel: +1 (775) 786-1188

info@baobabpress.com

https://baobabpress.com

ADULT
  Fiction
    Graphic Novels: General
    Novels: Contemporary; Literary
    Short Fiction: Contemporary; Literary
  Nonfiction
    Essays: General
    Short Nonfiction: Memoir
  Poetry > *Poetry Collections*
CHILDREN'S > **Fiction**
  Board Books; *Picture Books*

How to send: Submittable

Constantly strives to discover, cultivate, and nurture authors working in all genres. Publishes Creative Nonfiction, Short-Story, Novel, and Comic/Visual Narrative manuscripts (Comic/Visual Narrative manuscripts will not be considered without artwork). Also publishes children's picture and board books (send text with or without artwork). Submit via online submission system. Submit no more than one submission at a time.

P055 Barbican Press
Book Publisher
United Kingdom

martin@barbicanpress.com

https://barbicanpress.com
https://twitter.com/BarbicanPress1
https://www.instagram.com/barbicanpress/

ADULT
  Fiction > *Novels*
    General, and in particular: Historical

Fiction; LGBTQIA; Science Fiction; Women's Fiction

Poetry in Translation
Nonfiction Books: General, and in particular: Sailing; Ships
Poetry Collections: Classics / Ancient World

Poetry > *Poetry Collections*

Scripts > *Theatre Scripts*: Drama

CHILDREN'S
Fiction
Graphic Novels; *Short Fiction Collections*
Scripts > *Theatre Scripts*: Drama

Closed to approaches.

Many of our titles were written as the creative elements of PhDs in Creative Writing. Universities can offer safe harbour for writers, challenging them with regular and expert feedback, giving them years in which their books achieve full voice without the necessity to compromise. Understandably, mainstream publishers tend to seek work that resembles other books that have made money. Breakout originality is harder to place. Those are the books we give a home to.

P056 Barbour Publishing
Book Publisher
United States
Tel: +1 (800) 852-8010

submissions@barbourbooks.com

https://www.barbourbooks.com
https://www.facebook.com/BarbourPublishing/
https://twitter.com/barbourbuzz
https://www.youtube.com/user/BarbourPublishing1
https://www.instagram.com/barbourbooks/

ADULT
Fiction > *Novels*
Amish; Contemporary; Historical Fiction; Romance; Suspense

Nonfiction
Nonfiction Books: Bible Studies; Bibles; Christian Living; Christianity; Evangelism; Inspirational
Puzzles: General

CHILDREN'S > **Nonfiction**
Activity Books: General
Nonfiction Books: Bible Stories; Bible Studies; Bibles
Puzzles: General

How to send: Through a literary agent

Publishes a range of fiction and nonfiction, but all must demonstrate a conservative, evangelical Christian world view, and speak to broad segments of the evangelical Christian market.

P057 Basalt Books
Publishing Imprint
WSU Press, Cooper Publications Building, PO Box 645910, Pullman, WA 99164-5910, 509-335-7630
United States

https://wsupress.wsu.edu/basalt-books-submission-guidelines/

Book Publisher: Washington State University Press (**P501**)

ADULT > **Nonfiction** > *Nonfiction Books*
Arts; Biography; Cookery; Culture; Environment; Food; History; Memoir; Nature; Pacific Northwest; Science

CHILDREN'S > **Nonfiction** > *Nonfiction Books*
Arts; Biography; Cookery; Culture; Environment; Food; History; Memoir; Nature; Pacific Northwest; Science

Send: Query; Market info; Table of Contents; Writing sample; Author bio
How to send: Email

Welcomes proposals for book projects anchored in the Pacific Northwest, particularly those focusing on the people, places, and cultures of the greater Northwest region. We encourage both established and first-time writers to contact us with your ideas. We are committed to publishing well-written and well-told stories.

P058 Basic Books
Publishing Imprint
United States

https://www.basicbooks.com
https://www.hachettebookgroup.com/imprint/basic-books/

Book Publisher: Perseus Books

Nonfiction > *Nonfiction Books*
Current Affairs; History; Politics; Psychology; Science; Sociology

Publishes award-winning books in history, science, sociology, psychology, politics, and current affairs.

P059 Basic Health Publications, Inc.
Publishing Imprint
United States

submissions@turnerpublishing.com

https://turnerbookstore.com/collections/basic-health

Book Publisher: Turner Publishing (**P462**)

Nonfiction > *Nonfiction Books*: Health

Send: Full text; Author bio; Market info
How to send: Word file email attachment; PDF file email attachment

Submit by email, including your manuscript as an attached Word Doc or PDF to your email (a completed manuscript is preferred, but partial manuscripts or detailed outlines/pitches are also accepted); author details including platform, following, qualifications, etc.; and pertinent marketing details, including intended audience and the sales angle of the book.

P060 Baylor University Press
Book Publisher
1920 S. 4th St., Waco, TX 76706
United States
Tel: +1 (254) 710-3164

BUP_Acquisitions@baylor.edu

https://www.baylorpress.com
https://www.facebook.com/BaylorPress/
https://x.com/Baylor_Press

ACADEMIC > **Nonfiction** > *Nonfiction Books*
Anthropology; Christianity; Culture; History; Islam; Judaism; Literature; Philosophy; Politics; Religion; Science; Sociology

Send: Query
How to send: Email

The Press publishes technical scholarship for researchers, tools for teachers, and textbooks for students. All Press publications under our primary academic imprint enjoy rigorous peer review and project development. The list focuses on scriptural, historical, and theological studies of Christianity, Judaism, and Islam. Press publications also investigate the relationship between religion and politics, the sciences, sociology, anthropology, literature, philosophy, history, and culture.

P061 Bentley Publishers
Book Publisher
United States

http://www.bentleypublishers.com
https://www.facebook.com/bentleypubs
https://www.youtube.com/bentleypublishers

Nonfiction
Nonfiction Books: Cars
Reference: Cars

Publishes books for motoring enthusiasts, including technical, motor sports, and service manuals.

P062 Berghahn Books Ltd
Book Publisher
3 Newtec Place, Magdalen Rd, Oxford, OX4 1RE
United Kingdom
Tel: +44 (0) 1865 250011

editorial@berghahnbooks.com

https://www.berghahnbooks.com
https://www.facebook.com/BerghahnBooks
https://twitter.com/berghahnbooks
https://www.youtube.com/channel/UCuh-

JFDwm_HfzX1zJ92tzcw
https://www.instagram.com/berghahnbooks/

ACADEMIC > **Nonfiction** > *Nonfiction Books*
Anthropology; Archaeology; Culture; Education; Environment; Films; Gender; History; Politics; Sociology; TV; Warfare

Send: Query; Submission Form; Outline
How to send: Email attachment

Academic publisher of books and journals covering the social sciences. Download New Book Outline form from website, complete, and submit by email with an outline and/or chapter summary.

Editor: Marion Berghahn

P063 Berrett-Koehler Publishers

Book Publisher
1333 Broadway, Suite P-100, Oakland, CA 94612
United States
Tel: +1 (510) 817-2277
Fax: +1 (510) 817-2278

submissions@bkpub.com
bkpub@bkpub.com

https://www.bkconnection.com
https://www.facebook.com/BerrettKoehler
https://twitter.com/Bkpub
https://www.linkedin.com/company/berrett-koehler-publishers/
https://www.pinterest.com/berrettkoehler/
https://www.youtube.com/berrettkoehler

Nonfiction > *Nonfiction Books*
Business; Career Development; Communication; Creativity; Economics; Equality; Leadership; Management

Send: Proposal; Outline; Writing sample; Market info
How to send: PDF file email attachment; Word file email attachment

Connecting people and ideas to create a world that works for all. Publishes titles that promote positive change at personal, organizational, and societal levels.

P064 Bess Press

Book Publisher
3565 Harding Avenue, Honolulu, HI 96816
United States
Tel: +1 (808) 734-7159
Fax: +1 (808) 732-3627

https://www.besspress.com

ACADEMIC > **Nonfiction** > *Nonfiction Books*
Hawai'i; Pacific

ADULT
Fiction > *Novels*
Hawai'i; Pacific

Nonfiction > *Nonfiction Books*
Biography; Hawai'i; Memoir; Pacific

CHILDREN'S > **Fiction**
Activity Books: Hawai'i; Pacific
Board Books: Hawai'i; Pacific
Picture Books: Hawai'i; Pacific

How to send: Online submission system

Publishes books about Hawai'i and the Pacific. All submissions should be sent via the online form. See website for full guidelines.

P065 BFI Publishing

Book Publisher
United Kingdom

https://www.bfi.org.uk
https://www.bfi.org.uk/bfi-book-releases-trade-sales
https://www.bloomsbury.com/uk/discover/bloomsbury-academic/authors/contacts-for-authors/

Book Publisher: Bloomsbury Academic (**P071**)

ACADEMIC > **Nonfiction** > *Nonfiction Books*
Film Industry; Films

Publishes film and television-related books and resources, both for schools and academic readerships, and more generally.

P066 Bird Eye Books

Publishing Imprint
United Kingdom

https://birdeyebooks.com
https://twitter.com/BirdEyeBooks/

Book Publisher: Graffeg (**P190**)

Nonfiction > *Illustrated Books*
Architecture; Crafts; Photography; Visual Arts; Visual Culture

How to send: Online submission system

Imprint publishing high quality illustrated books about the visual arts. We plan to work with authors, artists, sculptors, ceramicists, photographers, illustrators, crafts people, architects and other creatives to publish beautiful books about our visual culture.

P067 Birlinn Ltd

Book Publisher
West Newington House, 10 Newington Road, Edinburgh, EH9 1QS
United Kingdom
Tel: +44 (0) 1316 684371

info@birlinn.co.uk

http://birlinn.co.uk
https://www.facebook.com/birlinnbooks/
https://twitter.com/BirlinnBooks
https://www.youtube.com/channel/UChVAhFnMniUb_3XiVmXPT7Q
https://www.instagram.com/birlinnbooks/

Fiction
Novels: Comedy / Humour; Crime; Historical Fiction; Thrillers
Short Fiction Collections: General

Nonfiction > *Nonfiction Books*
Art History; Arts; Biography; Business; Comedy / Humour; Crime; Current Affairs; Folklore, Myths, and Legends; Food; Gaelic; Gardening; Geology; Local History; Memoir; Nature; Photography; Politics; Scotland; Sport; Traditional Music; Travel

Send: Query; Synopsis; Writing sample
How to send: Email
How not to send: Post

Focuses on Scottish material: local, military, and Highland history; humour, adventure; reference, guidebooks, and folklore. No longer accepting submissions for fiction, poetry, or children's books. Submissions for these areas must be made through a literary agent. Continues to accept direct submissions for nonfiction.

Publishing Imprint: Polygon (**P360**)

P068 Blackstaff Press

Book Publisher
Jubilee Business Park, 21 Jubilee Road, Newtownards, BT23 4YH
United Kingdom
Tel: +44 (0) 28 9182 0505

sales@colourpoint.co.uk

https://blackstaffpress.com
https://facebook.com/Blackstaffpressni
https://twitter.com/BlackstaffNI

Book Publisher: Colourpoint Educational (**P119**)

Fiction > *Novels*

Nonfiction > *Nonfiction Books*
General, and in particular: Biography; History; Ireland; Memoir; Northern Ireland; Politics; Sport

Does not want:

> **Fiction** > *Novels*
> Erotic; Fantasy; Horror; Science Fiction

Closed to approaches.

Focuses on subjects of interest to the Irish market, both north and south. Not taking on any new projects.

P069 Bloodaxe Books

Book Publisher
Eastburn, South Park, Hexham, Northumberland, NE46 1BS
United Kingdom
Tel: +44 (0) 01434 611581

editor@bloodaxebooks.com
submissions@bloodaxebooks.com

https://www.bloodaxebooks.com

Poetry > *Poetry Collections*

Closed to approaches.

Submit poetry only if you have a track record of publication in magazines. If so, send sample of up to a dozen poems with SAE. No submissions by email or on disk. Poems from the UK sent without return postage will be recycled unread; submissions by email will be deleted unread. No longer accepting poets who have already published a full-length collection with another publisher. Considers poets from beyond the UK and Ireland by invitation or recommendation only. See website for full details.

Editorial Director: Neil Astley

P070 Bloodhound Books
Book Publisher
Nine Hills Road, Cambridge, CB2 1GE
United Kingdom

info@bloodhoundbooks.com
submissions@bloodhoundbooks.com

https://www.bloodhoundbooks.com
https://www.facebook.com/bloodhoundbooks/
https://twitter.com/Bloodhoundbook
https://www.instagram.com/bloodhound.books/

Professional Bodies: Independent Publishers Guild (IPG); The Crime Writers' Association

Fiction > *Novels*
Contemporary Romance; Cozy Mysteries; Crime; Domestic Suspense; Historical Fiction; Literary; Police Procedural; Psychological Thrillers; Romantic Comedy; Saga; Thrillers; Women's Fiction

Nonfiction > *Nonfiction Books*: Crime

Send: Query; Synopsis; Full text
How to send: Word file email attachment

Looking for entertaining, fresh and distinctive fiction that stands out from the crowd. We accept unsolicited submissions, manuscripts from agents, previously published authors, including self-published authors, and debut writers. We're looking for gripping, commercial stories with memorable characters. If your style of storytelling is unique, and readers are going to remember your novel, we want to hear from you.

P071 Bloomsbury Academic
Book Publisher
50 Bedford Square, London, WC1B 3DP
United Kingdom
Tel: +44 (0) 20 7631 5600

contact@bloomsbury.com

http://www.bloomsburyacademic.com

Book Publisher: Bloomsbury Publishing Plc

ACADEMIC > **Nonfiction** > *Nonfiction Books*
Africa; Archaeology; Architecture; Arts; Asia; Business; Classics / Ancient World; Computer Science; Crime; Design; Drama; Economics; Education; Engineering; Environment; Ethnic Groups; Fashion; Films; Food; Gender; Health; History; Information Science; Interior Design; Language; Legal; Literature; Management; Mathematics; Media; Medicine; Middle East; Music; Nursing; Philosophy; Politics; Psychology; Psychotherapy; Religion; Science; Sexuality; Society; Sociology; Sport; Technology; Visual Culture; Wellbeing

Publishes books for students, researchers, and independent thinkers.

Book Publishers: ABC-CLIO (**P008**); BFI Publishing (**P065**)

P072 Bloomsbury Professional
Book Publisher
50 Bedford Square, London, WC1B 3DP
United Kingdom
Tel: +44 (0) 20 7631 5600

contact@bloomsbury.com

https://www.bloomsburyprofessional.com
https://twitter.com/BloomsburyPro
https://www.linkedin.com/company/bloomsbury-professional

Book Publisher: Bloomsbury Publishing Plc

PROFESSIONAL > **Nonfiction** > *Nonfiction Books*
Accounting; Legal; Taxation

Publishes high quality books and digital products for lawyers, tax practitioners, accountants and business professionals.

P073 Blue Jeans Books
Publishing Imprint
United Kingdom

submissions@sunpenny.com

https://www.sunpenny.com/imprints/

Book Publisher: Sunpenny Publishing (**P435**)

Fiction > *Novels*: Romance

Does not want:

Fiction > *Novels*: Christian Romance

Romance genre imprint, non-Christian based.

P074 Blue Poppy Enterprises
Book Publisher
4804 SE 69th Avenue, Portland, OR 97206
United States
Tel: +1 (503) 650-6077
Fax: +1 (503) 650-6076

info@bluepoppy.com

https://www.bluepoppy.com
https://www.facebook.com/bluepoppy1
https://www.youtube.com/channel/UCSDGdeyprhpKC3imL9JCVcw
https://instagram.com/bluepoppyenterprises

ADULT > **Nonfiction** > *Nonfiction Books*
Acupuncture; Chinese Medicine; Chinese Philosophy

PROFESSIONAL > **Nonfiction** > *Nonfiction Books*
Acupuncture; Chinese Medicine; Chinese Philosophy

Publishes books on acupuncture, oriental medicine, and Chinese philosophy, for professional practitioners and lay readers.

Editor-in-Chief: Bob Flaws

P075 Blue Star Press
Book Publisher
Bend, OR
United States
Tel: +1 (458) 202-9530

submissions@bluestarpress.com
contact@bluestarpress.com

https://www.bluestarpress.com
https://www.instagram.com/bluestarpress/
https://www.facebook.com/bluestarpresslegacy/
https://www.tiktok.com/@bluestarpress
https://www.pinterest.com/bluestarpress/

Nonfiction > *Nonfiction Books*
Arts; Comedy / Humour; Creativity; Wellbeing

Send: Submission Form
How to send: Email

Focuses on the arts, creative processes, wellness, and witty non-fiction.

P076 BOA Editions, Ltd
Book Publisher
250 North Goodman Street, Suite 306, Rochester, NY 14607
United States
Tel: +1 (585) 546-3410

contact@boaeditions.org

https://www.boaeditions.org

Fiction > *Short Fiction Collections*: Literary

Nonfiction > *Nonfiction Books*
Literature; Poetry as a Subject

Poetry in Translation > *Poetry Collections*

Poetry > *Poetry Collections*

Send: Full text
How to send: Submittable

Publisher of literary fiction, poetry, and prose about poetry and poetics. Specific reading periods (see website). Also runs annual poetry and fiction competitions. See website for more details.

P077 Boathooks Books
Publishing Imprint
United Kingdom

submissions@sunpenny.com

https://www.sunpenny.com/imprints/

Book Publisher: Sunpenny Publishing (**P435**)

Nonfiction > *Nonfiction Books*
   Boats; Sailing

Send: Query; Author bio; Marketing Plan; Synopsis; Full text
How to send: Email
How not to send: Post

Publishes books on boating of all kinds.

P078 Bookouture
Book Publisher
United Kingdom

http://www.bookouture.com
https://twitter.com/bookouture

Book Publisher: Hachette UK

Fiction > *Novels*
   General, and in particular: Book Club Fiction; Contemporary Romance; Cozy Mysteries; Crime; Domestic Suspense; Fantasy; Historical Fiction; Multicultural; Police Procedural; Psychological Thrillers; Romantic Comedy; Science Fiction; Thrillers; Women's Fiction

Send: Full text
How to send: Online submission system

Publishes commercial fiction.

For most authors outside the bestseller lists, traditional publishers simply aren't adding enough value to justify low royalty rates. And because authors aren't all experts in editing, design, or marketing, self-publishing doesn't get the most out of their books or time. Digital publishing offers incredible opportunities to connect with readers all over the world – but finding the help you need to make the most of them can be tricky.

That's why we bring both big publisher experience and small team creativity. We genuinely understand and invest in brands – developing long-term strategies, marketing plans and websites for each of our authors.

And we work with the most brilliant editorial, design and marketing professionals in the business to make sure that everything we do is perfectly tailored to you and ridiculously good.

Combine all of that with an incredible 45% royalty rate we think we're simply the perfect combination of high returns and inspirational publishing.

P079 Books of Chapel Hill
Publishing Imprint
United States

Book Publisher: Workman Publishing (**P519**)

P080 Bramble
Publishing Imprint
United States

Publishing Imprint: Tor Publishing Group (**P456**)

P081 Brewin Books Ltd
Book Publisher
19 Enfield Ind. Estate, Redditch, Worcestershire, B97 6BY
United Kingdom
Tel: +44 (0) 1527 854228
Fax: +44 (0) 1527 60451

admin@brewinbooks.com

https://www.brewinbooks.com
http://www.facebook.com/brewinbooks
http://www.twitter.com/brewinbooks

ADULT
   Fiction > *Novels*
      Contemporary; Ghost Stories

   Nonfiction > *Nonfiction Books*
      Arts; Biography; Comedy / Humour; Creativity; Family; Health; History; Memoir; Military History; Military; Music; Police; Social History; Sport; The Midlands; Transport; Travel; Wellbeing

CHILDREN'S
   Fiction
      Novels; *Picture Books*
   Nonfiction > *Nonfiction Books*

Send: Query; Synopsis; Author bio
How to send: Email; Post

Publishes regional books on Midland history in the areas of the police, hospitals, the military, family, social and biographies. Also publishes contemporary fiction and books for children. Welcomes submissions from aspiring authors.

Authors: Rob Blakeman; Carl Chinn; Alton Douglas; Brian Drew; Audrey Duggan; Jean Field; Jill Fraser; Gwen Freeman; Patrick Hayes; Nick Owen; Shirley Thompson

Publishing Imprints: Breedon Books; Brewin Books; History into Print; Hunt End Books; Richards Publishing

P082 Bright Press
Publishing Imprint
18 Circus Street, Brighton, BN2 9QF
United Kingdom
Tel: +44 (0) 1273 727268

marketinguk@quarto.com

https://www.quartoknows.com/Bright-Press

Book Publisher: The Quarto Group, Inc. (**P367**)

Nonfiction > *Illustrated Books*
   Activities; Arts; Crafts; Culture; Food and Drink; Gardening; Lifestyle; Science

Dedicated to producing beautiful books that will inspire a wide range of enthusiasts, from beer lovers and science geeks to gardeners and artists.

P083 The British Academy
Book Publisher
10–11 Carlton House Terrace, London, SW1Y 5AH
United Kingdom
Tel: +44 (0) 20 7969 5200

publishing@thebritishacademy.ac.uk

https://www.thebritishacademy.ac.uk
https://www.thebritishacademy.ac.uk/publishing/

ACADEMIC > **Nonfiction** > *Nonfiction Books*
   Archaeology; Culture; History; Philosophy; Society

Registered charity publishing not for profit. Publishes humanities and social sciences, particularly history, philosophy, and archaeology.

P084 The British Museum Press
Book Publisher
British Museum, Great Russell Street, London, WC1B 3DG
United Kingdom

publicity@britishmuseum.org

https://www.britishmuseum.org/commercial/british-museum-press

ACADEMIC > **Nonfiction** > *Nonfiction Books*
   Archaeology; Arts; Culture; History

ADULT > **Nonfiction** > *Nonfiction Books*
   Archaeology; Arts; Culture; History

Publishes books inspired by the collections of the British Museum, covering fine and decorative arts, history, archaeology and world cultures.

P085 Broadview Press
Book Publisher
PO Box 1243, Peterborough, ON, K9J 7H5
Canada
Tel: +1 (705) 482-5915
Fax: +1 (705) 743-8353

customerservice@broadviewpress.com

https://broadviewpress.com
https://www.facebook.com/thebroadviewpress/
https://twitter.com/broadviewpress
https://www.instagram.com/broadviewpress/

ACADEMIC > Nonfiction > *Nonfiction Books*
   History; Literature; Philosophy; Politics; Writing

Send: Query
Don't send: Proposal; Full text
How to send: Email

Publishes academic books on literature, philosophy, and history. Before sending a proposal send an email query to the appropriate editor (see website).

P086 Brown, Son & Ferguson, Ltd
Book Publisher
Unit 1A, 426 Drumoyne Road, Glasgow, G51 4DA
United Kingdom
Tel: +44 (0) 1418 830141
Fax: +44 (0) 1418 105931

info@skipper.co.uk

https://www.skipper.co.uk

ADULT > Nonfiction > *Nonfiction Books*
   History; Model Ships and Boats; Sailing; Ships

PROFESSIONAL > Nonfiction > *Nonfiction Books*
   Sailing; Shipping; Ships

Nautical publishers, printers and ships' stationers since 1832. Publishes technical and non-technical nautical textbooks, books about the sea, historical books, information on old sailing ships and how to build model ships.

P087 Burning Eye Books
Book Publisher
United Kingdom

https://burningeyebooks.wordpress.com

Poetry > *Performance Poetry*

Closed to approaches.

Aims to create an inclusive representation of the best and most promising performance poets. Welcomes submissions from all human beings regardless of gender, race, religion, or any definition of origin or ethnicity. The only thing requirement is that you are active as a poet in the UK. No sexism / genderism, transphobia / homophobia, racism, ableism, or apologists for sexual assault and rape.

P088 C&T Publishing
Book Publisher
1651 Challenge Drive, Concord, CA 94520-5206
United States

ctinfo@ctpub.com

https://www.ctpub.com

Nonfiction > *Nonfiction Books*
   Embroidery; Quilting; Sewing

Publishes books on sewing and related crafts.

Publishing Imprints: Crosley-Griffith; FunStitch Studio; Kansas City Star Quilts; Stash Books

P089 Cadno
Publishing Imprint
United Kingdom

https://graffeg.com

Book Publisher: Graffeg (**P190**)

CHILDREN'S > Fiction > *Middle Grade*

How to send: Online submission system

Imprint handling middle grade fiction. Submissions welcome using online submission system (see website).

P090 Caitlin Press Inc.
Book Publisher; Ebook Publisher
3375 Ponderosa Way, Qualicum Beach, BC, V9K 2J8
Canada
Tel: +1 (604) 741-4200

vici@caitlin-press.com

https://caitlin-press.com
http://facebook.com/caitlinbooks
http://twitter.com/caitlinpress
http://instagram.com/caitlinpress.daggereditions

ADULT
   Fiction
      Novels; Short Fiction Collections
   Nonfiction > *Nonfiction Books*
      Arts; Biography; British Columbia; Environment; Feminism; History; LGBTQIA; Memoir; Outdoor Activities; Photography; Travel
   Poetry > *Poetry Collections*

CHILDREN'S > Fiction > *Novels*

Send: Query; Outline; Author bio; Writing sample
Don't send: Full text
How to send: Post
How not to send: Email

Publishes books on topics concerning or by writers from the British Columbia Interior and stories about and by British Columbia women. No submissions by email. See website for full guidelines.

Editors: Sarah Corsie; Vici Johnstone

P091 Calkins Creek
Publishing Imprint
United States

Book Publisher: Astra Publishing House (**P037**)

P092 Candlemark & Gleam
Book Publisher
United States

eloi@candlemarkandgleam.com
Morlocks@candlemarkandgleam.com

https://www.candlemarkandgleam.com

Fiction > *Novels*
   Alternative History; Fantasy; Magical Realism; Science Fiction; Speculative

How to send: By referral

We specialize in speculative fiction—we're eager to explore infinite possibilities. We believe wholeheartedly in the power of the imagination, and we want to shape speculative fiction (science fiction, fantasy, magical realism, alternative history) as it deserves to develop: not a genre, but a way of looking at things with fresh eyes.

P093 Candy Jar Books
Book Publisher
Mackintosh House, 136 Newport Road, Cardiff, CF24 1DJ
United Kingdom
Tel: +44 (0) 2921 157202

hello@candyjarbooks.co.uk
submissions@candyjarbooks.co.uk

https://www.candy-jar.co.uk

ADULT
   Fiction > *Novels*
   Nonfiction > *Nonfiction Books*

CHILDREN'S > Fiction > *Middle Grade*

YOUNG ADULT > Fiction > *Novels*

Send: Query; Synopsis; Writing sample
How to send: Email; Post

Costs: Offers services that writers have to pay for. Also offers self publishing services through a sister imprint.

We are always on the lookout for new ideas and talent, for stories that are fresh and engaging. We'd love to read what you have been working on. If you have an agent, great, but don't worry if not; we welcome unsolicited manuscripts. We do not accept children's picture books.

Publishing Director: Shaun Russell

P094 Canterbury Press
Publishing Imprint
Hymns Ancient and Modern Ltd, 3rd Floor, Invicta House, 110 Golden Lane, London, EC1Y 0TG
United Kingdom
Tel: +44 (0) 20 7776 7540
Fax: +44 (0) 20 7776 7556

https://canterburypress.hymnsam.co.uk
https://twitter.com/canterburypress
https://www.facebook.com/Canterbury-Press-176777199005586/

Book Publisher: Hymns Ancient & Modern Ltd

Nonfiction > *Nonfiction Books*
Biography; Christianity; Comedy / Humour; Spirituality; Travel

Supplier of popular religious books. Publishes a wide range of titles, covering liturgy, worship, mission, ministry, spirituality, biography, travel and even humour.

P095 Captivate Press
Book Publisher
United States

captivatepress@gmail.com

https://captivatepress.site

Fiction > *Novels*

Nonfiction > *Nonfiction Books*

Does not want:

> **Fiction** > *Novels*
> Erotic Romance; Science Fiction; Thrillers

Send: Query; Market info; Writing sample
How to send: Email

We are accepting manuscripts from writers in the U.S. and Canada only and are particularly interested in writers who have an advance social media presence. Please do not send Sci-fi, Smutty Romance, or Thrillers. We accept un-agented submissions. We do not require exclusive submissions. Please be sure that your manuscript is properly formatted according to basic manuscript format guidelines.

P096 Cassell
Publishing Imprint
United Kingdom

https://www.octopusbooks.co.uk/imprint/octopus/cassell/page/cassell/

Book Publisher: Octopus Publishing Group Limited

Nonfiction
Illustrated Books: Entertainment; Popular Culture; Sport
Nonfiction Books: Business; Current Affairs; Narrative Nonfiction; Popular Psychology; Popular Science

Publishes illustrated non-fiction specialising in popular culture, entertainment, sport and reference titles, and non-illustrated narrative non-fiction, including popular science, business narrative, popular psychology and current affairs.

P097 Celadon Books
Publishing Imprint
United States

Book Publisher: Macmillan Publishers

P098 CGI (Chartered Governance Institute) Publishing
Book Publisher
Saffron House, 6–10 Kirby Street, London, EC1N 8TS
United Kingdom
Tel: +44 (0) 20 7580 4741

https://www.cgi.org.uk
https://www.cgi.org.uk/shop
https://www.linkedin.com/school/cgiuki
https://www.facebook.com/CGIUKI
https://twitter.com/CGIUKI
https://www.flickr.com/photos/icsaglobal

PROFESSIONAL > **Nonfiction** > *Nonfiction Books*: Business

Practical governance books and media on business skills; boards; risk and compliance; company secretarial practice; governance; and study texts.

P099 Chapman Publishing
Book Publisher
4 Broughton Place, Edinburgh, EH1 3RX
United Kingdom
Tel: +44 (0) 131 557 2207

chapman-pub@blueyonder.co.uk

http://www.chapman-pub.co.uk

Fiction > *Short Fiction Collections*

Poetry > *Poetry Collections*

Scripts > *Theatre Scripts*

Closed to approaches.

Note: No new books being undertaken as at August 2022. Check website for current status.

Publishes one or two books of short stories, drama, and (mainly) poetry by established and rising Scottish writers per year. No novels. Only considers writers who have previously been published in the press's magazine. Only publishes plays that have been previously performed. No unsolicited MSS.

Magazine: Chapman (**M081**)

P100 Charisma House
Publishing Imprint
600 Rinehart Rd, Lake Mary, FL 32746
United States
Tel: +1 (407) 333-0600

info@charismamedia.com

https://charismahouse.com
https://www.facebook.com/CharismaHouse/
https://twitter.com/charismahouse
https://www.instagram.com/charismahousebooks/

Media Company: Charisma Media

Fiction > *Novels*: Christianity

Nonfiction > *Nonfiction Books*
Christian Living; Christianity; Politics

Through the power of the Holy Spirit we inspire people to radically change their world. Providing Spirit-Filled Christians globally with resources to empower them to change their world through the power of the Holy Spirit.

P101 Charles River Press
Book Publisher
United States
Tel: +1 (508) 364-9851

info@charlesriverpress.com

http://www.charlesriverpress.com
https://www.facebook.com/charles.r.press/
https://twitter.com/CharlesRiverLLC
https://www.youtube.com/user/CharlesRiverPress/

Fiction > *Novels*: Erotic

Nonfiction > *Nonfiction Books*: Sport

Send: Author bio; Market info; Synopsis; Full text

Costs: Offers services that writers have to pay for. Also offers editing and design services.

Currently accepting sports and erotica manuscripts.

Authors: Richard Herrick; John McMullen; Mike Ryan; Tony Schiavone; Jonathan Womack; Rowena Womack

P102 Charlesbridge Publishing
Book Publisher
9 Galen Street, Watertown, MA 02472
United States
Tel: +1 (617) 926-0329

tradeeditorial@charlesbridge.com

https://www.charlesbridge.com
https://twitter.com/charlesbridge
https://www.facebook.com/CharlesbridgePublishingInc
https://www.pinterest.com/charlesbridge/
https://www.instagram.com/charlesbridgepublishing/
https://charlesbridgebooks.tumblr.com/
https://www.youtube.com/user/Charlesbridge1

CHILDREN'S
Fiction
Board Books; *Early Readers*; *Middle Grade*; *Picture Books*
Nonfiction
Board Books: General
Early Readers: General
Middle Grade: Arts; Biography; History; Mathematics; Nature; Science; Social Issues
Picture Books: General

Send: Full text
How to send: Word file email attachment; PDF

file email attachment
How not to send: In the body of an email

Publishes books for children, with teen and adult imprints. No text or art generated by artificial intelligence.

Publishing Imprints: Charlesbridge Teen (**P103**); Imagine Publishing (**P234**)

P103 Charlesbridge Teen
Publishing Imprint
9 Galen Street, Watertown, MA 02472
United States
Tel: +1 (800) 225-3214

ya.submissions@charlesbridge.com

https://charlesbridgeteen.com
https://twitter.com/CharlesbridgeYA
https://www.facebook.com/CharlesbridgePublishingInc/
https://www.pinterest.com/charlesbridge/
https://www.instagram.com/charlesbridgeteen/
http://charlesbridgebooks.tumblr.com/

Book Publisher: Charlesbridge Publishing (**P102**)

YOUNG ADULT
  Fiction > *Novels*
  Nonfiction > *Nonfiction Books*

Send: Query; Synopsis; Writing sample; Proposal; Outline
How to send: Email attachment

Features storytelling that presents new ideas and an evolving world. Our carefully curated stories give voice to unforgettable characters with unique perspectives. We publish books that inspire teens to cheer or sigh, laugh or reflect, reread or share with a friend, and ultimately, pick up another book. Our mission – to make reading irresistible!

P104 Chartered Institute of Personnel and Development (CIPD) Publishing
Book Publisher
151 The Broadway, London, SW19 1JQ
United Kingdom
Tel: +44 (0) 20 8612 6202

https://www.cipd.co.uk
https://www.cipd.co.uk/learn/bookshop

ACADEMIC > **Nonfiction** > *Nonfiction Books*
  Business; Personal Development

PROFESSIONAL > **Nonfiction** > *Nonfiction Books*
  Business; Personal Development

Publishes professional and academic books, looseleafs, and online subscription products, covering topics relating to personnel, training, and management.

Publishing Director: Stephen Dunn

P105 Chelsea House Publishers
Publishing Imprint
132 West 31st Street, 16th Floor, New York, NY 10001
United States
Tel: +1 (800) 322-8755
Fax: +1 (800) 678-3633

CustServ@Infobase.com

https://chelseahouse.infobasepublishing.com

Book Publisher: Infobase Publishing

ACADEMIC > **Nonfiction** > *Nonfiction Books*
  Biography; Contemporary; Geography; Health; History; Science; Sociology

Publishes curriculum-based nonfiction books for middle school and high school students, spanning historical and contemporary biographies, social studies, geography, science, health, high-interest titles, and more. Provides educators and librarians with colorful, engaging books and eBooks that can be used as supplemental reading for the school curriculum and as solid resources for research projects.

P106 Cherry Lake Publishing Group
Book Publisher
2395 South Huron Parkway, Suite 200, Ann Arbor, MI 48104
United States
Tel: +1 (866) 918-3956

submissions@sleepingbearpress.com

https://cherrylakepublishing.com
https://www.facebook.com/CherryLakePublishing
https://www.instagram.com/cherrylakepublishing

CHILDREN'S
  Fiction
    Board Books; Early Readers; Middle Grade; Picture Books
  Nonfiction
    Board Books; Early Readers; Middle Grade; Picture Books

Send: Query; Author bio; Outline
How to send: In the body of an email

We are a publisher of quality children's books. We publish a wide range of books, including board books, beginning readers, picture books, and select middle grade titles. We accept both fiction and nonfiction submissions. We are committed to the principles of diversity, equity and inclusion and welcome stories from diverse authors. Please browse our website or catalog for examples of the types of books we publish.

Publishing Imprint: Tilbury House Publishers (**P450**)

P107 Child's Play (International) Ltd
Book Publisher
Ashworth Road, Bridgemead, Swindon, Wiltshire, SN5 7YD
United Kingdom
Tel: +44 (0) 1793 616286

office@childs-play.com

http://www.childs-play.com
https://www.facebook.com/ChildsPlayBooks/
https://twitter.com/ChildsPlayBooks
http://pinterest.com/childsplaybooks/
http://www.instagram.com/childsplaybooks/
https://www.youtube.com/channel/UCik8Eew5rGc2LfpggFgX4Qg

CHILDREN'S
  Fiction
    Activity Books; Board Books; Picture Books
  Poetry > *Picture Books*

Send: Query; Full text
How to send: Email

Specialises in publishing books that allow children to learn through play. No novels. No AI-generated stories.

P108 Choc Lit
Book Publisher
United Kingdom

choc-lit@joffebooks.com

https://www.choc-lit.com
https://twitter.com/choclituk
https://www.facebook.com/Choc-Lit-30680012481/
https://www.instagram.com/choclituk/
https://www.youtube.com/channel/UCLZBZ2qeR5gtOyDoqEjMbQw

Book Publisher: Joffe Books (**P248**)

Fiction > *Novels*
  Book Club Women's Fiction; Contemporary Romance; Domestic Noir; Family Saga; Historical Fiction; Historical Romance; Psychological Thrillers; Romance; Romantasy; Romantic Comedy; Romantic Suspense; Suspense; Time Travel; Timeslip Romance; World War II

Send: Query; Synopsis; Submission Form; Author bio
How to send: Email attachment

Our favourite genres include contemporary uplit, spicy grump-sunshine, laugh-out-loud romantic comedy, cosy village romance, beachy escapes, time travel romantasy, sweeping historical sagas and WWII romances, spicy happily-ever-afters, and gripping women's book club fiction. We also love psychological thrillers, suspense and domestic noir. We want to read #OwnVoices submissions that bring characters who represent the same marginalised identities as their author, including but not limited to

BIPOC, LGBT+ and differently abled people, people living in underrepresented cultures and socioeconomic backgrounds, and more. We encourage authors from diverse backgrounds to submit their work and make their voices heard. We especially look for great stories, fresh ideas, excellent writing and original voices; in short authors who say something interesting about the world as they see it. We publish writers we believe in, from debut novelists and agented authors, to self-represented writers and authors who are already well-established. Submissions are welcome from anywhere in the world, however, we only publish books in the English language. We accept submissions from agents, previously published authors (including self-published authors) with long backlists, first-time writers with only one book under their belt, and anyone in between. We do NOT publish non-fiction, poetry, YA fiction, children's fiction, sci-fi or erotica. If these are your genres, we are probably not the publisher for you.

Author: Juliet Archer

Publishing Imprint: Ruby Fiction (**P384**)

P109 Chosen Books
Book Publisher

Book Publisher: Baker Publishing Group

Closed to approaches.

P110 ChristLight Books
Publishing Imprint
United Kingdom

https://www.sunpenny.com/imprints/

Book Publisher: Sunpenny Publishing (**P435**)

Fiction > *Novels*: Christianity

Nonfiction > *Nonfiction Books*: Christianity

Send: Query; Author bio; Marketing Plan; Synopsis; Full text
How to send: Email

Publishes Christian fiction and nonfiction books.

P111 Chronicle Books LLC
Book Publisher
680 Second Street, San Francisco, California 94107
United States
Tel: +1 (415) 537 4200

submissions@chroniclebooks.com

https://www.chroniclebooks.com
https://facebook.com/ChronicleBooks
https://twitter.com/ChronicleBooks
https://pinterest.com/ChronicleBooks
https://instagram.com/ChronicleBooks

ADULT > **Nonfiction** > *Nonfiction Books*
 Arts; Beauty; Cookery; Design; Fashion; Interior Design; Photography; Popular Culture; Relationships

CHILDREN'S
Fiction
 Activity Books; *Board Books*; *Chapter Books*; *Early Readers*; *Middle Grade*; *Picture Books*
Nonfiction
 Activity Books; *Board Books*; *Chapter Books*; *Early Readers*; *Middle Grade*; *Picture Books*

Send: Query; Outline; Writing sample; Market info; Author bio
How to send: Word file email attachment; PDF file email attachment

Publishes nonfiction for adults, and fiction and nonfiction for children. See website for full guidelines.

P112 Cinnamon Press
Book Publisher
Office 49019, PO Box 15113, Birmingham, B2 2NJ
United Kingdom

jan@cinnamonpress.com

https://www.cinnamonpress.com

Fiction > *Novels*

Nonfiction > *Nonfiction Books*

Poetry > *Poetry Collections*

Small-press publisher of full length poetry collections, unique and imaginative novels, and practical and informative nonfiction with wide appeal. Willing to consider most genres as long as writing is thought-provoking, enjoyable, and accessible; but does not publish genre fiction (romantic, erotica, horror or crime), biography, autobiography, academic, technical or how-to. No unsolicited MSS. See website for submission details.

Editor: Jan Fortune

P113 Claret Press
Book Publisher
51 Iveley Road, London, SW4 0EN
United Kingdom
Tel: +44 (0) 7736 716927

contact@claretpress.com

https://www.claretpress.com
https://www.facebook.com/ClaretPublisher
https://twitter.com/ClaretPress

Fiction > *Novels*
 Mystery; Thrillers

Nonfiction > *Nonfiction Books*
 Memoir; Politics; Travel

Closed to approaches.

A Micro Publisher specialising in narratives that encourage conversations about contemporary politics, issues and places. We love a great read about our shared world, about politics, people and places. Our page turners percolate with ideas, entertain and enlighten.

We're London-based and the majority of our books are about Britain. But our travelogues take you around the world. So do many of our thrillers. Hearts and minds are opened by our memoirs and novels.

P114 Classical Comics
Book Publisher
PO Box 177, Ludlow, SY8 9DL
United Kingdom

https://www.classicalcomics.com
https://www.facebook.com/ClassicalComics/
https://www.instagram.com/classcomeducation

CHILDREN'S > **Fiction** > *Graphic Novels*: Literature

Closed to approaches.

Publishes graphic novel adaptations of classical literature.

Creative Director: Jo Wheeler

Managing Director: Gary Bryant

P115 Cleis Press
Book Publisher
221 River St, 9th Fl, Hoboken, NJ 07030
United States
Tel: +1 (212) 431-5455

cleis@cleispress.com
acquisitions@cleispress.com

https://cleispress.com
https://instagram.com/cleis_press
https://twitter.com/cleispress
https://www.facebook.com/CleisPress.Page
https://www.pinterest.com/cleispress/
https://cleispress.tumblr.com/

Fiction > *Novels*
 Erotic Romance; Erotic

Nonfiction > *Nonfiction Books*
 Feminism; Health; LGBTQIA; Memoir; Relationships; Self Help; Sex; Sexuality; Women's Studies

How to send: Through a literary agent

The largest independent sexuality publishing company in the United States. With a focus on LGBTQ, BDSM, romance, and erotic writing for all sexual preferences. Agented approaches only.

P116 Coaches Choice
Book Publisher
311 – 21st Street, Camanche, IA 52730
United States
Tel: +1 (888) 229-5745

submissions@coacheschoice.com

https://coacheschoice.com

ADULT > **Nonfiction** > *Nonfiction Books*: Sports Coaching

PROFESSIONAL > **Nonfiction** > *Nonfiction Books*: Sports Coaching

Send: Query
How to send: Email

Always looking for people passionate about about sports instruction with the goal of improvement for coaches of all sports in all facets of their lives.

P117 College Press Publishing
Book Publisher
1307 W 20th Street, Joplin, MO 64804
United States

collpressjoplin@gmail.com

https://collegepress.com
https://www.facebook.com/collpresspublishing/

Nonfiction > *Nonfiction Books*
  Bible Studies; Biography; Christianity; Evangelism; History

Send: Query; Proposal
How to send: Post; Email

Publishes Bible studies, topical studies (biblically based), apologetic studies, historical biographies of Christians, Sunday/Bible School curriculum (adult electives). No poetry, game or puzzle books, books on prophecy from a premillennial or dispensational viewpoint, or any books that do not contain a Christian message.

Publishing Imprint: HeartSpring Publishing

P118 Collins
Book Publisher
Westerhill Road, Bishopbriggs, Glasgow, G64 2QT
United Kingdom

education@harpercollins.co.uk

https://collins.co.uk

Book Publisher: HarperCollins UK

ACADEMIC > **Nonfiction** > *Nonfiction Books*: Education

ADULT > **Nonfiction** > *Reference*
  Atlases; Dictionaries

Send: Author bio; Outline; Market info

Publishes reference books and educational resources.

P119 Colourpoint Educational
Book Publisher
Colourpoint House, Jubilee Business Park, 21 Jubilee Road, Newtownards, Northern Ireland, BT23 4YH
United Kingdom
Tel: +44 (0) 28 9182 0505

sales@colourpoint.co.uk

https://colourpointeducational.com
https://twitter.com/ColourpointEdu

ACADEMIC > **Nonfiction** > *Nonfiction Books*
  Biology; Chemistry; Design; Digital Technology; Education; French; Gaelic; Geography; Health; History; Home Economics / Domestic Science; Legal; Lifestyle; Mathematics; Physical Education; Physics; Politics; Religion; Technology

Send: Query
How to send: Email

Provides textbooks, ebooks and digital resources for Northern Ireland students at Key Stage 3 level, and the CCEA revised specification at GCSE and AS/A2/A-level.

Book Publisher: Blackstaff Press (**P068**)

Editor: Wesley Johnston

P120 Comma Press
Book Publisher
Studio 510a, 5th Floor, Hope Mill, 113 Pollard Street, Manchester, M4 7JA
United Kingdom

ra.page@commapress.co.uk

http://commapress.co.uk
https://facebook.com/commapressmcr
https://twitter.com/commapress
https://instagram.com/commapress

Fiction > *Short Fiction*

A not-for-profit publisher and development agency specialising in short fiction from the UK and beyond.

P121 Compassiviste Publishing
Book Publisher
United Kingdom

submissions@compassivistepublishing.com

https://compassivistepublishing.com
https://x.com/compassiviste
https://www.tiktok.com/@compassiviste
https://www.instagram.com/compassiviste/
https://www.facebook.com/CompassivisteOfficial/
https://www.linkedin.com/company/compassiviste

Fiction
  Novels: Adventure; Commercial; Contemporary; Drama; Experimental; Fantasy; Literary; Mainstream; Popular; Science Fiction; Thrillers; Traditional
  Short Fiction Collections: General

Nonfiction > *Nonfiction Books*
  Anthropology; Arts; Autobiography; Biography; Comedy / Humour; Culture; Current Affairs; Entertainment; Health; History; How To; Leisure; Lifestyle; Literature; Men's Interests; Music; Nature; New Age; Philosophy; Photography; Politics; Psychology; Science; Self Help; Sociology; Spirituality; Technology; Travel; Women's Interests

Send: Query; Synopsis; Outline; Author bio; Writing sample
How to send: Email; Online submission system

Welcomes unsolicited full-length manuscripts and submissions to our quarterly anthology. We welcome writers at any stage of their career, and support authors from disadvantaged and diverse backgrounds. Our work includes fiction and non-fiction books across a wide range of genres, covering important social, cultural and environmental topics aligned with our foundation's charitable causes. We invest 100% of our net profits back into the charity.

P122 Convergent
Publishing Imprint

Book Publisher: Random House

P123 Cornell Maritime Press
Publishing Imprint
United States

https://schifferbooks.com/pages/schiffer-imprints

Book Publisher: Schiffer Publishing (**P398**)

PROFESSIONAL > **Nonfiction** > *Nonfiction Books*
  Boats; Legal; Maritime History; Regional; Sailing

Titles for personnel in marine businesses, including texts for the Merchant Marine Academies, boating, water safety, maritime law, salvage, navigation, and regional maritime history.

P124 Countryside Books
Book Publisher
35a Kingfisher Court, Hambridge Road, Newbury, Berkshire, RG14 5SJ
United Kingdom
Tel: +44 (0) 1635 43816

info@countrysidebooks.co.uk

https://countrysidebooks.co.uk
https://twitter.com/countrysidebook
https://www.facebook.com/CountrysideBooks/
https://www.instagram.com/countrysidebooks/

Nonfiction > *Nonfiction Books*
  Architecture; Aviation; Comedy / Humour; Crime; Cycling; Dialects; Ghosts; History; Local History; Mystery; Nostalgia; Railways; Supernatural / Paranormal; Walking; World War I; World War II

Publishes nonfiction only, mostly regional books relating to specific English counties. Covers topics such as local history, walks, photography, dialect, genealogy, military and aviation, and some transport; but not interested in natural history books or personal memories. No fiction or poetry.

P125 Coyote Arts
Book Publisher
PO Box 6690, Albuquerque, NM 87197-6690
United States

sales@coyote-arts.com

https://coyote-arts.com
https://www.facebook.com/coyoteartsllc/
https://twitter.com/coyoteartsllc
https://instagram.com/coyoteartsllc
https://www.pinterest.com/coyoteartsllc/

Fiction > *Novels*
   Arts; Literary

Nonfiction > *Nonfiction Books*: Arts

Poetry > *Any Poetic Form*

A literary arts publisher dedicated to the power of words and images to transform human lives and the environment we inhabit. Publishes works in the genres of poetry, fiction, non-fiction, and drama that engage the sense of wonder and possibility.

P126 Crabtree Publishing
Book Publisher
347 Fifth Ave, Suite 1402-145, New York, NY 10016
United States
Tel: +1 (800) 387-7650

https://crabtreebooks.com

ACADEMIC > **Nonfiction** > *Nonfiction Books*
   Arts; Biography; Earth Science; Economics; Finance; Geography; Health; History; Mathematics; Science; Sociology; Space; Technology; Visual Culture

CHILDREN'S
   Fiction
      Board Books: General
      Chapter Books: General
      Early Readers: Comedy / Humour; Fairy Tales; Fantasy; Horror; Magical Realism; Mystery
      Graphic Novels: General
      Picture Books: General
   Nonfiction > *Nonfiction Books*

Closed to approaches.

Publishes educational books for children. No unsolicited mss. All material is generated in-house.

P127 Croner-i Limited
Book Publisher
240 Blackfriars Road, London, SE1 8NW
United Kingdom
Tel: +44 (0) 800 231 5199

https://www.croneri.co.uk

PROFESSIONAL > **Nonfiction** > *Nonfiction Books*
   Accounting; Business; Taxation

Publishes books and resources for business professionals covering tax and accounting, human resources, health and safety, and compliance.

Online Magazine: Accountancy Daily (**M011**)

P128 Crossway
Publishing Imprint
1300 Crescent Street, Wheaton, IL 60187
United States
Tel: +1 (630) 682-4300

info@crossway.org

http://www.crossway.org

ACADEMIC > **Nonfiction** > *Nonfiction Books*
   Bible Studies; Christianity; Church History

ADULT > **Nonfiction** > *Nonfiction Books*
   Christian Living; Christianity

PROFESSIONAL > **Nonfiction** > *Nonfiction Books*: Christianity

Send: Query
How to send: Email

Publishes nonfiction books that engage believers' minds, stir their affections, and motivate their wills. Focuses on key issues facing Christians; Christian life; the Christian worldview; and academic and professional volumes directed toward college and seminary students, pastors, and others in full-time Christian work.

P129 Crown
Publishing Imprint
United States

https://crownpublishing.com/archives/imprint/crown-publishers
https://www.instagram.com/crownpublishing
https://twitter.com/CrownPublishing
https://www.facebook.com/CrownPublishing

Book Publisher: The Crown Publishing Group (**P131**)

Nonfiction > *Nonfiction Books*
   Biography; Business; Cultural Criticism; Current Affairs; Economics; History; Politics; Psychology; Science; Social Justice

Publishes across a wide range of nonfiction genres with an emphasis on politics, current affairs, social justice, personal narrative, biography, history, economics, business, cultural criticism, science, social science, and psychology. As a team, we are committed to publishing a diverse array of leading and emerging voices who enlarge our understanding of the world; help us navigate and succeed in a rapidly evolving climate; challenge legacy narratives; and harness the power of storytelling to illuminate, entertain, inspire, and connect readers everywhere.

P130 Crown Currency
Publishing Imprint

Book Publisher: The Crown Publishing Group (**P131**)

P131 The Crown Publishing Group
Book Publisher
United States

customerservice@prh.com

https://crownpublishing.com
https://www.facebook.com/CrownPublishing
https://twitter.com/crownpublishing
http://instagram.com/crownpublishing
http://www.goodreads.com/user/show/2504245-crown-publishing-group
https://www.pinterest.com/crownpublishing/

Book Publisher: Penguin Random House

Fiction > *Novels*

Nonfiction
   Gift Books: General
   Nonfiction Books: Arts; Biography; Business; Comedy / Humour; Cookery; Crafts; Fitness; Gardening; Health; History; Hobbies; Memoir; Politics; Self Help

Division of large international publisher.

Publishing Imprints: 4 Color Books; Clarkson Potter; Crown (**P129**); Crown Currency (**P130**); Currency; Ten Speed Graphic (**P443**); Ten Speed Press (**P444**); Watson-Guptill Publications

P132 Dahlia Books
Book Publisher
United Kingdom

submissions@dahliapublishing.co.uk

http://www.dahliapublishing.co.uk
https://twitter.com/dahliabooks

Fiction > *Short Fiction Collections*
   Contemporary; Diversity; Regional

Send: Query; Outline; Writing sample
How to send: Word file email attachment

We only accept proposals for short fiction and short stories when presented as a collection from UK based writers. Please do not send us single short stories. We are particularly keen on publishing diverse voices and actively encourage submissions from first-time writers.

Print Magazine: Present Tense (**M296**)

P133 Dancing Girl Press
Book Publisher
United States

dancinggirlpress@yahoo.com

http://www.dancinggirlpress.com

Poetry > *Chapbooks*

Send: Full text

Publishes chapbooks by female poets between 12 and 32 pages. No payment, but free 10 copies and 40% discount on further copies.

P134 Daunt Books Publishing
Book Publisher
207-209 Kentish Town Rd, London, NW5 2JU
United Kingdom

publishing@dauntbooks.co.uk

https://dauntbookspublishing.co.uk
https://twitter.com/dauntbookspub

Fiction in Translation
Novels: Literary
Short Fiction Collections: Literary

Fiction
Novels: Literary
Short Fiction Collections: Literary

Nonfiction in Translation
Essays: General
Nonfiction Books: Memoir; Narrative Nonfiction

Nonfiction
Essays: General
Nonfiction Books: Memoir; Narrative Nonfiction

Closed to approaches.

We publish the finest and most exciting new writing in English and in translation, whether that's literary fiction – novels and short stories – or narrative non-fiction including essays and memoir. We also publish modern classics, reviving authors who have been overlooked and publishing them in bold editions with introductions from the best contemporary writers.

P135 DAW Books
Publishing Imprint
United States

https://astrapublishinghouse.com/imprints/daw-books/

Book Publisher: Astra Publishing House **(P037)**

Fiction > *Novels*
  Fantasy; Science Fiction

The first publishing company ever devoted exclusively to science fiction and fantasy. Seeks to publish a wide range of voices and stories.

P136 Dedalus Ltd
Book Publisher
Langford Lodge, St Judith's Lane, Sawtry, PE28 5XE
United Kingdom
Tel: +44 (0) 1487 832382

info@dedalusbooks.com

https://www.dedalusbooks.com

https://www.facebook.com/profile.php?id=100063653493212
https://twitter.com/dedalusbooks
http://vimeo.com/dedalusbooks

Fiction in Translation > *Novels*
  Contemporary; Literary

Fiction > *Novels*
  Contemporary; Literary

Send: Query; Writing sample; Self-Addressed Stamped Envelope (SASE)
How to send: Post

Publisher of literary fiction, including contemporary English language fiction and translated European fiction. Most books are translations.

Book Publisher: Dedalus European Classics

P137 Del Rey
Publishing Imprint
United States

Book Publisher: Random House

P138 Denis Kitchen Publishing Company Co., LLC
Book Publisher
P.O. Box 2250, Amherst, MA 01004
United States
Tel: +1 (413) 259-1627

help@deniskitchen.com

http://deniskitchenpublishing.com

Fiction
  Cartoons; Comics; Graphic Novels
Nonfiction > *Nonfiction Books*
  Arts; Comic Books

Publishes comics and graphic novels and books on the subject.

P139 DeVorss & Company
Book Publisher
PO Box 1389, Camarillo, CA 93011-1389
United States

editorial@devorss.com

https://www.devorss.com

ADULT > **Nonfiction** > *Nonfiction Books*
  Alternative Health; Inspirational; Lifestyle; Mind, Body, Spirit; Religion; Self Help; Spirituality

CHILDREN'S > **Nonfiction** > *Nonfiction Books*

Send: Query; Outline; Table of Contents; Market info; Author bio
How to send: Email

Publishes New Thought, spirituality, self-improvement, alternative health and lifestyle, religion, children's books, and positive thinking. No poetry.

P140 The Dial Press
Publishing Imprint

Book Publisher: Random House

P141 DK Publishing
Book Publisher
1745 Broadway, 20th Floor, New York, NY 10019
United States

ecustomerservice@randomhouse.com

http://www.dk.com

Book Publisher: DK (Dorling Kindersley Ltd)

ADULT > **Nonfiction**
  Nonfiction Books: Food; Gardening; Hobbies; Lifestyle; Travel; Wellbeing
  Reference: General

CHILDREN'S > **Nonfiction**
  Board Books; *Early Readers*; *Middle Grade*; *Picture Books*

How to send: Through a literary agent

Publishes highly visual nonfiction for children. Assumes no responsibility for unsolicited mss. Approach through an established literary agent.

P142 Dodo Ink
Book Publisher
United Kingdom

dodopublishingco@gmail.com

http://www.dodoink.com
https://twitter.com/DodoInk
https://www.facebook.com/profile.php?id=100064126986391

Fiction > *Novels*: Literary

Closed to approaches.

Independent UK publisher aiming to publish three novels per year, in paperback and digital formats. Publishes risk-taking, imaginative novels, that don't fall into easy marketing categories. Closed to submissions as at August 2023.

Editor: Sam Mills

P143 Doubleday (UK)
Publishing Imprint
United Kingdom

https://www.penguin.co.uk/company/publishers/transworld#Doubleday

Book Publisher: Transworld Publishers

Fiction > *Novels*

Nonfiction > *Nonfiction Books*: Narrative Nonfiction

A boutique literary imprint with a vibrant and dynamic list that publishes prize winners, international bestsellers and fresh new voices with passion and creative flair. We seek out ground-breaking books that engage the heart and mind; that speak to the zeitgeist but will also resonate for years to come.

Authors: Kate Atkinson; Sue Black; John Boyne; Bill Bryson; Nicola Dinan; Lottie Hazell; Rachel Joyce; Tracy King; John Lewis-Stempel; Catherine Newman; Elliot Page; Terry Pratchett; Hallie Rubenhold; Curtis Sittenfeld; Christopher Somerville; Clover Stroud

P144 Dreamspinner Press
Book Publisher
PO Box 1245, Woodville, FL 32362
United States
Tel: +1 (800) 970-3759
Fax: +1 (888) 308-3739

contact@dreamspinnerpress.com
submissions@dreamspinnerpress.com

https://www.dreamspinnerpress.com
https://www.facebook.com/dreamspinnerpress/
https://twitter.com/dreamspinners
https://www.instagram.com/dreamspinner_press/

Fiction > *Novels*
 Gay; Romance

Send: Synopsis; Full text
How to send: Email

Publishes gay male romance in all genres. While works do not need to be graphic, they must contain a primary or strong secondary romance plotline and focus on the interaction between two or more male characters. The main characters of the story must end in a gay or gay polyamorous relationship. Other relationships (heterosexual, lesbian, mixed gender polyamory) are acceptable in secondary pairings or as part of the development of a main character.

Authors: M. Jules Aedin; Rhianne Aile; Maria Albert; Eric Arvin; Mickie B. Ashling; Connie Bailey; Alix Bekins; Nicki Bennett; Sienna Bishop; Scarlett Blackwell; S. Blaise; Steven Blue-Williams; Anne Brooke; Bethany Brown; Janey Chapel; J. M. Colail; Jaymz Connelly; Lisa Marie Davis; Remmy Duchene; Giselle Ellis; Catt Ford; Lacey-Anne Frye; Reve Garrison; Andrew Grey; Felicitas Ivey; Ashlyn Kane; Sean Kennedy; V.B. Kildaire; Shay Kincaid; Marguerite Labbe; Clare London; Dar Mavison; Anais Morten; Chrissy Munder; Zahra Owens; D. G. Parker; Michael Powers; Angela Romano; Abigail Roux; Isabella Rowan; Steve Sampson; Ian Sentelik; Jane Seville; John Simpson; Jenna Hilary Sinclair; Dan Skinner; Sasha Skye; Sonja Spencer; Jaxx Steele; Jaelyn Storm; Rowena Sudbury; Fae Sutherland; Ariel Tachna; Madeleine Urban; G.S. Wiley

Publishing Imprints: DSP Publications (**P145**); Harmony Ink Press (**P205**)

P145 DSP Publications
Publishing Imprint
PO Box 1245, Woodville, FL 32362
United States
Tel: +1 (800) 970-3759
Fax: +1 (888) 308-3739

contact@dreamspinnerpress.com

https://www.dsppublications.com
https://twitter.com/DSPPublications
https://www.facebook.com/dsppublications/

Book Publisher: Dreamspinner Press (**P144**)

Fiction > *Novels*
 Fantasy; Historical Fiction; Horror; Mystery; Science Fiction; Spirituality; Supernatural / Paranormal

We are a boutique imprint producing quality fiction that pushes the envelope to present immersive, unique, and unforgettable reading experiences. We choose stories that beg to be told, tales that depart from mainstream concepts to create fantastic and compelling journeys of the mind.

P146 Duncan Petersen Publishing Limited
Book Publisher
United Kingdom

http://duncanpetersen.blogspot.com

Nonfiction > *Nonfiction Books*
 Cycling; Travel; Walking Guides

Travel publishing house. Publishes Hotel Guides, along with a variety of walking and cycling guides for Britain.

P147 Dynasty Press
Book Publisher
19 New Road, Brighton, BN1 1UF
United Kingdom
Tel: +44 (0) 7970 066894

admin@dynastypress.co.uk

http://www.dynastypress.co.uk
https://www.facebook.com/dynastypress

Nonfiction > *Nonfiction Books*
 Biography; History; Royalty

Publishes books connected to royalty, dynasties and people of influence.

P148 Eerdmans Books for Young Readers
Publishing Imprint
4035 Park East Court SE, Grand Rapids, Michigan 49546
United States
Tel: +1 (800) 253-7521

customerservice@eerdmans.com

https://www.eerdmans.com/youngreaders/

Book Publisher: William B. Eerdmans Publishing Co.

CHILDREN'S > **Fiction**
 Board Books; *Middle Grade*; *Picture Books*
YOUNG ADULT
 Fiction > *Novels*
 Nonfiction > *Nonfiction Books*

Send: Query; Synopsis; Writing sample; Full text
Don't send: Self-Addressed Stamped Envelope (SASE)
How to send: Post

Publishes board books, picture books, novels, and nonfiction. Seeks manuscripts that are honest, wise, and hopeful; but also publishes stories that simply delight with their storyline, characters, or good humor. Stories that celebrate diversity, stories of historical significance, and stories that relate to contemporary social issues are of special interest at this time. Currently publishes 18 to 20 books a year. Submit by post only but do not include SASE. No return of materials or response unless interested.

P149 Elliott & Thompson
Book Publisher
2 John Street, London, WC1N 2ES
United Kingdom
Tel: +44 (0) 7973 956107

info@eandtbooks.com

http://www.eandtbooks.com
https://twitter.com/eandtbooks
https://www.instagram.com/elliottandthompson/

Fiction > *Novels*

Nonfiction
 Gift Books: General
 Nonfiction Books: Arts; Biography; Business; Comedy / Humour; Economics; History; Language; Music; Nature; Politics; Science; Sport

Publishes original and bestselling nonfiction and carefully selected fiction.

P150 Elsevier Ltd
Book Publisher
125 London Wall, London, EC2Y 5AS
United Kingdom
Tel: +44 (0) 20 7424 4200
Fax: +44 (0) 20 7483 2293

https://www.elsevier.com

ACADEMIC > **Nonfiction** > *Nonfiction Books*
 Health; Medicine; Science; Technology
PROFESSIONAL > **Nonfiction** > *Nonfiction Books*
 Health; Medicine; Science; Technology

Send: Query
Don't send: Full text

Publisher of medical, scientific, and technical books for the professional and academic markets.

Book Publisher: Morgan Kaufmann Publishers

P151 Encyclopedia Britannica (UK) Ltd
Book Publisher
2nd Floor, Unity Wharf, Mill Street, London, SE1 2BH
United Kingdom
Tel: +44 (0) 20 7500 7800
Fax: +44 (0) 20 7500 7878

enqbol@britannica.co.uk

https://britannica.co.uk

ACADEMIC > **Nonfiction** > *Reference*

ADULT > **Nonfiction** > *Reference*

Global digital educational publisher, publishing information and instructional products used in schools, universities, homes, libraries and workplaces throughout the world.

P152 Engram Books
Publishing Imprint
United Kingdom

submissions@sunpenny.com

https://www.sunpenny.com/imprints/

Book Publisher: Sunpenny Publishing (**P435**)

Nonfiction > *Nonfiction Books*
    Autobiography; Biography; Disabilities; Memoir

Send: Author bio; Marketing Plan; Synopsis; Full text
How to send: Email
How not to send: Post

Imprint to focus on memoirs, auto-biographies, and biographies – including books about the challenges of disabilities. Especially interested in books that will be uplifting for the disabled community; that will reach out to others and let them know they are not alone, that others have gone through similar issues; how to deal with those issues; where to find help – and similar.

P153 Enitharmon Editions
Book Publisher
United Kingdom
Tel: +44 (0) 20 7430 0844

info@enitharmon.co.uk

https://www.enitharmon.co.uk
https://www.facebook.com/EnitharmonEditions/
https://twitter.com/enitharmonpress
https://instagram.com/enitharmon.editions
https://www.youtube.com/channel/UCIRq9ScqeBrQ4_HdqELUzaw
https://www.pinterest.co.uk/enitharmoneditions/

Fiction > *Short Fiction Collections*

Nonfiction
    Illustrated Books: Arts; Photography
    Nonfiction Books: Arts; Literary Criticism; Literary
Poetry > *Poetry Collections*

Closed to approaches.

An independent British publisher. We specialise in artists' books, artworks and literary editions. Our artists' books, which are in the tradition of the livre d'artiste, contain loose-leaf signed limited edition prints by such artists as Peter Blake, Jim Dine and Duane Michals. The artworks we publish include etchings, lithographs, photographs and paintings by artists including David Hockney, Paula Rego and Caroline Walker.

P154 Enslow Publishers, Inc.
Book Publisher
2544 Clinton Street, Buffalo, NY 14224
United States

CustomerService@enslow.com

https://www.enslow.com

ACADEMIC > **Nonfiction** > *Nonfiction Books*
    Biography; Current Affairs; Drugs; Health; History; Holidays; Mathematics; Politics; Recreation; Science; Sport; Technology

Send: Query
How to send: Email

Publishes high-quality educational nonfiction books for children and young adults, who will access these materials in schools and public libraries. Our goals are that readers will be able to trust our products and that the books will satisfy their needs. The primary markets are school and public libraries. Books cover subjects including biography, contemporary issues, health & drug education, history and government, holidays and customs, math, science and technology, science projects and experiments, sports and recreation.

P155 EPTA Books
Publishing Imprint
United Kingdom

submissions@sunpenny.com

https://www.sunpenny.com/imprints/

Book Publisher: Sunpenny Publishing (**P435**)

Nonfiction > *Coffee Table Books*

Send: Query; Author bio; Marketing Plan; Synopsis; Full text
How to send: Email
How not to send: Post

Imprint for non-fiction books and coffee-table beauties.

P156 Essence Press
Book Publisher
United Kingdom

essencepress@btinternet.com

https://www.juliejohnstone.com/essence-press/

Poetry > *Poetry Collections*

Publishes the work of the editor, and occasionally the work of other poets and artists, usually working in collaboration to create handbound poem-objects or artists' books.

Editor: Julie Johnstone

P157 Evan-Moor Educational Publishers
Book Publisher
10 Harris Court, Ste C-3, Monterey, CA 93940
United States
Tel: +1 (800) 777-4362
Fax: +1 (800) 777-4332

customerservice@evan-moor.com

http://www.evan-moor.com
http://www.facebook.com/evanmoorcorp
https://twitter.com/evanmoor
https://www.youtube.com/channel/UCW1uyTjhrULw-vnU8PRwk0A
https://www.instagram.com/evanmoor_publisher/?hl=en

CHILDREN'S > **Nonfiction** > *Nonfiction Books*: Education

PROFESSIONAL > **Nonfiction** > *Nonfiction Books*: Education

Publishes practical, creative, and engaging PreK-8 educational materials.

P158 Everything With Words
Book Publisher
United Kingdom

info@everythingwithwords.com

http://www.everythingwithwords.com

ADULT > **Fiction** > *Novels*: Literary

CHILDREN'S > **Fiction** > *Novels*

Send: Query; Outline; Author bio; Writing sample
How to send: Email

We are open to submissions from both agents and authors.

At the moment, we don't publish picture books and we're not very interested in books with a strong moral or didactic aim — fine books do change people's view of the world but we find that books where the author's views are the main driving force tend to be heavy and predictable.

We don't publish adult horror fiction or crime.

Your book must be full length which means at least forty thousand words.

We try to respond to every query but we do receive a lot of submissions.

Please send a brief summary, something about yourself and three chapters or the first fifty pages.

P159 Facet Publishing
Book Publisher
Room 150, C/O British Library, 96 Euston Road, NW1 2DB
United Kingdom

info@facetpublishing.co.uk

https://www.facetpublishing.co.uk
https://www.facebook.com/facetpublishing
https://twitter.com/facetpublishing
https://www.youtube.com/user/facetpublishing
https://www.linkedin.com/company/facet-publishing

PROFESSIONAL > **Nonfiction** > *Nonfiction Books*
Data and Information Systems; Information Science

Describes itself as the leading publisher of books for library, information and heritage professionals worldwide.

P160 Fairlight Books
Book Publisher; Online Publisher
Summertown Pavilion, 18-24 Middle Way, Oxford, OX2 7LG
United Kingdom
Tel: +44 (0) 1865 957790

contact@fairlightbooks.com
Submissions@FairlightBooks.com

https://www.fairlightbooks.co.uk
https://www.facebook.com/FairlightBooks/
https://twitter.com/FairlightBooks
https://www.instagram.com/fairlightbooks/

Fiction
Novellas: Literary
Novels: Literary
Short Fiction: Literary

Closed to approaches.

Publishes literary fiction. Accepts novels and novellas for print publication and short stories up to 10,000 words (including flash fiction) for online publication. Send query by email with synopsis and writing sample up to 10,000 words for long fiction, or full text for short stories.

P161 Farrar, Straus & Giroux
Publishing Imprint
United States

Book Publisher: Macmillan Publishers

P162 Fathom Books
Book Publisher
United States

editor@fathombooks.org

http://fathombooks.org
https://sharkpackpoetry.com/fathom-books/
https://spr.submittable.com/submit

Fiction > *Novels*
Experimental; LGBTQIA; Literary; Philosophy; Women

Poetry > *Any Poetic Form*

Closed to approaches.

Costs: Offers services that writers have to pay for. Free to submit, but fee for expedited response.

Independent small press publishing volumes of poetry, very experimental fiction, hybrids, poetics, speculation, etc. Primary interest is text by women and queers. Accepts submissions via online submission system during specific windows only.

P163 The Feminist Press
Book Publisher
365 Fifth Avenue, Suite 5406, New York, NY 10016
United States

editor@feministpress.org

https://www.feministpress.org
https://www.facebook.com/FeministPress/
http://thefeministpress.tumblr.com/
https://www.youtube.com/channel/UCClCd_SsorK5JGKCE7rD7vw
https://twitter.com/FeministPress
https://www.instagram.com/feministpress/

ADULT
Fiction
Graphic Novels: Feminism
Novels: Contemporary; Fantasy; Feminism; Literary; Mystery; Speculative
Nonfiction > *Nonfiction Books*
Activism; Africa; African American; Arts; Asia; Asian American; Biography; Education; Feminism; Films; Health; History; Italian American; Italy; Journalism; Judaism; LGBTQIA; Legal; Media; Medicine; Memoir; Middle East; Popular Culture; Postcolonialism; Science; Sexuality; South America

Poetry > *Poetry Collections*: Feminism

CHILDREN'S > **Fiction** > *Novels*: Feminism

Closed to approaches.

Feminist publisher, publishing an array of genres including cutting-edge fiction, activist nonfiction, literature in translation, hybrid memoirs, children's books, and more.

P164 Fernwood Publishing
Book Publisher
2970 Oxford Street, Halifax, NS, B3L 2W4
Canada
Tel: +1 (902) 857-1388

editorial@fernpub.ca

https://fernwoodpublishing.ca
https://twitter.com/fernpub
https://www.facebook.com/fernwood.publishing
https://instagram.com/fernpub

ACADEMIC > **Nonfiction** > *Nonfiction Books*
Activism; African Diaspora; Biography; Canada; Climate Science; Crime; Culture; Disabilities; Economics; Education; Family; Feminism; Gender; Health; History; Legal; Memoir; Politics; Postcolonialism; Racism; Sexuality; Social Class; Social Issues; Sociology; Urban

Send: Proposal
Don't send: Full text
How to send: Email

A non-fiction publisher specializing in books that provide a critical analysis of society. Publishes books that address issues of activism and social change, Indigenous resistance and decolonization, global justice, law, politics, social work, sociology, anti-racism, feminism, social theory, and more.

Acquisitions Editors: Tanya Andrusieczko; Wayne Antony; Jazz Cook; Fiona Jeffries; Fazeela Jiwa; Errol Sharpe

Managing Editor: Beverley Rach

Publishing Imprint: Roseway (**P382**)

P165 Fighting High
Book Publisher
23 Hitchin Road, Stotfold, Hitchin, Herts, SG5 4HP
United Kingdom
Tel: +44 (0) 7936 415843

fightinghigh@btinternet.com

https://fighting-high-books.myshopify.com
https://twitter.com/FightingHigh
https://www.facebook.com/groups/24337176057

Nonfiction > *Nonfiction Books*
Adventure; Military History

Send: Query; Proposal; Synopsis; Writing sample
Don't send: Full text
How to send: Email

We specialise in non-fiction books that focus on human endeavour, particularly in a historical military setting. We also consider other stories of human enterprise and adventure.

P166 Filter Press
Book Publisher
400 Shy Circle, Westcliffe, CO 81252
United States
Tel: +1 (719) 481-2420

info@filterpressbooks.com
publisher@filterpressbooks.com

https://www.filterpressbooks.com
https://www.instagram.com/filterpressbooks/
https://twitter.com/filterpressllc

ADULT
Fiction > *Novels*
Colorado; Historical Fiction; Southwestern United States

Nonfiction > *Nonfiction Books*
Biography; Colorado; History; Travel

Poetry > *Any Poetic Form*
Colorado; Southwestern United States

CHILDREN'S > **Fiction**
Chapter Books: Colorado; Historical Fiction; Southwestern United States
Early Readers: Colorado; Historical Fiction; Southwestern United States
Middle Grade: Colorado; Historical Fiction; Southwestern United States
Picture Books: Colorado; Historical Fiction; Southwestern United States

Closed to approaches.

The publishing focus is on quality nonfiction and historical fiction with Southwest settings.

P167 Firefly
Book Publisher
Britannia House, Caerphilly Business Park, Van Road, Caerphilly, CF83 3GG
United Kingdom

submissions@fireflypress.co.uk
hello@fireflypress.co.uk

https://fireflypress.co.uk
https://www.facebook.com/FireflyPress/
https://twitter.com/FireflyPress
https://www.instagram.com/fireflypress/
https://www.youtube.com/channel/UCqzaLmXCoGJEQuaooZcnb4Q

CHILDREN'S > **Fiction**
Early Readers; *Middle Grade*
TEEN > **Fiction** > *Novels*
YOUNG ADULT > **Fiction** > *Novels*

Closed to approaches.

Publishes fiction and nonfiction for children and young adults aged 5-19. Not currently accepting nonfiction submissions. Fiction submissions through agents only. Not currently publishing any picture books or colour illustrated book for any age group.

P168 Fiscal Publications
Book Publisher
United Kingdom
Tel: +44 (0) 800 678 5934

info@fiscalpublications.com

https://www.fiscalpublications.com

ACADEMIC > **Nonfiction** > *Nonfiction Books*
Economics; Finance; Taxation

PROFESSIONAL > **Nonfiction** > *Nonfiction Books*
Economics; Finance; Taxation

Send: Query
How to send: Email

Publishes academic and professional books specialising in taxation, public finance and public economics. Materials are relevant worldwide to policy-makers, administrators, lecturers and students of the economics, politics, law and practice of taxation.

P169 Forge
Publishing Imprint
United States

https://us.macmillan.com/tomdohertyassociates/
https://www.torforgeblog.com/
https://www.facebook.com/forgereads/

Publishing Imprint: Tor Publishing Group (**P456**)

Fiction > *Novels*
Mystery; Thrillers; Westerns

Closed to approaches.

Publisher of Fiction, Thrillers, Mysteries, Westerns, and more. Open submission policy currently suspended due to COVID-19.

P170 Fortress Press
Publishing Imprint
411 Washington Ave N, 3rd Floor, Minneapolis, MN 55401
United States
Tel: +1 (844) 993-3812
Fax: +1 (800) 722-7766

https://www.fortresspress.com
https://www.facebook.com/fortresspress/
https://twitter.com/fortresspress
https://www.youtube.com/user/FortressPress

Book Publisher: 1517 Media

ACADEMIC > **Nonfiction** > *Nonfiction Books*
Bible Studies; Christianity; Culture; History; Literature; Philosophy; Social Justice

PROFESSIONAL > **Nonfiction** > *Nonfiction Books*: Christianity

Publisher of compelling theological, biblical, and ethical engagements for the church and the world in which it lives.

P171 Forum Books
Publishing Imprint

Book Publisher: Random House

P172 Franklin Watts
Publishing Imprint

Book Publisher: Hachette Children's Group

P173 Free Association Books Ltd
Book Publisher
1 Angel Cottages, Milespit Hill, London, NW7 1RD
United Kingdom

freeassociationbooks@gmail.com

https://freeassociationpublishing.com

Nonfiction > *Nonfiction Books*
Health; History; Politics; Psychotherapy; Social Issues

Send: Query; Synopsis; Outline; Writing sample
How to send: Email; Post

Send submissions by post or by email. Publishes books on a wide range of topics including psychotherapy, social work, health studies, history, public policy and more.

P174 Free Spirit Publishing
Book Publisher
Attn: Acquisitions, 9850 51st Ave. N, Suite 100, Minneapolis, MN 55442
United States
Tel: +1 (714) 891-2273
Fax: +1 (888) 877-7606

acquisitions@freespirit.com

https://www.freespirit.com
https://freespiritpublishing.submittable.com/submit
https://www.facebook.com/freespiritpublishing
https://twitter.com/FreeSpiritBooks
http://www.pinterest.com/freespiritbooks
https://www.instagram.com/freespiritpublishing
http://www.youtube.com/user/FreeSpiritPublishing

CHILDREN'S
Fiction
Board Books: Bullying; Disabilities; Personal Development; Wellbeing
Novels: Bullying; Depression; Disabilities; Family; Health; Personal Development; Wellbeing
Picture Books: Bullying; Disabilities; Personal Development; Wellbeing
Nonfiction
Board Books: Bullying; Disabilities; Education; Personal Development; Wellbeing
Nonfiction Books: Bullying; Depression; Disabilities; Education; Family; Health; Personal Development; Social Justice; Wellbeing
Picture Books: Biography; Bullying; Disabilities; Education; Personal Development; Wellbeing
TEEN
Fiction > *Novels*
Bullying; Depression; Disabilities; Family; Health; LGBTQIA; Personal Development; Wellbeing

Nonfiction > *Nonfiction Books*
Bullying; Depression; Disabilities; Education; Family; Health; LGBTQIA; Personal Development; Social Justice; Wellbeing

Send: Proposal
How to send: Post; Submittable

Publishes nonfiction books and learning materials for children and teens, parents, educators, counselors, and others who live and work with young people. Also publishes fiction relevant to the mission of providing children and teens with the tools they need to succeed in life, e.g.: self-esteem; conflict resolution, etc. No general fiction or storybooks; books with animal or mythical characters; books with religious or New Age content; or single biographies, autobiographies, or memoirs. Submit by proposals by post or through online submission system. See website for full submission guidelines.

P175 Friends United Press
Book Publisher
101 Quaker Hill Drive, Richmond, IN 47374
United States
Tel: +1 (765) 962-7573

info@fum.org

https://bookstore.friendsunitedmeeting.org/collections/friends-united-press
https://www.facebook.com/friendsunitedmeeting/
https://www.instagram.com/friendsunitedmeeting/

Nonfiction > *Nonfiction Books*: Quakerism

Publishes books by Quakers on Quaker history, spirituality, and doctrine.

P176 FrontLine
Publishing Imprint
United States

Media Company: Charisma Media

P177 Gale
Book Publisher
27555 Executive Dr. Ste 270, Farmington Hills, MI 48331
United States
Tel: +1 (800) 877-4253
Fax: +1 (877) 363-4253

gale.customerexperience@cengage.com

https://www.gale.com
https://www.facebook.com/GaleCengage
https://www.linkedin.com/company/gale
https://twitter.com/galecengage
https://www.youtube.com/user/GaleCengage

Book Publisher: Cengage

ACADEMIC > Nonfiction
Nonfiction Books: Business; Chemistry; Computer Science; Earth Science; Economics; Education; Finance; Health; History; Legal; Literature; Mathematics; Medicine; Physics; Science; Sociology; Technology
Reference: General

ADULT > Nonfiction
Nonfiction Books: Agriculture; Antiques; Arts; Astronomy; Business; Chemistry; Crafts; Earth Science; Economics; Education; Finance; Gardening; Health; History; Hobbies; Legal; Literature; Medicine; Science; Sport; Technology
Reference: General

PROFESSIONAL > Nonfiction
Nonfiction Books: Business; Economics; Education; Finance; Health; Legal; Medicine; Science; Sociology; Technology
Reference: General

Supplies businesses, schools, and libraries with books and electronic reference materials.

Book Publisher: KidHaven Press

Publishing Imprints: The Taft Group; Blackbird Press; Charles Scribner & Sons; Five Star; G.K. Hall & Co.; Graham & Whiteside Ltd; Greenhaven Publishing; KG Saur Verlag GmbH & Co. KG; Lucent Books; Macmillan Reference USA; Primary Source Media; Schirmer Reference; St James Press; Thorndike Press; Twayne Publishers; UXL; Wheeler Publishing

P178 Geared Up Publications
Publishing Imprint
United States

https://schifferbooks.com/pages/schiffer-imprints

Book Publisher: Schiffer Publishing (**P398**)

Nonfiction > *Nonfiction Books*: Deep Sea Fishing

Books on deep sea fishing and techniques for a robust catch.

P179 Gertrude Press
Book Publisher
United States

editor@gertrudepress.org

https://www.gertrudepress.org

Types: Fiction; Nonfiction; Poetry
Formats: Short Fiction
Subjects: Literary
Markets: Adult

Closed to approaches.

Publishes work by writers identifying as LGBTQ, both in online journal form and as chapbooks. Considers work for chapbook publication through its annual contests only. See website for details.

Online Magazine: Gertrude (**M164**)

P180 Gill
Book Publisher
Ireland

https://www.gill.ie

Publishing Imprints: Gill Books (**P181**); Gill Education (**P182**)

P181 Gill Books
Publishing Imprint
Hume Avenue, Park West, Dublin, D12 YV96
Ireland
Tel: +353 (01) 500 9500

https://www.gillbooks.ie
http://www.facebook.com/GillBooks
http://www.twitter.com/Gill_Books
http://www.instagram.com/GillBooks

Book Publisher: Gill (**P180**)

ADULT > Nonfiction
Gift Books: Ireland
Nonfiction Books: Biography; Comedy / Humour; Crafts; Crime; Current Affairs; Food and Drink; History; Hobbies; Ireland; Lifestyle; Mind, Body, Spirit; Nature; Parenting; Politics; Sport
Reference: General, and in particular: Ireland
CHILDREN'S
Fiction > *Novels*
Nonfiction > *Nonfiction Books*

Send: Query; Outline; Synopsis; Table of Contents; Writing sample; Author bio
How to send: Online submission system; Post

Publishes adult nonfiction and children's fiction and nonfiction. No adult fiction, poetry, short stories or plays. In general, focuses on books of Irish interest. Prefers proposals through online submission system, but will also accept proposals by post. See website for full submission guidelines.

P182 Gill Education
Publishing Imprint
Hume Avenue, Park West, D12 YV96
Ireland
Tel: +353 (1) 500 9500

primarysubmissions@gill.ie
secondarysubmissions@gill.ie

https://www.gilleducation.ie
https://www.facebook.com/GillEducation
https://twitter.com/GillEducation
https://www.instagram.com/GillEducation

Book Publisher: Gill (**P180**)

ACADEMIC > Nonfiction > *Nonfiction Books*
Accounting; Arts; Building / Construction; Business; Communication; Computer Programming; Design; Economics; Education; English; French; Geography; German; Graphic Design; Health; History; Home Economics / Domestic Science; Information Science; Irish (Gaeilge); Legal; Management; Marketing; Mathematics;

Music; Nursing; Physical Education; Physics; Politics; Psychology; Religion; Science; Sociology

Send: Proposal
How to send: Email

Publishes books for the primary, secondary, and further education markets. Welcomes proposals from first time and experienced authors alike. All subject areas are of interest. See website for full guidelines.

P183 Glass Poetry Press
Book Publisher
United States

chaps@glass-poetry.com
editor@glass-poetry.com

https://www.glass-poetry.com
https://www.glass-poetry.com/submissions.html

Poetry > *Chapbooks*

Publishes poetry chapbooks between 15 and 25 pages. Open to submissions between October 1 and October 31 each year.

P184 The Globe Pequot Press
Book Publisher
64 South Main Street, Essex, CT 06426
United States

GPSubmissions@rowman.com

http://www.globepequot.com
https://rowman.com/Page/GlobePequot
https://www.facebook.com/globepequot/
https://twitter.com/globepequot

Book Publisher: Rowman & Littlefield Publishing Group

Nonfiction > *Nonfiction Books*
Biography; Business; Cookery; Gardening; History; Mind, Body, Spirit; Nature; Travel

Send: Outline; Table of Contents; Writing sample; Author bio; Market info
How to send: Email; Post

Publishes books about iconic brands and people, regional interest, history, lifestyle, cooking and food culture, and folklore – books that hit the intersection of a reader's interest in a specific place and their passion for a specific topic.

Book Publisher: Backbeat Books (**P046**)

Publishing Imprints: Applause; Astragal Press; Down East Books; FalconGuides; Lyons Press; Mcbooks Press; Muddy Boots; Pineapple Press (**P356**); Prometheus; Skip Jack Press; Stackpole Books; TwoDot; Union Park Press

P185 Gold SF
Publishing Imprint
United States

goldsmithspress@gold.ac.uk

https://www.gold.ac.uk/goldsmiths-press/submissions/

Book Publisher: Goldsmiths Press (**P186**)

Fiction > *Novels*
Economics; Environment; Ethnic Groups; Experimental; Gender; Intersectional Feminism; LGBTQIA; Politics; Postcolonialism; Science Fiction; Sexuality; Social Class; Social Justice; Speculative

Send: Proposal; Writing sample
How to send: Email

Dedicated to discovering and publishing new intersectional feminist science fiction, promoting voices that answer to the unprecedented times in which we find ourselves, and orientated towards to social, economic, and environmental justice.

P186 Goldsmiths Press
Book Publisher
Room 108, Deptford Town Hall, Lewisham Way, New Cross, London, SE14 6NW
United Kingdom

goldsmithspress@gold.ac.uk

https://www.gold.ac.uk/goldsmiths-press

ACADEMIC > **Nonfiction** > *Nonfiction Books*

Send: Query
Don't send: Full text

University press aiming to cut across disciplinary boundaries and blur the distinctions between theory, practice, fiction and non-fiction. See website for proposal forms and submit by email.

Editors: Adrian Driscoll; Sarah Kember; Ellen Parnavelas; Guy Sewell

Publishing Imprint: Gold SF (**P185**)

P187 Goodman Beck Publishing
Book Publisher
United States

info@goodmanbeck.com

https://www.goodmanbeck.com
https://www.facebook.com/goodmanbeck
https://twitter.com/goodmanbeck

Fiction > *Novels*

Nonfiction > *Nonfiction Books*
Mental Health; Personal Development; Psychology; Self Help; Spirituality

Does not want:

Fiction > *Novels*
Fantasy; Romance; Science Fiction

Nonfiction > *Nonfiction Books*
How To; Politics; Religion

Send: Query
How to send: Email
How not to send: Post

Interested in helping people feel better about themselves and their lives. Focuses on mental health, personal growth, aging well, positive psychology, accessible spirituality, and overall self-help. Not interested in science fiction, fantasy, religious or political works, romance novels, textbooks, or how-to books.

Editor: Michael Pearson

P188 Goose Lane Editions
Book Publisher
Suite 330, 500 Beaverbrook Court, Fredericton, NB, E3B 5X4
Canada
Tel: +1 (506) 450-4251
Fax: +1 (888) 926-8377

info@gooselane.com

https://gooselane.com
https://www.twitter.com/goose_lane
https://www.facebook.com/GooseLaneEditions/
https://www.instagram.com/goose_lane

Fiction > *Novels*

Nonfiction > *Nonfiction Books*
Architecture; Arts; LGBTQIA; Military History; New Brunswick; Walking Guides

Send: Query; Author bio; Synopsis; Writing sample
How to send: Online submission system

Publishes literary fiction and nonfiction (and poetry through its poetry imprint) by established and up-and-coming Canadian authors. Submissions will only be considered from outside Canada if the author is Canadian and the book is of extraordinary interest to Canadian readers. No unsolicited MSS, children's, or young adult. See website for full submission details.

Editor: Angela Williams

Publishing Imprint: Icehouse (**P226**)

P189 Goss & Crested China Club
Book Publisher
Forestside House, Broadwalk, Forestside, Rowlands Castle, PO9 6EE
United Kingdom
Tel: +44 (0) 7738 842856

http://www.gosschinaclub.co.uk

ADULT > **Nonfiction** > *Reference*
Antiques; Collectibles

PROFESSIONAL > **Nonfiction** > *Reference*
Antiques; Collectibles

Publishes books on crested heraldic china and antique porcelain.

Managing Director: Andrew Pine

P190 Graffeg
Book Publisher
24 Stradey Park Business Centre, Mwrwg Road, Llangennech, Llanelli, SA14 8YP
United Kingdom
Tel: +44 (0) 1554 824000

croeso@graffeg.com

https://graffeg.com
https://www.facebook.com/graffegbooks
https://twitter.com/graffeg_books
https://www.pinterest.co.uk/GraffegBooks/
http://instagram.com/graffegbooks
https://www.youtube.com/channel/UCqnEBIarxraMZEYD8llXh-A

Nonfiction > *Illustrated Books*
 Food; History; Nature

Send: Outline; Full text; Table of Contents; Author bio
How to send: Online submission system

Always pleased to receive submissions from new and published authors. Publishes illustrated books on nature, heritage and food. Imprints welcome submissions for children's books up to young adult reads. Books with the potential of being serialised are also of special interest.

Publishing Imprints: Bird Eye Books (**P066**); Cadno (**P089**); Graffeg Childrens (**P191**)

P191 Graffeg Childrens
Publishing Imprint
United Kingdom

https://graffeg.com

Book Publisher: Graffeg (**P190**)

CHILDREN'S
 Fiction > *Picture Books*
 Nonfiction > *Illustrated Books*

Send: Outline; Full text; Table of Contents; Author bio
How to send: Online submission system

Welcomes submissions for children's books.

P192 Granta Books
Book Publisher
12 Addison Avenue, London, W11 4QR
United Kingdom
Tel: +44 (0) 20 7605 1360

info@granta.com

https://granta.com/books/
https://www.facebook.com/grantamag/
https://twitter.com/GrantaMag
https://www.instagram.com/granta_magazine/

Fiction > *Novels*: Literary

Nonfiction > *Nonfiction Books*
 Autobiography; Culture; History; Literary Criticism; Nature; Politics; Social Issues; Travel

Closed to approaches.

Publishes around 70% nonfiction / 30% fiction. In nonfiction publishes serious cultural, political and social history, narrative history, or memoir. Rarely publishes straightforward biographies. No genre fiction. Not accepting unsolicited submissions.

P193 Graywolf Press
Book Publisher
212 Third Avenue North, Suite 485, Minneapolis, MN 55401
United States
Tel: +1 (651) 641-0077
Fax: +1 (651) 641-0036

wolves@graywolfpress.org

https://www.graywolfpress.org
https://graywolfpress.submittable.com/submit
https://www.facebook.com/GraywolfPress/
https://twitter.com/GraywolfPress
https://www.instagram.com/graywolfpress/

Fiction
 Novels: Literary
 Short Fiction Collections: Literary

Nonfiction
 Essays: Creative Writing; Cultural Criticism; Literary Criticism; Literary
 Nonfiction Books: Creative Writing; Cultural Criticism; Literary Criticism; Memoir
Poetry > *Poetry Collections*

Closed to approaches.

Publishes about 30 books annually, mostly poetry, memoirs, essays, novels, and short stories. Accepts submissions through literary agents, or via competitions during specific windows.

Online Magazine: Graywolf Lab (**M172**)

P194 Guinness World Records
Book Publisher
Ground Floor, The Rookery, 2 Dyott Street, London, WC1A 1DE
United Kingdom

https://www.guinnessworldrecords.com

Nonfiction > *Reference*

Publishes books of amazing facts, figures, and feats of outstanding human endeavour.

P195 Guppy Books
Book Publisher
United Kingdom

https://guppybooks.co.uk
https://twitter.com/guppybooks
https://www.instagram.com/guppypublishin/

CHILDREN'S > **Fiction**
 Chapter Books; *Early Readers*; *Middle Grade*

How to send: Through a literary agent

A small and independent publisher of children's fiction. No nonfiction or picture books. No submissions from unagented or unpublished authors.

P196 Hachette Book Group
Book Publisher
United States

https://www.hachettebookgroup.com

Book Publisher: Hachette Livre

Fiction > *Novels*

Nonfiction > *Nonfiction Books*

How to send: Through a literary agent

Includes 24 imprints covering the entire array of contemporary fiction and nonfiction, from the most popular to the most literary.

Book Publishers: Grand Central Publishing; Little, Brown and Company; Perseus Books; Workman Publishing (**P519**)

P197 Half Mystic Press
Book Publisher
United States

hello@halfmystic.com

https://www.halfmystic.com
https://halfmystic.submittable.com/submit

Fiction
 Novellas; *Novels*; *Short Fiction Collections*
Nonfiction > *Nonfiction Books*
 Memoir; Music

Poetry > *Poetry Collections*

How to send: Submittable

Publishes poetry, essay, and short story collections; drama; memoirs; novellas; full-length novels; experimental work. Publishes full-length manuscripts only—no chapbooks. See website for full submission guidelines.

Print Magazine: Half Mystic Journal (**M175**)

P198 Hammersmith Books
Book Publisher
4/4A Bloomsbury Square, London, WC1A 2RP
United Kingdom

https://www.hammersmithbooks.co.uk
https://www.facebook.com/HammersmithHealthBooks
http://twitter.com/HHealthBooks
https://www.instagram.com/hhealthbooks/?hl=en
https://www.pinterest.com/hhealthbooks/

ACADEMIC > **Nonfiction** > *Nonfiction Books*
 Diet; Health; Medicine; Mental Health; Nutrition; Wellbeing

ADULT > **Nonfiction** > *Nonfiction Books*
 Diet; Health; Medicine; Mental Health; Nutrition; Wellbeing

PROFESSIONAL > Nonfiction > *Nonfiction Books*
   Diet; Health; Medicine; Mental Health; Nutrition; Wellbeing

Publisher of health, medicine, and nutrition books for the general public, health professionals, and academic markets.

Editor: Georgina Bentliff

P199 Handspring Publishing
Publishing Imprint
United Kingdom

Publishing Imprint: Jessica Kingsley Publishers (**P246**)

P200 Happy Yak
Publishing Imprint
1 Triptych Place, Second Floor, London, SE1 9SH
United Kingdom
Tel: +44 (0) 20 7700 9000

https://www.quartoknows.com/happy-yak

Book Publisher: The Quarto Group, Inc. (**P367**)

CHILDREN'S
   Fiction
      Board Books; Picture Books
   Nonfiction > *Nonfiction Books*

Send: Proposal
How to send: Email

A publisher of innovative preschool concepts, laugh-out-loud picture books, and illustrated nonfiction titles. If you have a book idea in one of our focus areas that you'd like to share with us, we'd love to hear it.

P201 Hardie Grant UK
Book Publisher
United Kingdom

https://www.hardiegrant.com
https://www.instagram.com/hardiegrantmedia/

Nonfiction > *Nonfiction Books*

An independent publishing and media business working with authors and brands to create high-quality books, magazines, websites and content across platforms.

P202 Harlequin Desire
Book Publisher
195 Broadway, 24th floor, New York, NY 10007
United States
Tel: +1 (212) 207-7000

submissions@harlequin.com
https://www.harlequin.com

Types: Fiction
Subjects: Contemporary; Romance
Markets: Adult

Closed to approaches.

Publishes contemporary romances up to 50,000 words, featuring strong-but-vulnerable alpha heroes and dynamic, successful heroines, set in a world of wealth and glamour. See website for more details and to submit via online submission system.

Editor: Stacy Boyd

P203 Harlequin Mills & Boon Ltd
Book Publisher
Harlequin, 1 London Bridge Street, London, SE1 9GF
United Kingdom

info@millsandboon.co.uk

https://www.millsandboon.co.uk
https://www.instagram.com/millsandboonuk/
https://www.facebook.com/millsandboon/
https://twitter.com/MillsandBoon
https://harlequin.submittable.com/submit

Fiction > *Novels:* Romance

How to send: Submittable

Major publisher with extensive romance list and various romance imprints. Submit via online submission system.

Publishing Imprints: Harlequin MIRA; Mills & Boon Historical; Mills & Boon Medical; Mills & Boon Modern Romance; Mills & Boon Riva; Mills and Boon Cherish

P204 Harmony
Publishing Imprint

Book Publisher: Random House

P205 Harmony Ink Press
Publishing Imprint
United States

https://www.harmonyinkpress.com

Book Publisher: Dreamspinner Press (**P144**)

NEW ADULT > Fiction > *Novels*
   Fantasy; LGBTQIA; Mystery; Romance; Science Fiction; Supernatural / Paranormal

TEEN > Fiction > *Novels*
   Fantasy; LGBTQIA; Mystery; Romance; Science Fiction; Supernatural / Paranormal

Publishes Teen and New Adult fiction featuring significant personal growth of unforgettable characters across the LGBTQ+ spectrum.

P206 Harvard University Press
Book Publisher
79 Garden Street, Cambridge, MA 02138
United States
Tel: +1 (617) 495-2600

contact_hup@harvard.edu

https://www.hup.harvard.edu
https://www.facebook.com/HarvardPress
https://twitter.com/Harvard_Press
https://www.instagram.com/harvardpress/
https://www.linkedin.com/company/harvard-university-press-hup/
https://medium.com/@hup

ACADEMIC > Nonfiction
   Nonfiction Books: Architecture; Arts; Biography; Business; Classics / Ancient World; Economics; Education; Health; History; Legal; Literature; Media; Medicine; Music; Nature; Performing Arts; Philosophy; Politics; Popular Culture; Psychology; Religion; Science; Sociology
   Reference: General

Publishes humanities, sciences, social sciences, etc. Academic nonfiction only. See website for manuscript guidelines and appropriate editorial contacts.

Publishing Imprint: Belknap Press

P207 Hashtag Press
Book Publisher
United Kingdom

info@hashtagpress.co.uk
submissions@hashtagpress.co.uk

https://www.hashtagpress.co.uk
https://twitter.com/hashtag_press
https://www.instagram.com/hashtag_press/
https://www.tiktok.com/@hashtag_press
https://www.facebook.com/hashtagpressbooks

ADULT > Nonfiction > *Nonfiction Books*
   Memoir; Parenting; Self Help

CHILDREN'S > Fiction > *Middle Grade*
   Adventure; Comedy / Humour; Coming of Age; Friends; Mental Health

YOUNG ADULT > Fiction > *Novels*

Send: Query; Pitch; Synopsis; Writing sample; Author bio
How to send: Word file email attachment

We are looking for excellent writers with brilliant diverse stories to tell.

Please read the about us before submitting to us. We would prefer books that haven't been published already.

We love diverse and inclusive books! We are open to debut authors especially those from an underrepresented background. We publish commercial fiction books for young people that are plot driven with relatable, inspiring characters.

We are a tiny publishing house, so we are incredibly selective.

Any books that are not diverse or inclusive will be a no.

P208 Haus Publishing
Book Publisher
4 Cinnamon Row, Plantation Wharf, London, SW11 3TW

United Kingdom
Tel: +44 (0) 20 3637 9729

submissions@hauspublishing.com
haus@hauspublishing.com

https://www.hauspublishing.com
https://www.facebook.com/hauspublishing
https://www.twitter.com/hauspublishing
https://www.instagram.com/hauspublishing/
https://www.youtube.com/channel/UCDSWSrh_wI5t_rflbyI3O7w

Fiction > *Novels*

Nonfiction > *Nonfiction Books*
Arts; Biography; Current Affairs; History; Memoir; Politics; Travel

Send: Query; Proposal; Synopsis; Writing sample; Author bio
How to send: Email; Through a literary agent

Accepts fiction submissions through literary agents only. Nonfiction submissions may be submitted direct by authors.

Book Publisher: The Armchair Traveller at the bookHaus

Editor: Emma Henderson

Publishing Imprints: Armchair Traveller; Haus Fiction; HausBooks; Life&Times

P209 Hawthorne Books
Book Publisher
2201 NE 23rd Avenue Third Floor, Portland, OR 97212
United States
Tel: +1 (503) 327-8849

rhughes@hawthornebooks.com

http://www.hawthornebooks.com
https://www.facebook.com/HawthorneBooks
http://twitter.com//hawthornebooks
http://pinterest.com/hawthornebooks/

Fiction > *Novels*: Literary

Nonfiction > *Nonfiction Books*
Memoir; Narrative Essays

Closed to approaches.

An independent literary press based in Portland, Oregon, with a national scope and deep regional roots. Focuses on literary fiction and nonfiction with innovative and varied approaches to the relationships between essay, memoir, and narrative.

Authors: Kassten Alonso; Poe Ballantine; Peter Donahue; Monica Drake; D'Arcy Fallon; Peter Fogtdal; Jeff Meyers; Mark Mordue; Scott Nadelson; Toby Olson; Gin Phillips; Lynne Sharon Schwartz; Tom Spanbauer; Michael Strelow; Richard Wiley

P210 Hay House Publishers
Book Publisher
The Sixth Floor, Watson House, 54 Baker Street, London, W1U 7BU
United Kingdom

Tel: +44 (0) 20 3927 7290
Fax: +44 (0) 20 3675 2451

submissions@hayhouse.co.uk

https://www.hayhouse.co.uk
https://www.facebook.com/hayhouse
https://www.instagram.com/hayhouseuk
https://twitter.com/hayhouseuk

Nonfiction > *Nonfiction Books*
Alternative Health; Angels; Anxiety Disorders; Astrology; Business; Communication; Finance; Health; New Age; Parenting; Personal Development; Pets; Psychological Trauma; Relationships; Self Help; Spirituality; Tarot; Vegetarianism

Send: Query; Synopsis
How to send: Online submission system

Describes itself as the world's leading mind body and spirit publisher. Approach via form on website. See website for full submission guidelines.

P211 Hazel Press
Book Publisher
United Kingdom

https://hazelpress.co.uk
https://zirk.us/@hazelpress
https://twitter.com/hazel_press
https://www.instagram.com/hazelpresspublisher/
https://www.youtube.com/channel/UCOVRNv8pZw_l5DaoJ62IZug

Fiction > *Short Fiction*
Arts; Climate Science; Environment; Feminism

Nonfiction > *Essays*
Arts; Climate Science; Environment; Feminism

Poetry > *Poetry Collections*
Arts; Climate Science; Environment; Feminism

Closed to approaches.

An independent publisher focusing on the environment, the realities of the climate crisis, feminism and the arts. Publishes short books of poetry, essays and interdisciplinary work that is intelligent, inspiring and has a strong sense of place. Seeks to engage with ecological issues in a collaborative and provocative way.

P212 Hearing Eye
Book Publisher
Box 1, 99 Torriano Avenue, London, NW5 2RX
United Kingdom
Tel: +44 (0) 7519 917915

https://hearingeye.org
https://www.facebook.com/hearingeyepoetry

Poetry > *Poetry Collections*

Small independent poetry publisher. Rarely publishes unsolicited material.

P213 Hell's Hundred
Publishing Imprint
United States

Book Publisher: Soho Press (**P417**)

P214 Henley Hall Press
Book Publisher
United Kingdom

https://henleyhallpress.co.uk
https://twitter.com/HenleyHallPress

Nonfiction > *Nonfiction Books*
Farming; Gardening; History; Politics

Send: Pitch
How to send: Online contact form

An independent publisher of thought-provoking non-fiction books.

Our categories are: farming, politics, history, garden design and that all-encompassing category 'misc'.

No cancel culture here. We are happy to publish books that challenge received wisdom – or wokedom – and we support the work of the Free Speech Union.

We aim to publish just two to four books a year. This is to devote the time to help your book succeed in a crowded market.

P215 Henry Holt & Co.
Publishing Imprint
United States

Book Publisher: Macmillan Publishers

P216 High Stakes Publishing
Publishing Imprint
Harpenden, AL5 1EQ
United Kingdom
Tel: +44 (0) 1582 766348

https://highstakespublishing.co.uk

Book Publisher: Oldcastle Books Group (**P326**)

Nonfiction > *Nonfiction Books*: Gambling

Imprint publishing books on gambling.

P217 High Tide Press
Book Publisher
101 Hempstead Place Suite 1A, Joliet, Il 60433
United States
Tel: +1 (779) 702-5540

Submissions@HighTidePress.org
Greetings@HighTidePress.org

https://hightidepress.org
https://www.facebook.com/HighTidePress/
https://twitter.com/hightidepress

Nonfiction > *Nonfiction Books*
Leadership; Management; Mental Disorders; Personal Development; Psychology; Wellbeing

Send: Query; Outline; Market info; Author bio
Don't send: Full text
How to send: In the body of an email; Post
How not to send: Email attachment

Publishes titles on Person-Centered Planning; Behavioral Health; Intellectual and developmental disabilities; Positive Psychology; Nonprofit management; Leadership and management.

P218 Hippo Park
Publishing Imprint
United States

Book Publisher: Astra Publishing House **(P037)**

P219 Hippocrene Books, Inc.
Book Publisher
171 Madison Avenue, Suite 1300, New York, NY 10016
United States

editorial@hippocrenebooks.com
info@hippocrenebooks.com

https://www.hippocrenebooks.com
https://www.facebook.com/pages/Hippocrene-Books-Inc/129993534671
https://twitter.com/hippocrenebooks
https://pinterest.com/hippocrenebooks

Nonfiction
  Nonfiction Books: Cookery; Ethnic
  Reference: Language

How to send: Email

Publishes general nonfiction, particularly foreign language reference books and ethnic cookbooks. No fiction. Send submissions by email.

P220 Hiraeth Books
Book Publisher; Ebook Publisher; Online Publisher
United States

hireath.sff@gmail.com
hiraethsubs@yahoo.com

https://www.hiraethsffh.com/
https://www.facebook.com/HiraethPublishing
https://twitter.com/HiraethSf

Fiction
  Chapbooks: Fantasy; Horror; Science Fiction; Speculative; Supernatural / Paranormal
  Colouring Books: Fantasy; Horror; Science Fiction; Speculative; Supernatural / Paranormal
  Novellas: Fantasy; Horror; Science Fiction; Speculative; Supernatural / Paranormal
  Novels: Fantasy; Horror; Science Fiction; Speculative; Supernatural / Paranormal
  Short Fiction Collections: Fantasy; Horror; Science Fiction; Speculative; Supernatural / Paranormal

  Short Fiction: Fantasy; Horror; Science Fiction; Speculative; Supernatural / Paranormal
Poetry > *Poetry Collections*
  Fantasy; Horror; Science Fiction; Speculative; Supernatural / Paranormal

Send: Synopsis; Writing sample
How to send: Email attachment

We publish what we consider the very best in speculative fiction: science fiction, fantasy, horror, paranormal, anything out of the ordinary. We welcome new and established authors and artists equally, as talent is often found in out-of-the-way places. We are a family friendly company, but we don't shy away from strong language or tough situations if the story or artwork calls for it.

We publish novels, novellas, chapbooks, coloring books, anthologies, collections, even short stories online in the effort to showcase the many talented writers and artists how have entrusted us with their creations. We do our best to present their work in an attractive package that will gain the most attention and entertain the most readers.

Online Magazine / Print Magazine: Scifaikuest **(M323)**

P221 The History Press
Book Publisher
United Kingdom

submissions@thehistorypress.co.uk

https://www.thehistorypress.co.uk
https://www.facebook.com/thehistorypressuk/
https://twitter.com/TheHistoryPress/
https://www.pinterest.com/thehistorypress/

Nonfiction > *Nonfiction Books*
  General, and in particular: Archaeology; Aviation; Biography; Crime; Culture; Entertainment; Folklore, Myths, and Legends; History; Local History; Maritime History; Memoir; Military; Nature; Society; Sport; Transport

Send: Query; Synopsis; Author bio; Market info; Proposal
Don't send: Full text
How to send: Email

Publishes books on history, from local to international, and general nonfiction. Welcomes submissions from both new and established authors. Send query by email. No unsolicited mss. See website for full guidelines.

Publishing Imprint: Phillimore

P222 Hodder & Stoughton Ltd
Book Publisher
Carmelite House, 50 Victoria Embankment, London, EC4Y 0DZ
United Kingdom
Tel: +44 (0) 20 3122 6777

enquiries@hachette.co.uk

https://www.hodder.co.uk
https://www.facebook.com/HODDERBOOKS/
https://twitter.com/HodderBooks
https://www.instagram.com/hodderbooks/

Fiction > *Novels*

Nonfiction > *Nonfiction Books*

How to send: Through a literary agent

Large London-based publisher of nonfiction and fiction.

Book Publisher: Hodder Faith

Publishing Imprint: Nicholas Brealey Publishing

P223 HopeRoad
Book Publisher
PO Box 55544, Exhibition Road, London, SW7 2DB
United Kingdom

info@hoperoadpublishing.com

https://www.hoperoadpublishing.com
https://www.facebook.com/HopeRoadPublishing
https://twitter.com/hoperoadpublish
https://www.instagram.com/hoperoadpublishing/
https://www.youtube.com/channel/UCd3aU4rc8zWAnB3dgnV-xhw?view_as=subscriber

ADULT > **Fiction** > *Novels*
  Africa; Asia; Caribbean; Culture; Disabilities; Social Justice

YOUNG ADULT > **Fiction** > *Novels*
  Africa; Asia; Caribbean; Culture; Disabilities; Social Justice

How to send: Through a literary agent

Promotes the best writing from and about Africa, Asia and the Caribbean, with themes of identity, cultural stereotyping, disability and injustices of particular interest.

P224 Host Publications
Book Publisher
PO BOX 302920, Austin, TX 78703
United States

editors@hostpublications.com

https://hostpublications.com
https://hostpublications.submittable.com/submit
http://instagram.com/HostPublications

Fiction in Translation > *Short Fiction Collections*

Fiction > *Short Fiction Collections*

Poetry in Translation > *Poetry Collections*

Poetry > *Poetry Collections*

Closed to approaches.

Publishes literature from across the United States and around the world, including Nobel Prize winners. In 2018, shifted its focus from international authors to authors based in the United States, and committed to creating a seat at the table for marginalized groups: primarily women, people of color, immigrants, and LGBTQ+ writers.

P225 Howgate Publishing
Book Publisher
United Kingdom

info@howgatepublishing.com

https://www.howgatepublishing.com
https://twitter.com/kirstin_howgate

Nonfiction > *Nonfiction Books*
 Military; Warfare

Send: Proposal; Table of Contents; Synopsis; Author bio; Market info
How to send: Email

Our vision is simple: to positively impact the way we collectively think about war and warfare, to provide a specific resource and expertise for authors and readers, to be the 'go-to' place for military thought.

P226 Icehouse
Publishing Imprint
Canada

https://gooselane.com/pages/poetry-submission

Book Publisher: Goose Lane Editions (**P188**)

Poetry > *Poetry Collections*

Closed to approaches.

Publishes full-length poetry collections of roughly 48-100 pages, by new and established writers. Consider submissions by Canadian citizens or permanent residents only. Accepts submissions annually between April 1 and June 30.

P227 Icon Books Ltd
Book Publisher
Omnibus Business Centre, 39-41 North Road, London, N7 9DP
United Kingdom
Tel: +44 (0) 20 7697 9695
Fax: +44 (0) 20 7697 9501

info@iconbooks.com
submissions@iconbooks.net

https://iconbooks.com
https://twitter.com/iconbooks
https://www.facebook.com/iconbooks
https://www.instagram.com/iconbooks/
http://www.youtube.com/iconbooksuk

Nonfiction > *Nonfiction Books*
 Biography; Business; Crime; Cultural History; Current Affairs; Economics; Environment; Health; History; Language; Lifestyle; Literature; Mathematics; Memoir; Military History; Nature; Philosophy; Politics; Popular Science; Psychology; Religion; Self Help; Social History; Sport; Transport; Travel

Send: Submission Form
How to send: Email
How not to send: Post

We are an adult non-fiction publisher and are happy to read manuscripts from potential new authors. We accept unsolicited adult non-fiction manuscripts only. We do not accept adult fiction, poetry, or children's fiction. If you would like to submit, please download and fill in our submissions form, and send it by email.

P228 IDW Publishing
Book Publisher
2355 Northside Drive, Suite 140, San Diego, CA 92108
United States

info@idwpublishing.com

https://www.idwpublishing.com

ADULT > **Fiction**
 Comics; *Graphic Novels*; *Novels*
CHILDREN'S > **Fiction**
 Comics; *Graphic Novels*; *Novels*
YOUNG ADULT > **Fiction**
 Comics; *Graphic Novels*; *Novels*

Publisher of comic books and graphic novels based on well known intellectual properties, for both children and adults.

P229 Idyll Arbor
Book Publisher
2432 39th Street, Bedford, IN 47421
United States
Tel: +1 (812) 675-6623

editors@idyllarbor.com

https://www.idyllarbor.com

ADULT > **Nonfiction** > *Nonfiction Books*: Health

PROFESSIONAL > **Nonfiction** > *Nonfiction Books*
 Health; Medicine

How to send: Email

Provides information and tools you can use for Recreational Therapists, Activity Professionals, and Allied Therapists. We have texts for educators and students; books for specific areas of your practice; assessments for patients, clients, and residents; and therapeutic games.

We also have books that will improve your personal health and the health of people you work with. Other books from our imprint look at ways we can work to heal our culture.

As we move forward, we continue our commitment to provide material that tracks the trends in the fields we cover and helps you find the energy, ideas, and inspiration you need to succeed in your practice.

P230 Ig Publishing
Book Publisher
PO Box 2547, New York, NY 10163
United States
Tel: +1 (718) 797-0676

robert@igpub.com

https://www.igpub.com
https://twitter.com/Igpublishing
https://www.facebook.com/pages/Ig-Publishing/176428769078839
https://www.pinterest.com/igpublishing/
https://www.instagram.com/igpublishing/

Fiction > *Novels*: Literary

Nonfiction > *Nonfiction Books*
 Culture; Politics

Send: Query
How to send: Email

A New York-based award-winning independent press dedicated to publishing original literary fiction and political and cultural nonfiction. Send query by email only.

Editor-in-Chief: Robert Lasner

Publishing Imprint: IgKids (**P231**)

P231 IgKids
Publishing Imprint
United States

https://www.igpub.com/
https://www.igpub.com/category/titles/igkids/

Book Publisher: Ig Publishing (**P230**)

CHILDREN'S > **Fiction** > *Middle Grade*
YOUNG ADULT > **Fiction** > *Novels*

Send: Query
How to send: Email

Publishes a curated list of middle grade and YA fiction.

P232 Igloo Books Limited
Book Publisher
United Kingdom

inquire@igloobooks.com

https://igloobooks.com
https://www.facebook.com/igloobooks/
https://instagram.com/igloobooks/
https://www.tiktok.com/@igloobooks

ADULT > **Nonfiction**
 Activity Books; *Colouring Books*; *Gift Books*; *Puzzles*
CHILDREN'S
 Fiction
  Board Books; *Picture Books*
 Nonfiction
  Activity Books; *Board Books*; *Reference*

Publishes nonfiction and gift and puzzle books for adults, and fiction, nonfiction, and novelty books for children.

Publishing Imprint: Autumn Publishing Ltd (**P042**)

P233 Image
Publishing Imprint

Book Publisher: Random House

P234 Imagine Publishing
Publishing Imprint
United States

https://www.imaginebooks.net
https://twitter.com/Imagine_CB
https://www.facebook.com/ImaginePress/
https://www.pinterest.com/charlesbridge/adult-books-from-imagine-publishing/
https://www.instagram.com/imagine_cb/

Book Publisher: Charlesbridge Publishing (**P102**)

Nonfiction
  Coffee Table Books: General
  Nonfiction Books: Arts; Comedy / Humour; Cookery; History; Nature; Politics; Women's Studies
  Puzzles: General

Closed to approaches.

Publishes 8-10 titles a year, primarily focused on history, politics, women's studies, and nature.

P235 Indiana University Press
Book Publisher
IU Office of Scholarly Publishing, Herman B Wells Library E350, 1320 E 10th Street E4, Bloomington, IN 47405-3907
United States
Tel: +1 (812) 855-8817

https://iupress.org
https://www.facebook.com/iupress
https://twitter.com/iupress
https://www.instagram.com/iu.press/
https://www.youtube.com/c/IndianaUniversityPress/videos

ACADEMIC > **Nonfiction** > *Nonfiction Books*
  Africa; American Civil War; American Midwest; Eastern Europe; Films; Folklore, Myths, and Legends; Gender; International; Ireland; Jewish Holocaust; Judaism; Media; Middle East; Military History; Music; Paleontology; Performing Arts; Philosophy; Railways; Refugees; Regional; Religion; Russia; Sexuality; Transport

Send: Proposal; Outline; Table of Contents; Writing sample; Author bio
How to send: Online submission system

Submit proposals via online proposal submission form.

P236 Indigo Dreams Publishing
Book Publisher
24 Forest Houses, Halwill, Beaworthy, Devon, EX21 5UU
United Kingdom

publishing@indigodreams.co.uk

https://www.indigodreams.co.uk
https://twitter.com/IndigoDreamsPub

Poetry > *Poetry Collections*

Closed to approaches.

Publishes poetry collections up to 60/70 pages and poetry pamphlets up to 36 pages. See website for submission guidelines.

Authors: Roselle Angwin; Frances Galleymore; Paula Rae Gibson; Seema Gill; Charlie Hill; James Lawless; Robert Leach; Dennis Loccoriere; Angela Locke; Char March; Ann Pilling; Cyril Tawney

Editor: Ronnie Goodyer

Magazines: The Dawntreader (**M115**); Reach

P237 Influx Press
Book Publisher
United Kingdom

https://www.influxpress.com
http://instagram.com/influxpress
http://twitter.com/influxpress

Fiction > *Novels*: Gender

Nonfiction > *Nonfiction Books*: Creative Nonfiction

Closed to approaches.

Publishes innovative and challenging fiction, poetry and creative non-fiction from across the UK and beyond.

P238 Information Today, Inc.
Book Publisher
143 Old Marlton Pike, Medford, NJ 08055-8750
United States
Tel: +1 (609) 654-6266
Fax: +1 (609) 654-4309

custserv@infotoday.com

https://www.infotoday.com

Nonfiction > *Nonfiction Books*
  Computers; Data and Information Systems; Information Science; Technology

Publishes books and magazines on information technology.

P239 Ink & Willow
Publishing Imprint

Book Publisher: Random House

P240 Inkandescent
Book Publisher
United Kingdom

https://www.inkandescent.co.uk
https://www.facebook.com/InkandescentPublishing/
https://twitter.com/InkandescentUK
https://www.instagram.com/inkandescentuk/
https://www.youtube.com/channel/UC65iDI_gjHKDzJfQSeyDdPA

Fiction
  Novellas; *Novels*
Nonfiction > *Nonfiction Books*

Poetry > *Poetry Collections*

Closed to approaches.

We are committed to outsider voices underrepresented in mainstream publishing. In the context of what we do, that primarily means writers who identify as LGBTQ+ or working class, or come from BAME backgrounds. We discover and celebrate original and diverse writing that challenges the status quo. We welcome submissions from new talent and not so new talent, particularly in the form of novellas and short novels.

P241 Integrity Media
Book Publisher
85 Great Portland Street, First Floor, London, W1W 7LT
United Kingdom
Tel: +44 (0) 20 3745 0658

enquiries@integrity-media.co.uk

http://www.integrity-media.co.uk

A publishing company with a unique objective. We aim to provide a platform and portal for those suffering poor mental health, to find release, acceptance and growth through literature. Whether they wish to write an autobiographical work or simple write creatively.

While the above is our primary motivation, we accept submissions from all authors who fit within our areas of interest.

Online Magazine: Authentic Shorts (**M040**)

Publishing Imprints: Authentic Ideas (**P040**); Authentic Life (**P041**)

P242 International Society for Technology in Education (ISTE)
Book Publisher
2111 Wilson Boulevard, Suite 300, Arlington, VA 22201
United States
Tel: +1 (503) 342-2848
Fax: +1 (541) 302-3778

iste@iste.org

https://www.iste.org
https://www.iste.org/professional-development/books

https://twitter.com/iste
https://www.instagram.com/isteconnects/
https://www.facebook.com/ISTEconnects
https://www.iste.org/youtube

ACADEMIC > **Nonfiction** > *Nonfiction Books*
Computer Programming; Digital Technology

PROFESSIONAL > **Nonfiction** > *Nonfiction Books*
Computer Programming; Digital Technology; Education

Publishes books and resources focused on technology in education.

P243 InterVarsity Press (IVP)
Book Publisher
Studio 101, The Record Hall, 16-16A Baldwins Gardens, London, EC1N 7RJ
United Kingdom
Tel: +44 (0) 20 7592 3900

submissions@ivpbooks.com

https://ivpbooks.com
https://www.facebook.com/ivpbooks
https://www.instagram.com/ivpbooks/
https://twitter.com/IVPbookcentre

ACADEMIC > **Nonfiction** > *Nonfiction Books*: Religion

ADULT > **Nonfiction** > *Nonfiction Books*
Biography; Christian Living; Church History; Contemporary Culture; Religion

Closed to approaches.

Aims to produce quality, Evangelical books for the digital age. Send query through form on website.

P244 Jain Publishing Company, Inc.
Book Publisher
Fremont, CA 94539
United States
Tel: +1 (510) 659-8272

mail@jainpub.com

https://www.jainpub.com

ACADEMIC > **Nonfiction** > *Reference*: Asia

ADULT > **Nonfiction** > *Nonfiction Books*: Asia

Send: Query; Proposal; Market info; Outline; Author bio
Don't send: Full text

Primarily publishes Asia related scholarly / academic references, and books for general readers. Complete manuscripts should only be sent on request. Send proposal in first instance. See website for full guidelines.

Editor: M. Jain

P245 Jamii Publishing
Book Publisher
United States

https://jamiipublishing.com
https://jamiipublishing.submittable.com/submit
https://twitter.com/jamiipub
https://www.facebook.com/jamiipublishing/

ADULT
Fiction > *Short Fiction Collections*
Nonfiction > *Essays*: Lyric Essays
Poetry > *Poetry Collections*
Literary; Slipstream

CHILDREN'S > **Poetry** > *Poetry Collections*

Closed to approaches.

Publishes literary poetry, including slipstream, hybrid, children's poetry, multiple authors, short story, lyric essay, visual/textual. Manuscripts must be a part of a larger community based project. No royalties.

Editor: Nikia Chaney

P246 Jessica Kingsley Publishers
Publishing Imprint
Carmelite House, 50 Victoria Embankment, London, EC4Y 0DZ
United Kingdom
Tel: +44 (0) 20 3122 6000

hello@jkp.com
proposals@jkp.com

https://www.jkp.com
https://jkp.submittable.com/submit
https://www.facebook.com/jessicakingsleypublishers
https://twitter.com/JKPBooks
http://www.pinterest.com/jkpbooks
http://instagram.com/JKPbooks

Book Publisher: John Murray Press (**P249**)

ACADEMIC > **Nonfiction** > *Nonfiction Books*
Autism; Culture; Gender Issues; Health; Mental Health; Parenting; Religion; Social Issues

CHILDREN'S > **Nonfiction** > *Nonfiction Books*

PROFESSIONAL > **Nonfiction** > *Nonfiction Books*
Autism; Culture; Gender Issues; Health; Mental Health; Parenting; Religion; Social Issues

Send: Proposal
How to send: Submittable

Publishes books on autism, social work and arts therapies.

Publishing Imprints: Handspring Publishing (*P199*); Singing Dragon (**P409**)

P247 JMD Media / DB Publishing
Book Publisher
United Kingdom
Tel: +44 (0) 7914 647382

https://www.jmdmedia.co.uk

Fiction > *Novels*

Nonfiction > *Nonfiction Books*
Autobiography; Biography; Comedy / Humour; Crime; Football / Soccer; Ghosts; Local History; Local; Magic; Motorsports; Social History; Sport; Supernatural / Paranormal; Travel; Walking

Send: Query; Outline; Author bio
How to send: Email
How not to send: Post

Considers all types of books, but focuses on local interest, sport, biography, autobiography and social history. Approach by email or phone – no submissions by post. See website for full guidelines.

Editor: Steve Caron

P248 Joffe Books
Book Publisher
United Kingdom

submissions@joffebooks.com

https://www.joffebooks.com
https://www.facebook.com/joffebooks
https://twitter.com/joffebooks
https://www.instagram.com/joffebooks

Fiction > *Novels*
Cozy Mysteries; Crime; Domestic Noir; Fantasy; Historical Fiction; Mystery; Police Procedural; Psychological Thrillers; Romance; Saga; Suspense; Women's Fiction; World War II

Send: Full text; Synopsis; Author bio
How to send: Email

Publishes crime fiction, mysteries, psychological thrillers, cosy crime, police procedurals, chillers, suspense and domestic noir. Will also consider women's fiction, fantasy, historical fiction and romance novels, including WWII romances and sagas. Manuscripts must be at least 60,000 words. Send query by email with complete manuscript as an attachment, a synopsis in the body of the email, and 100 words about yourself. Include "submission" in the subject line. Reply not guaranteed unless interested. See website for full guidelines.

Book Publisher: Choc Lit (**P108**)

Editor: Jasper Joffe

P249 John Murray Press
Book Publisher
Carmelite House, 50 Victoria Embankment, London, EC4Y 0DZ

United Kingdom
Tel: +44 (0) 20 3122 7222

enquiries@hachette.co.uk

https://www.johnmurraypress.co.uk

Book Publisher: Hachette UK

Fiction > *Novels*

Nonfiction > *Nonfiction Books*

Publisher of fiction and nonfiction, founded in the eighteenth century.

Publishing Imprints: Chambers; Jessica Kingsley Publishers (**P246**)

P250 The Johns Hopkins University Press
Book Publisher
2715 North Charles Street, Baltimore, Maryland 21218-4363
United States
Tel: +1 (410) 516-6900

https://www.press.jhu.edu
https://twitter.com/JHUPress
https://www.facebook.com/JohnsHopkinsUniversityPress
https://www.youtube.com/user/JHUPJournals
https://www.pinterest.com/jhupress/

ACADEMIC > **Nonfiction** > *Nonfiction Books*
 Architecture; Arts; Business; Classics / Ancient World; Economics; Education; Health; History; Language; Legal; Literature; Mathematics; Medicine; Music; Politics; Recreation; Religion; Science; Sociology; Sport

Publishes titles in history, science, higher education, health and wellness, humanities, classics, and public health. Provides authors with a reputable forum for evidence-based discourse and exposure to a worldwide audience.

Editor-in-Chief: Trevor Lipscombe

Magazine: African American Review (**M014**)

P251 Kane Press
Publishing Imprint
United States

kpsubmissions@astrapublishinghouse.com

https://astrapublishinghouse.com/imprints/kane-press/

Book Publisher: Astra Publishing House (**P037**)

CHILDREN'S
 Fiction
  Chapter Books; *Early Readers*; *Middle Grade*; *Picture Books*
 Nonfiction > *Nonfiction Books*
  Arts; Engineering; Mathematics; Science; Technology

Send: Proposal
How to send: Email; Through a literary agent

An award-winning publisher of illustrated STEAM and literacy titles. Fiction and nonfiction books for ages 3–11 feature fun stories with curriculum connections and are the perfect springboard for learning in classrooms, libraries, and homes. Currently accepting proposals for series only, from published authors and literary agents.

P252 The Kates Hill Press
Book Publisher
8 Chapel Street, Wall Heath, Kingswinford, West Midlands, DY6 0JU
United Kingdom
Tel: +44 (0) 1384 254719

kateshillpress1992@gmail.com

https://kateshillpress.com

Fiction
 Novels; *Short Fiction Collections*
Nonfiction > *Nonfiction Books*
 History; Local History; Memoir

Poetry > *Poetry Collections*

Small independent publisher producing short runs of fiction and social history books with a west midlands theme or by a west midlands writer. Also publishes booklets of poetry and dialect verse by Black Country/West Midlands poets.

P253 Kensington Publishing Corp.
Book Publisher
900 Third Avenue, 26th Floor, New York, NY 10022
United States
Tel: +1 (800) 221-2647

https://www.kensingtonbooks.com
https://www.facebook.com/kensingtonpublishing
https://twitter.com/KensingtonBooks
https://www.instagram.com/kensingtonbooks/
https://www.youtube.com/user/KensingtonPublishing
https://www.pinterest.co.uk/kensingtonbooks/
https://www.tiktok.com/@kensingtonbooks

ADULT
 Fiction
  Comics: General
  Graphic Novels: General
  Novels: Cozy Mysteries; Fantasy; Literary; Mystery; Romance; Thrillers; Westerns
 Nonfiction
  Nonfiction Books: Activities; Autobiography; Biography; Business; Comedy / Humour; Computers; Cookery; Crafts; Crime; Economics; Education; Engineering; Family; Fitness; Games; Gardening; Health; History; Hobbies; Houses and Homes; Language; Legal; Medicine; Mind, Body, Spirit; Music; Nature; Performing Arts; Pets; Philosophy; Photography; Politics; Psychology; Recreation; Relationships; Religion; Science; Self Help; Sociology; Sport; Technology; Transport; Travel
  Reference: General

CHILDREN'S > **Fiction** > *Novels*

YOUNG ADULT
 Fiction > *Novels*
 Nonfiction > *Nonfiction Books*

Send: Query
Don't send: Full text
How to send: In the body of an email

Send query only, in the body of the email. Submit to one editor only. See website for full guidelines and individual editor contact details.

Editor: John Scognamiglio

Publishing Imprints: Aphrodisia; Brava; Citadel Press; Dafina; Holloway House; John Scognamiglio Books; KTeen; KTeen Dafina; Kensington Hardcover; Kensington Mass-Market; Kensington Trade Paperback; Lyle Stuart Books; Lyrical Caress; Lyrical Liaison; Lyrical Press (**P277**); Lyrical Shine; Lyrical Underground; Pinnacle; Rebel Base Books; Zebra; Zebra Shout

P254 Kitchen Press
Book Publisher
1 Windsor Place, Dundee, DD2 1BG
United Kingdom
Tel: +44 (0) 1382 660890

https://kitchenpress.co.uk
https://www.facebook.com/kitchenpress

Nonfiction > *Nonfiction Books*
 Cookery; Food and Drink

Send: Outline; Author bio
Don't send: Full text
How to send: Online contact form

Cookbook publisher founded in 2011. We work with food writers, chefs and restaurants throughout the UK. We take our food and drink seriously. Our aim is to publish the freshest food writing, with recipes that work and images that make you hungry.

P255 Kogan Page Ltd
Book Publisher
45 Gee Street, 2nd Floor, London, EC1V 3RS
United Kingdom
Tel: +44 (0) 20 7278 0433

kpinfo@koganpage.com

https://www.koganpage.com
https://www.facebook.com/KoganPage
https://twitter.com/Koganpage
https://www.instagram.com/koganpage/
https://www.linkedin.com/company/kogan-page_2/
https://www.youtube.com/user/KoganPageBooks

Nonfiction > *Nonfiction Books*
  Business; Career Development; Finance

Publishes award-winning content from the world's leading business experts to help organizations and professionals develop the skills, competencies and knowledge to thrive.

P256 Kore Press
Book Publisher
PO Box 40682, Tucson, AZ 85717
United States

https://www.facebook.com/korepress

Fiction > *Novels*

Nonfiction > *Nonfiction Books*

Poetry > *Poetry Collections*

Closed to approaches.

Publishes fiction, poetry, nonfiction, hybrid, and cultural criticism. Accepts submissions both through open submission windows and competitions.

Managing Editor: Ann Dernier

P257 Korero Press
Book Publisher
London
United Kingdom
Fax: +44 (0) 7906 314098

info@koreropress.com
contact@koreropress.com

https://www.koreropress.com
https://www.facebook.com/koreropress
https://twitter.com/KoreroPress
http://www.pinterest.com/koreropress
https://instagram.com/koreropress/

Nonfiction > *Illustrated Books*
  Arts; Drawing; Erotic; Fantasy; Horror; How To; Painting; Popular Culture; Science Fiction

Send: Query; Outline; Author bio; Market info
How to send: Email

A London-based publisher with a love of lowbrow and kustom kulture. List is mainly made up of pop culture, street art, erotica and horror titles. Publishes illustrated books only. No novels.

P258 Kube Publishing
Book Publisher
MCC, Ratby Lane, Markfield, Leicestershire, LE67 9SY
United Kingdom
Tel: +44 (0) 1530 249230

info@kubepublishing.com

https://www.kubepublishing.com
https://kubepublishing.submittable.com/submit
https://www.facebook.com/kubepublishing
https://twitter.com/Kube_Publishing
http://pinterest.com/kubepub/
https://www.instagram.com/kubepublishing/

http://www.youtube.com/user/KubeVideos/feed
https://www.tiktok.com/@kubepublishing?lang=en

ACADEMIC > Nonfiction > *Nonfiction Books*: Islam

ADULT > Nonfiction > *Nonfiction Books*
  Biography; Creativity; Culture; Current Affairs; History; Islam; Memoir; Politics; Spirituality

CHILDREN'S
Fiction
  Board Books: Islam
  Chapter Books: Islam
  Early Readers: Islam
  Middle Grade: Islam
  Picture Books: Islam

Nonfiction
  Activity Books: Islam
  Nonfiction Books: Islam
  Picture Books: Islam

Poetry > *Any Poetic Form*: Islam

Send: Query
How to send: Submittable

Independent publisher of general interest, academic, and children's books on Islam and the Muslim experience. Publishes nonfiction for children, young people, and adults, but fiction and poetry for children. See website for full guidelines.

P259 Langmarc Publishing
Book Publisher
PO Box 90488, Austin, Texas 78709-0488
United States
Tel: +1 (512) 394-0989

langmarc@booksails.com

https://www.langmarc.com

Fiction > *Novels*

Nonfiction > *Nonfiction Books*

Closed to approaches.

Started primarily as a publishing house for church resources and inspirational/motivational books. Now publishes novels and nonfiction.

Publishing Imprints: Harbor Lights Series; North Sea Press

P260 Lantana Publishing
Book Publisher
Clavier House, 21 Fifth Road, Newbury, RG14 6DN
United Kingdom

submissions@lantanapublishing.com

https://www.lantanapublishing.com
https://www.instagram.com/lantana_publishing/
https://www.facebook.com/lantanapublishing
https://twitter.com/lantanapub

https://www.youtube.com/channel/UC_edBCMh3Y2wDID2X9qMSkA

CHILDREN'S
Fiction
  Chapter Books; *Early Readers*; *Graphic Novels*; *Middle Grade*; *Picture Books*
Nonfiction > *Nonfiction Books*

Poetry > *Any Poetic Form*

Send: Full text
How to send: Email

We are looking for manuscripts and book dummies by authors and illustrators from under-represented groups. We particularly love stories that make us laugh, cry or move us in some way.

P261 Laurence King Publishing
Publishing Imprint
Carmelite House, 50 Victoria Embankment, London, EC4Y 0DZ
United Kingdom
Tel: +44 (0)20 3122 6444

commissioning@laurenceking.com

https://www.laurenceking.com
https://twitter.com/LaurenceKingPub
https://www.instagram.com/LaurenceKingPub/
https://www.facebook.com/LaurenceKingPublishing
https://www.pinterest.co.uk/LaurenceKingPub/
https://vimeo.com/laurencekingpublishing
https://www.youtube.com/user/laurencekingpub

Book Publishers: Hachette UK; Hachette Children's Group

ACADEMIC > Nonfiction > *Nonfiction Books*
  Architecture; Arts; Beauty; Design; Fashion; Films; Music; Nature; Photography; Popular Culture; Popular Science

ADULT > Nonfiction > *Nonfiction Books*
  Architecture; Arts; Beauty; Design; Fashion; Films; Music; Nature; Photography; Popular Culture; Popular Science

CHILDREN'S > Nonfiction > *Illustrated Books*

Send: Query; Synopsis; Market info; Author bio
How to send: Email

Publisher of books on the creative arts. Send proposal by email.

P262 Leamington Books
Book Publisher
32 Leamington Terrace, Edinburgh, EH10 4JL
United Kingdom

https://leamingtonbooks.com

Fiction > *Novels*
  Commercial; Crime; Literary

Nonfiction > *Nonfiction Books*
Poetry > *Poetry Collections*

Closed to approaches.

Founded in 2020 to publish new fiction and poetry, and since 2021 has published debut novels each year, in the commercial, literary and crime styles. We have published two poetry collections each year, a mixture of new and established authors and performers, in Scottish Gaelic as well as English. We have published six anthologies, on diverse themes and non-fiction titles on Nordic runes, cryptocurrency, and the lyrics of Bob Dylan.

P263 Leapfrog Press
Book Publisher
PO Box 1293, Dunkirk, NY 14048
United States

leapfrog@leapfrogpress.com

https://leapfrogpress.com
https://www.facebook.com/Leapfrogpress
https://twitter.com/leapfrogpress1
https://instagram.com/leapfrogpress

ADULT
 Fiction > *Novels*
 Nonfiction > *Nonfiction Books*
 Poetry > *Poetry Collections*

CHILDREN'S > **Fiction** > *Middle Grade*

YOUNG ADULT > **Fiction** > *Novels*

Publisher with an eclectic list of fiction, poetry, and nonfiction, including paperback originals of adult, young adult and middle-grade fiction, and nonfiction.

P264 Lerner Publishing Group
Book Publisher
241 First Avenue North, Minneapolis, MN 55401-1607
United States
Tel: +1 (800) 328-4929

custserve@lernerbooks.com

https://lernerbooks.com
https://www.facebook.com/lernerbooks
https://twitter.com/lernerbooks

CHILDREN'S
 Fiction
  Audiobooks; *Ebooks*; *Graphic Novels*; *Middle Grade*; *Novels*; *Picture Books*
 Nonfiction
  Audiobooks; *Ebooks*; *Nonfiction Books*
YOUNG ADULT
 Fiction
  Audiobooks; *Ebooks*; *Novels*
 Nonfiction
  Audiobooks; *Ebooks*; *Nonfiction Books*

How to send: Through a literary agent; By referral

Publishes fiction and nonfiction for children and young adults. No submissions or queries from unagented or unreferred authors.

Publishing Imprints: Carolrhoda Books; Carolrhoda Lab; Darby Creek; Ediciones Lerner; First Avenue Editions; Graphic Universe; Kar-Ben Publishing; Lerner Digital; Lerner Publications; LernerClassroom; Millbrook Press; Twenty-First Century Books; Zest Books

P265 LexisNexis
Book Publisher
Lexis House, 30 Farringdon Street, EC4A 4HH
United Kingdom
Tel: +44 (0) 330 161 1234

BIS@lexisnexis.co.uk

https://www.lexisnexis.com/en-gb

PROFESSIONAL > **Nonfiction** > *Reference*: Legal

Publishes books, looseleafs, journals etc. for legal professionals.

Book Publisher: Jordan Publishing

P266 Lightning Books
Publishing Imprint
United Kingdom

dan@eye-books.com

https://www.eye-books.com

Book Publisher: Eye Books

Fiction > *Novels*

Send: Query; Pitch; Synopsis; Writing sample
How to send: Word file email attachment

Query by email with the word SUBMISSION in capitals at the beginning of the subject field, followed by your name and book title. Attach a single Word file containing a pitch of up to 250 words, a synopsis of up to 500 words, and the first three chapters, up to 10,000 words.

P267 Liguori Publications
Book Publisher
One Liguori Drive, Liguori, MO 63057-9999
United States
Tel: +1 (800) 325-9521

manuscript_submission@liguori.org

https://www.liguori.org

Nonfiction > *Nonfiction Books*: Catholicism

Send: Query; Author bio; Outline; Table of Contents; Writing sample; Market info
How to send: Email attachment

Publishes books founded in the Roman Catholic belief and tradition, including meditations on the seasons of the Church Year (Advent/Christmas, Lent/Easter) or on liturgical readings and texts; stories on, or reflections with, the life, words, and works of the saints; and studies, guides, and books for receiving, ministering and experiencing the sacraments.

Editor: Daniel Michaels

P268 The Lilliput Press
Book Publisher
62-63 Sitric Road, Arbour Hill, Dublin 7
Ireland

editorial@lilliputpress.ie
contact@lilliputpress.ie

https://www.lilliputpress.ie
https://www.facebook.com/thelilliputpress/
https://twitter.com/LilliputPress
https://www.instagram.com/lilliputpress/

Fiction > *Novels*: Ireland

Nonfiction
 Nonfiction Books: Architecture; Arts; Biography; Cultural Criticism; Environment; Food; Genealogy; History; Ireland; Literary Criticism; Literature; Local History; Memoir; Mind, Body, Spirit; Music; Nature; Philosophy; Photography; Travel
 Reference: Ireland

Poetry > *Any Poetic Form*: Ireland

Closed to approaches.

Publishes books broadly focused on Irish themes. No genre literature, such as children's literature, crime fiction or science fiction. See website for full guidelines.

P269 Llewellyn Worldwide Ltd
Book Publisher
Acquisitions Department, 2143 Wooddale Drive, Woodbury, MN 55125
United States
Tel: +1 (612) 291-1970
Fax: +1 (612) 291-1908

submissions@llewellyn.com

http://www.llewellyn.com

Nonfiction > *Nonfiction Books*
 Alternative Health; Angels; Astral Projection; Astrology; Chakras; Cryptozoology; Ghost Hunting; Kabbalah; Meditation; Mind, Body, Spirit; Paganism; Psychic Abilities; Reiki; Reincarnation; Shamanism; Spirit Guides; Spirituality; Tarot; UFOs; Wicca; Witchcraft; Yoga

Send: Query; Proposal; Full text; Outline; Table of Contents; Market info; Author bio; Writing sample
How to send: Word file email attachment; Post; PDF file email attachment

As the world's oldest and largest independent publisher of books for body, mind, and spirit, we are dedicated to bringing our readers the very best in metaphysical books and resources. Since 1901, we've been at the forefront of holistic and metaphysical publishing and thought. We've been a source of illumination, instruction, and new perspectives on a wealth of topics, including astrology, tarot, wellness, earth-based spirituality, magic, and the paranormal.

P270 Loft Press, Inc.
Book Publisher
9293 Fort Valley Road, Fort Valley, VA 22652
United States
Tel: +1 (540) 933-6210
Fax: +1 (540) 933-6523

books@loftpress.com

http://www.loftpress.com

ADULT
  Fiction > *Novels*

  Nonfiction > *Nonfiction Books*
    History; Memoir; Philosophy

  Poetry > *Poetry Collections*

PROFESSIONAL > **Nonfiction** > *Nonfiction Books*
    Business; Logistics; Supply Chain Management; Transport; Warehousing

Does not want:

> Fiction > *Novels*
>   Coming of Age; Fantasy; Feminism; Gender; Science Fiction; Women's Fiction

Send: Query; Writing sample; Outline; Market info; Self-Addressed Stamped Envelope (SASE)
How to send: Post
How not to send: Email

Publishes books for both the business community and the general reading public. Business books specialize in transportation loss and damage, logistics, warehousing, and supply chain management. For the general reading public, publishes Poetry, history, philosophy, and memoirs. Publishes very little fiction. No "coming of age" works, science fiction, fantasy, feminist-, gender-, or women-oriented works, or any manuscript with inappropriate coarse language.

P271 Logaston Press
Book Publisher
The Holme, Church Road, Eardisley, Herefordshire, HR3 6NJ
United Kingdom
Tel: +44 (0) 1544 327182

info@logastonpress.co.uk

https://logastonpress.co.uk
https://twitter.com/LogastonPress

Nonfiction > *Nonfiction Books*
  Archaeology; Architecture; Biography; Breconshire; Gloucestershire; Herefordshire; Local History; Montgomeryshire; Radnorshire; Shropshire; Walking Guides; Worcestershire

Send: Query; Submission Form; Table of Contents; Writing sample; Author bio
How to send: Email

Publishes local history, biography, archaeology, architecture, landscape and topography, and walk guides; and also books about the Southern Marches region: the English counties of Herefordshire, Shropshire, Worcestershire and Gloucestershire, and the Welsh counties of Radnorshire, Breconshire and Montgomeryshire.

Publishing Imprint: Fircone Books Ltd

P272 Loyola Press
Book Publisher
8770 W Bryn Mawr Ave, Suite 1125, Chicago, IL 60631
United States
Tel: +1 (773) 281-1818
Fax: +1 (773) 281-0152

submissions@loyolapress.com

https://www.loyolapress.com
https://www.facebook.com/LoyolaPress
https://twitter.com/loyolapress
https://instagram.com/loyolapress/
https://www.youtube.com/user/LoyolaPress

Nonfiction > *Nonfiction Books*
  Catholicism; Ignation Spirituality

Send: Query
How to send: Email; Post

Provides resources for readers of all ages interested in Ignatian spirituality and prayer, and supports parish ministry leaders and catechists especially in their roles of fostering and passing on a living faith.

Publishing Imprint: Loyola Classics

P273 LSU Press
Book Publisher
338 Johnston Hall, Louisiana State University, Baton Rouge, LA 70803
United States
Tel: +1 (225) 578-6294

https://lsupress.org
https://www.facebook.com/LSUPress/
https://twitter.com/lsupress
https://www.instagram.com/lsupress/

ACADEMIC > **Nonfiction** > *Nonfiction Books*
    African American; American Civil War; American History; Architecture; Caribbean History; Culture; Environment; Food; History; Literature; Louisiana; Media; Roots Music; Social Justice; World War II

ADULT > **Poetry** > *Poetry Collections*

Send: Query; Proposal; Writing sample; Author bio; Table of Contents; Self-Addressed Stamped Envelope (SASE)
How to send: Email; Post

Publishes works of scholarly and creative excellence, amplifying diverse voices while promoting dialogue about the rich and varied cultures of Louisiana, the South, and the world beyond.

P274 Lund Humphries Limited
Publishing Imprint
The Alphabeta Building, 18 Finsbury Square, London, EC2A 1AH
United Kingdom
Tel: +44 (0) 20 7440 7530

info@lundhumphries.com

https://www.lundhumphries.com
http://facebook.com/LHArtBooks
https://www.twitter.com/LHArtBooks
https://instagram.com/lhartbooks
https://www.youtube.com/channel/UCt-2V5NDuUGTzJOxNGSqR7w

Book Publisher: Ashgate Publishing Ltd

ACADEMIC > **Nonfiction** > *Nonfiction Books*
    Architecture; Arts; Design

ADULT > **Nonfiction** > *Nonfiction Books*
    Architecture; Arts; Design

PROFESSIONAL > **Nonfiction** > *Nonfiction Books*
    Architecture; Arts; Design

Send: Query; Proposal
How to send: Email

Publishes books on art, art history, and design. See website for guidelines on submitting a proposal.

Editor: Lucy Clark

P275 The Lutterworth Press
Publishing Imprint
PO Box 60, Cambridge, CB1 2NT
United Kingdom
Tel: +44 (0) 1223 350865
Fax: +44 (0) 1223 366951

publishing@lutterworth.com

https://www.lutterworth.com
https://lutterworthpress.wordpress.com
https://twitter.com/LuttPress
https://www.facebook.com/JamesClarkeandCo
https://www.instagram.com/lutterworthpress

Book Publisher: James Clarke & Co.

ADULT > **Nonfiction** > *Nonfiction Books*
  Anthropology; Antiques; Archaeology; Architecture; Arts; Biography; British History; Church Architecture; Church Art; Church History; Classics / Ancient World; Crafts; Education; Environment; European History; Games; History; Leisure; Literary Criticism; Literature; Nature; New Age; Philosophy; Poetry as a Subject; Politics; Psychology; Religion; Science; Sociology; Sport; Technology

CHILDREN'S
  Fiction > *Novels*

  Nonfiction > *Nonfiction Books*: Religion

Send: Submission Form
How to send: Post; Fax; Email

Publisher of religious books. Handles nonfiction for adults, and fiction and nonfiction for children. No adult fiction, cookery books, or drama or poetry.

Not currently accepting children's books.

P276 LW Books
Publishing Imprint
United States

https://schifferbooks.com/pages/schiffer-imprints

Book Publisher: Schiffer Publishing (**P398**)

Nonfiction > *Nonfiction Books*
  Ceramics; Collectibles

Specialized books with price guides for collectibles, especially ceramics.

P277 Lyrical Press
Publishing Imprint
United States

https://www.kensingtonbooks.com

Book Publisher: Kensington Publishing Corp. (**P253**)

Fiction > *Novels*
  Cozy Mysteries; Erotic; Historical Romance; Thrillers

A digital first imprint that offers readers a prolific catalogue of titles ranging from sweeping historical romances and edgy erotic titles to chilling thrillers and cozy mysteries.

Editor: John Scognamiglio

P278 M. Evans & Company
Publishing Imprint
United States

https://rowman.com/action/search/cop/m.%20evans%20&%20company

Book Publisher: Rowman & Littlefield Publishing Group

Nonfiction > *Nonfiction Books*
  General, and in particular: Health; Psychology

Publishes general nonfiction, but best known for popular psychology and health books.

P279 Macmillan Children's Books
Publishing Imprint
United Kingdom

https://www.panmacmillan.com/mcb
https://twitter.com/MacmillanKidsUK
https://www.facebook.com/panmacmillanbooks/
https://www.instagram.com/panmacmillan
https://www.tiktok.com/@panmacmillan

Book Publisher: Pan Macmillan

CHILDREN'S > **Fiction**
  Board Books; *Chapter Books*; *Middle Grade*; *Picture Books*
YOUNG ADULT > **Fiction** > *Novels*

How to send: Through a literary agent

One of the UK's leading children's publishers, creating and publishing absorbing and exciting stories for children of all ages for over 150 years.

P280 Manilla Press
Publishing Imprint
United Kingdom

https://www.bonnierbooks.co.uk/imprints/manilla-press/

Book Publisher: Bonnier Books (UK)

Fiction > *Novels*

Nonfiction > *Nonfiction Books*

How to send: Through a literary agent

A boutique literary imprint dedicated to publishing unique author-led fiction and non-fiction. Boasting a carefully curated list and international reach, our books aspire to capture the mood of the times and the hearts and minds of our readers.

A home for novelists, journalists, memoirists, thinkers, dreamers, influencers, and experts. We are driven by our passion for bold and distinctive storytelling – seeking out a broad range of voices and underrepresented talents as we publish for readers from all walks of life.

P281 Margaret K. McElderry Books
Publishing Imprint
United States

https://www.simonandschuster.biz/m/mkm/margaret-mcelderry

Book Publisher: Simon & Schuster Children's Publishing

CHILDREN'S
  Fiction
    Middle Grade: Contemporary; Historical Fiction; Literary Fantasy
    Picture Books: General
  Poetry > *Any Poetic Form*
TEEN
  Fiction > *Novels*
    Contemporary; Historical Fiction; Literary Fantasy
  Poetry > *Any Poetic Form*

Publisher of literary author-driven fiction and nonfiction for the teen, middle grade, picture book, and poetry markets. Specializes in high quality literary fantasy, contemporary, and historical fiction, as well as character-driven picture books and poetry for all ages.

P282 Marion Boyars Publishers
Book Publisher
26 Parke Road, London, SW13 9NG
United Kingdom

jjoyce@equinoxpub.com

http://www.marionboyars.co.uk

Types: Fiction; Nonfiction
Formats: Film Scripts; Theatre Scripts
Subjects: Anthropology; Autobiography; Culture; Drama; Literary Criticism; Music; Philosophy; Psychology; Sociology; Women's Interests
Markets: Adult; Children's

Closed to approaches.

Not accepting new submissions as at April 2024. Check website for current status.

Editor: Catheryn Kilgarriff

P283 MB Media
Book Publisher
United States

mbmediafamily@gmail.com

https://mbmediacorp.com/

Provides publishing and related services to individuals and professionals within and outside the writing industry. Whether you're an individual seeking editing services before self-publishing your book, a company in need of a website, a writer looking for a publishing offer, or anything in between, we're here to help!

Publishing Imprint: Oh MG Press (**P322**)

P284 MCD Books
Publishing Imprint
United States

https://www.mcdbooks.com
https://twitter.com/mcdbooks
https://www.instagram.com/mcdbooks/
https://www.facebook.com/MCDBooks/

Book Publisher: Macmillan Publishers

P285 McGraw Hill EMEA
Book Publisher
Unit 4, Foundation Park, Roxborough Way, Maidenhead, SL6 3UD
United Kingdom
Tel: +44 (0) 1628 502500

emea_uk_ireland@mheducation.com
emea_me@mheducation.com
emea_europe@mheducation.com

https://www.mheducation.co.uk
https://www.facebook.com/mheducationemea
https://twitter.com/mhe_emea
https://www.linkedin.com/showcase/27094331/admin/
https://www.youtube.com/channel/UCmbIrRJdSlo0J99kFa5uYfA

Book Publisher: McGraw-Hill Education

ACADEMIC > **Nonfiction** > *Nonfiction Books*: Education

PROFESSIONAL > **Nonfiction** > *Nonfiction Books*
  Engineering; Health; Medicine; Science

Publisher of books for the professional and academic markets, particularly healthcare, medical, engineering, and science.

P286 McNidder & Grace
Book Publisher; Ebook Publisher
21 Bridge Street, Carmarthen, SA31 3JS
United Kingdom
Tel: +44 (0) 7788 219370

andy@mcnidderandgrace.co.uk

https://mcnidderandgrace.com
https://www.instagram.com/mcniddergrace/
https://twitter.com/McNidderGrace
https://www.facebook.com/mcnidder.grace

Fiction > *Novels*
  General, and in particular: Crime; Popular Culture; Thrillers

Nonfiction > *Nonfiction Books*
  General, and in particular: Arts; Biography; Country Lifestyle; Health; History; Music; Photography; Popular Culture; Wellbeing

How to send: Email

We specialise in non-fiction and fiction titles for adults. With a particular emphasis on popular culture, our non-fiction list includes books on photography, art, music, biography, history, country pursuits and more recently health and well-being. Our fiction list concentrates primarily on Crime and Thrillers.

P287 Media Lab Books
Publishing Imprint

https://us.macmillan.com/publishers/media-lab-books

Book Publisher: Macmillan Publishers

A premier publishing imprint in New York City that partners with expert authors and high-profile brands like Smithsonian, John Wayne, Hasbro, Steve Spangler, Disney and more in order to publish a wide variety of titles designed to inform, educate and entertain readers around the world.

P288 Medical Physics Publishing
Book Publisher; Ebook Publisher
4555 Helgesen Drive, Madison, WI 53718
United States
Tel: +1 (608) 224-4508
Fax: +1 (608) 224-5016

bobbett@medicalphysics.org
mpp@medicalphysics.org

https://medicalphysics.org
https://www.facebook.com/medicalphysics
https://www.linkedin.com/company/medical-physics-publishing-inc

PROFESSIONAL > **Nonfiction** > *Nonfiction Books*
  Medicine; Physics

Send: Query
How to send: Email

Aims to provide affordable books in medical physics and related fields. A nonprofit, tax-exempt 501(c)3 organization. Books are written by and for physicists, residents, radiologists, and technologists.

P289 Medina Publishing
Book Publisher
50 High Street, Cowes, Isle Of Wight, PO31 7RR
United Kingdom

info@medinapublishing.com
submissions@medinapublishing.com

https://medinapublishing.com

Nonfiction > *Nonfiction Books*
  General, and in particular: Comedy / Humour; Memoir; Travel

Closed to approaches.

We specialise in non-fiction, particularly travel memoirs, and also publish humour under our imprint. Always interested in daring new literature. Whether you are an up-and-coming author or a well-established hand with something a little different up your sleeve, get in touch.

P290 Menasha Ridge Press
Publishing Imprint
United States

https://adventurewithkeen.com/menasha-ridge-press-submissions-form/

Book Publisher: AdventureKEEN (**P013**)

Nonfiction > *Nonfiction Books*
  Cookery; Food; History; Outdoor Activities; Travel; Wilderness Sports; Wildlife

Send: Query; Pitch; Outline
How to send: Online submission system

Independent publisher covering the outdoors, wilderness sports, wildlife, cooking, history, dining, and travel worldwide.

P291 Mensch Publishing
Book Publisher
United Kingdom

enquiries@menschpublishing.com

https://menschpublishing.com

Nonfiction > *Nonfiction Books*

No mission statement nor other worthy but meaningless platitudes. Its aim is simply to help authors reach readers with minimal intervention and maximum impact and to reward them proportionately.

P292 Mentor Books
Book Publisher
43 Furze Road, Sandyford Industrial Estate, Dublin 18
Ireland
Tel: 01 2952112

admin@mentorbooks.ie

https://www.mentorbooks.ie

ACADEMIC > **Nonfiction** > *Nonfiction Books*
  Biology; Business; Economics; English; French; Geography; German; History; Irish (Gaeilge); Physical Education; Religion; Science; Spanish

PROFESSIONAL > **Nonfiction** > *Nonfiction Books*: Education

Publishes educational books.

P293 Merriam Press
Book Publisher; Ebook Publisher
489 South Street, Hoosick Falls NY 12090
United States
Tel: +1 (866) 357-7377

merriampress@gmail.com

https://www.merriam-press.com
https://www.facebook.com/MerriamPress

Nonfiction > *Nonfiction Books*
  Military History; World War II

Closed to approaches.

Military history publisher, focusing on World War II.

P294 Methuen Publishing Ltd
Book Publisher
1 Wheelgate, Malton, YO17 7HT
United Kingdom

methuenenquiries@methuen.co.uk

http://www.methuen.co.uk
https://twitter.com/MethuenandCo

Fiction > *Novels*

Nonfiction
  Essays: General
  Nonfiction Books: Autobiography; Biography; Classics / Ancient World; Literature; Politics; Sport; Theatre; Travel; World War II

Send: Query
How to send: Email
How not to send: Phone

If you would like to check whether our publishing list is a fit for your manuscript, please send a brief enquiry only. Thank you. Please note that we do not publish works for children or young adults (including science fiction).

P295 Metro Publications Ltd
Book Publisher
United Kingdom
Tel: +44 (0) 20 8533 7777

info@metropublications.com

https://metropublications.com
https://twitter.com/metrolondon
https://www.instagram.com/metropublications/
https://www.linkedin.com/company/metro-publications-limited

Nonfiction > *Nonfiction Books*
Arts; Culture; Food; London; Walking Guides

Publisher of guide books on many aspects of London life.

P296 Milkweed Editions
Book Publisher
1011 Washington Avenue South, Open Book, Suite 300, Minneapolis, MN 55415
United States

orders@milkweed.org

https://milkweed.org
http://www.facebook.com/milkweed.books
http://twitter.com/#!/Milkweed_Books
https://www.instagram.com/milkweed_books/
http://www.youtube.com/MilkweedEditions
https://www.pinterest.com/Milkfolk/

Fiction > *Novels*

Nonfiction > *Nonfiction Books*

Poetry > *Poetry Collections*

Closed to approaches.

An independent publisher of fiction, nonfiction, and poetry.

P297 Mills & Boon
Publishing Imprint
1 London Bridge Street, London, SE1 9GF
United Kingdom

info@millsandboon.co.uk
submissions@harlequin.com

https://www.millsandboon.co.uk
https://harlequin.submittable.com/submit
https://www.facebook.com/millsandboon
https://twitter.com/MillsandBoon
https://www.instagram.com/millsandboonuk/
https://www.tiktok.com/@millsandboonuk

Book Publishers: Harlequin Enterprises; HarperCollins UK

Fiction > *Novels*
Adventure; Crime; Historical Romance; Medicine; Romance; Romantic Suspense; Romantic Thrillers

How to send: Submittable

Across every romance genre, from historical to contemporary, rom-com to erotica, our compelling, uplifting romances guarantee an instant escape to fantasy worlds, and the heart-warming reassurance of 'happily ever after'. We are proud to publish over 1,300 authors, 700 new titles a year, with manuscripts from 200 authors living in the UK and a further 1,300 worldwide.

P298 MineditionUS
Publishing Imprint
United States

Book Publisher: Astra Publishing House (**P037**)

P299 Minnesota Historical Society Press
Book Publisher
345 Kellogg Blvd. West, Saint Paul, MN 55102-1906
United States
Tel: +1 (651) 259-3205
Fax: +1 (651) 297-1345

https://www.mnhs.org/mnhspress
https://www.facebook.com/Mnhspress
https://twitter.com/MNHSPress
https://www.youtube.com/playlist?list=PLRrmlN6cO7LvpRkbuLYO6paOGLjrKCoXP

Nonfiction > *Nonfiction Books*
American Midwest; Culture; History; Minnesota

Send: Query; Market info; Author bio; Table of Contents; Outline; Writing sample
How to send: Email; Post

Publishes books on the history and culture of America's Upper Midwest. Submit proposal by post including author info, working title, description of the book, table of contents/outline, intended readership, outline of the market and potential competition, the book's length, your schedule for completing it, and 15-25 sample pages. See website for detailed guidelines.

Publishing Imprint: Borealis Books

P300 Minotaur Books
Publishing Imprint
United States

Book Publisher: Macmillan Publishers

P301 Mirror Books
Book Publisher
One Canada Square, Canary Wharf, London, E14 5AP
United Kingdom

submissions@mirrorbooks.co.uk

https://mirrorbooks.co.uk

Nonfiction > *Nonfiction Books*
Celebrity; Crime; Memoir; Nostalgia

Send: Query; Outline; Synopsis; Table of Contents; Writing sample; Author bio; Marketing Plan
How to send: Email

Currently accepting submissions with a focus on nonfiction real-life (memoir, crime, nostalgia, personalities and celebrities). Send submissions by email.

P302 Missouri Historical Society Press
Book Publisher
PO Box 775460, St. Louis, MO 63177
United States

https://mohistory.org
https://mohistory.org/publications/submissions

Nonfiction > *Nonfiction Books*
History; St Louis

Send: Query; Full text; Outline
How to send: Word file email attachment

Welcomes book submissions that illuminate the history of the St Louis region and its people in an accessible way for the general public.

Publishing Director: Lauren Mitchell

P303 The MIT Press
Book Publisher
255 Main Street, 9th Floor, Cambridge, MA 02142
United States
Tel: +1 (617) 253-5646

https://mitpress.mit.edu
https://www.facebook.com/mitpress
https://twitter.com/mitpress
https://www.linkedin.com/company/11587565/
https://www.pinterest.com/mitpress/
https://www.instagram.com/mitpress/
https://www.youtube.com/c/TheMITPress

ACADEMIC > **Nonfiction** > *Nonfiction Books*
Arts; Design; Science; Sociology; Technology

University press publishing books and journals at the intersection of science, technology, art, social science, and design.

Acquisitions Editors: Matthew Browne; Susan Buckley; Beth Clevenger; Katie Helke; Victoria Hindley; Justin Kehoe; Philip Laughlin; Marc Lowenthal; Gita Manaktala; Jermey Matthews; Robert Prior; Elizabeth Swayze; Emily Taber; Thomas Weaver

P304 The Monacelli Press
Publishing Imprint
Attn: Acquisitions, 111 Broadway, Suite 301, New York, New York 10006
United States

submissions@monacellipress.com

https://www.phaidon.com/store/the-monacelli-press/

Book Publisher: Phaidon Press

Nonfiction > *Nonfiction Books*
Architecture; Arts; Gardening; Interior Design; Photography

How to send: Post; Email

Will review book proposals in the fields of architecture and landscape architecture, fine and decorative arts, design, and photography.

P305 Moody Publishers
Book Publisher
820 North LaSalle Boulevard, Chicago, IL 60610
United States
Tel: +1 (800) 678-8812

moody.publishers@moody.edu
Submissions@moody.edu

https://www.moodypublishers.com
https://www.instagram.com/moodypublishers/
https://www.facebook.com/moodypublishers/
https://twitter.com/MoodyPublishers
https://www.youtube.com/user/MoodyPro

ADULT > **Nonfiction** > *Nonfiction Books*
Bible Studies; Christian Living; Christianity

CHILDREN'S
  Fiction > *Middle Grade*: Christianity
  Nonfiction > *Nonfiction Books*
    Bible Stories; Bible Studies

TEEN > **Nonfiction** > *Nonfiction Books*
Christian Living; Christianity; Relationships

Send: Query; Author bio; Synopsis; Table of Contents; Outline; Market info; Writing sample
How to send: Email; Through a literary agent; By referral; Conferences

Titles are designed to glorify God in content and style. Titles are selected for publication based upon fit with this goal, quality of writing, and potential for market success. Accepts unsolicited manuscripts, but priority given to submissions sent through a professional literary agent, an author already published by the company, an associate who works for a ministry, or personal contact at a writers' conference.

Publishing Imprints: Lift Every Voice; Northfield Publishing

P306 Mudfog Press
Book Publisher
C/o Arts and Events, Culture and Tourism, P.O Box 99A, Civic Centre, Middlesbrough, TS1 2QQ
United Kingdom

paulinepoethughes@gmail.com

https://www.mudfog.co.uk

Fiction > *Short Fiction Collections*

Poetry > *Poetry Collections*

Send: Writing sample; Synopsis
How to send: Post; Email

Publishes poetry and short fiction by writers in the Tees Valley area. Send query with 15-20 poems or 2-3 stories, or a sample of 10-15 pages for other genres, with synopsis.

P307 Multnomah
Publishing Imprint

Book Publisher: Random House

P308 Murdoch Books Australia
Book Publisher
Sydney
Australia

fridaypitch@allenandunwin.com

https://www.murdochbooks.com

Book Publisher: Allen & Unwin (**P018**)

Nonfiction > *Nonfiction Books*
Family; Food; Health; Houses and Homes; Personal Development; Sustainable Living

Send: Submission Form; Proposal; Synopsis
How to send: Email

We publish commercially appealing and visually outstanding books written by fresh, brave authors and creatives with unique points of view. Our bestselling and award-winning titles span our four pillars: Food, Home, Gift and Life. While we are Australian owned and operated, we are an international publisher, with offices in London, Auckland, as well as Sydney, and an extensive network of international publishing partners including in the US and across more than 20 languages.

Book Publisher: Murdoch Books UK Ltd

P309 The Mysterious Press
Publishing Imprint
United States

https://www.mysteriouspress.com
https://penzlerpublishers.com/product-category/mysterious-press/
https://twitter.com/eMysteries
https://www.facebook.com/MysteriousPressCom

Book Publisher: Penzler Publishers (**P345**)

Fiction > *Novels*
  Crime; Mystery

Publishes the very best in crime fiction from around the globe.

P310 NAHB BuilderBooks
Book Publisher
United States
Tel: +1 (800) 888-4741

https://www.builderbooks.com
https://www.facebook.com/NAHBhome

PROFESSIONAL > **Nonfiction** > *Nonfiction Books*: Building / Construction

Publishes education and training products aimed at professionals in the construction industry.

P311 Native Ink Press
Book Publisher
United States

Submissions@nativeinkpress.com

http://nativeinkpress.com
https://www.facebook.com/nativeinkpress
https://twitter.com/NativeInkPress

ADULT > **Nonfiction** > *Nonfiction Books*
General, and in particular: Biography; Cookery; Crafts; Creativity; Environment; Gardening; Memoir; Narrative Essays; Self Help

CHILDREN'S > **Fiction**
Chapter Books; *Early Readers*; *Middle Grade*; *Picture Books*

Send: Query; Author bio; Synopsis; Marketing Plan; Writing sample; Full text
How to send: Email

Publishes nonfiction and children's fiction, including picture books, picture storybooks, easy readers, early chapter books, and middle grade novels. Accepts submissions from US authors only. Send query by email. See website for full guidelines.

P312 NBM Publishing
Book Publisher
160 Broadway, Suite 700 East Wing, New York, NY 10038
United States

tnantier@nbmpub.com

https://nbmpub.com
https://twitter.com/NBMPUB
https://www.facebook.com/NBMGraphicNovels
https://www.instagram.com/nbmgraphicnovels/
https://www.tiktok.com/@nbmgraphicnovels
https://www.youtube.com/@NBMGraphicNovels

Fiction > *Graphic Novels*
General, and in particular: Comedy / Humour; Erotic; Fantasy; Historical Fiction; Literary; Mystery; Science Fiction

Nonfiction > *Graphic Nonfiction*
General, and in particular: Autobiography; Biography; Crime; How To; Journalism

Send: Query; Synopsis; Self-Addressed Stamped Envelope (SASE)
How to send: Email; Post

We are interested in literary fiction, non-fiction and biographies. We are not interested in superheroes or any genre. We have no need for illustrations alone including covers. To submit please send a one-page synopsis of your story which will include any pertinent background and some character development. For the art, please send copies of a few finished pages or pencils for the project or at least of previous work in the same style you plan on using. Please do not at first send a complete finished story as that will only delay an answer greatly. To submit electronically: Send a low-resolution pdf of no more than 10 megs as attachment. You may submit a link to a website as an extra source but not by itself. If sending by mail and you want anything back, including an answer, please include a SASE.

Editor: Terry Nantier

P313 Nell James Publishers
Book Publisher
United Kingdom

info@nelljames.co.uk

https://nelljames.co.uk
https://twitter.com/NJamesPublisher

Nonfiction > *Nonfiction Books*
  Contemporary; Social Issues

Send: Outline; Synopsis; Pitch; Market info; Author bio; Submission Form
How to send: Email

An independent publisher of nonfiction books, bringing awareness to issues in modern society. Download submission form from website and return by email.

Currently closed to fiction and poetry submissions.

P314 New Harbinger Publications
Book Publisher
5720 Shattuck Avenue, Oakland, CA 94609
United States

proposals@newharbinger.com

https://www.newharbinger.com
https://www.facebook.com/NewHarbinger
https://www.instagram.com/newharbinger/
https://twitter.com/NewHarbinger
https://www.linkedin.com/company/new-harbinger-publications/
https://www.youtube.com/newharbinger

ADULT > **Nonfiction** > *Nonfiction Books*
  Health; Mental Health; Psychology; Self Help

PROFESSIONAL > **Nonfiction** > *Nonfiction Books*
  Health; Mental Health; Psychology

Send: Query; Proposal; Market info; Author bio; Writing sample
How to send: Email

Publishes psychology and health self-help books that must be simple and easy to understand, but also complete and authoritative. Most authors for this publisher are therapists or other helping professionals. See website for extensive author guidelines.

P315 New Walk Editions
Book Publisher
c/o Nick Everett, School of English, Leicester University, University Road, Leicester, LE1 7RH
United Kingdom

newwalkmagazine@gmail.com

https://newwalkmagazine.com

Poetry > *Poetry Collections*

Send: Full text; Author bio
How to send: Word file email attachment; Post

A small press specialising in extremely high quality poetry pamphlets. Interested in poetic plurality: equally interested in established and new poets, and a broad church stylistically and thematically. Send 12-24 pages of poems by email or by post.

Editor: Nick Everett

P316 Nightfire
Publishing Imprint
United States

nightfiresubmissions@tor.com

https://us.macmillan.com/tomdohertyassociates/
https://nightfire.moksha.io/publication/nightfire/guidelines

Publishing Imprint: Tor Publishing Group (**P456**)

Fiction > *Novels*
  Dark Fantasy; Horror; Supernatural / Paranormal

Closed to approaches.

Publishes fiction that unsettles and delights, exploring the full range of horror, dark fantasy, and the supernatural.

P317 Nine Arches Press
Book Publisher
Unit 14, Frank Whittle Business Centre, Great Central Way, Rugby, Warwickshire, CV21 3XH
United Kingdom
Tel: +44 (0) 1788 226005

mail@ninearchespress.com

https://ninearchespress.com
https://ninearchespress.submittable.com/submit
https://twitter.com/NineArchesPress

Poetry > *Poetry Collections*

Closed to approaches.

Publishes poetry collections. Accepts submissions during specific submission windows. See website for details.

Magazine: Under the Radar (**M384**)

P318 No Starch Press, Inc.
Book Publisher
329 Primrose Road, #42, Burlingame, CA 94010-4093
United States
Tel: +1 (415) 863-9900
Fax: +1 (415) 863-9950

editors@nostarch.com
support@nostarch.com

https://nostarch.com

ADULT > **Nonfiction** > *Nonfiction Books*
  Arts; Computer Programming; Computer Science; Computers; Design

CHILDREN'S > **Nonfiction** > *Nonfiction Books*
  Arts; Computer Programming; Computer Science; Computers; Design

Send: Query; Outline; Synopsis; Market info; Author bio
How to send: Email

Publishes unique books on computer programming, security, hacking, alternative operating systems, STEM, and LEGO.

P319 Nosy Crow
Book Publisher
The Crow's Nest, 14 Baden Place, Crosby Row, London, SE1 1YW
United Kingdom
Tel: +44 (0) 20 7089 7575

hello@nosycrow.com

https://nosycrow.com
https://www.facebook.com/NosyCrow
https://www.instagram.com/nosycrow/
https://twitter.com/nosycrow
https://www.youtube.com/user/NosyCrow

CHILDREN'S
  Fiction
    Board Books; Chapter Books; Middle Grade; Picture Books
  Nonfiction > *Nonfiction Books*

Closed to approaches.

Publishes child-focused, parent-friendly children's books for ages 0-12. No submissions from white people.

P320 Oak Tree Press
Book Publisher
Suite 309, NSC Campus Mahon, Cork, T12 XY2N
Ireland
Tel: +353 21 230 7021

info@oaktreepress.com

https://oaktreepress.ie

PROFESSIONAL > **Nonfiction** > *Nonfiction Books*: Business

How to send: Online submission system

Publishes books on business, particularly for small business owners and managers.

P321 Oghma Creative Media
Book Publisher
United States

submissions@oghmacreative.net

https://oghmacreative.com

ADULT
  Fiction > *Novels*
    Contemporary Romance; Contemporary; Crime; Diversity; Environment; Fantasy; High / Epic Fantasy; Historical Fiction; Historical Romance; Horror; LGBTQIA; Mainstream; Military; Mystery; Nautical; Police Procedural; Romance; Romantic Comedy; Romantic Thrillers; Science Fiction; Secret Intelligence; Space Opera; Supernatural / Paranormal; Thrillers; Traditional; Westerns

  Nonfiction > *Nonfiction Books*
    Biography; Entertainment; History; Military; Mind, Body, Spirit; Music; TV

CHILDREN'S > *Fiction*
  Chapter Books; Middle Grade; Picture Books
NEW
ADULT > *Fiction* > *Novels*: Contemporary Romance

YOUNG ADULT > *Fiction* > *Novels*

Send: Query; Synopsis; Full text
How to send: Email; Through a literary agent

A traditional publisher reaching out to authors who don't want to take the self-publishing route. Provides a team of editors, designers, and marketers to help bring your work to its finished form. Aims to develop long-term relationships with authors and artists. Closed to submissions between November 1 and April 1.

Currently only accepting submissions from agents and authors who have already published with them.

P322 Oh MG Press
Publishing Imprint
United States

ohmgpress@gmail.com

https://ohmgpress.com
https://www.facebook.com/OhMGPress/
https://x.com/OhMGpress

Book Publisher: MB Media (**P283**)

CHILDREN'S > *Fiction* > *Middle Grade*

Does not want:

> **CHILDREN'S** > *Fiction* > *Middle Grade*
>   Dark Magic; Gender; Science Fiction; Sex; Witchcraft

Send: Full text
How to send: Email

Costs: Offers services that writers have to pay for. Offers manuscript editing services.

Traditional middle grade publisher. No advance. High royalties. Welcomes submissions from authors based in the United States and Canada exclusively. Accepts early middle grade fiction between 16,000 and 30,000 words, and middle grade fiction between 30,000 and 65,000 words. Offers manuscript editing services for a fee.

P323 The Ohio State University Press
Book Publisher
United States
Tel: +1 (773) 702-7000

OSUPInfo@osu.edu

https://ohiostatepress.org

ACADEMIC > **Nonfiction** > *Nonfiction Books*
  19th Century; Central America; Classics / Ancient World; Comic Books; Communication; Creative Nonfiction; Culture; Disabilities; Ethnic Groups; Films; Gender; History; Language; Literature; Media; Medieval; Ohio; Politics; Sexuality; South America; United States

ADULT
  Fiction > *Novels*
  Poetry > *Poetry Collections*

Send: Query; Outline; Table of Contents; Writing sample; Market info; Author bio
How to send: Email attachment

Publishes mainly academic nonfiction, but also has imprints for regional books that are of interest to the citizens of the state of Ohio, primarily about their history, environment, and culture; and creative works, including the winners of the poetry and prose prizes.

Acquisitions Editor: Ana Maria Jimenez-Moreno

Acquisitions Editor / Managing Editor: Tara Cyphers

Associate Editor: Becca Bostock

Editorial Director: Kristen Elias Rowley

Publishing Director: Tony Sanfilippo

P324 Ohio University Press
Book Publisher
Alden Library, Suite 101, 30 Park Place, Athens, OH 45701-2909
United States
Tel: +1 (740) 593-1154

https://www.ohioswallow.com

ACADEMIC > **Nonfiction** > *Nonfiction Books*
  Africa; American History; American Midwest; Anthropology; Appalachia; Art History; Arts; Asia; Central America; Crafts; Environment; Europe; Films; Food; Gender; Health; History; Hobbies; Japan; Journalism; Language; Legal; Literature; Media; Nature; North America; Ohio; Performing Arts; Philosophy; Poetry as a Subject; Politics; Religion; South America; Sport; TV; Theatre; Women; Writing

Send: Query; Table of Contents; Writing sample; Author bio
Don't send: Full text
How to send: Email

Publishes primarily nonfiction. See website for full guidelines.

Editor: Ricky S. Huard

Publishing Imprint: Swallow Press

P325 Old Street Publishing Ltd
Book Publisher
Notaries House, Exeter, EX1 1AJ
United Kingdom

info@oldstreetpublishing.co.uk

http://www.oldstreetpublishing.co.uk
https://twitter.com/oldstpublishing

Fiction > *Novels*

Nonfiction > *Nonfiction Books*

Send: Query; Outline
Don't send: Full text
How to send: Email

Independent British publisher of fiction and nonfiction.

P326 Oldcastle Books Group
Book Publisher
18 Coleswood Road, Harpenden, Hertfordshire, AL5 1EQ
United Kingdom

publicity@oldcastlebooks.com

http://www.oldcastlebooks.co.uk

Fiction > *Novels*

Nonfiction > *Nonfiction Books*

How to send: Through a literary agent

Accepts submissions through literary agents only.

Publishing Imprints: Creative Essentials; Crime & Mystery Club; High Stakes Publishing (**P216**); Kamera Books; No Exit Press; Oldcastle Books; Pocketessentials; Pulp! The Classics

P327 Oneworld Publications
Book Publisher
10 Bloomsbury Street, London, WC1B 3SR
United Kingdom
Tel: +44 (0) 20 7307 8900

submissions@oneworld-publications.com

https://oneworld-publications.com
https://www.facebook.com/oneworldpublications
https://twitter.com/OneworldNews
https://www.instagram.com/oneworldpublications/
https://www.youtube.com/user/oneworldpublications

ADULT
  Fiction in Translation > *Novels*

  Fiction > *Novels*
    General, and in particular: Crime; Thrillers

  Nonfiction
    Gift Books: General
    Nonfiction Books: Anthropology; Arts; Baha'i; Biography; Buddhism; Business; Christianity; Comedy / Humour; Current Affairs; Economics; Feminism; Gender; Health; Hinduism; History; Islam; Judaism; Literature; Memoir; Middle East; Nature; Philosophy; Politics; Popular Psychology; Popular Science; Psychology; Religion; Science; Self Help; Spirituality

CHILDREN'S > **Fiction** > *Novels*

Send: Query; Submission Form
How to send: Email

Not accepting fiction submissions as at May 2022. Hopes this will change in the near future, but has been hoping this since at least 2018. Check website for current status.

Nonfiction authors must be academics and/or experts in their field. Approaches for fiction must provide a clear and concise synopsis, outlining the novel's main themes. See website for full submission guidelines, and forms for fiction and nonfiction, which should be submitted by email.

P328 Ooligan Press
Book Publisher
PO Box 751, Portland, OR 97207
United States
Tel: +1 (503) 725-9748
Fax: +1 (503) 725-3561

ooligan@ooliganpress.pdx.edu
publisher@ooliganpress.pdx.edu

https://www.ooliganpress.com
https://ooliganpress.submittable.com/submit
https://www.facebook.com/ooliganpress/
https://twitter.com/ooliganpress
https://www.instagram.com/ooliganpress
https://www.youtube.com/user/OoliganPress
https://sk.pinterest.com/ooliganpress/_saved/

ADULT
  Fiction > *Novels*: Literary

  Nonfiction > *Nonfiction Books*
    General, and in particular: Publishing; Sustainable Living; Writing

YOUNG ADULT > **Fiction** > *Novels*

Does not want:

> **Nonfiction** > *Nonfiction Books*
> Memoir; Religion; Self Help

Send: Query; Proposal; Writing sample
How to send: Submittable
How not to send: Through a literary agent

A student-run trade press rooted in the Pacific Northwest dedicated to cultivating the next generation of publishing professionals. Prioritizes literary equity and inclusion. Strives to publish culturally relevant titles from local, marginalized voices in order to make literature accessible and redefine who has a place within its pages.

P329 Orenda Books
Book Publisher
16 Carson Road, West Dulwich, London, SE21 8HU
United Kingdom

info@orendabooks.co.uk
submissions@orendabooks.co.uk

https://orendabooks.co.uk
https://twitter.com/orendabooks
https://www.facebook.com/orendabooks
https://www.instagram.com/orendabooks

Fiction in Translation > *Novels*

Fiction
  Novels: Adventure; Comedy / Humour; Crime; Ghost Stories; Historical Fiction; Horror; Legal Thrillers; Literary; Mystery; Political Thrillers; Psychological Thrillers; Romance; Suspense; Thrillers
  Short Fiction Collections: General

Closed to approaches.

Publishes literary fiction and upmarket genre fiction (in particular, crime fiction) only. No nonfiction, screenplays, children's books, or young adult. Send one-page synopsis and full ms (or three-chapter sample) by email.

P330 Otago University Press
Book Publisher
PO Box 56, Dunedin 9054
New Zealand
Tel: +64 3 479 8807

oup.submissions@otago.ac.nz

https://www.otago.ac.nz
https://www.otago.ac.nz/press/index.html

ACADEMIC > **Nonfiction** > *Nonfiction Books*
  Arts; Biography; Contemporary; Creative Nonfiction; History; Literature; Maori; Memoir; Narrative Essays; Nature; Pacific

ADULT > **Poetry** > *Poetry Collections*

Send: Table of Contents; Synopsis; Writing sample; Full text; Proposal; Market info; Author bio

How to send: Email
How not to send: Post

Publishes books of scholarly and cultural significance that enrich society. Produces a range of non-fiction books on New Zealand and the Pacific, focusing on history, Māori/Pacific, natural history, contemporary issues, biography/memoir, essays and creative non-fiction, literature and the arts. Also publishes a small amount of poetry as well as New Zealand's longest-running and leading journal of new writing and art.

Magazine: Landfall (**M215**)

P331 Ouen Press
Book Publisher
United Kingdom

submissions@ouenpress.com

http://www.ouenpress.com
https://www.facebook.com/ouenpress
https://twitter.com/ouenp

Fiction > *Novels*: Contemporary

Nonfiction > *Nonfiction Books*
  Biography; Travel

Send: Query; Outline; Author bio; Writing sample
How to send: Email
How not to send: Post; Email attachment

Seeking to publish well written Contemporary Fiction, Travel Literature, and Biography if edgy! No genre, no children's books, no poetry, no single short stories, no guide books, no recipe books. Response only if interested. If no response after 60 days, assume rejection.

P332 Out-Spoken Press
Book Publisher
United Kingdom

press@outspokenldn.com

https://www.outspokenldn.com
https://out-spoken.submittable.com/submit
https://www.facebook.com/outspokenldn
https://twitter.com/OutSpokenLDN
https://instagram.com/outspokenldn

Poetry > *Poetry Collections*

Closed to approaches.

A London-based independent publisher of poetry and critical writing. Founded in 2015 with the aim of challenging a lack of diversity in publishing, the press was shortlisted for the British Book Awards' Small Publisher of the Year three years running in 2020, 2021 and 2022.

P333 Oxbow Books
Book Publisher
The Wheelhouse, Angel Court, 81 St Clement's Street, Oxford, OX4 1AW
United Kingdom

Tel: +44 (0) 1865 241249
Fax: +44 (0) 1865 794449

bookadmin@Oxbowbooks.com

https://www.oxbowbooks.com
https://www.facebook.com/oxbowbooks
https://www.twitter.com/oxbowbooks
https://www.linkedin.com/company/oxbow-books

ACADEMIC > **Nonfiction** > *Nonfiction Books*
   Archaeology; Classics / Ancient World; Medieval

Publisher of academic books on archaeology, ancient history and medieval studies.

Editor: Richard Purslow

Publishing Imprint: Aris & Phillips

P334 Pacific Press Publishing Association
Book Publisher
1350 North Kings Road, Nampa, ID 83687
United States
Tel: +1 (208) 465-2500
Fax: +1 (208) 465-2531

booksubmissions@pacificpress.com

https://www.pacificpress.com

ADULT > **Nonfiction** > *Nonfiction Books*
   Bible Studies; Biography; Christian Living; Christianity; Church History; Cookery; Health; Parenting; Relationships

CHILDREN'S
   Fiction
      Chapter Books: Christianity
      Middle Grade: Christianity
      Picture Books: Christianity
   Nonfiction
      Chapter Books: Christianity
      Middle Grade: Christianity
      Picture Books: Christianity

Send: Query
How to send: Email
How not to send: Post

Seventh-day Adventist publisher publishing mainly nonfiction, but some fiction especially children's fiction. All titles are religious and Christian and confirm to Seventh-day Adventist beliefs. Send query by email only.

P335 Pan Macmillan Australia
Book Publisher
Australia
Tel: +61 2 92859100

pan.reception@macmillan.com.au

https://www.panmacmillan.com.au

Book Publisher: Pan Macmillan

ADULT
   Fiction > *Novels*
      Contemporary; Crime; Drama; Historical Fiction; Literary; Psychological Suspense; Saga; Thrillers
   Nonfiction > *Nonfiction Books*
      Contemporary; Crime; Health; History; Lifestyle; Memoir; Mind, Body, Spirit; Narrative Nonfiction

CHILDREN'S > **Fiction** > *Middle Grade*

YOUNG ADULT > **Fiction** > *Novels*

Send: Query; Author bio; Market info; Synopsis; Proposal; Writing sample
How to send: Online submission system

Accepts submissions via online submission system.

P336 Parthian Books
Book Publisher
The Old Surgery, Napier Street, Cardigan, SA43 1ED
United Kingdom
Tel: +44 (0) 7890 968246

parthiansubmissions@gmail.com

https://www.parthianbooks.com

Fiction
   Novels: Literary
   Short Fiction: Literary

Nonfiction > *Nonfiction Books*

Poetry > *Poetry Collections*

Closed to approaches.

Publisher of poetry, fiction, and creative nonfiction, of Welsh origin, in the English language. Also publishes English language translations of Welsh language work. Send query with SAE, and (for fiction) a one-page synopsis and first 30 pages, or (for poetry) a sample of 15-20 poems. No email submissions, genre fiction of any kind, or children's / teenage fiction. See website for full submission guidelines.

Author: Richard Owain Roberts

P337 Patrician Press
Book Publisher
Manningtree, Essex
United Kingdom

patricia@patricianpress.com

https://patricianpress.com
https://www.facebook.com/PatricianPress

Fiction
   Novels: General, and in particular: Italy
   Short Fiction Collections: General, and in particular: Italy; Politics
Nonfiction > *Essays*
   General, and in particular: Italy; Politics
Poetry > *Poetry Collections*
   General, and in particular: Italy; Politics

Closed to approaches.

From 2023, the press is no longer publishing any new titles, except for updated editions.

Publishing Imprint: Pudding Press

P338 Pavilion Books
Book Publisher
The News Building, 1 London Bridge St, London, SE1 9GF
United Kingdom
Tel: +44 (0) 20 8741 7070

https://www.pavilionbooks.com
https://www.instagram.com/pavilionbooks/
https://twitter.com/PavilionBooks
https://uk.pinterest.com/pavilionbook

Book Publisher: HarperCollins UK

ADULT > **Nonfiction** > *Illustrated Books*
   Arts; Comedy / Humour; Crafts; Design; Fashion; Food and Drink; Games; Gardening; History; Lifestyle; Popular Culture

CHILDREN'S
   Fiction
      Board Books; Early Readers; Picture Books
   Nonfiction
      Activity Books; Colouring Books

Closed to approaches.

A London-based publisher specialising in illustrated books for the UK and international markets. At the core of the business are specialist lists such as craft, cookery and children's.

Publishing Imprints: Batsford; Collins & Brown; National Trust; Pavilion Children's; Portico

P339 Pavilion Poetry
Publishing Imprint
United Kingdom

reviewslup@liverpool.ac.uk

https://www.liverpooluniversitypress.co.uk/topic/imprints/pavilion-poetry/
https://twitter.com/PavilionPoetry

Book Publisher: Liverpool University Press

Poetry > *Poetry Collections*

Closed to approaches.

Seeks to publish the very best in contemporary poetry. Always international in its reach, it publishes poetry that takes a risk. Whether by new or established and award-winning writers, this is poetry sure to challenge and delight.

P340 Paycock Press
Book Publisher; Magazine Publisher
3819 13th St N, Arlington, VA 22201
United States
Tel: +1 (703) 380-4893

rchrdpeabody9@gmail.com

https://gargoylemagazine.com/books/

Fiction
  Novellas; *Short Fiction Collections*
Poetry > *Poetry Collections*

A very small indie press interested in publishing fiction books in the 100–200 page range. That means manuscripts of 20,000–40,000 words. Shorter is fine, too. For poetry volumes we prefer the standard 64-page book. We're not really interested in most genre fiction or mainstream lit.

Online Magazine: Gargoyle Online (**M161**)

P341 Peepal Tree Press
Book Publisher
17 King's Avenue, Leeds, LS6 1QS
United Kingdom
Tel: +44 (0) 113 245 1703

contact@peepaltreepress.com

https://www.peepaltreepress.com

Fiction > *Short Fiction Collections*
  Black People; Caribbean Diaspora; Caribbean

Nonfiction > *Nonfiction Books*
  Arts; Black People; Caribbean Diaspora; Caribbean; Cultural Criticism; Literary Criticism; Memoir

Poetry > *Poetry Collections*
  Black People; Caribbean Diaspora; Caribbean

Closed to approaches.

Publishes international Caribbean, Black British, and south Asian writing. Submit through online submission system.

P342 Pen & Ink Designs Publishing
Book Publisher; Self Publishing Service; Editorial Service
United Kingdom

https://www.penandinkdesigns.co.uk

ADULT
  Fiction
    Novels: Crime; Historical Fiction; Mystery
    Short Fiction Collections: General

  Nonfiction > *Nonfiction Books*: Self Help

  Poetry > *Poetry Collections*

CHILDREN'S > **Fiction**
  Chapter Books; *Colouring Books*; *Novels*; *Picture Books*; *Short Fiction Collections*
YOUNG ADULT > **Nonfiction** > *Nonfiction Books*: Self Help

Send: Query
How to send: Online contact form

Costs: Offers services that writers have to pay for.

The publisher has been operating since 2012 on a small basis originally by publishing a selection of children's picture books and other short story books. This was followed by the publication of an award winning historical novel and due to a physical move of the business to Wales the company began working with another small independent publisher. Due to the pandemic this publisher had to retire from the business leaving the business to continue under the ownership of the original proprietor. Since then the publisher has become a member of and been accepted as a small independent Welsh Publisher by the CCPW Group (backed by Literature Wales). They have published a small quantity of manuscripts both fiction and non-fiction and offer a variety of services aimed at assisting new and developing writers.

P343 Pen & Sword Books Ltd
Book Publisher
George House, Units 12 & 13, Beevor Street, Off Pontefract Road, Barnsley, South Yorkshire, S71 1HN
United Kingdom
Tel: +44 (0) 1226 734222

editorialoffice@pen-and-sword.co.uk

https://www.pen-and-sword.co.uk

Nonfiction > *Nonfiction Books*
  Local History; Maritime History; Military Aviation; Military History

Send: Query
Don't send: Full text

Publishes across a number of areas including military history, naval and maritime history, aviation, local history, family history, transport, discovery and exploration, collectables and antiques, nostalgia and true crime. In 2017, launched a new lifestyle imprint which publishes books on areas such as health and diet, hobbies and sport, gardening and wildlife and space. Submit proposal using form on website.

Editor: Lisa Hooson

Publishing Imprints: Frontline Books; Leo Cooper; Pen & Sword Aviation; Pen & Sword Maritime; Remember When; Wharncliffe Books; White Owl

P344 Penguin Random House Verlagsgruppe
Book Publisher
Germany

https://www.penguinrandomhouse.de

Book Publisher: Penguin Random House

Book Publisher: Prestel Publishing Ltd (**P362**)

P345 Penzler Publishers
Book Publisher
United States

https://penzlerpublishers.com
https://twitter.com/PenzlerPub
https://www.instagram.com/PenzlerPub/

Fiction > *Novels*
  Mystery; Suspense; Thrillers

An independent publisher of mysteries, thrillers, and suspense.

Publishing Imprints: American Mystery Classics (**P023**); The Mysterious Press (**P309**); Scarlet (**P393**)

P346 Peter Lang
Book Publisher
John Eccles House, Science Park, Robert Robinson Avenue, Littlemore, OX4 4GP
United Kingdom

Publishing@peterlang.com
info@peterlang.com

https://www.peterlang.com
https://www.facebook.com/pages/Peter-Lang-Oxford/260315267419469
https://twitter.com/peterlangoxford
http://peterlangoxford.wordpress.com/

Book Publisher: Peter Lang Group (**P347**)

ACADEMIC > **Nonfiction** > *Nonfiction Books*
  Arts; Communication; Culture; Economics; Education; English; France; Germany; History; Italy; Language; Legal; Management; Media; Philosophy; Politics; Religion; Romania; Science; Slavs; Society; Spain

Send: Query
How to send: Email

Select appropriate editor from website and query by email.

Editor: Na Li

Publishing Director: Lucy Melville

Senior Editors: Tony Mason; Dr Laurel Plapp

P347 Peter Lang Group
Book Publisher
Place de la Gare 12, 1003 Lausanne
Switzerland

https://www.peterlang.com

Book Publisher: Peter Lang (**P346**)

P348 Peter Lang Publishing
Book Publisher
80 Broad St, Fl 5, New York, NY 10004-4145
United States
Tel: +1 (844) 882-0928

editorial@peterlang.com

https://www.peterlang.com
https://www.facebook.com/PeterLangPublishingUSA
https://twitter.com/PeterLangUSA

https://www.instagram.com/peterlangpublishing

ACADEMIC > Nonfiction > *Nonfiction Books*
Arts; Communication; Culture; Economics; Education; English; France; Germany; History; Italy; Language; Legal; Management; Media; Philosophy; Politics; Religion; Romania; Science; Slavs; Society; Spain

Send: Query
How to send: Online submission system

International academic publisher. Submit query via web form.

P349 Peter Owen Publishers
Book Publisher
Somerset House, Strand, London, WC2R 1LA
United Kingdom

books@pushkinpress.com

https://www.peterowen.com
https://twitter.com/PeterOwenPubs
https://www.facebook.com/peter.owen.publishers
https://www.instagram.com/peterowenpublishing

Book Publisher: Pushkin Press

Fiction > *Novels*
International; Literary

Nonfiction > *Nonfiction Books*

Does not want:

> **Nonfiction >** *Nonfiction Books*
> Memoir; Self Help; Spirituality; Sport

Closed to approaches.

Publishes general nonfiction and international literary fiction. No first novels, short stories, poetry, plays, sport, spirituality, self-help, or children's or genre fiction. Accepts query by email only, including cover letter, synopsis, and one or two sample chapters. No submissions by post. Prefers fiction to come from an agent or translator as appropriate.

Editorial Director: Antonia Owen

P350 Peter Pauper Press
Book Publisher
3 International Drive, Suite 310, Rye Brook, NY 10573-7501
United States
Tel: +1 (914) 681-0144
Fax: +1 (914) 681-0389

customerservice@peterpauper.com
orders@peterpauper.com

https://www.peterpauper.com
https://www.facebook.com/pages/Peter-Pauper-Press-Inc/137389080124

https://twitter.com/PeterPauperPres
https://pinterest.com/peterpauperpres/

ADULT > Nonfiction > *Gift Books*
CHILDREN'S > Nonfiction > *Activity Books*

Closed to approaches.

Described as a preeminent gift and stationery publisher.

P351 Phoenix Moirai
Book Publisher
United States

https://whimsillusion.com
https://twitter.com/whimsillusion

ADULT > Fiction
Novellas; Novels; Short Fiction Collections; Short Fiction
CHILDREN'S > Fiction
Chapter Books; Middle Grade
YOUNG ADULT > Fiction
Novellas; Novels; Short Fiction Collections; Short Fiction

How to send: Online submission system
How not to send: Email

Started in 2014 as a graphic design, writing, and video production company, with a goal of growing into a full publisher. They have reached that goal and are currently accepting manuscripts from all writers, including unagented and first-time authors. They also created a forum for writers and readers to come together to be and find beta readers for their works in progress. This is also the platform in which writers submit their manuscripts for publication. No membership to the site is needed or requested to submit. Submissions are open to all genre writers, regardless of social media following or manuscript length. Simply wants to read and publish fresh new voices who may not fit in a simple genre bubble, and writers struggling to find a way to have their voices heard.

P352 Piatkus Books
Publishing Imprint
50 Victoria Embankment, London, EC4Y 0DZ
United Kingdom
Tel: +44 (0) 20 3122 7000

info@littlebrown.co.uk

https://www.littlebrown.co.uk/imprint/piatkus/page/lbbg-imprint-piatkus/
https://business.facebook.com/piatkusfiction/?business_id=873802706096561
https://twitter.com/PiatkusBooks

Publishing Imprint: Little, Brown Book Group

Fiction > *Novels*
Fantasy; Historical Fiction; Popular; Romance; Supernatural / Paranormal; Suspense

Nonfiction > *Nonfiction Books*
Business; Health; Mind, Body, Spirit; Parenting; Personal Development; Popular Psychology; Self Help

How to send: Through a literary agent

No longer accepts unsolicited submissions. Accepts material through a literary agent only.

P353 Picador
Publishing Imprint
United States

Book Publisher: Macmillan Publishers

P354 Piccadilly Press
Publishing Imprint
United Kingdom
Tel: +44 (0) 20 3770 8888

hello@bonnierbooks.co.uk

https://www.bonnierbooks.co.uk/imprints/piccadilly-press/
https://www.instagram.com/piccadilly.press/
https://twitter.com/piccadillypress
https://www.facebook.com/piccadillypressbooks/

CHILDREN'S > Fiction
Chapter Books; Early Readers; Middle Grade

Publishes books primarily for readers aged 5 to 12 years old. Publishes fun, engaging, family-orientated stories in any genre that will capture the imagination of readers and listeners.

P355 Pinata Books
Publishing Imprint
Arte Publico Press, University of Houston, 4902 Gulf Fwy, Bldg 19, Rm100, Houston, TX 77204-2004
United States
Fax: +1 (713) 743-2847

submapp@uh.edu

https://artepublicopress.com/pinata-books/

Book Publisher: Arte Publico Press (**P033**)

CHILDREN'S > Fiction > *Novels*
Central America; Culture; South America
YOUNG ADULT > Fiction > *Novels*
Central America; Culture; South America

Send: Query; Synopsis; Writing sample
How to send: Online submission system

Publishes children's and young adult literature that authentically and realistically portrays themes, characters, and customs unique to US Hispanic culture. Submit via form on website.

P356 Pineapple Press
Publishing Imprint
64 South Main Street, Essex, CT 06426
United States

http://pineapplepress.com
https://www.facebook.com/PineapplePress/

Book Publisher: The Globe Pequot Press (**P184**)

ADULT
  Fiction > *Novels*
    Florida; Folklore, Myths, and Legends
  Nonfiction
    Nonfiction Books: Animals; Arts; Florida; Gardening; History; Nature; Travel
    Reference: Florida

CHILDREN'S
  Fiction > *Novels*: Florida
  Nonfiction > *Nonfiction Books*: Florida

Send: Query; Outline; Table of Contents; Writing sample; Author bio; Market info
How to send: Email; Post

Publishes quality books that educate and entertain while making the real Florida accessible to readers nationwide. Topics include gardening, nature, art, folklore, history, travel, and children's books and fiction that feature the sunshine state.

P357 Plexus Publishing Limited
Book Publisher
United Kingdom

editorialassistant@plexusbooks.com

http://www.plexusbooks.com
https://www.instagram.com/plexusbooks/
https://twitter.com/plexusbooks

Nonfiction > *Illustrated Books*
  Biography; Films; Music; Popular Culture

Publishes illustrated nonfiction books specialising in biography, popular culture, movies and music.

P358 Pluto Press
Book Publisher
New Wing, Somerset House, Strand, London, WC2R 1LA
United Kingdom
Tel: +44 (0) 20 8348 2724

pluto@plutobooks.com
submissions@plutobooks.com

https://www.plutobooks.com

Nonfiction > *Nonfiction Books*
  Africa; Asia; Caribbean; Economics; Environment; Ethnic Groups; Feminism; Gender; History; Middle East; Police; Politics; Science; Sexuality; Socio-Political; Sociology; South America; Technology; United States; Warfare

Send: Query; Proposal; Synopsis; Table of Contents; Market info; Author bio
How to send: Email

An independent, radical publisher of non-fiction books. No poetry collections or novels. Send proposal by email to relevant editor. See website for individual editor subject areas and email addresses.

Associate Editors: Ken Barlow; Anne Beech; Jakob Horstmann

Editorial Director: David Castle

Editors: David Shulman; Neda Tehrani

P359 Pocket Mountains
Book Publisher
The Old Church, Annanside, Moffat, DG10 9HB
United Kingdom
Tel: +44 (0) 1683 221641

https://pocketmountains.com
https://www.facebook.com/Pocket-Mountains-Ltd-107054847745288/
https://twitter.com/pocketmountains
https://www.instagram.com/pocketmountainsltd/

Nonfiction > *Nonfiction Books*
  Adventure; Cycling; Nature; Running; Walking Guides

Publishes accessible and inspiring pocket-sized guidebooks for anyone who likes a bit of an adventure, including cycling, easy walking, wildlife and running guides to various parts of Scotland, England and Wales.

Editors: Robbie Porteous; April Simmons

P360 Polygon
Publishing Imprint
West Newington House, 10 Newington Road, Edinburgh, EH9 1QS
United Kingdom
Tel: +44 (0) 1316 684371

info@birlinn.co.uk

https://birlinn.co.uk/polygon/

Book Publisher: Birlinn Ltd (**P067**)

Fiction > *Novels*
  Book Club Fiction; Commercial; Literary

Nonfiction > *Nonfiction Books*
  Crime; Films; Memoir; Music; Narrative Nonfiction; Nature; Popular Culture; Travel

Poetry > *Poetry Collections*

Send: Query; Synopsis; Writing sample; Author bio
How to send: Email; Online submission system

Publishes literary fiction and poetry, both classic and modern. Send query by email with synopsis and sample material.

P361 Press 53
Book Publisher
560 N. Trade Street, Suite 103, Winston-Salem, NC 27101
United States
Tel: +1 (336) 770-5353

editor@press53.com

https://www.press53.com

Fiction > *Short Fiction Collections*

Poetry > *Poetry Collections*

Publishes collections of poetry and short stories by US-based authors. No novels or book length fiction. Finds authors through its competitions, and through writers being active in the literary community and literary magazines.

Editor: Kevin Morgan Watson

P362 Prestel Publishing Ltd
Book Publisher
First Floor, 15 Adeline Place, London, WC1B 3AJ
United Kingdom
Tel: +44 (0) 20 7323 5004

sales@prestel-uk.co.uk

https://prestelpublishing.penguinrandomhouse.de

Book Publisher: Penguin Random House Verlagsgruppe (**P344**)

Nonfiction > *Nonfiction Books*
  Architecture; Arts; Design; Photography

Send: Proposal
How to send: Email

One of the world's leading publishers in the fields of art, architecture, photography and design. The company has its headquarters in Munich, offices in New York and London, and an international sales network.

P363 Prufrock Press
Publishing Imprint
United States

https://www.routledge.com/go/prufrock-press

Book Publisher: Routledge

ACADEMIC > **Nonfiction** > *Nonfiction Books*
  Arts; Language; Mathematics; Science; Society

CHILDREN'S > **Nonfiction** > *Nonfiction Books*

PROFESSIONAL > **Nonfiction** > *Nonfiction Books*
  Arts; Education; Language; Mathematics; Science; Society

Publisher of professional learning resources, gifted child identification instruments, and curricula designed for gifted students, advanced learners, and twice-exceptional children. Comprehensive line of more than 500 titles across the areas of Language Arts, Math, Science, Social Studies, Children's Nonfiction, and more, Offers teachers and parents exciting, research-based resources for helping gifted, advanced, and special needs learners succeed.

Editor: Misha Kydd

P364 Purdue University Press
Book Publisher
504 Mitch Daniels Blvd., West Lafayette, IN 47907-2058
United States
Tel: +1 (765) 494-2038

pupress@purdue.edu

https://thepress.purdue.edu
https://www.facebook.com/purduepress
https://twitter.com/purduepress

ACADEMIC > **Nonfiction** > *Nonfiction Books*
Agriculture; Animals; Central Europe; Culture; Dementia; Engineering; Environment; Genocide; History; Indiana; Jewish Holocaust; Literature; Politics; Public Health; Science; Technology

ADULT > **Nonfiction** > *Nonfiction Books*
Agriculture; Animals; Central Europe; Culture; Dementia; Engineering; Environment; Genocide; History; Indiana; Jewish Holocaust; Literature; Politics; Public Health; Science; Technology

Send: Query; Author bio; Table of Contents; Proposal; Writing sample
How to send: Email

Dedicated to publishing works for academic and general readers. Welcomes proposals in its core subjects, which should be emailed to the Director.

Editorial Directors: Andrea Gapsch; Justin Race

Publishing Imprint: PuP

P365 Pureplay Press
Book Publisher
United States

info@pureplaypress.com

https://www.pureplaypress.com

Fiction > *Novels*

Nonfiction > *Nonfiction Books*
Cuba; Culture; History; Politics

Poetry > *Poetry Collections*

Send: Query
Don't send: Full text
How to send: Email

Publishes books with Cuban themes, in English and Spanish, and is beginning to publish on other subjects. No unsolicited MSS. Send query of up to 250 words, similar to the book blurb you would expect on the back of a book.

P366 Quadrant Books
Book Publisher
Suite 2, 7 Dyer Street, Cirencester, Gloucestershire, GL7 2PF
United Kingdom
Tel: +44 (0) 20 3290 0920

info@quadrant-books.com

https://www.quadrant-books.com
https://www.tumblr.com/blog/quadrantbooks
https://quadrant-books.blogspot.com/
https://www.linkedin.com/in/quadrant-books-581696217/
https://www.pinterest.co.uk/1512f8253dcb0516b636f64a1af470/_saved/
https://vimeo.com/userquadrantbooks
https://www.facebook.com/QuadrantBooks
https://twitter.com/BooksQuadrant

Fiction > *Novels*

Nonfiction > *Nonfiction Books*

A small independent publishing house based in rural Gloucestershire and dedicated to publishing the best in up-and-coming fiction and non-fiction from talented authors from the UK and overseas.

P367 The Quarto Group, Inc.
Book Publisher
1 Triptych Place 2nd Floor, 185 Park Street, London, SE1 9BL
United Kingdom
Tel: +44 (0) 20 7700 9000

https://www.quarto.com
https://www.instagram.com/quartobooksus
https://www.youtube.com/channel/UCg6_9Q3TbEXRPspas_bqPHw
https://www.pinterest.com/quartoknows
https://www.tiktok.com/@quartobooks

ADULT > **Nonfiction** > *Nonfiction Books*

CHILDREN'S > **Nonfiction** > *Nonfiction Books*

Publisher of illustrated nonfiction books for adults and children.

Publishing Imprints: Book Sales; Bright Press (**P082**); Burgess Lea Press; Cool Springs Press; Epic Ink; Fair Winds Press; Frances Lincoln Children's Books; Happy Yak (**P200**); Harvard Common Press; Iqon Editions; Ivy Kids; Ivy Press; Leaping Hare Press; Lincoln First Editions; Motorbooks; Quarry; Quarto Children's Books; Quarto Publishing; Race Point Publishing; Rock Point Gift & Stationery; Rockport Publishing; SmartLab Toys; Union Books; Voyageur Press; Walter Foster Jr.; Walter Foster Publishing; Wellfleet Press; White Lion Publishing; Wide-Eyed Editions (**P509**); Words & Pictures (**P515**); becker&mayer! books; becker&mayer! kids; small world creations

P368 Quill Driver Books
Publishing Imprint
2006 South Mary Street, Fresno, CA 93721
United States
Tel: +1 (800) 345-4447
Fax: +1 (559) 233-6933

kent@lindenpub.com

https://quilldriverbooks.com

Book Publisher: Linden Publishing

Types: Nonfiction
Subjects: Architecture; Arts; Biography; Business; Comedy / Humour; Crime; Health; Hobbies; Lifestyle; Self Help; Spirituality; Technology; Travel
Markets: Adult

Closed to approaches.

Publishes nonfiction only. Send a book proposal including synopsis; commercial info; author platform; and sample chapters or supporting materials. See website for full guidelines.

Editor: Kent Sorsky

P369 Quirk Books
Book Publisher
215 Church Street, Philadelphia, PA 19106
United States
Tel: +1 (215) 627-3581
Fax: +1 (215) 627-5220

https://www.quirkbooks.com
https://www.facebook.com/QuirkBooks/
https://twitter.com/quirkbooks
https://www.tiktok.com/@quirkbooks
https://www.pinterest.com/quirkbooks
http://www.youtube.com/irreference
https://instagram.com/quirkbooks

ADULT
  Fiction > *Novels*
    General, and in particular: Romance

  Nonfiction > *Nonfiction Books*
    Comedy / Humour; Crafts; Food and Drink; Games; Gardening; History; Horror; LGBTQIA; Parenting; Pets; Popular Culture; Relationships; Sport

CHILDREN'S
  Fiction > *Middle Grade*
  Nonfiction > *Nonfiction Books*

How to send: Through a literary agent

Publishes unconventional books across a broad range of categories. Agents should approach individual editors directly. Unagented submissions should be directed to the unsolicited submissions inbox, which is only open at certain times (see website for current status).

P370 R D Publishers
Book Publisher
Robert D. Reed Publishers, POB 1992,
Bandon, OR 97411,
United States
Tel: +1 (541) 347-9882
Fax: +1 (531) 347-9883

4bobreed@msn.com

https://rdrpublishers.com

Types: Fiction; Nonfiction; Scripts
Formats: Film Scripts; TV Scripts
Subjects: Arts; Comedy / Humour; Commercial; Drama; Entertainment; Fantasy; Lifestyle; Media; Psychology; Romance; Science; Science Fiction
Markets: Adult; Children's; Young Adult

Closed to approaches.

This company is looking for developing authors with a drive and the talent to submit ready manuscripts in for film, television, and print publication. They have a proven track record of success and are willing to work with the right author who has the right ideas for a saleable market.

Authors: Arun Gandhi; Daniel Quinn; Bernie Siegel

P371 Rand McNally
Book Publisher
United States
Tel: +1 (877) 446-4863

tndsupport@randmcnally.com

https://www.randmcnally.com
https://www.randmcnally.com/publishing

ADULT > **Nonfiction** > *Reference*
  Road Atlases; Travel

CHILDREN'S > **Nonfiction** > *Activity Books*: Travel

Publishes road atlases and activity books for children, focusing on travel.

P372 Random House Worlds
Publishing Imprint

Book Publisher: Random House

P373 Ransom Publishing Ltd
Book Publisher
Unit 7, Brocklands Farm, West Meon,
Hampshire, GU32 1JN
United Kingdom
Tel: +44 (0) 1730 829091

ransom@ransom.co.uk

https://www.ransom.co.uk

ADULT
  Fiction > *Short Fiction*: High-Low Literacy
  Nonfiction > *Nonfiction Books*: High-Low Literacy

CHILDREN'S
  Fiction > *Middle Grade*: High-Low Literacy
  Nonfiction > *Nonfiction Books*: High-Low Literacy

YOUNG ADULT
  Fiction > *Short Fiction*: High-Low Literacy
  Nonfiction > *Nonfiction Books*: High-Low Literacy

Send: Author bio
How to send: Email

An independent specialist publisher of high quality, inspirational books that encourage and help children, young adults, and adults to develop their reading skills. Books are intended to have content which is age appropriate and engaging, but reading levels that would normally be appropriate for younger readers. Writers with experience in writing phonics or guided readers, or hi lo readers, may send their CV by email.

Editor: Steve Rickard

P374 Ravenstone
Publishing Imprint
Canada

info@turnstonepress.com

https://www.turnstonepress.com/books/ravenstone.html
https://www.facebook.com/turnstone.press.3
https://twitter.com/turnstonepress
http://www.pinterest.com/turnstonepress/
https://www.instagram.com/turnstone_press/
https://www.youtube.com/user/TurnstonePress
http://www.goodreads.com/user/show/16275125-turnstone-press

Book Publisher: Turnstone Press

Fiction > *Novels*
  Mystery; Noir; Thrillers

Send: Full text
How to send: Online submission system

Publishes literary mysteries, thrillers, noir, speculative fiction, and urban fantasy.

P375 Red Feather
Publishing Imprint
United States

proposals@schifferbooks.com

https://redfeathermbs.com
https://www.facebook.com/REDFeatherMindBodySpirit/
https://www.instagram.com/redfeather.mbs/
https://www.youtube.com/channel/UCbx_ahvb0yoOUgUKhYV5vng
https://twitter.com/RedFeatherMBS

Book Publisher: Schiffer Publishing (**P398**)

Nonfiction > *Nonfiction Books*
  Astrology; Fortune Telling and Divination; Health; Lifestyle; Meditation; Mind, Body, Spirit; Numerology; Palmistry; Psychic Abilities; Spirituality

Send: Pitch; Author bio; Table of Contents; Writing sample
How to send: Email

Seeks to create groundbreaking sacred tools with a purpose that are made with pride, giving honor to the subject matter of each and every project.

P376 Renard Press Ltd
Book Publisher
124 City Road, London, EC1V 2NX
United Kingdom
Tel: +44 (0) 20 8050 2928

info@renardpress.com

https://renardpress.com
https://querymanager.com/query/renardpress
https://twitter.com/renardpress/
https://www.instagram.com/renardpress/
https://www.facebook.com/therenardpress
https://www.pinterest.co.uk/renardpress/

Fiction > *Novels*: Literary

Nonfiction > *Nonfiction Books*: Literary

Poetry > *Poetry Collections*

Scripts > *Theatre Scripts*

Closed to approaches.

We're currently considering both non-fiction and fiction with a literary bent, as well as poetry (collections only) and playscripts. Generally speaking, we're not looking for science-fiction, romance or crime – but if you feel your work is literary and only partially defined by one of these categories, please feel free to send it our way.

P377 Roc Lit 101
Publishing Imprint

Book Publisher: Random House

P378 Rocky Mountain Books
Book Publisher
Canada

don@rmbooks.com

https://rmbooks.com
https://www.facebook.com/rmbooks/

ADULT > **Nonfiction** > *Nonfiction Books*
  Adventure; Arts; Culture; Environment; History; Nature; Outdoor Activities; Photography; Travel; Walking Guides

CHILDREN'S > **Nonfiction** > *Nonfiction Books*
  Adventure; Arts; Culture; Environment; History; Nature; Outdoor Activities; Photography; Travel; Walking Guides

Send: Query
How to send: Email

Established to specialize primarily in guidebooks for hikers, climbers and skiers, this publisher has repositioned itself for the 21st century and now publishes and promotes a dynamic, growing list of provocative, engaging and award-winning books on mountain history, adventure travel, outdoor lifestyle, environmental consciousness, Indigenous culture, and contemporary photography—as well as a growing selection of bestselling books for children.

Editor: Fraser Seely

P379 Rocky Nook
Book Publisher
1010 B Street, Ste 350, San Rafael, CA 94901
United States

editorial@rockynook.com
info@rockynook.com

https://rockynook.com
https://www.facebook.com/rockynookinc/
https://rockynook.com/wp-content/uploads/2017/05/tw-rn.png
https://www.instagram.com/rocky_nook/

Nonfiction > *Nonfiction Books*
  Crafts; Drawing; Graphic Design; Painting; Photography

Send: Author bio; Query; Outline; Writing sample; Market info
How to send: Email

A small, independent publishing company with the goal of helping photographers of all levels improve their skills in capturing those moments that matter. Creates books that help you master the technology, find inspiration, and hone your craft in order to create better pictures. Also now publishing books on drawing, painting, graphic design, crafts, and much more.

P380 Rodale
Publishing Imprint

Book Publisher: Random House

P381 Rose and Crown Books
Publishing Imprint
United Kingdom

submissions@sunpenny.com

https://www.sunpenny.com/imprints

Book Publisher: Sunpenny Publishing (**P435**)

Fiction > *Novels*
  Christian Romance; Inspirational

Send: Author bio; Marketing Plan; Synopsis; Full text
How to send: Email
How not to send: Post

We were the first publishers in the UK to start publishing Christian / Inspirational Romance as a genre. Later, others followed, but we were proud to be the first.

P382 Roseway
Publishing Imprint
2970 Oxford Street, Halifax, NS, B3L 2W4
Canada
Tel: +1 (902) 857-1388

roseway@fernpub.ca

https://fernwoodpublishing.ca/publish/roseway

Book Publisher: Fernwood Publishing (**P164**)

Fiction > *Novels*
  General, and in particular: Politics

Nonfiction > *Nonfiction Books*
  Biography; Creative Nonfiction; Memoir; Politics

Poetry > *Poetry Collections*

Send: Proposal; Author bio; Pitch; Market info; Marketing Plan; Writing sample; Full text
How to send: Email attachment

Publishes works of fiction, creative nonfiction, poetry, memoirs, biographies, and politically infused literary compositions. Publishes primarily for an adult audience but has occasionally published material for younger readers. Through diverse content, aims to spark critical thought and inclusively engage readers.

P383 Round Hall
Publishing Imprint; Magazine Publisher
Spaces, Office 313, 77 Sir John Rogerson's Quay, Block C, Dublin 2, D02YK60
Ireland

https://www.sweetandmaxwell.co.uk/roundhall/

Book Publisher: Thomson Reuters

PROFESSIONAL > **Nonfiction**
  Articles: Legal
  Nonfiction Books: Legal

Send: Query
How to send: Email

Publishes information on Irish law in the form of books, journals, periodicals, looseleaf services, CD-ROMs and online services. Contact by email.

Company Director: Martin McCann
Editor: Pamela Moran

P384 Ruby Fiction
Publishing Imprint
Finsgate, 5-7 Cranwood Street, London, EC1V 9EE
United Kingdom

info@rubyfiction.com
submissions@rubyfiction.com

https://www.rubyfiction.com
https://twitter.com/rubyfiction
https://www.facebook.com/pages/RubyFiction

Book Publisher: Choc Lit (**P108**)

Fiction > *Novels*
  Romance; Thrillers; Women's Fiction

Send: Author bio; Synopsis
How to send: Online submission system

Publishes thrillers, women's fiction and romances without the hero's point of view, between 60,000 and 100,000 words, suitable for a female adult audience.

P385 RYA (Royal Yachting Association)
Book Publisher
RYA House, Ensign Way, Hamble, Southampton, Hampshire, SO31 4YA
United Kingdom
Tel: +44 (0) 23 8060 4100

https://www.rya.org.uk/
https://www.facebook.com/RoyalYachtingAssociation
https://twitter.com/rya
https://www.youtube.com/user/RYA1875
https://www.instagram.com/royalyachtingassociation/
https://www.linkedin.com/company/royal-yachting-association

Nonfiction > *Nonfiction Books*
  Boats; Sailing; Yachts

Publisher of books on boating and sailing.

Editor: Phil Williams-Ellis

P386 Safari Press
Book Publisher
15621 Chemical Lane, Huntington Beach, CA 92649
United States

info@safaripress.com

https://www.safaripress.com
https://www.facebook.com/SafariPress

Nonfiction > *Nonfiction Books*
  Firearms; Hunting

Publisher of big-game hunting, wingshooting, and sporting-firearms books.

P387 Saga Press
Publishing Imprint

Book Publisher: Simon & Schuster Adult Publishing

P388 Saguaro Books, LLC
Book Publisher
16201 E. Keymar Drive, Fountain Hills, AZ 85268
United States
Tel: +1 (480) 372-1362
Fax: +1 (480) 284-4855

mjnickum@saguarobooks.com

https://www.saguarobooks.com

CHILDREN'S > **Fiction** > *Middle Grade*

YOUNG ADULT > Fiction > Novels
Send: Query
How to send: Email

Publishes books for children and young adults aged 10-18, by first-time authors over the age of 18. Send query by email describing your submission in first instance. Exclusive submissions only. No fan fiction or submissions from literary agents.

Editor: Mary Nickum

P389 Salt Publishing
Book Publisher
12 Norwich Road, CROMER, Norfolk, NR27 0AX
United Kingdom

submissions@saltpublishing.com

https://www.saltpublishing.com
https://twitter.com/saltpublishing
https://www.facebook.com/SaltPublishing
https://instagram.com/saltpublishing/

Fiction > Novels
General, and in particular: Comedy / Humour; Dark; Gothic; Northern England

Nonfiction > Nonfiction Books
Climate Science; Creative Writing; Culture; Finance; Health; Narrative Nonfiction; Nature; Northern England; Social Issues

Send: Query; Synopsis; Author bio; Writing sample
How to send: Through a literary agent; Word file email attachment
How not to send: Post

We are particularly interested in dark, uncanny and edgy fiction, comic fiction, eerie novels and Gothic novels. We have an active interest in supporting writers from, and novels about, the North of England. We have a particular interest in narrative non-fiction writing about the natural world. We are also happy to consider life-writing projects, creative writing guides, and works that centre on the North of England. We are also happy to consider introductory or brief polemical works on key issues of the day – for example, ageing, climate change, cultural capital, energy security, health, housing, identity, social mobility, and wealth.

P390 Saqi Books
Book Publisher
Gable House, 18-24 Turnham Green Terrace, London, W4 1QP
United Kingdom
Tel: +44 (0) 20 7221 9347

submissions@saqibooks.com

https://saqibooks.com
http://www.twitter.com/SaqiBooks
https://www.facebook.com/SaqiBooks/
https://www.youtube.com/channel/UCqvwvEp1N5rHauJEmmXq16g
http://instagram.com/saqibooks

ACADEMIC > Nonfiction > Nonfiction Books
Middle East; North Africa

ADULT > Nonfiction > Nonfiction Books
Middle East; North Africa

Send: Query; Synopsis; Table of Contents; Writing sample; Author bio; Market info
How to send: Email

Publisher of books related to the Arab world and the Middle East. See website for full submission guidelines.

Publishing Imprint: Telegram Books

P391 Sasquatch Books
Book Publisher
1904 Third Avenue, Suite 710, Seattle, Washington 98101
United States

editorialdepartment@sasquatchbooks.com

https://sasquatchbooks.com
https://www.facebook.com/SasquatchBooksSeattle/
https://twitter.com/sasquatchbooks
https://www.instagram.com/sasquatchbooks/

Nonfiction > Nonfiction Books
Arts; Business; Family; Food; Gardening; Literature; Nature; Politics; Wine

Send: Query; Proposal; Full text
How to send: Email

Publishes books by the most gifted writers, artists, chefs, naturalists, and thought leaders in the Pacific Northwest and on the West Coast, and brings their talents to a national audience. Welcomes agented and unagented submissions from both debut and experienced writers.

Publishing Imprints: Little Bigfoot; Spruce Books

P392 Scala Arts & Heritage Publishers
Book Publisher
43 Great Ormond Street, London, SW2 5UA
United Kingdom

https://scalapublishers.com

Nonfiction > Illustrated Books
Antiques; Architecture; Arts; History

Specialises in producing illustrated books for museums, galleries, libraries, cathedrals, heritage sites and educational institutions.

P393 Scarlet
Publishing Imprint
United States

https://penzlerpublishers.com/product-category/scarlet/

Book Publisher: Penzler Publishers (**P345**)

Fiction > Novels
Domestic Thriller; Psychological Suspense

Aims to bring audiences fresh voices in psychological suspense and domestic thrillers.

P394 Schiffer Craft
Publishing Imprint
4880 Lower Valley Road, Atglen, PA 19310
United States
Tel: +1 (610) 593-1777
Fax: +1 (610) 593-2002

proposals@schifferbooks.com

https://www.schiffercraft.com
https://www.facebook.com/schiffercraft/
https://www.instagram.com/schiffercraft/

Book Publisher: Schiffer Publishing (**P398**)

Nonfiction > Nonfiction Books: Crafts

Send: Outline; Pitch; Author bio; Table of Contents; Writing sample; Market info
How to send: Email

Publishes to help energize maker and craft communities worldwide. Dedicated to publishing high quality books and kits that inspire, instruct, and educate. Aims to enrich lives through craft.

P395 Schiffer Fashion Press
Publishing Imprint
United States

https://schifferbooks.com/pages/schiffer-imprints

Book Publisher: Schiffer Publishing (**P398**)

Nonfiction > Nonfiction Books: Fashion

An imprint of fashion-related books that provides inspiration, historical reference, and instruction to all areas of the fashion community.

P396 Schiffer Kids
Publishing Imprint
4880 Lower Valley Road, Atglen, PA 19310
United States
Tel: +1 (610) 593-1777
Fax: +1 (610) 593-2002

proposals@schifferbooks.com

https://www.schiffer-kids.com
https://www.facebook.com/schifferkids/
https://twitter.com/schifferkids
https://www.instagram.com/schifferkids/

Book Publisher: Schiffer Publishing (**P398**)

CHILDREN'S
  Fiction
    Activity Books; Board Books; Early Readers; Graphic Novels; Middle Grade; Picture Books
  Nonfiction
    Activity Books; Board Books; Early

Readers; Middle Grade; Picture Books

Send: Query; Outline; Pitch; Author bio; Table of Contents; Writing sample; Market info
How to send: Email

Our mission is to build the knowledge base for SEED and STEAM learning through content that promotes critical thinking, opens up conversations, and ultimately inspires young minds. Our award-winning titles explore concepts such as managing emotions, forming positive relationships, and making informed behavioral decisions. As a platform for the leading voices in social and emotional education, we support the SEED learning process by elevating their voices.

P397 Schiffer Military History
Publishing Imprint
United States

proposals@schifferbooks.com

https://www.schiffermilitary.com
https://schifferbooks.com/pages/schiffer-imprints

Book Publisher: Schiffer Publishing (**P398**)

Nonfiction > *Nonfiction Books*
 Aviation; History; Military

Send: Query; Outline; Pitch; Author bio; Table of Contents; Writing sample; Market info
How to send: Email

Dedicated to publishing definitive books on military and aviation history by the world's leading historians.

P398 Schiffer Publishing
Book Publisher
4880 Lower Valley Road, Atglen, PA 19310
United States
Tel: +1 (610) 593-1777
Fax: +1 (610) 593-2002

proposals@schifferbooks.com

https://schifferbooks.com
https://www.facebook.com/schifferpublishing
https://twitter.com/Schifferbooks
https://www.instagram.com/SchifferPublishing/
https://www.youtube.com/user/SchifferPublishing1
https://schifferpublishing.tumblr.com/
https://pinterest.com/schifferbooks/

Nonfiction > *Nonfiction Books*
 Antiques; Architecture; Arts; Fashion; Health; Lifestyle; Popular Culture; Regional; Transport

Send: Query; Outline; Pitch; Author bio; Table of Contents; Writing sample; Market info
How to send: Email

Focused on creating publications that inspire, educate, and inform inquisitive readers seeking trusted content to enrich their lives and passions.

Publishing Imprints: Cornell Maritime Press (**P123**); Geared Up Publications (**P178**); LW Books (**P276**); Red Feather (**P375**); Schiffer Craft (**P394**); Schiffer Fashion Press (**P395**); Schiffer Kids (**P396**); Schiffer Military History (**P397**); Tidewater Publishers (**P449**); Whitford Press (**P508**)

P399 Scholastic
Book Publisher
557 Broadway, New York, NY 10012
United States

TeachingResources@Scholastic.com

https://www.scholastic.com
https://scholastic.force.com/scholasticfaqs/s/article/How-do-I-submit-a-manuscript-for-teaching-ideas

CHILDREN'S
Fiction
 Chapter Books; *Early Readers*; *Middle Grade*; *Novels*; *Picture Books*
Nonfiction
 Chapter Books; *Early Readers*; *Illustrated Books*; *Middle Grade*
PROFESSIONAL > **Nonfiction** > *Nonfiction Books*: Education

How to send: Through a literary agent

The world's largest publisher and distributor of children's books. Provides professional services, classroom magazines, and produces educational and popular children's media.

Book Publishers: Arthur A. Levine Books; Chicken House Publishing; Scholastic UK (**P400**)

Publishing Imprints: AFK; Cartwheel Books; Graphix; Klutz; Orchard Books; PUSH; Scholastic Audio; Scholastic Focus; Scholastic Inc.; Scholastic Press; Scholastic Reference

P400 Scholastic UK
Book Publisher
Euston House, 1 London Bridge, London, SE1 9BG, WITNEY:, Unit 18F, Thorney Leys Park, Witney, OXON, OX28 4GE, SOUTHAM:, Westfield Road, Southam, Warwickshire, CV47 0RA
United Kingdom
Tel: +44 (0) 800 212281

enquiries@scholastic.co.uk

https://www.scholastic.co.uk
https://www.facebook.com/ScholasticUK
https://twitter.com/scholasticuk
https://instagram.com/scholastic_uk
https://www.pinterest.co.uk/scholasticuk
https://www.youtube.com/user/scholasticfilmsuk

Book Publisher: Scholastic (**P399**)

CHILDREN'S
Fiction
 Board Books; *Chapter Books*; *Early* *Readers*; *Middle Grade*; *Novels*; *Picture Books*
Nonfiction
 Board Books; *Chapter Books*; *Early Readers*; *Middle Grade*; *Nonfiction Books*; *Picture Books*

Publisher of fiction and nonfiction for children, as well as educational material for primary schools.

Book Publisher: Scholastic Children's Books

P401 SCM Press
Publishing Imprint
United Kingdom

https://scmpress.hymnsam.co.uk

Book Publisher: Hymns Ancient & Modern Ltd

Nonfiction > *Nonfiction Books*: Christianity

Publishes books which engage academic theology with the wider church and with society. We release around 40 new books a year across biblical studies, practical theology, ecclesiology and ethics.

P402 Scratching Shed Publishing
Book Publisher; Magazine Publisher
47 Street Lane, Leeds, West Yorkshire, LS8 1AP
United Kingdom
Tel: +44 (0) 0113 225 9797
Fax: +44 (0) 0113 225 2515

admin@scratchingshedpublishing.com

https://www.scratchingshedpublishing.com
https://www.facebook.com/scratching.shed

ADULT
Fiction > *Novels*
 Northern England; Sport

Nonfiction > *Nonfiction Books*
 General, and in particular: Autobiography; Biography; Boxing; Children; Comedy / Humour; Cricket; Current Affairs; Football / Soccer; History; Horse Racing; Local History; Music; Northern England; Performing Arts; Politics; Rugby League; Sport; Travel

CHILDREN'S
Fiction > *Picture Books*: Sport

Poetry > *Poetry Collections*: Comedy / Humour

Send: Query; Author bio; Synopsis; Outline; Market info; Writing sample; Self-Addressed Stamped Envelope (SASE)
How to send: Email; Post

Primary aim is to produce high-quality books inspired by aspects of northern English culture, though in recent years that brief has widened considerably to include several national and

P403 Seaworthy Publications
Book Publisher
6300 N Wickham Road, Unit #130-416,
Melbourne, FL 32940
United States
Tel: +1 (321) 389-2506

queries@seaworthy.com

http://www.seaworthy.com

Nonfiction > *Articles*
  Boats; Sailing

Send: Full text

Nautical book publisher specialising in recreational boating. Send query by email outlining your work and attaching sample table of contents and two or three sample chapters. See website for full submission guidelines.

P404 Sentient Publications
Book Publisher
PO Box 1851, Boulder, CO 80306
United States
Tel: +1 (303) 443-2188

submissions@sentientpublications.com

https://www.sentientpublications.com

Fiction > *Novels*: Literary

Nonfiction > *Nonfiction Books*
  Education; Holistic Health; Spirituality

Send: Query; Author bio; Synopsis; Full text; Writing sample
How to send: Email

We have typically published titles with content related to the areas of holistic health, alternative education, and spirituality. While our primary focus is non-fiction in those genres, we're open to evaluating very well-written literary fiction and other work which may cross over into new territory for us.

P405 Seren Books
Book Publisher
Suite 6, 4 Derwen Road, Bridgend, CF31 1LH
United Kingdom
Tel: +44 (0) 1656 663018

seren@serenbooks.com
poetrysubmissions@serenbooks.com
mickfelton@serenbooks.com

https://www.serenbooks.com
https://www.facebook.com/SerenBooks
http://www.twitter.com/SerenBooks
http://www.pinterest.com/SerenBooks

Fiction
  Novels: Literary
  Short Fiction: Literary

Nonfiction > *Nonfiction Books*
  Arts; Biography; Current Affairs; Drama; History; Literary Criticism; Memoir; Music; Photography; Sport; Travel

Poetry > *Poetry Collections*

Send: Query; Full text; Proposal; Author bio; Synopsis; Outline; Market info
How to send: Email; Post

Publishes fiction, nonfiction, and poetry. Specialises in English-language writing from Wales and aims to bring Welsh culture, art, literature, and politics to a wider audience. Accepts nonfiction submissions by post or by email. Prefers poetry submissions by email, but will accept hard copies. Accepts fiction only from authors with whom there is an existing publishing relationship.

Poetry Editor: Amy Wack

Publisher: Mick Felton

P406 Shipwreckt Books Publishing Company
Book Publisher
153 Franklin Street, Winona, MN 55987
United States

contact@shipwrecktbooks.com

https://shipwrecktbooks.press
https://shipwrecktbooks.submittable.com/submit
https://www.facebook.com/SWBPC/
https://twitter.com/shipwrecktbook/

Fiction
  Novels; *Short Fiction Collections*
Nonfiction
  Essays: General
  Nonfiction Books: General, and in particular: Biography; Family; Memoir
Poetry > *Poetry Collections*

Closed to approaches.

Publishes books and literary magazine. Submit query letter, brief bio, synopsis, and/or writing sample via online submission system.

Print Magazine: Lost Lake Folk Opera Magazine (**M227**)

Publishing Imprints: Lost Lake Folk Art; Rocket Science Press; Up On Big Rock Poetry

P407 Sigma Press
Book Publisher
Stobart House, Pontyclerc, Penybanc Road, Ammanford, Carmarthenshire, SA18 3HP
United Kingdom
Tel: +44 (0) 1269 593100

info@sigmapress.co.uk

https://www.sigmapress.co.uk
https://www.facebook.com/sigmawalkingbooks/
https://twitter.com/Sigma_Press

Nonfiction > *Nonfiction Books*
  Cycling Guides; Regional; Walking Guides

An independent publisher of regional walking and cycling guides and local interest books.

Editors: Jane Evans; Nigel Evans

P408 Siloam
Publishing Imprint
United States

Media Company: Charisma Media

P409 Singing Dragon
Publishing Imprint
Carmelite House, 50 Victoria Embankment, London, EC4Y 0DZ
United Kingdom
Tel: +44 (0) 20 3122 6000

hello@singingdragon.com
proposals@jkp.com

https://uk.singingdragon.com
https://jkp.submittable.com/submit
https://twitter.com/Singing_Dragon_
https://www.facebook.com/SingingDragon
http://instagram.com/singingdragonbooks

Publishing Imprint: Jessica Kingsley Publishers (**P246**)

ADULT > **Nonfiction**
  Graphic Nonfiction: Alternative Health; Health; Wellbeing
  Nonfiction Books: Alternative Health; Aromatherapy; Ayurveda; Childbirth; Chinese Medicine; Culture; Ethnic Groups; Fertility; Health; Herbal Remedies; Lifestyle; Martial Arts; Nutrition; Pregnancy; Qigong; Tai Chi; Taoism / Daoism; Wellbeing; Yoga
CHILDREN'S > **Nonfiction** > *Nonfiction Books*
  Depression; Mental Health; Wellbeing

PROFESSIONAL > **Nonfiction** > *Nonfiction Books*
  Career Development; Health; Medicine

Send: Proposal
How to send: Submittable
How not to send: Post

Publishes authoritative books on complementary and alternative health, Tai Chi, Qigong and ancient wisdom traditions for health, wellbeing, and professional and personal development. Our books are for professionals and general readers. We also publish graphic novels across our subject areas, and books for children on issues such as bereavement, depression and anger.

P410 Sinister Stoat Press
Publishing Imprint
United States

https://www.weaselpress.com/sinisterstoatpress

https://www.facebook.com/sinisterstoat
https://twitter.com/sinisterstoat

Fiction
Chapbooks: Dark Fantasy; Furries; Ghost Stories; Horror; LGBTQIA; Psychological Horror; Science Fiction; Sex; Supernatural / Paranormal Horror; Vampires; Werewolves
Novellas: Dark Fantasy; Furries; Ghost Stories; Horror; LGBTQIA; Psychological Horror; Science Fiction; Sex; Supernatural / Paranormal Horror; Vampires; Werewolves
Novels: Dark Fantasy; Furries; Ghost Stories; Horror; LGBTQIA; Psychological Horror; Science Fiction; Sex; Supernatural / Paranormal Horror; Vampires; Werewolves
Short Fiction Collections: Dark Fantasy; Furries; Ghost Stories; Horror; LGBTQIA; Psychological Horror; Science Fiction; Sex; Supernatural / Paranormal Horror; Vampires; Werewolves

Closed to approaches.

Horror publisher publishing Furry works, Queer Horror, Extreme Horror, Splatter Punk, Slashers, Paranormal Horror, Weird Horror, Vampires, Werewolves, Monsters, Cryptids (within reason), Sci-Fi horror, and Dark Fantasy. Only accepting work from Authors of Color, Authors who Identify as LGBTQ+, Authors with Disabilities, and Current and Former Sex Workers.

P411 Slope Editions
Book Publisher
United States

https://www.slopeeditions.org
https://twitter.com/SlopeEditions
http://slopeeditions.tumblr.com/
http://instagram.com/slopeeditions
https://www.facebook.com/slopeeditions

Poetry
Chapbooks; *Poetry Collections*

Aims to present readers with a fine and eclectic array of poetry being written in English today. Releases each year one to two well-chosen and stylistically diverse softcover, perfect-bound books and chapbooks that defy convention and categorization.

Editor-in-Chief: Ethan Paquin

P412 SmashBear Publishing
Book Publisher
Office 6945, London, W1A 6US
United Kingdom

info@smashbearpublishing.co.uk

https://www.smashbearpublishing.com
https://www.linkedin.com/company/smashbearpublishing
https://www.facebook.com/smashbearpublishing
https://x.com/SmashBearPH
https://www.instagram.com/smashbearpublishing/

Fiction > *Novels*
Fantasy; Horror; Science Fiction; Supernatural / Paranormal Romance; Urban Fantasy

We specialise in urban fantasy, fantasy, and paranormal romance but will also consider horror and Sci-Fi.

P413 Smokestack Books
Book Publisher
School Farm, Nether Silton, Thirsk, North Yorkshire, YO7 2JZ
United Kingdom
Tel: +44 (0) 1765 658917

info@smokestack-books.co.uk

https://smokestack-books.co.uk

Poetry > *Poetry Collections*

Closed to approaches.

Publishes poetry which is unconventional, unfashionable, radical or left-field. No fiction, short-stories, drama, nonfiction, or books for children.

Editor: Andy Croft

P414 Society for Promoting Christian Knowledge (SPCK)
Book Publisher
The Record Hall, 16-16A Baldwins Gardens, London
United Kingdom

contact@spck.org.uk

https://spckpublishing.co.uk
https://www.facebook.com/pages/SPCK-Publishing/205059496214486
https://www.instagram.com/spck_publishing/
https://twitter.com/SPCKPublishing

ADULT
Fiction > *Novels*: Christianity

Nonfiction > *Nonfiction Books*
Arts; Bible Studies; Biography; Christian Living; Christianity; Culture; Family; Health; History; Meditation; Personal Development; Relationships; Society; Spirituality

CHILDREN'S > **Fiction** > *Picture Books*: Christianity

Send: Query; Table of Contents; Outline; Market info
How to send: Online submission system

A recognised market-leader in the areas of Theology and Christian Spirituality. Nearly all books are commissioned so rarely accepts unsolicited projects for publication.

P415 Society of Genealogists
Book Publisher
40 Wharf Road, London, N1 7GS
United Kingdom
Tel: +44 (0) 20 7251 8799

hello@sog.org.uk

https://www.sog.org.uk
https://facebook.com/societyofgenealogists
https://twitter.com/soggenealogist
https://www.pinterest.co.uk/societyofgeneal/

Nonfiction > *Nonfiction Books*
Genealogy; History

Publishes a wide variety of family history and genealogy publications.

P416 Soho Crime
Publishing Imprint
United States

Book Publisher: Soho Press (**P417**)

P417 Soho Press
Book Publisher
United States

https://sohopress.com
https://twitter.com/soho_press
https://www.facebook.com/SohoPress

ADULT > **Fiction** > *Novels*
Crime; Literary

YOUNG ADULT > **Fiction** > *Novels*

An independent book publisher based in Manhattan. Founded in 1986, Soho publishes 80-100 books a year across its imprints, and is known for introducing bold literary voices, award-winning crime fiction, and ground-breaking young adult fiction.

Publishing Imprints: Hell's Hundred (*P213*); Soho Crime (*P416*); Soho Teen (*P418*)

P418 Soho Teen
Publishing Imprint
United States

Book Publisher: Soho Press (**P417**)

P419 Sparsile Books
Book Publisher
United Kingdom
Tel: +44 (0) 7938 864485

enquiries@sparsilebooks.com
Submissions@sparsilebooks.com

https://www.sparsilebooks.com
https://www.facebook.com/sparsilebooks/
https://twitter.com/SparsileBooks
https://www.instagram.com/sparsile_books_ltd/

Fiction > *Novels*
Contemporary; Crime; Historical Fiction; Literary; Scotland; Thrillers

Nonfiction > *Nonfiction Books*
General, and in particular: Scotland

Send: Query; Synopsis; Writing sample; Market info; Author bio
How to send: Email

A small boutique publisher, specializing in literary fiction and high quality non-fiction. We have an old-fashioned approach, which sees publishing in terms of an art. We have undertaken only to publish original and beautifully-crafted works with attention to historical detail and the poetry of language.

P420 Spout Press
Book Publisher
PO Box 581067, Minneapolis, MN 55458-1067
United States

spoutpress@gmail.com

https://www.spoutpress.org

Fiction
  Novels: Contemporary; Experimental; Literary
  Short Fiction Collections: Contemporary; Experimental; Literary
Poetry > *Poetry Collections*
  Contemporary; Experimental; Literary

Closed to approaches.

A small, all-volunteer, non-profit literary publisher. Publishes and promotes the finest in contemporary experimental writing — mentoring young writers and bringing new and/or under-appreciated voices to the attention of a larger audience. This is accomplished through the publishing of books and the production of live events within the community. Both strive to combine artistic genres to facilitate dialogue between the film, music, visual art, and literary communities creating synergy that expands possibilities for both artists and audiences.

P421 SRL Publishing
Book Publisher
Office 47396, PO Box 6945, London, W1A 6US
United Kingdom

admin@srlpublishing.co.uk
submissions@srlpublishing.co.uk

https://srlpublishing.co.uk
https://www.facebook.com/srlpublishing
https://www.instagram.com/srlpublishing
https://twitter.com/srlpublishing
https://www.tiktok.com/@srlpublishing
https://www.threads.net/@srlpublishing
https://www.linkedin.com/company/srlpublishing

Fiction > *Novels*

Nonfiction > *Nonfiction Books*

Does not want:

> **Fiction** > *Novels*
>   Erotic; Religion
> **Nonfiction** > *Nonfiction Books*
>   Religion; Self Help

Send: Query; Author bio; Synopsis; Full text; Pitch
How to send: Word file email attachment

We don't care about your colour; we care about your words.

Writers will never be asked their sexuality, race, or religion – only if the author wishes to disclose, and we will never use this information to generate sales. We advise anyone who is thinking of submitting their work to us, to not put their race in the subject heading. We view all submissions as equal and will not prioritise any submissions from certain minority groups.

We love stories – fiction or non-fiction. We will consider most genres, topics, or formats.

No graphic or eroticised incest/rape; necrophilia; paedophilia; bestiality; erotica, fetishes or porn; or anything that encourages violence, hate, or racism. No poetry, self-help titles, short story collections, anthologies, or faith-based books. No AI-generated submissions in any form. These include works that are written or co-written by AI technology.

P422 St Martin's Press
Publishing Imprint
United States

Book Publisher: Macmillan Publishers

P423 St. Martin's Essentials
Publishing Imprint
United States

Book Publisher: Macmillan Publishers

P424 St. Martin's Griffin
Publishing Imprint
United States

Book Publisher: Macmillan Publishers

P425 St. Martin's Publishing Group
Publishing Imprint
United States

Book Publisher: Macmillan Publishers

P426 Stainer & Bell Ltd
Book Publisher
Victoria House, 23 Gruneisen Road, London, England, N3 1DZ
United Kingdom
Tel: +44 (0) 20 8343 3303

post@stainer.co.uk

https://stainer.co.uk

Nonfiction > *Nonfiction Books*: Music

An independent music publisher with a catalogue of choral, orchestral, vocal and instrumental music representing the highest achievements of British composers from the sixteenth century to the present, an extensive list of contemporary hymnody and religious song, and a range of collected editions.

P427 Stanford University Press
Book Publisher
485 Broadway, First Floor, Redwood City CA 94063-8460
United States
Tel: +1 (650) 723-9434

https://www.sup.org
http://www.facebook.com/stanforduniversitypress
http://www.twitter.com/stanfordpress
https://www.youtube.com/channel/UCmd8xj7yu0WGeLRqL39UjLA
http://instagram.com/stanfordupress

ACADEMIC > **Nonfiction** > *Nonfiction Books*
  Anthropology; Asia; Business; History; Judaism; Legal; Literature; Media; Middle East; Philosophy; Politics; Religion; Sociology; South America

Send: Query; Proposal; Author bio; Table of Contents
How to send: Email; Post

Submit proposals by post, or see website for list of editors and submit proposal to the appropriate editor by email.

P428 Steerforth Press
Book Publisher
31 Hanover Street, Suite 1, Lebanon, NH 03766
United States
Tel: +1 (603) 643-4787

submissions@steerforth.com
info@steerforth.com

https://steerforth.com
https://twitter.com/SteerforthPress
https://www.instagram.com/steerforthpress/
https://www.facebook.com/steerforthpress

Nonfiction > *Nonfiction Books*
  Crime; History; Investigative Journalism; Literary Journalism; Narrative Nonfiction

Send: Query; Proposal
Don't send: Full text
How to send: Email

Exclusively considering works of narrative nonfiction, such as investigative or literary journalism, true crime and history for a general audience.

Fiction Editor / Poetry Editor: Roland Pease

Publishing Imprints: For Beginners; Playboy Press; Zoland Books; Zoland Poetry

P429 Steward House Publishers
Book Publisher
2307 Steamboat Lp E #202, Port Orchard, WA 98366
United States

query@stewardhouse.com
submissions@stewardhouse.com

https://www.stewardhouse.com

Fiction > *Novels*

Nonfiction > *Nonfiction Books*

Send: Full text; Query; Synopsis; Writing sample
How to send: Email attachment

Generally publishes works between 15,000 and 150,000 words in length, and is open to a variety of genres, both fiction and non-fiction, if the writing shows skill and care with words. Not accepting book proposals: only finished manuscripts will be considered for publication. All submissions must contain either a full manuscript (preferred) or a partial manuscript that includes at least three sample chapters, a cover letter, and a synopsis of the whole manuscript.

P430 Stewed Rhubarb Press
Book Publisher
United Kingdom

https://stewedrhubarb.org

Poetry > *Poetry Collections*

Closed to approaches.

A small independent Scottish press with its roots in Edinburgh. We are an inclusive, friendly press that champions new and diverse poetry written across a wide range of styles, always with a strong (but not exclusive!) interest in spoken word performance. Poetry pamphlets are our mainstay.

P431 Stipes Publishing
Book Publisher
204 W. University Avenue, Champaign, IL 61820
United States
Tel: +1 (217) 356-8391
Fax: +1 (217) 356-5753

stipes01@sbcglobal.net

https://stipes.com

ACADEMIC > **Nonfiction** > *Nonfiction Books*
  Agriculture; American Literature; Anatomy; Architecture; Arts; Audio Visual Technology; Building / Construction; Business Law; Chemistry; Classics / Ancient World; Computer Science; Creativity; Economics; Engineering; Environment; French; Health; Journalism; Mathematics; Music; Physics; Physiology; Police; Science; Sociology; Spanish

A trusted source for quality educational materials at the university, college, community college, and high school levels. Founded in the 1920s, it is a second and third generation family business and one of the few remaining family-owned and operated educational publishers in the United States.

P432 Summit Books
Publishing Imprint

Book Publisher: Simon & Schuster Adult Publishing

P433 Sunbelt Publications, Inc.
Book Publisher
664 Marsat Court, Suite A, Chula Vista, CA 91911
United States
Tel: +1 (619) 258-4911
Fax: +1 (619) 258-4916

info@sunbeltpub.com

https://sunbeltpublications.com
https://www.facebook.com/SunbeltPub/
https://twitter.com/sunbeltpub

ADULT
  Fiction > *Novels*
    California; Southwestern United States; United States

  Nonfiction > *Nonfiction Books*
    Biography; California; Central America; Cookery; Finance; Folklore, Myths, and Legends; Gardening; Health; History; Houses and Homes; Legal; Native Americans; Nature; Science; Self Help; United States

CHILDREN'S > **Nonfiction**
  Colouring Books: California; Nature
  Nonfiction Books: California; Native Americans; Nature
  Picture Books: California; Native Americans; Nature

Publishes and distributes award-winning books, specializing in regional interest for the Pacific Southwest including Baja California.

Editor: Jennifer Redmond

P434 Sunberry Books
Publishing Imprint
United Kingdom

submissions@sunpenny.com

https://www.sunpenny.com/imprints/

Book Publisher: Sunpenny Publishing (**P435**)

CHILDREN'S > **Fiction** > *Novels*

YOUNG ADULT > **Fiction** > *Novels*

Send: Author bio; Marketing Plan; Synopsis; Full text
How to send: Email
How not to send: Post

Imprint set up for children's books and YA (Young Adults).

P435 Sunpenny Publishing
Book Publisher
United Kingdom

submissions@sunpenny.com

https://www.sunpenny.com

ADULT
  Fiction > *Novels*
    General, and in particular: Christian Romance; Christianity; Inspirational; Romance

  Nonfiction > *Nonfiction Books*
    General, and in particular: Boats; Christianity

CHILDREN'S > **Fiction** > *Novels*

TEEN > **Fiction** > *Novels*

Send: Author bio; Marketing Plan; Synopsis; Full text
How to send: Email
How not to send: Post

An independent small publishing house focusing particularly on encouraging and developing new talent in writing – in fiction and non-fiction, and in Christian and romantic works.

We have a soft spot for travel, sailing, adventure, crime/detective, courage and overcoming, self-help, gift books and coffee-table books. We enjoy wit and humour, entertainment, upliftment. Sunpenny promotes beauty and excellence in publishing. Books do not have to be Christian in either topic or nature, but they do have to keep to acceptable value standards.

What we won't even consider: Unless it is suitably within an overall context of "overcoming", we do not accept depressive or self-contemplative styles, 'black comedy', racism, gratuitous sex or violence or foul language, or anything else that does not conform to good mainstream family values (and we get to be the judge!) ... our taste also does not run to the gothic – vampires, werewolves, and the like, or horror generally; nor do we enjoy the crass and the crude, no matter how witty. If it's seedy or seamy, please don't even try. And let's not even go into the futuristic games-type wild fantasy adventure "I have the power!" stuff. Intelligent sci-fi, yes. Silliness, no. Aliens, probably not. And if you have a book that expounds theories/religions such as The Big Bang, Evolution and suchlike – why even waste your time sending it to a Christian publisher? Save yourself the money. :-)

Please visit our web site and read ALL our guidelines carefully before querying.

Authors: Cheryl Cain; Rowland Evans; JS Holloway; Lucy McCarraher; Julie McGowan; Terri Tiffany

Editor: Jo Holloway

Publishing Imprints: Blue Jeans Books (**P073**); Boathooks Books (**P077**); ChristLight Books (**P110**); EPTA Books (**P155**); Engram Books (**P152**); Rose and Crown Books (**P381**); Sunberry Books (**P434**)

P436 Sweet & Maxwell
Publishing Imprint
United Kingdom

https://www.sweetandmaxwell.co.uk

Book Publisher: Thomson Reuters

PROFESSIONAL > **Nonfiction** > *Nonfiction Books*: Legal

Send: Proposal
How to send: Email

Our branded legal business in the UK has over 200 years of heritage in legal publishing and is well-recognised for its commitment to quality in the legal industry, both in the UK and globally. Send proposal by email.

Editorial Manager: Judith Hudson

P437 Sweet Cherry Publishing
Book Publisher
Unit 4U18, The Book Brothers Business Park, Tolwell Road, Leicester, LE4 1BR
United Kingdom
Tel: +44 (0) 1162 536796

submissions@sweetcherrypublishing.com

https://www.sweetcherrypublishing.com
http://www.facebook.com/sweetcherrypublishing
https://twitter.com/sweetcherrypub
https://www.instagram.com/sweetcherrypublishing/

CHILDREN'S > **Fiction**
Board Books; Chapter Books; Middle Grade; Picture Books
YOUNG ADULT > **Fiction** > *Novels*

Send: Query; Writing sample; Synopsis; Author bio
How to send: Email

Publishes picture and board books, chapter books, middle-grade fiction, and young adult fiction. Specialises in sets and series, so unlikely to take on a stand-alone title. Send submissions by email. See website for full submission guidelines.

Editor: Abdul Thadha

P438 Sweetgum Press
Book Publisher
United States

https://sweetgumpress.com

Fiction > *Short Fiction Collections*
American Midwest; Historical Fiction; Missouri

Poetry > *Poetry Collections*
American Midwest; History; Missouri

Closed to approaches.

Publishes book-length works (70-250 pages) by writers from the Midwest, particularly Missouri. The editors look for manuscripts that are unlikely to attract mainstream publishers but are worthy of publication because of one or more qualities, among them originality, authenticity, beauty, regional or historical appeal.

P439 Tailwinds Press
Book Publisher
PO Box 2283, Radio City Station, New York, NY 10101-2283
United States

submissions@tailwindspress.com

http://www.tailwindspress.com

Fiction > *Novels*: Literary

Closed to approaches.

New York City-based independent press specialising in high-quality literary fiction and nonfiction. Send submissions by post or email. See website for full guidelines.

P440 Tall-Lighthouse
Book Publisher
United Kingdom

tall.lighthouse@yahoo.com

https://tall-lighthouse.co.uk
https://www.facebook.com/talllighthousekeeper/

Poetry > *Poetry Collections*

Closed to approaches.

An independent poetry press renowned for publishing exciting new poets.

P441 Taylor & Francis Group
Book Publisher
4 Park Square, Milton Park, Abingdon, OX14 4RN
United Kingdom
Tel: +44 (0) 20 8052 0500

enquiries@taylorandfrancis.com

https://taylorandfrancis.com
https://www.facebook.com/TaylorandFrancisGroup
https://twitter.com/weareandf
https://www.linkedin.com/company/taylor-&-francis-group/

Book Publisher: Informa PLC

ACADEMIC > **Nonfiction** > *Nonfiction Books*
Agriculture; Arts; Biomedical Science; Business; Chemistry; Computer Science; Earth Science; Economics; Education; Engineering; Environment; Finance; Geography; Health; History; Information Science; Language; Legal; Literature; Management; Mathematics; Medicine; Nursing; Philosophy; Physics; Politics; Psychiatry; Psychology; Religion; Science; Sociology; Statistics; Sustainable Living; Technology

PROFESSIONAL > **Nonfiction** > *Nonfiction Books*
Agriculture; Biomedical Science; Business; Chemistry; Computer Science; Earth Science; Economics; Education; Engineering; Environment; Finance; Geography; Health; History; Information Science; Language; Legal; Literature; Management; Mathematics; Medicine; Nursing; Philosophy; Physics; Politics; Psychiatry; Psychology; Religion; Science; Sociology; Statistics; Sustainable Living; Technology

One of the leading research publishers in the world, serving academia and professionals in industry and government.

Book Publishers: Ashgate Publishing Limited; Focal Press; Routledge

Publishing Imprint: Psychology Press

P442 Templar Books
Publishing Imprint
United Kingdom
Tel: +44 (0) 20 3770 8888

hello@bonnierbooks.co.uk

https://www.bonnierbooks.co.uk/childrens-imprints/templar-books/
https://www.instagram.com/templarbooks/
https://twitter.com/templarbooks
https://www.facebook.com/templarbooks/
https://www.tiktok.com/@booksforkidsuk

Book Publisher: Bonnier Books (UK)

CHILDREN'S
Fiction > *Picture Books*

Nonfiction
Board Books; Gift Books; Illustrated Books

From vibrant board and picture books for early readers to beautiful gift and novelty books that capture the imagination of the whole family, has become one of the world's most respected children's imprints, building a reputation for innovation and creativity over nearly forty-five years.

Renowned for its cleverly-conceived concept publishing with an emphasis on paper innovation, stylish design, and contemporary illustration for an international audience, its stories are truly immersive, playful reading experiences that get inside the world of a child.

P443 Ten Speed Graphic
Publishing Imprint

Book Publisher: The Crown Publishing Group (**P131**)

P444 Ten Speed Press
Publishing Imprint
United States

https://crownpublishing.com/archives/imprint/ten-speed-press

Book Publisher: The Crown Publishing Group (**P131**)

Nonfiction > *Illustrated Books*
   Design; Food and Drink; Gardening; Health; Popular Culture

Known for creating beautiful illustrated books with innovative design and award-winning content. Actively seeks out new and established authors who are authorities and tastemakers in the world of food, drink, pop culture, graphic novels, illustration, design, reference, gardening, and health.

Publishing Imprint: Crossing Press

P445 Texas A&M University Press
Book Publisher; Ebook Publisher
John H. Lindsey Building, Lewis Street, College Station, Texas 77843-4354
United States
Tel: +1 (800) 826-8911

tamupressproposals@gmail.com

https://www.tamupress.com
https://twitter.com/TAMUPress
https://www.instagram.com/tamupress
https://www.goodreads.com/user/show/82064706-texas-a-m-university-press

ACADEMIC > **Nonfiction** > *Nonfiction Books*
   African American; Agriculture; American History; Anthropology; Archaeology; Arts; Biography; Cookery; Culture; Environment; Ethnic; Food; Gardening; History; Immigration; Military History; Music; Nature; Political History; Politics; Science; Sport; Texas; Veterinary; Women's Studies

ADULT
   Fiction > *Novels*

   Nonfiction > *Nonfiction Books*
      African American; Agriculture; American History; Anthropology; Archaeology; Arts; Biography; Cookery; Culture; Environment; Food; Gardening; Health; Military History; Music; Nature; Political History; Politics; Science; Sport; Texas; Veterinary

   Poetry > *Poetry Collections*

Send: Query
How to send: Email

Publishes fifty to sixty new titles a year, including both works of science and scholarship and books that educate and entertain the general reader. All books are published simultaneously in print and ebook editions and sold all over the world.

P446 Thames & Hudson Inc.
Book Publisher
500 Fifth Avenue, New York, NY 10110
United States
Tel: +1 (212) 354-3763
Fax: +1 (212) 398-1252

bookinfo@thames.wwnorton.com

https://www.thamesandhudsonusa.com
https://www.instagram.com/thamesandhudsonusa
https://twitter.com/ThamesHudsonUSA
https://www.facebook.com/ThamesandHudsonUSA

Book Publisher: Thames and Hudson Ltd

ADULT > **Nonfiction**
   Nonfiction Books: Anthropology; Antiques; Archaeology; Architecture; Arts; Biography; Business; Classics / Ancient World; Comedy / Humour; Comic Books; Computer and Video Games; Crafts; Design; Drawing; Evolution; Fashion; Food; History; Interior Design; Lifestyle; Literary Criticism; Medicine; Military History; Music; Performing Arts; Philosophy; Photography; Popular Culture; Religion; Science; Spirituality; Sport; TV; Travel
   Reference: General

CHILDREN'S
   Fiction
      Chapter Books; *Early Readers*; *Picture Books*
   Nonfiction
      Activity Books; *Nonfiction Books*; *Picture Books*
YOUNG ADULT > **Nonfiction** > *Nonfiction Books*

Send: Query
Don't send: Full text
How to send: In the body of an email
How not to send: Email attachment

Send proposals up to six pages by email. No attachments or unsolicited mss.

P447 Thinkwell Books, UK
Book Publisher
United Kingdom

https://thinkwellbooks.org

Fiction > *Novels*
   Commercial; Literary; Science Fiction; Warfare

Nonfiction > *Nonfiction Books*
   Politics; Social Issues; Sport

Send: Query; Synopsis; Full text
How to send: Email

We welcome fiction, sport and political/social works that make us sit up and thirst for the next line, the next profound, humorous, emotional, devastating or stupefying glimpse of originality.

Publishing Imprint: Scruff Whan

P448 Thistle Publishing
Book Publisher
London
United Kingdom

info@thistlepublishing.co.uk

http://www.thistlepublishing.co.uk
http://twitter.com/ThistleBooks
https://www.facebook.com/ThistlePublishing/

Fiction > *Novels*

Nonfiction > *Nonfiction Books*

Send: Query; Synopsis; Author bio; Writing sample; Outline
How to send: Email

London-based publisher of quality fiction and nonfiction. Welcomes submissions. For nonfiction, send synopsis, author profile, sample chapter, and brief chapter summaries; for fiction, send synopsis and three sample chapters.

P449 Tidewater Publishers
Publishing Imprint
United States

https://schifferbooks.com/pages/schiffer-imprints

Book Publisher: Schiffer Publishing (**P398**)

ADULT > **Nonfiction** > *Nonfiction Books*
   Chesapeake Bay; History; Lifestyle

CHILDREN'S > **Nonfiction** > *Nonfiction Books*
   Chesapeake Bay; History; Lifestyle

Life and history in the Chesapeake Bay region for children and adults.

P450 Tilbury House Publishers
Publishing Imprint
United States

submissions@sleepingbearpress.com

https://www.tilburyhouse.com

Book Publisher: Cherry Lake Publishing Group (**P106**)

CHILDREN'S
   Fiction
      Board Books; *Early Readers*; *Middle Grade*; *Picture Books*
   Nonfiction
      Board Books; *Early Readers*; *Middle Grade*; *Picture Books*

How to send: Email
How not to send: Post

Publishes a wide range of children's books, including board books, beginning readers, picture books, and middle grade titles. Publishes both fiction and nonfiction. Committed to the principles of diversity, equity, and inclusion, and welcomes stories from diverse authors.

P451 Tiny Owl
Book Publisher
366 Woodstock Road, Oxford, OX2 8AE
United Kingdom

info@tinyowl.co.uk

https://tinyowl.co.uk
https://www.facebook.com/tinyowlpublishing/
https://twitter.com/tinyowl_books
https://www.youtube.com/channel/UCJkMec_cxEVzTf2iUGvk2Pg
https://www.instagram.com/tiny_owl_publishing/

CHILDREN'S > **Fiction** > *Picture Books*

Closed to approaches.

Publisher of picture books for children.

P452 Tippermuir Books
Book Publisher
Perth, Scotland
United Kingdom

https://tippermuirbooks.co.uk
https://www.facebook.com/profile.php?id=100076236727041
https://www.instagram.com/tippermuirbooks/
https://x.com/tippermuirbooks

ADULT
  Fiction > *Novels*
    General, and in particular: Scotland

  Nonfiction > *Nonfiction Books*
    General, and in particular: Scotland

CHILDREN'S > **Fiction**
  Early Readers: General, and in particular: Scotland
  Picture Books: General, and in particular: Scotland

Our mission is to add to the cultural life of Scotland by publishing interesting and worthy books in English and Scots. The company's strength is our smallness (actually, we are not that small anymore) and love of the written word. We publish books that appeal to us and/or we feel are important culturally, socially, and most importantly, because they are great reads.

P453 Toad Hall Editions
Book Publisher; Self Publishing Service; Magazine Publisher
United States

hello@toadhalleditions.ink

https://www.toadhalleditions.ink

https://www.instagram.com/toadhalleditions/

Fiction
  Novels; *Short Fiction Collections*
Nonfiction > *Nonfiction Books*
  Creative Nonfiction; Memoir; Personal Essays

Poetry > *Poetry Collections*

Does not want:

> **Fiction** > *Novels*
>   Fantasy; Historical Fiction; Horror; Mystery; Romance; Science Fiction; Thrillers
>
> **Nonfiction** > *Nonfiction Books*
>   Finance; Motivational Self-Help

Costs: Offers services that writers have to pay for.

Small press publisher that also provides self-publishing services. Publishes 1-3 per year, written by women or gender-diverse people.

Magazine: Kerning (**M211**)

P454 Toon Books
Publishing Imprint
United States

Book Publisher: Astra Publishing House (**P037**)

P455 Tor
Publishing Imprint
United States

https://us.macmillan.com/tomdohertyassociates/
https://www.torforgeblog.com/

Publishing Imprint: Tor Publishing Group (**P456**)

Fiction > *Novels*
  Fantasy; Science Fiction

Closed to approaches.

Particular emphasis on science fiction and fantasy. Open submission policy currently suspended due to COVID-19.

Publishing Imprints: Orb; Tor; Tor/Seven Seas

P456 Tor Publishing Group
Publishing Imprint
120 Broadway, New York, NY 10271
United States

https://us.macmillan.com/torpublishinggroup/
https://www.facebook.com/torbooks
https://twitter.com/torbooks
https://www.youtube.com/user/torforge

Book Publisher: Macmillan Publishers

ADULT > **Fiction** > *Novels*
  Fantasy; Horror; Mystery; Science Fiction; Thrillers

TEEN > **Fiction** > *Novels*
  Fantasy; Science Fiction; Speculative

Publisher of Science Fiction, Fantasy, Horror, Mystery, Thriller and Suspense, and Other Speculative Fiction.

Publishing Imprints: Bramble (*P080*); Forge (**P169**); Nightfire (**P316**); Tor (**P455**); Tor Teen (**P457**); Tor.com Publishing (**P458**)

P457 Tor Teen
Publishing Imprint
United States

torteenpublicity@torteenbooks.com

https://torteen.com
https://www.instagram.com/torteen/
https://twitter.com/torteen
https://www.facebook.com/torteen
http://torteen.tumblr.com/

Publishing Imprint: Tor Publishing Group (**P456**)

TEEN > **Fiction** > *Novels*
  General, and in particular: Fantasy; Science Fiction

YOUNG ADULT > **Fiction** > *Novels*
  General, and in particular: Fantasy; Science Fiction

Launched as an imprint dedicated to publishing quality science fiction, fantasy, and general fiction for young adults.

P458 Tor.com Publishing
Publishing Imprint
United States

https://publishing.tor.com

Publishing Imprint: Tor Publishing Group (**P456**)

Fiction
  Novellas: Fantasy; Science Fiction
  Novels: Fantasy; Science Fiction

An imprint for science fiction and fantasy novellas and novels, a line that provides a home for emerging and established writers to tell focused, engaging stories in exactly the number of words they choose. Most titles are available globally in print and DRM-free ebook format.

P459 Torrey House Press, LLC
Book Publisher
370 S 300 E, Suite 103, Salt Lake City, UT 84111
United States

Gray@TorreyHouse.org

https://www.torreyhouse.org
https://torreyhousepress.submittable.com/submit/
https://www.facebook.com/TorreyHousePress/
https://twitter.com/torreyhouse
https://www.instagram.com/torreyhousepress

ADULT
Fiction
Graphic Novels: General
Novels: Contemporary; Fantasy; Futurism; Historical Fiction; Horror; LGBTQIA; Literary; Magical Realism; Mystery; Romance; Science Fiction; Thrillers; Urban
Short Fiction Collections: General

Nonfiction
Essays: General
Nonfiction Books: Creative Nonfiction; Investigative Journalism; Literary Journalism; Memoir
Poetry > *Poetry Collections*

YOUNG ADULT > **Fiction** > *Novels*

How to send: Submittable

Interested in great writing that engages, in a wide variety of ways, with place, the natural world, and/or issues that link the Western United States to the past, present, and future of the ever-changing Earth. Originally founded with a specific focus on the Intermountain West but, over the past thirteen years, has expanded its scope to include literature from the plains to the Pacific. (And yes, that includes Alaska and Hawaii!)

Editors: Kirsten Johanna Allen; Mark Bailey

P460 Torva
Publishing Imprint
United Kingdom

https://www.penguin.co.uk/company/publishers/transworld#Torva

Book Publisher: Transworld Publishers

Nonfiction > *Nonfiction Books*

Imprint for bold ideas that ignite debate. Publishes expert voices who challenge how we live and work, and books that tackle some of the biggest questions about our world, from the birth of the universe to how we have a good life.

Authors: Dawn Butler; Helen Czerski; Hannah Fry; Emma Gannon; Viv Groskop; Jonathan Kennedy; Monty Lyman; Thomas Hertog

P461 Troika Books
Book Publisher
United Kingdom
Tel: +44 (0) 7710 412830

kidglovesbooks@gmail.com

https://www.troikabooks.com
https://twitter.com/TroikaBooks
https://youtube.com/channel/UCmc3CUxge0slDJwLs57WLJw

CHILDREN'S
Fiction
Novels; *Picture Books*
Poetry > *Any Poetic Form*

Closed to approaches.

Publishes picture books, fiction, and poetry for children.

Editor: Martin West

P462 Turner Publishing
Book Publisher
Nashville, TN
United States

submissions@turnerpublishing.com

https://turnerbookstore.com
https://www.facebook.com/turner.publishing/
https://twitter.com/TurnerPub
https://www.pinterest.com/turnerpub
https://www.instagram.com/turnerpub/
https://www.youtube.com/@turnerpublishing3277

ADULT
Fiction > *Novels*
Contemporary Romance; Dystopian Fiction; Fantasy; Historical Fiction; Horror; Literary; Mystery; Romance; Romantasy; Science Fiction; Suspense; Thrillers

Nonfiction > *Nonfiction Books*
Animals; Autobiography; Biography; Business; Cookery; Crafts; Crime; Current Affairs; Drinks; Economics; Entertainment; Family; Genealogy; Health; History; Hobbies; Medicine; Mind, Body, Spirit; Nature; Pets; Politics; Psychology; Relationships; Religion; Science; Travel; Wellbeing

CHILDREN'S
Fiction
Chapter Books; *Comics*; *Graphic Novels*; *Middle Grade*; *Novels*; *Picture Books*
Nonfiction > *Nonfiction Books*

TEEN > **Fiction** > *Novels*

YOUNG ADULT > **Fiction** > *Novels*

Send: Proposal; Full text; Author bio; Outline; Pitch; Market info
How to send: Word file email attachment; PDF file email attachment

An award-winning, independent publisher of books. The company is in the top 101 independent publishing companies in the U.S. as compiled by Bookmarket.com and has been named five times to Publishers Weekly's Fastest Growing Publishers List. Currently accepting submissions of fiction and non-fiction manuscripts. Submissions can be made by agents or authors directly.

Publishing Imprints: Basic Health Publications, Inc. (**P059**); Jewish Lights Publishing

P463 Turtle Press
Book Publisher
United States

https://www.turtlepress.com
https://www.youtube.com/channel/UCQg1AWsmVgRPFTB-CQOVoyQ

Nonfiction > *Nonfiction Books*
Martial Arts; Mind, Body, Spirit; Philosophy

Publisher of books on martial arts.

P464 Two Fine Crows Books
Publishing Imprint
United States

https://twofinecrowsbooks.com
https://saddleroadpress.submittable.com/submit

Book Publisher / Ebook Publisher: Saddle Road Press

Nonfiction > *Nonfiction Books*
Nature; Spirituality

Publishes books of nature and spirit.

P465 Tyndale House Publishers, Inc.
Book Publisher
351 Executive Drive, Carol Stream, IL 60188
United States
Tel: +1 (855) 277-9400
Fax: +1 (866) 622-9474

https://www.tyndale.com
https://facebook.com/TyndaleHouse
https://twitter.com/TyndaleHouse
https://pinterest.com/TyndaleHouse/
https://instagram.com/tyndalehouse/
https://youtube.com/user/TyndaleHP/

ADULT
Fiction > *Novels*
Allegory; Christianity; Contemporary Romance; Contemporary; Historical Fiction; Mystery; Romantic Suspense; Suspense; Thrillers; Westerns

Nonfiction
Nonfiction Books: Archaeology; Arts; Autobiography; Biography; Business; Christian Living; Christianity; Comedy / Humour; Culture; Current Affairs; Education; Finance; Health; History; Judaism; Leadership; Leisure; Memoir; Mental Health; Personal Development; Politics; Sport; Travel
Reference: Christianity

CHILDREN'S
Fiction
Chapbooks: Christianity
Picture Books: Christianity

Nonfiction > *Nonfiction Books*
Christian Living; Christianity

TEEN
Fiction > *Novels*: Christianity

Nonfiction > *Nonfiction Books*
Christian Living; Christianity; Relationships; Sex

How to send: Through a literary agent

Christian publisher, publishing bibles, nonfiction, fiction, and books for kids and teens.

P466 Ugly Duckling Presse
Book Publisher
The Old American Can Factory, 232 Third Street, #E303 (corner Third Avenue), Brooklyn, NY 11215
United States
Tel: +1 (347) 948-5170

office@uglyducklingpresse.org

https://uglyducklingpresse.org

Nonfiction > *Nonfiction Books*: Experimental

Poetry in Translation > *Poetry Collections*

Poetry > *Poetry Collections*

Closed to approaches.

Nonprofit publisher of poetry, translation, experimental nonfiction, performance texts, and books by artists. Check website for specific calls for submissions.

Print Magazine: Second Factory (**M328**)

P467 Ulverscroft Ltd
Book Publisher
The Green, Bradgate Road, Anstey, Leicester, LE7 7FU
United Kingdom
Tel: +44 (0) 116 236 4325

customersupport@ulverscroft.co.uk

https://www.ulverscroft.com
https://www.facebook.com/Ulverscroft
https://www.instagram.com/ulverscroftltd

Fiction > *Novels*

Nonfiction > *Nonfiction Books*

Publishes a wide variety of large print titles in hard and soft cover formats, as well as abridged and unabridged audio books. Many titles are written by the world's favourite authors.

Editor: Mark Merrill

P468 Unbound Press
Book Publisher
20 St Thomas Street, London, SE1 9RS
United Kingdom

support@unbound.com

https://unbound.com
https://facebook.com/unbound
https://twitter.com/unbounders
https://instagram.com/unbounders

Fiction > *Novels*

Nonfiction > *Nonfiction Books*

Send: Full text

Crowdfunding publisher. Submit manuscripts via form on website.

P469 Unicorn
Publishing Imprint
United Kingdom

https://www.unicornpublishing.org/page/about/

Book Publisher: Unicorn Publishing Group (**P470**)

Nonfiction > *Nonfiction Books*
Cultural History; Visual Arts

Send: Query
How to send: Email

We are always looking for new and exciting projects relating to the visual arts and cultural history. Email the chairman in the first instance.

Chair: Ian Macpherson

P470 Unicorn Publishing Group
Book Publisher
Charleston Studio, Meadow Business Centre, Ringmer, Lewes, East Sussex, BN8 5RW
United Kingdom
Tel: +44 (0) 1273 812066

ian@unicornpublishing.org

https://www.unicornpublishing.org
https://www.facebook.com/UnicornPressLtd/
https://www.linkedin.com/company/unicorn-publishing-group/
https://twitter.com/UnicornPubGroup/
https://www.instagram.com/UnicornPubGroup/

Fiction > *Novels*: Historical Fiction

Nonfiction > *Nonfiction Books*
Cultural History; Health; Military History; Philosophy; Visual Arts

How to send: Email; Post

Publishes books on the visual arts and cultural history, military history, and historical fiction, through four separate imprints. Approach by email or by post.

Chair: Ian Macpherson

Publishing Director: Lucy Duckworth

Publishing Imprints: Unicorn (**P469**); Uniform (**P471**); Unify (**P472**); Universe (**P474**)

P471 Uniform
Publishing Imprint
United Kingdom

https://www.unicornpublishing.org/page/about/

Book Publisher: Unicorn Publishing Group (**P470**)

Nonfiction > *Nonfiction Books*: Military History

P472 Unify
Publishing Imprint
United Kingdom

https://www.unicornpublishing.org/page/about/

Book Publisher: Unicorn Publishing Group (**P470**)

Nonfiction > *Nonfiction Books*
Health; Philosophy

Imprint publishing health and philosophy titles.

P473 Unity
Book Publisher
1901 NW Blue Parkway, Unity Village, MO 64065--0001
United States
Tel: +1 (816) 524-3550

unitycustomerservice@unityonline.org

https://www.unity.org

Nonfiction > *Nonfiction Books*
Health; Lifestyle; Philosophy; Relationships; Self Help; Spirituality

Publisher of books on Spirituality, New Thought, personal growth, spiritual leadership, mind-body-spirit, and spiritual self-help.

P474 Universe
Publishing Imprint
United Kingdom

https://www.unicornpublishing.org/page/about/

Book Publisher: Unicorn Publishing Group (**P470**)

Fiction > *Novels*: Historical Fiction

P475 The University of Akron Press
Book Publisher
185 E. Mill St., University of Akron, Akron, OH 44325-1703
United States

uapress@uakron.edu

https://www.uakron.edu/uapress/
https://theuniversityofakronpress.submittable.com/submit

ACADEMIC > **Nonfiction** > *Nonfiction Books*
Culture; History; Ohio; Poetry as a Subject; Politics; Psychology

ADULT
Nonfiction > *Nonfiction Books*
Cookery; Culture; Food; History; Ohio; Sport

Poetry > *Poetry Collections*

Send: Query; Submission Form
Don't send: Full text
How to send: Submittable; Post; Email

For nonfiction, download and complete form on website, or submit through online submission system. Also publishes books of poetry, mainly through its annual competition.

P476 University of Alaska Press

Book Publisher
Editorial Department, University of Alaska Press, PO Box 756240, 104 Eielson Building, Fairbanks, AK 99775-6240
United States
Tel: +1 (720) 406-8849
Fax: +1 (720) 406-3443

https://upcolorado.com/university-of-alaska-press

ACADEMIC > **Nonfiction** > *Nonfiction Books*
Alaska; Biography; Culture; History; Language; Memoir; Nature; Politics; Science

ADULT
Fiction > *Short Fiction Collections*: Alaska

Poetry > *Poetry Collections*: Alaska

Send: Query; Proposal
How to send: Online submission system

Publishing books on politics and history, Native languages and cultures, science and natural history, biography and memoir, poetry, fiction and anthologies, and original translations, all with an emphasis on the state of Alaska.

P477 University of Alberta Press

Book Publisher
1-16 Rutherford Library South, 11204 89 Avenue NW, Edmonton, AB, T6G 2J4
Canada
Tel: +1 (780) 492-3662

https://ualbertapress.ca
https://ualbertapress.submittable.com/submit
https://www.facebook.com/UAlbertaPress
https://x.com/UAlbertaPress
https://www.instagram.com/ualbertapress/

ACADEMIC > **Nonfiction** > *Nonfiction Books*
Activism; Africa; Alberta; Animals; Anthropology; Arts; Asia; Australasia / Oceania; Canada; City and Town Planning; Climate Science; Crime; Culture; Design; Disabilities; Education; Environment; Ethnic Groups; Europe; Films; Food; Gender; Geography; Health; History; Immigration; LGBTQIA; Language; Legal; Literary Criticism; Literature; Medicine; Middle East; Native Americans; Nature; Performing Arts; Philosophy; Politics; Psychology; Racism; Refugees; Religion; Science; Sexuality; Society; Sociology; Sport; TV; Technology; Urban

ADULT
Fiction > *Short Fiction Collections*

Nonfiction > *Nonfiction Books*
Autobiography; Literary; Memoir; Travel

Poetry > *Poetry Collections*

Send: Query; Proposal; Full text
How to send: Submittable

A contemporary, award-winning publisher of scholarly and creative books distinguished by their editorial care, exceptional design, and global reach. We publish scholarly work by established and emerging authors in the Humanities and Social Sciences, as well as works of poetry and literary nonfiction. We actively work to diversify our publishing program, and welcome submissions by authors from diverse and marginalized backgrounds.

P478 University of California Press

Book Publisher
United States

krobinson@ucpress.edu

https://www.ucpress.edu
https://twitter.com/ucpress
https://www.facebook.com/ucpress
https://www.instagram.com/uc_press/
https://www.youtube.com/channel/UCX5V8BHO32jgshduh7nbR8Q
https://www.linkedin.com/company/university-of-california-press

ACADEMIC > **Nonfiction** > *Nonfiction Books*
Africa; Anthropology; Arts; Asia; Classics / Ancient World; Crime; Economics; Environment; Films; Food; Gender; Geography; Health; History; Language; Legal; Literature; Media; Middle East; Music; Philosophy; Politics; Religion; Science; Sexuality; Sociology; South America; Technology; United States; Wine

Scholarly publisher based in California.

Acquisitions Editors: Naja Pulliam Collins; Niels Hooper; LeKeisha Hughes; Chloe Layman; Michelle Lipinski; Kate Marshall; Enrique Ochoa-Kaup; Raina Polivka; Maura Roessner; Eric A. Schmidt; Naomi Schneider

Editorial Director: Kim Robinson

P479 University of Georgia Press

Book Publisher
Main Library, Third Floor, 320 South Jackson Street, Athens, GA 30602
United States

books@uga.edu

https://ugapress.org
https://www.facebook.com/UGAPress
https://twitter.com/UGAPress
https://www.instagram.com/ugapress/
https://www.goodreads.com/user/show/23695305-university-of-georgia-press
https://ugapress.wordpress.com/

ACADEMIC > **Nonfiction** > *Nonfiction Books*
African American; American History; American Literature; Current Affairs; Environment; Food; Geography; Georgia (US State); National Security; Nature; US Southern States; United States; Urban

ADULT > **Nonfiction** > *Nonfiction Books*
African American; American History; American Literature; Current Affairs; Environment; Food; Geography; Georgia (US State); National Security; Nature; US Southern States; United States; Urban

Send: Query; Proposal; Author bio; Market info
How to send: Email

Publishes scholarly and general-interest books in the areas indicated. See website for full submission guidelines.

P480 University of Iowa Press

Book Publisher
119 West Park Road, 100 Kuhl House, Iowa City IA 52242-1000
United States
Tel: +1 (319) 335-2000

uipress@uiowa.edu

https://www.uipress.uiowa.edu

ACADEMIC > **Nonfiction** > *Nonfiction Books*
American Midwest; Archaeology; Books; Culture; Food; History; Literature; Nature; Poetry as a Subject; Theatre; Writing

ADULT
Fiction
Novels; *Short Fiction*
Poetry > *Any Poetic Form*

Send: Outline; Market info; Table of Contents; Writing sample; Author bio
How to send: Email; Through a contest

Send proposals for nonfiction by email. Accepts short fiction and poetry through annual competitions only. Also publishes novels.

P481 University of Maine Press

Book Publisher
5729 Fogler Library, Orono, ME 04469-5729
United States
Tel: +1 (207) 581-1643

Betsy.Rose@maine.edu

https://umaine.edu/umpress/

ACADEMIC > **Nonfiction** > *Nonfiction Books*
Arts; Maine; Science

ADULT > **Fiction** > *Novels*: Maine

Closed to approaches.

Publishes scholarly books and original writing in science, the arts and the humanities, focusing on the intellectual concerns of the Maine region. Occasionally publishes regional fiction. Send query by email or by post with SASE between September 1 and October 31.

P482 University of Massachusetts Press

Book Publisher
East Experiment Station, 671 N. Pleasant St,
Amherst, MA 01003
United States
Fax: +1 (413) 545-1226

admin@umpress.umass.edu

https://www.umasspress.com
https://www.facebook.com/umasspress/
https://twitter.com/umasspress

ACADEMIC > **Nonfiction** > *Nonfiction Books*
  19th Century; 20th Century; African American; American Civil War; Anthropology; Architecture; Arts; Autobiography; Biography; Children; Cultural History; Culture; Disabilities; Drama; Education; Environment; Films; Food; Health; History; Journalism; Judaism; LGBTQIA; Legal; Literature; Media; Medicine; Military History; Music; Native Americans; New England; Political History; Popular Culture; Recreation; Religion; Renaissance; Science; Social Class; Sociology; Sport; Technology; United States; Urban

ADULT
  Fiction > *Novels*

  Nonfiction > *Nonfiction Books*
    General, and in particular: Creative Nonfiction

  Poetry > *Poetry Collections*

Focuses primarily on books in the field of American studies, including books that explore the history, politics, literature, culture, and environment of the United States – as well as works with a transnational perspective. In addition to publishing works of scholarship, the Press produces books of more general interest for a wider readership. Also publishes poetry and fiction via its annual competitions only.

Editor-in-Chief: Matt Becker

P483 The University of Michigan Press

Book Publisher
4190 Shapiro Library, 919 S. University Avenue, Ann Arbor, MI 48109-1185
United States
Tel: +1 (734) 764-4388
Fax: +1 (734) 615-1540

http://www.press.umich.edu

ACADEMIC > **Nonfiction**
  Nonfiction Books: Africa; African American; Anthropology; Archaeology; Arts; Asia; Biography; Business; Caribbean; Classics / Ancient World; Cookery; Culture; Dance; Disabilities; Economics; Education; Engineering; Environment; Ethnic Groups; Gender; German; Health; History; Ireland; Islam; Judaism; Language; Legal; Literature; Mathematics; Media; Medicine; Medieval; Memoir; Michigan; Middle East; Music; Native Americans; Nature; Philosophy; Politics; Psychology; Religion; Renaissance; Sexuality; Social Class; Sociology; South America; Sport; Theatre; Travel; United States; Urban; Women's Studies; Writing
  Reference: General

ADULT > **Fiction** > *Novels*

Send query with table of contents, outline of chapters, overview, and CV. Queries should include statements on the rationale of your book, similar and competing books in the field, your target audience, why you think it is right for this list, the length of MS, number of illustrations, and what your anticipated date of completion is. Send queries and proposals by email to specific editor (guidelines on website). See website for particular guidelines relating to fiction and certain series published by the press.

P484 University of Nevada Press

Book Publisher
Mail Stop 0166, Reno, NV 89557-0166
United States

cvickers@unpress.nevada.edu

https://www.unpress.nevada.edu
https://twitter.com/UNVPress
https://www.facebook.com/universityofnevadapress
https://www.instagram.com/universitynevadapress
https://www.linkedin.com/company/74920592/admin/

ACADEMIC > **Nonfiction** > *Nonfiction Books*
  American West; Architecture; Arts; Autobiography; Biography; Business; Drama; Economics; Education; Engineering; Family; Gambling; Games; History; Language; Legal; Literary Criticism; Medicine; Nature; Nevada; Performing Arts; Philosophy; Politics; Psychology; Relationships; Technology; Transport

ADULT
  Fiction
    Novels: American West; Nevada
    Short Fiction Collections: American West; Nevada

  Nonfiction > *Nonfiction Books*
    American West; Cookery; Fitness; Health; Mind, Body, Spirit; Nevada; Recreation; Sport; Travel

  Poetry > *Any Poetic Form*
    American West; Nevada

Send: Outline; Market info; Proposal; Author bio; Table of Contents; Writing sample
How to send: Online submission system

Publishes regionally focused works that contribute to our understanding of Nevada, the Great Basin, and American West. Also publishes scholarly books in the humanities and social sciences in the fields of environmental studies, public health, mining studies, Native American studies, urban studies, Basque studies, and gambling and commercial gaming. The Press publishes select fiction as well. Submit a book proposal, which includes a CV, detailed table of contents, and sample chapter.

Editor: JoAnne Banducci

P485 University of North Texas Press

Book Publisher
1155 Union Circle #311336, Denton, TX 76203-5017
United States
Tel: +1 (940) 565-2142

https://untpress.unt.edu
https://www.facebook.com/UniversityOfNorthTexasPress/
https://twitter.com/untpress/
https://www.pinterest.com/untpress0263/

ACADEMIC > **Nonfiction** > *Nonfiction Books*
  Crime; Culture; Environment; Folklore, Myths, and Legends; Food History; History; Legal; Military History; Multicultural; Music; Nature; Texas; Women's Studies

ADULT
  Fiction > *Short Fiction*
  Poetry > *Any Poetic Form*

Send: Query
How to send: Post; Email
How not to send: Phone

Publishes in the humanities and social sciences, with an emphasis on Texas. Also publishes fiction and poetry through its annual competitions. See website for more details.

P486 University of Pennsylvania Press

Book Publisher
3905 Spruce Street, Philadelphia, PA 19104-4112
United States

custserv@pobox.upenn.edu

https://www.upenn.edu/pennpress

ACADEMIC > Nonfiction > *Nonfiction Books*
African Diaspora; Atlantic; Culture; History; Intellectual History; Judaism; Literary Criticism; Medieval; North America; Political History; Renaissance; South America

Send: Query
How to send: Email

Send query by email to appropriate editor.

Associate Editor: Jenny Tan

Editor-in-Chief: Walter Biggins

Senior Editor: Robert Lockhart

P487 University of Tennessee Press

Book Publisher
Hodges Library 323, 1015 Volunteer Blvd, Knoxville, TN 37996-4108
United States
Tel: +1 (865) 974-3321

utpress@utk.edu

https://utpress.org
https://www.facebook.com/utennpress/
https://twitter.com/utennpress

ACADEMIC > Nonfiction > *Nonfiction Books*
American Civil War; American History; Anthropology; Folklore, Myths, and Legends; Literature; Music; Popular Culture; Religion; Sport

Send: Query; Table of Contents; Writing sample; Author bio

The press is committed to preserving knowledge about Tennessee and the region and, by expanding its unique publishing program, it promotes a broad base of cultural understanding and, ultimately, improves life in the state.

Acquisitions Editor: Scot Danforth

P488 University of Texas Press

Book Publisher
3001 Lake Austin Blvd, 2.200, Stop E4800, Austin, TX 78703-4206
United States

https://utpress.utexas.edu

ACADEMIC > Nonfiction > *Nonfiction Books*
Anthropology; Archaeology; Architecture; Arts; Biography; Caribbean; Classics / Ancient World; Comic Books; Cookery; Environment; Films; Food; Gender; History; Judaism; Literary Criticism; Literature; Media; Middle East; Music; Nature; Photography; Sexuality; South America; Southwestern United States; Texas; United States

ADULT > Nonfiction > *Nonfiction Books*
Art History; Arts; Culture; Current Affairs; Food; History; Music; Nature; Texas

Send: Query; Proposal; Table of Contents; Writing sample; Author bio; Submission Form
How to send: Email

Send query with proposal, table of contents, sample chapter, and CV. Publishes scholarly books and some general readership nonfiction. See website for full details.

P489 University of Virginia Press

Book Publisher
P.O. Box 400318, Charlottesville, VA 22904-4318
United States
Tel: +1 (434) 924-3468
Fax: +1 (434) 982-2655

vapress@virginia.edu

https://www.upress.virginia.edu/

ACADEMIC > Nonfiction > *Nonfiction Books*
18th Century; Africa; African American; American Civil War; American History; Anthropology; Archaeology; Architecture; Arts; Autobiography; Biography; Business; Caribbean; Cookery; Culture; Current Affairs; Education; Environment; European History; Food; Geography; History; Legal; Literary Criticism; Literature; Memoir; Nature; Philosophy; Photography; Politics; Publishing; Religion; Science; Sociology; Technology; Virginia; Women's Studies

ADULT
Nonfiction > *Nonfiction Books*: Virginia

Poetry > *Any Poetic Form*

Send: Submission Form

Has a reputation for publishing quality scholarship in American history and government, eighteenth-century and Victorian literature, Afro-Caribbean studies, cultural religion, architectural and environmental history, and trade books of regional interest.

P490 The University of Wisconsin Press

Book Publisher
728 State Street, Suite 443, Madison, WI 53706
United States
Tel: +1 (608) 263-1110
Fax: +1 (608) 263-1173

uwiscpress@uwpress.wisc.edu

https://uwpress.wisc.edu
https://www.facebook.com/universityofwisconsinpress
https://twitter.com/UWiscPress
https://www.instagram.com/uwiscpress
https://www.goodreads.com/user/show/24113667-university-of-wisconsin-press
https://uwpress.wisc.edu/blog.html

ACADEMIC > Nonfiction > *Nonfiction Books*
Africa; African American; American Civil War; American Midwest; Anthropology; Asia; Autobiography; Brazil; Caribbean; Cinemas / Movie Theaters; Classics / Ancient World; Dance; Earth Science; Eastern Europe; Environment; Ethnography; Folklore, Myths, and Legends; Germany; History; Ireland; Judaism; LGBTQIA; Media; Native Americans; Outdoor Activities; Politics; Popular Culture; Russia; Scandinavia; South America; Travel; Wisconsin

ADULT
Fiction > *Novels*
General, and in particular: Mystery

Poetry > *Any Poetic Form*

Publishes scholarly, general interest nonfiction books and books featuring the American midwest, along with a limited number of novels and short story and poetry collections.

P491 University Press of Colorado

Book Publisher
1580 N Logan St, Ste 660, PMB 39883, Denver, CO, 80203-1942
United States
Tel: +1 (720) 406-8849

https://upcolorado.com
https://twitter.com/UPColorado
https://www.facebook.com/profile.php?id=100069378078836

ACADEMIC > Nonfiction > *Nonfiction Books*
American West; Anthropology; Archaeology; Colorado; Environment; Ethnic; History; Native Americans; Science

Send: Proposal; Table of Contents; Market info; Author bio
How to send: Online submission system

Currently accepting manuscript proposals in anthropology, archaeology, ethnohistory, environmental justice, history of the American West, indigenous studies, and the natural sciences as well as projects about the state of Colorado and the Rocky Mountain region.

Publishing Imprint: Utah State University Press

P492 Unseen Press

Book Publisher
United States

https://www.unseenpress.com
https://www.facebook.com/ghostoursIN/
https://twitter.com/ghosts_IN
https://www.youtube.com/channel/

UCinXzwCZ2_qj-xRO62SULaw
https://instagram.com/ghosts_in/

Nonfiction
Colouring Books: Crime; Folklore, Myths, and Legends; Ghosts; History; Indiana; Supernatural / Paranormal
Nonfiction Books: Crime; Folklore, Myths, and Legends; Ghosts; History; Indiana; Supernatural / Paranormal

Dedicated to bringing the information about ghosts to the public. Promotes ghost research as a source of folklore and also as viable scientific area of study.

P493 Valley Press
Book Publisher; Publishing Service
Woodend, The Crescent, Scarborough, YO11 2PW
United Kingdom

hello@valleypressuk.com

https://www.valleypressuk.com
https://www.facebook.com/valleypress
https://twitter.com/valleypress
https://www.pinterest.com/valleypress

Fiction
Novels; Short Fiction Collections
Nonfiction > *Nonfiction Books*
Memoir; Travel

Poetry > *Poetry Collections*

Closed to approaches.

Costs: Offers services that writers have to pay for.

Publishes poetry, fiction, and nonfiction.

P494 VanderWyk & Burnham
Book Publisher
1610 Long Leaf Circle, St. Louis, MO 63146
United States
Tel: +1 (314) 432-3435
Fax: +1 (314) 993-4485

quickpublishing@sbcglobal.net

http://www.vandb.com

Nonfiction > *Nonfiction Books*
Alzheimer's; Animals; Cookery; Disabilities; Education; Family; Memoir; Nature; Nursing; Personal Development; Pets; Society; Spirituality; Stress Management; Travel

Closed to approaches.

Not accepting unsolicited proposals or submissions as at May 2023.

P495 Vane Women Press
Book Publisher
United Kingdom

submissions@vanewomen.co.uk

https://www.vanewomen.co.uk
https://www.facebook.com/profile.php?id=100064798383906

Fiction > *Short Fiction Collections*

Poetry > *Poetry Collections*

Closed to approaches.

Publishes poetry by women of the North East. Send query by email in first instance. You will then be provided with a postal address to which you will need to send a hard copy submission. See website for full details.

P496 Velocity Press
Book Publisher
United Kingdom

info@velocitypress.uk

https://velocitypress.uk
https://twitter.com/PressVelocity
https://www.instagram.com/velocitypress/
https://www.facebook.com/velocitypressbooks
https://www.youtube.com/channel/UC2BdIfx5ljzDKwp49tDO_Vw
https://soundcloud.com/velocitypress

Fiction > *Novels*: Electronic Music

Nonfiction > *Nonfiction Books*: Electronic Music

Send: Query; Outline; Table of Contents
How to send: Email

Publishes fiction and nonfiction about the history and innovation of electronic music and club culture.

P497 Vinspire Publishing
Book Publisher
107 Clearview Circle, Goose Creek, SC 29445
United States
Tel: +1 (843) 695-7530

vinspirepublishingeic@gmail.com

https://www.vinspirepublishing.com

ADULT
Fiction > *Novels*
African American; Contemporary Romance; Historical Fiction; Historical Romance; Inspirational; Literary; Mystery; Romance; Supernatural / Paranormal Romance

Nonfiction > *Nonfiction Books*

CHILDREN'S > **Fiction**
Middle Grade; Picture Books
YOUNG ADULT > **Fiction** > *Novels*

Send: Query; Author bio; Outline; Synopsis
How to send: In the body of an email

At present, we are accepting agented and unagented submissions for historical novels and our romances with mature heroes and heroines. We are closed to all other submissions at this time.

P498 Virago Books
Publishing Imprint
50 Victoria Embankment, London, EC4Y 0DZ
United Kingdom
Tel: +44 (0) 20 3122 7000

https://www.virago.co.uk
https://www.facebook.com/ViragoPress
https://twitter.com/viragobooks
https://www.instagram.com/viragopress/

Publishing Imprint: Little, Brown Book Group

Fiction
Graphic Novels: Women
Novels: Women's Fiction; Women's Issues; Women
Nonfiction > *Nonfiction Books*
Feminism; Women's Issues; Women's Studies; Women

How to send: Through a literary agent

Publishes books by women. Founded in 1973 to put women centre stage; to explore the untold stories of their lives; above all to champion women's talent. Publishes award-winning fiction, agenda-setting non-fiction, a rich list of rediscovered classics – and most recently a boutique list of graphic novels.

Authors: Maya Angelou; Margaret Atwood; Jennifer Belle; Waris Dirie; Sarah Dunant; Germaine Greer; Daphne du Maurier; Michele Roberts; Gillian Slovo; Talitha Stevenson; Natasha Walter; Sarah Waters; Edith Wharton

Publishing Imprints: Virago Modern Classics; Virago.

P499 W.W. Norton & Company Ltd
Book Publisher
15 Carlisle Street, London, W1D 3BS
United Kingdom
Tel: +44 (0) 20 7323 1579

crussell1@wwnorton.com

https://wwnorton.co.uk
https://twitter.com/wwnortonUK
https://www.instagram.com/wwnortonuk/
https://medium.com/@W.W.NortonUK
https://www.pinterest.com/wwnortonuk/

ACADEMIC > **Nonfiction** > *Nonfiction Books*
African American; Anthropology; Astronomy; Biology; Chemistry; Classics / Ancient World; Computer Science; Films; Geology; History; Literature; Music; Philosophy; Physics; Politics; Psychology; Religion; Sociology; Statistics

ADULT
Fiction
Graphic Novels; Novels
Nonfiction
Essays: General
Nonfiction Books: Adventure; African American; Archaeology; Architecture;

Arts; Astronomy; Biography; Business; Classics / Ancient World; Comedy / Humour; Crafts; Crime; Culture; Current Affairs; Design; Drama; Economics; Education; Environment; Films; Folklore, Myths, and Legends; Food and Drink; Games; Gardening; Health; History; Hobbies; Houses and Homes; LGBTQIA; Legal; Literature; Medicine; Memoir; Music; Nature; Neuropsychology; Neuroscience; Oceanography; Parenting; Pets; Philosophy; Photography; Politics; Psychology; Psychotherapy; Religion; Self Help; Sociology; Sport; Statistics; Technology; Transport; Travel; Women's Studies; Writing

Poetry > *Poetry Collections*

CHILDREN'S
Fiction
Chapter Books; *Early Readers*; *Picture Books*
Nonfiction > *Nonfiction Books*

PROFESSIONAL > **Nonfiction** > *Nonfiction Books*
Addiction; Anxiety Disorders; Architecture; Autism; Child Psychotherapy; Couple Therapy; Depression; Design; Diversity; Eating Disorders; Education; Family Therapy; Genetics; Geriatrics; Health; Hypnosis; Juvenile Psychotherapy; Medicine; Multicultural; Neurobiology; Neuropsychology; Neuroscience; Personal Coaching; Post Traumatic Stress Disorder; Psychiatry; Psychoanalysis; Psychological Trauma; Psychotherapy; Self Help; Sexuality; Writing

UK branch of a US publisher. No editorial office in the UK – contact the main office in New York (see separate listing).

P500 W.W. Norton & Company, Inc.
Book Publisher
500 Fifth Avenue, New York, NY 10110
United States
Tel: +1 (212) 354-5500
Fax: +1 (212) 869-0856

https://wwnorton.com
https://www.facebook.com/wwnorton/
https://twitter.com/wwnorton
https://www.instagram.com/w.w.norton/

ACADEMIC > **Nonfiction** > *Nonfiction Books*
Anthropology; Architecture; Arts; Astronomy; Biology; Chemistry; Communication; Computer Science; Design; Economics; Education; English; Films; Geology; History; Literature; Mathematics; Music; Science; Sociology

ADULT
Fiction
Graphic Novels: General

Novels: Adventure; African American; Alternative History; Animals; Asian American; Coming of Age; Crime; Culture; Disabilities; Dystopian Fiction; Epistolary; Erotic; Family; Fantasy; Folklore, Myths, and Legends; Mystery; Thrillers
Short Fiction Collections: General

Nonfiction
Nonfiction Books: Architecture; Biography; Business; Comedy / Humour; Cookery; Design; Economics; Education; History; Hobbies; Houses and Homes; Legal; Literary Criticism; Mathematics; Memoir; Mental Health; Mind, Body, Spirit; Performing Arts; Philosophy; Politics; Psychology; Religion; Visual Arts
Reference: General

Poetry > *Poetry Collections*

PROFESSIONAL > **Nonfiction** > *Nonfiction Books*: Education

How to send: Through a literary agent

No longer accepts submissions directly – submissions through a literary agent only.

P501 Washington State University Press
Book Publisher
Cooper Publications Building, PO Box 645910, Pullman, WA 99164-5910
United States
Tel: +1 (509) 335-7630
Fax: +1 (509) 335-8568

wsupress@wsu.edu
https://wsupress.wsu.edu

Types: Nonfiction
Subjects: Biography; Cookery; Culture; History; Nature; Politics; Westerns
Markets: Academic; Adult

Send: Query
Don't send: Full text

Send query by post or by email (preferred) with author CV, summary of proposed work, sample bio, and one or two sample chapters. Specialises in the American West, particularly the prehistory, history, environment, politics, and culture of the greater Northwest region. No fiction, poetry, or literary criticism. See website for full guidelines.

Editor-in-Chief: Linda Bathgate

Publishing Imprint: Basalt Books (**P057**)

P502 Waterbrook
Publishing Imprint

Book Publisher: Random House

P503 Watkins Publishing
Book Publisher
Unit 11, Shepperton House, 89 Shepperton Road, London, N1 3DF
United Kingdom
Tel: +44 (0) 20 3813 6940

enquiries@watkinspublishing.com
https://www.watkinspublishing.com

Book Publisher: Watkins Media

Types: Nonfiction
Subjects: History; Lifestyle; Religion; Self Help
Markets: Adult

Closed to approaches.

Publishes books in the field of Mind, Body and Spirit. Not accepting submissions as at April 2019. Check website for current status.

P504 Wayne State University Press
Book Publisher
4809 Woodward Avenue, Detroit, Michigan 48201-1309
United States

https://www.wsupress.wayne.edu

ACADEMIC > **Nonfiction** > *Nonfiction Books*
African American; Detroit; Fairy Tales; Films; Health; Judaism; Media; Michigan; Regional; TV

ADULT
Fiction > *Short Fiction Collections*

Nonfiction > *Nonfiction Books*: Creative Nonfiction

Poetry > *Poetry Collections*

Send: Query; Proposal; Author bio; Writing sample
Don't send: Full text
How to send: Email

Actively acquiring books in African American studies, media studies, fairy-tale studies, Jewish studies, citizenship studies, and regional studies: books about the state of Michigan, the city of Detroit, and the Great Lakes region. Send query to appropriate acquisitions editor (see website for details and individual contact details).

P505 Weidenfeld & Nicolson
Book Publisher
United Kingdom

https://www.weidenfeldandnicolson.co.uk
https://twitter.com/wnbooks/
https://www.facebook.com/WeidenfeldandNicolson/
https://www.instagram.com/orionbooks/?hl=en

Book Publisher: The Orion Publishing Group Limited

Fiction > *Novels*: Literary

Nonfiction > *Nonfiction Books*

Describes itself as one of the most prestigious and dynamic literary imprints in British and international publishing, home to a wide range of literary fiction and non-fiction, modern classics, prizewinning debuts and worldwide bestsellers.

P506 Wesleyan University Press
Book Publisher
215 Long Lane, Middletown, CT 06459
United States
Tel: +1 (860) 685-7727
Fax: +1 (860) 685-7712

stamminen@wesleyan.edu

https://www.weslpress.org

ACADEMIC > **Nonfiction** > *Nonfiction Books*
Dance; Music

ADULT > **Poetry** > *Poetry Collections*

Send: Query; Proposal
Don't send: Full text
How to send: Email; Submittable

Accepting proposals in the areas of poetry, dance and music. See website for submission guidelines.

P507 Whitecap Books Ltd
Book Publisher
Suite 209, 314 West Cordova Street,
Vancouver, BC, V6B 1E8
Canada

hdoll@fitzhenry.ca

https://www.whitecap.ca
http://www.pinterest.com/whitecapbooks/
https://twitter.com/whitecapbooks
https://www.facebook.com/whitecapbooks

Nonfiction > *Nonfiction Books*
Food; Health; Regional History; Wellbeing; Wine

Closed to approaches.

Publishes visually appealing books on food, wine, health and well-being, regional history, and regional guidebooks.

P508 Whitford Press
Publishing Imprint
United States

https://schifferbooks.com/pages/schiffer-imprints

Book Publisher: Schiffer Publishing (**P398**)

Nonfiction > *Nonfiction Books*
Mind, Body, Spirit; Supernatural / Paranormal

Publishes books on paranormal activities and mind and spirit lifestyles.

P509 Wide-Eyed Editions
Publishing Imprint
1 Triptych Place, Second Floor, London,
SE1 9SH
United Kingdom
Tel: +44 (0) 20 7700 9000

QuartoExploresSubmissions@Quartous.com

https://www.quartoknows.com/Wide-Eyed-Editions

Book Publisher: The Quarto Group, Inc. (**P367**)

CHILDREN'S > **Nonfiction** > *Nonfiction Books*
Arts; Nature; Travel

Send: Query
Don't send: Full text

Publishes books on the arts, natural history and armchair travel. Send query with proposal by email. See website for full guidelines.

P510 Wild Places Publishing
Book Publisher
PO Box 100, Abergavenny, NP7 9WY
United Kingdom
Tel: +44 (0) 1873 737707

books@wildplaces.co.uk

https://wildplaces.co.uk

Nonfiction > *Nonfiction Books*: Caving and Potholing

Publisher specialising in caving-related publications.

P511 Windhorse Publications Ltd
Book Publisher
38 Newmarket Road, Cambridge, CB5 8DT
United Kingdom

info@windhorsepublications.com
dhammamegha@windhorsepublications.com

https://www.windhorsepublications.com
https://www.facebook.com/windhorse.publications/
https://twitter.com/WindhorsePubs
https://www.instagram.com/windhorsepubs/
https://issuu.com/windhorsepublications
https://vimeo.com/windhorsepublications
https://soundcloud.com/windhorsepublications
https://thebuddhistcentre.com/windhorsepublications?display=latest

Nonfiction > *Nonfiction Books*: Buddhism

Send: Query; Proposal
Don't send: Full text
How to send: Email

An independent publisher of English-language non-fiction books on Buddhism, meditation and mindfulness. Based in the UK, we publish and distribute internationally. We publish books for practitioners at all stages in the path as well as for a wider non-Buddhist readership. We are also interested in books exploring new directions in Buddhist scholarship.

P512 Wisdom Publications
Book Publisher
199 Elm Street, Somerville, MA 02144
United States

submissions@wisdompubs.org

https://wisdomexperience.org
https://twitter.com/wisdompubs
https://www.facebook.com/wisdompubs
https://instagram.com/wisdompubs
https://www.youtube.com/channel/UCKrdx4usaugOhLzjvYmzpIg

Nonfiction > *Nonfiction Books*: Buddhism

Send: Submission Form
How to send: Email

Will only consider books directly related to Buddhism, written by people with relevant credentials. Download submission questionnaire from website, then complete and return by email.

P513 Wolfpack Publishing
Book Publisher
1707 E. Diana Street, Tampa, FL 33610
United States

submissions@wolfpackpublishing.com

https://wolfpackpublishing.com
https://www.goodreads.com/group/show/138635-wolfpack-publishing
https://www.facebook.com/WolfpackPub/
https://twitter.com/wolfpackpub

Fiction > *Novels*
Adventure; Crime; Historical Fiction; Thrillers; Westerns

Closed to approaches.

An award winning indie publisher that began life as a small Western Fiction publishing company, but which now publishes across a variety of genres.

P514 WordCrafts Press
Book Publisher
912 E. Lincoln St, Tullahoma, TN 37388
United States
Tel: +1 (615) 397-8376

wordcrafts@wordcrafts.net

https://www.wordcrafts.net

ADULT
Fiction > *Novels*
Christianity; Contemporary; Dystopian Fiction; Fantasy; Historical Fiction; Horror; Literary; Mystery; Romance; Suspense; Women's Fiction

Nonfiction > *Nonfiction Books*
Animals; Bible Studies; Biography; Business; Cars; Christian Living; Comedy / Humour; Education; History; Memoir; Philosophy; Self Help; Sport; Travel

Poetry > *Poetry Collections*
General, and in particular: Christianity

Scripts > Theatre Scripts
CHILDREN'S > Fiction
Middle Grade; Picture Books
YOUNG ADULT > Fiction > *Novels*
General, and in particular: Fantasy

Send: Proposal
How to send: Query Manager

We publish fiction, nonfiction, and stage plays for both the Christian market and the general market. We do not publish erotica.

Acquisitions Editors: Kristen Ownby; Mike Parker; Shanda Perkins

Authors: Gail Kittleson; Dan Kulp; Robert G. Lee; Jason Lee McKinney; Joey Monteleone; Carrie Anne Noble; Darden North; Paula K. Parker

P515 Words & Pictures
Publishing Imprint
1 Triptych Place, Second Floor, London, SE1 9SH
United Kingdom
Tel: +44 (0) 20 770 9000

QuartoHomesSubmissions@Quarto.com

https://www.quartoknows.com/words-pictures

Book Publisher: The Quarto Group, Inc. (**P367**)

CHILDREN'S > Fiction > *Picture Books*

How to send: Email

Always on the lookout for authors and artists with creative ideas to enhance and broaden their list of children's books. See website for submission guidelines.

Publisher: Holly Willsher

P516 WordSong
Publishing Imprint
815 Church Street, Honesdale, PA 18431
United States
Tel: +1 (570) 253-1164

submissions@boydsmillspress.com

https://www.boydsmillspress.com

Book Publisher: Astra Publishing House (**P037**)

Types: Poetry
Markets: Children's

Send: Full text

Describes itself as "the only children's imprint in the United States specifically dedicated to poetry". Send book-length collection of poetry by post with SASE. Do not make initial query prior to submission.

P517 Wordsonthestreet
Book Publisher; Magazine Publisher
Six San Antonio Park, Salthill, Galway
Ireland

publisher@wordsonthestreet.com

http://www.wordsonthestreet.com

Fiction
Novellas; Novels; Short Fiction Collections
Poetry > *Poetry Collections*

How to send: Post
How not to send: Email

Independent publisher based in Galway, Ireland, publishing novels, novellas, short story and poetry collections, and Ireland's premier fiction and poetry magazine.

Editor: Tony O'Dwyer

Magazine: Crannog Magazine (**M103**)

Publishing Imprint: 6th House

P518 Wordsworth Editions
Book Publisher
PO Box 13147, Stansted, CM21 1BT
United Kingdom
Tel: +44 (0) 1920 465167

enquiries@wordsworth-editions.com

http://www.wordsworth-editions.com
https://twitter.com/WordsworthEd
https://en-gb.facebook.com/wordsworth.editions/

ADULT
Fiction > *Novels*
Poetry > *Poetry Collections*

CHILDREN'S > Fiction > *Novels*

Closed to approaches.

Publishes out-of-copyright titles.

Managing Director: Helen Trayler

P519 Workman Publishing
Book Publisher
1290 Avenue of the Americas, New York, NY 10104
United States
Tel: +1 (800) 759-0190
Fax: +1 (212) 364-0950

Workman-Inquiry@hbgusa.com

https://www.workman.com
https://www.instagram.com/workmanpub/
https://www.tiktok.com/@workmanpub
https://twitter.com/workmanpub
https://www.facebook.com/WorkmanPublishing/
https://www.linkedin.com/company/workman-publishing/
https://www.pinterest.com/workmanpub/

Book Publisher: Hachette Book Group (**P196**)

ADULT
Fiction > *Novels*

Nonfiction
Gift Books: General
Nonfiction Books: Comedy / Humour; Cookery; Country Lifestyle; Gardening; Parenting; Pregnancy

CHILDREN'S > Nonfiction > *Nonfiction Books*

We are publishers of award-winning cookbooks, parenting/pregnancy guides, books on gardening, country living, and humor, as well as children's books, gift books, fiction, and the bestselling calendar line in the business.

Publishing Imprints: Algonquin Books (**P016**); Algonquin Young Readers (**P017**); Artisan Books; Books of Chapel Hill (**P079**); Storey Publishing; Timber Press

P520 Yale University Press (London)
Book Publisher
47 Bedford Square, London, WC1B 3DP
United Kingdom
Tel: +44 (0) 20 7079 4900

sales@yaleup.co.uk

https://www.yalebooks.co.uk

ADULT > Nonfiction
Nonfiction Books: Architecture; Arts; Biography; Business; Computers; Current Affairs; Economics; Fashion; Health; History; Language; Legal; Literature; Mathematics; Medicine; Memoir; Music; Philosophy; Politics; Religion; Science; Society; Sociology; Technology; Wellbeing
Reference: General

CHILDREN'S > Nonfiction > *Nonfiction Books:* Education

Send: Query; Author bio; Market info; Table of Contents; Writing sample
How to send: Post; Email

Publishes world class scholarship for a broad readership.

Editors: Mark Eastment; Joanna Godfrey; Julian Loose; Heather McCallum; Sophie Neve

P521 YesYes Books
Book Publisher
1631 Broadway St #121, Portland, OR 97232-1425
United States
Tel: +1 (503) 446-3851

info@yesyesbooks.com

https://www.yesyesbooks.com
https://yesyesbooks.submittable.com/submit
https://www.facebook.com/yesyesbooks/
https://twitter.com/YesYesBooks
https://www.instagram.com/yesyesbooks

Fiction
Novellas; Novels; Short Fiction Collections
Poetry > *Poetry Collections*

Closed to approaches.

A dynamic independent press that publishes poetry and prose collections from bold fresh voices.

P522 Zibby Books
Book Publisher
United States

info@zibbybooks.com
submissions@zibbybooks.com

https://www.zibbybooks.com
https://www.instagram.com/zibbybooks
https://www.facebook.com/zibbybooks
https://twitter.com/zibbybooks

Fiction > *Novels*

Nonfiction > *Nonfiction Books*: Memoir

How to send: Email

A publishing home for fiction and memoir.

P523 ZigZag Education
Book Publisher
Unit 3, Greenway Business Centre, Doncaster Road, Bristol, BS10 5PY
United Kingdom
Tel: +44 (0) 1179 503199

support@ZigZagEducation.co.uk

https://zigzageducation.co.uk

ACADEMIC > **Nonfiction** > *Nonfiction Books*

Arts; Business; Classics / Ancient World; Computer Science; Crime; Design; Drama; Economics; English; Films; Food; Geography; Health; History; Language; Legal; Mathematics; Media; Music; Nutrition; Philosophy; Physical Education; Politics; Psychology; Religion; Science; Sociology; Technology; Travel

Educational publisher publishing photocopiable and digital teaching resources for schools and colleges. Register on publisher's author support website if interested in writing or contributing to resources.

Index

17th Century
See more broadly: History
18th Century
See more broadly: History
University of Virginia Press..................... P489
19th Century
See more broadly: History
Ohio State University Press, The............... P323
University of Massachusetts Press P482
20th Century
See more broadly: History
Power Cut Lite M294
University of Massachusetts Press P482
Walsh, Kate L646
Williams, Laura L662
ADHD
See more broadly: Neurodiversity
Academic
ABC-CLIO P008
Agricultural History M017
Badger Learning P048
Baylor University Press P060
Berghahn Books Ltd P062
Bess Press P064
BFI Publishing P065
BFS Journal M060
Bloomsbury Academic P071
British Academy, The P083
British Museum Press, The P084
Broadview Press P085
Chartered Institute of Personnel and
    Development (CIPD) Publishing P104
Chelsea House Publishers P105
Collins P118
Colourpoint Educational P119
Crabtree Publishing P126
Crossway P128
Elsevier Ltd P150
Encyclopedia Britannica (UK) Ltd............. P151
Enslow Publishers, Inc. P154
Evans, David... L203
Feminist Studies....................................... M139
Fernwood Publishing P164
Fiscal Publications P168
Fortress Press P170
Gale P177
Geographical Journal, The M162
Gill Education P182
Goldsmiths Press P186
Hammersmith Books P198
Harvard University Press P206
Indiana University Press P235
International Piano M200
International Society for Technology in
    Education (ISTE).............................. P242
InterVarsity Press (IVP) P243
Jain Publishing Company, Inc................... P244
Jessica Kingsley Publishers P246
Johns Hopkins University Press, The P250
Kube Publishing....................................... P258
Laurence King Publishing P261
LSU Press P273
Lund Humphries Limited......................... P274
Manoa.. M233
McGraw Hill EMEA P285
Mentor Books P292
MIT Press, The P303

Moving Worlds: A Journal of
    Transcultural Writings M247
Ohio State University Press, The............... P323
Ohio University Press............................... P324
Otago University Press P330
Oxbow Books... P333
Peter Lang... P346
Peter Lang Publishing P348
Prufrock Press P363
Purdue University Press P364
Rosenberg Group, The............................. L549
Saqi Books P390
Science Factory, The L569
Stanford University Press P427
Stipes Publishing P431
Taylor & Francis Group P441
Texas A&M University Press P445
Tocher... M378
University of Akron Press, The P475
University of Alaska Press P476
University of Alberta Press...................... P477
University of California Press.................. P478
University of Georgia Press..................... P479
University of Iowa Press.......................... P480
University of Maine Press P481
University of Massachusetts Press........... P482
University of Michigan Press, The P483
University of Nevada Press P484
University of North Texas Press.............. P485
University of Pennsylvania Press............. P486
University of Tennessee Press P487
University of Texas Press P488
University of Virginia Press P489
University of Wisconsin Press, The.......... P490
University Press of Colorado................... P491
W.W. Norton & Company Ltd P499
W.W. Norton & Company, Inc................. P500
Wallace Stevens Journal, The.................. M396
Washington State University Press......... P501
Wayne State University Press.................. P504
Wesleyan University Press P506
ZigZag Education P523
Accounting
See more broadly: Finance
Accountancy Age M010
Accountancy Daily M011
Bloomsbury Professional......................... P072
Croner-i Limited..................................... P127
Gill Education P182
Activism
See more broadly: Politics; Society
Borstel, Stefanie Sanchez Von................. L071
Feminist Press, The P163
Fernwood Publishing P164
Maw, Jane Graham L434
Oxford Review of Books M271
University of Alberta Press...................... P477
Activities
See more specifically: Outdoor Activities
Arcadia Publishing P031
Bright Press... P082
Cobblestone... M087
Kensington Publishing Corp.................... P253
Activity Books
Autumn Publishing Ltd P042
Barbour Publishing................................. P056
Bess Press.. P064

Child's Play (International) Ltd P107
Chronicle Books LLC P111
Igloo Books Limited P232
Kube Publishing...................................... P258
Pavilion Books P338
Peter Pauper Press.................................. P350
Rand McNally.. P371
Schiffer Kids.. P396
Thames & Hudson Inc. P446
Acupuncture
See more broadly: Alternative Health
Blue Poppy Enterprises........................... P074
Addiction
See more broadly: Social Issues
W.W. Norton & Company Ltd P499
Adventure
4RV Tenacious P005
Abuzz Press P010
AdventureBox M013
AdventureKEEN P013
Armada, Kurestin L030
Caprio, Alice.. L103
Carroll, Megan L110
Compassiviste Publishing P121
Crystal Magazine M110
Diana Finch Literary Agency L167
Dodd, Saffron L172
Doug Grad Literary Agency L177
Eberly, Chelsea.. L187
Ellor, Zabé L198
Ferguson, T.S... L218
Fighting High P165
Gisondi, Katie L261
Gordon, Andrew L270
Gunic, Masha.. L284
Haley, Jolene L289
Hashtag Press... P207
Hensley, Chelsea..................................... L307
Hodges, Jodie... L315
Irvine, Lucy L325
Karinch, Maryann L351
Kimber, Natalie....................................... L368
Kirby, Robert L370
Langton, Becca L383
Leon, Nina L394
Marshall, Jen... L427
Mills & Boon P297
Miranda, Caroline................................... L454
Orenda Books P329
Ostby, Kristin L494
Pages, Saribel.. L496
Parker, Elana Roth L499
Paul S. Levine Literary Agency L502
Pocket Mountains P359
Rocky Mountain Books P378
Sanchez, Kaitlyn L561
Scoular, Rosemary L570
Sierra M336
Sluytman, Antoinette Van....................... L588
Soloway, Jennifer March L590
Story Unlikely... M356
Takikawa, Marin L618
Thorneycroft, Euan L628
Trudel, Jes... L634
Victoria Sanders & Associates LLC.......... L642
W.W. Norton & Company Ltd P499
W.W. Norton & Company, Inc. P500

Claim your free access to www.firstwriter.com: See p.403

Weiman, Paula L649
Whatnall, Michaela............................L655
Wickers, Chandler L659
Williamson, Jo...................................L664
Wolfpack Publishing P513
Advertising
See more broadly: Marketing
Campaign M079
Africa
See more broadly: Regional
See more specifically: African Diaspora; North Africa
Better Than Starbucks M058
Bloomsbury Academic P071
Feminist Press, The P163
HopeRoad...P223
Indiana University Press..................P235
Ohio University Press......................P324
Pluto Press..P358
University of Alberta Press..............P477
University of California Press.........P478
University of Michigan Press, The..P483
University of Virginia Press P489
University of Wisconsin Press, The.P490
Woodhouse, James............................L670
African American
See more broadly: Ethnic Groups
See more specifically: African American Issues
African American Review M014
Feminist Press, The P163
LSU Press P273
Texas A&M University Press..........P445
University of Georgia Press P479
University of Massachusetts Press...P482
University of Michigan Press, The..P483
University of Virginia Press P489
University of Wisconsin Press, The.P490
Vinspire Publishing P497
W.W. Norton & Company Ltd P499
W.W. Norton & Company, Inc.......P500
Wayne State University Press..........P504
Zack Company, Inc, The L678
African American Issues
See more broadly: African American
African Diaspora
See more broadly: Africa
Fernwood Publishing........................P164
Obsidian: Literature in the African Diaspora...................................... M265
University of Pennsylvania Press.....P486
Agriculture
See more specifically: Farming; Self-Sufficiency; Smallholdings
Agricultural History......................... M017
Gale P177
Purdue University Press...................P364
Stipes Publishing..............................P431
Taylor & Francis Group...................P441
Texas A&M University Press P445
Air Travel
See more broadly: Travel
Pilot... M284
Alaska
See more broadly: United States
Amato Books....................................P021
University of Alaska Press...............P476
Albemarle
See more broadly: Virginia
See more specifically: Charlottesville
CharlottesvilleFamily M082
Alberta
See more broadly: Canada
University of Alberta Press..............P477
Alien Fiction
See more broadly: Science Fiction
See more specifically: Alien Invasion

Mozley, Jack......................................L465
Alien Invasion
See more broadly: Alien Fiction
Allegory
MMB Creative L455
Tyndale House Publishers, Inc. P465
Alternative Health
See more broadly: Health
See more specifically: Acupuncture; Aromatherapy; Ayurveda; Chinese Medicine; Herbal Remedies; Reiki
DeVorss & Company P139
Freymann, Sarah Jane L242
Hay House Publishers......................P210
Llewellyn Worldwide Ltd P269
Singing Dragon P409
Zack Company, Inc, The L678
Alternative History
See more broadly: Speculative
Candlemark & Gleam P092
Harris, Erin L300
Mozley, Jack......................................L465
Mustelier, James................................L471
Pierce, Rosie L517
W.W. Norton & Company, Inc. P500
Alternative Lifestyles
See more broadly: Lifestyle
Alzheimer's
See more broadly: Dementia
VanderWyk & Burnham P494
Amateur Investigator
See more broadly: Mystery
Amateur Radio
See more broadly: Radio Technology
Amateur Winemaking
See more broadly: Winemaking
American Civil War
See more broadly: Warfare
Indiana University Press P235
LSU Press P273
University of Massachusetts Press ...P482
University of Tennessee Press..........P487
University of Virginia Press.............P489
University of Wisconsin Press, The .P490
American History
See more broadly: History
Arcadia Publishing P031
Brattle Agency LLC, The.................L080
Cobblestone M087
LSU Press P273
Ohio University Press......................P324
Texas A&M University Press.......... P445
Thayer, Henry L626
University of Georgia Press P479
University of Tennessee Press..........P487
University of Virginia Press P489
Zack Company, Inc, The L678
American Literature
See more broadly: Literature
Stipes Publishing.............................. P431
University of Georgia Press P479
American Midwest
See more broadly: United States
Indiana University Press P235
Kotchman, Katie L374
Minnesota Historical Society Press ..P299
Ohio University Press......................P324
Sweetgum Press................................P438
University of Iowa Press P480
University of Wisconsin Press, The .P490
American Revolution
See more broadly: Warfare
American West
See more broadly: United States
Cowboys & Indians.......................... M101
Horse & Rider.................................. M188

Saddlebag Dispatches M319
University of Nevada Press..............P484
University Press of Colorado P491
Americana
See more broadly: United States
Amish
See more broadly: Christianity
Barbour Publishing P056
Amish Romance
See more broadly: Christian Romance
Anatomy
See more broadly: Medicine
Stipes Publishing..............................P431
Angels
See more broadly: Religion
Hay House Publishers......................P210
Llewellyn Worldwide Ltd................P269
Animal Husbandry
See more broadly: Farming
See more specifically: Apiculture (Beekeeping)
Animal Rights
See more broadly: Animals
Animals
See more broadly: Nature
See more specifically: Animal Rights; Birds; Deer; Furries; Horses; Pets; Prehistoric Animals; Veterinary; Wildlife
Anderson, Darley..............................L022
Maltese, Alyssa.................................L422
Mortimer, Michele............................L462
Pass, Marina de.................................L500
Pineapple Press.................................P356
Purdue University Press...................P364
River Hills Traveler M313
Roberts, Soumeya Bendimerad........L540
Rushall, Kathleen..............................L556
Turner Publishing.............................P462
University of Alberta Press..............P477
VanderWyk & Burnham P494
W.W. Norton & Company, Inc.......P500
Weiss, Alexandra..............................L650
WordCrafts Press..............................P514
Zack Company, Inc, The L678
Animation Scripts
Sheil Land Associates Ltd L577
Antarctica
See more broadly: Regional
Anthropology
Armstrong, Susan.............................L032
Baylor University Press P060
Berghahn Books Ltd P062
Compassiviste Publishing P121
Lambert, Sophie................................L380
London Review of Books M225
Lutterworth Press, The P275
Marion Boyars Publishers................P282
Ohio University Press......................P324
Oneworld Publications P327
Stanford University Press P427
Texas A&M University Press P445
Thames & Hudson Inc.....................P446
University of Alberta Press..............P477
University of California Press.........P478
University of Massachusetts Press ..P482
University of Michigan Press, The..P483
University of Tennessee Press.........P487
University of Texas Press P488
University of Virginia Press P489
University of Wisconsin Press, The.P490
University Press of Colorado P491
W.W. Norton & Company Ltd P499
W.W. Norton & Company, Inc.......P500
Antiques
Arcadia Publishing P031
Gale P177
Goss & Crested China Club.............P189

Access more listings online at www.firstwriter.com

Graham, Stacey	L272
Homes & Antiques	M187
Lutterworth Press, The	P275
Scala Arts & Heritage Publishers	P392
Schiffer Publishing	P398
Thames & Hudson Inc.	P446

Anxiety Disorders
See more broadly: Psychology

Hay House Publishers	P210
W.W. Norton & Company Ltd	P499

Any Poetic Form

2River View, The	M001
30 North	M002
32 Poems	M003
aaduna	M005
About Place Journal	M007
Abridged	M008
Account, The	M009
Acumen	M012
African American Review	M014
African Voices	M015
Agni	M016
Alaska Quarterly Review	M019
Allegro Poetry Magazine	M021
Amethyst Review	M024
Angela Poetry Magazine	M025
Antigonish Review, The	M026
Arboreal	M027
Arc	M028
Asimov's Science Fiction	M033
Atlanta Review	M036
Atrium	M038
Babybug	M041
Bacopa Literary Review	M042
Baffler, The	M043
Bald and Bonkers Network LLC	P050
Bandit Fiction	M045
Banipal	M046
Barren Magazine	M047
Bear Deluxe Magazine, The	M052
Belmont Story Review	M054
Better Than Starbucks	M058
BFS Horizons	M059
Black Moon Magazine	M064
Black Warrior Review	M066
Blue Earth Review	M067
Blue Mesa Review	M068
Bookseeker Agency	L070
Boston Review	M071
Boyfriend Village	M073
Butcher's Dog	M077
Chang, Nicola	L116
Chapman	M081
Chautauqua Literary Journal	M083
Cheshire	M084
Cincinnati Review, The	M086
Cobblestone	M087
Cocoa Girl	M088
Coil, The	M089
Cola	M090
Commonweal	M091
Concho River Review	M092
Conjunctions	M093
Conjunctions Online	M094
Coyote Arts	P125
Crab Orchard Review	M102
Crannog Magazine	M103
Crazyhorse / Swamp Pink	M104
Cream City Review	M105
Critical Quarterly	M108
Crystal Magazine	M110
CutBank	M111
Cyphers	M112
Dalhousie Review, The	M113
Dark Horse, The	M114
Dawntreader, The	M115
Dream Catcher	M123
Ecotone	M127
Eddison Pearson Ltd	L188
Ekphrastic Review, The	M128
El Portal	M129
Event	M133
Fathom Books	P162
Faultline	M137
Feminist Studies	M139
Fiddlehead, The	M141
Filter Press	P166
First Line, The	M143
Five Points	M144
Folio	M147
Fortnightly Review, The	M149
Fourteen Poems	M152
Fourth River, The	M153
Fresh Words – An International Literary Magazine	M154
Fugue	M155
Future Fire, The	M158
Gargoyle Online	M161
Georgia Review, The	M163
Gertrude	M164
Ginosko Literary Journal	M165
Glacier, The	M166
Grain Literary Magazine	M170
Granta	M171
Graywolf Lab	M172
Gulf Coast: A Journal of Literature and Fine Arts	M173
Gutter Magazine	M174
Half Mystic Journal	M175
Hanging Loose	M177
Harpur Palate	M179
Hedgerow: A Journal of Small Poems	M182
Helix, The	M183
Here Comes Everyone	M184
Hotel Amerika	M189
Hudson Review, The	M190
Hunger Mountain	M191
I-70 Review	M192
Idaho Review	M193
Identity Theory	M194
Image	M195
Indiana Review	M196
Ink Sweat and Tears	M197
Irish Pages	M203
Island	M204
Journal, The	M207
Kavya Kishor	M208
Kenyon Review, The	M210
Kerning	M211
Kube Publishing	P258
Lake, The	M213
Landfall	M215
Lantana Publishing	P260
Lighthouse	M218
Lilliput Press, The	P268
Literary Mama	M220
London Grip New Poetry	M223
London Magazine, The	M224
London Review of Books	M225
Lost Lake Folk Opera Magazine	M227
Louisiana Literature	M228
MacGuffin, The	M229
Magma	M231
Malahat Review, The	M232
Manoa	M233
Margaret K. McElderry Books	P281
Massachusetts Review, The	M237
Meetinghouse	M238
Michigan Quarterly Review	M240
Mid-American Review	M241
Midsummer Dream House	M242
Midway Journal	M243
Missouri Review, The	M245
Modern Poetry in Translation	M246
Moving Worlds: A Journal of Transcultural Writings	M247
MQR Mixtape	M248
Nashville Review	M251
Neon	M253
New England Review	M255
New Orleans Review	M257
New Welsh Reader	M259
North, The	M262
Northern Gravy	M263
Obsidian: Literature in the African Diaspora	M265
Old Red Kimono	M267
On Spec	M268
Orbis International Literary Journal	M269
Oxford Poetry	M270
Oxford Review of Books	M271
Oyez Review	M272
Pacifica Literary Review	M273
Panorama	M274
Paris Review, The	M275
Passionfruit Review, The	M277
Pennine Ink Magazine	M280
Pleiades	M285
Ploughshares	M286
PN Review	M287
Poetry Ireland Review	M288
Poetry London	M289
Poetry Review, The	M290
Poetry Wales	M291
Popshot Quarterly	M293
Power Cut Lite	M294
Present Tense	M296
Prole	M299
Pulsar Poetry Magazine	M300
Pushing Out the Boat	M301
Qu Literary Magazine	M302
Rabble Review	M303
Radar Poetry	M305
Rialto, The	M311
River Styx	M314
Riverbed Review	M315
Saddlebag Dispatches	M319
Second Factory	M328
Shearsman	M330
Shenandoah	M331
Shooter Literary Magazine	M333
Shoreline of Infinity	M334
Shorts Magazine	M335
Sinister Wisdom	M337
Snowflake Magazine	M338
Soho Review, The	M339
South	M343
South Carolina Review	M344
Southern Humanities Review	M345
Southern Review, The	M346
Southwest Review	M348
Southword Journal	M349
Spelt Magazine	M352
Spitball	M353
Stinging Fly, The	M355
Strange Horizons	M357
Structo Magazine	M359
Studio One	M360
Sunspot Literary Journal	M364
Supplement, The	M365
Takahe	M369
Tears in the Fence	M371
Temz Review, The	M372
Thin Air Magazine	M374
Third Coast	M375
This England	M376
Threepenny Review, The	M377
Tributaries	M380

Troika Books ... P461
Tusculum Review, The ... M381
UCity Review ... M382
Under the Radar ... M384
Understorey Magazine ... M385
University of Iowa Press ... P480
University of Nevada Press ... P484
University of North Texas Press ... P485
University of Virginia Press ... P489
University of Wisconsin Press, The ... P490
Vagabond City ... M386
Vallum ... M387
Virginia Quarterly Review, The ... M389
Waccamaw ... M394
Wallace Stevens Journal, The ... M396
Wasafiri ... M398
West Branch ... M400
WestWard Quarterly ... M403
White Review, The ... M404
Windsor Review ... M405
Yale Review, The ... M409
Yes Poetry Magazine ... M412
Zone 3 ... M419

Apiculture (Beekeeping)
See more broadly: Animal Husbandry
Rosenberg Group, The ... L549

Appalachia
See more broadly: United States
Ohio University Press ... P324

Archaeology
Berghahn Books Ltd ... P062
Bloomsbury Academic ... P071
British Academy, The ... P083
British Museum Press, The ... P084
Grossman, Loren R. ... L280
History Press, The ... P221
Logaston Press ... P271
Lutterworth Press, The ... P275
Oxbow Books ... P333
Texas A&M University Press ... P445
Thames & Hudson Inc. ... P446
Tyndale House Publishers, Inc. ... P465
University of Iowa Press ... P480
University of Michigan Press, The ... P483
University of Texas Press ... P488
University of Virginia Press ... P489
University Press of Colorado ... P491
W.W. Norton & Company Ltd ... P499

Archery
See more broadly: Sport
Bowhunter ... M072

Architecture
See more specifically: Church Architecture; City and Town Planning
Arcadia Publishing ... P031
Architectural Review, The ... M029
Bird Eye Books ... P066
Bloomsbury Academic ... P071
Cottage Life ... M099
Countryside Books ... P124
Goose Lane Editions ... P188
Grossman, Loren R. ... L280
Harvard University Press ... P206
Johns Hopkins University Press, The ... P250
Laurence King Publishing ... P261
Lilliput Press, The ... P268
Logaston Press ... P271
LSU Press ... P273
Lund Humphries Limited ... P274
Lutterworth Press, The ... P275
Metropolis Magazine ... M239
Monacelli Press, The ... P304
Prestel Publishing Ltd ... P362
Quill Driver Books ... P368
Regina Ryan Books ... L531
Scala Arts & Heritage Publishers ... P392

Schiffer Publishing ... P398
Stipes Publishing ... P431
Thames & Hudson Inc. ... P446
University of Massachusetts Press ... P482
University of Nevada Press ... P484
University of Texas Press ... P488
University of Virginia Press ... P489
Virginia Wine & Country Life ... M390
W.W. Norton & Company Ltd ... P499
W.W. Norton & Company, Inc. ... P500
Wallpaper ... M397
Yale University Press (London) ... P520

Arctic
See more broadly: Regional

Arizona
See more broadly: United States

Aromatherapy
See more broadly: Alternative Health
Singing Dragon ... P409

Art Criticism
See more broadly: Arts
Amling, Eric ... L021
Gulf Coast: A Journal of Literature and Fine Arts ... M173

Art History
See more broadly: Arts; History
Birlinn Ltd ... P067
Brattle Agency LLC, The ... L080
Charnace, Edwina de ... L117
Curran, Sabhbh ... L145
Derviskadic, Dado ... L164
MMB Creative ... L455
Ohio University Press ... P324
University of Texas Press ... P488

Articles
417 Magazine ... M004
AARP The Magazine ... M006
Accountancy Age ... M010
Acumen ... M012
Agricultural History ... M017
Air & Space Quarterly ... M018
Arc ... M028
Architectural Review, The ... M029
Art Monthly ... M030
Art Papers ... M031
Art Quarterly ... M032
Astronomy Now ... M034
Atlanta Magazine ... M035
Baffler, The ... M043
Balance ... M044
BBC Doctor Who Magazine ... M048
BBC History Magazine ... M049
BBC Science Focus ... M050
Bear Deluxe Magazine, The ... M052
Bella ... M053
Best of British ... M056
Better Homes and Gardens ... M057
BFS Journal ... M060
Birds & Blooms ... M062
Black Belt ... M063
Bluegrass Unlimited ... M069
Bookseller, The ... M070
Bowhunter ... M072
Britain Magazine ... M075
Business Traveller ... M076
Campaign ... M079
Carolina Woman ... M080
Chapman ... M081
CharlottesvilleFamily ... M082
Cobblestone ... M087
Cocoa Girl ... M088
Commonweal ... M091
Conversation (UK), The ... M095
Corridor of Uncertainty, The ... M097
Cotswold Life ... M098
Cottage Life ... M099

Country Smallholding ... M100
Cowboys & Indians ... M101
Creem ... M107
Cruising World ... M109
Crystal Magazine ... M110
Dawntreader, The ... M115
Descent ... M118
Devon Life ... M119
Diver ... M120
Economist, The ... M126
Ekphrastic Review, The ... M128
Entrepreneur ... M131
Essex Life ... M132
Facts & Fiction ... M135
Fate ... M136
Fee: Foundation for Economic Education ... M138
Feminist Studies ... M139
First For Women ... M142
Flaneur ... M145
Flyfishing & Tying Journal ... M146
Fortean Times: The Journal of Strange Phenomena ... M148
Forty20 ... M150
Foundation: The International Review of Science Fiction ... M151
Funeral Business Solutions ... M156
Garden Answers ... M159
Garden News ... M160
Geographical Journal, The ... M162
Go World Travel Magazine ... M167
Good Homes ... M168
Good Ski Guide, The ... M169
Graywolf Lab ... M172
Harper's Magazine ... M178
Healthy ... M180
Here Comes Everyone ... M184
History Today ... M186
Homes & Antiques ... M187
Horse & Rider ... M188
Hudson Review, The ... M190
Inque ... M198
Insurance Age ... M199
International Piano ... M200
Ireland's Own ... M202
Island ... M204
Jazz Journal ... M206
Kavya Kishor ... M208
Kent Life ... M209
Kids Alive! ... M212
Lancashire Life ... M214
Landfall ... M215
Leisure Group Travel ... M216
Leisure Painter ... M217
Linguist, The ... M219
London Grip ... M222
London Grip New Poetry ... M223
London Review of Books ... M225
marie claire ... M234
marie claire (UK) ... M235
Marlin ... M236
Massachusetts Review, The ... M237
Metropolis Magazine ... M239
Michigan Quarterly Review ... M240
MiniWorld Magazine ... M244
My Weekly ... M249
NB Magazine ... M252
New Internationalist ... M256
New Statesman ... M258
Norfolk & Suffolk Bride ... M260
OK! Magazine ... M266
Orbis International Literary Journal ... M269
Oxford Poetry ... M270
Park Home and Holiday Living ... M276
PC Gamer ... M278
PC Pro ... M279

Pennine Ink Magazine	M280	
Pensacola Magazine	M281	
Pilot	M284	
Poetry Ireland Review	M288	
Poetry Wales	M291	
Political Quarterly, The	M292	
Practising Midwife, The	M295	
Preservation Magazine	M297	
Pride	M298	
Racecar Engineering	M304	
Rail Express	M306	
Reactor	M307	
Reader, The	M308	
Red Magazine	M309	
Redbook Magazine	M310	
Riposte	M312	
River Hills Traveler	M313	
Rock & Gem	M316	
Round Hall	P383	
Rugby World	M317	
Ruralite	M318	
Saddlebag Dispatches	M319	
SAIL Magazine	M320	
Sailing Today	M321	
Savannah Magazine	M322	
Scifaikuest	M323	
Scots Magazine, The	M324	
Scottish Farmer, The	M325	
Scottish Field	M326	
Seaworthy Publications	P403	
Seventeen	M329	
Ships Monthly Magazine	M332	
Sierra	M336	
Snowflake Magazine	M338	
SOMA	M340	
Somerset Life	M341	
Southern Theatre	M347	
Southwest Review	M348	
Spa Magazine	M350	
Speciality Food	M351	
Square Mile Magazine	M354	
Strange Horizons	M357	
Strategic Finance	M358	
Successful Meetings	M361	
Supplement, The	M365	
Swimming Pool News	M367	
That's Life!	M373	
This England	M376	
Threepenny Review, The	M377	
Tocher	M378	
Uncut	M383	
Virginia Wine & Country Life	M390	
Virginia Wine & Country Weddings	M391	
Viz	M392	
Vogue	M393	
Walk Magazine	M395	
Wallace Stevens Journal, The	M396	
Wallpaper	M397	
Wasafiri	M398	
Welsh Country	M399	
Westchester Magazine	M402	
Wine Enthusiast	M406	
Woman & Home	M407	
Yachting Monthly	M408	
Yankee Magazine	M410	
Yorkshire Life	M413	
Yorkshire Women's Life Magazine	M414	
Your Cat	M415	
Yours	M416	

Arts

See more specifically: Art Criticism; Art History; Church Art; Drawing; Painting; Performing Arts; Photography; Practical Art; Visual Arts

African American Review	M014
Alcock, Michael	L014
Anvil Press Publishers	P028
Arcadia Publishing	P031
Art Monthly	M030
Art Papers	M031
Art Quarterly	M032
Atlanta Magazine	M035
Aurora Metro Press	P039
Bal, Emma	L038
Barr, Anjanette	L045
Basalt Books	P057
Bear Deluxe Magazine, The	M052
Bernardi, Amanda	L062
Birlinn Ltd	P067
Bloomsbury Academic	P071
Blue Star Press	P075
Brailsford, Karen	L077
Brattesani, Hannah	L079
Brewin Books Ltd	P081
Brick	M074
Bright Press	P082
British Museum Press, The	P084
Caitlin Press Inc.	P090
Charlesbridge Publishing	P102
Chase Literary Agency	L118
Chronicle Books LLC	P111
Compassiviste Publishing	P121
Conversation (UK), The	M095
Conville, Clare	L137
Cotswold Life	M098
Cowboys & Indians	M101
Coyote Arts	P125
Crabtree Publishing	P126
Crown Publishing Group, The	P131
Curran, Sabhbh	L145
Denis Kitchen Publishing Company Co., LLC	P138
Devon Life	M119
Draper, Claire	L178
Ekphrastic Review, The	M128
Elliott & Thompson	P149
Enitharmon Editions	P153
Feminist Press, The	P163
Feminist Studies	M139
Flaneur	M145
Frances Goldin Literary Agency, Inc.	L238
Future Fire, The	M158
Gale	P177
Galustian, Natalie	L251
Gill Education	P182
Global Lion Intellectual Property Management, Inc.	L264
Goose Lane Editions	P188
Graywolf Lab	M172
Grossman, Loren R.	L280
Harvard University Press	P206
Haus Publishing	P208
Hazel Press	P211
Hudson Review, The	M190
Image	M195
Imagine Publishing	P234
Inque	M198
Island Online	M205
Johns Hopkins University Press, The	P250
Kane Press	P251
Kent Life	M209
Kim, Julia	L367
Korero Press	P257
Lambert, Sophie	L380
Landfall	M215
Laurence King Publishing	P261
Lilliput Press, The	P268
Limelight Management	L400
London Grip	M222
London Review of Books	M225
Lund Humphries Limited	P274
Lutterworth Press, The	P275
Marshall, Jen	L427
Massachusetts Review, The	M237
McCormick Literary	L436
McNidder & Grace	P286
Metro Publications Ltd	P295
Metropolis Magazine	M239
MIT Press, The	P303
Monacelli Press, The	P304
Morrell, Imogen	L460
Muscato, Nate	L469
New England Review	M255
New Statesman	M258
No Starch Press, Inc.	P318
Ohio University Press	P324
Oneworld Publications	P327
Otago University Press	P330
Pavilion Books	P338
Peepal Tree Press	P341
Pelham, Imogen	L504
Peter Lang	P346
Peter Lang Publishing	P348
Pineapple Press	P356
Power Cut Lite	M294
Prestel Publishing Ltd	P362
Prufrock Press	P363
Quill Driver Books	P368
R D Publishers	P370
Ramer, Susan	L528
Reilly, Milly	L533
Riposte	M312
Rocky Mountain Books	P378
Sasquatch Books	P391
Scala Arts & Heritage Publishers	P392
Schiffer Publishing	P398
Scoular, Rosemary	L570
Seren Books	P405
Seymour, Charlotte	L575
Society for Promoting Christian Knowledge (SPCK)	P414
SOMA	M340
Southwest Review	M348
Square Mile Magazine	M354
Stipes Publishing	P431
Sunshine Artist	M363
Taylor & Francis Group	P441
Texas A&M University Press	P445
Thames & Hudson Inc.	P446
Thayer, Henry	L626
Threepenny Review, The	M377
Trudel, Jes.	L634
Tyndale House Publishers, Inc.	P465
University of Alberta Press	P477
University of California Press	P478
University of Maine Press	P481
University of Massachusetts Press	P482
University of Michigan Press, The	P483
University of Nevada Press	P484
University of Texas Press	P488
University of Virginia Press	P489
Victoria Sanders & Associates LLC	L642
Virginia Quarterly Review, The	M389
Virginia Wine & Country Life	M390
Vogue	M393
W.W. Norton & Company Ltd	P499
W.W. Norton & Company, Inc.	P500
Wallpaper	M397
Welsh Country	M399
White Review, The	M404
Wide-Eyed Editions	P509
Yale Review, The	M409
Yale University Press (London)	P520
Yankee Magazine	M410
ZigZag Education	P523
Zuraw-Friedland, Ayla	L681

Asia

See more broadly: Regional

See more specifically: East Asia; Japan; South-East Asia
Bloomsbury Academic P071
Feminist Press, The P163
HopeRoad P223
Jain Publishing Company, Inc. P244
Manoa M233
Ohio University Press P324
Pluto Press P358
Stanford University Press P427
University of Alberta Press P477
University of California Press P478
University of Michigan Press, The P483
University of Wisconsin Press, The P490

Asian American
See more broadly: Ethnic Groups
Feminist Press, The P163
W.W. Norton & Company, Inc. P500

Astral Projection
See more broadly: Psychic Abilities
Llewellyn Worldwide Ltd. P269

Astrology
See more broadly: Fortune Telling and Divination
Hay House Publishers P210
Llewellyn Worldwide Ltd. P269
Red Feather P375
Rushall, Kathleen L556

Astronomy
See more broadly: Science
Armstrong, Susan L032
Astronomy Now M034
Gale P177
W.W. Norton & Company Ltd P499
W.W. Norton & Company, Inc. P500

Atlanta
See more broadly: Georgia (US State)
Atlanta Magazine M035

Atlantic
See more broadly: Regional
University of Pennsylvania Press P486

Atlantic Northeast
See more broadly: North America
Atlantic Northeast M037

Atlases
Collins P118

Audio Technology
See more broadly: Audio Visual Technology
See more specifically: Radio Technology

Audio Visual Technology
See more broadly: Technology
See more specifically: Audio Technology
Stipes Publishing P431

Audiobooks
Lerner Publishing Group P264

Augmented Reality
See more broadly: Technology

Australasia / Oceania
See more broadly: Regional
See more specifically: New Zealand
University of Alberta Press P477

Austria
See more broadly: Europe

Autism
See more broadly: Neuropsychology
Jessica Kingsley Publishers P246
W.W. Norton & Company Ltd P499

AutoHotKey
See more broadly: Computer Programming

Autobiography
See more broadly: Biography
See more specifically: Autofiction; Memoir; Personal Essays; Personal Experiences
Arcadia Publishing P031
Asabi Publishing P034
Authentic Life P041
Backbeat Books P046

Canterbury Literary Agency L101
Compassiviste Publishing P121
Dillsworth, Elise L170
Engram Books P152
Frances Goldin Literary Agency, Inc. L238
Glenister, Emily L263
Granta Books P192
Grossman, Loren R. L280
Irish Pages M203
JMD Media / DB Publishing P247
Joy Harris Literary Agency, Inc. L340
Kensington Publishing Corp. P253
Limelight Management L400
Marion Boyars Publishers P282
Methuen Publishing Ltd P294
MMB Creative L455
NBM Publishing P312
Robert Smith Literary Agency Ltd L539
Robertson Murray Literary Agency L541
Scratching Shed Publishing P402
Strachan Literary Agency L602
Turner Publishing P462
Tyndale House Publishers, Inc. P465
University of Alberta Press P477
University of Massachusetts Press P482
University of Nevada Press P484
University of Virginia Press P489
University of Wisconsin Press, The P490
Victoria Sanders & Associates LLC L642
Zack Company, Inc, The L678

Autofiction
See more broadly: Autobiography
Goldstein, Veronica L268
MMB Creative L455
Tolka M379
Yeoh, Rachel L675

Avant-Garde
Midsummer Dream House M242

Aviation
See more broadly: Transport
See more specifically: Military Aviation
Air & Space Quarterly M018
Countryside Books P124
History Press, The P221
Schiffer Military History P397
Zack Company, Inc, The L678

Ayurveda
See more broadly: Alternative Health
Singing Dragon P409

Baha'i
See more broadly: Religion
Oneworld Publications P327

Baseball
See more broadly: Sport
Spitball M353

Basketball
See more broadly: Sport
Thayer, Henry L626

Beat Generation
See more broadly: Literature

Beauty
See more specifically: Hairstyles; Make-Up
Chronicle Books LLC P111
Finan, Ciara L223
First For Women M142
Healthy M180
Laurence King Publishing P261
marie claire M234
marie claire (UK) M235
My Weekly M249
Pride M298
Red Magazine M309
Redbook Magazine M310
Scottish Field M326
Seventeen M329
Vogue M393

Wallpaper M397
Woman & Home M407
Yours M416

Beer
See more broadly: Drinks
See more specifically: Beer Making

Beer Making
See more broadly: Beer
Virginia Wine & Country Life M390

Bible Stories
See more broadly: Christianity
Barbour Publishing P056
Moody Publishers P305

Bible Studies
See more broadly: Christianity
Barbour Publishing P056
Brown, Megan L088
College Press Publishing P117
Crossway P128
Fortress Press P170
Moody Publishers P305
Pacific Press Publishing Association P334
Society for Promoting Christian
   Knowledge (SPCK) P414
WordCrafts Press P514

Bibles
See more broadly: Christianity
Barbour Publishing P056

Bigfoot
See more broadly: Folklore, Myths, and Legends

Biker Lifestyle
See more broadly: Lifestyle

Biochemistry
See more broadly: Biology; Chemistry

Bioethics
See more broadly: Biology

Biography
See more specifically: Autobiography
Alcock, Michael L014
Allison & Busby Ltd L019
Ammonite Press P024
Arcadia Publishing P031
Asabi Publishing P034
Atyeo, Charlotte L034
Aurora Metro Press P039
Authentic Life P041
Backbeat Books P046
Barr, Anjanette L045
Bartholomew, Jason L047
Basalt Books P057
Bess Press P064
Betsy Amster Literary Enterprises L063
Birlinn Ltd P067
Blackstaff Press P068
Bradford Literary Agency L075
Brailsford, Karen L077
Brannan, Maria L078
Brewin Books Ltd P081
Caitlin Press Inc P090
Canterbury Literary Agency L101
Canterbury Press P094
Carter, Rebecca L111
Charlesbridge Publishing P102
Chase Literary Agency L118
Chelsea House Publishers P105
Clarke, Catherine L129
College Press Publishing P117
Compassiviste Publishing P121
Coombs Moylett & Maclean Literary
   Agency L139
Crabtree Publishing P126
Crown P129
Crown Publishing Group, The P131
Cynthia Cannell Literary Agency L150
Dana Newman Literary, LLC L152
Darga, Jon Michael L155

Access more listings online at www.firstwriter.com

Derviskadic, Dado L164
Dixon, Isobel L171
Dolby, Trevor L173
Doug Grad Literary Agency L177
Dunham, Jennie L180
Dynasty Press P147
Eisenmann, Caroline L192
Elliott & Thompson P149
Emily Sweet Associates L199
Engram Books L152
Enslow Publishers, Inc. P154
Feminist Press, The P163
Fernwood Publishing P164
Filter Press P166
Frances Collin Literary Agent ... L237
Free Spirit Publishing P174
Furniss, Eugenie L249
Galustian, Natalie L251
Geiger, Ellen L255
Gill Books P181
Glenister, Emily L263
Globe Pequot Press, The P184
Gordon, Andrew L270
Greyhound Literary L278
Harvard University Press P206
Haus Publishing P208
History Press, The P221
Holloway, Sally L318
Icon Books Ltd P227
InterVarsity Press (IVP) P243
JMD Media / DB Publishing P247
Joelle Delbourgo Associates, Inc. ... L334
Jonathan Pegg Literary Agency ... L337
Kensington Publishing Corp. P253
Kim, Julia L367
Kube Publishing P258
Lazin, Sarah L388
Lilliput Press, The P268
Limelight Management L400
Logaston Press P271
London Review of Books M225
Lutterworth Press, The P275
Malahat Review, The M232
McCormick Literary L436
McNidder & Grace P286
Methuen Publishing Ltd P294
Michel, Caroline L446
Mihell, Natasha L448
Mills, Rachel L452
Moorhead, Max L459
Mundy, Toby L466
Murray, Judith L468
Native Ink Press P311
NBM Publishing P312
O'Grady, Faith L485
Oghma Creative Media P321
Oneworld Publications P327
Otago University Press P330
Ouen Press P331
Pacific Press Publishing Association ... P334
Pande, Ayesha L497
Perez Literary & Entertainment ... L506
Perez, Kristina L507
Pestritto, Carrie L511
Plexus Publishing Limited P357
Quill Driver Books P368
Reid, Janet L532
Robert Smith Literary Agency Ltd ... L539
Roseway P382
Rutman, Jim L558
Salvo, Katie L560
Scifaikuest M323
Scratching Shed Publishing P402
Seren Books P405
Sheil Land Associates Ltd L577
Sheree Bykofsky Associates, Inc. ... L579

Shipwreckt Books Publishing
  Company P406
Society for Promoting Christian
  Knowledge (SPCK) P414
Sunbelt Publications, Inc. P433
Sweet, Emily L614
Texas A&M University Press ... P445
Thames & Hudson Inc. P446
Thayer, Henry L626
Turner Publishing P462
Tyndale House Publishers, Inc. ... P465
University of Alaska Press P476
University of Massachusetts Press ... P482
University of Michigan Press, The ... P483
University of Nevada Press P484
University of Texas Press P488
University of Virginia Press P489
Viney Agency, The L643
W.W. Norton & Company Ltd ... P499
W.W. Norton & Company, Inc. ... P500
Wallace Stevens Journal, The ... M396
Washington State University Press ... P501
Willms, Kathryn L665
WordCrafts Press P514
Wordserve Literary L673
Yale University Press (London) ... P520
Zack Company, Inc, The L678
Biology
See more broadly: Science
See more specifically: Biochemistry; Bioethics;
  Biomedical Science; Evolution; Human
  Biology; Neurobiology; Paleontology
Colourpoint Educational P119
Conrad, Claire Paterson L136
Mentor Books P292
W.W. Norton & Company Ltd ... P499
W.W. Norton & Company, Inc. ... P500
Biomedical Science
See more broadly: Biology; Medicine
Taylor & Francis Group P441
Birds
See more broadly: Animals
Birds & Blooms M062
Regina Ryan Books L531
Black People
See more broadly: Ethnic Groups
Cocoa Girl M088
Peepal Tree Press P341
Bluegrass
See more broadly: Music
Bluegrass Unlimited M069
Board Books
Allen & Unwin P018
Arcadia Publishing P031
Ascend Books, LLC P035
Baobab Press P054
Bess Press P064
Caroline Sheldon Literary Agency ... L106
Charlesbridge Publishing P102
Cherry Lake Publishing Group ... P106
Child's Play (International) Ltd ... P107
Chronicle Books LLC P111
Crabtree Publishing P126
DK Publishing P141
Eerdmans Books for Young Readers ... P148
Free Spirit Publishing P174
Happy Yak P200
Hare, Jessica L296
Holroyde, Penny L319
Igloo Books Limited P232
Kube Publishing P258
Macmillan Children's Books P279
Nosy Crow P319
Pavilion Books P338
Schiffer Kids P396
Scholastic UK P400

Susan Schulman Literary Agency ... L610
Sweet Cherry Publishing P437
Templar Books P442
Tilbury House Publishers P450
Trudel, Jes L634
Walsh, Caroline L645
Boats
See more broadly: Vehicles
See more specifically: Motor Boats; Shipping;
  Yachts
Boathooks Books P077
Cornell Maritime Press P123
Cottage Life M099
Cruising World M109
Marlin M236
River Hills Traveler M313
RYA (Royal Yachting Association) ... P385
SAIL Magazine M320
Seaworthy Publications P403
Sunpenny Publishing P435
Book Club Fiction
See more specifically: Book Club Women's Fiction
Armstrong, Susan L032
Baxter, Veronique L052
Berdinsky, Kendall L060
Bolton, Camilla L069
Bookouture P078
Brace, Samantha L074
Brannan, Maria L078
Brewer, Amy L081
Buckley, Louise L091
Caprio, Alice L103
Carroll, Megan L110
Caskie, Robert L113
Chanchani, Sonali L115
Cho, Catherine L124
Crowley, Sheila L144
Curran, Sabhbh L145
Danaczko, Melissa L153
Davies, Elinor L160
Dawson, Liza L162
Dunn, Ben L181
Evans, Kiya L205
Fabien, Samantha L207
Ferguson, Hannah L217
Fergusson, Julie L219
Finan, Ciara L223
Forrester, Jemima L232
Foster, Clara L233
Foxx, Kat L235
Friedman, Claire L243
Glenister, Emily L263
Greenstreet, Katie L277
Grunewald, Hattie L282
Haggerty, Taylor L287
Hardman, Caroline L295
Harper, Logan L299
Harris, Erin L300
Hayden, Viola L305
Hordern, Kate L320
Hornsley, Sarah L321
Kaliszewska, Joanna L347
Kate Barker Literary, TV, & Film
  Agency L352
Kavanagh, Jade L355
Keane Kataria Literary Agency ... L358
Leeke, Jessica L391
Lightner, Kayla L399
MacDonald, Emily L412
Macdougall, Laura L413
Maidment, Olivia L421
Marini, Victoria L423
Mehren, Jane von L440
Milburn, Madeleine L449
Mileo, Jessica L451
Moore, Mary C. L457

Mushens, Juliet.....................................L470
Napolitano, Maria..................................L473
Nash, Justin..L474
Neely, Rachel......................................L476
Niumata, Erin......................................L480
O'Grady, Niamh....................................L486
Pass, Marina de...................................L500
Perez Literary & Entertainment.................L506
Perez, Kristina.....................................L507
Pickering, Juliet...................................L516
Plitt, Carrie..L520
Polygon..P360
Power, Anna.......................................L523
Preston, Amanda..................................L526
Ramer, Susan......................................L528
Schofield, Hannah.................................L567
Seymour, Charlotte................................L575
Sheil Land Associates Ltd........................L577
Simons, Tanera....................................L585
Simpson, Cara Lee................................L586
Soler, Shania N....................................L589
Steed, Hayley......................................L595
Thorneycroft, Euan................................L628
Thwaites, Steph...................................L629
Topping, Antony...................................L632
Walsh, Caroline....................................L645
Yeoh, Rachel.......................................L675

Book Club Women's Fiction
See more broadly: Book Club Fiction; Women's Fiction
Burke, Kate..L093
Choc Lit...P108
Eberly, Chelsea....................................L187

Book Publishing
See more broadly: Publishing
Bookseller, The....................................M070
NB Magazine......................................M252

Books
See more broadly: Media
Acumen..M012
African American Review........................M014
Banipal...M046
Black Moon Magazine............................M064
Bookseller, The....................................M070
Boston Review.....................................M071
Concho River Review.............................M092
Dalhousie Review, The...........................M113
Event...M133
Foundation: The International Review of Science Fiction.............................M151
Fresh Words – An International Literary Magazine..........................M154
Fugue..M155
Future Fire, The...................................M158
Georgia Review, The..............................M163
Gulf Coast: A Journal of Literature and Fine Arts..................................M173
Hudson Review, The..............................M190
Ireland's Own......................................M202
Landfall..M215
Literary Mama.....................................M220
London Grip.......................................M222
Long Poem Magazine.............................M226
Malahat Review, The..............................M232
Mid-American Review............................M241
Missouri Review, The.............................M245
New Statesman....................................M258
Oxford Review of Books.........................M271
Pleiades..M285
Poetry Wales......................................M291
Political Quarterly, The..........................M292
Reactor..M307
Red Magazine.....................................M309
Sierra..M336
Sinister Wisdom..................................M337
South Carolina Review...........................M344
Spitball...M353
Square Mile Magazine............................M354
Stinging Fly, The..................................M355
Supplement, The..................................M365
Takahe...M369
Tusculum Review, The...........................M381
University of Iowa Press.........................P480
Vagabond City....................................M386
Wallace Stevens Journal, The...................M396

Boxing
See more broadly: Sport
Scratching Shed Publishing......................P402
Square Mile Magazine............................M354

Boy Books
Kimber, Natalie....................................L368

Brazil
See more broadly: South America
University of Wisconsin Press, The............P490

Breconshire
See more broadly: Wales
Logaston Press....................................P271

British Columbia
See more broadly: Canada
See more specifically: Vancouver Island
Arsenal Pulp Press................................P032
Caitlin Press Inc...................................P090

British History
See more broadly: History
Lutterworth Press, The...........................P275
Zack Company, Inc, The.........................L678

Buddhism
See more broadly: Religion
See more specifically: Mahayana Buddhism; Theravada Buddhism
Ericka T. Phillips..................................L200
Oneworld Publications...........................P327
Windhorse Publications Ltd.....................P511
Wisdom Publications.............................P512

Building / Construction
See more broadly: Business
See more specifically: Electrical Contracting
Cottage Life.......................................M099
Gill Education.....................................P182
NAHB BuilderBooks..............................P310
Stipes Publishing..................................P431

Buildings
See more specifically: Houses and Homes

Bullying
See more broadly: Social Issues
Free Spirit Publishing............................P174

Burton upon Trent
See more broadly: Staffordshire

Business
See more specifically: Building / Construction; Business Law; Entrepreneurship; Film Industry; Funeral Industry; Insurance; Investments; Logistics; Management; Marketing; Procurement; Publishing; Trade; Warehousing; Women in Business
Accountancy Age.................................M010
Accountancy Daily................................M011
Arcadia Publishing................................P031
Backbeat Books...................................P046
Banter Press.......................................P053
Baumer, Jan.......................................L051
Berrett-Koehler Publishers......................P063
Birlinn Ltd...P067
Bloomsbury Academic...........................P071
Bradford Literary Agency.......................L075
Business Traveller.................................M076
Campaign..M079
Campos, Vanessa.................................L100
Cassell...P096
CGI (Chartered Governance Institute) Publishing....................................P098
Chartered Institute of Personnel and Development (CIPD) Publishing........P104
Chase Literary Agency...........................L118
Christie, Jennifer..................................L126
Conversation (UK), The.........................M095
Croner-i Limited..................................P127
Crown..P129
Crown Publishing Group, The.................P131
Dana Newman Literary, LLC...................L152
Diana Finch Literary Agency...................L167
Dickerson, Donya.................................L168
Dijkstra, Sandra...................................L169
Doug Grad Literary Agency....................L177
Economist, The...................................M126
Elliott & Thompson..............................P149
Entrepreneur......................................M131
Felicia Eth Literary Representation..........L214
Fogg, Jack...L230
Frankel, Valerie...................................L239
Funny Times......................................M157
Gale..P177
Garamond Agency, Inc., The..................L253
Getzler, Josh......................................L256
Gill Education.....................................P182
Global Lion Intellectual Property Management, Inc..........................L264
Globe Pequot Press, The........................P184
Gordon, Andrew..................................L270
Harmsworth, Esmond............................L297
Harvard University Press........................P206
Hay House Publishers...........................P210
Hiyate, Sam.......................................L313
Hoffman, Scott...................................L316
Holloway, Sally...................................L318
Icon Books Ltd...................................P227
Irene Goodman Literary Agency (IGLA)....................................L324
Jeff Herman Agency, LLC, The................L331
Johns Hopkins University Press, The.........P250
Jonathan Pegg Literary Agency................L337
Karinch, Maryann.................................L351
Kensington Publishing Corp....................P253
Killingley, Jessica..................................L365
Knight Features..................................L373
Kogan Page Ltd..................................P255
Kotchman, Katie..................................L374
Langtons International..........................L384
Leisure Group Travel.............................M216
Limelight Management..........................L400
Loft Press, Inc....................................P270
Marshall, Jen......................................L427
Mehren, Jane von................................L440
Mentor Books....................................P292
New Statesman....................................M258
Oak Tree Press...................................P320
Oneworld Publications...........................P327
Paul S. Levine Literary Agency................L502
Pensacola Magazine.............................M281
Perry Literary....................................L509
Piatkus Books....................................P352
Quill Driver Books...............................P368
Regina Ryan Books..............................L531
Riposte..M312
Rudy Agency, The................................L553
Sasquatch Books.................................P391
Schwartz, Steve..................................L568
Sheree Bykofsky Associates, Inc..............L579
Spa Magazine....................................M350
Speciality Food...................................M351
Stanford University Press.......................P427
Successful Meetings.............................M361
Taylor & Francis Group.........................P441
Thames & Hudson Inc..........................P446
Turner Publishing................................P462
Tyndale House Publishers, Inc.................P465
University of Michigan Press, The............P483

Index | Chick Lit

University of Nevada Press P484
University of Virginia Press P489
Usselman, Laura L639
W.W. Norton & Company Ltd P499
W.W. Norton & Company, Inc. P500
Westchester Magazine M402
Willms, Kathryn L665
WordCrafts Press P514
Writer's Side L674
Yale University Press (London) P520
ZigZag Education P523

Business Law
See more broadly: Business; Legal
Stipes Publishing P431

CIA
See more broadly: Secret Intelligence

California
See more broadly: United States
Sunbelt Publications, Inc. P433

Cambridgeshire
See more broadly: England

Camping
See more broadly: Outdoor Activities
River Hills Traveler M313

Campus Novels
See more specifically: Dark Academia

Canada
See more broadly: North America
See more specifically: Alberta; British Columbia; New Brunswick; Yukon
Fernwood Publishing P164
University of Alberta Press P477

Cannabis
See more broadly: Drugs

Canoeing
See more broadly: Sport

Caravans
See more broadly: Vehicles
Park Home and Holiday Living M276

Career Development
See more broadly: Personal Development
Berrett-Koehler Publishers P063
Betsy Amster Literary Enterprises L063
Kogan Page Ltd P255
marie claire M234
Pride M298
Singing Dragon P409
Zack Company, Inc, The L678

Caribbean
See more broadly: Regional
See more specifically: Cuba
HopeRoad P223
Peepal Tree Press P341
Pluto Press P358
University of Michigan Press, The P483
University of Texas Press P488
University of Virginia Press P489
University of Wisconsin Press, The P490

Caribbean Diaspora
See more broadly: Ethnic Groups
Peepal Tree Press P341

Caribbean History
See more broadly: History
LSU Press P273

Cars
See more broadly: Vehicles
See more specifically: Classic Cars; Mini Cars; Racecars; Sports Cars
Bentley Publishers P061
Doug Grad Literary Agency L177
Square Mile Magazine M354
WordCrafts Press P514

Cartoons
Beano, The M051
Black Warrior Review M066
Denis Kitchen Publishing Company Co., LLC P138
Funny Times M157
Kids Alive! M212
Oakland Arts Review, The M264
Soho Review, The M339
Viz M392

Catholicism
See more broadly: Christianity
See more specifically: Ignation Spirituality
Liguori Publications P267
Loyola Press P272

Cats
See more broadly: Pets
Rutherford, Laetitia L557
Your Cat M415

Caving and Potholing
See more broadly: Outdoor Activities
Descent M118
Wild Places Publishing P510

Celebrity
See more broadly: Entertainment
See more specifically: Sports Celebrity
Bella M053
Essex Life M132
Granger, David L275
Heymont, Lane L309
Kent Life M209
Kruger Cowne L376
marie claire M234
marie claire (UK) M235
Mirror Books P301
Nolan, Laura L481
OK! Magazine M266
Pierce, Rosie L517
Seventeen M329
YMU Books L676
Yours M416

Celebrity Memoir
See more broadly: Memoir
Richter, Rick L537

Central America
See more broadly: Regional
Arte Publico Press P033
Ohio State University Press, The P323
Ohio University Press P324
Phillips, Aemilia L515
Pinata Books P355
Sunbelt Publications, Inc. P433

Central Europe
See more broadly: Europe
Purdue University Press P364

Ceramics
See more broadly: Collectibles; Crafts
LW Books P276

Chakras
See more broadly: Psychic Abilities
Llewellyn Worldwide Ltd P269

Chapbooks
Anhinga Press P027
Dancing Girl Press P133
Glass Poetry Press P183
Hiraeth Books P220
Sinister Stoat Press P410
Slope Editions P411
Tyndale House Publishers, Inc. P465

Chapter Books
4RV Publishing P004
Alex Adsett Literary L016
Allen & Unwin P018
Alternating Current Press P020
Arcadia Publishing P031
Armada, Kurestin L030
Badger Learning P048
Bent Agency (UK), The L057
Bent Agency, The L058
Bright Agency (UK), The L082
Bright Agency (US), The L083
Brooks, Savannah L084
Caroline Sheldon Literary Agency L106
Chronicle Books LLC P111
Cooper, Gemma L140
Crabtree Publishing P126
Dunow, Carlson & Lerner Agency L184
Filter Press P166
Flynn, Amy Thrall L229
Guppy Books P195
Hare, Jessica L296
Harwell, Hilary L301
Hawk, Susan L303
Holroyde, Penny L319
Irvine, Lucy L325
Kane Press P251
Kube Publishing P258
Lakosil, Natalie L379
Lantana Publishing P260
Macmillan Children's Books P279
Native Ink Press P311
Nosy Crow P319
O'Grady, Faith L485
Oghma Creative Media P321
Ostby, Kristin L494
Pacific Press Publishing Association P334
Pen & Ink Designs Publishing P342
Petty, Rachel L512
Phoenix Moirai P351
Piccadilly Press P354
Richter, Rick L537
Rofe, Jennifer L545
Scholastic P399
Scholastic UK P400
Susan Schulman Literary Agency L610
Sutherland, Kari L611
Sweet Cherry Publishing P437
Terlip, Paige L624
Thames & Hudson Inc. P446
Trudel, Jes. L634
Turner Publishing P462
W.W. Norton & Company Ltd P499
Walsh, Caroline L645

Charlottesville
See more broadly: Albemarle
CharlottesvilleFamily M082

Chemistry
See more broadly: Science
See more specifically: Biochemistry
Colourpoint Educational P119
Gale P177
Stipes Publishing P431
Taylor & Francis Group P441
W.W. Norton & Company Ltd P499
W.W. Norton & Company, Inc. P500

Chesapeake Bay
See more broadly: United States
Tidewater Publishers P449

Cheshire
See more broadly: England
See more specifically: Chester

Chess
See more broadly: Games

Chester
See more broadly: Cheshire

Chicago
See more broadly: Illinois

Chick Lit
See more broadly: Women's Fiction
Coombs Moylett & Maclean Literary Agency L139
Leon, Nina L394
Pestritto, Carrie L511
Tran, Jennifer Chen L633
Zack Company, Inc, The L678

Claim your free access to www.firstwriter.com: See p.403

330 Index | Child Psychotherapy

Child Psychotherapy
See more broadly: Juvenile Psychotherapy
W.W. Norton & Company Ltd P499
Childbirth
See more broadly: Pregnancy
Foxx, Kat..................L235
Singing Dragon P409
Childcare
See more broadly: Children
Zack Company, Inc, The L678
Children
See more broadly: Family
See more specifically: Childcare
Scratching Shed Publishing P402
University of Massachusetts Press..................P482
Children's
3 Seas Literary Agency..................L001
4RV Publishing P004
Above the Line Agency..................L003
AdventureBox M013
Agency (London) Ltd, The..................L009
Albert Whitman & Company..................P015
Alex Adsett Literary..................L016
Alice Williams Literary..................L017
Allen & Unwin..................P018
Alternating Current Press P020
Anderson, Darley..................L022
Andrade, Hannah..................L023
Andrew Nurnberg Associates, Ltd..................L024
Andrews McMeel Publishing P026
Anne Clark Literary Agency L028
Arcadia Publishing P031
Armada, Kurestin L030
Arms, Victoria Wells..................L031
Arsenal Pulp Press..................P032
Asabi Publishing..................P034
Ascend Books, LLC P035
Atyeo, Charlotte L034
Autumn Publishing Ltd P042
Babybug M041
Badger Learning..................P048
Baobab Press P054
Barbican Press..................P055
Barbour Publishing..................P056
Baror International, Inc...................L044
Barr, Anjanette L045
Basalt Books..................P057
Bath Literary Agency L049
Bauman, Erica..................L050
Baxter, Veronique L052
BBC Doctor Who Magazine..................M048
Beano, The M051
Belton, Maddy..................L055
Bent Agency (UK), The..................L057
Bent Agency, The..................L058
Bess Press..................P064
Better Than Starbucks M058
Borstel, Stefanie Sanchez Von..................L071
Bradford Literary Agency..................L075
Bradford, Laura..................L076
Brewin Books Ltd P081
Bright Agency (UK), The..................L082
Bright Agency (US), The..................L083
Brooks, Savannah..................L084
Burns, Camille..................L094
C&W (Conville & Walsh)..................L096
CAA (London) L098
Cadno..................P089
Caitlin Press Inc..................P090
Candy Jar Books..................P093
Caprio, Alice..................L103
Caroline Sheldon Literary Agency..................L106
Carroll, Megan L110
Carter, Rebecca L111
Cartey, Claire L112
Charlesbridge Publishing..................P102
Cherry Lake Publishing Group..................P106
Child's Play (International) Ltd..................P107
Chiotti, Danielle..................L123
Chronicle Books LLC..................P111
Cichello, Kayla L127
Clarke, Catherine L129
Classical Comics..................P114
Cobblestone M087
Cocoa Girl M088
Colwill, Charlotte..................L132
Comparato, Andrea..................L134
Cooper, Gemma..................L140
Crabtree Publishing..................P126
Crandall, Becca..................L142
Curtis Brown..................L146
Cusick, John..................L148
DeVorss & Company..................P139
DHH Literary Agency Ltd L166
DK Publishing P141
Dodd, Saffron L172
Dominguez, Adriana..................L174
Draper, Claire L178
Dunham Literary, Inc...................L179
Dunham, Jennie L180
Dunow, Carlson & Lerner Agency..................L184
Eberly, Chelsea..................L187
Eddison Pearson Ltd L188
Eerdmans Books for Young Readers..................P148
Eisenbraun, Nicole..................L191
Ellor, Zabé..................L198
Eunice McMullen Children's Literary Agent Ltd L201
Evan-Moor Educational Publishers..................P157
Everything With Words P158
Fabien, Samantha..................L207
Fairbank Literary Representation L208
Fazzari, Hillary L210
Feldmann, Kait Lee..................L212
Fellows, Abi..................L216
Feminist Press, The..................P163
Ferguson, T.S..................L218
Fernandez, Rochelle..................L220
Figueroa, Melanie L221
Fillingham Weston Associates..................L222
Filter Press P166
Finegan, Stevie L226
Firefly P167
Flannery Literary L228
Flynn, Amy Thrall L229
Frances Goldin Literary Agency, Inc. L238
Fraser Ross Associates..................L240
Free Spirit Publishing..................P174
Friedman, Claire L243
Fuller, Lisa..................L248
Gahan, Isobel L250
Gauntlett, Adam..................L254
Getzler, Josh L256
Ghahremani, Lilly L257
Gilbert, Tara..................L258
Gill Books..................P181
Gisondi, Katie..................L261
Glass Literary Management LLC..................L262
Goetz, Adria..................L265
Goff, Anthony..................L266
Goff, Ellen L267
Good Literary Agency, The L269
Graffeg Childrens P191
Grajkowski, Kara..................L273
Grajkowski, Michelle..................L274
Greyhound Literary..................L278
Gruber, Pam..................L281
Gunic, Masha..................L284
Guppy Books P195
Hakim, Serene..................L288
Haley, Jolene..................L289
Hannah Sheppard Literary Agency L291
Hannigan, Carrie L292
Happy Yak P200
Hare, Jessica..................L296
Harwell, Hilary..................L301
Hashtag Press P207
Hawk, Susan..................L303
Hawn, Molly Ker..................L304
Hensley, Chelsea..................L307
Hernando, Paloma L308
Hodges, Jodie L315
Holroyde, Penny..................L319
Hordern, Kate..................L320
IDW Publishing..................P228
IgKids..................P231
Igloo Books Limited..................P232
Inscriptions Literary Agency L323
Irvine, Lucy L325
Jamieson, Molly L329
Jamii Publishing P245
Janklow & Nesbit UK Ltd L330
Jessica Kingsley Publishers P246
Jo Unwin Literary Agency..................L333
Joelle Delbourgo Associates, Inc...................L334
K2 Literary..................L344
Kahn, Ella Diamond L345
Kane Press..................P251
Kate Nash Literary Agency L353
Kathryn Green Literary Agency, LLC L354
Kean, Taylor Martindale..................L357
Kensington Publishing Corp...................P253
Kids Alive! M212
Knigge, Sheyla L372
KT Literary..................L377
Kube Publishing P258
Lakosil, Natalie L379
Landis, Sarah..................L381
Langlee, Lina..................L382
Langton, Becca..................L383
Lantana Publishing P260
Latshaw, Katherine..................L386
Laurence King Publishing P261
Leapfrog Press..................P263
Lechon, Shannon L390
Lees, Jordan..................L392
Leon, Nina..................L394
Lerner Publishing Group P264
Lindsay Literary Agency..................L401
Lutterworth Press, The P275
MacLeod, Lauren L418
Macmillan Children's Books..................P279
Madeleine Milburn Literary, TV & Film Agency L420
Margaret K. McElderry Books P281
Marion Boyars Publishers..................P282
Marr, Jill..................L425
Marshall, Jen L427
Mattson, Jennifer..................L432
Maurer, Shari..................L433
McBride, Juliana L435
Megibow, Sara L439
Mihell, Natasha L448
Mileo, Jessica..................L451
Miranda, Caroline..................L454
Moody Publishers..................P305
Moore, Penny L458
Morris, Natascha L461
Mustelier, James..................L471
Nathan, Abigail L475
Native Ink Press P311
Nelson Literary Agency, LLC L477
No Starch Press, Inc. P318
Northern Gravy M263
Nosy Crow P319
O'Brien, Lee L484
O'Grady, Faith..................L485
O'Neill, Molly L487

Access more listings online at **www.firstwriter.com**

Column 1	Column 2	Column 3

Oghma Creative Media P321
Oh MG Press P322
Olswanger, Anna L491
Oneworld Publications P327
Ostby, Kristin L494
Pacific Press Publishing Association P334
Pages, Saribel L496
Pan Macmillan Australia P335
Parker, Elana Roth L499
Paul S. Levine Literary Agency L502
Pavilion Books P338
Pen & Ink Designs Publishing P342
Pestritto, Carrie L511
Peter Pauper Press P350
Petty, Rachel L512
Phelan, Beth L514
Phoenix Moirai P351
Piccadilly Press P354
Pinata Books P355
Pineapple Press P356
Plant, Zoe L519
Posner, Marcy L522
Prasanna, Tanusri L525
Prufrock Press P363
Quarto Group, Inc., The P367
Quirk Books P369
R D Publishers P370
Rand McNally P371
Ransom Publishing Ltd P373
Regina Ryan Books L531
Reino, Jessica L534
Richter, Rick L537
Robertson Murray Literary Agency L541
Robinson, Quressa L542
Rocky Mountain Books P378
Rofe, Jennifer L545
Rogers, Coleridge & White Ltd L546
Ross, Whitney L551
Rubin Pfeffer Content, LLC L552
Rudy Agency, The L553
Rushall, Kathleen L556
Saguaro Books, LLC P388
Salvo, Katie L560
Sanchez, Kaitlyn L561
Sant, Kelly Van L563
Scarfe, Rory L566
Schiffer Kids P396
Scholastic P399
Scholastic UK P400
Scratching Shed Publishing P402
Seager, Chloe L571
Shaw Agency, The L576
Sheil Land Associates Ltd L577
Shestopal, Camilla L581
Singing Dragon P409
Siobhan, Aiden L587
Society for Promoting Christian
  Knowledge (SPCK) P414
Soler, Shania N. L589
Soloway, Jennifer March L590
Sophie Hicks Agency L591
Spring Literary L594
Stephens, Jenny L596
Stewart, Douglas L599
StoryWise L601
Strachan Literary Agency L602
Stringer Literary Agency LLC, The L603
Sunbelt Publications, Inc. P433
Sunberry Books P434
Sunpenny Publishing P435
Susan Schulman Literary Agency L610
Sutherland, Kari L611
Sweet Cherry Publishing P437
SYLA – Susan Yearwood Literary
  Agency L616
Symonds, Laurel L617

Talbot, Emily L619
Templar Books P442
Terlip, Paige L624
Thames & Hudson Inc. P446
Thwaites, Steph L629
Tidewater Publishers P449
Tilbury House Publishers P450
Tiny Owl P451
Tippermuir Books P452
Tran, Jennifer Chen L633
Troika Books P461
Trudel, Jes L634
Turner Publishing P462
Two Piers Literary Agency, The L636
Tyndale House Publishers, Inc. P465
Unwin, Jo L638
Victoria Sanders & Associates LLC L642
Viney Agency, The L643
Vinspire Publishing P497
W.W. Norton & Company Ltd P499
Walsh, Caroline L645
Watson, Little Ltd L647
Watterson, Jessica L648
Weiman, Paula L649
Weiss, Alexandra L650
Weitzner, Tess L651
Westin, Erin Casey L654
Whatnall, Michaela L655
Whispering Buffalo Literary Agency .. L657
Wide-Eyed Editions P509
Williams, Laura L662
Williamson, Jo L664
Wilson, Desiree L667
Woods, Bryony L671
WordCrafts Press P514
Words & Pictures P515
Wordserve Literary L673
WordSong P516
Wordsworth Editions P518
Workman Publishing P519
Yale University Press (London) P520
Zacker, Marietta B. L679

China
See more broadly: South-East Asia

Chinese Medicine
See more broadly: Alternative Health
Blue Poppy Enterprises P074
Singing Dragon P409

Chinese Philosophy
See more broadly: Philosophy
Blue Poppy Enterprises P074

Choral Music
See more broadly: Music

Christian Living
See more broadly: Christianity
Barbour Publishing P056
Brown, Megan L088
Charisma House P100
Crossway P128
InterVarsity Press (IVP) P243
Moody Publishers P305
Pacific Press Publishing Association ... P334
Society for Promoting Christian
  Knowledge (SPCK) P414
Stone, Geoffrey L600
Tyndale House Publishers, Inc. P465
WordCrafts Press P514

Christian Romance
See more broadly: Romance
See more specifically: Amish Romance
Inscriptions Literary Agency L323
Rose and Crown Books P381
Sunpenny Publishing P435

Christianity
See more broadly: Religion

See more specifically: Amish; Bible Stories; Bible Studies; Bibles; Catholicism; Christian Living; Evangelism; Methodism; Mormonism; Quakerism
4RV Publishing P004
Abuzz Press P010
Ambassador Speakers Bureau &
  Literary Agency L019
Balow, Dan L039
Barbour Publishing P056
Baylor University Press P060
Brown, Megan L088
Canterbury Press P094
Charisma House P100
ChristLight Books P110
College Press Publishing P117
Crossway P128
Eason, Lynette L186
Fortress Press P170
Inscriptions Literary Agency L323
Kids Alive! M212
MacGregor & Luedeke L414
Moody Publishers P305
Oneworld Publications P327
Pacific Press Publishing Association .. P334
SCM Press P401
Society for Promoting Christian
  Knowledge (SPCK) P414
Sunpenny Publishing P435
Tyndale House Publishers, Inc. P465
WordCrafts Press P514
Wordserve Literary L673

Church Architecture
See more broadly: Architecture
Lutterworth Press, The P275

Church Art
See more broadly: Arts
Lutterworth Press, The P275

Church History
See more broadly: History
Crossway P128
InterVarsity Press (IVP) P243
Lutterworth Press, The P275
Pacific Press Publishing Association .. P334

Church Music
See more broadly: Music
See more specifically: Hymnals

Cider
See more broadly: Drinks

Cinemas / Movie Theaters
See more broadly: Film Industry
University of Wisconsin Press, The ... P490

City and Town Planning
See more broadly: Architecture
Brick M074
Metropolis Magazine M239
University of Alberta Press P477

Civil Rights
See more broadly: Politics
New Internationalist M256

Classic Cars
See more broadly: Cars

Classical Music
See more broadly: Music
Edenborough, Sam L189

Classics / Ancient World
Barbican Press P055
Bloomsbury Academic P071
Fazzari, Hillary L210
Foxx, Kat L235
Harvard University Press P206
Johns Hopkins University Press, The . P250
London Review of Books M225
Lutterworth Press, The P275
Methuen Publishing Ltd P294
Nash, Justin L474

332 Index | Climate Science

Ohio State University Press, The P323
Oxbow Books P333
Oxford Review of Books M271
Stipes Publishing P431
Thames & Hudson Inc. P446
University of California Press P478
University of Michigan Press, The P483
University of Texas Press P488
University of Wisconsin Press, The P490
W.W. Norton & Company Ltd P499
Zack Company, Inc, The L678
ZigZag Education P523

Climate Science

See more broadly: Earth Science; Environment

Cooper, Maggie L141
Fernwood Publishing P164
Hazel Press P211
Mendia, Isabel L441
Salt Publishing P389
Sierra M336
University of Alberta Press P477
Weiss, Alexandra L650

Climbing

See more broadly: Sport

Coffee Table Books

EPTA Books P155
Imagine Publishing P234

Cognitive Science

See more broadly: Science

Collectibles

See more specifically: Ceramics

Arcadia Publishing P031
Goss & Crested China Club P189
LW Books P276

College / University

See more broadly: School

See more specifically: Harvard

Colorado

See more broadly: United States

Filter Press P166
University Press of Colorado P491

Colouring Books

Abuzz Press P010
Hiraeth Books P220
Igloo Books Limited P232
Pavilion Books P338
Pen & Ink Designs Publishing P342
Sunbelt Publications, Inc. P433
Unseen Press P492

Comedy / Humour

See more specifically: Dark Humour; Romantic Comedy; Satire

Allison & Busby Ltd P019
Andrews McMeel Publishing P026
Arcadia Publishing P031
Armada, Kurestin L030
Authentic Ideas P040
Baffler, The M043
Barr, Nicola L046
Baumer, Jan L051
Baxter, Veronique L052
Beano, The M051
Belton, Maddy L055
Better Than Starbucks M058
Birlinn Ltd P067
Blue Star Press P075
Bowlin, Sarah L073
Bradford Literary Agency L075
Brattesani, Hannah L079
Brewer, Amy L081
Brewin Books Ltd P081
Canterbury Press P094
Carroll, Megan L110
Chase Literary Agency L118
Chiotti, Danielle L123
Christie, Jennifer L126
Cichello, Kayla L127
Colwill, Charlotte L132
Compassiviste Publishing P121
Countryside Books P124
Crabtree Publishing P126
Crown Publishing Group, The P131
Crystal Magazine M110
Cusick, John L148
Danko, Margaret L154
Dawson, Liza L162
Dolby, Trevor L173
Doug Grad Literary Agency L177
Dunham, Jennie L180
Eberly, Chelsea L187
Elliott & Thompson P149
Ellor, Zabé L198
Fairbank Literary Representation L208
Forrester, Jemima L232
Fuentes, Sarah L247
Funny Times M157
Furniss, Eugenie L249
Galustian, Natalie L251
Getzler, Josh L256
Ghahremani, Lilly L257
Gilbert, Tara L258
Gill Books P181
Graham, Stacey L272
Greyhound Literary L278
Gunic, Masha L284
Haley, Jolene L289
Hannah Sheppard Literary Agency L291
Hannigan, Carrie L292
Hashtag Press P207
Hernando, Paloma L308
Hodges, Jodie L315
Imagine Publishing P234
Irvine, Lucy L325
JMD Media / DB Publishing P247
Jonathan Pegg Literary Agency L337
Joy Harris Literary Agency, Inc. L340
Kahn, Jody L346
Kathryn Green Literary Agency, LLC L354
Kensington Publishing Corp. P253
Lechon, Shannon L390
Levitt, Sarah L396
Macdougall, Laura L413
Mack, Kate L415
Marr, Jill L425
Medina Publishing P289
NBM Publishing P312
O'Grady, Faith L485
O'Grady, Niamh L486
O'Neill, Molly L487
O'Shea, Amy L488
Oneworld Publications P327
Orenda Books P329
Ostby, Kristin L494
Parker, Elana Roth L499
Pavilion Books P338
Quill Driver Books P368
Quirk Books P369
R D Publishers P370
Reilly, Milly L533
Reino, Jessica L534
Robert Smith Literary Agency Ltd L539
Robertson Murray Literary Agency L541
Rutherford, Laetitia L557
Salt Publishing P389
Sanchez, Kaitlyn L561
Schwartz, Steve L568
Scratching Shed Publishing P402
Sheil Land Associates Ltd L577
Sheree Bykofsky Associates, Inc. L579
Soho Review, The M339
Soler, Shania N. L589
Soloway, Jennifer March L590
Square Mile Magazine M354
Story Unlikely M356
Strachan Literary Agency L602
Swainson, Joanna L613
Thames & Hudson Inc. P446
Topping, Antony L632
Tyndale House Publishers, Inc. P465
Vance, Lisa Erbach L641
Victoria Sanders & Associates LLC L642
Viz M392
W.W. Norton & Company Ltd P499
W.W. Norton & Company, Inc. P500
Watterson, Jessica L648
Wells, Karmen L652
Whelan, Maria L656
Williams, Katie L661
Williams, Laura L662
Williamson, Jo L664
WordCrafts Press P514
Workman Publishing P519
Young, Claudia L677
Zack Company, Inc, The L678

Comic Books

Denis Kitchen Publishing Company Co., LLC P138
Ohio State University Press, The P323
Thames & Hudson Inc. P446
University of Texas Press P488

Comics

Denis Kitchen Publishing Company Co., LLC P138
Hodges, Jodie L315
IDW Publishing P228
Kensington Publishing Corp. P253
Nashville Review M251
Shenandoah M331
Turner Publishing P462

Coming of Age

Brace, Samantha L074
Carroll, Megan L110
Chanchani, Sonali L115
Ellis-Martin, Sian L197
Gahan, Isobel L250
Gruber, Pam L281
Haley, Jolene L289
Hashtag Press P207
Maltese, Alyssa L422
Miranda, Caroline L454
Pierce, Rosie L517
Plitt, Carrie L520
Prasanna, Tanusri L525
Sanchez, Kaitlyn L561
W.W. Norton & Company, Inc. P500
Weiss, Alexandra L650
Wells, Karmen L652
Wickers, Chandler L659

Commentary

See more specifically: Cultural Commentary; Social Commentary

Commercial

See more specifically: Commercial Fantasy; Commercial Women's Fiction; Upmarket Commercial Fiction

Adsett, Alex L006
Afonso, Thais L008
Alex Adsett Literary L016
Andrade, Hannah L023
Andrew, Nelle L025
Avon P044
Baror International, Inc. L044
Barr, Nicola L046
Bates, Tim L048
Bauman, Erica L050
Bent, Jenny L059
Brannan, Maria L078
Brotherstone Creative Management L085

Brotherstone, Charlie	L086	
Browne & Miller Literary Associates	L089	
Bucci, Chris	L090	
Buckley, Louise	L091	
Campbell, Charlie	L099	
Caprio, Alice	L103	
Carroll, Megan	L110	
Caskie, Robert	L113	
Cavanagh, Claire	L114	
Chase Literary Agency	L118	
Cichello, Kayla	L127	
Compassiviste Publishing	P121	
Conrad, Claire Paterson	L136	
Conville, Clare	L137	
Coombs Moylett & Maclean Literary Agency	L139	
Crowley, Sheila	L144	
Danaczko, Melissa	L153	
Darga, Jon Michael	L155	
Darley Anderson Agency, The	L157	
Davies, Elinor	L160	
Dijkstra, Sandra	L169	
Dunow, Carlson & Lerner Agency	L184	
Eberly, Chelsea	L187	
Edwards, Max	L190	
Ellis-Martin, Sian	L197	
Ellor, Zabé	L198	
Emily Sweet Associates	L199	
Evans, Kiya	L205	
Evans, Stephany	L206	
Fabien, Samantha	L207	
Fazzari, Hillary	L210	
Fellows, Abi	L216	
Ferguson, Hannah	L217	
Fernandez, Rochelle	L220	
Figueroa, Melanie	L221	
Finan, Ciara	L223	
Finch, Rebeka	L225	
for Authors, A	L231	
Forrester, Jemima	L232	
Fox, Aram	L234	
Foxx, Kat	L235	
Frances Goldin Literary Agency, Inc.	L238	
Friedman, Claire	L243	
Friedman, Rebecca	L244	
Galustian, Natalie	L251	
Glenister, Emily	L263	
Global Lion Intellectual Property Management, Inc.	L264	
Goff, Anthony	L266	
Gordon, Andrew	L270	
Graham, Stacey	L272	
Greenstreet, Katie	L277	
Greyhound Literary	L278	
Gruber, Pam	L281	
Grunewald, Hattie	L282	
Gunic, Masha	L284	
Haggerty, Taylor	L287	
Hayden, Viola	L305	
Heymont, Lane	L309	
Hordern, Kate	L320	
Hornsley, Sarah	L321	
Irvine, Lucy	L325	
Jamieson, Molly	L329	
Janklow & Nesbit UK Ltd	L330	
Joelle Delbourgo Associates, Inc.	L334	
Joy Harris Literary Agency, Inc.	L340	
Judith Murdoch Literary Agency	L341	
Kate Barker Literary, TV, & Film Agency	L352	
Kate Nash Literary Agency	L353	
Keren, Eli	L362	
Kimber, Natalie	L368	
Kirby, Robert	L370	
Lambert, Sophie	L380	
Langlee, Lina	L382	
Latshaw, Katherine	L386	
Laxfield Literary Associates	L387	
Leamington Books	P262	
Lees, Jordan	L392	
Leon, Nina	L394	
Lutyens and Rubinstein	L410	
Macdougall, Laura	L413	
MacKenzie, Joanna	L416	
Marr, Jill	L425	
Marshall, Jen	L427	
McBride, Juliana	L435	
McCormick Literary	L436	
Merullo, Annabel	L443	
Milburn, Madeleine	L449	
Mileo, Jessica	L451	
Mills, Rachel	L452	
Movable Type Management	L464	
Mustelier, James	L471	
Napolitano, Maria	L473	
Nathan, Abigail	L475	
Nelson, Kristin	L478	
Niumata, Erin	L480	
O'Brien, Lee	L484	
Parker, Elana Roth	L499	
Pass, Marina de	L500	
Perez Literary & Entertainment	L506	
Perez, Kristina	L507	
Pestritto, Carrie	L511	
Phillips, Aemilia	L515	
Pickering, Juliet	L516	
Pierce, Rosie	L517	
Plant, Zoe	L519	
Polygon	P360	
Preston, Amanda	L526	
R D Publishers	P370	
Reid, Janet	L532	
Riccardi, Francesca	L535	
Richter, Rick	L537	
Robertson Murray Literary Agency	L541	
Robinson, Quressa	L542	
Rocking Chair Books	L544	
Rofe, Jennifer	L545	
Rogers, Coleridge & White Ltd	L546	
Ruppin Agency, The	L555	
Sarah Jane Freymann Literary Agency	L564	
Scarfe, Rory	L566	
Schofield, Hannah	L567	
Selectric Artists	L573	
Shaw Agency, The	L576	
Signorelli, Michael	L582	
Silk, Julia	L583	
Simons, Tanera	L585	
Soloway, Jennifer March	L590	
Steed, Hayley	L595	
Stewart, Douglas	L599	
Strachan Literary Agency	L602	
Stringer, Marlene	L604	
Susan Schulman Literary Agency	L610	
Swainson, Joanna	L613	
Symonds, Laurel	L617	
Tannenbaum, Amy	L620	
Teresa Chris Literary Agency Ltd	L623	
Thinkwell Books, UK	P447	
Thorneycroft, Euan	L628	
Thwaites, Steph	L629	
Todd, Hannah	L631	
Tran, Jennifer Chen	L633	
Trudel, Jes	L634	
Vance, Lisa Erbach	L641	
Victoria Sanders & Associates LLC	L642	
Walsh, Caroline	L645	
Walsh, Kate	L646	
Wells, Karmen	L652	
Whelan, Maria	L656	
Whispering Buffalo Literary Agency	L657	
Williams, Laura	L662	
Williams, Sarah	L663	
Wilson, Ed	L668	
Wood, Caroline	L669	
Woodhouse, James	L670	
Woods, Bryony	L671	
Writer's Side	L674	
YMU Books	L676	

Commercial Fantasy
See more broadly: Commercial; Fantasy

Commercial Women's Fiction
See more broadly: Commercial; Women's Fiction

Alex Adsett Literary	L016
Barr, Nicola	L046
Carr, Jamie	L108
Cavanagh, Claire	L114
Curtis Brown	L146
Keane Kataria Literary Agency	L358
Langtry, Elena	L385
Limelight Management	L400
Niumata, Erin	L480
Sheil Land Associates Ltd	L577
Teresa Chris Literary Agency Ltd	L623
Unwin, Jo	L638
Zack Company, Inc, The	L678

Communication

Banter Press	P053
Berrett-Koehler Publishers	P063
Gill Education	P182
Hay House Publishers	P210
Knight Features	L373
Ohio State University Press, The	P323
Peter Lang	P346
Peter Lang Publishing	P348
W.W. Norton & Company, Inc.	P500

Computer Programming
See more broadly: Computers
See more specifically: AutoHotKey

Gill Education	P182
International Society for Technology in Education (ISTE)	P242
No Starch Press, Inc.	P318

Computer Science
See more broadly: Computers

Bloomsbury Academic	P071
Gale	P177
No Starch Press, Inc.	P318
Stipes Publishing	P431
Taylor & Francis Group	P441
W.W. Norton & Company Ltd	P499
W.W. Norton & Company, Inc.	P500
ZigZag Education	P523

Computer and Video Games
See more broadly: Computers; Games

PC Gamer	M278
Thames & Hudson Inc.	P446

Computers
See more broadly: Technology
See more specifically: Computer Programming; Computer Science; Computer and Video Games; Cyber Security; Data and Information Systems; Internet; Software

Information Today, Inc.	P238
Kensington Publishing Corp.	P253
No Starch Press, Inc.	P318
PC Gamer	M278
PC Pro	M279
Yale University Press (London)	P520

Conservative
See more broadly: Politics

Contemporary
See more specifically: Contemporary Crime; Contemporary Culture; Contemporary Fantasy; Contemporary Politics; Contemporary Women's Fiction; Upmarket Contemporary Fiction

Abridged	M008

334 Index | Contemporary Crime

Alekseii, Keir L015
Allegro Poetry Magazine M021
Allison & Busby Ltd P019
Angela Poetry Magazine M025
Armada, Kurestin L030
Armstrong, Susan L032
Art Papers M031
Baobab Press P054
Barbour Publishing P056
Barr, Nicola L046
Bent, Jenny L059
Borstel, Stefanie Sanchez Von L071
Brewin Books Ltd P081
Brooks, Savannah L084
Buckley, Louise L091
Burke, Kate L093
Carroll, Megan L110
Chase Literary Agency L118
Chelsea House Publishers P105
Christensen, Erica L125
Colwill, Charlotte L132
Compassiviste Publishing P121
Coombs Moylett & Maclean Literary Agency L139
Cooper, Gemma L140
Cusick, John L148
Cynthia Cannell Literary Agency L150
Dahlia Books P132
Danaczko, Melissa L153
Dawson, Liza L162
Dedalus Ltd P136
Dixon, Isobel L171
Dodd, Saffron L172
Eberly, Chelsea L187
Eddison Pearson Ltd L188
Ellis-Martin, Sian L197
Ellor, Zabé L198
Feminist Press, The P163
Figueroa, Melanie L221
Getzler, Josh L256
Gilbert, Tara L258
Glenister, Emily L263
Goldstein, Veronica L268
Good Literary Agency, The L269
Grajkowski, Kara L273
Grimm, Katie L279
Gunic, Masha L284
Hakim, Serene L288
Haley, Jolene L289
Hannigan, Carrie L292
Hansen, Stephanie L293
Harlequin Desire P202
Harris, Erin L300
Hensley, Chelsea L307
Holloway, Sally L318
Kahn, Ella Diamond L345
Kate Barker Literary, TV, & Film Agency L352
Kean, Taylor Martindale L357
Keane Kataria Literary Agency L358
Langton, Becca L383
Leigh Feldman Literary L393
Leon, Nina L394
Maidment, Olivia L421
Maltese, Alyssa L422
Margaret K. McElderry Books P281
Marini, Victoria L423
Maurer, Shari L433
McBride, Juliana L435
Midsummer Dream House M242
Milusich, Grace L453
Nell James Publishers P313
North, The M262
Oghma Creative Media P321
Ostby, Kristin L494
Otago University Press P330
Ouen Press P331
Pages, Saribel L496
Pan Macmillan Australia P335
Parker, Elana Roth L499
Pass, Marina de L500
Paul S. Levine Literary Agency L502
Pestritto, Carrie L511
Phelan, Beth L514
Posner, Marcy L522
Prasanna, Tanusri L525
Preston, Amanda L526
Ramer, Susan L528
Reino, Jessica L534
Robinson, Quressa L542
Rofe, Jennifer L545
Ross, Whitney L551
Rushall, Kathleen L556
Rutherford, Laetitia L557
Sheil Land Associates Ltd L577
Siobhan, Aiden L587
Soloway, Jennifer March L590
Sparsile Books P419
Spout Press P420
Stringer, Marlene L604
Swainson, Joanna L613
Symonds, Laurel L617
Takikawa, Marin L618
Topping, Antony L632
Torrey House Press, LLC P459
Tran, Jennifer Chen L633
Trudel, Jes L634
Tyndale House Publishers, Inc. P465
Vallum M387
Victoria Sanders & Associates LLC L642
Weiman, Paula L649
Weiss, Alexandra L650
Weitzner, Tess L651
Whatnall, Michaela L655
Williams, Laura L662
Williamson, Jo L664
Wilson, Desiree L667
WordCrafts Press P514
Young, Claudia L677
Zone 3 M419

Contemporary Crime
See more broadly: Contemporary; Crime

Contemporary Culture
See more broadly: Contemporary; Culture
Hudson Review, The M190
InterVarsity Press (IVP) P243

Contemporary Fantasy
See more broadly: Contemporary; Fantasy
Belton, Maddy L055
Good Literary Agency, The L269
Hensley, Chelsea L307

Contemporary Politics
See more broadly: Contemporary; Politics

Contemporary Romance
See more broadly: Romance
Afonso, Thais L008
Avon Books P045
Bloodhound Books P070
Bookouture P078
Bradford Literary Agency L075
Bradford, Laura L076
Choc Lit P108
Cichello, Kayla L127
Fabien, Samantha L207
Friedman, Rebecca L244
Harper, Logan L299
Inscriptions Literary Agency L323
Leon, Nina L394
Lindsay Literary Agency L401
Lineberry, Isabel L402
Maltese, Alyssa L422
Nichols, Mariah L479
Oghma Creative Media P321
Petty, Rachel L512
Reino, Jessica L534
Tannenbaum, Amy L620
Turner Publishing P462
Tyndale House Publishers, Inc. P465
Vinspire Publishing P497
Williamson, Jo L664

Contemporary Women's Fiction
See more broadly: Contemporary; Women's Fiction
Eason, Lynette L186

Cookery
See more broadly: Food and Drink
See more specifically: Recipes; Regional Cooking; Vegetarian Cooking
Amling, Eric L021
Arcadia Publishing P031
Bal, Emma L038
Basalt Books P057
Baumer, Jan L051
Bernardi, Amanda L062
Betsy Amster Literary Enterprises L063
Better Homes and Gardens M057
Bradford Literary Agency L075
Chang, Nicola L116
Chiotti, Danielle L123
Chronicle Books LLC P111
Clarke, Caro L128
Crown Publishing Group, The P131
Danko, Margaret L154
Darga, Jon Michael L155
DeBlock, Liza L163
Derviskadic, Dado L164
Doug Grad Literary Agency L177
Draper, Claire L178
Ekus Group, The L193
Ekus, Sally L194
Ellis-Martin, Sian L197
Emily Sweet Associates L199
Evans, Kate L204
Felicia Eth Literary Representation L214
Freymann, Sarah Jane L242
Galustian, Natalie L251
Galvin, Lori L252
Globe Pequot Press, The P184
Graham, Stacey L272
Greyhound Literary L278
Hippocrene Books, Inc. P219
Hobbs, Victoria L314
Imagine Publishing P234
Ireland's Own M202
Irene Goodman Literary Agency (IGLA) L324
Joelle Delbourgo Associates, Inc. L334
Kensington Publishing Corp. P253
Kimber, Natalie L368
Kitchen Press P254
Latshaw, Katherine L386
Lewinsohn Literary L397
Limelight Management L400
Loughman, Morwenna L408
MacLeod, Lauren L418
McCormick Literary L436
Menasha Ridge Press P290
Murgolo, Karen L467
My Weekly M249
Native Ink Press P311
Nichols, Mariah L479
Niumata, Erin L480
Pacific Press Publishing Association P334
Peddle, Kay L503
Pelham, Imogen L504
People's Friend, The M283
Perry Literary L509
Pickering, Juliet L516

Access more listings online at www.firstwriter.com

Regina Ryan Books L531
Robertson Murray Literary Agency L541
Ross, Whitney L551
Rutherford, Laetitia L557
Sarah Jane Freymann Literary Agency L564
Seymour, Charlotte L575
Sheil Land Associates Ltd L577
Sheree Bykofsky Associates, Inc. L579
Stephens, Jenny L596
Stone, Geoffrey L600
Strachan Literary Agency L602
Sunbelt Publications, Inc P433
Sweet, Emily L614
Texas A&M University Press P445
Turner Publishing P462
University of Akron Press, The P475
University of Michigan Press, The P483
University of Nevada Press P484
University of Texas Press P488
University of Virginia Press P489
VanderWyk & Burnham P494
W.W. Norton & Company, Inc. P500
Washington State University Press P501
Wood, Caroline L669
Workman Publishing P519
Young, Claudia L677
Zack Company, Inc, The L678

Cotswolds

See more broadly: England

Cotswold Life M098

Country Lifestyle

See more broadly: Countryside; Lifestyle

Country Smallholding M100
McNidder & Grace P286
Virginia Wine & Country Life M390
Workman Publishing P519

Countryside

See more specifically: Country Lifestyle; Rural Living

Cotswold Life M098
Country Smallholding M100
Devon Life M119
Kent Life M209

Couple Therapy

See more broadly: Relationships

W.W. Norton & Company Ltd P499

Courtroom Dramas

See more broadly: Crime

Alfred Hitchcock Mystery Magazine M020

Cozy Fantasy

See more broadly: Fantasy

Belton, Maddy L055
Buckley, Louise L091
Cooper, Maggie L141
Finan, Ciara L223
Goetz, Adria L265
Nathan, Abigail L475
Weiss, Alexandra L650

Cozy Mysteries

See more broadly: Mystery

Bloodhound Books P070
Bookouture P078
Buckley, Louise L091
Davies, Elinor L160
Gisondi, Katie L261
Good Literary Agency, The L269
Haley, Jolene L289
Joffe Books P248
Kathryn Green Literary Agency, LLC L354
Keane Kataria Literary Agency L358
Kensington Publishing Corp. P253
Lakosil, Natalie L379
Lyrical Press P277
Nathan, Abigail L475
Ostby, Kristin L494
Pestritto, Carrie L511
Terlip, Paige L624
Tibbets, Anne L630
Todd, Hannah L631
Zack Company, Inc, The L678

Crafts

See more specifically: Ceramics; Crocheting; Embroidery; Knitting; Lacemaking; Model Making; Quilting; Sewing

Arcadia Publishing P031
Arsenal Pulp Press P032
Bajek, Lauren L037
Bird Eye Books P066
Bright Press P082
Crown Publishing Group, The P131
Draper, Claire L178
Fairbank Literary Representation L208
Fogg, Jack L230
Gale P177
Gill Books P181
Graham, Stacey L272
Kensington Publishing Corp. P253
Limelight Management L400
Lutterworth Press, The P275
My Weekly M249
Native Ink Press P311
Ohio University Press P324
Pavilion Books P338
People's Friend, The M283
Quirk Books P369
Roberts, Soumeya Bendimerad L540
Rocky Nook P379
Schiffer Craft P394
Sunshine Artist M363
Thames & Hudson Inc. P446
Turner Publishing P462
W.W. Norton & Company Ltd P499
Welsh Country M399

Creative Nonfiction

30 North M002
About Place Journal M007
Account, The M009
Antigonish Review, The M026
Atlantic Northeast M037
Bacopa Literary Review M042
Barren Magazine M047
Belmont Story Review M054
Better Than Starbucks M058
Big Fiction M061
Blue Earth Review M067
Blue Mesa Review M068
Carter, Rebecca L111
Chautauqua Literary Journal M083
Cincinnati Review, The M086
Concho River Review M092
Conjunctions M093
Conjunctions Online M094
Conrad, Claire Paterson L136
Cooper, Maggie L141
Crazyhorse / Swamp Pink M104
Cream City Review M105
Creative Nonfiction M106
CutBank M111
El Portal M129
Event M133
Faultline M137
Fiddlehead, The M141
Folio M147
Fourth River, The M153
Gertrude M164
Ginosko Literary Journal M165
Gutter Magazine M174
Half Mystic Journal M175
Harpur Palate M179
Hunger Mountain M191
Idaho Review M193
Identity Theory M194
Influx Press P237
Irish Pages M203
Kerning M211
Kimber, Natalie L368
Laxfield Literary Associates L387
Literary Mama M220
Louisiana Literature M228
MacGuffin, The M229
Malahat Review, The M232
Midway Journal M243
Nashville Review M251
New Welsh Reader M259
Oakland Arts Review, The M264
Ohio State University Press, The P323
Otago University Press P330
Oyez Review M272
Pacifica Literary Review M273
Passionfruit Review, The M277
Pleiades M285
Present Tense M296
Prole M299
Rabble Review M303
River Styx M314
Roseway P382
Shenandoah M331
Silver, Janet L584
Sonder Magazine M342
South Carolina Review M344
Southern Humanities Review M345
Spelt Magazine M352
Story Unlikely M356
Studio One M360
Tears in the Fence M371
Third Coast M375
Toad Hall Editions P453
Torrey House Press, LLC P459
Understorey Magazine M385
University of Massachusetts Press P482
Vagabond City M386
Virginia Quarterly Review, The M389
Wayne State University Press P504
Windsor Review M405
Zone 3 .... M419

Creative Writing

See more broadly: Writing

Graywolf Press P193
Salt Publishing P389
Scifaikuest M323
Stinging Fly, The M355

Creativity

Berrett-Koehler Publishers P063
Blue Star Press P075
Brewin Books Ltd P081
Kube Publishing P258
Literary Mama M220
Native Ink Press P311
O'Neill, Molly L487
Stipes Publishing P431
Susan Schulman Literary Agency L610

Cricket

See more broadly: Sport

Corridor of Uncertainty, The M097
Scratching Shed Publishing P402

Crime

See more specifically: Contemporary Crime; Courtroom Dramas; Crime Thrillers; Detective Fiction; Domestic Noir; Hardboiled Crime; High Concept Crime; Historical Crime; Noir; Organised Crime; Police; Police Procedural; Upmarket Crime

4RV Tenacious P005
Adams, Seren L005
Adsett, Alex L006
Alex Adsett Literary L016
Alfred Hitchcock Mystery Magazine M020
Allison & Busby Ltd P019

Claim your free access to **www.firstwriter.com**: See p.403

Andrade, Hannah	L023	
Andrew, Nelle	L025	
Arcadia Publishing	P031	
Armstrong, Susan	L032	
Arthurson, Wayne	L033	
Asabi Publishing	P034	
Authentic Ideas	P040	
Avon	P044	
Barr, Nicola	L046	
Bartholomew, Jason	L047	
Baxter, Veronique	L052	
Berlyne, John	L061	
Birlinn Ltd	P067	
Bloodhound Books	P070	
Bloomsbury Academic	P071	
Bolton, Camilla	L069	
Bookouture	P078	
Brace, Samantha	L074	
Buckley, Louise	L091	
Burke, Kate	L093	
Campbell, Charlie	L099	
Carter, Rebecca	L111	
Clarke, Caro	L128	
Cochran, Alexander	L130	
Coombes, Clare	L138	
Coombs Moylett & Maclean Literary Agency	L139	
Countryside Books	P124	
Curtis Brown	L146	
Danko, Margaret	L154	
Darley Anderson Agency, The	L157	
Davies, Elinor	L160	
Dixon, Isobel	L171	
Doug Grad Literary Agency	L177	
Edwards, Max	L190	
Ellery Queen Mystery Magazine	M130	
Ellis-Martin, Sian	L197	
Evans, Stephany	L206	
Ferguson, Hannah	L217	
Fernandez, Rochelle	L220	
Fernwood Publishing	P164	
Finan, Ciara	L223	
for Authors, A	L231	
Forrester, Jemima	L232	
Foxx, Kat	L235	
Frances Goldin Literary Agency, Inc.	L238	
Furniss, Eugenie	L249	
Future Fire, The	M158	
Gauntlett, Adam	L254	
Getzler, Josh	L256	
Gill Books	P181	
Glenister, Emily	L263	
Grunewald, Hattie	L282	
Haley, Jolene	L289	
Hardman, Caroline	L295	
Harmsworth, Esmond	L297	
Harper, Logan	L299	
Hayden, Viola	L305	
History Press, The	P221	
Hiyate, Sam	L313	
Hobbs, Victoria	L314	
Hordern, Kate	L320	
Icon Books Ltd	P227	
Inscriptions Literary Agency	L323	
Jeff Herman Agency, LLC, The	L331	
JMD Media / DB Publishing	L247	
Joffe Books	P248	
Judith Murdoch Literary Agency	L341	
Kahn, Ella Diamond	L345	
Kaliszewska, Joanna	L347	
Kane Literary Agency	L348	
Karinch, Maryann	L351	
Kensington Publishing Corp.	P253	
Keren, Eli	L362	
Kim, Julia	L367	
Lakosil, Natalie	L379	
Lambert, Sophie	L380	
Langlee, Lina	L382	
Langtons International	L384	
Langtry, Elena	L385	
Leamington Books	P262	
Lees, Jordan	L392	
Leon, Nina	L394	
Limelight Management	L400	
MacDonald, Emily	L412	
Macdougall, Laura	L413	
MacGregor & Luedeke	L414	
MacLeod, Lauren	L418	
Marr, Jill	L425	
Marshall, Jen	L427	
McNidder & Grace	P286	
Milburn, Madeleine	L449	
Mills & Boon	P297	
Mirror Books	P301	
Molloy, Jess	L456	
Morrell, Imogen	L460	
Mortimer, Michele	L462	
Murray, Judith	L468	
Mushens, Juliet	L470	
Mysterious Press, The	P309	
Nash, Justin	L474	
Nathan, Abigail	L475	
NBM Publishing	P312	
Neely, Rachel	L476	
O'Shea, Amy	L488	
Oghma Creative Media	P321	
Oneworld Publications	P327	
Orenda Books	P329	
Pan Macmillan Australia	P335	
Pass, Marina de	L500	
Pen & Ink Designs Publishing	P342	
Perez Literary & Entertainment	L506	
Perez, Kristina	L507	
Perry Literary	L509	
Pine, Gideon	L518	
Polygon	P360	
Power, Anna	L523	
Preston, Amanda	L526	
Quill Driver Books	P368	
Regina Ryan Books	L531	
Reid, Janet	L532	
Riccardi, Francesca	L535	
Richter, Rick	L537	
Robert Smith Literary Agency Ltd	L539	
Rogers, Coleridge & White Ltd	L546	
Ruppin Agency, The	L555	
Schofield, Hannah	L567	
Schwartz, Steve	L568	
Seymour, Charlotte	L575	
Sheil Land Associates Ltd	L577	
Shestopal, Camilla	L581	
Silk, Julia	L583	
Soho Press	P417	
Soloway, Jennifer March	L590	
Sparsile Books	P419	
Steerforth Press	P428	
Story Unlikely	M356	
Strachan Literary Agency	L602	
Stringer, Marlene	L604	
Swainson, Joanna	L613	
Teresa Chris Literary Agency Ltd	L623	
Thorneycroft, Euan	L628	
Todd, Hannah	L631	
Topping, Antony	L632	
Turner Publishing	P462	
University of Alberta Press	P477	
University of California Press	P478	
University of North Texas Press	P485	
Unseen Press	P492	
Victoria Sanders & Associates LLC	L642	
W.W. Norton & Company Ltd	P499	
W.W. Norton & Company, Inc.	P500	
Williams, Laura	L662	
Wilson, Ed	L668	
Wolfpack Publishing	P513	
Wood, Caroline	L669	
Young, Claudia	L677	
Zack Company, Inc, The	L678	
ZigZag Education	P523	

Crime Thrillers
See more broadly: *Crime; Thrillers*
Hannah Sheppard Literary Agency L291

Crocheting
See more broadly: *Crafts*

Cryptozoology
See more broadly: *Supernatural / Paranormal*
Llewellyn Worldwide Ltd P269

Cuba
See more broadly: *Caribbean*
Pureplay Press P365

Cultural Commentary
See more broadly: *Commentary; Culture*
Carter, Rebecca L111
Pande, Ayesha L497
Whelan, Maria L656

Cultural Criticism
See more broadly: *Culture*
American Book Review M022
Combemale, Chris L133
Crown P129
Eisenmann, Caroline L192
Feminist Studies M139
Fuentes, Sarah L247
Graywolf Press P193
Lewis, Alison L398
Lilliput Press, The P268
McQuilkin, Rob L438
Mendia, Isabel L441
New England Review M255
Peepal Tree Press P341
Pelham, Imogen L504
Phillips, Aemilia L515
Power, Anna L523
Rabble Review M303
Stephens, Jenny L596
Takahe M369
Usselman, Laura L639
Virginia Quarterly Review, The M389
Yale Review, The M409

Cultural History
See more broadly: *Culture; History*
Asabi Publishing P034
Derviskadic, Dado L164
Icon Books Ltd P227
Keren, Eli L362
Kirby, Robert L370
McCormick Literary L436
Moorhead, Max L459
Perez Literary & Entertainment L506
Perez, Kristina L507
Ramer, Susan L528
Seymour, Charlotte L575
Takikawa, Marin L618
Unicorn P469
Unicorn Publishing Group P470
University of Massachusetts Press P482
Zack Company, Inc, The L678

Culture
See more specifically: *Contemporary Culture; Cultural Commentary; Cultural Criticism; Cultural History; Ethnic; Folklore, Myths, and Legends; Jewish Culture; Multicultural; Popular Culture; Postcolonialism; Sub-Culture; Visual Culture; Youth Culture*
African American Review M014
Antigonish Review, The M026
Arsenal Pulp Press P032
Art Papers M031

Arte Publico Press P033
Asabi Publishing P034
Atlanta Magazine M035
Atlantic Northeast M037
Baffler, The M043
Barr, Anjanette L045
Basalt Books P057
Baylor University Press P060
Bear Deluxe Magazine, The M052
Berghahn Books Ltd P062
Boston Review M071
Brattle Agency LLC, The L080
Bright Press P082
Britain Magazine M075
British Academy, The P083
British Museum Press, The P084
Burns, Camille L094
Capron, Elise L104
Carr, Jamie L108
Cavanagh, Claire L114
Chanchani, Sonali L115
Clarke, Caro L128
Cocoa Girl M088
Commonweal M091
Compassiviste Publishing P121
Conversation (UK), The M095
Cooper, Maggie L141
Cowboys & Indians M101
Critical Quarterly M108
Davies, Elinor L160
Dawson, Liza L162
Edenborough, Sam L189
Evans, David L203
Evans, Kiya L205
Fee: Foundation for Economic Education M138
Fellows, Abi L216
Feminist Studies M139
Fernwood Publishing P164
Fortress Press P170
Frances Collin Literary Agent L237
Frances Goldin Literary Agency, Inc. L238
Geiger, Ellen L255
Ghahremani, Lilly L257
Goldstein, Veronica L268
Granger, David L275
Granta Books P192
Hakim, Serene L288
Harmsworth, Esmond L297
Harper's Magazine M178
Heymont, Lane L309
History Press, The P221
HopeRoad P223
Ig Publishing P230
Image M195
Island Online M205
Jessica Kingsley Publishers P246
Joy Harris Literary Agency, Inc. L340
Kahn, Jody L346
Kent Life M209
Kim, Jennifer L366
Kim, Julia L367
Kotchman, Katie L374
Krienke, Mary L375
Kube Publishing P258
Landfall M215
Lightner, Kayla L399
London Grip M222
London Review of Books M225
LSU Press P273
Macdougall, Laura L413
Mack, Kate L415
Manoa M233
marie claire M234
Marion Boyars Publishers P282
Metro Publications Ltd P295
Metropolis Magazine M239
Minnesota Historical Society Press P299
Morrell, Imogen L460
Mortimer, Michele L462
Moving Worlds: A Journal of Transcultural Writings M247
New Statesman M258
Nolan, Laura L481
O'Neill, Molly L487
Ohio State University Press, The P323
Oxford Review of Books M271
Pensacola Magazine M281
Peter Lang P346
Peter Lang Publishing P348
Phillips, Aemilia L515
Pinata Books P355
Posner, Marcy L522
Power Cut Lite M294
Purdue University Press P364
Pureplay Press P365
Rocky Mountain Books P378
Salt Publishing P389
Sanders, Rayhane L562
Savannah Magazine M322
Scottish Field M326
Sierra M336
Signorelli, Michael L582
Singing Dragon P409
Society for Promoting Christian Knowledge (SPCK) P414
Spackman, James L593
Square Mile Magazine M354
Sweren, Becky L615
Texas A&M University Press P445
This England M376
Threepenny Review, The M377
Tocher M378
Tyndale House Publishers, Inc. P465
University of Akron Press, The P475
University of Alaska Press P476
University of Alberta Press P477
University of Iowa Press P480
University of Massachusetts Press P482
University of Michigan Press, The P483
University of North Texas Press P485
University of Pennsylvania Press P486
University of Texas Press P488
University of Virginia Press P489
Victoria Sanders & Associates LLC L642
W.W. Norton & Company Ltd P499
W.W. Norton & Company, Inc. P500
Wasafiri M398
Washington State University Press P501
Welsh Country M399
Whelan, Maria L656
Willms, Kathryn L665
Yankee Magazine M410
Yorkshire Life M413

Current Affairs

Alcock, Michael L014
Bartholomew, Jason L047
Basic Books P058
Baxter, Veronique L052
Birlinn Ltd P067
Brouckaert, Justin L087
Cassell P096
Chase Literary Agency L118
Chiotti, Danielle L123
Cochran, Alexander L130
Compassiviste Publishing P121
Concepcion, Cristina L135
Coombs Moylett & Maclean Literary Agency L139
Crown P129
Curran, Sabhbh L145
Dana Newman Literary, LLC L152
Dijkstra, Sandra L169
Dunham, Jennie L180
Economist, The M126
Emily Sweet Associates L199
Enslow Publishers, Inc. P154
Faulks, Holly L209
Frances Goldin Literary Agency, Inc. L238
Funny Times M157
Gill Books P181
Gordon, Andrew L270
Hanbury Agency, The L290
Hardman, Caroline L295
Harper's Magazine M178
Haus Publishing P208
Icon Books Ltd P227
Joelle Delbourgo Associates, Inc. L334
Jonathan Pegg Literary Agency L337
Kim, Julia L367
Kube Publishing P258
Lazin, Sarah L388
Marr, Jill L425
Massachusetts Review, The M237
Mundy, Toby L466
New Statesman M258
Oneworld Publications P327
Oxford Review of Books M271
Peddle, Kay L503
Perez Literary & Entertainment L506
Perez, Kristina L507
Power, Anna L523
Rabble Review M303
Robert Smith Literary Agency Ltd L539
Robertson Murray Literary Agency L541
Schwartz, Steve L568
Scratching Shed Publishing P402
Seren Books P405
Sheree Bykofsky Associates, Inc. L579
Signorelli, Michael L582
Southwest Review M348
Strothman, Wendy L608
Sweet, Emily L614
Thayer, Henry L626
Turner Publishing P462
Tyndale House Publishers, Inc. P465
University of Georgia Press P479
University of Texas Press P488
University of Virginia Press P489
Victoria Sanders & Associates LLC L642
W.W. Norton & Company Ltd P499
Walsh, Kate L646
Wordserve Literary L673
Yale University Press (London) P520
Yankee Magazine M410
Zack Company, Inc, The L678

Cyber Security

See more broadly: Computers

Cyberpunk

See more broadly: Science Fiction

Afonso, Thais L008
Edenborough, Sam L189

Cycling

See more broadly: Sport

See more specifically: Cycling Guides

Countryside Books P124
Duncan Petersen Publishing Limited P146
Pocket Mountains P359

Cycling Guides

See more broadly: Cycling

Sigma Press P407

Dance

See more broadly: Performing Arts

Bowlin, Sarah L073
Brick M074
Hudson Review, The M190
University of Michigan Press, The P483
University of Wisconsin Press, The P490

Wesleyan University Press P506
Dark
See more specifically: Dark Academia; Dark Fantasy; Dark Humour; Dark Thrillers
Belton, Maddy L055
Black Static M065
Brattesani, Hannah L079
Burke, Kate L093
Curran, Sabhbh L145
Fellows, Abi L216
Ferguson, T.S. L218
Fuentes, Sarah L247
Hensley, Chelsea L307
Kavanagh, Jade L355
Kenny, Julia L361
Lechon, Shannon L390
Lees, Jordan L392
Lovell, Jake L409
Neon M253
Phillips, Aemilia L515
Salt Publishing P389
Steed, Hayley L595
Takikawa, Marin L618
Williams, Laura L662
Williamson, Jo L664

Dark Academia
See more broadly: Campus Novels; Dark
Buckley, Louise L091
Fazzari, Hillary L210
Pass, Marina de L500
Pierce, Rosie L517
Steed, Hayley L595

Dark Fantasy
See more broadly: Dark; Fantasy
Andrade, Hannah L023
Nightfire P316
Sinister Stoat Press P410
Sluytman, Antoinette Van L588

Dark Humour
See more broadly: Comedy / Humour; Dark
Andrade, Hannah L023
Carroll, Megan L110
Charnace, Edwina de L117
Cichello, Kayla L127
Mustelier, James L471

Dark Magic
See more broadly: Magic
Woods, Bryony L671

Dark Thrillers
See more broadly: Dark; Thrillers
Cochran, Alexander L130

Darts
See more broadly: Sport

Data and Information Systems
See more broadly: Computers
Facet Publishing P159
Information Today, Inc. P238

Decorating
See more broadly: Interior Design
Good Homes M168
Homes & Antiques M187
Red Magazine M309

Deep Sea Fishing
See more broadly: Fishing
Geared Up Publications P178

Deer
See more broadly: Animals

Dementia
See more broadly: Mental Health
See more specifically: Alzheimer's
Purdue University Press P364

Depression
See more broadly: Psychology
Free Spirit Publishing P174
Singing Dragon P409
W.W. Norton & Company Ltd P499

Derbyshire
See more broadly: England

Design
See more specifically: Graphic Design; Interior Design
Arcadia Publishing P031
Architectural Review, The M029
Atlanta Magazine M035
Bernardi, Amanda L062
Bloomsbury Academic P071
Carter, Rebecca L111
Chronicle Books LLC P111
Colourpoint Educational P119
Cottage Life M099
Fairbank Literary Representation L208
Fogg, Jack L230
Gill Education P182
Laurence King Publishing P261
Lund Humphries Limited P274
Marshall, Jen L427
Metropolis Magazine L239
MIT Press, The P303
No Starch Press, Inc. P318
Pavilion Books P338
Prestel Publishing Ltd P362
Redbook Magazine M310
Riposte M312
Roberts, Soumeya Bendimerad L540
Ross, Whitney L551
Sarah Jane Freymann Literary Agency L564
SOMA M340
Ten Speed Press P444
Thames & Hudson Inc. P446
University of Alberta Press P477
W.W. Norton & Company Ltd P499
W.W. Norton & Company, Inc. P500
Wallpaper M397
ZigZag Education P523

Detective Fiction
See more broadly: Crime; Mystery
Lees, Jordan L392
Moore, Mary C. L457
Riccardi, Francesca L535

Detroit
See more broadly: Michigan
Wayne State University Press P504

Devon
See more broadly: England
Devon Life M119

Diabetes
See more broadly: Health
Balance M044

Dialects
See more broadly: Language
Countryside Books P124

Dictionaries
Collins P118

Diet
See more broadly: Food and Drink; Health
Bella M053
First For Women M142
Hammersmith Books P198
Regina Ryan Books L531
Zack Company, Inc, The L678

Digital Technology
See more broadly: Technology
Colourpoint Educational P119
International Society for Technology in Education (ISTE) P242

Dinosaurs
See more broadly: Prehistoric Animals

Disabilities
See more broadly: Health
Buckley, Louise L091
Engram Books P152
Fernwood Publishing P164

Free Spirit Publishing P174
HopeRoad P223
Krienke, Mary L375
Matte, Rebecca L431
Ohio State University Press, The P323
University of Alberta Press P477
University of Massachusetts Press P482
University of Michigan Press, The P483
VanderWyk & Burnham P494
W.W. Norton & Company, Inc. P500

Discrimination
See more broadly: Social Issues
See more specifically: Racism

Diverse Romance
See more broadly: Romance
Petty, Rachel L512

Diversity
See more broadly: Social Issues
Arsenal Pulp Press P032
Dahlia Books P132
Nichols, Mariah L479
Oghma Creative Media P321
Prasanna, Tanusri L525
W.W. Norton & Company Ltd P499

Diving
See more broadly: Outdoor Activities
See more specifically: Scuba Diving

Dogs
See more broadly: Pets
Doug Grad Literary Agency L177
Pass, Marina de L500

Domestic
See more specifically: Domestic Mystery; Domestic Noir; Domestic Suspense; Domestic Thriller
Baxter, Veronique L052
Hodges, Jodie L315
Tibbets, Anne L630

Domestic Mystery
See more broadly: Domestic; Mystery
Tibbets, Anne L630

Domestic Noir
See more broadly: Crime; Domestic
Choc Lit P108
Joffe Books P248

Domestic Suspense
See more broadly: Domestic; Suspense
Bent, Jenny L059
Bloodhound Books P070
Bookouture P078
Fergusson, Julie L219
Galvin, Lori L252
Harper, Logan L299
Keren, Eli L362
Maltese, Alyssa L422
Reid, Janet L532
Vance, Lisa Erbach L641

Domestic Thriller
See more broadly: Domestic; Thrillers
Kane Literary Agency L348
Scarlet P393
Selectric Artists L573

Dorset
See more broadly: England

Drama
Alaska Quarterly Review M019
Anvil Press Publishers P028
Authentic Ideas P040
Barbican Press P055
Bloomsbury Academic P071
Compassiviste Publishing P121
Galustian, Natalie L251
London Grip M222
Marion Boyars Publishers P282
Marshall, Jen L427
Massachusetts Review, The M237

Index | English

New England Review M255
Pan Macmillan Australia P335
R D Publishers P370
Seren Books P405
Story Unlikely M356
Tennyson Agency, The L622
Tusculum Review, The M381
University of Massachusetts Press P482
University of Nevada Press P484
W.W. Norton & Company Ltd P499
Wells, Karmen L652
Williams, Katie L661
ZigZag Education P523

Drawing
See more broadly: Arts
Korero Press P257
Rocky Nook P379
Thames & Hudson Inc. P446

Drinks
See more broadly: Food and Drink
See more specifically: Beer; Cider; Whisky; Wine
Turner Publishing P462

Drugs
See more specifically: Cannabis
Enslow Publishers, Inc. P154

Dystopian Fiction
See more broadly: Speculative
Bennett, Laura L056
Fazzari, Hillary L210
Hensley, Chelsea L307
Liverpool Literary Agency, The L404
Mozley, Jack L465
Soler, Shania N. L589
Steed, Hayley L595
Turner Publishing P462
W.W. Norton & Company, Inc. P500
Wells, Karmen L652
WordCrafts Press P514

Early Readers
4RV Publishing P004
AdventureBox M013
Allen & Unwin P018
Arcadia Publishing P031
Badger Learning P048
Caroline Sheldon Literary Agency L106
Charlesbridge Publishing P102
Cherry Lake Publishing Group P106
Chronicle Books LLC P111
Crabtree Publishing P126
Curtis Brown L146
DK Publishing P141
Dunow, Carlson & Lerner Agency L184
Filter Press P166
Finegan, Stevie L226
Firefly P167
Flynn, Amy Thrall L229
Guppy Books P195
Hare, Jessica L296
Holroyde, Penny L319
Irvine, Lucy L325
Kane Press P251
Kube Publishing P258
Lantana Publishing P260
Native Ink Press P311
Pavilion Books P338
Petty, Rachel L512
Piccadilly Press P354
Richter, Rick L537
Schiffer Kids P396
Scholastic P399
Scholastic UK P400
Thames & Hudson Inc. P446
Tilbury House Publishers P450
Tippermuir Books P452
W.W. Norton & Company Ltd P499

Earth Science
See more broadly: Science
See more specifically: Climate Science; Geology; Oceanography
Crabtree Publishing P126
Gale P177
Taylor & Francis Group P441
University of Wisconsin Press, The P490

East Asia
See more broadly: Asia
Charnace, Edwina de L117

Eastern Europe
See more broadly: Europe
Indiana University Press P235
University of Wisconsin Press, The P490

Eating Disorders
See more broadly: Psychology
W.W. Norton & Company Ltd P499

Ebooks
Lerner Publishing Group P264

Economics
Arcadia Publishing P031
Berrett-Koehler Publishers P063
Bloomsbury Academic P071
Campbell, Charlie L099
Christie, Jennifer L126
Combemale, Chris L133
Conversation (UK), The M095
Crabtree Publishing P126
Crown P129
Elliott & Thompson P149
Evans, Kate L204
Fernwood Publishing P164
Finan, Ciara L223
Fiscal Publications P168
Gale P177
Gill Education P182
Gold SF P185
Gordon, Andrew L270
Harvard University Press P206
Holloway, Sally L318
Icon Books Ltd P227
Johns Hopkins University Press, The P250
Kensington Publishing Corp. P253
London Review of Books M225
Mentor Books P292
MMB Creative L455
Oneworld Publications P327
Peter Lang P346
Peter Lang Publishing P348
Pluto Press P358
Stipes Publishing P431
Susan Schulman Literary Agency L610
Taylor & Francis Group P441
Turner Publishing P462
University of California Press P478
University of Michigan Press, The P483
University of Nevada Press P484
W.W. Norton & Company Ltd P499
W.W. Norton & Company, Inc. P500
Yale University Press (London) P520
Zack Company, Inc, The L678
ZigZag Education P523

Education
See more specifically: Physical Education; Reading
Arcadia Publishing P031
Berghahn Books Ltd P062
Bloomsbury Academic P071
CharlottesvilleFamily M082
Collins P118
Colourpoint Educational P119
Conversation (UK), The M095
Evan-Moor Educational Publishers P157
Feminist Press, The P163
Fernwood Publishing P164

Free Spirit Publishing P174
Gale P177
Gill Education P182
Global Lion Intellectual Property Management, Inc. L264
Grossman, Loren R. L280
Harvard University Press P206
International Society for Technology in Education (ISTE) P242
Johns Hopkins University Press, The P250
Kensington Publishing Corp. P253
Lutterworth Press, The P275
McGraw Hill EMEA P285
Mentor Books P292
Muscato, Nate L469
Peter Lang P346
Peter Lang Publishing P348
Prufrock Press P363
Scholastic P399
Sentient Publications P404
Taylor & Francis Group P441
Tyndale House Publishers, Inc. P465
University of Alberta Press P477
University of Massachusetts Press P482
University of Michigan Press, The P483
University of Nevada Press P484
University of Virginia Press P489
VanderWyk & Burnham P494
W.W. Norton & Company Ltd P499
W.W. Norton & Company, Inc. P500
WordCrafts Press P514
Yale University Press (London) P520

Electrical Contracting
See more broadly: Building / Construction

Electronic Music
See more broadly: Music
Velocity Press P496

Embroidery
See more broadly: Crafts; Hobbies
C&T Publishing P088

Emergency Services
See more specifically: Search and Rescue

Energy
See more broadly: Technology
Ruralite M318

Engineering
Arcadia Publishing P031
Bloomsbury Academic P071
Kane Press P251
Kensington Publishing Corp. P253
McGraw Hill EMEA P285
Purdue University Press P364
Racecar Engineering M304
Stipes Publishing P431
Symonds, Laurel L617
Taylor & Francis Group P441
University of Michigan Press, The P483
University of Nevada Press P484
Wilson, Desiree L667

England
See more broadly: United Kingdom
See more specifically: Cambridgeshire; Cheshire; Cotswolds; Derbyshire; Devon; Dorset; Essex; Gloucestershire; Herefordshire; Kent; Lancashire; Lincolnshire; London; Norfolk; Northern England; Shropshire; Somerset; Staffordshire; Suffolk; The Midlands; West Country; Worcestershire; Yorkshire
This England M376

English
See more broadly: Language
Autumn Publishing Ltd P042
Badger Learning P048
Gill Education P182
Mentor Books P292

Claim your free access to www.firstwriter.com: See p.403

Peter Lang	P346
Peter Lang Publishing	P348
W.W. Norton & Company, Inc.	P500
ZigZag Education	P523

Entertainment
See more specifically: Celebrity

Ascend Books, LLC	P035
Brailsford, Karen	L077
Cassell	P096
Compassiviste Publishing	P121
Cowboys & Indians	M101
FRA (Futerman, Rose, & Associates)	L236
Frances Goldin Literary Agency, Inc.	L238
History Press, The	P221
Ireland's Own	M202
marie claire (UK)	M235
Oghma Creative Media	P321
Pensacola Magazine	M281
Pride	M298
R D Publishers	P370
Turner Publishing	P462
Virginia Wine & Country Life	M390
Zack Company, Inc, The	L678

Entrepreneurship
See more broadly: Business

Campos, Vanessa	L100
Entrepreneur	M131
Kruger Cowne	L376
Trudel, Jes	L634
Zack Company, Inc, The	L678

Environment
See more broadly: Nature
See more specifically: Climate Science; Sustainable Living

Basalt Books	P057
Bear Deluxe Magazine, The	M052
Berghahn Books Ltd	P062
Bernardi, Amanda	L062
Bloomsbury Academic	P071
Brattesani, Hannah	L079
Caitlin Press Inc	P090
Carter, Rebecca	L111
Conrad, Claire Paterson	L136
Conversation (UK), The	M095
Coombs Moylett & Maclean Literary Agency	L139
Cottage Life	M099
Danko, Margaret	L154
Dawntreader, The	M115
Dawson, Liza	L162
Diana Finch Literary Agency	L167
Future Fire, The	M158
Gold SF	P185
Harper's Magazine	M178
Hazel Press	P211
Icon Books Ltd	P227
Island Online	M205
Kirby, Robert	L370
Lambert, Sophie	L380
Lilliput Press, The	P268
LSU Press	P273
Lutterworth Press, The	P275
Morrell, Imogen	L460
Native Ink Press	P311
New England Review	M255
New Internationalist	M256
Oghma Creative Media	P321
Ohio University Press	P324
Pluto Press	P358
Posner, Marcy	L522
Preston, Amanda	L526
Purdue University Press	P364
Regina Ryan Books	L531
Riposte	M312
Rocky Mountain Books	P378
Rushall, Kathleen	L556
Sierra	M336
Sorg, Arley	L592
Stephens, Jenny	L596
Stipes Publishing	P431
Takikawa, Marin	L618
Taylor & Francis Group	P441
Texas A&M University Press	P445
Trudel, Jes	L634
University of Alberta Press	P477
University of California Press	P478
University of Georgia Press	P479
University of Massachusetts Press	P482
University of Michigan Press, The	P483
University of North Texas Press	P485
University of Texas Press	P488
University of Virginia Press	P489
University of Wisconsin Press, The	P490
University Press of Colorado	P491
W.W. Norton & Company Ltd	P499
Weiss, Alexandra	L650
Willms, Kathryn	L665
Zack Company, Inc, The	L678

Epistolary

W.W. Norton & Company, Inc.	P500

Equality
See more broadly: Social Issues

Atyeo, Charlotte	L034
Berrett-Koehler Publishers	P063

Equestrian
See more broadly: Sport

Erotic
See more specifically: Erotic Romance

Asabi Publishing	P034
Charles River Press	P101
Cleis Press	P115
Curtis Brown	L146
Knigge, Sheyla	L372
Korero Press	P257
Lyrical Press	P277
Maclean, Jamie	L417
NBM Publishing	P312
W.W. Norton & Company, Inc.	P500
Zack Company, Inc, The	L678

Erotic Romance
See more broadly: Erotic; Romance

Barone Literary Agency	L043
Bradford Literary Agency	L075
Bradford, Laura	L076
Cleis Press	P115

Essays

aaduna	M005
AARP The Magazine	M006
About Place Journal	M007
Acumen	M012
African American Review	M014
Agni	M016
Antigonish Review, The	M026
Arboreal	M027
Arc	M028
Auroras & Blossoms PoArtMo Anthology	M039
Baobab Press	P054
Big Fiction	M061
Blue Earth Review	M067
Boston Review	M071
Brattesani, Hannah	L079
Brick	M074
Cheshire	M084
Clarke, Caro	L128
Coil, The	M089
Combemale, Chris	L133
Concho River Review	M092
Crab Orchard Review	M102
Creative Nonfiction	M106
Critical Quarterly	M108
Dalhousie Review, The	M113
Daunt Books Publishing	P134
Dublin Review, The	M124
Eisenmann, Caroline	L192
Feminist Studies	M139
First Line, The	M143
Five Points	M144
Folio	M147
Fortnightly Review, The	M149
Fresh Words – An International Literary Magazine	M154
Fugue	M155
Galustian, Natalie	L251
Georgia Review, The	M163
Gertrude	M164
Graywolf Press	P193
Gulf Coast: A Journal of Literature and Fine Arts	M173
Gutter Magazine	M174
Harper's Magazine	M178
Hazel Press	P211
Hotel Amerika	M189
Hudson Review, The	M190
Idaho Review	M193
Identity Theory	M194
Image	M195
Indiana Review	M196
Irish Pages	M203
Island	M204
Island Online	M205
Jamii Publishing	P245
Kavya Kishor	M208
Kenyon Review, The	M210
Kerning	M211
Landfall	M215
Latshaw, Katherine	L386
Literary Mama	M220
Long Poem Magazine	M226
Lost Lake Folk Opera Magazine	M227
Louisiana Literature	M228
Malahat Review, The	M232
Manoa	M233
Massachusetts Review, The	M237
Methuen Publishing Ltd	P294
Michigan Quarterly Review	M240
Mid-American Review	M241
Midway Journal	M243
Missouri Review, The	M245
MMB Creative	L455
Moving Worlds: A Journal of Transcultural Writings	M247
Nashville Review	M251
New England Review	M255
New Welsh Reader	M259
Oxford Poetry	M270
Oxford Review of Books	M271
Patrician Press	P337
PN Review	M287
Poetry Ireland Review	M288
Poetry Review, The	M290
Power Cut Lite	M294
Qu Literary Magazine	M302
Rabble Review	M303
Reactor	M307
Riposte	M312
Rutman, Jim	L558
Shenandoah	M331
Shipwreckt Books Publishing Company	P406
Shooter Literary Magazine	M333
Shorts Magazine	M335
Sinister Wisdom	M337
Snowflake Magazine	M338
South Carolina Review	M344
Southern Humanities Review	M345
Southern Review, The	M346
Stinging Fly, The	M355

Strange Horizons M357
Sunspot Literary Journal M364
Tahoma Literary Review.......................... M368
Takahe M369
Tears in the Fence M371
Tolka M379
Torrey House Press, LLC......................... P459
Tusculum Review, The M381
Vagabond City M386
Vallum M387
W.W. Norton & Company Ltd................. P499
Waccamaw M394
Wallace Stevens Journal, The M396
Wasafiri M398
West Branch M400
White Review, The M404
Windsor Review M405
Woods, Bryony L671
Yale Review, The M409
Yes Poetry Magazine M412

Essex
See more broadly: England
Essex Life M132

Ethnic
See more broadly: Culture
Hippocrene Books, Inc............................ P219
Texas A&M University Press P445
University Press of Colorado P491

Ethnic Groups
See more broadly: Society
See more specifically: African American; Asian American; Black People; Caribbean Diaspora; Italian American; Maori; Native Americans; Slavs
Bloomsbury Academic............................. P071
Chanchani, Sonali L115
Dawson, Liza L162
Ellis-Martin, Sian..................................... L197
Gold SF P185
Macdougall, Laura L413
Ohio State University Press, The............. P323
Pluto Press P358
Pride M298
Sanders, Rayhane..................................... L562
Simpson, Cara Lee L586
Singing Dragon P409
University of Alberta Press P477
University of Michigan Press, The........... P483

Ethnography
See more broadly: Sociology
University of Wisconsin Press, The P490

Europe
See more broadly: Regional
See more specifically: Austria; Central Europe; Eastern Europe; France; Germany; Ireland; Italy; Romania; Russia; Scandinavia; Spain; Switzerland; United Kingdom
Barr, Nicola L046
Ohio University Press P324
University of Alberta Press P477

European History
See more broadly: History
Brattle Agency LLC, The......................... L080
Lutterworth Press, The........................... P275
University of Virginia Press..................... P489
Zack Company, Inc, The......................... L678

Evangelism
See more broadly: Christianity
Barbour Publishing P056
Brown, Megan L088
College Press Publishing P117

Events
See more specifically: Weddings
Devon Life M119

Evolution
See more broadly: Biology

Thames & Hudson Inc.............................. P446

Exercise
See more broadly: Fitness
Balance.. M044

Experimental
Abridged M008
Alaska Quarterly Review.......................... M019
Black Warrior Review.............................. M066
Carter, Rebecca L111
Compassiviste Publishing........................ P121
Conrad, Claire Paterson L136
Fathom Books P162
Fiction M140
Glacier, The... M166
Gold SF P185
Goldstein, Veronica L268
Half Mystic Journal M175
Island.. M204
Island Online M205
Joy Harris Literary Agency, Inc................ L340
Midsummer Dream House...................... M242
Moving Worlds: A Journal of Transcultural Writings M247
Second Factory M328
Spout Press P420
Tahoma Literary Review M368
Ugly Duckling Presse P466
Wilson, Ed... L668

Experimental Poetry
Better Than Starbucks M058
Half Mystic Journal M175
MacGuffin, The....................................... M229
Oakland Arts Review, The M264

FBI
See more broadly: Police

Fabulism
See more broadly: Magical Realism
Cooper, Maggie L141
Harris, Erin... L300
MMB Creative L455
O'Neill, Molly... L487
Rutherford, Laetitia L557

Fairy Tales
Belton, Maddy L055
Crabtree Publishing P126
Eisenbraun, Nicole L191
Ferguson, T.S.. L218
Harris, Erin... L300
Hensley, Chelsea L307
Mustelier, James...................................... L471
Strong, Amy L605
Wayne State University Press.................. P504
Wilson, Desiree L667
Woods, Bryony L671

Falconry
See more broadly: Sport

Family
See more broadly: Relationships
See more specifically: Children; Family Therapy; Parenting
Andrew, Nelle L025
Arcadia Publishing P031
Brace, Samantha L074
Brewin Books Ltd P081
Brown, Megan L088
Burke, Kate L093
Carroll, Megan L110
Chanchani, Sonali.................................... L115
CharlottesvilleFamily M082
Cho, Catherine L124
Cooper, Gemma L140
Crowley, Sheila L144
Danaczko, Melissa L153
Danko, Margaret L154
Davies, Elinor.. L160
Dunham, Jennie L180

Ellis-Martin, Sian..................................... L197
Fernwood Publishing P164
Free Spirit Publishing P174
Greenstreet, Katie L277
Haley, Jolene L289
Hannah Sheppard Literary Agency L291
Kensington Publishing Corp. P253
Lewinsohn Literary L397
Macdougall, Laura L413
MacKenzie, Joanna.................................. L416
Maidment, Olivia L421
Murdoch Books Australia P308
O'Grady, Niamh L486
O'Neill, Molly... L487
Plitt, Carrie L520
Redbook Magazine M310
Riccardi, Francesca L535
Roberts, Soumeya Bendimerad L540
Sasquatch Books P391
Shipwreckt Books Publishing Company P406
Society for Promoting Christian Knowledge (SPCK) P414
Soloway, Jennifer March L590
Steed, Hayley L595
Thwaites, Steph....................................... L629
Trussell, Caroline L635
Turner Publishing P462
University of Nevada Press...................... P484
Vance, Lisa Erbach L641
VanderWyk & Burnham P494
W.W. Norton & Company, Inc. P500
Wordserve Literary L673

Family Saga
Armstrong, Susan L032
Baxter, Veronique L052
Charnace, Edwina de L117
Choc Lit P108
Ellis-Martin, Sian..................................... L197
Evans, Kate L204
Figueroa, Melanie L221
Harris, Erin... L300
Kim, Jennifer L366
Lightner, Kayla L399
Macdougall, Laura L413
Maidment, Olivia L421
Milburn, Madeleine L449
MMB Creative L455
Pass, Marina de L500
People's Friend Pocket Novels M282
Pierce, Rosie L517
Rushall, Kathleen L556
Sheil Land Associates Ltd........................ L577
Simpson, Cara Lee L586
Takikawa, Marin L618
Tran, Jennifer Chen................................. L633
Wickers, Chandler L659
Williams, Sarah....................................... L663

Family Therapy
See more broadly: Family
W.W. Norton & Company Ltd................. P499

Fantasy
See more specifically: Commercial Fantasy; Contemporary Fantasy; Cozy Fantasy; Dark Fantasy; Gaslamp Fantasy; Grounded Fantasy; High / Epic Fantasy; Historical Fantasy; Light Fantasy; Literary Fantasy; Low Fantasy; Magic; Magical Realism; Romantasy; Science Fantasy; Slipstream; Superhero Fantasy; Sword and Sorcery; Urban Fantasy
3 Seas Literary Agency L001
4RV Publishing.. P004
4RV Tenacious P005
Aardwolf Press.. P007
Adsett, Alex L006

Claim your free access to www.firstwriter.com: See p.403

342 Index | *Farm Equipment*

Afonso, Thais L008
Alekseii, Keir L015
Alex Adsett Literary L016
Allison & Busby Ltd P019
Armada, Kurestin L030
Armstrong, Susan L032
Arthurson, Wayne L033
Asimov's Science Fiction M033
Authentic Ideas P040
Baen Books P049
Bajek, Lauren L037
Baror International, Inc L044
Belton, Maddy L055
Bennett, Laura L056
Bent, Jenny L059
Berlyne, John L061
BFS Horizons M059
BFS Journal M060
Bhasin, Tamanna L064
Boker, Sidney L067
Bookouture P078
Bradford Literary Agency L075
Brannan, Maria L078
Burns, Camille L094
Candlemark & Gleam P092
Caprio, Alice L103
Carr, Michael L109
Carroll, Megan L110
Chase Literary Agency L118
Chevais, Jennifer L122
Cho, Catherine L124
Clarke, Caro L128
Cochran, Alexander L130
Colwill, Charlotte L132
Compassiviste Publishing P121
Crabtree Publishing P126
Crystal Magazine M110
Curtis Brown L146
Cusick, John L148
DAW Books P135
Dodd, Saffron L172
DSP Publications P145
Eberly, Chelsea L187
Edenborough, Sam L189
Edwards, Max L190
Ellor, Zabé L198
Fabien, Samantha L207
Feminist Press, The P163
Fernandez, Rochelle L220
Figueroa, Melanie L221
Finan, Ciara L223
Fitzgerald, Bea L227
Forrester, Jemima L232
Frances Collin Literary Agent L237
Gahan, Isobel L250
Gilbert, Tara L258
Gisondi, Katie L261
Global Lion Intellectual Property Management, Inc L264
Goff, Ellen L267
Good Literary Agency, The L269
Gunic, Masha L284
Hakim, Serene L288
Hannigan, Carrie L292
Harmony Ink Press P205
Hawn, Molly Ker L304
Hensley, Chelsea L307
Hiraeth Books P220
Hodges, Jodie L315
Hogrebe, Christina L317
Interzone M201
Irvine, Lucy L325
Jamieson, Molly L329
Joelle Delbourgo Associates, Inc. L334
Joffe Books P248
Julie Crisp Literary Agency L343
Kean, Taylor Martindale L357
Kensington Publishing Corp. P253
Killingley, Jessica L365
Kim, Jennifer L366
Knigge, Sheyla L372
Korero Press P257
Landis, Sarah L381
Langlee, Lina L382
Langton, Becca L383
Lechon, Shannon L390
Lees, Jordan L392
Leon, Nina L394
Lightner, Kayla L399
Lineberry, Isabel L402
Liverpool Literary Agency, The L404
Magazine of Fantasy & Science Fiction, The M230
Maltese, Alyssa L422
Marini, Victoria L423
Marr, Jill L425
Matte, Rebecca L431
Megibow, Sara L439
Mihell, Natasha L448
Milusich, Grace L453
Miranda, Caroline L454
MMB Creative L455
Molloy, Jess L456
Murray, Judith L468
Muscato, Nate L469
Mushens, Juliet L470
Mustelier, James L471
Nash, Justin L474
Nathan, Abigail L475
NBM Publishing P312
Neely, Rachel L476
Nelson, Kristin L478
O'Brien, Lee L484
Oghma Creative Media P321
On Spec M268
Pages, Saribel L496
Perez Literary & Entertainment L506
Perez, Kristina L507
Perotto-Wills, Martha L508
Pestritto, Carrie L511
Petty, Rachel L512
Phelan, Beth L514
Piatkus Books P352
Plant, Zoe L519
Posner, Marcy L522
R D Publishers P370
Reactor M307
Reino, Jessica L534
Robinson, Quressa L542
Rofe, Jennifer L545
Ross, Whitney L551
Rutherford, Laetitia L557
Salazar, Des L559
Selectric Artists L573
Sheil Land Associates Ltd L577
Shoreline of Infinity M334
Siobhan, Aiden L587
SmashBear Publishing P412
Soloway, Jennifer March L590
Sorg, Arley L592
Sternig & Byrne Literary Agency L598
Story Unlikely M356
Strange Horizons M357
Stringer, Marlene L604
Strong, Amy L605
Symonds, Laurel L617
Terlip, Paige L624
Tibbets, Anne L630
Tor P455
Tor Publishing Group P456
Tor Teen P457
Tor.com Publishing P458
Torrey House Press, LLC P459
Trussell, Caroline L635
Turner Publishing P462
Udden, Jennifer L637
Victoria Sanders & Associates LLC L642
W.W. Norton & Company, Inc. P500
Watterson, Jessica L648
Weiman, Paula L649
Weiss, Alexandra L650
Whatnall, Michaela L655
Wilson, Desiree L667
Wilson, Ed L668
Woods, Bryony L671
WordCrafts Press P514
Zack Company, Inc, The L678
Zeno Agency L680

Farm Equipment

See more broadly: Farming

Virginia Wine & Country Life M390

Farming

See more broadly: Agriculture

See more specifically: Animal Husbandry; Farm Equipment; Urban Farming

Henley Hall Press P214
Scottish Farmer, The M325
Spelt Magazine M352

Fashion

See more specifically: Hairstyles

Bella M053
Bloomsbury Academic P071
Cavanagh, Claire L114
Chronicle Books LLC P111
Cotswold Life M098
Cowboys & Indians M101
Curran, Sabhbh L145
Derviskadic, Dado L164
Essex Life M132
First For Women M142
Laurence King Publishing P261
Mack, Kate L415
marie claire M234
marie claire (UK) M235
Marshall, Jen L427
My Weekly M249
Norfolk & Suffolk Bride M260
Pavilion Books P338
Pensacola Magazine M281
Pride M298
Ramer, Susan L528
Red Magazine M309
Ross, Whitney L551
Schiffer Fashion Press P395
Schiffer Publishing P398
Scottish Field M326
Seventeen M329
SOMA M340
Thames & Hudson Inc. P446
Vogue M393
Wallpaper M397
Woman & Home M407
Yale University Press (London) P520
Yorkshire Women's Life Magazine M414
Yours M416

Feminism

See more broadly: Gender

See more specifically: Intersectional Feminism

Atyeo, Charlotte L034
Barr, Nicola L046
Baxter, Veronique L052
Caitlin Press Inc. P090
Cleis Press P115
Conrad, Claire Paterson L136
Draper, Claire L178
Eberly, Chelsea L187
Evans, Kiya L205
Fazzari, Hillary L210

Access more listings online at ***www.firstwriter.com***

Feminist Press, The	P163	
Feminist Studies	M139	
Fernwood Publishing	P164	
Finan, Ciara	L223	
Finegan, Stevie	L226	
Forrester, Jemima	L232	
Future Fire, The	M158	
Hannah Sheppard Literary Agency	L291	
Hardman, Caroline	L295	
Hazel Press	P211	
Latshaw, Katherine	L386	
Mortimer, Michele	L462	
New Internationalist	M256	
Oneworld Publications	P327	
Perez Literary & Entertainment	L506	
Perez, Kristina	L507	
Phillips, Aemilia	L515	
Pluto Press	P358	
Understorey Magazine	M385	
Virago Books	P498	

Feminist Romance
See more broadly: Romance
Cooper, Maggie L141

Fertility
See more broadly: Health
Singing Dragon P409

Fiction

3 Seas Literary Agency	L001
30 North	M002
404 Ink	P002
4RV Publishing	P004
4RV Tenacious	P005
A.M. Heath & Company Limited, Author's Agents	L002
aaduna	M005
Aardwolf Press	P007
Able Muse Press	P009
About Place Journal	M007
Abuzz Press	P010
Account, The	M009
Acheampong, Kwaku	L004
Ad Hoc Fiction	P011
Adams, Seren	L005
Adsett, Alex	L006
AdventureBox	M013
Afonso, Thais	L008
African American Review	M014
African Voices	M015
Afterglow Books	P014
Agency (London) Ltd, The	L009
Agni	M016
Ahearn Agency, Inc, The	L011
Alaska Quarterly Review	M019
Albert Whitman & Company	P015
Alekseii, Keir	L015
Alex Adsett Literary	L016
Alfred Hitchcock Mystery Magazine	M020
Algonquin Books	P016
Alice Williams Literary	L017
Allen & Unwin	P018
Allison & Busby Ltd	P019
Alternating Current Press	P020
Ambassador Speakers Bureau & Literary Agency	L019
Ambrosi, Beniamino	L020
American Mystery Classics	P023
American Short Fiction	M023
Amethyst Review	M024
Amling, Eric	L021
And Other Stories	P025
Anderson, Darley	L022
Andrade, Hannah	L023
Andrew Nurnberg Associates, Ltd	L024
Andrew, Nelle	L025
Andrews McMeel Publishing	P026
Anne Clark Literary Agency	L028

Antigonish Review, The	M026
Antony Harwood Limited	L029
Anvil Press Publishers	P028
Arachne Press	P030
Arboreal	M027
Arcadia Publishing	P031
Armada, Kurestin	L030
Arms, Victoria Wells	L031
Armstrong, Susan	L032
Arsenal Pulp Press	P032
Arte Publico Press	P033
Arthurson, Wayne	L033
Asabi Publishing	P034
Ascend Books, LLC	P035
Asimov's Science Fiction	M033
Atlantic Northeast	M037
Atyeo, Charlotte	L034
Aurora Metro Press	P039
Auroras & Blossoms PoArtMo Anthology	M039
Authentic Ideas	P040
Authentic Shorts	M040
Avon	P044
Avon Books	P045
Babybug	M041
Bacopa Literary Review	M042
Bad Press Ink	P047
Badger Learning	P048
Baen Books	P049
Baffler, The	M043
Bajek, Lauren	L037
Bald and Bonkers Network LLC	P050
Bandit Fiction	M045
Baobab Press	P054
Barbara, Stephen	L041
Barbican Press	P055
Barbour Publishing	P056
Barone Literary Agency	L043
Baror International, Inc.	L044
Barr, Anjanette	L045
Barr, Nicola	L046
Barren Magazine	M047
Bartholomew, Jason	L047
Bates, Tim	L048
Bath Literary Agency	L049
Bauman, Erica	L050
Baxter, Veronique	L052
Beano, The	M051
Bear Deluxe Magazine, The	L052
Begum, Salma	L053
Belmont Story Review	M054
Beloit Fiction Journal	M055
Belton, Maddy	L055
Bennett, Laura	L056
Bent Agency (UK), The	L057
Bent Agency, The	L058
Bent, Jenny	L059
Berdinsky, Kendall	L060
Berlyne, John	L061
Bess Press	P064
Betsy Amster Literary Enterprises	L063
Better Than Starbucks	M058
BFS Horizons	M059
Bhasin, Tamanna	L064
Big Fiction	M061
Birlinn Ltd	L067
Black Moon Magazine	M064
Black Static	M065
Black Warrior Review	M066
Blackstaff Press	P068
Blake Friedmann Literary Agency Ltd	L066
Bloodhound Books	P070
Blue Earth Review	M067
Blue Jeans Books	P073
Blue Mesa Review	M068
BOA Editions, Ltd.	P076

Boker, Sidney	L067
Bolton, Camilla	L069
Bookouture	P078
Bookseeker Agency	L070
Borstel, Stefanie Sanchez Von	L071
Boston Review	M071
Bowlin, Sarah	L073
Boyfriend Village	M073
Brace, Samantha	L074
Bradford Literary Agency	L075
Bradford, Laura	L076
Brannan, Maria	L078
Brattesani, Hannah	L079
Brattle Agency LLC, The	L080
Brewer, Amy	L081
Brewin Books Ltd	P081
Bright Agency (UK), The	L082
Bright Agency (US), The	L083
Brooks, Savannah	L084
Brotherstone Creative Management	L085
Brotherstone, Charlie	L086
Browne & Miller Literary Associates	L089
Bucci, Chris	L090
Buckley, Louise	L091
Bukowski, Danielle	L092
Burke, Kate	L093
Burns, Camille	L094
C&W (Conville & Walsh)	L096
CAA (London)	L098
Cadno	P089
Cafe Irreal, The	M078
Caitlin Press Inc.	P090
Campbell, Charlie	L099
Candlemark & Gleam	P092
Candy Jar Books	P093
Canterbury Literary Agency	L101
Caprio, Alice	L103
Capron, Elise	L104
Captivate Press	P095
Caroline Sheldon Literary Agency	L106
Carr, Jamie	L108
Carr, Michael	L109
Carroll, Megan	L110
Carter, Rebecca	L111
Cartey, Claire	L112
Caskie, Robert	L113
Cavanagh, Claire	L114
Chanchani, Sonali	L115
Chang, Nicola	L116
Chapman	M081
Chapman Publishing	P099
Charisma House	P100
Charles River Press	P101
Charlesbridge Publishing	P102
Charlesbridge Teen	P103
Charnace, Edwina de	L117
Chase Literary Agency	L118
Chautauqua Literary Journal	M083
Cherry Lake Publishing Group	P106
Cheshire	M084
Chevais, Jennifer	L122
Child's Play (International) Ltd	P107
Chiotti, Danielle	L123
Cho, Catherine	L124
Choc Lit	P108
Christensen, Erica	L125
ChristLight Books	P110
Chronicle Books LLC	P111
Cichello, Kayla	L127
Cincinnati Review, The	M086
Cinnamon Press	P112
Claret Press	P113
Clarke, Caro	L128
Clarke, Catherine	L129
Classical Comics	P114
Cleis Press	P115

Cobblestone	M087	
Cochran, Alexander	L130	
Coil, The	M089	
Cola	M090	
Colwill, Charlotte	L132	
Combemale, Chris	L133	
Comma Press	P120	
Comparato, Andrea	L134	
Compassiviste Publishing	P121	
Concepcion, Cristina	L135	
Concho River Review	M092	
Conjunctions	M093	
Conjunctions Online	M094	
Conrad, Claire Paterson	L136	
Conville, Clare	L137	
Coombes, Clare	L138	
Coombs Moylett & Maclean Literary Agency	L139	
Cooper, Gemma	L140	
Cooper, Maggie	L141	
Coyote Arts	P125	
Crab Orchard Review	M102	
Crabtree Publishing	P126	
Crandall, Becca	L142	
Crannog Magazine	M103	
Crazyhorse / Swamp Pink	M104	
Cream City Review	M105	
Critical Quarterly	M108	
Crowley, Sheila	L144	
Crown Publishing Group, The	P131	
Crystal Magazine	M110	
Curran, Sabhbh	L145	
Curtis Brown	L146	
Curtis Brown (Australia) Pty Ltd	L147	
Cusick, John	L148	
CutBank	M111	
Cynthia Cannell Literary Agency	L150	
Cyphers	M112	
Dahlia Books	P132	
Dalhousie Review, The	M113	
Dana Newman Literary, LLC	L152	
Danaczko, Melissa	L153	
Danko, Margaret	L154	
Darga, Jon Michael	L155	
Darhansoff & Verrill Literary Agents	L156	
Darley Anderson Agency, The	L157	
Daunt Books Publishing	P134	
David Godwin Associates	L158	
Davies, Elinor	L160	
DAW Books	P135	
Dawntreader, The	M115	
Dawson, Liza	L162	
DeBlock, Liza	L163	
Dedalus Ltd	P136	
Deep Overstock Magazine	M116	
Denis Kitchen Publishing Company Co., LLC	P138	
DHH Literary Agency Ltd	L166	
Dijkstra, Sandra	L169	
Dillsworth, Elise	L170	
Dixon, Isobel	L171	
Dodd, Saffron	L172	
Dodo Ink	P142	
Dominguez, Adriana	L174	
Don Congdon Associates, Inc.	L175	
Donald Maass Literary Agency	L176	
Doubleday (UK)	P143	
Doug Grad Literary Agency	L177	
Draper, Claire	L178	
Dream Catcher	M123	
Dreamspinner Press	P144	
DSP Publications	P145	
Dublin Review, The	M124	
Dunham Literary, Inc.	L179	
Dunham, Jennie	L180	
Dunn, Ben	L181	
DunnFogg	L182	
Dunow, Carlson & Lerner Agency	L184	
Eason, Lynette	L186	
Eberly, Chelsea	L187	
Ecotone	M127	
Eddison Pearson Ltd	L188	
Edenborough, Sam	L189	
Edwards, Max	L190	
Eerdmans Books for Young Readers	P148	
Eisenbraun, Nicole	L191	
Eisenmann, Caroline	L192	
Ekphrastic Review, The	M128	
El Portal	M129	
Elaine Markson Literary Agency	L195	
Elaine Steel	L196	
Ellery Queen Mystery Magazine	M130	
Elliott & Thompson	P149	
Ellis-Martin, Sian	L197	
Ellor, Zabé	L198	
Emily Sweet Associates	L199	
Enitharmon Editions	P153	
Eunice McMullen Children's Literary Agent Ltd	L201	
Evan Marshall Agency, The	L202	
Evans, David	L203	
Evans, Kate	L204	
Evans, Kiya	L205	
Evans, Stephany	L206	
Event	M133	
Everything With Words	P158	
Fabien, Samantha	L207	
Fabula Argentea	M134	
Fairbank Literary Representation	L208	
Fairlight Books	P160	
Fathom Books	P162	
Faulks, Holly	L209	
Faultline	M137	
Fazzari, Hillary	L210	
Feldmann, Kait Lee	L212	
Feldstein, Rebecca	L213	
Felicia Eth Literary Representation	L214	
Felicity Bryan Associates	L215	
Fellows, Abi	L216	
Feminist Press, The	P163	
Feminist Studies	M139	
Ferguson, Hannah	L217	
Ferguson, T.S.	L218	
Fergusson, Julie	L219	
Fernandez, Rochelle	L220	
Fiction	M140	
Fiddlehead, The	M141	
Figueroa, Melanie	L221	
Filter Press	P166	
Finan, Ciara	L223	
Finch, Rebeka	L225	
Finegan, Stevie	L226	
Firefly	P167	
First Line, The	M143	
Fitzgerald, Bea	L227	
Five Points	M144	
Flannery Literary	L228	
Flynn, Amy Thrall	L229	
Fogg, Jack	L230	
Folio	M147	
for Authors, A	L231	
Forge	P169	
Forrester, Jemima	L232	
Fortnightly Review, The	M149	
Foster, Clara	L233	
Fourth River, The	M153	
Fox, Aram	L234	
Foxx, Kat	L235	
Frances Collin Literary Agent	L237	
Frances Goldin Literary Agency, Inc.	L238	
Frankel, Valerie	L239	
Fraser Ross Associates	L240	
Free Spirit Publishing	P174	
Fresh Words – An International Literary Magazine	M154	
Freymann, Sarah Jane	L242	
Friedman, Claire	L243	
Friedman, Rebecca	L244	
Friedrich Agency LLC, The	L245	
Fuentes, Sarah	L247	
Fugue	M155	
Fuller, Lisa	L248	
Funny Times	M157	
Furniss, Eugenie	L249	
Future Fire, The	M158	
Gahan, Isobel	L250	
Galustian, Natalie	L251	
Galvin, Lori	L252	
Gargoyle Online	M161	
Gauntlett, Adam	L254	
Geiger, Ellen	L255	
Georgia Review, The	M163	
Gertrude	M164	
Gertrude Press	P179	
Getzler, Josh	L256	
Ghahremani, Lilly	L257	
Gilbert, Tara	L258	
Gill Books	P181	
Gillam, Bianca	L259	
Ginosko Literary Journal	M165	
Gisondi, Katie	L261	
Glacier, The	M166	
Glass Literary Management LLC	L262	
Glenister, Emily	L263	
Global Lion Intellectual Property Management, Inc.	L264	
Goetz, Adria	L265	
Goff, Anthony	L266	
Goff, Ellen	L267	
Gold SF	P185	
Goldstein, Veronica	L268	
Good Literary Agency, The	L269	
Goodman Beck Publishing	P187	
Goose Lane Editions	P188	
Gordon, Andrew	L270	
Graffeg Childrens	P191	
Graham, Stacey	L272	
Grain Literary Magazine	M170	
Grajkowski, Kara	L273	
Grajkowski, Michelle	L274	
Granta	M171	
Granta Books	P192	
Graywolf Lab	M172	
Graywolf Press	P193	
Greene & Heaton Ltd	L276	
Greenstreet, Katie	L277	
Greyhound Literary	L278	
Grimm, Katie	L279	
Gruber, Pam	L281	
Grunewald, Hattie	L282	
Gulf Coast: A Journal of Literature and Fine Arts	M173	
Gunic, Masha	L284	
Guppy Books	P195	
Gutter Magazine	M174	
Hachette Book Group	P196	
Haggerty, Taylor	L287	
Hakim, Serene	L288	
Haley, Jolene	L289	
Half Mystic Journal	M175	
Half Mystic Press	P197	
Hanbury Agency, The	L290	
Hanging Loose	M177	
Hannah Sheppard Literary Agency	L291	
Hannigan, Carrie	L292	
Hansen, Stephanie	L293	
Happy Yak	P200	
Hardman, Caroline	L295	

Hare, Jessica	L296
Harlequin Desire	P202
Harlequin Mills & Boon Ltd	P203
Harmony Ink Press	P205
Harmsworth, Esmond	L297
Harold Ober Associates, Inc.	L298
Harper's Magazine	M178
Harper, Logan	L299
Harpur Palate	M179
Harris, Erin	L300
Harwell, Hilary	L301
Hashtag Press	P207
Haus Publishing	P208
Hawk, Susan	L303
Hawn, Molly Ker	L304
Hawthorne Books	P209
Hayden, Viola	L305
Hazel Press	P211
Headley, David H.	L306
Heavy Traffic	M181
Hedgerow: A Journal of Small Poems	M182
Helix, The	M183
Hensley, Chelsea	L307
Here Comes Everyone	M184
Hernando, Paloma	L308
Heymont, Lane	L309
Hiraeth Books	P220
Hiyate, Sam	L313
Hobbs, Victoria	L314
Hodder & Stoughton Ltd	P222
Hodges, Jodie	L315
Hogrebe, Christina	L317
Holroyde, Penny	L319
HopeRoad	P223
Hordern, Kate	L320
Hornsley, Sarah	L321
Host Publications	P224
Hotel Amerika	M189
Hudson Review, The	M190
Hunger Mountain	M191
Hwang, Annie	L322
I-70 Review	M192
Idaho Review	M193
Identity Theory	M194
IDW Publishing	P228
Ig Publishing	P230
IgKids	P231
Igloo Books Limited	P232
Image	M195
Indiana Review	M196
Influx Press	P237
Inkandescent	P240
Inque	M198
Inscriptions Literary Agency	L323
Interzone	M201
Ireland's Own	M202
Irene Goodman Literary Agency (IGLA)	L324
Irish Pages	M203
Irvine, Lucy	L325
Island	M204
Island Online	M205
Jamieson, Molly	L329
Jamii Publishing	P245
Janklow & Nesbit UK Ltd	L330
JMD Media / DB Publishing	P247
Jo Unwin Literary Agency	L333
Joelle Delbourgo Associates, Inc.	L334
Joffe Books	P248
John Murray Press	P249
Jonathan Clowes Ltd	L336
Jonathan Pegg Literary Agency	L337
Jones, Philip Gwyn	L339
Joy Harris Literary Agency, Inc.	L340
Judith Murdoch Literary Agency	L341
Julie Crisp Literary Agency	L343
K2 Literary	L344
Kahn, Ella Diamond	L345
Kahn, Jody	L346
Kaliszewska, Joanna	L347
Kane Literary Agency	L348
Kane Press	P251
Kantor, Camille	L349
Kardon, Julia	L350
Karinch, Maryann	L351
Kate Barker Literary, TV, & Film Agency	L352
Kate Nash Literary Agency	L353
Kates Hill Press, The	P252
Kathryn Green Literary Agency, LLC	L354
Kavanagh, Jade	L355
Kavya Kishor	M208
Kean, Taylor Martindale	L357
Keane Kataria Literary Agency	L358
Kenny, Julia	L361
Kensington Publishing Corp.	P253
Kenyon Review, The	M210
Keren, Eli	L362
Kerning	M211
Ki Agency Ltd	L364
Kids Alive!	M212
Killingley, Jessica	L365
Kim, Jennifer	L366
Kim, Julia	L367
Kimber, Natalie	L368
Kimberley Cameron & Associates	L369
Kirby, Robert	L370
Knigge, Sheyla	L372
Kore Press	P256
Kotchman, Katie	L374
Krienke, Mary	L375
KT Literary	L377
Kube Publishing	P258
Labyrinth Literary Agency, The	L378
Lakosil, Natalie	L379
Lambert, Sophie	L380
Landfall	M215
Landis, Sarah	L381
Langlee, Lina	L382
Langmarc Publishing	P259
Langton, Becca	L383
Langtons International	L384
Langtry, Elena	L385
Lantana Publishing	P260
Latshaw, Katherine	L386
Laxfield Literary Associates	L387
Leach, Saskia	L389
Leamington Books	P262
Leapfrog Press	P263
Lechon, Shannon	L390
Leeke, Jessica	L391
Lees, Jordan	L392
Leigh Feldman Literary	L393
Leon, Nina	L394
Lerner Publishing Group	P264
Levitt, Sarah	L396
Lewinsohn Literary	L397
Lewis, Alison	L398
Lighthouse	M218
Lightner, Kayla	L399
Lightning Books	P266
Lilliput Press, The	P268
Limelight Management	L400
Lindsay Literary Agency	L401
Lineberry, Isabel	L402
Liss, Laurie	L403
Literary Mama	M220
Litro Magazine	M221
Liverpool Literary Agency, The	L404
Liza Dawson Associates	L405
Loft Press, Inc.	P270
London Magazine, The	M224
Lost Lake Folk Opera Magazine	M227
Lotus Lane Literary	L407
Loughman, Morwenna	L408
Louisiana Literature	M228
Lovell, Jake	L409
Lutterworth Press, The	P275
Lutyens and Rubinstein	L410
Lyrical Press	P277
MacDonald, Emily	L412
Macdougall, Laura	L413
MacGregor & Luedeke	L414
MacGuffin, The	M229
MacKenzie, Joanna	L416
Maclean, Jamie	L417
MacLeod, Lauren	L418
Macmillan Children's Books	P279
Madan, Neeti	L419
Madeleine Milburn Literary, TV & Film Agency	L420
Magazine of Fantasy & Science Fiction, The	M230
Maidment, Olivia	L421
Malahat Review, The	M232
Maltese, Alyssa	L422
Manilla Press	P280
Manoa	M233
Margaret K. McElderry Books	P281
Marini, Victoria	L423
Marion Boyars Publishers	P282
Marr, Jill	L425
Marsh Agency, The	L426
Marshall, Jen	L427
Massachusetts Review, The	M237
Massie, Maria	L430
Matte, Rebecca	L431
Mattson, Jennifer	L432
Maurer, Shari	L433
McBride, Juliana	L435
McCormick Literary	L436
McNidder & Grace	P286
McQuilkin, Rob	L438
Meetinghouse	M238
Megibow, Sara	L439
Mehren, Jane von	L440
Meridian Artists	L442
Merullo, Annabel	L443
Metamorphosis Literary Agency	L444
Methuen Publishing Ltd	P294
Mic Cheetham Literary Agency	L445
Michel, Caroline	L446
Michigan Quarterly Review	M240
Mid-American Review	M241
Midsummer Dream House	M242
Midway Journal	M243
Mihell, Natasha	L448
Milburn, Madeleine	L449
Mildred Marmur Associates, Ltd.	L450
Mileo, Jessica	L451
Milkweed Editions	P296
Mills & Boon	P297
Milusich, Grace	L453
Miranda, Caroline	L454
Missouri Review, The	M245
MMB Creative	L455
Molloy, Jess	L456
Moody Publishers	P305
Moore, Mary C.	L457
Moore, Penny	L458
Moorhead, Max	L459
Morrell, Imogen	L460
Morris, Natascha	L461
Mortimer, Michele	L462
Motala, Tasneem	L463
Movable Type Management	L464
Moving Worlds: A Journal of Transcultural Writings	M247

Mozley, Jack	L465
MQR Mixtape	M248
Mudfog Press	P306
Mundy, Toby	L466
Murray, Judith	L468
Muscato, Nate	L469
Mushens, Juliet	L470
Mustelier, James	L471
My Weekly	M249
Mysterious Press, The	P309
Mystery Magazine	M250
Napolitano, Maria	L473
Nash, Justin	L474
Nashville Review	M251
Nathan, Abigail	L475
Native Ink Press	P311
NBM Publishing	P312
Neely, Rachel	L476
Nelson Literary Agency, LLC	L477
Nelson, Kristin	L478
Neon	M253
New Accelerator, The	M254
New England Review	M255
New Orleans Review	M257
New Welsh Reader	M259
Nichols, Mariah	L479
Nightfire	P316
Niumata, Erin	L480
Northbank Talent Management	L482
Northern Gravy	M263
Nosy Crow	P319
O'Brien, Lee	L484
O'Grady, Faith	L485
O'Grady, Niamh	L486
O'Neill, Molly	L487
Oakland Arts Review, The	M264
Obsidian: Literature in the African Diaspora	M265
Oghma Creative Media	P321
Ogtrop, Kristin van	L489
Oh MG Press	P322
Ohio State University Press, The	P323
Old Red Kimono	M267
Old Street Publishing Ltd	P325
Oldcastle Books Group	P326
Olswanger, Anna	L491
On Spec	M268
Oneworld Publications	P327
Ooligan Press	P328
Orbis International Literary Journal	M269
Orenda Books	P329
Ostby, Kristin	L494
Ouen Press	P331
Oxford Review of Books	M271
Oyez Review	M272
Pacific Press Publishing Association	P334
Pacifica Literary Review	M273
Pages, Saribel	L496
Pan Macmillan Australia	P335
Pande, Ayesha	L497
Panorama	M274
Paradigm Talent and Literary Agency	L498
Paris Review, The	M275
Parker, Elana Roth	L499
Parthian Books	P336
Pass, Marina de	L500
Passionfruit Review, The	M277
Patrician Press	P337
Patterson, Emma	L501
Paul S. Levine Literary Agency	L502
Pavilion Books	P338
Paycock Press	P340
Peepal Tree Press	P341
Pelham, Imogen	L504
Pen & Ink Designs Publishing	P342
Pennine Ink Magazine	M280
Penzler Publishers	P345
People's Friend Pocket Novels	M282
People's Friend, The	M283
Perez Literary & Entertainment	L506
Perez, Kristina	L507
Perotto-Wills, Martha	L508
Pestritto, Carrie	L511
Peter Owen Publishers	P349
Petty, Rachel	L512
Phelan, Beth	L514
Phillips, Aemilia	L515
Phoenix Moirai	P351
Piatkus Books	P352
Piccadilly Press	P354
Pickering, Juliet	L516
Pierce, Rosie	L517
Pinata Books	P355
Pine, Gideon	L518
Pineapple Press	P356
Plant, Zoe	L519
Pleiades	M285
Plitt, Carrie	L520
Ploughshares	M286
Polygon	P360
Popshot Quarterly	M293
Portobello Literary	L521
Posner, Marcy	L522
Power Cut Lite	M294
Power, Anna	L523
Prasanna, Tanusri	L525
Present Tense	M296
Press 53	P361
Preston, Amanda	L526
Prole	M299
Pureplay Press	P365
Pushing Out the Boat	M301
Qu Literary Magazine	M302
Quadrant Books	P366
Quirk Books	P369
R D Publishers	P370
Rabble Review	M303
Ramer, Susan	L528
Ransom Publishing Ltd	P373
Ravenstone	P374
Redhammer	L530
Reid, Janet	L532
Reilly, Milly	L533
Reino, Jessica	L534
Renard Press Ltd	P376
Riccardi, Francesca	L535
Richard Curtis Associates, Inc.	L536
Richter, Rick	L537
River Styx	M314
Riverbed Review	M315
Roberts, Soumeya Bendimerad	L540
Robertson Murray Literary Agency	L541
Robinson, Quressa	L542
Rocking Chair Books	L544
Rofe, Jennifer	L545
Rogers, Coleridge & White Ltd	L546
Root, Holly	L548
Rose and Crown Books	P381
Rosenberg Group, The	L549
Roseway	P382
Ross, Whitney	L551
Rubin Pfeffer Content, LLC	L552
Ruby Fiction	P384
Rudy Agency, The	L553
Rupert Crew Ltd	L554
Ruppin Agency, The	L555
Rushall, Kathleen	L556
Rutherford, Laetitia	L557
Rutman, Jim	L558
Saddlebag Dispatches	M319
Saguaro Books, LLC	P388
Salazar, Des	L559
Salt Publishing	P389
Salvo, Katie	L560
Sanchez, Kaitlyn	L561
Sanders, Rayhane	L562
Sant, Kelly Van	L563
Sarah Jane Freymann Literary Agency	L564
Sayle Literary Agency, The	L565
Scarfe, Rory	L566
Scarlet	P393
Schiffer Kids	P396
Schofield, Hannah	L567
Scholastic	P399
Scholastic UK	P400
Schwartz, Steve	L568
Scratching Shed Publishing	P402
Scribble	M327
Seager, Chloe	L571
Sebes & Bisseling	L572
Second Factory	M328
Selectric Artists	L573
Sentient Publications	P404
Seren Books	P405
Serra, Maria Cardona	L574
Seymour, Charlotte	L575
Shaw Agency, The	L576
Sheil Land Associates Ltd	L577
Shenandoah	M331
Shesto Literary	L580
Shestopal, Camilla	L581
Shipwreckt Books Publishing Company	P406
Shooter Literary Magazine	M333
Shoreline of Infinity	M334
Shorts Magazine	M335
Signorelli, Michael	L582
Silk, Julia	L583
Silver, Janet	L584
Simons, Tanera	L585
Simpson, Cara Lee	L586
Sinister Stoat Press	P410
Sinister Wisdom	M337
Siobhan, Aiden	L587
Sluytman, Antoinette Van	L588
SmashBear Publishing	P412
Snowflake Magazine	M338
Society for Promoting Christian Knowledge (SPCK)	P414
Soho Press	P417
Soho Review, The	M339
Soler, Shania N.	L589
Soloway, Jennifer March	L590
Sonder Magazine	M342
Sophie Hicks Agency	L591
Sorg, Arley	L592
South Carolina Review	M344
Southern Humanities Review	M345
Southern Review, The	M346
Southwest Review	M348
Southword Journal	M349
Spackman, James	L593
Sparsile Books	P419
Spitball	M353
Spout Press	P420
Spring Literary	L594
SRL Publishing	P421
Steed, Hayley	L595
Sternig & Byrne Literary Agency	L598
Steward House Publishers	P429
Stewart, Douglas	L599
Stinging Fly, The	M355
Story Unlikely	M356
StoryWise	L601
Strachan Literary Agency	L602
Strange Horizons	M357
Stringer Literary Agency LLC, The	L603
Stringer, Marlene	L604

Index | Film Scripts

Strong, Amy... L605
Structo Magazine... M359
Stuart Krichevsky Literary Agency, Inc.... L609
Studio One... M360
Sunbelt Publications, Inc.... P433
Sunberry Books... P434
Sunpenny Publishing... P435
Sunspot Literary Journal... M364
Supplement, The... M365
Susan Schulman Literary Agency... L610
Sutherland, Kari... L611
Swainson, Joanna... L613
Sweet Cherry Publishing... P437
Sweetgum Press... P438
SYLA – Susan Yearwood Literary Agency... L616
Symonds, Laurel... L617
Tahoma Literary Review... M368
Tailwinds Press... P439
Takahe... M369
Takikawa, Marin... L618
Talbot, Emily... L619
Tannenbaum, Amy... L620
Tears in the Fence... M371
Templar Books... P442
Temz Review, The... M372
Teresa Chris Literary Agency Ltd... L623
Terlip, Paige... L624
Texas A&M University Press... P445
Thames & Hudson Inc.... P446
Thayer, Henry... L626
Theseus Agency, The... L627
Thin Air Magazine... M374
Thinkwell Books, UK... P447
Third Coast... M375
Thistle Publishing... P448
Thorneycroft, Euan... L628
Threepenny Review, The... M377
Thwaites, Steph... L629
Tibbets, Anne... L630
Tilbury House Publishers... P450
Tiny Owl... P451
Tippermuir Books... P452
Toad Hall Editions... P453
Tocher... M378
Todd, Hannah... L631
Tolka... M379
Topping, Antony... L632
Tor... P455
Tor Publishing Group... P456
Tor Teen... P457
Tor.com Publishing... P458
Torrey House Press, LLC... P459
Tran, Jennifer Chen... L633
Tributaries... M380
Troika Books... P461
Trudel, Jes... L634
Trussell, Caroline... L635
Turner Publishing... P462
Tusculum Review, The... M381
Two Piers Literary Agency, The... L636
Tyndale House Publishers, Inc.... P465
Udden, Jennifer... L637
Ulverscroft Ltd.... P467
Unbound Press... P468
Under the Radar... M384
Understorey Magazine... M385
Unicorn Publishing Group... P470
Universe... P474
University of Alaska Press... P476
University of Alberta Press... P477
University of Iowa Press... P480
University of Maine Press... P481
University of Massachusetts Press... P482
University of Michigan Press, The... P483
University of Nevada Press... P484
University of North Texas Press... P485
University of Wisconsin Press, The... P490
Unwin, Jo... L638
Usselman, Laura... L639
Vagabond City... M386
Valley Press... P493
Vance, Lisa Erbach... L641
Vane Women Press... P495
Velocity Press... P496
Vestal Review... M388
Victoria Sanders & Associates LLC... L642
Viney Agency, The... L643
Viney, Charlie... L644
Vinspire Publishing... P497
Virago Books... P498
Virginia Quarterly Review, The... M389
Viz... M392
W.W. Norton & Company Ltd... P499
W.W. Norton & Company, Inc.... P500
Waccamaw... M394
Walsh, Caroline... L645
Wasafiri... M398
Watson, Little Ltd... L647
Watterson, Jessica... L648
Wayne State University Press... P504
Weidenfeld & Nicolson... P505
Weiman, Paula... L649
Weiss, Alexandra... L650
Weitzner, Tess... L651
Wells, Karmen... L652
West Branch... M400
Westin, Erin Casey... L654
Whatnall, Michaela... L655
Whelan, Maria... L656
Whispering Buffalo Literary Agency... L657
White Review, The... M404
Wickers, Chandler... L659
Williams, Laura... L662
Williams, Sarah... L663
Williamson, Jo... L664
Willms, Kathryn... L665
Wilson, Desiree... L667
Wilson, Ed.... L668
Windsor Review... M405
Wolfpack Publishing... P513
Wood, Caroline... L669
Woodhouse, James... L670
Woods, Bryony... L671
Woollard, Jessica... L672
WordCrafts Press... P514
Words & Pictures... P515
Wordserve Literary... L673
Wordsonthestreet... P517
Wordsworth Editions... P518
Workman Publishing... P519
Writer's Side... L674
Yale Review, The... M409
Yellow Mama Webzine... M411
Yeoh, Rachel... L675
Yes Poetry Magazine... M412
YesYes Books... P521
Young, Claudia... L677
Yours Fiction – Women's Special Series... M417
Zack Company, Inc, The... L678
Zacker, Marietta B.... L679
Zeno Agency... L680
Zibby Books... P522
Zoetrope: All-Story... M418
Zone 3... M419
Zuraw-Friedland, Ayla... L681

Fiction as a Subject
See more broadly: Literature
American Book Review... M022
Big Fiction... M061

Fiction in Translation
Ambrosi, Beniamino... L020
American Short Fiction... M023
And Other Stories... P025
Antigonish Review, The... M026
Banipal... M046
Charnace, Edwina de... L117
Cincinnati Review, The... M086
Cyphers... M112
Daunt Books Publishing... P134
Dedalus Ltd... P136
Faultline... M137
Fiction... M140
Five Points... M144
Future Fire, The... M158
Gulf Coast: A Journal of Literature and Fine Arts... M173
Half Mystic Journal... M175
Host Publications... P224
Hunger Mountain... M191
Indiana Review... M196
Interzone... M201
Irish Pages... M203
Kenyon Review, The... M210
Kim, Jennifer... L366
Manoa... M233
Massachusetts Review, The... M237
Michigan Quarterly Review... M240
Mid-American Review... M241
Moving Worlds: A Journal of Transcultural Writings... M247
Nashville Review... M251
Oneworld Publications... P327
Orbis International Literary Journal... M269
Orenda Books... P329
Shenandoah... M331
Southern Review, The... M346
Stinging Fly, The... M355
Structo Magazine... M359
Sunspot Literary Journal... M364
Tocher... M378
Tributaries... M380
White Review, The... M404

Film Industry
See more broadly: Business
See more specifically: Cinemas / Movie Theaters
BFI Publishing... P065
Global Lion Intellectual Property Management, Inc.... L264

Film Scripts
Above the Line Agency... L003
Agency (London) Ltd, The... L009
AHA Talent Ltd... L010
Alan Brodie Representation... L013
Aurora Metro Press... P039
AVAnti Productions & Management... L035
Barnard, Arthur... L042
Bell, Eva... L054
Bolger, Maeve... L068
Cincinnati Review, The... M086
Comparato, Andrea... L134
Curtis Brown... L146
Elaine Steel... L196
Fillingham Weston Associates... L222
Frances Goldin Literary Agency, Inc.... L238
Hickman, Emily... L311
Inscriptions Literary Agency... L323
JFL Agency... L332
Judy Daish Associates Ltd... L342
Kelleher, Sophie... L359
Ki Agency Ltd... L364
Lyon, Rebecca... L411
Marion Boyars Publishers... P282
Meridian Artists... L442
Middleton, Leah... L447
Oakland Arts Review, The... M264

Paradigm Talent and Literary Agency L498
Qu Literary Magazine M302
R D Publishers P370
Rochelle Stevens & Co. L543
Scarfe, Rory L566
Sheil Land Associates Ltd L577
Sunspot Literary Journal M364
Tennyson Agency, The L622
Valerie Hoskins Associates L640
Victoria Sanders & Associates LLC L642
Williams, Katie L661

Films

See more broadly: Media

African American Review M014
Berghahn Books Ltd P062
BFI Publishing P065
Bloomsbury Academic P071
Cavanagh, Claire L114
Derviskadic, Dado L164
Doug Grad Literary Agency L177
Feminist Press, The P163
Flaneur M145
Future Fire, The M158
Gordon, Andrew L270
Hudson Review, The M190
Indiana University Press P235
Ireland's Own M202
Kim, Julia L367
Laurence King Publishing P261
My Weekly M249
New England Review M255
Ohio State University Press, The P323
Ohio University Press P324
Oxford Review of Books M271
Plexus Publishing Limited P357
Polygon P360
Power Cut Lite M294
Red Magazine M309
Rutman, Jim L558
Sheree Bykofsky Associates, Inc. L579
Sierra M336
SOMA M340
Square Mile Magazine M354
Supplement, The M365
Thayer, Henry L626
Uncut M383
University of Alberta Press P477
University of California Press P478
University of Massachusetts Press P482
University of Texas Press P488
W.W. Norton & Company Ltd P499
W.W. Norton & Company, Inc. P500
Wayne State University Press P504
Yale Review, The M409
Zack Company, Inc, The L678
ZigZag Education P523

Finance

See more specifically: Accounting; Investments; Personal Finance; Taxation

Accountancy Age M010
Accountancy Daily M011
Carr, Jamie L108
Cottage Life M099
Crabtree Publishing P126
Dawson, Liza L162
Economist, The M126
Entrepreneur M131
Fiscal Publications P168
Furniss, Eugenie L249
Gale P177
Hay House Publishers P210
Kogan Page Ltd P255
Lightner, Kayla L399
marie claire M234
Salt Publishing P389
Strategic Finance M358
Sunbelt Publications, Inc. P433
Susan Schulman Literary Agency L610
Taylor & Francis Group P441
Tyndale House Publishers, Inc. P465
Wordserve Literary L673
Yours M416
Zack Company, Inc, The L678

Firearms

See more broadly: Weapons

Safari Press P386

Fishing

See more broadly: Hunting

See more specifically: Deep Sea Fishing; Fly Fishing; Offshore Gamefishing

Amato Books P021
River Hills Traveler M313

Fitness

See more broadly: Health

See more specifically: Exercise; Running

AARP The Magazine M006
Arcadia Publishing P031
Crown Publishing Group, The P131
Dana Newman Literary, LLC L152
Evans, Stephany L206
Healthy M180
Hoffman, Scott L316
Kensington Publishing Corp. P253
marie claire M234
Red Magazine M309
Redbook Magazine M310
Robert Smith Literary Agency Ltd L539
Square Mile Magazine M354
University of Nevada Press P484
Yours M416
Zack Company, Inc, The L678

Florida

See more broadly: United States

See more specifically: Pensacola

Pineapple Press P356

Fly Fishing

See more broadly: Fishing

Amato Books P021
Flyfishing & Tying Journal M146

Folk Horror

See more broadly: Horror

Jamieson, Molly L329
Swainson, Joanna L613

Folklore, Myths, and Legends

See more broadly: Culture

See more specifically: Bigfoot

Afonso, Thais L008
Andrade, Hannah L023
Armstrong, Susan L032
Barr, Anjanette L045
Bauman, Erica L050
Belton, Maddy L055
Birlinn Ltd P067
Cho, Catherine L124
Dawntreader, The M115
Eberly, Chelsea L187
Edenborough, Sam L189
Ferguson, T.S. L218
Foster, Clara L233
Gruber, Pam L281
Haley, Jolene L289
Harris, Erin L300
Hensley, Chelsea L307
History Press, The P221
Indiana University Press P235
Irvine, Lucy L325
Knigge, Sheyla L372
Lechon, Shannon L390
Lightner, Kayla L399
Marr, Jill L425
Mustelier, James L471
Nash, Justin L474
Pass, Marina de L500
Pineapple Press P356
Scots Magazine, The M324
Soler, Shania N. L589
Strong, Amy L605
Sunbelt Publications, Inc. P433
Swainson, Joanna L613
Takikawa, Marin L618
Tocher M378
University of North Texas Press P485
University of Tennessee Press P487
University of Wisconsin Press, The P490
Unseen Press P492
W.W. Norton & Company Ltd P499
W.W. Norton & Company, Inc. P500
Weiss, Alexandra L650
Williamson, Jo L664

Food

See more broadly: Food and Drink

See more specifically: Food History; Vegetarian Food

417 Magazine M004
AARP The Magazine M006
Alcock, Michael L014
Arms, Victoria Wells L031
Bal, Emma L038
Basalt Books P057
Bates, Tim L048
Baxter, Veronique L052
Birlinn Ltd P067
Bloomsbury Academic P071
Bradford Literary Agency L075
Brattesani, Hannah L079
Brick M074
Carr, Jamie L108
Chang, Nicola L116
CharlottesvilleFamily M082
Chiotti, Danielle L123
Clarke, Caro L128
Combemale, Chris L133
Coombs Moylett & Maclean Literary Agency L139
Cooper, Maggie L141
Curran, Sabhbh L145
Derviskadic, Dado L164
DK Publishing P141
Ellis-Martin, Sian L197
Evans, Kate L204
Fairbank Literary Representation L208
First For Women M142
Fogg, Jack L230
Foxx, Kat L235
Funny Times M157
Galvin, Lori L252
Goff, Ellen L267
Graffeg P190
Granger, David L275
Healthy M180
Hiyate, Sam L313
Hobbs, Victoria L314
Joelle Delbourgo Associates, Inc. L334
Kahn, Jody L346
Kim, Julia L367
Lambert, Sophie L380
Lilliput Press, The P268
LSU Press P273
MacLeod, Lauren L418
Marr, Jill L425
Menasha Ridge Press P290
Metro Publications Ltd P295
Mills, Rachel L452
Morrell, Imogen L460
Murdoch Books Australia P308
Ohio University Press P324
Peddle, Kay L503
Pickering, Juliet L516

Index | Gender 349

Power, Anna ... L523
Ramer, Susan ... L528
Red Magazine ... M309
Reilly, Milly ... L533
Richter, Rick ... L537
Rutherford, Laetitia ... L557
Sasquatch Books ... P391
Savannah Magazine ... M322
Scoular, Rosemary ... L570
Seymour, Charlotte ... L575
Somerset Life ... M341
Stephens, Jenny ... L596
Texas A&M University Press ... P445
Thames & Hudson Inc. ... P446
Topping, Antony ... L632
University of Akron Press, The ... P475
University of Alberta Press ... P477
University of California Press ... P478
University of Georgia Press ... P479
University of Iowa Press ... P480
University of Massachusetts Press ... P482
University of Texas Press ... P488
University of Virginia Press ... P489
Whitecap Books Ltd ... P507
Woman & Home ... M407
Yankee Magazine ... M410
Yours ... M416
Zack Company, Inc, The ... L678
ZigZag Education ... P523

Food History
See more broadly: Food
Bowlin, Sarah ... L073
University of North Texas Press ... P485

Food Journalism
See more broadly: Food and Drink; Journalism
Young, Claudia ... L677

Food and Drink
See more specifically: Cookery; Diet; Drinks; Food; Food Journalism; Nutrition; Restaurants
Andrews McMeel Publishing ... P026
Atlanta Magazine ... M035
Bright Press ... P082
Cotswold Life ... M098
Cowboys & Indians ... M101
Devon Life ... M119
Essex Life ... M132
Evans, Stephany ... L206
Flaneur ... M145
Gill Books ... P181
Kent Life ... M209
Kitchen Press ... P254
Lancashire Life ... M214
marie claire ... M234
My Weekly ... M249
Pavilion Books ... P338
Quirk Books ... P369
Redbook Magazine ... M310
Scottish Field ... M326
Speciality Food ... M351
Square Mile Magazine ... M354
Sweet, Emily ... L614
Ten Speed Press ... P444
Virginia Wine & Country Life ... M390
W.W. Norton & Company Ltd ... P499
Welsh Country ... M399
Westchester Magazine ... M402
Willms, Kathryn ... L665
Yorkshire Life ... M413

Football / Soccer
See more broadly: Sport
JMD Media / DB Publishing ... P247
Scratching Shed Publishing ... P402

Formal Poetry
Better Than Starbucks ... M058
Oakland Arts Review, The ... M264
Tahoma Literary Review ... M368

Formula One
See more broadly: Motorsports
Square Mile Magazine ... M354

Fortune Telling and Divination
See more broadly: Mysticism
See more specifically: Astrology; Horoscopes; Numerology; Palmistry; Tarot
Red Feather ... P375

Fossils
See more broadly: Geology
Rock & Gem ... M316

France
See more broadly: Europe
Irene Goodman Literary Agency (IGLA) ... L324
Peter Lang ... P346
Peter Lang Publishing ... P348

Free Verse
Better Than Starbucks ... M058
MacGuffin, The ... M229
Oakland Arts Review, The ... M264
Tahoma Literary Review ... M368

French
See more broadly: Language
Colourpoint Educational ... P119
Gill Education ... P182
Mentor Books ... P292
Stipes Publishing ... P431

Friends
See more broadly: Social Groups
Chanchani, Sonali ... L115
Chang, Nicola ... L116
Cooper, Gemma ... L140
Danaczko, Melissa ... L153
Davies, Elinor ... L160
Ellis-Martin, Sian ... L197
Hannah Sheppard Literary Agency ... L291
Hashtag Press ... P207
Lewinsohn Literary ... L397
Macdougall, Laura ... L413
MacKenzie, Joanna ... L416
O'Neill, Molly ... L487
Ostby, Kristin ... L494
Pierce, Rosie ... L517
Plitt, Carrie ... L520
Redbook Magazine ... M310
Riccardi, Francesca ... L535
Sanchez, Kaitlyn ... L561
Vance, Lisa Erbach ... L641
Williams, Laura ... L662
Woods, Bryony ... L671

Funeral Industry
See more broadly: Business
Funeral Business Solutions ... M156

Furries
See more broadly: Animals
Sinister Stoat Press ... P410

Futurism
Kruger Cowne ... L376
Torrey House Press, LLC ... P459

Gaelic
See more broadly: Language
Birlinn Ltd ... P067
Colourpoint Educational ... P119

Gambling
High Stakes Publishing ... P216
University of Nevada Press ... P484

Games
See more broadly: Leisure
See more specifically: Chess; Computer and Video Games
Arcadia Publishing ... P031
Asabi Publishing ... P034
Kensington Publishing Corp. ... P253
Lutterworth Press, The ... P275
Pavilion Books ... P338
Quirk Books ... P369
Sheree Bykofsky Associates, Inc. ... L579
University of Nevada Press ... P484
W.W. Norton & Company Ltd ... P499

Gardening
See more broadly: Hobbies
Arcadia Publishing ... P031
Atlanta Magazine ... M035
Betsy Amster Literary Enterprises ... L063
Better Homes and Gardens ... M057
Birds & Blooms ... M062
Birlinn Ltd ... P067
Bright Press ... P082
Cotswold Life ... M098
Country Smallholding ... M100
Crown Publishing Group, The ... P131
DK Publishing ... P141
Doug Grad Literary Agency ... L177
Essex Life ... M132
Gale ... P177
Garden Answers ... M159
Garden News ... M160
Globe Pequot Press, The ... P184
Grossman, Loren R. ... L280
Henley Hall Press ... P214
Kensington Publishing Corp. ... P253
Kent Life ... M209
Macdougall, Laura ... L413
Monacelli Press, The ... P304
My Weekly ... M249
Native Ink Press ... P311
Pavilion Books ... P338
Pineapple Press ... P356
Quirk Books ... P369
Regina Ryan Books ... L531
Sasquatch Books ... P391
Scottish Field ... M326
Sheil Land Associates Ltd ... L577
Somerset Life ... M341
Strachan Literary Agency ... L602
Sunbelt Publications, Inc ... P433
Ten Speed Press ... P444
Texas A&M University Press ... P445
Virginia Wine & Country Life ... M390
W.W. Norton & Company Ltd ... P499
Welsh Country ... M399
Workman Publishing ... P519
Yours ... M416
Zack Company, Inc, The ... L678

Gaslamp Fantasy
See more broadly: Fantasy; Historical Fiction

Gay
See more broadly: LGBTQIA
Dreamspinner Press ... P144

Gems
See more broadly: Geology
Rock & Gem ... M316

Gender
See more broadly: Social Groups
See more specifically: Feminism; Gender Politics; Women; Women's Studies
Berghahn Books Ltd ... P062
Bloomsbury Academic ... P071
Chanchani, Sonali ... L115
Cooper, Maggie ... L141
Fernwood Publishing ... P164
Goff, Ellen ... L267
Gold SF ... P185
Indiana University Press ... P235
Influx Press ... P237
Macdougall, Laura ... L413
Ohio State University Press, The ... P323
Ohio University Press ... P324
Oneworld Publications ... P327
Pluto Press ... P358

Simpson, Cara Lee L586
University of Alberta Press......................P477
University of California Press...................P478
University of Michigan Press, The............P483
University of Texas Press P488
Weiss, Alexandra.....................................L650
Wilson, Desiree L667
Gender Issues
See more broadly: Social Issues
Atyeo, Charlotte L034
Jessica Kingsley Publishers P246
Gender Politics
See more broadly: Gender
Maclean, Jamie..................................L417
Genealogy
See more broadly: History
Grossman, Loren R.............................L280
Lilliput Press, The P268
Society of Genealogists P415
Turner Publishing P462
Genetics
See more broadly: Science
W.W. Norton & Company Ltd P499
Genocide
See more broadly: History
Purdue University Press......................P364
Geography
See more specifically: Rivers
Chelsea House Publishers...................P105
Colourpoint Educational P119
Crabtree Publishing P126
Geographical Journal, The...................M162
Gill Education P182
Mentor Books P292
Taylor & Francis Group........................P441
University of Alberta Press...................P477
University of California Press...............P478
University of Georgia Press P479
University of Virginia Press P489
ZigZag Education P523
Geology
See more broadly: Earth Science
See more specifically: Fossils; Gems; Lapidary; Minerals; Rocks
Birlinn Ltd...P067
W.W. Norton & Company Ltd P499
W.W. Norton & Company, Inc. P500
Georgia (US State)
See more broadly: United States
See more specifically: Atlanta; Savannah, GA
University of Georgia Press P479
Geriatrics
See more broadly: Medicine
W.W. Norton & Company Ltd P499
German
See more broadly: Language
Gill Education P182
Mentor Books P292
University of Michigan Press, The........P483
Germany
See more broadly: Europe
Peter Lang P346
Peter Lang Publishing.........................P348
University of Wisconsin Press, The P490
Ghost Hunting
See more broadly: Ghosts
Llewellyn Worldwide Ltd......................P269
Ghost Stories
See more broadly: Supernatural / Paranormal
Andrade, Hannah L023
Brewin Books Ltd P081
Glenister, Emily..................................L263
Goff, Ellen...L267
Haley, Jolene.....................................L289
Hannah Sheppard Literary Agency.......L291
Kim, Jennifer.....................................L366

Orenda Books P329
Pierce, Rosie L517
Sheil Land Associates Ltd......................L577
Shestopal, Camilla L581
Sinister Stoat Press P410
Soloway, Jennifer March L590
Swainson, Joanna L613
Takikawa, Marin....................................L618
Vance, Lisa Erbach L641
Williams, Laura L662
Yours Fiction – Women's Special Series..M417
Ghosts
See more broadly: Supernatural / Paranormal
See more specifically: Ghost Hunting
23 House Publishing P001
Countryside Books P124
JMD Media / DB Publishing P247
Unseen Press.....................................P492
Gift Books
Allison & Busby Ltd P019
Ammonite Press P024
Andrews McMeel Publishing P026
Betsy Amster Literary Enterprises L063
Crown Publishing Group, The..............P131
Elliott & Thompson P149
Fairbank Literary Representation L208
Ghahremani, Lilly L257
Gill Books..P181
Igloo Books Limited P232
Jonathan Pegg Literary Agency............L337
Lewinsohn Literary.............................L397
Oneworld Publications P327
Peter Pauper Press.............................P350
Sheil Land Associates Ltd...................L577
Templar Books...................................P442
Willms, Kathryn..................................L665
Workman Publishing...........................P519
Glasgow
See more broadly: Scotland
Gloucestershire
See more broadly: England
Logaston Press P271
Golf
See more broadly: Sport
Square Mile Magazine M354
Gothic
See more broadly: Horror
Afonso, Thais.....................................L008
Armstrong, Susan...............................L032
Barr, Anjanette...................................L045
Brannan, Maria L078
Buckley, Louise..................................L091
Burke, Kate L093
Evans, Kiya L205
Foxx, Kat L235
Glenister, Emily..................................L263
Goff, Ellen...L267
Jamieson, Molly L329
Kim, Jennifer.....................................L366
Lechon, Shannon L390
Leon, Nina L394
Lightner, Kayla L399
Lovell, Jake L409
Marr, Jill L425
Milusich, Grace L453
Miranda, Caroline L454
Murray, Judith L468
Mushens, Juliet L470
Neely, Rachel.....................................L476
Plant, Zoe L519
Salt Publishing P389
Soler, Shania N. L589
Takikawa, Marin..................................L618
Williams, Laura L662

Graphic Design
See more broadly: Design
Gill Education P182
Rocky Nook P379
Graphic Nonfiction
Arsenal Pulp Press P032
Black Warrior Review M066
Eberly, Chelsea..................................L187
Lechon, Shannon L390
NBM Publishing P312
Oakland Arts Review, The....................M264
Selectric Artists L573
Singing Dragon P409
Siobhan, Aiden L587
Spackman, James...............................L593
Graphic Novels
Andrade, Hannah L023
Armada, Kurestin L030
Arsenal Pulp Press P032
Baobab Press P054
Barbican Press P055
Bauman, Erica L050
Bent Agency (UK), The........................L057
Bent Agency, The L058
Boker, Sidney L067
Bradford Literary Agency L075
Bradford, Laura L076
Brattle Agency LLC, The L080
Bright Agency (UK), The L082
Bright Agency (US), The L083
Chase Literary Agency L118
Chevais, Jennifer L122
Classical Comics P114
Cooper, Gemma L140
Crabtree Publishing P126
Crandall, Becca L142
Denis Kitchen Publishing Company Co., LLC..P138
Doug Grad Literary Agency L177
Draper, Claire L178
Dunham, Jennie.................................L180
Eberly, Chelsea..................................L187
Ellor, Zabé L198
Fazzari, Hillary L210
Feldmann, Kait Lee L212
Feminist Press, The P163
Ferguson, T.S. L218
Finegan, Stevie L226
Gahan, Isobel....................................L250
Gilbert, Tara L258
Gisondi, Katie L261
Goetz, Adria L265
Goff, Ellen...L267
Graham, Stacey L272
Grimm, Katie L279
Gruber, Pam L281
Hannah Sheppard Literary Agency.......L291
Hannigan, Carrie L292
Harwell, Hilary L301
Hawn, Molly Ker.................................L304
Hernando, Paloma L308
Hodges, Jodie L315
IDW Publishing..................................P228
Kensington Publishing Corp. P253
Kimber, Natalie L368
Langton, Becca L383
Lantana Publishing P260
Lechon, Shannon L390
Lerner Publishing Group P264
Lewinsohn Literary.............................L397
Lightner, Kayla L399
Marshall, Jen.....................................L427
Mileo, Jessica L451
Morris, Natascha L461
Motala, Tasneem L463
NBM Publishing P312

Oakland Arts Review, The M264
Olswanger, Anna L491
Pages, Saribel L496
Paul S. Levine Literary Agency L502
Power, Anna L523
Rocking Chair Books L544
Sanchez, Kaitlyn L561
Schiffer Kids P396
Selectric Artists L573
Siobhan, Aiden L587
Sluytman, Antoinette Van L588
Spackman, James L593
Sunspot Literary Journal M364
Sutherland, Kari L611
Symonds, Laurel L617
Torrey House Press, LLC P459
Tran, Jennifer Chen L633
Turner Publishing P462
Virago Books P498
W.W. Norton & Company Ltd P499
W.W. Norton & Company, Inc. P500
Weiss, Alexandra L650
Westin, Erin Casey L654
Whatnall, Michaela L655
Wilson, Desiree L667
Zack Company, Inc, The L678
Zacker, Marietta B. L679
Zuraw-Friedland, Ayla L681

Graphic Poems
Neon M253

Graphic Short Fiction
Stinging Fly, The M355
Sunspot Literary Journal M364

Greenock
See more broadly: Inverclyde

Grimdark
See more broadly: Speculative

Grimsby
See more broadly: Lincolnshire

Grounded Fantasy
See more broadly: Fantasy
Bent, Jenny L059
DeBlock, Liza L163
Gruber, Pam L281
Whatnall, Michaela L655

Grounded Science Fiction
See more broadly: Science Fiction
Evans, Kiya L205

Haibun
Hedgerow: A Journal of Small Poems ... M182
Ink Sweat and Tears M197
Scifaikuest M323

Haiga
Hedgerow: A Journal of Small Poems ... M182
Ink Sweat and Tears M197

Haiku
Better Than Starbucks M058
Hedgerow: A Journal of Small Poems ... M182
Ink Sweat and Tears M197
Scifaikuest M323

Hairstyles
See more broadly: Beauty; Fashion
marie claire (UK) M235
Pride M298
Red Magazine M309
Redbook Magazine M310

Hard Science Fiction
See more broadly: Science Fiction
Edenborough, Sam L189
Willms, Kathryn L665
Zack Company, Inc, The L678

Hardboiled Crime
See more broadly: Crime
Inscriptions Literary Agency L323

Harvard
See more broadly: College / University

Hauliers
See more broadly: Transport

Hawai'i
See more broadly: United States
Bess Press P064

Health
See more specifically: Alternative Health; Diabetes; Diet; Disabilities; Fertility; Fitness; Holistic Health; Medicine; Mental Health; Mind, Body, Spirit; Nursing; Nutrition; Public Health; Wellbeing; Women's Health
AARP The Magazine M006
Alcock, Michael L014
Arcadia Publishing P031
Atlanta Magazine M035
Authentic Life P041
Autumn Publishing Ltd P042
Balance M044
Basic Health Publications, Inc. P059
Baumer, Jan L051
Bernardi, Amanda L062
Betsy Amster Literary Enterprises L063
Bloomsbury Academic P071
Brailsford, Karen L077
Brewin Books Ltd P081
CharlottesvilleFamily M082
Chelsea House Publishers P105
Cleis Press P115
Colourpoint Educational P119
Compassiviste Publishing P121
Conversation (UK), The M095
Crabtree Publishing P126
Crown Publishing Group, The P131
Dana Newman Literary, LLC L152
Derviskadic, Dado L164
Doug Grad Literary Agency L177
Ekus, Sally L194
Elsevier Ltd P150
Enslow Publishers, Inc. P154
Ericka T. Phillips L200
Evans, Stephany L206
Feminist Press, The P163
Fernwood Publishing P164
Finan, Ciara L223
First For Women M142
Frankel, Valerie L239
Free Association Books Ltd P173
Free Spirit Publishing P174
Freymann, Sarah Jane L242
Gale P177
Gill Education P182
Good Literary Agency, The L269
Grossman, Loren R. L280
Hammersmith Books P198
Hardman, Caroline L295
Harvard University Press P206
Hay House Publishers P210
Healthy M180
Hiyate, Sam L313
Hobbs, Victoria L314
Hoffman, Scott L316
Icon Books Ltd P227
Idyll Arbor P229
Ireland's Own M202
Irene Goodman Literary Agency (IGLA) L324
Jeff Herman Agency, LLC, The L331
Jessica Kingsley Publishers P246
Joelle Delbourgo Associates, Inc. L334
Johns Hopkins University Press, The P250
Karinch, Maryann L351
Kensington Publishing Corp. P253
Krienke, Mary L375
Latshaw, Katherine L386
Lazin, Sarah L388

Lightner, Kayla L399
Limelight Management L400
M. Evans & Company P278
marie claire M234
marie claire (UK) M235
Marr, Jill L425
Marshall, Jen L427
McGraw Hill EMEA P285
McNidder & Grace P286
Murdoch Books Australia P308
Murgolo, Karen L467
My Weekly M249
New Harbinger Publications P314
Ohio University Press P324
Oneworld Publications P327
Pacific Press Publishing Association P334
Pan Macmillan Australia P335
Pensacola Magazine M281
Piatkus Books P352
Pine, Gideon L518
Pride M298
Quill Driver Books P368
Red Feather P375
Red Magazine M309
Regina Ryan Books L531
Reilly, Milly L533
Reino, Jessica L534
Robert Smith Literary Agency Ltd L539
Rudy Agency, The L553
Salt Publishing P389
Savannah Magazine M322
Schiffer Publishing P398
Science Factory, The L569
Seventeen M329
Sheree Bykofsky Associates, Inc. L579
Silk, Julia L583
Singing Dragon P409
Society for Promoting Christian Knowledge (SPCK) P414
Stipes Publishing P431
Strachan Literary Agency L602
Sunbelt Publications, Inc. P433
Susan Schulman Literary Agency L610
Taylor & Francis Group P441
Ten Speed Press P444
Texas A&M University Press P445
Turner Publishing P462
Tyndale House Publishers, Inc. P465
Unicorn Publishing Group P470
Unify P472
Unity P473
University of Alberta Press P477
University of California Press P478
University of Massachusetts Press P482
University of Michigan Press, The P483
University of Nevada Press P484
W.W. Norton & Company Ltd P499
Wayne State University Press P504
Whitecap Books Ltd P507
Willms, Kathryn L665
Woman & Home M407
Wordserve Literary L673
Yale University Press (London) P520
Yours M416
Zack Company, Inc, The L678
ZigZag Education P523

Heavy Metal
See more broadly: Music

Hemp
See more broadly: Plants

Herbal Remedies
See more broadly: Alternative Health
Singing Dragon P409

Herefordshire
See more broadly: England
Logaston Press P271

High / Epic Fantasy
See more broadly: Fantasy

Armada, Kurestin	L030
Belton, Maddy	L055
Carroll, Megan	L110
Finegan, Stevie	L226
Headley, David H.	L306
Hensley, Chelsea	L307
Hernando, Paloma	L308
Lindsay Literary Agency	L401
Mustelier, James	L471
Oghma Creative Media	P321
Parker, Elana Roth	L499
Sluytman, Antoinette Van	L588
Soler, Shania N.	L589
Weiman, Paula	L649
Zack Company, Inc, The	L678

High Concept
See more specifically: High Concept Crime; High Concept Romance; High Concept Thrillers

Adams, Seren	L005
Baxter, Veronique	L052
Begum, Salma	L053
Bent, Jenny	L059
Brannan, Maria	L078
Caprio, Alice	L103
Carroll, Megan	L110
Chase Literary Agency	L118
Cho, Catherine	L124
Colwill, Charlotte	L132
Cooper, Gemma	L140
Davies, Elinor	L160
DeBlock, Liza	L163
Dunn, Ben	L181
Edwards, Max	L190
Fabien, Samantha	L207
Fazzari, Hillary	L210
Ferguson, T.S.	L218
Forrester, Jemima	L232
Foster, Clara	L233
Gauntlett, Adam	L254
Ghahremani, Lilly	L257
Gisondi, Katie	L261
Grimm, Katie	L279
Gunic, Masha	L284
Hannah Sheppard Literary Agency	L291
Harris, Erin	L300
Headley, David H.	L306
Holloway, Sally	L318
Kantor, Camille	L349
Kate Barker Literary, TV, & Film Agency	L352
Killingley, Jessica	L365
Landis, Sarah	L381
Langlee, Lina	L382
Lees, Jordan	L392
Lindsay Literary Agency	L401
MacDonald, Emily	L412
Marini, Victoria	L423
Mileo, Jessica	L451
Miranda, Caroline	L454
Mozley, Jack	L465
Mushens, Juliet	L470
Napolitano, Maria	L473
Nelson, Kristin	L478
O'Brien, Lee	L484
Parker, Elana Roth	L499
Pestritto, Carrie	L511
Petty, Rachel	L512
Plant, Zoe	L519
Rushall, Kathleen	L556
Steed, Hayley	L595
Terlip, Paige	L624
Trudel, Jes	L634
Weiss, Alexandra	L650
Wells, Karmen	L652
Wilson, Desiree	L667
Wilson, Ed	L668

High Concept Crime
See more broadly: Crime; High Concept

Gordon, Andrew	L270

High Concept Romance
See more broadly: High Concept; Romance

Evans, Kiya	L205

High Concept Thrillers
See more broadly: High Concept; Thrillers

Burke, Kate	L093
Preston, Amanda	L526
Todd, Hannah	L631

High School
See more broadly: School

High Society
See more broadly: Society

High-Low Literacy
See more broadly: Reading

Ransom Publishing Ltd	P373

Hinduism
See more broadly: Religion

Oneworld Publications	P327

Historical Crime
See more broadly: Crime; Historical Fiction

Maclean, Jamie	L417

Historical Fantasy
See more broadly: Fantasy; Historical Fiction

Foxx, Kat	L235
Gahan, Isobel	L250
Gilbert, Tara	L258

Historical Fiction
See more specifically: Gaslamp Fantasy; Historical Crime; Historical Fantasy; Historical Literary; Historical Mystery Fiction; Historical Romance; Historical Thrillers; Saga; Vikings Fiction

4RV Tenacious	P005
Allison & Busby Ltd	P019
Andrade, Hannah	L023
Andrew, Nelle	L025
Armada, Kurestin	L030
Armstrong, Susan	L032
Asabi Publishing	P034
Barbican Press	P055
Barbour Publishing	P056
Barone Literary Agency	L043
Baror International, Inc.	L044
Baxter, Veronique	L052
Belton, Maddy	L055
Berlyne, John	L061
Bhasin, Tamanna	L064
Birlinn Ltd	P067
Bloodhound Books	P070
Boker, Sidney	L067
Bookouture	P078
Borstel, Stefanie Sanchez Von	L071
Brace, Samantha	L074
Bradford, Laura	L076
Bucci, Chris	L090
Buckley, Louise	L091
Burke, Kate	L093
Burns, Camille	L094
Carr, Michael	L109
Chang, Nicola	L116
Chase Literary Agency	L118
Cho, Catherine	L124
Choc Lit	P108
Colwill, Charlotte	L132
Coombes, Clare	L138
Coombs Moylett & Maclean Literary Agency	L139
Cooper, Maggie	L141
Curran, Sabhbh	L145
Curtis Brown	L146
Danaczko, Melissa	L153
Danko, Margaret	L154
Darley Anderson Agency, The	L157
Davies, Elinor	L160
Dawson, Liza	L162
DeBlock, Liza	L163
Dixon, Isobel	L171
Doug Grad Literary Agency	L177
DSP Publications	P145
Dunham, Jennie	L180
Eason, Lynette	L186
Eddison Pearson Ltd	L188
Ellis-Martin, Sian	L197
Evans, Kiya	L205
Fazzari, Hillary	L210
Felicia Eth Literary Representation	L214
Fellows, Abi	L216
Figueroa, Melanie	L221
Filter Press	P166
Finan, Ciara	L223
for Authors, A	L231
Forrester, Jemima	L232
Foxx, Kat	L235
Frances Collin Literary Agent	L237
Furniss, Eugenie	L249
Gauntlett, Adam	L254
Geiger, Ellen	L255
Getzler, Josh	L256
Glenister, Emily	L263
Greenstreet, Katie	L277
Grimm, Katie	L279
Grunewald, Hattie	L282
Gunic, Masha	L284
Hardman, Caroline	L295
Harmsworth, Esmond	L297
Harris, Erin	L300
Hayden, Viola	L305
Hensley, Chelsea	L307
Hodges, Jodie	L315
Hordern, Kate	L320
Hornsley, Sarah	L321
Irene Goodman Literary Agency (IGLA)	L324
Irvine, Lucy	L325
Joffe Books	P248
Jonathan Pegg Literary Agency	L337
Kahn, Ella Diamond	L345
Karinch, Maryann	L351
Kate Barker Literary, TV, & Film Agency	L352
Kathryn Green Literary Agency, LLC	L354
Kean, Taylor Martindale	L357
Keane Kataria Literary Agency	L358
Keren, Eli	L362
Kim, Julia	L367
Kimber, Natalie	L368
Leigh Feldman Literary	L393
Leon, Nina	L394
Lightner, Kayla	L399
Limelight Management	L400
Macdougall, Laura	L413
Maidment, Olivia	L421
Maltese, Alyssa	L422
Margaret K. McElderry Books	P281
Marr, Jill	L425
Maurer, Shari	L433
Mehren, Jane von	L440
Milburn, Madeleine	L449
MMB Creative	L455
Morrell, Imogen	L460
Mortimer, Michele	L462
Murray, Judith	L468
Mushens, Juliet	L470
Mustelier, James	L471
Nash, Justin	L474
NBM Publishing	P312
Neely, Rachel	L476

Index | History

Nelson, Kristin L478
Niumata, Erin L480
Oghma Creative Media P321
Orenda Books P329
Ostby, Kristin L494
Pan Macmillan Australia P335
Pass, Marina de L500
Patterson, Emma L501
Pen & Ink Designs Publishing P342
Pestritto, Carrie L511
Piatkus Books P352
Posner, Marcy L522
Power Cut Lite M294
Power, Anna L523
Preston, Amanda L526
Rofe, Jennifer L545
Ruppin Agency, The L555
Rutherford, Laetitia L557
Schofield, Hannah L567
Schwartz, Steve L568
Sheil Land Associates Ltd L577
Shestopal, Camilla L581
Silk, Julia L583
Simons, Tanera L585
Siobhan, Aiden L587
Sluytman, Antoinette Van L588
Soler, Shania N. L589
Sparsile Books P419
Steed, Hayley L595
Story Unlikely M356
Stringer, Marlene L604
Swainson, Joanna L613
Sweetgum Press P438
Symonds, Laurel L617
Tannenbaum, Amy L620
Thorneycroft, Euan L628
Torrey House Press, LLC P459
Tran, Jennifer Chen L633
Turner Publishing P462
Tyndale House Publishers, Inc. P465
Unicorn Publishing Group P470
Universe P474
Vinspire Publishing P497
Whatnall, Michaela L655
Williams, Laura L662
Wolfpack Publishing P513
WordCrafts Press P514
Wordserve Literary L673
Young, Claudia L677
Yours Fiction – Women's Special Series M417
Zack Company, Inc, The L678

Historical Literary
See more broadly: Historical Fiction; Literary
Topping, Antony L632

Historical Mystery Fiction
See more broadly: Historical Fiction; Mystery
Thorneycroft, Euan L628
Williams, Laura L662

Historical Romance
See more broadly: Historical Fiction; Romance
Adsett, Alex L006
Armada, Kurestin L030
Avon Books P045
Bradford Literary Agency L075
Bradford, Laura L076
Choc Lit P108
Foster, Clara L233
Leon, Nina L394
Lyrical Press P277
Mills & Boon P297
Nathan, Abigail L475
Oghma Creative Media P321
Ostby, Kristin L494
Udden, Jennifer L637
Vinspire Publishing P497

Historical Thrillers
See more broadly: Historical Fiction; Thrillers
Topping, Antony L632

History
See more specifically: 17th Century; 18th Century; 19th Century; 20th Century; American History; Art History; British History; Caribbean History; Church History; Cultural History; European History; Genealogy; Genocide; Intellectual History; Jewish Holocaust; Local History; Maritime History; Medieval; Military History; Modern History; Narrative History; Nostalgia; Political History; Popular History; Regional History; Renaissance; Revisionist History; Social History
ABC-CLIO P008
Agricultural History M017
Alcock, Michael L014
Amato Books P021
Amber Books Ltd P022
Ammonite Press P024
Andrew, Nelle L025
Antigonish Review, The M026
Arcadia Publishing P031
Arte Publico Press P033
Atlantic Northeast M037
Aurora Metro Press P039
Backbeat Books P046
Badger Learning P048
Barr, Anjanette L045
Bartholomew, Jason L047
Basalt Books P057
Basic Books P058
Baxter, Veronique L052
Baylor University Press P060
BBC History Magazine M049
Berghahn Books Ltd P062
Best of British M056
Betsy Amster Literary Enterprises L063
Blackstaff Press P068
Bloomsbury Academic P071
Borstel, Stefanie Sanchez Von L071
Bowlin, Sarah L073
Bradford Literary Agency L075
Brannan, Maria L078
Brewin Books Ltd P081
Brick M074
Britain Magazine M075
British Academy P083
British Museum Press, The P084
Broadview Press P085
Brouckaert, Justin L087
Brown, Son & Ferguson, Ltd. P086
Bucci, Chris L090
Caitlin Press Inc. P090
Capron, Elise L104
Carter, Rebecca L111
Charlesbridge Publishing P102
Chase Literary Agency L118
Chelsea House Publishers P105
Christie, Jennifer L126
Clarke, Catherine L129
Cochran, Alexander L130
Coil, The M089
College Press Publishing P117
Colourpoint Educational P119
Compassiviste Publishing P121
Conville, Clare L137
Coombs Moylett & Maclean Literary Agency L139
Cooper, Gemma L140
Cotswold Life M098
Countryside Books P124
Crabtree Publishing P126
Crown P129
Crown Publishing Group, The P131
Curran, Sabhbh L145
Dana Newman Literary, LLC L152
Danaczko, Melissa L153
Darga, Jon Michael L155
Devon Life M119
Diana Finch Literary Agency L167
Dickerson, Donya L168
Dijkstra, Sandra L169
Doug Grad Literary Agency L177
Dunham, Jennie L180
Dynasty Press P147
Eberly, Chelsea L187
Edenborough, Sam L189
Edwards, Max L190
Eisenmann, Caroline L192
Elliott & Thompson P149
Ellis-Martin, Sian L197
Ellor, Zabé L198
Emily Sweet Associates L199
Enslow Publishers, Inc. P154
Evans, David L203
Evans, Kate L204
Fazzari, Hillary L210
Fee: Foundation for Economic Education M138
Fellows, Abi L216
Feminist Press, The P163
Fernwood Publishing P164
Filter Press P166
Finan, Ciara L223
Fortress Press P170
Fox, Aram L234
Frances Collin Literary Agent L237
Frances Goldin Literary Agency, Inc. L238
Free Association Books Ltd P173
Fuentes, Sarah L247
Gale P177
Galustian, Natalie L251
Garamond Agency, Inc., The L253
Gauntlett, Adam L254
Geiger, Ellen L255
Getzler, Josh L256
Gill Books P181
Gill Education P182
Glenister, Emily L263
Globe Pequot Press, The P184
Gordon, Andrew L270
Graffeg P190
Granta Books P192
Greyhound Literary L278
Grimm, Katie L279
Hanbury Agency, The L290
Harmsworth, Esmond L297
Harvard University Press P206
Haus Publishing P208
Henley Hall Press P214
Hernando, Paloma L308
Heymont, Lane L309
History Press, The P221
History Today M186
Hoffman, Scott L316
Holloway, Sally L318
Hordern, Kate L320
Icon Books Ltd P227
Imagine Publishing P234
Ireland's Own M202
Irene Goodman Literary Agency (IGLA) L324
Irish Pages M203
Jeff Herman Agency, LLC, The L331
Joelle Delbourgo Associates, Inc. L334
Johns Hopkins University Press, The P250
Jonathan Pegg Literary Agency L337
Joy Harris Literary Agency, Inc. L340
Kahn, Jody L346

Claim your free access to www.firstwriter.com: See p.403

354 Index | Hobbies

Kardon, Julia L350
Karinch, Maryann L351
Kate Barker Literary, TV, & Film Agency L352
Kates Hill Press, The P252
Kathryn Green Literary Agency, LLC L354
Kensington Publishing Corp. P253
Kim, Jennifer L366
Kim, Julia L367
Kube Publishing P258
Lambert, Sophie L380
Lazin, Sarah L388
Levitt, Sarah L396
Lewis, Alison L398
Lightner, Kayla L399
Lilliput Press, The P268
Loft Press, Inc. P270
London Review of Books M225
Lovell, Jake L409
LSU Press P273
Lutterworth Press, The P275
MacDonald, Emily L412
Macdougall, Laura L413
Mack, Kate L415
MacLeod, Lauren L418
Malahat Review, The M232
Marr, Jill L425
Marshall, Jen L427
McNidder & Grace P286
McQuilkin, Rob L438
Mehren, Jane von L440
Menasha Ridge Press P290
Mendia, Isabel L441
Mentor Books P292
Michel, Caroline L446
Minnesota Historical Society Press P299
Miranda, Caroline L454
Missouri Historical Society Press P302
MMB Creative L455
Morrell, Imogen L460
Mundy, Toby L466
Murray, Judith L468
Nash, Justin L474
O'Grady, Faith L485
O'Shea, Amy L488
Oghma Creative Media P321
Ohio State University Press, The P323
Ohio University Press P324
Oneworld Publications P327
Otago University Press P330
Oxford Review of Books M271
Pan Macmillan Australia P335
Pande, Ayesha L497
Pavilion Books P338
Peddle, Kay L503
Pelham, Imogen L504
Peter Lang P346
Peter Lang Publishing P348
Pine, Gideon L518
Pineapple Press P356
Plitt, Carrie L520
Pluto Press P358
Power Cut Lite M294
Power, Anna L523
Preservation Magazine M297
Preston, Amanda L526
Purdue University Press P364
Pureplay Press P365
Quirk Books P369
Regina Ryan Books L531
Reid, Janet L532
Richter, Rick L537
Robert Smith Literary Agency Ltd L539
Robertson Murray Literary Agency L541
Rocky Mountain Books P378
Rosenberg Group, The L549
Rudy Agency, The L553
Rutman, Jim L558
Salvo, Katie L560
Scala Arts & Heritage Publishers P392
Schiffer Military History P397
Schofield, Hannah L567
Science Factory, The L569
Scots Magazine, The M324
Scoular, Rosemary L570
Scratching Shed Publishing P402
Seren Books P405
Signorelli, Michael L582
Society for Promoting Christian Knowledge (SPCK) P414
Society of Genealogists P415
Somerset Life M341
Southwest Review M348
Stanford University Press P427
Steerforth Press P428
Stephens, Jenny L596
Stone, Geoffrey L600
Strothman, Wendy L608
Sunbelt Publications, Inc. P433
Susan Schulman Literary Agency L610
Sweet, Emily L614
Sweetgum Press P438
Sweren, Becky L615
Symonds, Laurel L617
Taylor & Francis Group P441
Texas A&M University Press P445
Thames & Hudson Inc. P446
Thayer, Henry L626
This England M376
Thorneycroft, Euan L628
Tidewater Publishers P449
Topping, Antony L632
Turner Publishing P462
Tyndale House Publishers, Inc. P465
University of Akron Press, The P475
University of Alaska Press P476
University of Alberta Press P477
University of California Press P478
University of Iowa Press P480
University of Massachusetts Press P482
University of Michigan Press, The P483
University of Nevada Press P484
University of North Texas Press P485
University of Pennsylvania Press P486
University of Texas Press P488
University of Virginia Press P489
University of Wisconsin Press, The P490
University Press of Colorado P491
Unseen Press P492
Victoria Sanders & Associates LLC L642
Virginia Quarterly Review, The M389
W.W. Norton & Company Ltd P499
W.W. Norton & Company, Inc. P500
Walsh, Kate L646
Washington State University Press P501
Watkins Publishing P503
Welsh Country M399
Wickers, Chandler L659
Williams, Laura L662
Willms, Kathryn L665
Wilson, Desiree L667
Wilson, Ed L668
WordCrafts Press P514
Wordserve Literary L673
Yale Review, The M409
Yale University Press (London) P520
Yankee Magazine M410
ZigZag Education P523

Hobbies
See more specifically: Embroidery; Gardening; Knitting; Motorcycling; Numismatics (Coin / Currency Collecting); Quilting; Rock Collecting / Rockhounding; Sewing; Stamp Collecting
Arcadia Publishing P031
Crown Publishing Group, The P131
DK Publishing P141
Gale P177
Gill Books P181
Kensington Publishing Corp. P253
Ohio University Press P324
Quill Driver Books P368
Turner Publishing P462
W.W. Norton & Company Ltd P499
W.W. Norton & Company, Inc. P500

Hockey
See more broadly: Sport

Holiday Homes
See more broadly: Holidays
Park Home and Holiday Living M276

Holidays
See more specifically: Holiday Homes
Enslow Publishers, Inc. P154

Holistic Health
See more broadly: Health
Sentient Publications P404

Home Economics / Domestic Science
Colourpoint Educational P119
Gill Education P182

Home Improvement
See more broadly: Houses and Homes
Better Homes and Gardens M057
Draper, Claire L178
Redbook Magazine M310
Zack Company, Inc, The L678

Homelessness
See more broadly: Social Issues

Horoscopes
See more broadly: Fortune Telling and Divination
marie claire M234

Horror
See more specifically: Folk Horror; Gothic; Literary Horror; Psychological Horror; Speculative Horror; Supernatural / Paranormal Horror; Werewolves; Zombies
Aardwolf Press P007
Afonso, Thais L008
Alekseii, Keir L015
Armada, Kurestin L030
Armstrong, Susan L032
Asabi Publishing P034
Authentic Ideas P040
Bajek, Lauren L037
Barone Literary Agency L043
Baxter, Veronique L052
Begum, Salma L053
Bent, Jenny L059
Berlyne, John L061
BFS Horizons M059
Black Static M065
Brannan, Maria L078
Brattesani, Hannah L079
Brooks, Savannah L084
Buckley, Louise L091
Carroll, Megan L110
Charnace, Edwina de L117
Chase Literary Agency L118
Chevais, Jennifer L122
Coombs Moylett & Maclean Literary Agency L139
Crabtree Publishing P126
Crystal Magazine M110
Curtis Brown L146
Cusick, John L148
Danko, Margaret L154
DSP Publications P145
Edenborough, Sam L189
Evans, Kiya L205

Access more listings online at www.firstwriter.com

Fabien, Samantha	L207	
Ferguson, T.S.	L218	
Figueroa, Melanie	L221	
Gilbert, Tara	L258	
Glenister, Emily	L263	
Gunic, Masha	L284	
Haley, Jolene	L289	
Hannah Sheppard Literary Agency	L291	
Harmsworth, Esmond	L297	
Harper, Logan	L299	
Harris, Erin	L300	
Heymont, Lane	L309	
Hiraeth Books	P220	
Interzone	M201	
Jamieson, Molly	L329	
Kavanagh, Jade	L355	
Kim, Jennifer	L366	
Kim, Julia	L367	
Korero Press	P257	
Langlee, Lina	L382	
Lechon, Shannon	L390	
Lees, Jordan	L392	
Leon, Nina	L394	
Lovell, Jake	L409	
Maidment, Olivia	L421	
Maltese, Alyssa	L422	
Marr, Jill	L425	
Marshall, Jen	L427	
Mihell, Natasha	L448	
Miranda, Caroline	L454	
MMB Creative	L455	
Morrell, Imogen	L460	
Mortimer, Michele	L462	
Murray, Judith	L468	
Mustelier, James	L471	
Nightfire	P316	
Oghma Creative Media	P321	
On Spec	M268	
Orenda Books	P329	
Pages, Saribel	L496	
Perotto-Wills, Martha	L508	
Pestritto, Carrie	L511	
Petty, Rachel	L512	
Pierce, Rosie	L517	
Pine, Gideon	L518	
Plant, Zoe	L519	
Quirk Books	P369	
Reino, Jessica	L534	
Richter, Rick	L537	
Salazar, Des	L559	
Scifaikuest	M323	
Sheil Land Associates Ltd	L577	
Shestopal, Camilla	L581	
Sinister Stoat Press	P410	
Sluytman, Antoinette Van	L588	
SmashBear Publishing	P412	
Soler, Shania N.	L589	
Sorg, Arley	L592	
Steed, Hayley	L595	
Story Unlikely	M356	
Swainson, Joanna	L613	
Tibbets, Anne	L630	
Tor Publishing Group	P456	
Torrey House Press, LLC	P459	
Trussell, Caroline	L635	
Turner Publishing	P462	
Udden, Jennifer	L637	
Weiss, Alexandra	L650	
Weitzner, Tess	L651	
Wells, Karmen	L652	
Whatnall, Michaela	L655	
Williams, Laura	L662	
Wilson, Desiree	L667	
WordCrafts Press	P514	
Yellow Mama Webzine	M411	
Zack Company, Inc, The	L678	

Zeno Agency	L680	
Horse Racing		
See more broadly: Sport		
Scratching Shed Publishing	P402	
Horses		
See more broadly: Animals		
Horse & Rider	M188	
Houses and Homes		
See more broadly: Buildings		
See more specifically: Home Improvement; Ranches; Spas and Hot Tubs		
Arcadia Publishing	P031	
Barr, Nicola	L046	
Bernardi, Amanda	L062	
CharlottesvilleFamily	M082	
Cowboys & Indians	M101	
Devon Life	M119	
Kensington Publishing Corp.	P253	
Kent Life	M209	
Murdoch Books Australia	P308	
Savannah Magazine	M322	
Somerset Life	M341	
Sunbelt Publications, Inc.	P433	
W.W. Norton & Company Ltd	P499	
W.W. Norton & Company, Inc.	P500	
Westchester Magazine	M402	
Yankee Magazine	M410	
Yorkshire Life	M413	
How To		
Abuzz Press	P010	
Amato Books	P021	
Compassiviste Publishing	P121	
Coombs Moylett & Maclean Literary Agency	L139	
Cottage Life	M099	
Doug Grad Literary Agency	L177	
Entrepreneur	M131	
Graham, Stacey	L272	
Jeff Herman Agency, LLC, The	L331	
Korero Press	P257	
Maclean, Jamie	L417	
Marlin	M236	
NBM Publishing	P312	
Nichols, Mariah	L479	
Paul S. Levine Literary Agency	L502	
Rock & Gem	M316	
Rutherford, Laetitia	L557	
Human Biology		
See more broadly: Biology		
Hardman, Caroline	L295	
Hunting		
See more broadly: Sport		
See more specifically: Fishing		
Amato Books	P021	
Bowhunter	M072	
River Hills Traveler	M313	
Safari Press	P386	
Hymnals		
See more broadly: Church Music		
Hypnosis		
See more broadly: Psychology		
W.W. Norton & Company Ltd	P499	
Ignation Spirituality		
See more broadly: Catholicism		
Loyola Press	P272	
Illinois		
See more broadly: United States		
See more specifically: Chicago		
Illustrated Books		
Amber Books Ltd	P022	
Bird Eye Books	P066	
Bright Press	P082	
Cassell	P096	
Chase Literary Agency	L118	
Cooper, Gemma	L140	
Doug Grad Literary Agency	L177	

Enitharmon Editions	P153	
Ghahremani, Lilly	L257	
Graffeg	P190	
Graffeg Childrens	P191	
Korero Press	P257	
Krienke, Mary	L375	
Latshaw, Katherine	L386	
Laurence King Publishing	P261	
Lewinsohn Literary	L397	
Macdougall, Laura	L413	
Mack, Kate	L415	
Ogtrop, Kristin van	L489	
Pavilion Books	P338	
Pickering, Juliet	L516	
Plexus Publishing Limited	P357	
Rudy Agency, The	L553	
Scala Arts & Heritage Publishers	P392	
Scholastic	P399	
Stephens, Jenny	L596	
Templar Books	P442	
Ten Speed Press	P444	
Immigration		
See more broadly: Social Issues		
Mendia, Isabel	L441	
Sanders, Rayhane	L562	
Texas A&M University Press	P445	
University of Alberta Press	P477	
Immunology		
See more broadly: Medicine		
Indiana		
See more broadly: United States		
Purdue University Press	P364	
Unseen Press	P492	
Information Science		
See more broadly: Science		
Bloomsbury Academic	P071	
Facet Publishing	P159	
Gill Education	P182	
Information Today, Inc.	P238	
Taylor & Francis Group	P441	
Inspirational		
See more broadly: Religion		
See more specifically: Inspirational Memoir		
404 Ink	P002	
Barbour Publishing	P056	
Borstel, Stefanie Sanchez Von	L071	
DeVorss & Company	P139	
Robert Smith Literary Agency Ltd	L539	
Rose and Crown Books	P381	
Sunpenny Publishing	P435	
Vinspire Publishing	P497	
Zack Company, Inc, The	L678	
Inspirational Memoir		
See more broadly: Inspirational; Memoir		
Insurance		
See more broadly: Business		
Insurance Age	M199	
Intellectual History		
See more broadly: History		
University of Pennsylvania Press	P486	
Interior Design		
See more broadly: Design		
See more specifically: Decorating		
Bloomsbury Academic	P071	
Chronicle Books LLC	P111	
Cotswold Life	M098	
Essex Life	M132	
Good Homes	M168	
Homes & Antiques	M187	
Metropolis Magazine	M239	
Monacelli Press, The	P304	
Red Magazine	M309	
Scottish Field	M326	
Thames & Hudson Inc.	P446	
Virginia Wine & Country Life	M390	
Westchester Magazine	M402	

International
- Better Than Starbucks ... M058
- Danaczko, Melissa ... L153
- Dillsworth, Elise ... L170
- Fairbank Literary Representation ... L208
- Gutter Magazine ... M174
- Hakim, Serene ... L288
- Indiana University Press ... P235
- Peter Owen Publishers ... P349
- Tibbets, Anne ... L630
- Zack Company, Inc, The ... L678

Internet
See more broadly: Computers
See more specifically: Internet Culture
- Lightner, Kayla ... L399
- Pierce, Rosie ... L517
- Weiss, Alexandra ... L650

Internet Culture
See more broadly: Internet
- Brouckaert, Justin ... L087
- Lightner, Kayla ... L399

Intersectional Feminism
See more broadly: Feminism
- Clarke, Caro ... L128
- Goff, Ellen ... L267
- Gold SF ... P185

Interviews
- African American Review ... M014
- Arc ... M028
- Art Monthly ... M030
- Banipal ... M046
- BFS Journal ... M060
- Black Moon Magazine ... M064
- Bluegrass Unlimited ... M069
- Brick ... M074
- Cocoa Girl ... M088
- Coil, The ... M089
- Dream Catcher ... M123
- Ekphrastic Review, The ... M128
- Essex Life ... M132
- Facts & Fiction ... M135
- Forty20 ... M150
- Fresh Words – An International Literary Magazine ... M154
- Funeral Business Solutions ... M156
- Gulf Coast: A Journal of Literature and Fine Arts ... M173
- Identity Theory ... M194
- Inque ... M198
- Journal, The ... M207
- Kavya Kishor ... M208
- Midway Journal ... M243
- OK! Magazine ... M266
- Oxford Poetry ... M270
- Oxford Review of Books ... M271
- Paris Review, The ... M275
- Poetry Ireland Review ... M288
- Red Magazine ... M309
- Riposte ... M312
- Snowflake Magazine ... M338
- Stinging Fly, The ... M355
- Strange Horizons ... M357
- Tears in the Fence ... M371
- Temz Review, The ... M372
- Vagabond City ... M386
- Vallum ... M387
- Vestal Review ... M388
- White Review, The ... M404
- Yes Poetry Magazine ... M412
- Yorkshire Life ... M413
- Yours ... M416

Inverclyde
See more broadly: Scotland
See more specifically: Greenock

Investigative Journalism
See more broadly: Journalism
- Andrade, Hannah ... L023
- Bal, Emma ... L038
- Bernardi, Amanda ... L062
- Chanchani, Sonali ... L115
- Charnace, Edwina de ... L117
- Fogg, Jack ... L230
- Fuentes, Sarah ... L247
- Geiger, Ellen ... L255
- Goldstein, Veronica ... L268
- Holloway, Sally ... L318
- Karinch, Maryann ... L351
- Marshall, Jen ... L427
- Marsiglia, Caroline ... L428
- Nolan, Laura ... L481
- Patterson, Emma ... L501
- Pelham, Imogen ... L504
- Pine, Gideon ... L518
- Plitt, Carrie ... L520
- Rudy Agency, The ... L553
- Scoular, Rosemary ... L570
- Steerforth Press ... P428
- Sweren, Becky ... L615
- Torrey House Press, LLC ... P459
- Zack Company, Inc, The ... L678

Investments
See more broadly: Business; Finance
- AARP The Magazine ... M006
- Square Mile Magazine ... M354

Ireland
See more broadly: Europe
- Blackstaff Press ... P068
- Gill Books ... P181
- Indiana University Press ... P235
- Ireland's Own ... M202
- Lilliput Press, The ... P268
- Molloy, Jess ... L456
- University of Michigan Press, The ... P483
- University of Wisconsin Press, The ... P490

Irish (Gaeilge)
See more broadly: Language
- Gill Education ... P182
- Mentor Books ... P292

Islam
See more broadly: Religion
See more specifically: Sufism
- Baylor University Press ... P060
- Kube Publishing ... P258
- Oneworld Publications ... P327
- University of Michigan Press, The ... P483

Islamic Philosophy
See more broadly: Philosophy

Italian American
See more broadly: Ethnic Groups
- Feminist Press, The ... P163

Italy
See more broadly: Europe
- Feminist Press, The ... P163
- Patrician Press ... P337
- Peter Lang ... P346
- Peter Lang Publishing ... P348

Japan
See more broadly: Asia
- Ohio University Press ... P324

Jazz
See more broadly: Music
- Edenborough, Sam ... L189
- Jazz Journal ... M206

Jewish Culture
See more broadly: Culture

Jewish Holocaust
See more broadly: History
- Indiana University Press ... P235
- Purdue University Press ... P364

Jokes
- Soho Review, The ... M339

Journalism
See more specifically: Food Journalism; Investigative Journalism; Literary Journalism; Narrative Journalism; Science Journalism
- Begum, Salma ... L053
- Carr, Jamie ... L108
- Chase Literary Agency ... L118
- Doug Grad Literary Agency ... L177
- Edwards, Max ... L190
- Evans, David ... L203
- Felicia Eth Literary Representation ... L214
- Feminist Press, The ... P163
- Freymann, Sarah Jane ... L242
- Friedman, Rebecca ... L244
- Granger, David ... L275
- Harper's Magazine ... M178
- Kahn, Jody ... L346
- Kardon, Julia ... L350
- Kim, Jennifer ... L366
- Kruger Cowne ... L376
- Lazin, Sarah ... L388
- Levitt, Sarah ... L396
- Lewis, Alison ... L398
- Madan, Neeti ... L419
- Moorhead, Max ... L459
- NBM Publishing ... P312
- Ohio University Press ... P324
- Peddle, Kay ... L503
- Perry Literary ... L509
- Phillips, Aemilia ... L515
- Posner, Marcy ... L522
- Rutman, Jim ... L558
- Sarah Jane Freymann Literary Agency ... L564
- Seymour, Charlotte ... L575
- Silk, Julia ... L583
- Stipes Publishing ... P431
- University of Massachusetts Press ... P482
- Wickers, Chandler ... L659

Judaism
See more broadly: Religion
See more specifically: Kabbalah
- Baylor University Press ... P060
- Carr, Jamie ... L108
- Feminist Press, The ... P163
- Indiana University Press ... P235
- Irene Goodman Literary Agency (IGLA) ... L324
- Oneworld Publications ... P327
- Stanford University Press ... P427
- Tyndale House Publishers, Inc. ... P465
- University of Massachusetts Press ... P482
- University of Michigan Press, The ... P483
- University of Pennsylvania Press ... P486
- University of Texas Press ... P488
- University of Wisconsin Press, The ... P490
- Wayne State University Press ... P504
- Zack Company, Inc, The ... L678

Juvenile Psychotherapy
See more broadly: Psychotherapy
See more specifically: Child Psychotherapy
- W.W. Norton & Company Ltd ... P499

Kabbalah
See more broadly: Judaism
- Llewellyn Worldwide Ltd ... P269

Kent
See more broadly: England
- Kent Life ... M209

Knitting
See more broadly: Crafts; Hobbies

LGBTQIA
See more broadly: Sexuality
See more specifically: Gay
- Afonso, Thais ... L008
- Arsenal Pulp Press ... P032
- Asabi Publishing ... P034

Barbican Press P055
Belton, Maddy L055
Brewer, Amy L081
Caitlin Press Inc. P090
Cavanagh, Claire L114
Clarke, Caro L128
Cleis Press P115
Cooper, Maggie L141
Draper, Claire L178
Dunham, Jennie L180
Ellis-Martin, Sian L197
Evans, Kiya L205
Fathom Books P162
Feminist Press, The P163
Ferguson, T.S. L218
Finegan, Stevie L226
Fourteen Poems M152
Free Spirit Publishing P174
Future Fire, The M158
Gertrude M164
Gold SF P185
Goose Lane Editions P188
Harmony Ink Press P205
Hernando, Paloma L308
Irvine, Lucy L325
Keren, Eli L362
Knigge, Sheyla L372
Langton, Becca L383
Leon, Nina L394
Macdougall, Laura L413
Morrell, Imogen L460
O'Brien, Lee L484
Oghma Creative Media P321
Quirk Books P369
Salazar, Des L559
Salvo, Katie L560
Sinister Stoat Press P410
Sinister Wisdom M337
Siobhan, Aiden L587
Snowflake Magazine M338
Todd, Hannah L631
Torrey House Press, LLC P459
University of Alberta Press P477
University of Massachusetts Press P482
University of Wisconsin Press, The P490
W.W. Norton & Company Ltd P499
Weiss, Alexandra L650
Wells, Karmen L652
Williams, Laura L662
Wilson, Desiree L667
Zuraw-Friedland, Ayla L681
Lacemaking
See more broadly: Crafts
Lancashire
See more broadly: England
Lancashire Life M214
Language
See more specifically: Dialects; English; French; Gaelic; German; Irish (Gaeilge); Slang; Spanish; Writing
Arcadia Publishing P031
Bloomsbury Academic P071
Doug Grad Literary Agency L177
Elliott & Thompson P149
Faulks, Holly L209
Hippocrene Books, Inc. P219
Icon Books Ltd P227
Johns Hopkins University Press, The P250
Kensington Publishing Corp. P253
Linguist, The M219
Ohio State University Press, The P323
Ohio University Press P324
Peter Lang P346
Peter Lang Publishing P348
Prufrock Press P363
Robert Smith Literary Agency Ltd L539

Taylor & Francis Group P441
University of Alaska Press P476
University of Alberta Press P477
University of California Press P478
University of Michigan Press, The P483
University of Nevada Press P484
Yale University Press (London) P520
ZigZag Education P523
Lapidary
See more broadly: Geology
Rock & Gem M316
Leadership
See more broadly: Personal Development
Berrett-Koehler Publishers P063
High Tide Press P217
Ki Agency Ltd L364
Tyndale House Publishers, Inc. P465
Zack Company, Inc, The L678
Left Wing Politics
See more broadly: Politics
Baffler, The M043
Legal
See more specifically: Business Law; Legal Thrillers; Taxation
Arcadia Publishing P031
Bloomsbury Academic P071
Bloomsbury Professional P072
Colourpoint Educational P119
Cornell Maritime Press P123
Feminist Press, The P163
Fernwood Publishing P164
Frances Goldin Literary Agency, Inc. L238
Gale P177
Gill Education P182
Grossman, Loren R. L280
Harvard University Press P206
Johns Hopkins University Press, The P250
Kensington Publishing Corp. P253
LexisNexis P265
London Review of Books M225
Ohio University Press P324
Paul S. Levine Literary Agency L502
Peter Lang P346
Peter Lang Publishing P348
Round Hall P383
Rudy Agency, The L553
Stanford University Press P427
Sunbelt Publications, Inc. P433
Susan Schulman Literary Agency L610
Sweet & Maxwell P436
Taylor & Francis Group P441
University of Alberta Press P477
University of California Press P478
University of Massachusetts Press P482
University of Michigan Press, The P483
University of Nevada Press P484
University of North Texas Press P485
University of Virginia Press P489
Usselman, Laura L639
Victoria Sanders & Associates LLC L642
W.W. Norton & Company Ltd P499
W.W. Norton & Company, Inc. P500
Wordserve Literary L673
Yale University Press (London) P520
ZigZag Education P523
Legal Thrillers
See more broadly: Legal; Thrillers
Orenda Books P329
Reino, Jessica L534
Leisure
See more specifically: Games; Pubs; Recreation; Sailing; Skiing; Snowboarding
Arcadia Publishing P031
CharlottesvilleFamily M082
Compassiviste Publishing P121
Lutterworth Press, The P275

Regina Ryan Books L531
Tyndale House Publishers, Inc. P465
Lifestyle
See more specifically: Alternative Lifestyles; Biker Lifestyle; Country Lifestyle; Luxury Lifestyle; Mountain Lifestyle; Ranch Lifestyle; Retirement; Rural Living; Self-Sufficiency; Vegetarianism
417 Magazine M004
Alive Literary Agency L018
Atlanta Magazine M035
Bent, Jenny L059
Betsy Amster Literary Enterprises L063
Bright Press P082
Carolina Woman M080
CharlottesvilleFamily M082
Chiotti, Danielle L123
Colourpoint Educational P119
Compassiviste Publishing P121
Coombs Moylett & Maclean Literary
   Agency L139
Cottage Life M099
Danko, Margaret L154
Devon Life M119
DeVorss & Company P139
Diana Finch Literary Agency L167
DK Publishing P141
Ekus, Sally L194
Essex Life M132
Evans, Stephany L206
Fairbank Literary Representation L208
Faulks, Holly L209
Forrester, Jemima L232
Frankel, Valerie L239
Freymann, Sarah Jane L242
Gill Books P181
Good Literary Agency, The L269
Graham, Stacey L272
Greyhound Literary L278
Grunewald, Hattie L282
Hardman, Caroline L295
Healthy M180
Hiyate, Sam L313
Icon Books Ltd P227
Irene Goodman Literary Agency
   (IGLA) L324
Jonathan Pegg Literary Agency L337
Kate Barker Literary, TV, & Film
   Agency L352
Kent Life M209
Kim, Julia L367
Latshaw, Katherine L386
Loughman, Morwenna L408
Maclean, Jamie L417
Madan, Neeti L419
marie claire (UK) M235
My Weekly M249
Nichols, Mariah L479
O'Grady, Faith L485
O'Shea, Amy L488
Ogtrop, Kristin van L489
OK! Magazine M266
Pan Macmillan Australia P335
Park Home and Holiday Living M276
Pavilion Books P338
Pensacola Magazine M281
People's Friend, The M283
Pride M298
Quill Driver Books P368
R D Publishers P370
Red Feather P375
Redbook Magazine M310
Regina Ryan Books L531
River Hills Traveler M313
Roberts, Soumeya Bendimerad L540
Robertson Murray Literary Agency L541

358 Index | Light Fantasy

Ruralite M318
Sarah Jane Freymann Literary Agency L564
Savannah Magazine M322
Schiffer Publishing P398
Scottish Field M326
Seventeen M329
Shaw Agency, The L576
Sheil Land Associates Ltd L577
Silk, Julia L583
Singing Dragon P409
Somerset Life M341
Stephens, Jenny L596
Strachan Literary Agency L602
Sweet, Emily L614
Thames & Hudson Inc. P446
That's Life! M373
Tidewater Publishers P449
Unity P473
Virginia Wine & Country Weddings M391
Vogue M393
Watkins Publishing P503
Westchester Magazine M402
Willms, Kathryn L665
Woman & Home M407
Yankee Magazine M410
Yorkshire Life M413
Yorkshire Women's Life Magazine M414

Light Fantasy

See more broadly: Fantasy

Ostby, Kristin L494
Steed, Hayley L595

Lincolnshire

See more broadly: England

See more specifically: Grimsby

Literary

See more specifically: Historical Literary; Literary Fantasy; Literary Horror; Literary Journalism; Literary Mystery; Literary Suspense; Literary Thrillers

30 North M002
About Place Journal M007
Adams, Seren L005
Adsett, Alex L006
Alaska Quarterly Review M019
Alex Adsett Literary L016
Ambrosi, Beniamino L020
Amling, Eric L021
And Other Stories P025
Andrew, Nelle L025
Antigonish Review, The M026
Armada, Kurestin L030
Armstrong, Susan L032
Arsenal Pulp Press P032
Arthurson, Wayne L033
Atyeo, Charlotte L034
Authentic Ideas P040
Bacopa Literary Review M042
Bajek, Lauren L037
Baobab Press P054
Baror International, Inc. L044
Barr, Nicola L046
Baxter, Veronique L052
Begum, Salma L053
Beloit Fiction Journal M055
Bent, Jenny L059
Betsy Amster Literary Enterprises L063
Bloodhound Books P070
BOA Editions, Ltd P076
Bowlin, Sarah L073
Brace, Samantha L074
Bradford Literary Agency L075
Brattesani, Hannah L079
Brattle Agency LLC, The L080
Brick M074
Brotherstone Creative Management L085
Brotherstone, Charlie L086
Bucci, Chris L090
Buckley, Louise L091
Cafe Irreal, The M078
Campbell, Charlie L099
Capron, Elise L104
Carr, Jamie L108
Caskie, Robert L113
Cavanagh, Claire L114
Chanchani, Sonali L115
Chang, Nicola L116
Chapman M081
Chase Literary Agency L118
Chiotti, Danielle L123
Cho, Catherine L124
Cichello, Kayla L127
Cincinnati Review, The M086
Clarke, Caro L128
Cochran, Alexander L130
Coil, The M089
Cola M090
Colwill, Charlotte L132
Combemale, Chris L133
Compassiviste Publishing P121
Conjunctions M093
Conrad, Claire Paterson L136
Conville, Clare L137
Coombs Moylett & Maclean Literary Agency L139
Cooper, Maggie L141
Coyote Arts P125
Crannog Magazine M103
Curran, Sabhbh L145
Curtis Brown L146
Dalhousie Review, The M113
Dana Newman Literary, LLC L152
Danaczko, Melissa L153
Danko, Margaret L154
Daunt Books Publishing P134
Dawson, Liza L162
DeBlock, Liza L163
Dedalus Ltd P136
Dijkstra, Sandra L169
Dillsworth, Elise L170
Dixon, Isobel L171
Dodo Ink P142
Dunham, Jennie L180
Dunow, Carlson & Lerner Agency L184
Eberly, Chelsea L187
Eisenmann, Caroline L192
Ellis-Martin, Sian L197
Emily Sweet Associates L199
Enitharmon Editions P153
Evans, David L203
Evans, Kate L204
Evans, Kiya L205
Evans, Stephany L206
Everything With Words P158
Fairbank Literary Representation L208
Fairlight Books P160
Fathom Books P162
Faulks, Holly L209
Felicia Eth Literary Representation L214
Fellows, Abi L216
Feminist Press, The P163
Ferguson, Hannah L217
Fergusson, Julie L219
Fiction M140
Figueroa, Melanie L221
Five Points M144
Fogg, Jack L230
Folio M147
for Authors, A L231
Forrester, Jemima L232
Foster, Clara L233
Fourth River, The M153
Fox, Aram L234
Frances Collin Literary Agent L237
Frances Goldin Literary Agency, Inc. L238
Freymann, Sarah Jane L242
Friedman, Rebecca L244
Fuentes, Sarah L247
Galustian, Natalie L251
Georgia Review, The M163
Gertrude Press P179
Goff, Anthony L266
Goldstein, Veronica L268
Gordon, Andrew L270
Grain Literary Magazine M170
Granta Books P192
Graywolf Press P193
Greyhound Literary L278
Grimm, Katie L279
Gruber, Pam L281
Gunic, Masha L284
Gutter Magazine M174
Hakim, Serene L288
Hardman, Caroline L295
Harmsworth, Esmond L297
Harper, Logan L299
Harris, Erin L300
Hawthorne Books P209
Hiyate, Sam L313
Hotel Amerika M189
Hunger Mountain M191
Hwang, Annie L322
Idaho Review M193
Ig Publishing P230
Image M195
Indiana Review M196
Inque M198
Island M204
Island Online M205
Jamii Publishing P245
Janklow & Nesbit UK Ltd L330
Joelle Delbourgo Associates, Inc. L334
Jonathan Pegg Literary Agency L337
Joy Harris Literary Agency, Inc. L340
Judith Murdoch Literary Agency L341
Kahn, Jody L346
Kaliszewska, Joanna L347
Kantor, Camille L349
Kardon, Julia L350
Kate Barker Literary, TV, & Film Agency L352
Kean, Taylor Martindale L357
Kenny, Julia L361
Kensington Publishing Corp. P253
Keren, Eli L362
Kim, Jennifer L366
Kim, Julia L367
Kimber, Natalie L368
Kotchman, Katie L374
Krienke, Mary L375
Lambert, Sophie L380
Landfall M215
Langlee, Lina L382
Laxfield Literary Associates L387
Leamington Books P262
Lechon, Shannon L390
Lees, Jordan L392
Leigh Feldman Literary L393
Leon, Nina L394
Levitt, Sarah L396
Lewis, Alison L398
Lightner, Kayla L399
Louisiana Literature M228
Lutyens and Rubinstein L410
MacDonald, Emily L412
Macdougall, Laura L413
MacGregor & Luedeke L414
Maidment, Olivia L421
Marsh Agency, The L426

Marshall, Jen	L427
Massachusetts Review, The	M237
Massie, Maria	L430
Maurer, Shari	L433
McBride, Juliana	L435
McCormick Literary	L436
Mehren, Jane von	L440
Merullo, Annabel	L443
Mid-American Review	M241
Midsummer Dream House	M242
Milburn, Madeleine	L449
MMB Creative	L455
Moorhead, Max	L459
Morrell, Imogen	L460
Mortimer, Michele	L462
Mozley, Jack	L465
Mundy, Toby	L466
Murray, Judith	L468
Muscato, Nate	L469
Mustelier, James	L471
NBM Publishing	P312
Nelson, Kristin	L478
Neon	M253
New Orleans Review	M257
New Welsh Reader	M259
O'Grady, Niamh	L486
Oakland Arts Review, The	M264
Ogtrop, Kristin van	L489
Ooligan Press	P328
Orenda Books	P329
Oyez Review	M272
Pan Macmillan Australia	P335
Pande, Ayesha	L497
Panorama	M274
Paris Review, The	M275
Parthian Books	P336
Pass, Marina de	L500
Patterson, Emma	L501
Pelham, Imogen	L504
Perotto-Wills, Martha	L508
Pestritto, Carrie	L511
Peter Owen Publishers	P349
Phillips, Aemilia	L515
Pickering, Juliet	L516
Pierce, Rosie	L517
Pine, Gideon	L518
Plitt, Carrie	L520
Polygon	P360
Popshot Quarterly	M293
Power, Anna	L523
Prole	M299
Pushing Out the Boat	M301
Qu Literary Magazine	M302
Ramer, Susan	L528
Reid, Janet	L532
Reilly, Milly	L533
Renard Press Ltd	P376
Riverbed Review	M315
Roberts, Soumeya Bendimerad	L540
Robertson Murray Literary Agency	L541
Robinson, Quressa	L542
Rocking Chair Books	L544
Rofe, Jennifer	L545
Rogers, Coleridge & White Ltd	L546
Ruppin Agency, The	L555
Rutherford, Laetitia	L557
Rutman, Jim	L558
Salazar, Des	L559
Sarah Jane Freymann Literary Agency	L564
Sentient Publications	P404
Seren Books	P405
Serra, Maria Cardona	L574
Seymour, Charlotte	L575
Shaw Agency, The	L576
Sheil Land Associates Ltd	L577
Signorelli, Michael	L582
Silk, Julia	L583
Silver, Janet	L584
Simpson, Cara Lee	L586
Soho Press	P417
Soloway, Jennifer March	L590
Sorg, Arley	L592
Southern Humanities Review	M345
Sparsile Books	P419
Spout Press	P420
Stewart, Douglas	L599
Story Unlikely	M356
Strachan Literary Agency	L602
Stringer, Marlene	L604
Susan Schulman Literary Agency	L610
Swainson, Joanna	L613
Symonds, Laurel	L617
Tahoma Literary Review	M368
Tailwinds Press	P439
Takahe	M369
Takikawa, Marin	L618
Tannenbaum, Amy	L620
Temz Review, The	M372
Teresa Chris Literary Agency Ltd	L623
Thayer, Henry	L626
Thin Air Magazine	M374
Thinkwell Books, UK	P447
Thorneycroft, Euan	L628
Threepenny Review, The	M377
Torrey House Press, LLC	P459
Tran, Jennifer Chen	L633
Turner Publishing	P462
Tusculum Review, The	M381
University of Alberta Press	P477
Unwin, Jo	L638
Usselman, Laura	L639
Vance, Lisa Erbach	L641
Victoria Sanders & Associates LLC	L642
Vinspire Publishing	P497
Waccamaw	M394
Wasafiri	M398
Weidenfeld & Nicolson	P505
Weiss, Alexandra	L650
Weitzner, Tess	L651
Wells, Karmen	L652
Whelan, Maria	L656
Whispering Buffalo Literary Agency	L657
White Review, The	M404
Wickers, Chandler	L659
Williams, Laura	L662
Williams, Sarah	L663
Willms, Kathryn	L665
Wilson, Ed	L668
Wood, Caroline	L669
Woodhouse, James	L670
Woods, Bryony	L671
Woollard, Jessica	L672
WordCrafts Press	P514
Wordserve Literary	L673
Writer's Side	L674
Yale Review, The	M409
Yellow Mama Webzine	M411
Yeoh, Rachel	L675
Young, Claudia	L677
Zack Company, Inc, The	L678
Zone 3	M419
Zuraw-Friedland, Ayla	L681

Literary Criticism
See more broadly: Literature

American Book Review	M022
Arcadia Publishing	P031
Chapman	M081
Critical Quarterly	M108
Enitharmon Editions	P153
Feminist Studies	M139
First Line, The	M143
Granta Books	P192
Graywolf Press	P193
Hudson Review, The	M190
Lilliput Press, The	P268
London Review of Books	M225
Lutterworth Press, The	P275
Marion Boyars Publishers	P282
MMB Creative	L455
Moving Worlds: A Journal of Transcultural Writings	M247
New England Review	M255
Peepal Tree Press	P341
Rutman, Jim	L558
Seren Books	P405
Thames & Hudson Inc.	P446
University of Alberta Press	P477
University of Nevada Press	P484
University of Pennsylvania Press	P486
University of Texas Press	P488
University of Virginia Press	P489
Virginia Quarterly Review, The	M389
W.W. Norton & Company, Inc.	P500
Wallace Stevens Journal, The	M396
Yale Review, The	M409

Literary Fantasy
See more broadly: Fantasy; Literary

Margaret K. McElderry Books	P281

Literary Horror
See more broadly: Horror; Literary

Colwill, Charlotte	L132
Tibbets, Anne	L630

Literary Journalism
See more broadly: Journalism; Literary

Irish Pages	M203
Litro Magazine	M221
Southern Humanities Review	M345
Steerforth Press	P428
Torrey House Press, LLC	P459

Literary Memoir
See more broadly: Memoir

Andrew, Nelle	L025
Eisenmann, Caroline	L192
Fellows, Abi	L216
Fuentes, Sarah	L247
Kahn, Jody	L346
Lewis, Alison	L398
Peddle, Kay	L503
Ramer, Susan	L528
Robinson, Quressa	L542

Literary Mystery
See more broadly: Literary; Mystery

Chanchani, Sonali	L115
Harris, Erin	L300

Literary Suspense
See more broadly: Literary; Suspense

Evans, Kate	L204
Greenstreet, Katie	L277

Literary Thrillers
See more broadly: Literary; Thrillers

Chang, Nicola	L116
Geiger, Ellen	L255
Pelham, Imogen	L504

Literature
See more specifically: American Literature; Beat Generation; Fiction as a Subject; Literary Criticism; Medieval Literature; Metaphysical; Poetry as a Subject

African American Review	M014
Baylor University Press	P060
Black Moon Magazine	M064
Bloomsbury Academic	P071
BOA Editions, Ltd	P076
Brick	M074
Broadview Press	P085
Charnace, Edwina de	L117
Classical Comics	P114
Compassiviste Publishing	P121

Crystal Magazine	M110
Ekphrastic Review, The	M128
Flaneur	M145
Fortress Press	P170
Fresh Words – An International Literary Magazine	M154
Gale	P177
Graywolf Lab	M172
Gulf Coast: A Journal of Literature and Fine Arts	M173
Harvard University Press	P206
Holloway, Sally	L318
Icon Books Ltd	P227
Image	M195
Ink Sweat and Tears	M197
Inque	M198
Ireland's Own	M202
Johns Hopkins University Press, The	P250
Lilliput Press, The	P268
London Review of Books	M225
LSU Press	P273
Lutterworth Press, The	P275
Manoa	M233
Massachusetts Review, The	M237
Methuen Publishing Ltd	P294
Moving Worlds: A Journal of Transcultural Writings	M247
New Orleans Review	M257
Ohio State University Press, The	P323
Ohio University Press	P324
Oneworld Publications	P327
Otago University Press	P330
Oxford Poetry	M270
Power Cut Lite	M294
Purdue University Press	P364
Rabble Review	M303
Reader, The	M308
Sasquatch Books	P391
Southwest Review	M348
Stanford University Press	P427
Taylor & Francis Group	P441
Temz Review, The	M372
Threepenny Review, The	M377
University of Alberta Press	P477
University of California Press	P478
University of Iowa Press	P480
University of Massachusetts Press	P482
University of Michigan Press, The	P483
University of Tennessee Press	P487
University of Texas Press	P488
University of Virginia Press	P489
Victoria Sanders & Associates LLC	L642
Virginia Wine & Country Life	M390
W.W. Norton & Company Ltd	P499
W.W. Norton & Company, Inc.	P500
Wallace Stevens Journal, The	M396
Wasafiri	M398
White Review, The	M404
Windsor Review	M405
Yale University Press (London)	P520

Live Music
See more broadly: Music

Local
See more broadly: Regional

| JMD Media / DB Publishing | P247 |
| Landfall | M215 |

Local History
See more broadly: History

AdventureKEEN	P013
Birlinn Ltd	P067
Countryside Books	P124
History Press, The	P221
JMD Media / DB Publishing	P247
Kates Hill Press, The	P252
Kent Life	M209
Lilliput Press, The	P268
Logaston Press	P271
Pen & Sword Books Ltd	P343
Scratching Shed Publishing	P402

Logistics
See more broadly: Business

| Loft Press, Inc. | P270 |

London
See more broadly: England

| Metro Publications Ltd | P295 |
| Square Mile Magazine | M354 |

Long Form Poetry

| Long Poem Magazine | M226 |
| Tahoma Literary Review | M368 |

Louisiana
See more broadly: United States

| LSU Press | P273 |

Love
See more broadly: Relationships

| Ellis-Martin, Sian | L197 |
| Passionfruit Review, The | M277 |

Low Fantasy
See more broadly: Fantasy

Gilbert, Tara	L258
Soler, Shania N.	L589
Trudel, Jes	L634
Weiss, Alexandra	L650

Luxury Lifestyle
See more broadly: Lifestyle

Lyric Essays

Identity Theory	M194
Jamii Publishing	P245
Southern Humanities Review	M345
Tahoma Literary Review	M368

Lyrical

| Glacier, The | M166 |

Mafia
See more broadly: Organised Crime

Magazines
See more broadly: Media

| Future Fire, The | M158 |

Magic
See more broadly: Fantasy
See more specifically: Dark Magic

Bauman, Erica	L050
Belton, Maddy	L055
Bent, Jenny	L059
Buckley, Louise	L091
Cooper, Gemma	L140
Danaczko, Melissa	L153
Dodd, Saffron	L172
Forrester, Jemima	L232
Haley, Jolene	L289
Harris, Erin	L300
Hernando, Paloma	L308
JMD Media / DB Publishing	P247
Knigge, Sheyla	L372
Leon, Nina	L394
Phillips, Aemilia	L515
Plant, Zoe	L519
Rofe, Jennifer	L545
Rushall, Kathleen	L556
Sanchez, Kaitlyn	L561
Terlip, Paige	L624
Weiman, Paula	L649
Williams, Laura	L662

Magical Realism
See more broadly: Fantasy
See more specifically: Fabulism

Andrew, Nelle	L025
Armstrong, Susan	L032
Barr, Anjanette	L045
Candlemark & Gleam	P092
Cho, Catherine	L124
Cichello, Kayla	L127
Cooper, Maggie	L141
Crabtree Publishing	P126
Danko, Margaret	L154
Davies, Elinor	L160
Eberly, Chelsea	L187
Evans, Kiya	L205
Felicia Eth Literary Representation	L214
Figueroa, Melanie	L221
Foxx, Kat	L235
Glenister, Emily	L263
Gunic, Masha	L284
Haley, Jolene	L289
Julie Crisp Literary Agency	L343
Kean, Taylor Martindale	L357
Keren, Eli	L362
Leon, Nina	L394
Lightner, Kayla	L399
Maidment, Olivia	L421
Marr, Jill	L425
O'Neill, Molly	L487
Reino, Jessica	L534
Soler, Shania N.	L589
Stringer, Marlene	L604
Takikawa, Marin	L618
Torrey House Press, LLC	P459
Trussell, Caroline	L635
Weiss, Alexandra	L650
Weitzner, Tess	L651
Whelan, Maria	L656
Williams, Laura	L662
Wilson, Desiree	L667
Yeoh, Rachel	L675

Mahayana Buddhism
See more broadly: Buddhism
See more specifically: Zen

Maine
See more broadly: United States

| University of Maine Press | P481 |

Mainstream

Compassiviste Publishing	P121
Freymann, Sarah Jane	L242
Oghma Creative Media	P321
Paul S. Levine Literary Agency	L502
Wordserve Literary	L673

Make-Up
See more broadly: Beauty

| Redbook Magazine | M310 |

Management
See more broadly: Business
See more specifically: Project Management; Service Management; Supply Chain Management

Berrett-Koehler Publishers	P063
Bloomsbury Academic	P071
Gill Education	P182
High Tide Press	P217
Peter Lang	P346
Peter Lang Publishing	P348
Taylor & Francis Group	P441
Zack Company, Inc, The	L678

Maori
See more broadly: Ethnic Groups

| Otago University Press | P330 |

Maritime History
See more broadly: History

Cornell Maritime Press	P123
History Press, The	P221
Pen & Sword Books Ltd	P343

Marketing
See more broadly: Business
See more specifically: Advertising

Banter Press	P053
Campaign	M079
Gill Education	P182

Martial Arts
See more broadly: Sport
See more specifically: Qigong; Tai Chi

| Black Belt | M063 |

Index | Memoir 361

Singing Dragon ... P409
Turtle Press ... P463

Marxism

See more broadly: Philosophy; Politics

Maryland

See more broadly: United States

Mathematics

See more specifically: Statistics

Autumn Publishing Ltd ... P042
Badger Learning ... P048
Bloomsbury Academic ... P071
Charlesbridge Publishing ... P102
Colourpoint Educational ... P119
Crabtree Publishing ... P126
Diana Finch Literary Agency ... L167
Enslow Publishers, Inc. ... P154
Gale ... P177
Gill Education ... P182
Icon Books Ltd ... P227
Johns Hopkins University Press, The ... P250
Kane Press ... P251
Marshall, Jen ... L427
Prufrock Press ... P363
Science Factory, The ... L569
Stipes Publishing ... P431
Symonds, Laurel ... L617
Taylor & Francis Group ... P441
University of Michigan Press, The ... P483
W.W. Norton & Company, Inc. ... P500
Wilson, Desiree ... L667
Yale University Press (London) ... P520
ZigZag Education ... P523

Media

See more specifically: Books; Films; Magazines; Social Media; TV; Theatre

Bloomsbury Academic ... P071
Campaign ... M079
Draper, Claire ... L178
Feminist Press, The ... P163
FRA (Futerman, Rose, & Associates) ... L236
Harvard University Press ... P206
Hernando, Paloma ... L308
Indiana University Press ... P235
Joy Harris Literary Agency, Inc. ... L340
LSU Press ... P273
Ohio State University Press, The ... P323
Ohio University Press ... P324
Peter Lang ... P346
Peter Lang Publishing ... P348
R D Publishers ... P370
Stanford University Press ... P427
University of California Press ... P478
University of Massachusetts Press ... P482
University of Michigan Press, The ... P483
University of Texas Press ... P488
University of Wisconsin Press, The ... P490
Wayne State University Press ... P504
Weiss, Alexandra ... L650
ZigZag Education ... P523

Medicine

See more broadly: Health

See more specifically: Anatomy; Biomedical Science; Geriatrics; Immunology; Physiology; Psychiatry

Arcadia Publishing ... P031
Betsy Amster Literary Enterprises ... L063
Bloomsbury Academic ... P071
Elsevier Ltd ... P150
Feminist Press, The ... P163
Gale ... P177
Glenister, Emily ... L263
Grossman, Loren R. ... L280
Hammersmith Books ... P198
Hardman, Caroline ... L295
Harvard University Press ... P206
Idyll Arbor ... P229
Johns Hopkins University Press, The ... P250
Karinch, Maryann ... L351
Kensington Publishing Corp. ... P253
Lechon, Shannon ... L390
McGraw Hill EMEA ... P285
Medical Physics Publishing ... P288
Mills & Boon ... P297
Nolan, Laura ... L481
Reilly, Milly ... L533
Rudy Agency, The ... L553
Science Factory, The ... L569
Singing Dragon ... P409
Taylor & Francis Group ... P441
Thames & Hudson Inc. ... P446
Turner Publishing ... P462
University of Alberta Press ... P477
University of Massachusetts Press ... P482
University of Michigan Press, The ... P483
University of Nevada Press ... P484
W.W. Norton & Company Ltd ... P499
Yale University Press (London) ... P520

Medieval

See more broadly: History

Fazzari, Hillary ... L210
Nash, Justin ... L474
Ohio State University Press, The ... P323
Oxbow Books ... P333
University of Michigan Press, The ... P483
University of Pennsylvania Press ... P486
Zack Company, Inc, The ... L678

Medieval Literature

See more broadly: Literature

Meditation

See more broadly: Mind, Body, Spirit

Llewellyn Worldwide Ltd ... P269
Red Feather ... P375
Society for Promoting Christian Knowledge (SPCK) ... P414
Zack Company, Inc, The ... L678

Memoir

See more broadly: Autobiography

See more specifically: Celebrity Memoir; Inspirational Memoir; Literary Memoir

Allison & Busby Ltd ... P019
Antigonish Review, The ... M026
Arthurson, Wayne ... L033
Asabi Publishing ... P034
Atyeo, Charlotte ... L034
Bal, Emma ... L038
Baobab Press ... P054
Barr, Anjanette ... L045
Bartholomew, Jason ... L047
Basalt Books ... P057
Baumer, Jan ... L051
Baxter, Veronique ... L052
Begum, Salma ... L053
Bess Press ... P064
Birlinn Ltd ... P067
Blackstaff Press ... P068
Blue Earth Review ... M067
Bradford Literary Agency ... L075
Brailsford, Karen ... L077
Brewin Books Ltd ... P081
Brick ... M074
Caitlin Press Inc. ... P090
Capron, Elise ... L104
Carter, Rebecca ... L111
Caskie, Robert ... L113
Cavanagh, Claire ... L114
Chase Literary Agency ... L118
Chevais, Jennifer ... L122
Chiotti, Danielle ... L123
Christie, Jennifer ... L126
Claret Press ... P113
Clarke, Caro ... L128
Clarke, Catherine ... L129
Cleis Press ... P115
Comparato, Andrea ... L134
Conville, Clare ... L137
Creative Nonfiction ... M106
Crown Publishing Group, The ... P131
Curtis Brown ... L146
Cynthia Cannell Literary Agency ... L150
Dana Newman Literary, LLC ... L152
Danaczko, Melissa ... L153
Daunt Books Publishing ... P134
Dawson, Liza ... L162
Diana Finch Literary Agency ... L167
Dillsworth, Elise ... L170
Dixon, Isobel ... L171
Dolby, Trevor ... L173
Doug Grad Literary Agency ... L177
Draper, Claire ... L178
Dublin Review, The ... M124
Dunham, Jennie ... L180
Dunn, Ben ... L181
Edwards, Max ... L190
Engram Books ... P152
Evans, Kate ... L204
Evans, Stephany ... L206
Fairbank Literary Representation ... L208
Faulks, Holly ... L209
Felicia Eth Literary Representation ... L214
Feminist Press, The ... P163
Fernandez, Rochelle ... L220
Fernwood Publishing ... P164
Fogg, Jack ... L230
Fox, Aram ... L234
Foxx, Kat ... L235
Frances Collin Literary Agent ... L237
Frankel, Valerie ... L239
Freymann, Sarah Jane ... L242
Friedman, Rebecca ... L244
Furniss, Eugenie ... L249
Galustian, Natalie ... L251
Galvin, Lori ... L252
Gauntlett, Adam ... L254
Gertrude ... M164
Glenister, Emily ... L263
Goldstein, Veronica ... L268
Gordon, Andrew ... L270
Graywolf Press ... P193
Greenstreet, Katie ... L277
Greyhound Literary ... L278
Grimm, Katie ... L279
Half Mystic Press ... P197
Hardman, Caroline ... L295
Harris, Erin ... L300
Hashtag Press ... P207
Haus Publishing ... P208
Hawthorne Books ... P209
Hayden, Viola ... L305
History Press, The ... P221
Hiyate, Sam ... L313
Hordern, Kate ... L320
Icon Books Ltd ... P227
Identity Theory ... M194
Inscriptions Literary Agency ... L323
Irish Pages ... M203
Jeff Herman Agency, LLC, The ... L331
Joelle Delbourgo Associates, Inc. ... L334
Jonathan Pegg Literary Agency ... L337
Kardon, Julia ... L350
Kate Barker Literary, TV, & Film Agency ... L352
Kates Hill Press, The ... P252
Kathryn Green Literary Agency, LLC ... L354
Kim, Julia ... L367
Kimber, Natalie ... L368
Kotchman, Katie ... L374
Kube Publishing ... P258
Lambert, Sophie ... L380

362 Index | *Men's Interests*

Langtons International ... L384
Latshaw, Katherine ... L386
Laxfield Literary Associates ... L387
Lazin, Sarah ... L388
Lechon, Shannon ... L390
Leigh Feldman Literary ... L393
Levitt, Sarah ... L396
Lewinsohn Literary ... L397
Lightner, Kayla ... L399
Lilliput Press, The ... P268
Litro Magazine ... M221
Loft Press, Inc. ... P270
London Review of Books ... M225
MacDonald, Emily ... L412
MacGregor & Luedeke ... L414
MacLeod, Lauren ... L418
Madan, Neeti ... L419
Malahat Review, The ... M232
Marr, Jill ... L425
Marsiglia, Caroline ... L428
Massie, Maria ... L430
Maurer, Shari ... L433
Maw, Jane Graham ... L434
McCormick Literary ... L436
McQuilkin, Rob ... L438
Medina Publishing ... P289
Mehren, Jane von ... L440
Mihell, Natasha ... L448
Mirror Books ... P301
Moorhead, Max ... L459
Mortimer, Michele ... L462
Mundy, Toby ... L466
Murgolo, Karen ... L467
Murray, Judith ... L468
Nashville Review ... M251
Native Ink Press ... P311
Niumata, Erin ... L480
O'Grady, Faith ... L485
O'Shea, Amy ... L488
Oakland Arts Review, The ... M264
Ogtrop, Kristin van ... L489
Oneworld Publications ... P327
Otago University Press ... P330
Pan Macmillan Australia ... P335
Pande, Ayesha ... L497
Patterson, Emma ... L501
Peepal Tree Press ... P341
Pelham, Imogen ... L504
Perry Literary ... L509
Pestritto, Carrie ... L511
Pierce, Rosie ... L517
Plitt, Carrie ... L520
Polygon ... P360
Power, Anna ... L523
Prasanna, Tanusri ... L525
Preston, Amanda ... L526
Reid, Janet ... L532
Richter, Rick ... L537
Roberts, Soumeya Bendimerad ... L540
Roseway ... P382
Ruppin Agency, The ... L555
Sarah Jane Freymann Literary Agency ... L564
Schofield, Hannah ... L567
Scoular, Rosemary ... L570
Selectric Artists ... L573
Seren Books ... P405
Sheil Land Associates Ltd ... L577
Shenandoah ... M331
Shestopal, Camilla ... L581
Shipwreckt Books Publishing Company ... P406
Shooter Literary Magazine ... M333
Signorelli, Michael ... L582
Silk, Julia ... L583
Simpson, Cara Lee ... L586
Southern Humanities Review ... M345
Story Unlikely ... M356
Susan Schulman Literary Agency ... L610
Swainson, Joanna ... L613
Sweet, Emily ... L614
Sweren, Becky ... L615
Thorneycroft, Euan ... L628
Toad Hall Editions ... P453
Tolka ... M379
Topping, Antony ... L632
Torrey House Press, LLC ... P459
Tyndale House Publishers, Inc. ... P465
University of Alaska Press ... P476
University of Alberta Press ... P477
University of Michigan Press, The ... P483
University of Virginia Press ... P489
Usselman, Laura ... L639
Valley Press ... P493
VanderWyk & Burnham ... P494
W.W. Norton & Company Ltd ... P499
W.W. Norton & Company, Inc. ... P500
Williams, Laura ... L662
Williams, Sarah ... L663
Wilson, Ed ... L668
Wood, Caroline ... L669
Woods, Bryony ... L671
Woollard, Jessica ... L672
WordCrafts Press ... P514
Wordserve Literary ... L673
Yale Review, The ... M409
Yale University Press (London) ... P520
Yeoh, Rachel ... L675
Zack Company, Inc, The ... L678
Zibby Books ... P522

Men's Interests
Compassiviste Publishing ... P121

Men's Issues
See more broadly: Social Issues
Freymann, Sarah Jane ... L242

Menopause
See more broadly: Women's Health
First For Women ... M142
Macdougall, Laura ... L413

Mental Disorders
See more broadly: Psychiatry
High Tide Press ... P217

Mental Health
See more broadly: Health
See more specifically: Dementia
Authentic Life ... P041
Danko, Margaret ... L154
Finegan, Stevie ... L226
Goodman Beck Publishing ... P187
Grunewald, Hattie ... L282
Hammersmith Books ... P198
Hashtag Press ... P207
Jessica Kingsley Publishers ... P246
Krienke, Mary ... L375
Lechon, Shannon ... L390
Lightner, Kayla ... L399
Maltese, Alyssa ... L422
New Harbinger Publications ... P314
Nichols, Mariah ... L479
Singing Dragon ... P409
Soloway, Jennifer March ... L590
Trudel, Jes ... L634
Tyndale House Publishers, Inc. ... P465
W.W. Norton & Company, Inc. ... P500
Weiss, Alexandra ... L650
Williams, Laura ... L662
Wilson, Desiree ... L667

Metaphysical
See more broadly: Literature

Methodism
See more broadly: Christianity

Michigan
See more broadly: United States
See more specifically: Detroit
University of Michigan Press, The ... P483
Wayne State University Press ... P504

Middle East
See more broadly: Regional
Bloomsbury Academic ... P071
Feminist Press, The ... P163
Ghahremani, Lilly ... L257
Indiana University Press ... P235
Oneworld Publications ... P327
Pluto Press ... P358
Saqi Books ... P390
Stanford University Press ... P427
University of Alberta Press ... P477
University of California Press ... P478
University of Michigan Press, The ... P483
University of Texas Press ... P488

Middle Grade
3 Seas Literary Agency ... L001
4RV Publishing ... P004
Agency (London) Ltd, The ... L009
Albert Whitman & Company ... P015
Alex Adsett Literary ... L016
Alice Williams Literary ... L017
Allen & Unwin ... P018
Andrade, Hannah ... L023
Andrews McMeel Publishing ... P026
Anne Clark Literary Agency ... L028
Arcadia Publishing ... P031
Armada, Kurestin ... L030
Arms, Victoria Wells ... L031
Atyeo, Charlotte ... L034
Badger Learning ... P048
Baror International, Inc. ... L044
Bath Literary Agency ... L049
Baxter, Veronique ... L052
Belton, Maddy ... L055
Bent Agency (UK), The ... L057
Bent Agency, The ... L058
Borstel, Stefanie Sanchez Von ... L071
Bradford, Laura ... L076
Bright Agency (UK), The ... L082
Bright Agency (US), The ... L083
Brooks, Savannah ... L084
Burns, Camille ... L094
Cadno ... P089
Candy Jar Books ... P093
Caprio, Alice ... L103
Caroline Sheldon Literary Agency ... L106
Carroll, Megan ... L110
Charlesbridge Publishing ... P102
Cherry Lake Publishing Group ... P106
Chiotti, Danielle ... L123
Chronicle Books LLC ... P111
Cichello, Kayla ... L127
Colwill, Charlotte ... L132
Comparato, Andrea ... L134
Cooper, Gemma ... L140
Crandall, Becca ... L142
Curtis Brown ... L146
Cusick, John ... L148
DK Publishing ... P141
Dodd, Saffron ... L172
Dominguez, Adriana ... L174
Draper, Claire ... L178
Dunham, Jennie ... L180
Dunow, Carlson & Lerner Agency ... L184
Eberly, Chelsea ... L187
Eerdmans Books for Young Readers ... P148
Eisenbraun, Nicole ... L191
Ellor, Zabé ... L198
Eunice McMullen Children's Literary Agent Ltd ... L201
Fabien, Samantha ... L207
Fairbank Literary Representation ... L208
Fazzari, Hillary ... L210

Index | Missouri

Fellows, Abi	L216
Ferguson, T.S.	L218
Fernandez, Rochelle	L220
Figueroa, Melanie	L221
Filter Press	P166
Finegan, Stevie	L226
Firefly	P167
Flannery Literary	L228
Flynn, Amy Thrall	L229
Gahan, Isobel	L250
Gauntlett, Adam	L254
Getzler, Josh	L256
Ghahremani, Lilly	L257
Gisondi, Katie	L261
Goetz, Adria	L265
Goff, Ellen	L267
Good Literary Agency, The	L269
Grajkowski, Michelle	L274
Gruber, Pam	L281
Gunic, Masha	L284
Guppy Books	P195
Hakim, Serene	L288
Haley, Jolene	L289
Hannah Sheppard Literary Agency	L291
Hare, Jessica	L296
Harwell, Hilary	L301
Hashtag Press	P207
Hawk, Susan	L303
Hawn, Molly Ker	L304
Hensley, Chelsea	L307
Hernando, Paloma	L308
Hodges, Jodie	L315
Holroyde, Penny	L319
Hordern, Kate	L320
IgKids	P231
Inscriptions Literary Agency	L323
Irvine, Lucy	L325
Joelle Delbourgo Associates, Inc.	L334
Kahn, Ella Diamond	L345
Kane Press	P251
Kate Nash Literary Agency	L353
Kathryn Green Literary Agency, LLC	L354
Kean, Taylor Martindale	L357
Knigge, Sheyla	L372
KT Literary	L377
Kube Publishing	P258
Lakosil, Natalie	L379
Landis, Sarah	L381
Langlee, Lina	L382
Langton, Becca	L383
Lantana Publishing	P260
Latshaw, Katherine	L386
Leapfrog Press	P263
Lechon, Shannon	L390
Lees, Jordan	L392
Leon, Nina	L394
Lerner Publishing Group	P264
Lindsay Literary Agency	L401
MacLeod, Lauren	L418
Macmillan Children's Books	P279
Margaret K. McElderry Books	P281
Mattson, Jennifer	L432
Maurer, Shari	L433
McBride, Juliana	L435
Megibow, Sara	L439
Mihell, Natasha	L448
Miranda, Caroline	L454
Moody Publishers	P305
Moore, Penny	L458
Mustelier, James	L471
Nathan, Abigail	L475
Native Ink Press	P311
Nelson Literary Agency, LLC	L477
Nosy Crow	P319
O'Grady, Faith	L485
O'Neill, Molly	L487
Oghma Creative Media	P321
Oh MG Press	P322
Ostby, Kristin	L494
Pacific Press Publishing Association	P334
Pan Macmillan Australia	P335
Parker, Elana Roth	L499
Pestritto, Carrie	L511
Petty, Rachel	L512
Phelan, Beth	L514
Phoenix Moirai	P351
Piccadilly Press	P354
Plant, Zoe	L519
Posner, Marcy	L522
Prasanna, Tanusri	L525
Quirk Books	P369
Ransom Publishing Ltd	P373
Reino, Jessica	L534
Richter, Rick	L537
Robinson, Quressa	L542
Rofe, Jennifer	L545
Ross, Whitney	L551
Rushall, Kathleen	L556
Saguaro Books, LLC	P388
Salvo, Katie	L560
Sanchez, Kaitlyn	L561
Sant, Kelly Van	L563
Schiffer Kids	P396
Scholastic	P399
Scholastic UK	P400
Seager, Chloe	L571
Shestopal, Camilla	L581
Siobhan, Aiden	L587
Soler, Shania N.	L589
Soloway, Jennifer March	L590
StoryWise	L601
Stringer Literary Agency LLC, The	L603
Susan Schulman Literary Agency	L610
Sutherland, Kari	L611
Sweet Cherry Publishing	P437
Symonds, Laurel	L617
Talbot, Emily	L619
Terlip, Paige	L624
Thwaites, Steph	L629
Tilbury House Publishers	P450
Tran, Jennifer Chen	L633
Trudel, Jes	L634
Turner Publishing	P462
Two Piers Literary Agency, The	L636
Unwin, Jo	L638
Vinspire Publishing	P497
Walsh, Caroline	L645
Weiman, Paula	L649
Weiss, Alexandra	L650
Weitzner, Tess	L651
Westin, Erin Casey	L654
Whatnall, Michaela	L655
Williams, Laura	L662
Williamson, Jo	L664
Wilson, Desiree	L667
Woods, Bryony	L671
WordCrafts Press	P514
Wordserve Literary	L673
Zacker, Marietta B.	L679

Midwifery
See more broadly: Nursing

Macdougall, Laura	L413
Practising Midwife, The	M295

Military
See more broadly: Warfare
See more specifically: Military Aviation; Military Vehicles; Special Forces

Amber Books Ltd	P022
Brewin Books Ltd	P081
Brown, Megan	L088
Doug Grad Literary Agency	L177
History Press, The	P221
Howgate Publishing	P225
Knight Features	L373
Lovell, Jake	L409
Nash, Justin	L474
Oghma Creative Media	P321
Robert Smith Literary Agency Ltd	L539
Schiffer Military History	P397
Wordserve Literary	L673
Zack Company, Inc, The	L678

Military Aviation
See more broadly: Aviation; Military

Air & Space Quarterly	M018
Pen & Sword Books Ltd	P343

Military History
See more broadly: History; Warfare

Brewin Books Ltd	P081
Dolby, Trevor	L173
Fighting High	P165
Goose Lane Editions	P188
Icon Books Ltd	P227
Indiana University Press	P235
Merriam Press	P293
Pen & Sword Books Ltd	P343
Texas A&M University Press	P445
Thames & Hudson Inc.	P446
Unicorn Publishing Group	P470
Uniform	P471
University of Massachusetts Press	P482
University of North Texas Press	P485
Zack Company, Inc, The	L678

Military Vehicles
See more broadly: Military; Vehicles

Millennial

Carr, Jamie	L108
Watterson, Jessica	L648

Mind, Body, Spirit
See more broadly: Health
See more specifically: Meditation; Yoga

Arcadia Publishing	P031
Curran, Sabhbh	L145
Dana Newman Literary, LLC	L152
DeVorss & Company	P139
Ericka T. Phillips	L200
Gill Books	P181
Globe Pequot Press, The	P184
Haley, Jolene	L289
Joelle Delbourgo Associates, Inc.	L334
Kensington Publishing Corp.	P253
Lilliput Press, The	P268
Llewellyn Worldwide Ltd	P269
Oghma Creative Media	P321
Pan Macmillan Australia	P335
Paul S. Levine Literary Agency	L502
Piatkus Books	P352
Red Feather	P375
Sheil Land Associates Ltd	L577
Susan Schulman Literary Agency	L610
Terlip, Paige	L624
Turner Publishing	P462
Turtle Press	P463
University of Nevada Press	P484
W.W. Norton & Company, Inc.	P500
Whitford Press	P508
Zack Company, Inc, The	L678

Minerals
See more broadly: Geology

Rock & Gem	M316

Mini Cars
See more broadly: Cars

MiniWorld Magazine	M244

Minnesota
See more broadly: United States

Minnesota Historical Society Press	P299

Missouri
See more broadly: United States
See more specifically: St Louis

417 Magazine M004
River Hills Traveler M313
Sweetgum Press................................... P438
Model Aircraft
See more broadly: Model Making
Model Making
See more broadly: Crafts
See more specifically: Model Aircraft; Model Ships and Boats
Model Ships and Boats
See more broadly: Model Making
Brown, Son & Ferguson, Ltd P086
Modern History
See more broadly: History
Montgomeryshire
See more broadly: Wales
Logaston Press..................................... P271
Mormonism
See more broadly: Christianity
Motherhood
See more broadly: Parenting
Buckley, Louise L091
Foxx, Kat... L235
Literary Mama M220
Roberts, Soumeya Bendimerad L540
Motivational Self-Help
See more broadly: Self Help
Derviskadic, Dado L164
Kotchman, Katie L374
Motor Boats
See more broadly: Boats
Motorbikes
See more broadly: Vehicles
Square Mile Magazine M354
Motorcycling
See more broadly: Hobbies
Motorhomes
See more broadly: Vehicles
Motorsports
See more broadly: Sport
See more specifically: Formula One; NASCAR
JMD Media / DB Publishing P247
O'Grady, Faith L485
Mountain Lifestyle
See more broadly: Lifestyle
Multicultural
See more broadly: Culture
Bookouture P078
Cho, Catherine L124
Felicia Eth Literary Representation L214
Freymann, Sarah Jane L242
Geiger, Ellen L255
Jeff Herman Agency, LLC, The L331
Moving Worlds: A Journal of Transcultural Writings M247
Sheree Bykofsky Associates, Inc. L579
Tran, Jennifer Chen L633
University of North Texas Press P485
W.W. Norton & Company Ltd P499
Music
See more specifically: Bluegrass; Choral Music; Church Music; Classical Music; Electronic Music; Heavy Metal; Jazz; Live Music; Musical Instruments; Popular Music; Punk; Rock Music; Roots Music; Traditional Music
A-R Editions P006
Arcadia Publishing P031
Atyeo, Charlotte L034
Backbeat Books P046
Begum, Salma L053
Bloomsbury Academic P071
Brattle Agency LLC, The L080
Brewin Books Ltd P081
Brick M074
Cavanagh, Claire L114
Compassiviste Publishing P121

Doug Grad Literary Agency L177
Edenborough, Sam L189
Elliott & Thompson P149
Flaneur M145
FRA (Futerman, Rose, & Associates) L236
Galustian, Natalie................................ L251
Gill Education P182
Gordon, Andrew L270
Graywolf Lab M172
Greyhound Literary L278
Half Mystic Journal M175
Half Mystic Press P197
Harvard University Press P206
Hudson Review, The M190
Indiana University Press P235
Johns Hopkins University Press, The P250
Kensington Publishing Corp. P253
Kim, Jennifer L366
Laurence King Publishing P261
Lilliput Press, The P268
Mack, Kate... L415
Marion Boyars Publishers P282
Marr, Jill L425
Massachusetts Review, The M237
McNidder & Grace P286
Mortimer, Michele L462
Nolan, Laura L481
Oghma Creative Media P321
Plexus Publishing Limited P357
Polygon P360
Ramer, Susan L528
Red Magazine M309
Richter, Rick L537
Riposte M312
Rutman, Jim L558
Scratching Shed Publishing P402
Seren Books P405
Sheree Bykofsky Associates, Inc. L579
SOMA M340
Southwest Review M348
Spackman, James L593
Square Mile Magazine M354
Stainer & Bell Ltd P426
Stipes Publishing P431
Texas A&M University Press P445
Thames & Hudson Inc. P446
Tocher M378
Topping, Antony L632
Uncut M383
University of California Press P478
University of Massachusetts Press P482
University of Michigan Press, The P483
University of North Texas Press P485
University of Tennessee Press P487
University of Texas Press P488
Victoria Sanders & Associates LLC L642
Virginia Wine & Country Life M390
W.W. Norton & Company Ltd P499
W.W. Norton & Company, Inc. P500
Walsh, Kate L646
Wesleyan University Press P506
Yale Review, The M409
Yale University Press (London) P520
Zack Company, Inc, The L678
ZigZag Education P523
Musical Instruments
See more broadly: Music
See more specifically: Piano
Backbeat Books P046
Musicals
See more broadly: Theatre
Mystery
See more specifically: Amateur Investigator; Cozy Mysteries; Detective Fiction; Domestic Mystery; Historical Mystery Fiction; Literary Mystery; Romantic Mystery

4RV Tenacious P005
Adsett, Alex L006
Afonso, Thais L008
Alex Adsett Literary L016
Alfred Hitchcock Mystery Magazine M020
Allison & Busby Ltd P019
American Mystery Classics P023
Andrade, Hannah L023
Armada, Kurestin L030
Asabi Publishing P034
Authentic Ideas P040
Baxter, Veronique L052
Betsy Amster Literary Enterprises L063
Bolton, Camilla L069
Brace, Samantha L074
Bradford Literary Agency L075
Bradford, Laura L076
Brooks, Savannah L084
Bucci, Chris L090
Burke, Kate L093
Cichello, Kayla L127
Claret Press P113
Comparato, Andrea L134
Coombs Moylett & Maclean Literary Agency L139
Countryside Books P124
Crabtree Publishing P126
Crowley, Sheila L144
Crystal Magazine M110
Davies, Elinor L160
Dawson, Liza L162
Dodd, Saffron L172
Doug Grad Literary Agency L177
DSP Publications P145
Dunham, Jennie L180
Eason, Lynette L186
Eberly, Chelsea L187
Ellery Queen Mystery Magazine M130
Ellor, Zabé L198
Evans, Kiya L205
Evans, Stephany L206
Fabien, Samantha L207
Fate M136
Feminist Press, The P163
Fernandez, Rochelle L220
Figueroa, Melanie L221
Forge P169
Foxx, Kat L235
Frankel, Valerie L239
Future Fire, The M158
Galvin, Lori L252
Getzler, Josh L256
Gisondi, Katie L261
Graham, Stacey L272
Grimm, Katie L279
Gunic, Masha L284
Haley, Jolene L289
Harmony Ink Press L205
Harmsworth, Esmond L297
Harper, Logan L299
Hensley, Chelsea L307
Hiyate, Sam L313
Inscriptions Literary Agency L323
Irene Goodman Literary Agency (IGLA) L324
Irvine, Lucy L325
Joelle Delbourgo Associates, Inc. L334
Joffe Books P248
Joy Harris Literary Agency, Inc. L340
Karinch, Maryann L351
Kensington Publishing Corp. P253
Keren, Eli L362
Kim, Julia L367
Langtons International L384
Lechon, Shannon L390
Leon, Nina L394

Index | *Narrative Nonfiction* **365**

Limelight Management ... L400
MacKenzie, Joanna ... L416
Maclean, Jamie ... L417
Marr, Jill ... L425
Maurer, Shari ... L433
Milusich, Grace ... L453
Mortimer, Michele ... L462
Mustelier, James ... L471
Mysterious Press, The ... P309
Mystery Magazine ... M250
Nathan, Abigail ... L475
NBM Publishing ... P312
Niumata, Erin ... L480
Oghma Creative Media ... P321
Orenda Books ... P329
Ostby, Kristin ... L494
Pages, Saribel ... L496
Parker, Elana Roth ... L499
Pass, Marina de ... L500
Paul S. Levine Literary Agency ... L502
Pen & Ink Designs Publishing ... P342
Penzler Publishers ... P345
Pestritto, Carrie ... L511
Pierce, Rosie ... L517
Pine, Gideon ... L518
Plant, Zoe ... L519
Posner, Marcy ... L522
Ravenstone ... P374
Reid, Janet ... L532
Reino, Jessica ... L534
Ruppin Agency, The ... L555
Salazar, Des ... L559
Sheil Land Associates Ltd ... L577
Shestopal, Camilla ... L581
Soloway, Jennifer March ... L590
Steed, Hayley ... L595
Story Unlikely ... M356
Strachan Literary Agency ... L602
Stringer, Marlene ... L604
Takikawa, Marin ... L618
Tibbets, Anne ... L630
Tor Publishing Group ... P456
Torrey House Press, LLC ... P459
Tran, Jennifer Chen ... L633
Trudel, Jes ... L634
Turner Publishing ... P462
Tyndale House Publishers, Inc. ... P465
Udden, Jennifer ... L637
University of Wisconsin Press, The ... P490
Victoria Sanders & Associates LLC ... L642
Vinspire Publishing ... P497
W.W. Norton & Company, Inc. ... P500
Weiss, Alexandra ... L650
Williams, Laura ... L662
WordCrafts Press ... P514
Yours Fiction – Women's Special Series ... M417
Zack Company, Inc, The ... L678

Mysticism
See more broadly: Supernatural / Paranormal
See more specifically: Fortune Telling and Divination
Dawntreader, The ... M115

NASCAR
See more broadly: Motorsports

Narrative Essays
See more broadly: Narrative Nonfiction
See more specifically: Personal Essays
Hawthorne Books ... P209
Native Ink Press ... P311
Otago University Press ... P330
Plitt, Carrie ... L520

Narrative History
See more broadly: History; Narrative Nonfiction
Dawson, Liza ... L162
Dixon, Isobel ... L171
Dolby, Trevor ... L173

Narrative Journalism
See more broadly: Journalism; Narrative Nonfiction
Mendia, Isabel ... L441
Strothman, Wendy ... L608

Narrative Nonfiction
See more specifically: Narrative Essays; Narrative History; Narrative Journalism
Adams, Seren ... L005
Adsett, Alex ... L006
Alex Adsett Literary ... L016
And Other Stories ... P025
Andrade, Hannah ... L023
Andrew, Nelle ... L025
Armstrong, Susan ... L032
Arthurson, Wayne ... L033
Asabi Publishing ... P034
Bal, Emma ... L038
Bartholomew, Jason ... L047
Bates, Tim ... L048
Baumer, Jan ... L051
Berdinsky, Kendall ... L060
Betsy Amster Literary Enterprises ... L063
Bowlin, Sarah ... L073
Brattesani, Hannah ... L079
Brouckaert, Justin ... L087
Bucci, Chris ... L090
Capron, Elise ... L104
Carr, Jamie ... L108
Caskie, Robert ... L113
Cassell ... P096
Chanchani, Sonali ... L115
Chiotti, Danielle ... L123
Cho, Catherine ... L124
Clarke, Caro ... L128
Cochran, Alexander ... L130
Combemale, Chris ... L133
Concepcion, Cristina ... L135
Coombs Moylett & Maclean Literary Agency ... L139
Curran, Sabhbh ... L145
Dana Newman Literary, LLC ... L152
Daunt Books Publishing ... P134
Diana Finch Literary Agency ... L167
Dominguez, Adriana ... L174
Doubleday (UK) ... P143
Dunham Literary, Inc. ... L179
Dunham, Jennie ... L180
Dunn, Ben ... L181
Ellis-Martin, Sian ... L197
Evans, Kate ... L204
Evans, Kiya ... L205
Evans, Stephany ... L206
Fairbank Literary Representation ... L208
Ferguson, Hannah ... L217
Fogg, Jack ... L230
Fox, Aram ... L234
Frances Collin Literary Agent ... L237
Freymann, Sarah Jane ... L242
Friedman, Claire ... L243
Galustian, Natalie ... L251
Garamond Agency, Inc., The ... L253
Gauntlett, Adam ... L254
Gillam, Bianca ... L259
Gordon, Andrew ... L270
Grimm, Katie ... L279
Gruber, Pam ... L281
Hannah Sheppard Literary Agency ... L291
Hardman, Caroline ... L295
Harris, Erin ... L300
Hayden, Viola ... L305
Hobbs, Victoria ... L314
Holloway, Sally ... L318
Hwang, Annie ... L322
Irving, Dotti ... L326
Jeff Herman Agency, LLC, The ... L331
Joelle Delbourgo Associates, Inc. ... L334
Kahn, Jody ... L346
Kardon, Julia ... L350
Kotchman, Katie ... L374
Krienke, Mary ... L375
Lambert, Sophie ... L380
Latshaw, Katherine ... L386
Leigh Feldman Literary ... L393
Levitt, Sarah ... L396
Lightner, Kayla ... L399
Loughman, Morwenna ... L408
MacDonald, Emily ... L412
Macdougall, Laura ... L413
MacLeod, Lauren ... L418
Maidment, Olivia ... L421
Malahat Review, The ... M232
Maltese, Alyssa ... L422
Marr, Jill ... L425
Marshall, Jen ... L427
Marsiglia, Caroline ... L428
Massie, Maria ... L430
Maurer, Shari ... L433
Maw, Jane Graham ... L434
McCormick Literary ... L436
Mileo, Jessica ... L451
Mills, Rachel ... L452
Miranda, Caroline ... L454
Molloy, Jess ... L456
Moorhead, Max ... L459
Morrell, Imogen ... L460
Mortimer, Michele ... L462
Mundy, Toby ... L466
Murgolo, Karen ... L467
Niumata, Erin ... L480
O'Grady, Faith ... L485
O'Grady, Niamh ... L486
O'Neill, Molly ... L487
Pan Macmillan Australia ... P335
Pande, Ayesha ... L497
Pass, Marina de ... L500
Patterson, Emma ... L501
Peddle, Kay ... L503
Perry Literary ... L509
Pestritto, Carrie ... L511
Phillips, Aemilia ... L515
Pickering, Juliet ... L516
Pierce, Rosie ... L517
Pine, Gideon ... L518
Plitt, Carrie ... L520
Polygon ... P360
Posner, Marcy ... L522
Prasanna, Tanusri ... L525
Preston, Amanda ... L526
Ramer, Susan ... L528
Regina Ryan Books ... L531
Reid, Janet ... L532
Richter, Rick ... L537
Roberts, Soumeya Bendimerad ... L540
Robinson, Quressa ... L542
Ruppin Agency, The ... L555
Rutman, Jim ... L558
Salt Publishing ... P389
Sarah Jane Freymann Literary Agency ... L564
Schofield, Hannah ... L567
Selectric Artists ... L573
Serra, Maria Cardona ... L574
Shaw Agency, The ... L576
Shestopal, Camilla ... L581
Sierra ... M336
Silk, Julia ... L583
Simpson, Cara Lee ... L586
Steerforth Press ... P428
Stephens, Jenny ... L596
Stewart, Douglas ... L599
Story Unlikely ... M356

Strothman, Wendy L608
Swainson, Joanna L613
Tahoma Literary Review M368
Takikawa, Marin L618
Terlip, Paige L624
Vance, Lisa Erbach..................................L641
Viney Agency, The..................................L643
Weitzner, Tess..L651
Wells, Karmen...L652
Whatnall, Michaela.................................L655
Williams, Laura.......................................L662
Willms, Kathryn L665
Wilson, Desiree.......................................L667
Woollard, Jessica L672
Writer's Side L674

National Security
See more broadly: Warfare
University of Georgia Press....................P479
Zack Company, Inc, The L678

Native Americans
See more broadly: Ethnic Groups
Sunbelt Publications, Inc. P433
University of Alberta Press.....................P477
University of Massachusetts Press..........P482
University of Michigan Press, The.........P483
University of Wisconsin Press, The P490
University Press of Colorado..................P491
Zack Company, Inc, The L678

Nature
See more specifically: Animals; Environment
Adams, Seren L005
AdventureKEEN P013
Arcadia Publishing P031
Atyeo, Charlotte L034
Autumn Publishing Ltd P042
Bajek, Lauren..L037
Bal, Emma L038
Barr, Anjanette..L045
Basalt Books..P057
Bates, Tim L048
Bernardi, Amanda L062
Birlinn Ltd...P067
Brannan, Maria L078
Britain Magazine M075
Caskie, Robert...L113
Charlesbridge Publishing........................P102
Chase Literary Agency L118
Clarke, Caro L128
Clarke, Catherine....................................L129
Compassiviste Publishing P121
Conrad, Claire Paterson..........................L136
Conville, Clare..L137
Cottage Life M099
Crystal Magazine....................................M110
Dawntreader, The M115
Dolby, Trevor..L173
Dunn, Ben L181
Edwards, Max...L190
Elliott & Thompson P149
Evans, David...L203
Evans, Kate L204
Fogg, Jack L230
Fox, Aram L234
Frances Collin Literary Agent L237
Frances Goldin Literary Agency, Inc.....L238
Freymann, Sarah Jane L242
Gill Books P181
Globe Pequot Press, The.........................P184
Goldstein, Veronica L268
Graffeg..P190
Granta Books..P192
Harvard University Press P206
History Press, The P221
Hobbs, Victoria.......................................L314
Icon Books Ltd P227
Imagine Publishing.................................P234

Irish Pages...M203
Island Online...M205
Jonathan Pegg Literary Agency..............L337
Kantor, Camille L349
Kate Barker Literary, TV, & Film
  Agency...L352
Kensington Publishing Corp. P253
Kent Life...M209
Lambert, Sophie......................................L380
Laurence King Publishing......................P261
Laxfield Literary Associates L387
Lewinsohn Literary L397
Lilliput Press, The...................................P268
Limelight Management L400
Lutterworth Press, The...........................P275
MacDonald, Emily..................................L412
Macdougall, Laura..................................L413
Maltese, Alyssa.......................................L422
Morrell, Imogen......................................L460
Mortimer, Michele..................................L462
Ohio University Press P324
Oneworld Publications...........................P327
Otago University Press...........................P330
Panorama M274
Peddle, Kay L503
Pineapple Press.......................................P356
Plitt, Carrie..L520
Pocket Mountains P359
Polygon P360
Posner, Marcy...L522
Preston, Amanda.....................................L526
Regina Ryan Books L531
Reilly, Milly L533
River Hills Traveler................................M313
Roberts, Soumeya Bendimerad...............L540
Rocky Mountain Books..........................P378
Ruppin Agency, The...............................L555
Rutherford, Laetitia................................L557
Salt Publishing P389
Sasquatch Books.....................................P391
Science Factory, The...............................L569
Scoular, Rosemary..................................L570
Seymour, Charlotte L575
Sierra M336
Simpson, Cara Lee..................................L586
Stephens, Jenny.......................................L596
Strothman, Wendy..................................L608
Sunbelt Publications, Inc........................P433
Swainson, Joanna L613
Texas A&M University Press.................P445
This England...M376
Thorneycroft, Euan.................................L628
Topping, Antony.....................................L632
Turner Publishing P462
Two Fine Crows Books P464
University of Alaska Press P476
University of Alberta Press.....................P477
University of Georgia Press....................P479
University of Iowa Press P480
University of Michigan Press, The.........P483
University of Nevada Press....................P484
University of North Texas Press.............P485
University of Texas Press.......................P488
University of Virginia Press...................P489
VanderWyk & Burnham.........................P494
W.W. Norton & Company Ltd...............P499
Washington State University Press........P501
Welsh Country..M399
Wide-Eyed Editions................................P509
Williams, Sarah......................................L663
Willms, Kathryn.....................................L665
Wilson, Ed L668
Yeoh, Rachel...L675
Zack Company, Inc, The L678

Nautical
Adlard Coles P012

Oghma Creative Media...........................P321
Neurobiology
See more broadly: Biology
W.W. Norton & Company Ltd P499
Neurodiversity
See more broadly: Psychology
See more specifically: ADHD
Neuropsychology
See more broadly: Psychology
See more specifically: Autism
W.W. Norton & Company Ltd P499
Neuroscience
See more broadly: Science
Buckley, Louise L091
W.W. Norton & Company Ltd P499
Nevada
See more broadly: United States
University of Nevada Press....................P484
New Adult
Acheampong, Kwaku L004
Barone Literary Agency L043
Brannan, Maria L078
Dunham, Jennie......................................L180
Fazzari, Hillary.......................................L210
Finch, Rebeka L225
Harmony Ink Press P205
Leon, Nina L394
Lineberry, Isabel.....................................L402
Madeleine Milburn Literary, TV &
  Film Agency L420
Oghma Creative Media...........................P321
Preston, Amanda.....................................L526
Salazar, Des L559
Soler, Shania N.......................................L589
Tran, Jennifer Chen L633
New Age
See more broadly: Spirituality
Compassiviste Publishing P121
Danko, Margaret.....................................L154
Hay House Publishers............................P210
Lutterworth Press, The...........................P275
New Brunswick
See more broadly: Canada
Goose Lane Editions...............................P188
New England
See more broadly: United States
University of Massachusetts Press..........P482
Yankee Magazine M410
New Jersey
See more broadly: United States
New York City
See more broadly: New York State
New York State
See more broadly: United States
See more specifically: New York City; Westchester County
New Zealand
See more broadly: Australasia / Oceania
Landfall..M215
Takahe..M369
News
Accountancy Daily M011
Astronomy Now M034
Atlanta Magazine M035
Balance...M044
BBC Science Focus M050
Bluegrass Unlimited M069
Campaign M079
Conversation (UK), The.........................M095
Crystal Magazine....................................M110
Economist, The.......................................M126
Facts & Fiction M135
Forty20 ....M150
Funeral Business Solutions.....................M156
Insurance Age...M199
Jazz Journal M206
New Internationalist M256

Access more listings online at www.firstwriter.com

OK! Magazine M266
PC Gamer M278
Practising Midwife, The M295
Pride M298
Racecar Engineering M304
River Hills Traveler M313
Rugby World M317
Scottish Farmer, The M325
Spa Magazine M350
Speciality Food M351
Supplement, The M365
That's Life! M373
Wallace Stevens Journal, The M396
Welsh Country M399

Noir
See more broadly: Crime
Asabi Publishing P034
Future Fire, The M158
Kane Literary Agency L348
Ravenstone P374

Nonfiction
23 House Publishing P001
30 North M002
32 Poems M003
404 Ink P002
417 Magazine M004
4RV Publishing P004
4RV Tenacious P005
A-R Editions P006
A.M. Heath & Company Limited,
   Author's Agents L002
aaduna M005
AARP The Magazine M006
ABC-CLIO P008
Able Muse Press P009
About Place Journal M007
Abuzz Press P010
Account, The M009
Accountancy Age M010
Accountancy Daily M011
Acheampong, Kwaku L004
Acumen M012
Adams, Seren L005
Adlard Coles P012
Adsett, Alex L006
AdventureKEEN P013
African American Review M014
Agni M016
Agricultural History M017
Air & Space Quarterly M018
Alaska Quarterly Review M019
Alcock, Michael L014
Alex Adsett Literary L016
Algonquin Books P016
Alice Williams Literary L017
Alive Literary Agency L018
Allen & Unwin P018
Allison & Busby Ltd P019
Alternating Current Press P020
Amato Books P021
Ambassador Speakers Bureau &
   Literary Agency L019
Amber Books Ltd P022
Ambrosi, Beniamino L020
American Book Review M022
Amethyst Review M024
Amling, Eric L021
Ammonite Press P024
And Other Stories P025
Andrade, Hannah L023
Andrew Nurnberg Associates, Ltd ... L024
Andrew, Nelle L025
Andrews McMeel Publishing P026
Anne Clark Literary Agency L028
Antigonish Review, The M026
Antony Harwood Limited L029

Anvil Press Publishers P028
Apa Publications Group P029
Arboreal M027
Arc M028
Arcadia Publishing P031
Architectural Review, The M029
Arms, Victoria Wells L031
Arsenal Pulp Press P032
Art Monthly M030
Art Papers M031
Art Quarterly M032
Arte Publico Press P033
Arthurson, Wayne L033
Asabi Publishing P034
Ascend Books, LLC P035
Astronomy Now M034
Atlanta Magazine M035
Atlantic Northeast M037
Atyeo, Charlotte L034
Aurora Metro Press P039
Auroras & Blossoms PoArtMo
   Anthology M039
Authentic Life M041
Autumn Publishing Ltd P042
Babybug M041
Backbeat Books P046
Bacopa Literary Review M042
Badger Learning P048
Baffler, The M043
Bajek, Lauren L037
Bal, Emma L038
Balance M044
Bald and Bonkers Network LLC P050
Balow, Dan L039
Banipal M046
Banter Press P053
Baobab Press P054
Barbara, Stephen L041
Barbour Publishing P056
Baror International, Inc. L044
Barr, Anjanette L045
Barr, Nicola L046
Barren Magazine M047
Bartholomew, Jason L047
Basalt Books P057
Basic Books P058
Basic Health Publications, Inc. P059
Bates, Tim L048
Bath Literary Agency L049
Baumer, Jan L051
Baxter, Veronique L052
Baylor University Press P060
BBC Doctor Who Magazine M048
BBC History Magazine M049
BBC Science Focus M050
Bear Deluxe Magazine, The M052
Begum, Salma L053
Bella M053
Belmont Story Review M054
Belton, Maddy L055
Bent Agency (UK), The L057
Bent Agency, The L058
Bent, Jenny L059
Bentley Publishers P061
Berdinsky, Kendall L060
Berghahn Books Ltd P062
Bernardi, Amanda L062
Berrett-Koehler Publishers P063
Bess Press P064
Best of British M056
Betsy Amster Literary Enterprises .. L063
Better Homes and Gardens M057
Better Than Starbucks M058
BFI Publishing P065
BFS Journal M060
Big Fiction M061

Bird Eye Books P066
Birds & Blooms M062
Birlinn Ltd P067
Black Belt M063
Black Moon Magazine M064
Black Warrior Review M066
Blackstaff Press P068
Blake Friedmann Literary Agency Ltd L066
Bloodhound Books P070
Bloomsbury Academic P071
Bloomsbury Professional P072
Blue Earth Review M067
Blue Mesa Review M068
Blue Poppy Enterprises P074
Blue Star Press P075
Bluegrass Unlimited M069
BOA Editions, Ltd P076
Boathooks Books P077
Bookseller, The M070
Borstel, Stefanie Sanchez Von L071
Boston Review M071
Bowhunter M072
Bowlin, Sarah L073
Boyfriend Village M073
Bradford Literary Agency L075
Bradford, Laura L076
Brailsford, Karen L077
Brannan, Maria L078
Brattesani, Hannah L079
Brattle Agency LLC, The L080
Brewin Books Ltd P081
Brick M074
Bright Agency (UK), The L082
Bright Agency (US), The L083
Bright Press P082
Britain Magazine M075
British Academy, The P083
British Museum Press, The P084
Broadview Press P085
Brooks, Savannah L084
Brotherstone Creative Management L085
Brotherstone, Charlie L086
Brouckaert, Justin L087
Brown, Megan L088
Brown, Son & Ferguson, Ltd P086
Browne & Miller Literary Associates L089
Bucci, Chris L090
Buckley, Louise L091
Bukowski, Danielle L092
Burns, Camille L094
Business Traveller M076
C&T Publishing P088
C&W (Conville & Walsh) L096
CAA (London) L098
Caitlin Press Inc. P090
Campaign M079
Campbell, Charlie L099
Campos, Vanessa L100
Candy Jar Books P093
Canterbury Literary Agency L101
Canterbury Press P094
Capron, Elise L104
Captivate Press P095
Carolina Woman M080
Carr, Jamie L108
Carr, Michael L109
Carroll, Megan L110
Carter, Rebecca L111
Cartey, Claire L112
Caskie, Robert L113
Cassell P096
Cavanagh, Claire L114
CGI (Chartered Governance Institute)
   Publishing P098
Chanchani, Sonali L115
Chang, Nicola L116

Chapman	M081
Charisma House	P100
Charles River Press	P101
Charlesbridge Publishing	P102
Charlesbridge Teen	P103
CharlottesvilleFamily	M082
Charnace, Edwina de	L117
Chartered Institute of Personnel and Development (CIPD) Publishing	P104
Chase Literary Agency	L118
Chautauqua Literary Journal	M083
Chelsea House Publishers	P105
Cherry Lake Publishing Group	P106
Cheshire	M084
Chevais, Jennifer	L122
Chiotti, Danielle	L123
Cho, Catherine	L124
Christie, Jennifer	L126
ChristLight Books	P110
Chronicle Books LLC	P111
Cincinnati Review, The	M086
Cinnamon Press	P112
Claret Press	P113
Clarke, Caro	L128
Clarke, Catherine	L129
Cleis Press	P115
Coaches Choice	P116
Cobblestone	M087
Cochran, Alexander	L130
Cocoa Girl	M088
Coil, The	M089
College Press Publishing	P117
Collins	P118
Colourpoint Educational	P119
Colwill, Charlotte	L132
Combemale, Chris	L133
Commonweal	M091
Comparato, Andrea	L134
Compassiviste Publishing	P121
Concepcion, Cristina	L135
Concho River Review	M092
Conjunctions	M093
Conjunctions Online	M094
Conrad, Claire Paterson	L136
Conversation (UK), The	M095
Conville, Clare	L137
Coombs Moylett & Maclean Literary Agency	L139
Cooper, Gemma	L140
Cooper, Maggie	L141
Cornell Maritime Press	P123
Corridor of Uncertainty, The	M097
Cotswold Life	M098
Cottage Life	M099
Country Smallholding	M100
Countryside Books	P124
Cowboys & Indians	M101
Coyote Arts	P125
Crab Orchard Review	M102
Crabtree Publishing	P126
Crandall, Becca	L142
Crazyhorse / Swamp Pink	M104
Cream City Review	M105
Creative Nonfiction	M106
Creem	M107
Critical Quarterly	M108
Croner-i Limited	P127
Crossway	P128
Crowley, Sheila	L144
Crown	P129
Crown Publishing Group, The	P131
Cruising World	M109
Crystal Magazine	M110
Curran, Sabhbh	L145
Curtis Brown	L146
Curtis Brown (Australia) Pty Ltd	L147
CutBank	M111
Cynthia Cannell Literary Agency	L150
Dalhousie Review, The	M113
Dana Newman Literary, LLC	L152
Danaczko, Melissa	L153
Danko, Margaret	L154
Darga, Jon Michael	L155
Darhansoff & Verrill Literary Agents	L156
Daunt Books Publishing	P134
David Godwin Associates	L158
Dawntreader, The	M115
Dawson, Liza	L162
DeBlock, Liza	L163
Denis Kitchen Publishing Company Co., LLC	P138
Derviskadic, Dado	L164
Descent	M118
Devon Life	M119
DeVorss & Company	P139
DHH Literary Agency Ltd	L166
Diana Finch Literary Agency	L167
Dickerson, Donya	L168
Dijkstra, Sandra	L169
Dillsworth, Elise	L170
Diver	M120
Dixon, Isobel	L171
DK Publishing	P141
Dolby, Trevor	L173
Dominguez, Adriana	L174
Don Congdon Associates, Inc.	L175
Donald Maass Literary Agency	L176
Doubleday (UK)	P143
Doug Grad Literary Agency	L177
Draper, Claire	L178
Dream Catcher	M123
Dublin Review, The	M124
Duncan Petersen Publishing Limited	P146
Dunham Literary, Inc.	L179
Dunham, Jennie	L180
Dunn, Ben	L181
DunnFogg	L182
Dunow, Carlson & Lerner Agency	L184
Dynasty Press	P147
Eason, Lynette	L186
Eberly, Chelsea	L187
Economist, The	M126
Ecotone	M127
Edenborough, Sam	L189
Edwards, Max	L190
Eerdmans Books for Young Readers	P148
Eisenmann, Caroline	L192
Ekphrastic Review, The	M128
Ekus Group, The	L193
Ekus, Sally	L194
El Portal	M129
Elaine Markson Literary Agency	L195
Elaine Steel	L196
Elliott & Thompson	P149
Ellis-Martin, Sian	L197
Ellor, Zabé	L198
Elsevier Ltd	P150
Emily Sweet Associates	L199
Encyclopedia Britannica (UK) Ltd	P151
Engram Books	P152
Enitharmon Editions	P153
Enslow Publishers, Inc.	P154
Entrepreneur	M131
EPTA Books	P155
Ericka T. Phillips	L200
Essex Life	M132
Evan Marshall Agency, The	L202
Evan-Moor Educational Publishers	P157
Evans, David	L203
Evans, Kate	L204
Evans, Kiya	L205
Evans, Stephany	L206
Event	M133
Facet Publishing	P159
Facts & Fiction	M135
Fairbank Literary Representation	L208
Fate	M136
Faulks, Holly	L209
Faultline	M137
Fazzari, Hillary	L210
Fee: Foundation for Economic Education	M138
Feldstein Agency, The	L213
Felicia Eth Literary Representation	L214
Felicity Bryan Associates	L215
Fellows, Abi	L216
Feminist Press, The	P163
Feminist Studies	M139
Ferguson, Hannah	L217
Fernandez, Rochelle	L220
Fernwood Publishing	P164
Fiddlehead, The	M141
Fighting High	P165
Filter Press	P166
Finan, Ciara	L223
Finegan, Stevie	L226
First For Women	M142
First Line, The	M143
Fiscal Publications	P168
Five Points	M144
Flaneur	M145
Flannery Literary	L228
Flyfishing & Tying Journal	M146
Fogg, Jack	L230
Folio	M147
Forrester, Jemima	L232
Fortean Times: The Journal of Strange Phenomena	M148
Fortnightly Review, The	M149
Fortress Press	P170
Forty20	M150
Foundation: The International Review of Science Fiction	M151
Fourth River, The	M153
Fox, Aram	L234
Foxx, Kat	L235
FRA (Futerman, Rose, & Associates)	L236
Frances Collin Literary Agent	L237
Frances Goldin Literary Agency, Inc.	L238
Frankel, Valerie	L239
Fraser Ross Associates	L240
Free Association Books Ltd	P173
Free Spirit Publishing	P174
Fresh Words – An International Literary Magazine	M154
Freymann, Sarah Jane	L242
Friedman, Claire	L243
Friedman, Rebecca	L244
Friedrich Agency LLC, The	L245
Friends United Press	P175
Frog Literary Agency	L246
Fuentes, Sarah	L247
Fugue	M155
Funeral Business Solutions	M156
Furniss, Eugenie	L249
Future Fire, The	M158
Gahan, Isobel	L250
Gale	P177
Galustian, Natalie	L251
Galvin, Lori	L252
Garamond Agency, Inc., The	L253
Garden Answers	M159
Garden News	M160
Gauntlett, Adam	L254
Geared Up Publications	P178
Geiger, Ellen	L255
Geographical Journal, The	M162
Georgia Review, The	M163

Index | Nonfiction

Gertrude	M164
Gertrude Press	P179
Getzler, Josh	L256
Ghahremani, Lilly	L257
Gill Books	P181
Gill Education	P182
Gillam, Bianca	L259
Ginosko Literary Journal	M165
Glass Literary Management LLC	L262
Glenister, Emily	L263
Global Lion Intellectual Property Management, Inc.	L264
Globe Pequot Press, The	P184
Go World Travel Magazine	M167
Goff, Anthony	L266
Goff, Ellen	L267
Goldsmiths Press	P186
Goldstein, Veronica	L268
Good Homes	M168
Good Literary Agency, The	L269
Good Ski Guide, The	M169
Goodman Beck Publishing	P187
Goose Lane Editions	P188
Gordon, Andrew	L270
Goss & Crested China Club	P189
Graffeg	P190
Graffeg Childrens	P191
Graham Maw Christie Literary Agency	L271
Graham, Stacey	L272
Grain Literary Magazine	M170
Grajkowski, Michelle	L274
Granger, David	L275
Granta	M171
Granta Books	P192
Graywolf Lab	M172
Graywolf Press	P193
Greene & Heaton Ltd	L276
Greenstreet, Katie	L277
Greyhound Literary	L278
Grimm, Katie	L279
Grossman, Loren R.	L280
Gruber, Pam	L281
Grunewald, Hattie	L282
Guinness World Records	P194
Guinsler, Robert	L283
Gulf Coast: A Journal of Literature and Fine Arts	M173
Gutter Magazine	M174
Hachette Book Group	P196
Haley, Jolene	L289
Half Mystic Journal	M175
Half Mystic Press	P197
Hammersmith Books	P198
Hanbury Agency, The	L290
Hannah Sheppard Literary Agency	L291
Hannigan, Carrie	L292
Hansen, Stephanie	L293
Happy Yak	P200
Hardie Grant UK	P201
Hardman, Caroline	L295
Hare, Jessica	L296
Harmsworth, Esmond	L297
Harold Ober Associates, Inc.	L298
Harper's Magazine	M178
Harpur Palate	M179
Harris, Erin	L300
Harvard University Press	P206
Hashtag Press	P207
Haus Publishing	P208
Hawk, Susan	L303
Hawn, Molly Ker	L304
Hawthorne Books	P209
Hay House Publishers	P210
Hayden, Viola	L305
Hazel Press	P211
Healthy	M180
Helix, The	M183
Henley Hall Press	P214
Here Comes Everyone	M184
Hernando, Paloma	L308
Heymont, Lane	L309
High Stakes Publishing	P216
High Tide Press	P217
Hippocrene Books, Inc.	P219
History Press, The	P221
History Today	M186
Hiyate, Sam	L313
Hobbs, Victoria	L314
Hodder & Stoughton Ltd	P222
Hoffman, Scott	L316
Holloway, Sally	L318
Holroyde, Penny	L319
Homes & Antiques	M187
Hordern, Kate	L320
Hornsley, Sarah	L321
Horse & Rider	M188
Hotel Amerika	M189
Howgate Publishing	P225
Hudson Review, The	M190
Hunger Mountain	M191
Hwang, Annie	L322
Icon Books Ltd	P227
Idaho Review	M193
Identity Theory	M194
Idyll Arbor	P229
Ig Publishing	P230
Igloo Books Limited	P232
Image	M195
Imagine Publishing	P234
Indiana Review	M196
Indiana University Press	P235
Influx Press	P237
Information Today, Inc.	P238
Ink Sweat and Tears	M197
Inkandescent	P240
Inque	M198
Inscriptions Literary Agency	L323
Insurance Age	M199
International Piano	M200
International Society for Technology in Education (ISTE)	P242
InterVarsity Press (IVP)	P243
Ireland's Own	M202
Irene Goodman Literary Agency (IGLA)	L324
Irish Pages	M203
Irving, Dotti	L326
Island	M204
Island Online	M205
Jacobson, Rachel	L328
Jain Publishing Company, Inc.	P244
Jamii Publishing	P245
Janklow & Nesbit UK Ltd	L330
Jazz Journal	M206
Jeff Herman Agency, LLC, The	L331
Jessica Kingsley Publishers	P246
JMD Media / DB Publishing	P247
Jo Unwin Literary Agency	L333
Joelle Delbourgo Associates, Inc.	L334
John Murray Press	P249
Johns Hopkins University Press, The	P250
Jonathan Clowes Ltd	L336
Jonathan Pegg Literary Agency	L337
Journal, The	M207
Joy Harris Literary Agency, Inc.	L340
Kahn, Ella Diamond	L345
Kahn, Jody	L346
Kane Press	P251
Kantor, Camille	L349
Kardon, Julia	L350
Karinch, Maryann	L351
Kate Barker Literary, TV, & Film Agency	L352
Kate Nash Literary Agency	L353
Kates Hill Press, The	P252
Kathryn Green Literary Agency, LLC	L354
Kavya Kishor	M208
Kellerman, Carly	L360
Kensington Publishing Corp.	P253
Kent Life	M209
Kenyon Review, The	M210
Keren, Eli	L362
Kerning	M211
Ki Agency Ltd	L364
Kids Alive!	M212
Killingley, Jessica	L365
Kim, Jennifer	L366
Kim, Julia	L367
Kimber, Natalie	L368
Kimberley Cameron & Associates	L369
Kirby, Robert	L370
Kitchen Press	P254
Knight Features	L373
Kogan Page Ltd	P255
Kore Press	P256
Korero Press	P257
Kotchman, Katie	L374
Krienke, Mary	L375
Kruger Cowne	L376
Kube Publishing	P258
Labyrinth Literary Agency, The	L378
Lakosil, Natalie	L379
Lambert, Sophie	L380
Lancashire Life	M214
Landfall	M215
Langmarc Publishing	P259
Langtons International	L384
Langtry, Elena	L385
Lantana Publishing	P260
Latshaw, Katherine	L386
Laurence King Publishing	P261
Laxfield Literary Associates	L387
Lazin, Sarah	L388
Leamington Books	P262
Leapfrog Press	P263
Lechon, Shannon	L390
Lees, Jordan	L392
Leigh Feldman Literary	L393
Leisure Group Travel	M216
Leisure Painter	M217
Lerner Publishing Group	P264
Levitt, Sarah	L396
Lewinsohn Literary	L397
Lewis, Alison	L398
LexisNexis	P265
Lightner, Kayla	L399
Liguori Publications	P267
Lilliput Press, The	P268
Limelight Management	L400
Linguist, The	M219
Liss, Laurie	L403
Literary Mama	M220
Litro Magazine	M221
Liza Dawson Associates	L405
Llewellyn Worldwide Ltd	P269
Loft Press, Inc.	P270
Logaston Press	P271
London Grip	M222
London Grip New Poetry	M223
London Magazine, The	M224
London Review of Books	M225
Long Poem Magazine	M226
Lost Lake Folk Opera Magazine	M227
Lotus Lane Literary	L407
Loughman, Morwenna	L408
Louisiana Literature	M228
Lovell, Jake	L409

Loyola Press	P272
LSU Press	P273
Lund Humphries Limited	P274
Lutterworth Press, The	P275
Lutyens and Rubinstein	L410
LW Books	P276
M. Evans & Company	P278
MacDonald, Emily	L412
Macdougall, Laura	L413
MacGregor & Luedeke	L414
MacGuffin, The	M229
Mack, Kate	L415
Maclean, Jamie	L417
MacLeod, Lauren	L418
Madan, Neeti	L419
Madeleine Milburn Literary, TV & Film Agency	L420
Magma	M231
Maidment, Olivia	L421
Malahat Review, The	M232
Maltese, Alyssa	L422
Manilla Press	P280
Manoa	M233
marie claire	M234
marie claire (UK)	M235
Marion Boyars Publishers	P282
Marlin	M236
Marr, Jill	L425
Marsh Agency, The	L426
Marshall, Jen	L427
Marsiglia, Caroline	L428
Massachusetts Review, The	M237
Massie, Maria	L430
Maurer, Shari	L433
Maw, Jane Graham	L434
McCormick Literary	L436
McGraw Hill EMEA	P285
McNicol, Andy	L437
McNidder & Grace	P286
McQuilkin, Rob	L438
Medical Physics Publishing	P288
Medina Publishing	P289
Mehren, Jane von	L440
Menasha Ridge Press	P290
Mendia, Isabel	L441
Mensch Publishing	P291
Mentor Books	P292
Meridian Artists	L442
Merriam Press	P293
Merullo, Annabel	L443
Metamorphosis Literary Agency	L444
Methuen Publishing Ltd	P294
Metro Publications Ltd	P295
Metropolis Magazine	M239
Mic Cheetham Literary Agency	L445
Michel, Caroline	L446
Michigan Quarterly Review	M240
Mid-American Review	M241
Midsummer Dream House	M242
Midway Journal	M243
Mihell, Natasha	L448
Mildred Marmur Associates, Ltd.	L450
Mileo, Jessica	L451
Milkweed Editions	P296
Mills, Rachel	L452
MiniWorld Magazine	M244
Minnesota Historical Society Press	P299
Miranda, Caroline	L454
Mirror Books	P301
Missouri Historical Society Press	P302
Missouri Review, The	M245
MIT Press, The	P303
MMB Creative	L455
Molloy, Jess	L456
Monacelli Press, The	P304
Moody Publishers	P305
Moore, Penny	L458
Moorhead, Max	L459
Morrell, Imogen	L460
Mortimer, Michele	L462
Movable Type Management	L464
Moving Worlds: A Journal of Transcultural Writings	M247
Mundy, Toby	L466
Murdoch Books Australia	P308
Murgolo, Karen	L467
Murray, Judith	L468
Muscato, Nate	L469
Musteleir, James	L471
My Weekly	M249
NAHB BuilderBooks	P310
Nash, Justin	L474
Nashville Review	M251
Native Ink Press	P311
NB Magazine	M252
NBM Publishing	P312
Nell James Publishers	P313
New England Review	M255
New Harbinger Publications	P314
New Internationalist	M256
New Orleans Review	M257
New Statesman	M258
New Welsh Reader	M259
Nichols, Mariah	L479
Niumata, Erin	L480
No Starch Press, Inc.	P318
Nolan, Laura	L481
Norfolk & Suffolk Bride	M260
Northbank Talent Management	L482
Nosy Crow	P319
O'Grady, Faith	L485
O'Grady, Niamh	L486
O'Neill, Molly	L487
O'Shea, Amy	L488
Oak Tree Press	P320
Oakland Arts Review, The	M264
Oghma Creative Media	P321
Ogtrop, Kristin van	L489
Ohio State University Press, The	P323
Ohio University Press	P324
OK! Magazine	M266
Old Street Publishing Ltd	P325
Oldcastle Books Group	P326
Oneworld Publications	P327
Ooligan Press	P328
Orbis International Literary Journal	M269
Otago University Press	P330
Ouen Press	P331
Oxbow Books	P333
Oxford Poetry	M270
Oxford Review of Books	M271
Oyez Review	M272
Pacific Press Publishing Association	P334
Pacifica Literary Review	M273
Pan Macmillan Australia	P335
Pande, Ayesha	L497
Panorama	M274
Paradigm Talent and Literary Agency	L498
Paris Review, The	M275
Park Home and Holiday Living	M276
Parthian Books	P336
Pass, Marina de	L500
Passionfruit Review, The	M277
Patrician Press	P337
Patterson, Emma	L501
Paul S. Levine Literary Agency	L502
Pavilion Books	P338
PC Gamer	M278
PC Pro	M279
Peddle, Kay	L503
Peepal Tree Press	P341
Pelham, Imogen	L504
Pen & Ink Designs Publishing	P342
Pen & Sword Books Ltd	P343
Pennine Ink Magazine	M280
Pensacola Magazine	M281
People's Friend, The	M283
Perez Literary & Entertainment	L506
Perez, Kristina	L507
Perotto-Wills, Martha	L508
Perry Literary	L509
Pestritto, Carrie	L511
Peter Lang	P346
Peter Lang Publishing	P348
Peter Owen Publishers	P349
Peter Pauper Press	P350
Petty, Rachel	L512
Phelan, Beth	L514
Phillips, Aemilia	L515
Piatkus Books	P352
Pickering, Juliet	L516
Pierce, Rosie	L517
Pilot	M284
Pine, Gideon	L518
Pineapple Press	P356
Pleiades	M285
Plexus Publishing Limited	P357
Plitt, Carrie	L520
Ploughshares	M286
Pluto Press	P358
PN Review	M287
Pocket Mountains	P359
Poetry Ireland Review	M288
Poetry Review, The	M290
Poetry Wales	M291
Political Quarterly, The	M292
Polygon	P360
Portobello Literary	L521
Posner, Marcy	L522
Power Cut Lite	M294
Power, Anna	L523
Practising Midwife, The	M295
Prasanna, Tanusri	L525
Present Tense	M296
Preservation Magazine	M297
Prestel Publishing Ltd	P362
Preston, Amanda	L526
Pride	M298
Prole	M299
Prufrock Press	P363
Purdue University Press	P364
Pureplay Press	P365
Qu Literary Magazine	M302
Quadrant Books	P366
Quarto Group, Inc., The	P367
Quill Driver Books	P368
Quirk Books	P369
R D Publishers	P370
Rabble Review	M303
Racecar Engineering	M304
Rail Express	M306
Ramer, Susan	L528
Rand McNally	P371
Ransom Publishing Ltd	P373
Reactor	M307
Reader, The	M308
Red Feather	P375
Red Magazine	M309
Redbook Magazine	M310
Redhammer	L530
Regina Ryan Books	L531
Reid, Janet	L532
Reilly, Milly	L533
Reino, Jessica	L534
Renard Press Ltd	P376
Richard Curtis Associates, Inc.	L536
Richter, Rick	L537
Riposte	M312

River Hills Traveler	M313
River Styx	M314
Robert Smith Literary Agency Ltd	L539
Roberts, Soumeya Bendimerad	L540
Robertson Murray Literary Agency	L541
Robinson, Quressa	L542
Rock & Gem	M316
Rocking Chair Books	L544
Rocky Mountain Books	P378
Rocky Nook	P379
Rosenberg Group, The	L549
Roseway	P382
Ross, Whitney	L551
Round Hall	P383
Rubin Pfeffer Content, LLC	L552
Rudy Agency, The	L553
Rugby World	M317
Rupert Crew Ltd	L554
Ruppin Agency, The	L555
Ruralite	M318
Rutherford, Laetitia	L557
Rutman, Jim	L558
RYA (Royal Yachting Association)	P385
Saddlebag Dispatches	M319
Safari Press	P386
SAIL Magazine	M320
Sailing Today	M321
Salt Publishing	P389
Salvo, Katie	L560
Sanchez, Kaitlyn	L561
Sanders, Rayhane	L562
Saqi Books	P390
Sarah Jane Freymann Literary Agency	L564
Sasquatch Books	P391
Savannah Magazine	M322
Sayle Literary Agency, The	L565
Scala Arts & Heritage Publishers	P392
Scarfe, Rory	L566
Schiffer Craft	P394
Schiffer Fashion Press	P395
Schiffer Kids	P396
Schiffer Military History	P397
Schiffer Publishing	P398
Schofield, Hannah	L567
Scholastic	P399
Scholastic UK	P400
Schwartz, Steve	L568
Science Factory, The	L569
Scifaikuest	M323
SCM Press	P401
Scots Magazine, The	M324
Scottish Farmer, The	M325
Scottish Field	M326
Scoular, Rosemary	L570
Scratching Shed Publishing	P402
Seager, Chloe	L571
Seaworthy Publications	P403
Sebes & Bisseling	L572
Second Factory	M328
Selectric Artists	L573
Sentient Publications	P404
Seren Books	P405
Serra, Maria Cardona	L574
Seventeen	M329
Seymour, Charlotte	L575
Shaw Agency, The	L576
Sheil Land Associates Ltd	L577
Shenandoah	M331
Sheree Bykofsky Associates, Inc.	L579
Shesto Literary	L580
Shestopal, Camilla	L581
Ships Monthly Magazine	M332
Shipwreckt Books Publishing Company	P406
Shooter Literary Magazine	M333
Shorts Magazine	M335
Sierra	M336
Sigma Press	P407
Signorelli, Michael	L582
Silk, Julia	L583
Silver, Janet	L584
Simpson, Cara Lee	L586
Singing Dragon	P409
Sinister Wisdom	M337
Siobhan, Aiden	L587
Snowflake Magazine	M338
Society for Promoting Christian Knowledge (SPCK)	P414
Society of Genealogists	P415
SOMA	M340
Somerset Life	M341
Sonder Magazine	M342
Sophie Hicks Agency	L591
South Carolina Review	M344
Southern Humanities Review	M345
Southern Review, The	M346
Southern Theatre	M347
Southwest Review	M348
Spa Magazine	M350
Spackman, James	L593
Sparsile Books	P419
Speciality Food	M351
Spelt Magazine	M352
Spitball	M353
Spring Literary	L594
Square Mile Magazine	M354
SRL Publishing	P421
Stainer & Bell Ltd	P426
Stanford University Press	P427
Steerforth Press	P428
Stephens, Jenny	L596
Steward House Publishers	P429
Stewart, Douglas	L599
Stinging Fly, The	M355
Stipes Publishing	P431
Stone, Geoffrey	L600
Story Unlikely	M356
StoryWise	L601
Strachan Literary Agency	L602
Strange Horizons	M357
Strategic Finance	M358
Strothman, Wendy	L608
Stuart Krichevsky Literary Agency, Inc.	L609
Studio One	M360
Successful Meetings	M361
Sunbelt Publications, Inc.	P433
Sunpenny Publishing	P435
Sunshine Artist	M363
Sunspot Literary Journal	M364
Supplement, The	M365
Susan Schulman Literary Agency	L610
Swainson, Joanna	L613
Sweet & Maxwell	P436
Sweet, Emily	L614
Sweren, Becky	L615
Swimming Pool News	M367
SYLA – Susan Yearwood Literary Agency	L616
Symonds, Laurel	L617
Tahoma Literary Review	M368
Takahe	M369
Take a Break's Take a Puzzle	M370
Takikawa, Marin	L618
Talbot, Emily	L619
Taylor & Francis Group	P441
Tears in the Fence	M371
Templar Books	P442
Temz Review, The	M372
Ten Speed Press	P444
Terlip, Paige	L624
Texas A&M University Press	P445
Thames & Hudson Inc.	P446
That's Life!	M373
Thayer, Henry	L626
Theseus Agency, The	L627
Thin Air Magazine	M374
Thinkwell Books, UK	P447
Third Coast	M375
This England	M376
Thistle Publishing	P448
Thorneycroft, Euan	L628
Threepenny Review, The	M377
Thwaites, Steph	L629
Tidewater Publishers	P449
Tilbury House Publishers	P450
Tippermuir Books	P452
Toad Hall Editions	P453
Tocher	M378
Tolka	M379
Topping, Antony	L632
Torrey House Press, LLC	P459
Torva	P460
Tributaries	M380
Trudel, Jes	L634
Turner Publishing	P462
Turtle Press	P463
Tusculum Review, The	M381
Two Fine Crows Books	P464
Two Piers Literary Agency, The	L636
Tyndale House Publishers, Inc.	P465
Ugly Duckling Presse	P466
Ulverscroft Ltd	P467
Unbound Press	P468
Uncut	M383
Understorey Magazine	M385
Unicorn	P469
Unicorn Publishing Group	P470
Uniform	P471
Unify	P472
Unity	P473
University of Akron Press, The	P475
University of Alaska Press	P476
University of Alberta Press	P477
University of California Press	P478
University of Georgia Press	P479
University of Iowa Press	P480
University of Maine Press	P481
University of Massachusetts Press	P482
University of Michigan Press, The	P483
University of Nevada Press	P484
University of North Texas Press	P485
University of Pennsylvania Press	P486
University of Tennessee Press	P487
University of Texas Press	P488
University of Virginia Press	P489
University of Wisconsin Press, The	P490
University Press of Colorado	P491
Unseen Press	P492
Usselman, Laura	L639
Vagabond City	M386
Valley Press	P493
Vallum	M387
Vance, Lisa Erbach	L641
VanderWyk & Burnham	P494
Velocity Press	P496
Vestal Review	M388
Victoria Sanders & Associates LLC	L642
Viney Agency, The	L643
Viney, Charlie	L644
Vinspire Publishing	P497
Virago Books	P498
Virginia Quarterly Review, The	M389
Virginia Wine & Country Life	M390
Virginia Wine & Country Weddings	M391
Viz	M392
Vogue	M393
W.W. Norton & Company Ltd	P499

W.W. Norton & Company, Inc.	P500
Waccamaw	M394
Walk Magazine	M395
Wallace Stevens Journal, The	M396
Wallpaper	M397
Walsh, Caroline	L645
Walsh, Kate	L646
Wasafiri	M398
Washington State University Press	P501
Watkins Publishing	P503
Watson, Little Ltd.	L647
Watterson, Jessica	L648
Wayne State University Press	P504
Weidenfeld & Nicolson	P505
Weiss, Alexandra	L650
Weitzner, Tess	L651
Wells, Karmen	L652
Welsh Country	M399
Wesleyan University Press	P506
West Branch	M400
Westchester Magazine	M402
Westin, Erin Casey	L654
Whatnall, Michaela	L655
Whelan, Maria	L656
Whispering Buffalo Literary Agency	L657
White Review, The	M404
Whitecap Books Ltd	P507
Whitford Press	P508
Wickers, Chandler	L659
Wide-Eyed Editions	P509
Wild Places Publishing	P510
Williams, Laura	L662
Williams, Sarah	L663
Willms, Kathryn	L665
Wilson, Desiree	L667
Wilson, Ed	L668
Windhorse Publications Ltd.	P511
Windsor Review	M405
Wine Enthusiast	M406
Wisdom Publications	P512
Woman & Home	M407
Wood, Caroline	L669
Woods, Bryony	L671
Woollard, Jessica	L672
WordCrafts Press	P514
Wordserve Literary	L673
Workman Publishing	P519
Writer's Side	L674
Yachting Monthly	M408
Yale Review, The	M409
Yale University Press (London)	P520
Yankee Magazine	M410
Yeoh, Rachel	L675
Yes Poetry Magazine	M412
YMU Books	L676
Yorkshire Life	M413
Yorkshire Women's Life Magazine	M414
Young, Claudia	L677
Your Cat	M415
Yours	M416
Zack Company, Inc, The	L678
Zacker, Marietta B.	L679
Zeno Agency	L680
Zibby Books	P522
ZigZag Education	P523
Zone 3	M419
Zuraw-Friedland, Ayla	L681

Nonfiction Books

23 House Publishing	P001
404 Ink	P002
4RV Publishing	P004
4RV Tenacious	P005
A-R Editions	P006
A.M. Heath & Company Limited, Author's Agents	L002
Able Muse Press	P009
Abuzz Press	P010
Acheampong, Kwaku	L004
Adams, Seren	L005
Adlard Coles	P012
Adsett, Alex	L006
AdventureKEEN	P013
Alcock, Michael	L014
Alex Adsett Literary	L016
Algonquin Books	P016
Alice Williams Literary	L017
Alive Literary Agency	L018
Allen & Unwin	P018
Allison & Busby Ltd	P019
Alternating Current Press	P020
Amato Books	P021
Ambassador Speakers Bureau & Literary Agency	L019
Ambrosi, Beniamino	L020
Amling, Eric	L021
Ammonite Press	P024
And Other Stories	P025
Andrade, Hannah	L023
Andrew Nurnberg Associates, Ltd	L024
Andrew, Nelle	L025
Andrews McMeel Publishing	P026
Anne Clark Literary Agency	L028
Antony Harwood Limited	L029
Anvil Press Publishers	P028
Apa Publications Group	P029
Arcadia Publishing	P031
Arms, Victoria Wells	L031
Armstrong, Susan	L032
Arsenal Pulp Press	P032
Arte Publico Press	P033
Arthurson, Wayne	L033
Asabi Publishing	P034
Ascend Books, LLC	P035
Atyeo, Charlotte	L034
Aurora Metro Press	P039
Authentic Life	P041
Autumn Publishing Ltd	P042
Backbeat Books	P046
Badger Learning	P048
Bajek, Lauren	L037
Bal, Emma	L038
Bald and Bonkers Network LLC	P050
Balow, Dan	L039
Banter Press	P053
Barbara, Stephen	L041
Barbican Press	P055
Barbour Publishing	P056
Baror International, Inc.	L044
Barr, Anjanette	L045
Barr, Nicola	L046
Barren Magazine	M047
Bartholomew, Jason	L047
Basalt Books	P057
Basic Books	P058
Basic Health Publications, Inc.	P059
Bates, Tim	L048
Bath Literary Agency	L049
Baumer, Jan	L051
Baxter, Veronique	L052
Baylor University Press	P060
Begum, Salma	L053
Belton, Maddy	L055
Bent Agency (UK), The	L057
Bent Agency, The	L058
Bent, Jenny	L059
Bentley Publishers	P061
Berdinsky, Kendall	L060
Berghahn Books Ltd	P062
Bernardi, Amanda	L062
Berrett-Koehler Publishers	P063
Bess Press	P064
Betsy Amster Literary Enterprises	L063
BFI Publishing	P065
Birlinn Ltd	P067
Blackstaff Press	P068
Blake Friedmann Literary Agency Ltd	L066
Bloodhound Books	P070
Bloomsbury Academic	P071
Bloomsbury Professional	P072
Blue Poppy Enterprises	P074
Blue Star Press	P075
BOA Editions, Ltd.	P076
Boathooks Books	P077
Borstel, Stefanie Sanchez Von	L071
Bowlin, Sarah	L073
Bradford Literary Agency	L075
Bradford, Laura	L076
Brailsford, Karen	L077
Brannan, Maria	L078
Brattesani, Hannah	L079
Brattle Agency LLC, The	L080
Brewin Books Ltd	P081
Bright Agency (UK), The	L082
Bright Agency (US), The	L083
British Academy, The	P083
British Museum Press, The	P084
Broadview Press	P085
Brooks, Savannah	L084
Brotherstone Creative Management	L085
Brotherstone, Charlie	L086
Brouckaert, Justin	L087
Brown, Megan	L088
Brown, Son & Ferguson, Ltd	P086
Browne & Miller Literary Associates	L089
Bucci, Chris	L090
Buckley, Louise	L091
Bukowski, Danielle	L092
Burns, Camille	L094
C&T Publishing	P088
C&W (Conville & Walsh)	L096
CAA (London)	L098
Caitlin Press Inc.	P090
Campbell, Charlie	L099
Campos, Vanessa	L100
Candy Jar Books	P093
Canterbury Literary Agency	L101
Canterbury Press	P094
Capron, Elise	L104
Captivate Press	P095
Carr, Jamie	L108
Carr, Michael	L109
Carroll, Megan	L110
Carter, Rebecca	L111
Cartey, Claire	L112
Caskie, Robert	L113
Cassell	P096
Cavanagh, Claire	L114
CGI (Chartered Governance Institute) Publishing	P098
Chanchani, Sonali	L115
Chang, Nicola	L116
Charisma House	P100
Charles River Press	P101
Charlesbridge Teen	P103
Charnace, Edwina de	L117
Chartered Institute of Personnel and Development (CIPD) Publishing	P104
Chase Literary Agency	L118
Chelsea House Publishers	P105
Chevais, Jennifer	L122
Chiotti, Danielle	L123
Cho, Catherine	L124
Christie, Jennifer	L126
ChristLight Books	P110
Chronicle Books LLC	P111
Cinnamon Press	P112
Claret Press	P113
Clarke, Caro	L128

Index | Nonfiction Books

Clarke, Catherine	L129
Cleis Press	P115
Coaches Choice	P116
Cochran, Alexander	L130
College Press Publishing	P117
Collins	P118
Colourpoint Educational	P119
Colwill, Charlotte	L132
Combemale, Chris	L133
Comparato, Andrea	L134
Compassiviste Publishing	P121
Concepcion, Cristina	L135
Conrad, Claire Paterson	L136
Conville, Clare	L137
Coombs Moylett & Maclean Literary Agency	L139
Cooper, Gemma	L140
Cooper, Maggie	L141
Cornell Maritime Press	P123
Countryside Books	P124
Coyote Arts	P125
Crabtree Publishing	P126
Crandall, Becca	L142
Croner-i Limited	P127
Crossway	P128
Crowley, Sheila	L144
Crown	P129
Crown Publishing Group, The	P131
Curran, Sabhbh	L145
Curtis Brown	L146
Curtis Brown (Australia) Pty Ltd	L147
Cynthia Cannell Literary Agency	L150
Dana Newman Literary, LLC	L152
Danaczko, Melissa	L153
Danko, Margaret	L154
Darga, Jon Michael	L155
Darhansoff & Verrill Literary Agents	L156
Daunt Books Publishing	P134
David Godwin Associates	L158
Dawson, Liza	L162
DeBlock, Liza	L163
Denis Kitchen Publishing Company Co., LLC	P138
Derviskadic, Dado	L164
DeVorss & Company	P139
DHH Literary Agency Ltd	L166
Diana Finch Literary Agency	L167
Dickerson, Donya	L168
Dijkstra, Sandra	L169
Dillsworth, Elise	L170
Dixon, Isobel	L171
DK Publishing	P141
Dolby, Trevor	L173
Dominguez, Adriana	L174
Don Congdon Associates, Inc.	L175
Donald Maass Literary Agency	L176
Doubleday (UK)	P143
Doug Grad Literary Agency	L177
Draper, Claire	L178
Duncan Petersen Publishing Limited	P146
Dunham Literary, Inc.	L179
Dunham, Jennie	L180
Dunn, Ben	L181
DunnFogg	L182
Dunow, Carlson & Lerner Agency	L184
Dynasty Press	P147
Eason, Lynette	L186
Eberly, Chelsea	L187
Edenborough, Sam	L189
Edwards, Max	L190
Eerdmans Books for Young Readers	P148
Eisenmann, Caroline	L192
Ekus Group, The	L193
Ekus, Sally	L194
Elaine Markson Literary Agency	L195
Elaine Steel	L196
Elliott & Thompson	P149
Ellis-Martin, Sian	L197
Ellor, Zabé	L198
Elsevier Ltd	P150
Engram Books	P152
Enitharmon Editions	P153
Enslow Publishers, Inc.	P154
Ericka T. Phillips	L200
Evan-Moor Educational Publishers	P157
Evans, David	L203
Evans, Kate	L204
Evans, Kiya	L205
Evans, Stephany	L206
Facet Publishing	P159
Fairbank Literary Representation	L208
Faulks, Holly	L209
Fazzari, Hillary	L210
Feldstein Agency, The	L213
Felicia Eth Literary Representation	L214
Felicity Bryan Associates	L215
Fellows, Abi	L216
Feminist Press, The	P163
Ferguson, Hannah	L217
Fernandez, Rochelle	L220
Fernwood Publishing	P164
Fighting High	P165
Filter Press	P166
Finan, Ciara	L223
Finegan, Stevie	L226
Fiscal Publications	P168
Flannery Literary	L228
Fogg, Jack	L230
Forrester, Jemima	L232
Fortress Press	P170
Fox, Aram	L234
Foxx, Kat	L235
FRA (Futerman, Rose, & Associates)	L236
Frances Collin Literary Agent	L237
Frankel, Valerie	L239
Fraser Ross Associates	L240
Free Association Books Ltd	P173
Free Spirit Publishing	P174
Freymann, Sarah Jane	L242
Friedman, Claire	L243
Friedman, Rebecca	L244
Friedrich Agency LLC, The	L245
Friends United Press	P175
Frog Literary Agency	L246
Fuentes, Sarah	L247
Furniss, Eugenie	L249
Gahan, Isobel	L250
Gale	P177
Galustian, Natalie	L251
Galvin, Lori	L252
Garamond Agency, Inc., The	L253
Gauntlett, Adam	L254
Geared Up Publications	P178
Geiger, Ellen	L255
Getzler, Josh	L256
Ghahremani, Lilly	L257
Gill Books	P181
Gill Education	P182
Gillam, Bianca	L259
Glass Literary Management LLC	L262
Glenister, Emily	L263
Global Lion Intellectual Property Management, Inc.	L264
Globe Pequot Press, The	P184
Goff, Anthony	L266
Goff, Ellen	L267
Goldsmiths Press	P186
Goldstein, Veronica	L268
Good Literary Agency, The	L269
Goodman Beck Publishing	P187
Goose Lane Editions	P188
Gordon, Andrew	L270
Graham Maw Christie Literary Agency	L271
Graham, Stacey	L272
Grajkowski, Michelle	L274
Granger, David	L275
Granta Books	P192
Graywolf Press	P193
Greene & Heaton Ltd	L276
Greenstreet, Katie	L277
Greyhound Literary	L278
Grimm, Katie	L279
Grossman, Loren R.	L280
Gruber, Pam	L281
Grunewald, Hattie	L282
Guinsler, Robert	L283
Hachette Book Group	P196
Haley, Jolene	L289
Half Mystic Press	P197
Hammersmith Books	P198
Hanbury Agency, The	L290
Hannah Sheppard Literary Agency	L291
Hannigan, Carrie	L292
Hansen, Stephanie	L293
Happy Yak	P200
Hardie Grant UK	P201
Hardman, Caroline	L295
Hare, Jessica	L296
Harmsworth, Esmond	L297
Harold Ober Associates, Inc.	L298
Harris, Erin	L300
Harvard University Press	P206
Hashtag Press	P207
Haus Publishing	P208
Hawk, Susan	L303
Hawn, Molly Ker	L304
Hawthorne Books	P209
Hay House Publishers	P210
Hayden, Viola	L305
Henley Hall Press	P214
Hernando, Paloma	L308
Heymont, Lane	L309
High Stakes Publishing	P216
High Tide Press	P217
Hippocrene Books, Inc.	P219
History Press, The	P221
Hiyate, Sam	L313
Hobbs, Victoria	L314
Hodder & Stoughton Ltd	P222
Hoffman, Scott	L316
Holloway, Sally	L318
Holroyde, Penny	L319
Hordern, Kate	L320
Hornsley, Sarah	L321
Howgate Publishing	P225
Hwang, Annie	L322
Icon Books Ltd	P227
Idyll Arbor	P229
Ig Publishing	P230
Imagine Publishing	P234
Indiana University Press	P235
Influx Press	P237
Information Today, Inc.	P238
Inkandescent	P240
Inscriptions Literary Agency	L323
International Society for Technology in Education (ISTE)	P242
InterVarsity Press (IVP)	P243
Irene Goodman Literary Agency (IGLA)	L324
Irving, Dotti	L326
Jacobson, Rachel	L328
Jain Publishing Company, Inc.	P244
Janklow & Nesbit UK Ltd	L330
Jeff Herman Agency, LLC, The	L331
Jessica Kingsley Publishers	P246
JMD Media / DB Publishing	P247
Jo Unwin Literary Agency	L333

Claim your free access to www.firstwriter.com: See p.403

Joelle Delbourgo Associates, Inc. L334
John Murray Press P249
Johns Hopkins University Press, The P250
Jonathan Clowes Ltd L336
Jonathan Pegg Literary Agency L337
Kahn, Ella Diamond L345
Kahn, Jody L346
Kane Press P251
Kantor, Camille L349
Kardon, Julia L350
Karinch, Maryann L351
Kate Barker Literary, TV, & Film Agency L352
Kate Nash Literary Agency L353
Kates Hill Press, The P252
Kathryn Green Literary Agency, LLC L354
Kellerman, Carly L360
Kensington Publishing Corp. P253
Keren, Eli L362
Ki Agency Ltd L364
Killingley, Jessica L365
Kim, Jennifer L366
Kim, Julia L367
Kimber, Natalie L368
Kimberley Cameron & Associates L369
Kirby, Robert L370
Kitchen Press P254
Knight Features L373
Kogan Page Ltd P255
Kore Press P256
Kotchman, Katie L374
Krienke, Mary L375
Kruger Cowne L376
Kube Publishing P258
Labyrinth Literary Agency, The L378
Lakosil, Natalie L379
Lambert, Sophie L380
Langmarc Publishing P259
Langtons International L384
Langtry, Elena L385
Lantana Publishing P260
Latshaw, Katherine L386
Laurence King Publishing P261
Laxfield Literary Associates L387
Lazin, Sarah L388
Leamington Books P262
Leapfrog Press P263
Lechon, Shannon L390
Lees, Jordan L392
Leigh Feldman Literary L393
Lerner Publishing Group P264
Levitt, Sarah L396
Lewinsohn Literary L397
Lewis, Alison L398
Lightner, Kayla L399
Liguori Publications P267
Lilliput Press, The P268
Limelight Management L400
Liss, Laurie L403
Liza Dawson Associates L405
Llewellyn Worldwide Ltd P269
Loft Press, Inc. P270
Logaston Press P271
Lotus Lane Literary L407
Loughman, Morwenna L408
Lovell, Jake L409
Loyola Press P272
LSU Press P273
Lund Humphries Limited P274
Lutterworth Press, The P275
Lutyens and Rubinstein L410
LW Books P276
M. Evans & Company P278
MacDonald, Emily L412
Macdougall, Laura L413
MacGregor & Luedeke L414
Mack, Kate L415
Maclean, Jamie L417
MacLeod, Lauren L418
Madan, Neeti L419
Madeleine Milburn Literary, TV & Film Agency L420
Maidment, Olivia L421
Maltese, Alyssa L422
Manilla Press P280
Marr, Jill L425
Marshall, Jen L427
Marsiglia, Caroline L428
Massie, Maria L430
Maurer, Shari L433
Maw, Jane Graham L434
McCormick Literary L436
McGraw Hill EMEA P285
McNicol, Andy L437
McNidder & Grace P286
McQuilkin, Rob L438
Medical Physics Publishing P288
Medina Publishing P289
Mehren, Jane von L440
Menasha Ridge Press P290
Mendia, Isabel L441
Mensch Publishing P291
Mentor Books P292
Meridian Artists L442
Merriam Press P293
Merullo, Annabel L443
Metamorphosis Literary Agency L444
Methuen Publishing Ltd P294
Metro Publications Ltd P295
Mic Cheetham Literary Agency L445
Michel, Caroline L446
Mihell, Natasha L448
Mildred Marmur Associates, Ltd. L450
Mileo, Jessica L451
Milkweed Editions P296
Mills, Rachel L452
Minnesota Historical Society Press P299
Miranda, Caroline L454
Mirror Books P301
Missouri Historical Society Press P302
MIT Press, The P303
MMB Creative L455
Molloy, Jess L456
Monacelli Press, The P304
Moody Publishers P305
Moore, Penny L458
Moorhead, Max L459
Morrell, Imogen L460
Mortimer, Michele L462
Movable Type Management L464
Mundy, Toby L466
Murdoch Books Australia P308
Murgolo, Karen L467
Murray, Judith L468
Muscato, Nate L469
Mustelier, James L471
NAHB BuilderBooks P310
Nash, Justin L474
Native Ink Press P311
Nell James Publishers P313
New Harbinger Publications P314
Nichols, Mariah L479
Niumata, Erin L480
No Starch Press, Inc. P318
Nolan, Laura L481
Northbank Talent Management L482
Nosy Crow P319
O'Grady, Faith L485
O'Grady, Niamh L486
O'Neill, Molly L487
O'Shea, Amy L488
Oak Tree Press P320
Oghma Creative Media P321
Ogtrop, Kristin van L489
Ohio State University Press, The P323
Ohio University Press P324
Old Street Publishing Ltd P325
Oldcastle Books Group P326
Oneworld Publications P327
Ooligan Press P328
Otago University Press P330
Ouen Press P331
Oxbow Books P333
Pacific Press Publishing Association P334
Pan Macmillan Australia P335
Pande, Ayesha L497
Paradigm Talent and Literary Agency L498
Parthian Books P336
Pass, Marina de L500
Patterson, Emma L501
Paul S. Levine Literary Agency L502
Peddle, Kay L503
Peepal Tree Press P341
Pelham, Imogen L504
Pen & Ink Designs Publishing P342
Pen & Sword Books Ltd P343
People's Friend, The M283
Perez Literary & Entertainment L506
Perez, Kristina L507
Perotto-Wills, Martha L508
Perry Literary L509
Pestritto, Carrie L511
Peter Lang P346
Peter Lang Publishing P348
Peter Owen Publishers P349
Petty, Rachel L512
Phelan, Beth L514
Phillips, Aemilia L515
Piatkus Books P352
Pickering, Juliet L516
Pierce, Rosie L517
Pine, Gideon L518
Pineapple Press P356
Plitt, Carrie L520
Pluto Press P358
Pocket Mountains P359
Polygon P360
Portobello Literary L521
Posner, Marcy L522
Power, Anna L523
Prasanna, Tanusri L525
Prestel Publishing Ltd P362
Preston, Amanda L526
Prufrock Press P363
Purdue University Press P364
Pureplay Press P365
Quadrant Books P366
Quarto Group, Inc., The P367
Quirk Books P369
Ramer, Susan L528
Ransom Publishing Ltd P373
Red Feather P375
Redhammer L530
Regina Ryan Books L531
Reid, Janet L532
Reilly, Milly L533
Reino, Jessica L534
Renard Press Ltd P376
Richard Curtis Associates, Inc. L536
Richter, Rick L537
Robert Smith Literary Agency Ltd L539
Roberts, Soumeya Bendimerad L540
Robinson, Quressa L542
Rocking Chair Books L544
Rocky Mountain Books P378
Rocky Nook P379
Rosenberg Group, The L549
Roseway P382

*Access more listings online at **www.firstwriter.com***

Ross, Whitney	L551
Round Hall	P383
Rudy Agency, The	L553
Rupert Crew Ltd	L554
Ruppin Agency, The	L555
Rutherford, Laetitia	L557
Rutman, Jim	L558
RYA (Royal Yachting Association)	P385
Safari Press	P386
Salt Publishing	P389
Salvo, Katie	L560
Sanchez, Kaitlyn	L561
Sanders, Rayhane	L562
Saqi Books	P390
Sarah Jane Freymann Literary Agency	L564
Sasquatch Books	P391
Sayle Literary Agency, The	L565
Scarfe, Rory	L566
Schiffer Craft	P394
Schiffer Fashion Press	P395
Schiffer Military History	P397
Schiffer Publishing	P398
Schofield, Hannah	L567
Scholastic	P399
Scholastic UK	P400
Schwartz, Steve	L568
Science Factory, The	L569
SCM Press	P401
Scoular, Rosemary	L570
Scratching Shed Publishing	P402
Seager, Chloe	L571
Sebes & Bisseling	L572
Selectric Artists	L573
Sentient Publications	P404
Seren Books	P405
Serra, Maria Cardona	L574
Seymour, Charlotte	L575
Shaw Agency, The	L576
Sheil Land Associates Ltd	L577
Sheree Bykofsky Associates, Inc.	L579
Shesto Literary	L580
Shestopal, Camilla	L581
Shipwreckt Books Publishing Company	P406
Sigma Press	P407
Signorelli, Michael	L582
Silk, Julia	L583
Silver, Janet	L584
Simpson, Cara Lee	L586
Singing Dragon	P409
Society for Promoting Christian Knowledge (SPCK)	P414
Society of Genealogists	P415
Sophie Hicks Agency	L591
Spackman, James	L593
Sparsile Books	P419
Spring Literary	L594
SRL Publishing	P421
Stainer & Bell Ltd	P426
Stanford University Press	P427
Steerforth Press	P428
Stephens, Jenny	L596
Steward House Publishers	P429
Stewart, Douglas	L599
Stipes Publishing	P431
Stone, Geoffrey	L600
StoryWise	L601
Strothman, Wendy	L608
Stuart Krichevsky Literary Agency, Inc.	L609
Sunbelt Publications, Inc.	P433
Sunpenny Publishing	P435
Susan Schulman Literary Agency	L610
Swainson, Joanna	L613
Sweet & Maxwell	P436
Sweet, Emily	L614
Sweren, Becky	L615
SYLA – Susan Yearwood Literary Agency	L616
Symonds, Laurel	L617
Takikawa, Marin	L618
Talbot, Emily	L619
Taylor & Francis Group	P441
Terlip, Paige	L624
Texas A&M University Press	P445
Thames & Hudson Inc.	P446
Thayer, Henry	L626
Theseus Agency, The	L627
Thinkwell Books, UK	P447
Thistle Publishing	P448
Thorneycroft, Euan	L628
Thwaites, Steph	L629
Tidewater Publishers	P449
Tippermuir Books	P452
Toad Hall Editions	P453
Topping, Antony	L632
Torrey House Press, LLC	P459
Torva	P460
Trudel, Jes	L634
Turner Publishing	P462
Turtle Press	P463
Two Fine Crows Books	P464
Two Piers Literary Agency, The	L636
Tyndale House Publishers, Inc.	P465
Ugly Duckling Presse	P466
Ulverscroft Ltd	P467
Unbound Press	P468
Unicorn	P469
Unicorn Publishing Group	P470
Uniform	P471
Unify	P472
Unity	P473
University of Akron Press, The	P475
University of Alaska Press	P476
University of Alberta Press	P477
University of California Press	P478
University of Georgia Press	P479
University of Iowa Press	P480
University of Maine Press	P481
University of Massachusetts Press	P482
University of Michigan Press, The	P483
University of Nevada Press	P484
University of North Texas Press	P485
University of Pennsylvania Press	P486
University of Tennessee Press	P487
University of Texas Press	P488
University of Virginia Press	P489
University of Wisconsin Press, The	P490
University Press of Colorado	P491
Unseen Press	P492
Usselman, Laura	L639
Valley Press	P493
Vance, Lisa Erbach	L641
VanderWyk & Burnham	P494
Velocity Press	P496
Viney Agency, The	L643
Viney, Charlie	L644
Vinspire Publishing	P497
Virago Books	P498
W.W. Norton & Company Ltd	P499
W.W. Norton & Company, Inc.	P500
Walsh, Caroline	L645
Walsh, Kate	L646
Watson, Little Ltd	L647
Watterson, Jessica	L648
Wayne State University Press	P504
Weidenfeld & Nicolson	P505
Weiss, Alexandra	L650
Weitzner, Tess	L651
Wells, Karmen	L652
Wesleyan University Press	P506
Westin, Erin Casey	L654
Whatnall, Michaela	L655
Whelan, Maria	L656
Whispering Buffalo Literary Agency	L657
Whitecap Books Ltd	P507
Whitford Press	P508
Wickers, Chandler	L659
Wide-Eyed Editions	P509
Wild Places Publishing	P510
Williams, Laura	L662
Williams, Sarah	L663
Willms, Kathryn	L665
Wilson, Desiree	L667
Wilson, Ed	L668
Windhorse Publications Ltd	P511
Wisdom Publications	P512
Wood, Caroline	L669
Woods, Bryony	L671
Woollard, Jessica	L672
WordCrafts Press	P514
Wordserve Literary	L673
Workman Publishing	P519
Writer's Side	L674
Yale University Press (London)	P520
Yeoh, Rachel	L675
YMU Books	L676
Young, Claudia	L677
Zack Company, Inc, The	L678
Zacker, Marietta B.	L679
Zeno Agency	L680
Zibby Books	P522
ZigZag Education	P523
Zuraw-Friedland, Ayla	L681

Nonfiction in Translation

Ambrosi, Beniamino	L020
And Other Stories	P025
Armstrong, Susan	L032
Charnace, Edwina de	L117
Daunt Books Publishing	P134
Faultline	M137
Five Points	M144
Half Mystic Journal	M175
Hunger Mountain	M191
Indiana Review	M196
Irish Pages	M203
Kenyon Review, The	M210
Massachusetts Review, The	M237
Nashville Review	M251
New England Review	M255
Shenandoah	M331
Southern Review, The	M346
Tributaries	M380

Norfolk
See more broadly: England
| Norfolk & Suffolk Bride | M260 |

North Africa
See more broadly: Africa
| Saqi Books | P390 |

North America
See more broadly: Regional
See more specifically: Atlantic Northeast; Canada; United States
| Ohio University Press | P324 |
| University of Pennsylvania Press | P486 |

North Pacific Rim
See more broadly: Pacific

Northern England
See more broadly: England
| Salt Publishing | P389 |
| Scratching Shed Publishing | P402 |

Northern Ireland
See more broadly: United Kingdom
| Blackstaff Press | P068 |

Nostalgia
See more broadly: History
| Best of British | M056 |
| Countryside Books | P124 |

376 Index | Novel Excerpts

Essex Life M132
Foxx, Kat L235
Mirror Books P301

Novel Excerpts

aaduna M005
African Voices M015
Alaska Quarterly Review M019
Coil, The M089
Fiddlehead, The M141
Idaho Review M193
Kenyon Review, The M210
New England Review M255
Pacifica Literary Review M273
Shenandoah M331
Stinging Fly, The M355

Novelettes

Big Fiction M061
Sunspot Literary Journal M364

Novellas

Alaska Quarterly Review M019
Fairlight Books P160
Half Mystic Press P197
Hiraeth Books P220
Inkandescent P240
New England Review M255
Paycock Press P340
People's Friend Pocket Novels M282
Phoenix Moirai P351
Sinister Stoat Press P410
Sunspot Literary Journal M364
Tor.com Publishing P458
Wordsonthestreet P517
YesYes Books P521

Novels

3 Seas Literary Agency L001
404 Ink P002
4RV Publishing P004
4RV Tenacious P005
A.M. Heath & Company Limited, Author's Agents L002
Aardwolf Press P007
Able Muse Press P009
Abuzz Press P010
Acheampong, Kwaku L004
Adams, Seren L005
Adsett, Alex L006
Afonso, Thais L008
Afterglow Books P014
Agency (London) Ltd, The L009
Ahearn Agency, Inc, The L011
Albert Whitman & Company P015
Alekseii, Keir L015
Alex Adsett Literary L016
Algonquin Books P016
Alice Williams Literary L017
Allen & Unwin P018
Allison & Busby Ltd P019
Alternating Current Press P020
Ambassador Speakers Bureau & Literary Agency L019
Ambrosi, Beniamino L020
American Mystery Classics P023
Amling, Eric L021
And Other Stories P025
Anderson, Darley L022
Andrade, Hannah L023
Andrew Nurnberg Associates, Ltd L024
Andrew, Nelle L025
Anne Clark Literary Agency L028
Antony Harwood Limited L029
Anvil Press Publishers P028
Arcadia Publishing P031
Armada, Kurestin L030
Arms, Victoria Wells L031
Armstrong, Susan L032
Arsenal Pulp Press P032
Arte Publico Press P033
Arthurson, Wayne L033
Asabi Publishing P034
Atyeo, Charlotte L034
Aurora Metro Press P039
Authentic Ideas P040
Avon P044
Avon Books P045
Bad Press Ink P047
Badger Learning P048
Baen Books P049
Bajek, Lauren L037
Bald and Bonkers Network LLC P050
Baobab Press P054
Barbara, Stephen L041
Barbican Press P055
Barbour Publishing P056
Barone Literary Agency L043
Baror International, Inc. L044
Barr, Anjanette L045
Barr, Nicola L046
Bartholomew, Jason L047
Bates, Tim L048
Bath Literary Agency L049
Bauman, Erica L050
Baxter, Veronique L052
Begum, Salma L053
Belton, Maddy L055
Bennett, Laura L056
Bent Agency (UK), The L057
Bent Agency, The L058
Bent, Jenny L059
Berdinsky, Kendall L060
Berlyne, John L061
Bess Press P064
Betsy Amster Literary Enterprises L063
Bhasin, Tamanna L064
Birlinn Ltd P067
Blackstaff Press P068
Blake Friedmann Literary Agency Ltd L066
Bloodhound Books P070
Blue Jeans Books P073
Boker, Sidney L067
Bolton, Camilla L069
Bookouture P078
Bookseeker Agency L070
Bowlin, Sarah L073
Brace, Samantha L074
Bradford Literary Agency L075
Bradford, Laura L076
Brannan, Maria L078
Brattesani, Hannah L079
Brattle Agency LLC, The L080
Brewer, Amy L081
Brewin Books Ltd P081
Brooks, Savannah L084
Brotherstone Creative Management L085
Brotherstone, Charlie L086
Browne & Miller Literary Associates L089
Bucci, Chris L090
Buckley, Louise L091
Bukowski, Danielle L092
Burke, Kate L093
Burns, Camille L094
C&W (Conville & Walsh) L096
CAA (London) L098
Caitlin Press Inc. P090
Campbell, Charlie L099
Candlemark & Gleam P092
Candy Jar Books P093
Canterbury Literary Agency L101
Caprio, Alice L103
Capron, Elise L104
Captivate Press P095
Caroline Sheldon Literary Agency L106
Carr, Jamie L108
Carr, Michael L109
Carroll, Megan L110
Carter, Rebecca L111
Cartey, Claire L112
Caskie, Robert L113
Cavanagh, Claire L114
Chanchani, Sonali L115
Chang, Nicola L116
Charisma House P100
Charles River Press P101
Charlesbridge Teen P103
Charnace, Edwina de L117
Chase Literary Agency L118
Chevais, Jennifer L122
Chiotti, Danielle L123
Cho, Catherine L124
Choc Lit P108
Christensen, Erica L125
ChristLight Books P110
Cichello, Kayla L127
Cinnamon Press P112
Claret Press P113
Clarke, Caro L128
Clarke, Catherine L129
Cleis Press P115
Cochran, Alexander L130
Colwill, Charlotte L132
Combemale, Chris L133
Comparato, Andrea L134
Compassiviste Publishing P121
Concepcion, Cristina L135
Conrad, Claire Paterson L136
Conville, Clare L137
Coombes, Clare L138
Coombs Moylett & Maclean Literary Agency L139
Cooper, Gemma L140
Cooper, Maggie L141
Coyote Arts P125
Crandall, Becca L142
Crowley, Sheila L144
Crown Publishing Group, The P131
Curran, Sabhbh L145
Curtis Brown L146
Curtis Brown (Australia) Pty Ltd L147
Cusick, John L148
Cynthia Cannell Literary Agency L150
Dana Newman Literary, LLC L152
Danaczko, Melissa L153
Danko, Margaret L154
Darga, Jon Michael L155
Darhansoff & Verrill Literary Agents L156
Darley Anderson Agency, The L157
Daunt Books Publishing P134
David Godwin Associates L158
Davies, Elinor L160
DAW Books P135
Dawson, Liza L162
DeBlock, Liza L163
Dedalus Ltd P136
DHH Literary Agency Ltd L166
Dijkstra, Sandra L169
Dillsworth, Elise L170
Dixon, Isobel L171
Dodd, Saffron L172
Dodo Ink P142
Don Congdon Associates, Inc. L175
Donald Maass Literary Agency L176
Doubleday (UK) P143
Doug Grad Literary Agency L177
Draper, Claire L178
Dreamspinner Press P144
DSP Publications P145
Dunham Literary, Inc. L179
Dunham, Jennie L180
Dunn, Ben L181

DunnFogg	L182	
Dunow, Carlson & Lerner Agency	L184	
Eason, Lynette	L186	
Eberly, Chelsea	L187	
Eddison Pearson Ltd	L188	
Edenborough, Sam	L189	
Edwards, Max	L190	
Eerdmans Books for Young Readers	P148	
Eisenbraun, Nicole	L191	
Eisenmann, Caroline	L192	
Elaine Markson Literary Agency	L195	
Elaine Steel	L196	
Elliott & Thompson	P149	
Ellis-Martin, Sian	L197	
Ellor, Zabé	L198	
Eunice McMullen Children's Literary Agent Ltd	L201	
Evans, David	L203	
Evans, Kate	L204	
Evans, Kiya	L205	
Evans, Stephany	L206	
Everything With Words	P158	
Fabien, Samantha	L207	
Fairbank Literary Representation	L208	
Fairlight Books	P160	
Fathom Books	P162	
Faulks, Holly	L209	
Fazzari, Hillary	L210	
Feldstein Agency, The	L213	
Felicia Eth Literary Representation	L214	
Felicity Bryan Associates	L215	
Fellows, Abi	L216	
Feminist Press, The	P163	
Ferguson, Hannah	L217	
Ferguson, T.S.	L218	
Fergusson, Julie	L219	
Fernandez, Rochelle	L220	
Figueroa, Melanie	L221	
Filter Press	P166	
Finan, Ciara	L223	
Finch, Rebeka	L225	
Finegan, Stevie	L226	
Firefly	P167	
Fitzgerald, Bea	L227	
Flannery Literary	L228	
Flynn, Amy Thrall	L229	
Fogg, Jack	L230	
for Authors, A	L231	
Forge	P169	
Forrester, Jemima	L232	
Foster, Clara	L233	
Fox, Aram	L234	
Foxx, Kat	L235	
Frances Collin Literary Agent	L237	
Frankel, Valerie	L239	
Fraser Ross Associates	L240	
Free Spirit Publishing	P174	
Freymann, Sarah Jane	L242	
Friedman, Claire	L243	
Friedman, Rebecca	L244	
Friedrich Agency LLC, The	L245	
Fuentes, Sarah	L247	
Fuller, Lisa	L248	
Furniss, Eugenie	L249	
Gahan, Isobel	L250	
Galustian, Natalie	L251	
Galvin, Lori	L252	
Gauntlett, Adam	L254	
Geiger, Ellen	L255	
Getzler, Josh	L256	
Ghahremani, Lilly	L257	
Gilbert, Tara	L258	
Gill Books	P181	
Gillam, Bianca	L259	
Gisondi, Katie	L261	
Glass Literary Management LLC	L262	
Glenister, Emily	L263	
Global Lion Intellectual Property Management, Inc.	L264	
Goetz, Adria	L265	
Goff, Anthony	L266	
Goff, Ellen	L267	
Gold SF	P185	
Goldstein, Veronica	L268	
Good Literary Agency, The	L269	
Goodman Beck Publishing	P187	
Goose Lane Editions	P188	
Gordon, Andrew	L270	
Graham, Stacey	L272	
Grajkowski, Kara	L273	
Grajkowski, Michelle	L274	
Granta Books	P192	
Graywolf Press	P193	
Greene & Heaton Ltd	L276	
Greenstreet, Katie	L277	
Greyhound Literary	L278	
Grimm, Katie	L279	
Gruber, Pam	L281	
Grunewald, Hattie	L282	
Gunic, Masha	L284	
Hachette Book Group	P196	
Haggerty, Taylor	L287	
Hakim, Serene	L288	
Haley, Jolene	L289	
Half Mystic Press	P197	
Hanbury Agency, The	L290	
Hannah Sheppard Literary Agency	L291	
Hannigan, Carrie	L292	
Hansen, Stephanie	L293	
Hardman, Caroline	L295	
Harlequin Mills & Boon Ltd	P203	
Harmony Ink Press	P205	
Harmsworth, Esmond	L297	
Harold Ober Associates, Inc.	L298	
Harper, Logan	L299	
Harris, Erin	L300	
Harwell, Hilary	L301	
Hashtag Press	P207	
Haus Publishing	P208	
Hawk, Susan	L303	
Hawn, Molly Ker	L304	
Hawthorne Books	P209	
Hayden, Viola	L305	
Headley, David H.	L306	
Hensley, Chelsea	L307	
Hernando, Paloma	L308	
Heymont, Lane	L309	
Hiraeth Books	P220	
Hiyate, Sam	L313	
Hobbs, Victoria	L314	
Hodder & Stoughton Ltd	P222	
Hogrebe, Christina	L317	
HopeRoad	P223	
Hordern, Kate	L320	
Hornsley, Sarah	L321	
Hwang, Annie	L322	
IDW Publishing	P228	
Ig Publishing	P230	
IgKids	P231	
Influx Press	P237	
Inkandescent	P240	
Inscriptions Literary Agency	L323	
Irene Goodman Literary Agency (IGLA)	L324	
Irvine, Lucy	L325	
Jamieson, Molly	L329	
Janklow & Nesbit UK Ltd	L330	
JMD Media / DB Publishing	P247	
Jo Unwin Literary Agency	L333	
Joelle Delbourgo Associates, Inc.	L334	
Joffe Books	P248	
John Murray Press	P249	
Jonathan Clowes Ltd	L336	
Jonathan Pegg Literary Agency	L337	
Jones, Philip Gwyn	L339	
Judith Murdoch Literary Agency	L341	
Julie Crisp Literary Agency	L343	
K2 Literary	L344	
Kahn, Ella Diamond	L345	
Kahn, Jody	L346	
Kaliszewska, Joanna	L347	
Kane Literary Agency	L348	
Kantor, Camille	L349	
Kardon, Julia	L350	
Karinch, Maryann	L351	
Kate Barker Literary, TV, & Film Agency	L352	
Kate Nash Literary Agency	L353	
Kates Hill Press, The	P252	
Kathryn Green Literary Agency, LLC	L354	
Kavanagh, Jade	L355	
Kean, Taylor Martindale	L357	
Keane Kataria Literary Agency	L358	
Kenny, Julia	L361	
Kensington Publishing Corp.	P253	
Keren, Eli	L362	
Ki Agency Ltd	L364	
Killingley, Jessica	L365	
Kim, Jennifer	L366	
Kim, Julia	L367	
Kimber, Natalie	L368	
Kimberley Cameron & Associates	L369	
Kirby, Robert	L370	
Knigge, Sheyla	L372	
Kore Press	P256	
Kotchman, Katie	L374	
Krienke, Mary	L375	
KT Literary	L377	
Labyrinth Literary Agency, The	L378	
Lakosil, Natalie	L379	
Lambert, Sophie	L380	
Landis, Sarah	L381	
Langlee, Lina	L382	
Langmarc Publishing	P259	
Langton, Becca	L383	
Langtons International	L384	
Langtry, Elena	L385	
Latshaw, Katherine	L386	
Laxfield Literary Associates	L387	
Leach, Saskia	L389	
Leamington Books	P262	
Leapfrog Press	P263	
Lechon, Shannon	L390	
Leeke, Jessica	L391	
Lees, Jordan	L392	
Leigh Feldman Literary	L393	
Leon, Nina	L394	
Lerner Publishing Group	P264	
Levitt, Sarah	L396	
Lewinsohn Literary	L397	
Lewis, Alison	L398	
Lightner, Kayla	L399	
Lightning Books	P266	
Lilliput Press, The	P268	
Limelight Management	L400	
Lindsay Literary Agency	L401	
Lineberry, Isabel	L402	
Liss, Laurie	L403	
Liverpool Literary Agency, The	L404	
Liza Dawson Associates	L405	
Loft Press, Inc.	P270	
Lotus Lane Literary	L407	
Loughman, Morwenna	L408	
Lovell, Jake	L409	
Lutterworth Press, The	P275	
Lutyens and Rubinstein	L410	
Lyrical Press	P277	
MacDonald, Emily	L412	

Claim your free access to www.firstwriter.com: See p.403

Macdougall, Laura	L413
MacGregor & Luedeke	L414
MacKenzie, Joanna	L416
Maclean, Jamie	L417
MacLeod, Lauren	L418
Macmillan Children's Books	P279
Madan, Neeti	L419
Madeleine Milburn Literary, TV & Film Agency	L420
Maidment, Olivia	L421
Maltese, Alyssa	L422
Manilla Press	P280
Margaret K. McElderry Books	P281
Marini, Victoria	L423
Marr, Jill	L425
Marshall, Jen	L427
Massie, Maria	L430
Matte, Rebecca	L431
Mattson, Jennifer	L432
Maurer, Shari	L433
McBride, Juliana	L435
McCormick Literary	L436
McNidder & Grace	P286
McQuilkin, Rob	L438
Megibow, Sara	L439
Mehren, Jane von	L440
Meridian Artists	L442
Merullo, Annabel	L443
Metamorphosis Literary Agency	L444
Methuen Publishing Ltd	P294
Mic Cheetham Literary Agency	L445
Michel, Caroline	L446
Mihell, Natasha	L448
Milburn, Madeleine	L449
Mildred Marmur Associates, Ltd.	L450
Mileo, Jessica	L451
Milkweed Editions	P296
Mills & Boon	P297
Milusich, Grace	L453
Miranda, Caroline	L454
MMB Creative	L455
Molloy, Jess	L456
Moore, Mary C.	L457
Moore, Penny	L458
Moorhead, Max	L459
Morrell, Imogen	L460
Morris, Natascha	L461
Mortimer, Michele	L462
Motala, Tasneem	L463
Movable Type Management	L464
Mozley, Jack	L465
Mundy, Toby	L466
Murray, Judith	L468
Muscato, Nate	L469
Mushens, Juliet	L470
Mustelier, James	L471
Mysterious Press, The	P309
Napolitano, Maria	L473
Nash, Justin	L474
Nathan, Abigail	L475
Neely, Rachel	L476
Nelson Literary Agency, LLC	L477
Nelson, Kristin	L478
Nichols, Mariah	L479
Nightfire	P316
Niumata, Erin	L480
Northbank Talent Management	L482
O'Brien, Lee	L484
O'Grady, Faith	L485
O'Grady, Niamh	L486
O'Neill, Molly	L487
Oghma Creative Media	P321
Ogtrop, Kristin van	L489
Ohio State University Press, The	P323
Old Street Publishing Ltd	P325
Oldcastle Books Group	P326
Oneworld Publications	P327
Ooligan Press	P328
Orenda Books	P329
Ostby, Kristin	L494
Ouen Press	P331
Pan Macmillan Australia	P335
Pande, Ayesha	L497
Paradigm Talent and Literary Agency	L498
Parker, Elana Roth	L499
Parthian Books	P336
Pass, Marina de	L500
Patrician Press	P337
Patterson, Emma	L501
Paul S. Levine Literary Agency	L502
Pelham, Imogen	L504
Pen & Ink Designs Publishing	P342
Penzler Publishers	P345
Perez Literary & Entertainment	L506
Perez, Kristina	L507
Perotto-Wills, Martha	L508
Pestritto, Carrie	L511
Peter Owen Publishers	P349
Petty, Rachel	L512
Phelan, Beth	L514
Phillips, Aemilia	L515
Phoenix Moirai	P351
Piatkus Books	P352
Pickering, Juliet	L516
Pierce, Rosie	L517
Pinata Books	P355
Pine, Gideon	L518
Pineapple Press	P356
Plant, Zoe	L519
Plitt, Carrie	L520
Polygon	P360
Portobello Literary	L521
Posner, Marcy	L522
Power, Anna	L523
Prasanna, Tanusri	L525
Preston, Amanda	L526
Pureplay Press	P365
Quadrant Books	P366
Quirk Books	P369
Ramer, Susan	L528
Ravenstone	P374
Redhammer	L530
Reid, Janet	L532
Reilly, Milly	L533
Reino, Jessica	L534
Renard Press Ltd	P376
Riccardi, Francesca	L535
Richard Curtis Associates, Inc.	L536
Richter, Rick	L537
Roberts, Soumeya Bendimerad	L540
Robinson, Quressa	L542
Rocking Chair Books	L544
Rogers, Coleridge & White Ltd	L546
Root, Holly	L548
Rose and Crown Books	P381
Rosenberg Group, The	L549
Roseway	P382
Ross, Whitney	L551
Ruby Fiction	P384
Rudy Agency, The	L553
Rupert Crew Ltd	L554
Ruppin Agency, The	L555
Rushall, Kathleen	L556
Rutherford, Laetitia	L557
Rutman, Jim	L558
Saguaro Books, LLC	P388
Salazar, Des	L559
Salt Publishing	P389
Salvo, Katie	L560
Sanders, Rayhane	L562
Sant, Kelly Van	L563
Sarah Jane Freymann Literary Agency	L564
Sayle Literary Agency, The	L565
Scarfe, Rory	L566
Scarlet	P393
Schofield, Hannah	L567
Scholastic	P399
Scholastic UK	P400
Schwartz, Steve	L568
Scratching Shed Publishing	P402
Seager, Chloe	L571
Sebes & Bisseling	L572
Selectric Artists	L573
Sentient Publications	P404
Seren Books	P405
Serra, Maria Cardona	L574
Seymour, Charlotte	L575
Shaw Agency, The	L576
Sheil Land Associates Ltd	L577
Shesto Literary	L580
Shestopal, Camilla	L581
Shipwreckt Books Publishing Company	P406
Signorelli, Michael	L582
Silk, Julia	L583
Silver, Janet	L584
Simons, Tanera	L585
Simpson, Cara Lee	L586
Sinister Stoat Press	P410
Siobhan, Aiden	L587
Sluytman, Antoinette Van	L588
SmashBear Publishing	P412
Society for Promoting Christian Knowledge (SPCK)	P414
Soho Press	P417
Soler, Shania N.	L589
Soloway, Jennifer March	L590
Sophie Hicks Agency	L591
Sorg, Arley	L592
Sparsile Books	P419
Spout Press	P420
Spring Literary	L594
SRL Publishing	P421
Steed, Hayley	L595
Sternig & Byrne Literary Agency	L598
Steward House Publishers	P429
Stewart, Douglas	L599
Stringer Literary Agency LLC, The	L603
Stringer, Marlene	L604
Strong, Amy	L605
Stuart Krichevsky Literary Agency, Inc.	L609
Sunbelt Publications, Inc.	P433
Sunberry Books	P434
Sunpenny Publishing	P435
Susan Schulman Literary Agency	L610
Sutherland, Kari	L611
Swainson, Joanna	L613
Sweet Cherry Publishing	P437
SYLA – Susan Yearwood Literary Agency	L616
Symonds, Laurel	L617
Tailwinds Press	P439
Takikawa, Marin	L618
Talbot, Emily	L619
Tannenbaum, Amy	L620
Teresa Chris Literary Agency Ltd	L623
Terlip, Paige	L624
Texas A&M University Press	P445
Thayer, Henry	L626
Theseus Agency, The	L627
Thinkwell Books, UK	P447
Thistle Publishing	P448
Thorneycroft, Euan	L628
Thwaites, Steph	L629
Tibbets, Anne	L630
Tippermuir Books	P452
Toad Hall Editions	P453

Todd, Hannah L631
Topping, Antony L632
Tor P455
Tor Publishing Group P456
Tor Teen P457
Tor.com Publishing P458
Torrey House Press, LLC P459
Tran, Jennifer Chen L633
Troika Books P461
Trudel, Jes. L634
Trussell, Caroline L635
Turner Publishing P462
Two Piers Literary Agency, The L636
Tyndale House Publishers, Inc. P465
Udden, Jennifer L637
Ulverscroft Ltd. P467
Unbound Press P468
Unicorn Publishing Group P470
Universe P474
University of Iowa Press P480
University of Maine Press P481
University of Massachusetts Press P482
University of Michigan Press, The P483
University of Nevada Press P484
University of Wisconsin Press, The P490
Unwin, Jo L638
Usselman, Laura L639
Valley Press P493
Vance, Lisa Erbach L641
Velocity Press P496
Viney Agency, The L643
Viney, Charlie L644
Vinspire Publishing P497
Virago Books P498
W.W. Norton & Company Ltd P499
W.W. Norton & Company, Inc. P500
Walsh, Caroline L645
Watson, Little Ltd L647
Watterson, Jessica L648
Weidenfeld & Nicolson P505
Weiman, Paula L649
Weiss, Alexandra L650
Weitzner, Tess L651
Wells, Karmen L652
Westin, Erin Casey L654
Whatnall, Michaela L655
Whelan, Maria L656
Whispering Buffalo Literary Agency L657
Wickers, Chandler L659
Williams, Laura L662
Williams, Sarah L663
Williamson, Jo L664
Willms, Kathryn L665
Wilson, Desiree L667
Wilson, Ed L668
Wolfpack Publishing P513
Wood, Caroline L669
Woodhouse, James L670
Woods, Bryony L671
Woollard, Jessica L672
WordCrafts Press P514
Wordserve Literary L673
Wordsonthestreet P517
Wordsworth Editions P518
Workman Publishing P519
Writer's Side L674
Yeoh, Rachel L675
YesYes Books P521
Young, Claudia L677
Zack Company, Inc, The L678
Zacker, Marietta B. L679
Zeno Agency L680
Zibby Books P522
Zuraw-Friedland, Ayla L681
Novels in Verse
  Borstel, Stefanie Sanchez Von L071

Ostby, Kristin L494
Numerology
  See more broadly: Fortune Telling and Divination
  Red Feather P375
Numismatics (Coin / Currency Collecting)
  See more broadly: Hobbies
Nursing
  See more broadly: Health
  See more specifically: Midwifery
  Bloomsbury Academic P071
  Gill Education P182
  Taylor & Francis Group P441
  VanderWyk & Burnham P494
Nutrition
  See more broadly: Food and Drink; Health
  AARP The Magazine M006
  Betsy Amster Literary Enterprises L063
  Derviskadic, Dado L164
  Hammersmith Books P198
  Marr, Jill L425
  Redbook Magazine M310
  Singing Dragon P409
  Zack Company, Inc, The L678
  ZigZag Education P523
Oceanography
  See more broadly: Earth Science
  W.W. Norton & Company Ltd P499
Offshore Gamefishing
  See more broadly: Fishing
  Amato Books P021
  Marlin M236
Ohio
  See more broadly: United States
  Ohio State University Press, The P323
  Ohio University Press P324
  University of Akron Press, The P475
Organised Crime
  See more broadly: Crime
  See more specifically: Mafia
Outdoor Activities
  See more broadly: Activities
  See more specifically: Camping; Caving and Potholing; Diving; Outdoor Survival Skills; Walking
  417 Magazine M004
  AdventureKEEN P013
  Caitlin Press Inc. P090
  Menasha Ridge Press P290
  River Hills Traveler M313
  Rocky Mountain Books P378
  Scots Magazine, The M324
  Scottish Field M326
  University of Wisconsin Press, The P490
  Yorkshire Life M413
  Zack Company, Inc, The L678
Outdoor Survival Skills
  See more broadly: Outdoor Activities
  Asabi Publishing P034
Ozarks
  See more broadly: United States
  River Hills Traveler M313
Pacific
  See more broadly: Regional
  See more specifically: North Pacific Rim; South Pacific
  Bess Press P064
  Manoa M233
  Otago University Press P330
Pacific Northwest
  See more broadly: United States
  Basalt Books P057
Paganism
  See more broadly: Religion
  See more specifically: Wicca
  Llewellyn Worldwide Ltd P269

Painting
  See more broadly: Arts
  Korero Press P257
  Leisure Painter M217
  Rocky Nook P379
  Zack Company, Inc, The L678
Paleontology
  See more broadly: Biology
  Armstrong, Susan L032
  Indiana University Press P235
Palmistry
  See more broadly: Fortune Telling and Divination
  Red Feather P375
Parenting
  See more broadly: Family
  See more specifically: Motherhood; Pregnancy
  Baumer, Jan L051
  Bernardi, Amanda L062
  Betsy Amster Literary Enterprises L063
  Bradford Literary Agency L075
  CharlottesvilleFamily M082
  Dana Newman Literary, LLC L152
  Dickerson, Donya L168
  Draper, Claire L178
  Dunham, Jennie L180
  Felicia Eth Literary Representation L214
  Foxx, Kat L235
  Freymann, Sarah Jane L242
  Gill Books P181
  Hashtag Press P207
  Hay House Publishers P210
  Jeff Herman Agency, LLC, The L331
  Jessica Kingsley Publishers P246
  Joelle Delbourgo Associates, Inc. L334
  Kathryn Green Literary Agency, LLC L354
  Lazin, Sarah L388
  Macdougall, Laura L413
  Maurer, Shari L433
  Pacific Press Publishing Association P334
  Perry Literary L509
  Piatkus Books P352
  Quirk Books P369
  Red Magazine M309
  Redbook Magazine M310
  Regina Ryan Books L531
  Reino, Jessica L534
  Sheree Bykofsky Associates, Inc. L579
  Usselman, Laura L639
  W.W. Norton & Company Ltd P499
  Workman Publishing P519
  Zack Company, Inc, The L678
Pennsylvania
  See more broadly: United States
  See more specifically: Pittsburgh
Pensacola
  See more broadly: Florida
  Pensacola Magazine M281
Performance Poetry
  Burning Eye Books P087
Performing Arts
  See more broadly: Arts
  See more specifically: Dance; Storytelling
  Arcadia Publishing P031
  Brick M074
  Harvard University Press P206
  Indiana University Press P235
  Kensington Publishing Corp. P253
  Nolan, Laura L481
  Ohio University Press P324
  Scratching Shed Publishing P402
  Thames & Hudson Inc. P446
  University of Alberta Press P477
  University of Nevada Press P484
  W.W. Norton & Company, Inc. P500
Personal Coaching
  See more broadly: Personal Development

380 Index | *Personal Development*

Ki Agency Ltd ... L364
W.W. Norton & Company Ltd ... P499

Personal Development

See more specifically: Career Development; Leadership; Personal Coaching; Self Help

Alive Literary Agency ... L018
Ammonite Press ... P024
Charnace, Edwina de ... L117
Chartered Institute of Personnel and Development (CIPD) Publishing ... P104
Christie, Jennifer ... L126
Cynthia Cannell Literary Agency ... L150
Dickerson, Donya ... L168
Evans, Kate ... L204
Free Spirit Publishing ... P174
Goodman Beck Publishing ... P187
Grunewald, Hattie ... L282
Hardman, Caroline ... L295
Hay House Publishers ... P210
High Tide Press ... P217
Hiyate, Sam ... L313
Ki Agency Ltd ... L364
Killingley, Jessica ... L365
MMB Creative ... L455
Murdoch Books Australia ... P308
Piatkus Books ... P352
Robert Smith Literary Agency Ltd ... L539
Schofield, Hannah ... L567
Sheil Land Associates Ltd ... L577
Sheree Bykofsky Associates, Inc. ... L579
Society for Promoting Christian Knowledge (SPCK) ... P414
Strachan Literary Agency ... L602
Tyndale House Publishers, Inc. ... P465
VanderWyk & Burnham ... P494
Willms, Kathryn ... L665
Zack Company, Inc, The ... L678

Personal Essays

See more broadly: Autobiography; Narrative Essays

AARP The Magazine ... M006
Blue Earth Review ... M067
Creative Nonfiction ... M106
Identity Theory ... M194
Malahat Review, The ... M232
New England Review ... M255
Roberts, Soumeya Bendimerad ... L540
Southern Humanities Review ... M345
Toad Hall Editions ... P453
Tolka ... M379

Personal Experiences

See more broadly: Autobiography

Christie, Jennifer ... L126

Personal Finance

See more broadly: Finance

AARP The Magazine ... M006
First For Women ... M142
My Weekly ... M249
Zack Company, Inc, The ... L678

Pet Fish

See more broadly: Pets

Pets

See more broadly: Animals

See more specifically: Cats; Dogs; Pet Fish

Arcadia Publishing ... P031
Funny Times ... M157
Graham, Stacey ... L272
Hay House Publishers ... P210
Kensington Publishing Corp. ... P253
Quirk Books ... P369
Redbook Magazine ... M310
Turner Publishing ... P462
VanderWyk & Burnham ... P494
W.W. Norton & Company Ltd ... P499
Yours ... M416
Zack Company, Inc, The ... L678

Philosophy

See more specifically: Chinese Philosophy; Islamic Philosophy; Marxism; Taoism / Daoism

Arcadia Publishing ... P031
Authentic Life ... P041
Baylor University Press ... P060
Bloomsbury Academic ... P071
British Academy, The ... P083
Broadview Press ... P085
Christie, Jennifer ... L126
Clarke, Catherine ... L129
Combemale, Chris ... L133
Compassiviste Publishing ... P121
Derviskadic, Dado ... L164
Evans, David ... L203
Evans, Kate ... L204
Fathom Books ... P162
Fee: Foundation for Economic Education ... M138
Fortress Press ... P170
Frances Goldin Literary Agency, Inc. ... L238
Harvard University Press ... P206
Icon Books Ltd ... P227
Indiana University Press ... P235
Kensington Publishing Corp. ... P253
Lilliput Press, The ... P268
Loft Press, Inc. ... P270
London Review of Books ... M225
Lutterworth Press, The ... P275
Macdougall, Laura ... L413
Marion Boyars Publishers ... P282
Massachusetts Review, The ... M237
Ohio University Press ... P324
Oneworld Publications ... P327
Oxford Review of Books ... M271
Peter Lang ... P346
Peter Lang Publishing ... P348
Science Factory, The ... L569
Stanford University Press ... P427
Taylor & Francis Group ... P441
Thames & Hudson Inc. ... P446
Turtle Press ... P463
Unicorn Publishing Group ... P470
Unify ... P472
Unity ... P473
University of Alberta Press ... P477
University of California Press ... P478
University of Michigan Press, The ... P483
University of Nevada Press ... P484
University of Virginia Press ... P489
W.W. Norton & Company Ltd ... P499
W.W. Norton & Company, Inc. ... P500
WordCrafts Press ... P514
Yale University Press (London) ... P520
Yeoh, Rachel ... L675
ZigZag Education ... P523

Photography

See more broadly: Arts

Ammonite Press ... P024
Anvil Press Publishers ... P028
Arcadia Publishing ... P031
Bird Eye Books ... P066
Birlinn Ltd ... P067
Brick ... M074
Caitlin Press Inc. ... P090
Chase Literary Agency ... L118
Chronicle Books LLC ... P111
Compassiviste Publishing ... P121
Darga, Jon Michael ... L155
Doug Grad Literary Agency ... L177
Enitharmon Editions ... P153
Ghahremani, Lilly ... L257
Kensington Publishing Corp. ... P253
Laurence King Publishing ... P261
Lilliput Press, The ... P268
McNidder & Grace ... P286
Monacelli Press, The ... P304
Power Cut Lite ... M294
Prestel Publishing Ltd ... P362
Rocky Mountain Books ... P378
Rocky Nook ... P379
Ruralite ... M318
Seren Books ... P405
Square Mile Magazine ... M354
Thames & Hudson Inc. ... P446
University of Texas Press ... P488
University of Virginia Press ... P489
W.W. Norton & Company Ltd ... P499

Physical Education

See more broadly: Education

Colourpoint Educational ... P119
Gill Education ... P182
Mentor Books ... P292
ZigZag Education ... P523

Physics

See more broadly: Science

Colourpoint Educational ... P119
Gale ... P177
Gill Education ... P182
Medical Physics Publishing ... P288
Stipes Publishing ... P431
Taylor & Francis Group ... P441
W.W. Norton & Company Ltd ... P499

Physiology

See more broadly: Medicine

Stipes Publishing ... P431

Piano

See more broadly: Musical Instruments

International Piano ... M200

Picture Books

4RV Publishing ... P004
Agency (London) Ltd, The ... L009
Albert Whitman & Company ... P015
Alice Williams Literary ... L017
Allen & Unwin ... P018
Arcadia Publishing ... P031
Armada, Kurestin ... L030
Arms, Victoria Wells ... L031
Ascend Books, LLC ... P035
Atyeo, Charlotte ... L034
Baobab Press ... P054
Barr, Anjanette ... L045
Bath Literary Agency ... L049
Bess Press ... P064
Bradford Literary Agency ... L075
Brewin Books Ltd ... P081
Bright Agency (UK), The ... L082
Bright Agency (US), The ... L083
Brooks, Savannah ... L084
CAA (London) ... L098
Caroline Sheldon Literary Agency ... L106
Cartey, Claire ... L112
Charlesbridge Publishing ... P102
Cherry Lake Publishing Group ... P106
Child's Play (International) Ltd ... P107
Chronicle Books LLC ... P111
Cichello, Kayla ... L127
Comparato, Andrea ... L134
Crabtree Publishing ... P126
Crandall, Becca ... L142
Curtis Brown ... L146
DK Publishing ... P141
Dominguez, Adriana ... L174
Dunham Literary, Inc. ... L179
Dunham, Jennie ... L180
Eberly, Chelsea ... L187
Eddison Pearson Ltd ... L188
Eerdmans Books for Young Readers ... P148
Eunice McMullen Children's Literary Agent Ltd ... L201
Fairbank Literary Representation ... L208

Index | Poetry 381

Feldmann, Kait Lee L212
Fernandez, Rochelle L220
Filter Press P166
Finegan, Stevie L226
Flynn, Amy Thrall L229
Fraser Ross Associates L240
Free Spirit Publishing P174
Ghahremani, Lilly L257
Goetz, Adria L265
Goff, Ellen L267
Graffeg Childrens P191
Happy Yak P200
Hare, Jessica L296
Harwell, Hilary L301
Hawk, Susan L303
Hensley, Chelsea L307
Hodges, Jodie L315
Holroyde, Penny L319
Igloo Books Limited P232
Inscriptions Literary Agency L323
Irvine, Lucy L325
Joelle Delbourgo Associates, Inc. L334
Kane Press P251
Kube Publishing P258
Lakosil, Natalie L379
Lantana Publishing P260
Lerner Publishing Group P264
Lindsay Literary Agency L401
Macmillan Children's Books P279
Margaret K. McElderry Books P281
Marr, Jill L425
Maurer, Shari L433
Moore, Penny L458
Morris, Natascha L461
Native Ink Press P311
Nelson Literary Agency, LLC L477
Nosy Crow P319
Oghma Creative Media P321
Olswanger, Anna L491
Pacific Press Publishing Association P334
Pages, Saribel L496
Pavilion Books P338
Pen & Ink Designs Publishing P342
Petty, Rachel L512
Prasanna, Tanusri L525
Regina Ryan Books L531
Richter, Rick L537
Rofe, Jennifer L545
Rudy Agency, The L553
Rushall, Kathleen L556
Sanchez, Kaitlyn L561
Schiffer Kids P396
Scholastic P399
Scholastic UK P400
Scratching Shed Publishing P402
Society for Promoting Christian Knowledge (SPCK) P414
Soloway, Jennifer March L590
Spring Literary L594
StoryWise L601
Stringer Literary Agency LLC, The L603
Sunbelt Publications, Inc P433
Susan Schulman Literary Agency L610
Sutherland, Kari L611
Sweet Cherry Publishing P437
Symonds, Laurel L617
Talbot, Emily L619
Templar Books P442
Terlip, Paige L624
Thames & Hudson Inc. P446
Tilbury House Publishers P450
Tiny Owl P451
Tippermuir Books P452
Troika Books P461
Trudel, Jes L634
Turner Publishing P462
Tyndale House Publishers, Inc. P465
Vinspire Publishing P497
W.W. Norton & Company Ltd P499
Walsh, Caroline L645
Weiss, Alexandra L650
Westin, Erin Casey L654
Whatnall, Michaela L655
Williamson, Jo L664
WordCrafts Press P514
Words & Pictures P515
Zacker, Marietta B. L679

Piloting
See more broadly: Planes
Pilot M284

Pittsburgh
See more broadly: Pennsylvania

Planes
See more broadly: Vehicles
See more specifically: Piloting

Plants
See more specifically: Hemp
Draper, Claire L178

Poetry
2River View, The M001
30 North M002
32 Poems M003
404 Ink P002
4RV Poetry P003
4RV Publishing P004
aaduna M005
Able Muse Press P009
About Place Journal M007
Abridged M008
Account, The M009
Acumen M012
African American Review M014
African Voices M015
Agni M016
Alaska Quarterly Review M019
Allegro Poetry Magazine M021
Amethyst Review M024
Amling, Eric L021
And Other Stories P025
Andrews McMeel Publishing P026
Angela Poetry Magazine M025
Anhinga Press P027
Antigonish Review, The M026
Anvil Press Publishers P028
Arachne Press P030
Arboreal M027
Arc M028
Arcadia Publishing P031
Asimov's Science Fiction M033
Atlanta Review M036
Atrium M038
Babybug M041
Bacopa Literary Review M042
Baffler, The M043
Bald and Bonkers Network LLC P050
Bandit Fiction M045
Baobab Press P054
Barbican Press P055
Barren Magazine M047
Bath Literary Agency L049
Bear Deluxe Magazine, The M052
Begum, Salma L053
Belmont Story Review M054
Better Than Starbucks M058
BFS Horizons M059
Black Moon Magazine M064
Black Warrior Review M066
Bloodaxe Books P069
Blue Earth Review M067
Blue Mesa Review M068
BOA Editions, Ltd P076
Bookseeker Agency L070
Borstel, Stefanie Sanchez Von L071
Boston Review M071
Boyfriend Village M073
Burning Eye Books P087
Butcher's Dog M077
Caitlin Press Inc. P090
Chang, Nicola L116
Chapman M081
Chapman Publishing P099
Chautauqua Literary Journal M083
Cheshire M084
Child's Play (International) Ltd P107
Cincinnati Review, The M086
Cinnamon Press P112
Cobblestone M087
Cocoa Girl M088
Coil, The M089
Cola M090
Commonweal M091
Concho River Review M092
Conjunctions M093
Conjunctions Online M094
Coyote Arts P125
Crab Orchard Review M102
Crannog Magazine M103
Crazyhorse / Swamp Pink M104
Cream City Review M105
Critical Quarterly M108
Crystal Magazine M110
CutBank M111
Cyphers M112
Dalhousie Review, The M113
Dancing Girl Press P133
Dark Horse, The M114
Dawntreader, The M115
Dream Catcher M123
Ecotone M127
Eddison Pearson Ltd L188
Ekphrastic Review, The M128
El Portal M129
Enitharmon Editions P153
Essence Press P156
Event M133
Fathom Books P162
Faultline M137
Feminist Press, The P163
Feminist Studies M139
Fiddlehead, The M141
Filter Press P166
First Line, The M143
Five Points M144
Folio M147
Fortnightly Review, The M149
Fourteen Poems M152
Fourth River, The M153
Frances Goldin Literary Agency, Inc. L238
Fresh Words – An International Literary Magazine M154
Fugue M155
Future Fire, The M158
Gargoyle Online M161
Georgia Review, The M163
Gertrude M164
Gertrude Press P179
Ginosko Literary Journal M165
Glacier, The M166
Glass Poetry Press P183
Grain Literary Magazine M170
Granta M171
Graywolf Lab M172
Graywolf Press P193
Gulf Coast: A Journal of Literature and Fine Arts M173
Gutter Magazine M174
Half Mystic Journal M175
Half Mystic Press P197

Hanging Loose	M177
Harpur Palate	M179
Harris, Erin	L300
Hazel Press	P211
Hearing Eye	P212
Hedgerow: A Journal of Small Poems	M182
Helix, The	M183
Here Comes Everyone	M184
Hiraeth Books	P220
Host Publications	P224
Hotel Amerika	M189
Hudson Review, The	M190
Hunger Mountain	M191
Hwang, Annie	L322
I-70 Review	M192
Icehouse	P226
Idaho Review	M193
Identity Theory	M194
Image	M195
Indiana Review	M196
Indigo Dreams Publishing	P236
Ink Sweat and Tears	M197
Inkandescent	P240
Irish Pages	M203
Island	M204
Jamii Publishing	P245
Journal, The	M207
Kates Hill Press, The	P252
Kavya Kishor	M208
Kenyon Review, The	M210
Kerning	M211
Kore Press	P256
Kube Publishing	P258
Lake, The	M213
Landfall	M215
Lantana Publishing	P260
Leamington Books	P262
Leapfrog Press	P263
Lighthouse	M218
Lilliput Press, The	P268
Literary Mama	M220
Loft Press, Inc.	P270
London Grip New Poetry	M223
London Magazine, The	M224
London Review of Books	M225
Long Poem Magazine	M226
Lost Lake Folk Opera Magazine	M227
Louisiana Literature	M228
LSU Press	P273
MacGuffin, The	M229
Magma	M231
Malahat Review, The	M232
Manoa	M233
Margaret K. McElderry Books	P281
Massachusetts Review, The	M237
McQuilkin, Rob	L438
Meetinghouse	M238
Michigan Quarterly Review	M240
Mid-American Review	M241
Midsummer Dream House	M242
Midway Journal	M243
Milkweed Editions	P296
Missouri Review, The	M245
Moving Worlds: A Journal of Transcultural Writings	M247
MQR Mixtape	M248
Mudfog Press	P306
Nashville Review	M251
Neon	M253
New England Review	M255
New Orleans Review	M257
New Walk Editions	P315
New Welsh Reader	M259
Nine Arches Press	P317
North, The	M262
Northern Gravy	M263
Oakland Arts Review, The	M264
Obsidian: Literature in the African Diaspora	M265
Ohio State University Press, The	P323
Old Red Kimono	M267
On Spec	M268
Orbis International Literary Journal	M269
Ostby, Kristin	L494
Otago University Press	P330
Out-Spoken Press	P332
Oxford Poetry	M270
Oxford Review of Books	M271
Oyez Review	M272
Pacifica Literary Review	M273
Panorama	M274
Paris Review, The	M275
Parthian Books	P336
Passionfruit Review, The	M277
Patrician Press	P337
Pavilion Poetry	P339
Paycock Press	P340
Peepal Tree Press	P341
Pen & Ink Designs Publishing	P342
Pennine Ink Magazine	M280
Pleiades	M285
Ploughshares	M286
PN Review	M287
Poetry Ireland Review	M288
Poetry London	M289
Poetry Review, The	M290
Poetry Wales	M291
Polygon	P360
Popshot Quarterly	M293
Power Cut Lite	M294
Present Tense	M296
Press 53	P361
Prole	M299
Pulsar Poetry Magazine	M300
Pureplay Press	P365
Pushing Out the Boat	P301
Qu Literary Magazine	M302
Rabble Review	M303
Radar Poetry	M305
Renard Press Ltd	P376
Rialto, The	M311
River Styx	M314
Riverbed Review	M315
Roseway	P382
Saddlebag Dispatches	P319
Scifaikuest	M323
Scratching Shed Publishing	P402
Second Factory	M328
Seren Books	P405
Shearsman	M330
Shenandoah	M331
Shipwreckt Books Publishing Company	P406
Shooter Literary Magazine	M333
Shoreline of Infinity	M334
Shorts Magazine	M335
Silver, Janet	L584
Sinister Wisdom	M337
Slope Editions	P411
Smokestack Books	P413
Snowflake Magazine	M338
Soho Review, The	M339
South	M343
South Carolina Review	M344
Southern Humanities Review	M345
Southern Review, The	M346
Southwest Review	M348
Southword Journal	M349
Spelt Magazine	M352
Spitball	M353
Spout Press	P420
Stewed Rhubarb Press	P430
Stinging Fly, The	M355
Strange Horizons	M357
Structo Magazine	M359
Studio One	M360
Sunspot Literary Journal	M364
Supplement, The	M365
Sweetgum Press	P438
Tahoma Literary Review	M368
Takahe	M369
Tall-Lighthouse	P440
Tears in the Fence	M371
Temz Review, The	M372
Texas A&M University Press	P445
Thin Air Magazine	M374
Third Coast	M375
This England	M376
Threepenny Review, The	M377
Toad Hall Editions	P453
Torrey House Press, LLC	P459
Tributaries	M380
Troika Books	P461
Tusculum Review, The	M381
UCity Review	M382
Ugly Duckling Presse	P466
Under the Radar	M384
Understorey Magazine	M385
University of Akron Press, The	P475
University of Alaska Press	P476
University of Alberta Press	P477
University of Iowa Press	P480
University of Massachusetts Press	P482
University of Nevada Press	P484
University of North Texas Press	P485
University of Virginia Press	P489
University of Wisconsin Press, The	P490
Vagabond City	M386
Valley Press	P493
Vallum	M387
Vane Women Press	P495
Virginia Quarterly Review, The	M389
W.W. Norton & Company Ltd	P499
W.W. Norton & Company, Inc.	P500
Waccamaw	M394
Wallace Stevens Journal, The	M396
Walsh, Caroline	L645
Wasafiri	M398
Wayne State University Press	P504
Wesleyan University Press	P506
West Branch	M400
WestWard Quarterly	M403
White Review, The	M404
Windsor Review	M405
WordCrafts Press	P514
WordSong	P516
Wordsonthestreet	P517
Wordsworth Editions	P518
Yale Review, The	M409
Yes Poetry Magazine	M412
YesYes Books	P521
Zone 3	M419

Poetry Collections

404 Ink	P002
4RV Poetry	P003
4RV Publishing	P004
Able Muse Press	P009
Amling, Eric	L021
And Other Stories	P025
Andrews McMeel Publishing	P026
Anhinga Press	P027
Anvil Press Publishers	P028
Arachne Press	P030
Arcadia Publishing	P031
Baobab Press	P054
Barbican Press	P055
Begum, Salma	L053
Bloodaxe Books	P069

Index | Politics 383

BOA Editions, Ltd P076
Caitlin Press Inc. P090
Chapman Publishing P099
Cinnamon Press P112
Enitharmon Editions P153
Essence Press P156
Feminist Press, The P163
Graywolf Press P193
Half Mystic Press P197
Harris, Erin L300
Hazel Press P211
Hearing Eye P212
Hiraeth Books P220
Host Publications P224
Hwang, Annie L322
Icehouse P226
Indigo Dreams Publishing P236
Inkandescent P240
Jamii Publishing P245
Kates Hill Press, The P252
Kore Press P256
Leamington Books P262
Leapfrog Press P263
Loft Press, Inc. P270
LSU Press P273
McQuilkin, Rob L438
Milkweed Editions P296
Mudfog Press P306
New Walk Editions P315
Nine Arches Press P317
Ohio State University Press, The P323
Otago University Press P330
Out-Spoken Press P332
Parthian Books P336
Patrician Press P337
Pavilion Poetry P339
Paycock Press P340
Peepal Tree Press P341
Pen & Ink Designs Publishing P342
Polygon P360
Press 53 .... P361
Pureplay Press P365
Renard Press Ltd P376
Roseway P382
Scratching Shed Publishing P402
Seren Books P405
Shipwreckt Books Publishing Company P406
Silver, Janet L584
Slope Editions P411
Smokestack Books P413
Spout Press P420
Stewed Rhubarb Press P430
Sweetgum Press P438
Tall-Lighthouse P440
Texas A&M University Press P445
Toad Hall Editions P453
Torrey House Press, LLC P459
Ugly Duckling Presse P466
University of Akron Press, The P475
University of Alaska Press P476
University of Alberta Press P477
University of Massachusetts Press P482
Valley Press P493
Vane Women Press P495
W.W. Norton & Company Ltd P499
W.W. Norton & Company, Inc. P500
Walsh, Caroline L645
Wayne State University Press P504
Wesleyan University Press P506
WordCrafts Press P514
Wordsonthestreet P517
Wordsworth Editions P518
YesYes Books P521

Poetry as a Subject
See more broadly: Literature
32 Poems M003
Acumen M012
American Book Review M022
Arc M028
BOA Editions, Ltd P076
Ink Sweat and Tears M197
Journal, The M207
London Grip New Poetry M223
Long Poem Magazine M226
Lutterworth Press, The P275
Magma M231
Ohio University Press P324
Oxford Review of Books M271
PN Review M287
Poetry Ireland Review M288
Poetry Review, The M290
Poetry Wales M291
Scifaikuest M323
University of Akron Press, The P475
University of Iowa Press P480
Wallace Stevens Journal, The M396

Poetry in Translation
Acumen M012
Antigonish Review, The M026
Banipal M046
Barbican Press P055
Better Than Starbucks M058
BOA Editions, Ltd P076
Cincinnati Review, The M086
Cyphers M112
Ekphrastic Review, The M128
Faultline M137
Five Points M144
Future Fire, The M158
Gulf Coast: A Journal of Literature and Fine Arts M173
Half Mystic Journal M175
Host Publications P224
Hunger Mountain M191
Indiana Review M196
Irish Pages M203
Journal, The M207
Kenyon Review, The M210
Manoa M233
Massachusetts Review, The M237
Michigan Quarterly Review M240
Mid-American Review M241
Modern Poetry in Translation M246
Moving Worlds: A Journal of Transcultural Writings M247
Nashville Review M251
Orbis International Literary Journal M269
Oxford Poetry M270
Poetry London M289
Poetry Review, The M290
Shenandoah M331
Southern Review, The M346
Stinging Fly, The M355
Structo Magazine M359
Sunspot Literary Journal M364
Tributaries M380
Ugly Duckling Presse P466
White Review, The M404

Police
See more broadly: Crime
See more specifically: FBI; Police History
Brewin Books Ltd P081
Pluto Press P358
Stipes Publishing P431

Police History
See more broadly: Police

Police Procedural
See more broadly: Crime
Alfred Hitchcock Mystery Magazine M020
Bloodhound Books P070
Bookouture P078
Joffe Books P248
Kane Literary Agency L348
Oghma Creative Media P321
Pass, Marina de L500
Thorneycroft, Euan L628
Tibbets, Anne L630
Williams, Laura L662

Political History
See more broadly: History; Politics
Texas A&M University Press P445
University of Massachusetts Press P482
University of Pennsylvania Press P486

Political Thrillers
See more broadly: Politics; Thrillers
Andrew, Nelle L025
Orenda Books P329

Politics
See more specifically: Activism; Civil Rights; Conservative; Contemporary Politics; Left Wing Politics; Marxism; Political History; Political Thrillers; Progressive Politics; Socio-Political
404 Ink P002
Andrew, Nelle L025
Arcadia Publishing P031
Arsenal Pulp Press P032
Arte Publico Press P033
Baffler, The M043
Bartholomew, Jason L047
Basic Books P058
Baylor University Press P060
Berghahn Books Ltd P062
Birlinn Ltd P067
Blackstaff Press P068
Bloomsbury Academic P071
Boston Review M071
Brattle Agency LLC, The L080
Broadview Press P085
Brouckaert, Justin L087
Bucci, Chris L090
Carter, Rebecca L111
Caskie, Robert L113
Chanchani, Sonali L115
Charisma House P100
Claret Press P113
Colourpoint Educational P119
Commonweal M091
Compassiviste Publishing P121
Conversation (UK), The M095
Coombs Moylett & Maclean Literary Agency L139
Cottage Life M099
Crown P129
Crown Publishing Group, The P131
Danko, Margaret L154
Dawson, Liza L162
Diana Finch Literary Agency L167
Dijkstra, Sandra L169
Doug Grad Literary Agency L177
Dunham, Jennie L180
Economist, The M126
Elliott & Thompson P149
Ellis-Martin, Sian L197
Enslow Publishers, Inc. P154
Evans, David L203
Evans, Kate L204
Faulks, Holly L209
Fee: Foundation for Economic Education M138
Fernwood Publishing P164
Finan, Ciara L223
Finegan, Stevie L226
Flaneur M145
Fox, Aram L234
FRA (Futerman, Rose, & Associates) L236
Frances Goldin Literary Agency, Inc. L238

Claim your free access to **www.firstwriter.com**: See p.403

Free Association Books Ltd	P173
Funny Times	M157
Furniss, Eugenie	L249
Garamond Agency, Inc., The	L253
Geiger, Ellen	L255
Getzler, Josh	L256
Gill Books	P181
Gill Education	P182
Gold SF	P185
Goldstein, Veronica	L268
Gordon, Andrew	L270
Granger, David	L275
Granta Books	P192
Greyhound Literary	L278
Harmsworth, Esmond	L297
Harper's Magazine	M178
Harvard University Press	P206
Haus Publishing	P208
Henley Hall Press	P214
Hobbs, Victoria	L314
Icon Books Ltd	P227
Ig Publishing	P230
Imagine Publishing	P234
Irene Goodman Literary Agency (IGLA)	L324
Johns Hopkins University Press, The	P250
Kensington Publishing Corp.	P253
Kim, Jennifer	L366
Kim, Julia	L367
Kube Publishing	P258
Lazin, Sarah	L388
London Review of Books	M225
Lutterworth Press, The	P275
Macdougall, Laura	L413
marie claire	M234
Marr, Jill	L425
McCormick Literary	L436
Mendia, Isabel	L441
Methuen Publishing Ltd	P294
MMB Creative	L455
Moorhead, Max	L459
Morrell, Imogen	L460
Muscato, Nate	L469
New Internationalist	M256
New Statesman	M258
Ohio State University Press, The	P323
Ohio University Press	P324
Oneworld Publications	P327
Oxford Review of Books	M271
Patrician Press	P337
Paul S. Levine Literary Agency	L502
Peddle, Kay	L503
Peter Lang	P346
Peter Lang Publishing	P348
Phillips, Aemilia	L515
Pluto Press	P358
Political Quarterly, The	M292
Purdue University Press	P364
Pureplay Press	P365
Rabble Review	M303
Regina Ryan Books	L531
Reilly, Milly	L533
Richter, Rick	L537
Riposte	M312
Roseway	P382
Rudy Agency, The	L553
Sasquatch Books	P391
Scoular, Rosemary	L570
Scratching Shed Publishing	P402
Seventeen	M329
Sheil Land Associates Ltd	L577
Signorelli, Michael	L582
Stanford University Press	P427
Susan Schulman Literary Agency	L610
Taylor & Francis Group	P441
Texas A&M University Press	P445
Thayer, Henry	L626
Thinkwell Books, UK	P447
Thorneycroft, Euan	L628
Turner Publishing	P462
Tyndale House Publishers, Inc.	P465
University of Akron Press, The	P475
University of Alaska Press	P476
University of Alberta Press	P477
University of California Press	P478
University of Michigan Press, The	P483
University of Nevada Press	P484
University of Virginia Press	P489
University of Wisconsin Press, The	P490
Victoria Sanders & Associates LLC	L642
Virginia Quarterly Review, The	M389
W.W. Norton & Company Ltd	P499
W.W. Norton & Company, Inc.	P500
Washington State University Press	P501
Wilson, Ed	L668
Yale Review, The	M409
Yale University Press (London)	P520
Yeoh, Rachel	L675
Zack Company, Inc, The	L678
ZigZag Education	P523

Popular
See more specifically: Popular Culture; Popular History; Popular Music; Popular Psychology; Popular Science

Compassiviste Publishing	P121
Joelle Delbourgo Associates, Inc.	L334
Piatkus Books	P352
Regina Ryan Books	L531
Schwartz, Steve	L568

Popular Culture
See more broadly: Culture; Popular

Ammonite Press	P024
Aurora Metro Press	P039
Bates, Tim	L048
Bernardi, Amanda	L062
Betsy Amster Literary Enterprises	L063
Bowlin, Sarah	L073
Bradford Literary Agency	L075
Bucci, Chris	L090
Cassell	P096
Cavanagh, Claire	L114
Chronicle Books LLC	P111
Curran, Sabhbh	L145
Dana Newman Literary, LLC	L152
Darga, Jon Michael	L155
Derviskadic, Dado	L164
Dickerson, Donya	L168
Dolby, Trevor	L173
Ellis-Martin, Sian	L197
Evans, Kate	L204
Fairbank Literary Representation	L208
Felicia Eth Literary Representation	L214
Feminist Press, The	P163
Forrester, Jemima	L232
Glenister, Emily	L263
Goldstein, Veronica	L268
Gordon, Andrew	L270
Graham, Stacey	L272
Hanbury Agency, The	L290
Harvard University Press	P206
Heymont, Lane	L309
Holloway, Sally	L318
Irene Goodman Literary Agency (IGLA)	L324
Joelle Delbourgo Associates, Inc.	L334
Kathryn Green Literary Agency, LLC	L354
Kim, Jennifer	L366
Kim, Julia	L367
Kimber, Natalie	L368
Korero Press	P257
Kotchman, Katie	L374
Latshaw, Katherine	L386
Laurence King Publishing	P261
Lazin, Sarah	L388
Levitt, Sarah	L396
Lewinsohn Literary	L397
MacLeod, Lauren	L418
Madan, Neeti	L419
Maltese, Alyssa	L422
Marr, Jill	L425
Marshall, Jen	L427
McNidder & Grace	P286
Mehren, Jane von	L440
Mortimer, Michele	L462
Mundy, Toby	L466
Muscato, Nate	L469
O'Grady, Faith	L485
Paul S. Levine Literary Agency	L502
Pavilion Books	P338
Perry Literary	L509
Pickering, Juliet	L516
Pierce, Rosie	L517
Plexus Publishing Limited	P357
Polygon	P360
Quirk Books	P369
Ramer, Susan	L528
Reino, Jessica	L534
Richter, Rick	L537
Robert Smith Literary Agency Ltd	L539
Schiffer Publishing	P398
Susan Schulman Literary Agency	L610
Ten Speed Press	P444
Thames & Hudson Inc.	P446
Thayer, Henry	L626
University of Massachusetts Press	P482
University of Tennessee Press	P487
University of Wisconsin Press, The	P490
Watterson, Jessica	L648
Wells, Karmen	L652
Wickers, Chandler	L659
Williams, Laura	L662
Wilson, Ed	L668
Wordserve Literary	L673

Popular History
See more broadly: History; Popular

Bernardi, Amanda	L062
Evans, Kiya	L205
Furniss, Eugenie	L249
Patterson, Emma	L501
Swainson, Joanna	L613

Popular Music
See more broadly: Music; Popular

Thayer, Henry	L626

Popular Psychology
See more broadly: Popular; Psychology

Cassell	P096
Holloway, Sally	L318
Jonathan Pegg Literary Agency	L337
Kate Barker Literary, TV, & Film Agency	L352
Loughman, Morwenna	L408
Oneworld Publications	P327
Piatkus Books	P352
Plitt, Carrie	L520

Popular Science
See more broadly: Popular; Science

Alcock, Michael	L014
Barr, Anjanette	L045
Bernardi, Amanda	L062
Bucci, Chris	L090
Cassell	P096
Christie, Jennifer	L126
Clarke, Caro	L128
Combemale, Chris	L133
Conrad, Claire Paterson	L136
Coombs Moylett & Maclean Literary Agency	L139
Curran, Sabhbh	L145

Access more listings online at www.firstwriter.com

Danko, Margaret L154
DeBlock, Liza L163
Derviskadic, Dado L164
Dolby, Trevor L173
Dunn, Ben L181
Evans, Kate L204
Faulks, Holly L209
Felicia Eth Literary Representation L214
Fuentes, Sarah L247
Gauntlett, Adam L254
Gordon, Andrew L270
Hardman, Caroline L295
Holloway, Sally L318
Icon Books Ltd P227
Jonathan Pegg Literary Agency L337
Kantor, Camille L349
Keren, Eli L362
Kotchman, Katie L374
Langtry, Elena L385
Laurence King Publishing P261
Levitt, Sarah L396
Limelight Management L400
Loughman, Morwenna L408
Macdougall, Laura L413
Maurer, Shari L433
Mills, Rachel L452
Mundy, Toby L466
Oneworld Publications P327
Peddle, Kay L503
Perez Literary & Entertainment L506
Perez, Kristina L507
Plitt, Carrie L520
Power, Anna L523
Robinson, Quressa L542
Scoular, Rosemary L570
Seymour, Charlotte L575
Sheil Land Associates Ltd L577
Walsh, Kate L646
Williams, Laura L662
Zack Company, Inc, The L678

Post Traumatic Stress Disorder
See more broadly: Psychological Trauma
W.W. Norton & Company Ltd P499

Post-Apocalyptic
See more broadly: Science Fiction
Bennett, Laura L056
Liverpool Literary Agency, The L404
Mozley, Jack L465
Zack Company, Inc, The L678

Postcolonialism
See more broadly: Culture; Society
Feminist Press, The P163
Fernwood Publishing P164
Future Fire, The M158
Gold SF P185
Roberts, Soumeya Bendimerad L540
Takikawa, Marin L618
Yeoh, Rachel L675

Poverty
See more broadly: Social Issues
Barr, Anjanette L045

Practical Art
See more broadly: Arts

Pregnancy
See more broadly: Parenting
See more specifically: Childbirth
Foxx, Kat L235
Singing Dragon P409
Workman Publishing P519

Prehistoric Animals
See more broadly: Animals
See more specifically: Dinosaurs

Preschool
See more broadly: School

Prescriptive Nonfiction
Baumer, Jan L051

Krienke, Mary L375
Latshaw, Katherine L386
Maltese, Alyssa L422
Mileo, Jessica L451
Niumata, Erin L480
O'Shea, Amy L488
Ogtrop, Kristin van L489
Stephens, Jenny L596

Procurement
See more broadly: Business

Professional
Accountancy Age M010
Accountancy Daily M011
Architectural Review, The M029
Bloomsbury Professional P072
Blue Poppy Enterprises P074
Bookseller, The M070
Brown, Son & Ferguson, Ltd P086
Campaign M079
CGI (Chartered Governance Institute)
   Publishing P098
Chartered Institute of Personnel and
   Development (CIPD) Publishing P104
Coaches Choice P116
Cornell Maritime Press P123
Croner-i Limited P127
Crossway P128
Elsevier Ltd P150
Evan-Moor Educational Publishers P157
Facet Publishing P159
Fiscal Publications P168
Fortress Press P170
Funeral Business Solutions M156
Gale P177
Goss & Crested China Club P189
Hammersmith Books P198
Idyll Arbor P229
Insurance Age M199
International Piano M200
International Society for Technology in
   Education (ISTE) P242
Jessica Kingsley Publishers P246
Leisure Group Travel M216
LexisNexis P265
Linguist, The M219
Loft Press, Inc. P270
Lund Humphries Limited P274
McGraw Hill EMEA P285
Medical Physics Publishing P288
Mentor Books P292
NAHB BuilderBooks P310
New Harbinger Publications P314
Oak Tree Press P320
PC Pro M279
Pilot M284
Practising Midwife, The M295
Prufrock Press P363
Round Hall P383
Scholastic P399
Scottish Farmer, The M325
Ships Monthly Magazine M332
Singing Dragon P409
Spa Magazine M350
Speciality Food M351
Strategic Finance M358
Successful Meetings M361
Sunshine Artist M363
Sweet & Maxwell P436
Swimming Pool News M367
Taylor & Francis Group P441
W.W. Norton & Company Ltd P499
W.W. Norton & Company, Inc. P500

Progressive Politics
See more broadly: Politics
Mendia, Isabel L441

Project Management
See more broadly: Management

Property / Real Estate
Atlanta Magazine M035
Cotswold Life M098
Cottage Life M099
Essex Life M132
Lancashire Life M214
Square Mile Magazine M354
Westchester Magazine M402

Prose Poetry
Better Than Starbucks M058
Hedgerow: A Journal of Small Poems M182
Ink Sweat and Tears M197
Orbis International Literary Journal M269
Tears in the Fence M371

Prostitution
See more broadly: Sex

Psychiatry
See more broadly: Medicine
See more specifically: Mental Disorders
Taylor & Francis Group P441
W.W. Norton & Company Ltd P499

Psychic Abilities
See more broadly: Supernatural / Paranormal
See more specifically: Astral Projection; Chakras
Llewellyn Worldwide Ltd P269
Red Feather P375

Psychoanalysis
See more broadly: Psychology
W.W. Norton & Company Ltd P499

Psychological Horror
See more broadly: Horror
Sinister Stoat Press P410
Siobhan, Aiden L587
Soloway, Jennifer March L590
Stringer, Marlene L604
Tibbets, Anne L630
Trussell, Caroline L635
Udden, Jennifer L637

Psychological Suspense
See more broadly: Suspense
See more specifically: Psychological Suspense Thrillers
Brace, Samantha L074
Curran, Sabhbh L145
Forrester, Jemima L232
Greenstreet, Katie L277
Hordern, Kate L320
Kavanagh, Jade L355
Marr, Jill L425
Pan Macmillan Australia P335
Pierce, Rosie L517
Posner, Marcy L522
Scarlet P393
Soloway, Jennifer March L590
Tannenbaum, Amy L620
Terlip, Paige L624
Thorneycroft, Euan L628
Vance, Lisa Erbach L641

Psychological Suspense Thrillers
See more broadly: Psychological Suspense; Psychological Thrillers

Psychological Thrillers
See more broadly: Thrillers
See more specifically: Psychological Suspense Thrillers
Andrew, Nelle L025
Berdinsky, Kendall L060
Bloodhound Books P070
Bookouture P078
Charnace, Edwina de L117
Choc Lit P108
Coombes, Clare L138
Danaczko, Melissa L153
Evans, Kiya L205

Fergusson, Julie L219
Finan, Ciara L223
Galvin, Lori L252
Glenister, Emily L263
Harper, Logan L299
Joffe Books P248
Kane Literary Agency L348
Langtry, Elena L385
Maltese, Alyssa L422
Nichols, Mariah L479
Orenda Books P329
Reino, Jessica L534
Richter, Rick L537
Shestopal, Camilla L581
Trussell, Caroline L635
Williams, Laura L662
Williamson, Jo L664

Psychological Trauma
See more broadly: Psychology
See more specifically: Post Traumatic Stress Disorder
Hay House Publishers P210
W.W. Norton & Company Ltd P499

Psychology
See more specifically: Anxiety Disorders; Depression; Eating Disorders; Hypnosis; Neurodiversity; Neuropsychology; Popular Psychology; Psychoanalysis; Psychological Trauma; Psychotherapy; Stress Management
Arcadia Publishing P031
Authentic Life P041
Basic Books P058
Baxter, Veronique L052
Betsy Amster Literary Enterprises .. L063
Bloomsbury Academic P071
Christie, Jennifer L126
Compassiviste Publishing P121
Crown P129
Curran, Sabhbh L145
Dana Newman Literary, LLC L152
Derviskadic, Dado L164
Felicia Eth Literary Representation .. L214
Fogg, Jack L230
Freymann, Sarah Jane L242
Garamond Agency, Inc., The L253
Gauntlett, Adam L254
Geiger, Ellen L255
Gill Education P182
Goodman Beck Publishing P187
Gordon, Andrew L270
Hardman, Caroline L295
Harmsworth, Esmond L297
Harvard University Press P206
High Tide Press L217
Hoffman, Scott L316
Icon Books Ltd P227
Jeff Herman Agency, LLC, The L331
Joelle Delbourgo Associates, Inc. ... L334
Kensington Publishing Corp. P253
Kirby, Robert L370
Kotchman, Katie L374
London Review of Books M225
Lutterworth Press, The P275
M. Evans & Company P278
Macdougall, Laura L413
Maltese, Alyssa L422
Marion Boyars Publishers P282
Maw, Jane Graham L434
Mills, Rachel L452
MMB Creative L455
Molloy, Jess L456
Murgolo, Karen L467
Mushens, Juliet L470
New Harbinger Publications P314
Nolan, Laura L481
Oneworld Publications P327

Pelham, Imogen L504
Perry Literary L509
Pierce, Rosie L517
Posner, Marcy L522
Power, Anna L523
Preston, Amanda L526
R D Publishers P370
Regina Ryan Books L531
Reilly, Milly L533
Rosenberg Group, The L549
Schwartz, Steve L568
Sheil Land Associates Ltd L577
Sheree Bykofsky Associates, Inc. .. L579
Susan Schulman Literary Agency .. L610
Taylor & Francis Group P441
Turner Publishing P462
University of Akron Press, The P475
University of Alberta Press P477
University of Michigan Press, The .. P483
University of Nevada Press P484
Victoria Sanders & Associates LLC .. L642
W.W. Norton & Company Ltd P499
W.W. Norton & Company, Inc. P500
Willms, Kathryn L665
Wordserve Literary L673
ZigZag Education P523

Psychotherapy
See more broadly: Psychology
See more specifically: Juvenile Psychotherapy
Bloomsbury Academic P071
Free Association Books Ltd P173
W.W. Norton & Company Ltd P499

Public Health
See more broadly: Health
Purdue University Press P364

Publishing
See more broadly: Business
See more specifically: Book Publishing; Small Press
Ooligan Press P328
University of Virginia Press P489

Pubs
See more broadly: Leisure
Square Mile Magazine M354

Punk
See more broadly: Music

Puzzles
Andrews McMeel Publishing P026
Barbour Publishing P056
Cobblestone M087
Igloo Books Limited P232
Imagine Publishing P234
Take a Break's Take a Puzzle M370

Qigong
See more broadly: Martial Arts
Singing Dragon P409

Quakerism
See more broadly: Christianity
Friends United Press P175

Queer Romance
See more broadly: Romance
Matte, Rebecca L431

Quilting
See more broadly: Crafts; Hobbies
C&T Publishing P088

Racecars
See more broadly: Cars
Racecar Engineering M304

Racism
See more broadly: Discrimination
Fernwood Publishing P164
Mendia, Isabel L441
University of Alberta Press P477

Radio Control
See more broadly: Technology

Radio Scripts
AHA Talent Ltd L010
Alan Brodie Representation L013
Bolger, Maeve L068
Elaine Steel L196
JFL Agency L332
Judy Daish Associates Ltd L342
Oakland Arts Review, The M264
Rochelle Stevens & Co. L543
Tennyson Agency, The L622
Valerie Hoskins Associates L640

Radio Technology
See more broadly: Audio Technology
See more specifically: Amateur Radio

Radnorshire
See more broadly: Wales
Logaston Press P271

Railways
See more broadly: Transport
Countryside Books P124
Indiana University Press P235
Rail Express M306

Ranch Lifestyle
See more broadly: Lifestyle
Cowboys & Indians M101

Ranches
See more broadly: Houses and Homes
Cowboys & Indians M101

Reading
See more broadly: Education
See more specifically: High-Low Literacy

Real Life Stories
Bella M053
Colwill, Charlotte L132
My Weekly M249
Robert Smith Literary Agency Ltd .. L539
Simpson, Cara Lee L586
Yours M416

Realistic
Mortimer, Michele L462
Soloway, Jennifer March L590

Recipes
See more broadly: Cookery
Balance M044
Better Homes and Gardens M057
Kent Life M209
Ruralite M318
Yours M416

Recreation
See more broadly: Leisure
See more specifically: Recreational Vehicles
Arcadia Publishing P031
Enslow Publishers, Inc. P154
Johns Hopkins University Press, The .. P250
Kensington Publishing Corp. P253
University of Massachusetts Press . P482
University of Nevada Press P484

Recreational Vehicles
See more broadly: Recreation; Vehicles

Reference
ABC-CLIO P008
Arcadia Publishing P031
Bentley Publishers P061
Brown, Megan L088
Collins P118
DK Publishing P141
Encyclopedia Britannica (UK) Ltd .. P151
Gale P177
Gill Books P181
Goss & Crested China Club P189
Guinness World Records P194
Harvard University Press P206
Hippocrene Books, Inc. P219
Igloo Books Limited P232
Jain Publishing Company, Inc. P244
Jeff Herman Agency, LLC, The L331

Joelle Delbourgo Associates, Inc. L334
Kensington Publishing Corp. P253
Lazin, Sarah L388
LexisNexis P265
Lilliput Press, The P268
Pineapple Press P356
Rand McNally P371
Regina Ryan Books L531
Thames & Hudson Inc. P446
Tyndale House Publishers, Inc. P465
University of Michigan Press, The P483
W.W. Norton & Company, Inc. P500
Yale University Press (London) P520

Refugees
See more broadly: Social Issues
Indiana University Press P235
University of Alberta Press P477

Regency Romance
See more broadly: Romance

Regional
See more specifically: Africa; Antarctica; Arctic; Asia; Atlantic; Australasia / Oceania; Caribbean; Central America; Europe; Local; Middle East; North America; Pacific; Regional History; South America
23 House Publishing P001
Arsenal Pulp Press P032
Cornell Maritime Press P123
Dahlia Books P132
Indiana University Press P235
MacDonald, Emily L412
Schiffer Publishing P398
Sigma Press P407
Wayne State University Press P504

Regional Cooking
See more broadly: Cookery

Regional History
See more broadly: History; Regional
Whitecap Books Ltd P507

Reiki
See more broadly: Alternative Health
Llewellyn Worldwide Ltd P269

Reincarnation
See more broadly: Supernatural / Paranormal
Llewellyn Worldwide Ltd P269

Relationships
See more specifically: Couple Therapy; Family; Love; Sex; Sexuality
AARP The Magazine M006
Arcadia Publishing P031
Bradford Literary Agency L075
Chiotti, Danielle L123
Cho, Catherine L124
Chronicle Books LLC P111
Cleis Press P115
Dunham, Jennie L180
Ellis-Martin, Sian L197
Finan, Ciara L223
Funny Times M157
Hay House Publishers P210
Kensington Publishing Corp. P253
Lewinsohn Literary L397
Maclean, Jamie L417
marie claire M234
marie claire (UK) M235
McBride, Juliana L435
Moody Publishers P305
O'Grady, Niamh L486
Pacific Press Publishing Association P334
Paul S. Levine Literary Agency L502
Pickering, Juliet L516
Quirk Books P369
Red Magazine M309
Redbook Magazine M310
Simpson, Cara Lee L586

Society for Promoting Christian
  Knowledge (SPCK) P414
Soloway, Jennifer March L590
Turner Publishing P462
Tyndale House Publishers, Inc. P465
Unity P473
University of Nevada Press P484
Vance, Lisa Erbach L641
Wilson, Desiree L667
Yours M416
Zack Company, Inc, The L678

Religion
See more broadly: Spirituality
See more specifically: Angels; Baha'i; Buddhism; Christianity; Hinduism; Inspirational; Islam; Judaism; Paganism; Shamanism; Voodoo
Alive Literary Agency L018
Arcadia Publishing P031
Barr, Anjanette L045
Baumer, Jan L051
Baylor University Press P060
Bloomsbury Academic P071
Colourpoint Educational P119
Commonweal M091
Derviskadic, Dado L164
DeVorss & Company P139
Dijkstra, Sandra L169
Doug Grad Literary Agency L177
Funny Times M157
Geiger, Ellen L255
Gill Education P182
Harvard University Press P206
Icon Books Ltd P227
Image M195
Indiana University Press P235
InterVarsity Press (IVP) P243
Irish Pages M203
Jessica Kingsley Publishers P246
Johns Hopkins University Press, The P250
Kensington Publishing Corp. P253
Lutterworth Press, The P275
Mentor Books P292
Milusich, Grace L453
Ohio University Press P324
Oneworld Publications P327
Peter Lang P346
Peter Lang Publishing P348
Richter, Rick L537
Stanford University Press P427
Strachan Literary Agency L602
Taylor & Francis Group P441
Thames & Hudson Inc. P446
Turner Publishing P462
University of Alberta Press P477
University of California Press P478
University of Massachusetts Press P482
University of Michigan Press, The P483
University of Tennessee Press P487
University of Virginia Press P489
W.W. Norton & Company Ltd P499
W.W. Norton & Company, Inc. P500
Watkins Publishing P503
Yale University Press (London) P520
Zack Company, Inc, The L678
ZigZag Education P523

Renaissance
See more broadly: History
University of Massachusetts Press P482
University of Michigan Press, The P483
University of Pennsylvania Press P486

Restaurants
See more broadly: Food and Drink
Somerset Life M341
Westchester Magazine M402

Retirement
See more broadly: Lifestyle

Retropunk
See more broadly: Science Fiction

Reviews
32 Poems M003
Acumen M012
African American Review M014
American Book Review M022
Arc M028
Art Monthly M030
Banipal M046
BFS Journal M060
Big Fiction M061
Black Moon Magazine M064
Bluegrass Unlimited M069
Boston Review M071
Coil, The M089
Concho River Review M092
Creem M107
Dalhousie Review, The M113
Ekphrastic Review, The M128
Event M133
Facts & Fiction M135
Fortnightly Review, The M149
Foundation: The International Review
  of Science Fiction M151
Fresh Words – An International
  Literary Magazine M154
Fugue M155
Funeral Business Solutions M156
Future Fire, The M158
Georgia Review, The M163
Gulf Coast: A Journal of Literature and
  Fine Arts M173
Hudson Review, The M190
Ink Sweat and Tears M197
Jazz Journal M206
Journal, The M207
Kavya Kishor M208
Landfall M215
Literary Mama M220
London Grip M222
London Grip New Poetry M223
London Review of Books M225
Long Poem Magazine M226
Magma M231
Malahat Review, The M232
Mid-American Review M241
Missouri Review, The M245
New Orleans Review M257
Oxford Poetry M270
Oxford Review of Books M271
PC Gamer M278
Pleiades M285
PN Review M287
Poetry Review, The M290
Poetry Wales M291
Political Quarterly, The M292
Power Cut Lite M294
Reactor M307
Red Magazine M309
Sierra M336
Sinister Wisdom M337
Somerset Life M341
South Carolina Review M344
Spitball M353
Strange Horizons M357
Sunshine Artist M363
Supplement, The M365
Takahe M369
Tears in the Fence M371
Temz Review, The M372
Tusculum Review, The M381
Uncut M383
Vagabond City M386

Vallum.. M387
Vestal Review................................... M388
Wallace Stevens Journal, The.................. M396
West Branch.. M400
Yes Poetry Magazine............................. M412
Revisionist History
See more broadly: History
Rivers
See more broadly: Geography
Riverbed Review................................. M315
Road Atlases
See more broadly: Travel
Rand McNally..................................... P371
Road Trips
See more broadly: Travel
Robots
See more broadly: Technology
Rock Collecting / Rockhounding
See more broadly: Hobbies
Rock & Gem...................................... M316
Rock Music
See more broadly: Music
Creem.. M107
Rocks
See more broadly: Geology
Rock & Gem...................................... M316
Romance
*See more specifically: Christian Romance;
Contemporary Romance; Diverse Romance;
Erotic Romance; Feminist Romance; High
Concept Romance; Historical Romance;
Queer Romance; Regency Romance;
Romantasy; Romantic Comedy; Romantic
Mystery; Romantic Suspense; Romantic
Thrillers; Speculative Romance;
Supernatural / Paranormal Romance;
Timeslip Romance; Upmarket Romance*
3 Seas Literary Agency.........................L001
4RV Publishing....................................P004
4RV Tenacious....................................P005
Afterglow Books..................................P014
Alex Adsett Literary.............................L016
Allison & Busby Ltd............................P019
Anderson, Darley.................................L022
Armada, Kurestin.................................L030
Avon Books...P045
Barbour Publishing...............................P056
Barone Literary Agency.......................L043
Begum, Salma.....................................L053
Belton, Maddy.....................................L055
Bent, Jenny..L059
Bhasin, Tamanna..................................L064
Blue Jeans Books.................................P073
Bradford Literary Agency....................L075
Bradford, Laura....................................L076
Brannan, Maria....................................L078
Brewer, Amy.......................................L081
Burns, Camille.....................................L094
Caprio, Alice.......................................L103
Carroll, Megan.....................................L110
Chang, Nicola......................................L116
Choc Lit..P108
Christensen, Erica................................L125
Cichello, Kayla....................................L127
Colwill, Charlotte................................L132
Crowley, Sheila....................................L144
Crystal Magazine.................................M110
Curtis Brown.......................................L146
Cusick, John..L148
Darley Anderson Agency, The.............L157
Davies, Elinor......................................L160
Doug Grad Literary Agency.................L177
Draper, Claire......................................L178
Dreamspinner Press.............................P144
Eberly, Chelsea....................................L187
Ellis-Martin, Sian.................................L197
Ellor, Zabé..L198
Evans, Kate..L204
Evans, Kiya...L205
Evans, Stephany...................................L206
Fazzari, Hillary....................................L210
Figueroa, Melanie................................L221
Finan, Ciara...L223
Finch, Rebeka.....................................L225
Foster, Clara..L233
Foxx, Kat...L235
Frankel, Valerie...................................L239
Friedman, Claire..................................L243
Gilbert, Tara..L258
Gisondi, Katie.....................................L261
Glenister, Emily...................................L263
Goff, Ellen...L267
Good Literary Agency, The.................L269
Grajkowski, Michelle..........................L274
Greenstreet, Katie...............................L277
Haggerty, Taylor..................................L287
Haley, Jolene.......................................L289
Hannah Sheppard Literary Agency......L291
Harlequin Desire..................................P202
Harlequin Mills & Boon Ltd................P203
Harmony Ink Press..............................P205
Hensley, Chelsea.................................L307
Hernando, Paloma...............................L308
Hogrebe, Christina..............................L317
Hornsley, Sarah...................................L321
Irene Goodman Literary Agency
  (IGLA)..L324
Irvine, Lucy..L325
Jamieson, Molly..................................L329
Joffe Books...P248
Keane Kataria Literary Agency...........L358
Kensington Publishing Corp................P253
Knigge, Sheyla....................................L372
Langlee, Lina......................................L382
Leon, Nina..L394
Lewinsohn Literary..............................L397
Macdougall, Laura..............................L413
MacGregor & Luedeke.......................L414
Maltese, Alyssa...................................L422
Marr, Jill...L425
Marshall, Jen......................................L427
Matte, Rebecca...................................L431
Megibow, Sara....................................L439
Mills & Boon......................................P297
MMB Creative....................................L455
Molloy, Jess..L456
Mortimer, Michele..............................L462
Murray, Judith....................................L468
Nathan, Abigail...................................L475
Neely, Rachel.....................................L476
Nichols, Mariah..................................L479
Niumata, Erin.....................................L480
Oghma Creative Media......................P321
Orenda Books.....................................P329
Ostby, Kristin......................................L494
Parker, Elana Roth..............................L499
Paul S. Levine Literary Agency...........L502
People's Friend Pocket Novels............M282
Perez Literary & Entertainment...........L506
Perez, Kristina....................................L507
Pestritto, Carrie..................................L511
Petty, Rachel......................................L512
Piatkus Books.....................................P352
Plitt, Carrie...L520
Posner, Marcy....................................L522
Preston, Amanda................................L526
Quirk Books.......................................P369
R D Publishers...................................P370
Reino, Jessica.....................................L534
Rosenberg Group, The.......................L549
Ross, Whitney....................................L551
Ruby Fiction......................................P384
Rushall, Kathleen................................L556
Salazar, Des..L559
Salvo, Katie..L560
Serra, Maria Cardona..........................L574
Sheil Land Associates Ltd...................L577
Simons, Tanera...................................L585
Siobhan, Aiden...................................L587
Soler, Shania N...................................L589
Soloway, Jennifer March.....................L590
Steed, Hayley.....................................L595
Story Unlikely....................................M356
Stringer, Marlene................................L604
Sunpenny Publishing..........................P435
Todd, Hannah.....................................L631
Torrey House Press, LLC....................P459
Tran, Jennifer Chen.............................L633
Trudel, Jes..L634
Trussell, Caroline................................L635
Turner Publishing...............................P462
Udden, Jennifer..................................L637
Vinspire Publishing............................P497
Watterson, Jessica..............................L648
Williams, Laura..................................L662
Williams, Sarah..................................L663
Williamson, Jo....................................L664
Wilson, Desiree..................................L667
Wood, Caroline..................................L669
Woods, Bryony...................................L671
WordCrafts Press................................P514
Wordserve Literary.............................L673
Yours Fiction – Women's Special
  Series..M417
Zack Company, Inc, The.....................L678
Romania
See more broadly: Europe
Peter Lang..P346
Peter Lang Publishing.........................P348
Romantasy
See more broadly: Fantasy; Romance
Adsett, Alex..L006
Afonso, Thais.....................................L008
Armada, Kurestin...............................L030
Bradford Literary Agency...................L075
Carroll, Megan....................................L110
Charnace, Edwina de..........................L117
Choc Lit...P108
Darley Anderson Agency, The............L157
DeBlock, Liza.....................................L163
Evans, Kiya..L205
Fazzari, Hillary...................................L210
Finan, Ciara..L223
Finch, Rebeka....................................L225
Fitzgerald, Bea...................................L227
Foster, Clara.......................................L233
Gillam, Bianca....................................L259
Gisondi, Katie....................................L261
Goff, Ellen..L267
Hannah Sheppard Literary Agency......L291
Lechon, Shannon................................L390
Leon, Nina...L394
Lindsay Literary Agency....................L401
Lineberry, Isabel.................................L402
Marr, Jill...L425
Matte, Rebecca...................................L431
Milusich, Grace..................................L453
Murray, Judith....................................L468
Nathan, Abigail...................................L475
Schofield, Hannah..............................L567
Soler, Shania N...................................L589
Steed, Hayley.....................................L595
Trussell, Caroline................................L635
Turner Publishing...............................P462
Udden, Jennifer..................................L637
Zack Company, Inc, The.....................L678
Romantic Comedy
See more broadly: Comedy / Humour; Romance

Index | *Science* **389**

Adsett, Alex L006
Afonso, Thais L008
Alex Adsett Literary L016
Andrew, Nelle L025
Avon Books P045
Bauman, Erica L050
Bent, Jenny L059
Bloodhound Books P070
Bookouture P078
Bradford Literary Agency L075
Brannan, Maria L078
Brooks, Savannah L084
Choc Lit P108
Cichello, Kayla L127
Cooper, Gemma L140
Cusick, John L148
Danko, Margaret L154
Darley Anderson Agency, The L157
Dodd, Saffron L172
Ellis-Martin, Sian L197
Evans, Kiya L205
Fabien, Samantha L207
Fazzari, Hillary L210
Fellows, Abi L216
Fergusson, Julie L219
Fernandez, Rochelle L220
Finan, Ciara L223
Finch, Rebeka L225
Foxx, Kat L235
Gilbert, Tara L258
Gillam, Bianca L259
Gisondi, Katie L261
Glenister, Emily L263
Goetz, Adria L265
Good Literary Agency, The L269
Graham, Stacey L272
Haley, Jolene L289
Harper, Logan L299
Langton, Becca L383
Lewinsohn Literary L397
MacDonald, Emily L412
Marr, Jill L425
Mileo, Jessica L451
Murray, Judith L468
Napolitano, Maria L473
Nathan, Abigail L475
Neely, Rachel L476
Nichols, Mariah L479
Niumata, Erin L480
O'Brien, Lee L484
Oghma Creative Media P321
Parker, Elana Roth L499
Pierce, Rosie L517
Robinson, Quressa L542
Schofield, Hannah L567
Simons, Tanera L585
Steed, Hayley L595
Thwaites, Steph L629
Todd, Hannah L631
Trussell, Caroline L635
Vance, Lisa Erbach L641
Weiman, Paula L649
Weiss, Alexandra L650
Whatnall, Michaela L655
Williams, Laura L662
Williamson, Jo L664
Wilson, Desiree L667

Romantic Mystery
See more broadly: Mystery; Romance
Adsett, Alex L006
Foster, Clara L233
Milburn, Madeleine L449
Nathan, Abigail L475

Romantic Suspense
See more broadly: Romance; Suspense
Bradford Literary Agency L075
Bradford, Laura L076
Choc Lit P108
Eason, Lynette L186
Haley, Jolene L289
Leon, Nina L394
Mills & Boon P297
Shestopal, Camilla L581
Tyndale House Publishers, Inc. P465
Zack Company, Inc, The L678

Romantic Thrillers
See more broadly: Romance; Thrillers
Leon, Nina L394
Mills & Boon P297
Oghma Creative Media P321

Roots Music
See more broadly: Music
LSU Press P273

Royalty
Britain Magazine M075
Dynasty Press P147
Glenister, Emily L263

Rugby
See more broadly: Sport
See more specifically: Rugby League
Rugby World M317

Rugby League
See more broadly: Rugby
Forty20 ..... M150
Scratching Shed Publishing P402

Running
See more broadly: Fitness
Evans, Stephany L206
Pocket Mountains P359

Rural Living
See more broadly: Countryside; Lifestyle
Spelt Magazine M352

Russia
See more broadly: Europe
Indiana University Press P235
University of Wisconsin Press, The P490

Saga
See more broadly: Historical Fiction
Allison & Busby Ltd P019
Avon P044
Bloodhound Books P070
Chang, Nicola L116
Crowley, Sheila L144
Joffe Books P248
Keane Kataria Literary Agency L358
Macdougall, Laura L413
Pan Macmillan Australia P335
Todd, Hannah L631
Yours Fiction – Women's Special Series M417

Sailing
See more broadly: Leisure; Travel
Barbican Press P055
Boathooks Books P077
Brown, Son & Ferguson, Ltd P086
Cornell Maritime Press P123
Cruising World M109
RYA (Royal Yachting Association) P385
SAIL Magazine M320
Sailing Today M321
Seaworthy Publications P403
Yachting Monthly M408

Satire
See more broadly: Comedy / Humour
Baffler, The M043
Joy Harris Literary Agency, Inc L340
Victoria Sanders & Associates LLC L642
Viz M392

Savannah, GA
See more broadly: Georgia (US State)
Savannah Magazine M322

Scandinavia
See more broadly: Europe
University of Wisconsin Press, The P490

School
See more specifically: College / University; High School; Preschool
Prasanna, Tanusri L525

Science
See more specifically: Astronomy; Biology; Chemistry; Cognitive Science; Earth Science; Genetics; Information Science; Neuroscience; Physics; Popular Science; Science Journalism; Space
Arcadia Publishing P031
Autumn Publishing Ltd P042
Badger Learning P048
Bajek, Lauren L037
Bal, Emma L038
Basalt Books P057
Basic Books P058
Baylor University Press P060
BBC Science Focus M050
Bloomsbury Academic P071
Brannan, Maria L078
Brick M074
Bright Press P082
Brouckaert, Justin L087
Buckley, Louise L091
Capron, Elise L104
Charlesbridge Publishing P102
Chase Literary Agency L118
Chelsea House Publishers P105
Christie, Jennifer L126
Compassiviste Publishing P121
Conversation (UK), The M095
Cooper, Gemma L140
Crabtree Publishing P126
Crown P129
Danaczko, Melissa L153
Diana Finch Literary Agency L167
Dickerson, Donya L168
Dijkstra, Sandra L169
Dunham, Jennie L180
Edenborough, Sam L189
Elliott & Thompson P149
Ellor, Zabé L198
Elsevier Ltd P150
Enslow Publishers, Inc. P154
Evans, David L203
Evans, Kate L204
Fate M136
Feminist Press, The P163
Frances Goldin Literary Agency, Inc. L238
Freymann, Sarah Jane L242
Gale P177
Garamond Agency, Inc., The L253
Gill Education P182
Goldstein, Veronica L268
Grimm, Katie L279
Grossman, Loren R. L280
Harmsworth, Esmond L297
Harvard University Press P206
Heymont, Lane L309
Ireland's Own M202
Irish Pages M203
Joelle Delbourgo Associates, Inc. L334
Johns Hopkins University Press, The P250
Kane Press P251
Kate Barker Literary, TV, & Film Agency L352
Kensington Publishing Corp. P253
Kimber, Natalie L368
Kirby, Robert L370
Lewis, Alison L398
London Review of Books M225
Lutterworth Press, The P275

Macdougall, Laura	L413	
Maltese, Alyssa	L422	
Marr, Jill	L425	
Marshall, Jen	L427	
Massachusetts Review, The	M237	
McGraw Hill EMEA	P285	
Mehren, Jane von	L440	
Mendia, Isabel	L441	
Mentor Books	P292	
Michel, Caroline	L446	
Miranda, Caroline	L454	
MIT Press, The	P303	
MMB Creative	L455	
Murgolo, Karen	L467	
Oneworld Publications	P327	
Pelham, Imogen	L504	
Perry Literary	L509	
Peter Lang	P346	
Peter Lang Publishing	P348	
Pluto Press	P358	
Preston, Amanda	L526	
Prufrock Press	P363	
Purdue University Press	P364	
R D Publishers	P370	
Regina Ryan Books	L531	
Reid, Janet	L532	
Richter, Rick	L537	
Robertson Murray Literary Agency	L541	
Rudy Agency, The	L553	
Ruppin Agency, The	L555	
Science Factory, The	L569	
Signorelli, Michael	L582	
Stipes Publishing	P431	
Strothman, Wendy	L608	
Sunbelt Publications, Inc.	P433	
Susan Schulman Literary Agency	L610	
Swainson, Joanna	L613	
Symonds, Laurel	L617	
Taylor & Francis Group	P441	
Texas A&M University Press	P445	
Thames & Hudson Inc.	P446	
Thayer, Henry	L626	
Thorneycroft, Euan	L628	
Topping, Antony	L632	
Turner Publishing	P462	
University of Alaska Press	P476	
University of Alberta Press	P477	
University of California Press	P478	
University of Maine Press	P481	
University of Massachusetts Press	P482	
University of Virginia Press	P489	
University Press of Colorado	P491	
W.W. Norton & Company, Inc.	P500	
Weiss, Alexandra	L650	
Williams, Sarah	L663	
Willms, Kathryn	L665	
Wilson, Desiree	L667	
Yale University Press (London)	P520	
Zack Company, Inc, The	L678	
ZigZag Education	P523	

Science Fantasy
See more broadly: Fantasy; Science Fiction
Lechon, Shannon L390

Science Fiction
See more specifically: Alien Fiction; Cyberpunk; Grounded Science Fiction; Hard Science Fiction; Post-Apocalyptic; Retropunk; Science Fantasy; Slipstream; Soft Science Fiction; Space Opera; Steampunk; Time Travel

3 Seas Literary Agency	L001
4RV Publishing	P004
4RV Tenacious	P005
Aardwolf Press	P007
Adsett, Alex	L006
Afonso, Thais	L008
Alekseii, Keir	L015
Alex Adsett Literary	L016
Armada, Kurestin	L030
Armstrong, Susan	L032
Arthurson, Wayne	L033
Asimov's Science Fiction	M033
Authentic Ideas	P040
Baen Books	P049
Bajek, Lauren	L037
Barbican Press	P055
Baror International, Inc.	L044
BBC Doctor Who Magazine	M048
Belton, Maddy	L055
Bennett, Laura	L056
Berlyne, John	L061
Boker, Sidney	L067
Bookouture	P078
Bradford Literary Agency	L075
Candlemark & Gleam	P092
Carr, Michael	L109
Chevais, Jennifer	L122
Cochran, Alexander	L130
Colwill, Charlotte	L132
Compassiviste Publishing	P121
Crystal Magazine	M110
Curtis Brown	L146
Cusick, John	L148
DAW Books	P135
Doug Grad Literary Agency	L177
DSP Publications	P145
Edwards, Max	L190
Ellor, Zabé	L198
Fazzari, Hillary	L210
Fernandez, Rochelle	L220
Figueroa, Melanie	L221
Fitzgerald, Bea	L227
Foundation: The International Review of Science Fiction	M151
Frances Collin Literary Agent	L237
Gahan, Isobel	L250
Global Lion Intellectual Property Management, Inc.	L264
Gold SF	P185
Gunic, Masha	L284
Harmony Ink Press	P205
Harris, Erin	L300
Hawn, Molly Ker	L304
Hensley, Chelsea	L307
Hernando, Paloma	L308
Hiraeth Books	P220
Inscriptions Literary Agency	L323
Interzone	M201
Irvine, Lucy	L325
Jamieson, Molly	L329
Joelle Delbourgo Associates, Inc.	L334
Julie Crisp Literary Agency	L343
Kim, Jennifer	L366
Kimber, Natalie	L368
Korero Press	P257
Langlee, Lina	L382
Lechon, Shannon	L390
Lees, Jordan	L392
Leon, Nina	L394
Lightner, Kayla	L399
Liverpool Literary Agency, The	L404
Magazine of Fantasy & Science Fiction, The	M230
Matte, Rebecca	L431
Megibow, Sara	L439
Mihell, Natasha	L448
Miranda, Caroline	L454
MMB Creative	L455
Mozley, Jack	L465
Murray, Judith	L468
Muscato, Nate	L469
Mushens, Juliet	L470
Mustelier, James	L471
Nash, Justin	L474
Nathan, Abigail	L475
NBM Publishing	P312
Nelson, Kristin	L478
New Accelerator, The	M254
Nichols, Mariah	L479
Oghma Creative Media	P321
On Spec	M268
Perotto-Wills, Martha	L508
Plant, Zoe	L519
Posner, Marcy	L522
R D Publishers	P370
Reactor	M307
Reino, Jessica	L534
Robinson, Quressa	L542
Ross, Whitney	L551
Salazar, Des	L559
Scifaikuest	M323
Selectric Artists	L573
Sheil Land Associates Ltd	L577
Shoreline of Infinity	M334
Sinister Stoat Press	P410
Sluytman, Antoinette Van	L588
SmashBear Publishing	P412
Sorg, Arley	L592
Sternig & Byrne Literary Agency	L598
Story Unlikely	M356
Strange Horizons	M357
Terlip, Paige	L624
Thinkwell Books, UK	P447
Tibbets, Anne	L630
Tor	P455
Tor Publishing Group	P456
Tor Teen	P457
Tor.com Publishing	P458
Torrey House Press, LLC	P459
Turner Publishing	P462
Udden, Jennifer	L637
Wells, Karmen	L652
Whatnall, Michaela	L655
Wilson, Desiree	L667
Wilson, Ed	L668
Woods, Bryony	L671
Zack Company, Inc, The	L678
Zeno Agency	L680

Science Journalism
See more broadly: Journalism; Science

Scotland
See more broadly: United Kingdom
See more specifically: Glasgow; Inverclyde; Shetland

Birlinn Ltd	P067
Gutter Magazine	M174
MacDonald, Emily	L412
Macdougall, Laura	L413
Scots Magazine, The	M324
Scottish Farmer, The	M325
Scottish Field	M326
Sparsile Books	P419
Tippermuir Books	P452
Tocher	M378

Scripts

Above the Line Agency	L003
African Voices	M015
Agency (London) Ltd, The	L009
AHA Talent Ltd	L010
Alan Brodie Representation	L013
Alaska Quarterly Review	M019
Anvil Press Publishers	P028
Aurora Metro Press	P039
AVAnti Productions & Management	L035
Barbican Press	P055
Barnard, Arthur	L042
Bell, Eva	L054
Bolger, Maeve	L068

Index | Short Fiction 391

Chapman Publishing P099
Cincinnati Review, The M086
Comparato, Andrea L134
Curtis Brown L146
Elaine Steel L196
Fillingham Weston Associates L222
Freedman, Robert L241
Gurman Agency, LLC L285
Hickman, Emily L311
Inscriptions Literary Agency L323
JFL Agency L332
Judy Daish Associates Ltd L342
Kelleher, Sophie L359
Kenyon Review, The M210
Ki Agency Ltd L364
Lost Lake Folk Opera Magazine M227
Lyon, Rebecca L411
Meridian Artists L442
Middleton, Leah L447
New England Review M255
Oakland Arts Review, The M264
Obsidian: Literature in the African Diaspora M265
Paradigm Talent and Literary Agency L498
Praeger, Marta L524
Pushing Out the Boat M301
Qu Literary Magazine M302
R D Publishers P370
Renard Press Ltd P376
River Styx M314
Rochelle Stevens & Co. L543
Scarfe, Rory L566
Sheil Land Associates Ltd L577
Sunspot Literary Journal M364
Tennyson Agency, The L622
Third Coast M375
Tusculum Review, The M381
Valerie Hoskins Associates L640
Williams, Katie L661
WordCrafts Press P514

Scuba Diving
See more broadly: Diving
Diver M120

Search and Rescue
See more broadly: Emergency Services

Secret Intelligence
See more broadly: Warfare
See more specifically: CIA
Oghma Creative Media P321
Zack Company, Inc, The L678

Self Help
See more broadly: Personal Development
See more specifically: Motivational Self-Help
Ammonite Press P024
Arcadia Publishing P031
Authentic Life P041
Baumer, Jan L051
Bent, Jenny L059
Betsy Amster Literary Enterprises L063
Bradford Literary Agency L075
Campos, Vanessa L100
Charnace, Edwina de L117
Chase Literary Agency L118
Cleis Press P115
Compassiviste Publishing P121
Coombs Moylett & Maclean Literary Agency L139
Crown Publishing Group, The P131
DeVorss & Company P139
Dickerson, Donya L168
Doug Grad Literary Agency L177
Fellows, Abi L216
Freymann, Sarah Jane L242
Global Lion Intellectual Property Management, Inc. L264
Goodman Beck Publishing P187
Hashtag Press P207
Hay House Publishers P210
Icon Books Ltd P227
Jeff Herman Agency, LLC, The L331
Kensington Publishing Corp. P253
MacGregor & Luedeke L414
Marsiglia, Caroline L428
MMB Creative L455
Native Ink Press P311
New Harbinger Publications P314
Nichols, Mariah L479
O'Grady, Faith L485
Oneworld Publications P327
Paul S. Levine Literary Agency L502
Pen & Ink Designs Publishing P342
Perry Literary L509
Piatkus Books P352
Quill Driver Books P368
Richter, Rick L537
Sarah Jane Freymann Literary Agency L564
Schwartz, Steve L568
Shestopal, Camilla L581
Sunbelt Publications, Inc. P433
Terlip, Paige L624
Unity P473
W.W. Norton & Company Ltd P499
Watkins Publishing P503
WordCrafts Press P514
Wordserve Literary L673

Self-Sufficiency
See more broadly: Agriculture; Lifestyle
Country Smallholding M100

Senryu
Hedgerow: A Journal of Small Poems M182
Scifaikuest M323

Service Management
See more broadly: Management

Sewing
See more broadly: Crafts; Hobbies
C&T Publishing P088

Sex
See more broadly: Relationships
See more specifically: Prostitution
Cleis Press P115
Ellis-Martin, Sian L197
Maltese, Alyssa L422
marie claire M234
marie claire (UK) M235
Red Magazine M309
Redbook Magazine M310
Sinister Stoat Press P410
Tyndale House Publishers, Inc. P465
Zack Company, Inc, The L678

Sexuality
See more broadly: Relationships
See more specifically: LGBTQIA
Bloomsbury Academic P071
Cleis Press P115
Ellis-Martin, Sian L197
Feminist Press, The P163
Fernwood Publishing P164
Gold SF P185
Indiana University Press P235
Krienke, Mary L375
Macdougall, Laura L413
Ohio State University Press, The P323
Pluto Press P358
Sanders, Rayhane L562
Soloway, Jennifer March L590
University of Alberta Press P477
University of California Press P478
University of Michigan Press, The P483
University of Texas Press P488
W.W. Norton & Company Ltd P499

Shamanism
See more broadly: Religion
Llewellyn Worldwide Ltd P269

Shetland
See more broadly: Scotland

Shipping
See more broadly: Boats
Brown, Son & Ferguson, Ltd P086
Ships Monthly Magazine M332

Ships
See more broadly: Vehicles
Barbican Press P055
Brown, Son & Ferguson, Ltd P086
Ships Monthly Magazine M332

Shooting
See more broadly: Sport

Short Fiction
30 North M002
aaduna M005
About Place Journal M007
Account, The M009
African American Review M014
African Voices M015
Agni M016
Alaska Quarterly Review M019
Alfred Hitchcock Mystery Magazine M020
American Short Fiction M023
Amethyst Review M024
Antigonish Review, The M026
Arboreal M027
Asimov's Science Fiction M033
Atlantic Northeast M037
Aurora Metro Press P039
Auroras & Blossoms PoArtMo Anthology M039
Authentic Shorts M040
Babybug M041
Bacopa Literary Review M042
Baffler, The M043
Bandit Fiction M045
Banipal M046
Baobab Press P054
Barren Magazine M047
Bear Deluxe Magazine, The M052
Belmont Story Review M054
Beloit Fiction Journal M055
Better Than Starbucks M058
BFS Horizons M059
Black Moon Magazine M064
Black Static M065
Black Warrior Review M066
Blue Earth Review M067
Blue Mesa Review M068
Boston Review M071
Boyfriend Village M073
Cafe Irreal, The M078
Chapman M081
Chautauqua Literary Journal M083
Cheshire M084
Cincinnati Review, The M086
Cobblestone M087
Coil, The M089
Cola M090
Comma Press P120
Concho River Review M092
Conjunctions M093
Conjunctions Online M094
Crab Orchard Review M102
Crannog Magazine M103
Crazyhorse / Swamp Pink M104
Cream City Review M105
Critical Quarterly M108
Crystal Magazine M110
CutBank M111
Cyphers M112
Dalhousie Review, The M113
Dawntreader, The M115
Deep Overstock Magazine M116

Claim your free access to **www.firstwriter.com**: See p.403

Dream Catcher	M123
Dublin Review, The	M124
Ecotone	M127
Ekphrastic Review, The	M128
El Portal	M129
Ellery Queen Mystery Magazine	M130
Evans, David	L203
Event	M133
Fabula Argentea	M134
Fairlight Books	P160
Faultline	M137
Feminist Studies	M139
Fiction	M140
Fiddlehead, The	M141
First Line, The	M143
Five Points	M144
Folio	M147
Fortnightly Review, The	M149
Fourth River, The	M153
Fresh Words – An International Literary Magazine	M154
Fugue	M155
Funny Times	M157
Future Fire, The	M158
Galustian, Natalie	L251
Gargoyle Online	M161
Georgia Review, The	M163
Gertrude	M164
Gertrude Press	P179
Ginosko Literary Journal	M165
Glacier, The	M166
Grain Literary Magazine	M170
Granta	M171
Graywolf Lab	M172
Gulf Coast: A Journal of Literature and Fine Arts	M173
Gutter Magazine	M174
Half Mystic Journal	M175
Hanging Loose	M177
Harper's Magazine	M178
Harpur Palate	M179
Hazel Press	P211
Heavy Traffic	M181
Hedgerow: A Journal of Small Poems	M182
Helix, The	M183
Here Comes Everyone	M184
Hiraeth Books	P220
Hotel Amerika	M189
Hudson Review, The	M190
Hunger Mountain	M191
I-70 Review	M192
Idaho Review	M193
Identity Theory	M194
Image	M195
Indiana Review	M196
Inque	M198
Interzone	M201
Ireland's Own	M202
Irish Pages	M203
Island	M204
Island Online	M205
Joy Harris Literary Agency, Inc.	L340
Kavya Kishor	M208
Kenyon Review, The	M210
Kerning	M211
Landfall	M215
Lighthouse	M218
Literary Mama	M220
Litro Magazine	M221
London Magazine, The	M224
Lost Lake Folk Opera Magazine	M227
Louisiana Literature	M228
MacGuffin, The	M229
Magazine of Fantasy & Science Fiction, The	M230
Malahat Review, The	M232
Manoa	M233
Massachusetts Review, The	M237
Meetinghouse	M238
Michigan Quarterly Review	M240
Mid-American Review	M241
Midsummer Dream House	M242
Midway Journal	M243
Missouri Review, The	M245
Moving Worlds: A Journal of Transcultural Writings	M247
MQR Mixtape	M248
My Weekly	M249
Mystery Magazine	M250
Nashville Review	M251
Neon	M253
New Accelerator, The	M254
New England Review	M255
New Orleans Review	M257
New Welsh Reader	M259
Northern Gravy	M263
Oakland Arts Review, The	M264
Obsidian: Literature in the African Diaspora	M265
Old Red Kimono	M267
On Spec	M268
Orbis International Literary Journal	M269
Oxford Review of Books	M271
Oyez Review	M272
Pacifica Literary Review	M273
Panorama	M274
Paris Review, The	M275
Parthian Books	P336
Passionfruit Review, The	M277
Pennine Ink Magazine	M280
People's Friend, The	M283
Phoenix Moirai	P351
Pleiades	M285
Ploughshares	M286
Popshot Quarterly	M293
Power Cut Lite	M294
Present Tense	M296
Prole	M299
Pushing Out the Boat	M301
Qu Literary Magazine	M302
Rabble Review	M303
Ransom Publishing Ltd	P373
River Styx	M314
Riverbed Review	M315
Saddlebag Dispatches	M319
Scribble	M327
Second Factory	M328
Seren Books	P405
Shenandoah	M331
Shooter Literary Magazine	M333
Shoreline of Infinity	M334
Shorts Magazine	M335
Sinister Wisdom	M337
Snowflake Magazine	M338
Soho Review, The	M339
Sonder Magazine	M342
South Carolina Review	M344
Southern Humanities Review	M345
Southern Review, The	M346
Southwest Review	M348
Southword Journal	M349
Spitball	M353
Stinging Fly, The	M355
Story Unlikely	M356
Strange Horizons	M357
Structo Magazine	M359
Studio One	M360
Sunspot Literary Journal	M364
Supplement, The	M365
Tahoma Literary Review	M368
Takahe	M369
Tears in the Fence	M371
Temz Review, The	M372
Thin Air Magazine	M374
Third Coast	M375
Threepenny Review, The	M377
Tocher	M378
Tolka	M379
Tributaries	M380
Tusculum Review, The	M381
Under the Radar	M384
Understorey Magazine	M385
University of Iowa Press	P480
University of North Texas Press	P485
Vagabond City	M386
Vestal Review	M388
Virginia Quarterly Review, The	M389
Waccamaw	M394
Wasafiri	M398
West Branch	M400
White Review, The	M404
Wilson, Desiree	L667
Windsor Review	M405
Yale Review, The	M409
Yes Poetry Magazine	M412
Yours Fiction – Women's Special Series	M417
Zoetrope: All-Story	M418
Zone 3	M419

Short Fiction Collections

404 Ink	P002
Ad Hoc Fiction	P011
Arachne Press	P030
Barbican Press	P055
Birlinn Ltd	P067
BOA Editions, Ltd.	P076
Brooks, Savannah	L084
Caitlin Press Inc.	P090
Chang, Nicola	L116
Chapman Publishing	P099
Compassiviste Publishing	P121
Conville, Clare	L137
Dahlia Books	P132
Daunt Books Publishing	P134
Enitharmon Editions	P153
Felicia Eth Literary Representation	L214
Glenister, Emily	L263
Graywolf Press	P193
Grimm, Katie	L279
Half Mystic Press	P197
Hiraeth Books	P220
Host Publications	P224
Jamii Publishing	P245
Kates Hill Press, The	P252
Miranda, Caroline	L454
Motala, Tasneem	L463
Mudfog Press	P306
Orenda Books	P329
Patrician Press	P337
Paycock Press	P340
Peepal Tree Press	P341
Pen & Ink Designs Publishing	P342
Phoenix Moirai	P351
Plitt, Carrie	L520
Press 53	P361
Shipwreckt Books Publishing Company	P406
Sinister Stoat Press	P410
Spout Press	P420
Sweetgum Press	P438
Thwaites, Steph	L629
Toad Hall Editions	P453
Torrey House Press, LLC	P459
University of Alaska Press	P476
University of Alberta Press	P477
University of Nevada Press	P484
Valley Press	P493
Vane Women Press	P495

Index | Social Media 393

W.W. Norton & Company, Inc. ... P500
Wayne State University Press ... P504
Wordsonthestreet ... P517
YesYes Books ... P521

Short Nonfiction

30 North ... M002
About Place Journal ... M007
Account, The ... M009
Alaska Quarterly Review ... M019
Amethyst Review ... M024
Atlantic Northeast ... M037
Babybug ... M041
Bacopa Literary Review ... M042
Baobab Press ... P054
Belmont Story Review ... M054
Better Than Starbucks ... M058
Big Fiction ... M061
Black Warrior Review ... M066
Blue Earth Review ... M067
Blue Mesa Review ... M068
Boyfriend Village ... M073
Brick ... M074
Chautauqua Literary Journal ... M083
Cincinnati Review, The ... M086
Concho River Review ... M092
Conjunctions ... M093
Conjunctions Online ... M094
Crazyhorse / Swamp Pink ... M104
Cream City Review ... M105
CutBank ... M111
Dublin Review, The ... M124
Ecotone ... M127
Ekphrastic Review, The ... M128
El Portal ... M129
Event ... M133
Faultline ... M137
Fiddlehead, The ... M141
Five Points ... M144
Fourth River, The ... M153
Fresh Words – An International Literary Magazine ... M154
Gertrude ... M164
Ginosko Literary Journal ... M165
Grain Literary Magazine ... M170
Granta ... M171
Half Mystic Journal ... M175
Harpur Palate ... M179
Helix, The ... M183
Hunger Mountain ... M191
Idaho Review ... M193
Identity Theory ... M194
Irish Pages ... M203
Kerning ... M211
Literary Mama ... M220
Litro Magazine ... M221
London Magazine, The ... M224
MacGuffin, The ... M229
Malahat Review, The ... M232
Midsummer Dream House ... M242
Midway Journal ... M243
Nashville Review ... M251
New England Review ... M255
New Orleans Review ... M257
New Welsh Reader ... M259
Oakland Arts Review, The ... M264
Oyez Review ... M272
Pacifica Literary Review ... M273
Panorama ... M274
Paris Review, The ... M275
Passionfruit Review, The ... M277
Pleiades ... M285
Ploughshares ... M286
Present Tense ... M296
Prole ... M299
River Styx ... M314
Second Factory ... M328
Shenandoah ... M331
Shooter Literary Magazine ... M333
Sonder Magazine ... M342
South Carolina Review ... M344
Spelt Magazine ... M352
Spitball ... M353
Story Unlikely ... M356
Studio One ... M360
Tahoma Literary Review ... M368
Tears in the Fence ... M371
Thin Air Magazine ... M374
Third Coast ... M375
Tolka ... M379
Tributaries ... M380
Understorey Magazine ... M385
Virginia Quarterly Review, The ... M389
Windsor Review ... M405
Yours ... M416
Zone 3 ... M419

Shropshire

See more broadly: England

Logaston Press ... P271

Skiing

See more broadly: Leisure; Sport

Good Ski Guide, The ... M169

Slang

See more broadly: Language

Slavs

See more broadly: Ethnic Groups

Peter Lang ... P346
Peter Lang Publishing ... P348

Slipstream

See more broadly: Fantasy; Science Fiction

Asimov's Science Fiction ... M033
Jamii Publishing ... P245
Strange Horizons ... M357

Small Press

See more broadly: Publishing

Supplement, The ... M365

Smallholdings

See more broadly: Agriculture

Country Smallholding ... M100

Snowboarding

See more broadly: Leisure; Sport

Social Class

See more broadly: Social Groups

Chanchani, Sonali ... L115
Dawson, Liza ... L162
Ellis-Martin, Sian ... L197
Fernwood Publishing ... P164
Gold SF ... P185
Macdougall, Laura ... L413
Simpson, Cara Lee ... L586
University of Massachusetts Press ... P482
University of Michigan Press, The ... P483
Zuraw-Friedland, Ayla ... L681

Social Commentary

See more broadly: Commentary; Society

Carter, Rebecca ... L111
Davies, Elinor ... L160
Faulks, Holly ... L209
MacDonald, Emily ... L412
Malahat Review, The ... M232
Marr, Jill ... L425
Mozley, Jack ... L465
Roberts, Soumeya Bendimerad ... L540
Simpson, Cara Lee ... L586
Yeoh, Rachel ... L675

Social Groups

See more broadly: Society

See more specifically: Friends; Gender; Social Class; Working Class

Social History

See more broadly: History

Brewin Books Ltd ... P081
DeBlock, Liza ... L163
Fuentes, Sarah ... L247
Icon Books Ltd ... P227
JMD Media / DB Publishing ... P247
Pickering, Juliet ... L516
Ramer, Susan ... L528
Schofield, Hannah ... L567
Seymour, Charlotte ... L575
Takikawa, Marin ... L618

Social Issues

See more broadly: Society

See more specifically: Addiction; Bullying; Discrimination; Diversity; Equality; Gender Issues; Homelessness; Immigration; Men's Issues; Poverty; Refugees; Women's Issues

404 Ink ... P002
Barr, Nicola ... L046
Betsy Amster Literary Enterprises ... L063
Bradford Literary Agency ... L075
Caskie, Robert ... L113
Charlesbridge Publishing ... P102
Christie, Jennifer ... L126
Dana Newman Literary, LLC ... L152
Eisenmann, Caroline ... L192
Evans, Kate ... L204
Felicia Eth Literary Representation ... L214
Fernwood Publishing ... P164
Finegan, Stevie ... L226
Free Association Books Ltd ... P173
Geiger, Ellen ... L255
Granta Books ... P192
Grimm, Katie ... L279
Hoffman, Scott ... L316
Jessica Kingsley Publishers ... P246
Kotchman, Katie ... L374
Lazin, Sarah ... L388
Lechon, Shannon ... L390
Nell James Publishers ... P313
New Internationalist ... M256
Pelham, Imogen ... L504
Plitt, Carrie ... L520
Posner, Marcy ... L522
Pride ... M298
Ruppin Agency, The ... L555
Salt Publishing ... P389
Susan Schulman Literary Agency ... L610
Takikawa, Marin ... L618
Thinkwell Books, UK ... P447

Social Justice

See more broadly: Society

Bernardi, Amanda ... L062
Chanchani, Sonali ... L115
Cooper, Maggie ... L141
Crown ... P129
Eberly, Chelsea ... L187
Fortress Press ... P170
Free Spirit Publishing ... P174
Gold SF ... P185
HopeRoad ... P223
Kahn, Jody ... L346
LSU Press ... P273
Marshall, Jen ... L427
New Internationalist ... M256
Peddle, Kay ... L503
Phillips, Aemilia ... L515
Prasanna, Tanusri ... L525
Richter, Rick ... L537
Riposte ... M312
Sierra ... M336
Stephens, Jenny ... L596
Trudel, Jes ... L634
Willms, Kathryn ... L665

Social Media

See more broadly: Media

Begum, Salma ... L053

Society

See more specifically: Activism; Ethnic Groups; High Society; Postcolonialism; Social Commentary; Social Groups; Social Issues; Social Justice; Socio-Political; Sociology

Bloomsbury Academic P071
British Academy, The P083
Cavanagh, Claire L114
Chanchani, Sonali L115
Conversation (UK), The M095
Davies, Elinor L160
Evans, Kiya L205
Faulks, Holly L209
Frances Goldin Literary Agency, Inc. L238
Goldstein, Veronica L268
Harper's Magazine M178
History Press, The P221
Island Online M205
MMB Creative L455
Peter Lang P346
Peter Lang Publishing P348
Prufrock Press P363
Reilly, Milly L533
Robertson Murray Literary Agency L541
Society for Promoting Christian
    Knowledge (SPCK) P414
University of Alberta Press P477
VanderWyk & Burnham P494
Victoria Sanders & Associates LLC L642
Whelan, Maria L656
Yale University Press (London) P520

Socio-Political
See more broadly: Politics; Society
Pluto Press P358

Sociology
See more broadly: Society
See more specifically: Ethnography
ABC-CLIO P008
Arcadia Publishing P031
Arsenal Pulp Press P032
Basic Books P058
Baylor University Press P060
Berghahn Books Ltd P062
Bernardi, Amanda L062
Bloomsbury Academic P071
Chelsea House Publishers P105
Compassiviste Publishing P121
Crabtree Publishing P126
Fernwood Publishing P164
Fogg, Jack L230
Gale P177
Garamond Agency, Inc., The L253
Gill Education P182
Goldstein, Veronica L268
Grossman, Loren R. L280
Harvard University Press P206
Johns Hopkins University Press, The P250
Kensington Publishing Corp. P253
Lutterworth Press, The P275
Marion Boyars Publishers P282
MIT Press, The P303
Mortimer, Michele L462
Muscato, Nate L469
Perry Literary L509
Pluto Press P358
Stanford University Press P427
Stipes Publishing P431
Taylor & Francis Group P441
University of Alberta Press P477
University of California Press P478
University of Massachusetts Press P482
University of Michigan Press, The P483
University of Virginia Press P489
W.W. Norton & Company Ltd P499
W.W. Norton & Company, Inc. P500
Yale University Press (London) P520

ZigZag Education P523

Soft Science Fiction
See more broadly: Science Fiction
Brannan, Maria L078
Finegan, Stevie L226
Weiss, Alexandra L650

Software
See more broadly: Computers
See more specifically: Software Development

Software Development
See more broadly: Software

Somerset
See more broadly: England
Somerset Life M341

South America
See more broadly: Regional
See more specifically: Brazil
Arte Publico Press P033
Feminist Press, The P163
Ohio State University Press, The P323
Ohio University Press P324
Phillips, Aemilia L515
Pinata Books P355
Pluto Press P358
Stanford University Press P427
University of California Press P478
University of Michigan Press, The P483
University of Pennsylvania Press P486
University of Texas Press P488
University of Wisconsin Press, The P490

South Pacific
See more broadly: Pacific
Takahe M369

South-East Asia
See more broadly: Asia
See more specifically: China

Southeastern United States
See more broadly: United States

Southwestern United States
See more broadly: United States
Filter Press P166
Sunbelt Publications, Inc. P433
University of Texas Press P488

Space
See more broadly: Science
Air & Space Quarterly M018
Crabtree Publishing P126
Weiss, Alexandra L650

Space Opera
See more broadly: Science Fiction
Armada, Kurestin L030
Berlyne, John L061
Gahan, Isobel L250
Gunic, Masha L284
Headley, David H. L306
Oghma Creative Media P321

Spain
See more broadly: Europe
Peter Lang P346
Peter Lang Publishing P348

Spanish
See more broadly: Language
Mentor Books P292
Stipes Publishing P431

Spas and Hot Tubs
See more broadly: Houses and Homes
Spa Magazine M350
Swimming Pool News M367

Special Forces
See more broadly: Military

Speculative
See more specifically: Alternative History; Dystopian Fiction; Grimdark; Speculative Horror; Speculative Romance; Speculative Thrillers; Utopian Fiction
Aardwolf Press P007

Afonso, Thais L008
Andrew, Nelle L025
Armada, Kurestin L030
Armstrong, Susan L032
Bajek, Lauren L037
Bauman, Erica L050
Baxter, Veronique L052
Bent, Jenny L059
Bradford, Laura L076
Brannan, Maria L078
Brooks, Savannah L084
Burns, Camille L094
Candlemark & Gleam P092
Chanchani, Sonali L115
Cho, Catherine L124
Clarke, Caro L128
Cochran, Alexander L130
Cusick, John L148
DeBlock, Liza L163
Dunn, Ben L181
Eason, Lynette L186
Edenborough, Sam L189
Ellor, Zabé L198
Evans, Kiya L205
Fabien, Samantha L207
Feminist Press, The P163
Fergusson, Julie L219
Figueroa, Melanie L221
Fogg, Jack L230
Forrester, Jemima L232
Friedman, Claire L243
Fuentes, Sarah L247
Fuller, Lisa L248
Future Fire, The M158
Gilbert, Tara L258
Gold SF P185
Goldstein, Veronica L268
Grimm, Katie L279
Gruber, Pam L281
Hannah Sheppard Literary Agency L291
Harris, Erin L300
Hawn, Molly Ker L304
Hiraeth Books P220
Hordern, Kate L320
Hornsley, Sarah L321
Kahn, Ella Diamond L345
Kavanagh, Jade L355
Keren, Eli L362
Killingley, Jessica L365
Kim, Jennifer L366
Kirby, Robert L370
Landis, Sarah L381
Langlee, Lina L382
Lechon, Shannon L390
Lees, Jordan L392
Lightner, Kayla L399
Lovell, Jake L409
MacKenzie, Joanna L416
Maidment, Olivia L421
Maltese, Alyssa L422
Marr, Jill L425
McBride, Juliana L435
Miranda, Caroline L454
Moore, Mary C. L457
Morrell, Imogen L460
Mozley, Jack L465
Mustelier, James L471
Napolitano, Maria L473
Nelson, Kristin L478
Neon M253
On Spec M268
Pages, Saribel L496
Pass, Marina de L500
Petty, Rachel L512
Plant, Zoe L519
Preston, Amanda L526

Simpson, Cara Lee...................................L586
Siobhan, Aiden..L587
Sluytman, Antoinette Van.........................L588
Sorg, Arley..L592
Steed, Hayley..L595
Strange Horizons......................................M357
Swainson, Joanna.....................................L613
Takikawa, Marin.......................................L618
Tannenbaum, Amy....................................L620
Tor Publishing Group................................P456
Trudel, Jes...L634
Vance, Lisa Erbach...................................L641
Weiss, Alexandra......................................L650
Whatnall, Michaela..................................L655
Whelan, Maria..L656
Williams, Laura..L662
Willms, Kathryn.......................................L665
Wilson, Desiree...L667
Wilson, Ed...L668

Speculative Horror
See more broadly: Horror; Speculative
Julie Crisp Literary Agency......................L343

Speculative Romance
See more broadly: Romance; Speculative
Hannah Sheppard Literary Agency...........L291
Ostby, Kristin..L494
Zack Company, Inc, The...........................L678

Speculative Thrillers
See more broadly: Speculative; Thrillers

Spirit Guides
See more broadly: Spirituality
Llewellyn Worldwide Ltd.........................P269

Spirituality
See more specifically: New Age; Religion; Spirit Guides
Amethyst Review......................................M024
Authentic Life...P041
Baumer, Jan..L051
Brailsford, Karen......................................L077
Brown, Megan..L088
Canterbury Press.......................................P094
Compassiviste Publishing.........................P121
Cynthia Cannell Literary Agency.............L150
Danko, Margaret.......................................L154
Dawntreader, The.....................................M115
Derviskadic, Dado....................................L164
DeVorss & Company................................P139
DSP Publications......................................P145
Ericka T. Phillips......................................L200
Evans, Stephany.......................................L206
Freymann, Sarah Jane...............................L242
Goodman Beck Publishing.......................P187
Haley, Jolene...L289
Hay House Publishers..............................P210
Image..M195
Jeff Herman Agency, LLC, The................L331
Joy Harris Literary Agency, Inc...............L340
Kimber, Natalie..L368
Kube Publishing.......................................P258
Llewellyn Worldwide Ltd........................P269
MacGregor & Luedeke.............................L414
Murgolo, Karen..L467
Oneworld Publications.............................P327
Quill Driver Books...................................P368
Red Feather...P375
Regina Ryan Books..................................L531
Sarah Jane Freymann Literary Agency....L564
Sentient Publications................................P404
Sheree Bykofsky Associates, Inc.............L579
Society for Promoting Christian
     Knowledge (SPCK).............................P414
Thames & Hudson Inc..............................P446
Two Fine Crows Books............................P464
Unity..P473
VanderWyk & Burnham............................P494
Zack Company, Inc, The..........................L678

Sport
See more specifically: Archery; Baseball; Basketball; Boxing; Canoeing; Climbing; Cricket; Cycling; Darts; Equestrian; Falconry; Football / Soccer; Golf; Hockey; Horse Racing; Hunting; Martial Arts; Motorsports; Rugby; Shooting; Skiing; Snowboarding; Sports Coaching; Swimming; Water Sports; Wilderness Sports
AdventureKEEN..P013
Antigonish Review, The...........................M026
Arcadia Publishing....................................P031
Ascend Books, LLC..................................P035
Atyeo, Charlotte..L034
Barr, Nicola...L046
Bates, Tim...L048
Bernardi, Amanda.....................................L062
Birlinn Ltd...P067
Blackstaff Press...P068
Bloomsbury Academic..............................P071
Brattle Agency LLC, The..........................L080
Brewin Books Ltd.....................................P081
Brick..M074
Brouckaert, Justin.....................................L087
Bucci, Chris..L090
Campbell, Charlie.....................................L099
Cassell...P096
Charles River Press...................................P101
Dana Newman Literary, LLC...................L152
Doug Grad Literary Agency.....................L177
Elliott & Thompson..................................P149
Enslow Publishers, Inc.............................P154
Felicia Eth Literary Representation..........L214
Flaneur..M145
Fogg, Jack...L230
Frances Goldin Literary Agency, Inc.......L238
Gale...P177
Gill Books...P181
Gordon, Andrew.......................................L270
Greyhound Literary..................................L278
History Press, The....................................P221
Icon Books Ltd...P227
Ireland's Own...M202
JMD Media / DB Publishing....................P247
Johns Hopkins University Press, The......P250
Kahn, Jody..L346
Karinch, Maryann.....................................L351
Kensington Publishing Corp.....................P253
Limelight Management.............................L400
Lutterworth Press, The.............................P275
Macdougall, Laura....................................L413
Marr, Jill..L425
Methuen Publishing Ltd...........................P294
Mortimer, Michele....................................L462
Mundy, Toby...L466
Ohio University Press...............................P324
Paul S. Levine Literary Agency...............L502
Perry Literary..L509
Quirk Books..P369
Regina Ryan Books..................................L531
Reino, Jessica...L534
Robertson Murray Literary Agency.........L541
Rudy Agency, The....................................L553
Rutman, Jim..L558
Schwartz, Steve..L568
Scratching Shed Publishing......................P402
Seren Books..P405
Signorelli, Michael...................................L582
Spackman, James......................................L593
Square Mile Magazine..............................M354
Stone, Geoffrey...L600
Texas A&M University Press...................P445
Thames & Hudson Inc..............................P446
Thayer, Henry...L626
Thinkwell Books, UK...............................P447
Tyndale House Publishers, Inc................P465
University of Akron Press, The................P475
University of Alberta Press.......................P477
University of Massachusetts Press...........P482
University of Michigan Press, The..........P483
University of Nevada Press......................P484
University of Tennessee Press..................P487
W.W. Norton & Company Ltd.................P499
Wilson, Ed...L668
WordCrafts Press......................................P514

Sports Cars
See more broadly: Cars

Sports Celebrity
See more broadly: Celebrity
FRA (Futerman, Rose, & Associates).....L236
Richter, Rick...L537
Zack Company, Inc, The..........................L678

Sports Coaching
See more broadly: Sport
Coaches Choice..P116

Spy Thrillers
See more broadly: Thrillers
Armada, Kurestin......................................L030
Dawson, Liza..L162
Pass, Marina de..L500
Thorneycroft, Euan...................................L628

St Louis
See more broadly: Missouri
Missouri Historical Society Press............P302

Staffordshire
See more broadly: England
See more specifically: Burton upon Trent

Stamp Collecting
See more broadly: Hobbies

Statistics
See more broadly: Mathematics
Taylor & Francis Group............................P441
W.W. Norton & Company Ltd.................P499

Steam Engines
See more broadly: Steam Power; Vehicles

Steam Power
See more broadly: Technology
See more specifically: Steam Engines

Steampunk
See more broadly: Science Fiction
Bennett, Laura...L056
Liverpool Literary Agency, The..............L404

Storytelling
See more broadly: Performing Arts
Facts & Fiction...M135

Stress Management
See more broadly: Psychology
VanderWyk & Burnham............................P494

Sub-Culture
See more broadly: Culture
Cavanagh, Claire.......................................L114
Danaczko, Melissa....................................L153
Derviskadic, Dado....................................L164
Eisenmann, Caroline.................................L192
Nolan, Laura...L481
Roberts, Soumeya Bendimerad................L540

Suffolk
See more broadly: England
Norfolk & Suffolk Bride..........................M260

Sufism
See more broadly: Islam

Superhero Fantasy
See more broadly: Fantasy

Supernatural / Paranormal
See more specifically: Cryptozoology; Ghost Stories; Ghosts; Mysticism; Psychic Abilities; Reincarnation; Supernatural / Paranormal Horror; Supernatural / Paranormal Romance; Supernatural / Paranormal Thrillers; UFOs; Vampires; Witchcraft; Witches
Armstrong, Susan......................................L032

Buckley, Louise L091
Countryside Books P124
DSP Publications P145
Fate M136
Fortean Times: The Journal of Strange
   Phenomena M148
Harmony Ink Press P205
Hiraeth Books P220
JMD Media / DB Publishing P247
Leon, Nina L394
Lovell, Jake L409
Nightfire P316
Oghma Creative Media P321
Ostby, Kristin L494
Piatkus Books P352
Reino, Jessica L534
Shestopal, Camilla L581
Siobhan, Aiden L587
Unseen Press P492
Vance, Lisa Erbach L641
Whitford Press P508
Wordserve Literary L673

Supernatural / Paranormal Horror
  See more broadly: Horror; Supernatural /
    Paranormal
  Foxx, Kat L235
  Hensley, Chelsea L307
  Sinister Stoat Press P410

Supernatural / Paranormal Romance
  See more broadly: Romance; Supernatural /
    Paranormal
  Avon Books P045
  Bradford Literary Agency L075
  Cooper, Gemma L140
  Leon, Nina L394
  Nichols, Mariah L479
  SmashBear Publishing P412
  Vinspire Publishing P497
  Zack Company, Inc, The L678

Supernatural / Paranormal Thrillers
  See more broadly: Supernatural / Paranormal;
    Thrillers
  Afonso, Thais L008
  Davies, Elinor L160

Supply Chain Management
  See more broadly: Management
  Loft Press, Inc. P270

Surfing
  See more broadly: Water Sports

Surreal
  Asimov's Science Fiction M033
  Neon M253
  Rutherford, Laetitia L557

Suspense
  See more specifically: Domestic Suspense;
    Literary Suspense; Psychological Suspense;
    Romantic Suspense
  4RV Tenacious P005
  Afonso, Thais L008
  Ahearn Agency, Inc, The L011
  Alfred Hitchcock Mystery Magazine M020
  Andrew, Nelle L025
  Armstrong, Susan L032
  Avon P044
  Barbour Publishing P056
  Baror International, Inc. L044
  Bent, Jenny L059
  Bolton, Camilla L069
  Brooks, Savannah L084
  Cho, Catherine L124
  Choc Lit P108
  Cichello, Kayla L127
  Comparato, Andrea L134
  Coombs Moylett & Maclean Literary
    Agency L139
  Crowley, Sheila L144

Crystal Magazine M110
Cusick, John L148
Dana Newman Literary, LLC L152
Danko, Margaret L154
Fabien, Samantha L207
Felicia Eth Literary Representation L214
Figueroa, Melanie L221
Fogg, Jack L230
Foxx, Kat L235
Friedman, Claire L243
Friedman, Rebecca L244
Harmsworth, Esmond L297
Harris, Erin L300
Hayden, Viola L305
Hornsley, Sarah L321
Inscriptions Literary Agency L323
Joffe Books P248
Jonathan Pegg Literary Agency L337
Joy Harris Literary Agency, Inc. L340
Kavanagh, Jade L355
Kenny, Julia L361
Leon, Nina L394
Limelight Management L400
Milburn, Madeleine L449
Orenda Books P329
Penzler Publishers P345
Piatkus Books P352
Power, Anna L523
Prasanna, Tanusri L525
Reino, Jessica L534
Schofield, Hannah L567
Seymour, Charlotte L575
Shestopal, Camilla L581
Soloway, Jennifer March L590
Story Unlikely M356
Strachan Literary Agency L602
Stringer, Marlene L604
Tibbets, Anne L630
Trudel, Jes. L634
Turner Publishing P462
Tyndale House Publishers, Inc. P465
Victoria Sanders & Associates LLC L642
Weiman, Paula L649
Weiss, Alexandra L650
WordCrafts Press P514
Wordserve Literary L673
Zack Company, Inc, The L678

Sustainable Living
  See more broadly: Environment
  Cooper, Maggie L141
  Evans, Stephany L206
  Kimber, Natalie L368
  Metropolis Magazine M239
  Murdoch Books Australia P308
  Ooligan Press P328
  Regina Ryan Books L531
  Sierra M336
  Taylor & Francis Group P441

Swimming
  See more broadly: Sport
  See more specifically: Swimming Pools

Swimming Pools
  See more broadly: Swimming
  Swimming Pool News M367

Switzerland
  See more broadly: Europe

Sword and Sorcery
  See more broadly: Fantasy

TV
  See more broadly: Media
  BBC Doctor Who Magazine M048
  Berghahn Books Ltd P062
  Cavanagh, Claire L114
  Flaneur M145
  Global Lion Intellectual Property
    Management, Inc. L264

Kim, Julia L367
My Weekly M249
Oghma Creative Media P321
Ohio University Press P324
Oxford Review of Books M271
Red Magazine M309
Square Mile Magazine M354
Thames & Hudson Inc. P446
University of Alberta Press P477
Wayne State University Press P504
Yale Review, The M409
Zack Company, Inc, The L678

TV Scripts
  Above the Line Agency L003
  Agency (London) Ltd, The L009
  AHA Talent Ltd L010
  Alan Brodie Representation L013
  Barnard, Arthur L042
  Bell, Eva L054
  Bolger, Maeve L068
  Curtis Brown L146
  Elaine Steel L196
  Fillingham Weston Associates L222
  Hickman, Emily L311
  JFL Agency L332
  Judy Daish Associates Ltd L342
  Kelleher, Sophie L359
  Ki Agency Ltd L364
  Lyon, Rebecca L411
  Meridian Artists L442
  Middleton, Leah L447
  Oakland Arts Review, The M264
  Paradigm Talent and Literary Agency L498
  Qu Literary Magazine M302
  R D Publishers P370
  Rochelle Stevens & Co. L543
  Scarfe, Rory L566
  Sheil Land Associates Ltd L577
  Tennyson Agency, The L622
  Valerie Hoskins Associates L640
  Williams, Katie L661

Tai Chi
  See more broadly: Martial Arts
  Singing Dragon P409

Tanka
  Hedgerow: A Journal of Small Poems M182
  Scifaikuest M323

Taoism / Daoism
  See more broadly: Philosophy
  Singing Dragon P409

Tarot
  See more broadly: Fortune Telling and Divination
  Haley, Jolene L289
  Hay House Publishers P210
  Llewellyn Worldwide Ltd P269
  Rushall, Kathleen L556

Taxation
  See more broadly: Finance; Legal
  Bloomsbury Professional P072
  Croner-i Limited P127
  Fiscal Publications P168

Technology
  See more specifically: Audio Visual Technology;
    Augmented Reality; Computers; Digital
    Technology; Energy; Radio Control; Robots;
    Steam Power
  Arcadia Publishing P031
  Bloomsbury Academic P071
  Carter, Rebecca L111
  Colourpoint Educational P119
  Combemale, Chris L133
  Compassiviste Publishing P121
  Conversation (UK), The M095
  Crabtree Publishing P126
  Dana Newman Literary, LLC L152
  Dickerson, Donya L168

Index | *Thrillers* 397

Dunham, Jennie L180
Elsevier Ltd P150
Enslow Publishers, Inc. P154
Frances Goldin Literary Agency, Inc. L238
Funny Times M157
Gale P177
Global Lion Intellectual Property Management, Inc. L264
Goldstein, Veronica L268
Grossman, Loren R. L280
Information Today, Inc. P238
Kane Press P251
Kensington Publishing Corp. P253
Lightner, Kayla L399
London Review of Books M225
Lutterworth Press, The P275
Marshall, Jen L427
Metropolis Magazine M239
MIT Press, The P303
Muscato, Nate L469
Perry Literary L509
Pluto Press P358
Purdue University Press P364
Quill Driver Books P368
Science Factory, The L569
Signorelli, Michael L582
Square Mile Magazine M354
Symonds, Laurel L617
Taylor & Francis Group P441
Thorneycroft, Euan L628
University of Alberta Press P477
University of California Press P478
University of Massachusetts Press P482
University of Nevada Press P484
University of Virginia Press P489
W.W. Norton & Company Ltd P499
Wallpaper M397
Wickers, Chandler L659
Wilson, Desiree L667
Yale University Press (London) P520
Zack Company, Inc, The L678
ZigZag Education P523
Zuraw-Friedland, Ayla L681

Teen
4RV Publishing P004
Agency (London) Ltd, The L009
Asabi Publishing P034
Auroras & Blossoms PoArtMo Anthology M039
Badger Learning P048
Eunice McMullen Children's Literary Agent Ltd L201
Firefly P167
Free Spirit Publishing P174
Haggerty, Taylor L287
Harmony Ink Press P205
Hawk, Susan L303
Langton, Becca L383
Madeleine Milburn Literary, TV & Film Agency L420
Margaret K. McElderry Books P281
Moody Publishers P305
Seager, Chloe L571
Shaw Agency, The L576
Sunpenny Publishing P435
Tor Publishing Group P456
Tor Teen P457
Turner Publishing P462
Tyndale House Publishers, Inc. P465
Walsh, Caroline L645

Tennessee
See more broadly: United States

Texas
See more broadly: United States
Texas A&M University Press P445
University of North Texas Press P485
University of Texas Press P488

The Midlands
See more broadly: England
Brewin Books Ltd P081

Theatre
See more broadly: Media
See more specifically: Musicals
African American Review M014
Doug Grad Literary Agency L177
Flaneur M145
Hudson Review, The M190
Methuen Publishing Ltd P294
Ohio University Press P324
Southern Theatre M347
University of Iowa Press P480
University of Michigan Press, The P483

Theatre Scripts
African Voices M015
Agency (London) Ltd, The L009
AHA Talent Ltd L010
Alan Brodie Representation L013
Alaska Quarterly Review M019
Anvil Press Publishers P028
Aurora Metro Press P039
Barbican Press P055
Barnard, Arthur L042
Bell, Eva L054
Bolger, Maeve L068
Chapman Publishing P099
Cincinnati Review, The M086
Curtis Brown L146
Elaine Steel L196
Fillingham Weston Associates L222
Freedman, Robert L241
Gurman Agency, LLC L285
Hickman, Emily L311
JFL Agency L332
Judy Daish Associates Ltd L342
Kelleher, Sophie L359
Kenyon Review, The M210
Ki Agency Ltd L364
Lost Lake Folk Opera Magazine M227
Lyon, Rebecca L411
Marion Boyars Publishers P282
New England Review M255
Oakland Arts Review, The M264
Obsidian: Literature in the African Diaspora M265
Paradigm Talent and Literary Agency L498
Praeger, Marta L524
Pushing Out the Boat M301
Qu Literary Magazine M302
Renard Press Ltd P376
River Styx M314
Rochelle Stevens & Co L543
Sheil Land Associates Ltd L577
Sunspot Literary Journal M364
Tennyson Agency, The L622
Third Coast M375
Tusculum Review, The M381
Victoria Sanders & Associates LLC L642
Williams, Katie L661
WordCrafts Press P514

Theravada Buddhism
See more broadly: Buddhism

Thrillers
See more specifically: Crime Thrilllers; Dark Thrillers; Domestic Thriller; High Concept Thrillers; Historical Thrillers; Legal Thrillers; Literary Thrillers; Political Thrillers; Psychological Thrillers; Romantic Thrillers; Speculative Thrillers; Spy Thrilllers; Supernatural / Paranormal Thrillers; Upmarket Thrillers
3 Seas Literary Agency L001
Afonso, Thais L008
Allison & Busby Ltd P019
Anderson, Darley L022
Andrew, Nelle L025
Armstrong, Susan L032
Asabi Publishing P034
Authentic Ideas P040
Avon P044
Baror International, Inc. L044
Bartholomew, Jason L047
Baxter, Veronique L052
Belton, Maddy L055
Berlyne, John L061
Betsy Amster Literary Enterprises L063
Birlinn Ltd P067
Bloodhound Books P070
Bolton, Camilla L069
Bookouture P078
Brace, Samantha L074
Bradford Literary Agency L075
Bradford, Laura L076
Brannan, Maria L078
Brooks, Savannah L084
Bucci, Chris L090
Buckley, Louise L091
Burke, Kate L093
Campbell, Charlie L099
Carroll, Megan L110
Chanchani, Sonali L115
Chevais, Jennifer L122
Christensen, Erica L125
Claret Press P113
Cochran, Alexander L130
Compassiviste Publishing P121
Coombs Moylett & Maclean Literary Agency L139
Crowley, Sheila L144
Crystal Magazine M110
Curtis Brown L146
Cusick, John L148
Dana Newman Literary, LLC L152
Darley Anderson Agency, The L157
Dawson, Liza L162
DeBlock, Liza L163
Dixon, Isobel L171
Dodd, Saffron L172
Doug Grad Literary Agency L177
Dunham, Jennie L180
Dunn, Ben L181
Eason, Lynette L186
Eberly, Chelsea L187
Ellis-Martin, Sian L197
Ellor, Zabé L198
Evans, Kiya L205
Evans, Stephany L206
Fabien, Samantha L207
Faulks, Holly L209
Ferguson, Hannah L217
Figueroa, Melanie L221
Finan, Ciara L223
for Authors, A L231
Forge P169
Forrester, Jemima L232
Foxx, Kat L235
Frances Goldin Literary Agency, Inc. L238
Frankel, Valerie L239
Friedman, Claire L243
Gauntlett, Adam L254
Getzler, Josh L256
Gillam, Bianca L259
Goetz, Adria L265
Gordon, Andrew L270
Grunewald, Hattie L282
Gunic, Masha L284
Haley, Jolene L289
Hannah Sheppard Literary Agency L291
Hansen, Stephanie L293

Hardman, Caroline	L295
Harmsworth, Esmond	L297
Hensley, Chelsea	L307
Hiyate, Sam	L313
Hobbs, Victoria	L314
Hogrebe, Christina	L317
Hornsley, Sarah	L321
Irene Goodman Literary Agency (IGLA)	L324
Joelle Delbourgo Associates, Inc.	L334
Jonathan Pegg Literary Agency	L337
Kaliszewska, Joanna	L347
Kane Literary Agency	L348
Karinch, Maryann	L351
Kavanagh, Jade	L355
Kensington Publishing Corp.	P253
Keren, Eli	L362
Lakosil, Natalie	L379
Lambert, Sophie	L380
Landis, Sarah	L381
Langlee, Lina	L382
Langtons International	L384
Lechon, Shannon	L390
Lees, Jordan	L392
Leon, Nina	L394
Limelight Management	L400
Lovell, Jake	L409
Lyrical Press	P277
MacDonald, Emily	L412
MacKenzie, Joanna	L416
Maclean, Jamie	L417
Marr, Jill	L425
McNidder & Grace	P286
Milburn, Madeleine	L449
Milusich, Grace	L453
Morrell, Imogen	L460
Mortimer, Michele	L462
Mundy, Toby	L466
Murray, Judith	L468
Mushens, Juliet	L470
Napolitano, Maria	L473
Nash, Justin	L474
Nathan, Abigail	L475
Neely, Rachel	L476
Nelson, Kristin	L478
Nichols, Mariah	L479
Niumata, Erin	L480
O'Brien, Lee	L484
Oghma Creative Media	P321
Oneworld Publications	P327
Orenda Books	P329
Ostby, Kristin	L494
Pan Macmillan Australia	P335
Parker, Elana Roth	L499
Pass, Marina de	L500
Paul S. Levine Literary Agency	L502
Penzler Publishers	P345
Perez Literary & Entertainment	L506
Perez, Kristina	L507
Pestritto, Carrie	L511
Petty, Rachel	L512
Pierce, Rosie	L517
Pine, Gideon	L518
Plant, Zoe	L519
Posner, Marcy	L522
Ravenstone	P374
Reid, Janet	L532
Riccardi, Francesca	L535
Rogers, Coleridge & White Ltd	L546
Ruby Fiction	P384
Ruppin Agency, The	L555
Salazar, Des	L559
Schofield, Hannah	L567
Schwartz, Steve	L568
Seymour, Charlotte	L575
Sheil Land Associates Ltd	L577
Shestopal, Camilla	L581
Soloway, Jennifer March	L590
Sparsile Books	P419
Steed, Hayley	L595
Story Unlikely	M356
Strachan Literary Agency	L602
Stringer, Marlene	L604
Swainson, Joanna	L613
Tannenbaum, Amy	L620
Terlip, Paige	L624
Thorneycroft, Euan	L628
Thwaites, Steph	L629
Tibbets, Anne	L630
Todd, Hannah	L631
Topping, Antony	L632
Tor Publishing Group	P456
Torrey House Press, LLC	P459
Trudel, Jes	L634
Trussell, Caroline	L635
Turner Publishing	P462
Tyndale House Publishers, Inc.	P465
Udden, Jennifer	L637
Vance, Lisa Erbach	L641
Victoria Sanders & Associates LLC	L642
W.W. Norton & Company, Inc.	P500
Weiman, Paula	L649
Weiss, Alexandra	L650
Williams, Sarah	L663
Wilson, Desiree	L667
Wilson, Ed	L668
Wolfpack Publishing	P513
Wood, Caroline	L669
Young, Claudia	L677
Zack Company, Inc, The	L678

Time Travel
See more broadly: Science Fiction

| Begum, Salma | L053 |
| Choc Lit | P108 |

Timeslip Romance
See more broadly: Romance

| Choc Lit | P108 |

Trade
See more broadly: Business

Traditional

Alaska Quarterly Review	M019
Compassiviste Publishing	P121
Midsummer Dream House	M242
Oghma Creative Media	P321

Traditional Music
See more broadly: Music

| Birlinn Ltd | P067 |

Trains
See more broadly: Vehicles

Translations

Frances Goldin Literary Agency, Inc.	L238
Joy Harris Literary Agency, Inc.	L340
Victoria Sanders & Associates LLC	L642

Transport
See more specifically: Aviation; Hauliers; Railways; Vehicles

Arcadia Publishing	P031
Brewin Books Ltd	P081
History Press, The	P221
Icon Books Ltd	P227
Indiana University Press	P235
Kensington Publishing Corp.	P253
Loft Press, Inc.	P270
Schiffer Publishing	P398
University of Nevada Press	P484
W.W. Norton & Company Ltd	P499
Wallpaper	M397

Travel
See more specifically: Air Travel; Road Atlases; Road Trips; Sailing

AARP The Magazine	M006
AdventureKEEN	P013
Antigonish Review, The	M026
Apa Publications Group	P029
Arcadia Publishing	P031
Asabi Publishing	P034
Atlanta Magazine	M035
Aurora Metro Press	P039
Bal, Emma	L038
Baxter, Veronique	L052
Bella	M053
Betsy Amster Literary Enterprises	L063
Birlinn Ltd	P067
Brewin Books Ltd	P081
Brick	M074
Britain Magazine	M075
Business Traveller	M076
Caitlin Press Inc	P090
Campbell, Charlie	L099
Canterbury Press	P094
Carter, Rebecca	L111
Claret Press	P113
Clarke, Caro	L128
Compassiviste Publishing	P121
Cowboys & Indians	M101
Crystal Magazine	M110
Curran, Sabhbh	L145
Devon Life	M119
DK Publishing	P141
Doug Grad Literary Agency	L177
Duncan Petersen Publishing Limited	P146
Essex Life	M132
Felicia Eth Literary Representation	L214
Filter Press	P166
Flaneur	M145
Foxx, Kat	L235
Frances Collin Literary Agent	L237
Frances Goldin Literary Agency, Inc.	L238
Fresh Words – An International Literary Magazine	M154
Freymann, Sarah Jane	L242
Globe Pequot Press, The	P184
Go World Travel Magazine	M167
Good Ski Guide, The	M169
Granta Books	P192
Haus Publishing	P208
Horse & Rider	M188
Icon Books Ltd	P227
JMD Media / DB Publishing	P247
Kensington Publishing Corp.	P253
Kent Life	M209
Lambert, Sophie	L380
Lancashire Life	M214
Laxfield Literary Associates	L387
Leisure Group Travel	M216
Lilliput Press, The	P268
Limelight Management	L400
Litro Magazine	M221
Malahat Review, The	M232
marie claire	M234
Marlin	M236
Medina Publishing	P289
Menasha Ridge Press	P290
Methuen Publishing Ltd	P294
My Weekly	M249
Nash, Justin	L474
New England Review	M255
Ouen Press	P331
Panorama	M274
Peddle, Kay	L503
Pineapple Press	P356
Plitt, Carrie	L520
Polygon	P360
Preservation Magazine	M297
Quill Driver Books	P368
Rand McNally	P371
Red Magazine	M309
Regina Ryan Books	L531

River Hills Traveler	M313
Rocky Mountain Books	P378
Ruralite	M318
Schwartz, Steve	L568
Scottish Field	M326
Scoular, Rosemary	L570
Scratching Shed Publishing	P402
Seren Books	P405
Sheil Land Associates Ltd	L577
Sierra	M336
Somerset Life	M341
Southern Humanities Review	M345
Square Mile Magazine	M354
Strachan Literary Agency	L602
Thames & Hudson Inc.	P446
Tolka	M379
Turner Publishing	P462
Tyndale House Publishers, Inc.	P465
University of Alberta Press	P477
University of Michigan Press, The	P483
University of Nevada Press	P484
University of Wisconsin Press, The	P490
Valley Press	P493
VanderWyk & Burnham	P494
W.W. Norton & Company Ltd	P499
Wide-Eyed Editions	P509
Williams, Sarah	L663
Woman & Home	M407
WordCrafts Press	P514
Yankee Magazine	M410
Yorkshire Life	M413
Yorkshire Women's Life Magazine	M414
Young, Claudia	L677
Yours	M416
ZigZag Education	P523

UFOs
See more broadly: Supernatural / Paranormal

Llewellyn Worldwide Ltd	P269
Lovell, Jake	L409

US Southern States
See more broadly: United States

4RV Tenacious	P005
Dawson, Liza	L162
University of Georgia Press	P479

United Kingdom
See more broadly: Europe
See more specifically: England; Northern Ireland; Scotland; Wales

Best of British	M056
Britain Magazine	M075

United States
See more broadly: North America
See more specifically: Alaska; American Midwest; American West; Americana; Appalachia; Arizona; California; Chesapeake Bay; Colorado; Florida; Georgia (US State); Hawai'i; Illinois; Indiana; Louisiana; Maine; Maryland; Michigan; Minnesota; Missouri; Nevada; New England; New Jersey; New York State; Ohio; Ozarks; Pacific Northwest; Pennsylvania; Southeastern United States; Southwestern United States; Tennessee; Texas; US Southern States; Utah; Virginia; Wisconsin

Ohio State University Press, The	P323
Pluto Press	P358
Sunbelt Publications, Inc.	P433
University of California Press	P478
University of Georgia Press	P479
University of Massachusetts Press	P482
University of Michigan Press, The	P483
University of Texas Press	P488

Upmarket
See more specifically: Upmarket Commercial Fiction; Upmarket Contemporary Fiction; Upmarket Crime; Upmarket Romance; Upmarket Thrillers; Upmarket Women's Fiction

Armada, Kurestin	L030
Bajek, Lauren	L037
Brannan, Maria	L078
Brattesani, Hannah	L079
Buckley, Louise	L091
Carroll, Megan	L110
Chevais, Jennifer	L122
Cichello, Kayla	L127
Dana Newman Literary, LLC	L152
Danko, Margaret	L154
Davies, Elinor	L160
DeBlock, Liza	L163
Edenborough, Sam	L189
Eisenmann, Caroline	L192
Evans, Kiya	L205
Fabien, Samantha	L207
Faulks, Holly	L209
Figueroa, Melanie	L221
Forrester, Jemima	L232
Foster, Clara	L233
Friedman, Claire	L243
Fuentes, Sarah	L247
Getzler, Josh	L256
Gilbert, Tara	L258
Goetz, Adria	L265
Greenstreet, Katie	L277
Grunewald, Hattie	L282
Harper, Logan	L299
Jonathan Pegg Literary Agency	L337
Kahn, Ella Diamond	L345
Kahn, Jody	L346
Kardon, Julia	L350
Keren, Eli	L362
Krienke, Mary	L375
Lakosil, Natalie	L379
Leeke, Jessica	L391
Lees, Jordan	L392
Leon, Nina	L394
Lightner, Kayla	L399
Lovell, Jake	L409
MacDonald, Emily	L412
Marr, Jill	L425
Milburn, Madeleine	L449
Mills, Rachel	L452
Moore, Mary C.	L457
Morrell, Imogen	L460
Napolitano, Maria	L473
Ostby, Kristin	L494
Pass, Marina de	L500
Patterson, Emma	L501
Pelham, Imogen	L504
Perez Literary & Entertainment	L506
Perez, Kristina	L507
Ramer, Susan	L528
Roberts, Soumeya Bendimerad	L540
Rutherford, Laetitia	L557
Serra, Maria Cardona	L574
Sutherland, Kari	L611
Takikawa, Marin	L618
Terlip, Paige	L624
Topping, Antony	L632
Tran, Jennifer Chen	L633
Walsh, Caroline	L645
Weitzner, Tess	L651
Whatnall, Michaela	L655
Wickers, Chandler	L659
Wilson, Desiree	L667
Yeoh, Rachel	L675

Upmarket Commercial Fiction
See more broadly: Commercial; Upmarket

Armstrong, Susan	L032
Barr, Nicola	L046
Betsy Amster Literary Enterprises	L063
Bradford Literary Agency	L075

Carr, Jamie	L108
Chiotti, Danielle	L123
Combemale, Chris	L133
Gauntlett, Adam	L254
Glenister, Emily	L263
Hardman, Caroline	L295
Hiyate, Sam	L313
Kaliszewska, Joanna	L347
Williams, Laura	L662

Upmarket Contemporary Fiction
See more broadly: Contemporary; Upmarket

Ellor, Zabé	L198
Woods, Bryony	L671

Upmarket Crime
See more broadly: Crime; Upmarket

Serra, Maria Cardona	L574
Silk, Julia	L583

Upmarket Romance
See more broadly: Romance; Upmarket

Berdinsky, Kendall	L060
Carroll, Megan	L110

Upmarket Thrillers
See more broadly: Thrillers; Upmarket

Silk, Julia	L583

Upmarket Women's Fiction
See more broadly: Upmarket; Women's Fiction

Bent, Jenny	L059
Betsy Amster Literary Enterprises	L063
Eberly, Chelsea	L187
Evans, Stephany	L206
Grimm, Katie	L279
Hordern, Kate	L320
Lakosil, Natalie	L379
Mortimer, Michele	L462
Parker, Elana Roth	L499
Pestritto, Carrie	L511
Whelan, Maria	L656

Urban

Begum, Salma	L053
Fernwood Publishing	P164
Torrey House Press, LLC	P459
University of Alberta Press	P477
University of Georgia Press	P479
University of Massachusetts Press	P482
University of Michigan Press, The	P483

Urban Fantasy
See more broadly: Fantasy

Bennett, Laura	L056
Berlyne, John	L061
DeBlock, Liza	L163
Glenister, Emily	L263
Leon, Nina	L394
Liverpool Literary Agency, The	L404
SmashBear Publishing	P412
Trussell, Caroline	L635
Wilson, Desiree	L667
Zack Company, Inc, The	L678

Urban Farming
See more broadly: Farming

Utah
See more broadly: United States

Utopian Fiction
See more broadly: Speculative

Mozley, Jack	L465

Vampires
See more broadly: Supernatural / Paranormal

DeBlock, Liza	L163
Sinister Stoat Press	P410

Vancouver Island
See more broadly: British Columbia

Veganism
See more broadly: Vegetarianism

Vegetarian Cooking
See more broadly: Cookery; Vegetarianism

Vegetarian Food
See more broadly: Food; Vegetarianism

Vegetarianism
See more broadly: Lifestyle
See more specifically: Veganism; Vegetarian Cooking; Vegetarian Food
Hay House Publishers P210

Vehicles
See more broadly: Transport
See more specifically: Boats; Caravans; Cars; Military Vehicles; Motorbikes; Motorhomes; Planes; Recreational Vehicles; Ships; Steam Engines; Trains

Veterinary
See more broadly: Animals
Texas A&M University Press P445

Vikings Fiction
See more broadly: Historical Fiction
Pass, Marina de L500

Virginia
See more broadly: United States
See more specifically: Albemarle
University of Virginia Press P489
Virginia Wine & Country Life M390
Virginia Wine & Country Weddings M391

Visual Arts
See more broadly: Arts
Bird Eye Books P066
Graywolf Lab M172
Unicorn P469
Unicorn Publishing Group P470
W.W. Norton & Company, Inc. P500

Visual Culture
See more broadly: Culture
African American Review M014
Bird Eye Books P066
Bloomsbury Academic P071
Crabtree Publishing P126

Visual Poetry
Black Warrior Review M066

Voodoo
See more broadly: Religion

Wales
See more broadly: United Kingdom
See more specifically: Breconshire; Montgomeryshire; Radnorshire
Welsh Country M399

Walking
See more broadly: Outdoor Activities
See more specifically: Walking Guides
Amato Books P021
Countryside Books P124
Devon Life M119
Essex Life M132
JMD Media / DB Publishing P247
Walk Magazine M395
Welsh Country M399
Yorkshire Life M413

Walking Guides
See more broadly: Walking
Duncan Petersen Publishing Limited P146
Goose Lane Editions P188
Kent Life M209
Logaston Press P271
Metro Publications Ltd P295
Pocket Mountains P359
Rocky Mountain Books P378
Sigma Press P407

Warehousing
See more broadly: Business
Loft Press, Inc. P270

Warfare
See more specifically: American Civil War; American Revolution; Military; Military History; National Security; Secret Intelligence; World War I; World War II
Berghahn Books Ltd P062
Howgate Publishing P225

Pluto Press P358
Robert Smith Literary Agency Ltd L539
Thinkwell Books, UK P447
Wickers, Chandler L659

Water Sports
See more broadly: Sport
See more specifically: Surfing

Weapons
See more specifically: Firearms

Weddings
See more broadly: Events
Norfolk & Suffolk Bride M260
Savannah Magazine M322
Virginia Wine & Country Weddings M391

Wellbeing
See more broadly: Health
Ammonite Press P024
Atlanta Magazine M035
Aurora Metro Press P039
Baumer, Jan L051
Bernardi, Amanda L062
Bloomsbury Academic P071
Blue Star Press P075
Brailsford, Karen L077
Brewin Books Ltd P081
Dana Newman Literary, LLC L152
DK Publishing P141
Ekus, Sally L194
Evans, Stephany L206
First For Women M142
Frankel, Valerie L239
Free Spirit Publishing P174
Greyhound Literary L278
Hammersmith Books P198
Hardman, Caroline L295
High Tide Press P217
Hoffman, Scott L316
Kate Barker Literary, TV, & Film Agency L352
Latshaw, Katherine L386
McNidder & Grace P286
Mills, Rachel L452
Mortimer, Michele L462
Murgolo, Karen L467
Pine, Gideon L518
Preston, Amanda L526
Red Magazine M309
Regina Ryan Books L531
Seventeen M329
Shaw Agency, The L576
Silk, Julia L583
Singing Dragon P409
Stephens, Jenny L596
Turner Publishing P462
Whitecap Books Ltd P507
Willms, Kathryn L665
Woman & Home M407
Yale University Press (London) P520
Yorkshire Women's Life Magazine M414
Zack Company, Inc, The L678

Werewolves
See more broadly: Horror
DeBlock, Liza L163
Sinister Stoat Press P410

West Country
See more broadly: England

Westchester County
See more broadly: New York State
Westchester Magazine M402

Westerns
Armada, Kurestin L030
Crystal Magazine M110
Doug Grad Literary Agency L177
Forge P169
Kensington Publishing Corp. P253
Lovell, Jake L409

Oghma Creative Media P321
Robinson, Quressa L542
Story Unlikely M356
Tyndale House Publishers, Inc. P465
Washington State University Press P501
Wolfpack Publishing P513

Whisky
See more broadly: Drinks
Square Mile Magazine M354

Wicca
See more broadly: Paganism
Llewellyn Worldwide Ltd P269

Wilderness Sports
See more broadly: Sport
Menasha Ridge Press P290

Wildlife
See more broadly: Animals
Menasha Ridge Press P290
Scots Magazine, The M324
Sierra M336

Wine
See more broadly: Drinks
See more specifically: Winemaking
Bowlin, Sarah L073
Chiotti, Danielle L123
Fairbank Literary Representation L208
Foxx, Kat L235
Rosenberg Group, The L549
Sasquatch Books P391
Square Mile Magazine M354
University of California Press P478
Virginia Wine & Country Life M390
Whitecap Books Ltd P507
Wine Enthusiast M406

Winemaking
See more broadly: Wine
See more specifically: Amateur Winemaking

Wisconsin
See more broadly: United States
University of Wisconsin Press, The P490

Witchcraft
See more broadly: Supernatural / Paranormal
Foxx, Kat L235
Haley, Jolene L289
Llewellyn Worldwide Ltd P269

Witches
See more broadly: Supernatural / Paranormal
Buckley, Louise L091
DeBlock, Liza L163
Foxx, Kat L235
Haley, Jolene L289
Rushall, Kathleen L556
Williams, Laura L662

Women
See more broadly: Gender
Fathom Books P162
Fazzari, Hillary L210
Glenister, Emily L263
Ohio University Press P324
Riposte M312
Understorey Magazine M385
Virago Books P498
Yours M416

Women in Business
See more broadly: Business

Women's Fiction
See more specifically: Book Club Women's Fiction; Chick Lit; Commercial Women's Fiction; Contemporary Women's Fiction; Upmarket Women's Fiction
3 Seas Literary Agency L001
4RV Tenacious P005
Afonso, Thais L008
Ahearn Agency, Inc, The L011
Andrew, Nelle L025
Armstrong, Susan L032

Index | *Young Adult* **401**

Barbican Press ... P055
Barone Literary Agency ... L043
Bloodhound Books ... P070
Bolton, Camilla ... L069
Bookouture ... P078
Bradford Literary Agency ... L075
Bradford, Laura ... L076
Brewer, Amy ... L081
Burke, Kate ... L093
Carr, Michael ... L109
Chanchani, Sonali ... L115
Coombes, Clare ... L138
Coombs Moylett & Maclean Literary Agency ... L139
Danko, Margaret ... L154
Davies, Elinor ... L160
Doug Grad Literary Agency ... L177
Dunham, Jennie ... L180
Dunn, Ben ... L181
Evans, Stephany ... L206
Fabien, Samantha ... L207
Ferguson, Hannah ... L217
Figueroa, Melanie ... L221
Finch, Rebeka ... L225
Forrester, Jemima ... L232
Frances Collin Literary Agent ... L237
Friedman, Rebecca ... L244
Getzler, Josh ... L256
Gillam, Bianca ... L259
Grajkowski, Michelle ... L274
Hornsley, Sarah ... L321
Joelle Delbourgo Associates, Inc. ... L334
Joffe Books ... P248
Kotchman, Katie ... L374
Langtons International ... L384
Leon, Nina ... L394
MacKenzie, Joanna ... L416
Mileo, Jessica ... L451
Nichols, Mariah ... L479
Niumata, Erin ... L480
Paul S. Levine Literary Agency ... L502
Pelham, Imogen ... L504
People's Friend, The ... M283
Posner, Marcy ... L522
Reino, Jessica ... L534
Rosenberg Group, The ... L549
Ruby Fiction ... P384
Salvo, Katie ... L560
Schofield, Hannah ... L567
Shestopal, Camilla ... L581
Steed, Hayley ... L595
Stringer, Marlene ... L604
Susan Schulman Literary Agency ... L610
Tannenbaum, Amy ... L620
Todd, Hannah ... L631
Tran, Jennifer Chen ... L633
Trussell, Caroline ... L635
Virago Books ... P498
Williamson, Jo ... L664
WordCrafts Press ... P514
Wordserve Literary ... L673
Zack Company, Inc, The ... L678

Women's Health
See more broadly: Health
See more specifically: Menopause

Women's Interests
Canterbury Literary Agency ... L101
Carolina Woman ... M080
Compassiviste Publishing ... P121
Dana Newman Literary, LLC ... L152
Joy Harris Literary Agency, Inc. ... L340
marie claire ... M234
Marion Boyars Publishers ... P282
My Weekly ... M249
OK! Magazine ... M266
People's Friend, The ... M283
Red Magazine ... M309
Sheree Bykofsky Associates, Inc. ... L579
Strachan Literary Agency ... L602
Victoria Sanders & Associates LLC ... L642
Woman & Home ... M407

Women's Issues
See more broadly: Social Issues
Betsy Amster Literary Enterprises ... L063
Dawson, Liza ... L162
Felicia Eth Literary Representation ... L214
Freymann, Sarah Jane ... L242
Geiger, Ellen ... L255
Kim, Julia ... L367
Posner, Marcy ... L522
Ramer, Susan ... L528
Regina Ryan Books ... L531
Serra, Maria Cardona ... L574
Understorey Magazine ... M385
Virago Books ... P498
Willms, Kathryn ... L665
Wordserve Literary ... L673
Yorkshire Women's Life Magazine ... M414
Zack Company, Inc, The ... L678

Women's Studies
See more broadly: Gender
Cleis Press ... P115
Imagine Publishing ... P234
Texas A&M University Press ... P445
University of Michigan Press, The ... P483
University of North Texas Press ... P485
University of Virginia Press ... P489
Virago Books ... P498
W.W. Norton & Company Ltd ... P499

Worcestershire
See more broadly: England
Logaston Press ... P271

Working Class
See more broadly: Social Groups

World War I
See more broadly: Warfare
Countryside Books ... P124

World War II
See more broadly: Warfare
Choc Lit ... P108
Countryside Books ... P124
Joffe Books ... P248
LSU Press ... P273
Merriam Press ... P293
Methuen Publishing Ltd ... P294

Writing
See more broadly: Language
See more specifically: Creative Writing
Banipal ... M046
Banter Press ... P053
Brick ... M074
Broadview Press ... P085
Literary Mama ... M220
Ohio University Press ... P324
Ooligan Press ... P328
Susan Schulman Literary Agency ... L610
University of Iowa Press ... P480
University of Michigan Press, The ... P483
W.W. Norton & Company Ltd ... P499

Yachts
See more broadly: Boats
RYA (Royal Yachting Association) ... P385
Square Mile Magazine ... M354
Yachting Monthly ... M408

Yoga
See more broadly: Mind, Body, Spirit
Llewellyn Worldwide Ltd ... P269
Singing Dragon ... P409
Zack Company, Inc, The ... L678

Yorkshire
See more broadly: England
Yorkshire Life ... M413
Yorkshire Women's Life Magazine ... M414

Young Adult
3 Seas Literary Agency ... L001
4RV Publishing ... P004
Adsett, Alex ... L006
Afonso, Thais ... L008
Agency (London) Ltd, The ... L009
Albert Whitman & Company ... P015
Alekseii, Keir ... L015
Alex Adsett Literary ... L016
Alice Williams Literary ... L017
Allen & Unwin ... P018
Andrade, Hannah ... L023
Anne Clark Literary Agency ... L028
Arcadia Publishing ... P031
Arms, Victoria Wells ... L031
Arsenal Pulp Press ... P032
Arthurson, Wayne ... L033
Asabi Publishing ... P034
Atyeo, Charlotte ... L034
Aurora Metro Press ... P039
Badger Learning ... P048
Barbara, Stephen ... L041
Barone Literary Agency ... L043
Baror International, Inc. ... L044
Barr, Nicola ... L046
Bath Literary Agency ... L049
Bauman, Erica ... L050
Belton, Maddy ... L055
Bennett, Laura ... L056
Bent Agency (UK), The ... L057
Bent Agency, The ... L058
Bent, Jenny ... L059
Berlyne, John ... L061
Bhasin, Tamanna ... L064
Boker, Sidney ... L067
Bradford Literary Agency ... L075
Bradford, Laura ... L076
Brannan, Maria ... L078
Brooks, Savannah ... L084
Burns, Camille ... L094
C&W (Conville & Walsh) ... L096
Candy Jar Books ... P093
Caprio, Alice ... L103
Carroll, Megan ... L110
Charlesbridge Teen ... P103
Chiotti, Danielle ... L123
Cho, Catherine ... L124
Christensen, Erica ... L125
Cichello, Kayla ... L127
Colwill, Charlotte ... L132
Coombs Moylett & Maclean Literary Agency ... L139
Cooper, Gemma ... L140
Crandall, Becca ... L142
Curtis Brown ... L146
Cusick, John ... L148
Darhansoff & Verrill Literary Agents ... L156
DHH Literary Agency Ltd ... L166
Dodd, Saffron ... L172
Donald Maass Literary Agency ... L176
Draper, Claire ... L178
Dunham, Jennie ... L180
Eason, Lynette ... L186
Eberly, Chelsea ... L187
Eddison Pearson Ltd ... L188
Eerdmans Books for Young Readers ... P148
Eisenbraun, Nicole ... L191
Ellor, Zabé ... L198
Evan Marshall Agency, The ... L202
Fabien, Samantha ... L207
Fazzari, Hillary ... L210
Felicia Eth Literary Representation ... L214
Fellows, Abi ... L216
Ferguson, T.S. ... L218
Figueroa, Melanie ... L221

*Claim your free access to **www.firstwriter.com**: See p.403*

Fillingham Weston Associates	L222
Firefly	P167
Fitzgerald, Bea	L227
Flannery Literary	L228
Flynn, Amy Thrall	L229
Foster, Clara	L233
Foxx, Kat	L235
Frances Goldin Literary Agency, Inc.	L238
Frankel, Valerie	L239
Freymann, Sarah Jane	L242
Friedman, Claire	L243
Friedman, Rebecca	L244
Fuller, Lisa	L248
Gahan, Isobel	L250
Ghahremani, Lilly	L257
Gilbert, Tara	L258
Gisondi, Katie	L261
Goff, Ellen	L267
Good Literary Agency, The	L269
Graham, Stacey	L272
Grajkowski, Kara	L273
Grimm, Katie	L279
Gruber, Pam	L281
Gunic, Masha	L284
Hakim, Serene	L288
Haley, Jolene	L289
Hannah Sheppard Literary Agency	L291
Hansen, Stephanie	L293
Harris, Erin	L300
Harwell, Hilary	L301
Hashtag Press	P207
Hawk, Susan	L303
Hawn, Molly Ker	L304
Hensley, Chelsea	L307
Hernando, Paloma	L308
Heymont, Lane	L309
HopeRoad	P223
IDW Publishing	P228
IgKids	P231
Irene Goodman Literary Agency (IGLA)	L324
Irvine, Lucy	L325
Janklow & Nesbit UK Ltd	L330
Jo Unwin Literary Agency	L333
Joelle Delbourgo Associates, Inc.	L334
Joy Harris Literary Agency, Inc.	L340
Kahn, Ella Diamond	L345
Kate Nash Literary Agency	L353
Kathryn Green Literary Agency, LLC	L354
Kean, Taylor Martindale	L357
Kensington Publishing Corp.	P253
Kimber, Natalie	L368
Knigge, Sheyla	L372
KT Literary	L377
Lakosil, Natalie	L379
Langlee, Lina	L382
Langton, Becca	L383
Latshaw, Katherine	L386
Leapfrog Press	P263
Lechon, Shannon	L390
Leigh Feldman Literary	L393
Leon, Nina	L394
Lerner Publishing Group	P264
Lindsay Literary Agency	L401
Lineberry, Isabel	L402
Liverpool Literary Agency, The	L404
MacLeod, Lauren	L418
Macmillan Children's Books	P279
Madeleine Milburn Literary, TV & Film Agency	L420
Maltese, Alyssa	L422
Marini, Victoria	L423
Marsh Agency, The	L426
Matte, Rebecca	L431
Mattson, Jennifer	L432
Maurer, Shari	L433
McBride, Juliana	L435
McCormick Literary	L436
Megibow, Sara	L439
Metamorphosis Literary Agency	L444
Mihell, Natasha	L448
Milusich, Grace	L453
Miranda, Caroline	L454
Moore, Penny	L458
Morris, Natascha	L461
Mortimer, Michele	L462
Motala, Tasneem	L463
Mustelier, James	L471
Nathan, Abigail	L475
Nelson Literary Agency, LLC	L477
Nelson, Kristin	L478
Nichols, Mariah	L479
Northbank Talent Management	L482
Northern Gravy	M263
O'Brien, Lee	L484
O'Neill, Molly	L487
Oghma Creative Media	P321
Ooligan Press	P328
Ostby, Kristin	L494
Pan Macmillan Australia	P335
Pande, Ayesha	L497
Parker, Elana Roth	L499
Pass, Marina de	L500
Paul S. Levine Literary Agency	L502
Pen & Ink Designs Publishing	P342
Perez Literary & Entertainment	L506
Perez, Kristina	L507
Perotto-Wills, Martha	L508
Pestritto, Carrie	L511
Petty, Rachel	L512
Phelan, Beth	L514
Phoenix Moirai	P351
Pinata Books	P355
Plant, Zoe	L519
Posner, Marcy	L522
Prasanna, Tanusri	L525
Preston, Amanda	L526
R D Publishers	P370
Ransom Publishing Ltd	P373
Reino, Jessica	L534
Richter, Rick	L537
Robertson Murray Literary Agency	L541
Robinson, Quressa	L542
Rogers, Coleridge & White Ltd	L546
Ross, Whitney	L551
Rubin Pfeffer Content, LLC	L552
Rudy Agency, The	L553
Rushall, Kathleen	L556
Saguaro Books, LLC	P388
Salazar, Des	L559
Salvo, Katie	L560
Sant, Kelly Van	L563
Sarah Jane Freymann Literary Agency	L564
Schofield, Hannah	L567
Seager, Chloe	L571
Selectric Artists	L573
Seventeen	M329
Sheil Land Associates Ltd	L577
Shestopal, Camilla	L581
Siobhan, Aiden	L587
Sluytman, Antoinette Van	L588
Soho Press	P417
Soler, Shania N.	L589
Soloway, Jennifer March	L590
Spring Literary	L594
Stewart, Douglas	L599
Strachan Literary Agency	L602
Stringer Literary Agency LLC, The	L603
Stringer, Marlene	L604
Stuart Krichevsky Literary Agency, Inc.	L609
Sunberry Books	P434
Susan Schulman Literary Agency	L610
Sutherland, Kari	L611
Sweet Cherry Publishing	P437
SYLA – Susan Yearwood Literary Agency	L616
Symonds, Laurel	L617
Takikawa, Marin	L618
Talbot, Emily	L619
Terlip, Paige	L624
Thames & Hudson Inc.	P446
Thwaites, Steph	L629
Tor Teen	P457
Torrey House Press, LLC	P459
Tran, Jennifer Chen	L633
Trudel, Jes	L634
Turner Publishing	P462
Two Piers Literary Agency, The	L636
Unwin, Jo	L638
Victoria Sanders & Associates LLC	L642
Vinspire Publishing	P497
Walsh, Caroline	L645
Weiman, Paula	L649
Weiss, Alexandra	L650
Weitzner, Tess	L651
Westin, Erin Casey	L654
Whatnall, Michaela	L655
Whispering Buffalo Literary Agency	L657
Williams, Laura	L662
Williamson, Jo	L664
Wilson, Desiree	L667
Woods, Bryony	L671
WordCrafts Press	P514
Wordserve Literary	L673
Zacker, Marietta B.	L679

Youth Culture
See more broadly: Culture

Arsenal Pulp Press	P032

Yukon
See more broadly: Canada

Zen
See more broadly: Mahayana Buddhism

Zombies
See more broadly: Horror

Get Free Access to the firstwriter.com Website

To claim your free access to the firstwriter.com website simply go to the website at https://www.firstwriter.com/subscribe and begin the subscription process as normal. On the second page, enter the required details (such as your name and address, etc.) then for "Voucher / coupon number" enter the following promotional code:

- **5JBG-72PV**

This will reduce the cost of creating a subscription by up to $18 / £15 / €18, making it free to create a monthly, quarterly, or combination subscription. Alternatively, you can use the discount to take out an annual or life subscription at a reduced rate.

Continue the process until your account is created. Please note that you will need to provide your payment details, even if there is no up-front payment. This is in case you choose to leave your subscription running after the free initial period, but there is no obligation for you to do so.

When you use this code to take out a free subscription you are under no obligation to make any payments whatsoever and you are free to cancel your account before you make any payments if you wish.

If you need any assistance, please email support@firstwriter.com.

If you have found this book useful, please consider leaving a review on the website where you bought it.

What you get

Once you have set up access to the site you will be able to benefit from all the following features:

Databases
All our databases are updated almost every day, and include powerful search facilities to help you find exactly what you need. Searches that used to take you hours or even days in print books or on search engines can now be done in seconds, and produce more accurate and up-to-date information. Our agents database also includes independent reports from at least three separate sources, showing you which are the top agencies and helping you avoid the scams that are all over the internet. You can try out any of our databases before you subscribe:

- Search dozens of **current competitions**.
- Search **over 2,400 literary agents and agencies**.
- Search **over 2,200 magazines**.
- Search **over 2,700 book publishers** that **don't** charge fees.

Plus advanced features to help you with your search:

- Save searches and save time – set multiple search parameters specific to your work, save them, and then access the search results with a single click whenever you log in. You can even save multiple different searches if you have different types of work you are looking to place.
- Add personal notes to listings, visible only to you and fully searchable – helping you to organise your actions.
- Set reminders on listings to notify you when to submit your work, when to follow up, when to expect a reply, or any other custom action.
- Track which listings you've viewed and when, to help you organise your search – any listings which have changed since you last viewed them will be highlighted for your attention!

Daily email updates
As a subscriber you will be able to take advantage of our email alert service, meaning you can specify your particular interests and we'll send you automatic email updates when we change or add a listing that matches them. So if you're interested in agents dealing in romantic fiction in the United States you can have us send you emails with the latest updates about them – keeping you up to date without even having to log in.

User feedback
Our agent, publisher, and magazine databases all include a user feedback feature that allows our subscribers to leave feedback on each listing – giving you not only the chance to have your say about the markets you contact, but giving a unique authors' perspective on the listings.

Save on copyright protection fees
If you're sending your work away to publishers, competitions, or literary agents, it's vital that you first protect your copyright. As a subscriber to firstwriter.com you can do this through our site and save 10% on the copyright registration fees normally payable for protecting your work internationally through the Intellectual Property Rights Office.

Monthly newsletter
When you subscribe to firstwriter.com you also receive our monthly email newsletter – described by one publishing company as "the best in the business" – including articles, news, and interviews for writers. And the best part is that you can continue to receive the newsletter even after you stop your paid subscription – at no cost!

Terms and conditions

The promotional code contained in this publication may be used by the owner of the book only to create one subscription to firstwriter.com at a reduced cost, or for free. It may not be used by or disseminated to third parties. Should the code be misused then the owner of the book will be liable for any costs incurred, including but not limited to payment in full at the standard rate for the subscription in question. The code may be used at any time until the end of the calendar year named in the title of the publication, after which time it will become invalid. The code may be redeemed against the creation of a new account only – it cannot be redeemed against the ongoing costs of keeping a subscription open. In order to create a subscription a method of payment must be provided, but there is no obligation to make any payment. Subscriptions may be cancelled at any time, and if an account is cancelled before any payment becomes due then no payment will be made. Once a subscription has been created, the normal schedule of payments will begin on a monthly, quarterly, or annual basis, unless a life Subscription is selected, or the subscription is cancelled prior to the first payment becoming due. Subscriptions may be cancelled at any time, but if they are left open beyond the date at which the first payment becomes due and is processed then payments will not be refundable.

www.ingramcontent.com/pod-product-compliance
Lightning Source LLC
Chambersburg PA
CBHW081152020426
42333CB00020B/2487